CHIRON

1887 - 2000

CAO TIMES
BOX 75, OLD CHELSEA STATION
NEW YORK, N. Y. 10113

Facsimile of excerpt, reduced.

SMITHSONIAN INSTITUTION
ASTROPHYSICAL OBSERVATORY
60 GARDEN STREET CAMBRIDGE, MASSACHUSETTS 02138
TELEPHONE 617 495-7000

1982 October 22

Mr. Al H. Morrison
Box 75, Old Chelsea Sta.
New York, NY 10011

Dear Mr. Morrison:

The enclosed positions have been corrected for precession, and are thus for the mean ecliptic of date. The error in the positions should be good to 1 arcmin, as quite accurate elements at 200-day intervals (epochs) were used.

Sincerely,

Daniel Green
Minor Planet Center

CONTENTS:

EDITOR'S NOTES:

The best references for the mythological character of Chiron are to be found in the numerous editions of the scholarly works of Robert Graves.

The principal center or collection point for empirical observations of the workings of Chiron today is the Association For Studying Chiron. Write to:

Zane B. Stein K 201
757 East Main Street
Lansdale PA 19446

Send a contribution for a sample copy of The Key.

This ephemeris is distributed as a service to the astrological community.

A contribution of $4 per copy is needed to cover costs of publishing and distribution.

Published and distributed by CAO TIMES
Box 75, Old Chelsea Station
New York NY 10113

Ephemeris of Chiron

0 hour Ephemeris Time

Computed by Daniel Green.

Zodiac symbols added by Editor.

0 = 0 Aries		180 = 0 Libra	
30 = 0 Taurus		210 = 0 Scorpio	
60 = 0 Gemini		240 = 0 Sagittarius	
90 = 0 Cancer		270 = 0 Capricorn	
120 = 0 Leo		300 = 0 Aquarius	
150 = 0 Virgo		330 = 0 Pisces	

Example: 1982 10 18 56 43 -03 11 is read:

1982 18 October 26♉43 latitude 3 S 11

Date		Long.	Lat.
1887 01 29	♊	78 27	-05 54
1887 02 08		78 12	-05 51
1887 02 18		78 04	-05 47
1887 02 28		78 04	-05 44
1887 03 10		78 12	-05 40
1887 03 20		78 29	-05 36
1887 03 30		78 52	-05 33
1887 04 09		79 23	-05 30
1887 04 19		80 00	-05 27
1887 04 29		80 42	-05 25
1887 05 09		81 29	-05 23
1887 05 19		82 19	-05 22
1887 05 29		83 12	-05 22
1887 06 08		84 07	-05 22
1887 06 18		85 03	-05 22
1887 06 28		85 59	-05 23
1887 07 08		86 54	-05 25
1887 07 18		87 47	-05 27
1887 07 28		88 37	-05 30
1887 08 07		89 24	-05 34
1887 08 17	♋	90 07	-05 38
1887 08 27		90 44	-05 43
1887 09 06		91 15	-05 48
1887 09 16		91 39	-05 53
1887 09 26		91 55	-05 59
1887 10 06		92 04	-06 05
1887 10 16		92 04	-06 11
1887 10 26		91 56	-06 16
1887 11 05		91 40	-06 22
1887 11 15		91 17	-06 27
1887 11 25		90 47	-06 31
1887 12 05		90 13	-06 34
1887 12 15	♊	89 34	-06 36
1887 12 25		88 55	-06 38
1888 01 04		88 16	-06 37
1888 01 14		87 40	-06 36
1888 01 24		87 08	-06 34
1888 02 03		86 42	-06 31
1888 02 13		86 24	-06 28
1888 02 23		86 13	-06 23
1888 03 04		86 11	-06 19
1888 03 14		86 16	-06 14
1888 03 24		86 33	-06 10
1888 04 03		86 56	-06 06
1888 04 13		87 27	-06 02
1888 04 23		88 04	-05 58
1888 05 03		88 48	-05 55
1888 05 13		89 36	-05 53
1888 05 23	♋	90 29	-05 51
1888 06 02		91 24	-05 50
1888 06 12		92 22	-05 49
1888 06 22		93 22	-05 49
1888 07 02		94 22	-05 50
1888 07 12		95 21	-05 52
1888 07 22		96 19	-05 54
1888 08 01		97 14	-05 57
1888 08 11		98 07	-06 00
1888 08 21		98 55	-06 04

Date		Long.	Lat.
1888 08 31	♋	99 38	-06 09
1888 09 10		100 15	-06 14
1888 09 20		100 45	-06 20
1888 09 30		101 07	-06 26
1888 10 10		101 21	-06 33
1888 10 20		101 27	-06 39
1888 10 30		101 23	-06 46
1888 11 09		101 11	-06 52
1888 11 19		100 51	-06 58
1888 11 29		100 23	-07 03
1888 12 09		99 49	-07 06
1888 12 19		99 10	-07 09
1888 12 29		98 29	-07 11
1889 01 08		97 48	-07 11
1889 01 18		97 09	-07 10
1889 01 28		96 34	-07 08
1889 02 07		96 04	-07 04
1889 02 17		95 42	-07 00
1889 02 27		95 28	-06 55
1889 03 09		95 23	-06 50
1889 03 19		95 27	-06 45
1889 03 29		95 40	-06 39
1889 04 08		96 01	-06 34
1889 04 18		96 31	-06 29
1889 04 28		97 09	-06 24
1889 05 08		97 53	-06 20
1889 05 18		98 42	-06 17
1889 05 28		99 37	-06 14
1889 06 07		100 35	-06 12
1889 06 17		101 36	-06 11
1889 06 27		102 39	-06 10
1889 07 07		103 44	-06 11
1889 07 17		104 48	-06 12
1889 07 27		105 51	-06 13
1889 08 06		106 53	-06 16
1889 08 16		107 51	-06 19
1889 08 26		108 46	-06 23
1889 09 05		109 36	-06 28
1889 09 15		110 21	-06 33
1889 09 25		110 56	-06 39
1889 10 05		111 28	-06 45
1889 10 15		111 49	-06 52
1889 10 25		112 02	-06 59
1889 11 04		112 05	-07 06
1889 11 14		111 59	-07 13
1889 11 24		111 43	-07 19
1889 12 04		111 19	-07 25
1889 12 14		110 47	-07 29
1889 12 24		110 10	-07 33
1890 01 03		109 28	-07 35
1890 01 13		108 45	-07 36
1890 01 23		108 03	-07 35
1890 02 02		107 24	-07 33
1890 02 12		106 49	-07 29
1890 02 22		106 22	-07 25
1890 03 04		106 03	-07 19
1890 03 14		105 53	-07 13
1890 03 24		105 53	-07 07

Date		Long.	Lat.
1890 04 03	♋	106 03	-07 00
1890 04 13		106 21	-06 54
1890 04 23		106 49	-06 46
1890 05 03		107 25	-06 42
1890 05 13		108 09	-06 37
1890 05 23		108 59	-06 33
1890 06 02		109 55	-06 29
1890 06 12		110 55	-06 26
1890 06 22		112 00	-06 23
1890 07 02		113 07	-06 22
1890 07 12		114 15	-06 21
1890 07 22		115 25	-06 21
1890 08 01		116 34	-06 22
1890 08 11		117 42	-06 24
1890 08 21		118 48	-06 26
1890 08 31		119 50	-06 30
1890 09 10	♌	120 49	-06 34
1890 09 20		121 42	-06 39
1890 09 30		122 26	-06 44
1890 10 10		123 06	-06 50
1890 10 20		123 39	-06 57
1890 10 30		124 00	-07 04
1890 11 09		124 13	-07 11
1890 11 19		124 15	-07 18
1890 11 29		124 06	-07 25
1890 12 09		123 46	-07 31
1890 12 19		123 21	-07 37
1890 12 29		122 47	-07 41
1891 01 08		122 07	-07 44
1891 01 18		121 23	-07 46
1891 01 28		120 38	-07 45
1891 02 07	♋	119 55	-07 43
1891 02 17		119 15	-07 40
1891 02 27		118 42	-07 35
1891 03 09		118 17	-07 29
1891 03 19		118 00	-07 23
1891 03 29		117 54	-07 16
1891 04 08		117 58	-07 08
1891 04 18		118 12	-07 01
1891 04 28		118 36	-06 54
1891 05 08		119 09	-06 47
1891 05 18		119 50	-06 40
1891 05 28		120 40	-06 35
1891 06 07		121 35	-06 29
1891 06 17		122 37	-06 25
1891 06 27		123 43	-06 21
1891 07 07		124 53	-06 19
1891 07 17		126 06	-06 17
1891 07 27		127 20	-06 16
1891 08 06		128 35	-06 15
1891 08 16		129 50	-06 16
1891 08 26		131 03	-06 17
1891 09 05		132 14	-06 19
1891 09 15		133 21	-06 22
1891 09 25		134 24	-06 26
1891 10 05		135 21	-06 30
1891 10 15		136 12	-06 36
1891 10 25		136 54	-06 41

Date		Long.	Lat.
1891 11 04	♌	137 28	-06 48
1891 11 14		137 51	-06 54
1891 11 24		138 05	-07 01
1891 12 04		138 07	-07 08
1891 12 14		137 59	-07 14
1891 12 24		137 40	-07 20
1892 01 03		137 12	-07 25
1892 01 13		136 36	-07 29
1892 01 23		135 54	-07 31
1892 02 02		135 08	-07 31
1892 02 12		134 22	-07 30
1892 02 22		133 38	-07 27
1892 03 03		132 58	-07 23
1892 03 13		132 25	-07 17
1892 03 23		132 00	-07 11
1892 04 02		131 45	-07 03
1892 04 12		131 41	-06 55
1892 04 22		131 47	-06 47
1892 05 02		132 04	-06 39
1892 05 12		132 32	-06 31
1892 05 22		133 09	-06 23
1892 06 01		133 55	-06 16
1892 06 11		134 48	-06 10
1892 06 21		135 49	-06 04
1892 07 01		136 55	-05 59
1892 07 11		138 06	-05 55
1892 07 21		139 21	-05 51
1892 07 31		140 39	-05 49
1892 08 10		141 59	-05 47
1892 08 20		143 19	-05 46
1892 08 30		144 40	-05 45
1892 09 09		145 58	-05 46
1892 09 19		147 15	-05 47
1892 09 29		148 28	-05 49
1892 10 09		149 36	-05 52
1892 10 19	♍	150 38	-05 56
1892 10 29		151 33	-06 00
1892 11 08		152 20	-06 04
1892 11 18		152 57	-06 10
1892 11 28		153 24	-06 15
1892 12 08		153 41	-06 21
1892 12 18		153 46	-06 26
1892 12 28		153 39	-06 32
1893 01 07		153 21	-06 36
1893 01 17		152 54	-06 40
1893 01 27		152 18	-06 43
1893 02 06		151 35	-06 44
1893 02 16		150 49	-06 43
1893 02 26		150 01	-06 41
1893 03 08	♌	149 16	-06 38
1893 03 18		148 35	-06 33
1893 03 28		148 01	-06 27
1893 04 07		147 35	-06 19
1893 04 17		147 20	-06 11
1893 04 27		147 16	-06 03
1893 05 07		147 23	-05 54
1893 05 17		147 41	-05 46
1893 05 27		148 10	-05 38

Chiron

Date		Long.	Lat.
1893 06 06		148 49	-05 30
1893 06 16	♌	149 37	-05 23
1893 06 26	♍	150 33	-05 16
1893 07 06		151 36	-05 10
1893 07 16		152 46	-05 04
1893 07 26		154 01	-05 00
1893 08 05		155 20	-04 55
1893 08 15		156 42	-04 52
1893 08 25		158 06	-04 49
1893 09 04		159 31	-04 47
1893 09 14		160 55	-04 46
1893 09 24		162 19	-04 45
1893 10 04		163 40	-04 45
1893 10 14		164 58	-04 46
1893 10 24		166 11	-04 47
1893 11 03		167 19	-04 49
1893 11 13		168 19	-04 51
1893 11 23		169 11	-04 54
1893 12 03		169 53	-04 57
1893 12 13		170 25	-05 01
1893 12 23		170 45	-05 04
1894 01 02		170 54	-05 08
1894 01 12		170 51	-05 11
1894 01 22		170 36	-05 14
1894 02 01		170 11	-05 16
1894 02 11		169 36	-05 17
1894 02 21		168 54	-05 17
1894 03 03		168 08	-05 15
1894 03 13		167 20	-05 13
1894 03 23		166 34	-05 09
1894 04 02		165 51	-05 04
1894 04 12		165 15	-04 57
1894 04 22		164 48	-04 50
1894 05 02		164 31	-04 43
1894 05 12		164 24	-04 35
1894 05 22		164 30	-04 27
1894 06 01		164 46	-04 19
1894 06 11		165 14	-04 12
1894 06 21		165 52	-04 04
1894 07 01		166 39	-03 58
1894 07 11		167 36	-03 51
1894 07 21		168 39	-03 45
1894 07 31		169 50	-03 40
1894 08 10		171 06	-03 35
1894 08 20		172 26	-03 30
1894 08 30		173 50	-03 27
1894 09 09		175 16	-03 23
1894 09 19		176 44	-03 20
1894 09 29		178 12	-03 18
1894 10 09		179 38	-03 16
1894 10 19	♎	181 03	-03 15
1894 10 29		182 25	-03 14
1894 11 08		183 41	-03 13
1894 11 18		184 53	-03 13
1894 11 28		185 57	-03 13
1894 12 08		186 53	-03 13
1894 12 18		187 40	-03 14
1894 12 28		188 16	-03 15
1895 01 07		188 41	-03 15
1895 01 17		188 54	-03 16
1895 01 27		188 55	-03 17
1895 02 06		188 44	-03 17
1895 02 16		188 21	-03 17
1895 02 26		187 50	-03 16
1895 03 08		187 10	-03 14
1895 03 18		186 25	-03 11
1895 03 28		185 37	-03 08
1895 04 07		184 50	-03 04
1895 04 17		184 06	-02 59
1895 04 27		183 28	-02 54
1895 05 07		182 58	-02 48
1895 05 17		182 37	-02 42
1895 05 27		182 27	-02 36
1895 06 06		182 29	-02 30
1895 06 16		182 42	-02 23
1895 06 26		183 06	-02 17
1895 07 06	♎	183 41	-02 12
1895 07 16		184 25	-02 06
1895 07 26		185 18	-02 01
1895 08 05		186 20	-01 56
1895 08 15		187 28	-01 51
1895 08 25		188 43	-01 47
1895 09 04		190 02	-01 43
1895 09 14		191 25	-01 39
1895 09 24		192 51	-01 36
1895 10 04		194 19	-01 33
1895 10 14		195 46	-01 30
1895 10 24	♎	197 14	-01 27
1895 11 03		198 39	-01 24
1895 11 13		200 02	-01 22
1895 11 23		201 20	-01 20
1895 12 03		202 33	-01 18
1895 12 13		203 39	-01 16
1895 12 23		204 37	-01 14
1896 01 02		205 26	-01 12
1896 01 12		206 05	-01 10
1896 01 22		206 33	-01 08
1896 02 01		206 49	-01 06
1896 02 11		206 53	-01 03
1896 02 21		206 45	-01 01
1896 03 02		206 27	-00 58
1896 03 12		205 58	-00 55
1896 03 22		205 21	-00 52
1896 04 01		204 38	-00 49
1896 04 11		203 51	-00 45
1896 04 21		203 05	-00 41
1896 05 01		202 20	-00 37
1896 05 11		201 40	-00 33
1896 05 21		201 07	-00 29
1896 05 31		200 43	-00 25
1896 06 10		200 30	-00 21
1896 06 20		200 27	-00 17
1896 06 30		200 35	-00 13
1896 07 10		200 54	-00 10
1896 07 20		201 24	-00 06
1896 07 30		202 04	-00 03
1896 08 09		202 52	+00 01
1896 08 19		203 50	+00 04
1896 08 29		204 54	+00 07
1896 09 08		206 05	+00 10
1896 09 18		207 20	+00 13
1896 09 28		208 40	+00 15
1896 10 08	♏	210 03	+00 18
1896 10 18		211 28	+00 21
1896 10 28		212 53	+00 24
1896 11 07		214 19	+00 27
1896 11 17		215 42	+00 30
1896 11 27		217 03	+00 33
1896 12 07		218 20	+00 37
1896 12 17		219 31	+00 40
1896 12 27		220 36	+00 44
1897 01 06		221 34	+00 47
1897 01 16		222 22	+00 51
1897 01 26		223 01	+00 55
1897 02 05		223 30	+01 00
1897 02 15		223 47	+01 04
1897 02 25		223 53	+01 09
1897 03 07		223 47	+01 13
1897 03 17		223 30	+01 18
1897 03 27		223 04	+01 22
1897 04 06		222 29	+01 27
1897 04 16		221 48	+01 31
1897 04 26		221 04	+01 35
1897 05 06		220 18	+01 38
1897 05 16		219 33	+01 41
1897 05 26		218 53	+01 44
1897 06 05		218 19	+01 46
1897 06 15		217 52	+01 48
1897 06 25		217 36	+01 50
1897 07 05		217 29	+01 51
1897 07 15		217 33	+01 52
1897 07 25		217 47	+01 53
1897 08 04		218 12	+01 54
1897 08 14		218 47	+01 55
1897 08 24		219 31	+01 56
1897 09 03		220 23	+01 57
1897 09 13		221 23	+01 58
1897 09 23		222 29	+01 59
1897 10 03	♏	223 40	+02 01
1897 10 13		224 55	+02 02
1897 10 23		226 13	+02 04
1897 11 02		227 34	+02 06
1897 11 12		228 55	+02 09
1897 11 22		230 16	+02 11
1897 12 02		231 35	+02 15
1897 12 12		232 52	+02 18
1897 12 22		234 05	+02 22
1898 01 01		235 13	+02 26
1898 01 11		236 14	+02 30
1898 01 21		237 09	+02 35
1898 01 31		237 55	+02 41
1898 02 10		238 31	+02 46
1898 02 20		238 58	+02 52
1898 03 02		239 13	+02 58
1898 03 12		239 18	+03 04
1898 03 22		239 12	+03 09
1898 04 01		238 56	+03 15
1898 04 11		238 31	+03 21
1898 04 21		237 58	+03 25
1898 05 01		237 19	+03 30
1898 05 11		236 36	+03 33
1898 05 21		235 51	+03 36
1898 05 31		235 08	+03 38
1898 06 10		234 28	+03 40
1898 06 20	♏	233 54	+03 40
1898 06 30		233 27	+03 40
1898 07 10		233 09	+03 40
1898 07 20		233 00	+03 39
1898 07 30		233 01	+03 38
1898 08 09		233 13	+03 36
1898 08 19		233 34	+03 35
1898 08 29		234 05	+03 34
1898 09 08		234 45	+03 33
1898 09 18		235 32	+03 32
1898 09 28		236 27	+03 31
1898 10 08		237 28	+03 31
1898 10 18		238 34	+03 31
1898 10 28		239 45	+03 31
1898 11 07	♐	240 58	+03 32
1898 11 17		242 14	+03 33
1898 11 27		243 30	+03 35
1898 12 07		244 45	+03 38
1898 12 17		246 00	+03 41
1898 12 27		247 11	+03 44
1899 01 06		248 19	+03 48
1899 01 16		249 21	+03 52
1899 01 26		250 18	+03 57
1899 02 05		251 07	+04 03
1899 02 15		251 48	+04 09
1899 02 25		252 20	+04 15
1899 03 07		252 43	+04 21
1899 03 17		252 56	+04 28
1899 03 27		252 58	+04 34
1899 04 06		252 50	+04 41
1899 04 16		252 33	+04 47
1899 04 26		252 07	+04 52
1899 05 06		251 35	+04 57
1899 05 16		250 56	+05 01
1899 05 26		250 15	+05 05
1899 06 05		249 32	+05 07
1899 06 15		248 51	+05 08
1899 06 25		248 13	+05 08
1899 07 05		247 40	+05 07
1899 07 15		247 14	+05 05
1899 07 25		246 56	+05 03
1899 08 04		246 47	+05 01
1899 08 14		246 47	+04 58
1899 08 24		246 57	+04 55
1899 09 03		247 17	+04 52
1899 09 13		247 45	+04 49
1899 09 23		248 22	+04 46
1899 10 03		249 07	+04 44
1899 10 13		249 58	+04 42
1899 10 23		250 55	+04 40
1899 11 02		251 57	+04 39
1899 11 12		253 03	+04 39
1899 11 22		254 12	+04 39
1899 12 02		255 22	+04 40
1899 12 12		256 33	+04 41
1899 12 22		257 43	+04 43
1900 01 01	♐	258 51	+04 46
1900 01 11		259 57	+04 49
1900 01 21		260 59	+04 53
1900 01 31		261 55	+04 58
1900 02 10		262 45	+05 03
1900 02 20		263 29	+05 08
1900 03 02		264 04	+05 15
1900 03 12		264 31	+05 21
1900 03 22		264 48	+05 28
1900 04 01		264 56	+05 34
1900 04 11		264 55	+05 41
1900 04 21		264 44	+05 47
1900 05 01		264 25	+05 53
1900 05 11		263 58	+05 58
1900 05 21		263 25	+06 03
1900 05 31		262 47	+06 06
1900 06 10		262 07	+06 09
1900 06 20		261 26	+06 10
1900 06 30		260 47	+06 10
1900 07 10		260 11	+06 09
1900 07 20		259 40	+06 07
1900 07 30		259 16	+06 04
1900 08 09		259 00	+06 01
1900 08 19		258 53	+05 57
1900 08 29		258 54	+05 53
1900 09 08		259 04	+05 49
1900 09 18		259 23	+05 44
1900 09 28		259 51	+05 40
1900 10 08		260 27	+05 37
1900 10 18		261 09	+05 34
1900 10 28		261 58	+05 31
1900 11 07		262 53	+05 29
1900 11 17		263 52	+05 27
1900 11 27		264 54	+05 26
1900 12 07		265 58	+05 26
1900 12 17		267 04	+05 27
1900 12 27		268 09	+05 28
1901 01 06		269 14	+05 30
1901 01 16	♑	270 17	+05 32
1901 01 26	♑	271 16	+05 36
1901 02 05		272 11	+05 40
1901 02 15		273 01	+05 44
1901 02 25		273 45	+05 49
1901 03 07		274 22	+05 55
1901 03 17		274 51	+06 01
1901 03 27		275 11	+06 07
1901 04 06		275 23	+06 14
1901 04 16		275 26	+06 20
1901 04 26		275 20	+06 27
1901 05 06		275 05	+06 33
1901 05 16		274 43	+06 38
1901 05 26		274 15	+06 43
1901 06 05		273 41	+06 46
1901 06 15		273 04	+06 49
1901 06 25		272 25	+06 50
1901 07 05		271 46	+06 50
1901 07 15		271 09	+06 50
1901 07 25		270 36	+06 48
1901 08 04		270 09	+06 45
1901 08 14	♐	269 48	+06 41
1901 08 24		269 35	+06 37
1901 09 03		269 30	+06 32
1901 09 13		269 33	+06 27
1901 09 23		269 45	+06 22
1901 10 03	♑	270 05	+06 18
1901 10 13		270 34	+06 13
1901 10 23		271 09	+06 09
1901 11 02		271 51	+06 06
1901 11 12		272 39	+06 03
1901 11 22		273 31	+06 00
1901 12 02		274 27	+05 58
1901 12 12		275 26	+05 57
1901 12 22		276 27	+05 57
1902 01 01		277 28	+05 58
1902 01 11		278 29	+05 59
1902 01 21		279 28	+06 01
1902 01 31		280 25	+06 03
1902 02 10		281 18	+06 07
1902 02 20		282 07	+06 11
1902 03 02		282 50	+06 15
1902 03 12		283 27	+06 20
1902 03 22		283 57	+06 26
1902 04 01		284 19	+06 32
1902 04 11		284 33	+06 38
1902 04 21		284 39	+06 44
1902 05 01		284 36	+06 50
1902 05 11		284 25	+06 56
1902 05 21		284 07	+07 01
1902 05 31		283 42	+07 06
1902 06 10		283 12	+07 10
1902 06 20		282 38	+07 12
1902 06 30		282 01	+07 14
1902 07 10		281 23	+07 14
1902 07 20		280 47	+07 14
1902 07 30		280 13	+07 12
1902 08 09		279 43	+07 09
1902 08 19		279 20	+07 05
1902 08 29		279 03	+07 01
1902 09 08		278 53	+06 56
1902 09 18		278 52	+06 51
1902 09 28		278 58	+06 46
1902 10 08		279 13	+06 41
1902 10 18		279 35	+06 36
1902 10 28		280 05	+06 31
1902 11 07		280 41	+06 27
1902 11 17		281 23	+06 24
1902 11 27		282 10	+06 21
1902 12 07		283 01	+06 18
1902 12 17		283 55	+06 17
1902 12 27		284 52	+06 16
1903 01 06		285 49	+06 16
1903 01 16		286 46	+06 16
1903 01 26		287 42	+06 18
1903 02 05		288 36	+06 20
1903 02 15		289 27	+06 23
1903 02 25		290 14	+06 26
1903 03 07		290 56	+06 30
1903 03 17		291 33	+06 35
1903 03 27		292 03	+06 40
1903 04 06		292 25	+06 45
1903 04 16		292 41	+06 51
1903 04 26		292 48	+06 57
1903 05 06		292 48	+07 02
1903 05 16		292 40	+07 08
1903 05 26		292 24	+07 13
1903 06 05		292 02	+07 17
1903 06 15		291 35	+07 21
1903 06 25		291 03	+07 24
1903 07 05		290 28	+07 25
1903 07 15		289 52	+07 26
1903 07 25		289 16	+07 25
1903 08 04		288 43	+07 24
1903 08 14		288 12	+07 21
1903 08 24		287 47	+07 18
1903 09 03		287 28	+07 13

1903 09 13	♑	287 15	+07 09
1903 09 23		287 10	+07 03
1903 10 03		287 13	+06 58
1903 10 13		287 23	+06 53
1903 10 23		287 41	+06 48
1903 11 02		288 06	+06 43
1903 11 12		288 38	+06 39
1903 11 22		289 15	+06 35
1903 12 02		289 58	+06 31
1903 12 12		290 44	+06 29
1903 12 22		291 34	+06 27
1904 01 01		292 27	+06 25
1904 01 11		293 20	+06 25
1904 01 21		294 14	+06 25
1904 01 31		295 07	+06 26
1904 02 10		295 59	+06 28
1904 02 20		296 47	+06 30
1904 03 01		297 33	+06 33
1904 03 11		298 13	+06 37
1904 03 21		298 49	+06 41
1904 03 31		299 18	+06 45
1904 04 10		299 41	+06 50
1904 04 20		299 57	+06 55
1904 04 30	♒	300 06	+07 01
1904 05 10		300 07	+07 06
1904 05 20		300 01	+07 11
1904 05 30	♑	299 47	+07 16
1904 06 09		299 28	+07 20
1904 06 19		299 02	+07 24
1904 06 29	♑	298 32	+07 26
1904 07 09		298 00	+07 28
1904 07 19		297 25	+07 29
1904 07 29		296 50	+07 28
1904 08 08		296 17	+07 27
1904 08 18		295 47	+07 24
1904 08 28		295 20	+07 21
1904 09 07		295 00	+07 17
1904 09 17		294 45	+07 12
1904 09 27		294 38	+07 07
1904 10 07		294 38	+07 02
1904 10 17		294 45	+06 57
1904 10 27		294 59	+06 52
1904 11 06		295 21	+06 47
1904 11 16		295 49	+06 42
1904 11 26		296 22	+06 38
1904 12 06		297 01	+06 35
1904 12 16		297 44	+06 32
1904 12 26		298 31	+06 30
1905 01 05		299 20	+06 28
1905 01 15	♒	300 10	+06 27
1905 01 25		301 01	+06 27
1905 02 04		301 52	+06 28
1905 02 14		302 41	+06 29
1905 02 24		303 27	+06 31
1905 03 06		304 11	+06 33
1905 03 16		304 50	+06 37
1905 03 26		305 24	+06 40
1905 04 05		305 53	+06 45
1905 04 15		306 16	+06 49
1905 04 25		306 32	+06 54
1905 05 05		306 41	+06 59
1905 05 15		306 43	+07 04
1905 05 25		306 38	+07 08
1905 06 04		306 26	+07 13
1905 06 14		306 08	+07 17
1905 06 24		305 44	+07 20
1905 07 04		305 16	+07 23
1905 07 14		304 45	+07 24
1905 07 24		304 12	+07 25
1905 08 03		303 38	+07 25
1905 08 13		303 06	+07 23
1905 08 23		302 35	+07 21
1905 09 02		302 09	+07 18
1905 09 12		301 47	+07 14
1905 09 22		301 32	+07 10
1905 10 02		301 23	+07 05
1905 10 12		301 20	+07 00
1905 10 22		301 25	+06 55
1905 11 01		301 37	+06 50
1905 11 11		301 56	+06 45
1905 11 21		302 21	+06 40
1905 12 01		302 52	+06 36
1905 12 11		303 28	+06 33
1905 12 21		304 08	+06 30
1905 12 31		304 52	+06 27
1906 01 10		305 38	+06 26
1906 01 20		306 26	+06 24
1906 01 30		307 14	+06 24
1906 02 09		308 02	+06 24
1906 02 19		308 49	+06 25
1906 03 01		309 33	+06 27
1906 03 11		310 15	+06 29
1906 03 21		310 53	+06 32
1906 03 31		311 26	+06 35
1906 04 10		311 54	+06 39
1906 04 20		312 16	+06 43
1906 04 30	♒	312 32	+06 48
1906 05 10		312 41	+06 52
1906 05 20		312 44	+06 57
1906 05 30		312 39	+07 01
1906 06 09		312 29	+07 05
1906 06 19		312 12	+07 09
1906 06 29		311 50	+07 12
1906 07 09		311 23	+07 14
1906 07 19		310 53	+07 16
1906 07 29		310 21	+07 17
1906 08 08		309 48	+07 16
1906 08 18		309 16	+07 15
1906 08 28		308 47	+07 13
1906 09 07		308 20	+07 10
1906 09 17		307 56	+07 06
1906 09 27	♒	307 42	+07 02
1906 10 07		307 32	+06 58
1906 10 17		307 28	+06 53
1906 10 27		307 32	+06 48
1906 11 06		307 42	+06 43
1906 11 16		307 58	+06 38
1906 11 26		308 21	+06 34
1906 12 06		308 50	+06 30
1906 12 16		309 24	+06 26
1906 12 26		310 01	+06 23
1907 01 05		310 43	+06 21
1907 01 15		311 26	+06 19
1907 01 25		312 12	+06 18
1907 02 04		312 58	+06 17
1907 02 14		313 44	+06 17
1907 02 24		314 29	+06 18
1907 03 06		315 12	+06 19
1907 03 16		315 52	+06 21
1907 03 26		316 28	+06 24
1907 04 05		317 00	+06 27
1907 04 15		317 27	+06 30
1907 04 25		317 49	+06 34
1907 05 05		318 04	+06 38
1907 05 15		318 13	+06 42
1907 05 25		318 16	+06 46
1907 06 04		318 12	+06 50
1907 06 14		318 02	+06 54
1907 06 24		317 46	+06 56
1907 07 04		317 25	+07 00
1907 07 14		316 59	+07 03
1907 07 24		316 30	+07 04
1907 08 03		315 59	+07 05
1907 08 13		315 27	+07 04
1907 08 23		314 56	+07 03
1907 09 02		314 27	+07 01
1907 09 12		314 01	+06 56
1907 09 22		313 39	+06 55
1907 10 02		313 22	+06 51
1907 10 12		313 12	+06 47
1907 10 22		313 07	+06 42
1907 11 01		313 09	+06 37
1907 11 11		313 18	+06 33
1907 11 21		313 33	+06 28
1907 12 01		313 55	+06 24
1907 12 11		314 21	+06 20
1907 12 21		314 53	+06 16
1907 12 31		315 29	+06 13
1908 01 10		316 08	+06 11
1908 01 20		316 50	+06 09
1908 01 30		317 34	+06 08
1908 02 09		318 18	+06 07
1908 02 19		319 02	+06 07
1908 02 29		319 45	+06 08
1908 03 10		320 26	+06 09
1908 03 20		321 05	+06 11
1908 03 30		321 40	+06 13
1908 04 09		322 11	+06 16
1908 04 19		322 37	+06 19
1908 04 29		322 57	+06 22
1908 05 09		323 12	+06 26
1908 05 19		323 21	+06 30
1908 05 29		323 24	+06 33
1908 06 08		323 20	+06 37
1908 06 18		323 10	+06 41
1908 06 28		322 55	+06 44
1908 07 08		322 35	+06 46
1908 07 18		322 10	+06 48
1908 07 28		321 42	+06 50
1908 08 07		321 12	+06 50
1908 08 17		320 41	+06 50
1908 08 27		320 10	+06 49
1908 09 06		319 42	+06 47
1908 09 16		319 16	+06 44
1908 09 26		318 54	+06 41
1908 10 06		318 37	+06 37
1908 10 16		318 26	+06 33
1908 10 26		318 21	+06 29
1908 11 05		318 23	+06 24
1908 11 15		318 31	+06 20
1908 11 25		318 45	+06 15
1908 12 05		319 05	+06 11
1908 12 15		319 30	+06 07
1908 12 25	♒	320 01	+06 04
1909 01 04		320 35	+06 01
1909 01 14		321 13	+05 59
1909 01 24		321 53	+05 57
1909 02 03		322 35	+05 56
1909 02 13		323 18	+05 55
1909 02 23		324 00	+05 55
1909 03 05		324 42	+05 55
1909 03 15		325 21	+05 56
1909 03 25		325 58	+05 58
1909 04 04		326 32	+06 00
1909 04 14		327 02	+06 02
1909 04 24		327 27	+06 05
1909 05 04		327 47	+06 08
1909 05 14		328 01	+06 12
1909 05 24		328 10	+06 15
1909 06 03		328 12	+06 19
1909 06 13		328 08	+06 22
1909 06 23		327 59	+06 25
1909 07 03		327 44	+06 28
1909 07 13		327 24	+06 30
1909 07 23		327 00	+06 32
1909 08 02		326 33	+06 33
1909 08 12		326 03	+06 34
1909 08 22		325 33	+06 33
1909 09 01		325 03	+06 32
1909 09 11		324 35	+06 30
1909 09 21		324 10	+06 28
1909 10 01		323 48	+06 25
1909 10 11		323 32	+06 21
1909 10 21		323 21	+06 17
1909 10 31		323 16	+06 13
1909 11 10		323 17	+06 09
1909 11 20		323 24	+06 04
1909 11 30		323 37	+06 00
1909 12 10		323 56	+05 56
1909 12 20		324 21	+05 53
1909 12 30		324 50	+05 50
1910 01 09		325 23	+05 47
1910 01 19		326 00	+05 45
1910 01 29		326 39	+05 43
1910 02 08		327 19	+05 42
1910 02 18		328 00	+05 41
1910 02 28		328 41	+05 41
1910 03 10		329 22	+05 41
1910 03 20		330 00	+05 42
1910 03 30	♓	330 36	+05 43
1910 04 09		331 08	+05 45
1910 04 19		331 37	+05 47
1910 04 29		332 01	+05 50
1910 05 09		332 20	+05 53
1910 05 19		332 34	+05 56
1910 05 29		332 42	+05 59
1910 06 08		332 44	+06 02
1910 06 18		332 40	+06 05
1910 06 28		332 31	+06 08
1910 07 08		332 16	+06 11
1910 07 18		331 56	+06 13
1910 07 28		331 33	+06 14
1910 08 07		331 06	+06 15
1910 08 17		330 37	+06 16
1910 08 27		330 08	+06 15
1910 09 06	♒	329 39	+06 14
1910 09 16		329 11	+06 12
1910 09 26		328 46	+06 10
1910 10 06		328 25	+06 07
1910 10 16		328 09	+06 04
1910 10 26		327 58	+06 00
1910 11 05		327 53	+05 56
1910 11 15		327 54	+05 52
1910 11 25		328 01	+05 48
1910 12 05		328 13	+05 44
1910 12 15		328 32	+05 40
1910 12 25		328 56	+05 37
1911 01 04	♒	329 24	+05 34
1911 01 14		329 56	+05 31
1911 01 24	♓	330 32	+05 29
1911 02 03		331 10	+05 27
1911 02 13		331 49	+05 26
1911 02 23		332 29	+05 25
1911 03 05		333 09	+05 25
1911 03 15		333 48	+05 26
1911 03 25		334 25	+05 26
1911 04 04		335 00	+05 28
1911 04 14		335 31	+05 29
1911 04 24		335 59	+05 31
1911 05 04		336 22	+05 33
1911 05 14		336 40	+05 36
1911 05 24		336 53	+05 39
1911 06 03		337 01	+05 42
1911 06 13		337 02	+05 45
1911 06 23		336 58	+05 47
1911 07 03		336 49	+05 50
1911 07 13		336 34	+05 52
1911 07 23		336 15	+05 54
1911 08 02	♓	335 51	+05 55
1911 08 12		335 25	+05 56
1911 08 22		334 57	+05 56
1911 09 01		334 28	+05 56
1911 09 11		333 59	+05 55
1911 09 21		333 32	+05 53
1911 10 01		333 08	+05 51
1911 10 11		332 47	+05 48
1911 10 21		332 31	+05 45
1911 10 31		332 21	+05 41
1911 11 10		332 16	+05 37
1911 11 20		332 16	+05 34
1911 11 30		332 23	+05 30
1911 12 10		332 36	+05 26
1911 12 20		332 54	+05 23
1911 12 30		333 18	+05 19
1912 01 09		333 45	+05 17
1912 01 19		334 17	+05 14
1912 01 29		334 51	+05 12
1912 02 08		335 28	+05 10
1912 02 18		336 07	+05 09
1912 02 28		336 46	+05 09
1912 03 09		337 24	+05 08
1912 03 19		338 02	+05 09
1912 03 29		338 38	+05 09
1912 04 08		339 12	+05 10
1912 04 18		339 43	+05 12
1912 04 28		340 09	+05 14
1912 05 08		340 32	+05 16
1912 05 18		340 49	+05 18
1912 05 28		341 01	+05 21
1912 06 07		341 08	+05 23
1912 06 17		341 10	+05 26
1912 06 27		341 05	+05 28
1912 07 07		340 55	+05 31
1912 07 17		340 41	+05 33
1912 07 27		340 21	+05 34
1912 08 06		339 58	+05 36
1912 08 16		339 32	+05 36
1912 08 26		339 04	+05 36
1912 09 05		338 36	+05 36
1912 09 15		338 08	+05 35
1912 09 25		337 41	+05 33
1912 10 05		337 18	+05 31
1912 10 15		336 57	+05 28
1912 10 25		336 42	+05 25
1912 11 04		336 31	+05 22
1912 11 14		336 27	+05 18
1912 11 24		336 28	+05 14
1912 12 04		336 35	+05 11
1912 12 14		336 47	+05 07
1912 12 24		337 05	+05 04
1913 01 03		337 28	+05 01
1913 01 13	♓	337 56	+04 58
1913 01 23		338 27	+04 56
1913 02 02		339 00	+04 54
1913 02 12		339 37	+04 53
1913 02 22		340 14	+04 52
1913 03 04		340 52	+04 51
1913 03 14		341 30	+04 51
1913 03 24		342 07	+04 51
1913 04 03		342 42	+04 52
1913 04 13		343 15	+04 52
1913 04 23		343 45	+04 54
1913 05 03		344 10	+04 55
1913 05 13		344 32	+04 57
1913 05 23		344 49	+04 59
1913 06 02		345 00	+05 02
1913 06 12		345 07	+05 04
1913 06 22		345 07	+05 06
1913 07 02		345 03	+05 09
1913 07 12		344 53	+05 11
1913 07 22		344 38	+05 12
1913 08 01		344 18	+05 14
1913 08 11		343 55	+05 15
1913 08 21		343 30	+05 15
1913 08 31		343 02	+05 15
1913 09 10		342 34	+05 15
1913 09 20		342 06	+05 14
1913 09 30		341 40	+05 12
1913 10 10		341 17	+05 10
1913 10 20		340 57	+05 07
1913 10 30		340 42	+05 04
1913 11 09		340 32	+05 01
1913 11 19		340 28	+04 58
1913 11 29		340 29	+04 54
1913 12 09		340 36	+04 51
1913 12 19		340 49	+04 48

Chiron

Chiron

1913	12	29	♓	341	07	+04	45
1914	01	08		341	30	+04	42
1914	01	18		341	57	+04	40
1914	01	28		342	27	+04	37
1914	02	07		343	01	+04	36
1914	02	17		343	37	+04	34
1914	02	27		344	13	+04	33
1914	03	09		344	51	+04	32
1914	03	19		345	28	+04	32
1914	03	29		346	04	+04	32
1914	04	08		346	38	+04	33
1914	04	18		347	10	+04	34
1914	04	28		347	39	+04	35
1914	05	08		348	04	+04	36
1914	05	18		348	25	+04	38
1914	05	28		348	41	+04	40
1914	06	07		348	52	+04	42
1914	06	17		348	57	+04	44
1914	06	27		348	57	+04	46
1914	07	07		348	52	+04	48
1914	07	17		348	42	+04	50
1914	07	27		348	27	+04	51
1914	08	06		348	07	+04	53
1914	08	16		347	44	+04	54
1914	08	26		347	19	+04	54
1914	09	05		346	52	+04	54
1914	09	15		346	24	+04	53
1914	09	25		345	56	+04	52
1914	10	05		345	31	+04	50
1914	10	15		345	08	+04	48
1914	10	25		344	49	+04	46
1914	11	04		344	34	+04	43
1914	11	14		344	25	+04	40
1914	11	24		344	21	+04	37
1914	12	04		344	23	+04	34
1914	12	14		344	30	+04	31
1914	12	24		344	43	+04	28
1915	01	03		345	01	+04	25
1915	01	13		345	24	+04	22
1915	01	23		345	51	+04	20
1915	02	02		346	21	+04	18
1915	02	12		346	54	+04	16
1915	02	22		347	29	+04	15
1915	03	04		348	06	+04	14
1915	03	14		348	43	+04	13
1915	03	24		349	19	+04	13
1915	04	03		349	54	+04	13
1915	04	13	♓	350	28	+04	14
1915	04	23		350	59	+04	14
1915	05	03		351	27	+04	15
1915	05	13		351	51	+04	17
1915	05	23		352	11	+04	18
1915	06	02		352	26	+04	20
1915	06	12		352	37	+04	22
1915	06	22		352	42	+04	23
1915	07	02		352	41	+04	25
1915	07	12		352	36	+04	27
1915	07	22		352	25	+04	29
1915	08	01		352	10	+04	30
1915	08	11		351	50	+04	31
1915	08	21		351	27	+04	32
1915	08	31		351	01	+04	32
1915	09	10		350	34	+04	32
1915	09	20		350	07	+04	31
1915	09	30		349	40	+04	30
1915	10	10		349	15	+04	28
1915	10	20		348	52	+04	26
1915	10	30		348	34	+04	24
1915	11	09		348	20	+04	21
1915	11	19		348	11	+04	18
1915	11	29		348	07	+04	16
1915	12	09		348	09	+04	13
1915	12	19		348	17	+04	10
1915	12	29		348	30	+04	07
1916	01	08		348	49	+04	04
1916	01	18		349	12	+04	02
1916	01	28		349	38	+04	00
1916	02	07		350	09	+03	58
1916	02	17		350	42	+03	56
1916	02	27		351	16	+03	55
1916	03	08		351	52	+03	54
1916	03	18		352	29	+03	53
1916	03	28		353	05	+03	53
1916	04	07		353	39	+03	53
1916	04	17		354	12	+03	54
1916	04	27		354	43	+03	54
1916	05	07		355	10	+03	55
1916	05	17		355	33	+03	56

1916	05	27	♓	355	52	+03	58
1916	06	06		356	07	+03	59
1916	06	16		356	17	+04	01
1916	06	26		356	21	+04	02
1916	07	06		356	20	+04	04
1916	07	16		356	14	+04	05
1916	07	26		356	03	+04	07
1916	08	05		355	47	+04	08
1916	08	15		355	27	+04	09
1916	08	25		355	04	+04	09
1916	09	04		354	39	+04	09
1916	09	14		354	12	+04	09
1916	09	24		353	44	+04	08
1916	10	04		353	18	+04	07
1916	10	14		352	53	+04	05
1916	10	24		352	31	+04	04
1916	11	03		352	13	+04	01
1916	11	13		352	00	+03	59
1916	11	23		351	51	+03	56
1916	12	03		351	48	+03	53
1916	12	13		351	51	+03	51
1916	12	23		351	59	+03	48
1917	01	02		352	13	+03	45
1917	01	12		352	31	+03	43
1917	01	22		352	54	+03	41
1917	02	01		353	21	+03	39
1917	02	11		353	51	+03	37
1917	02	21		354	24	+03	36
1917	03	03		354	59	+03	34
1917	03	13		355	34	+03	33
1917	03	23		356	10	+03	33
1917	04	02		356	46	+03	33
1917	04	12		357	20	+03	33
1917	04	22		357	52	+03	33
1917	05	02		358	22	+03	34
1917	05	12		358	49	+03	34
1917	05	22		359	11	+03	35
1917	06	01		359	30	+03	36
1917	06	11		359	44	+03	38
1917	06	21		359	53	+03	39
1917	07	01		359	56	+03	40
1917	07	11	♓	359	55	+03	42
1917	07	21		359	48	+03	43
1917	07	31		359	37	+03	44
1917	08	10		359	21	+03	45
1917	08	20		359	00	+03	46
1917	08	30		358	37	+03	46
1917	09	09		358	11	+03	46
1917	09	19		357	45	+03	46
1917	09	29		357	17	+03	45
1917	10	09		356	51	+03	44
1917	10	19		356	27	+03	42
1917	10	29		356	05	+03	40
1917	11	08		355	48	+03	38
1917	11	18		355	35	+03	36
1917	11	28		355	27	+03	34
1917	12	08		355	25	+03	31
1917	12	18		355	28	+03	28
1917	12	28		355	37	+03	26
1918	01	07		355	51	+03	24
1918	01	17		356	10	+03	21
1918	01	27		356	33	+03	19
1918	02	06		357	00	+03	17
1918	02	16		357	30	+03	16
1918	02	26		358	03	+03	14
1918	03	08		358	38	+03	13
1918	03	18		359	13	+03	12
1918	03	28		359	49	+03	12
1918	04	07	♈	0	24	+03	12
1918	04	17		0	57	+03	12
1918	04	27		1	29	+03	12
1918	05	07		1	58	+03	12
1918	05	17		2	24	+03	13
1918	05	27		2	46	+03	14
1918	06	06		3	04	+03	15
1918	06	16		3	18	+03	16
1918	06	26		3	26	+03	17
1918	07	06		3	29	+03	18
1918	07	16		3	27	+03	19
1918	07	26		3	20	+03	20
1918	08	05		3	08	+03	21
1918	08	15		2	51	+03	22
1918	08	25		2	30	+03	22
1918	09	04		2	07	+03	23
1918	09	14		1	41	+03	22
1918	09	24		1	14	+03	22
1918	10	04		0	47	+03	21
1918	10	14		0	21	+03	20
1918	10	24	♓	359	57	+03	18
1918	11	03		359	36	+03	17
1918	11	13		359	19	+03	15
1918	11	23		359	07	+03	13
1918	12	03		359	00	+03	10
1918	12	13		358	58	+03	08
1918	12	23		359	02	+03	06

1919	01	02	♓	359	11	+03	03
1919	01	12		359	26	+03	01
1919	01	22		359	45	+02	59
1919	02	01	♈	0	09	+02	57
1919	02	11		0	36	+02	55
1919	02	21		1	07	+02	54
1919	03	03		1	39	+02	53
1919	03	13		2	14	+02	52
1919	03	23		2	49	+02	51
1919	04	02		3	24	+02	50
1919	04	12		3	59	+02	50
1919	04	22		4	32	+02	50
1919	05	02		5	04	+02	50
1919	05	12		5	37	+02	51
1919	05	22		5	58	+02	51
1919	06	01		6	19	+02	52
1919	06	11		6	37	+02	52
1919	06	21		6	49	+02	53
1919	07	01		6	57	+02	54
1919	07	11		6	59	+02	55
1919	07	21		6	57	+02	56
1919	07	31		6	49	+02	57
1919	08	10		6	36	+02	58
1919	08	20		6	19	+02	58
1919	08	30		5	59	+02	58
1919	09	09		5	35	+02	58
1919	09	19		5	09	+02	58
1919	09	29		4	42	+02	58
1919	10	09	♈	4	15	+02	57
1919	10	19		3	49	+02	56
1919	10	29		3	25	+02	54
1919	11	08		3	05	+02	53
1919	11	18		2	49	+02	51
1919	11	28		2	37	+02	49
1919	12	08		2	30	+02	47
1919	12	18		2	29	+02	44
1919	12	28		2	34	+02	42
1920	01	07		2	44	+02	40
1920	01	17		2	59	+02	38
1920	01	27		3	18	+02	36
1920	02	06		3	43	+02	35
1920	02	16		4	10	+02	33
1920	02	26		4	41	+02	32
1920	03	07		5	14	+02	31
1920	03	17		5	48	+02	30
1920	03	27		6	23	+02	29
1920	04	06		6	59	+02	28
1920	04	16		7	33	+02	28
1920	04	26		8	06	+02	28
1920	05	06		8	37	+02	28
1920	05	16		9	05	+02	28
1920	05	26		9	30	+02	28
1920	06	05		9	51	+02	29
1920	06	15		10	08	+02	30
1920	06	25		10	20	+02	30
1920	07	05		10	27	+02	31
1920	07	15		10	29	+02	32
1920	07	25		10	26	+02	32
1920	08	04		10	18	+02	33
1920	08	14		10	04	+02	33
1920	08	24		9	47	+02	34
1920	09	03		9	26	+02	34
1920	09	13		9	02	+02	34
1920	09	23		8	35	+02	33
1920	10	03		8	08	+02	33
1920	10	13		7	41	+02	32
1920	10	23		7	16	+02	31
1920	11	02		6	52	+02	29
1920	11	12		6	32	+02	28
1920	11	22		6	17	+02	26
1920	12	02		6	05	+02	24
1920	12	12		6	00	+02	22
1920	12	22		5	59	+02	20
1921	01	01		6	04	+02	18
1921	01	11		6	15	+02	17
1921	01	21		6	31	+02	15
1921	01	31		6	51	+02	13
1921	02	10		7	15	+02	12
1921	02	20		7	44	+02	10
1921	03	02		8	15	+02	09
1921	03	12		8	48	+02	08
1921	03	22		9	22	+02	07
1921	04	01		9	57	+02	06
1921	04	11		10	33	+02	06
1921	04	21		11	07	+02	05
1921	05	01		11	40	+02	05
1921	05	11		12	10	+02	05
1921	05	21		12	38	+02	05
1921	05	31		13	03	+02	05
1921	06	10		13	23	+02	06
1921	06	20		13	40	+02	06
1921	06	30		13	51	+02	07
1921	07	10		13	58	+02	07
1921	07	20		13	59	+02	07
1921	07	30		13	55	+02	08

1921	08	09	♈	13	46	+02	08
1921	08	19		13	32	+02	09
1921	08	29		13	14	+02	09
1921	09	08		12	53	+02	09
1921	09	18		12	28	+02	08
1921	09	28		12	02	+02	08
1921	10	08		11	35	+02	07
1921	10	18		11	08	+02	06
1921	10	28		10	42	+02	05
1921	11	07		10	19	+02	04
1921	11	17		10	00	+02	03
1921	11	27		9	44	+02	01
1921	12	07		9	34	+01	59
1921	12	17		9	29	+01	58
1921	12	27		9	29	+01	56
1922	01	06	♈	9	35	+01	54
1922	01	16		9	46	+01	52
1922	01	26		10	02	+01	51
1922	02	05		10	23	+01	49
1922	02	15		10	49	+01	48
1922	02	25		11	17	+01	47
1922	03	07		11	48	+01	46
1922	03	17		12	22	+01	45
1922	03	27		12	57	+01	44
1922	04	06		13	32	+01	43
1922	04	16		14	07	+01	42
1922	04	26		14	41	+01	42
1922	05	06		15	14	+01	42
1922	05	16		15	44	+01	42
1922	05	26		16	12	+01	42
1922	06	05		16	36	+01	42
1922	06	15		16	56	+01	42
1922	06	25		17	12	+01	42
1922	07	05		17	23	+01	42
1922	07	15		17	29	+01	42
1922	07	25		17	30	+01	43
1922	08	04		17	26	+01	43
1922	08	14		17	16	+01	43
1922	08	24		17	02	+01	43
1922	09	03		16	43	+01	43
1922	09	13		16	21	+01	43
1922	09	23		15	56	+01	42
1922	10	03		15	30	+01	42
1922	10	13		15	02	+01	41
1922	10	23		14	35	+01	40
1922	11	02		14	10	+01	39
1922	11	12		13	47	+01	38
1922	11	22		13	28	+01	37
1922	12	02		13	13	+01	35
1922	12	12		13	03	+01	34
1922	12	22		12	59	+01	32
1923	01	01		13	00	+01	31
1923	01	11		13	07	+01	29
1923	01	21		13	19	+01	28
1923	01	31		13	36	+01	26
1923	02	10		13	57	+01	25
1923	02	20		14	23	+01	24
1923	03	02		14	52	+01	23
1923	03	12		15	24	+01	22
1923	03	22		15	57	+01	21
1923	04	01		16	32	+01	20
1923	04	11		17	08	+01	19
1923	04	21		17	43	+01	19
1923	05	01		18	17	+01	18
1923	05	11		18	50	+01	18
1923	05	21		19	20	+01	18
1923	05	31		19	48	+01	17
1923	06	10		20	12	+01	17
1923	06	20		20	32	+01	17
1923	06	30		20	47	+01	17
1923	07	10		20	58	+01	17
1923	07	20		21	03	+01	17
1923	07	30		21	03	+01	17
1923	08	09		20	58	+01	17
1923	08	19		20	48	+01	17
1923	08	29		20	34	+01	17
1923	09	08		20	14	+01	17
1923	09	18		19	52	+01	16
1923	09	28		19	27	+01	16
1923	10	08		19	00	+01	15
1923	10	18		18	32	+01	14
1923	10	28		18	05	+01	13
1923	11	07		17	40	+01	12
1923	11	17		17	18	+01	11
1923	11	27		16	59	+01	10
1923	12	07		16	44	+01	09
1923	12	17		16	35	+01	08
1923	12	27		16	31	+01	06
1924	01	06		16	33	+01	05
1924	01	16		16	40	+01	04
1924	01	26		16	53	+01	02
1924	02	05		17	11	+01	01
1924	02	15		17	33	+01	00
1924	02	25		17	59	+00	59
1924	03	06		18	29	+00	58

20 ♈ 14
Lat 1 N 17

1924 03 16		19 01	+00 57
1924 03 26	♈	19 35	+00 56
1924 04 05		20 11	+00 56
1924 04 15		20 47	+00 55
1924 04 25		21 22	+00 54
1924 05 05		21 56	+00 54
1924 05 15		22 29	+00 53
1924 05 25		22 59	+00 53
1924 06 04		23 27	+00 52
1924 06 14		23 51	+00 52
1924 06 24		24 10	+00 52
1924 07 04		24 25	+00 52
1924 07 14		24 35	+00 51
1924 07 24		24 41	+00 51
1924 08 03		24 40	+00 51
1924 08 13		24 35	+00 51
1924 08 23		24 24	+00 50
1924 09 02		24 09	+00 50
1924 09 12		23 49	+00 49
1924 09 22		23 26	+00 49
1924 10 02		23 00	+00 48
1924 10 12		22 33	+00 48
1924 10 22		22 05	+00 47
1924 11 01		21 38	+00 46
1924 11 11		21 13	+00 45
1924 11 21		20 51	+00 44
1924 12 01		20 32	+00 43
1924 12 11		20 19	+00 42
1924 12 21		20 10	+00 41
1924 12 31		20 07	+00 40
1925 01 10		20 09	+00 39
1925 01 20		20 17	+00 38
1925 01 30		20 31	+00 37
1925 02 09		20 49	+00 36
1925 02 19		21 12	+00 35
1925 03 01		21 39	+00 34
1925 03 11		22 10	+00 33
1925 03 21		22 42	+00 32
1925 03 31		23 17	+00 31
1925 04 10		23 53	+00 30
1925 04 20		24 29	+00 30
1925 04 30		25 05	+00 29
1925 05 10		25 39	+00 29
1925 05 20		26 12	+00 28
1925 05 30		26 43	+00 27
1925 06 09		27 10	+00 27
1925 06 19		27 34	+00 26
1925 06 29		27 53	+00 26
1925 07 09		28 08	+00 25
1925 07 19		28 18	+00 25
1925 07 29		28 23	+00 24
1925 08 08		28 22	+00 24
1925 08 18		28 16	+00 23
1925 08 28		28 05	+00 23
1925 09 07		27 49	+00 22
1925 09 17		27 29	+00 21
1925 09 27		27 05	+00 21
1925 10 07		26 39	+00 20
1925 10 17		26 11	+00 19
1925 10 27		25 43	+00 19
1925 11 06		25 16	+00 18
1925 11 16		24 51	+00 17
1925 11 26		24 29	+00 16
1925 12 06		24 11	+00 15
1925 12 16		23 57	+00 14
1925 12 26		23 49	+00 13
1926 01 05		23 47	+00 13
1926 01 15		23 50	+00 12
1926 01 25		23 59	+00 11
1926 02 04		24 13	+00 10
1926 02 14		24 32	+00 09
1926 02 24		24 56	+00 08
1926 03 06		25 24	+00 08
1926 03 16		25 55	+00 07
1926 03 26		26 28	+00 06
1926 04 05		27 04	+00 05
1926 04 15		27 40	+00 05
1926 04 25		28 16	+00 04
1926 05 05		28 53	+00 03
1926 05 15		29 28	+00 03
1926 05 25	♉	30 01	+00 02
1926 06 04		30 31	+00 01
1926 06 14		30 59	+00 01
1926 06 24	♉	31 22	00 00
1926 07 04		31 42	-00 01
1926 07 14		31 57	-00 02
1926 07 24		32 06	-00 02
1926 08 03		32 11	-00 03
1926 08 13		32 10	-00 04
1926 08 23		32 03	-00 05
1926 09 02		31 52	-00 06
1926 09 12		31 35	-00 06
1926 09 22		31 14	-00 07
1926 10 02		30 50	-00 08
1926 10 12		30 24	-00 09
1926 10 22	♈	29 56	-00 10
1926 11 01		29 27	-00 11
1926 11 11		29 00	-00 11
1926 11 21		28 35	-00 12
1926 12 01		28 13	-00 13
1926 12 11		27 55	-00 13
1926 12 21		27 42	-00 14
1926 12 31		27 34	-00 15
1927 01 10		27 32	-00 15
1927 01 20		27 36	-00 16
1927 01 30		27 46	-00 17
1927 02 09		28 01	-00 17
1927 02 19		28 21	-00 18
1927 03 01		28 46	-00 18
1927 03 11		29 14	-00 19
1927 03 21		29 46	-00 20
1927 03 31	♉	30 20	-00 20
1927 04 10		30 56	-00 21
1927 04 20		31 33	-00 22
1927 04 30		32 10	-00 22
1927 05 10		32 47	-00 23
1927 05 20		33 22	-00 24
1927 05 30		33 56	-00 25
1927 06 09		34 27	-00 26
1927 06 19		34 54	-00 27
1927 06 29		35 16	-00 27
1927 07 09		35 38	-00 28
1927 07 19		35 53	-00 29
1927 07 29		36 02	-00 31
1927 08 08		36 06	-00 32
1927 08 18		36 05	-00 33
1927 08 28		35 58	-00 34
1927 09 07		35 46	-00 35
1927 09 17		35 29	-00 36
1927 09 27		35 08	-00 37
1927 10 07		34 43	-00 38
1927 10 17		34 16	-00 39
1927 10 27		33 47	-00 40
1927 11 06		33 19	-00 40
1927 11 16		32 51	-00 41
1927 11 26		32 26	-00 42
1927 12 06		32 04	-00 42
1927 12 16		31 46	-00 43
1927 12 26		31 33	-00 43
1928 01 05		31 26	-00 44
1928 01 15		31 25	-00 44
1928 01 25		31 30	-00 44
1928 02 04		31 40	-00 45
1928 02 14		31 56	-00 45
1928 02 24		32 17	-00 46
1928 03 05		32 42	-00 46
1928 03 15		33 12	-00 46
1928 03 25		33 44	-00 47
1928 04 04		34 19	-00 47
1928 04 14		34 56	-00 48
1928 04 24		35 34	-00 49
1928 05 04		36 12	-00 49
1928 05 14		36 49	-00 50
1928 05 24		37 25	-00 51
1928 06 03		37 59	-00 52
1928 06 13		38 30	-00 53
1928 06 23		38 59	-00 54
1928 07 03	♉	39 23	-00 56
1928 07 13		39 43	-00 57
1928 07 23		39 57	-00 58
1928 08 02		40 07	-01 00
1928 08 12		40 11	-01 01
1928 08 22		40 09	-01 02
1928 09 01		40 02	-01 04
1928 09 11		39 50	-01 05
1928 09 21		39 32	-01 06
1928 10 01		39 11	-01 08
1928 10 11		38 45	-01 09
1928 10 21		38 17	-01 10
1928 10 31		37 48	-01 11
1928 11 10		37 19	-01 11
1928 11 20		36 51	-01 12
1928 11 30		36 26	-01 13
1928 12 10		36 04	-01 13
1928 12 20		35 46	-01 13
1928 12 30		35 34	-01 13
1929 01 09		35 27	-01 14
1929 01 19		35 26	-01 14
1929 01 29		35 31	-01 14
1929 02 08		35 43	-01 14
1929 02 18		35 59	-01 14
1929 02 28		36 21	-01 14
1929 03 10		36 48	-01 14
1929 03 20		37 18	-01 15
1929 03 30		37 51	-01 15
1929 04 09		38 27	-01 15
1929 04 19		39 05	-01 16
1929 04 29		39 43	-01 17
1929 05 09		40 22	-01 17
1929 05 19		41 00	-01 18
1929 05 29	♉	41 37	-01 19
1929 06 08		42 12	-01 20
1929 06 18		42 44	-01 22
1929 06 28		43 13	-01 23
1929 07 08		43 37	-01 25
1929 07 18		43 57	-01 26
1929 07 28		44 13	-01 28
1929 08 07		44 22	-01 29
1929 08 17		44 27	-01 31
1929 08 27		44 25	-01 33
1929 09 06		44 17	-01 35
1929 09 16		44 05	-01 36
1929 09 26		43 47	-01 38
1929 10 06		43 24	-01 39
1929 10 16		42 58	-01 41
1929 10 26		42 30	-01 42
1929 11 05		42 00	-01 43
1929 11 15		41 31	-01 43
1929 11 25		41 02	-01 44
1929 12 05		40 36	-01 44
1929 12 15		40 14	-01 44
1929 12 25		39 56	-01 45
1930 01 04		39 44	-01 44
1930 01 14		39 38	-01 44
1930 01 24		39 37	-01 44
1930 02 03		39 43	-01 44
1930 02 13		39 55	-01 44
1930 02 23		40 13	-01 43
1930 03 05		40 36	-01 43
1930 03 15		41 03	-01 43
1930 03 25		41 34	-01 43
1930 04 04		42 09	-01 44
1930 04 14		42 46	-01 44
1930 04 24		43 24	-01 45
1930 05 04		44 04	-01 45
1930 05 14		44 44	-01 46
1930 05 24		45 23	-01 47
1930 06 03		46 01	-01 48
1930 06 13		46 36	-01 49
1930 06 23		47 09	-01 51
1930 07 03		47 39	-01 53
1930 07 13	♉	48 04	-01 54
1930 07 23		48 25	-01 56
1930 08 02		48 40	-01 58
1930 08 12		48 50	-02 00
1930 08 22		48 55	-02 02
1930 09 01		48 53	-02 04
1930 09 11		48 46	-02 06
1930 09 21		48 33	-02 08
1930 10 01		48 14	-02 10
1930 10 11		47 51	-02 12
1930 10 21		47 25	-02 13
1930 10 31		46 56	-02 15
1930 11 10		46 25	-02 16
1930 11 20		45 55	-02 16
1930 11 30		45 26	-02 17
1930 12 10		45 00	-02 17
1930 12 20		44 37	-02 17
1930 12 30		44 19	-02 17
1931 01 09		44 07	-02 16
1931 01 19		44 01	-02 16
1931 01 29		44 01	-02 15
1931 02 08		44 08	-02 15
1931 02 18		44 20	-02 14
1931 02 28		44 39	-02 14
1931 03 10		45 02	-02 13
1931 03 20		45 31	-02 13
1931 03 30		46 03	-02 13
1931 04 09		46 39	-02 13
1931 04 19		47 17	-02 13
1931 04 29		47 56	-02 14
1931 05 09		48 37	-02 15
1931 05 19		49 18	-02 15
1931 05 29		49 58	-02 17
1931 06 08		50 37	-02 18
1931 06 18		51 14	-02 19
1931 06 28		51 48	-02 21
1931 07 08		52 19	-02 23
1931 07 18		52 45	-02 25
1931 07 28		53 07	-02 27
1931 08 07		53 23	-02 29
1931 08 17		53 34	-02 32
1931 08 27		53 38	-02 34
1931 09 06		53 37	-02 37
1931 09 16		53 30	-02 39
1931 09 26		53 16	-02 42
1931 10 06		52 58	-02 44
1931 10 16		52 34	-02 46
1931 10 26		52 07	-02 47
1931 11 05		51 37	-02 49
1931 11 15		51 06	-02 50
1931 11 25		50 35	-02 51
1931 12 05		50 05	-02 51
1931 12 15		49 38	-02 51
1931 12 25		49 15	-02 51
1932 01 04	♉	48 57	-02 50
1932 01 14		48 45	-02 50
1932 01 24		48 39	-02 49
1932 02 03		48 39	-02 48
1932 02 13		48 46	-02 47
1932 02 23		49 00	-02 46
1932 03 04		49 19	-02 45
1932 03 14		49 43	-02 44
1932 03 24		50 13	-02 44
1932 04 03		50 46	-02 44
1932 04 13		51 23	-02 44
1932 04 23		52 02	-02 44
1932 05 03		52 44	-02 44
1932 05 13		53 26	-02 45
1932 05 23		54 08	-02 46
1932 06 02		54 50	-02 47
1932 06 12		55 30	-02 48
1932 06 22		56 08	-02 50
1932 07 02		56 44	-02 52
1932 07 12		57 16	-02 54
1932 07 22		57 43	-02 56
1932 08 01		58 06	-02 59
1932 08 11		58 23	-03 01
1932 08 21		58 35	-03 04
1932 08 31		58 40	-03 07
1932 09 10		58 39	-03 10
1932 09 20		58 32	-03 13
1932 09 30		58 19	-03 16
1932 10 10	♉	58 00	-03 18
1932 10 20		57 36	-03 20
1932 10 30		57 08	-03 22
1932 11 09		56 38	-03 24
1932 11 19		56 06	-03 25
1932 11 29		55 34	-03 26
1932 12 09		55 03	-03 26
1932 12 19		54 35	-03 26
1932 12 29		54 12	-03 25
1933 01 08		53 53	-03 25
1933 01 18		53 41	-03 24
1933 01 28		53 35	-03 22
1933 02 07		53 35	-03 21
1933 02 17		53 43	-03 20
1933 02 27		53 56	-03 18
1933 03 09		54 16	-03 17
1933 03 19		54 42	-03 16
1933 03 29		55 12	-03 15
1933 04 08		55 47	-03 15
1933 04 18		56 25	-03 15
1933 04 28		57 06	-03 15
1933 05 08		57 49	-03 15
1933 05 18		58 32	-03 15
1933 05 28		59 16	-03 16
1933 06 07	♊	60 00	-03 17
1933 06 17		60 42	-03 19
1933 06 27		61 22	-03 21
1933 07 07		61 59	-03 23
1933 07 17		62 33	-03 25
1933 07 27		63 02	-03 28
1933 08 06		63 26	-03 31
1933 08 16		63 45	-03 34
1933 08 26		63 58	-03 37
1933 09 05		64 04	-03 41
1933 09 15		64 04	-03 44
1933 09 25		63 57	-03 47
1933 10 05		63 44	-03 51
1933 10 15		63 25	-03 54
1933 10 25		63 01	-03 56
1933 11 04		62 33	-03 58
1933 11 14		62 01	-04 00
1933 11 24		61 28	-04 01
1933 12 04		60 55	-04 02
1933 12 14		60 24	-04 02
1933 12 24	♉	59 55	-04 02
1934 01 03		59 31	-04 01
1934 01 13		59 11	-04 00
1934 01 23		58 58	-03 59
1934 02 02		58 52	-03 57
1934 02 12		58 52	-03 55
1934 02 22		59 00	-03 53
1934 03 04		59 14	-03 52
1934 03 14		59 35	-03 50
1934 03 24	♊	60 01	-03 49
1934 04 03		60 33	-03 47
1934 04 13		61 09	-03 47
1934 04 23		61 48	-03 46
1934 05 03		62 31	-03 46
1934 05 13		63 15	-03 46

Chiron ⚷

Chiron

1934 05 23	♊	64 01	-03 46
1934 06 02		64 47	-03 47
1934 06 12		65 32	-03 49
1934 06 22		66 17	-03 50
1934 07 02		66 59	-03 52
1934 07 12		67 38	-03 55
1934 07 22		68 14	-03 57
1934 08 01		68 45	-04 00
1934 08 11		69 11	-04 04
1934 08 21		69 32	-04 07
1934 08 31		69 46	-04 11
1934 09 10		69 54	-04 15
1934 09 20		69 55	-04 19
1934 09 30		69 50	-04 23
1934 10 10		69 37	-04 26
1934 10 20		69 18	-04 30
1934 10 30		68 54	-04 33
1934 11 09		68 25	-04 35
1934 11 19		67 53	-04 37
1934 11 29		67 19	-04 39
1934 12 09		66 45	-04 39
1934 12 19		66 12	-04 39
1934 12 29		65 42	-04 39
1935 01 08	♊	65 16	-04 38
1935 01 18		64 56	-04 36
1935 01 28		64 42	-04 34
1935 02 07		64 35	-04 32
1935 02 17		64 36	-04 30
1935 02 27		64 43	-04 28
1935 03 09		64 58	-04 25
1935 03 19		65 19	-04 23
1935 03 29		65 46	-04 21
1935 04 08		66 19	-04 20
1935 04 18		66 56	-04 19
1935 04 28		67 37	-04 18
1935 05 08		68 21	-04 17
1935 05 18		69 08	-04 17
1935 05 28		69 55	-04 18
1935 06 07		70 44	-04 18
1935 06 17		71 32	-04 20
1935 06 27		72 18	-04 21
1935 07 07		73 03	-04 24
1935 07 17		73 45	-04 26
1935 07 27		74 23	-04 29
1935 08 06		74 57	-04 32
1935 08 16		75 26	-04 36
1935 08 26		75 49	-04 40
1935 09 05		76 06	-04 44
1935 09 15		76 16	-04 49
1935 09 25		76 19	-04 53
1935 10 05		76 15	-04 58
1935 10 15		76 03	-05 02
1935 10 25		75 45	-05 06
1935 11 04		75 21	-05 09
1935 11 14		74 52	-05 12
1935 11 24		74 19	-05 14
1935 12 04		73 44	-05 16
1935 12 14		73 08	-05 17
1935 12 24		72 34	-05 17
1936 01 03		72 02	-05 16
1936 01 13		71 35	-05 15
1936 01 23		71 13	-05 13
1936 02 02		70 58	-05 10
1936 02 12		70 50	-05 08
1936 02 22		70 50	-05 05
1936 03 03		70 57	-05 02
1936 03 13		71 12	-04 59
1936 03 23		71 33	-04 57
1936 04 02		72 01	-04 54
1936 04 12		72 35	-04 52
1936 04 22		73 14	-04 50
1936 05 02		73 57	-04 49
1936 05 12		74 43	-04 48
1936 05 22		75 31	-04 48
1936 06 01		76 21	-04 48
1936 06 11		77 12	-04 49
1936 06 21		78 03	-04 50
1936 07 01		78 53	-04 52
1936 07 11		79 41	-04 54
1936 07 21		80 26	-04 57
1936 07 31		81 07	-05 00
1936 08 10		81 45	-05 04
1936 08 20		82 17	-05 08
1936 08 30		82 43	-05 12
1936 09 09		83 03	-05 17
1936 09 19		83 16	-05 22
1936 09 29		83 22	-05 27
1936 10 09		83 19	-05 32
1936 10 19	♊	83 10	-05 37
1936 10 29		82 53	-05 41
1936 11 08		82 29	-05 45
1936 11 18		82 00	-05 49
1936 11 28		81 27	-05 51
1936 12 08		80 51	-05 53
1936 12 18		80 14	-05 54
1936 12 28		79 38	-05 54
1937 01 07		79 04	-05 53
1937 01 17		78 35	-05 52
1937 01 27		78 11	-05 49
1937 02 06		77 54	-05 46
1937 02 16		77 45	-05 43
1937 02 26		77 43	-05 40
1937 03 08		77 50	-05 36
1937 03 18		78 04	-05 32
1937 03 28		78 26	-05 29
1937 04 07	♊	78 54	-05 26
1937 04 17		79 29	-05 23
1937 04 27		80 09	-05 21
1937 05 07		80 53	-05 19
1937 05 17		81 41	-05 18
1937 05 27		82 32	-05 18
1937 06 06		83 25	-05 17
1937 06 16		84 19	-05 18
1937 06 26		85 13	-05 19
1937 07 06		86 06	-05 20
1937 07 16		86 58	-05 23
1937 07 26		87 47	-05 25
1937 08 05		88 33	-05 29
1937 08 15		89 14	-05 33
1937 08 25		89 51	-05 37
1937 09 04	♋	90 21	-05 42
1937 09 14		90 45	-05 47
1937 09 24		91 02	-05 52
1937 10 04		91 11	-05 58
1937 10 14		91 12	-06 04
1937 10 24		91 05	-06 09
1937 11 03		90 50	-06 14
1937 11 13		90 28	-06 19
1937 11 23	♊	89 59	-06 23
1937 12 03		89 26	-06 26
1937 12 13		88 49	-06 29
1937 12 23		88 11	-06 30
1938 01 02		87 32	-06 30
1938 01 12		86 57	-06 29
1938 01 22		86 25	-06 27
1938 02 01		85 59	-06 24
1938 02 11		85 39	-06 21
1938 02 21		85 26	-06 17
1938 03 03		85 24	-06 13
1938 03 13		85 29	-06 08
1938 03 23		85 43	-06 04
1938 04 02		86 04	-06 00
1938 04 12		86 33	-05 56
1938 04 22		87 08	-05 53
1938 05 02		87 49	-05 50
1938 05 12		88 35	-05 47
1938 05 22		89 25	-05 46
1938 06 01	♋	90 19	-05 44
1938 06 11		91 15	-05 44
1938 06 21		92 12	-05 44
1938 07 01		93 10	-05 45
1938 07 11		94 07	-05 46
1938 07 21		95 03	-05 48
1938 07 31		95 57	-05 51
1938 08 10		96 47	-05 54
1938 08 20		97 34	-05 58
1938 08 30		98 16	-06 02
1938 09 09		98 51	-06 07
1938 09 19		99 21	-06 13
1938 09 29		99 43	-06 19
1938 10 09		99 56	-06 25
1938 10 19		100 02	-06 31
1938 10 29		99 59	-06 37
1938 11 08		99 47	-06 43
1938 11 18		99 28	-06 49
1938 11 28		99 01	-06 53
1938 12 08		98 28	-06 57
1938 12 18		97 51	-07 00
1938 12 28		97 11	-07 01
1939 01 07		96 31	-07 02
1939 01 17		95 52	-07 01
1939 01 27		95 18	-06 59
1939 02 06		94 48	-06 56
1939 02 16		94 25	-06 52
1939 02 26		94 11	-06 47
1939 03 08		94 05	-06 42
1939 03 18		94 07	-06 37
1939 03 28		94 19	-06 32
1939 04 07		94 39	-06 27
1939 04 17		95 07	-06 22
1939 04 27		95 42	-06 18
1939 05 07		96 24	-06 14
1939 05 17		97 12	-06 11
1939 05 27		98 04	-06 08
1939 06 06		99 00	-06 06
1939 06 16		99 59	-06 05
1939 06 26		100 59	-06 05
1939 07 06	♋	102 01	-06 05
1939 07 16		103 03	-06 06
1939 07 26		104 04	-06 07
1939 08 05		105 04	-06 10
1939 08 15		106 00	-06 13
1939 08 25		106 53	-06 17
1939 09 04		107 41	-06 21
1939 09 14		108 23	-06 26
1939 09 24		108 59	-06 32
1939 10 04		109 28	-06 38
1939 10 14		109 48	-06 44
1939 10 24		110 00	-06 51
1939 11 03		110 03	-06 58
1939 11 13		109 56	-07 04
1939 11 23		109 41	-07 10
1939 12 03		109 17	-07 16
1939 12 13		108 46	-07 20
1939 12 23		108 10	-07 24
1940 01 02		107 29	-07 26
1940 01 12		106 47	-07 27
1940 01 22		106 06	-07 26
1940 02 01		105 28	-07 24
1940 02 11		104 54	-07 21
1940 02 21		104 27	-07 16
1940 03 02		104 08	-07 11
1940 03 12		103 58	-07 05
1940 03 22		103 57	-06 59
1940 04 01		104 06	-06 53
1940 04 11		104 23	-06 47
1940 04 21		104 50	-06 42
1940 05 01		105 24	-06 36
1940 05 11		106 06	-06 31
1940 05 21		106 54	-06 27
1940 05 31		107 48	-06 24
1940 06 10		108 46	-06 21
1940 06 20		109 48	-06 19
1940 06 30		110 52	-06 17
1940 07 10		111 58	-06 17
1940 07 20		113 05	-06 17
1940 07 30		114 12	-06 18
1940 08 09		115 17	-06 19
1940 08 19		116 20	-06 22
1940 08 29		117 20	-06 25
1940 09 08		118 16	-06 29
1940 09 18		119 06	-06 34
1940 09 28		119 51	-06 39
1940 10 08	♌	120 28	-06 45
1940 10 18		120 57	-06 52
1940 10 28		121 17	-06 58
1940 11 07		121 27	-07 05
1940 11 17		121 28	-07 12
1940 11 27		121 19	-07 19
1940 12 07		121 01	-07 25
1940 12 17		120 34	-07 30
1940 12 27		120 00	-07 34
1941 01 06	♋	119 20	-07 37
1941 01 16		118 37	-07 39
1941 01 26		117 53	-07 38
1941 02 05		117 11	-07 37
1941 02 15		116 33	-07 33
1941 02 25		116 01	-07 29
1941 03 07		115 36	-07 24
1941 03 17		115 20	-07 17
1941 03 27		115 14	-07 11
1941 04 06		115 18	-07 04
1941 04 16		115 32	-06 56
1941 04 26		115 55	-06 50
1941 05 06		116 27	-06 43
1941 05 16		117 07	-06 37
1941 05 26		117 55	-06 32
1941 06 05		118 49	-06 27
1941 06 15		119 49	-06 23
1941 06 25	♌	120 53	-06 20
1941 07 05		122 00	-06 17
1941 07 15		123 10	-06 15
1941 07 25		124 22	-06 15
1941 08 04		125 34	-06 14
1941 08 14		126 46	-06 15
1941 08 24		127 56	-06 17
1941 09 03		129 04	-06 19
1941 09 13		130 09	-06 22
1941 09 23		131 08	-06 26
1941 10 03	♌	132 02	-06 31
1941 10 13		132 49	-06 36
1941 10 23		133 29	-06 42
1941 11 02		133 59	-06 48
1941 11 12		134 20	-06 55
1941 11 22		134 31	-07 01
1941 12 02		134 32	-07 08
1941 12 12		134 22	-07 14
1941 12 22		134 02	-07 20
1942 01 01		133 33	-07 25
1942 01 11		132 56	-07 28
1942 01 21	♌	132 15	-07 30
1942 01 31		131 30	-07 31
1942 02 10		130 45	-07 30
1942 02 20		130 02	-07 27
1942 03 02		129 23	-07 23
1942 03 12		128 52	-07 17
1942 03 22		128 29	-07 11
1942 04 01		128 15	-07 03
1942 04 11		128 12	-06 56
1942 04 21		128 19	-06 48
1942 05 01		128 36	-06 40
1942 05 11		129 04	-06 33
1942 05 21		129 41	-06 25
1942 05 31		130 26	-06 19
1942 06 10		131 18	-06 13
1942 06 20		132 18	-06 08
1942 06 30		133 23	-06 03
1942 07 10		134 32	-05 59
1942 07 20		135 45	-05 56
1942 07 30		137 01	-05 54
1942 08 09		138 18	-05 52
1942 08 19		139 36	-05 52
1942 08 29		140 53	-05 52
1942 09 08		142 09	-05 53
1942 09 18		143 22	-05 54
1942 09 28		144 31	-05 57
1942 10 08		145 36	-06 00
1942 10 18		146 34	-06 04
1942 10 28		147 25	-06 08
1942 11 07		148 09	-06 13
1942 11 17		148 42	-06 19
1942 11 27		149 06	-06 25
1942 12 07		149 19	-06 30
1942 12 17		149 21	-06 36
1942 12 27		149 11	-06 42
1943 01 06		148 51	-06 46
1943 01 16		148 22	-06 50
1943 01 26		147 45	-06 53
1943 02 05		147 02	-06 54
1943 02 15		146 16	-06 53
1943 02 25		145 30	-06 51
1943 03 07		144 45	-06 48
1943 03 17		144 06	-06 43
1943 03 27		143 35	-06 37
1943 04 06		143 12	-06 29
1943 04 16		142 59	-06 22
1943 04 26		142 56	-06 13
1943 05 06		143 05	-06 05
1943 05 16		143 25	-05 57
1943 05 26		143 55	-05 49
1943 06 05		144 34	-05 42
1943 06 15		145 23	-05 35
1943 06 25		146 19	-05 28
1943 07 05		147 22	-05 22
1943 07 15		148 31	-05 17
1943 07 25		149 45	-05 13
1943 08 04	♍	151 02	-05 09
1943 08 14		152 22	-05 06
1943 08 24		153 44	-05 04
1943 09 03		155 07	-05 02
1943 09 13		156 30	-05 02
1943 09 23		157 50	-05 01
1943 10 03		159 09	-05 02
1943 10 13		160 23	-05 03
1943 10 23		161 33	-05 05
1943 11 02		162 36	-05 07
1943 11 12		163 33	-05 10
1943 11 22		164 20	-05 14
1943 12 02		164 58	-05 18
1943 12 12		165 26	-05 22
1943 12 22		165 43	-05 26
1944 01 01	♍	165 47	-05 30
1944 01 11		165 40	-05 34
1944 01 21		165 22	-05 37
1944 01 31		164 54	-05 39
1944 02 10		164 18	-05 40
1944 02 20		163 35	-05 40
1944 03 01		162 48	-05 39
1944 03 11		162 01	-05 36
1944 03 21		161 16	-05 32
1944 03 31		160 35	-05 27
1944 04 10		160 02	-05 20
1944 04 20		159 38	-05 13
1944 04 30		159 24	-05 06
1944 05 10		159 21	-04 58
1944 05 20		159 29	-04 50
1944 05 30		159 48	-04 42
1944 06 09		160 18	-04 34
1944 06 19		160 58	-04 27
1944 06 29		161 47	-04 20
1944 07 09		162 45	-04 14
1944 07 19		163 49	-04 08
1944 07 29		165 00	-04 03
1944 08 08		166 16	-03 58
1944 08 18		167 37	-03 54
1944 08 28		169 00	-03 50

1944 09 07	♍	170 25	-03 47
1944 09 17		171 51	-03 45
1944 09 27		173 17	-03 43
1944 10 07		174 42	-03 42
1944 10 17		176 05	-03 41
1944 10 27		177 23	-03 40
1944 11 06		178 37	-03 40
1944 11 16		179 45	-03 41
1944 11 26	♎	180 46	-03 42
1944 12 06		181 38	-03 43
1944 12 16		182 21	-03 44
1944 12 26		182 53	-03 46
1945 01 05		183 13	-03 47
1945 01 15		183 22	-03 49
1945 01 25		183 19	-03 50
1945 02 04		183 04	-03 51
1945 02 14		182 39	-03 51
1945 02 24		182 04	-03 51
1945 03 06		181 23	-03 49
1945 03 16		180 37	-03 47
1945 03 26	♍	179 49	-03 44
1945 04 05		179 03	-03 40
1945 04 15		178 21	-03 35
1945 04 25		177 46	-03 29
1945 05 05		177 19	-03 23
1945 05 15		177 02	-03 16
1945 05 25		176 56	-03 09
1945 06 04		177 01	-03 03
1945 06 14		177 18	-02 56
1945 06 24		177 45	-02 50
1945 07 04		178 23	-02 44
1945 07 14		179 11	-02 38
1945 07 24	♎	180 07	-02 32
1945 08 03		181 10	-02 27
1945 08 13		182 21	-02 22
1945 08 23		183 36	-02 18
1945 09 02		184 57	-02 14
1945 09 12		186 21	-02 10
1945 09 22		187 47	-02 07
1945 10 02		189 14	-02 04
1945 10 12		190 42	-02 01
1945 10 22		192 08	-01 59
1945 11 01		193 32	-01 56
1945 11 11		194 53	-01 55
1945 11 21		196 10	-01 53
1945 12 01		197 20	-01 51
1945 12 11		198 24	-01 50
1945 12 21		199 19	-01 49
1945 12 31		200 05	-01 47
1946 01 10	♎	200 40	-01 46
1946 01 20		201 04	-01 45
1946 01 30		201 17	-01 44
1946 02 09		201 17	-01 42
1946 02 19		201 06	-01 40
1946 03 01		200 43	-01 38
1946 03 11		200 12	-01 36
1946 03 21		199 32	-01 33
1946 03 31		198 46	-01 30
1946 04 10		198 01	-01 26
1946 04 20		197 15	-01 22
1946 04 30		196 31	-01 18
1946 05 10		195 54	-01 14
1946 05 20		195 24	-01 09
1946 05 30		195 04	-01 04
1946 06 09		194 54	-01 00
1946 06 19		194 55	-00 55
1946 06 29		195 07	-00 51
1946 07 09		195 31	-00 46
1946 07 19		196 05	-00 42
1946 07 29		196 46	-00 38
1946 08 08		197 41	-00 35
1946 08 18		198 41	-00 31
1946 08 28		199 46	-00 27
1946 09 07		201 01	-00 24
1946 09 17		202 19	-00 21
1946 09 27		203 41	-00 18
1946 10 07		205 05	-00 15
1946 10 17		206 31	-00 12
1946 10 27		207 57	-00 09
1946 11 06		209 23	-00 06
1946 11 16	♏	210 46	-00 03
1946 11 26		212 07	00 00
1946 12 06		213 23	+00 03
1946 12 16		214 34	+00 06
1946 12 26		215 37	+00 10
1947 01 05		216 33	+00 13
1947 01 15		217 20	+00 16
1947 01 25		217 56	+00 20
1947 02 04		218 22	+00 24
1947 02 14		218 36	+00 27
1947 02 24		218 39	+00 31
1947 03 06		218 30	+00 35
1947 03 16		218 10	+00 39
1947 03 26		217 41	+00 43
1947 04 05		217 04	+00 48
1947 04 15		216 22	+00 51
1947 04 25	♏	215 36	+00 55
1947 05 05		214 50	+00 59
1947 05 15		214 07	+01 02
1947 05 25		213 28	+01 05
1947 06 04		212 56	+01 08
1947 06 14		212 33	+01 10
1947 06 24		212 20	+01 12
1947 07 04		212 17	+01 14
1947 07 14		212 25	+01 16
1947 07 24		212 43	+01 18
1947 08 03		213 13	+01 20
1947 08 13		213 51	+01 21
1947 08 23		214 39	+01 23
1947 09 02		215 35	+01 24
1947 09 12		216 37	+01 26
1947 09 22		217 46	+01 28
1947 10 02		219 00	+01 30
1947 10 12		220 18	+01 32
1947 10 22		221 38	+01 34
1947 11 01		223 01	+01 37
1947 11 11		224 23	+01 39
1947 11 21		225 46	+01 42
1947 12 01		227 06	+01 45
1947 12 11		228 24	+01 49
1947 12 21		229 37	+01 53
1947 12 31		230 45	+01 57
1948 01 10		231 46	+02 01
1948 01 20	♏	232 40	+02 06
1948 01 30		233 25	+02 11
1948 02 09		234 00	+02 16
1948 02 19		234 25	+02 21
1948 02 29		234 39	+02 27
1948 03 10		234 42	+02 32
1948 03 20		234 34	+02 38
1948 03 30		234 15	+02 43
1948 04 09		233 48	+02 48
1948 04 19		233 13	+02 53
1948 04 29		232 32	+02 57
1948 05 09		231 48	+03 01
1948 05 19		231 03	+03 04
1948 05 29		230 20	+03 06
1948 06 08		229 42	+03 08
1948 06 18		229 09	+03 09
1948 06 28		228 44	+03 09
1948 07 08		228 29	+03 09
1948 07 18		228 23	+03 09
1948 07 28		228 28	+03 08
1948 08 07		228 42	+03 07
1948 08 17		229 07	+03 07
1948 08 27		229 42	+03 06
1948 09 06		230 25	+03 05
1948 09 16		231 16	+03 05
1948 09 26		232 14	+03 05
1948 10 06		233 18	+03 05
1948 10 16		234 27	+03 06
1948 10 26		235 40	+03 06
1948 11 05		236 56	+03 08
1948 11 15		238 14	+03 09
1948 11 25		239 32	+03 12
1948 12 05	♐	240 49	+03 14
1948 12 15		242 05	+03 17
1948 12 25		243 18	+03 21
1949 01 04		244 26	+03 25
1949 01 14		245 30	+03 29
1949 01 24		246 27	+03 34
1949 02 03		247 16	+03 40
1949 02 13		247 57	+03 45
1949 02 23		248 29	+03 52
1949 03 05		248 51	+03 58
1949 03 15		249 03	+04 04
1949 03 25		249 04	+04 11
1949 04 04		248 55	+04 17
1949 04 14		248 36	+04 23
1949 04 24		248 09	+04 29
1949 05 04		247 34	+04 33
1949 05 14		246 55	+04 37
1949 05 24		246 12	+04 41
1949 06 03		245 29	+04 43
1949 06 13		244 48	+04 44
1949 06 23		244 10	+04 44
1949 07 03		243 38	+04 44
1949 07 13		243 13	+04 42
1949 07 23		242 57	+04 40
1949 08 02		242 50	+04 38
1949 08 12		242 53	+04 36
1949 08 22		243 06	+04 33
1949 09 01		243 28	+04 30
1949 09 11		244 00	+04 28
1949 09 21		244 39	+04 26
1949 10 01		245 27	+04 24
1949 10 11		246 21	+04 22
1949 10 21		247 21	+04 21
1949 10 31		248 25	+04 21
1949 11 10		249 34	+04 21
1949 11 20		250 45	+04 21
1949 11 30		251 57	+04 22
1949 12 10	♐	253 10	+04 24
1949 12 20		254 22	+04 26
1949 12 30		255 32	+04 29
1950 01 09		256 39	+04 32
1950 01 19		257 42	+04 36
1950 01 29		258 40	+04 41
1950 02 08		259 31	+04 46
1950 02 18		260 15	+04 52
1950 02 28		260 51	+04 58
1950 03 10		261 18	+05 05
1950 03 20		261 35	+05 11
1950 03 30		261 43	+05 18
1950 04 09		261 41	+05 25
1950 04 19	♐	261 29	+05 31
1950 04 29		261 09	+05 37
1950 05 09		260 41	+05 42
1950 05 19		260 06	+05 47
1950 05 29		259 28	+05 50
1950 06 08		258 47	+05 53
1950 06 18		258 05	+05 54
1950 06 28		257 26	+05 54
1950 07 08		256 50	+05 53
1950 07 18		256 20	+05 51
1950 07 28		255 57	+05 49
1950 08 07		255 42	+05 46
1950 08 17		255 35	+05 42
1950 08 27		255 38	+05 38
1950 09 06		255 51	+05 34
1950 09 16		256 12	+05 30
1950 09 26		256 42	+05 27
1950 10 06		257 20	+05 23
1950 10 16		258 05	+05 20
1950 10 26		258 56	+05 18
1950 11 05		259 52	+05 16
1950 11 15		260 53	+05 15
1950 11 25		261 58	+05 14
1950 12 05		263 04	+05 14
1950 12 15		264 12	+05 15
1950 12 25		265 19	+05 16
1951 01 04		266 26	+05 18
1951 01 14		267 30	+05 21
1951 01 24		268 31	+05 24
1951 02 03		269 27	+05 29
1951 02 13	♑	270 19	+05 33
1951 02 23		271 03	+05 39
1951 03 05		271 41	+05 44
1951 03 15		272 11	+05 51
1951 03 25		272 32	+05 57
1951 04 04		272 44	+06 04
1951 04 14		272 46	+06 10
1951 04 24		272 40	+06 17
1951 05 04		272 25	+06 23
1951 05 14		272 03	+06 28
1951 05 24		271 33	+06 33
1951 06 03		270 59	+06 37
1951 06 13		270 21	+06 39
1951 06 23	♐	269 41	+06 41
1951 07 03		269 01	+06 41
1951 07 13		268 24	+06 40
1951 07 23		267 51	+06 38
1951 08 02		267 24	+06 36
1951 08 12		267 03	+06 32
1951 08 22		266 51	+06 28
1951 09 01		266 47	+06 23
1951 09 11		266 51	+06 19
1951 09 21		267 04	+06 14
1951 10 01		267 26	+06 09
1951 10 11		267 56	+06 05
1951 10 21		268 33	+06 01
1951 10 31		269 17	+05 58
1951 11 10	♑	270 06	+05 55
1951 11 20		271 00	+05 52
1951 11 30		271 58	+05 51
1951 12 10		272 59	+05 50
1951 12 20		274 01	+05 50
1951 12 30		275 04	+05 50
1952 01 09		276 07	+05 52
1952 01 19		277 08	+05 54
1952 01 29		278 06	+05 57
1952 02 08		279 01	+06 00
1952 02 18		279 51	+06 04
1952 02 28		280 36	+06 09
1952 03 09		281 14	+06 14
1952 03 19		281 44	+06 20
1952 03 29		282 07	+06 26
1952 04 08		282 22	+06 32
1952 04 18		282 28	+06 39
1952 04 28		282 26	+06 45
1952 05 08		282 15	+06 51
1952 05 18		281 56	+06 56
1952 05 28		281 31	+07 01
1952 06 07		281 00	+07 05
1952 06 17		280 25	+07 08
1952 06 27		279 47	+07 09
1952 07 07		279 09	+07 10
1952 07 17	♑	278 32	+07 09
1952 07 27		277 58	+07 07
1952 08 06		277 28	+07 05
1952 08 16		277 04	+07 01
1952 08 26		276 47	+06 57
1952 09 05		276 38	+06 52
1952 09 15		276 37	+06 47
1952 09 25		276 44	+06 42
1952 10 05		277 00	+06 37
1952 10 15		277 23	+06 32
1952 10 25		277 54	+06 27
1952 11 04		278 31	+06 23
1952 11 14		279 15	+06 20
1952 11 24		280 03	+06 17
1952 12 04		280 55	+06 14
1952 12 14		281 51	+06 13
1952 12 24		282 49	+06 12
1953 01 03		283 47	+06 12
1953 01 13		284 46	+06 13
1953 01 23		285 44	+06 14
1953 02 02		286 39	+06 16
1953 02 12		287 32	+06 19
1953 02 22		288 20	+06 23
1953 03 04		289 04	+06 27
1953 03 14		289 41	+06 32
1953 03 24		290 12	+06 37
1953 04 03		290 36	+06 43
1953 04 13		290 52	+06 48
1953 04 23		291 00	+06 54
1953 05 03		291 01	+07 00
1953 05 13		290 53	+07 06
1953 05 23		290 37	+07 11
1953 06 02		290 15	+07 16
1953 06 12		289 48	+07 20
1953 06 22		289 15	+07 23
1953 07 02		288 40	+07 24
1953 07 12		288 03	+07 25
1953 07 22		287 27	+07 25
1953 08 01		286 52	+07 23
1953 08 11		286 22	+07 20
1953 08 21		285 56	+07 17
1953 08 31		285 36	+07 13
1953 09 10		285 24	+07 08
1953 09 20		285 19	+07 03
1953 09 30		285 21	+06 57
1953 10 10		285 32	+06 52
1953 10 20		285 51	+06 47
1953 10 30		286 16	+06 42
1953 11 09		286 48	+06 38
1953 11 19		287 27	+06 34
1953 11 29		288 10	+06 30
1953 12 09		288 58	+06 28
1953 12 19		289 49	+06 26
1953 12 29		290 43	+06 24
1954 01 08		291 37	+06 24
1954 01 18		292 33	+06 24
1954 01 28		293 27	+06 25
1954 02 07		294 20	+06 27
1954 02 17		295 10	+06 29
1954 02 27		295 57	+06 32
1954 03 09		296 39	+06 36
1954 03 19		297 16	+06 40
1954 03 29		297 46	+06 45
1954 04 08		298 10	+06 50
1954 04 18		298 27	+06 55
1954 04 28		298 37	+07 01
1954 05 08		298 38	+07 06
1954 05 18		298 33	+07 12
1954 05 28		298 20	+07 16
1954 06 07		298 00	+07 21
1954 06 17		297 35	+07 25
1954 06 27		297 05	+07 27
1954 07 07		296 31	+07 29
1954 07 17		295 56	+07 30
1954 07 27		295 21	+07 30
1954 08 06		294 47	+07 28
1954 08 16		294 16	+07 26
1954 08 26		293 49	+07 23
1954 09 05		293 28	+07 19
1954 09 15		293 13	+07 14
1954 09 25		293 05	+07 09
1954 10 05		293 05	+07 04
1954 10 15	♑	293 12	+06 58
1954 10 25		293 27	+06 53
1954 11 04		293 48	+06 48
1954 11 14		294 17	+06 43
1954 11 24		294 51	+06 39

Chiron ⚷

1954 12 04	♑	295 31	+06 36
1954 12 14	♑	296 14	+06 33
1954 12 24		297 02	+06 31
1955 01 03		297 52	+06 29
1955 01 13		298 43	+06 28
1955 01 23		299 35	+06 28
1955 02 02	♒	300 27	+06 28
1955 02 12	♒	301 17	+06 30
1955 02 22		302 05	+06 32
1955 03 04		302 50	+06 34
1955 03 14		303 30	+06 38
1955 03 24		304 06	+06 41
1955 04 03		304 36	+06 46
1955 04 13		305 00	+06 50
1955 04 23		305 17	+06 55
1955 05 03		305 27	+07 00
1955 05 13		305 30	+07 05
1955 05 23		305 25	+07 10
1955 06 02		305 14	+07 15
1955 06 12		304 56	+07 19
1955 06 22		304 33	+07 22
1955 07 02		304 05	+07 25
1955 07 12		303 33	+07 27
1955 07 22		303 00	+07 28
1955 08 01		302 26	+07 28
1955 08 11		301 52	+07 26
1955 08 21		301 21	+07 24
1955 08 31		300 54	+07 21
1955 09 10		300 32	+07 17
1955 09 20		300 16	+07 13
1955 09 30		300 06	+07 08
1955 10 10		300 04	+07 03
1955 10 20		300 08	+06 57
1955 10 30		300 20	+06 52
1955 11 09		300 39	+06 47
1955 11 19		301 04	+06 43
1955 11 29		301 35	+06 39
1955 12 09		302 11	+06 35
1955 12 19		302 52	+06 32
1955 12 29		303 36	+06 29
1956 01 08		304 23	+06 28
1956 01 18		305 12	+06 26
1956 01 28		306 01	+06 26
1956 02 07		306 50	+06 26
1956 02 17		307 38	+06 27
1956 02 27		308 24	+06 29
1956 03 08		309 07	+06 31
1956 03 18		309 46	+06 34
1956 03 28		310 20	+06 37
1956 04 07		310 49	+06 41
1956 04 17		311 13	+06 45
1956 04 27		311 30	+06 50
1956 05 07		311 40	+06 55
1956 05 17		311 43	+06 59
1956 05 27		311 40	+07 04
1956 06 06		311 30	+07 08
1956 06 16		311 13	+07 12
1956 06 26		310 51	+07 15
1956 07 06		310 25	+07 18
1956 07 16		309 55	+07 19
1956 07 26		309 23	+07 20
1956 08 05		308 49	+07 20
1956 08 15		308 17	+07 19
1956 08 25		307 47	+07 17
1956 09 04		307 20	+07 14
1956 09 14		306 57	+07 10
1956 09 24		306 40	+07 06
1956 10 04		306 29	+07 01
1956 10 14		306 25	+06 56
1956 10 24		306 28	+06 51
1956 11 03		306 37	+06 46
1956 11 13		306 54	+06 42
1956 11 23		307 17	+06 37
1956 12 03		307 45	+06 33
1956 12 13		308 19	+06 29
1956 12 23		308 57	+06 26
1957 01 02		309 39	+06 24
1957 01 12	♒	310 23	+06 22
1957 01 22	♒	311 09	+06 21
1957 02 01		311 56	+06 20
1957 02 11		312 43	+06 20
1957 02 21		313 29	+06 21
1957 03 03		314 13	+06 22
1957 03 13		314 54	+06 24
1957 03 23		315 31	+06 27
1957 04 02		316 05	+06 30
1957 04 12		316 33	+06 33
1957 04 22	♒	316 55	+06 37
1957 05 02	♒	317 12	+06 41
1957 05 12		317 22	+06 45
1957 05 22		317 26	+06 49
1957 06 01		317 23	+06 54
1957 06 11		317 14	+06 58
1957 06 21		316 58	+07 01
1957 07 01		316 37	+07 04
1957 07 11		316 12	+07 06
1957 07 21		315 43	+07 08
1957 07 31		315 12	+07 09
1957 08 10		314 40	+07 09
1957 08 20		314 08	+07 08
1957 08 30		313 39	+07 06
1957 09 09		313 12	+07 03
1957 09 19		312 49	+06 59
1957 09 29		312 32	+06 55
1957 10 09		312 20	+06 51
1957 10 19		312 15	+06 46
1957 10 29		312 17	+06 42
1957 11 08		312 25	+06 37
1957 11 18		312 40	+06 32
1957 11 28		313 00	+06 28
1957 12 08		313 27	+06 24
1957 12 18		313 59	+06 20
1957 12 28		314 35	+06 17
1958 01 07		315 14	+06 14
1958 01 17		315 57	+06 13
1958 01 27		316 41	+06 11
1958 02 06		317 25	+06 11
1958 02 16		318 10	+06 10
1958 02 26		318 54	+06 11
1958 03 08		319 36	+06 12
1958 03 18		320 16	+06 14
1958 03 28		320 52	+06 16
1958 04 07		321 24	+06 19
1958 04 17		321 51	+06 22
1958 04 27		322 13	+06 25
1958 05 07		322 29	+06 29
1958 05 17		322 39	+06 33
1958 05 27		322 43	+06 37
1958 06 06		322 40	+06 41
1958 06 16		322 31	+06 44
1958 06 26		322 17	+06 46
1958 07 06		321 57	+06 50
1958 07 16		321 32	+06 52
1958 07 26		321 05	+06 54
1958 08 05		320 34	+06 55
1958 08 15		320 03	+06 54
1958 08 25		319 32	+06 53
1958 09 04		319 03	+06 52
1958 09 14		318 37	+06 49
1958 09 24		318 14	+06 46
1958 10 04		317 57	+06 42
1958 10 14		317 45	+06 38
1958 10 24		317 39	+06 33
1958 11 03		317 40	+06 29
1958 11 13		317 47	+06 24
1958 11 23		318 00	+06 20
1958 12 03		318 20	+06 15
1958 12 13		318 45	+06 12
1958 12 23		319 15	+06 08
1959 01 02		319 50	+06 05
1959 01 12		320 27	+06 03
1959 01 22		321 08	+06 01
1959 02 01		321 50	+05 59
1959 02 11		322 33	+05 59
1959 02 21		323 16	+05 58
1959 03 03		323 59	+05 59
1959 03 13		324 39	+06 00
1959 03 23		325 17	+06 01
1959 04 02		325 52	+06 03
1959 04 12	♒	326 23	+06 06
1959 04 22	♒	326 49	+06 09
1959 05 02		327 11	+06 12
1959 05 12		327 26	+06 15
1959 05 22		327 36	+06 19
1959 06 01		327 39	+06 22
1959 06 11		327 36	+06 26
1959 06 21		327 28	+06 29
1959 07 01		327 13	+06 32
1959 07 11		326 54	+06 34
1959 07 21		326 30	+06 36
1959 07 31		326 03	+06 38
1959 08 10		325 34	+06 38
1959 08 20		325 04	+06 38
1959 08 30		324 34	+06 37
1959 09 09		324 05	+06 35
1959 09 19		323 39	+06 33
1959 09 29		323 17	+06 30
1959 10 09		322 59	+06 26
1959 10 19		322 47	+06 22
1959 10 29		322 41	+06 18
1959 11 08		322 41	+06 14
1959 11 18		322 48	+06 09
1959 11 28	♒	323 01	+06 05
1959 12 08	♒	323 19	+06 01
1959 12 18		323 43	+05 57
1959 12 28		324 12	+05 54
1960 01 07		324 45	+05 51
1960 01 17		325 22	+05 49
1960 01 27		326 01	+05 47
1960 02 06		326 41	+05 45
1960 02 16		327 23	+05 45
1960 02 26		328 05	+05 44
1960 03 07		328 46	+05 45
1960 03 17		329 25	+05 46
1960 03 27	♓	330 02	+05 47
1960 04 06	♓	330 35	+05 49
1960 04 16		331 05	+05 51
1960 04 26		331 30	+05 54
1960 05 06		331 51	+05 56
1960 05 16		332 05	+05 59
1960 05 26		332 14	+06 03
1960 06 05		332 18	+06 06
1960 06 15		332 15	+06 09
1960 06 25		332 06	+06 12
1960 07 05		331 52	+06 15
1960 07 15		331 33	+06 17
1960 07 25		331 10	+06 19
1960 08 04		330 44	+06 20
1960 08 14		330 15	+06 20
1960 08 24	♒	329 45	+06 20
1960 09 03	♒	329 16	+06 19
1960 09 13		328 48	+06 17
1960 09 23		328 22	+06 15
1960 10 03		328 00	+06 12
1960 10 13		327 43	+06 09
1960 10 23		327 31	+06 05
1960 11 02		327 25	+06 01
1960 11 12		327 25	+05 57
1960 11 22		327 31	+05 53
1960 12 02		327 43	+05 49
1960 12 12		328 01	+05 45
1960 12 22		328 25	+05 41
1961 01 01		328 53	+05 38
1961 01 11		329 25	+05 35
1961 01 21	♓	330 00	+05 33
1961 01 31	♓	330 38	+05 31
1961 02 10		331 17	+05 30
1961 02 20		331 58	+05 29
1961 03 02		332 38	+05 29
1961 03 12		333 18	+05 29
1961 03 22		333 56	+05 30
1961 04 01		334 31	+05 31
1961 04 11		335 04	+05 33
1961 04 21		335 32	+05 35
1961 05 01		335 57	+05 37
1961 05 11		336 16	+05 40
1961 05 21		336 30	+05 43
1961 05 31		336 39	+05 45
1961 06 10		336 42	+05 48
1961 06 20		336 39	+05 51
1961 06 30		336 30	+05 54
1961 07 10	♓	336 16	+05 56
1961 07 20	♓	335 57	+05 58
1961 07 30		335 34	+06 00
1961 08 09		335 09	+06 01
1961 08 19		334 40	+06 01
1961 08 29		334 11	+06 01
1961 09 08		333 42	+06 00
1961 09 18		333 15	+05 58
1961 09 28		332 50	+05 56
1961 10 08		332 28	+05 53
1961 10 18		332 12	+05 50
1961 10 28		332 00	+05 46
1961 11 07		331 54	+05 43
1961 11 17		331 54	+05 39
1961 11 27		332 00	+05 35
1961 12 07		332 12	+05 31
1961 12 17		332 29	+05 27
1961 12 27		332 52	+05 24
1962 01 06		333 19	+05 21
1962 01 16		333 50	+05 19
1962 01 26		334 25	+05 16
1962 02 05		335 02	+05 15
1962 02 15		335 40	+05 13
1962 02 25		336 19	+05 13
1962 03 07		336 59	+05 12
1962 03 17		337 37	+05 13
1962 03 27		338 14	+05 13
1962 04 06		338 48	+05 14
1962 04 16		339 20	+05 16
1962 04 26		339 47	+05 17
1962 05 06		340 11	+05 20
1962 05 16		340 30	+05 22
1962 05 26		340 43	+05 24
1962 06 05		340 51	+05 27
1962 06 15		340 53	+05 30
1962 06 25		340 50	+05 32
1962 07 05	♓	340 41	+05 35
1962 07 15	♓	340 27	+05 37
1962 07 25		340 09	+05 39
1962 08 04		339 46	+05 40
1962 08 14		339 20	+05 41
1962 08 24		338 53	+05 41
1962 09 03		338 24	+05 41
1962 09 13		337 56	+05 40
1962 09 23		337 29	+05 38
1962 10 03		337 04	+05 36
1962 10 13		336 43	+05 33
1962 10 23		336 27	+05 30
1962 11 02		336 15	+05 27
1962 11 12		336 10	+05 23
1962 11 22		336 10	+05 20
1962 12 02		336 16	+05 16
1962 12 12		336 27	+05 12
1962 12 22		336 45	+05 09
1963 01 01		337 07	+05 06
1963 01 11		337 34	+05 03
1963 01 21		338 04	+05 01
1963 01 31		338 38	+04 59
1963 02 10		339 14	+04 57
1963 02 20		339 52	+04 56
1963 03 02		340 30	+04 55
1963 03 12		341 08	+04 55
1963 03 22		341 46	+04 55
1963 04 01		342 22	+04 55
1963 04 11		342 55	+04 56
1963 04 21		343 26	+04 58
1963 05 01		343 52	+04 59
1963 05 11		344 15	+05 01
1963 05 21		344 33	+05 03
1963 05 31		344 46	+05 06
1963 06 10		344 53	+05 08
1963 06 20		344 55	+05 10
1963 06 30		344 51	+05 13
1963 07 10		344 42	+05 15
1963 07 20	♓	344 28	+05 17
1963 07 30	♓	344 09	+05 18
1963 08 09		343 47	+05 19
1963 08 19		343 21	+05 20
1963 08 29		342 54	+05 20
1963 09 08		342 26	+05 20
1963 09 18		341 58	+05 19
1963 09 28		341 31	+05 17
1963 10 08		341 07	+05 15
1963 10 18		340 47	+05 12
1963 10 28		340 31	+05 10
1963 11 07		340 20	+05 06
1963 11 17		340 15	+05 03
1963 11 27		340 15	+05 00
1963 12 07		340 21	+04 56
1963 12 17		340 33	+04 53
1963 12 27		340 50	+04 50
1964 01 06		341 12	+04 47
1964 01 16		341 38	+04 44
1964 01 26		342 09	+04 42
1964 02 05		342 42	+04 40
1964 02 15		343 17	+04 38
1964 02 25		343 54	+04 37
1964 03 06		344 32	+04 37
1964 03 16		345 09	+04 36
1964 03 26		345 46	+04 36
1964 04 05		346 21	+04 37
1964 04 15		346 53	+04 38
1964 04 25		347 23	+04 39
1964 05 05		347 49	+04 40
1964 05 15		348 11	+04 42
1964 05 25		348 28	+04 44
1964 06 04		348 40	+04 46
1964 06 14		348 46	+04 48
1964 06 24		348 48	+04 50
1964 07 04		348 44	+04 52
1964 07 14		348 34	+04 54
1964 07 24		348 20	+04 56
1964 08 03		348 01	+04 57
1964 08 13		347 39	+04 58
1964 08 23		347 13	+04 59
1964 09 02		346 46	+04 59
1964 09 12		346 18	+04 58
1964 09 22		345 51	+04 57
1964 10 02		345 25	+04 55
1964 10 12		345 01	+04 53
1964 10 22		344 41	+04 51
1964 11 01		344 26	+04 48
1964 11 11		344 15	+04 45
1964 11 21		344 10	+04 42
1964 12 01		344 11	+04 39
1964 12 11		344 17	+04 36
1964 12 21		344 29	+04 33
1964 12 31		344 46	+04 30
1965 01 10		345 08	+04 27
1965 01 20		345 35	+04 24
1965 01 30		346 05	+04 22

1965 02 09	♓	346 37	+04 21
1965 02 19		347 12	+04 19
1965 03 01		347 49	+04 18
1965 03 11		348 26	+04 17
1965 03 21		349 03	+04 17
1965 03 31		349 38	+04 17
1965 04 10		350 12	+04 18
1965 04 20		350 44	+04 18
1965 04 30		351 13	+04 19
1965 05 10		351 38	+04 21
1965 05 20		351 59	+04 22
1965 05 30		352 15	+04 24
1965 06 09		352 27	+04 26
1965 06 19		352 33	+04 28
1965 06 29		352 33	+04 29
1965 07 09		352 29	+04 31
1965 07 19		352 19	+04 33
1965 07 29	♓	352 04	+04 34
1965 08 08		351 46	+04 35
1965 08 18		351 23	+04 36
1965 08 28		350 58	+04 37
1965 09 07		350 31	+04 36
1965 09 17		350 03	+04 36
1965 09 27		349 36	+04 35
1965 10 07		349 10	+04 33
1965 10 17		348 47	+04 31
1965 10 27		348 28	+04 29
1965 11 06		348 13	+04 26
1965 11 16		348 03	+04 24
1965 11 26		347 58	+04 21
1965 12 06		348 00	+04 18
1965 12 16		348 06	+04 15
1965 12 26		348 18	+04 12
1966 01 05		348 36	+04 09
1966 01 15		348 58	+04 06
1966 01 25		349 24	+04 04
1966 02 04		349 54	+04 02
1966 02 14		350 26	+04 01
1966 02 24		351 01	+03 59
1966 03 06		351 37	+03 58
1966 03 16		352 13	+03 58
1966 03 26		352 50	+03 57
1966 04 05		353 25	+03 57
1966 04 15		353 58	+03 58
1966 04 25		354 29	+03 58
1966 05 05		354 57	+03 59
1966 05 15		355 21	+04 00
1966 05 25		355 42	+04 02
1966 06 04		355 57	+04 03
1966 06 14		356 08	+04 05
1966 06 24		356 13	+04 06
1966 07 04		356 13	+04 08
1966 07 14		356 08	+04 10
1966 07 24		355 58	+04 11
1966 08 03		355 43	+04 12
1966 08 13		355 24	+04 13
1966 08 23		355 01	+04 14
1966 09 02		354 36	+04 14
1966 09 12		354 09	+04 14
1966 09 22		353 42	+04 13
1966 10 02		353 15	+04 12
1966 10 12		352 50	+04 10
1966 10 22		352 27	+04 09
1966 11 01		352 08	+04 06
1966 11 11		351 54	+04 04
1966 11 21		351 44	+04 01
1966 12 01		351 40	+03 59
1966 12 11		351 42	+03 56
1966 12 21		351 49	+03 53
1966 12 31		352 02	+03 50
1967 01 10		352 19	+03 48
1967 01 20		352 42	+03 45
1967 01 30		353 08	+03 43
1967 02 09		353 38	+03 42
1967 02 19		354 10	+03 40
1967 03 01		354 44	+03 39
1967 03 11		355 20	+03 38
1967 03 21		355 56	+03 37
1967 03 31		356 32	+03 37
1967 04 10		357 06	+03 37
1967 04 20		357 39	+03 37
1967 04 30		358 09	+03 38
1967 05 10		358 37	+03 38
1967 05 20		359 00	+03 39
1967 05 30		359 20	+03 41
1967 06 09		359 35	+03 42
1967 06 19		359 45	+03 43
1967 06 29		359 49	+03 45
1967 07 09		359 49	+03 46
1967 07 19		359 43	+03 47
1967 07 29		359 33	+03 49
1967 08 08		359 17	+03 50
1967 08 18		358 58	+03 50
1967 08 28		358 35	+03 51
1967 09 07		358 10	+03 51
1967 09 17		357 43	+03 50
1967 09 27		357 16	+03 50
1967 10 07		356 49	+03 49
1967 10 17		356 24	+03 47
1967 10 27	♓	356 02	+03 45
1967 11 06		355 44	+03 43
1967 11 16		355 30	+03 41
1967 11 26		355 21	+03 39
1967 12 06		355 18	+03 36
1967 12 16		355 20	+03 33
1967 12 26		355 27	+03 31
1968 01 05		355 40	+03 28
1968 01 15		355 56	+03 26
1968 01 25		356 21	+03 24
1968 02 04		356 47	+03 22
1968 02 14		357 17	+03 20
1968 02 24		357 49	+03 19
1968 03 05		358 24	+03 18
1968 03 15		358 59	+03 17
1968 03 25		359 35	+03 16
1968 04 04	♈	0 10	+03 16
1968 04 14		0 44	+03 16
1968 04 24		1 16	+03 16
1968 05 04		1 46	+03 16
1968 05 14		2 13	+03 17
1968 05 24		2 36	+03 18
1968 06 03		2 54	+03 19
1968 06 13		3 09	+03 20
1968 06 23		3 18	+03 21
1968 07 03		3 22	+03 22
1968 07 13		3 21	+03 24
1968 07 23		3 15	+03 25
1968 08 02		3 04	+03 26
1968 08 12		2 48	+03 26
1968 08 22		2 28	+03 27
1968 09 01		2 05	+03 27
1968 09 11		1 40	+03 27
1968 09 21		1 13	+03 27
1968 10 01		0 46	+03 26
1968 10 11		0 19	+03 25
1968 10 21	♓	359 55	+03 23
1968 10 31		359 33	+03 22
1968 11 10		359 15	+03 20
1968 11 20		359 02	+03 18
1968 11 30		358 54	+03 15
1968 12 10		358 51	+03 13
1968 12 20		358 54	+03 11
1968 12 30		359 02	+03 08
1969 01 09		359 16	+03 06
1969 01 19		359 34	+03 04
1969 01 29		359 57	+03 02
1969 02 08	♈	0 23	+03 00
1969 02 18		0 53	+02 59
1969 02 28		1 26	+02 57
1969 03 10		2 00	+02 56
1969 03 20		2 35	+02 55
1969 03 30		3 10	+02 55
1969 04 09		3 45	+02 54
1969 04 19		4 19	+02 54
1969 04 29		4 51	+02 54
1969 05 09		5 20	+02 55
1969 05 19		5 46	+02 55
1969 05 29		6 09	+02 56
1969 06 08		6 27	+02 57
1969 06 18		6 40	+02 58
1969 06 28		6 49	+02 59
1969 07 08		6 53	+02 59
1969 07 18		6 51	+03 00
1969 07 28		6 44	+03 01
1969 08 07		6 32	+03 02
1969 08 17		6 16	+03 03
1969 08 27		5 56	+03 03
1969 09 06		5 33	+03 03
1969 09 16		5 07	+03 03
1969 09 26		4 40	+03 02
1969 10 06		4 13	+03 02
1969 10 16		3 47	+03 01
1969 10 26		3 23	+02 59
1969 11 05		3 02	+02 58
1969 11 15		2 45	+02 56
1969 11 25		2 32	+02 54
1969 12 05		2 24	+02 52
1969 12 15		2 22	+02 49
1969 12 25		2 26	+02 47
1970 01 04		2 34	+02 45
1970 01 14		2 48	+02 43
1970 01 24	♈	3 07	+02 41
1970 02 03		3 31	+02 39
1970 02 13		3 58	+02 38
1970 02 23		4 28	+02 36
1970 03 05		5 00	+02 35
1970 03 15		5 34	+02 34
1970 03 25		6 09	+02 33
1970 04 04		6 45	+02 33
1970 04 14		7 19	+02 32
1970 04 24	♈	7 53	+02 32
1970 05 04		8 24	+02 32
1970 05 14		8 53	+02 32
1970 05 24		9 19	+02 33
1970 06 03		9 40	+02 33
1970 06 13		9 56	+02 34
1970 06 23		10 11	+02 35
1970 07 03		10 19	+02 35
1970 07 13		10 22	+02 36
1970 07 23		10 20	+02 37
1970 08 02		10 12	+02 37
1970 08 12		10 00	+02 38
1970 08 22		9 43	+02 38
1970 09 01		9 23	+02 38
1970 09 11		8 59	+02 38
1970 09 21		8 34	+02 38
1970 10 01		8 07	+02 38
1970 10 11		7 40	+02 37
1970 10 21		7 14	+02 36
1970 10 31		6 50	+02 34
1970 11 10		6 29	+02 33
1970 11 20		6 12	+02 31
1970 11 30		6 00	+02 29
1970 12 10		5 53	+02 27
1970 12 20		5 52	+02 25
1970 12 30		5 56	+02 23
1971 01 09		6 05	+02 21
1971 01 19		6 20	+02 20
1971 01 29		6 40	+02 18
1971 02 08		7 03	+02 16
1971 02 18		7 31	+02 15
1971 02 28		8 01	+02 14
1971 03 10		8 34	+02 12
1971 03 20		9 08	+02 11
1971 03 30		9 43	+02 11
1971 04 09		10 18	+02 10
1971 04 19		10 53	+02 10
1971 04 29		11 26	+02 10
1971 05 09		11 57	+02 09
1971 05 19		12 25	+02 10
1971 05 29		12 51	+02 10
1971 06 08		13 12	+02 10
1971 06 18		13 29	+02 11
1971 06 28		13 41	+02 11
1971 07 08		13 49	+02 11
1971 07 18		13 51	+02 12
1971 07 28		13 48	+02 12
1971 08 07		13 40	+02 13
1971 08 17		13 28	+02 13
1971 08 27		13 10	+02 13
1971 09 06		12 50	+02 13
1971 09 16		12 26	+02 13
1971 09 26		12 00	+02 13
1971 10 06		11 33	+02 12
1971 10 16		11 06	+02 11
1971 10 26		10 40	+02 10
1971 11 05		10 16	+02 09
1971 11 15		9 56	+02 08
1971 11 25		9 40	+02 06
1971 12 05		9 28	+02 04
1971 12 15		9 22	+02 03
1971 12 25		9 21	+02 01
1972 01 04		9 26	+01 59
1972 01 14		9 36	+01 57
1972 01 24		9 52	+01 56
1972 02 03		10 12	+01 54
1972 02 13		10 36	+01 53
1972 02 23		11 04	+01 51
1972 03 04		11 34	+01 50
1972 03 14		12 07	+01 49
1972 03 24		12 42	+01 48
1972 04 03		13 17	+01 48
1972 04 13		13 52	+01 47
1972 04 23	♈	14 27	+01 47
1972 05 03		14 59	+01 46
1972 05 13		15 30	+01 46
1972 05 23		15 59	+01 46
1972 06 02		16 23	+01 46
1972 06 12		16 44	+01 46
1972 06 22		17 01	+01 47
1972 07 02		17 13	+01 47
1972 07 12		17 20	+01 47
1972 07 22		17 22	+01 47
1972 08 01		17 18	+01 48
1972 08 11		17 10	+01 48
1972 08 21		16 56	+01 48
1972 08 31		16 39	+01 48
1972 09 10		16 17	+01 48
1972 09 20		15 53	+01 47
1972 09 30		15 27	+01 47
1972 10 10		15 00	+01 46
1972 10 20		14 33	+01 45
1972 10 30		14 07	+01 44
1972 11 09		13 44	+01 43
1972 11 19		13 24	+01 42
1972 11 29		13 08	+01 40
1972 12 09	♈	12 57	+01 39
1972 12 19		12 52	+01 37
1972 12 29		12 52	+01 36
1973 01 08		12 57	+01 34
1973 01 18		13 08	+01 33
1973 01 28		13 24	+01 31
1973 02 07		13 45	+01 30
1973 02 17		14 09	+01 29
1973 02 27		14 38	+01 28
1973 03 09		15 09	+01 26
1973 03 19		15 42	+01 26
1973 03 29		16 17	+01 25
1973 04 08		16 52	+01 24
1973 04 18		17 27	+01 23
1973 04 28		18 02	+01 23
1973 05 08		18 35	+01 23
1973 05 18		19 05	+01 22
1973 05 28		19 33	+01 22
1973 06 07		19 58	+01 22
1973 06 17		20 18	+01 22
1973 06 27		20 35	+01 22
1973 07 07		20 46	+01 22
1973 07 17		20 53	+01 22
1973 07 27		20 54	+01 22
1973 08 06		20 50	+01 22
1973 08 16		20 41	+01 22
1973 08 26		20 27	+01 22
1973 09 05		20 09	+01 22
1973 09 15		19 47	+01 21
1973 09 25		19 22	+01 21
1973 10 05		18 56	+01 20
1973 10 15		18 28	+01 20
1973 10 25		18 01	+01 19
1973 11 04		17 36	+01 18
1973 11 14		17 13	+01 17
1973 11 24		16 53	+01 16
1973 12 04		16 38	+01 14
1973 12 14		16 28	+01 13
1973 12 24		16 23	+01 12
1974 01 03		16 24	+01 10
1974 01 13		16 30	+01 09
1974 01 23		16 41	+01 08
1974 02 02		16 58	+01 06
1974 02 12		17 19	+01 05
1974 02 22		17 45	+01 04
1974 03 04		18 14	+01 03
1974 03 14		18 45	+01 02
1974 03 24		19 19	+01 01
1974 04 03		19 54	+01 00
1974 04 13		20 30	+01 00
1974 04 23		21 05	+00 59
1974 05 03		21 40	+00 59
1974 05 13		22 12	+00 58
1974 05 23		22 43	+00 58
1974 06 02		23 11	+00 57
1974 06 12		23 35	+00 57
1974 06 22		23 56	+00 57
1974 07 02		24 12	+00 57
1974 07 12		24 23	+00 57
1974 07 22	♈	24 29	+00 56
1974 08 01		24 29	+00 56
1974 08 11		24 25	+00 56
1974 08 21		24 15	+00 56
1974 08 31		24 01	+00 55
1974 09 10		23 42	+00 55
1974 09 20		23 20	+00 54
1974 09 30		22 55	+00 54
1974 10 10		22 28	+00 53
1974 10 20		22 00	+00 53
1974 10 30		21 33	+00 52
1974 11 09		21 08	+00 51
1974 11 19		20 45	+00 50
1974 11 29		20 26	+00 49
1974 12 09		20 11	+00 48
1974 12 19		20 01	+00 46
1974 12 29		19 57	+00 45
1975 01 08		19 58	+00 44
1975 01 18		20 05	+00 43
1975 01 28		20 18	+00 42
1975 02 07		20 35	+00 41
1975 02 17		20 57	+00 40
1975 02 27		21 23	+00 39
1975 03 09		21 53	+00 38
1975 03 19		22 25	+00 37
1975 03 29		22 59	+00 36
1975 04 08		23 35	+00 36
1975 04 18		24 10	+00 35
1975 04 28		24 46	+00 34

Chiron 

⚷ Chiron

Date	Sign	Position	Declination
1975 05 08	♈	25 21	+00 34
1975 05 18		25 54	+00 33
1975 05 28		26 25	+00 33
1975 06 07		26 52	+00 32
1975 06 17		27 17	+00 32
1975 06 27		27 37	+00 31
1975 07 07		27 52	+00 31
1975 07 17		28 03	+00 30
1975 07 27		28 09	+00 30
1975 08 06		28 09	+00 29
1975 08 16		28 04	+00 29
1975 08 26		27 54	+00 29
1975 09 05		27 39	+00 28
1975 09 15		27 20	+00 27
1975 09 25		26 57	+00 27
1975 10 05		26 31	+00 26
1975 10 15		26 04	+00 25
1975 10 25		25 36	+00 25
1975 11 04		25 09	+00 24
1975 11 14		24 43	+00 23
1975 11 24		24 21	+00 22
1975 12 04		24 02	+00 21
1975 12 14		23 48	+00 20
1975 12 24		23 38	+00 19
1976 01 03		23 35	+00 18
1976 01 13		23 37	+00 18
1976 01 23		23 45	+00 17
1976 02 02		23 58	+00 16
1976 02 12		24 16	+00 15
1976 02 22		24 39	+00 14
1976 03 03		25 06	+00 13
1976 03 13		25 36	+00 13
1976 03 23		26 09	+00 12
1976 04 02		26 43	+00 11
1976 04 12		27 19	+00 10
1976 04 22		27 56	+00 10
1976 05 02		28 32	+00 09
1976 05 12		29 07	+00 08
1976 05 22		29 40	+00 08
1976 06 01		30 11	+00 07
1976 06 11	♉	30 38	+00 06
1976 06 21		31 03	+00 06
1976 07 01		31 23	+00 05
1976 07 11		31 38	+00 04
1976 07 21		31 49	+00 04
1976 07 31		31 54	+00 03
1976 08 10		31 54	+00 02
1976 08 20		31 49	+00 01
1976 08 30		31 38	+00 01
1976 09 09		31 22	00 00
1976 09 19		31 03	-00 01
1976 09 29		30 39	-00 02
1976 10 09		30 13	-00 03
1976 10 19	♈	29 45	-00 03
1976 10 29		29 17	-00 04
1976 11 08		28 50	-00 05
1976 11 18		28 24	-00 06
1976 11 28		28 02	-00 06
1976 12 08		27 43	-00 07
1976 12 18		27 29	-00 08
1976 12 28		27 21	-00 09
1977 01 07		27 18	-00 09
1977 01 17		27 20	-00 10
1977 01 27		27 29	-00 11
1977 02 06		27 43	-00 11
1977 02 16		28 02	-00 12
1977 02 26		28 25	-00 12
1977 03 08		28 53	-00 13
1977 03 18		29 24	-00 14
1977 03 28		29 57	-00 14
1977 04 07	♉	30 33	-00 15
1977 04 17		31 09	-00 16
1977 04 27		31 46	-00 16
1977 05 07		32 23	-00 17
1977 05 17		32 56	-00 18
1977 05 27		33 32	-00 19
1977 06 06		34 03	-00 20
1977 06 16		34 31	-00 20
1977 06 26		34 55	-00 21
1977 07 06		35 15	-00 22
1977 07 16		35 31	-00 23
1977 07 26		35 41	-00 24
1977 08 05		35 46	-00 25
1977 08 15		35 46	-00 26
1977 08 25		35 40	-00 27
1977 09 04		35 29	-00 28
1977 09 14		35 12	-00 29
1977 09 24		34 52	-00 30
1977 10 04	♉	34 28	-00 31
1977 10 14		34 01	-00 32
1977 10 24		33 33	-00 33
1977 11 03		33 05	-00 34
1977 11 13		32 37	-00 34
1977 11 23		32 11	-00 35
1977 12 03		31 49	-00 36
1977 12 13		31 30	-00 36
1977 12 23		31 17	-00 37
1978 01 02		31 09	-00 37
1978 01 12		31 06	-00 38
1978 01 22		31 10	-00 38
1978 02 01		31 19	-00 38
1978 02 11		31 34	-00 39
1978 02 21		31 54	-00 39
1978 03 03		32 16	-00 40
1978 03 13		32 47	-00 40
1978 03 23		33 18	-00 41
1978 04 02		33 53	-00 41
1978 04 12		34 29	-00 42
1978 04 22		35 06	-00 42
1978 05 02		35 43	-00 43
1978 05 12		36 20	-00 44
1978 05 22		36 56	-00 45
1978 06 01		37 30	-00 46
1978 06 11		38 02	-00 47
1978 06 21		38 30	-00 48
1978 07 01		38 55	-00 49
1978 07 11		39 15	-00 50
1978 07 21		39 31	-00 51
1978 07 31		39 41	-00 53
1978 08 10		39 46	-00 54
1978 08 20		39 45	-00 55
1978 08 30		39 39	-00 57
1978 09 09		39 27	-00 58
1978 09 19		39 11	-00 59
1978 09 29		38 50	-01 00
1978 10 09		38 25	-01 01
1978 10 19		37 58	-01 02
1978 10 29		37 29	-01 03
1978 11 08		37 00	-01 04
1978 11 18		36 32	-01 05
1978 11 28		36 06	-01 05
1978 12 08		35 44	-01 06
1978 12 18		35 26	-01 06
1978 12 28		35 12	-01 06
1979 01 07		35 04	-01 07
1979 01 17	♉	35 03	-01 07
1979 01 27		35 07	-01 07
1979 02 06		35 17	-01 07
1979 02 16		35 32	-01 07
1979 02 26		35 53	-01 07
1979 03 08		36 18	-01 08
1979 03 18		36 48	-01 08
1979 03 28		37 20	-01 08
1979 04 07		37 55	-01 09
1979 04 17		38 32	-01 09
1979 04 27		39 10	-01 10
1979 05 07		39 49	-01 11
1979 05 17		40 26	-01 12
1979 05 27		41 03	-01 13
1979 06 06		41 38	-01 14
1979 06 16		42 10	-01 15
1979 06 26		42 39	-01 16
1979 07 06		43 04	-01 17
1979 07 16		43 24	-01 19
1979 07 26		43 40	-01 20
1979 08 05		43 50	-01 22
1979 08 15		43 55	-01 24
1979 08 25		43 54	-01 25
1979 09 04		43 48	-01 27
1979 09 14		43 36	-01 28
1979 09 24		43 19	-01 30
1979 10 04		42 57	-01 31
1979 10 14		42 32	-01 33
1979 10 24		42 04	-01 34
1979 11 03		41 35	-01 35
1979 11 13		41 06	-01 35
1979 11 23		40 37	-01 36
1979 12 03		40 11	-01 37
1979 12 13		39 48	-01 37
1979 12 23		39 30	-01 37
1980 01 02		39 17	-01 37
1980 01 12		39 09	-01 37
1980 01 22		39 08	-01 37
1980 02 01		39 13	-01 37
1980 02 11		39 24	-01 36
1980 02 21		39 40	-01 36
1980 03 02		40 02	-01 36
1980 03 12		40 28	-01 36
1980 03 22		40 58	-01 36
1980 04 01		41 32	-01 37
1980 04 11		42 08	-01 37
1980 04 21		42 46	-01 37
1980 05 01		43 25	-01 38
1980 05 11		44 04	-01 39
1980 05 21	♉	44 43	-01 40
1980 05 31		45 20	-01 41
1980 06 10		45 56	-01 42
1980 06 20		46 28	-01 44
1980 06 30		46 58	-01 45
1980 07 10		47 24	-01 47
1980 07 20		47 45	-01 48
1980 07 30		48 01	-01 50
1980 08 09		48 11	-01 52
1980 08 19		48 16	-01 54
1980 08 29		48 16	-01 56
1980 09 08		48 09	-01 58
1980 09 18		47 57	-02 00
1980 09 28		47 39	-02 02
1980 10 08		47 17	-02 03
1980 10 18		46 51	-02 05
1980 10 28		46 23	-02 06
1980 11 07		45 53	-02 07
1980 11 17		45 23	-02 08
1980 11 27		44 54	-02 08
1980 12 07		44 27	-02 09
1980 12 17		44 04	-02 09
1980 12 27		43 46	-02 09
1981 01 06		43 33	-02 08
1981 01 16		43 25	-02 08
1981 01 26	♉	43 25	-02 08
1981 02 05		43 30	-02 07
1981 02 15		43 41	-02 07
1981 02 25		43 59	-02 06
1981 03 07		44 21	-02 06
1981 03 17		44 48	-02 06
1981 03 27		45 20	-02 06
1981 04 06		45 54	-02 06
1981 04 16		46 31	-02 06
1981 04 26		47 10	-02 06
1981 05 06		47 50	-02 07
1981 05 16		48 31	-02 08
1981 05 26		49 11	-02 09
1981 06 05		49 49	-02 10
1981 06 15		50 26	-02 11
1981 06 25		51 00	-02 13
1981 07 05		51 30	-02 15
1981 07 15		51 56	-02 17
1981 07 25		52 18	-02 19
1981 08 04		52 35	-02 21
1981 08 14		52 46	-02 23
1981 08 24		52 51	-02 26
1981 09 03		52 51	-02 28
1981 09 13		52 44	-02 30
1981 09 23		52 31	-02 33
1981 10 03		52 14	-02 35
1981 10 13		51 51	-02 37
1981 10 23		51 25	-02 38
1981 11 02		50 55	-02 40
1981 11 12		50 25	-02 41
1981 11 22		49 54	-02 41
1981 12 02		49 24	-02 42
1981 12 12		48 57	-02 42
1981 12 22		48 34	-02 42
1982 01 01		48 15	-02 41
1982 01 11		48 02	-02 41
1982 01 21		47 55	-02 40
1982 01 31		47 55	-02 39
1982 02 10		48 00	-02 38
1982 02 20		48 12	-02 36
1982 03 02		48 30	-02 37
1982 03 12		48 54	-02 36
1982 03 22		49 22	-02 36
1982 04 01		49 54	-02 36
1982 04 11		50 30	-02 36
1982 04 21		51 09	-02 36
1982 05 01		51 49	-02 36
1982 05 11		52 30	-02 37
1982 05 21		53 12	-02 37
1982 05 31		53 53	-02 39
1982 06 10		54 33	-02 40
1982 06 20		55 11	-02 41
1982 06 30		55 46	-02 43
1982 07 10		56 18	-02 45
1982 07 20		56 45	-02 48
1982 07 30		57 08	-02 50
1982 08 09		57 25	-02 52
1982 08 19		57 37	-02 55
1982 08 29		57 43	-02 58
1982 09 08		57 43	-03 01
1982 09 18		57 36	-03 03
1982 09 28		57 24	-03 06
1982 10 08		57 06	-03 08
1982 10 18		56 43	-03 11
1982 10 28		56 16	-03 13
1982 11 07		55 46	-03 14
1982 11 17		55 14	-03 15
1982 11 27		54 42	-03 16
1982 12 07		54 12	-03 16
1982 12 17		53 44	-03 16
1982 12 27		53 20	-03 16
1983 01 06		53 01	-03 15
1983 01 16		52 48	-03 14
1983 01 26		52 41	-03 13
1983 02 05	♉	52 41	-03 12
1983 02 15		52 47	-03 11
1983 02 25		53 00	-03 10
1983 03 07		53 18	-03 08
1983 03 17		53 43	-03 08
1983 03 27		54 12	-03 07
1983 04 06		54 46	-03 06
1983 04 16		55 23	-03 06
1983 04 26		56 02	-03 06
1983 05 06		56 44	-03 06
1983 05 16		57 27	-03 07
1983 05 26		58 10	-03 08
1983 06 05		58 53	-03 09
1983 06 15		59 34	-03 10
1983 06 25	♊	60 14	-03 12
1983 07 05		60 50	-03 14
1983 07 15		61 24	-03 16
1983 07 25		61 53	-03 19
1983 08 04		62 17	-03 22
1983 08 14		62 36	-03 25
1983 08 24		62 49	-03 28
1983 09 03		62 55	-03 31
1983 09 13		62 56	-03 34
1983 09 23		62 49	-03 37
1983 10 03		62 37	-03 40
1983 10 13		62 19	-03 43
1983 10 23		61 55	-03 46
1983 11 02		61 28	-03 48
1983 11 12		60 57	-03 50
1983 11 22		60 25	-03 51
1983 12 02	♉	59 52	-03 52
1983 12 12		59 21	-03 52
1983 12 22		58 52	-03 52
1984 01 01		58 27	-03 51
1984 01 11		58 08	-03 50
1984 01 21		57 54	-03 49
1984 01 31		57 47	-03 47
1984 02 10		57 47	-03 45
1984 02 20		57 53	-03 44
1984 03 01		58 06	-03 42
1984 03 11		58 26	-03 41
1984 03 21		58 51	-03 39
1984 03 31		59 21	-03 38
1984 04 10		59 56	-03 38
1984 04 20	♊	60 35	-03 37
1984 04 30		61 16	-03 37
1984 05 10		61 59	-03 37
1984 05 20		62 44	-03 37
1984 05 30		63 29	-03 38
1984 06 09		64 13	-03 40
1984 06 19		64 57	-03 41
1984 06 29		65 38	-03 43
1984 07 09		66 17	-03 45
1984 07 19		66 52	-03 48
1984 07 29		67 23	-03 51
1984 08 08		67 49	-03 54
1984 08 18		68 09	-03 57
1984 08 28		68 23	-04 01
1984 09 07		68 31	-04 04
1984 09 17		68 33	-04 08
1984 09 27		68 27	-04 12
1984 10 07		68 15	-04 15
1984 10 17		67 57	-04 18
1984 10 27		67 34	-04 21
1984 11 06		67 06	-04 24
1984 11 16		66 34	-04 26
1984 11 26		66 01	-04 27
1984 12 06		65 27	-04 28
1984 12 16		64 55	-04 28
1984 12 26		64 25	-04 28
1985 01 05		63 59	-04 27
1985 01 15		63 39	-04 25
1985 01 25		63 24	-04 24
1985 02 04		63 17	-04 22
1985 02 14		63 16	-04 20
1985 02 24		63 23	-04 17
1985 03 06		63 36	-04 15
1985 03 16		63 56	-04 13
1985 03 26		64 23	-04 12
1985 04 05		64 54	-04 10
1985 04 15		65 30	-04 09
1985 04 25		66 10	-04 08
1985 05 05	♊	66 53	-04 08
1985 05 15		67 36	-04 08
1985 05 25		68 25	-04 08
1985 06 04		69 12	-04 09
1985 06 14		69 59	-04 10
1985 06 24		70 44	-04 12
1985 07 04		71 28	-04 14
1985 07 14		72 09	-04 16
1985 07 24		72 46	-04 19
1985 08 03		73 20	-04 22
1985 08 13		73 48	-04 26

1985 08 23	♊	74 11	-04 30
1985 09 02		74 27	-04 34
1985 09 12		74 37	-04 38
1985 09 22		74 40	-04 42
1985 10 02		74 36	-04 46
1985 10 12		74 25	-04 50
1985 10 22		74 07	-04 54
1985 11 01		73 43	-04 57
1985 11 11		73 15	-05 00
1985 11 21		72 43	-05 03
1985 12 01		72 08	-05 04
1985 12 11		71 33	-05 05
1985 12 21		71 00	-05 05
1985 12 31		70 28	-05 04
1986 01 10		70 01	-05 03
1986 01 20		69 40	-05 01
1986 01 30		69 24	-04 59
1986 02 09		69 16	-04 57
1986 02 19		69 15	-04 54
1986 03 01		69 21	-04 51
1986 03 11		69 35	-04 49
1986 03 21		69 55	-04 46
1986 03 31		70 22	-04 44
1986 04 10		70 55	-04 42
1986 04 20		71 32	-04 41
1986 04 30		72 14	-04 40
1986 05 10		72 59	-04 39
1986 05 20		73 46	-04 39
1986 05 30		74 35	-04 39
1986 06 09		75 24	-04 39
1986 06 19		76 13	-04 41
1986 06 29		77 02	-04 42
1986 07 09		77 48	-04 44
1986 07 19		78 32	-04 47
1986 07 29		79 13	-04 50
1986 08 08		79 49	-04 54
1986 08 18		80 20	-04 57
1986 08 28		80 46	-05 02
1986 09 07		81 05	-05 06
1986 09 17		81 17	-05 11
1986 09 27		81 23	-05 16
1986 10 07		81 20	-05 20
1986 10 17		81 11	-05 25
1986 10 27		80 54	-05 29
1986 11 06		80 31	-05 33
1986 11 16		80 02	-05 36
1986 11 26		79 30	-05 39
1986 12 06		78 54	-05 41
1986 12 16		78 18	-05 42
1986 12 26		77 43	-05 42
1987 01 05		77 10	-05 41
1987 01 15		76 41	-05 40
1987 01 25		76 17	-05 38
1987 02 04		76 00	-05 35
1987 02 14		75 51	-05 32
1987 02 24		75 49	-05 29
1987 03 06		75 55	-05 25
1987 03 16		76 08	-05 22
1987 03 26		76 29	-05 19
1987 04 05		76 56	-05 16
1987 04 15		77 30	-05 14
1987 04 25		78 09	-05 12
1987 05 05		78 52	-05 10
1987 05 15		79 38	-05 09
1987 05 25		80 28	-05 08
1987 06 04		81 19	-05 08
1987 06 14		82 12	-05 09
1987 06 24		83 04	-05 10
1987 07 04		83 56	-05 11
1987 07 14		84 46	-05 13
1987 07 24		85 33	-05 16
1987 08 03	♊	86 17	-05 19
1987 08 13		86 57	-05 23
1987 08 23		87 32	-05 27
1987 09 02		88 02	-05 32
1987 09 12		88 24	-05 37
1987 09 22		88 40	-05 42
1987 10 02		88 48	-05 47
1987 10 12		88 49	-05 53
1987 10 22		88 41	-05 58
1987 11 01		88 26	-06 03
1987 11 11		88 04	-06 07
1987 11 21		87 36	-06 11
1987 12 01		87 03	-06 14
1987 12 11		86 27	-06 17
1987 12 21		85 50	-06 18
1987 12 31		85 12	-06 18
1988 01 10		84 37	-06 17
1988 01 20		84 06	-06 15
1988 01 30		83 40	-06 13
1988 02 09		83 21	-06 10
1988 02 19		83 10	-06 06
1988 02 29		83 07	-06 02
1988 03 10		83 11	-05 58
1988 03 20		83 24	-05 54
1988 03 30		83 45	-05 50
1988 04 09	♊	84 12	-05 47
1988 04 19		84 46	-05 43
1988 04 29		85 26	-05 41
1988 05 09		86 11	-05 39
1988 05 19		87 00	-05 37
1988 05 29		87 52	-05 36
1988 06 08		88 46	-05 35
1988 06 18		89 41	-05 36
1988 06 28	♋	90 37	-05 36
1988 07 08		91 33	-05 38
1988 07 18		92 27	-05 40
1988 07 28		93 18	-05 42
1988 08 07		94 07	-05 46
1988 08 17		94 52	-05 50
1988 08 27		95 31	-05 54
1988 09 06		96 05	-05 59
1988 09 16		96 33	-06 04
1988 09 26		96 53	-06 10
1988 10 06		97 06	-06 16
1988 10 16		97 10	-06 22
1988 10 26		97 06	-06 28
1988 11 05		96 54	-06 33
1988 11 15		96 34	-06 38
1988 11 25		96 07	-06 43
1988 12 05		95 34	-06 47
1988 12 15		94 58	-06 49
1988 12 25		94 19	-06 51
1989 01 04		93 39	-06 51
1989 01 14		93 02	-06 50
1989 01 24		92 28	-06 48
1989 02 03		91 59	-06 45
1989 02 13		91 38	-06 42
1989 02 23		91 23	-06 37
1989 03 05		91 18	-06 33
1989 03 15		91 20	-06 28
1989 03 25		91 32	-06 23
1989 04 04		91 51	-06 19
1989 04 14		92 19	-06 14
1989 04 24		92 53	-06 10
1989 05 04		93 34	-06 07
1989 05 14		94 20	-06 04
1989 05 24		95 11	-06 01
1989 06 03		96 05	-06 00
1989 06 13		97 02	-05 59
1989 06 23		98 01	-05 58
1989 07 03		99 01	-05 59
1989 07 13		100 01	-06 00
1989 07 23		101 00	-06 02
1989 08 02		101 56	-06 04
1989 08 12		102 51	-06 07
1989 08 22		103 41	-06 11
1989 09 01		104 26	-06 15
1989 09 11		105 06	-06 20
1989 09 21		105 40	-06 26
1989 10 01		106 06	-06 32
1989 10 11		106 24	-06 38
1989 10 21		106 34	-06 45
1989 10 31	♋	106 35	-06 51
1989 11 10		106 27	-06 57
1989 11 20		106 10	-07 03
1989 11 30		105 46	-07 08
1989 12 10		105 15	-07 13
1989 12 20		104 38	-07 16
1989 12 30		103 58	-07 18
1990 01 09		103 17	-07 19
1990 01 19		102 37	-07 18
1990 01 29		102 00	-07 16
1990 02 08		101 28	-07 13
1990 02 18		101 02	-07 09
1990 02 28		100 44	-07 04
1990 03 10		100 35	-06 59
1990 03 20		100 35	-06 53
1990 03 30		100 44	-06 47
1990 04 09		101 01	-06 42
1990 04 19		101 28	-06 36
1990 04 29		102 02	-06 31
1990 05 09		102 43	-06 27
1990 05 19		103 30	-06 23
1990 05 29		104 22	-06 20
1990 06 08		105 19	-06 17
1990 06 18		106 19	-06 16
1990 06 28		107 21	-06 15
1990 07 08		108 25	-06 14
1990 07 18		109 30	-06 15
1990 07 28		110 34	-06 16
1990 08 07		111 37	-06 18
1990 08 17		112 37	-06 20
1990 08 27		113 34	-06 24
1990 09 06		114 26	-06 28
1990 09 16		115 14	-06 33
1990 09 26		115 55	-06 38
1990 10 06		116 29	-06 44
1990 10 16		116 54	-06 51
1990 10 26		117 11	-06 58
1990 11 05		117 19	-07 04
1990 11 15		117 17	-07 11
1990 11 25	♋	117 06	-07 18
1990 12 05		116 46	-07 24
1990 12 15		116 18	-07 29
1990 12 25		115 43	-07 33
1991 01 04		115 03	-07 35
1991 01 14		114 21	-07 36
1991 01 24		113 38	-07 36
1991 02 03		112 58	-07 34
1991 02 13		112 21	-07 31
1991 02 23		111 50	-07 27
1991 03 05		111 28	-07 22
1991 03 15		111 13	-07 16
1991 03 25		111 09	-07 09
1991 04 04		111 14	-07 03
1991 04 14		111 28	-06 56
1991 04 24		111 52	-06 50
1991 05 04		112 24	-06 43
1991 05 14		113 05	-06 38
1991 05 24		113 52	-06 33
1991 06 03		114 45	-06 29
1991 06 13		115 43	-06 25
1991 06 23		116 46	-06 22
1991 07 03		117 52	-06 20
1991 07 13		119 00	-06 19
1991 07 23	♌	120 09	-06 18
1991 08 02		121 19	-06 19
1991 08 12		122 28	-06 20
1991 08 22		123 35	-06 22
1991 09 01		124 40	-06 24
1991 09 11		125 40	-06 28
1991 09 21		126 36	-06 32
1991 10 01		127 26	-06 37
1991 10 11		128 09	-06 42
1991 10 21		128 45	-06 49
1991 10 31		129 11	-06 55
1991 11 10		129 28	-07 02
1991 11 20		129 35	-07 09
1991 11 30		129 32	-07 16
1991 12 10		129 19	-07 22
1991 12 20		128 57	-07 27
1991 12 30		128 26	-07 32
1992 01 09		127 48	-07 35
1992 01 19		127 06	-07 37
1992 01 29	♌	126 22	-07 38
1992 02 08		125 38	-07 36
1992 02 18		124 56	-07 34
1992 02 28		124 20	-07 29
1992 03 09		123 51	-07 24
1992 03 19		123 30	-07 17
1992 03 29		123 19	-07 10
1992 04 08		123 18	-07 03
1992 04 18		123 27	-06 55
1992 04 28		123 47	-06 48
1992 05 08		124 15	-06 41
1992 05 18		124 53	-06 34
1992 05 28		125 39	-06 28
1992 06 07		126 31	-06 23
1992 06 17		127 30	-06 18
1992 06 27		128 34	-06 14
1992 07 07		129 43	-06 10
1992 07 17		130 54	-06 08
1992 07 27		132 08	-06 06
1992 08 06		133 23	-06 05
1992 08 16		134 38	-06 05
1992 08 26		135 52	-06 05
1992 09 05		137 05	-06 07
1992 09 15		138 14	-06 09
1992 09 25		139 20	-06 12
1992 10 05		140 20	-06 16
1992 10 15		141 14	-06 21
1992 10 25		142 00	-06 26
1992 11 04		142 39	-06 31
1992 11 14		143 08	-06 37
1992 11 24		143 26	-06 44
1992 12 04		143 34	-06 50
1992 12 14		143 31	-06 56
1992 12 24		143 18	-07 02
1993 01 03		142 54	-07 07
1993 01 13		142 22	-07 10
1993 01 23		141 43	-07 13
1993 02 02		140 59	-07 14
1993 02 12		140 13	-07 13
1993 02 22		139 28	-07 11
1993 03 04		138 46	-07 07
1993 03 14		138 10	-07 02
1993 03 24		137 41	-06 56
1993 04 03		137 21	-06 49
1993 04 13		137 12	-06 41
1993 04 23		137 13	-06 33
1993 05 03		137 25	-06 25
1993 05 13		137 47	-06 17
1993 05 23		138 19	-06 09
1993 06 02		139 01	-06 02
1993 06 12		139 51	-05 55
1993 06 22		140 48	-05 49
1993 07 02		141 52	-05 44
1993 07 12	♌	143 00	-05 39
1993 07 22		144 14	-05 35
1993 08 01		145 30	-05 32
1993 08 11		146 49	-05 30
1993 08 21		148 10	-05 28
1993 08 31		149 30	-05 27
1993 09 10	♍	150 50	-05 27
1993 09 20		152 08	-05 27
1993 09 30		153 23	-05 29
1993 10 10		154 33	-05 31
1993 10 20		155 39	-05 33
1993 10 30		156 37	-05 37
1993 11 09		157 29	-05 41
1993 11 19		158 11	-05 45
1993 11 29		158 44	-05 50
1993 12 09		159 06	-05 55
1993 12 19		159 16	-06 00
1993 12 29		159 16	-06 04
1994 01 08		159 04	-06 09
1994 01 18		158 41	-06 12
1994 01 28		158 09	-06 15
1994 02 07		157 30	-06 16
1994 02 17		156 45	-06 16
1994 02 27		155 58	-06 15
1994 03 09		155 12	-06 12
1994 03 19		154 28	-06 07
1994 03 29		153 51	-06 02
1994 04 08		153 21	-05 55
1994 04 18		153 01	-05 48
1994 04 28	♍	152 51	-05 40
1994 05 08		152 53	-05 32
1994 05 18		153 05	-05 23
1994 05 28		153 29	-05 15
1994 06 07		154 03	-05 08
1994 06 17		154 46	-05 00
1994 06 27		155 38	-04 54
1994 07 07		156 38	-04 47
1994 07 17		157 44	-04 42
1994 07 27		158 56	-04 37
1994 08 06		160 13	-04 32
1994 08 16		161 33	-04 28
1994 08 26		162 56	-04 25
1994 09 05		164 21	-04 23
1994 09 15		165 46	-04 21
1994 09 25		167 10	-04 20
1994 10 05		168 33	-04 19
1994 10 15		169 52	-04 19
1994 10 25		171 08	-04 19
1994 11 04		172 18	-04 20
1994 11 14		173 22	-04 22
1994 11 24		174 18	-04 24
1994 12 04		175 05	-04 26
1994 12 14		175 42	-04 29
1994 12 24		176 08	-04 31
1995 01 03		176 23	-04 34
1995 01 13		176 26	-04 37
1995 01 23		176 17	-04 39
1995 02 02		175 57	-04 41
1995 02 12		175 27	-04 41
1995 02 22		174 49	-04 41
1995 03 04		174 05	-04 40
1995 03 14		173 18	-04 38
1995 03 24		172 30	-04 34
1995 04 03		171 46	-04 30
1995 04 13		171 07	-04 24
1995 04 23		170 35	-04 18
1995 05 03		170 13	-04 11
1995 05 13		170 01	-04 04
1995 05 23		170 00	-03 57
1995 06 02		170 11	-03 49
1995 06 12		170 33	-03 42
1995 06 22		171 06	-03 35
1995 07 02		171 48	-03 28
1995 07 12		172 40	-03 22
1995 07 22		173 39	-03 16
1995 08 01		174 46	-03 11
1995 08 11		175 59	-03 06
1995 08 21		177 17	-03 02
1995 08 31		178 39	-02 58
1995 09 10	♎	180 04	-02 54
1995 09 20		181 30	-02 51
1995 09 30		182 58	-02 48
1995 10 10		184 25	-02 46
1995 10 20		185 56	-02 44
1995 10 30		187 13	-02 42
1995 11 09		188 32	-02 41
1995 11 19		189 46	-02 40
1995 11 29		190 53	-02 40

Chiron ⚷

Chiron

Date		Longitude	Declination
1995 12 09	♎	191 53	-02 39
1995 12 19		192 44	-02 39
1995 12 29		193 25	-02 39
1996 01 08		193 56	-02 39
1996 01 18		194 14	-02 39
1996 01 28		194 21	-02 39
1996 02 07		194 16	-02 38
1996 02 17		193 59	-02 37
1996 02 27		193 32	-02 36
1996 03 08		192 56	-02 34
1996 03 18		192 14	-02 32
1996 03 28		191 26	-02 29
1996 04 07		190 40	-02 25
1996 04 17		189 55	-02 21
1996 04 27		189 14	-02 16
1996 05 07		188 40	-02 11
1996 05 17		188 14	-02 06
1996 05 27		187 59	-02 00
1996 06 06		187 55	-01 54
1996 06 16		188 02	-01 49
1996 06 26		188 20	-01 43
1996 07 06		188 49	-01 36
1996 07 16		189 28	-01 33
1996 07 26	♎	190 17	-01 26
1996 08 05		191 14	-01 24
1996 08 15		192 19	-01 20
1996 08 25		193 30	-01 15
1996 09 04		194 46	-01 12
1996 09 14		196 07	-01 08
1996 09 24		197 31	-01 05
1996 10 04		198 57	-01 02
1996 10 14		200 24	-00 58
1996 10 24		201 51	-00 56
1996 11 03		203 17	-00 53
1996 11 13		204 40	-00 50
1996 11 23		206 00	-00 48
1996 12 03		207 15	-00 45
1996 12 13		208 24	-00 43
1996 12 23		209 25	-00 40
1997 01 02	♏	210 16	-00 37
1997 01 12		211 01	-00 35
1997 01 22		211 34	-00 32
1997 02 01		211 55	-00 29
1997 02 11		212 05	-00 27
1997 02 21		212 03	-00 23
1997 03 03		211 49	-00 20
1997 03 13		211 25	-00 17
1997 03 23		210 52	-00 13
1997 04 02		210 12	-00 10
1997 04 12		209 27	-00 06
1997 04 22		208 40	-00 02
1997 05 02		207 55	+00 01
1997 05 12		207 13	+00 05
1997 05 22		206 36	+00 09
1997 06 01		206 06	+00 12
1997 06 11		205 49	+00 15
1997 06 21		205 41	+00 19
1997 07 01		205 44	+00 22
1997 07 11		205 57	+00 25
1997 07 21		206 22	+00 27
1997 07 31		206 56	+00 30
1997 08 10		207 40	+00 33
1997 08 20		208 33	+00 35
1997 08 30		209 34	+00 36
1997 09 09		210 41	+00 40
1997 09 19		211 53	+00 43
1997 09 29		213 11	+00 45
1997 10 09		214 31	+00 46
1997 10 19		215 55	+00 51
1997 10 29		217 19	+00 53
1997 11 08		218 43	+00 56
1997 11 18		220 07	+00 59
1997 11 28		221 28	+01 02
1997 12 08		222 46	+01 06
1997 12 18		223 59	+01 09
1997 12 28		225 06	+01 13
1998 01 07		226 07	+01 17
1998 01 17		226 59	+01 22
1998 01 27		227 41	+01 26
1998 02 06		228 14	+01 31
1998 02 16		228 36	+01 36
1998 02 26		228 46	+01 41
1998 03 08		228 45	+01 46
1998 03 18		228 33	+01 51
1998 03 28		228 11	+01 55
1998 04 07		227 40	+02 00
1998 04 17		227 02	+02 05
1998 04 27		226 19	+02 09
1998 05 07		225 34	+02 12
1998 05 17		224 49	+02 15
1998 05 27		224 07	+02 18
1998 06 06		223 30	+02 20
1998 06 16		223 00	+02 21
1998 06 26		222 39	+02 22
1998 07 06	♏	222 27	+02 23
1998 07 16		222 26	+02 23
1998 07 26		222 36	+02 24
1998 08 05		222 55	+02 24
1998 08 15		223 25	+02 24
1998 08 25		224 05	+02 25
1998 09 04		224 53	+02 25
1998 09 14		225 48	+02 25
1998 09 24		226 50	+02 26
1998 10 04		227 58	+02 27
1998 10 14		229 11	+02 28
1998 10 24		230 27	+02 30
1998 11 03		231 46	+02 31
1998 11 13		233 06	+02 34
1998 11 23		234 26	+02 36
1998 12 03		235 45	+02 39
1998 12 13		237 03	+02 42
1998 12 23		238 16	+02 46
1999 01 02		239 25	+02 50
1999 01 12	♐	240 29	+02 55
1999 01 22		241 26	+03 00
1999 02 01		242 14	+03 05
1999 02 11		242 54	+03 10
1999 02 21		243 24	+03 16
1999 03 03		243 44	+03 22
1999 03 13		243 53	+03 29
1999 03 23		243 51	+03 35
1999 04 02		243 39	+03 41
1999 04 12		243 18	+03 47
1999 04 22		242 48	+03 52
1999 05 02		242 11	+03 56
1999 05 12		241 29	+04 00
1999 05 22		240 46	+04 03
1999 06 01		240 02	+04 06
1999 06 11	♏	239 21	+04 07
1999 06 21		238 44	+04 07
1999 07 01		238 14	+04 07
1999 07 11		237 52	+04 06
1999 07 21		237 39	+04 05
1999 07 31		237 36	+04 03
1999 08 10		237 43	+04 02
1999 08 20		238 00	+04 00
1999 08 30		238 26	+03 58
1999 09 09		239 02	+03 56
1999 09 19		239 46	+03 55
1999 09 29	♐	240 37	+03 53
1999 10 09		241 35	+03 52
1999 10 19		242 38	+03 52
1999 10 29		243 46	+03 52
1999 11 08		244 57	+03 52
1999 11 18		246 11	+03 53
1999 11 28		247 26	+03 55
1999 12 08		248 41	+03 57
1999 12 18		249 55	+04 00
1999 12 28		251 07	+04 03
2000 01 07		252 15	+04 06
2000 01 17		253 19	+04 11
2000 01 27		254 17	+04 16
2000 02 06		255 08	+04 21
2000 02 16		255 52	+04 27
2000 02 26		256 27	+04 33
2000 03 07		256 53	+04 39
2000 03 17		257 09	+04 46
2000 03 27		257 15	+04 53
2000 04 06		257 11	+04 59
2000 04 16		256 57	+05 06
2000 04 26		256 34	+05 11
2000 05 06		256 04	+05 17
2000 05 16		255 28	+05 21
2000 05 26		254 48	+05 24
2000 06 05		254 06	+05 27
2000 06 15	♐	253 24	+05 28
2000 06 25		252 44	+05 28
2000 07 05		252 09	+05 27
2000 07 15		251 41	+05 26
2000 07 25		251 19	+05 24
2000 08 04		251 07	+05 21
2000 08 14		251 03	+05 17
2000 08 24		251 09	+05 14
2000 09 03		251 25	+05 10
2000 09 13		251 49	+05 07
2000 09 23		252 22	+05 04
2000 10 03		253 04	+05 01
2000 10 13		253 52	+04 59
2000 10 23		254 46	+04 57
2000 11 02		255 46	+04 55
2000 11 12		256 49	+04 54
2000 11 22		257 56	+04 54
2000 12 02		259 05	+04 55
2000 12 12		260 15	+04 56
2000 12 22		261 25	+04 57

CHRONOLOGY OF ASTROLOGICAL INTEREST IN CHIRON

1920 - 1940: Maurice Wemyss deduces empirically an approximately correct ephemeris covering one orbit of Chiron, publishes it in Wheel of Life.

Since then many other astrologers have sensed some undiscovered planet's workings while interpreting horoscopes. One of these is Charles A. Jayne, Jr.

29 August 1977: Cover of CAO TIMES predicts a new planet discovery by facsimile of a painting showing a building crane lifting it into orbit. Ranelle Wolf, artist, on commission from editor.

Volume 3, No. 1, published 29 August, 1977, predicting the imminent discovery of Chiron.

18 - 19 October 1977: Charles Kowal of Caltech, at Mt. Palomar CA, makes plates during the nights.

1 November 1977, circa 10 AM PST, Charles Kowal is convinced that he sees a small new body with orbit of a planet. Joelle K. D. Mahoney, Director of the accredited school, Astrological Research Centre -- ARC -- interviews Charles Kowal by phone

International Astronomic Union - IAU - confirms by telegram soon after. Elements of orbit are created by Dr. Brian G. Marsden, Director of Smithsonian Institute Astrophysics Observatory. This is an achievement unrivalled in the history of astronomy. Never before has such information been derived so fully, so accurately, and so quickly. Dr. Marsden's place in the history of brilliant science is assured.

1977: James Neely begins work on a program to make an astrological ephemeris from Dr. Marsden's work, the elements of Chiron's orbit, as given in the IAU telegram.

1977: Zane B. Stein persuades Dr. Marsden to make an ephemeris, 1937 - 1954 in right ascension/declination. Joelle K. D. Mahoney organizes volunteers and gets the computer work underway.

11 June 1978: The world's first astrological ephemeris of Chiron, 1937 - 1954 is published at a meeting of Astrologers' Guild of America, Inc., in New York City.

All the various symbols previously suggested, including several depicted in a Canadian publication * Phenomena, CAO NEWSLETTER and The Astrological Review, were considered and a formal vote taken. The key-like symbol now in general worldwide use thus became the first planetary symbol adopted by democratic voting by astrological organizations.

August 1978: Dr. Marsden encourages CAO to select and adopt an astrological symbol for Chiron. IAU no longer adopts planetary symbols, but labels minor planets with a number in parentheses. (2060) Chiron is classed as a minor planet by IAU.

1979-1980: Mark Pottenger computes an ephemeris in once a month positions, with stations, 1685 - 1889.

18 August 1978: CAO General Convention at San Diego CA votes to adopt the present symbol. Another proposed by Riverside Astrologers (Memphis TN) got a third of the vote. The artist was Joyce Greer.

September 1978: Ephemeris of Chiron 1890 - 1979 is published by CAO TIMES for Chiron Committee, subsuming previous installments.

13 November 1978: Zane B. Stein founds Association for Studying Chiron, at Philadelphia PA.

December 1978: Phenomena Publications (Canada) has in print an ephemeris, including right/ascension / declination and heliocentric positions, artwork and other materials. The figures are computed by Eric Tarkington from a program created by James Neely from the elements originated by Dr. Brian Marsden,

16 December 1979: Zane B. Stein lectures on Chiron at meeting of Astrologers' Guild of America, Inc. This is the first known formal discussion at anv astrological meeting. This text is now distributed by CAO TIMES worldwide.

6 June 1980: Chiron Committee completes its work, extends ephemeris 1979-2000.

18 October 1982: Daniel Green computes this ephemeris in longitude & latitude from a program developed 1982 by Dr. Brian Marsden and Dr. Green.

5 November 1982: This 1887-2000 ephemeris is published by CAO TIMES.

20 May 1985: This ephemeris is reprinted once more, for those responding to outstanding offers for sale.

This ephemeris is very soon to be superseded by a new edition giving daily positions from 3 March 1891 to 20 October 2000. Declinations are also given.

If you would rather have the new edition, return this one for credit toward purchase of the new edition, in saleable condition.

THE DAILY POSITION EPHEMERIS OF CHIRON is **$20.** postpaid. Order from CAO TIMES, Box 75 Old Chelsea Station, New York NY 10113.

Remittances from Canada and other countries should be in currency, either the equivalent sum in foreign currency or US dollars.

If you must send a check, it must be drawn against a US bank in US dollars.

In some countries US Postal Money Orders are available. If you use these, you must advise CAO TIMES that you are doing so, as these remittances take several weeks and usually have the name and address garbled.

You can also order from Chiron Verlag, Postfach 29, 7409 DUSSLINGEN, West Germany. [Distributors]

The magazine CAO TIMES continues to include articles on Chiron, some of which will be reprinted as separate pamphlets/books later. Subscription rates: 4 issues [48 pages 8½x11] US $20: Canada & Mexico $22: Overseas $26. It is intended that there should be four issues in an average year, but the dates of publication vary.

CAO TIMES, Box 75 Old Chelsea Station, New York NY 10113 USA

NOTE: This chart should be rectified. What Charles Kowal said in answer to the question was "about" ten o'clock. Four clock minutes earlier gives a chart which fits events since then much better, and also relates more exactly to the charts of those who are concerned with the astrology of Chiron.

PLANET	SIGN	LONG	HSE	DECL	LAT	GEOCENTRIC N-NODE	S-NODE	DIS	SPEED
SUN	Scp	9 12 15	11	14S34	0 00	N-NODE	S-NODE	73	60' 3"
MOON R	Can	12 31 22	7	17N39	5S14	13L145	13Ar45	5	11°53'=>SLOW
MERC	Scp	17 46.9	11	17S50	0S43	05Sc09	11Sc59	3	93'38"
VENU R	Lib	19 29.8	10	6S12	1N33	23V103	24Sc51	11	74 51
MARS	Leo	2 26.8	8	21N 3	1N28	08Ge53	15Sc25	69	23 34
JUPI E	Can	6 1.6R	7	22N58	0S21	19Ca58	01Cp01	78	-1 41
SATU D	Leo	29 7.5	8	12N54	1N12	29Ca18	17Cp51	51	4 8
URAN E	Scp	11 55.9	11	15S 3	0N23	15Ge50	12Sa25	40	3 45
NEPT	Sag	14 33.6	12	21S 8	1N26	13Le23	09Aq37	9	1 56
PLUT	Lib	15 3.4	10	9N22	16N34	21Ca42	18Cp48	88	2 12
ASC	Sag	26 3.3	1	23S23					
MC	Lib	13 51.7	10	5S28					
NODE*	Lib	14 58.3	10						
PFOR	Leo	29 22.4							
VERTEX	Leo	8 58.5							
EASTPT	Cpr	11 44.1							

MUTUAL RECEPTION SUN AND MARS

R=RULE D=DETRIMENT
E=EXALTED F=FALL
*TRUE NODE
☉/☽ ANGLE=243.32°

ASTRO COMPUTING SERVICE
from
NEIL F MICHELSEN
P O Box 16430
San Diego, CA 92116
714 / 297-5648
DATE=10/15/81

	CARD	FIX	MUT
FIRE	0	2	1
EARTH	0	0	0
AIR	2	0	0
WATER	2	3	0

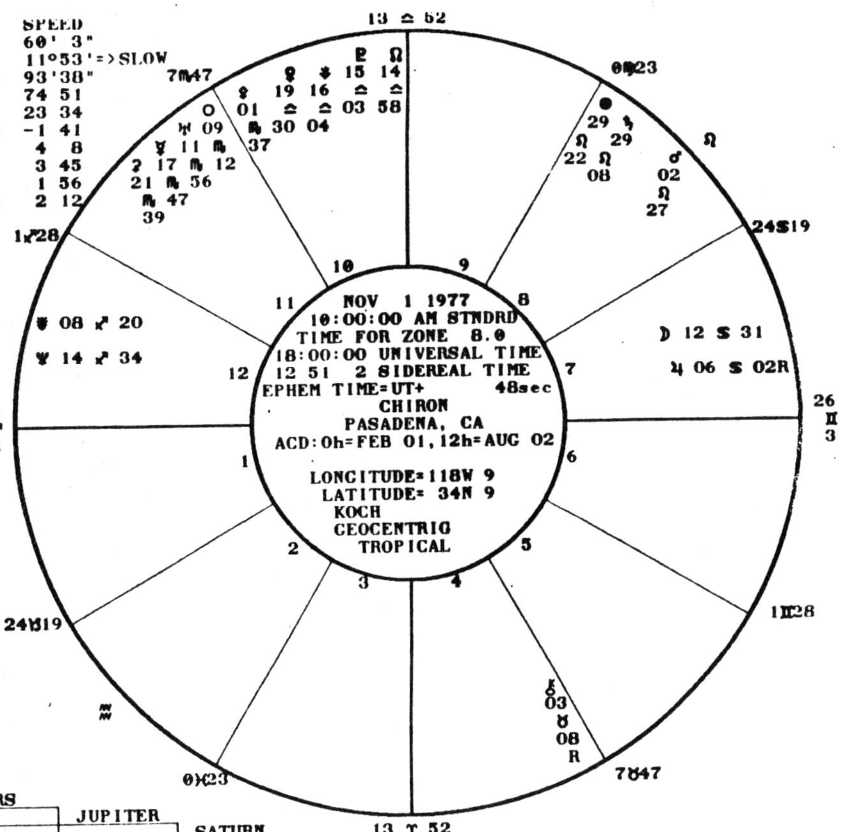

NATAL ASPECTS

	ANGLE	ORB	#		ANGLE	ORB	#
CON=Conjunction	0	10	10	TRI=Trine	120	10	6
SSX=Semisextile	30	3	5	SQQ=Sesquiquad	135	4	2
SSQ=Semi-Square	45	4	6	BQT=Biquintile	144	3	1
SXT=Sextile	60	6	4	QCX=Quincunx	150	3	1
QTL=Quintile	72	3	8	OPP=Opposition	180	10	1
SQR=Square	90	10	9	/ =Parallel or Contraparallel	0	1	5

A=Applying S=Separating

TOTAL ASPECTS = 58

	SUN	MOON	MERCURY	VENUS	MARS	JUPITER	SATURN	URANUS	NEPTUNE	PLUTO	ASC	MC
MOON	TRI 3 19S											
MERC	CON 8 35S	TRI 5/15A										
VENU		SQR 6 58A	SSX 1 43A									
MARS	SQR 6 45S											
JUPI	TRI 3 11S	CON 6 30S	SQQ 3 15A									
SATU	QTL 1 55A	SSQ 1 36A										
URAN	CON 2/44A	TRI 0 35S	CON 5 51S		SQR 9 29A	TRI 5 54S	QTL 0 48A					
NEPT		QCX 2 02A		SXT 4 56S	SQQ 2/53S			SSX 2 38A				
PLUT		SQR 2 32A	SSX 2 43S	CON 4 26S	QTL 0 37A	SQR 9 02S	SSQ 0 56A		SXT 0 30S			
ASC	SSQ 1 51				BQT 0 24	OPP 9/58	TRI 3 04	SSQ 0 53		QTL 1 00		
MC		SQR 1 20		CON 5/38	QTL 0 35	SQR 7 50	SSQ 0 16	SSX 1 56	SXT 0 42	CON 1 12	QTL 0 12	
NODE		SQR 2 27	SSX 2 49	CON 4 32	QTL 0 31	SQR 8 57	SSQ 0 51		SXT 0 25	CON 0 05	QTL 0 55	CON 1 07

*** MID POINTS SORTED INTO ZODIACAL SEQUENCE ***

⚷ 03♉08	M/⚷ 23♋30	♃/♇ 25♌32	♂/♇ 08♍45	♄/♇ 22♍05	☿/♄ 08♎27	♀/☊ 17♎14	♅/♇ 28♎30	☉/☿ 13♏30	♀/A 22♏47	☉/⚷ 06♒10
♃/⚷ 04♊35	☊/⚷ 24 03	♀/♃ 27 46	♃/♅ 08 59	♂/♅ 22 11	♂/♆ 08 30	♀/♇ 17 17	☉/♀ 29 21	♆/M 14 13	☉/♆ 26 53	♅/⚷ 07 32
☽/⚷ 07 50	♇/⚷ 24 06	☽/M 28 12	☉/☽ 10 52	♀/♄ 24 19	M 13 52	♀ 19 30	♀/♅ 00♏43	♆/☊ 14 46	♅/♆ 28 15	☿/⚷ 10 28
♂/⚷ 17 48	♀/⚷ 26 19	☽/☊ 28 45	♀/♂ 10 58	☿/♂ 25 07	♂/A 14 15	♄/♆ 21 51	☿/M 00 49	♆/♇ 14 48	☿/♆ 01♐10	♆/⚷ 23 51
♄/⚷ 01♋08	♂ 02♌27	☽/♇ 28 47	☿/♃ 11 54	♃/♆ 25 18	M/☊ 14 25	☉/M 26 32	☿/☊ 01 23	☿/♅ 14 51	☉/A 02 38	A/⚷ 29 36
♃ 06 02	♃/♄ 02 35	♄ 29 08	☽/♅ 12 14	☽/♆ 28 32	♇/M 14 28	☉/☊ 27 05	☿/♇ 01 25	♀/♆ 17 02	♅/A 04 00	
☽/♃ 09 16	☽/♄ 05 49	☽/♀ 01♍01	☽/☿ 15 09	♃/A 01♎02	☊ 14 58	☉/♇ 27 08	☿/♀ 03 38	☿ 17 47	☿/A 06 55	
☽ 12 31	♂/♄ 15 47	☉/♃ 07 37	☉/♂ 20 50	☉/♄ 04 10	♇/☊ 15 01	♄/A 27 35	☉ 09 12	A/M 19 57	♆ 14 34	
♂/♃ 19 14	♃/M 24 57	♂/M 08 09	♄/M 21 30	☽/A 04 17	♇ 15 03	♅/M 27 54	☉/♅ 10 34	A/☊ 20 31	♆/A 20 18	
☽/♂ 22 29	♃/☊ 25 30	♂/☊ 08 43	♄/☊ 22 03	♄/♅ 05 32	♀/M 16 41	♅/☊ 28 27	♅ 11 56	♇/A 20 33	A 26 03	

JULIAN DAY # = 2443449.250000 MEAN OBLIQUITY OF ECLIPTIC = 23°26'32" SIDEREAL AYANAMSHA (SVP) = Pic 5°34' 7"

The Continuing Discovery of CHIRON

Erminie Lantero
M.Div., Ph.D.

$8.95

In a style that speaks to both the serious student and professional astrologer, THE CONTINUING DISCOVERY OF CHIRON engages the reader in a rare opportunity—a chance to witness the way in which astrologers come to assign meaning to a new planetary body. Erminie Lantero presents the only comprehensive study of the recently discovered Chiron, and lets the reader participate in the astronomical research leading up to its sighting, its background in mythology, its literary referents, and its use as an indispensable tool in astrological charts. Through the use of case studies, the author exhaustively documents Chiron's first four years in our consciousness, and goes on to pinpoint how Chiron can be used by astrologers to better understand certain facets of personality in the natal chart.

> "Lantero is exploring some fascinating terrain when she talks about Chiron transits as healing crises whose quality is one of transition. I suspect most literature on healing makes unconscious Neptunian and/or Plutonian assumptions about the process: that a healing crisis is either of the whole-making, detoxifying, definitely disorienting and confusing Neptunian variety, or the intense death and re-birth Plutonian melodrama. She is encompassing something which has great subtlety and complexity when she is discussing the healing possibilities inherent in the nature of transition."

ABOUT THE AUTHOR: Erminie Lantero came to astrology rather late in life. A Ph.D. in Philosophy from Radcliffe, she began her religious studies at Mount Holyoke College and received a M.Div. from Union Theological Seminary in New York. She has been on the faculties of Sweet Briar and Wellesley Colleges, and served as an editor and participant at Pendle Hill, an experimental Center for Religious and Social Studies near Philadelphia. In the late 1960's she served as research assistant for a two-volume history of the Ecumenical Movement in the American Churches. Her official "retirement" led her to a long-delayed exploration of the occult, and finally (some fifty years late) she discovered astrology as the life work she would have preferred all along. Since finishing her book on Chiron, she has retired to a community run according to the principles of Rudolf Steiner.

Samuel Weiser, Inc. • Box 612 • York Beach, ME 03910

Cover design by Alden Cole

ISBN 0-87728-549-7

Interpreting Chiron

ZANE B. STEIN

SECOND EDITION

Published by

Association for Studying Chiron
757 East Main Street, Apt. K201
Lansdale, PA 19446

Zane B. Stein

I hope this gives you some insights in how to begin to use Chiron. Of course, we must continue researching it for many years to come. If you want more information, write to:

Zane B. Stein,
Director, Association for Studying Chiron
757 E. Main St.   K-201
Lansdale, PA 19446

Or, telephone me any evening at (215) 368-4387.

Chironically,

Zane B. Stein

Interpreting Chiron

ZANE B. STEIN

Chiron was discovered in 1977, and already we know a great deal about it—more, in fact, than we knew about Pluto only a few years after its discovery. But in order to really understand Chiron's nature, it must be viewed in relation to what other discoveries were made around the same general period of time. For, while Chiron definitely has a unique meaning, it is also part of a large picture of changes which are occurring in mankind's awareness.

In March of 1977, the world was astonished by a new discovery about the planet Uranus. Now, Uranus has always been a shocker. In 1781 it startled the world simply by being discovered! For thousands of years, Saturn was viewed as the final body—the absolute limit. Its rings were viewed as representing the limitations that Saturn stood for. So, when Uranus was found, it totally destroyed the existing pictures of the solar system. Upon further research, its very motion proved unconventional—for it was found to revolve in reverse motion in comparison to the other planets, and also to have its axis inclined at an angle almost ninety degrees from the angle of the axes of the other planets. Even its moons were named unconventionally—after Shakespearean characters instead of after mythological beings. It was thought to have absolutely nothing in common with the planet Saturn.

But in that fateful March, RINGS WERE DISCOVERED AROUND URANUS! Saturn no longer had a monopoly on them—and now, the two planets had something very definite in common. Thus, Uranus shocks again. What do they have in common? they both teach lessons of responsibility, and concern for the future; they both are concerned with time (Saturn with bringing the past into the present; Uranus with brining the present into the future); and they both have to do with self-definition—Saturn defining one's limits, and Uranus pointing the way to one's individuality. The fact that we now know that both have rings indicates that we now realize (or should realize) that the principles of both are inter-connected; that too much of one is just as bad as too much of the other; that when we go too far into Saturn, Uranus must come and bring about a balance (and vice versa); and that they are both necessary steps in the process of one's evolution.

Once the rings were discovered, the way was paved to discover Chiron, and this was done by astronomer Charles Kowal on November 1, 1977. Chiron was found to orbit between Saturn and Uranus!!! Its orbit was also found to be highly elliptical—even more so than Pluto. At aphelion—that is, when furthest from the sun—Chiron actually reaches the orbit of Uranus. Even more interesting is the fact that at perihelion—closest to the sun—Chiron crosses Saturn's orbit and thus comes closer to us than Saturn ever does! Thus, Chiron is found to act as a link, or bridge, between the two major planets, swinging back and forth between them once every cycle (which varies from 49 to 51 years, by the way). Now we can see why it was necessary for the rings of Uranus to be found first—so that we could appreciate the linking process that Chiron represents.

The third major piece of the puzzle was discovered in the following year. Pluto, which previous to Chiron had held the distinction of having the most elliptical orbit of all the major planets, was suddenly found to have a moon. This did drastic things to our perception of the size of Pluto—Pluto was suddenly MUCH smaller than previously thought! Some astronomers were beginning to wonder if it should be demoted in status from major planet to planetoid! In fact, had its actual size been known in the 1930's, when it was discovered, it is possible that astrologers would have ignored it totally, considering that anything that small, so far out, could not possibly have an influence.

But we all know just how powerful Pluto is. It would be difficult to imagine not including it in charts today. Thus, Pluto's moon (called Charon, by the way), was verification that even a small body has powerful influences. And thus, it made it much more plausible for Chiron, which is the size of a large asteroid, to have the influence of a major planet.

One more thing about Pluto. Dr. Brian G. Marsden, of the Smithsonian Institution's Astrophysical Observatory, has suggested that a special category be devised, and a new name invented, for the Orbit-crossers. They would not be classed as planets, or asteroids, or comets—but would be unique within this class. The members of said class would be Pluto (which crosses the orbit of Neptune), Chiron (which crosses the orbit of Saturn), and Hidalgo (previously called an asteroid, but which crosses the orbit of Jupiter). (Hidalgo, incidentally, is also being studied. It has a 14-year orbit, so ties into Saturn [7 × 4], Chiron [7 × 7], and Uranus [12 × 7].)

So, with the above frame of reference related to you, I now want to begin describing Chiron's specific meanings, as they have surfaced so far. Obviously, we are only beginning to understand Chiron, since it was discovered so recently. But the results of current research suggest certain themes repeatedly. I will, repeatedly, refer to Chiron's relationship to Saturn and Uranus, as described above, and occasionally to its relationship to Pluto and Hidalgo.

KEYWORDS

The most potent keyword representing Chiron is MAVERICK. This word came from Samuel A. Maverick, an American pioneer and rancher who did not brand his cattle, unlike all the other ranchers around him. The word came to mean one who takes a stand apart from his associates—an independent individual who refuses to conform to his own group—one who does not align himself with any party, faction, or particular stand—one without the mark of the herd branded into his side as it is in his contemporaries. Mavericks may make enemies among those who do belong to some particular group, for those people may feel, "If you are not with us, you are against us." Yet as far as the Maverick is concerned, he is neither for nor against their principles. This is where Chiron differs from both Saturn and Uranus. Saturn wants to uphold tradition, and defend traditional beliefs. Saturn creates an "us-or-them" division. Uranus wants to break down the old, often to the point of being an iconoclast. Uranus can easily get the urge to "blow up" the very structure of some group. But Chiron, the MAVERICK, neither defends nor overthrows the establishment—rather, it is apart from it.

HEALING and WHOLEMAKING are Chiron words. When one has an imbalance—too much or too little of something, one needs to rectify the situation as soon as possible. If not, then it can lead to health problems, either physical, or emotional—or even spiritual. If one is closed off, one may be keeping oneself from becoming whole by not even being aware of whole other worlds out there to explore and make one complete. Saturn can be a wall which keeps us protected from whatever is outside, yet also isolated from new experiences and necessary growth. Saturn can produce stagnation, or an impasse. On the other hand, Uranus can represent a new world, waiting on the other side of a wall—but if the person refuses to open to it, Uranus can become a devastating force, destroying the wall, and really wreaking havoc to one's health. Then one must rebuild, if one can, and it can be slow and painful. But Chiron is a KEY, opening a door in Saturn's wall, allowing us to enter through the doorway into Uranus' world, so that we can discover what we need to heal us or make us whole, without abruptly removing all of Saturn's protection. It may be that it removes something from our lives so that the impasse no longer exists. It is almost always a time which we look back on, and say, "It was a real turning point." The Chiron wholemaking can bring experiences and trials which enable us to counsel others when we have been through them. One can say that, due to Chiron's tendency to emphasize either Saturn or Uranus (whichever is underemphasized), that its healing brings change when there is too much stability, and stability when there is too much change. When Chiron comes, new worlds open up or old doors close forever.

Chiron represents COMMON GROUND. Let us view the walls of a house as Saturn, and everything outside of that house as Uranus. With doors and windows shut tight, someone in the house can have no knowledge of what is going on outside the walls. And, someone who is outside not only has no knowledge of what is inside—but unless he can find a key to the door, the only way he can get into the house is to break in. HOWEVER, if the door is unlocked and opened—someone from within can get out and explore, and someone outside can come in—without in anyway damaging the walls of the structure. Thus, if you think about it—the DOORWAY itself is common ground—once the door is opened, it allows access in both directions—so you can say that the doorway itself belongs to both Saturn and Uranus—or to neither.

When one is born, one's parents are preoccupied by certain problems that they feel *must* be solved—difficulties and obstacles that *must* be overcome—and these problems are made quite clear to the child as it grows up. The sign in which Chiron falls, at any given time, represents what the current preoccupation of the parents is—and thus, it shifts whenever Chiron enters a new sign. However, for the child who was born while the parents worried over the obstacles produced by a particular Chiron transit, the desire to overcome these obstacles does not fade when Chiron changes signs. Instead, it has become a PERSONAL IMPERATIVE, staying with the child all his life. He grows up feeling that these problems are always high priority; that nothing must stand in the way of resolving any difficulties which arise in these areas; and that the difficulties represented by Chiron's sign are those that everyone should consider important as well. Within the area (by sign and house) that is influenced by Chiron, the person believes that no wall, obstacle, rule or regulation is truly important enough to stop him from resolving a problem—thus in these areas, he will be most likely to go beyond Saturn if necesary, or ignore Saturn if he has to.

Through time, and experience, Chiron soon becomes the need to search for a meaning to life that is deeper than that represented by Jupiter, more durable than Saturn, and that will last in spite of the changes brought about by Uranus. It can become a personal QUEST, as a person searches everywhere for something that will be meaningful throughout all time, and in every place. It thus represents NOW—the link between the past and the future—and will show a concern to bridge any gap that exists between these two. And, as the person begins to discover life's deeper meanings, Chiron represents the TEACHER who desires to open new worlds for others, and instill in others the same spark to want to learn, and to want to begin their own quests. It can also be expressed as the desire of the parent to open worlds for the child, or as any person who acts to prepare a child to face the world, thus any foster parents.

It is time beyond chronological time—Chiron = Chiros—timeless time—when ordinary clock time ceases to have meaning. It is in these moments when major decisions are made, and when some of the most creative work is done. There appears to be a connection between Chiron, and the period of time known as Void-of-course-Moon, as well.

And Chiron represents a TURNING POINT—which can seem either good or bad at the time, but is definitely remembered as a period when one's life changed direction in some way, or had to adjust to some new circumstances. Usually, one remembers this as a time when a new world opened, or when some door closed which forced one to look in a new direction and thus avoid stagnation in some way.

Some things are kept in line by a system of checks and balances. This system keeps things from growing too fast, or too large, or possibly it keeps things working together so that they do not fall apart. If one part of the system goes bad, or is found to have been bad all along, the whole system might be looked upon as suspect. Temporarily, the checks and balances may break down, resulting in uncontrollable growth, or expansion, or breaking apart. Chiron can be this PULLING THE PLUG or REMOVING THE DAM, and initially, it can seem that there is no way to put a brake on whatever was unleashed. But Chiron has a specific purpose in removing the restraint. As human beings, we tend to rely too heavily upon a system, once we find that it works. Chiron comes along and reminds us that no system is perfect. But unlike the planet Uranus, Chiron does not destroy the whole system—it calls our attention to some weak spot, or to the way in which we are relying too heavily upon it. By correcting this, we soon find that we can return to a system of checks and balances again, although (hopefully) we will be much wiser this time.

What is more, when the plug was pulled, we had the opportunity to learn a great deal more about the true nature of whatever was unleashed. Thus, we now have the knowledge to make much better use of it, and to TAP its power. This period is a great teacher. If we are good students, we find we have a great deal more power in our own life now, which we can turn on and use, almost like turning on a faucet.

And Chiron represents LOOPHOLES, enabling one to get around the system, instead of being imprisoned by it.

RULERSHIP

This has not been decided; in fact, there seem to be several different views on this, each with its own group of 'believers.' But much research has yet to be done to establish this with any degree of certainty. The views so far: Libra, the whole region of Scorpio–Sagittarius, Sagittarius, Gemini, Virgo, the Libra decanate of Aquarius, and of course, no sign at all. Personally, I feel (from the evidence so far) that Chiron has most in common with the higher side of Libra—but I will reserve any final judgement. Oh, yes, one other view was submitted—that in the age of Aquarius, Chiron will rule *Tropical* Sagittarius but *Sidereal* Libra—for those two will coincide!

TRANSITS

A good idea of Chiron-transits can be achieved by reading the Keyword section. However, a few points must be discussed here. Chiron seems to bring both difficult AND easy situations by transit, whether the aspect is a conjunction, trine, square, or other. It will, more often, bring a door-opening to a person—unless in aspect to Mars or Saturn—then, it seems to more often bring a door-closing and the need to look beyond one's present environment. Although it is possible that it has an influence a few degrees away, I have not noticed any manner of influence from its transits when they were more than 3° away—and clear, distinct events only when within 1½° orb.

To me, the most interesting Chiron transits are the aspects it makes to its own natal place. First of all, Chiron has a *very* eccentric orbit—it is in Libra for only about 1¾ years, yet stays in Aries for over 8¼ years. This process produces drastic differences, depending on Chiron's sign, as to when it makes its first aspect to the natal position.

Now, with Saturn, the astrological literature is filled with articles about how Saturn-to-Saturn aspects divide mankind's life into regular sections of about seven years each—Saturn being so regular in its orbit, that you can tell without an ephemeris approximately what part of its cycle someone is in simply by asking his or her age. For example, first transit Saturn square natal Saturn happens to *everyone* at about 7 years of age, and first opposition around age 14. Thus, you can define what stage mankind is in at any time, by Saturn's aspects; you could use them to describe the archetypal human life.

But with Chiron, the story is different—drastically different. A person with Chiron in early Virgo will have the first square (with transit Chiron in early Sagittarius) when he is only about 5½ years of age. Yet a person who was born when Chiron was in early Pisces will not experience the first square (with transit Chiron in early Gemini) until he is past 23 years old! What a drastic difference. And with the other Chiron signs, various ages between these two extremes. Think of the ramifications and permutations. A 5½-year-old is still a child; his personality is still being formed (most scientists say that the personality is formed by about age 7—in other words, by the time of the first Saturn square); he is still living totally under the influence of his parents or other adults; he has seen almost nothing of the world; and has not even seen one whole Jupiter cycle yet! On the other hand, a person past the age of 23 is an adult, and has been considered so by society for a few years already; his personality has been long formed; in most cases, he no longer lives with his parents and is probably self-supporting, possibly married for a few years already; and he has already seen transit Saturn-square, opposition, and again square his natal Saturn, is soon to see his second Jupiter return, and has already experienced transit Uranus-square-natal Uranus! What a drastic difference. How differently must one be influenced by the first Chiron square, depending on what age one is in when it occurs.

To give you a clearer picture of how drastic the age difference is, look at the chart. Across the bottom, you will find each sign—find the sign your own Chiron is in, for example. Then, up and down the left of the graph, are the ages of the first Chiron square. So, after you have found the column for your sign, run your finger up until you find the graph line, then look for the age to the left of that point. If you know whether your Chiron was early or late in its sign, you can be more specific as to age. For example, I have Chiron at 0°01′ Capricorn, which means the first square occurred at a little past 17 years of age. My wife has Chiron at 18°51′ Capricorn, so the first square for her was about 19½ years of age. My sister has it at 13°37′ Leo, so she was only 5½ when Chiron made its first square.

What does all this mean? Well, the first square is a major lesson, which brings the turning point; a new world opens up to you, or something new will come into your world. The exact nature of the event depends on the natal house, the house the transiting Chiron is in, and, of course, other planets which are involved at that time. A few examples may help to shed light on this.

THE VERTICAL COLUMN ON THE LEFT REPRESENTS THE AGE WHEN CHIRON MAKES ITS FIRST SQUARE TO ITS NATAL PLACE

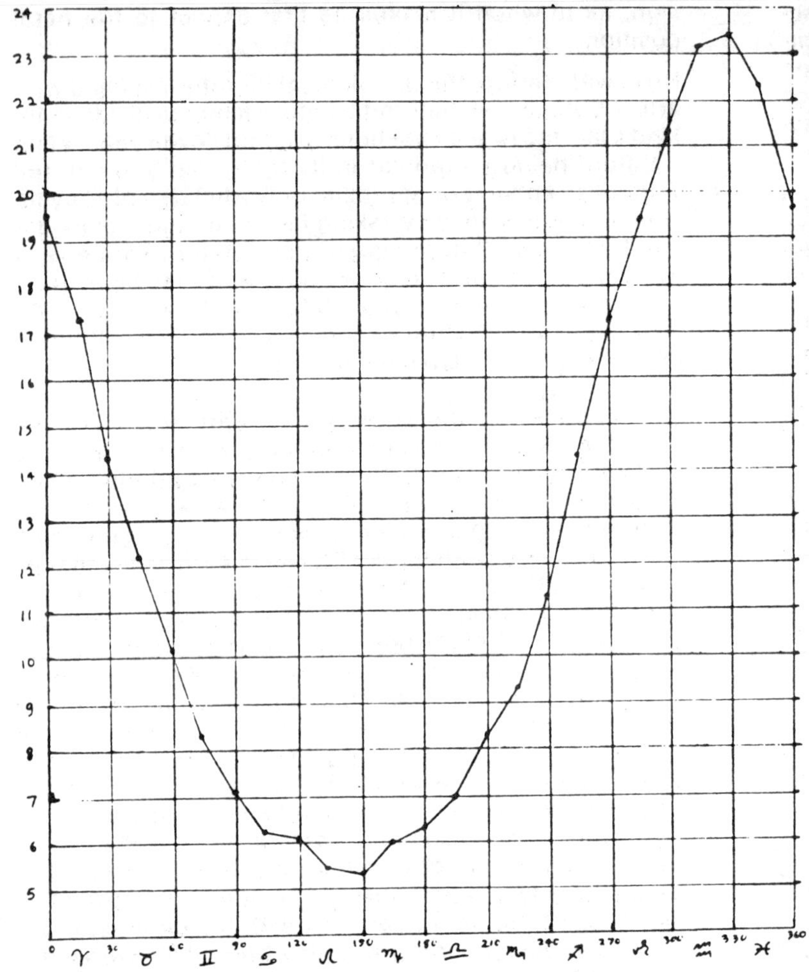

CHIRON'S SIGN POSITION

I. A very shy, introverted person, with difficulty communicating with others (yours truly as a child), had Chiron in Capricorn in the tenth house. At the time of my first square, I was informed that, since I was #3 in my graduating class in high school, and therefore Salutatorian, I had to give a speech at graduation. I had never talked to a large group before, and never had given any kind of speech. I was terrified, but went ahead, and got through it. My self-confidence grew; my ability to communicate grew as well.

Due to retrograde, the square happened twice more. The second time, I found suddenly found myself, for the first time, living away from home at a college, making my own hours, meeting people and cultures and philosophies I had never even dreamed of. The final time, I changed my major from botany to psychology. This was major, because I had wanted to be a botanist since age 7!

II. One person with Chiron in Leo in the fifth found that, at the time of her first square at age 5½, her parents moved her to a new neighborhood. In her old neighborhood, she had been an ordinary person, but now she was made fun of and picked on. She began to make friends with others who were also "underdogs," and feels that it was for this reason that she has always felt she has more in common with the underdogs in life.

III. A person with Chiron in Capricorn in the fourth met her fiance when Chiron in her seventh made the first square. At the retrograde square, they discovered that he had terminal cancer, but they married anyway. At the third square, his sickness became very severe and he died shortly thereafter.

IV. A person with Chiron in Libra in the second received a present from her parents at age 7 when Chiron made its first square—a piano. She later became a music teacher.

Also, the exact nature of the Chiron turning point depends upon one's age. For those Chiron-signs who make a first square before the first Saturn square, the Chiron lesson must be learned first, in order that the Saturn lesson be truly understood. This is a small group, as you can see by the graph, from Cancer to mid-Libra. However you define the first Saturn-square, it IS the first real test to one's reality-structure; it marks the first *real* awareness of the concept of time. Since Chiron denotes non-chronological time, perhaps people with these Chiron positions must discover "Chiros" before Chronos, so that the latter does not fit them into too tight a mold.

From age 7 to 14—and thus AFTER the first square of Saturn, but prior to the first opposition, we have a large segment of the population—Chiron in Taurus and Gemini, and then also mid-Libra to mid-Sagittarius. All of the people born with these Chiron positions need a basic grounding in Saturn's view of realityand time before they can take a look at Chiron's Chiros. Yet they must get a glimpse of Chiron's doorway into another world before the Saturn-opposition-Saturn brings their first confrontation with the reality structures of their peers. Perhaps, without the Chiron-square, these people would be unable to get truly beyond their own world enough to deal with other people at age 14.

From age 14 to 21—and thus between the opposition and second square of Saturn, we have Chiron in Aries, and then mid-Sagittarius through Capricorn. These people need the confrontation with the reality of others before they can begin to appreciate that any other world exists beyond their own.

Finally, age 21 to 23½—and past the second Saturn square, with only the Saturn return awaiting them before they have experienced an entire Saturn cycle. These people need as much Saturn influence as possible, before they are ready to look through the doorway into another world, or to experience another kind of time. Perhaps, because the rulers of Aquarius (Saturn/Uranus) and Pisces (Jupiter/Neptune) are on either side of Chiron, or perhaps because Uranus and Neptune teach of things that are way beyond Saturn's earthly structure and material viewpoint, these positions for Chiron need an extremely thorough, extensive grounding in Saturn before the Chiron square, so that the people don't get carried away into totally irrelevant directions.

Anyway, it is important to note that ALL Chiron positions have their first square BEFORE the Saturn return, and thus all people need to understand that there are things beyond one's reality before they can begin to build their own reality, separately from the past, at the Saturn return.

And, of course, transits of planets to one's natal Chiron are also quite significant. They are times when you can use the energy of the transiting body to cross over into uncharted areas, or accomplish something you have wanted to do for a long time, or when unusual circumstances arise giving you an opportunity to do something outside the normal routine. Sometimes, a transit of a planet to your Chiron coincides with an event that brings a major change in areas of life that are ruled by the house Chiron occupies.

A few examples of transits to natal Chirons:

Mars—an individual won an argument with someone, for the first time, to whom he had been losing arguments for years.

Mercury—when it passed over my tenth house Chiron, I received a letter from my father, from California (he lived in Pennsylvania, so the postmark surprised me). Inside was the news that my father's mother had died, and my parents had flown to California for the funeral—but they did not have time to let me know before they could catch the plane. Also inside was a note that they had made be beneficiary of the flight insurance—which made me a bit nervous.

Venus—an individual begins to teach astrology to a girl. What is so unusual is the fact that, a few years earlier, she had been more knowledgable about the subject than he, and was the person who got him involved in the first place.

Jupiter—an individual with Chiron in the tenth decided to search all around his neighborhood for the best prices on food, and found out that they existed in a store he had totally avoided before, because he did not like the outer appearance of that store.

Jupiter—when Jupiter crossed my tenth house Chiron, my first set of business cards arrived from a mail-order printer. Also on that day, I was called upon to help calm down an individual by explaining to him that he should not feel guilty for becoming paralyzed with fear while being a witness to a crime. I was truly able to help him get back to everyday life.

HOUSE POSITIONS

The house position of Chiron denotes a number of things. It points to major lessons one must learn, after one has learned the lessons of Saturn. It points to an area where one can best focus the energy of the Saturn/Uranus midpoint—even if it makes no aspect to this midpoint. The affairs of this house have an element of "NOW!" to them; when a problem arises here, you cannot wait until later to resolve it, and nothing must stand in your way when you are trying to overcome obstacles here. This house is where the greatest focus for healing and wholemaking lies; by using the positive energy of this house, one can help heal problems arising in the whole being. The people represented by this house are of special import to you; you feel that, at least in the areas and affairs represented by this house, you have something in common with everyone. And therefore you find it easiest, in this house, to relate to the common man as opposed to some "special interest group." In this house one is most likely to hold a maverick viewpoint—to believe in ideas which do not fit in with the accepted view, yet not be interested in tearing down the accepted view either. AND, Chiron can act like a doorway to the basic energy force of the house itself—enabling you to tap the particular power inherent in the house, and use it almost without limit or restriction (if you have first learned the lessons of Saturn which relate to that house). Finally, events in this house often do not fit any previously described set of conditions or rules; often they have a nature totally unrelated to any previous experiences which their associates may have had.

Some possibilities should be considered, but have not been researched yet:

The specific meaning of Chiron in a house may be altered depending upon what part of its orbit Chiron is in. For example, when Chiron is in Libra, it is at its closest point to the Sun, and can actually cross Saturn's orbit. Does its proximity to Saturn give it a different meaning in a house than when it is in, say, Aries, which is the sign Chiron occupies when it is closest to the orbit of Uranus? It has already been observed that world events are colored by Saturn or Uranus, whichever planet Chiron is moving closer to. For example, from 1920–1945, and currently since 1970 (until 1996), Chiron has been moving closer and closer to Saturn. We have seen the current cry for a return to traditional values, the reversal of a number of decisions made in the liberal '60s, the increasing demand for law and order. In the first period we had the rise of men like Hitler, and recently the rise of those like the Ayatollah Khomeini. On the other hand, look at 1945–1970, with Chiron moving gradually toward Uranus.

CHIRON IN HOUSES

First House: This person orients himself to the universe in a way that goes beyond any particular path, established viewpoint, or structured life-style. The first impression this person gives is that he cannot be categorized. He looks familiar sometimes, but you cannot put your finger on the reason. The eyes have a look about them as if the person were from another dimension—a stranger in a strange land. There is a refusal to let any obstacle interfere with the pursuit of his personal growth. If some such obstacle exists, he goes through it as if it did not—or tries to. Overcoming obstacles and resolving problems, in fact, is one way this person discovers himself. He believes he has something in common with everyone he meets, and that all people should also have such a belief. In the developed type, there is a special knack for opening doors for others, and a desire for all people to exist on the same level—thus, a hatred for inequality. Unless there are serious aspects to the contrary, these people are dynamic, radiating energy, and tend to be quite disarming. Their integrity is usually beyond question (unless the rest of the chart drastically disagrees). There is a strong "loner" quality to their personal lives, even though they may deal with people all the time. They often have the ability to get around the system, the unique ability to see beyond what others see, and often have a "wild" look in their eyes, which makes them quite attractive.

Norman Mailer, Rollo May, Mercedes McCambridge, Dan Rather, John Scali, Mike Schmidt, Anne Tyler, Archie Griffin, John DeLorean, Uri Geller, Rex Harrison, R. D. Laing, Vincent Price, Burt Reynolds, Rennie Davis, Kareem Abdul-Jabbar, Gregg Allman, Vida Blue, James Arness, Steve McQueen, Wilt Chamberlain, Huey P. Long, James Stewart, Marshal Tito, Adelle Davis, Joseph Alioto, Rosie Grier, Pete Townshend, Sally Fields.

Second House: Once these people become aware of what direction they are going in in life, they have the ability to draw upon unimaginable resources. Their desires are extremely powerful, and they truly feel that nothing should stand in the way of the gratification of those desires. On a lower level, there is a desire to control friendships and relationships. There is an ongoing search for people whose personal values are the same as theirs—and their attitude toward money and possessions is quite unique. There are lessons to be learned about money, possessions, values, and other forms of personal resources, but when they have learned these, there is often a need to help others who are poor or needy in some way. They are capable of a total immersion in their work, to the point where they become extremely skilled in one specific field. This position also gives them inventiveness, often a good deal of technical skill, and an increase in management ability. Once they have found something they truly value, or something they feel is truly worthwhile, they take it quite seriously, and it provides them with a great sense of personal power, and an air of authority. Usually they are quite observant. There also seems to be a great attraction for all eighth house affairs, such as power, sex, and the occult. Unles other things point to the contrary, they are usually "cool, calm" types.

William Lipscomb, Marsha Mason, Kate Millett, Walter Mondale, Jack Paar, James Wyeth, Marjoe Gortner, Mick Jagger, Mike Love, Cat Stevens, Alice Cooper, David Bowie, Johnny Wiessmuller, Bobby Fischer, Malcolm Dean, Benjamin Disraeli, Anthony Armstrong Jones, Jean Claude Killy, Sandy Koufax, Bela Lugosi, Henri Petain, Max Schmeling, Leopold Stokowski, Arturo Toscanini, Pearl S. Buck, Barry Goldwater, Eva Braun, Don Ameche, Kenneth Bergquist, Karen Black, Craig Breedlove, Garth Allen, "Mean" Joe Greene, John Updike, James Daly, Dianne Feinstein, Lauren Hutton, Sally Struthers, Sharon Tate.

Third House: Unless other things point to the contrary, here there is an innate belief, which goes back to childhood, that all things are possible. Relationships of all kinds are always on these people's minds. In the lower type, the sense of humor is very "pornographic" (dirty-minded), which stems from the importance of relationships. No matter what social level they are on, they have an ability to think like, and to communicate with, the common man. Even the people who have elevated their minds are usually noted for their good sense of humor. Basically they are of a liberal bent, often libertarians. They allow no limitations to stand in the way of their mental processes, and let their thoughts roam everywhere, even to the taboo. In fact, their logical minds are not confined to logic —they are very closely linked to their emotions, their instincts, and other areas, and their emotions are very easily aroused. Usually mental experimenters with fast minds, they tend to be mentally versatile, often controversial in thought and word, usually straightforward, possessed of a unique writing style, and often talkative.

Xaviera Hollander, Hugh Hefner, Larry Flynt, Gypsy Rose Lee, Jean Cocteau, Beverly Sills, Paul Newman, Robert Redford, O. J. Simpson, Clarence Lillehei, Roger Morton, George Steinbrenner, Casper Weinberger, Steve Cauthen, Phil Donahue, James Taylor, Arlo Guthrie, Algernon Swinburne, Joan Crawford, Betty Davis, Arthur Rimbaud, Ethel Merman, Dr. F. Regarde, Jean Paul Sartre, Robert Cummings, Betty Friedan, Erma Bombeck, Steve Allen, Ray Bradbury, Sigmund Freud, Alan Watts, Fritz Perls, Edgar Degas.

Fourth House: These people feel a very strong tie to humanity; they feel deeply inside that they share common roots with all mankind, and therefore have something in common with all people. There is usually a powerful desire to uplift others, either mentally, emotionally, or spiritually, and there is a powerful sympathy with the "little man"— the common man, who can be victimized by larger groups and corporations. These people don't want to start anything they feel might fail, for to them failure is failing mankind, not just themselves. They want to enlighten others, to build a world where everyone is treated equally, to bring joy to everyone they meet. But their powerful insecurity surfaces if they feel they have failed—they "can't fail!" If other things in the chart are unstable, this is a prime position for suicide when they feel they have failed. Also, these people are extremely upset when things are going on without their knowledge, or when things are going on which exclude them, or exclude someone they know. Theirs is a deep feeling that the whole world is a family— this gives them a strong community spirit. There are two basic types—the extremely undervalued type, often shy, tense, and nervous, whose fear of failure has kept him back somewhat; and the "tough under fire" type, who receives great respect, is quite popular, and is comfortable being controversial. Both types like to work!

Ken Kesey, Henry Lewis, Mickey Lolich, James Lovell, Marie McCarthy, Patricia Neal, William Rehnquist, Donna Summer, Helen Hayes, John Lindsay, Joan Baez, Carmen Delavallade, Bradford Dillman, David Carradine, Arthur Godfrey, Ernest Hemingway, Lenny Bruce, Herman Hesse, Oscar Wilde, Dr. Sam Sheppard, Albert Speer, Vincent Van Gogh, Paul Goebbels, Hal Holbrook, Elton John, Karl Krafft, Troy Perry, Clifford Odets, Zubin Mehta, Mark Goodson, Walt Disney, John Denver, Ralph Nader, Jerry Reed, Robert Kastenmeier, Toulouse-Lautrec, Bonnie Franklin, Red Skelton, Jon Voight.

Fifth House: These people want to be exclusively what they are—they don't want their creativity to be influenced by anyone else. They tend to be uninhibited and temperamental; there is frequently an "anything goes" attitude in the way they express themselves. The less evolved types have reputations for loose morals or as playboy types. No rules govern their creativity, and their style is totally their own. These people have a certain something that lives on after they die. There is something so totally unique about them that people know who you are talking about when you mention this quality, mannerism, or creation. These people have major lessons to learn through children and/or lovers, and these lessons will change their whole life-style, once learned. They often add a whole new career, after pursuing one career for many years, yet frequently keep the old one as well. They have a strong competitive streak, lots of enthusiasm for their field, and if they need to train for something, they train hard. Many are known for their sharp or caustic wit. There is often a strong bent toward trying to create a totally realistic style. They are true defenders of self-expression and freedom of thought, unless other things point to the contrary.

Eartha Kitt, George Lucas, Ross McDonald, Burgess Meredith, Kenneth Patchen, Valerie Perrine, Richard Pryor, Philip Roth, Shirley Temple-Black, Sarah Vaughan, Merle Haggard, Jules Lenier, Oscar Levant, Henry Miller, Chris Reeves, Arnold Schwarzenegger, Phoebe Snow, Ringo Starr, Simon Wiesenthal, Jacques Cousteau, John Derek, Barbara Streisand, Pierre Renoir, Bertrand Russell, Jean Harlow, Frank Sinatra, Melina Mercouri, Maria Callas, Tyrone Power, Rock Hudson, Robert Goulet, Art Arfons, Groucho Marx, Ruth Buzzi.

Sixth House: These people have unique health problems. Often, what seems to help others does nothing for them, or does the opposite of what it was meant to do. But health is a dominant concern for them. If these people come to terms with their own health problems, there is often a strong desire to help others in the medical field. They are hard-working people, determined, with a sense of duty and self-responsibility. They pay a lot of attention to detail, and often develop unique skills at some craft or handicraft. Whetever they decide is the best avenue for their skills, they want to be as expert and perfect as possible, and hate being restricted to any category within their field. They want freedom to try any and all techniques that may perfect their skills, and best do the job. Most of these people are shy and introverted as children. Often they are poor or indifferent students, in spite of the fact that they often have high intelligence. As adults they are often brooding, withdrawn, and leaning toward pessimism or realism; very few optimists have this position. They often appear to be cold, aloof, and into their own private worlds. In unevolved types, they consider everyone either inferior or superior to themselves. Two reasons for the last two sentences are: they fear the ending of any relationship because it is extremely painful to them, so they are afraid of getting too closely involved with anyone; and they have great lessons to learn in the way of service, and until they learn them, they fear not knowing how much of themselves to give (the fear of being used), so they may appear to be selfish. But, when they overcome these fears, they can be the most giving, helpful, and healing types.

Mia Farrow, James Goddard, Joel Grey, Alan Leo (opposition asc.), Janet Leigh, Daniel Nathans, Robert Wagner, Jackie Onassis, Bob Hope, Ingrid Bergman, Gwendolyn Brooks, Geraldine Chaplin Francis Ford Coppola, Jimmy Carter, A. E. Housman, Louis Pasteur, Maurice Ravel, Auguste Rodin, Joanne Woodward, Rita Hayworth, Lana Turner, Errol Flynn, Katherine Hepburn, Eleanor Bach, Stephen Crane, Sir William Crookes, Dr. Tom Dooley, Dennis Weaver, Clint Eastwood, Dustin Hoffman, Billy Rose, Martin Sheen, Cathy Rigby, John Knowles, Paul McCloskey, Liza Minelli, Pierre Salinger, Bruce Springsteen.

Seventh House: These people don't like having to deal with people in any set pattern or order; theirs is, typically, a nondiscriminatory approach to their dealings with others. But their need for contact with people is powerful, and especially contact with the opposite sex. Cooperation, however, is difficult and competitiveness is strong—especially with members of the same sex. They need to be seen as "just as good as" anyone else, and especially as good as anyone else in their own fields. Often high-strung, but almost always good in a debate, they are unyielding in their arguments. Many are strongly opinionated, and most have a crusading "urge." They are controversial, aggressive, often sharp tongued, usually loquacious, and candid. The ability to improvise is strong. They are often flamboyant, and have skill clowning around. The family is usually important. If they marry, it always opens up new worlds for them. Their enemies are always of a unique type, and they find it hard not have at least a few. They hate to get involved in any kind of party machinations, if they are in politics, and usually end up going against the machine or totally destroying it, thus becoming THE power.

Adlai Stevenson, Wendell Wilkie, John Anderson, Earl Warren, Richard Nixon, Fidel Castro, Benito Mussolini, Arthur Schlesinger, John Mitchell, Hamilton Jordan, Upton Sinclair, Redd Foxx, Brian Keith, Dennis Hopper, Kurt Russell, Yvette Mimieux, Susan St. James, John Cage, Eleanor Clark, Woody Herman, Ray Davies, John Entwhistle, Richard Basehart, John Barrymore, George Moscone, Carl Sandburg, Albert Schweitzer, Princess Grace of Monaco, William Blake, Rudolph Valentino, Mary Pickford, Rossano Brazzi, John Wayne, Gary Cooper, Charlton Heston, Sidney Poitier, Erwin Rommel, Bette Midler, Eleanor Smeal, Gloria Steinem, Gale Sayers, William Holden, Carol Channing.

Eighth House: These people usually have very strong instincts, and often have to work hard to re-channel a basic animal or "killer" instinct into something constructive. There is usually a basic "coolness" or sophistication; yet you can sense that, beneath it, they are quite volatile. These are the people who, if they work on themselves, develop great self-discipline, control, and "toughness"—yet there is still the "killer" instinct there. Often, as children, they are in trouble due to lack of self-control. These people try to concern themselves with simplicity, to get the basic "flavor" of something, or to get to the real roots of a situation. There is a desire for precision, and often a love and desire for research, with a knack for quickly penetrating a problem. They want to develop and sharpen their power and skills, and are quite capable of controlling others if they choose to do so. You can usually recognize them by their calm self-assurance, animal magnetism, and sense of utter conviction. They have the potential to tap and to channel vast energies and life forces, and to open doors to other worlds. Their sexual desires are often unique, but they are capable of transcending them in ways that others would not even think of. Their greatest lessons concern sex, power, and death.

Omar Sharif, Yul Brynner, Henry Winkler, James Dean, Stacy Keach, Richard Chamberlain, Robert Mitchum, Montgomery Clift, Robert Blake, Ryan O'Neal, Karl Malden, Bruce Lee, Joe Frazier, Jackie Robinson, Jack Nicklaus, Eddie Arcaro, Indira Gandhi, Mao Tse Tung, Dr. Louis Berman, C. C. Zain, William Masters, Bishop James Pike, Komar, F. Scott Fitzgerald, Christopher Isherwood, Jack Kerouac, John Steinbeck, Yoko Ono, Leonard Bernstein, Jimi Hendrix, Raquel Welch, Elizabeth Montgomery, Deborah Kerr, Christine Jorgensen, John Dunlop, Shirley Hufstedler, Lawton Chiles, Baudelaire.

Ninth House: In their direction of interest, these people have a talent for finding and understanding basic laws, general principles, and the underlying significance of a situation—the root, basic meanings which are often hidden from others. They also can work with these in ways that are quite unbelievable, synthesizing them into more complex patterns, or finding ways to explain them to others in words that an ordinary person can understand. Or, they may not use words as their medium, but find some other way of communicating their in-depth understanding of symbols. If often comes out as a talent for simplifying technical explanations, an ability to "tune-in" on the current of today, a talent for really identifying with the audience, a desire to teach, or a fantastic ability to persuade (or mold public opinion). They love challenges, are usually perceptive observers, good at ad-libbing, and outspoken with pronounced opinions. They have a powerful need to seek others with the same philosophies and beliefs and, usually, an equally powerful need to convince nonbelievers to believe in them. In its most negative expression, this produces a VERY narrow philosophy, a dislike or hatred of those who don't fit into this philosophy, and an almost "police mentality." Whether positively or negatively, they search for verification and clarification of what they believe in, in all areas of life.

Gay Talese, Paul Theroux, Tom Wicker, George Bernard Shaw, Andre Malraux, Alfred Hitchcock, Dane Rudhyar, John Addey, Marc Edmund Jones, Edgar Cayce, Nietzsche, David St. Clair, Judy Blume, John Clifford, Graham Nash, Jack Sheldon, Dolly Parton, Eric Satie, Edouard Manet, Andy Warhol, Howard Cosell, Julie Andrews, Goldie Hawn, Greta Garbo, Jim Bailey, Roddy McDowell, Candice Bergen, Ava Gardner, Shelley Fabares, Robert Stack, Ronald Reagan (if you use the Cancer-rising chart). William Colby, J. Edgar Hoover, Richard Daley, George Wallace, Ayatollah Khomeini, Adolf Hitler, Herman Goering, Everett LeRoy Jones, James Earl Ray, John W. Gacey, Enrico Fermi, Lotte Strahl, Stanley Hiller, Mary Wells, Arthur Okun.

Tenth House: These people drive themselves hard in their own field, often keeping grueling schedules. Yet they are usually known for being vital, alive and hard-working, with a singlemindedness of purpose, and a hatred of inactivity. When they talk about their purpose, they tend to lecture like a preacher. It is not unusual for them to reach a high position in some field without many of the requirements which are normally necessary to do so—such as a high-school graduate working at a job usually filled by a college graduate. In any event, they are usually in a position where they just don't seem to fit in with their co-workers—such as the only non-family member in a family-run business. Even if they choose a field where it is normal to be "different," they still seem to just not be like anyone else in the field. Thus, they are definitely conspicuous and capable of making quite an impact on their profession. They are known for having a "something extra" which makes them stand out as mavericks, *or* for NOT having something which others in the field have, which also makes them stand out. The public knows these people for their willingness to go beyond conventional methods in their careers, even if there is opposition from others, and they often disdain critics. Many have a great charisma. They usually have a fast wit, and tend to be known for their self-deprecating humor. They always feel they must have an immediate goal—and if they don't have one, they invent one. Often they find it difficult to concern themselves with long-range goals. They make good crusaders.

Jerry Lewis, Paul Lynde, Tom Poston, Jonathan Winters, Tom Smothers, Peter Ustinov, Flip Wilson, Tom Bosley, Dick Cavett, Truman Capote, Gale Storm, Loretta Young, Shirley MacLaine, Marilyn Monroe, Judy Garland, Joan Caufield, Diana Ross, Orson Welles, Willie Nelson, Sam Peckinpah, William Saroyan, Alfred Tennyson, Paul Verlaine, Giuseppe Verdi, Jack Anderson, Thomas Huxley, Isabelle Pagan, Alan Oken, Alice Anne Bailey, Nikola Tesla Michel Gauquelin, Georg Moore, Milton Shapp, Thomas Eagleton, Robert McNamara, Jerry Rubin, F. Lee Bailey, Leon Trotsky.

Eleventh House: Major lessons for these people include choosing friends and associates wisely, learning how to deal with the ways in which other people express their own unique abilities and talents, understanding children other than their own, and fitting versus non-fitting into society. One's Chiron can become submerged in this house—never seeming to surface—unless one finds a unique role in society. Then, one becomes very much the maverick. The urge to participate in society is unusually strong, and this group is quite aware of the needs and desires of their peers. In fact, once they find their own unique niche, they often become the hub or center for a whole group of people, leading the way down a different path, or bringing together people with a common goal. But for those who cannot find a totally unique role, there is an overpowering need to "fit," to be part of society, and this usually comes out in one of two ways—either a VERY marked conservative streak, or a total disillusionment with society, leading to a revolutionary tendency. In the former, there is a tendency to seem "solid" or "dull," and to appeal to a conservative crowd. Often one has a "loser" image, even if in no way a loser, and a tendency to be modest about one's achievements and, in general, to have a low-key or understated manner and a tendency toward self-deprecation. It is quite common for someone to start off as one of the above types, and then switch to another. One thing everyone in this position wants to be is a problem-solver, so many become interested in science. Their hopes and wishes are very powerful; they have strong ideals, and once they have a specific picture of the world they want to live in, they will let no closed doors keep them from getting there. In most, loyalty, team spirit, and sportsmanship are very strong.

Edith Custer, Herman Melville, William F. Buckley, Dr. Benjamin Spock, Robin Moore, O. Henry, Vance Packard, John Gardner, William Lamb, Robert Good, Luis Alvarez, Dr. Brian Marsden, Albert Einstein, Allard Lowenstein, Charles Duncan, Henry Kissinger, Gamal Abdul Nasser, Governor Jerry Brown, Yvonne Burke, Richard Alpert (Ram Dass), Anita Bryant, Jane Fonda, Diane Baker, Peter Graves, Phyllis Diller, Bob Crane, Linda Blair, Vivien Leigh, Jack Nicholson, Merv Griffin, Diane Keaton, Gregory Peck, Rick Nelson, Lawrence Welk, Tom Jones, B. J. Thomas, Jose Feliciano, Judy Collins.

Twelfth House: These people are experimenters and are multi-talented. They always have at least one goal to work on, and an unlimited desire to learn and to increase the foundation of knowledge. Most especially, they want to learn of the hidden truths behind the apparent reality—to the point where they have a fear that some door will open to them when they are unprepared—so they feel that they must always try to learn as much as they can on every subject, to prepare them for anything they may uncover. They have an interest in the past, and usually have a talent for bringing things from the past into the present to make them once again serve a useful purpose. Almost always they have many projects going on at the same time, so they are frequently in danger of overextending themselves. They usually have a very strong awareness of the unrealized potentials in both situations and people. Quite frequently they are known for their intellectual arrogance, and for the fact that they enjoy the role of dissenter. Yet it is quite common for them to not realize how they hinder themselves by holding maverick views. One of the most frequently experienced traits of this position is a tendency to not receive credit for things they have done, but at the same time they lack concern when this happens. There also exists a talent for "do-it-yourself," because often they cannot find anyone else to do what they want done. Most are moody. And most have a very strong awareness that the universe is filled with greater laws than those which are visible only throughthe five senses, and greater power then any which humans are capable of completely understanding.

Francoise Gauquelin, Neil Armstrong, Arthir Janov, Frank James Dixon, Pierre Teilhard de Chardin, Grigori Rasputin, Charles Richter, Al H. Morrison, Neil F. Michelsen, Noel Tyl, Richard Nolle, Kirk Oakes, Billy Graham, Toni Morrison, Jean Stafford, Joan Didion, Leo Guild, Marcel Proust, James Blish, Walt Whitman, Robert Smithson, George Gershwin, Harry Belafonte, Harry Bertoia, Rockwell Kent, Ottorino Respighi, Miles Davis, Ron Ely, Robert Culp, Richard Crenna, Jim Backus, Sally Kellerman, Elizabeth Ashley, George Peppard, Jackie Gleason, Barbara Stanwyck, Audrey Hepburn, Dean Martin, Robert Taft, Jack Valenti, Patricia Harris, Francisco Franco, Jack Kemp, Brendan Byrne, Robert Kennedy, Willy Brandt, Linda Lovelace.

ASPECTS

It would take a whole book to go into Chiron's every aspect with every planet, but I would like to discuss several points.

Orbs: For the purpose of research, I only used a one-degree orb for all Chiron aspects, except for three degrees for Sun and Moon. The only real exception to this was when Chiron was intimately involved in some aspect pattern, such as a grand square. But, from my own observations, I feel that the following is a good picture of true Chiron orbs in natal charts: Conjunction = 3°; square = 3°; opposition = 3°; trine = 3°; sextile = 1½°; semi-square = 1½°; sesquiquadrate = 1½°; quincunx = 1½°; semi-sextile = 1°; septile = 1°; *quintile* = 1°. I would add 2° for aspects to Sun or Moon if conjunction, square, opposition, or trine; 1½° if sextile, semi-square, or sesquadrate; and 1° if one of the others. I also give the extra orb to the ascendant, but I am not yet sure about the MC. As for Chiron's aspects to any of the asteroids, I cut all of the above orbs in half. Finally, for a major aspect of Chiron to a point, such as the ascendant/MC midpoint (a very sensitive point, by the way, along with its opposition and square points), I only allow a 1° orb.

Now I would like to discuss a few of Chiron's aspects that I find particularly interesting.

Chiron conjunct Sun: Three actresses who have this position are Gale Storm, Shirley Temple, and Doris Day. Except for Shirley (now Shirley Temple-Black), who went from show-business to being an ambassador, I do not know too much about the life-styles of these people. but all three presented, in their movies, the image of a wholesome, yet somewhat mischievous female, who was always getting into some type of trouble. From my personal research, as well as the list of other famous individuals with this aspect, I have concluded that this combination g... the following traits: a disregard for what others say can't be done, a need to express oneself which must not be hindered in any way, a need to express oneself in a way that separates one from his peers, an ability to see beyond the limits others remain within so that one can bring elements together which others may not even have considered, a concern for people's problems, and a tendency to divide people into two distinct groups—those that really like one, and those that dislike one (i.e., either you like this person with the conjunction or you don't; no indifference). A few other examples: Neil F. Michelsen, Jean Claude Killy, Huey P. Long, Vance Brand, Howard Cosell, Jean Cocteau, Jeff Bridges.

Chiron opposition Sun: These people are competitive, and quite full of spirit; they hate to be inactive, and are fighters at heart. In fact, once they discover a goal that is important to them, they become extremely active in the fight to obtain that goal. They have very definite viewpoints, and most of them are very people-conscious—even humanity-conscious. They seem to be unable to avoid making very definite enemies in life, and are very much interested in change. They have definite ideas of the way things could change for the better, and have no reservations about trying to make the ideas into reality. Some examples: Jane Fonda, Leon Trotsky, Melina Mercouri, George Bernard Shaw, Henry Cabot Lodge, Leon Spinks, John Koch, Roger Daltry.

Chiron quincunx Sun: Aloofness? Or at least it seems that way. These people are in their own world, seeing things from their own perspective, and it never quite matches the views of their associates. They may be liked, even loved, but a distance between them and others is nevertheless noticeable; it is quite difficult to get really close to them. This also often gives them a coolness, especially if Chiron is in an eighth house position to the Sun. This coolness can often make them even more attractive to others—they can represent the unattainable. Behind the aloofness, however, is a definite insecurity, especially in those with Chiron in a sixth house position to the Sun. It makes these people a bit nervous, or hyperactive, or jumpy, and gives them a very strong need to try to emphasize their sense of self—to emphasize whatever they identify as themselves. This can mean a need to emphasize the masculinity or femininity, if that is what they identify with. I suspect, deep down inside, that they have a large fear of being forced to change in some way, and a fear of not controlling their own lives. Some examples: George Peppard, Charles Bronson, James Daly, Tom Bosley, Bela Lugosi, Jack Valenti, Paul McClosky, Leonard Bernstein, Candice Bergen, Bonnie Franklin.

Chiron sextile Moon: These people tend to view others differently than the average person—they have a strong awareness of the needs, wants, and desires of others, and usually also of their weaknesses. There is, naturally, a temptation to use others with this aspect, but the more evolved souls resist it. Nevertheless, they are usually able to give people what they want. They have an instinct for giving things a unique, personal "twist," which makes them one-of-a-kind. They seem to have very strong survival instincts, and an absolute hatred for anything they perceive as unfair or unjust. They are perfectly willing to push against seemingly insurmountable odds if they feel there is something they need to do. Some examples: Billy Rose, Arnold Schwarzenegger, Luciano Pavarotti, Malcolm Dean, O. Henry, Betty Friedan, Mark Goodson, Nina Simone, Jane Fonda, Mickey Rooney, Henry Perot.

Chiron conjunct Mercury: Here are the innovators, the inventors, and those with a particularly unique way of communicating. If they write, or are in show business, they succeed in communicating far beyond simple words—they reach others on many other levels beyond just the verbal. Admittedly, they can be quite controversial, but they have an understanding of the common man's mind, and know how to reach it. Often there is a desire to open doors, previously closed to all but a very select few, for everyone; there is also a hatred of injustice and imbalance, and often of anything that restricts or limits others in any way, or that keeps people on a particular path. Some examples: Troy Perry, Clive Sinclair (inventor of the ZX81 and Timex/Sinclair 1000 computers), Ted Mack, Eugene McCarthy, B. J. Thomas, Benjamin Disraeli, Martin Sheen, Dwayne Hickman, Roman Gabriel, Yogi Berra.

Chiron square Venus: An extremely unique taste in art fits this aspect; if the person goes into the arts in any way, he often covers subjects that may be taboo, or that others simply have not considered. There is almost always an unusual sense of humor as well, and an appreciation for beauty where others do not perceive it. Their value system does not fit with society's, and many eventually develop the desire either to leave society or to ignore it. Others make the decision to try to change society's values. They have a very highly developed aesthetic sense, and a soft side—the males often will go overboard in asserting their masculinity, putting on a shell to protect themselves from being considered soft. Or, if they are not worried about being hurt, they may flaunt their soft, romantic side. Some examples: George Steinbrenner, Bruce Lee, Marjoe Gortner, Peter Fonda, Liberace, Adlai Stevenson, Charles Addams, Edgar Degas, Judy Collins, Brooke Shields, Sophia Loren, Le Petomane (known in Europe for "passing wind" in ways that imitated other sounds).

Chiron semi-square Mars: These people cannot stand the thought of being stopped if there is something they are trying to find out, or some task they are trying to accomplish. It seems that here, Chiron constantly eggs Mars on to go a little further, try a little more, try a different method, ignore this obstacle—and Mars seems unable to refuse. These people have a strong sense of self-assertiveness and usually have quite a temper, unless they are channeling it for some "cause." They also have very definite likes and dislikes and are usually quite frank in letting you know about them. Unless other things in the chart point to the contrary, they usually have a good deal of sex appeal. Some examples: Omar Sharif, Keith Emerson, Dr. Martin Luther King, Jr., Wilt Chamberlain, Bertrand Russell, Greta Garbo, Bishop James Pike, Redd Foxx, Madeline Kahn, Bette Midler.

Chiron square Jupiter: One thing that sets these people apart is their unique or unusual interpretations of situations or ideas. They are capable of perceiving meanings that are hidden from others, and of interpreting the most complex things so that even the common man can understand them—but this latter talent comes through experience. They go through continual upheaval in what they believe in and how they perceive life until they learn to accept change. At this point, they make the best teachers, interpreters, legislators, and excel in any position where they deal with basic meanings and symbols. However, if they refuse to accept the idea that all things change—if they refuse to integrate the concept of change into their belief system, the continual upheaval eventually can disrupt the very fabric of their life style. Some examples:

Rosalind Russell, Marcel Proust, Percy Bysshe Shelley, Rudolph Valentino, John Cage, Henry (Scoop) Jackson, Dan Rather.

Chiron sesquiquadrate Saturn: To these people, tradition, rules, and structures are all well and good, but are meant to be changed or gone beyond whenever the need arises. They always feel compelled to test the facts as they stand, and to go past them without much hesitation if necesary. They never see any structure or rule as always valid or always binding. There is a tendency to have a good bit of difficulty with authority, unless the authority gives them much freedom to forge ahead into the future. These people don't believe in the phrase, "You can't." Some examples: Francoise Gauquelin, Toulouse-Lautrec, Princess Grace of Monaco, Frank Borman, James Lovell, James Earl Ray.

Chiron opposition Uranus: I feel it is still too soon to arrive at a clear idea of the meaning of this aspect, as many people have it and some are still quite young. The one thing I can say is that these people have real spirit, and a very strong need to feel that their independence and individuality are not threatened. Some examples: Leon Spinks, Tracey Austin, Archie Griffin, Tatum O'Neal.

Chiron conjunct Neptune: While this intrigues me, I do not have enough cases to identify its meaning. It is interesting that two important figures in Communism, Joseph Stalin and Leon Trotsky, had this, as well as the blind singer Jose Feliciano, whose songs are full of emotion.

Chiron conjunct Pluto: Again, this intrigues me, but I have not enough examples. Karl Marx and Benito Mussolini had it, but so did Walt Whitman, and so does actor Michael Moriarity.

Chiron conjunct South Lunar Node: There seem to be two types—the unevolved type who is always getting in trouble or his eccentric or erratic behavior, and the evolved type who gets much pleasure out of sharing his unique insights and unusual life experiences with others. The former tend to fall back on Chiron's maverick nature whenever anything goes wrong in life, or whenever they are under stress—and thus express it negatively. The latter type has integrated Chiron, and thus instinctively knows how to use Chiron as part of the larger picture. Some examples: Craig Breedlove, Clifford Odets, Arthuro Toscanini, John Anderson, Merle Haggard, Dick Martin, Billy Carter.

Here are a few guidelines as to how Chiron acts in aspect to various planets:

CONJUNCTION: Unlike a regular conjunction, when Chiron is in conjunction with a planet, a fusion of the two bodies does not occur. Chiron does bring out the Maverick nature of the other planet, and seems to shape it so that it won't fit into any mold. Yet, the planet appears to have very little effect on shaping Chiron. Could that be because Chiron refuses to align itself with anything? There is a desire to equalize extremes, an ability to find something in common with everyone, and the ability to either open doors or go beyond obstacles for other people.

SEMI-SEXTILE: It seems to be more powerful than other planets in semi-sextile. While the person is not necessarily unconventional, he does seem to have an innate talent or knack for getting around obstacles, without putting forth much effort.

SEMI-SQUARE: The person feels compelled to use the planet that Chiron is aspecting—he cannot let it be idle. What is more, he feels the need to shape the planet, to control it, and accomplish things with it.

SEPTILE: Great potential to change society. The person seems to have Chiron activate automatically, the moment the other planet is activated—yet the two bodies may act independently of each other. It is just that he cannot use one, without the other body becoming active.

SEXTILE: Chiron refuses to remain still, and refuses to allow the other planet to be still as well; Chiron is always encouraging the other planet to go out, to solve problems, to be active—Chiron encourages the person to use the other planet as a tool to go out beyond the ordinary. There is a definite understanding of people and things that are not in the "norm."

QUINTILE: An ability to use the aspected planet to go way beyond one's present reality, to alternate realities, and then to bring back what one finds there into one's own world, and then to interrelate seemingly unrelated things.

SQUARE: This never produces stagnation, like other squares. On the contrary—ordinarily a planet tends to get into a rut, get set in its ways—but Chiron only lets this go on so long. Then, it "pulls the rug out from under you," and you are thrown off balance. You may end up falling down, but if you do, you will find that you have stumbled upon something really valuable that had been hidden from you before. (Perhaps there were diamonds under that rug, but you did not find them until the rug was removed, and you fell upon them.) Anyway, when Chiron throws you off balance, you have to learn to accept the fact that this planet must learn to adapt—must learn to change. Until one learns this, it seems that the planet goes back and forth to extremes, as the person must balance and rebalance. Once he learns that change is necessary for the growth of this planet, he welcomes change. In some people, a danger surfaces at this point—some people begin to thrill in change and new experiences so much that they live for them. These people must learn a new lesson—to welcome change, but it is not the end, only one part of the path.

TRINE: Untypical of a trine. Normally, we expect a trine to be easy and flowing—something we can take for granted. We do not expect any lessons to come from the areas 120 degrees away from a planet. But Chiron brings unexpected lessons from an area we thought we could feel quite comfortable in—it opens doors to worlds in areas we thought we knew quite well. Chiron in trine teaches us not to take anything for granted. Once we have learned this, we can now purposely use the aspected planet as a key to explore new worlds. We can express our own unique style with ease—and take for granted this part of ourselves. Of all Chiron aspects, the trine is least likely to get us into trouble for being different.

SESQUIQUADRATE: The planet in aspect to Chiron is quite often restless. It often finds itself in some situation where things suddenly come to a halt, and the person has to realign his energies. This aspect produces a resiliency, a spirited nature, and increases one's sense of humor.

QUINCUNX: There is an ability to observe the subtle forces behind things, the undercurrents, the twists and turns of life that others do not see. The person can use the aspected planet to draw other people out, and, to some extent,, to control others.

OPPOSITION: A need to go beyond ordinary methods of doing things, because the person cannot help perceiving alternate methods of doing things. However, there is often difficulty working within any structures, because the person sees so many alternatives. (One lesson here is, just because alternatives exist, it doesn't mean one has to choose them.) This is an aspect that brings challenges from Chiron's house to the planet, which the planet cannot ignore. It brings out the "fighting spirit" in the planet, or at least, a constant need to keep that planet active.

CHIRON'S SIGNS

Figuring out the meanings of Chiron in each sign is a complex affair. For one thing, Chiron has such an eccentric orbit that it stays in some signs a great deal longer than in others. Thus, we have had a much larger section of humanity to study with Chiron in Aries, for example (where it stayed for over eight years), than with Chiron in Libra (where it stayed less than two years).

For another thing, there is increasing evidence that it is not just Chiron's sign that is significant, but where Chiron is in relation to Saturn and Uranus. This factor can actually divide signs into two categories. For example, Chiron reaches perihelion in Libra. When it first enters that sign, it is moving away from Uranus. But after perihelion, it is still in Libra for awhile, yet now moving toward Uranus.

Nevertheless, certain definite traits are appearing for each Chiron sign position, and so here follows a brief description of Chiron through the signs.

ARIES: The best way to understand these people is to look at the two most recent periods in history with Chiron in Aries. The 1920s (The Roaring Twenties) with their "flappers," self-expression and uninhibitedness, and the 1970s, often termed the "Me Generation," were both very Arien times. Theirs is a personal imperative to push their potentials to the maximum, and a belief that everyone should express himself. There is a strong need to overcome any obstacles that may stand in the way of exploring new areas, especially if these areas lead to greater self-understanding. They have a strong need to make their own point of view understood, and believe the rights of the individual are paramount. They want to be first at *something.* Major lesson–controlling their aggressiveness and coping with the aggressiveness of other people.

TAURUS: Values change through time and cultures, but these people have a personal imperative to search for values that will remain, when everything else around them changes. All typical Taurean things, such as possessions and security, are extremely important, but they have unique viewpoints about them. They feel that nothing must stop them from acquiring what they feel they need to survive, and this includes material security. Many lessons come to them from this area of life, and as they evolve, they develop a great deal of concern for the needy. They feel that no one should be deprived of the necessities of life, and no one should becme wealthy at the expense of others. The less elevated types may not feel this way, but they are working out problems that will eventually lead them to this attitude. These people often are quite innovative in solving problems in the material world.

GEMINI: High on the list of priorities with these people is, as you might suspect, communication. It is especially important for them to understand why there is a communication breakdown, or why there is an obstacle to communication, and to do everything to resolve the situation. Therefore, these are the best people to have around as non-biased third parties in a dispute. They want very much to contact as many people as possible, and it hurts them if they are misunderstood. If they take up a cause, they can be quite fiery advocates. Learning is paramount to them, and they love to learn new ways of thinking, new ways of problem-solving. They are always testing, testing, testing, to see just what limitations their immediate environment puts on them, and on others.

CANCER: "Security!" Nothing must stand in their way, as they work to achieve this. Their family is paramount—and in the evolved types, the family is viewed as all of humanity. Thus, nothing must threaten whatever they define as family, and it is a personal imperative to protect the self and family at all costs. They have a hatred of aggression and animosity, as a rule, although a severely afflicted chart may conteract this trait. They are usually more in tune with their emotions than is the average person, and tuning in more all the time. One of their major lessons to learn is to control their emotions—not to let them run haywire, or to become lost in them. They have a knack of taking things from the past and bringing them into the present and future in a way that they become useful again—bridging the generations.

LEO: One thing almost everyone with this position has experienced is circumstances where he had to take control, because everyone else around was unable to cope with what was going on. One major lesson for these people is self-reliance. They have a personal imperative to be individualists, so it is very difficult for them to take advice. They have a unique sense of pride—they need to be called upon to do something "only you can do." They also must maintain their self-respect at all costs, and nothing must stand in the way of their doing this. They cannot stand any restrictions on their self-expression, not only for themselves, but for others. They usually have a strong affection for children, and for adults who still keep a childlike quality about them.

VIRGO: Many of these people have the soul of Don Quixote. They have a personal imperative to right wrongs, correct errors—and will not let anything stand in their way of doing so, once the errors are found. They are very much aware of all that is wrong in the world. One thing that irks these people more than anything else is to find that something has again gone wrong, once it has been corrected. There is a deep belief that no one should control another, no one should own another, and no one should keep anyone from being himself, and discovering his skills and abilities. They seem to have a knack for figuring out new ways of doing things, although in unevolved types, these "new ways" may not be socially acceptable.

LIBRA: One major lesson these people must learn is how to really tell when something is fair or just. They have a personal imperative to discover which side is correct, and a hatred of injustice—it must end NOW, not later. People are extremely important to them, and they feel that nothing must stand in the way of their trying to understand the viewpoints of other people. They also feel the reverse—that no one should close his mind to his own views. So they hate close-minded people, or people who shelter themselves from the views of others. Relationships all produce major lessons for them. Art, in some form, is a necessity; if they do not have a talent, they must have art or music or some aesthetic pleasure as an integral part of their lives. They must nourish their souls.

SCORPIO: The unevolved types feel that nothing must stand in the way of gratification of their desires. The evolved types feel that nothing must be in the way of understanding their desires, and working toward perfecting their higher selves. All types have a personal imperative to control their own lives at any cost. They have the ability to tune in to the universal energy and power, and use it for themselves. That is why many are involved in the occult, Eastern religions, and such. They have a powerful awareness of sex and sexual energy, which the higher types transmute to more powerful forces. The lower types tend to make enemies easily, for they feel that their own value system is easily superior to that of other people. The higher types search for common values that they can share with all mankind.

SAGITTARIUS: Want to get these people angry? Tell them somthing is "Off limits!" They cannot stand the thought that anything should be forbidden, especially if they feel it is something from which they can learn. They have a strong adventurous streak, and are always searching for something to believe in that will hold up, when everything else changes. They need to feel that they thoroughly understand the philosophy or religion in which they were brought up, and also what others believe in. When they find something to believe in, they have a very strong need to let no obstacles stand in the way of sharing it with others.

CAPRICORN: These people need to create some type of order or structure that will not fall apart when other things do, and which, it is hoped, will function after they are gone. They need to feel that they are on THE right path for them, and they deeply believe there is one specific path they must find for themselves. They also believe this is true for others—that each person has a correct path for himself. The more evolved types believe that each person's path is totally his own; the lesser types believe, once they find a path, that it is for everyone to follow. They hate anything that can sway them from their course, and feel the same is true for others. They have a strong need to succeed at their unique path, and can't stand failure.

AQUARIUS: The personal imperative for these people can be summed up in two words—THE FUTURE. They can't tolerate people who refuse to move forward, and they feel nothing must stop them from evolving, from discovering the new and the different. They have the souls of the Bohemians—free souls—and have a great deal of sympathy for those who stand out. They need people, and want to solve problems for others, as well as to bring people together. They cannot stand closed doors—they want (to steal a line from *Star Trek*) "to boldly go where no man has gone before."

PISCES: They have a personal imperative to feel that whatever they are involved in is THE truth, the important cause. They want to avoid involving themselves in anything that is not important, or not possible to achieve. In this last point, what qualifies "possible" is their evolutionary state, for the evolved ones believe that nothing is impossible. They want to be truly universal in lifestyle, and so will go beyond their world to become more whole. They have a deep optimism that they can make the world a better place—although this can be curtailed severely by heavy Saturn aspects. They are almost all quite psychic, and full of dreams. But one of the major lessons they have to learn is to avoid falling for wrong causes. They have an overpowering need to express love.

Progressions

So far, I have only studied the progressions of Chiron in the 'day-for-a-year' method. Obviously, Chiron itself does not progress very much this way, no matter how old someone gets. When Chiron does progress into a more exact aspect than at birth, the individual's Maverick qualities definitely become more prominent. When it becomes exact, the person can definitely expect some major crises, which results in his becoming much more aware of his potentials and his limitations.

But the more common event is a progression of another planet to one's natal Chiron. This always brings new experiences to the person, in the area of life represented by the progressing planet. And everyone who makes it to his first lunar return has had the moon over his Chiron, as well as the square, opposition, and other aspects. So the progressed moon-to-Chiron aspects are important to everyone.

My first experience with such an aspect was naturally in my own life. I wanted to be with my wife in the delivery room, for the birth of our second child. So, I had to take special classes, to make me eligible for such an honor. I finished the classes as the moon progressed in less than one degree from my Chiron; my wife started her contractions when the moon was on my Chiron; and I helped in the delivery while the moon was separating but still in orb.

Since then, I have seen many cases of progressed moon to natal Chiron, and the one common thread they all share is an experience that opens up another area of their life in a way that changes their opinion or image of themselves, and relates in some way to something connected with the moon. This could be a birth, or security, or food, or any of the many other lunar-ruled things.

All progressed aspects to Chiron appear to be significant. Sometimes one may happen at quite an early age. One mother told me that she was having trouble with her 2½-year-old son. She couldn't seem to toilet-train him, nor break him of his bottle-drinking. Then, she decided to try a new tactic—she told him he was getting to be a young man, and young men did not have "accidents" in their pants, and that they drank out of cups, not bottles. Overnight, he was completely toilet-trained, and never used the bottle again. His progressed sun was closely opposition this natal Chiron.

A young man was shy, and always getting "picked on" by his classmates. Finally, his parents took him to see a psychologist, as his progressed Mars came within 30′ of opposition to his natal Chiron. The therapy was quite successful, and he began to make friends (and stopped getting picked on) at the time the opposition was exact. His grades improved, he began to be able to defend himself if necessary, and he got his first real girlfriend, all before the progressed Mars moved more than 30′ past the opposition.

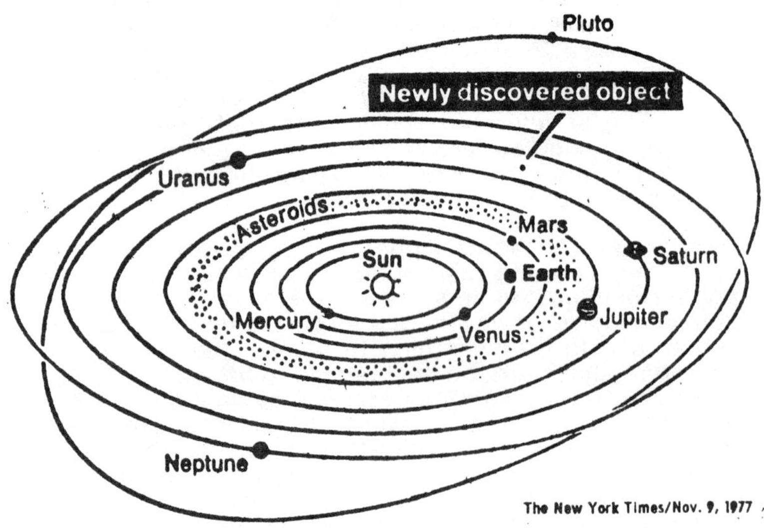

The New York Times/Nov. 9, 1977

Saturn and Uranus

Due to Chiron's special relationship with Saturn and Uranus, the aspects that Chiron makes with these two bodies are of particular importance. In light of this, I am including a special aspectarian for this century of the conjunctions, squares, and oppposi-tions Chiron makes with Saturn and with Uranus. The dates of the aspects are based on ephemeris time—the exact aspect may be a day earlier or later in your time zone.

As you can see, this is not a typical pattern of aspects. For example from 1935 to 1952, Chiron squares Saturn twenty-one times, before the distance between them begins to shrink significantly. Then, in 1966, these two bodies are conjunct—for the only time in this century. Uranus has just as unusual a relationship. In 1943, these two were square one time. Then, between 1952 and 1989, Chiron opposes Uranus forty-one times. Finally, these two square each other once, in 1997. One of the things this means is that we have very few examples of individuals with certain Chiron aspects to study, and an overabundance of others. (NO ONE born this century has Chiron in conjunction with Uranus.) Another thing this means is that whole generations of individuals can have certain Chiron/Saturn or Chiron/Uranus aspects—a good portion of the first half of the century has Chiron square Saturn—while the second half is almost all Chiron opposition Uranus. And another thing--the aspect seems to set the tone of the times. The Chiron/Uranus oppositions began in 1952, and seem to tie into the accelerated pace of scientific advancement during the second half of this century.

July 26, 1913: Chiron 90° Saturn	Aug. 7, 1954: Chiron 180° Uranus	Aug. 17, 1985: Chiron 180° Uranus
Jan. 14, 1914: Chiron 90° Saturn	Dec. 20, 1954: Chiron 180° Uranus	Oct. 1, 1985: Chiron 180° Uranus
May 19, 1914: Chiron 90° Saturn	Sep. 6, 1955: Chiron 180° Uranus	Feb. 25, 1986: Chiron 180° Saturn
Nov. 2, 1922: Chiron 180° Saturn	Dec. 5, 1955: Chiron 180° Uranus	Mar. 4, 1986: Chiron 180° Saturn
Apr. 15, 1935: Chiron 90° Saturn	Oct. 8, 1956: Chiron 180° Uranus	July 23, 1986: Chiron 180° Uranus
May 22, 1935: Chiron 90° Saturn	Nov. 15, 1956: Chiron 180° Uranus	Nov. 8, 1986: Chiron 180° Uranus
Feb. 16, 1936: Chiron 90° Saturn	Nov. 13, 1964: Chiron 180° Uranus	Jan. 13, 1987: Chiron 180° Saturn
Aug. 7, 1936: Chiron 90° Saturn	Dec. 31, 1964: Chiron 180° Uranus	May 14, 1987: Chiron 180° Saturn
Jan. 16, 1937: Chiron 90° Saturn	Nov. 1, 1965: Chiron 180° Uranus	July 4, 1987: Chiron 180° Uranus
Oct. 2, 1937: Chiron 90° Saturn	Jan. 22, 1966: Chiron 180° Uranus	Dec. 11, 1987: Chiron 180° Uranus
Dec. 17, 1937: Chiron 90° Saturn	Apr. 13, 1966: Chiron 0° Saturn	Dec. 30, 1987: Chiron 180° Saturn
Sep. 29, 1943: Chiron 90° Uranus	Oct. 23, 1966: Chiron 180° Uranus	June 14, 1988: Chiron 180° Uranus
Jan. 17, 1946: Chiron 90° Saturn	Feb. 9, 1967: Chiron 180° Uranus	June 16, 1988: Chiron 180° Saturn
Apr. 7, 1946: Chiron 90° Saturn	Oct. 15, 1967: Chiron 180° Uranus	Dec. 22, 1988: Chiron 180° Saturn
Jan. 8, 1947: Chiron 90° Saturn	Feb. 27, 1968: Chiron 180° Uranus	Jan. 18, 1989: Chiron 180° Uranus
May 20, 1947: Chiron 90° Saturn	Oct. 6, 1968: Chiron 180° Uranus	May 18, 1989: Chiron 180° Uranus
Jan. 8, 1948: Chiron 90° Saturn	Mar. 15, 1969: Chiron 180° Uranus	July 12, 1989: Chiron 180° Saturn
June 19, 1948: Chiron 90° Saturn	Sep. 29, 1969: Chiron 180° Uranus	Dec. 22, 1989: Chiron 180° Saturn
Jan. 13, 1949: Chiron 90° Saturn	Apr. 1, 1970: Chiron 180° Uranus	July 30, 1990: Chiron 180° Saturn
July 11, 1949: Chiron 90° Saturn	Sep. 22, 1970: Chiron 180° Uranus	Dec. 29, 1990: Chiron 180° Saturn
Jan. 28, 1950: Chiron 90° Saturn	Apr. 18, 1971: Chiron 180° Uranus	Aug. 11, 1991: Chiron 180° Saturn
July 21, 1950: Chiron 90° Saturn	Sep. 14, 1971: Chiron 180° Uranus	Jan. 14, 1992: Chiron 180° Saturn
Feb. 21, 1951: Chiron 90° Saturn	May 5, 1972: Chiron 180° Uranus	Aug. 15, 1992: Chiron 180° Saturn
July 22, 1951: Chiron 90° Saturn	Sep. 4, 1972: Chiron 180° Uranus	Feb. 7, 1993: Chiron 180° Saturn
Feb. 22, 1952: Chiron 180° Uranus	May 24, 1973: Chiron 180° Uranus	Aug. 14, 1993: Chiron 180° Saturn
Mar. 26, 1952: Chiron 90° Saturn	Aug. 26, 1973: Chiron 180° Uranus	Mar. 11, 1994: Chiron 180° Saturn
May 23, 1952: Chiron 180° Uranus	June 16, 1974: Chiron 180° Uranus	Aug. 9, 1994: Chiron 180° Saturn
July 10, 1952: Chiron 90° Saturn	Aug. 12, 1974: Chiron 180° Uranus	Apr. 23, 1995: Chiron 180° Saturn
Jan. 23, 1953: Chiron 180° Uranus	Aug. 27, 1975: Chiron 90° Saturn	July 28, 1995: Chiron 180° Saturn
July 5, 1953: Chiron 180° Uranus	Mar. 21, 1976: Chiron 90° Saturn	Oct. 10, 1997: Chiron 90° Uranus
Jan. 4, 1954: Chiron 180° Uranus	June 11, 1976: Chiron 90° Saturn	

QUESTIONNAIRE

In order to accelerate the discovery of Chiron's various influences, we have available a questionnaire in which yo can write down the effects that Chiron has had on your life. When we have enough questionnaires tabulated, the results will be published. To receive a copy ofthe questionnaire, send a self-addressed, stamped envelope, and we will be happy to mail one to you.

I hope this gives you some insights in how to begin to use Chiron. Of course, we must continue researching it for many years to come. If you want more information, write to:

Zane B. Stein,
Director, Association for Studying Chiron
757 E. Main St. K-201
Lansdale, PA 19446

Or, telephone me any evening at (215) 368-4387.

Chironically,

Zane B. Stein

The Continuing Discovery of CHIRON

Erminie Lantero
M.Div., Ph.D.

$8.95

In a style that speaks to both the serious student and professional astrologer, THE CONTINUING DISCOVERY OF CHIRON engages the reader in a rare opportunity—a chance to witness the way in which astrologers come to assign meaning to a new planetary body. Erminie Lantero presents the only comprehensive study of the recently discovered Chiron, and lets the reader participate in the astronomical research leading up to its sighting, its background in mythology, its literary referents, and its use as an indispensable tool in astrological charts. Through the use of case studies, the author exhaustively documents Chiron's first four years in our consciousness, and goes on to pinpoint how Chiron can be used by astrologers to better understand certain facets of personality in the natal chart.

> "Lantero is exploring some fascinating terrain when she talks about Chiron transits as healing crises whose quality is one of transition. I suspect most literature on healing makes unconscious Neptunian and/or Plutonian assumptions about the process: that a healing crisis is either of the whole-making, detoxifying, definitely disorienting and confusing Neptunian variety, or the intense death and re-birth Plutonian melodrama. She is encompassing something which has great subtlety and complexity when she is discussing the healing possibilities inherent in the nature of transition."

ABOUT THE AUTHOR: Erminie Lantero came to astrology rather late in life. A Ph.D. in Philosophy from Radcliffe, she began her religious studies at Mount Holyoke College and received a M.Div. from Union Theological Seminary in New York. She has been on the faculties of Sweet Briar and Wellesley Colleges, and served as an editor and participant at Pendle Hill, an experimental Center for Religious and Social Studies near Philadelphia. In the late 1960's she served as research assistant for a two-volume history of the Ecumenical Movement in the American Churches. Her official "retirement" led her to a long-delayed exploration of the occult, and finally (some fifty years late) she discovered astrology as the life work she would have preferred all along. Since finishing her book on Chiron, she has retired to a community run according to the principles of Rudolf Steiner.

Samuel Weiser, Inc. • Box 612 • York Beach, ME 03910

Cover design by Alden Cole

ISBN 0-87728-549-7

THE

DAILY POSITION

EPHEMERIS

OF

CHIRON

1891 - 2000

Computed by

EVE S. GREGORY

CAO TIMES
BOX 75 OLD CHELSEA STATION
NEW YORK NY 10113

THE
DAILY POSITION
EPHEMERIS
OF CHIRON
1891-2000

Computed by
Eve S. Gregory

This Daily Ephemeris of Chiron (2060) was computed on a Sanyo MBC 555-2 sixteen bit computer with a program written by Eve S. Gregory in consultation with Richard Moss, Ph.D., using orbital elements supplied by Dr. Brian G. Marsden at Smithsonian Institution Astrophysical Observatory.

The 10-day declinations of Chiron were computed in the same procedure.

Manufactured in United States of America

$20 per copy, postpaid

CAO TIMES
Box 75 Old Chelsea Station
New York NY 10113

Der Vertrieb in Europa efolgt durch den CHIRON VERLAG.
Bestellung sind zu richten an die folgende Adresse:

CHIRON VERLAG
Postfach 29
D-7409 Dusslingen
West Germany

ISBN 0-917573-03-X

CONTENTS INHALT

CHRONOLOGY OF ASTROLOGICAL INTEREST IN CHIRON

1920-1940: Maurice Wemyss deduces empirically an approximately correct ephemeris covering one orbit of Chiron, publishes in Wheel of Life.

Since then many other astrologers have sensed some undiscovered planet's workings while interpreting horoscopes. One of these is Charles A. Jayne Jr. in 1950.

29 August 1977: Cover of CAO TIMES is a facsimile of a painting showing a building crane lifting a new planet into orbit over New York City. Ranelle Wolfe, artist, on explicit commission from editor, Al H. Morrison

18 + 19 October 1977: Charles Kowal of Caltech, at Mt. Palomar CA, makes photo plates in a systematic search of the skies.

1 November 1977, "about 10 A.M." PST, Charles Kowal is convinced he sees a small new body with the orbit of a planet.

2 November 1977: Tom Gehrels of University of Arizona confirms the discovery.

8 November 1977: The discovery is announced. International Astronomical Union [IAU] has confirmed the discovery. A provisional orbit is calculated by Brian G. Marsden, Director of the Smithsonian Institution Astrophysical Observatory Minor Planet Center.

9 November 1977: The New York Times prints an article by John Noble Wilford announcing the discovery.

Joelle K.D. Mahoney, Director of Astrological Research Centre [a state-accredited school] interviews Charles Kowal by telephone. He does not know his birth hour, but answers queries about dates of events in his life. From this information and photos supplied by Charles Kowal, Joelle rectifies his chart 10 November 1977.

9 November 1977: An artist creates for Al H. Morrison a glyph for Chiron.

November 1977: Zane B. Stein persuades Dr. Marsden to compute an ephemeris. This turns out to be in right ascension/declination, covering 1937-1954. Chiron Committee is formed: Zane Stein, Al H. Morrison, Joelle K.D. Mahoney and Maria E. Bianco. Mahoney and Bianco write a program, Bianco computes an ephemeris in longitude and latitude.

11 June 1978: This world's first astrological ephemeris of Chiron 1937-1954 is published at a meeting of Astrologers' Guild of America Inc. It is discovered that both Charles Kowal and Maria E. Bianco have natal Chiron conjunct natal MC.

During that meeting all previously suggested glyphs for Chiron, including those depicted in a Canadian publication Phenomena, CAO NEWSLETTER and The Astrological Review, were considered and a formal vote taken, circa 2:38 PM EDT. The key-like glyph now in general worldwide use thus became the first planetary symbol adopted by democratic voting by an astrological organization, adopting a committee recommendation.

Chiron Committee further publishes this first ephemeris in CAO NEWSLETTER, mailed out by Astrologers' Guild of America Inc. as part of its participation in Congress of Astrological Organizations [CAO].

August 1978: Dr. Marsden encourages CAO to select a symbol for Chiron. IAU will tentatively class Chiron as a Minor Planet with a number: (2060), but will adopt no symbol.

18 August 1978: CAO in General Convention at San Diego CA takes a formal vote on the glyph chosen by the Guild and one proposed by Riverside Astrologers, Memphis, Tennessee [artist: Joyce Greer]. With Guild delegates abstaining, the key-like glyph again prevailed, by 2/3 majority.

September 1978: Chiron Committee publishes further ephemeris 1890-1979 [subsuming and correcting previous work] in CAO NEWSLETTER, again distributed by Astrologers' Guild of America Inc.

13 November 1978: Zane B. Stein founds The Association for Studying Chiron. There is a newsletter: The Key in which observations of Chiron are published.

December 1978: Phenomena Publications [Canada] puts into print a second ephemeris of Chiron. The figures are computed by Eric Tarkington from a program written by James Neely, based on the IAU announcements of Chiron's orbit.

1979: Marc Pottenger computes an ephemeris in monthly positions, with stations, 1685-1889. This one is distributed since 1980 by CAO TIMES.

1979: Weiser's Inc. commissions the first book on Chiron, to be written by Erminie Lantero.

16 December 1979: Zane B. Stein lectures a meeting of Astrologers' Guild of America Inc. in New York City on The Meaning of Chiron. This is the first known serious study of Chiron in horoscopes, the first known formal presentation at any organization meeting.

6 June 1980: Chiron Committee extends its ephemeris to include 1979-2000, completing its mission, dissolves.

September 1982: Phenomena Publications reprints its ephemeris of Chiron. There is no change in the figures. The text is slightly revised.

18 October 1982: Daniel Green at the Smithsonian Institution Astrophysical Observatory computes for CAO TIMES a new ephemeris of Chiron 1887-2000 in longitude/latitude, based on an updated program developed by Dr. Green and Dr. Marsden in 1982. As in all previous ephemerides, the positions are given at 10 day intervals.

5 November 1982: CAO TIMES publishes this latest ephemeris of Chiron 1887-2000.

1983: Zane B. Stein publishes a pamphlet: Interpreting Chiron. This is soon sold out and an expanded second edition published.

1983: The first-written text: The Continuing Discovery of Chiron is published by Weiser's.

26 October 1984: Dr. Hans Jörg Walter [Switzerland] presents a definitive study of Chiron at the 36th conference of Kosmobiologische Forschung in Stuttgart, Germany

1985: Chiron Verlag prints a translation of Zane B. Stein's work in German.

21 January 1985: CAO TIMES publishes an English translation of the key sections of Dr. Walter's thesis. [There are several additional articles in later issues].

November 1985: This Daily Position Ephemeris of Chiron is published by CAO TIMES, Box 75, Old Chelsea Station, New York NY 10113.

You can also order this ephemeris from CHIRON VERLAG Postfach 29, 2409 DUSSLINGEN, West Germany.

The list price is US$20, postpaid.

ISSN: 0146-3365

CAO TIMES

A QUARTERLY SURVEY OF CONTEMPORARY ASTROLOGY

Pedestrians watch as crane lifts another planet over N.Y.C.

Published 29 August 1977

[slightly reduced facsimile]

DIE CHRONOLOGIE DES ASTROLOGISCHEN INTERESSES AN CHIRON

1920-1940: Maurice Wemyss leitet empirisch eine annaehernd korrekte Ephemeride ab, welche eine Umlaufbahn Chirons erfasst. Er veoeffentlich sie in seiner Buchreihe: Wheel of Life.

Seitdem haben viele andere Astrologen bei Horoskopdeutungen gewisse Einfluesse durch einen unentdecketen Planeten gespuert. So auch Charles A. Jayne im Jahre 1950.

29. August 1977: Auf der Titelseite von CAO TIMES wird die Entdeckung eines neuen Planeten vorhergesagt. Das Faksimile eines Gemaeldes [vom Herausgeber Al H. Morrison in Auftrag gegeben] zeigt einen Baukran, welcher den Planeten ueber New York City in eine Umlaufbahn hochhebt. Die Kuenstlerin ist Ranelle Wolf.

18 + 19. Oktober 1977: Charles Kowal erstellt im Zuge einer systematischen Erforschung des Himmels photographische Platten. Mt. Palomar Observatorium, Caltech.

1. November 1977, 'ungefaehr um 10 Uhr': Charles Kowal ist ueberzeugt, dass er einen kleinen neuen Himmelskoerper mit einer planetaren Umlaufbahn sieht.

2. November 1977: Tom Gehrels von der 'University of Arizona' bestaetigt die Entdeckung.

8. November 1977: Charles Kowal gibt die Entdeckung bekannt. Die 'International Astronomical Union' [IAU] bestaetigt die Entdeckung. Eine provisorische Ephemeride wird sehr bald von Brian G. Marsden errechnet, dem Direktor des Astrophysikalischen Observatoriums der Smithsonian Institution.

9. November 1977: Die New York Times druckt auf der Titelseite einen Artikel von John Noble Wilford ab: Ein mysterioeses Objekt jenseits von Saturn koennte der 10. Planet des Sonnensystemes sein.'

Joelle K. D. Mahoney, Leiterin des 'Astrological Research Centre', einer anerkannten Schule, befragt Mr. Kowal telephonisch, erhaelt dessen Geburtsdaten un den Zeitpunkt der Endeckung Chirons. Sein Geburtshoroskop wurde an diesen Tag mit Hilfe der Progressionen von Lebensereignissen, wie sie Joelle am Telefon bericht wurden, korrigiert.

Ein Kuenstler unterbreitet Al H. Morrison, dem Herausgeber von CAO TIMES das erste Symbol fuer Chiron.

Der Astrologe Zane B. Stein ueberredet Dr. Marsden, eine Rektascension/Deklinations-Ephemeride fuer 1937-1954 zu berechnen. Die Daten gelangen ueber Al H. Morrison an Joelle K.D. Mahoney an Maria Bianco wer die Computerarbeit ergaenzt, um die Ephemeride fuer den astrologische Gebrauch in Laengen-und-Breitenangeben zu uebertragen.

11. Juni 1978, zirka 14.38 Uhr EDT: Die erste Chiron-Ephemeride der Welt wird bei einem Treffen der 'Astrologers' Guild of America Inc.' in New York City praesentiert. Man findet heraus, dass Mr. Kowals Radix-Chiron auf den zuvor von Joelle K.D. Mahoney korrigierten MC steht.

Ein Komitee stellt die vorgeschlagenen Symbole vor und es war darueber abgestimmt, wobei das allererste Symbol angenommen wird.Gleichzeitig wird die Ephemeride unter den anwesenden Astrologen verteilt.

Wenig spaeter veroeffentlicht das Chiron-Komitee die Ephemeride im CAO NEWSLETTER, welcher von der 'Astrologers' Guild of America Inc.' verschickt wird, einer Mitgliedsorganisation des 'Congress of Astrological Organizations [CAO]'.

August 1978: Dr. Marsden ermutig CAO dazu, ein Symbol auszuwaehlen und anzueignen. Die IAU will kein Symbol annehmen, sondern weist Chiron die Nummer eines Kleinplaneten zu: (2060).

18. August 1978: CAO stimmt bei der Generalversammlung in San Diego [Kalifornien] dafuer, das bisherige symbol anzunehmen. Ein Alternativvorschlag, der von den Riverside Astrologen aus Memphis, Tennessee unterbreitet wurde, erhielt ein Drittel der Stimmen. Die Kuenstlerin war Joyce Greer.

September 1978: Das Chiron-Komitee publiziert eine Ephemeride fuer 1890-1979 im CAO NEWSLETTER, der widerum der 'Astrologers' Guild of America Inc.' verschickt wird.

13 November 1978: Zane B. Stein gruendet 'The Association for Studying Chiron'. Es gibt einen Newsletter, The Key, in welchem monatlich von Beobachtungen ueber Chiron berichtet wird.

Dezember 1978: Eine zweite Ephemeride von Chiron wird durch Phenomena Publications [Kanada] herausgegeben. Sie wurde von Eric Tarkington auf der Basis eines Programmes errechnet, das von James Neely anhand der provisorischen Elemente, die urspruenglich von Dr. Marsden stammten, geschrieben wurde.

16. Dezember 1979: Zane B. Stein haelt einen Vortrag ueber Chiron bei einem Treffen der 'Astrologers' Guild of America Inc.' in New York City. Dies ist weltweit der erste formelle Bericht vor einer Versammlung irgendeiner astrologische Organisation. Dieser Text wird jetzt vertrieben von CAO TIMES und vom Chiron Verlag.

1979: Mark Pottenger entwickelt eine Ephemeride von Chiron fuer 1685-1889. Diese ist seite 1980 im Vertrieb von CAO TIMES.

6. Juni 1980: Das Chiron-Komitee vervollstaendigt seine Ephemeride von Chiron mit einem vorlaeufig letzten Teilabschnitt fuer 1979-2000. Veroeffenlicht und vertrieben durch CAO TIMES.

September 1982: 'Phenomena Publications' druckt seine Ephemeride von Chiron nach, mit denselben Zahlenwerten und leicht ueberarbeitete Text.

18. Oktober 1982: Daniel Green vom 'Smithsonian Astrophysical Obsrvatory' berechnet fuer CAO TIMES eine Chiron-Ephemeride in Laengen-und Breitenangaben anhand eines Programmes, das von Dr. Marsden und Dr. Green im Jahre 1982 entwickelt wurde. Wie bei den vorherigen Ephemeriden sind die Werte mit 10-taegigem Abstand angegeben.

5. November 1982: CAO TIMES veroeffentlicht diese letzte Ephemeride fuer 1887-2000.

1983: Zane B. Stein publiziert eine Broschuere: Interpreting Chiron.Diese ist bald ausverkauft und eine erweiterte zweite Auflage erscheint.

1983: Das erste Lehrbuch erscheint bei Samuel Weiser Inc.: The Continuing Discovery of Chiron, verfasst

[1980-81] von Erminie Lantero, M.Div., Ph.D. ISBN 0-87728-549-7

26. Oktober 1984: Dr. Hans Joerg Walter [Riehen, Schweiz] praesentiert eine ausgiebige Studie ueber Chiron bei der 36. Arbeitstagung fuer Kosmobiologische Forschung in Stuttgart.

1985: Beim Chiron Verlag erscheint Zane B. Steins Arbeit in Deutsch als Taschenbuch. ISBN 3-925100-01-6

21. Januar 1985: Eine englische Uebersetzung der wesentlichen Teile von Dr. Walters Vortrag erscheint in CAO TIMES, Vol. 6, No. 2. ISSN 0146-3365

Ein weiterer Artikel von Dr. Walter erscheint in Vol. 6, No.3.

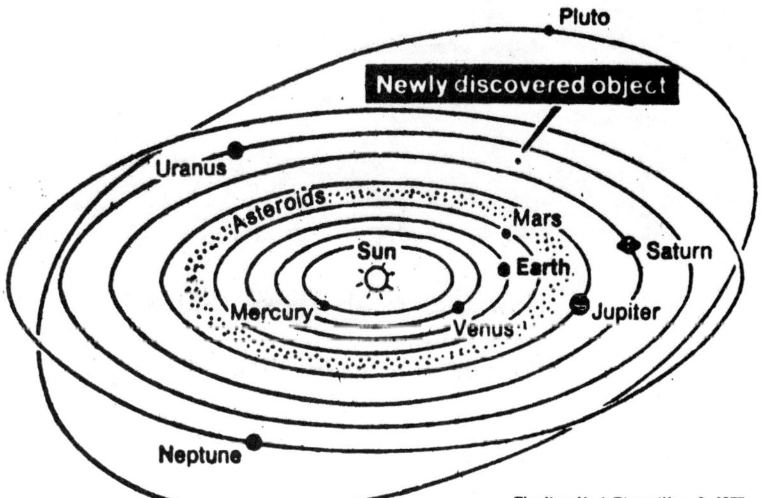

The New York Times/Nov. 9, 1977

NOTE: This chart should be rectified. What Charles Kowal said in answer to the question was "about" ten o'clock. Four clock minutes earlier gives a chart which fits events since then much better, and also relates more exactly to the charts of those who are concerned with the astrology of Chiron.

PLANET		SIGN	LONG	HSE	DECL	LAT	GEOCENTRIC		DIS	SPEED
SUN		Scp	9 12 15	11	14S34	0 00	N-NODE	S-NODE	73	60' 3"
MOON	R	Can	12 31 22	7	17N39	5S14	13L145	13Ar45	5	11°53'=>SLOW
MERC		Scp	17 46.9	11	17S50	0S43	05Sc09	11Sc59	3	93'38"
VENU	R	Lib	19 29.8	10	6S12	1N33	23V103	24Sc51	11	74 51
MARS		Leo	2 26.8	8	21N 3	1N28	08Ge53	15Sc25	69	23 34
JUPI	E	Can	6 1.6R	7	22N58	0S21	19Ca38	01Cp01	78	-1 41
SATU	D	Leo	29 7.5	8	12N54	1N12	29Ca18	17Cp51	51	4 8
URAN	E	Scp	11 55.9	11	15S 3	0N23	15Ge50	12Sa25	40	3 45
NEPT		Sag	14 33.6	12	21S 8	1N26	13Le23	09Aq37	9	1 56
PLUT		Lib	15 3.4	10	9N22	16N34	21Ca42	18Cp48	88	2 12
ASC		Sag	26 3.3	1	23S23					
MC		Lib	13 51.7	10	5S28					
NODE*		Lib	14 58.3	10						
PFOR		Leo	29 22.4							
VERTEX		Leo	8 58.5							
EASTPT		Cpr	11 44.1							

MUTUAL RECEPTION
SUN AND MARS

R=RULE D=DETRIMENT
E=EXALTED F=FALL
*TRUE NODE
☉/☽ ANGLE=243.32°

ASTRO COMPUTING SERVICE
from
NEIL F MICHELSEN
P O Box 16430
San Diego, CA 92116
714 / 297-5648
DATE=10/15/81

	CARD	FIX	MUT
FIRE	0	2	1
EARTH	0	0	0
AIR	2	0	0
WATER	2	3	0

6	4
0	0

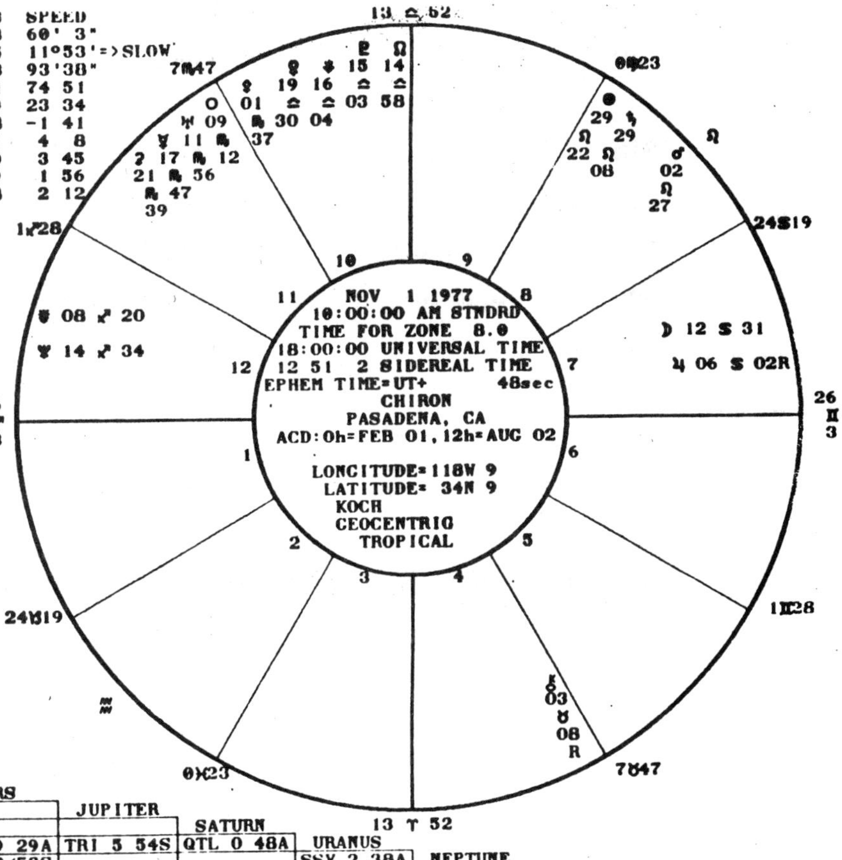

NATAL ASPECTS

	ANGLE	ORB	#		ANGLE	ORB	#
CON=Conjunction	0	10	10	TRI=Trine	120	10	6
SSX=Semisextile	30	3	5	SQQ=Sesquiquad	135	4	2
SSQ=Semi-Square	45	4	6	BQT=Biquintile	144	3	1
SXT=Sextile	60	6	4	QCX=Quincunx	150	3	1
QTL=Quintile	72	3	8	OPP=Opposition	180	10	1
SQR=Square	90	10	9	/ =Parallel or Contraparallel	0	1	5

A=Applying S=Separating

TOTAL ASPECTS = 58

	SUN	MOON	MERCURY	VENUS	MARS	JUPITER	SATURN	URANUS	NEPTUNE	PLUTO	ASC	MC
MOON	TRI 3 19S											
MERC	CON 8 35S	TRI 5/15A										
VENU		SQR 6 58A	SSX 1 43A									
MARS	SQR 6 45S											
JUPI	TRI 3 11S	CON 6 30S	SQQ 3 15A									
SATU	QTL 1 55A	SSQ 1 36A										
URAN	CON 2/44A	TRI 0 35S	CON 5 51S		SQR 9 29A	TRI 5 54S	QTL 0 48A					
NEPT		QCX 2 02A		SXT 4 56S	SQQ 2/53S			SSX 2 38A				
PLUT		SQR 2 32A	SSX 2 43S	CON 4 26S	QTL 0 37A	SQR 9 02S	SSQ 0 56A		SXT 0 30S			
ASC	SSQ 1 51				BQT 0 24	OPP 9/58	TRI 3 04	SSQ 0 53		QTL 1 00		
MC		SQR 1 20		CON 5/38	QTL 0 35	SQR 7 50	SSQ 0 16	SSX 1 56	SXT 0 42	CON 1 12	QTL 0 12	
NODE		SQR 2 27	SSX 2 49	CON 4 32	QTL 0 31	SQR 8 57	SSQ 0 51		SXT 0 25	CON 0 05	QTL 0 55	CON 1 07

*** MID POINTS SORTED INTO ZODIACAL SEQUENCE ***

⚷ 03♉08	M/⚷ 23♋30	♃/♇ 25♌32	♂/♇ 08♍45	♄/♇ 22♍05	☿/♄ 08♎27	♀/☊ 17♎14	♅/♇ 28♎30	☉/☿ 13♏30	♀/A 22♏47	☉/⚷ 06♒10
♃/⚷ 04♊35	☊/⚷ 24 03	♀/♃ 27 46	♃/♅ 08 59	♂/♅ 22 11	♂/♆ 08 30	♀/♇ 17 17	☉/♀ 29 21	♆/M 14 13	☉/♆ 26 53	♅/⚷ 07 32
☽/⚷ 07 50	♇/⚷ 24 06	☽/M 28 12	☉/☽ 10 52	♀/♄ 24 19	M 13 52	♀ 19 30	♀/♅ 00♏43	♆/☊ 14 46	♅/♆ 28 15	☿/⚷ 10 28
♂/⚷ 17 48	♀/⚷ 26 19	☽/☊ 28 45	♀/♂ 10 58	☿/♂ 25 07	♂/A 14 15	♄/♆ 21 51	☿/M 00 49	♆/♇ 14 48	☿/♆ 01♐10	♆/⚷ 23 51
♄/⚷ 01♋08	♂ 02♌27	☽/♇ 28 47	☿/♃ 11 54	♃/♆ 25 18	M/☊ 14 25	☉/M 26 32	☿/☊ 01 23	☿/♅ 14 51	☉/A 02 38	A/⚷ 29 36
♃ 06 02	♃/♄ 02 35	♄ 29 08	☽/♅ 12 14	☽/♆ 28 32	♇/M 14 28	☉/☊ 27 05	☿/♇ 01 25	♀/♆ 17 02	♅/A 04 00	
☽/♃ 09 16	☽/♄ 05 49	☽/♀ 01♍01	☽/☿ 15 09	♃/A 01♎02	☊ 14 58	☉/♇ 27 08	☿/♀ 03 38	☿ 17 47	☿/A 06 55	
☽ 12 31	♂/♄ 15 47	☉/♃ 07 37	☉/♂ 20 50	☉/♄ 04 10	♇/☊ 15 01	♄/A 27 35	☉ 09 12	A/M 19 57	♆ 14 34	
♂/♃ 19 14	♃/M 24 57	♂/M 08 09	♄/M 21 30	☽/A 04 17	♇ 15 03	♅/M 27 54	☉/♅ 10 34	A/☊ 20 31	♆/A 20 18	
☽/♂ 22 29	♃/☊ 25 30	♂/☊ 08 43	♄/☊ 22 03	♄/♅ 05 32	♀/M 16 41	♅/☊ 28 27	♅ 11 56	♇/A 20 33	A 26 03	

JULIAN DAY # = 2443449.250000 MEAN OBLIQUITY OF ECLIPTIC = 23°26'32" SIDEREAL AYANAMSHA (SVP) = Pic 5°34' 7"

How one reads these tables:

Wie man braucht diese Tabellen:

LONG.

0	= 0° Aries		0° Widder
30	= 0° Taurus		0° Stier
60	= 0° Gemini		0° Zwillinge
90	= 0° Cancer		0° Krebs
120	= 0° Leo		0° Loewe
150	= 0° Virgo		0° Jungfrau
180	= 0° Libra		0° Waage
210	= 0° Scorpio		0° Skorpion
240	= 0° Sagittarius		0° Schuetze
270	= 0° Capricorn		0° Steinbock
300	= 0° Aquarius		0° Wasserman
330	= 0° Pisces		0° Fische

All positions are for 0 hours Ephemeris Time

Alle Werte sind fuer 0 Stunden Ephemeris Zeit

Date ET	Long	Lat
1891 03 09	118 29	-7 29
1891 03 10	118 27	-7 28
1891 03 11	118 25	-7 28
1891 03 12	118 23	-7 27
1891 03 13	118 21	-7 26
1891 03 14	118 20	-7 26
1891 03 15	118 18	-7 25
1891 03 16	118 17	-7 24
1891 03 17	118 15	-7 24
1891 03 18	118 14	-7 23
1891 03 19	118 13	-7 22
1891 03 20	118 11	-7 22
1891 03 21	118 10	-7 21
1891 03 22	118 10	-7 20
1891 03 23	118 09	-7 20
1891 03 24	118 08	-7 19
1891 03 25	118 07	-7 18
1891 03 26	118 07	-7 17
1891 03 27	118 07	-7 17
1891 03 28	118 06	-7 16
1891 03 29	118 06	-7 15
1891 03 30	118 06	-7 14
1891 03 31	118 06	-7 14
1891 04 01	118 06	-7 13
1891 04 02	118 06	-7 12
1891 04 03	118 07	-7 12
1891 04 04	118 07	-7 11
1891 04 05	118 07	-7 10
1891 04 06	118 08	-7 09
1891 04 07	118 09	-7 09
1891 04 08	118 10	-7 08
1891 04 09	118 11	-7 07
1891 04 10	118 12	-7 06
1891 04 11	118 13	-7 06
1891 04 12	118 14	-7 05
1891 04 13	118 15	-7 04
1891 04 14	118 17	-7 03
1891 04 15	118 18	-7 03
1891 04 16	118 20	-7 02
1891 04 17	118 22	-7 01
1891 04 18	118 24	-7 00
1891 04 19	118 25	-7 00
1891 04 20	118 28	-6 59
1891 04 21	118 30	-6 58
1891 04 22	118 32	-6 57
1891 04 23	118 34	-6 57
1891 04 24	118 37	-6 56
1891 04 25	118 39	-6 55
1891 04 26	118 42	-6 55
1891 04 27	118 44	-6 54
1891 04 28	118 47	-6 53
1891 04 29	118 50	-6 52
1891 04 30	118 53	-6 52
1891 05 01	118 56	-6 51
1891 05 02	118 59	-6 50
1891 05 03	119 03	-6 50
1891 05 04	119 06	-6 49
1891 05 05	119 09	-6 48
1891 05 06	119 13	-6 48
1891 05 07	119 16	-6 47
1891 05 08	119 20	-6 46
1891 05 09	119 24	-6 46
1891 05 10	119 28	-6 45
1891 05 11	119 32	-6 44
1891 05 12	119 36	-6 44
1891 05 13	119 40	-6 43
1891 05 14	119 44	-6 42
1891 05 15	119 48	-6 42
1891 05 16	119 53	-6 41
1891 05 17	119 57	-6 40
1891 05 18	120 02	-6 40
1891 05 19	120 06	-6 39
1891 05 20	120 11	-6 39
1891 05 21	120 16	-6 38
1891 05 22	120 20	-6 37
1891 05 23	120 25	-6 37
1891 05 24	120 30	-6 36
1891 05 25	120 35	-6 36
1891 05 26	120 40	-6 35
1891 05 27	120 45	-6 35
1891 05 28	120 51	-6 34
1891 05 29	120 56	-6 34
1891 05 30	121 01	-6 33
1891 05 31	121 07	-6 32
1891 06 01	121 12	-6 32
1891 06 02	121 18	-6 31
1891 06 03	121 23	-6 31
1891 06 04	121 29	-6 30
1891 06 05	121 35	-6 30
1891 06 06	121 41	-6 29
1891 06 07	121 46	-6 29
1891 06 08	121 52	-6 28
1891 06 09	121 58	-6 28
1891 06 10	122 04	-6 28
1891 06 11	122 10	-6 27
1891 06 12	122 17	-6 27
1891 06 13	122 23	-6 26
1891 06 14	122 29	-6 26
1891 06 15	122 35	-6 25
1891 06 16	122 42	-6 25
1891 06 17	122 48	-6 25
1891 06 18	122 54	-6 24
1891 06 19	123 01	-6 24
1891 06 20	123 07	-6 23
1891 06 21	123 14	-6 23
1891 06 22	123 20	-6 23
1891 06 23	123 27	-6 22
1891 06 24	123 34	-6 22
1891 06 25	123 40	-6 22
1891 06 26	123 47	-6 21
1891 06 27	123 54	-6 21
1891 06 28	124 01	-6 21
1891 06 29	124 08	-6 20
1891 06 30	124 15	-6 20
1891 07 01	124 22	-6 20
1891 07 02	124 29	-6 19
1891 07 03	124 36	-6 19
1891 07 04	124 43	-6 19
1891 07 05	124 50	-6 19
1891 07 06	124 57	-6 18
1891 07 07	125 04	-6 18
1891 07 08	125 11	-6 18
1891 07 09	125 18	-6 18
1891 07 10	125 25	-6 17
1891 07 11	125 33	-6 17
1891 07 12	125 40	-6 17
1891 07 13	125 47	-6 17
1891 07 14	125 55	-6 17
1891 07 15	126 02	-6 16
1891 07 16	126 09	-6 16
1891 07 17	126 17	-6 16
1891 07 18	126 24	-6 16
1891 07 19	126 31	-6 16
1891 07 20	126 39	-6 16
1891 07 21	126 46	-6 16
1891 07 22	126 54	-6 15
1891 07 23	127 01	-6 15
1891 07 24	127 08	-6 15
1891 07 25	127 16	-6 15
1891 07 26	127 23	-6 15
1891 07 27	127 31	-6 15
1891 07 28	127 38	-6 15
1891 07 29	127 46	-6 15
1891 07 30	127 53	-6 15
1891 07 31	128 01	-6 15
1891 08 01	128 08	-6 15
1891 08 02	128 16	-6 15
1891 08 03	128 23	-6 15
1891 08 04	128 31	-6 15
1891 08 05	128 38	-6 15
1891 08 06	128 46	-6 15
1891 08 07	128 53	-6 15
1891 08 08	129 01	-6 15
1891 08 09	129 08	-6 15
1891 08 10	129 16	-6 15
1891 08 11	129 23	-6 15
1891 08 12	129 31	-6 15
1891 08 13	129 38	-6 15
1891 08 14	129 46	-6 15
1891 08 15	129 53	-6 15
1891 08 16	130 01	-6 15
1891 08 17	130 08	-6 15
1891 08 18	130 15	-6 15
1891 08 19	130 23	-6 15
1891 08 20	130 30	-6 15
1891 08 21	130 37	-6 16
1891 08 22	130 45	-6 16
1891 08 23	130 52	-6 16
1891 08 24	130 59	-6 16
1891 08 25	131 07	-6 16
1891 08 26	131 14	-6 16
1891 08 27	131 21	-6 17
1891 08 28	131 28	-6 17
1891 08 29	131 36	-6 17
1891 08 30	131 43	-6 17
1891 08 31	131 50	-6 17
1891 09 01	131 57	-6 18
1891 09 02	132 04	-6 18
1891 09 03	132 11	-6 18
1891 09 04	132 18	-6 18
1891 09 05	132 25	-6 18
1891 09 06	132 32	-6 19
1891 09 07	132 39	-6 19
1891 09 08	132 46	-6 19
1891 09 09	132 52	-6 20
1891 09 10	132 59	-6 20
1891 09 11	133 06	-6 20
1891 09 12	133 13	-6 20
1891 09 13	133 19	-6 21
1891 09 14	133 26	-6 21
1891 09 15	133 32	-6 21
1891 09 16	133 39	-6 22
1891 09 17	133 45	-6 22
1891 09 18	133 52	-6 22
1891 09 19	133 58	-6 23
1891 09 20	134 05	-6 23
1891 09 21	134 11	-6 24
1891 09 22	134 17	-6 24
1891 09 23	134 23	-6 24
1891 09 24	134 29	-6 25
1891 09 25	134 35	-6 25
1891 09 26	134 41	-6 26
1891 09 27	134 47	-6 26
1891 09 28	134 53	-6 26
1891 09 29	134 59	-6 27
1891 09 30	135 05	-6 27
1891 10 01	135 10	-6 28
1891 10 02	135 16	-6 28
1891 10 03	135 22	-6 29
1891 10 04	135 27	-6 29
1891 10 05	135 33	-6 30
1891 10 06	135 38	-6 30
1891 10 07	135 43	-6 31
1891 10 08	135 49	-6 31
1891 10 09	135 54	-6 32
1891 10 10	135 59	-6 32
1891 10 11	136 04	-6 33
1891 10 12	136 09	-6 33
1891 10 13	136 14	-6 34
1891 10 14	136 18	-6 34
1891 10 15	136 23	-6 35
1891 10 16	136 28	-6 35
1891 10 17	136 32	-6 36
1891 10 18	136 37	-6 36
1891 10 19	136 41	-6 37
1891 10 20	136 45	-6 38
1891 10 21	136 50	-6 38
1891 10 22	136 54	-6 39
1891 10 23	136 58	-6 39
1891 10 24	137 02	-6 40
1891 10 25	137 06	-6 41
1891 10 26	137 10	-6 41
1891 10 27	137 13	-6 42
1891 10 28	137 17	-6 42
1891 10 29	137 20	-6 43
1891 10 30	137 24	-6 44
1891 10 31	137 27	-6 44
1891 11 01	137 30	-6 45
1891 11 02	137 34	-6 46
1891 11 03	137 37	-6 46
1891 11 04	137 40	-6 47
1891 11 05	137 42	-6 48
1891 11 06	137 45	-6 48
1891 11 07	137 48	-6 49
1891 11 08	137 50	-6 50
1891 11 09	137 53	-6 50
1891 11 10	137 55	-6 51
1891 11 11	137 57	-6 52
1891 11 12	138 00	-6 52
1891 11 13	138 02	-6 53
1891 11 14	138 03	-6 54
1891 11 15	138 05	-6 54
1891 11 16	138 07	-6 55
1891 11 17	138 09	-6 56
1891 11 18	138 10	-6 56
1891 11 19	138 12	-6 57
1891 11 20	138 13	-6 58
1891 11 21	138 14	-6 58
1891 11 22	138 15	-6 59
1891 11 23	138 16	-7 00
1891 11 24	138 17	-7 00
1891 11 25	138 18	-7 01
1891 11 26	138 19	-7 02
1891 11 27	138 19	-7 02
1891 11 28	138 20	-7 03
1891 11 29	138 20	-7 04
1891 11 30	138 20	-7 04
1891 12 01	138 20	-7 05
1891 12 02	138 20	-7 06
1891 12 03	138 20	-7 06
1891 12 04	138 20	-7 07
1891 12 05	138 20	-7 08
1891 12 06	138 19	-7 08
1891 12 07	138 19	-7 09
1891 12 08	138 18	-7 10
1891 12 09	138 17	-7 10
1891 12 10	138 16	-7 11
1891 12 11	138 15	-7 12
1891 12 12	138 14	-7 12
1891 12 13	138 13	-7 13
1891 12 14	138 12	-7 14
1891 12 15	138 10	-7 14
1891 12 16	138 09	-7 15
1891 12 17	138 07	-7 15
1891 12 18	138 06	-7 16
1891 12 19	138 04	-7 17
1891 12 20	138 02	-7 17
1891 12 21	138 00	-7 18
1891 12 22	137 58	-7 18
1891 12 23	137 56	-7 19
1891 12 24	137 53	-7 19
1891 12 25	137 51	-7 20
1891 12 26	137 48	-7 20
1891 12 27	137 46	-7 21
1891 12 28	137 43	-7 21
1891 12 29	137 40	-7 22
1891 12 30	137 37	-7 22
1891 12 31	137 35	-7 23
1892 01 01	137 32	-7 23
1892 01 02	137 28	-7 24
1892 01 03	137 25	-7 24
1892 01 04	137 22	-7 25
1892 01 05	137 19	-7 25
1892 01 06	137 15	-7 25
1892 01 07	137 12	-7 26
1892 01 08	137 08	-7 26
1892 01 09	137 04	-7 27
1892 01 10	137 01	-7 27
1892 01 11	136 57	-7 27
1892 01 12	136 53	-7 28
1892 01 13	136 49	-7 28
1892 01 14	136 45	-7 28
1892 01 15	136 41	-7 28
1892 01 16	136 37	-7 29
1892 01 17	136 33	-7 29
1892 01 18	136 29	-7 29
1892 01 19	136 25	-7 29
1892 01 20	136 20	-7 30
1892 01 21	136 16	-7 30
1892 01 22	136 12	-7 30
1892 01 23	136 07	-7 30
1892 01 24	136 03	-7 30
1892 01 25	135 58	-7 30
1892 01 26	135 54	-7 30
1892 01 27	135 49	-7 31
1892 01 28	135 45	-7 31
1892 01 29	135 40	-7 31
1892 01 30	135 36	-7 31
1892 01 31	135 31	-7 31
1892 02 01	135 27	-7 31
1892 02 02	135 22	-7 31
1892 02 03	135 17	-7 31
1892 02 04	135 13	-7 31
1892 02 05	135 08	-7 30
1892 02 06	135 03	-7 30
1892 02 07	134 59	-7 30
1892 02 08	134 54	-7 30
1892 02 09	134 49	-7 30
1892 02 10	134 45	-7 30
1892 02 11	134 40	-7 30
1892 02 12	134 36	-7 30
1892 02 13	134 31	-7 29
1892 02 14	134 26	-7 29
1892 02 15	134 22	-7 29
1892 02 16	134 17	-7 29
1892 02 17	134 13	-7 28
1892 02 18	134 09	-7 28
1892 02 19	134 04	-7 28
1892 02 20	134 00	-7 27
1892 02 21	133 55	-7 27
1892 02 22	133 51	-7 27
1892 02 23	133 47	-7 26
1892 02 24	133 43	-7 26
1892 02 25	133 39	-7 26
1892 02 26	133 34	-7 25
1892 02 27	133 30	-7 25
1892 02 28	133 26	-7 24
1892 02 29	133 23	-7 24
1892 03 01	133 19	-7 23
1892 03 02	133 15	-7 23
1892 03 03	133 11	-7 22
1892 03 04	133 07	-7 22
1892 03 05	133 04	-7 21
1892 03 06	133 00	-7 21
1892 03 07	132 57	-7 20
1892 03 08	132 54	-7 20
1892 03 09	132 50	-7 19
1892 03 10	132 47	-7 18
1892 03 11	132 44	-7 18
1892 03 12	132 41	-7 17
1892 03 13	132 38	-7 17
1892 03 14	132 35	-7 16
1892 03 15	132 32	-7 15
1892 03 16	132 29	-7 15
1892 03 17	132 27	-7 14
1892 03 18	132 24	-7 13
1892 03 19	132 22	-7 13
1892 03 20	132 20	-7 12
1892 03 21	132 17	-7 11
1892 03 22	132 15	-7 11
1892 03 23	132 13	-7 10
1892 03 24	132 11	-7 09
1892 03 25	132 09	-7 08
1892 03 26	132 07	-7 08
1892 03 27	132 06	-7 07
1892 03 28	132 04	-7 06
1892 03 29	132 03	-7 05
1892 03 30	132 01	-7 05
1892 03 31	132 00	-7 04
1892 04 01	131 59	-7 03
1892 04 02	131 58	-7 02
1892 04 03	131 57	-7 01
1892 04 04	131 56	-7 01
1892 04 05	131 55	-7 00
1892 04 06	131 55	-6 59
1892 04 07	131 54	-6 58
1892 04 08	131 54	-6 57
1892 04 09	131 54	-6 57
1892 04 10	131 53	-6 56
1892 04 11	131 53	-6 55
1892 04 12	131 53	-6 54
1892 04 13	131 54	-6 53
1892 04 14	131 54	-6 53
1892 04 15	131 54	-6 52
1892 04 16	131 55	-6 51
1892 04 17	131 55	-6 50
1892 04 18	131 56	-6 49
1892 04 19	131 57	-6 49
1892 04 20	131 58	-6 48
1892 04 21	131 59	-6 47
1892 04 22	132 00	-6 46
1892 04 23	132 01	-6 45

Chiron

1892	04	24	132	02	-6	44
1892	04	25	132	04	-6	44
1892	04	26	132	05	-6	43
1892	04	27	132	07	-6	42
1892	04	28	132	09	-6	41
1892	04	29	132	10	-6	40
1892	04	30	132	12	-6	39
1892	05	01	132	14	-6	39
1892	05	02	132	17	-6	38
1892	05	03	132	19	-6	37
1892	05	04	132	21	-6	36
1892	05	05	132	24	-6	35
1892	05	06	132	26	-6	35
1892	05	07	132	29	-6	34
1892	05	08	132	32	-6	33
1892	05	09	132	35	-6	32
1892	05	10	132	38	-6	31
1892	05	11	132	41	-6	31
1892	05	12	132	44	-6	30
1892	05	13	132	47	-6	29
1892	05	14	132	50	-6	28
1892	05	15	132	54	-6	28
1892	05	16	132	57	-6	27
1892	05	17	133	01	-6	26
1892	05	18	133	05	-6	25
1892	05	19	133	09	-6	25
1892	05	20	133	13	-6	24
1892	05	21	133	17	-6	23
1892	05	22	133	21	-6	22
1892	05	23	133	25	-6	22
1892	05	24	133	29	-6	21
1892	05	25	133	33	-6	20
1892	05	26	133	38	-6	19
1892	05	27	133	42	-6	19
1892	05	28	133	47	-6	18
1892	05	29	133	52	-6	17
1892	05	30	133	56	-6	17
1892	05	31	134	01	-6	16
1892	06	01	134	06	-6	15
1892	06	02	134	11	-6	15
1892	06	03	134	16	-6	14
1892	06	04	134	21	-6	13
1892	06	05	134	27	-6	13
1892	06	06	134	32	-6	12
1892	06	07	134	37	-6	11
1892	06	08	134	43	-6	11
1892	06	09	134	48	-6	10
1892	06	10	134	54	-6	10
1892	06	11	135	00	-6	09
1892	06	12	135	05	-6	08
1892	06	13	135	11	-6	08
1892	06	14	135	17	-6	07
1892	06	15	135	23	-6	07
1892	06	16	135	29	-6	06
1892	06	17	135	35	-6	05
1892	06	18	135	41	-6	05
1892	06	19	135	47	-6	04
1892	06	20	135	54	-6	04
1892	06	21	136	00	-6	03
1892	06	22	136	06	-6	03
1892	06	23	136	13	-6	02
1892	06	24	136	19	-6	02
1892	06	25	136	26	-6	01
1892	06	26	136	33	-6	01
1892	06	27	136	39	-6	00
1892	06	28	136	46	-6	00
1892	06	29	136	53	-5	59
1892	06	30	136	59	-5	59
1892	07	01	137	06	-5	58
1892	07	02	137	13	-5	58
1892	07	03	137	20	-5	57
1892	07	04	137	27	-5	57
1892	07	05	137	34	-5	56
1892	07	06	137	41	-5	56
1892	07	07	137	49	-5	56
1892	07	08	137	56	-5	55
1892	07	09	138	03	-5	55
1892	07	10	138	10	-5	54
1892	07	11	138	17	-5	54
1892	07	12	138	25	-5	54
1892	07	13	138	32	-5	53
1892	07	14	138	40	-5	53
1892	07	15	138	47	-5	52
1892	07	16	138	55	-5	52
1892	07	17	139	02	-5	52
1892	07	18	139	10	-5	51
1892	07	19	139	17	-5	51
1892	07	20	139	25	-5	51
1892	07	21	139	32	-5	50
1892	07	22	139	40	-5	50
1892	07	23	139	48	-5	50
1892	07	24	139	56	-5	50
1892	07	25	140	03	-5	49
1892	07	26	140	11	-5	49
1892	07	27	140	19	-5	49
1892	07	28	140	27	-5	49
1892	07	29	140	35	-5	48
1892	07	30	140	42	-5	48
1892	07	31	140	50	-5	48
1892	08	01	140	58	-5	48
1892	08	02	141	06	-5	47

1892	08	03	141	14	-5	47
1892	08	04	141	22	-5	47
1892	08	05	141	30	-5	47
1892	08	06	141	38	-5	47
1892	08	07	141	46	-5	46
1892	08	08	141	54	-5	46
1892	08	09	142	02	-5	46
1892	08	10	142	10	-5	46
1892	08	11	142	18	-5	46
1892	08	12	142	26	-5	46
1892	08	13	142	34	-5	46
1892	08	14	142	42	-5	45
1892	08	15	142	50	-5	45
1892	08	16	142	58	-5	45
1892	08	17	143	06	-5	45
1892	08	18	143	14	-5	45
1892	08	19	143	22	-5	45
1892	08	20	143	30	-5	45
1892	08	21	143	39	-5	45
1892	08	22	143	47	-5	45
1892	08	23	143	55	-5	45
1892	08	24	144	03	-5	45
1892	08	25	144	11	-5	45
1892	08	26	144	19	-5	45
1892	08	27	144	27	-5	45
1892	08	28	144	35	-5	45
1892	08	29	144	43	-5	45
1892	08	30	144	51	-5	45
1892	08	31	144	59	-5	45
1892	09	01	145	07	-5	45
1892	09	02	145	15	-5	45
1892	09	03	145	22	-5	45
1892	09	04	145	30	-5	45
1892	09	05	145	38	-5	45
1892	09	06	145	46	-5	45
1892	09	07	145	54	-5	45
1892	09	08	146	02	-5	45
1892	09	09	146	10	-5	45
1892	09	10	146	17	-5	45
1892	09	11	146	25	-5	45
1892	09	12	146	33	-5	45
1892	09	13	146	40	-5	45
1892	09	14	146	48	-5	46
1892	09	15	146	56	-5	46
1892	09	16	147	03	-5	46
1892	09	17	147	11	-5	46
1892	09	18	147	18	-5	46
1892	09	19	147	26	-5	46
1892	09	20	147	33	-5	46
1892	09	21	147	41	-5	47
1892	09	22	147	48	-5	47
1892	09	23	147	56	-5	47
1892	09	24	148	03	-5	47
1892	09	25	148	10	-5	47
1892	09	26	148	17	-5	48
1892	09	27	148	25	-5	48
1892	09	28	148	32	-5	48
1892	09	29	148	39	-5	48
1892	09	30	148	46	-5	49
1892	10	01	148	53	-5	49
1892	10	02	149	00	-5	49
1892	10	03	149	07	-5	49
1892	10	04	149	14	-5	50
1892	10	05	149	20	-5	50
1892	10	06	149	27	-5	50
1892	10	07	149	34	-5	51
1892	10	08	149	40	-5	51
1892	10	09	149	47	-5	51
1892	10	10	149	53	-5	51
1892	10	11	150	00	-5	52
1892	10	12	150	06	-5	52
1892	10	13	150	13	-5	52
1892	10	14	150	19	-5	53
1892	10	15	150	25	-5	53
1892	10	16	150	31	-5	54
1892	10	17	150	37	-5	54
1892	10	18	150	43	-5	54
1892	10	19	150	49	-5	55
1892	10	20	150	55	-5	55
1892	10	21	151	01	-5	55
1892	10	22	151	07	-5	56
1892	10	23	151	12	-5	56
1892	10	24	151	18	-5	57
1892	10	25	151	23	-5	57
1892	10	26	151	29	-5	57
1892	10	27	151	34	-5	58
1892	10	28	151	39	-5	58
1892	10	29	151	44	-5	59
1892	10	30	151	50	-5	59
1892	10	31	151	55	-6	00
1892	11	01	151	59	-6	00
1892	11	02	152	04	-6	01
1892	11	03	152	09	-6	01
1892	11	04	152	14	-6	02
1892	11	05	152	18	-6	02
1892	11	06	152	23	-6	02
1892	11	07	152	27	-6	03
1892	11	08	152	31	-6	03
1892	11	09	152	36	-6	04
1892	11	10	152	40	-6	04
1892	11	11	152	44	-6	05
1892	11	12	152	48	-6	05
1892	11	13	152	52	-6	06
1892	11	14	152	55	-6	07
1892	11	15	152	59	-6	07
1892	11	16	153	02	-6	08

1892	11	17	153	06	-6	08
1892	11	18	153	09	-6	09
1892	11	19	153	12	-6	09
1892	11	20	153	16	-6	10
1892	11	21	153	19	-6	10
1892	11	22	153	22	-6	11
1892	11	23	153	24	-6	11
1892	11	24	153	27	-6	12
1892	11	25	153	30	-6	12
1892	11	26	153	32	-6	13
1892	11	27	153	34	-6	14
1892	11	28	153	37	-6	14
1892	11	29	153	39	-6	15
1892	11	30	153	41	-6	15
1892	12	01	153	43	-6	16
1892	12	02	153	45	-6	16
1892	12	03	153	46	-6	17
1892	12	04	153	48	-6	18
1892	12	05	153	50	-6	18
1892	12	06	153	51	-6	19
1892	12	07	153	52	-6	19
1892	12	08	153	53	-6	20
1892	12	09	153	54	-6	20
1892	12	10	153	55	-6	21
1892	12	11	153	56	-6	21
1892	12	12	153	57	-6	22
1892	12	13	153	57	-6	23
1892	12	14	153	58	-6	23
1892	12	15	153	58	-6	24
1892	12	16	153	58	-6	24
1892	12	17	153	58	-6	25
1892	12	18	153	58	-6	25
1892	12	19	153	58	-6	26
1892	12	20	153	58	-6	26
1892	12	21	153	58	-6	27
1892	12	22	153	57	-6	27
1892	12	23	153	57	-6	28
1892	12	24	153	56	-6	29
1892	12	25	153	55	-6	29
1892	12	26	153	54	-6	30
1892	12	27	153	53	-6	30
1892	12	28	153	52	-6	31
1892	12	29	153	51	-6	31
1892	12	30	153	49	-6	32
1892	12	31	153	48	-6	32
1893	01	01	153	46	-6	33
1893	01	02	153	45	-6	33
1893	01	03	153	43	-6	33
1893	01	04	153	41	-6	34
1893	01	05	153	39	-6	34
1893	01	06	153	37	-6	35
1893	01	07	153	35	-6	35
1893	01	08	153	32	-6	36
1893	01	09	153	30	-6	36
1893	01	10	153	27	-6	36
1893	01	11	153	25	-6	37
1893	01	12	153	22	-6	37
1893	01	13	153	19	-6	38
1893	01	14	153	16	-6	38
1893	01	15	153	13	-6	38
1893	01	16	153	10	-6	39
1893	01	17	153	07	-6	39
1893	01	18	153	04	-6	39
1893	01	19	153	01	-6	40
1893	01	20	152	57	-6	40
1893	01	21	152	54	-6	40
1893	01	22	152	50	-6	40
1893	01	23	152	46	-6	41
1893	01	24	152	43	-6	41
1893	01	25	152	39	-6	41
1893	01	26	152	35	-6	41
1893	01	27	152	31	-6	42
1893	01	28	152	27	-6	42
1893	01	29	152	23	-6	42
1893	01	30	152	19	-6	42
1893	01	31	152	15	-6	42
1893	02	01	152	11	-6	42
1893	02	02	152	06	-6	42
1893	02	03	152	02	-6	43
1893	02	04	151	58	-6	43
1893	02	05	151	53	-6	43
1893	02	06	151	49	-6	43
1893	02	07	151	44	-6	43
1893	02	08	151	40	-6	43
1893	02	09	151	35	-6	43
1893	02	10	151	30	-6	43
1893	02	11	151	26	-6	43
1893	02	12	151	21	-6	43
1893	02	13	151	16	-6	43
1893	02	14	151	12	-6	43
1893	02	15	151	07	-6	42
1893	02	16	151	02	-6	42
1893	02	17	150	58	-6	42
1893	02	18	150	53	-6	42
1893	02	19	150	48	-6	42
1893	02	20	150	43	-6	42
1893	02	21	150	39	-6	42
1893	02	22	150	34	-6	41
1893	02	23	150	29	-6	41
1893	02	24	150	24	-6	41
1893	02	25	150	20	-6	41
1893	02	26	150	15	-6	40
1893	02	27	150	10	-6	40
1893	02	28	150	06	-6	40
1893	03	01	150	01	-6	39
1893	03	02	149	56	-6	39

1893	03	03	149	52	-6	39
1893	03	04	149	47	-6	38
1893	03	05	149	43	-6	38
1893	03	06	149	38	-6	38
1893	03	07	149	34	-6	37
1893	03	08	149	29	-6	37
1893	03	09	149	25	-6	36
1893	03	10	149	21	-6	36
1893	03	11	149	16	-6	35
1893	03	12	149	12	-6	35
1893	03	13	149	08	-6	34
1893	03	14	149	04	-6	34
1893	03	15	149	00	-6	33
1893	03	16	148	56	-6	33
1893	03	17	148	52	-6	32
1893	03	18	148	48	-6	32
1893	03	19	148	44	-6	31
1893	03	20	148	41	-6	31
1893	03	21	148	37	-6	30
1893	03	22	148	34	-6	29
1893	03	23	148	30	-6	29
1893	03	24	148	27	-6	28
1893	03	25	148	23	-6	28
1893	03	26	148	20	-6	27
1893	03	27	148	17	-6	26
1893	03	28	148	14	-6	26
1893	03	29	148	11	-6	25
1893	03	30	148	08	-6	24
1893	03	31	148	05	-6	23
1893	04	01	148	03	-6	23
1893	04	02	148	00	-6	22
1893	04	03	147	58	-6	21
1893	04	04	147	55	-6	21
1893	04	05	147	53	-6	20
1893	04	06	147	51	-6	19
1893	04	07	147	49	-6	18
1893	04	08	147	47	-6	18
1893	04	09	147	45	-6	17
1893	04	10	147	43	-6	16
1893	04	11	147	41	-6	15
1893	04	12	147	40	-6	14
1893	04	13	147	38	-6	14
1893	04	14	147	37	-6	13
1893	04	15	147	35	-6	12
1893	04	16	147	34	-6	11
1893	04	17	147	33	-6	10
1893	04	18	147	32	-6	10
1893	04	19	147	31	-6	09
1893	04	20	147	31	-6	08
1893	04	21	147	30	-6	07
1893	04	22	147	30	-6	06
1893	04	23	147	29	-6	05
1893	04	24	147	29	-6	05
1893	04	25	147	29	-6	04
1893	04	26	147	29	-6	03
1893	04	27	147	29	-6	02
1893	04	28	147	29	-6	01
1893	04	29	147	29	-6	00
1893	04	30	147	30	-5	59
1893	05	01	147	30	-5	59
1893	05	02	147	31	-5	58
1893	05	03	147	32	-5	57
1893	05	04	147	32	-5	56
1893	05	05	147	33	-5	55
1893	05	06	147	34	-5	54
1893	05	07	147	36	-5	54
1893	05	08	147	37	-5	53
1893	05	09	147	38	-5	52
1893	05	10	147	40	-5	51
1893	05	11	147	41	-5	50
1893	05	12	147	43	-5	49
1893	05	13	147	45	-5	48
1893	05	14	147	47	-5	48
1893	05	15	147	49	-5	47
1893	05	16	147	51	-5	46
1893	05	17	147	53	-5	45
1893	05	18	147	56	-5	44
1893	05	19	147	58	-5	43
1893	05	20	148	01	-5	43
1893	05	21	148	04	-5	42
1893	05	22	148	06	-5	41
1893	05	23	148	09	-5	40
1893	05	24	148	12	-5	39
1893	05	25	148	16	-5	39
1893	05	26	148	19	-5	38
1893	05	27	148	22	-5	37
1893	05	28	148	25	-5	36
1893	05	29	148	29	-5	35
1893	05	30	148	33	-5	35
1893	05	31	148	36	-5	34
1893	06	01	148	40	-5	33
1893	06	02	148	44	-5	32
1893	06	03	148	48	-5	31
1893	06	04	148	52	-5	31
1893	06	05	148	56	-5	30
1893	06	06	149	01	-5	29
1893	06	07	149	05	-5	28
1893	06	08	149	09	-5	28
1893	06	09	149	14	-5	27
1893	06	10	149	19	-5	26
1893	06	11	149	23	-5	25
1893	06	12	149	28	-5	25
1893	06	13	149	33	-5	24
1893	06	14	149	38	-5	23
1893	06	15	149	43	-5	23
1893	06	16	149	48	-5	22

1893	06	17	149	54	-5	21
1893	06	18	149	59	-5	20
1893	06	19	150	04	-5	20
1893	06	20	150	10	-5	19
1893	06	21	150	15	-5	18
1893	06	22	150	21	-5	18
1893	06	23	150	27	-5	17
1893	06	24	150	33	-5	16
1893	06	25	150	38	-5	16
1893	06	26	150	44	-5	15
1893	06	27	150	50	-5	14
1893	06	28	150	56	-5	14
1893	06	29	151	03	-5	13
1893	06	30	151	09	-5	13
1893	07	01	151	15	-5	12
1893	07	02	151	22	-5	11
1893	07	03	151	28	-5	11
1893	07	04	151	34	-5	10
1893	07	05	151	41	-5	10
1893	07	06	151	48	-5	09
1893	07	07	151	54	-5	08
1893	07	08	152	01	-5	08
1893	07	09	152	08	-5	07
1893	07	10	152	15	-5	07
1893	07	11	152	22	-5	06
1893	07	12	152	29	-5	06
1893	07	13	152	36	-5	05
1893	07	14	152	43	-5	04
1893	07	15	152	50	-5	04
1893	07	16	152	57	-5	03
1893	07	17	153	04	-5	03
1893	07	18	153	12	-5	02
1893	07	19	153	19	-5	02
1893	07	20	153	26	-5	01
1893	07	21	153	34	-5	01
1893	07	22	153	41	-5	00
1893	07	23	153	49	-5	00
1893	07	24	153	56	-5	00
1893	07	25	154	04	-4	59
1893	07	26	154	12	-4	59
1893	07	27	154	19	-4	58
1893	07	28	154	27	-4	58
1893	07	29	154	35	-4	57
1893	07	30	154	43	-4	57
1893	07	31	154	51	-4	57
1893	08	01	154	59	-4	56
1893	08	02	155	06	-4	56
1893	08	03	155	14	-4	55
1893	08	04	155	22	-4	55
1893	08	05	155	31	-4	55
1893	08	06	155	39	-4	54
1893	08	07	155	47	-4	54
1893	08	08	155	55	-4	53
1893	08	09	156	03	-4	53
1893	08	10	156	11	-4	53
1893	08	11	156	19	-4	52
1893	08	12	156	28	-4	52
1893	08	13	156	36	-4	52
1893	08	14	156	44	-4	51
1893	08	15	156	52	-4	51
1893	08	16	157	01	-4	51
1893	08	17	157	09	-4	51
1893	08	18	157	17	-4	50
1893	08	19	157	26	-4	50
1893	08	20	157	34	-4	50
1893	08	21	157	43	-4	49
1893	08	22	157	51	-4	49
1893	08	23	157	59	-4	49
1893	08	24	158	08	-4	49
1893	08	25	158	16	-4	48
1893	08	26	158	25	-4	48
1893	08	27	158	33	-4	48
1893	08	28	158	42	-4	48
1893	08	29	158	50	-4	48
1893	08	30	158	59	-4	47
1893	08	31	159	07	-4	47
1893	09	01	159	16	-4	47
1893	09	02	159	24	-4	47
1893	09	03	159	33	-4	47
1893	09	04	159	41	-4	46
1893	09	05	159	50	-4	46
1893	09	06	159	58	-4	46
1893	09	07	160	07	-4	46
1893	09	08	160	15	-4	46
1893	09	09	160	24	-4	46
1893	09	10	160	32	-4	46
1893	09	11	160	41	-4	45
1893	09	12	160	49	-4	45
1893	09	13	160	58	-4	45
1893	09	14	161	06	-4	45
1893	09	15	161	15	-4	45
1893	09	16	161	23	-4	45
1893	09	17	161	32	-4	45
1893	09	18	161	40	-4	45
1893	09	19	161	48	-4	45
1893	09	20	161	57	-4	45
1893	09	21	162	05	-4	45
1893	09	22	162	13	-4	44
1893	09	23	162	22	-4	44
1893	09	24	162	30	-4	44
1893	09	25	162	38	-4	44
1893	09	26	162	46	-4	44
1893	09	27	162	55	-4	44
1893	09	28	163	03	-4	44
1893	09	29	163	11	-4	44
1893	09	30	163	19	-4	44
1893	10	01	163	27	-4	44
1893	10	02	163	35	-4	44
1893	10	03	163	43	-4	44
1893	10	04	163	51	-4	44
1893	10	05	163	59	-4	44
1893	10	06	164	07	-4	44
1893	10	07	164	15	-4	44
1893	10	08	164	23	-4	45
1893	10	09	164	31	-4	45
1893	10	10	164	39	-4	45
1893	10	11	164	46	-4	45
1893	10	12	164	54	-4	45
1893	10	13	165	02	-4	45
1893	10	14	165	09	-4	45
1893	10	15	165	17	-4	45
1893	10	16	165	24	-4	45
1893	10	17	165	32	-4	45
1893	10	18	165	39	-4	45
1893	10	19	165	47	-4	46
1893	10	20	165	54	-4	46
1893	10	21	166	01	-4	46
1893	10	22	166	08	-4	46
1893	10	23	166	15	-4	46
1893	10	24	166	22	-4	46
1893	10	25	166	29	-4	46
1893	10	26	166	36	-4	47
1893	10	27	166	43	-4	47
1893	10	28	166	50	-4	47
1893	10	29	166	57	-4	47
1893	10	30	167	04	-4	47
1893	10	31	167	10	-4	47
1893	11	01	167	17	-4	48
1893	11	02	167	23	-4	48
1893	11	03	167	30	-4	48
1893	11	04	167	36	-4	48
1893	11	05	167	43	-4	48
1893	11	06	167	49	-4	49
1893	11	07	167	55	-4	49
1893	11	08	168	01	-4	49
1893	11	09	168	07	-4	49
1893	11	10	168	13	-4	50
1893	11	11	168	19	-4	50
1893	11	12	168	24	-4	50
1893	11	13	168	30	-4	50
1893	11	14	168	36	-4	51
1893	11	15	168	41	-4	51
1893	11	16	168	47	-4	51
1893	11	17	168	52	-4	51
1893	11	18	168	57	-4	52
1893	11	19	169	02	-4	52
1893	11	20	169	07	-4	52
1893	11	21	169	12	-4	53
1893	11	22	169	17	-4	53
1893	11	23	169	22	-4	53
1893	11	24	169	27	-4	53
1893	11	25	169	31	-4	54
1893	11	26	169	36	-4	54
1893	11	27	169	40	-4	54
1893	11	28	169	45	-4	55
1893	11	29	169	49	-4	55
1893	11	30	169	53	-4	55
1893	12	01	169	57	-4	56
1893	12	02	170	01	-4	56
1893	12	03	170	05	-4	56
1893	12	04	170	08	-4	57
1893	12	05	170	12	-4	57
1893	12	06	170	15	-4	57
1893	12	07	170	19	-4	58
1893	12	08	170	22	-4	58
1893	12	09	170	25	-4	58
1893	12	10	170	28	-4	59
1893	12	11	170	31	-4	59
1893	12	12	170	34	-4	59
1893	12	13	170	37	-5	00
1893	12	14	170	39	-5	00
1893	12	15	170	42	-5	00
1893	12	16	170	44	-5	01
1893	12	17	170	46	-5	01
1893	12	18	170	48	-5	02
1893	12	19	170	51	-5	02
1893	12	20	170	52	-5	02
1893	12	21	170	54	-5	03
1893	12	22	170	56	-5	03
1893	12	23	170	57	-5	03
1893	12	24	170	59	-5	04
1893	12	25	171	00	-5	04
1893	12	26	171	01	-5	04
1893	12	27	171	02	-5	05
1893	12	28	171	03	-5	05
1893	12	29	171	04	-5	05
1893	12	30	171	05	-5	06
1893	12	31	171	06	-5	06
1894	01	01	171	06	-5	06
1894	01	02	171	06	-5	07
1894	01	03	171	07	-5	07
1894	01	04	171	07	-5	07
1894	01	05	171	07	-5	08
1894	01	06	171	07	-5	08
1894	01	07	171	06	-5	08
1894	01	08	171	06	-5	09
1894	01	09	171	06	-5	09
1894	01	10	171	05	-5	09
1894	01	11	171	04	-5	10
1894	01	12	171	03	-5	10
1894	01	13	171	03	-5	10
1894	01	14	171	01	-5	11
1894	01	15	171	00	-5	11
1894	01	16	170	59	-5	11
1894	01	17	170	58	-5	11
1894	01	18	170	56	-5	12
1894	01	19	170	54	-5	12
1894	01	20	170	53	-5	12
1894	01	21	170	51	-5	12
1894	01	22	170	49	-5	13
1894	01	23	170	47	-5	13
1894	01	24	170	45	-5	13
1894	01	25	170	42	-5	13
1894	01	26	170	40	-5	14
1894	01	27	170	38	-5	14
1894	01	28	170	35	-5	14
1894	01	29	170	32	-5	14
1894	01	30	170	30	-5	14
1894	01	31	170	27	-5	14
1894	02	01	170	24	-5	15
1894	02	02	170	21	-5	15
1894	02	03	170	17	-5	15
1894	02	04	170	14	-5	15
1894	02	05	170	11	-5	15
1894	02	06	170	07	-5	15
1894	02	07	170	04	-5	15
1894	02	08	170	00	-5	15
1894	02	09	169	57	-5	16
1894	02	10	169	53	-5	16
1894	02	11	169	49	-5	16
1894	02	12	169	45	-5	16
1894	02	13	169	41	-5	16
1894	02	14	169	37	-5	16
1894	02	15	169	33	-5	16
1894	02	16	169	29	-5	16
1894	02	17	169	25	-5	16
1894	02	18	169	21	-5	16
1894	02	19	169	16	-5	16
1894	02	20	169	12	-5	16
1894	02	21	169	08	-5	16
1894	02	22	169	03	-5	15
1894	02	23	168	59	-5	15
1894	02	24	168	54	-5	15
1894	02	25	168	49	-5	15
1894	02	26	168	45	-5	15
1894	02	27	168	40	-5	15
1894	02	28	168	36	-5	15
1894	03	01	168	31	-5	15
1894	03	02	168	26	-5	14
1894	03	03	168	21	-5	14
1894	03	04	168	17	-5	14
1894	03	05	168	12	-5	14
1894	03	06	168	07	-5	13
1894	03	07	168	02	-5	13
1894	03	08	167	57	-5	13
1894	03	09	167	53	-5	13
1894	03	10	167	48	-5	12
1894	03	11	167	43	-5	12
1894	03	12	167	38	-5	12
1894	03	13	167	33	-5	11
1894	03	14	167	29	-5	11
1894	03	15	167	24	-5	11
1894	03	16	167	19	-5	10
1894	03	17	167	14	-5	10
1894	03	18	167	10	-5	10
1894	03	19	167	05	-5	09
1894	03	20	167	00	-5	09
1894	03	21	166	56	-5	08
1894	03	22	166	51	-5	08
1894	03	23	166	47	-5	07
1894	03	24	166	42	-5	07
1894	03	25	166	38	-5	07
1894	03	26	166	33	-5	06
1894	03	27	166	29	-5	06
1894	03	28	166	25	-5	05
1894	03	29	166	21	-5	05
1894	03	30	166	16	-5	04
1894	03	31	166	12	-5	03
1894	04	01	166	08	-5	03
1894	04	02	166	04	-5	02
1894	04	03	166	00	-5	02
1894	04	04	165	56	-5	01
1894	04	05	165	52	-5	01
1894	04	06	165	49	-5	00
1894	04	07	165	45	-4	59
1894	04	08	165	42	-4	59
1894	04	09	165	38	-4	58
1894	04	10	165	35	-4	58
1894	04	11	165	31	-4	57
1894	04	12	165	28	-4	56
1894	04	13	165	25	-4	56
1894	04	14	165	22	-4	55
1894	04	15	165	19	-4	54
1894	04	16	165	16	-4	54
1894	04	17	165	13	-4	53
1894	04	18	165	10	-4	52
1894	04	19	165	08	-4	51
1894	04	20	165	05	-4	51
1894	04	21	165	03	-4	50
1894	04	22	165	01	-4	49
1894	04	23	164	58	-4	49
1894	04	24	164	56	-4	48
1894	04	25	164	54	-4	47
1894	04	26	164	52	-4	46
1894	04	27	164	51	-4	46
1894	04	28	164	49	-4	45
1894	04	29	164	47	-4	44
1894	04	30	164	46	-4	43
1894	05	01	164	44	-4	43
1894	05	02	164	43	-4	42
1894	05	03	164	42	-4	41
1894	05	04	164	41	-4	40
1894	05	05	164	40	-4	40
1894	05	06	164	39	-4	39
1894	05	07	164	39	-4	38
1894	05	08	164	38	-4	37
1894	05	09	164	37	-4	36
1894	05	10	164	37	-4	36
1894	05	11	164	37	-4	35
1894	05	12	164	37	-4	34
1894	05	13	164	37	-4	33
1894	05	14	164	37	-4	32
1894	05	15	164	37	-4	32
1894	05	16	164	37	-4	31
1894	05	17	164	38	-4	30
1894	05	18	164	38	-4	29
1894	05	19	164	39	-4	29
1894	05	20	164	40	-4	28
1894	05	21	164	41	-4	27
1894	05	22	164	42	-4	26
1894	05	23	164	43	-4	25
1894	05	24	164	44	-4	25
1894	05	25	164	45	-4	24
1894	05	26	164	47	-4	23
1894	05	27	164	48	-4	22
1894	05	28	164	50	-4	21
1894	05	29	164	52	-4	21
1894	05	30	164	54	-4	20
1894	05	31	164	56	-4	19
1894	06	01	164	58	-4	18
1894	06	02	165	00	-4	18
1894	06	03	165	03	-4	17
1894	06	04	165	05	-4	16
1894	06	05	165	08	-4	15
1894	06	06	165	10	-4	15
1894	06	07	165	13	-4	14
1894	06	08	165	16	-4	13
1894	06	09	165	19	-4	12
1894	06	10	165	22	-4	11
1894	06	11	165	25	-4	11
1894	06	12	165	29	-4	10
1894	06	13	165	32	-4	09
1894	06	14	165	36	-4	09
1894	06	15	165	39	-4	08
1894	06	16	165	43	-4	07
1894	06	17	165	47	-4	06
1894	06	18	165	51	-4	06
1894	06	19	165	55	-4	05
1894	06	20	165	59	-4	04
1894	06	21	166	03	-4	03
1894	06	22	166	07	-4	03
1894	06	23	166	12	-4	02
1894	06	24	166	16	-4	01
1894	06	25	166	21	-4	01
1894	06	26	166	26	-4	00
1894	06	27	166	30	-3	59
1894	06	28	166	35	-3	59
1894	06	29	166	40	-3	58
1894	06	30	166	45	-3	57
1894	07	01	166	50	-3	57
1894	07	02	166	56	-3	56
1894	07	03	167	01	-3	55
1894	07	04	167	06	-3	55
1894	07	05	167	12	-3	54
1894	07	06	167	17	-3	53
1894	07	07	167	23	-3	53
1894	07	08	167	29	-3	52
1894	07	09	167	35	-3	51
1894	07	10	167	40	-3	51
1894	07	11	167	46	-3	50
1894	07	12	167	52	-3	49
1894	07	13	167	59	-3	49
1894	07	14	168	05	-3	48
1894	07	15	168	11	-3	48
1894	07	16	168	17	-3	47
1894	07	17	168	24	-3	46
1894	07	18	168	30	-3	46
1894	07	19	168	37	-3	45
1894	07	20	168	43	-3	45
1894	07	21	168	50	-3	44
1894	07	22	168	57	-3	44
1894	07	23	169	04	-3	43
1894	07	24	169	10	-3	42
1894	07	25	169	17	-3	42
1894	07	26	169	24	-3	41
1894	07	27	169	31	-3	41
1894	07	28	169	39	-3	40
1894	07	29	169	46	-3	40
1894	07	30	169	53	-3	39
1894	07	31	170	00	-3	39
1894	08	01	170	08	-3	38
1894	08	02	170	15	-3	38
1894	08	03	170	22	-3	37
1894	08	04	170	30	-3	37
1894	08	05	170	37	-3	36
1894	08	06	170	45	-3	36
1894	08	07	170	53	-3	35
1894	08	08	171	00	-3	35
1894	08	09	171	08	-3	34

Chiron

1894	08	10	171	16	-3	34
1894	08	11	171	24	-3	33
1894	08	12	171	32	-3	33
1894	08	13	171	40	-3	32
1894	08	14	171	48	-3	32
1894	08	15	171	56	-3	32
1894	08	16	172	04	-3	31
1894	08	17	172	12	-3	31
1894	08	18	172	20	-3	30
1894	08	19	172	28	-3	30
1894	08	20	172	36	-3	29
1894	08	21	172	45	-3	29
1894	08	22	172	53	-3	29
1894	08	23	173	01	-3	28
1894	08	24	173	10	-3	28
1894	08	25	173	18	-3	27
1894	08	26	173	26	-3	27
1894	08	27	173	35	-3	27
1894	08	28	173	43	-3	26
1894	08	29	173	52	-3	26
1894	08	30	174	00	-3	26
1894	08	31	174	09	-3	25
1894	09	01	174	17	-3	25
1894	09	02	174	26	-3	24
1894	09	03	174	34	-3	24
1894	09	04	174	43	-3	24
1894	09	05	174	52	-3	23
1894	09	06	175	00	-3	23
1894	09	07	175	09	-3	23
1894	09	08	175	18	-3	22
1894	09	09	175	26	-3	22
1894	09	10	175	35	-3	22
1894	09	11	175	44	-3	22
1894	09	12	175	52	-3	21
1894	09	13	176	01	-3	21
1894	09	14	176	10	-3	21
1894	09	15	176	19	-3	20
1894	09	16	176	27	-3	20
1894	09	17	176	36	-3	20
1894	09	18	176	45	-3	20
1894	09	19	176	54	-3	19
1894	09	20	177	03	-3	19
1894	09	21	177	11	-3	19
1894	09	22	177	20	-3	19
1894	09	23	177	29	-3	18
1894	09	24	177	38	-3	18
1894	09	25	177	46	-3	18
1894	09	26	177	55	-3	18
1894	09	27	178	04	-3	17
1894	09	28	178	13	-3	17
1894	09	29	178	22	-3	17
1894	09	30	178	30	-3	17
1894	10	01	178	39	-3	17
1894	10	02	178	48	-3	16
1894	10	03	178	56	-3	16
1894	10	04	179	05	-3	16
1894	10	05	179	14	-3	16
1894	10	06	179	22	-3	16
1894	10	07	179	31	-3	15
1894	10	08	179	40	-3	15
1894	10	09	179	48	-3	15
1894	10	10	179	57	-3	15
1894	10	11	180	05	-3	15
1894	10	12	180	14	-3	15
1894	10	13	180	22	-3	14
1894	10	14	180	31	-3	14
1894	10	15	180	39	-3	14
1894	10	16	180	48	-3	14
1894	10	17	180	56	-3	14
1894	10	18	181	05	-3	14
1894	10	19	181	13	-3	14
1894	10	20	181	21	-3	14
1894	10	21	181	30	-3	13
1894	10	22	181	38	-3	13
1894	10	23	181	46	-3	13
1894	10	24	181	54	-3	13
1894	10	25	182	02	-3	13
1894	10	26	182	10	-3	13
1894	10	27	182	18	-3	13
1894	10	28	182	26	-3	13
1894	10	29	182	34	-3	13
1894	10	30	182	42	-3	13
1894	10	31	182	50	-3	12
1894	11	01	182	58	-3	12
1894	11	02	183	06	-3	12
1894	11	03	183	14	-3	12
1894	11	04	183	21	-3	12
1894	11	05	183	29	-3	12
1894	11	06	183	36	-3	12
1894	11	07	183	44	-3	12
1894	11	08	183	51	-3	12
1894	11	09	183	59	-3	12
1894	11	10	184	06	-3	12
1894	11	11	184	13	-3	12
1894	11	12	184	21	-3	12
1894	11	13	184	28	-3	12
1894	11	14	184	35	-3	12
1894	11	15	184	42	-3	12
1894	11	16	184	49	-3	12
1894	11	17	184	56	-3	12
1894	11	18	185	03	-3	12
1894	11	19	185	09	-3	12
1894	11	20	185	16	-3	12
1894	11	21	185	23	-3	12
1894	11	22	185	29	-3	12
1894	11	23	185	36	-3	12
1894	11	24	185	42	-3	12
1894	11	25	185	49	-3	12
1894	11	26	185	55	-3	12
1894	11	27	186	01	-3	12
1894	11	28	186	07	-3	12
1894	11	29	186	13	-3	12
1894	11	30	186	19	-3	12
1894	12	01	186	25	-3	12
1894	12	02	186	30	-3	12
1894	12	03	186	36	-3	12
1894	12	04	186	42	-3	12
1894	12	05	186	47	-3	12
1894	12	06	186	53	-3	12
1894	12	07	186	58	-3	12
1894	12	08	187	03	-3	12
1894	12	09	187	08	-3	12
1894	12	10	187	13	-3	12
1894	12	11	187	18	-3	12
1894	12	12	187	23	-3	12
1894	12	13	187	28	-3	13
1894	12	14	187	32	-3	13
1894	12	15	187	37	-3	13
1894	12	16	187	41	-3	13
1894	12	17	187	46	-3	13
1894	12	18	187	50	-3	13
1894	12	19	187	54	-3	13
1894	12	20	187	58	-3	13
1894	12	21	188	02	-3	13
1894	12	22	188	06	-3	13
1894	12	23	188	09	-3	13
1894	12	24	188	13	-3	13
1894	12	25	188	16	-3	13
1894	12	26	188	20	-3	13
1894	12	27	188	23	-3	14
1894	12	28	188	26	-3	14
1894	12	29	188	29	-3	14
1894	12	30	188	32	-3	14
1894	12	31	188	35	-3	14
1895	01	01	188	38	-3	14
1895	01	02	188	40	-3	14
1895	01	03	188	43	-3	14
1895	01	04	188	45	-3	14
1895	01	05	188	47	-3	14
1895	01	06	188	49	-3	14
1895	01	07	188	51	-3	14
1895	01	08	188	53	-3	14
1895	01	09	188	55	-3	14
1895	01	10	188	57	-3	15
1895	01	11	188	58	-3	15
1895	01	12	188	59	-3	15
1895	01	13	189	01	-3	15
1895	01	14	189	02	-3	15
1895	01	15	189	03	-3	15
1895	01	16	189	04	-3	15
1895	01	17	189	05	-3	15
1895	01	18	189	05	-3	15
1895	01	19	189	06	-3	15
1895	01	20	189	06	-3	15
1895	01	21	189	06	-3	15
1895	01	22	189	07	-3	15
1895	01	23	189	07	-3	15
1895	01	24	189	07	-3	15
1895	01	25	189	06	-3	15
1895	01	26	189	06	-3	15
1895	01	27	189	06	-3	16
1895	01	28	189	05	-3	16
1895	01	29	189	04	-3	16
1895	01	30	189	04	-3	16
1895	01	31	189	03	-3	16
1895	02	01	189	02	-3	16
1895	02	02	189	01	-3	16
1895	02	03	188	59	-3	16
1895	02	04	188	58	-3	16
1895	02	05	188	56	-3	16
1895	02	06	188	55	-3	16
1895	02	07	188	53	-3	16
1895	02	08	188	51	-3	16
1895	02	09	188	49	-3	16
1895	02	10	188	47	-3	16
1895	02	11	188	45	-3	16
1895	02	12	188	43	-3	16
1895	02	13	188	41	-3	15
1895	02	14	188	38	-3	15
1895	02	15	188	36	-3	15
1895	02	16	188	33	-3	15
1895	02	17	188	30	-3	15
1895	02	18	188	27	-3	15
1895	02	19	188	24	-3	15
1895	02	20	188	21	-3	15
1895	02	21	188	18	-3	15
1895	02	22	188	15	-3	15
1895	02	23	188	12	-3	15
1895	02	24	188	08	-3	15
1895	02	25	188	05	-3	15
1895	02	26	188	01	-3	14
1895	02	27	187	58	-3	14
1895	02	28	187	54	-3	14
1895	03	01	187	50	-3	14
1895	03	02	187	46	-3	14
1895	03	03	187	42	-3	14
1895	03	04	187	38	-3	13
1895	03	05	187	34	-3	13
1895	03	06	187	30	-3	13
1895	03	07	187	26	-3	13
1895	03	08	187	22	-3	13
1895	03	09	187	17	-3	13
1895	03	10	187	13	-3	12
1895	03	11	187	09	-3	12
1895	03	12	187	04	-3	12
1895	03	13	187	00	-3	12
1895	03	14	186	55	-3	11
1895	03	15	186	51	-3	11
1895	03	16	186	46	-3	11
1895	03	17	186	41	-3	11
1895	03	18	186	37	-3	10
1895	03	19	186	32	-3	10
1895	03	20	186	27	-3	10
1895	03	21	186	23	-3	09
1895	03	22	186	18	-3	09
1895	03	23	186	13	-3	09
1895	03	24	186	08	-3	08
1895	03	25	186	04	-3	08
1895	03	26	185	59	-3	08
1895	03	27	185	54	-3	07
1895	03	28	185	49	-3	07
1895	03	29	185	44	-3	07
1895	03	30	185	40	-3	06
1895	03	31	185	35	-3	06
1895	04	01	185	30	-3	06
1895	04	02	185	25	-3	05
1895	04	03	185	21	-3	05
1895	04	04	185	16	-3	04
1895	04	05	185	11	-3	04
1895	04	06	185	07	-3	03
1895	04	07	185	02	-3	03
1895	04	08	184	57	-3	03
1895	04	09	184	53	-3	02
1895	04	10	184	48	-3	02
1895	04	11	184	44	-3	01
1895	04	12	184	39	-3	01
1895	04	13	184	35	-3	00
1895	04	14	184	31	-3	00
1895	04	15	184	26	-2	59
1895	04	16	184	22	-2	59
1895	04	17	184	18	-2	58
1895	04	18	184	14	-2	58
1895	04	19	184	10	-2	57
1895	04	20	184	06	-2	57
1895	04	21	184	02	-2	56
1895	04	22	183	58	-2	56
1895	04	23	183	54	-2	55
1895	04	24	183	50	-2	55
1895	04	25	183	47	-2	54
1895	04	26	183	43	-2	54
1895	04	27	183	40	-2	53
1895	04	28	183	36	-2	52
1895	04	29	183	33	-2	52
1895	04	30	183	30	-2	51
1895	05	01	183	26	-2	51
1895	05	02	183	23	-2	50
1895	05	03	183	20	-2	50
1895	05	04	183	17	-2	49
1895	05	05	183	15	-2	48
1895	05	06	183	12	-2	48
1895	05	07	183	09	-2	47
1895	05	08	183	07	-2	47
1895	05	09	183	04	-2	46
1895	05	10	183	02	-2	45
1895	05	11	183	00	-2	45
1895	05	12	182	58	-2	44
1895	05	13	182	56	-2	44
1895	05	14	182	54	-2	43
1895	05	15	182	52	-2	42
1895	05	16	182	50	-2	42
1895	05	17	182	49	-2	41
1895	05	18	182	47	-2	41
1895	05	19	182	46	-2	40
1895	05	20	182	44	-2	39
1895	05	21	182	43	-2	39
1895	05	22	182	42	-2	38
1895	05	23	182	41	-2	37
1895	05	24	182	40	-2	37
1895	05	25	182	40	-2	36
1895	05	26	182	39	-2	36
1895	05	27	182	39	-2	35
1895	05	28	182	38	-2	34
1895	05	29	182	38	-2	34
1895	05	30	182	38	-2	33
1895	05	31	182	38	-2	32
1895	06	01	182	38	-2	32
1895	06	02	182	38	-2	31
1895	06	03	182	38	-2	31
1895	06	04	182	39	-2	30
1895	06	05	182	39	-2	29
1895	06	06	182	40	-2	29
1895	06	07	182	41	-2	28
1895	06	08	182	42	-2	27
1895	06	09	182	42	-2	27
1895	06	10	182	44	-2	26
1895	06	11	182	45	-2	26
1895	06	12	182	46	-2	25
1895	06	13	182	48	-2	24
1895	06	14	182	49	-2	24
1895	06	15	182	51	-2	23
1895	06	16	182	53	-2	22
1895	06	17	182	54	-2	22
1895	06	18	182	56	-2	21
1895	06	19	182	59	-2	21
1895	06	20	183	01	-2	20
1895	06	21	183	03	-2	19
1895	06	22	183	05	-2	19
1895	06	23	183	08	-2	18
1895	06	24	183	11	-2	18
1895	06	25	183	13	-2	17
1895	06	26	183	16	-2	16
1895	06	27	183	19	-2	16
1895	06	28	183	22	-2	15
1895	06	29	183	26	-2	15
1895	06	30	183	29	-2	14
1895	07	01	183	32	-2	14
1895	07	02	183	36	-2	13
1895	07	03	183	39	-2	12
1895	07	04	183	43	-2	12
1895	07	05	183	47	-2	11
1895	07	06	183	51	-2	11
1895	07	07	183	55	-2	10
1895	07	08	183	59	-2	10
1895	07	09	184	03	-2	09
1895	07	10	184	07	-2	08
1895	07	11	184	12	-2	08
1895	07	12	184	16	-2	07
1895	07	13	184	21	-2	07
1895	07	14	184	25	-2	06
1895	07	15	184	30	-2	06
1895	07	16	184	35	-2	05
1895	07	17	184	40	-2	05
1895	07	18	184	45	-2	04
1895	07	19	184	50	-2	04
1895	07	20	184	55	-2	03
1895	07	21	185	00	-2	02
1895	07	22	185	06	-2	02
1895	07	23	185	11	-2	01
1895	07	24	185	17	-2	01
1895	07	25	185	22	-2	00
1895	07	26	185	28	-2	00
1895	07	27	185	34	-1	59
1895	07	28	185	40	-1	59
1895	07	29	185	46	-1	58
1895	07	30	185	52	-1	58
1895	07	31	185	58	-1	57
1895	08	01	186	04	-1	57
1895	08	02	186	10	-1	56
1895	08	03	186	17	-1	56
1895	08	04	186	23	-1	55
1895	08	05	186	29	-1	55
1895	08	06	186	36	-1	55
1895	08	07	186	43	-1	54
1895	08	08	186	49	-1	54
1895	08	09	186	56	-1	53
1895	08	10	187	03	-1	53
1895	08	11	187	10	-1	52
1895	08	12	187	17	-1	52
1895	08	13	187	24	-1	51
1895	08	14	187	31	-1	51
1895	08	15	187	38	-1	50
1895	08	16	187	45	-1	50
1895	08	17	187	52	-1	49
1895	08	18	187	59	-1	49
1895	08	19	188	07	-1	49
1895	08	20	188	14	-1	48
1895	08	21	188	22	-1	48
1895	08	22	188	29	-1	47
1895	08	23	188	37	-1	47
1895	08	24	188	44	-1	47
1895	08	25	188	52	-1	46
1895	08	26	189	00	-1	46
1895	08	27	189	07	-1	45
1895	08	28	189	15	-1	45
1895	08	29	189	23	-1	44
1895	08	30	189	31	-1	44
1895	08	31	189	39	-1	44
1895	09	01	189	47	-1	43
1895	09	02	189	55	-1	43
1895	09	03	190	03	-1	42
1895	09	04	190	11	-1	42
1895	09	05	190	19	-1	42
1895	09	06	190	27	-1	41
1895	09	07	190	36	-1	41
1895	09	08	190	44	-1	41
1895	09	09	190	52	-1	40
1895	09	10	191	01	-1	40
1895	09	11	191	09	-1	39
1895	09	12	191	17	-1	39
1895	09	13	191	26	-1	39
1895	09	14	191	34	-1	38
1895	09	15	191	43	-1	38
1895	09	16	191	51	-1	38
1895	09	17	192	00	-1	37
1895	09	18	192	08	-1	37
1895	09	19	192	17	-1	37
1895	09	20	192	25	-1	36
1895	09	21	192	34	-1	36
1895	09	22	192	43	-1	36
1895	09	23	192	51	-1	35
1895	09	24	193	00	-1	35
1895	09	25	193	08	-1	35
1895	09	26	193	17	-1	34
1895	09	27	193	26	-1	34
1895	09	28	193	35	-1	34
1895	09	29	193	43	-1	33
1895	09	30	193	52	-1	33
1895	10	01	194	01	-1	33
1895	10	02	194	10	-1	32

1895 10 03	194 18	-1 32	1896 01 17	206 29	-1 08	1896 05 02	202 25	-0 36	1896 08 16	203 40	0 03
1895 10 04	194 27	-1 32	1896 01 18	206 32	-1 08	1896 05 03	202 21	-0 35	1896 08 17	203 45	0 04
1895 10 05	194 36	-1 31	1896 01 19	206 34	-1 08	1896 05 04	202 17	-0 35	1896 08 18	203 51	0 04
1895 10 06	194 45	-1 31	1896 01 20	206 37	-1 07	1896 05 05	202 13	-0 35	1896 08 19	203 57	0 04
1895 10 07	194 53	-1 31	1896 01 21	206 39	-1 07	1896 05 06	202 09	-0 34	1896 08 20	204 04	0 05
1895 10 08	195 02	-1 31	1896 01 22	206 41	-1 07	1896 05 07	202 05	-0 34	1896 08 21	204 10	0 05
1895 10 09	195 11	-1 30	1896 01 23	206 44	-1 07	1896 05 08	202 01	-0 33	1896 08 22	204 16	0 05
1895 10 10	195 20	-1 30	1896 01 24	206 46	-1 06	1896 05 09	201 57	-0 33	1896 08 23	204 22	0 05
1895 10 11	195 29	-1 30	1896 01 25	206 48	-1 06	1896 05 10	201 53	-0 33	1896 08 24	204 29	0 06
1895 10 12	195 37	-1 29	1896 01 26	206 49	-1 06	1896 05 11	201 50	-0 32	1896 08 25	204 35	0 06
1895 10 13	195 46	-1 29	1896 01 27	206 51	-1 06	1896 05 12	201 46	-0 32	1896 08 26	204 42	0 06
1895 10 14	195 55	-1 29	1896 01 28	206 53	-1 06	1896 05 13	201 43	-0 31	1896 08 27	204 48	0 07
1895 10 15	196 04	-1 29	1896 01 29	206 54	-1 05	1896 05 14	201 39	-0 31	1896 08 28	204 55	0 07
1895 10 16	196 13	-1 28	1896 01 30	206 55	-1 05	1896 05 15	201 36	-0 31	1896 08 29	205 02	0 07
1895 10 17	196 21	-1 28	1896 01 31	206 57	-1 05	1896 05 16	201 32	-0 30	1896 08 30	205 08	0 08
1895 10 18	196 30	-1 28	1896 02 01	206 58	-1 05	1896 05 17	201 29	-0 30	1896 08 31	205 15	0 08
1895 10 19	196 39	-1 27	1896 02 02	206 59	-1 05	1896 05 18	201 26	-0 29	1896 09 01	205 22	0 08
1895 10 20	196 48	-1 27	1896 02 03	207 00	-1 04	1896 05 19	201 23	-0 29	1896 09 02	205 29	0 08
1895 10 21	196 56	-1 27	1896 02 04	207 00	-1 04	1896 05 20	201 20	-0 28	1896 09 03	205 36	0 09
1895 10 22	197 05	-1 27	1896 02 05	207 01	-1 04	1896 05 21	201 17	-0 28	1896 09 04	205 43	0 09
1895 10 23	197 14	-1 26	1896 02 06	207 01	-1 04	1896 05 22	201 14	-0 28	1896 09 05	205 50	0 09
1895 10 24	197 22	-1 26	1896 02 07	207 02	-1 03	1896 05 23	201 11	-0 27	1896 09 06	205 58	0 10
1895 10 25	197 31	-1 26	1896 02 08	207 02	-1 03	1896 05 24	201 09	-0 27	1896 09 07	206 05	0 10
1895 10 26	197 40	-1 26	1896 02 09	207 02	-1 03	1896 05 25	201 06	-0 26	1896 09 08	206 12	0 10
1895 10 27	197 48	-1 25	1896 02 10	207 02	-1 03	1896 05 26	201 04	-0 26	1896 09 09	206 19	0 10
1895 10 28	197 57	-1 25	1896 02 11	207 02	-1 02	1896 05 27	201 01	-0 26	1896 09 10	206 27	0 11
1895 10 29	198 05	-1 25	1896 02 12	207 02	-1 02	1896 05 28	200 59	-0 25	1896 09 11	206 34	0 11
1895 10 30	198 14	-1 25	1896 02 13	207 02	-1 02	1896 05 29	200 57	-0 25	1896 09 12	206 42	0 11
1895 10 31	198 22	-1 24	1896 02 14	207 01	-1 02	1896 05 30	200 55	-0 24	1896 09 13	206 49	0 12
1895 11 01	198 31	-1 24	1896 02 15	207 01	-1 01	1896 05 31	200 53	-0 24	1896 09 14	206 57	0 12
1895 11 02	198 39	-1 24	1896 02 16	207 00	-1 01	1896 06 01	200 51	-0 24	1896 09 15	207 05	0 12
1895 11 03	198 48	-1 24	1896 02 17	206 59	-1 01	1896 06 02	200 49	-0 23	1896 09 16	207 12	0 13
1895 11 04	198 56	-1 23	1896 02 18	206 58	-1 01	1896 06 03	200 48	-0 23	1896 09 17	207 20	0 13
1895 11 05	199 04	-1 23	1896 02 19	206 57	-1 00	1896 06 04	200 46	-0 22	1896 09 18	207 28	0 13
1895 11 06	199 13	-1 23	1896 02 20	206 56	-1 00	1896 06 05	200 45	-0 22	1896 09 19	207 36	0 13
1895 11 07	199 21	-1 23	1896 02 21	206 55	-1 00	1896 06 06	200 43	-0 22	1896 09 20	207 43	0 14
1895 11 08	199 29	-1 22	1896 02 22	206 53	-1 00	1896 06 07	200 42	-0 21	1896 09 21	207 51	0 14
1895 11 09	199 38	-1 22	1896 02 23	206 52	-0 59	1896 06 08	200 41	-0 21	1896 09 22	207 59	0 14
1895 11 10	199 46	-1 22	1896 02 24	206 50	-0 59	1896 06 09	200 40	-0 20	1896 09 23	208 07	0 15
1895 11 11	199 54	-1 22	1896 02 25	206 48	-0 59	1896 06 10	200 39	-0 20	1896 09 24	208 15	0 15
1895 11 12	200 02	-1 21	1896 02 26	206 47	-0 59	1896 06 11	200 38	-0 20	1896 09 25	208 23	0 15
1895 11 13	200 10	-1 21	1896 02 27	206 45	-0 58	1896 06 12	200 37	-0 19	1896 09 26	208 31	0 15
1895 11 14	200 18	-1 21	1896 02 28	206 43	-0 58	1896 06 13	200 37	-0 19	1896 09 27	208 39	0 16
1895 11 15	200 26	-1 21	1896 02 29	206 41	-0 58	1896 06 14	200 36	-0 18	1896 09 28	208 48	0 16
1895 11 16	200 34	-1 21	1896 03 01	206 38	-0 58	1896 06 15	200 36	-0 18	1896 09 29	208 56	0 16
1895 11 17	200 42	-1 20	1896 03 02	206 36	-0 57	1896 06 16	200 36	-0 18	1896 09 30	209 04	0 17
1895 11 18	200 50	-1 20	1896 03 03	206 34	-0 57	1896 06 17	200 36	-0 17	1896 10 01	209 12	0 17
1895 11 19	200 58	-1 20	1896 03 04	206 31	-0 57	1896 06 18	200 35	-0 17	1896 10 02	209 20	0 17
1895 11 20	201 05	-1 20	1896 03 05	206 28	-0 56	1896 06 19	200 36	-0 17	1896 10 03	209 29	0 17
1895 11 21	201 13	-1 19	1896 03 06	206 26	-0 56	1896 06 20	200 36	-0 16	1896 10 04	209 37	0 18
1895 11 22	201 21	-1 19	1896 03 07	206 23	-0 56	1896 06 21	200 36	-0 16	1896 10 05	209 45	0 18
1895 11 23	201 28	-1 19	1896 03 08	206 20	-0 56	1896 06 22	200 36	-0 15	1896 10 06	209 54	0 18
1895 11 24	201 36	-1 19	1896 03 09	206 17	-0 55	1896 06 23	200 37	-0 15	1896 10 07	210 02	0 19
1895 11 25	201 43	-1 19	1896 03 10	206 14	-0 55	1896 06 24	200 38	-0 15	1896 10 08	210 10	0 19
1895 11 26	201 51	-1 18	1896 03 11	206 11	-0 55	1896 06 25	200 38	-0 14	1896 10 09	210 19	0 19
1895 11 27	201 58	-1 18	1896 03 12	206 07	-0 54	1896 06 26	200 39	-0 14	1896 10 10	210 27	0 19
1895 11 28	202 06	-1 18	1896 03 13	206 04	-0 54	1896 06 27	200 40	-0 14	1896 10 11	210 36	0 20
1895 11 29	202 13	-1 18	1896 03 14	206 01	-0 54	1896 06 28	200 41	-0 13	1896 10 12	210 44	0 20
1895 11 30	202 20	-1 18	1896 03 15	205 57	-0 53	1896 06 29	200 42	-0 13	1896 10 13	210 52	0 20
1895 12 01	202 27	-1 17	1896 03 16	205 54	-0 53	1896 06 30	200 44	-0 12	1896 10 14	211 01	0 21
1895 12 02	202 34	-1 17	1896 03 17	205 50	-0 53	1896 07 01	200 45	-0 12	1896 10 15	211 09	0 21
1895 12 03	202 41	-1 17	1896 03 18	205 46	-0 52	1896 07 02	200 47	-0 12	1896 10 16	211 18	0 21
1895 12 04	202 48	-1 17	1896 03 19	205 42	-0 52	1896 07 03	200 48	-0 11	1896 10 17	211 26	0 21
1895 12 05	202 55	-1 16	1896 03 20	205 38	-0 52	1896 07 04	200 50	-0 11	1896 10 18	211 35	0 22
1895 12 06	203 02	-1 16	1896 03 21	205 35	-0 51	1896 07 05	200 52	-0 11	1896 10 19	211 43	0 22
1895 12 07	203 08	-1 16	1896 03 22	205 31	-0 51	1896 07 06	200 54	-0 10	1896 10 20	211 52	0 22
1895 12 08	203 15	-1 16	1896 03 23	205 26	-0 51	1896 07 07	200 56	-0 10	1896 10 21	212 01	0 23
1895 12 09	203 22	-1 16	1896 03 24	205 22	-0 50	1896 07 08	200 58	-0 10	1896 10 22	212 09	0 23
1895 12 10	203 28	-1 15	1896 03 25	205 18	-0 50	1896 07 09	201 00	-0 09	1896 10 23	212 18	0 23
1895 12 11	203 35	-1 15	1896 03 26	205 14	-0 50	1896 07 10	201 03	-0 09	1896 10 24	212 26	0 23
1895 12 12	203 41	-1 15	1896 03 27	205 10	-0 49	1896 07 11	201 05	-0 08	1896 10 25	212 35	0 24
1895 12 13	203 47	-1 15	1896 03 28	205 05	-0 49	1896 07 12	201 08	-0 08	1896 10 26	212 43	0 24
1895 12 14	203 53	-1 15	1896 03 29	205 01	-0 49	1896 07 13	201 10	-0 08	1896 10 27	212 52	0 24
1895 12 15	204 00	-1 14	1896 03 30	204 57	-0 48	1896 07 14	201 13	-0 07	1896 10 28	213 00	0 25
1895 12 16	204 06	-1 14	1896 03 31	204 52	-0 48	1896 07 15	201 16	-0 07	1896 10 29	213 09	0 25
1895 12 17	204 12	-1 14	1896 04 01	204 48	-0 48	1896 07 16	201 19	-0 07	1896 10 30	213 17	0 25
1895 12 18	204 17	-1 14	1896 04 02	204 43	-0 47	1896 07 17	201 22	-0 06	1896 10 31	213 26	0 25
1895 12 19	204 23	-1 14	1896 04 03	204 39	-0 47	1896 07 18	201 26	-0 06	1896 11 01	213 34	0 26
1895 12 20	204 29	-1 13	1896 04 04	204 34	-0 47	1896 07 19	201 29	-0 06	1896 11 02	213 43	0 26
1895 12 21	204 34	-1 13	1896 04 05	204 29	-0 46	1896 07 20	201 32	-0 05	1896 11 03	213 51	0 26
1895 12 22	204 40	-1 13	1896 04 06	204 25	-0 46	1896 07 21	201 36	-0 05	1896 11 04	214 00	0 27
1895 12 23	204 45	-1 13	1896 04 07	204 20	-0 45	1896 07 22	201 39	-0 05	1896 11 05	214 08	0 27
1895 12 24	204 51	-1 13	1896 04 08	204 15	-0 45	1896 07 23	201 43	-0 04	1896 11 06	214 17	0 27
1895 12 25	204 56	-1 12	1896 04 09	204 11	-0 45	1896 07 24	201 47	-0 04	1896 11 07	214 25	0 28
1895 12 26	205 [illegible]	-1 12	1896 04 10	204 06	-0 44	1896 07 25	201 51	-0 04	1896 11 08	214 34	0 28
1895 12 27	205 06	-1 12	1896 04 11	204 01	-0 44	1896 07 26	201 55	-0 03	1896 11 09	214 42	0 28
1895 12 28	205 11	-1 12	1896 04 12	203 57	-0 44	1896 07 27	201 59	-0 03	1896 11 10	214 51	0 28
1895 12 29	205 16	-1 12	1896 04 13	203 52	-0 43	1896 07 28	202 03	-0 03	1896 11 11	214 59	0 29
1895 12 30	205 21	-1 12	1896 04 14	203 47	-0 43	1896 07 29	202 07	-0 02	1896 11 12	215 07	0 29
1895 12 31	205 25	-1 11	1896 04 15	203 42	-0 42	1896 07 30	202 12	-0 02	1896 11 13	215 16	0 29
1896 01 01	205 30	-1 11	1896 04 16	203 38	-0 42	1896 07 31	202 16	-0 02	1896 11 14	215 24	0 30
1896 01 02	205 35	-1 11	1896 04 17	203 33	-0 42	1896 08 01	202 21	-0 01	1896 11 15	215 32	0 30
1896 01 03	205 39	-1 11	1896 04 18	203 28	-0 41	1896 08 02	202 25	-0 01	1896 11 16	215 41	0 30
1896 01 04	205 43	-1 11	1896 04 19	203 24	-0 41	1896 08 03	202 30	-0 01	1896 11 17	215 49	0 31
1896 01 05	205 47	-1 10	1896 04 20	203 19	-0 41	1896 08 04	202 35	0 00	1896 11 18	215 57	0 31
1896 01 06	205 51	-1 10	1896 04 21	203 14	-0 40	1896 08 05	202 40	0 00	1896 11 19	216 05	0 31
1896 01 07	205 55	-1 10	1896 04 22	203 10	-0 40	1896 08 06	202 45	0 00	1896 11 20	216 13	0 32
1896 01 08	205 59	-1 10	1896 04 23	203 05	-0 39	1896 08 07	202 50	0 01	1896 11 21	216 21	0 32
1896 01 09	206 03	-1 10	1896 04 24	203 01	-0 39	1896 08 08	202 55	0 01	1896 11 22	216 30	0 32
1896 01 10	206 07	-1 09	1896 04 25	202 56	-0 39	1896 08 09	203 00	0 01	1896 11 23	216 38	0 32
1896 01 11	206 10	-1 09	1896 04 26	202 52	-0 38	1896 08 10	203 06	0 01	1896 11 24	216 46	0 33
1896 01 12	206 13	-1 09	1896 04 27	202 47	-0 38	1896 08 11	203 11	0 02			
1896 01 13	206 17	-1 09	1896 04 28	202 43	-0 37	1896 08 12	203 17	0 02			
1896 01 14	206 20	-1 09	1896 04 29	202 38	-0 37	1896 08 13	203 22	0 02			
1896 01 15	206 23	-1 08	1896 04 30	202 34	-0 37	1896 08 14	203 28	0 03			
1896 01 16	206 26	-1 08	1896 05 01	202 30	-0 36	1896 08 15	203 34	0 03			

1896	11	25	216	54	0	33
1896	11	26	217	02	0	33
1896	11	27	217	10	0	34
1896	11	28	217	17	0	34
1896	11	29	217	25	0	34
1896	11	30	217	33	0	35
1896	12	01	217	41	0	35
1896	12	02	217	48	0	35
1896	12	03	217	56	0	36
1896	12	04	218	04	0	36
1896	12	05	218	11	0	36
1896	12	06	218	19	0	37
1896	12	07	218	26	0	37
1896	12	08	218	34	0	37
1896	12	09	218	41	0	38
1896	12	10	218	48	0	38
1896	12	11	218	56	0	38
1896	12	12	219	03	0	39
1896	12	13	219	10	0	39
1896	12	14	219	17	0	39
1896	12	15	219	24	0	40
1896	12	16	219	31	0	40
1896	12	17	219	38	0	40
1896	12	18	219	45	0	41
1896	12	19	219	51	0	41
1896	12	20	219	58	0	42
1896	12	21	220	05	0	42
1896	12	22	220	11	0	42
1896	12	23	220	18	0	43
1896	12	24	220	24	0	43
1896	12	25	220	30	0	43
1896	12	26	220	37	0	44
1896	12	27	220	43	0	44
1896	12	28	220	49	0	44
1896	12	29	220	55	0	45
1896	12	30	221	01	0	45
1896	12	31	221	07	0	46
1897	01	01	221	13	0	46
1897	01	02	221	18	0	46
1897	01	03	221	24	0	47
1897	01	04	221	29	0	47
1897	01	05	221	35	0	47
1897	01	06	221	40	0	48
1897	01	07	221	46	0	48
1897	01	08	221	51	0	49
1897	01	09	221	56	0	49
1897	01	10	222	01	0	49
1897	01	11	222	06	0	50
1897	01	12	222	11	0	50
1897	01	13	222	15	0	51
1897	01	14	222	20	0	51
1897	01	15	222	25	0	51
1897	01	16	222	29	0	52
1897	01	17	222	33	0	52
1897	01	18	222	38	0	53
1897	01	19	222	42	0	53
1897	01	20	222	46	0	53
1897	01	21	222	50	0	54
1897	01	22	222	54	0	54
1897	01	23	222	57	0	55
1897	01	24	223	01	0	55
1897	01	25	223	05	0	55
1897	01	26	223	08	0	56
1897	01	27	223	11	0	56
1897	01	28	223	15	0	57
1897	01	29	223	18	0	57
1897	01	30	223	21	0	58
1897	01	31	223	24	0	58
1897	02	01	223	26	0	58
1897	02	02	223	29	0	59
1897	02	03	223	32	0	59
1897	02	04	223	34	1	00
1897	02	05	223	37	1	00
1897	02	06	223	39	1	01
1897	02	07	223	41	1	01
1897	02	08	223	43	1	01
1897	02	09	223	45	1	02
1897	02	10	223	47	1	02
1897	02	11	223	48	1	03
1897	02	12	223	50	1	03
1897	02	13	223	51	1	04
1897	02	14	223	53	1	04
1897	02	15	223	54	1	05
1897	02	16	223	55	1	05
1897	02	17	223	56	1	05
1897	02	18	223	57	1	06
1897	02	19	223	57	1	06
1897	02	20	223	58	1	07
1897	02	21	223	59	1	07
1897	02	22	223	59	1	08
1897	02	23	223	59	1	08
1897	02	24	223	59	1	09
1897	02	25	224	00	1	09
1897	02	26	223	59	1	10
1897	02	27	223	59	1	10
1897	02	28	223	59	1	10
1897	03	01	223	59	1	11
1897	03	02	223	58	1	11
1897	03	03	223	57	1	12
1897	03	04	223	57	1	12
1897	03	05	223	56	1	13
1897	03	06	223	55	1	13
1897	03	07	223	54	1	14
1897	03	08	223	53	1	14
1897	03	09	223	51	1	15
1897	03	10	223	50	1	15
1897	03	11	223	49	1	16
1897	03	12	223	47	1	16
1897	03	13	223	45	1	16
1897	03	14	223	43	1	17
1897	03	15	223	42	1	17
1897	03	16	223	39	1	18
1897	03	17	223	37	1	18
1897	03	18	223	35	1	19
1897	03	19	223	33	1	19
1897	03	20	223	30	1	20
1897	03	21	223	28	1	20
1897	03	22	223	25	1	21
1897	03	23	223	23	1	21
1897	03	24	223	20	1	21
1897	03	25	223	17	1	22
1897	03	26	223	14	1	22
1897	03	27	223	11	1	23
1897	03	28	223	08	1	23
1897	03	29	223	05	1	24
1897	03	30	223	02	1	24
1897	03	31	222	58	1	25
1897	04	01	222	55	1	25
1897	04	02	222	51	1	25
1897	04	03	222	48	1	26
1897	04	04	222	44	1	26
1897	04	05	222	40	1	27
1897	04	06	222	37	1	27
1897	04	07	222	33	1	28
1897	04	08	222	29	1	28
1897	04	09	222	25	1	28
1897	04	10	222	21	1	29
1897	04	11	222	17	1	29
1897	04	12	222	13	1	30
1897	04	13	222	09	1	30
1897	04	14	222	04	1	31
1897	04	15	222	00	1	31
1897	04	16	221	56	1	31
1897	04	17	221	51	1	32
1897	04	18	221	47	1	32
1897	04	19	221	43	1	33
1897	04	20	221	38	1	33
1897	04	21	221	34	1	33
1897	04	22	221	29	1	34
1897	04	23	221	25	1	34
1897	04	24	221	20	1	34
1897	04	25	221	16	1	35
1897	04	26	221	11	1	35
1897	04	27	221	07	1	36
1897	04	28	221	02	1	36
1897	04	29	220	57	1	36
1897	04	30	220	53	1	37
1897	05	01	220	48	1	37
1897	05	02	220	44	1	37
1897	05	03	220	39	1	38
1897	05	04	220	34	1	38
1897	05	05	220	30	1	38
1897	05	06	220	25	1	39
1897	05	07	220	21	1	39
1897	05	08	220	16	1	39
1897	05	09	220	12	1	40
1897	05	10	220	07	1	40
1897	05	11	220	03	1	40
1897	05	12	219	58	1	41
1897	05	13	219	54	1	41
1897	05	14	219	50	1	41
1897	05	15	219	45	1	41
1897	05	16	219	41	1	42
1897	05	17	219	37	1	42
1897	05	18	219	32	1	42
1897	05	19	219	28	1	43
1897	05	20	219	24	1	43
1897	05	21	219	20	1	43
1897	05	22	219	16	1	43
1897	05	23	219	12	1	44
1897	05	24	219	08	1	44
1897	05	25	219	04	1	44
1897	05	26	219	00	1	44
1897	05	27	218	57	1	45
1897	05	28	218	53	1	45
1897	05	29	218	49	1	45
1897	05	30	218	46	1	45
1897	05	31	218	42	1	46
1897	06	01	218	39	1	46
1897	06	02	218	36	1	46
1897	06	03	218	32	1	46
1897	06	04	218	29	1	46
1897	06	05	218	26	1	47
1897	06	06	218	23	1	47
1897	06	07	218	20	1	47
1897	06	08	218	17	1	47
1897	06	09	218	15	1	47
1897	06	10	218	12	1	48
1897	06	11	218	09	1	48
1897	06	12	218	07	1	48
1897	06	13	218	04	1	48
1897	06	14	218	02	1	48
1897	06	15	218	00	1	48
1897	06	16	217	58	1	49
1897	06	17	217	56	1	49
1897	06	18	217	54	1	49
1897	06	19	217	52	1	49
1897	06	20	217	50	1	49
1897	06	21	217	48	1	49
1897	06	22	217	47	1	50
1897	06	23	217	45	1	50
1897	06	24	217	44	1	50
1897	06	25	217	43	1	50
1897	06	26	217	42	1	50
1897	06	27	217	41	1	50
1897	06	28	217	40	1	50
1897	06	29	217	39	1	51
1897	06	30	217	38	1	51
1897	07	01	217	38	1	51
1897	07	02	217	37	1	51
1897	07	03	217	37	1	51
1897	07	04	217	36	1	51
1897	07	05	217	36	1	51
1897	07	06	217	36	1	51
1897	07	07	217	36	1	52
1897	07	08	217	36	1	52
1897	07	09	217	36	1	52
1897	07	10	217	37	1	52
1897	07	11	217	37	1	52
1897	07	12	217	38	1	52
1897	07	13	217	38	1	52
1897	07	14	217	39	1	52
1897	07	15	217	40	1	52
1897	07	16	217	41	1	53
1897	07	17	217	42	1	53
1897	07	18	217	43	1	53
1897	07	19	217	44	1	53
1897	07	20	217	46	1	53
1897	07	21	217	47	1	53
1897	07	22	217	49	1	53
1897	07	23	217	51	1	53
1897	07	24	217	52	1	53
1897	07	25	217	54	1	53
1897	07	26	217	56	1	54
1897	07	27	217	58	1	54
1897	07	28	218	01	1	54
1897	07	29	218	03	1	54
1897	07	30	218	05	1	54
1897	07	31	218	08	1	54
1897	08	01	218	11	1	54
1897	08	02	218	13	1	54
1897	08	03	218	16	1	54
1897	08	04	218	19	1	54
1897	08	05	218	22	1	54
1897	08	06	218	25	1	54
1897	08	07	218	28	1	55
1897	08	08	218	32	1	55
1897	08	09	218	35	1	55
1897	08	10	218	39	1	55
1897	08	11	218	42	1	55
1897	08	12	218	46	1	55
1897	08	13	218	50	1	55
1897	08	14	218	54	1	55
1897	08	15	218	58	1	55
1897	08	16	219	02	1	55
1897	08	17	219	06	1	55
1897	08	18	219	10	1	56
1897	08	19	219	14	1	56
1897	08	20	219	19	1	56
1897	08	21	219	23	1	56
1897	08	22	219	28	1	56
1897	08	23	219	33	1	56
1897	08	24	219	37	1	56
1897	08	25	219	42	1	56
1897	08	26	219	47	1	56
1897	08	27	219	52	1	56
1897	08	28	219	57	1	56
1897	08	29	220	02	1	57
1897	08	30	220	08	1	57
1897	08	31	220	13	1	57
1897	09	01	220	18	1	57
1897	09	02	220	24	1	57
1897	09	03	220	29	1	57
1897	09	04	220	35	1	57
1897	09	05	220	41	1	57
1897	09	06	220	46	1	57
1897	09	07	220	52	1	57
1897	09	08	220	58	1	58
1897	09	09	221	04	1	58
1897	09	10	221	10	1	58
1897	09	11	221	16	1	58
1897	09	12	221	22	1	58
1897	09	13	221	29	1	58
1897	09	14	221	35	1	58
1897	09	15	221	41	1	58
1897	09	16	221	48	1	58
1897	09	17	221	54	1	59
1897	09	18	222	01	1	59
1897	09	19	222	07	1	59
1897	09	20	222	14	1	59
1897	09	21	222	21	1	59
1897	09	22	222	28	1	59
1897	09	23	222	34	1	59
1897	09	24	222	41	1	59
1897	09	25	222	48	2	00
1897	09	26	222	55	2	00
1897	09	27	223	02	2	00
1897	09	28	223	09	2	00
1897	09	29	223	16	2	00
1897	09	30	223	23	2	00
1897	10	01	223	31	2	00
1897	10	02	223	38	2	01
1897	10	03	223	45	2	01
1897	10	04	223	53	2	01
1897	10	05	224	00	2	01
1897	10	06	224	07	2	01
1897	10	07	224	15	2	01
1897	10	08	224	22	2	02
1897	10	09	224	30	2	02
1897	10	10	224	37	2	02
1897	10	11	224	45	2	02
1897	10	12	224	53	2	02
1897	10	13	225	00	2	02
1897	10	14	225	08	2	03
1897	10	15	225	16	2	03
1897	10	16	225	24	2	03
1897	10	17	225	31	2	03
1897	10	18	225	39	2	03
1897	10	19	225	47	2	04
1897	10	20	225	55	2	04
1897	10	21	226	03	2	04
1897	10	22	226	11	2	04
1897	10	23	226	19	2	04
1897	10	24	226	27	2	05
1897	10	25	226	35	2	05
1897	10	26	226	43	2	05
1897	10	27	226	51	2	05
1897	10	28	226	59	2	05
1897	10	29	227	07	2	06
1897	10	30	227	15	2	06
1897	10	31	227	23	2	06
1897	11	01	227	31	2	06
1897	11	02	227	39	2	06
1897	11	03	227	47	2	07
1897	11	04	227	55	2	07
1897	11	05	228	03	2	07
1897	11	06	228	11	2	07
1897	11	07	228	19	2	08
1897	11	08	228	28	2	08
1897	11	09	228	36	2	08
1897	11	10	228	44	2	08
1897	11	11	228	52	2	09
1897	11	12	229	00	2	09
1897	11	13	229	08	2	09
1897	11	14	229	16	2	09
1897	11	15	229	24	2	10
1897	11	16	229	32	2	10
1897	11	17	229	41	2	10
1897	11	18	229	49	2	11
1897	11	19	229	57	2	11
1897	11	20	230	05	2	11
1897	11	21	230	13	2	11
1897	11	22	230	21	2	12
1897	11	23	230	29	2	12
1897	11	24	230	37	2	12
1897	11	25	230	45	2	13
1897	11	26	230	53	2	13
1897	11	27	231	01	2	13
1897	11	28	231	09	2	13
1897	11	29	231	17	2	14
1697	11	30	231	25	2	14
1897	12	01	231	32	2	14
1897	12	02	231	40	2	15
1897	12	03	231	48	2	15
1897	12	04	231	56	2	15
1897	12	05	232	04	2	16
1897	12	06	232	11	2	16
1897	12	07	232	19	2	16
1897	12	08	232	27	2	17
1897	12	09	232	34	2	17
1897	12	10	232	42	2	17
1897	12	11	232	49	2	18
1897	12	12	232	57	2	18
1897	12	13	233	04	2	19
1897	12	14	233	12	2	19
1897	12	15	233	19	2	19
1897	12	16	233	27	2	20
1897	12	17	233	34	2	20
1897	12	18	233	41	2	20
1897	12	19	233	48	2	21
1897	12	20	233	56	2	21
1897	12	21	234	03	2	22
1897	12	22	234	10	2	22
1897	12	23	234	17	2	22
1897	12	24	234	24	2	23
1897	12	25	234	31	2	23
1897	12	26	234	38	2	24
1897	12	27	234	44	2	24
1897	12	28	234	51	2	24
1897	12	29	234	58	2	25
1897	12	30	235	05	2	25
1897	12	31	235	11	2	26
1898	01	01	235	18	2	26
1898	01	02	235	24	2	26
1898	01	03	235	31	2	27
1898	01	04	235	37	2	27
1898	01	05	235	43	2	28
1898	01	06	235	49	2	28
1898	01	07	235	55	2	29
1898	01	08	236	02	2	29
1898	01	09	236	08	2	30
1898	01	10	236	13	2	30
1898	01	11	236	19	2	31
1898	01	12	236	25	2	31
1898	01	13	236	31	2	31

1898	01	14	236	36	2	32
1898	01	15	236	42	2	32
1898	01	16	236	47	2	33
1898	01	17	236	53	2	33
1898	01	18	236	58	2	34
1898	01	19	237	03	2	34
1898	01	20	237	09	2	35
1898	01	21	237	14	2	35
1898	01	22	237	19	2	36
1898	01	23	237	24	2	36
1898	01	24	237	28	2	37
1898	01	25	237	33	2	37
1898	01	26	237	38	2	38
1898	01	27	237	42	2	38
1898	01	28	237	47	2	39
1898	01	29	237	51	2	40
1898	01	30	237	55	2	40
1898	01	31	238	00	2	41
1898	02	01	238	04	2	41
1898	02	02	238	08	2	42
1898	02	03	238	12	2	42
1898	02	04	238	15	2	43
1898	02	05	238	19	2	43
1898	02	06	238	23	2	44
1898	02	07	238	26	2	44
1898	02	08	238	30	2	45
1898	02	09	238	33	2	45
1898	02	10	238	36	2	46
1898	02	11	238	39	2	47
1898	02	12	238	42	2	47
1898	02	13	238	45	2	48
1898	02	14	238	48	2	48
1898	02	15	238	51	2	49
1898	02	16	238	53	2	49
1898	02	17	238	56	2	50
1898	02	18	238	58	2	51
1898	02	19	239	00	2	51
1898	02	20	239	03	2	52
1898	02	21	239	05	2	52
1898	02	22	239	07	2	53
1898	02	23	239	09	2	54
1898	02	24	239	10	2	54
1898	02	25	239	12	2	55
1898	02	26	239	13	2	55
1898	02	27	239	15	2	56
1898	02	28	239	16	2	56
1898	03	01	239	17	2	57
1898	03	02	239	18	2	58
1898	03	03	239	19	2	58
1898	03	04	239	20	2	59
1898	03	05	239	21	2	59
1898	03	06	239	22	3	00
1898	03	07	239	22	3	01
1898	03	08	239	23	3	01
1898	03	09	239	23	3	02
1898	03	10	239	23	3	02
1898	03	11	239	23	3	03
1898	03	12	239	23	3	04
1898	03	13	239	23	3	04
1898	03	14	239	23	3	05
1898	03	15	239	23	3	05
1898	03	16	239	22	3	06
1898	03	17	239	22	3	07
1898	03	18	239	21	3	07
1898	03	19	239	21	3	08
1898	03	20	239	20	3	08
1898	03	21	239	19	3	09
1898	03	22	239	18	3	09
1898	03	23	239	17	3	10
1898	03	24	239	15	3	11
1898	03	25	239	14	3	11
1898	03	26	239	12	3	12
1898	03	27	239	11	3	12
1898	03	28	239	09	3	13
1898	03	29	239	07	3	13
1898	03	30	239	06	3	14
1898	03	31	239	04	3	15
1898	04	01	239	02	3	15
1898	04	02	238	59	3	16
1898	04	03	238	57	3	16
1898	04	04	238	55	3	17
1898	04	05	238	53	3	17
1898	04	06	238	50	3	18
1898	04	07	238	47	3	18
1898	04	08	238	45	3	19
1898	04	09	238	42	3	20
1898	04	10	238	39	3	20
1898	04	11	238	36	3	21
1898	04	12	238	33	3	21
1898	04	13	238	30	3	22
1898	04	14	238	27	3	22
1898	04	15	238	24	3	23
1898	04	16	238	21	3	23
1898	04	17	238	17	3	24
1898	04	18	238	14	3	24
1898	04	19	238	10	3	25
1898	04	20	238	07	3	25
1898	04	21	238	03	3	26
1898	04	22	238	00	3	26
1898	04	23	237	56	3	26
1898	04	24	237	52	3	27
1898	04	25	237	48	3	27
1898	04	26	237	44	3	28
1898	04	27	237	40	3	28
1898	04	28	237	36	3	29
1898	04	29	237	32	3	29
1898	04	30	237	28	3	29
1898	05	01	237	24	3	30
1898	05	02	237	20	3	30
1898	05	03	237	16	3	31
1898	05	04	237	11	3	31
1898	05	05	237	07	3	31
1898	05	06	237	03	3	32
1898	05	07	236	59	3	32
1898	05	08	236	54	3	32
1898	05	09	236	50	3	33
1898	05	10	236	46	3	33
1898	05	11	236	41	3	34
1898	05	12	236	37	3	34
1898	05	13	236	32	3	34
1898	05	14	236	28	3	34
1898	05	15	236	23	3	35
1898	05	16	236	19	3	35
1898	05	17	236	15	3	35
1898	05	18	236	10	3	36
1898	05	19	236	06	3	36
1898	05	20	236	01	3	36
1898	05	21	235	57	3	36
1898	05	22	235	52	3	37
1898	05	23	235	48	3	37
1898	05	24	235	44	3	37
1898	05	25	235	39	3	37
1898	05	26	235	35	3	38
1898	05	27	235	31	3	38
1898	05	28	235	26	3	38
1898	05	29	235	22	3	38
1898	05	30	235	18	3	38
1898	05	31	235	14	3	39
1898	06	01	235	09	3	39
1898	06	02	235	05	3	39
1898	06	03	235	01	3	39
1898	06	04	234	57	3	39
1898	06	05	234	53	3	39
1898	06	06	234	49	3	39
1898	06	07	234	45	3	40
1898	06	08	234	41	3	40
1898	06	09	234	38	3	40
1898	06	10	234	34	3	40
1898	06	11	234	30	3	40
1898	06	12	234	26	3	40
1898	06	13	234	23	3	40
1898	06	14	234	19	3	40
1898	06	15	234	16	3	40
1898	06	16	234	12	3	40
1898	06	17	234	09	3	40
1898	06	18	234	06	3	40
1898	06	19	234	03	3	40
1898	06	20	233	59	3	40
1898	06	21	233	56	3	40
1898	06	22	233	53	3	40
1898	06	23	233	51	3	41
1898	06	24	233	48	3	41
1898	06	25	233	45	3	41
1898	06	26	233	42	3	41
1898	06	27	233	40	3	40
1898	06	28	233	37	3	40
1898	06	29	233	35	3	40
1898	06	30	233	32	3	40
1898	07	01	233	30	3	40
1898	07	02	233	28	3	40
1898	07	03	233	26	3	40
1898	07	04	233	24	3	40
1898	07	05	233	22	3	40
1898	07	06	233	20	3	40
1898	07	07	233	19	3	40
1898	07	08	233	17	3	40
1898	07	09	233	16	3	40
1898	07	10	233	14	3	40
1898	07	11	233	13	3	40
1898	07	12	233	12	3	40
1898	07	13	233	10	3	40
1898	07	14	233	09	3	40
1898	07	15	233	08	3	39
1898	07	16	233	08	3	39
1898	07	17	233	07	3	39
1898	07	18	233	06	3	39
1898	07	19	233	06	3	39
1898	07	20	233	05	3	39
1898	07	21	233	05	3	39
1898	07	22	233	05	3	39
1898	07	23	233	05	3	39
1898	07	24	233	05	3	38
1898	07	25	233	05	3	38
1898	07	26	233	05	3	38
1898	07	27	233	05	3	38
1898	07	28	233	05	3	38
1898	07	29	233	06	3	38
1898	07	30	233	06	3	38
1898	07	31	233	07	3	38
1898	08	01	233	08	3	37
1898	08	02	233	09	3	37
1898	08	03	233	10	3	37
1898	08	04	233	11	3	37
1898	08	05	233	12	3	37
1898	08	06	233	13	3	37
1898	08	07	233	15	3	37
1898	08	08	233	16	3	37
1898	08	09	233	18	3	36
1898	08	10	233	19	3	36
1898	08	11	233	21	3	36
1898	08	12	233	23	3	36
1898	08	13	233	25	3	36
1898	08	14	233	27	3	36
1898	08	15	233	29	3	36
1898	08	16	233	32	3	35
1898	08	17	233	34	3	35
1898	08	18	233	36	3	35
1898	08	19	233	39	3	35
1898	08	20	233	42	3	35
1898	08	21	233	44	3	35
1898	08	22	233	47	3	35
1898	08	23	233	50	3	34
1898	08	24	233	53	3	34
1898	08	25	233	56	3	34
1898	08	26	233	59	3	34
1898	08	27	234	03	3	34
1898	08	28	234	06	3	34
1898	08	29	234	10	3	34
1898	08	30	234	13	3	34
1898	08	31	234	17	3	33
1898	09	01	234	21	3	33
1898	09	02	234	24	3	33
1898	09	03	234	28	3	33
1898	09	04	234	32	3	33
1898	09	05	234	36	3	33
1898	09	06	234	41	3	33
1898	09	07	234	45	3	33
1898	09	04	234	49	3	33
1898	09	05	234	54	3	32
1898	09	06	234	58	3	32
1898	09	07	235	03	3	32
1898	09	08	235	07	3	32
1898	09	09	235	12	3	32
1898	09	10	235	17	3	32
1898	09	11	235	22	3	32
1898	09	12	235	27	3	32
1898	09	13	235	32	3	32
1898	09	14	235	37	3	32
1898	09	15	235	42	3	32
1898	09	16	235	47	3	31
1898	09	17	235	52	3	31
1898	09	18	235	58	3	31
1898	09	19	236	03	3	31
1898	09	20	236	09	3	31
1898	09	21	236	14	3	31
1898	09	22	236	20	3	31
1898	09	23	236	26	3	31
1898	09	24	236	32	3	31
1898	09	25	236	37	3	31
1898	09	26	236	43	3	31
1898	10	27	236	49	3	31
1898	10	28	236	55	3	31
1898	10	29	237	01	3	31
1898	10	30	237	07	3	31
1898	10	31	237	14	3	31
1898	10	01	237	20	3	31
1898	10	02	237	26	3	31
1898	10	03	237	32	3	31
1898	10	04	237	39	3	31
1898	10	05	237	45	3	31
1898	10	06	237	52	3	31
1898	10	07	237	58	3	31
1898	10	08	238	05	3	31
1898	10	09	238	12	3	31
1898	10	10	238	18	3	31
1898	10	11	238	25	3	31
1898	10	12	238	32	3	31
1898	10	13	238	39	3	31
1898	10	14	238	45	3	31
1898	10	15	238	52	3	31
1898	10	16	238	59	3	31
1898	10	17	239	06	3	31
1898	10	18	239	13	3	31
1898	10	19	239	20	3	31
1898	10	20	239	27	3	31
1898	10	21	239	35	3	31
1898	10	22	239	42	3	31
1898	10	23	239	49	3	31
1898	10	24	239	56	3	31
1898	10	25	240	03	3	31
1898	10	26	240	11	3	31
1898	11	27	240	18	3	31
1898	11	28	240	25	3	31
1898	11	29	240	33	3	32
1898	11	30	240	40	3	32
1898	11	01	240	47	3	32
1898	11	02	240	55	3	32
1898	11	03	241	02	3	32
1898	11	04	241	10	3	32
1898	11	05	241	17	3	32
1898	11	06	241	25	3	32
1898	11	07	241	32	3	32
1898	11	08	241	40	3	33
1898	11	09	241	47	3	33
1898	11	10	241	55	3	33
1898	11	11	242	02	3	33
1898	11	12	242	10	3	33
1898	11	13	242	17	3	33
1898	11	14	242	25	3	34
1898	11	15	242	32	3	34
1898	11	16	242	40	3	34
1898	11	17	242	48	3	34
1898	11	18	242	55	3	34
1898	11	19	243	03	3	34
1898	11	20	243	10	3	35
1898	11	21	243	18	3	35
1898	11	22	243	26	3	35
1898	11	23	243	03	3	34
1898	11	24	243	11	3	35
1898	11	25	243	18	3	35
1898	11	26	243	26	3	35
1898	11	27	243	33	3	35
1898	11	28	243	41	3	35
1898	11	29	243	49	3	36
1898	11	30	243	56	3	36
1898	12	01	244	04	3	36
1898	12	02	244	11	3	36
1898	12	03	244	19	3	37
1898	12	04	244	26	3	37
1898	12	05	244	34	3	37
1898	12	06	244	41	3	37
1898	12	07	244	49	3	38
1898	12	08	244	56	3	38
1898	12	09	245	04	3	38
1898	12	10	245	11	3	38
1898	12	11	245	19	3	39
1898	12	12	245	26	3	39
1898	12	13	245	34	3	39
1898	12	14	245	41	3	40
1898	12	15	245	48	3	40
1898	12	16	245	56	3	40
1898	12	17	246	03	3	40
1898	12	18	246	10	3	41
1898	12	19	246	18	3	41
1898	12	20	246	25	3	41
1898	12	21	246	32	3	42
1898	12	22	246	39	3	42
1898	12	23	246	46	3	42
1898	12	24	246	53	3	43
1898	12	25	247	00	3	43
1898	12	26	247	08	3	43
1898	12	27	247	14	3	44
1898	12	28	247	21	3	44
1898	12	29	247	28	3	45
1898	12	30	247	35	3	45
1898	12	31	247	42	3	45
1899	01	01	247	49	3	46
1899	01	02	247	56	3	46
1899	01	03	248	02	3	47
1899	01	04	248	09	3	47
1899	01	05	248	16	3	47
1899	01	06	248	22	3	48
1899	01	07	248	29	3	48
1899	01	08	248	35	3	49
1899	01	09	248	41	3	49
1899	01	10	248	48	3	49
1899	01	11	248	54	3	50
1899	01	12	249	00	3	50
1899	01	13	249	06	3	51
1899	01	14	249	13	3	51
1899	01	15	249	19	3	52
1899	01	16	249	25	3	52
1899	01	17	249	31	3	53
1899	01	18	249	36	3	53
1899	01	19	249	42	3	54
1899	01	20	249	48	3	54
1899	01	21	249	54	3	55
1899	01	22	249	59	3	55
1899	01	23	250	05	3	56
1899	01	24	250	10	3	56
1899	01	25	250	16	3	57
1899	01	26	250	21	3	57
1899	01	27	250	26	3	58
1899	01	28	250	32	3	58
1899	01	29	250	37	3	59
1899	01	30	250	42	3	59
1899	01	31	250	47	4	00
1899	02	01	250	52	4	00
1899	02	02	250	56	4	01
1899	02	03	251	01	4	01
1899	02	04	251	06	4	02
1899	02	05	251	10	4	03
1899	02	06	251	15	4	03
1899	02	07	251	19	4	04
1899	02	08	251	24	4	04
1899	02	09	251	28	4	05
1899	02	10	251	32	4	05
1899	02	11	251	36	4	06
1899	02	12	251	40	4	07
1899	02	13	251	44	4	07
1899	02	14	251	48	4	08
1899	02	15	251	52	4	08
1899	02	16	251	55	4	09
1899	02	17	251	59	4	10
1899	02	18	252	02	4	10
1899	02	19	252	06	4	11
1899	02	20	252	09	4	11
1899	02	21	252	12	4	12
1899	02	22	252	15	4	13
1899	02	23	252	18	4	13
1899	02	24	252	21	4	14
1899	02	25	252	24	4	15
1899	02	26	252	27	4	15
1899	02	27	252	29	4	16
1899	02	28	252	32	4	16
1899	03	01	252	34	4	17
1899	03	02	252	37	4	18
1899	03	03	252	39	4	18
1899	03	04	252	41	4	19

1899 03 05	252 43	4 20
1899 03 06	252 45	4 20
1899 03 07	252 47	4 21
1899 03 08	252 48	4 22
1899 03 09	252 50	4 22
1899 03 10	252 51	4 23
1899 03 11	252 53	4 24
1899 03 12	252 54	4 24
1899 03 13	252 55	4 25
1899 03 14	252 57	4 26
1899 03 15	252 58	4 26
1899 03 16	252 58	4 27
1899 03 17	252 59	4 27
1899 03 18	253 00	4 28
1899 03 19	253 01	4 29
1899 03 20	253 01	4 29
1899 03 21	253 01	4 30
1899 03 22	253 02	4 31
1899 03 23	253 02	4 31
1899 03 24	253 02	4 32
1899 03 25	253 02	4 33
1899 03 26	253 02	4 33
1899 03 27	253 02	4 34
1899 03 28	253 01	4 35
1899 03 29	253 01	4 35
1899 03 30	253 00	4 36
1899 03 31	253 00	4 37
1899 04 01	252 59	4 37
1899 04 02	252 58	4 38
1899 04 03	252 57	4 39
1899 04 04	252 56	4 39
1899 04 05	252 55	4 40
1899 04 06	252 54	4 40
1899 04 07	252 53	4 41
1899 04 08	252 51	4 42
1899 04 09	252 50	4 42
1899 04 10	252 48	4 43
1899 04 11	252 47	4 44
1899 04 12	252 45	4 44
1899 04 13	252 43	4 45
1899 04 14	252 41	4 45
1899 04 15	252 39	4 46
1899 04 16	252 37	4 47
1899 04 17	252 35	4 47
1899 04 18	252 32	4 48
1899 04 19	252 30	4 48
1899 04 20	252 28	4 49
1899 04 21	252 25	4 49
1899 04 22	252 22	4 50
1899 04 23	252 20	4 51
1899 04 24	252 17	4 51
1899 04 25	252 14	4 52
1899 04 26	252 11	4 52
1899 04 27	252 08	4 53
1899 04 28	252 05	4 53
1899 04 29	252 02	4 54
1899 04 30	251 59	4 54
1899 05 01	251 56	4 55
1899 05 02	251 52	4 55
1899 05 03	251 49	4 56
1899 05 04	251 46	4 56
1899 05 05	251 42	4 57
1899 05 06	251 38	4 57
1899 05 07	251 35	4 57
1899 05 08	251 31	4 58
1899 05 09	251 28	4 58
1899 05 10	251 24	4 59
1899 05 11	251 20	4 59
1899 05 12	251 16	5 00
1899 05 13	251 12	5 00
1899 05 14	251 08	5 00
1899 05 15	251 04	5 01
1899 05 16	251 00	5 01
1899 05 17	250 56	5 01
1899 05 18	250 52	5 02
1899 05 19	250 48	5 02
1899 05 20	250 44	5 03
1899 05 21	250 40	5 03
1899 05 22	250 36	5 03
1899 05 23	250 32	5 03
1899 05 24	250 27	5 04
1899 05 25	250 23	5 04
1899 05 26	250 19	5 04
1899 05 27	250 15	5 05
1899 05 28	250 10	5 05
1899 05 29	250 06	5 05
1899 05 30	250 02	5 05
1899 05 31	249 58	5 05
1899 06 01	249 53	5 06
1899 06 02	249 49	5 06
1899 06 03	249 45	5 06
1899 06 04	249 41	5 06
1899 06 05	249 36	5 06
1899 06 06	249 32	5 07
1899 06 07	249 28	5 07
1899 06 08	249 24	5 07
1899 06 09	249 19	5 07
1899 06 10	249 15	5 07
1899 06 11	249 11	5 07
1899 06 12	249 07	5 07
1899 06 13	249 03	5 07
1899 06 14	248 59	5 07
1899 06 15	248 55	5 07
1899 06 16	248 51	5 08
1899 06 17	248 47	5 08
1899 06 18	248 43	5 08
1899 06 19	248 39	5 08
1899 06 20	248 35	5 08
1899 06 21	248 31	5 08
1899 06 22	248 28	5 08
1899 06 23	248 24	5 08
1899 06 24	248 20	5 08
1899 06 25	248 17	5 08
1899 06 26	248 13	5 08
1899 06 27	248 10	5 08
1899 06 28	248 06	5 07
1899 06 29	248 03	5 07
1899 06 30	247 59	5 07
1899 07 01	247 56	5 07
1899 07 02	247 53	5 07
1899 07 03	247 50	5 07
1899 07 04	247 47	5 07
1899 07 05	247 44	5 07
1899 07 06	247 41	5 07
1899 07 07	247 38	5 07
1899 07 08	247 35	5 06
1899 07 09	247 32	5 06
1899 07 10	247 30	5 06
1899 07 11	247 27	5 06
1899 07 12	247 25	5 06
1899 07 13	247 22	5 06
1899 07 14	247 20	5 05
1899 07 15	247 17	5 05
1899 07 16	247 15	5 05
1899 07 17	247 13	5 05
1899 07 18	247 11	5 05
1899 07 19	247 09	5 04
1899 07 20	247 07	5 04
1899 07 21	247 06	5 04
1899 07 22	247 04	5 04
1899 07 23	247 02	5 04
1899 07 24	247 01	5 03
1899 07 25	246 59	5 03
1899 07 26	246 58	5 03
1899 07 27	246 57	5 03
1899 07 28	246 56	5 02
1899 07 29	246 55	5 02
1899 07 30	246 54	5 02
1899 07 31	246 53	5 02
1899 08 01	246 52	5 01
1899 08 02	246 51	5 01
1899 08 03	246 51	5 01
1899 08 04	246 50	5 00
1899 08 05	246 50	5 00
1899 08 06	246 50	5 00
1899 08 07	246 50	5 00
1899 08 08	246 49	4 59
1899 08 09	246 49	4 59
1899 08 10	246 49	4 59
1899 08 11	246 50	4 58
1899 08 12	246 50	4 58
1899 08 13	246 50	4 58
1899 08 14	246 51	4 57
1899 08 15	246 51	4 57
1899 08 16	246 52	4 57
1899 08 17	246 53	4 57
1899 08 18	246 54	4 56
1899 08 19	246 55	4 56
1899 08 20	246 56	4 56
1899 08 21	246 57	4 55
1899 08 22	246 58	4 55
1899 08 23	246 59	4 55
1899 08 24	247 01	4 54
1899 08 25	247 02	4 54
1899 08 26	247 04	4 54
1899 08 27	247 06	4 53
1899 08 28	247 07	4 53
1899 08 29	247 09	4 53
1899 08 30	247 11	4 53
1899 08 31	247 13	4 52
1899 09 01	247 16	4 52
1899 09 02	247 18	4 52
1899 09 03	247 20	4 51
1899 09 04	247 23	4 51
1899 09 05	247 25	4 51
1899 09 06	247 28	4 50
1899 09 07	247 30	4 50
1899 09 08	247 33	4 50
1899 09 09	247 36	4 50
1899 09 10	247 39	4 49
1899 09 11	247 42	4 49
1899 09 12	247 45	4 49
1899 09 13	247 49	4 48
1899 09 14	247 52	4 48
1899 09 15	247 55	4 48
1899 09 16	247 59	4 48
1899 09 17	248 02	4 47
1899 09 18	248 06	4 47
1899 09 19	248 10	4 47
1899 09 20	248 13	4 46
1899 09 21	248 17	4 46
1899 09 22	248 21	4 46
1899 09 23	248 25	4 46
1899 09 24	248 29	4 45
1899 09 25	248 34	4 45
1899 09 26	248 38	4 45
1899 09 27	248 42	4 45
1899 09 28	248 47	4 44
1899 09 29	248 51	4 44
1899 09 30	248 56	4 44
1899 10 01	249 00	4 44
1899 10 02	249 05	4 44
1899 10 03	249 10	4 43
1899 10 04	249 15	4 43
1899 10 05	249 19	4 43
1899 10 06	249 24	4 43
1899 10 07	249 29	4 43
1899 10 08	249 35	4 42
1899 10 09	249 40	4 42
1899 10 10	249 45	4 42
1899 10 11	249 50	4 42
1899 10 12	249 56	4 42
1899 10 13	250 01	4 41
1899 10 14	250 06	4 41
1899 10 15	250 12	4 41
1899 10 16	250 18	4 41
1899 10 17	250 23	4 41
1899 10 18	250 29	4 41
1899 10 19	250 35	4 40
1899 10 20	250 40	4 40
1899 10 21	250 46	4 40
1899 10 22	250 52	4 40
1899 10 23	250 58	4 40
1899 10 24	251 04	4 40
1899 10 25	251 10	4 40
1899 10 26	251 16	4 40
1899 10 27	251 22	4 39
1899 10 28	251 29	4 39
1899 10 29	251 35	4 39
1899 10 30	251 41	4 39
1899 10 31	251 47	4 39
1899 11 01	251 54	4 39
1899 11 02	252 00	4 39
1899 11 03	252 06	4 39
1899 11 04	252 13	4 39
1899 11 05	252 19	4 39
1899 11 06	252 26	4 39
1899 11 07	252 33	4 39
1899 11 08	252 39	4 39
1899 11 09	252 46	4 39
1899 11 10	252 52	4 39
1899 11 11	252 59	4 39
1899 11 12	253 06	4 39
1899 11 13	253 13	4 39
1899 11 14	253 19	4 39
1899 11 15	253 26	4 39
1899 11 16	253 33	4 39
1899 11 17	253 40	4 39
1899 11 18	253 47	4 39
1899 11 19	253 54	4 39
1899 11 20	254 01	4 39
1899 11 21	254 07	4 39
1899 11 22	254 14	4 39
1899 11 23	254 21	4 39
1899 11 24	254 28	4 39
1899 11 25	254 35	4 39
1899 11 26	254 42	4 39
1899 11 27	254 49	4 39
1899 11 28	254 56	4 39
1899 11 29	255 03	4 39
1899 11 30	255 10	4 39
1899 12 01	255 18	4 39
1899 12 02	255 25	4 39
1899 12 03	255 32	4 40
1899 12 04	255 39	4 40
1899 12 05	255 46	4 40
1899 12 06	255 53	4 40
1899 12 07	256 00	4 40
1899 12 08	256 07	4 40
1899 12 09	256 14	4 40
1899 12 10	256 21	4 41
1899 12 11	256 28	4 41
1899 12 12	256 35	4 41
1899 12 13	256 42	4 41
1899 12 14	256 49	4 41
1899 12 15	256 56	4 41
1899 12 16	257 03	4 42
1899 12 17	257 10	4 42
1899 12 18	257 17	4 42
1899 12 19	257 24	4 42
1899 12 20	257 31	4 42
1899 12 21	257 38	4 43
1899 12 22	257 45	4 43
1899 12 23	257 52	4 43
1899 12 24	257 59	4 43
1899 12 25	258 06	4 44
1899 12 26	258 13	4 44
1899 12 27	258 20	4 44
1899 12 28	258 27	4 44
1899 12 29	258 33	4 45
1899 12 30	258 40	4 45
1899 12 31	258 47	4 45
1900 01 01	258 54	4 46
1900 01 02	259 01	4 46
1900 01 03	259 07	4 46
1900 01 04	259 14	4 47
1900 01 05	259 20	4 47
1900 01 06	259 27	4 47
1900 01 07	259 34	4 48
1900 01 08	259 40	4 48
1900 01 09	259 47	4 48
1900 01 10	259 53	4 49
1900 01 11	259 59	4 49
1900 01 12	260 06	4 49
1900 01 13	260 12	4 50
1900 01 14	260 18	4 50
1900 01 15	260 24	4 50
1900 01 16	260 31	4 51
1900 01 17	260 37	4 51
1900 01 18	260 43	4 52
1900 01 19	260 49	4 52
1900 01 20	260 55	4 52
1900 01 21	261 01	4 53
1900 01 22	261 07	4 53
1900 01 23	261 13	4 54
1900 01 24	261 18	4 54
1900 01 25	261 24	4 55
1900 01 26	261 30	4 55
1900 01 27	261 35	4 56
1900 01 28	261 41	4 56
1900 01 29	261 46	4 56
1900 01 30	261 52	4 57
1900 01 31	261 57	4 57
1900 02 01	262 03	4 58
1900 02 02	262 08	4 58
1900 02 03	262 13	4 59
1900 02 04	262 18	4 59
1900 02 05	262 23	5 00
1900 02 06	262 28	5 00
1900 02 07	262 33	5 01
1900 02 08	262 38	5 01
1900 02 09	262 43	5 02
1900 02 10	262 48	5 03
1900 02 11	262 52	5 03
1900 02 12	262 57	5 04
1900 02 13	263 01	5 04
1900 02 14	263 06	5 05
1900 02 15	263 10	5 05
1900 02 16	263 15	5 06
1900 02 17	263 19	5 06
1900 02 18	263 23	5 07
1900 02 19	263 27	5 08
1900 02 20	263 31	5 08
1900 02 21	263 35	5 09
1900 02 22	263 39	5 09
1900 02 23	263 42	5 10
1900 02 24	263 46	5 10
1900 02 25	263 50	5 11
1900 02 26	263 53	5 12
1900 02 27	263 57	5 12
1900 02 28	264 00	5 13
1900 03 01	264 03	5 14
1900 03 02	264 06	5 14
1900 03 03	264 09	5 15
1900 03 04	264 12	5 15
1900 03 05	264 15	5 16
1900 03 06	264 18	5 17
1900 03 07	264 21	5 17
1900 03 08	264 23	5 18
1900 03 09	264 26	5 19
1900 03 10	264 28	5 19
1900 03 11	264 31	5 20
1900 03 12	264 33	5 21
1900 03 13	264 35	5 21
1900 03 14	264 37	5 22
1900 03 15	264 39	5 23
1900 03 16	264 41	5 23
1900 03 17	264 43	5 24
1900 03 18	264 45	5 24
1900 03 19	264 46	5 25
1900 03 20	264 48	5 26
1900 03 21	264 49	5 26
1900 03 22	264 51	5 27
1900 03 23	264 52	5 28
1900 03 24	264 53	5 28
1900 03 25	264 54	5 29
1900 03 26	264 55	5 30
1900 03 27	264 56	5 31
1900 03 28	264 57	5 31
1900 03 29	264 57	5 32
1900 03 30	264 58	5 33
1900 03 31	264 58	5 33
1900 04 01	264 59	5 34
1900 04 02	264 59	5 35
1900 04 03	264 59	5 35
1900 04 04	264 59	5 36
1900 04 05	264 59	5 37
1900 04 06	264 59	5 37
1900 04 07	264 59	5 38
1900 04 08	264 59	5 39
1900 04 09	264 58	5 39
1900 04 10	264 58	5 40
1900 04 11	264 57	5 40
1900 04 12	264 57	5 41
1900 04 13	264 56	5 42
1900 04 14	264 55	5 42
1900 04 15	264 54	5 43
1900 04 16	264 53	5 44
1900 04 17	264 52	5 44
1900 04 18	264 51	5 45
1900 04 19	264 50	5 46
1900 04 20	264 48	5 46
1900 04 21	264 47	5 47
1900 04 22	264 45	5 47
1900 04 23	264 43	5 48

1900	04	24	264	42	5	49
1900	04	25	264	40	5	49
1900	04	26	264	38	5	50
1900	04	27	264	36	5	50
1900	04	28	264	34	5	51
1900	04	29	264	32	5	52
1900	04	30	264	30	5	52
1900	05	01	264	27	5	53
1900	05	02	264	25	5	53
1900	05	03	264	23	5	54
1900	05	04	264	20	5	54
1900	05	05	264	17	5	55
1900	05	06	264	15	5	55
1900	05	07	264	12	5	56
1900	05	08	264	09	5	56
1900	05	09	264	06	5	57
1900	05	10	264	04	5	58
1900	05	11	264	01	5	50
1900	05	12	263	57	5	58
1900	05	13	263	54	5	59
1900	05	14	263	51	5	59
1900	05	15	263	48	6	00
1900	05	16	263	45	6	00
1900	05	17	263	41	6	01
1900	05	18	263	38	6	01
1900	05	19	263	35	6	02
1900	05	20	263	31	6	02
1900	05	21	263	27	6	02
1900	05	22	263	24	6	03
1900	05	23	263	20	6	03
1900	05	24	263	17	6	04
1900	05	25	263	13	6	04
1900	05	26	263	09	6	04
1900	05	27	263	05	6	05
1900	05	28	263	02	6	05
1900	05	29	262	58	6	05
1900	05	30	262	54	6	06
1900	05	31	262	50	6	06
1900	06	01	262	46	6	06
1900	06	02	262	42	6	06
1900	06	03	262	38	6	07
1900	06	04	262	34	6	07
1900	06	05	262	30	6	07
1900	06	06	262	26	6	07
1900	06	07	262	22	6	08
1900	06	08	262	18	6	08
1900	06	09	262	14	6	08
1900	06	10	262	10	6	08
1900	06	11	262	06	6	08
1900	06	12	262	01	6	09
1900	06	13	261	57	6	09
1900	06	14	261	53	6	09
1900	06	15	261	49	6	09
1900	06	16	261	45	6	09
1900	06	17	261	41	6	09
1900	06	18	261	37	6	09
1900	06	19	261	33	6	09
1900	06	20	261	29	6	09
1900	06	21	261	25	6	09
1900	06	22	261	21	6	10
1900	06	23	261	17	6	10
1900	06	24	261	13	6	10
1900	06	25	261	09	6	10
1900	06	26	261	05	6	10
1900	06	27	261	01	6	10
1900	06	28	260	57	6	10
1900	06	29	260	53	6	10
1900	06	30	260	50	6	09
1900	07	01	260	46	6	09
1900	07	02	260	42	6	09
1900	07	03	260	38	6	09
1900	07	04	260	35	6	09
1900	07	05	260	31	6	09
1900	07	06	260	27	6	09
1900	07	07	260	24	6	09
1900	07	08	260	20	6	09
1900	07	09	260	17	6	09
1900	07	10	260	14	6	08
1900	07	11	260	10	6	08
1900	07	12	260	07	6	08
1900	07	13	260	04	6	08
1900	07	14	260	01	6	08
1900	07	15	259	58	6	08
1900	07	16	259	55	6	07
1900	07	17	259	52	6	07
1900	07	18	259	49	6	07
1900	07	19	259	46	6	07
1900	07	20	259	43	6	07
1900	07	21	259	40	6	06
1900	07	22	259	38	6	06
1900	07	23	259	35	6	06
1900	07	24	259	33	6	06
1900	07	25	259	30	6	05
1900	07	26	259	28	6	05
1900	07	27	259	25	6	05
1900	07	28	259	23	6	04
1900	07	29	259	21	6	04
1900	07	30	259	19	6	04
1900	07	31	259	17	6	03
1900	08	01	259	15	6	03
1900	08	02	259	13	6	03
1900	08	03	259	12	6	02
1900	08	04	259	10	6	02
1900	08	05	259	08	6	02
1900	08	06	259	07	6	01
1900	08	07	259	05	6	01

1900	08	08	259	04	6	01
1900	08	09	259	03	6	00
1900	08	10	259	02	6	00
1900	08	11	259	01	6	00
1900	08	12	259	00	5	59
1900	08	13	258	59	5	59
1900	08	14	258	58	5	58
1900	08	15	258	57	5	58
1900	08	16	258	57	5	58
1900	08	17	258	56	5	57
1900	08	18	258	56	5	57
1900	08	19	258	55	5	57
1900	08	20	258	55	5	56
1900	08	21	258	55	5	56
1900	08	22	258	55	5	55
1900	08	23	258	55	5	55
1900	08	24	258	55	5	54
1700	00	25	258	55	5	54
1900	08	26	258	55	5	54
1900	08	27	258	55	5	53
1900	08	28	258	56	5	53
1900	08	29	258	56	5	52
1900	08	30	258	57	5	52
1900	08	31	258	58	5	52
1900	09	01	258	59	5	51
1900	09	02	258	59	5	51
1900	09	03	259	00	5	50
1900	09	04	259	02	5	50
1900	09	05	259	03	5	49
1900	09	06	259	04	5	49
1900	09	07	259	05	5	49
1900	09	08	259	07	5	48
1900	09	09	259	08	5	48
1900	09	10	259	10	5	47
1900	09	11	259	12	5	47
1900	09	12	259	13	5	47
1900	09	13	259	15	5	46
1900	09	14	259	17	5	46
1900	09	15	259	19	5	45
1900	09	16	259	21	5	45
1900	09	17	259	24	5	44
1900	09	18	259	26	5	44
1900	09	19	259	28	5	44
1900	09	20	259	31	5	43
1900	09	21	259	33	5	43
1900	09	22	259	36	5	42
1900	09	23	259	39	5	42
1900	09	24	259	41	5	42
1900	09	25	259	44	5	41
1900	09	26	259	47	5	41
1900	09	27	259	50	5	40
1900	09	28	259	54	5	40
1900	09	29	259	57	5	40
1900	09	30	260	00	5	39
1900	10	01	260	03	5	39
1900	10	02	260	07	5	39
1900	10	03	260	10	5	38
1900	10	04	260	14	5	38
1900	10	05	260	18	5	38
1900	10	06	260	21	5	37
1900	10	07	260	25	5	37
1900	10	08	260	29	5	36
1900	10	09	260	33	5	36
1900	10	10	260	37	5	36
1900	10	11	260	41	5	35
1900	10	12	260	45	5	35
1900	10	13	260	49	5	35
1900	10	14	260	54	5	35
1900	10	15	260	58	5	34
1900	10	16	261	03	5	34
1900	10	17	261	07	5	34
1900	10	18	261	12	5	33
1900	10	19	261	16	5	33
1900	10	20	261	21	5	33
1900	10	21	261	26	5	32
1900	10	22	261	31	5	32
1900	10	23	261	35	5	32
1900	10	24	261	40	5	32
1900	10	25	261	45	5	31
1900	10	26	261	50	5	31
1900	10	27	261	55	5	31
1900	10	28	262	01	5	31
1900	10	29	262	06	5	30
1900	10	30	262	11	5	30
1900	10	31	262	16	5	30
1900	11	01	262	22	5	30
1700	11	02	262	27	5	29
1900	11	03	262	33	5	29
1900	11	04	262	38	5	29
1900	11	05	262	44	5	29
1900	11	06	262	49	5	29
1900	11	07	262	55	5	28
1900	11	08	263	01	5	28
1900	11	09	263	06	5	28
1900	11	10	263	12	5	28
1900	11	11	263	18	5	28
1900	11	12	263	24	5	28
1900	11	13	263	30	5	27
1900	11	14	263	36	5	27
1900	11	15	263	42	5	27
1900	11	16	263	48	5	27
1900	11	17	263	54	5	27
1900	11	18	264	00	5	27
1900	11	19	264	06	5	27
1900	11	20	264	12	5	27
1900	11	21	264	18	5	26

1900	11	22	264	24	5	26
1900	11	23	264	30	5	26
1900	11	24	264	37	5	26
1900	11	25	264	43	5	26
1900	11	26	264	49	5	26
1900	11	27	264	56	5	26
1900	11	28	265	02	5	26
1900	11	29	265	08	5	26
1900	11	30	265	15	5	26
1900	12	01	265	21	5	26
1900	12	02	265	28	5	26
1900	12	03	265	34	5	26
1900	12	04	265	40	5	26
1900	12	05	265	47	5	26
1900	12	06	265	53	5	26
1900	12	07	266	00	5	26
1900	12	08	266	06	5	26
1700	12	07	266	13	5	26
1900	12	10	266	20	5	26
1900	12	11	266	26	5	26
1900	12	12	266	33	5	26
1900	12	13	266	39	5	26
1900	12	14	266	46	5	26
1900	12	15	266	52	5	26
1900	12	16	266	59	5	26
1900	12	17	267	05	5	26
1900	12	18	267	12	5	26
1900	12	19	267	19	5	26
1900	12	20	267	25	5	27
1900	12	21	267	32	5	27
1900	12	22	267	38	5	27
1900	12	23	267	45	5	27
1900	12	24	267	51	5	27
1900	12	25	267	58	5	27
1900	12	26	268	05	5	27
1900	12	27	268	11	5	27
1900	12	28	268	18	5	28
1900	12	29	268	24	5	28
1900	12	30	268	31	5	28
1900	12	31	268	37	5	28
1901	01	01	268	44	5	28
1901	01	02	268	50	5	28
1901	01	03	268	56	5	29
1901	01	04	269	03	5	29
1901	01	05	269	09	5	29
1901	01	06	269	16	5	29
1901	01	07	269	22	5	30
1901	01	08	269	28	5	30
1901	01	09	269	35	5	30
1901	01	10	269	41	5	30
1901	01	11	269	47	5	31
1901	01	12	269	54	5	31
1901	01	13	270	00	5	31
1901	01	14	270	06	5	31
1901	01	15	270	12	5	32
1901	01	16	270	18	5	32
1901	01	17	270	24	5	32
1901	01	18	270	30	5	33
1901	01	19	270	36	5	33
1901	01	20	270	42	5	33
1901	01	21	270	48	5	34
1901	01	22	270	54	5	34
1901	01	23	271	00	5	34
1901	01	24	271	06	5	35
1901	01	25	271	12	5	35
1901	01	26	271	18	5	35
1901	01	27	271	23	5	36
1901	01	28	271	29	5	36
1901	01	29	271	35	5	36
1901	01	30	271	40	5	37
1901	01	31	271	46	5	37
1901	02	01	271	51	5	38
1901	02	02	271	57	5	38
1901	02	03	272	02	5	38
1901	02	04	272	07	5	39
1901	02	05	272	13	5	39
1901	02	06	272	18	5	40
1901	02	07	272	23	5	40
1901	02	08	272	28	5	40
1901	02	09	272	33	5	41
1901	02	10	272	38	5	41
1901	02	11	272	43	5	42
1901	02	12	272	48	5	42
1901	02	13	272	53	5	43
1901	02	14	272	58	5	43
1901	02	15	273	03	5	44
1901	02	16	273	07	5	44
1901	02	17	273	12	5	45
1901	02	18	273	17	5	45
1901	02	19	273	21	5	46
1901	02	20	273	25	5	46
1901	02	21	273	30	5	47
1901	02	22	273	34	5	47
1901	02	23	273	38	5	48
1901	02	24	273	42	5	48
1901	02	25	273	46	5	49
1901	02	26	273	50	5	49
1901	02	27	273	54	5	50
1901	02	28	273	58	5	51
1901	03	01	274	02	5	51
1901	03	02	274	06	5	52
1901	03	03	274	09	5	52
1901	03	04	274	13	5	53
1901	03	05	274	16	5	53
1901	03	06	274	20	5	54
1901	03	07	274	23	5	55

1901	03	08	274	26	5	55
1901	03	09	274	30	5	56
1901	03	10	274	33	5	56
1901	03	11	274	36	5	57
1901	03	12	274	39	5	58
1901	03	13	274	41	5	58
1901	03	14	274	44	5	59
1901	03	15	274	47	5	59
1901	03	16	274	49	6	00
1901	03	17	274	52	6	01
1901	03	18	274	54	6	01
1901	03	19	274	57	6	02
1901	03	20	274	59	6	02
1901	03	21	275	01	6	03
1901	03	22	275	03	6	04
1901	03	23	275	05	6	04
1901	03	24	275	07	6	05
1701	03	25	275	09	6	06
1901	03	26	275	11	6	06
1901	03	27	275	13	6	07
1901	03	28	275	14	6	08
1901	03	29	275	16	6	08
1901	03	30	275	17	6	09
1901	03	31	275	18	6	10
1901	04	01	275	20	6	10
1901	04	02	275	21	6	11
1901	04	03	275	22	6	11
1901	04	04	275	23	6	12
1901	04	05	275	24	6	13
1901	04	06	275	24	6	13
1901	04	07	275	25	6	14
1901	04	08	275	26	6	15
1901	04	09	275	26	6	15
1901	04	10	275	27	6	16
1901	04	11	275	27	6	17
1901	04	12	275	27	6	17
1901	04	13	275	27	6	18
1901	04	14	275	27	6	19
1901	04	15	275	27	6	19
1901	04	16	275	27	6	20
1901	04	17	275	27	6	21
1901	04	18	275	27	6	21
1901	04	19	275	26	6	22
1901	04	20	275	26	6	22
1901	04	21	275	25	6	23
1901	04	22	275	25	6	24
1901	04	23	275	24	6	24
1901	04	24	275	23	6	25
1901	04	25	275	22	6	26
1901	04	26	275	21	6	26
1901	04	27	275	20	6	27
1901	04	28	275	19	6	27
1901	04	29	275	18	6	28
1901	04	30	275	17	6	29
1901	05	01	275	15	6	29
1901	05	02	275	14	6	30
1901	05	03	275	12	6	30
1901	05	04	275	10	6	31
1901	05	05	275	09	6	32
1901	05	06	275	07	6	32
1901	05	07	275	05	6	33
1901	05	08	275	03	6	33
1901	05	09	275	01	6	34
1901	05	10	274	59	6	34
1901	05	11	274	57	6	35
1901	05	12	274	55	6	35
1901	05	13	274	52	6	36
1901	05	14	274	50	6	36
1901	05	15	274	48	6	37
1901	05	16	274	45	6	37
1901	05	17	274	42	6	38
1901	05	18	274	40	6	38
1901	05	19	274	37	6	39
1901	05	20	274	34	6	39
1901	05	21	274	31	6	40
1901	05	22	274	29	6	40
1901	05	23	274	26	6	41
1901	05	24	274	23	6	41
1901	05	25	274	20	6	42
1901	05	26	274	16	6	42
1901	05	27	274	13	6	42
1901	05	28	274	10	6	43
1901	05	29	274	07	6	43
1901	05	30	274	03	6	44
1901	05	31	274	00	6	44
1901	06	01	273	57	6	44
1901	06	02	273	53	6	45
1901	06	03	273	50	6	45
1901	06	04	273	46	6	45
1901	06	05	273	43	6	46
1901	06	06	273	39	6	46
1901	06	07	273	35	6	46
1901	06	08	273	32	6	47
1901	06	09	273	28	6	47
1901	06	10	273	24	6	47
1901	06	11	273	21	6	47
1901	06	12	273	17	6	48
1901	06	13	273	13	6	48
1901	06	14	273	09	6	48
1901	06	15	273	05	6	48
1901	06	16	273	02	6	48

1901	06	17	272	58	6	49
1901	06	18	272	54	6	49
1901	06	19	272	50	6	49
1901	06	20	272	46	6	49
1901	06	21	272	42	6	49
1901	06	22	272	38	6	49
1901	06	23	272	34	6	50
1901	06	24	272	30	6	50
1901	06	25	272	26	6	50
1901	06	26	272	22	6	50
1901	06	27	272	19	6	50
1901	06	28	272	15	6	50
1901	06	29	272	11	6	50
1901	06	30	272	07	6	50
1901	07	01	272	03	6	50
1901	07	02	271	59	6	50
1901	07	03	271	55	6	50
1901	07	04	271	51	6	50
1901	07	05	271	48	6	50
1901	07	06	271	44	6	50
1901	07	07	271	40	6	50
1901	07	08	271	36	6	50
1901	07	09	271	33	6	50
1901	07	10	271	29	6	50
1901	07	11	271	25	6	50
1901	07	12	271	22	6	49
1901	07	13	271	18	6	49
1901	07	14	271	14	6	49
1901	07	15	271	11	6	49
1901	07	16	271	07	6	49
1901	07	17	271	04	6	49
1901	07	18	271	00	6	49
1901	07	19	270	57	6	48
1901	07	20	270	54	6	48
1901	07	21	270	50	6	48
1901	07	22	270	47	6	48
1901	07	23	270	44	6	48
1901	07	24	270	41	6	47
1901	07	25	270	38	6	47
1901	07	26	270	35	6	47
1901	07	27	270	32	6	47
1901	07	28	270	29	6	46
1901	07	29	270	26	6	46
1901	07	30	270	23	6	46
1901	07	31	270	21	6	45
1901	08	01	270	18	6	45
1901	08	02	270	15	6	45
1901	08	03	270	13	6	44
1901	08	04	270	10	6	44
1901	08	05	270	08	6	44
1901	08	06	270	06	6	43
1901	08	07	270	03	6	43
1901	08	08	270	01	6	43
1901	08	09	269	59	6	42
1901	08	10	269	57	6	42
1901	08	11	269	55	6	42
1901	08	12	269	53	6	41
1901	08	13	269	51	6	41
1901	08	14	269	50	6	40
1901	08	15	269	48	6	40
1901	08	16	269	46	6	40
1901	08	17	269	45	6	39
1901	08	18	269	43	6	39
1901	08	19	269	42	6	38
1901	08	20	269	41	6	38
1901	08	21	269	39	6	38
1901	08	22	269	38	6	37
1901	08	23	269	37	6	37
1901	08	24	269	36	6	36
1901	08	25	269	35	6	36
1901	08	26	269	35	6	35
1901	08	27	269	34	6	35
1901	08	28	269	33	6	34
1901	08	29	269	33	6	34
1901	08	30	269	32	6	33
1901	08	31	269	32	6	33
1901	09	01	269	32	6	33
1901	09	02	269	31	6	32
1901	09	03	269	31	6	32
1901	09	04	269	31	6	31
1901	09	05	269	31	6	31
1901	09	06	269	31	6	30
1901	09	07	269	32	6	30
1901	09	08	269	32	6	29
1901	09	09	269	32	6	29
1901	09	10	269	33	6	28
1901	09	11	269	33	6	28
1901	09	12	269	34	6	27
1901	09	13	269	35	6	27
1901	09	14	269	35	6	26
1901	09	15	269	36	6	26
1901	09	16	269	37	6	25
1901	09	17	269	38	6	25
1901	09	18	269	40	6	24
1901	09	19	269	41	6	24
1901	09	20	269	42	6	23
1901	09	21	269	44	6	23
1901	09	22	269	45	6	22
1901	09	23	269	47	6	22
1901	09	24	269	48	6	21
1901	09	25	269	50	6	21
1901	09	26	269	52	6	20
1901	09	27	269	54	6	20
1901	09	28	269	56	6	20
1901	09	29	269	58	6	19
1901	09	30	270	00	6	19
1901	10	01	270	02	6	18
1901	10	02	270	05	6	18
1901	10	03	270	07	6	17
1901	10	04	270	09	6	17
1901	10	05	270	12	6	16
1901	10	06	270	15	6	16
1901	10	07	270	17	6	15
1901	10	08	270	20	6	15
1901	10	09	270	23	6	14
1901	10	10	270	26	6	14
1901	10	11	270	29	6	14
1901	10	12	270	32	6	13
1901	10	13	270	35	6	13
1901	10	14	270	38	6	12
1901	10	15	270	42	6	12
1901	10	16	270	45	6	11
1901	10	17	270	48	6	11
1901	10	18	270	52	6	11
1901	10	19	270	55	6	10
1901	10	20	270	59	6	10
1901	10	21	271	03	6	09
1901	10	22	271	07	6	09
1901	10	23	271	10	6	09
1901	10	24	271	14	6	08
1901	10	25	271	18	6	08
1901	10	26	271	22	6	08
1901	10	27	271	27	6	07
1901	10	28	271	31	6	07
1901	10	29	271	35	6	06
1901	10	30	271	39	6	06
1901	10	31	271	44	6	06
1901	11	01	271	48	6	05
1901	11	02	271	52	6	05
1901	11	03	271	57	6	05
1901	11	04	272	01	6	04
1901	11	05	272	06	6	04
1901	11	06	272	11	6	04
1901	11	07	272	16	6	04
1901	11	08	272	20	6	03
1901	11	09	272	25	6	03
1901	11	10	272	30	6	03
1901	11	11	272	35	6	02
1901	11	12	272	40	6	02
1901	11	13	272	45	6	02
1901	11	14	272	50	6	02
1901	11	15	272	55	6	01
1901	11	16	273	00	6	01
1901	11	17	273	06	6	01
1901	11	18	273	11	6	01
1901	11	19	273	16	6	00
1901	11	20	273	22	6	00
1901	11	21	273	27	6	00
1901	11	22	273	32	6	00
1901	11	23	273	38	6	00
1901	11	24	273	43	5	59
1901	11	25	273	49	5	59
1901	11	26	273	54	5	59
1901	11	27	274	00	5	59
1901	11	28	274	06	5	59
1901	11	29	274	11	5	58
1901	11	30	274	17	5	58
1901	12	01	274	23	5	58
1901	12	02	274	28	5	58
1901	12	03	274	34	5	58
1901	12	04	274	40	5	58
1901	12	05	274	46	5	58
1901	12	06	274	52	5	57
1901	12	07	274	58	5	57
1901	12	08	275	04	5	57
1901	12	09	275	09	5	57
1901	12	10	275	15	5	57
1901	12	11	275	21	5	57
1901	12	12	275	27	5	57
1901	12	13	275	33	5	57
1901	12	14	275	39	5	57
1901	12	15	275	45	5	57
1901	12	16	275	51	5	57
1901	12	17	275	58	5	57
1901	12	18	276	04	5	57
1901	12	19	276	10	5	57
1901	12	20	276	16	5	57
1901	12	21	276	22	5	57
1901	12	22	276	28	5	57
1901	12	23	276	34	5	57
1901	12	24	276	40	5	57
1901	12	25	276	46	5	57
1901	12	26	276	52	5	57
1901	12	27	276	59	5	57
1901	12	28	277	05	5	57
1901	12	29	277	11	5	57
1901	12	30	277	17	5	57
1901	12	31	277	23	5	57
1902	01	01	277	29	5	57
1902	01	02	277	35	5	57
1902	01	03	277	41	5	57
1902	01	04	277	48	5	57
1902	01	05	277	54	5	58
1902	01	06	278	00	5	58
1902	01	07	278	06	5	58
1902	01	08	278	12	5	58
1902	01	09	278	18	5	58
1902	01	10	278	24	5	58
1902	01	11	278	30	5	58
1902	01	12	278	36	5	58
1902	01	13	278	42	5	59
1902	01	14	278	48	5	59
1902	01	15	278	54	5	59
1902	01	16	279	00	5	59
1902	01	17	279	06	5	59
1902	01	18	279	12	6	00
1902	01	19	279	18	6	00
1902	01	20	279	23	6	00
1902	01	21	279	29	6	00
1902	01	22	279	35	6	00
1902	01	23	279	41	6	01
1902	01	24	279	47	6	01
1902	01	25	279	52	6	01
1902	01	26	279	58	6	01
1902	01	27	280	04	6	02
1902	01	28	280	09	6	02
1902	01	29	280	15	6	02
1902	01	30	280	20	6	03
1902	01	31	280	26	6	03
1902	02	01	280	32	6	03
1902	02	02	280	37	6	04
1902	02	03	280	42	6	04
1902	02	04	280	48	6	04
1902	02	05	280	53	6	04
1902	02	06	280	58	6	05
1902	02	07	281	04	6	05
1902	02	08	281	09	6	06
1902	02	09	281	14	6	06
1902	02	10	281	19	6	06
1902	02	11	281	24	6	07
1902	02	12	281	29	6	07
1902	02	13	281	34	6	07
1902	02	14	281	39	6	08
1902	02	15	281	44	6	08
1902	02	16	281	49	6	09
1902	02	17	281	54	6	09
1902	02	18	281	59	6	09
1902	02	19	282	03	6	10
1902	02	20	282	08	6	10
1902	02	21	282	12	6	11
1902	02	22	282	17	6	11
1902	02	23	282	21	6	12
1902	02	24	282	26	6	12
1902	02	25	282	30	6	12
1902	02	26	282	34	6	13
1902	02	27	282	39	6	13
1902	02	28	282	43	6	14
1902	03	01	282	47	6	14
1902	03	02	282	51	6	15
1902	03	03	282	55	6	15
1902	03	04	282	59	6	16
1902	03	05	283	03	6	16
1902	03	06	283	07	6	17
1902	03	07	283	10	6	17
1902	03	08	283	14	6	18
1902	03	09	283	17	6	18
1902	03	10	283	21	6	19
1902	03	11	283	24	6	19
1902	03	12	283	28	6	20
1902	03	13	283	31	6	21
1902	03	14	283	34	6	21
1902	03	15	283	38	6	22
1902	03	16	283	41	6	22
1902	03	17	283	44	6	23
1902	03	18	283	47	6	23
1902	03	19	283	50	6	24
1902	03	20	283	52	6	24
1902	03	21	283	55	6	25
1902	03	22	283	58	6	26
1902	03	23	284	00	6	26
1902	03	24	284	03	6	27
1902	03	25	284	05	6	27
1902	03	26	284	07	6	28
1902	03	27	284	10	6	28
1902	03	28	284	12	6	29
1902	03	29	284	14	6	30
1902	03	30	284	16	6	30
1902	03	31	284	18	6	31
1902	04	01	284	20	6	31
1902	04	02	284	22	6	32
1902	04	03	284	23	6	33
1902	04	04	284	25	6	33
1902	04	05	284	26	6	34
1902	04	06	284	28	6	35
1902	04	07	284	29	6	35
1902	04	08	284	31	6	36
1902	04	09	284	32	6	36
1902	04	10	284	33	6	37
1902	04	11	284	34	6	38
1902	04	12	284	35	6	38
1902	04	13	284	36	6	39
1902	04	14	284	37	6	39
1902	04	15	284	37	6	40
1902	04	16	284	38	6	41
1902	04	17	284	38	6	41
1902	04	18	284	39	6	42
1902	04	19	284	39	6	43
1902	04	20	284	39	6	43
1902	04	21	284	40	6	44
1902	04	22	284	40	6	44
1902	04	23	284	40	6	45
1902	04	24	284	40	6	46
1902	04	25	284	40	6	46
1902	04	26	284	39	6	47
1902	04	27	284	39	6	47
1902	04	28	284	39	6	48
1902	04	29	284	38	6	49
1902	04	30	284	38	6	49
1902	05	01	284	37	6	50
1902	05	02	284	36	6	50
1902	05	03	284	36	6	51
1902	05	04	284	35	6	52
1902	05	05	284	34	6	52
1902	05	06	284	33	6	53
1902	05	07	284	32	6	53
1902	05	08	284	30	6	54
1902	05	09	284	29	6	54
1902	05	10	284	28	6	55
1902	05	11	284	26	6	56
1902	05	12	284	25	6	56
1902	05	13	284	23	6	57
1902	05	14	284	22	6	57
1902	05	15	284	20	6	58
1902	05	16	284	18	6	58
1902	05	17	284	16	6	59
1902	05	18	284	14	6	59
1902	05	19	284	12	7	00
1902	05	20	284	10	7	00
1902	05	21	284	08	7	01
1902	05	22	284	06	7	01
1902	05	23	284	04	7	02
1902	05	24	284	01	7	02
1902	05	25	283	59	7	03
1902	05	26	283	56	7	03
1902	05	27	283	54	7	04
1902	05	28	283	51	7	04
1902	05	29	283	49	7	05
1902	05	30	283	46	7	05
1902	05	31	283	43	7	05
1902	06	01	283	40	7	06
1902	06	02	283	38	7	06
1902	06	03	283	35	7	07
1902	06	04	283	32	7	07
1902	06	05	283	29	7	07
1902	06	06	283	26	7	08
1902	06	07	283	23	7	08
1902	06	08	283	19	7	08
1902	06	09	283	16	7	09
1902	06	10	283	13	7	09
1902	06	11	283	10	7	09
1902	06	12	283	06	7	10
1902	06	13	283	03	7	10
1902	06	14	283	00	7	10
1902	06	15	282	56	7	11
1902	06	16	282	53	7	11
1902	06	17	282	49	7	11
1902	06	18	282	46	7	11
1902	06	19	282	42	7	12
1902	06	20	282	38	7	12
1902	06	21	282	35	7	12
1902	06	22	282	31	7	12
1902	06	23	282	28	7	12
1902	06	24	282	24	7	13
1902	06	25	282	20	7	13
1902	06	26	282	17	7	13
1902	06	27	282	13	7	13
1902	06	28	282	09	7	13
1902	06	29	282	05	7	13
1902	06	30	282	02	7	13
1902	07	01	281	58	7	13
1902	07	02	281	54	7	14
1902	07	03	281	50	7	14
1902	07	04	281	47	7	14
1902	07	05	281	43	7	14
1902	07	06	281	39	7	14
1902	07	07	281	35	7	14
1902	07	08	281	32	7	14
1902	07	09	281	28	7	14
1902	07	10	281	24	7	14
1902	07	11	281	20	7	14
1902	07	12	281	17	7	14
1902	07	13	281	13	7	14
1902	07	14	281	09	7	14
1902	07	15	281	06	7	14
1902	07	16	281	02	7	13
1902	07	17	280	58	7	13
1902	07	18	280	55	7	13
1902	07	19	280	51	7	13
1902	07	20	280	48	7	13
1902	07	21	280	44	7	13
1902	07	22	280	40	7	13
1902	07	23	280	37	7	13
1902	07	24	280	34	7	12
1902	07	25	280	30	7	12
1902	07	26	280	27	7	12
1902	07	27	280	24	7	12
1902	07	28	280	20	7	12
1902	07	29	280	17	7	11
1902	07	30	280	14	7	11
1902	07	31	280	11	7	11
1902	08	01	280	08	7	11
1902	08	02	280	04	7	10
1902	08	03	280	01	7	10
1902	08	04	279	58	7	10
1902	08	05	279	56	7	10
1902	08	06	279	53	7	09
1902	08	07	279	50	7	09
1902	08	08	279	47	7	09

15 VS 38

1902	08	09	279	44	7	08
1902	08	10	279	42	7	08
1902	08	11	279	39	7	08
1902	08	12	279	37	7	07
1902	08	13	279	34	7	07
1902	08	14	279	32	7	07
1902	08	15	279	29	7	06
1902	08	16	279	27	7	06
1902	08	17	279	25	7	06
1902	08	18	279	23	7	05
1902	08	19	279	21	7	05
1902	08	20	279	19	7	04
1902	08	21	279	17	7	04
1902	08	22	279	15	7	04
1902	08	23	279	13	7	03
1902	08	24	279	11	7	03
1902	08	25	279	10	7	02
1902	08	26	279	08	7	02
1902	08	27	279	07	7	01
1902	08	28	279	05	7	01
1902	08	29	279	04	7	00
1902	08	30	279	02	7	00
1902	08	31	279	01	6	59
1902	09	01	279	00	6	59
1902	09	02	278	59	6	59
1902	09	03	278	58	6	58
1902	09	04	278	57	6	58
1902	09	05	278	56	6	57
1902	09	06	278	55	6	57
1902	09	07	278	55	6	56
1902	09	08	278	54	6	56
1902	09	09	278	54	6	55
1902	09	10	278	53	6	55
1902	09	11	278	53	6	54
1902	09	12	278	53	6	54
1902	09	13	278	52	6	53
1902	09	14	278	52	6	53
1902	09	15	278	52	6	52
1902	09	16	278	52	6	52
1902	09	17	278	52	6	51
1902	09	18	278	53	6	51
1902	09	19	278	53	6	50
1902	09	20	278	53	6	50
1902	09	21	278	54	6	49
1902	09	22	278	54	6	48
1902	09	23	278	55	6	48
1902	09	24	278	56	6	47
1902	09	25	278	56	6	47
1902	09	26	278	57	6	46
1902	09	27	278	58	6	46
1902	09	28	278	59	6	45
1902	09	29	279	00	6	45
1902	09	30	279	02	6	44
1902	10	01	279	03	6	44
1902	10	02	279	04	6	43
1902	10	03	279	06	6	43
1902	10	04	279	07	6	42
1902	10	05	279	09	6	42
1902	10	06	279	10	6	41
1902	10	07	279	12	6	41
1902	10	08	279	14	6	40
1902	10	09	279	16	6	40
1902	10	10	279	18	6	39
1902	10	11	279	20	6	39
1902	10	12	279	22	6	38
1902	10	13	279	24	6	38
1902	10	14	279	26	6	37
1902	10	15	279	29	6	37
1902	10	16	279	31	6	36
1902	10	17	279	34	6	36
1902	10	18	279	36	6	35
1902	10	19	279	39	6	35
1902	10	20	279	42	6	34
1902	10	21	279	44	6	34
1902	10	22	279	47	6	33
1902	10	23	279	50	6	33
1902	10	24	279	53	6	33
1902	10	25	279	56	6	32
1902	10	26	279	59	6	32
1902	10	27	280	03	6	31
1902	10	28	280	06	6	31
1902	10	29	280	09	6	30
1902	10	30	280	13	6	30
1902	10	31	280	16	6	29
1902	11	01	280	20	6	29
1902	11	02	280	23	6	29
1902	11	03	280	27	6	28
1902	11	04	280	30	6	28
1902	11	05	280	34	6	27
1902	11	06	280	38	6	27
1902	11	07	280	42	6	27
1902	11	08	280	46	6	26
1902	11	09	280	50	6	26
1902	11	10	280	54	6	26
1902	11	11	280	58	6	25
1902	11	12	281	02	6	25
1902	11	13	281	07	6	24
1902	11	14	281	11	6	24
1902	11	15	281	15	6	24
1902	11	16	281	20	6	23
1902	11	17	281	24	6	23
1902	11	18	281	28	6	23
1902	11	19	281	33	6	22
1902	11	20	281	38	6	22
1902	11	21	281	42	6	22
1902	11	22	281	47	6	22

1902	11	23	281	52	6	21
1902	11	24	281	56	6	21
1902	11	25	282	01	6	21
1902	11	26	282	06	6	20
1902	11	27	282	11	6	20
1902	11	28	282	16	6	20
1902	11	29	282	21	6	20
1902	11	30	282	26	6	19
1902	12	01	282	31	6	19
1902	12	02	282	36	6	19
1902	12	03	282	41	6	19
1902	12	04	282	46	6	18
1902	12	05	282	52	6	18
1902	12	06	282	57	6	18
1902	12	07	283	02	6	18
1902	12	08	283	07	6	18
1902	12	09	283	13	6	17
1902	12	10	283	18	6	17
1902	12	11	283	23	6	17
1902	12	12	283	29	6	17
1902	12	13	283	34	6	17
1902	12	14	283	40	6	17
1902	12	15	283	45	6	16
1902	12	16	283	51	6	16
1902	12	17	283	56	6	16
1902	12	18	284	02	6	16
1902	12	19	284	07	6	16
1902	12	20	284	13	6	16
1902	12	21	284	18	6	16
1902	12	22	284	24	6	16
1902	12	23	284	30	6	16
1902	12	24	284	35	6	16
1902	12	25	234	41	6	15
1902	12	26	284	47	6	15
1902	12	27	284	52	6	15
1902	12	28	284	58	6	15
1902	12	29	285	04	6	15
1902	12	30	285	09	6	15
1902	12	31	285	15	6	15
1903	01	01	285	21	6	15
1903	01	02	285	26	6	15
1903	01	03	285	32	6	15
1903	01	04	285	38	6	15
1903	01	05	285	44	6	15
1903	01	06	285	49	6	15
1903	01	07	285	55	6	15
1903	01	08	286	01	6	15
1903	01	09	286	07	6	15
1903	01	10	286	12	6	15
1903	01	11	286	18	6	15
1903	01	12	286	24	6	16
1903	01	13	286	29	6	16
1903	01	14	286	35	6	16
1903	01	15	286	41	6	16
1903	01	16	286	47	6	16
1903	01	17	286	52	6	16
1903	01	18	286	58	6	16
1903	01	19	287	04	6	16
1903	01	20	287	09	6	16
1903	01	21	287	15	6	16
1903	01	22	287	20	6	17
1903	01	23	287	26	6	17
1903	01	24	287	32	6	17
1903	01	25	287	37	6	17
1903	01	26	287	43	6	17
1903	01	27	287	48	6	17
1903	01	28	287	54	6	18
1903	01	29	287	59	6	18
1903	01	30	288	05	6	18
1903	01	31	288	10	6	18
1903	02	01	288	15	6	18
1903	02	02	288	21	6	19
1903	02	03	288	26	6	19
1903	02	04	288	31	6	19
1903	02	05	288	37	6	19
1903	02	06	288	42	6	20
1903	02	07	288	47	6	20
1903	02	08	288	52	6	20
1903	02	09	288	57	6	20
1903	02	10	289	03	6	21
1903	02	11	289	08	6	21
1903	02	12	289	13	6	21
1903	02	13	289	18	6	21
1903	02	14	289	23	6	22
1903	02	15	289	28	6	22
1903	02	16	289	33	6	22
1903	02	17	289	37	6	23
1903	02	18	289	42	6	23
1903	02	19	289	47	6	23
1903	02	20	289	52	6	24
1903	02	21	289	56	6	24
1903	02	22	290	01	6	24
1903	02	23	290	06	6	25
1903	02	24	290	10	6	25
1903	02	25	290	15	6	26
1903	02	26	290	19	6	26
1903	02	27	290	23	6	26
1903	02	28	290	28	6	27
1903	03	01	290	32	6	27
1903	03	02	290	36	6	28
1903	03	03	290	41	6	28
1903	03	04	290	45	6	28
1903	03	05	290	49	6	29
1903	03	06	290	53	6	29
1903	03	07	290	57	6	30
1903	03	08	291	01	6	30

1903	03	09	291	04	6	31
1903	03	10	291	08	6	31
1903	03	11	291	12	6	31
1903	03	12	291	16	6	32
1903	03	13	291	19	6	32
1903	03	14	291	23	6	33
1903	03	15	291	26	6	33
1903	03	16	291	30	6	34
1903	03	17	291	33	6	34
1903	03	18	291	36	6	35
1903	03	19	291	40	6	35
1903	03	20	291	43	6	36
1903	03	21	291	46	6	36
1903	03	22	291	49	6	37
1903	03	23	291	52	6	37
1903	03	24	291	55	6	38
1903	03	25	291	57	6	38
1903	03	26	292	00	6	39
1903	03	27	292	03	6	39
1903	03	28	292	06	6	40
1903	03	29	292	08	6	40
1903	03	30	292	11	6	41
1903	03	31	292	13	6	41
1903	04	01	292	15	6	42
1903	04	02	292	18	6	43
1903	04	03	292	20	6	43
1903	04	04	292	22	6	44
1903	04	05	292	24	6	44
1903	04	06	292	26	6	45
1903	04	07	292	28	6	45
1903	04	08	292	29	6	46
1903	04	09	292	31	6	46
1903	04	10	292	33	6	47
1903	04	11	292	34	6	48
1903	04	12	292	36	6	48
1903	04	13	292	37	6	49
1903	04	14	292	39	6	49
1903	04	15	292	40	6	50
1903	04	16	292	41	6	50
1903	04	17	292	42	6	51
1903	04	18	292	43	6	52
1903	04	19	292	44	6	52
1903	04	20	292	45	6	53
1903	04	21	292	46	6	53
1903	04	22	292	47	6	54
1903	04	23	292	47	6	54
1903	04	24	292	48	6	55
1903	04	25	292	48	6	56
1903	04	26	292	49	6	56
1903	04	27	292	49	6	57
1903	04	28	292	49	6	57
1903	04	29	292	49	6	58
1903	04	30	292	49	6	59
1903	05	01	292	49	6	59
1903	05	02	292	49	7	00
1903	05	03	292	49	7	00
1903	05	04	292	49	7	01
1903	05	05	292	49	7	01
1903	05	06	292	48	7	02
1903	05	07	292	48	7	02
1903	05	08	292	47	7	03
1903	05	09	292	47	7	04
1903	05	10	292	46	7	04
1903	05	11	292	45	7	05
1903	05	12	292	44	7	05
1903	05	13	292	43	7	06
1903	05	14	292	42	7	06
1903	05	15	292	41	7	07
1903	05	16	292	40	7	07
1903	05	17	292	39	7	08
1903	05	18	292	38	7	08
1903	05	19	292	36	7	09
1903	05	20	292	35	7	09
1903	05	21	292	33	7	10
1903	05	22	292	32	7	10
1903	05	23	292	30	7	11
1903	05	24	292	28	7	11
1903	05	25	292	27	7	12
1903	05	26	292	25	7	12
1903	05	27	292	23	7	13
1903	05	28	292	21	7	13
1903	05	29	292	19	7	14
1903	05	30	292	17	7	14
1903	05	31	292	15	7	15
1903	06	01	292	12	7	15
1903	06	02	292	10	7	16
1903	06	03	292	08	7	16
1903	06	04	292	05	7	16
1903	06	05	292	03	7	17
1903	06	06	292	00	7	17
1903	06	07	291	58	7	18
1903	06	08	291	55	7	18
1903	06	09	291	52	7	18
1903	06	10	291	50	7	19
1903	06	11	291	47	7	19
1903	06	12	291	44	7	19
1903	06	13	291	41	7	20
1903	06	14	291	38	7	20
1903	06	15	291	35	7	20
1903	06	16	291	32	7	21
1903	06	17	291	29	7	21
1903	06	18	291	26	7	21
1903	06	19	291	23	7	22
1903	06	20	291	20	7	22
1903	06	21	291	17	7	22
1903	06	22	291	13	7	23

1903	06	23	291	10	7	23
1903	06	24	291	07	7	23
1903	06	25	291	03	7	23
1903	06	26	291	00	7	23
1903	06	27	290	57	7	24
1903	06	28	290	53	7	24
1903	06	29	290	50	7	24
1903	06	30	290	46	7	24
1903	07	01	290	43	7	24
1903	07	02	290	39	7	24
1903	07	03	290	36	7	25
1903	07	04	290	32	7	25
1903	07	05	290	29	7	25
1903	07	06	290	25	7	25
1903	07	07	290	21	7	25
1903	07	08	290	18	7	25
1903	07	09	290	14	7	25
1903	07	10	290	11	7	25
1903	07	11	290	07	7	25
1903	07	12	290	03	7	25
1903	07	13	290	00	7	25
1903	07	14	289	56	7	25
1903	07	15	289	53	7	25
1903	07	16	289	49	7	25
1903	07	17	289	45	7	25
1903	07	18	289	42	7	25
1903	07	19	289	38	7	25
1903	07	20	289	35	7	25
1903	07	21	289	31	7	25
1903	07	22	289	27	7	25
1903	07	23	289	24	7	25
1903	07	24	289	20	7	25
1903	07	25	289	17	7	25
1903	07	26	289	13	7	25
1903	07	27	289	10	7	25
1903	07	28	289	06	7	25
1903	07	29	289	03	7	24
1903	07	30	289	00	7	24
1903	07	31	288	56	7	24
1903	08	01	288	53	7	24
1903	08	02	288	50	7	24
1903	08	03	288	46	7	23
1903	08	04	288	43	7	23
1903	08	05	288	40	7	23
1903	08	06	288	37	7	23
1903	08	07	288	34	7	23
1903	08	08	288	30	7	22
1903	08	09	288	27	7	22
1903	08	10	288	24	7	22
1903	08	11	288	21	7	21
1903	08	12	288	19	7	21
1903	08	13	288	16	7	21
1903	08	14	288	13	7	21
1903	08	15	288	10	7	20
1903	08	16	288	07	7	20
1903	08	17	288	05	7	20
1903	08	18	288	02	7	19
1903	08	19	288	00	7	19
1903	08	20	287	57	7	19
1903	08	21	287	55	7	18
1903	08	22	287	52	7	18
1903	08	23	287	50	7	17
1903	08	24	287	48	7	17
1903	08	25	287	45	7	17
1903	08	26	287	43	7	16
1903	08	27	287	41	7	16
1903	08	28	287	39	7	15
1903	08	29	287	37	7	15
1903	08	30	287	35	7	15
1903	08	31	287	33	7	14
1903	09	01	287	32	7	14
1903	09	02	287	30	7	13
1903	09	03	287	28	7	13
1903	09	04	287	27	7	12
1903	09	05	287	25	7	12
1903	09	06	287	24	7	11
1903	09	07	287	22	7	11
1903	09	08	287	21	7	11
1903	09	09	287	20	7	10
1903	09	10	287	19	7	10
1903	09	11	287	18	7	09
1903	09	12	287	17	7	09
1903	09	13	287	16	7	08
1903	09	14	287	15	7	08
1903	09	15	287	14	7	07
1903	09	16	287	13	7	07
1903	09	17	287	13	7	06
1903	09	18	287	12	7	06
1903	09	19	287	12	7	05
1903	09	20	287	11	7	05
1903	09	21	287	11	7	04
1903	09	22	287	11	7	04
1903	09	23	287	11	7	03
1903	09	24	287	11	7	02
1903	09	25	287	11	7	02
1903	09	26	287	11	7	01
1903	09	27	287	11	7	01
1903	09	28	287	11	7	00
1903	09	29	287	11	7	00
1903	09	30	287	12	6	59
1903	10	01	287	12	6	59

Chiron

1903	10	02	287	13	6	58
1903	10	03	287	13	6	58
1903	10	04	287	14	6	57
1903	10	05	287	15	6	57
1903	10	06	287	16	6	56
1903	10	07	287	17	6	56
1903	10	08	287	18	6	55
1903	10	09	287	19	6	55
1903	10	10	287	20	6	54
1903	10	11	287	21	6	54
1903	10	12	287	22	6	53
1903	10	13	287	24	6	52
1903	10	14	287	25	6	52
1903	10	15	287	27	6	51
1903	10	16	287	28	6	51
1903	10	17	287	30	6	50
1903	10	18	287	32	6	50
1903	10	19	287	33	6	49
1903	10	20	287	35	6	49
1903	10	21	287	37	6	48
1903	10	22	287	39	6	48
1903	10	23	287	42	6	47
1903	10	24	287	44	6	47
1903	10	25	287	46	6	46
1903	10	26	287	48	6	46
1903	10	27	287	51	6	45
1903	10	28	287	53	6	45
1903	10	29	287	56	6	44
1903	10	30	287	58	6	44
1903	10	31	288	01	6	44
1903	11	01	288	04	6	43
1903	11	02	288	07	6	43
1903	11	03	288	09	6	42
1903	11	04	288	12	6	42
1903	11	05	288	15	6	41
1903	11	06	288	18	6	41
1903	11	07	288	22	6	40
1903	11	08	288	25	6	40
1903	11	09	288	28	6	39
1903	11	10	288	31	6	39
1903	11	11	288	35	6	39
1903	11	12	288	38	6	38
1903	11	13	288	42	6	38
1903	11	14	288	45	6	37
1903	11	15	288	49	6	37
1903	11	16	288	52	6	37
1903	11	17	288	56	6	36
1903	11	18	289	00	6	36
1903	11	19	289	04	6	35
1903	11	20	289	08	6	35
1903	11	21	289	12	6	35
1903	11	22	289	16	6	34
1903	11	23	289	20	6	34
1903	11	24	289	24	6	34
1903	11	25	289	28	6	33
1903	11	26	289	32	6	33
1903	11	27	289	36	6	33
1903	11	28	289	40	6	32
1903	11	29	289	45	6	32
1903	11	30	289	49	6	32
1903	12	01	289	54	6	31
1903	12	02	289	58	6	31
1903	12	03	290	03	6	31
1903	12	04	290	07	6	30
1903	12	05	290	12	6	30
1903	12	06	290	16	6	30
1903	12	07	290	21	6	30
1903	12	08	290	26	6	29
1903	12	09	290	30	6	29
1903	12	10	290	35	6	29
1903	12	11	290	40	6	29
1903	12	12	290	45	6	28
1903	12	13	290	50	6	28
1903	12	14	290	54	6	28
1903	12	15	290	59	6	28
1903	12	16	291	04	6	27
1903	12	17	291	09	6	27
1903	12	18	291	14	6	27
1903	12	19	291	19	6	27
1903	12	20	291	24	6	27
1903	12	21	291	30	6	26
1903	12	22	291	35	6	26
1903	12	23	291	40	6	26
1903	12	24	291	45	6	26
1903	12	25	291	50	6	26
1903	12	26	291	55	6	26
1903	12	27	292	01	6	26
1903	12	28	292	06	6	25
1903	12	29	292	11	6	25
1903	12	30	292	16	6	25
1903	12	31	292	22	6	25
1904	01	01	292	27	6	25
1904	01	02	292	32	6	25
1904	01	03	292	38	6	25
1904	01	04	292	43	6	25
1904	01	05	292	48	6	25
1904	01	06	292	54	6	25
1904	01	07	292	59	6	25
1904	01	08	293	04	6	25
1904	01	09	293	10	6	24
1904	01	10	293	15	6	24
1904	01	11	293	20	6	24
1904	01	12	293	26	6	24
1904	01	13	293	31	6	24
1904	01	14	293	37	6	24
1904	01	15	293	42	6	24
1904	01	16	293	47	6	24
1904	01	17	293	53	6	24
1904	01	18	293	58	6	24
1904	01	19	294	04	6	25
1904	01	20	294	09	6	25
1904	01	21	294	14	6	25
1904	01	22	294	20	6	25
1904	01	23	294	25	6	25
1904	01	24	294	30	6	25
1904	01	25	294	36	6	25
1904	01	26	294	41	6	25
1904	01	27	294	46	6	25
1904	01	28	294	52	6	25
1904	01	29	294	57	6	25
1904	01	30	295	02	6	25
1904	01	31	295	07	6	26
1904	02	01	295	13	6	26
1904	02	02	295	18	6	26
1904	02	03	295	23	6	26
1904	02	04	295	28	6	26
1904	02	05	295	33	6	26
1904	02	06	295	39	6	26
1904	02	07	295	44	6	27
1904	02	08	295	49	6	27
1904	02	09	295	54	6	27
1904	02	10	295	59	6	27
1904	02	11	296	04	6	27
1904	02	12	296	09	6	28
1904	02	13	296	14	6	28
1904	02	14	296	19	6	28
1904	02	15	296	24	6	28
1904	02	16	296	29	6	28
1904	02	17	296	33	6	29
1904	02	18	296	38	6	29
1904	02	19	296	43	6	29
1904	02	20	296	48	6	30
1904	02	21	296	52	6	30
1904	02	22	296	57	6	30
1904	02	23	297	02	6	30
1904	02	24	297	06	6	31
1904	02	25	297	11	6	31
1904	02	26	297	15	6	31
1904	02	27	297	20	6	32
1904	02	28	297	24	6	32
1904	02	29	297	28	6	32
1904	03	01	297	33	6	32
1904	03	02	297	37	6	33
1904	03	03	297	41	6	33
1904	03	04	297	46	6	34
1904	03	05	297	50	6	34
1904	03	06	297	54	6	34
1904	03	07	297	58	6	35
1904	03	08	298	02	6	35
1904	03	09	298	06	6	35
1904	03	10	298	10	6	36
1904	03	11	298	14	6	36
1904	03	12	298	17	6	36
1904	03	13	298	21	6	37
1904	03	14	298	25	6	37
1904	03	15	298	28	6	38
1904	03	16	298	32	6	38
1904	03	17	298	35	6	39
1904	03	18	298	39	6	39
1904	03	19	298	42	6	39
1904	03	20	298	46	6	40
1904	03	21	298	49	6	40
1904	03	22	298	52	6	41
1904	03	23	298	55	6	41
1904	03	24	298	58	6	42
1904	03	25	299	02	6	42
1904	03	26	299	05	6	42
1904	03	27	299	07	6	43
1904	03	28	299	10	6	43
1904	03	29	299	13	6	44
1904	03	30	299	16	6	44
1904	03	31	299	18	6	45
1904	04	01	299	21	6	45
1904	04	02	299	24	6	46
1904	04	03	299	26	6	46
1904	04	04	299	28	6	47
1904	04	05	299	31	6	47
1904	04	06	299	33	6	48
1904	04	07	299	35	6	48
1904	04	08	299	37	6	49
1904	04	09	299	39	6	49
1904	04	10	299	41	6	50
1904	04	11	299	43	6	50
1904	04	12	299	45	6	51
1904	04	13	299	47	6	51
1904	04	14	299	49	6	52
1904	04	15	299	50	6	52
1904	04	16	299	52	6	53
1904	04	17	299	53	6	53
1904	04	18	299	55	6	54
1904	04	19	299	56	6	54
1904	04	20	299	57	6	55
1904	04	21	299	58	6	56
1904	04	22	300	00	6	56
1904	04	23	300	01	6	57
1904	04	24	300	02	6	57
1904	04	25	300	02	6	58
1904	04	26	300	03	6	58
1904	04	27	300	04	6	59
1904	04	28	300	05	6	59
1904	04	29	300	05	7	00
1904	04	30	300	06	7	00
1904	05	01	300	06	7	01
1904	05	02	300	07	7	01
1904	05	03	300	07	7	02
1904	05	04	300	07	7	02
1904	05	05	300	07	7	03
1904	05	06	300	07	7	04
1904	05	07	300	07	7	04
1904	05	08	300	07	7	05
1904	05	09	300	07	7	05
1904	05	10	300	07	7	06
1904	05	11	300	07	7	06
1904	05	12	300	06	7	07
1904	05	13	300	06	7	07
1904	05	14	300	05	7	08
1904	05	15	300	05	7	08
1904	05	16	300	04	7	09
1904	05	17	300	03	7	09
1904	05	18	300	02	7	10
1904	05	19	300	02	7	10
1904	05	20	300	01	7	11
1904	05	21	300	00	7	11
1904	05	22	299	59	7	12
1904	05	23	299	57	7	12
1904	05	24	299	56	7	13
1904	05	25	299	55	7	13
1904	05	26	299	53	7	14
1904	05	27	299	52	7	14
1904	05	28	299	51	7	15
1904	05	29	299	49	7	15
1904	05	30	299	47	7	16
1904	05	31	299	46	7	16
1904	06	01	299	44	7	16
1904	06	02	299	42	7	17
1904	06	03	299	40	7	17
1904	06	04	299	38	7	18
1904	06	05	299	36	7	18
1904	06	06	299	34	7	19
1904	06	07	299	32	7	19
1904	06	08	299	30	7	19
1904	06	09	299	28	7	20
1904	06	10	299	25	7	20
1904	06	11	299	23	7	20
1904	06	12	299	21	7	21
1904	06	13	299	18	7	21
1904	06	14	299	16	7	22
1904	06	15	299	13	7	22
1904	06	16	299	10	7	22
1904	06	17	299	08	7	23
1904	06	18	299	05	7	23
1904	06	19	299	02	7	23
1904	06	20	299	00	7	24
1904	06	21	298	57	7	24
1904	06	22	298	54	7	24
1904	06	23	298	51	7	24
1904	06	24	298	48	7	25
1904	06	25	298	45	7	25
1904	06	26	298	42	7	25
1904	06	27	298	39	7	25
1904	06	28	298	36	7	26
1904	06	29	298	33	7	26
1904	06	30	298	29	7	26
1904	07	01	298	26	7	26
1904	07	02	298	23	7	27
1904	07	03	298	20	7	27
1904	07	04	298	16	7	27
1904	07	05	298	13	7	27
1904	07	06	298	10	7	27
1904	07	07	298	06	7	27
1904	07	08	298	03	7	27
1904	07	09	298	00	7	28
1904	07	10	297	56	7	28
1904	07	11	297	53	7	28
1904	07	12	297	49	7	28
1904	07	13	297	46	7	28
1904	07	14	297	43	7	28
1904	07	15	297	39	7	28
1904	07	16	297	36	7	28
1904	07	17	297	32	7	28
1904	07	18	297	29	7	28
1904	07	19	297	25	7	28
1904	07	20	297	22	7	28
1904	07	21	297	18	7	28
1904	07	22	297	15	7	28
1904	07	23	297	11	7	28
1904	07	24	297	08	7	28
1904	07	25	297	04	7	28
1904	07	26	297	01	7	28
1904	07	27	296	57	7	28
1904	07	28	296	54	7	28
1904	07	29	296	50	7	28
1904	07	30	296	47	7	28
1904	07	31	296	44	7	28
1904	08	01	296	40	7	27
1904	08	02	296	37	7	27
1904	08	03	296	33	7	27
1904	08	04	296	30	7	27
1904	08	05	296	27	7	27
1904	08	06	296	24	7	27
1904	08	07	296	20	7	27
1904	08	08	296	17	7	26
1904	08	09	296	14	7	26
1904	08	10	296	11	7	26
1904	08	11	296	08	7	26
1904	08	12	296	04	7	25
1904	08	13	296	01	7	25
1904	08	14	295	58	7	25
1904	08	15	295	55	7	25
1904	08	16	295	52	7	24
1904	08	17	295	50	7	24
1904	08	18	295	47	7	24
1904	08	19	295	44	7	24
1904	08	20	295	41	7	23
1904	08	21	295	38	7	23
1904	08	22	295	36	7	23
1904	08	23	295	33	7	22
1904	08	24	295	30	7	22
1904	08	25	295	28	7	22
1904	08	26	295	25	7	21
1904	08	27	295	23	7	21
1904	08	28	295	21	7	21
1904	08	29	295	18	7	20
1904	08	30	295	16	7	20
1904	08	31	295	14	7	19
1904	09	01	295	12	7	19
1904	09	02	295	09	7	19
1904	09	03	295	07	7	18
1904	09	04	295	05	7	18
1904	09	05	295	04	7	17
1904	09	06	295	02	7	17
1904	09	07	295	00	7	17
1904	09	08	294	58	7	16
1904	09	09	294	56	7	16
1904	09	10	294	55	7	15
1904	09	11	294	53	7	15
1904	09	12	294	52	7	14
1904	09	13	294	50	7	14
1904	09	14	294	49	7	13
1904	09	15	294	48	7	13
1904	09	16	294	47	7	12
1904	09	17	294	45	7	12
1904	09	18	294	44	7	11
1904	09	19	294	43	7	11
1904	09	20	294	42	7	10
1904	09	21	294	42	7	10
1904	09	22	294	41	7	09
1904	09	23	294	40	7	09
1904	09	24	294	39	7	08
1904	09	25	294	39	7	08
1904	09	26	294	38	7	07
1904	09	27	294	38	7	07
1904	09	28	294	38	7	06
1904	09	29	294	37	7	06
1904	09	30	294	37	7	05
1904	10	01	294	37	7	05
1904	10	02	294	37	7	04
1904	10	03	294	37	7	04
1904	10	04	294	37	7	03
1904	10	05	294	37	7	03
1904	10	06	294	37	7	02
1904	10	07	294	38	7	02
1904	10	08	294	38	7	01
1904	10	09	294	39	7	01
1904	10	10	294	39	7	00
1904	10	11	294	40	7	00
1904	10	12	294	40	6	59
1904	10	13	294	41	6	59
1904	10	14	294	42	6	58
1904	10	15	294	43	6	58
1904	10	16	294	44	6	57
1904	10	17	294	45	6	56
1904	10	18	294	46	6	56
1904	10	19	294	47	6	55
1904	10	20	294	48	6	55
1904	10	21	294	50	6	54
1904	10	22	294	51	6	54
1904	10	23	294	53	6	53
1904	10	24	294	54	6	53
1904	10	25	294	56	6	52
1904	10	26	294	58	6	52
1904	10	27	294	59	6	51
1904	10	28	295	01	6	51
1904	10	29	295	03	6	50
1904	10	30	295	05	6	50
1904	10	31	295	07	6	49
1904	11	01	295	09	6	49
1904	11	02	295	11	6	48
1904	11	03	295	14	6	48
1904	11	04	295	16	6	47
1904	11	05	295	18	6	47
1904	11	06	295	21	6	46
1904	11	07	295	23	6	46
1904	11	08	295	26	6	46
1904	11	09	295	29	6	45
1904	11	10	295	31	6	45
1904	11	11	295	34	6	44
1904	11	12	295	37	6	44
1904	11	13	295	40	6	43
1904	11	14	295	43	6	43
1904	11	15	295	46	6	42
1904	11	16	295	49	6	42
1904	11	17	295	52	6	42
1904	11	18	295	55	6	41
1904	11	19	295	58	6	41
1904	11	20	296	02	6	40
1904	11	21	296	05	6	40
1904	11	22	296	08	6	39

1904	11	23	296	12	6	39
1904	11	24	296	15	6	39
1904	11	25	296	19	6	38
1904	11	26	296	22	6	38
1904	11	27	296	26	6	38
1904	11	28	296	30	6	37
1904	11	29	296	34	6	37
1904	11	30	296	37	6	36
1904	12	01	296	41	6	36
1904	12	02	296	45	6	36
1904	12	03	296	49	6	35
1904	12	04	296	53	6	35
1904	12	05	296	57	6	35
1904	12	06	297	01	6	34
1904	12	07	297	05	6	34
1904	12	08	297	10	6	34
1904	12	09	297	14	6	33
1904	12	10	297	18	6	33
1904	12	11	297	22	6	33
1904	12	12	297	27	6	33
1904	12	13	297	31	6	32
1904	12	14	297	36	6	32
1904	12	15	297	40	6	32
1904	12	16	297	44	6	32
1904	12	17	297	49	6	31
1904	12	18	297	54	6	31
1904	12	19	297	58	6	31
1904	12	20	298	03	6	31
1904	12	21	298	07	6	30
1904	12	22	298	12	6	30
1904	12	23	298	17	6	30
1904	12	24	298	21	6	30
1904	12	25	298	26	6	29
1904	12	26	298	31	6	29
1904	12	27	298	36	6	29
1904	12	28	298	41	6	29
1904	12	29	298	45	6	29
1904	12	30	298	50	6	29
1904	12	31	298	55	6	28
1905	01	01	299	00	6	28
1905	01	02	299	05	6	28
1905	01	03	299	10	6	28
1905	01	04	299	15	6	28
1905	01	05	299	20	6	28
1905	01	06	299	25	6	28
1905	01	07	299	30	6	27
1905	01	08	299	35	6	27
1905	01	09	299	40	6	27
1905	01	10	299	45	6	27
1905	01	11	299	50	6	27
1905	01	12	299	55	6	27
1905	01	13	300	00	6	27
1905	01	14	300	05	6	27
1905	01	15	300	10	6	27
1905	01	16	300	15	6	27
1905	01	17	300	20	6	27
1905	01	18	300	26	6	27
1905	01	19	300	31	6	27
1905	01	20	300	36	6	27
1905	01	21	300	41	6	27
1905	01	22	300	46	6	27
1905	01	23	300	51	6	27
1905	01	24	300	56	6	27
1905	01	25	301	01	6	27
1905	01	26	301	06	6	27
1905	01	27	301	11	6	27
1905	01	28	301	16	6	27
1905	01	29	301	21	6	27
1905	01	30	301	27	6	27
1905	01	31	301	32	6	27
1905	02	01	301	37	6	27
1905	02	02	301	42	6	27
1905	02	03	301	47	6	27
1905	02	04	301	52	6	27
1905	02	05	301	57	6	27
1905	02	06	302	02	6	27
1905	02	07	302	07	6	28
1905	02	08	302	11	6	28
1905	02	09	302	16	6	28
1905	02	10	302	21	6	28
1905	02	11	302	26	6	28
1905	02	12	302	31	6	28
1905	02	13	302	36	6	28
1905	02	14	302	41	6	29
1905	02	15	302	45	6	29
1905	02	16	302	50	6	29
1905	02	17	302	55	6	29
1905	02	18	303	00	6	29
1905	02	19	303	04	6	29
1905	02	20	303	09	6	30
1905	02	21	303	14	6	30
1905	02	22	303	18	6	30
1905	02	23	303	23	6	30
1905	02	24	303	27	6	31
1905	02	25	303	32	6	31
1905	02	26	303	36	6	31
1905	02	27	303	41	6	31
1905	02	28	303	45	6	31
1905	03	01	303	49	6	32
1905	03	02	303	54	6	32
1905	03	03	303	58	6	32
1905	03	04	304	02	6	33
1905	03	05	304	06	6	33
1905	03	06	304	11	6	33
1905	03	07	304	15	6	33
1905	03	08	304	19	6	34
1905	03	09	304	23	6	34
1905	03	10	304	27	6	34
1905	03	11	304	31	6	35
1905	03	12	304	35	6	35
1905	03	13	304	39	6	35
1905	03	14	304	42	6	36
1905	03	15	304	46	6	36
1905	03	16	304	50	6	36
1905	03	17	304	54	6	37
1905	03	18	304	57	6	37
1905	03	19	305	01	6	37
1905	03	20	305	04	6	38
1905	03	21	305	08	6	38
1905	03	22	305	11	6	38
1905	03	23	305	14	6	39
1905	03	24	305	18	6	39
1705	03	25	305	21	6	40
1905	03	26	305	24	6	40
1905	03	27	305	27	6	40
1905	03	28	305	30	6	41
1905	03	29	305	33	6	41
1905	03	30	305	36	6	42
1905	03	31	305	39	6	42
1905	04	01	305	42	6	42
1905	04	02	305	45	6	43
1905	04	03	305	48	6	43
1905	04	04	305	50	6	44
1905	04	05	305	53	6	44
1905	04	06	305	56	6	45
1905	04	07	305	58	6	45
1905	04	08	306	01	6	45
1905	04	09	306	03	6	46
1905	04	10	306	05	6	46
1905	04	11	306	07	6	47
1905	04	12	306	10	6	47
1905	04	13	306	12	6	48
1905	04	14	306	14	6	48
1905	04	15	306	16	6	49
1905	04	16	306	18	6	49
1905	04	17	306	19	6	50
1905	04	18	306	21	6	50
1905	04	19	306	23	6	51
1905	04	20	306	25	6	51
1905	04	21	306	26	6	52
1905	04	22	306	28	6	52
1905	04	23	306	29	6	52
1905	04	24	306	30	6	53
1905	04	25	306	32	6	53
1905	04	26	306	33	6	54
1905	04	27	306	34	6	54
1905	04	28	306	35	6	55
1905	04	29	306	36	6	55
1905	04	30	306	37	6	56
1905	05	01	306	38	6	56
1905	05	02	306	39	6	57
1905	05	03	306	40	6	57
1905	05	04	306	40	6	58
1905	05	05	306	41	6	58
1905	05	06	306	41	6	59
1905	05	07	306	42	6	59
1905	05	08	306	42	7	00
1905	05	09	306	42	7	00
1905	05	10	306	43	7	01
1905	05	11	306	43	7	01
1905	05	12	306	43	7	02
1905	05	13	306	43	7	02
1905	05	14	306	43	7	03
1905	05	15	306	43	7	03
1905	05	16	306	43	7	04
1905	05	17	306	42	7	04
1905	05	18	306	42	7	05
1905	05	19	306	42	7	05
1905	05	20	306	41	7	06
1905	05	21	306	41	7	06
1905	05	22	306	40	7	07
1905	05	23	306	39	7	07
1905	05	24	306	38	7	08
1905	05	25	306	38	7	08
1905	05	26	306	37	7	08
1905	05	27	306	36	7	09
1905	05	28	306	35	7	09
1905	05	29	306	34	7	10
1905	05	30	306	33	7	10
1905	05	31	306	31	7	11
1905	06	01	306	30	7	11
1905	06	02	306	29	7	12
1905	06	03	306	27	7	12
1905	06	04	306	26	7	12
1905	06	05	306	24	7	13
1905	06	06	306	23	7	13
1905	06	07	306	21	7	14
1905	06	08	306	19	7	14
1905	06	09	306	18	7	14
1905	06	10	306	16	7	15
1905	06	11	306	14	7	15
1905	06	12	306	12	7	16
1905	06	13	306	10	7	16
1905	06	14	306	08	7	16
1905	06	15	306	06	7	17
1905	06	16	306	03	7	17
1905	06	17	306	01	7	17
1905	06	18	305	59	7	18
1905	06	19	305	57	7	18
1905	06	20	305	54	7	18
1905	06	21	305	52	7	19
1905	06	22	305	49	7	19
1905	06	23	305	47	7	19
1905	06	24	305	44	7	20
1905	06	25	305	42	7	20
1905	06	26	305	39	7	20
1905	06	27	305	36	7	21
1905	06	28	305	34	7	21
1905	06	29	305	31	7	21
1905	06	30	305	28	7	21
1905	07	01	305	25	7	22
1905	07	02	305	22	7	22
1905	07	03	305	19	7	22
1905	07	04	305	16	7	22
1905	07	05	305	13	7	22
1905	07	06	305	10	7	23
1905	07	07	305	07	7	23
1705	07	00	305	04	7	23
1905	07	09	305	01	7	23
1905	07	10	304	58	7	23
1905	07	11	304	55	7	23
1905	07	12	304	51	7	24
1905	07	13	304	48	7	24
1905	07	14	304	45	7	24
1905	07	15	304	42	7	24
1905	07	16	304	38	7	24
1905	07	17	304	35	7	24
1905	07	18	304	32	7	24
1905	07	19	304	28	7	24
1905	07	20	304	25	7	24
1905	07	21	304	22	7	24
1905	07	22	304	18	7	25
1905	07	23	304	15	7	25
1905	07	24	304	12	7	25
1905	07	25	304	08	7	25
1905	07	26	304	05	7	25
1905	07	27	304	02	7	25
1905	07	28	303	58	7	25
1905	07	29	303	55	7	25
1905	07	30	303	51	7	24
1905	07	31	303	48	7	24
1905	08	01	303	45	7	24
1905	08	02	303	41	7	24
1905	08	03	303	38	7	24
1905	08	04	303	35	7	24
1905	08	05	303	31	7	24
1905	08	06	303	28	7	24
1905	08	07	303	25	7	24
1905	08	08	303	21	7	24
1905	08	09	303	18	7	24
1905	08	10	303	15	7	23
1905	08	11	303	12	7	23
1905	08	12	303	09	7	23
1905	08	13	303	05	7	23
1905	08	14	303	02	7	23
1905	08	15	302	59	7	23
1905	08	16	302	56	7	22
1905	08	17	302	53	7	22
1905	08	18	302	50	7	22
1905	08	19	302	47	7	22
1905	08	20	302	44	7	21
1905	08	21	302	41	7	21
1905	08	22	302	38	7	21
1905	08	23	302	35	7	21
1905	08	24	302	32	7	20
1905	08	25	302	30	7	20
1905	08	26	302	27	7	20
1905	08	27	302	24	7	19
1905	08	28	302	21	7	19
1905	08	29	302	19	7	19
1905	08	30	302	16	7	19
1905	08	31	302	14	7	18
1905	09	01	302	11	7	18
1905	09	02	302	09	7	17
1905	09	03	302	06	7	17
1905	09	04	302	04	7	17
1905	09	05	302	02	7	16
1905	09	06	302	00	7	16
1905	09	07	301	57	7	16
1905	09	08	301	55	7	15
1905	09	09	301	53	7	15
1905	09	10	301	51	7	14
1905	09	11	301	49	7	14
1905	09	12	301	47	7	14
1905	09	13	301	45	7	13
1905	09	14	301	44	7	13
1905	09	15	301	42	7	12
1905	09	16	301	40	7	12
1905	09	17	301	39	7	12
1905	09	18	301	37	7	11
1905	09	19	301	36	7	11
1905	09	20	301	34	7	10
1905	09	21	301	33	7	10
1905	09	22	301	32	7	09
1905	09	23	301	30	7	09
1905	09	24	301	29	7	08
1905	09	25	301	28	7	08
1905	09	26	301	27	7	07
1905	09	27	301	26	7	07
1905	09	28	301	25	7	06
1905	09	29	301	25	7	06
1905	09	30	301	24	7	05
1905	10	01	301	23	7	05
1905	10	02	301	23	7	04
1905	10	03	301	22	7	04
1905	10	04	301	22	7	03
1905	10	05	301	21	7	03
1905	10	06	301	21	7	02
1905	10	07	301	21	7	02
1905	10	08	301	20	7	01
1905	10	09	301	20	7	01
1905	10	10	301	20	7	00
1905	10	11	301	20	7	00
1905	10	12	301	20	6	59
1905	10	13	301	21	6	59
1905	10	14	301	21	6	58
1905	10	15	301	21	6	58
1905	10	16	301	21	6	57
1905	10	17	301	22	6	57
1905	10	18	301	22	6	56
1905	10	19	301	23	6	56
1905	10	20	301	24	6	55
1905	10	21	301	24	6	55
1905	10	22	301	25	6	54
1905	10	23	301	26	6	54
1905	10	24	301	27	6	53
1905	10	25	301	28	6	53
1905	10	26	301	29	6	52
1905	10	27	301	30	6	52
1905	10	28	301	32	6	51
1905	10	29	301	33	6	51
1905	10	30	301	34	6	50
1905	10	31	301	36	6	50
1905	11	01	301	37	6	49
1905	11	02	301	39	6	49
1905	11	03	301	40	6	48
1905	11	04	301	42	6	48
1905	11	05	301	44	6	47
1905	11	06	301	46	6	47
1905	11	07	301	48	6	46
1905	11	08	301	50	6	46
1905	11	09	301	52	6	45
1905	11	10	301	54	6	45
1905	11	11	301	56	6	44
1905	11	12	301	58	6	44
1905	11	13	302	00	6	43
1905	11	14	302	03	6	43
1905	11	15	302	05	6	43
1905	11	16	302	08	6	42
1905	11	17	302	10	6	42
1905	11	18	302	13	6	41
1905	11	19	302	16	6	41
1905	11	20	302	18	6	40
1905	11	21	302	21	6	40
1905	11	22	302	24	6	39
1905	11	23	302	27	6	39
1905	11	24	302	30	6	39
1905	11	25	302	33	6	38
1905	11	26	302	36	6	38
1905	11	27	302	39	6	37
1905	11	28	302	42	6	37
1905	11	29	302	45	6	37
1905	11	30	302	49	6	36
1905	12	01	302	52	6	36
1905	12	02	302	55	6	35
1905	12	03	302	59	6	35
1905	12	04	303	02	6	35
1905	12	05	303	06	6	34
1905	12	06	303	09	6	34
1905	12	07	303	13	6	34
1905	12	08	303	17	6	33
1905	12	09	303	20	6	33
1905	12	10	303	24	6	33
1905	12	11	303	28	6	32
1905	12	12	303	32	6	32
1905	12	13	303	36	6	32
1905	12	14	303	39	6	31
1905	12	15	303	43	6	31
1905	12	16	303	47	6	31
1905	12	17	303	51	6	30
1905	12	18	303	56	6	30
1905	12	19	304	00	6	30
1905	12	20	304	04	6	30
1905	12	21	304	08	6	29
1905	12	22	304	12	6	29
1905	12	23	304	16	6	29
1905	12	24	304	21	6	28
1905	12	25	304	25	6	28
1905	12	26	304	29	6	28
1905	12	27	304	34	6	28
1905	12	28	304	38	6	28
1905	12	29	304	43	6	27
1905	12	30	304	47	6	27
1905	12	31	304	52	6	27
1906	01	01	304	56	6	27
1906	01	02	305	01	6	26
1906	01	03	305	05	6	26
1906	01	04	305	10	6	26
1906	01	05	305	14	6	26
1906	01	06	305	19	6	26
1906	01	07	305	24	6	26
1906	01	08	305	28	6	25
1906	01	09	305	33	6	25
1906	01	10	305	38	6	25
1906	01	11	305	42	6	25
1906	01	12	305	47	6	25

Chiron

1906	01	13	305	52	6	25
1906	01	14	305	57	6	25
1906	01	15	306	01	6	25
1906	01	16	306	06	6	24
1906	01	17	306	11	6	24
1906	01	18	306	16	6	24
1906	01	19	306	21	6	24
1906	01	20	306	25	6	24
1906	01	21	306	30	6	24
1906	01	22	306	35	6	24
1906	01	23	306	40	6	24
1906	01	24	306	45	6	24
1906	01	25	306	50	6	24
1906	01	26	306	54	6	24
1906	01	27	306	59	6	24
1906	01	28	307	04	6	24
1906	01	29	307	09	6	24
1906	01	30	307	14	6	24
1906	01	31	307	19	6	24
1906	02	01	307	23	6	24
1906	02	02	307	28	6	24
1906	02	03	307	33	6	24
1906	02	04	307	38	6	24
1906	02	05	307	43	6	24
1906	02	06	307	47	6	24
1906	02	07	307	52	6	24
1906	02	08	307	57	6	24
1906	02	09	308	02	6	24
1906	02	10	308	07	6	24
1906	02	11	308	11	6	24
1906	02	12	308	16	6	24
1906	02	13	308	21	6	24
1906	02	14	308	25	6	24
1906	02	15	308	30	6	25
1906	02	16	308	35	6	25
1906	02	17	308	39	6	25
1906	02	18	308	44	6	25
1906	02	19	308	49	6	25
1906	02	20	308	53	6	25
1906	02	21	308	58	6	25
1906	02	22	309	02	6	25
1906	02	23	309	07	6	26
1906	02	24	309	11	6	26
1906	02	25	309	16	6	26
1906	02	26	309	20	6	26
1906	02	27	309	24	6	26
1906	02	28	309	29	6	27
1906	03	01	309	33	6	27
1906	03	02	309	38	6	27
1906	03	03	309	42	6	27
1906	03	04	309	46	6	27
1906	03	05	309	50	6	28
1906	03	06	309	54	6	28
1906	03	07	309	59	6	28
1906	03	08	310	03	6	28
1906	03	09	310	07	6	28
1906	03	10	310	11	6	29
1906	03	11	310	15	6	29
1906	03	12	310	19	6	29
1906	03	13	310	23	6	29
1906	03	14	310	27	6	30
1906	03	15	310	30	6	30
1906	03	16	310	34	6	30
1906	03	17	310	38	6	31
1906	03	18	310	42	6	31
1906	03	19	310	45	6	31
1906	03	20	310	49	6	31
1906	03	21	310	53	6	32
1906	03	22	310	56	6	32
1906	03	23	311	00	6	32
1906	03	24	311	03	6	33
1906	03	25	311	07	6	33
1906	03	26	311	10	6	33
1906	03	27	311	13	6	34
1906	03	28	311	16	6	34
1906	03	29	311	20	6	34
1906	03	30	311	23	6	35
1906	03	31	311	26	6	35
1906	04	01	311	29	6	35
1906	04	02	311	32	6	36
1906	04	03	311	35	6	36
1906	04	04	311	38	6	37
1906	04	05	311	41	6	37
1906	04	06	311	43	6	37
1906	04	07	311	46	6	38
1906	04	08	311	49	6	38
1906	04	09	311	51	6	38
1906	04	10	311	54	6	39
1906	04	11	311	56	6	39
1906	04	12	311	59	6	40
1906	04	13	312	01	6	40
1906	04	14	312	03	6	40
1906	04	15	312	06	6	41
1906	04	16	312	08	6	41
1906	04	17	312	10	6	42
1906	04	18	312	12	6	42
1906	04	19	312	14	6	43
1906	04	20	312	16	6	43
1906	04	21	312	18	6	43
1906	04	22	312	20	6	44
1906	04	23	312	21	6	44
1906	04	24	312	23	6	45
1906	04	25	312	25	6	45
1906	04	26	312	26	6	46
1906	04	27	312	28	6	46
1906	04	28	312	29	6	46
1906	04	29	312	30	6	47
1906	04	30	312	32	6	47
1906	05	01	312	33	6	48
1906	05	02	312	34	6	48
1906	05	03	312	35	6	49
1906	05	04	312	36	6	49
1906	05	05	312	37	6	50
1906	05	06	312	38	6	50
1906	05	07	312	39	6	50
1906	05	08	312	40	6	51
1906	05	09	312	40	6	51
1906	05	10	312	41	6	52
1906	05	11	312	41	6	52
1906	05	12	312	42	6	53
1906	05	13	312	42	6	53
1906	05	14	312	43	6	54
1906	05	15	312	43	6	54
1906	05	16	312	43	6	55
1906	05	17	312	43	6	55
1906	05	18	312	43	6	55
1906	05	19	312	43	6	56
1906	05	20	312	43	6	56
1906	05	21	312	43	6	57
1906	05	22	312	43	6	57
1906	05	23	312	43	6	58
1906	05	24	312	42	6	58
1906	05	25	312	42	6	59
1906	05	26	312	42	6	59
1906	05	27	312	41	6	59
1906	05	28	312	40	7	00
1906	05	29	312	40	7	00
1906	05	30	312	39	7	01
1906	05	31	312	38	7	01
1906	06	01	312	37	7	02
1906	06	02	312	37	7	02
1906	06	03	312	36	7	02
1906	06	04	312	34	7	03
1906	06	05	312	33	7	03
1906	06	06	312	32	7	04
1906	06	07	312	31	7	04
1906	06	08	312	30	7	04
1906	06	09	312	28	7	05
1906	06	10	312	27	7	05
1906	06	11	312	25	7	06
1906	06	12	312	24	7	06
1906	06	13	312	22	7	06
1906	06	14	312	21	7	07
1906	06	15	312	19	7	07
1906	06	16	312	17	7	07
1906	06	17	312	15	7	08
1906	06	18	312	13	7	08
1906	06	19	312	11	7	09
1906	06	20	312	09	7	09
1906	06	21	312	07	7	09
1906	06	22	312	05	7	10
1906	06	23	312	03	7	10
1906	06	24	312	01	7	10
1906	06	25	311	59	7	10
1906	06	26	311	56	7	11
1906	06	27	311	54	7	11
1906	06	28	311	52	7	11
1906	06	29	311	49	7	12
1906	06	30	311	47	7	12
1906	07	01	311	44	7	12
1906	07	02	311	42	7	12
1906	07	03	311	39	7	13
1906	07	04	311	36	7	13
1906	07	05	311	34	7	13
1906	07	06	311	31	7	13
1906	07	07	311	28	7	14
1906	07	08	311	25	7	14
1906	07	09	311	23	7	14
1906	07	10	311	20	7	14
1906	07	11	311	17	7	14
1906	07	12	311	14	7	15
1906	07	13	311	11	7	15
1906	07	14	311	08	7	15
1906	07	15	311	05	7	15
1906	07	16	311	02	7	15
1906	07	17	310	59	7	15
1906	07	18	310	56	7	15
1906	07	19	310	53	7	16
1906	07	20	310	50	7	16
1906	07	21	310	46	7	16
1906	07	22	310	43	7	16
1906	07	23	310	40	7	16
1906	07	24	310	37	7	16
1906	07	25	310	34	7	16
1906	07	26	310	30	7	16
1906	07	27	310	27	7	16
1906	07	28	310	24	7	16
1906	07	29	310	21	7	16
1906	07	30	310	17	7	16
1906	07	31	310	14	7	16
1906	08	01	310	11	7	16
1906	08	02	310	08	7	16
1906	08	03	310	04	7	16
1906	08	04	310	01	7	16
1906	08	05	309	58	7	16
1906	08	06	309	55	7	16
1906	08	07	309	51	7	16
1906	08	08	309	48	7	16
1906	08	09	309	45	7	16
1906	08	10	309	42	7	16
1906	08	11	309	38	7	16
1906	08	12	309	35	7	16
1906	08	13	309	32	7	15
1906	08	14	309	29	7	15
1906	08	15	309	26	7	15
1906	08	16	309	22	7	15
1906	08	17	309	19	7	15
1906	08	18	309	16	7	15
1906	08	19	309	13	7	14
1906	08	20	309	10	7	14
1906	08	21	309	07	7	14
1906	08	22	309	04	7	14
1906	08	23	309	01	7	14
1906	08	24	308	58	7	13
1906	08	25	308	55	7	13
1906	08	26	308	52	7	13
1906	08	27	308	49	7	13
1906	08	28	308	46	7	13
1906	08	29	308	44	7	12
1906	08	30	308	41	7	12
1906	08	31	308	38	7	12
1906	09	01	308	35	7	11
1906	09	02	308	33	7	11
1906	09	03	308	30	7	11
1906	09	04	308	27	7	11
1906	09	05	308	25	7	10
1906	09	06	308	22	7	10
1906	09	07	308	20	7	10
1906	09	08	308	18	7	09
1906	09	09	308	15	7	09
1906	09	10	308	13	7	09
1906	09	11	308	11	7	08
1906	09	12	308	08	7	08
1906	09	13	308	06	7	07
1906	09	14	308	04	7	07
1906	09	15	308	02	7	07
1906	09	16	308	00	7	06
1906	09	17	307	58	7	06
1906	09	18	307	56	7	06
1906	09	19	307	54	7	05
1906	09	20	307	53	7	05
1906	09	21	307	51	7	04
1906	09	22	307	49	7	04
1906	09	23	307	48	7	03
1906	09	24	307	46	7	03
1906	09	25	307	45	7	03
1906	09	26	307	43	7	02
1906	09	27	307	42	7	02
1906	09	28	307	40	7	01
1906	09	29	307	39	7	01
1906	09	30	307	38	7	00
1906	10	01	307	37	7	00
1906	10	02	307	36	6	59
1906	10	03	307	35	6	59
1906	10	04	307	34	6	59
1906	10	05	307	33	6	58
1906	10	06	307	32	6	58
1906	10	07	307	32	6	57
1906	10	08	307	31	6	57
1906	10	09	307	30	6	56
1906	10	10	307	30	6	56
1906	10	11	307	29	6	55
1906	10	12	307	29	6	55
1906	10	13	307	29	6	54
1906	10	14	307	28	6	54
1906	10	15	307	28	6	53
1906	10	16	307	28	6	53
1906	10	17	307	28	6	52
1906	10	18	307	28	6	52
1906	10	19	307	28	6	51
1906	10	20	307	28	6	51
1906	10	21	307	29	6	50
1906	10	22	307	29	6	50
1906	10	23	307	29	6	49
1906	10	24	307	30	6	49
1906	10	25	307	30	6	48
1906	10	26	307	31	6	48
1906	10	27	307	31	6	47
1906	10	28	307	32	6	47
1906	10	29	307	33	6	46
1906	10	30	307	34	6	46
1906	10	31	307	35	6	45
1906	11	01	307	36	6	45
1906	11	02	307	37	6	44
1906	11	03	307	38	6	44
1906	11	04	307	39	6	43
1906	11	05	307	40	6	43
1906	11	06	307	41	6	42
1906	11	07	307	43	6	42
1906	11	08	307	44	6	42
1906	11	09	307	46	6	41
1906	11	10	307	47	6	41
1906	11	11	307	49	6	40
1906	11	12	307	51	6	40
1906	11	13	307	52	6	39
1906	11	14	307	54	6	39
1906	11	15	307	56	6	38
1906	11	16	307	58	6	38
1906	11	17	308	00	6	37
1906	11	18	308	02	6	37
1906	11	19	308	04	6	36
1906	11	20	308	07	6	36
1906	11	21	308	09	6	36
1906	11	22	308	11	6	35
1906	11	23	308	14	6	35
1906	11	24	308	16	6	34
1906	11	25	308	19	6	34
1906	11	26	308	21	6	33
1906	11	27	308	24	6	33
1906	11	28	308	26	6	33
1906	11	29	308	29	6	32
1906	11	30	308	32	6	32
1906	12	01	308	35	6	31
1906	12	02	308	38	6	31
1906	12	03	308	41	6	30
1906	12	04	308	44	6	30
1906	12	05	308	47	6	30
1906	12	06	308	50	6	29
1906	12	07	308	53	6	29
1906	12	08	308	56	6	29
1906	12	09	308	59	6	28
1906	12	10	309	03	6	28
1906	12	11	309	06	6	27
1906	12	12	309	09	6	27
1906	12	13	309	13	6	27
1906	12	14	309	16	6	26
1906	12	15	309	20	6	26
1906	12	16	309	23	6	26
1906	12	17	309	27	6	25
1906	12	18	309	30	6	25
1906	12	19	309	34	6	25
1906	12	20	309	38	6	25
1906	12	21	309	42	6	24
1906	12	22	309	45	6	24
1906	12	23	309	49	6	24
1906	12	24	309	53	6	23
1906	12	25	309	57	6	23
1906	12	26	310	01	6	23
1906	12	27	310	05	6	23
1906	12	28	310	09	6	22
1906	12	29	310	13	6	22
1906	12	30	310	17	6	22
1906	12	31	310	21	6	21
1907	01	01	310	25	6	21
1907	01	02	310	30	6	21
1907	01	03	310	34	6	21
1907	01	04	310	38	6	21
1907	01	05	310	42	6	20
1907	01	06	310	47	6	20
1907	01	07	310	51	6	20
1907	01	08	310	55	6	20
1907	01	09	311	00	6	20
1907	01	10	311	04	6	19
1907	01	11	311	08	6	19
1907	01	12	311	13	6	19
1907	01	13	311	17	6	19
1907	01	14	311	22	6	19
1907	01	15	311	26	6	19
1907	01	16	311	31	6	18
1907	01	17	311	35	6	18
1907	01	18	311	40	6	18
1907	01	19	311	44	6	18
1907	01	20	311	49	6	18
1907	01	21	311	53	6	18
1907	01	22	311	58	6	18
1907	01	23	312	02	6	18
1907	01	24	312	07	6	17
1907	01	25	312	11	6	17
1907	01	26	312	16	6	17
1907	01	27	312	21	6	17
1907	01	28	312	25	6	17
1907	01	29	312	30	6	17
1907	01	30	312	34	6	17
1907	01	31	312	39	6	17
1907	02	01	312	44	6	17
1907	02	02	312	48	6	17
1907	02	03	312	53	6	17
1907	02	04	312	58	6	17
1907	02	05	313	02	6	17
1907	02	06	313	07	6	17
1907	02	07	313	11	6	17
1907	02	08	313	16	6	17
1907	02	09	313	21	6	17
1907	02	10	313	25	6	17
1907	02	11	313	30	6	17
1907	02	12	313	34	6	17
1907	02	13	313	39	6	17
1907	02	14	313	44	6	17
1907	02	15	313	48	6	17
1907	02	16	313	53	6	17
1907	02	17	313	57	6	17
1907	02	18	314	02	6	17
1907	02	19	314	06	6	17
1907	02	20	314	11	6	17
1907	02	21	314	15	6	17
1907	02	22	314	19	6	18
1907	02	23	314	24	6	18
1907	02	24	314	28	6	18
1907	02	25	314	33	6	18
1907	02	26	314	37	6	18
1907	02	27	314	41	6	18
1907	02	28	314	46	6	18
1907	03	01	314	50	6	18
1907	03	02	314	54	6	19
1907	03	03	314	59	6	19

1907	03	04	315	03	6	19
1907	03	05	315	07	6	19
1907	03	06	315	11	6	19
1907	03	07	315	15	6	19
1907	03	08	315	19	6	20
1907	03	09	315	23	6	20
1907	03	10	315	28	6	20
1907	03	11	315	32	6	20
1907	03	12	315	36	6	20
1907	03	13	315	39	6	21
1907	03	14	315	43	6	21
1907	03	15	315	47	6	21
1907	03	16	315	51	6	21
1907	03	17	315	55	6	21
1907	03	18	315	59	6	22
1907	03	19	316	02	6	22
1907	03	20	316	06	6	22
1907	03	21	316	10	6	22
1907	03	22	316	13	6	23
1907	03	23	316	17	6	23
1907	03	24	316	21	6	23
1907	03	25	316	24	6	23
1907	03	26	316	28	6	24
1907	03	27	316	31	6	24
1907	03	28	316	34	6	24
1907	03	29	316	38	6	25
1907	03	30	316	41	6	25
1907	03	31	316	44	6	25
1907	04	01	316	47	6	25
1907	04	02	316	50	6	26
1907	04	03	316	54	6	26
1907	04	04	316	57	6	26
1907	04	05	317	00	6	27
1907	04	06	317	02	6	27
1907	04	07	317	05	6	27
1907	04	08	317	08	6	28
1907	04	09	317	11	6	28
1907	04	10	317	14	6	28
1907	04	11	317	16	6	29
1907	04	12	317	19	6	29
1907	04	13	317	22	6	29
1907	04	14	317	24	6	30
1907	04	15	317	27	6	30
1907	04	16	317	29	6	30
1907	04	17	317	31	6	31
1907	04	18	317	34	6	31
1907	04	19	317	36	6	32
1907	04	20	317	38	6	32
1907	04	21	317	40	6	32
1907	04	22	317	42	6	33
1907	04	23	317	44	6	33
1907	04	24	317	46	6	33
1907	04	25	317	48	6	34
1907	04	26	317	50	6	34
1907	04	27	317	52	6	35
1907	04	28	317	53	6	35
1907	04	29	317	55	6	35
1907	04	30	317	57	6	36
1907	05	01	317	58	6	36
1907	05	02	317	59	6	37
1907	05	03	318	01	6	37
1907	05	04	318	02	6	37
1907	05	05	318	03	6	38
1907	05	06	318	05	6	38
1907	05	07	318	06	6	39
1907	05	08	318	07	6	39
1907	05	09	318	08	6	39
1907	05	10	318	09	6	40
1907	05	11	318	10	6	40
1907	05	12	318	11	6	41
1907	05	13	318	11	6	41
1907	05	14	318	12	6	42
1907	05	15	318	13	6	42
1907	05	16	318	13	6	42
1907	05	17	318	14	6	43
1907	05	18	318	14	6	43
1907	05	19	318	14	6	44
1907	05	20	318	15	6	44
1907	05	21	318	15	6	44
1907	05	22	318	15	6	45
1907	05	23	318	15	6	45
1907	05	24	318	15	6	46
1907	05	25	318	15	6	46
1907	05	26	318	15	6	46
1907	05	27	318	15	6	47
1907	05	28	318	15	6	47
1907	05	29	318	14	6	48
1907	05	30	318	14	6	48
1907	05	31	318	14	6	49
1907	06	01	318	13	6	49
1907	06	02	318	13	6	49
1907	06	03	318	12	6	50
1907	06	04	318	11	6	50
1907	06	05	318	11	6	51
1907	06	06	318	10	6	51
1907	06	07	318	09	6	51
1907	06	08	318	08	6	52
1907	06	09	318	07	6	52
1907	06	10	318	06	6	52
1907	06	11	318	05	6	53
1907	06	12	318	04	6	53
1907	06	13	318	02	6	54
1907	06	14	318	01	6	54
1907	06	15	318	00	6	54
1907	06	16	317	58	6	55
1907	06	17	317	57	6	55
1907	06	18	317	55	6	55
1907	06	19	317	54	6	56
1907	06	20	317	52	6	56
1907	06	21	317	51	6	56
1907	06	22	317	49	6	57
1907	06	23	317	47	6	57
1907	06	24	317	45	6	57
1907	06	25	317	43	6	58
1907	06	26	317	41	6	58
1907	06	27	317	39	6	58
1907	06	28	317	37	6	58
1907	06	29	317	35	6	59
1907	06	30	317	33	6	59
1907	07	01	317	31	6	59
1907	07	02	317	29	7	00
1907	07	03	317	26	7	00
1907	07	04	317	24	7	00
1907	07	05	317	22	7	00
1907	07	06	317	19	7	01
1907	07	07	317	17	7	01
1907	07	08	317	14	7	01
1907	07	09	317	12	7	01
1907	07	10	317	09	7	02
1907	07	11	317	07	7	02
1907	07	12	317	04	7	02
1907	07	13	317	01	7	02
1907	07	14	316	58	7	02
1907	07	15	316	56	7	02
1907	07	16	316	53	7	03
1907	07	17	316	50	7	03
1907	07	18	316	47	7	03
1907	07	19	316	44	7	03
1907	07	20	316	41	7	03
1907	07	21	316	39	7	03
1907	07	22	316	36	7	04
1907	07	23	316	33	7	04
1907	07	24	316	30	7	04
1907	07	25	316	27	7	04
1907	07	26	316	24	7	04
1907	07	27	316	21	7	04
1907	07	28	316	17	7	04
1907	07	29	316	14	7	04
1907	07	30	316	11	7	04
1907	07	31	316	08	7	04
1907	08	01	316	05	7	04
1907	08	02	316	02	7	04
1907	08	03	315	59	7	04
1907	08	04	315	56	7	04
1907	08	05	315	52	7	04
1907	08	06	315	49	7	04
1907	08	07	315	46	7	04
1907	08	08	315	43	7	04
1907	08	09	315	40	7	04
1907	08	10	315	36	7	04
1907	08	11	315	33	7	04
1907	08	12	315	30	7	04
1907	08	13	315	27	7	04
1907	08	14	315	24	7	04
1907	08	15	315	21	7	04
1907	08	16	315	17	7	04
1907	08	17	315	14	7	04
1907	08	18	315	11	7	04
1907	08	19	315	08	7	03
1907	08	20	315	05	7	03
1907	08	21	315	02	7	03
1907	08	22	314	59	7	03
1907	08	23	314	56	7	03
1907	08	24	314	53	7	03
1907	08	25	314	50	7	03
1907	08	26	314	47	7	02
1907	08	27	314	44	7	02
1907	08	28	314	41	7	02
1907	08	29	314	38	7	02
1907	08	30	314	35	7	02
1907	08	31	314	32	7	01
1907	09	01	314	29	7	01
1907	09	02	314	27	7	01
1907	09	03	314	24	7	01
1907	09	04	314	21	7	00
1907	09	05	314	18	7	00
1907	09	06	314	16	7	00
1907	09	07	314	13	7	00
1907	09	08	314	10	6	59
1907	09	09	314	08	6	59
1907	09	10	314	05	6	59
1907	09	11	314	03	6	58
1907	09	12	314	00	6	58
1907	09	13	313	58	6	58
1907	09	14	313	56	6	57
1907	09	15	313	53	6	57
1907	09	16	313	51	6	57
1907	09	17	313	49	6	56
1907	09	18	313	47	6	56
1907	09	19	313	45	6	56
1907	09	20	313	43	6	55
1907	09	21	313	41	6	55
1907	09	22	313	39	6	55
1907	09	23	313	37	6	54
1907	09	24	313	35	6	54
1907	09	25	313	33	6	53
1907	09	26	313	31	6	53
1907	09	27	313	30	6	53
1907	09	28	313	28	6	52
1907	09	29	313	26	6	52
1907	09	30	313	25	6	51
1907	10	01	313	23	6	51
1907	10	02	313	22	6	51
1907	10	03	313	21	6	50
1907	10	04	313	19	6	50
1907	10	05	313	18	6	49
1907	10	06	313	17	6	49
1907	10	07	313	16	6	49
1907	10	08	313	15	6	48
1907	10	09	313	14	6	48
1907	10	10	313	13	6	47
1907	10	11	313	12	6	47
1907	10	12	313	11	6	46
1907	10	13	313	10	6	46
1907	10	14	313	10	6	45
1907	10	15	313	09	6	45
1907	10	16	313	09	6	44
1907	10	17	313	00	6	44
1907	10	18	313	08	6	44
1907	10	19	313	07	6	43
1907	10	20	313	07	6	43
1907	10	21	313	07	6	42
1907	10	22	313	07	6	42
1907	10	23	313	07	6	41
1907	10	24	313	07	6	41
1907	10	25	313	07	6	40
1907	10	26	313	07	6	40
1907	10	27	313	07	6	39
1907	10	28	313	07	6	39
1907	10	29	313	07	6	38
1907	10	30	313	08	6	38
1907	10	31	313	08	6	37
1907	11	01	313	09	6	37
1907	11	02	313	09	6	36
1907	11	03	313	10	6	36
1907	11	04	313	11	6	35
1907	11	05	313	12	6	35
1907	11	06	313	12	6	35
1907	11	07	313	13	6	34
1907	11	08	313	14	6	34
1907	11	09	313	15	6	33
1907	11	10	313	16	6	33
1907	11	11	313	18	6	32
1907	11	12	313	19	6	32
1907	11	13	313	20	6	31
1907	11	14	313	22	6	31
1907	11	15	313	23	6	30
1907	11	16	313	24	6	30
1907	11	17	313	26	6	29
1907	11	18	313	28	6	29
1907	11	19	313	29	6	29
1907	11	20	313	31	6	28
1907	11	21	313	33	6	28
1907	11	22	313	35	6	27
1907	11	23	313	37	6	27
1907	11	24	313	39	6	26
1907	11	25	313	41	6	26
1907	11	26	313	43	6	25
1907	11	27	313	45	6	25
1907	11	28	313	47	6	25
1907	11	29	313	49	6	24
1907	11	30	313	52	6	24
1907	12	01	313	54	6	23
1907	12	02	313	57	6	23
1907	12	03	313	59	6	23
1907	12	04	314	02	6	22
1907	12	05	314	04	6	22
1907	12	06	314	07	6	21
1907	12	07	314	10	6	21
1907	12	08	314	12	6	21
1907	12	09	314	15	6	20
1907	12	10	314	18	6	20
1907	12	11	314	21	6	19
1907	12	12	314	24	6	19
1907	12	13	314	27	6	19
1907	12	14	314	30	6	18
1907	12	15	314	33	6	18
1907	12	16	314	36	6	18
1907	12	17	314	39	6	17
1907	12	18	314	43	6	17
1907	12	19	314	46	6	17
1907	12	20	314	49	6	16
1907	12	21	314	53	6	16
1907	12	22	314	56	6	16
1907	12	23	315	00	6	15
1907	12	24	315	03	6	15
1907	12	25	315	07	6	15
1907	12	26	315	10	6	14
1907	12	27	315	14	6	14
1907	12	28	315	17	6	14
1907	12	29	315	21	6	14
1907	12	30	315	25	6	13
1907	12	31	315	29	6	13
1908	01	01	315	32	6	13
1908	01	02	315	36	6	13
1908	01	03	315	40	6	12
1908	01	04	315	44	6	12
1908	01	05	315	48	6	12
1908	01	06	315	52	6	12
1908	01	07	315	56	6	11
1908	01	08	316	00	6	11
1908	01	09	316	04	6	11
1908	01	10	316	08	6	11
1908	01	11	316	12	6	10
1908	01	12	316	16	6	10
1908	01	13	316	20	6	10
1908	01	14	316	24	6	10
1908	01	15	316	29	6	10
1908	01	16	316	33	6	10
1908	01	17	316	37	6	09
1908	01	18	316	41	6	09
1908	01	19	316	45	6	09
1908	01	20	316	50	6	09
1908	01	21	316	54	6	09
1908	01	22	316	58	6	09
1908	01	23	317	03	6	08
1908	01	24	317	07	6	08
1908	01	25	317	11	6	08
1908	01	26	317	16	6	08
1908	01	27	317	20	6	08
1908	01	28	317	24	6	08
1908	01	29	317	29	6	08
1908	01	30	317	33	6	08
1908	01	31	317	38	6	08
1908	02	01	317	42	6	07
1908	02	02	317	46	6	07
1908	02	03	317	51	6	07
1908	02	04	317	55	6	07
1908	02	05	318	00	6	07
1908	02	06	318	04	6	07
1908	02	07	318	09	6	07
1908	02	08	318	13	6	07
1908	02	09	318	17	6	07
1908	02	10	318	22	6	07
1908	02	11	318	26	6	07
1908	02	12	318	31	6	07
1908	02	13	318	35	6	07
1908	02	14	318	39	6	07
1908	02	15	318	44	6	07
1908	02	16	318	48	6	07
1908	02	17	318	53	6	07
1908	02	18	318	57	6	07
1908	02	19	319	01	6	07
1908	02	20	319	06	6	07
1908	02	21	319	10	6	07
1908	02	22	319	14	6	07
1908	02	23	319	19	6	07
1908	02	24	319	23	6	07
1908	02	25	319	27	6	07
1908	02	26	319	32	6	07
1908	02	27	319	36	6	07
1908	02	28	319	40	6	08
1908	02	29	319	44	6	08
1908	03	01	319	49	6	08
1908	03	02	319	53	6	08
1908	03	03	319	57	6	08
1908	03	04	320	01	6	08
1908	03	05	320	05	6	08
1908	03	06	320	09	6	08
1908	03	07	320	14	6	08
1908	03	08	320	18	6	09
1908	03	09	320	22	6	09
1908	03	10	320	26	6	09
1908	03	11	320	30	6	09
1908	03	12	320	34	6	09
1908	03	13	320	38	6	09
1908	03	14	320	41	6	09
1908	03	15	320	45	6	10
1908	03	16	320	49	6	10
1908	03	17	320	53	6	10
1908	03	18	320	57	6	10
1908	03	19	321	00	6	10
1908	03	20	321	04	6	11
1908	03	21	321	08	6	11
1908	03	22	321	11	6	11
1908	03	23	321	15	6	11
1908	03	24	321	19	6	11
1908	03	25	321	22	6	12
1908	03	26	321	26	6	12
1908	03	27	321	29	6	12
1908	03	28	321	33	6	12
1908	03	29	321	36	6	13
1908	03	30	321	39	6	13
1908	03	31	321	43	6	13
1908	04	01	321	46	6	13
1908	04	02	321	49	6	14
1908	04	03	321	52	6	14
1908	04	04	321	55	6	14
1908	04	05	321	58	6	14
1908	04	06	322	01	6	15
1908	04	07	322	04	6	15
1908	04	08	322	07	6	15
1908	04	09	322	10	6	16
1908	04	10	322	13	6	16
1908	04	11	322	16	6	16
1908	04	12	322	18	6	16
1908	04	13	322	21	6	17
1908	04	14	322	24	6	17
1908	04	15	322	26	6	17
1908	04	16	322	29	6	18
1908	04	17	322	31	6	18
1908	04	18	322	34	6	18
1908	04	19	322	36	6	19
1908	04	20	322	38	6	19
1908	04	21	322	41	6	19
1908	04	22	322	43	6	20

1908	04	23	322	45	6	20
1908	04	24	322	47	6	20
1908	04	25	322	49	6	21
1908	04	26	322	51	6	21
1908	04	27	322	53	6	21
1908	04	28	322	55	6	22
1908	04	29	322	57	6	22
1908	04	30	322	59	6	22
1908	05	01	323	00	6	23
1908	05	02	323	02	6	23
1908	05	03	323	04	6	23
1908	05	04	323	05	6	24
1908	05	05	323	07	6	24
1908	05	06	323	08	6	25
1908	05	07	323	09	6	25
1908	05	08	323	11	6	25
1908	05	09	323	12	6	26
1908	05	10	323	13	6	26
1908	05	11	323	14	6	26
1908	05	12	323	15	6	27
1908	05	13	323	16	6	27
1908	05	14	323	17	6	28
1908	05	15	323	18	6	28
1908	05	16	323	19	6	28
1908	05	17	323	19	6	29
1908	05	18	323	20	6	29
1908	05	19	323	21	6	29
1908	05	20	323	21	6	30
1908	05	21	323	22	6	30
1908	05	22	323	22	6	31
1908	05	23	323	22	6	31
1908	05	24	323	23	6	31
1908	05	25	323	23	6	32
1908	05	26	323	23	6	32
1908	05	27	323	23	6	32
1908	05	28	323	23	6	33
1908	05	29	323	23	6	33
1908	05	30	323	23	6	34
1908	05	31	323	23	6	34
1908	06	01	323	23	6	34
1908	06	02	323	22	6	35
1908	06	03	323	22	6	35
1908	06	04	323	22	6	35
1908	06	05	323	21	6	36
1908	06	06	323	21	6	36
1908	06	07	323	20	6	37
1908	06	08	323	20	6	37
1908	06	09	323	19	6	37
1908	06	10	323	18	6	38
1908	06	11	323	17	6	38
1908	06	12	323	16	6	38
1908	06	13	323	15	6	39
1908	06	14	323	14	6	39
1908	06	15	323	13	6	39
1908	06	16	323	12	6	40
1908	06	17	323	11	6	40
1908	06	18	323	10	6	40
1908	06	19	323	08	6	41
1908	06	20	323	07	6	41
1908	06	21	323	06	6	41
1908	06	22	323	04	6	42
1908	06	23	323	03	6	42
1908	06	24	323	01	6	42
1908	06	25	323	00	6	43
1908	06	26	322	58	6	43
1908	06	27	322	56	6	43
1908	06	28	322	54	6	43
1908	06	29	322	53	6	44
1908	06	30	322	51	6	44
1908	07	01	322	49	6	44
1908	07	02	322	47	6	45
1908	07	03	322	45	6	45
1908	07	04	322	43	6	45
1908	07	05	322	41	6	45
1908	07	06	322	38	6	46
1908	07	07	322	36	6	46
1908	07	08	322	34	6	46
1908	07	09	322	32	6	46
1908	07	10	322	29	6	47
1908	07	11	322	27	6	47
1908	07	12	322	24	6	47
1908	07	13	322	22	6	47
1908	07	14	322	20	6	47
1908	07	15	322	17	6	48
1908	07	16	322	14	6	48
1908	07	17	322	12	6	48
1908	07	18	322	09	6	48
1908	07	19	322	07	6	48
1908	07	20	322	04	6	48
1908	07	21	322	01	6	49
1908	07	22	321	58	6	49
1908	07	23	321	56	6	49
1908	07	24	321	53	6	49
1908	07	25	321	50	6	49
1908	07	26	321	47	6	49
1700	07	27	321	44	6	47
1908	07	28	321	41	6	49
1908	07	29	321	38	6	49
1908	07	30	321	35	6	50
1908	07	31	321	32	6	50
1908	08	01	321	29	6	50
1908	08	02	321	26	6	50
1908	08	03	321	23	6	50
1908	08	04	321	20	6	50
1908	08	05	321	17	6	50
1908	08	06	321	14	6	50
1908	08	07	321	11	6	50
1908	08	08	321	08	6	50
1908	08	09	321	05	6	50
1908	08	10	321	02	6	50
1908	08	11	320	59	6	50
1908	08	12	320	56	6	50
1908	08	13	320	53	6	50
1908	08	14	320	50	6	50
1908	08	15	320	46	6	50
1908	08	16	320	43	6	50
1908	08	17	320	40	6	50
1908	08	18	320	37	6	49
1908	08	19	320	34	6	49
1908	08	20	320	31	6	49
1908	08	21	320	28	6	49
1908	08	22	320	25	6	49
1908	08	23	320	22	6	49
1908	08	24	320	19	6	49
1908	08	25	320	16	6	49
1908	08	26	320	13	6	49
1908	08	27	320	10	6	48
1908	08	28	320	07	6	48
1908	08	29	320	04	6	48
1908	08	30	320	01	6	48
1908	08	31	319	58	6	48
1908	09	01	319	55	6	48
1908	09	02	319	52	6	47
1908	09	03	319	49	6	47
1908	09	04	319	47	6	47
1908	09	05	319	44	6	47
1908	09	06	319	41	6	47
1908	09	07	319	38	6	46
1908	09	08	319	36	6	46
1908	09	09	319	33	6	46
1908	09	10	319	30	6	46
1908	09	11	319	28	6	45
1908	09	12	319	25	6	45
1908	09	13	319	23	6	45
1908	09	14	319	20	6	44
1908	09	15	319	18	6	44
1908	09	16	319	15	6	44
1908	09	17	319	13	6	44
1908	09	18	319	11	6	43
1908	09	19	319	08	6	43
1908	09	20	319	06	6	43
1908	09	21	319	04	6	42
1908	09	22	319	02	6	42
1908	09	23	319	00	6	42
1908	09	24	318	58	6	41
1908	09	25	318	56	6	41
1908	09	26	318	54	6	41
1908	09	27	318	52	6	40
1908	09	28	318	50	6	40
1908	09	29	318	48	6	40
1908	09	30	318	46	6	39
1908	10	01	318	45	6	39
1908	10	02	318	43	6	38
1908	10	03	318	41	6	38
1908	10	04	318	40	6	38
1908	10	05	318	38	6	37
1908	10	06	318	37	6	37
1908	10	07	318	36	6	36
1908	10	08	318	34	6	36
1908	10	09	318	33	6	36
1908	10	10	318	32	6	35
1908	10	11	318	31	6	35
1908	10	12	318	30	6	34
1908	10	13	318	29	6	34
1908	10	14	318	28	6	34
1908	10	15	318	27	6	33
1908	10	16	318	26	6	33
1908	10	17	318	25	6	32
1908	10	18	318	24	6	32
1908	10	19	318	24	6	31
1908	10	20	318	23	6	31
1908	10	21	318	23	6	30
1908	10	22	318	22	6	30
1908	10	23	318	22	6	30
1908	10	24	318	21	6	29
1908	10	25	318	21	6	29
1908	10	26	318	21	6	28
1908	10	27	318	21	6	28
1908	10	28	318	21	6	27
1908	10	29	318	21	6	27
1908	10	30	318	21	6	26
1908	10	31	318	21	6	26
1908	11	01	318	21	6	26
1908	11	02	318	21	6	25
1908	11	03	318	22	6	25
1908	11	04	318	22	6	24
1908	11	05	318	22	6	24
1908	11	06	318	23	6	23
1908	11	07	318	24	6	23
1908	11	08	318	24	6	22
1908	11	09	318	25	6	22
1908	11	10	318	26	6	21
1908	11	11	318	26	6	21
1908	11	12	318	27	6	21
1908	11	13	318	28	6	20
1908	11	14	318	29	6	20
1908	11	15	318	30	6	19
1908	11	16	318	31	6	19
1908	11	17	318	33	6	18
1908	11	18	318	34	6	18
1908	11	19	318	35	6	17
1908	11	20	318	37	6	17
1908	11	21	318	38	6	17
1908	11	22	318	40	6	16
1908	11	23	318	41	6	16
1908	11	24	318	43	6	15
1908	11	25	318	44	6	15
1908	11	26	318	46	6	14
1908	11	27	318	48	6	14
1908	11	28	318	50	6	14
1908	11	29	318	52	6	13
1908	11	30	318	54	6	13
1908	12	01	318	56	6	12
1908	12	02	318	58	6	12
1908	12	03	319	00	6	12
1908	12	04	319	02	6	11
1908	12	05	319	05	6	11
1908	12	06	319	07	6	10
1908	12	07	319	09	6	10
1908	12	08	319	12	6	10
1908	12	09	319	14	6	09
1908	12	10	319	17	6	09
1908	12	11	319	19	6	09
1908	12	12	319	22	6	08
1908	12	13	319	24	6	08
1908	12	14	319	27	6	07
1908	12	15	319	30	6	07
1908	12	16	319	33	6	07
1908	12	17	319	36	6	06
1908	12	18	319	39	6	06
1908	12	19	319	42	6	06
1908	12	20	319	45	6	05
1908	12	21	319	48	6	05
1908	12	22	319	51	6	05
1908	12	23	319	54	6	04
1908	12	24	319	57	6	04
1908	12	25	320	00	6	04
1908	12	26	320	04	6	03
1908	12	27	320	07	6	03
1908	12	28	320	10	6	03
1908	12	29	320	14	6	03
1908	12	30	320	17	6	02
1908	12	31	320	20	6	02
1909	01	01	320	24	6	02
1909	01	02	320	28	6	01
1909	01	03	320	31	6	01
1909	01	04	320	35	6	01
1909	01	05	320	38	6	01
1909	01	06	320	42	6	00
1909	01	07	320	46	6	00
1909	01	08	320	49	6	00
1909	01	09	320	53	6	00
1909	01	10	320	57	5	59
1909	01	11	321	01	5	59
1909	01	12	321	05	5	59
1909	01	13	321	08	5	59
1909	01	14	321	12	5	59
1909	01	15	321	16	5	58
1909	01	16	321	20	5	58
1909	01	17	321	24	5	58
1909	01	18	321	28	5	58
1909	01	19	321	32	5	58
1909	01	20	321	36	5	57
1909	01	21	321	40	5	57
1909	01	22	321	44	5	57
1909	01	23	321	48	5	57
1909	01	24	321	53	5	57
1909	01	25	321	57	5	57
1909	01	26	322	01	5	56
1909	01	27	322	05	5	56
1909	01	28	322	09	5	56
1909	01	29	322	13	5	56
1909	01	30	322	18	5	56
1909	01	31	322	22	5	56
1909	02	01	322	26	5	56
1909	02	02	322	30	5	56
1909	02	03	322	34	5	55
1909	02	04	322	39	5	55
1909	02	05	322	43	5	55
1909	02	06	322	47	5	55
1909	02	07	322	51	5	55
1909	02	08	322	56	5	55
1909	02	09	323	00	5	55
1909	02	10	323	04	5	55
1909	02	11	323	08	5	55
1909	02	12	323	13	5	55
1909	02	13	323	17	5	55
1909	02	14	323	21	5	55
1909	02	15	323	26	5	55
1909	02	16	323	30	5	55
1909	02	17	323	34	5	55
1909	02	18	323	38	5	55
1909	02	19	323	43	5	55
1909	02	20	323	47	5	55
1909	02	21	323	51	5	55
1909	02	22	323	55	5	55
1909	02	23	323	59	5	55
1909	02	24	324	04	5	55
1909	02	25	324	08	5	55
1909	02	26	324	12	5	55
1909	02	27	324	16	5	55
1909	02	28	324	20	5	55
1909	03	01	324	25	5	55
1909	03	02	324	29	5	55
1909	03	03	324	33	5	55
1909	03	04	324	37	5	55
1909	03	05	324	41	5	55
1909	03	06	324	45	5	55
1909	03	07	324	49	5	55
1909	03	08	324	53	5	55
1909	03	09	324	57	5	56
1909	03	10	325	01	5	56
1909	03	11	325	05	5	56
1909	03	12	325	09	5	56
1909	03	13	325	13	5	56
1909	03	14	325	17	5	56
1909	03	15	325	21	5	56
1909	03	16	325	25	5	56
1909	03	17	325	28	5	56
1909	03	18	325	32	5	57
1909	03	19	325	36	5	57
1909	03	20	325	40	5	57
1909	03	21	325	43	5	57
1909	03	22	325	47	5	57
1909	03	23	325	51	5	57
1909	03	24	325	54	5	58
1909	03	25	325	58	5	58
1909	03	26	326	01	5	58
1909	03	27	326	05	5	58
1909	03	28	326	08	5	58
1909	03	29	326	12	5	59
1909	03	30	326	15	5	59
1909	03	31	326	19	5	59
1909	04	01	326	22	5	59
1909	04	02	326	25	5	59
1909	04	03	326	28	6	00
1909	04	04	326	32	6	00
1909	04	05	326	35	6	00
1909	04	06	326	38	6	00
1909	04	07	326	41	6	00
1909	04	08	326	44	6	01
1909	04	09	326	47	6	01
1909	04	10	326	50	6	01
1909	04	11	326	53	6	01
1909	04	12	326	56	6	02
1909	04	13	326	59	6	02
1909	04	14	327	01	6	02
1909	04	15	327	04	6	02
1909	04	16	327	07	6	03
1909	04	17	327	09	6	03
1909	04	18	327	12	6	03
1909	04	19	327	14	6	04
1909	04	20	327	17	6	04
1909	04	21	327	19	6	04
1909	04	22	327	22	6	04
1909	04	23	327	24	6	05
1909	04	24	327	26	6	05
1909	04	25	327	29	6	05
1909	04	26	327	31	6	06
1909	04	27	327	33	6	06
1909	04	28	327	35	6	06
1909	04	29	327	37	6	07
1909	04	30	327	39	6	07
1909	05	01	327	41	6	07
1909	05	02	327	43	6	08
1909	05	03	327	45	6	08
1909	05	04	327	46	6	08
1909	05	05	327	48	6	08
1909	05	06	327	50	6	09
1909	05	07	327	51	6	09
1909	05	08	327	53	6	09
1909	05	09	327	54	6	10
1909	05	10	327	56	6	10
1909	05	11	327	57	6	10
1909	05	12	327	58	6	11
1909	05	13	327	59	6	11
1909	05	14	328	01	6	11
1909	05	15	328	02	6	12
1909	05	16	328	03	6	12
1909	05	17	328	04	6	13
1909	05	18	328	05	6	13
1909	05	19	328	06	6	13
1909	05	20	328	06	6	14
1909	05	21	328	07	6	14
1909	05	22	328	08	6	14
1909	05	23	328	09	6	15
1909	05	24	328	09	6	15
1909	05	25	328	10	6	15
1909	05	26	328	10	6	16
1909	05	27	328	10	6	16
1909	05	28	328	11	6	16
1909	05	29	328	11	6	17
1909	05	30	328	11	6	17
1909	05	31	328	11	6	17
1909	06	01	328	11	6	18
1909	06	02	328	12	6	18
1909	06	03	328	11	6	18
1909	06	04	328	11	6	19
1909	06	05	328	11	6	19
1909	06	06	328	11	6	19
1909	06	07	328	11	6	20
1909	06	08	328	10	6	20
1909	06	09	328	10	6	20
1909	06	10	328	10	6	21

1909	06	11	328	09	6	21
1909	06	12	328	08	6	21
1909	06	13	328	08	6	22
1909	06	14	328	07	6	22
1909	06	15	328	06	6	22
1909	06	16	328	06	6	23
1909	06	17	328	05	6	23
1909	06	18	328	04	6	23
1909	06	19	328	03	6	24
1909	06	20	328	02	6	24
1909	06	21	328	01	6	24
1909	06	22	327	59	6	25
1909	06	23	327	58	6	25
1909	06	24	327	57	6	25
1909	06	25	327	56	6	26
1909	06	26	327	54	6	26
1909	06	27	327	53	6	26
1909	06	28	327	51	6	26
1909	06	29	327	50	6	27
1909	06	30	327	48	6	27
1909	07	01	327	47	6	27
1909	07	02	327	45	6	27
1909	07	03	327	43	6	28
1909	07	04	327	41	6	28
1909	07	05	327	40	6	28
1909	07	06	327	38	6	28
1909	07	07	327	36	6	29
1909	07	08	327	34	6	29
1909	07	09	327	32	6	29
1909	07	10	327	30	6	29
1909	07	11	327	28	6	30
1909	07	12	327	26	6	30
1909	07	13	327	23	6	30
1909	07	14	327	21	6	30
1909	07	15	327	19	6	30
1909	07	16	327	16	6	31
1909	07	17	327	14	6	31
1909	07	18	327	12	6	31
1909	07	19	327	09	6	31
1909	07	20	327	07	6	31
1909	07	21	327	04	6	32
1909	07	22	327	02	6	32
1909	07	23	326	59	6	32
1909	07	24	326	57	6	32
1909	07	25	326	54	6	32
1909	07	26	326	51	6	32
1909	07	27	326	49	6	32
1909	07	28	326	46	6	33
1909	07	29	326	43	6	33
1909	07	30	326	40	6	33
1909	07	31	326	38	6	33
1909	08	01	326	35	6	33
1909	08	02	326	32	6	33
1909	08	03	326	29	6	33
1909	08	04	326	26	6	33
1909	08	05	326	23	6	33
1909	08	06	326	20	6	33
1909	08	07	326	18	6	33
1909	08	08	326	15	6	33
1909	08	09	326	12	6	33
1909	08	10	326	09	6	33
1909	08	11	326	06	6	33
1909	08	12	326	03	6	33
1909	08	13	326	00	6	33
1909	08	14	325	57	6	33
1909	08	15	325	54	6	33
1909	08	16	325	51	6	33
1909	08	17	325	48	6	33
1909	08	18	325	45	6	33
1909	08	19	325	42	6	33
1909	08	20	325	39	6	33
1909	08	21	325	35	6	33
1909	08	22	325	32	6	33
1909	08	23	325	29	6	33
1909	08	24	325	26	6	33
1909	08	25	325	23	6	33
1909	08	26	325	20	6	33
1909	08	27	325	17	6	33
1909	08	28	325	14	6	33
1909	08	29	325	12	6	32
1909	08	30	325	09	6	32
1909	08	31	325	06	6	32
1909	09	01	325	03	6	32
1909	09	02	325	00	6	32
1909	09	03	324	57	6	32
1909	09	04	324	54	6	31
1909	09	05	324	51	6	31
1909	09	06	324	48	6	31
1909	09	07	324	46	6	31
1909	09	08	324	43	6	31
1909	09	09	324	40	6	31
1909	09	10	324	37	6	30
1909	09	11	324	35	6	30
1909	09	12	324	32	6	30
1909	09	13	324	29	6	30
1909	09	14	324	27	6	29
1909	09	15	324	24	6	29
1909	09	16	324	21	6	29
1909	09	17	324	19	6	29
1909	09	18	324	16	6	28
1909	09	19	324	14	6	28
1909	09	20	324	12	6	28
1909	09	21	324	09	6	28
1909	09	22	324	07	6	27
1909	09	23	324	05	6	27
1909	09	24	324	02	6	27
1909	09	25	324	00	6	26
1909	09	26	323	58	6	26
1909	09	27	323	56	6	26
1909	09	28	323	54	6	25
1909	09	29	323	52	6	25
1909	09	30	323	50	6	25
1909	10	01	323	48	6	25
1909	10	02	323	46	6	24
1909	10	03	323	44	6	24
1909	10	04	323	42	6	23
1909	10	05	323	41	6	23
1909	10	06	323	39	6	23
1909	10	07	323	37	6	22
1909	10	08	323	36	6	22
1909	10	09	323	34	6	22
1909	10	10	323	33	6	21
1909	10	11	323	31	6	21
1909	10	12	323	30	6	21
1909	10	13	323	29	6	20
1909	10	14	323	27	6	20
1909	10	15	323	26	6	19
1909	10	16	323	25	6	19
1909	10	17	323	24	6	19
1909	10	18	323	23	6	18
1909	10	19	323	22	6	18
1909	10	20	323	21	6	17
1909	10	21	323	20	6	17
1909	10	22	323	19	6	17
1909	10	23	323	19	6	16
1909	10	24	323	18	6	16
1909	10	25	323	17	6	15
1909	10	26	323	17	6	15
1909	10	27	323	16	6	14
1909	10	28	323	16	6	14
1909	10	29	323	16	6	14
1909	10	30	323	15	6	13
1909	10	31	323	15	6	13
1909	11	01	323	15	6	12
1909	11	02	323	15	6	12
1909	11	03	323	15	6	12
1909	11	04	323	15	6	11
1909	11	05	323	15	6	11
1909	11	06	323	15	6	10
1909	11	07	323	15	6	10
1909	11	08	323	15	6	09
1909	11	09	323	16	6	09
1909	11	10	323	16	6	08
1909	11	11	323	16	6	08
1909	11	12	323	17	6	08
1909	11	13	323	18	6	07
1909	11	14	323	18	6	07
1909	11	15	323	19	6	06
1909	11	16	323	20	6	06
1909	11	17	323	20	6	06
1909	11	18	323	21	6	05
1909	11	19	323	22	6	05
1909	11	20	323	23	6	04
1909	11	21	323	24	6	04
1909	11	22	323	26	6	03
1909	11	23	323	27	6	03
1909	11	24	323	28	6	03
1909	11	25	323	29	6	02
1909	11	26	323	31	6	02
1909	11	27	323	32	6	01
1909	11	28	323	34	6	01
1909	11	29	323	35	6	01
1909	11	30	323	37	6	00
1909	12	01	323	38	6	00
1909	12	02	323	40	5	59
1909	12	03	323	42	5	59
1909	12	04	323	44	5	59
1909	12	05	323	46	5	58
1909	12	06	323	48	5	58
1909	12	07	323	50	5	57
1909	12	08	323	52	5	57
1909	12	09	323	54	5	57
1909	12	10	323	56	5	56
1909	12	11	323	58	5	56
1909	12	12	324	00	5	55
1909	12	13	324	03	5	55
1909	12	14	324	05	5	55
1909	12	15	324	08	5	54
1909	12	16	324	10	5	54
1909	12	17	324	13	5	54
1909	12	18	324	15	5	53
1909	12	19	324	18	5	53
1909	12	20	324	20	5	53
1909	12	21	324	23	5	52
1909	12	22	324	26	5	52
1909	12	23	324	29	5	52
1909	12	24	324	32	5	51
1909	12	25	324	34	5	51
1909	12	26	324	37	5	51
1909	12	27	324	40	5	50
1909	12	28	324	43	5	50
1909	12	29	324	46	5	50
1909	12	30	324	50	5	49
1909	12	31	324	53	5	49
1910	01	01	324	56	5	49
1910	01	02	324	59	5	49
1910	01	03	325	02	5	48
1910	01	04	325	06	5	48
1910	01	05	325	09	5	48
1910	01	06	325	12	5	47
1910	01	07	325	16	5	47
1910	01	08	325	19	5	47
1910	01	09	325	23	5	47
1910	01	10	325	26	5	46
1910	01	11	325	30	5	46
1910	01	12	325	33	5	46
1910	01	13	325	37	5	46
1910	01	14	325	41	5	45
1910	01	15	325	44	5	45
1910	01	16	325	48	5	45
1910	01	17	325	52	5	45
1910	01	18	325	55	5	45
1910	01	19	325	59	5	44
1910	01	20	326	03	5	44
1910	01	21	326	07	5	44
1910	01	22	326	11	5	44
1910	01	23	326	14	5	44
1910	01	24	326	18	5	43
1910	01	25	326	22	5	43
1910	01	26	326	26	5	43
1910	01	27	326	30	5	43
1910	01	28	326	34	5	43
1910	01	29	326	38	5	43
1910	01	30	326	42	5	43
1910	01	31	326	46	5	42
1910	02	01	326	50	5	42
1910	02	02	326	54	5	42
1910	02	03	326	58	5	42
1910	02	04	327	02	5	42
1910	02	05	327	06	5	42
1910	02	06	327	10	5	42
1910	02	07	327	14	5	42
1910	02	08	327	19	5	41
1910	02	09	327	23	5	41
1910	02	10	327	27	5	41
1910	02	11	327	31	5	41
1910	02	12	327	35	5	41
1910	02	13	327	39	5	41
1910	02	14	327	43	5	41
1910	02	15	327	47	5	41
1910	02	16	327	51	5	41
1910	02	17	327	56	5	41
1910	02	18	328	00	5	41
1910	02	19	328	04	5	41
1910	02	20	328	08	5	41
1910	02	21	328	12	5	41
1910	02	22	328	16	5	41
1910	02	23	328	20	5	41
1910	02	24	328	24	5	41
1910	02	25	328	29	5	41
1910	02	26	328	33	5	41
1910	02	27	328	37	5	41
1910	02	28	328	41	5	41
1910	03	01	328	45	5	41
1910	03	02	328	49	5	41
1910	03	03	328	53	5	41
1910	03	04	328	57	5	41
1910	03	05	329	01	5	41
1910	03	06	329	05	5	41
1910	03	07	329	09	5	41
1910	03	08	329	13	5	41
1910	03	09	329	17	5	41
1910	03	10	329	21	5	41
1910	03	11	329	25	5	41
1910	03	12	329	29	5	41
1910	03	13	329	33	5	41
1910	03	14	329	37	5	41
1910	03	15	329	40	5	41
1910	03	16	329	44	5	41
1910	03	17	329	48	5	42
1910	03	18	329	52	5	42
1910	03	19	329	56	5	42
1910	03	20	329	59	5	42
1910	03	21	330	03	5	42
1910	03	22	330	07	5	42
1910	03	23	330	10	5	42
1910	03	24	330	14	5	42
1910	03	25	330	18	5	43
1910	03	26	330	21	5	43
1910	03	27	330	25	5	43
1910	03	28	330	28	5	43
1910	03	29	330	32	5	43
1910	03	30	330	35	5	43
1910	03	31	330	39	5	43
1910	04	01	330	42	5	44
1910	04	02	330	45	5	44
1910	04	03	330	49	5	44
1910	04	04	330	52	5	44
1910	04	05	330	55	5	44
1910	04	06	330	58	5	44
1910	04	07	331	02	5	45
1910	04	08	331	05	5	45
1910	04	09	331	08	5	45
1910	04	10	331	11	5	45
1910	04	11	331	14	5	45
1910	04	12	331	17	5	46
1910	04	13	331	20	5	46
1910	04	14	331	23	5	46
1910	04	15	331	25	5	46
1910	04	16	331	28	5	47
1910	04	17	331	31	5	47
1910	04	18	331	34	5	47
1910	04	19	331	36	5	47
1910	04	20	331	39	5	48
1910	04	21	331	42	5	48
1910	04	22	331	44	5	48
1910	04	23	331	47	5	48
1910	04	24	331	49	5	49
1910	04	25	331	51	5	49
1910	04	26	331	54	5	49
1910	04	27	331	56	5	49
1910	04	28	331	58	5	50
1910	04	29	332	01	5	50
1910	04	30	332	03	5	50
1910	05	01	332	05	5	50
1910	05	02	332	07	5	51
1910	05	03	332	09	5	51
1910	05	04	332	11	5	51
1910	05	05	332	13	5	52
1910	05	06	332	15	5	52
1910	05	07	332	16	5	52
1910	05	08	332	18	5	52
1910	05	09	332	20	5	53
1910	05	10	332	21	5	53
1910	05	11	332	23	5	53
1910	05	12	332	24	5	54
1910	05	13	332	26	5	54
1910	05	14	332	27	5	54
1910	05	15	332	29	5	54
1910	05	16	332	30	5	55
1910	05	17	332	31	5	55
1910	05	18	332	32	5	55
1910	05	19	332	33	5	56
1910	05	20	332	34	5	56
1910	05	21	332	35	5	56
1910	05	22	332	36	5	57
1910	05	23	332	37	5	57
1910	05	24	332	38	5	57
1910	05	25	332	39	5	58
1910	05	26	332	40	5	58
1910	05	27	332	40	5	58
1910	05	28	332	41	5	59
1910	05	29	332	41	5	59
1910	05	30	332	42	5	59
1910	05	31	332	42	5	59
1910	06	01	332	43	6	00
1910	06	02	332	43	6	00
1910	06	03	332	43	6	00
1910	06	04	332	43	6	01
1910	06	05	332	43	6	01
1910	06	06	332	43	6	01
1910	06	07	332	43	6	02
1910	06	08	332	43	6	02
1910	06	09	332	43	6	02
1910	06	10	332	43	6	03
1910	06	11	332	43	6	03
1910	06	12	332	43	6	03
1910	06	13	332	42	6	04
1910	06	14	332	42	6	04
1910	06	15	332	41	6	04
1910	06	16	332	41	6	04
1910	06	17	332	40	6	05
1910	06	18	332	40	6	05
1910	06	19	332	39	6	05
1910	06	20	332	38	6	06
1910	06	21	332	37	6	06
1910	06	22	332	36	6	06
1910	06	23	332	36	6	07
1910	06	24	332	35	6	07
1910	06	25	332	34	6	07
1910	06	26	332	32	6	07
1910	06	27	332	31	6	08
1910	06	28	332	30	6	08
1910	06	29	332	29	6	08
1910	06	30	332	28	6	08
1910	07	01	332	26	6	09
1910	07	02	332	25	6	09
1910	07	03	332	23	6	09
1910	07	04	332	22	6	09
1910	07	05	332	20	6	10
1910	07	06	332	19	6	10
1910	07	07	332	17	6	10
1910	07	08	332	15	6	10
1910	07	09	332	14	6	11
1910	07	10	332	12	6	11
1910	07	11	332	10	6	11
1910	07	12	332	08	6	11
1910	07	13	332	06	6	12
1910	07	14	332	04	6	12
1910	07	15	332	02	6	12
1910	07	16	332	00	6	12
1910	07	17	331	58	6	12
1910	07	18	331	56	6	13
1910	07	19	331	53	6	13
1910	07	20	331	51	6	13
1910	07	21	331	49	6	13
1910	07	22	331	47	6	13
1910	07	23	331	44	6	13
1910	07	24	331	42	6	14
1910	07	25	331	40	6	14
1910	07	26	331	37	6	14
1910	07	27	331	35	6	14
1910	07	28	331	32	6	14
1910	07	29	331	30	6	14
1910	07	30	331	27	6	14
1910	07	31	331	24	6	15

1910	08	01	331	22	6	15
1910	08	02	331	19	6	15
1910	08	03	331	16	6	15
1910	08	04	331	14	6	15
1910	08	05	331	11	6	15
1910	08	06	331	08	6	15
1910	08	07	331	05	6	15
1910	08	08	331	03	6	15
1910	08	09	331	00	6	15
1910	08	10	330	57	6	15
1910	08	11	330	54	6	15
1910	08	12	330	51	6	15
1910	08	13	330	48	6	15
1910	08	14	330	45	6	15
1910	08	15	330	43	6	15
1910	08	16	330	40	6	15
1910	08	17	330	37	6	15
1910	08	18	330	34	6	15
1910	08	19	330	31	6	15
1910	08	20	330	28	6	15
1910	08	21	330	25	6	15
1910	08	22	330	22	6	15
1910	08	23	330	19	6	15
1910	08	24	330	16	6	15
1910	08	25	330	13	6	15
1910	08	26	330	10	6	15
1910	08	27	330	07	6	15
1910	08	28	330	04	6	15
1910	08	29	330	01	6	15
1910	08	30	329	58	6	15
1910	08	31	329	55	6	15
1910	09	01	329	52	6	15
1910	09	02	329	49	6	14
1910	09	03	329	47	6	14
1910	09	04	329	44	6	14
1910	09	05	329	41	6	14
1910	09	06	329	38	6	14
1910	09	07	329	35	6	14
1910	09	08	329	32	6	14
1910	09	09	329	29	6	14
1910	09	10	329	27	6	13
1910	09	11	329	24	6	13
1910	09	12	329	21	6	13
1910	09	13	329	18	6	13
1910	09	14	329	16	6	13
1910	09	15	329	13	6	12
1910	09	16	329	10	6	12
1910	09	17	329	08	6	12
1910	09	18	329	05	6	12
1910	09	19	329	03	6	12
1910	09	20	329	00	6	11
1910	09	21	328	58	6	11
1910	09	22	328	55	6	11
1910	09	23	328	53	6	11
1910	09	24	328	50	6	10
1910	09	25	328	48	6	10
1910	09	26	328	46	6	10
1910	09	27	328	43	6	09
1910	09	28	328	41	6	09
1910	09	29	328	39	6	09
1910	09	30	328	37	6	09
1910	10	01	328	35	6	08
1910	10	02	328	32	6	08
1910	10	03	328	30	6	08
1910	10	04	328	28	6	07
1910	10	05	328	26	6	07
1910	10	06	328	25	6	07
1910	10	07	328	23	6	06
1910	10	08	328	21	6	06
1910	10	09	328	19	6	06
1910	10	10	328	17	6	05
1910	10	11	328	16	6	05
1910	10	12	328	14	6	05
1910	10	13	328	13	6	04
1910	10	14	328	11	6	04
1910	10	15	328	10	6	04
1910	10	16	328	08	6	03
1910	10	17	328	07	6	03
1910	10	18	328	06	6	03
1910	10	19	328	04	6	02
1910	10	20	328	03	6	02
1910	10	21	328	02	6	02
1910	10	22	328	01	6	01
1910	10	23	328	00	6	01
1910	10	24	327	59	6	00
1910	10	25	327	58	6	00
1910	10	26	327	57	6	00
1910	10	27	327	56	5	59
1910	10	28	327	56	5	59
1910	10	29	327	55	5	58
1910	10	30	327	54	5	58
1910	10	31	327	54	5	58
1910	11	01	327	53	5	57
1910	11	02	327	53	5	57
1910	11	03	327	53	5	56
1910	11	04	327	52	5	56
1910	11	05	327	52	5	56
1910	11	06	327	52	5	55
1910	11	07	327	52	5	55
1910	11	08	327	52	5	54
1910	11	09	327	52	5	54
1910	11	10	327	52	5	54
1910	11	11	327	52	5	53
1910	11	12	327	52	5	53
1910	11	13	327	52	5	52
1910	11	14	327	53	5	52
1910	11	15	327	53	5	52
1910	11	16	327	53	5	51
1910	11	17	327	54	5	51
1910	11	18	327	54	5	50
1910	11	19	327	55	5	50
1910	11	20	327	56	5	50
1910	11	21	327	56	5	49
1910	11	22	327	57	5	49
1910	11	23	327	58	5	48
1910	11	24	327	59	5	48
1910	11	25	328	00	5	48
1910	11	26	328	01	5	47
1910	11	27	328	02	5	47
1910	11	28	328	03	5	46
1910	11	29	328	04	5	46
1910	11	30	328	06	5	46
1910	12	01	328	07	5	45
1910	12	02	328	08	5	45
1910	12	03	328	10	5	44
1910	12	04	328	11	5	44
1910	12	05	328	13	5	44
1910	12	06	328	14	5	43
1910	12	07	328	16	5	43
1910	12	08	328	18	5	43
1910	12	09	328	20	5	42
1910	12	10	328	21	5	42
1910	12	11	328	23	5	41
1910	12	12	328	25	5	41
1910	12	13	328	27	5	41
1910	12	14	328	29	5	40
1910	12	15	328	31	5	40
1910	12	16	328	34	5	40
1910	12	17	328	36	5	39
1910	12	18	328	38	5	39
1910	12	19	328	40	5	39
1910	12	20	328	43	5	38
1910	12	21	328	45	5	38
1910	12	22	328	48	5	38
1910	12	23	328	50	5	37
1910	12	24	328	53	5	37
1910	12	25	328	55	5	37
1910	12	26	328	58	5	36
1910	12	27	329	00	5	36
1910	12	28	329	03	5	36
1910	12	29	329	06	5	35
1910	12	30	329	09	5	35
1910	12	31	329	12	5	35
1911	01	01	329	15	5	34
1911	01	02	329	18	5	34
1911	01	03	329	20	5	34
1911	01	04	329	24	5	34
1911	01	05	329	27	5	33
1911	01	06	329	30	5	33
1911	01	07	329	33	5	33
1911	01	08	329	36	5	32
1911	01	09	329	39	5	32
1911	01	10	329	42	5	32
1911	01	11	329	46	5	32
1911	01	12	329	49	5	31
1911	01	13	329	52	5	31
1911	01	14	329	56	5	31
1911	01	15	329	59	5	31
1911	01	16	330	03	5	30
1911	01	17	330	06	5	30
1911	01	18	330	10	5	30
1911	01	19	330	13	5	30
1911	01	20	330	17	5	30
1911	01	21	330	20	5	29
1911	01	22	330	24	5	29
1911	01	23	330	27	5	29
1911	01	24	330	31	5	29
1911	01	25	330	35	5	29
1911	01	26	330	39	5	28
1911	01	27	330	42	5	28
1911	01	28	330	46	5	28
1911	01	29	330	50	5	28
1911	01	30	330	54	5	28
1911	01	31	330	57	5	28
1911	02	01	331	01	5	27
1911	02	02	331	05	5	27
1911	02	03	331	09	5	27
1911	02	04	331	13	5	27
1911	02	05	331	17	5	27
1911	02	06	331	21	5	27
1911	02	07	331	25	5	27
1911	02	08	331	28	5	26
1911	02	09	331	32	5	26
1911	02	10	331	36	5	26
1911	02	11	331	40	5	26
1911	02	12	331	44	5	26
1911	02	13	331	48	5	26
1911	02	14	331	52	5	26
1911	02	15	331	56	5	26
1911	02	16	332	00	5	26
1911	02	17	332	04	5	26
1911	02	18	332	08	5	26
1911	02	19	332	12	5	25
1911	02	20	332	16	5	25
1911	02	21	332	20	5	25
1911	02	22	332	24	5	25
1911	02	23	332	28	5	25
1911	02	24	332	32	5	25
1911	02	25	332	36	5	25
1911	02	26	332	40	5	25
1911	02	27	332	44	5	25
1911	02	28	332	48	5	25
1911	03	01	332	52	5	25
1911	03	02	332	56	5	25
1911	03	03	333	00	5	25
1911	03	04	333	04	5	25
1911	03	05	333	08	5	25
1911	03	06	333	12	5	25
1911	03	07	333	16	5	25
1911	03	08	333	20	5	25
1911	03	09	333	24	5	25
1911	03	10	333	28	5	25
1911	03	11	333	32	5	25
1911	03	12	333	35	5	25
1911	03	13	333	39	5	25
1911	03	14	333	43	5	25
1911	03	15	333	47	5	25
1911	03	16	333	51	5	25
1911	03	17	333	55	5	25
1911	03	18	333	58	5	26
1911	03	19	334	02	5	26
1911	03	20	334	06	5	26
1911	03	21	334	10	5	26
1911	03	22	334	13	5	26
1911	03	23	334	17	5	26
1911	03	24	334	21	5	26
1911	03	25	334	24	5	26
1911	03	26	334	28	5	26
1911	03	27	334	31	5	26
1911	03	28	334	35	5	26
1911	03	29	334	38	5	27
1911	03	30	334	42	5	27
1911	03	31	334	45	5	27
1911	04	01	334	49	5	27
1911	04	02	334	52	5	27
1911	04	03	334	56	5	27
1911	04	04	334	59	5	27
1911	04	05	335	02	5	28
1911	04	06	335	06	5	28
1911	04	07	335	09	5	28
1911	04	08	335	12	5	28
1911	04	09	335	15	5	28
1911	04	10	335	18	5	28
1911	04	11	335	21	5	28
1911	04	12	335	24	5	29
1911	04	13	335	27	5	29
1911	04	14	335	30	5	29
1911	04	15	335	33	5	29
1911	04	16	335	36	5	29
1911	04	17	335	39	5	30
1911	04	18	335	42	5	30
1911	04	19	335	45	5	30
1911	04	20	335	48	5	30
1911	04	21	335	50	5	30
1911	04	22	335	53	5	31
1911	04	23	335	56	5	31
1911	04	24	335	58	5	31
1911	04	25	336	01	5	31
1911	04	26	336	03	5	31
1911	04	27	336	06	5	32
1911	04	28	336	08	5	32
1911	04	29	336	10	5	32
1911	04	30	336	13	5	32
1911	05	01	336	15	5	33
1911	05	02	336	17	5	33
1911	05	03	336	19	5	33
1911	05	04	336	21	5	33
1911	05	05	336	23	5	34
1911	05	06	336	25	5	34
1911	05	07	336	27	5	34
1911	05	08	336	29	5	34
1911	05	09	336	31	5	35
1911	05	10	336	33	5	35
1911	05	11	336	35	5	35
1911	05	12	336	36	5	35
1911	05	13	336	38	5	36
1911	05	14	336	40	5	36
1911	05	15	336	41	5	36
1911	05	16	336	43	5	36
1911	05	17	336	44	5	37
1911	05	18	336	46	5	37
1911	05	19	336	47	5	37
1911	05	20	336	48	5	38
1911	05	21	336	49	5	38
1911	05	22	336	51	5	38
1911	05	23	336	52	5	38
1911	05	24	336	53	5	39
1911	05	25	336	54	5	39
1911	05	26	336	55	5	39
1911	05	27	336	56	5	40
1911	05	28	336	56	5	40
1911	05	29	336	57	5	40
1911	05	30	336	58	5	40
1911	05	31	336	58	5	41
1911	06	01	336	59	5	41
1911	06	02	337	00	5	41
1911	06	03	337	00	5	42
1911	06	04	337	01	5	42
1911	06	05	337	01	5	42
1911	06	06	337	01	5	42
1911	06	07	337	01	5	43
1911	06	08	337	02	5	43
1911	06	09	337	02	5	43
1911	06	10	337	02	5	44
1911	06	11	337	02	5	44
1911	06	12	337	02	5	44
1911	06	13	337	02	5	44
1911	06	14	337	02	5	45
1911	06	15	337	01	5	45
1911	06	16	337	01	5	45
1911	06	17	337	01	5	46
1911	06	18	337	00	5	46
1911	06	19	337	00	5	46
1911	06	20	337	00	5	46
1911	06	21	336	59	5	47
1911	06	22	336	58	5	47
1911	06	23	336	58	5	47
1911	06	24	336	57	5	47
1911	06	25	336	56	5	48
1911	06	26	336	55	5	48
1911	06	27	336	55	5	48
1911	06	28	336	54	5	48
1911	06	29	336	53	5	49
1911	06	30	336	52	5	49
1911	07	01	336	51	5	49
1911	07	02	336	49	5	49
1911	07	03	336	48	5	50
1911	07	04	336	47	5	50
1911	07	05	336	46	5	50
1911	07	06	336	44	5	50
1911	07	07	336	43	5	51
1911	07	08	336	41	5	51
1911	07	09	336	40	5	51
1911	07	10	336	38	5	52
1911	07	11	336	37	5	52
1911	07	12	336	35	5	52
1911	07	13	336	33	5	52
1911	07	14	336	32	5	52
1911	07	15	336	30	5	53
1911	07	16	336	28	5	53
1911	07	17	336	26	5	53
1911	07	18	336	24	5	53
1911	07	19	336	22	5	53
1911	07	20	336	20	5	54
1911	07	21	336	18	5	54
1911	07	22	336	16	5	54
1911	07	23	336	14	5	54
1911	07	24	336	12	5	54
1911	07	25	336	10	5	54
1911	07	26	336	07	5	55
1911	07	27	336	05	5	55
1911	07	28	336	03	5	55
1911	07	29	336	00	5	55
1911	07	30	335	58	5	55
1911	07	31	335	56	5	55
1911	08	01	335	53	5	55
1911	08	02	335	51	5	55
1911	08	03	335	48	5	55
1911	08	04	335	46	5	55
1911	08	05	335	43	5	56
1911	08	06	335	40	5	56
1911	08	07	335	38	5	56
1911	08	08	335	35	5	56
1911	08	09	335	33	5	56
1911	08	10	335	30	5	56
1911	08	11	335	27	5	56
1911	08	12	335	24	5	56
1911	08	13	335	22	5	56
1911	08	14	335	19	5	56
1911	08	15	335	16	5	56
1911	08	16	335	13	5	56
1911	08	17	335	11	5	56
1911	08	18	335	08	5	56
1911	08	19	335	05	5	56
1911	08	20	335	02	5	56
1911	08	21	334	59	5	56
1911	08	22	334	56	5	56
1911	08	23	334	53	5	56
1911	08	24	334	50	5	56
1911	08	25	334	48	5	56
1911	08	26	334	45	5	56
1911	08	27	334	42	5	56
1911	08	28	334	39	5	56
1911	08	29	334	36	5	56
1911	08	30	334	33	5	56
1911	08	31	334	30	5	56
1911	09	01	334	27	5	56
1911	09	02	334	24	5	56
1911	09	03	334	21	5	56
1911	09	04	334	19	5	56
1911	09	05	334	16	5	55
1911	09	06	334	13	5	55
1911	09	07	334	10	5	55
1911	09	08	334	07	5	55
1911	09	09	334	04	5	55
1911	09	10	334	01	5	55
1911	09	11	333	59	5	55
1911	09	12	333	56	5	55
1911	09	13	333	53	5	54
1911	09	14	333	50	5	54
1911	09	15	333	48	5	54
1911	09	16	333	45	5	54
1911	09	17	333	42	5	54
1911	09	18	333	39	5	54
1911	09	19	333	37	5	53
1911	09	20	333	34	5	53
1911	09	21	333	32	5	53
1911	09	22	333	29	5	53
1911	09	23	333	26	5	53

1911	09	24	333	24	5	52
1911	09	25	333	21	5	52
1911	09	26	333	19	5	52
1911	09	27	333	17	5	52
1911	09	28	333	14	5	51
1911	09	29	333	12	5	51
1911	09	30	333	10	5	51
1911	10	01	333	07	5	51
1911	10	02	333	05	5	50
1911	10	03	333	03	5	50
1911	10	04	333	01	5	50
1911	10	05	332	59	5	50
1911	10	06	332	56	5	49
1911	10	07	332	54	5	49
1911	10	08	332	52	5	49
1911	10	09	332	50	5	48
1911	10	10	332	49	5	48
1911	10	11	332	47	5	48
1911	10	12	332	45	5	48
1911	10	13	332	43	5	47
1911	10	14	332	41	5	47
1911	10	15	332	40	5	47
1911	10	16	332	38	5	46
1911	10	17	332	37	5	46
1911	10	18	332	35	5	46
1911	10	19	332	34	5	45
1911	10	20	332	32	5	45
1911	10	21	332	31	5	45
1911	10	22	332	29	5	44
1911	10	23	332	28	5	44
1911	10	24	332	27	5	44
1911	10	25	332	26	5	43
1911	10	26	332	25	5	43
1911	10	27	332	24	5	43
1911	10	28	332	23	5	42
1911	10	29	332	22	5	42
1911	10	30	332	21	5	41
1911	10	31	332	20	5	41
1911	11	01	332	19	5	41
1911	11	02	332	18	5	40
1911	11	03	332	18	5	40
1911	11	04	332	17	5	40
1911	11	05	332	17	5	39
1911	11	06	332	16	5	39
1911	11	07	332	16	5	38
1911	11	08	332	15	5	38
1911	11	09	332	15	5	38
1911	11	10	332	15	5	37
1911	11	11	332	15	5	37
1911	11	12	332	15	5	37
1911	11	13	332	15	5	36
1911	11	14	332	15	5	36
1911	11	15	332	15	5	35
1911	11	16	332	15	5	35
1911	11	17	332	15	5	35
1911	11	18	332	15	5	34
1911	11	19	332	15	5	34
1911	11	20	332	16	5	34
1911	11	21	332	16	5	33
1911	11	22	332	17	5	33
1911	11	23	332	17	5	32
1911	11	24	332	18	5	32
1911	11	25	332	18	5	32
1911	11	26	332	19	5	31
1911	11	27	332	20	5	31
1911	11	28	332	21	5	30
1911	11	29	332	22	5	30
1911	11	30	332	23	5	30
1911	12	01	332	24	5	29
1911	12	02	332	25	5	29
1911	12	03	332	26	5	29
1911	12	04	332	27	5	28
1911	12	05	332	28	5	28
1911	12	06	332	30	5	27
1911	12	07	332	31	5	27
1911	12	08	332	32	5	27
1911	12	09	332	34	5	26
1911	12	10	332	35	5	26
1911	12	11	332	37	5	26
1911	12	12	332	39	5	25
1911	12	13	332	40	5	25
1911	12	14	332	42	5	25
1911	12	15	332	44	5	24
1911	12	16	332	46	5	24
1911	12	17	332	48	5	24
1911	12	18	332	50	5	23
1911	12	19	332	52	5	23
1911	12	20	332	54	5	23
1911	12	21	332	56	5	22
1911	12	22	332	58	5	22
1911	12	23	333	00	5	22
1911	12	24	333	02	5	21
1911	12	25	333	05	5	21
1911	12	26	333	07	5	21
1911	12	27	333	09	5	20
1911	12	28	333	12	5	20
1911	12	29	333	14	5	20
1911	12	30	333	17	5	19
1911	12	31	333	19	5	19
1912	01	01	333	22	5	19
1912	01	02	333	25	5	18
1912	01	03	333	27	5	18
1912	01	04	333	30	5	18
1912	01	05	333	33	5	18
1912	01	06	333	36	5	17
1912	01	07	333	39	5	17

1912	01	08	333	42	5	17
1912	01	09	333	45	5	16
1912	01	10	333	48	5	16
1912	01	11	333	51	5	16
1912	01	12	333	54	5	16
1912	01	13	333	57	5	15
1912	01	14	334	00	5	15
1912	01	15	334	03	5	15
1912	01	16	334	06	5	15
1912	01	17	334	10	5	14
1912	01	18	334	13	5	14
1912	01	19	334	16	5	14
1912	01	20	334	19	5	14
1912	01	21	334	23	5	14
1912	01	22	334	26	5	13
1912	01	23	334	30	5	13
1912	01	24	334	33	5	13
1912	01	25	334	37	5	13
1912	01	26	334	40	5	13
1912	01	27	334	44	5	12
1912	01	28	334	47	5	12
1912	01	29	334	51	5	12
1912	01	30	334	54	5	12
1912	01	31	334	58	5	12
1912	02	01	335	02	5	11
1912	02	02	335	05	5	11
1912	02	03	335	09	5	11
1912	02	04	335	13	5	11
1912	02	05	335	16	5	11
1912	02	06	335	20	5	11
1912	02	07	335	24	5	10
1912	02	08	335	28	5	10
1912	02	09	335	31	5	10
1912	02	10	335	35	5	10
1912	02	11	335	39	5	10
1912	02	12	335	43	5	10
1912	02	13	335	47	5	10
1912	02	14	335	50	5	10
1912	02	15	335	54	5	09
1912	02	16	335	58	5	09
1912	02	17	336	02	5	09
1912	02	18	336	06	5	09
1912	02	19	336	10	5	09
1912	02	20	336	14	5	09
1912	02	21	336	18	5	09
1912	02	22	336	21	5	09
1912	02	23	336	25	5	09
1912	02	24	336	29	5	09
1912	02	25	336	33	5	09
1912	02	26	336	37	5	09
1912	02	27	336	41	5	09
1912	02	28	336	45	5	09
1912	02	29	336	49	5	08
1912	03	01	336	53	5	08
1912	03	02	336	57	5	08
1912	03	03	337	00	5	08
1912	03	04	337	04	5	08
1912	03	05	337	08	5	08
1912	03	06	337	12	5	08
1912	03	07	337	16	5	08
1912	03	08	337	20	5	08
1912	03	09	337	24	5	08
1912	03	10	337	28	5	08
1912	03	11	337	31	5	08
1912	03	12	337	35	5	08
1912	03	13	337	39	5	08
1912	03	14	337	43	5	08
1912	03	15	337	47	5	08
1912	03	16	337	50	5	08
1912	03	17	337	54	5	08
1912	03	18	337	58	5	09
1912	03	19	338	02	5	09
1912	03	20	338	05	5	09
1912	03	21	338	09	5	09
1912	03	22	338	13	5	09
1912	03	23	338	16	5	09
1912	03	24	338	20	5	09
1912	03	25	338	24	5	09
1912	03	26	338	27	5	09
1912	03	27	338	31	5	09
1912	03	28	338	34	5	09
1912	03	29	338	38	5	09
1912	03	30	338	41	5	09
1912	03	31	338	45	5	09
1912	04	01	338	48	5	10
1912	04	02	338	52	5	10
1912	04	03	338	55	5	10
1912	04	04	338	58	5	10
1912	04	05	339	02	5	10
1912	04	06	339	05	5	10
1912	04	07	339	08	5	10
1912	04	08	339	11	5	10
1912	04	09	339	15	5	10
1912	04	10	339	18	5	11
1912	04	11	339	21	5	11
1912	04	12	339	24	5	11
1912	04	13	339	27	5	11
1912	04	14	339	30	5	11
1912	04	15	339	33	5	11
1912	04	16	339	36	5	12
1912	04	17	339	39	5	12
1912	04	18	339	42	5	12
1912	04	19	339	45	5	12
1912	04	20	339	48	5	12
1912	04	21	339	50	5	12

1912	04	22	339	53	5	13
1912	04	23	339	56	5	13
1912	04	24	339	58	5	13
1912	04	25	340	01	5	13
1912	04	26	340	04	5	13
1912	04	27	340	06	5	13
1912	04	28	340	09	5	14
1912	04	29	340	11	5	14
1912	04	30	340	13	5	14
1912	05	01	340	16	5	14
1912	05	02	340	18	5	14
1912	05	03	340	20	5	15
1912	05	04	340	23	5	15
1912	05	05	340	25	5	15
1912	05	06	340	27	5	15
1912	05	07	340	29	5	16
1912	05	08	340	31	5	16
1912	05	09	340	33	5	16
1912	05	10	340	35	5	16
1912	05	11	340	37	5	16
1912	05	12	340	39	5	17
1912	05	13	340	40	5	17
1912	05	14	340	42	5	17
1912	05	15	340	44	5	17
1912	05	16	340	45	5	18
1912	05	17	340	47	5	18
1912	05	18	340	48	5	18
1912	05	19	340	50	5	18
1912	05	20	340	51	5	19
1912	05	21	340	53	5	19
1912	05	22	340	54	5	19
1912	05	23	340	55	5	19
1912	05	24	340	57	5	20
1912	05	25	340	58	5	20
1912	05	26	340	59	5	20
1912	05	27	341	00	5	20
1912	05	28	341	01	5	21
1912	05	29	341	02	5	21
1912	05	30	341	03	5	21
1912	05	31	341	03	5	21
1912	06	01	341	04	5	22
1912	06	02	341	05	5	22
1912	06	03	341	06	5	22
1912	06	04	341	06	5	22
1912	06	05	341	07	5	23
1912	06	06	341	07	5	23
1912	06	07	341	08	5	23
1912	06	08	341	08	5	23
1912	06	09	341	08	5	24
1912	06	10	341	09	5	24
1912	06	11	341	09	5	24
1912	06	12	341	09	5	24
1912	06	13	341	09	5	25
1912	06	14	341	09	5	25
1912	06	15	341	09	5	25
1912	06	16	341	09	5	25
1912	06	17	341	09	5	26
1912	06	18	341	09	5	26
1912	06	19	341	08	5	26
1912	06	20	341	08	5	27
1912	06	21	341	08	5	27
1912	06	22	341	07	5	27
1912	06	23	341	07	5	27
1912	06	24	341	06	5	28
1912	06	25	341	06	5	28
1912	06	26	341	05	5	28
1912	06	27	341	05	5	28
1912	06	28	341	04	5	28
1912	06	29	341	03	5	29
1912	06	30	341	02	5	29
1912	07	01	341	01	5	29
1912	07	02	341	00	5	29
1912	07	03	340	59	5	30
1912	07	04	340	58	5	30
1912	07	05	340	57	5	30
1912	07	06	340	56	5	30
1912	07	07	340	55	5	31
1912	07	08	340	54	5	31
1912	07	09	340	52	5	31
1912	07	10	340	51	5	31
1912	07	11	340	49	5	31
1912	07	12	340	48	5	32
1912	07	13	340	46	5	32
1912	07	14	340	45	5	32
1912	07	15	340	43	5	32
1912	07	16	340	42	5	32
1912	07	17	340	40	5	33
1912	07	18	340	38	5	33
1912	07	19	340	36	5	33
1912	07	20	340	35	5	33
1912	07	21	340	33	5	33
1912	07	22	340	31	5	33
1912	07	23	340	29	5	34
1912	07	24	340	27	5	34
1912	07	25	340	25	5	34
1912	07	26	340	23	5	34
1912	07	27	340	21	5	34
1912	07	28	340	18	5	34
1912	07	29	340	16	5	35
1912	07	30	340	14	5	35
1912	07	31	340	12	5	35
1912	08	01	340	10	5	35
1912	08	02	340	07	5	35
1912	08	03	340	05	5	35
1912	08	04	340	02	5	35
1912	08	05	340	00	5	35

1912	08	06	339	58	5	35
1912	08	07	339	55	5	36
1912	08	08	339	53	5	36
1912	08	09	339	50	5	36
1912	08	10	339	47	5	36
1912	08	11	339	45	5	36
1912	08	12	339	42	5	36
1912	08	13	339	40	5	36
1912	08	14	339	37	5	36
1912	08	15	339	34	5	36
1912	08	16	339	32	5	36
1912	08	17	339	29	5	36
1912	08	18	339	26	5	36
1912	08	19	339	23	5	36
1912	08	20	339	21	5	36
1912	08	21	339	18	5	36
1912	08	22	339	15	5	36
1912	08	23	339	12	5	36
1912	08	24	339	09	5	36
1912	08	25	339	07	5	36
1912	08	26	339	[illegible]	5	36
1912	08	27	339	01	5	36
1912	08	28	338	58	5	36
1912	08	29	338	55	5	36
1912	08	30	338	52	5	36
1912	08	31	338	50	5	36
1912	09	01	338	47	5	36
1912	09	02	338	44	5	36
1912	09	03	338	41	5	36
1912	09	04	338	38	5	36
1912	09	05	338	35	5	36
1912	09	06	338	32	5	36
1912	09	07	338	30	5	36
1912	09	08	338	27	5	35
1912	09	09	338	24	5	35
1912	09	10	338	21	5	35
1912	09	11	338	18	5	35
1912	09	12	338	15	5	35
1912	09	13	338	13	5	35
1912	09	14	338	10	5	35
1912	09	15	338	07	5	35
1912	09	16	338	04	5	34
1912	09	17	338	02	5	34
1912	09	18	337	59	5	34
1912	09	19	337	56	5	34
1912	09	20	337	54	5	34
1912	09	21	337	51	5	34
1912	09	22	337	48	5	33
1912	09	23	337	46	5	33
1912	09	24	337	43	5	33
1912	09	25	337	41	5	33
1912	09	26	337	38	5	33
1912	09	27	337	36	5	32
1912	09	28	337	33	5	32
1912	09	29	337	31	5	32
1912	09	30	337	28	5	32
1912	10	01	337	26	5	32
1912	10	02	337	24	5	31
1912	10	03	337	21	5	31
1912	10	04	337	19	5	31
1912	10	05	337	17	5	31
1912	10	06	337	15	5	30
1912	10	07	337	12	5	30
1912	10	08	337	10	5	30
1912	10	09	337	08	5	30
1912	10	10	337	06	5	29
1912	10	11	337	04	5	29
1912	10	12	337	02	5	29
1912	10	13	337	00	5	29
1912	10	14	336	59	5	28
1912	10	15	336	57	5	28
1912	10	16	336	55	5	28
1912	10	17	336	53	5	27
1912	10	18	336	52	5	27
1912	10	19	336	50	5	27
1912	10	20	336	48	5	26
1912	10	21	336	47	5	26
1912	10	22	336	45	5	26
1912	10	23	336	44	5	26
1912	10	24	336	43	5	25
1912	10	25	336	41	5	25
1912	10	26	336	40	5	25
1912	10	27	336	39	5	24
1912	10	28	336	37	5	24
1912	10	29	336	36	5	24
1912	10	30	336	35	5	23
1912	10	31	336	34	5	23
1912	11	01	336	33	5	23
1912	11	02	336	32	5	22
1912	11	03	336	32	5	22
1912	11	04	336	31	5	22
1912	11	05	336	30	5	21
1912	11	06	336	29	5	21
1912	11	07	336	29	5	20
1912	11	08	336	28	5	20
1912	11	09	336	28	5	20
1912	11	10	336	27	5	19
1912	11	11	336	27	5	19
1912	11	12	336	26	5	19
1912	11	13	336	26	5	18
1912	11	14	336	26	5	18

Chiron ⚷

1912	11	15	336	26	5	18
1912	11	16	336	26	5	17
1912	11	17	336	26	5	17
1912	11	18	336	26	5	17
1912	11	19	336	26	5	16
1912	11	20	336	26	5	16
1912	11	21	336	26	5	15
1912	11	22	336	26	5	15
1912	11	23	336	27	5	15
1912	11	24	336	27	5	14
1912	11	25	336	27	5	14
1912	11	26	336	28	5	14
1912	11	27	336	29	5	13
1912	11	28	336	29	5	13
1912	11	29	336	30	5	13
1912	11	30	336	31	5	12
1912	12	01	336	31	5	12
1912	12	02	336	32	5	12
1912	12	03	336	33	5	11
1912	12	04	336	34	5	11
1912	12	05	336	35	5	10
1912	12	06	336	36	5	10
1912	12	07	336	37	5	10
1912	12	08	336	38	5	09
1912	12	09	336	40	5	09
1912	12	10	336	41	5	09
1912	12	11	336	42	5	08
1912	12	12	336	44	5	08
1912	12	13	336	45	5	08
1912	12	14	336	47	5	07
1912	12	15	336	48	5	07
1912	12	16	336	50	5	07
1912	12	17	336	51	5	06
1912	12	18	336	53	5	06
1912	12	19	336	55	5	06
1912	12	20	336	57	5	05
1912	12	21	336	59	5	05
1912	12	22	337	01	5	05
1912	12	23	337	03	5	04
1912	12	24	337	05	5	04
1912	12	25	337	07	5	04
1912	12	26	337	09	5	03
1912	12	27	337	11	5	03
1912	12	28	337	13	5	03
1912	12	29	337	16	5	03
1912	12	30	337	18	5	02
1912	12	31	337	20	5	02
1913	01	01	337	23	5	02
1913	01	02	337	25	5	01
1913	01	03	337	28	5	01
1913	01	04	337	30	5	01
1913	01	05	337	33	5	00
1913	01	06	337	35	5	00
1913	01	07	337	38	5	00
1913	01	08	337	41	5	00
1913	01	09	337	43	4	59
1913	01	10	337	46	4	59
1913	01	11	337	49	4	59
1913	01	12	337	52	4	59
1913	01	13	337	55	4	58
1913	01	14	337	58	4	58
1913	01	15	338	01	4	58
1913	01	16	338	04	4	58
1913	01	17	338	07	4	57
1913	01	18	338	10	4	57
1913	01	19	338	13	4	57
1913	01	20	338	16	4	57
1913	01	21	338	19	4	56
1913	01	22	338	23	4	56
1913	01	23	338	26	4	56
1913	01	24	338	29	4	56
1913	01	25	338	32	4	56
1913	01	26	338	36	4	55
1913	01	27	338	39	4	55
1913	01	28	338	43	4	55
1913	01	29	338	46	4	55
1913	01	30	338	49	4	55
1913	01	31	338	53	4	54
1913	02	01	338	56	4	54
1913	02	02	339	00	4	54
1913	02	03	339	03	4	54
1913	02	04	339	07	4	54
1913	02	05	339	10	4	54
1913	02	06	339	14	4	53
1913	02	07	339	18	4	53
1913	02	08	339	21	4	53
1913	02	09	339	25	4	53
1913	02	10	339	29	4	53
1913	02	11	339	32	4	53
1913	02	12	339	36	4	53
1913	02	13	339	40	4	52
1913	02	14	339	43	4	52
1913	02	15	339	47	4	52
1913	02	16	339	51	4	52
1913	02	17	339	55	4	52
1913	02	18	339	58	4	52
1913	02	19	340	02	4	52
1913	02	20	340	06	4	52
1913	02	21	340	10	4	52

1913	02	22	340	14	4	52
1913	02	23	340	17	4	51
1913	02	24	340	21	4	51
1913	02	25	340	25	4	51
1913	02	26	340	29	4	51
1913	02	27	340	33	4	51
1913	02	28	340	36	4	51
1913	03	01	340	40	4	51
1913	03	02	340	44	4	51
1913	03	03	340	48	4	51
1913	03	04	340	52	4	51
1913	03	05	340	55	4	51
1913	03	06	340	59	4	51
1913	03	07	341	03	4	51
1913	03	08	341	07	4	51
1913	03	09	341	11	4	51
1913	03	10	341	14	4	51
1913	03	11	341	18	4	51
1913	03	12	341	22	4	51
1913	03	13	341	26	4	51
1913	03	14	341	30	4	51
1913	03	15	341	33	4	51
1913	03	16	341	37	4	51
1913	03	17	341	41	4	51
1913	03	18	341	45	4	51
1913	03	19	341	48	4	51
1913	03	20	341	52	4	51
1913	03	21	341	56	4	51
1913	03	22	341	59	4	51
1913	03	23	342	03	4	51
1913	03	24	342	06	4	51
1913	03	25	342	10	4	51
1913	03	26	342	14	4	51
1913	03	27	342	17	4	51
1913	03	28	342	21	4	51
1913	03	29	342	24	4	51
1913	03	30	342	28	4	51
1913	03	31	342	31	4	51
1913	04	01	342	35	4	51
1913	04	02	342	38	4	51
1913	04	03	342	42	4	51
1913	04	04	342	45	4	52
1913	04	05	342	48	4	52
1913	04	06	342	52	4	52
1913	04	07	342	55	4	52
1913	04	08	342	58	4	52
1913	04	09	343	02	4	52
1913	04	10	343	05	4	52
1913	04	11	343	08	4	52
1913	04	12	343	11	4	52
1913	04	13	343	14	4	52
1913	04	14	343	17	4	53
1913	04	15	343	21	4	53
1913	04	16	343	24	4	53
1913	04	17	343	27	4	53
1913	04	18	343	30	4	53
1913	04	19	343	33	4	53
1913	04	20	343	35	4	53
1913	04	21	343	38	4	53
1913	04	22	343	41	4	54
1913	04	23	343	44	4	54
1913	04	24	343	47	4	54
1913	04	25	343	49	4	54
1913	04	26	343	52	4	54
1913	04	27	343	55	4	54
1913	04	28	343	57	4	55
1913	04	29	344	00	4	55
1913	04	30	344	02	4	55
1913	05	01	344	05	4	55
1913	05	02	344	07	4	55
1913	05	03	344	10	4	55
1913	05	04	344	12	4	56
1913	05	05	344	14	4	56
1913	05	06	344	17	4	56
1913	05	07	344	19	4	56
1913	05	08	344	21	4	56
1913	05	09	344	23	4	56
1913	05	10	344	25	4	57
1913	05	11	344	27	4	57
1913	05	12	344	29	4	57
1913	05	13	344	31	4	57
1913	05	14	344	33	4	57
1913	05	15	344	35	4	58
1913	05	16	344	37	4	58
1913	05	17	344	39	4	58
1913	05	18	344	40	4	58
1913	05	19	344	42	4	59
1913	05	20	344	44	4	59
1913	05	21	344	45	4	59
1913	05	22	344	47	4	59
1913	05	23	344	48	4	59
1913	05	24	344	49	5	00
1913	05	25	344	51	5	00
1913	05	26	344	52	5	00
1913	05	27	344	53	5	00
1913	05	28	344	55	5	01
1913	05	29	344	56	5	01
1913	05	30	344	57	5	01
1913	05	31	344	58	5	01
1913	06	01	344	59	5	01
1913	06	02	345	00	5	02
1913	06	03	345	01	5	02
1913	06	04	345	01	5	02
1913	06	05	345	02	5	02
1913	06	06	345	03	5	03

1913	06	07	345	03	5	03
1913	06	08	345	04	5	03
1913	06	09	345	05	5	03
1913	06	10	345	05	5	03
1913	06	11	345	06	5	04
1913	06	12	345	06	5	04
1913	06	13	345	06	5	04
1913	06	14	345	07	5	04
1913	06	15	345	07	5	05
1913	06	16	345	07	5	05
1913	06	17	345	07	5	05
1913	06	18	345	07	5	05
1913	06	19	345	07	5	06
1913	06	20	345	07	5	06
1913	06	21	345	07	5	06
1913	06	22	345	07	5	06
1913	06	23	345	06	5	07
1913	06	24	345	06	5	07
1913	06	25	345	06	5	07
1913	06	26	345	05	5	07
1913	06	27	345	05	5	07
1913	06	28	345	04	5	08
1913	06	29	345	04	5	08
1913	06	30	345	03	5	08
1913	07	01	345	03	5	08
1913	07	02	345	02	5	09
1913	07	03	345	01	5	09
1913	07	04	345	00	5	09
1913	07	05	344	59	5	09
1913	07	06	344	59	5	09
1913	07	07	344	58	5	10
1913	07	08	344	57	5	10
1913	07	09	344	55	5	10
1913	07	10	344	54	5	10
1913	07	11	344	53	5	10
1913	07	12	344	52	5	11
1913	07	13	344	51	5	11
1913	07	14	344	49	5	11
1913	07	15	344	48	5	11
1913	07	16	344	46	5	11
1913	07	17	344	45	5	11
1913	07	18	344	43	5	12
1913	07	19	344	42	5	12
1913	07	20	344	40	5	12
1913	07	21	344	39	5	12
1913	07	22	344	37	5	12
1913	07	23	344	35	5	13
1913	07	24	344	33	5	13
1913	07	25	344	32	5	13
1913	07	26	344	30	5	13
1913	07	27	344	28	5	13
1913	07	28	344	26	5	13
1913	07	29	344	24	5	13
1913	07	30	344	22	5	14
1913	07	31	344	20	5	14
1913	08	01	344	18	5	14
1913	08	02	344	15	5	14
1913	08	03	344	13	5	14
1913	08	04	344	11	5	14
1913	08	05	344	09	5	14
1913	08	06	344	07	5	14
1913	08	07	344	04	5	14
1913	08	08	344	02	5	15
1913	08	09	343	59	5	15
1913	08	10	343	57	5	15
1913	08	11	343	55	5	15
1913	08	12	343	52	5	15
1913	08	13	343	50	5	15
1913	08	14	343	47	5	15
1913	08	15	343	45	5	15
1913	08	16	343	42	5	15
1913	08	17	343	39	5	15
1913	08	18	343	37	5	15
1913	08	19	343	34	5	15
1913	08	20	343	32	5	15
1913	08	21	343	29	5	15
1913	08	22	343	26	5	15
1913	08	23	343	23	5	15
1913	08	24	343	21	5	15
1913	08	25	343	18	5	15
1913	08	26	343	15	5	15
1913	08	27	343	13	5	15
1913	08	28	343	10	5	15
1913	08	29	343	07	5	15
1913	08	30	343	04	5	15
1913	08	31	343	01	5	15
1913	09	01	342	59	5	15
1913	09	02	342	56	5	15
1913	09	03	342	53	5	15
1913	09	04	342	50	5	15
1913	09	05	342	47	5	15
1913	09	06	342	44	5	15
1913	09	07	342	42	5	15
1913	09	08	342	39	5	15
1913	09	09	342	36	5	15
1913	09	10	342	33	5	15
1913	09	11	342	30	5	15
1913	09	12	342	28	5	15
1913	09	13	342	25	5	14
1913	09	14	342	22	5	14
1913	09	15	342	19	5	14
1913	09	16	342	17	5	14
1913	09	17	342	14	5	14
1913	09	18	342	11	5	14
1913	09	19	342	08	5	14

1913	09	20	342	06	5	14
1913	09	21	342	03	5	13
1913	09	22	342	00	5	13
1913	09	23	341	58	5	13
1913	09	24	341	55	5	13
1913	09	25	341	52	5	13
1913	09	26	341	50	5	13
1913	09	27	341	47	5	12
1913	09	28	341	45	5	12
1913	09	29	341	42	5	12
1913	09	30	341	40	5	12
1913	10	01	341	37	5	12
1913	10	02	341	35	5	12
1913	10	03	341	32	5	11
1913	10	04	341	30	5	11
1913	10	05	341	28	5	11
1913	10	06	341	25	5	11
1913	10	07	341	23	5	10
1913	10	08	341	21	5	10
1913	10	09	341	18	5	10
1913	10	10	341	16	5	10
1913	10	11	341	14	5	10
1913	10	12	341	12	5	09
1913	10	13	341	10	5	09
1913	10	14	341	08	5	09
1913	10	15	341	06	5	09
1913	10	16	341	04	5	08
1913	10	17	341	02	5	08
1913	10	18	341	00	5	08
1913	10	19	340	58	5	07
1913	10	20	340	57	5	07
1913	10	21	340	55	5	07
1913	10	22	340	53	5	07
1913	10	23	340	52	5	06
1913	10	24	340	50	5	06
1913	10	25	340	49	5	06
1913	10	26	340	47	5	05
1913	10	27	340	46	5	05
1913	10	28	340	44	5	05
1913	10	29	340	43	5	05
1913	10	30	340	42	5	04
1913	10	31	340	40	5	04
1913	11	01	340	39	5	04
1913	11	02	340	38	5	03
1913	11	03	340	37	5	03
1913	11	04	340	36	5	03
1913	11	05	340	35	5	02
1913	11	06	340	34	5	02
1913	11	07	340	33	5	02
1913	11	08	340	32	5	01
1913	11	09	340	32	5	01
1913	11	10	340	31	5	01
1913	11	11	340	30	5	00
1913	11	12	340	30	5	00
1913	11	13	340	29	5	00
1913	11	14	340	29	4	59
1913	11	15	340	28	4	59
1913	11	16	340	28	4	59
1913	11	17	340	28	4	58
1913	11	18	340	27	4	58
1913	11	19	340	27	4	58
1913	11	20	340	27	4	57
1913	11	21	340	27	4	57
1913	11	22	340	27	4	57
1913	11	23	340	27	4	56
1913	11	24	340	27	4	56
1913	11	25	340	27	4	56
1913	11	26	340	28	4	55
1913	11	27	340	28	4	55
1913	11	28	340	28	4	55
1913	11	29	340	29	4	54
1913	11	30	340	29	4	54
1913	12	01	340	30	4	54
1913	12	02	340	30	4	53
1913	12	03	340	31	4	53
1913	12	04	340	31	4	53
1913	12	05	340	32	4	52
1913	12	06	340	33	4	52
1913	12	07	340	34	4	52
1913	12	08	340	35	4	51
1913	12	09	340	36	4	51
1913	12	10	340	37	4	51
1913	12	11	340	38	4	50
1913	12	12	340	39	4	50
1913	12	13	340	40	4	50
1913	12	14	340	41	4	49
1913	12	15	340	43	4	49
1913	12	16	340	44	4	49
1913	12	17	340	45	4	48
1913	12	18	340	47	4	48
1913	12	19	340	48	4	48
1913	12	20	340	50	4	47
1913	12	21	340	52	4	47
1913	12	22	340	53	4	47
1913	12	23	340	55	4	47
1913	12	24	340	57	4	46
1913	12	25	340	59	4	46
1913	12	26	341	00	4	46
1913	12	27	341	02	4	45
1913	12	28	341	04	4	45
1913	12	29	341	06	4	45
1913	12	30	341	08	4	44
1913	12	31	341	11	4	44
1914	01	01	341	13	4	44

1914	01	02	341	15	4	44
1914	01	03	341	17	4	43
1914	01	04	341	20	4	43
1914	01	05	341	22	4	43
1914	01	06	341	24	4	42
1914	01	07	341	27	4	42
1914	01	08	341	29	4	42
1914	01	09	341	32	4	42
1914	01	10	341	34	4	41
1914	01	11	341	37	4	41
1914	01	12	341	40	4	41
1914	01	13	341	42	4	41
1914	01	14	341	45	4	40
1914	01	15	341	48	4	40
1914	01	16	341	50	4	40
1914	01	17	341	53	4	40
1914	01	18	341	56	4	39
1914	01	19	341	59	4	39
1914	01	20	342	02	4	39
1914	01	21	342	05	4	39
1914	01	22	342	08	4	39
1914	01	23	342	11	4	38
1914	01	24	342	14	4	38
1914	01	25	342	17	4	38
1914	01	26	342	20	4	38
1914	01	27	342	24	4	37
1914	01	28	342	27	4	37
1914	01	29	342	30	4	37
1914	01	30	342	33	4	37
1914	01	31	342	37	4	37
1914	02	01	342	40	4	36
1914	02	02	342	43	4	36
1914	02	03	342	47	4	36
1914	02	04	342	50	4	36
1914	02	05	342	53	4	36
1914	02	06	342	57	4	36
1914	02	07	343	00	4	35
1914	02	08	343	04	4	35
1914	02	09	343	07	4	35
1914	02	10	343	11	4	35
1914	02	11	343	14	4	35
1914	02	12	343	18	4	35
1914	02	13	343	21	4	35
1914	02	14	343	25	4	34
1914	02	15	343	29	4	34
1914	02	16	343	32	4	34
1914	02	17	343	36	4	34
1914	02	18	343	40	4	34
1914	02	19	343	43	4	34
1914	02	20	343	47	4	34
1914	02	21	343	51	4	34
1914	02	22	343	54	4	33
1914	02	23	343	58	4	33
1914	02	24	344	02	4	33
1914	02	25	344	05	4	33
1914	02	26	344	09	4	33
1914	02	27	344	13	4	33
1914	02	28	344	16	4	33
1914	03	01	344	20	4	33
1914	03	02	344	24	4	33
1914	03	03	344	28	4	33
1914	03	04	344	31	4	33
1914	03	05	344	35	4	33
1914	03	06	344	39	4	32
1914	03	07	344	43	4	32
1914	03	08	344	46	4	32
1914	03	09	344	50	4	32
1914	03	10	344	54	4	32
1914	03	11	344	58	4	32
1914	03	12	345	01	4	32
1914	03	13	345	05	4	32
1914	03	14	345	09	4	32
1914	03	15	345	13	4	32
1914	03	16	345	16	4	32
1914	03	17	345	20	4	32
1914	03	18	345	24	4	32
1914	03	19	345	27	4	32
1914	03	20	345	31	4	32
1914	03	21	345	35	4	32
1914	03	22	345	38	4	32
1914	03	23	345	42	4	32
1914	03	24	345	46	4	32
1914	03	25	345	49	4	32
1914	03	26	345	53	4	32
1914	03	27	345	56	4	32
1914	03	28	346	00	4	32
1914	03	29	346	03	4	32
1914	03	30	346	07	4	32
1914	03	31	346	10	4	32
1914	04	01	346	14	4	32
1914	04	02	346	17	4	32
1914	04	03	346	21	4	32
1914	04	04	346	24	4	33
1914	04	05	346	28	4	33
1914	04	06	346	31	4	33
1914	04	07	346	34	4	33
1914	04	08	346	38	4	33
1914	04	09	346	41	4	33
1914	04	10	346	44	4	33
1914	04	11	346	48	4	33
1914	04	12	346	51	4	33
1914	04	13	346	54	4	33
1914	04	14	346	57	4	33
1914	04	15	347	00	4	33
1914	04	16	347	03	4	33
1914	04	17	347	07	4	34

1914	04	18	347	10	4	34
1914	04	19	347	13	4	34
1914	04	20	347	16	4	34
1914	04	21	347	19	4	34
1914	04	22	347	21	4	34
1914	04	23	347	24	4	34
1914	04	24	347	27	4	34
1914	04	25	347	30	4	34
1914	04	26	347	33	4	35
1914	04	27	347	36	4	35
1914	04	28	347	38	4	35
1914	04	29	347	41	4	35
1914	04	30	347	44	4	35
1914	05	01	347	46	4	35
1914	05	02	347	49	4	35
1914	05	03	347	51	4	36
1914	05	04	347	54	4	36
1914	05	05	347	56	4	36
1914	05	06	347	59	4	36
1914	05	07	348	01	4	36
1914	05	08	348	03	4	36
1914	05	09	348	06	4	36
1914	05	10	348	08	4	37
1914	05	11	348	10	4	37
1914	05	12	348	12	4	37
1914	05	13	348	14	4	37
1914	05	14	348	16	4	37
1914	05	15	348	18	4	38
1914	05	16	348	20	4	38
1914	05	17	348	22	4	38
1914	05	18	348	24	4	38
1914	05	19	348	26	4	38
1914	05	20	348	28	4	38
1914	05	21	348	29	4	39
1914	05	22	348	31	4	39
1914	05	23	348	33	4	39
1914	05	24	348	34	4	39
1914	05	25	348	36	4	39
1914	05	26	348	37	4	40
1914	05	27	348	39	4	40
1914	05	28	348	40	4	40
1914	05	29	348	41	4	40
1914	05	30	348	43	4	40
1914	05	31	348	44	4	41
1914	06	01	348	45	4	41
1914	06	02	348	46	4	41
1914	06	03	348	47	4	41
1914	06	04	348	48	4	41
1914	06	05	348	49	4	42
1914	06	06	348	50	4	42
1914	06	07	348	51	4	42
1914	06	08	348	52	4	42
1914	06	09	348	52	4	42
1914	06	10	348	53	4	43
1914	06	11	348	54	4	43
1914	06	12	348	54	4	43
1914	06	13	348	55	4	43
1914	06	14	348	55	4	43
1914	06	15	348	56	4	44
1914	06	16	348	56	4	44
1914	06	17	348	57	4	44
1914	06	18	348	57	4	44
1914	06	19	348	57	4	44
1914	06	20	348	57	4	45
1914	06	21	348	57	4	45
1914	06	22	348	57	4	45
1914	06	23	348	57	4	45
1914	06	24	348	57	4	45
1914	06	25	348	57	4	46
1914	06	26	348	57	4	46
1914	06	27	348	57	4	46
1914	06	28	348	57	4	46
1914	06	29	348	56	4	46
1914	06	30	348	56	4	47
1914	07	01	348	55	4	47
1914	07	02	348	55	4	47
1914	07	03	348	54	4	47
1914	07	04	348	54	4	47
1914	07	05	348	53	4	48
1914	07	06	348	52	4	48
1914	07	07	348	52	4	48
1914	07	08	348	51	4	48
1914	07	09	348	50	4	48
1914	07	10	348	49	4	49
1914	07	11	348	48	4	49
1914	07	12	348	47	4	49
1914	07	13	348	46	4	49
1914	07	14	348	45	4	49
1914	07	15	348	44	4	50
1914	07	16	348	43	4	50
1914	07	17	348	41	4	50
1914	07	18	348	40	4	50
1914	07	19	348	39	4	50
1914	07	20	348	37	4	50
1914	07	21	348	36	4	51
1914	07	22	348	34	4	51
1914	07	23	348	33	4	51
1914	07	24	348	31	4	51
1914	07	25	348	29	4	51
1914	07	26	348	28	4	51
1914	07	27	348	26	4	51
1914	07	28	348	24	4	52
1914	07	29	348	23	4	52
1914	07	30	348	21	4	52
1914	07	31	348	19	4	52
1914	08	01	348	17	4	52

1914	08	02	348	15	4	52
1914	08	03	348	13	4	52
1914	08	04	348	11	4	52
1914	08	05	348	09	4	53
1914	08	06	348	07	4	53
1914	08	07	348	05	4	53
1914	08	08	348	02	4	53
1914	08	09	348	00	4	53
1914	08	10	347	58	4	53
1914	08	11	347	56	4	53
1914	08	12	347	53	4	53
1914	08	13	347	51	4	53
1914	00	14	347	47	4	53
1914	08	15	347	46	4	53
1914	08	16	347	44	4	53
1914	08	17	347	41	4	54
1914	08	18	347	39	4	54
1914	08	19	347	36	4	54
1914	08	20	347	34	4	54
1914	08	21	347	31	4	54
1914	08	22	347	29	4	54
1914	08	23	347	26	4	54
1914	08	24	347	23	4	54
1914	08	25	347	21	4	54
1914	08	26	347	18	4	54
1914	08	27	347	15	4	54
1914	08	28	347	13	4	54
1914	08	29	347	10	4	54
1914	08	30	347	07	4	54
1914	08	31	347	05	4	54
1914	09	01	347	02	4	54
1914	09	02	346	59	4	54
1914	09	03	346	56	4	54
1914	09	04	346	54	4	54
1914	09	05	346	51	4	54
1914	09	06	346	48	4	54
1914	09	07	346	45	4	54
1914	09	08	346	42	4	54
1914	09	09	346	40	4	54
1914	09	10	346	37	4	53
1914	09	11	346	34	4	53
1914	09	12	346	31	4	53
1914	09	13	346	29	4	53
1914	09	14	346	26	4	53
1914	09	15	346	23	4	53
1914	09	16	346	20	4	53
1914	09	17	346	17	4	53
1914	09	18	346	15	4	53
1914	09	19	346	12	4	53
1914	09	20	346	09	4	53
1914	09	21	346	07	4	52
1914	09	22	346	04	4	52
1914	09	23	346	01	4	52
1914	09	24	345	58	4	52
1914	09	25	345	56	4	52
1914	09	26	345	53	4	52
1914	09	27	345	50	4	52
1914	09	28	345	48	4	52
1914	09	29	345	45	4	51
1914	09	30	345	43	4	51
1914	10	01	345	40	4	51
1914	10	02	345	38	4	51
1914	10	03	345	35	4	51
1914	10	04	345	33	4	51
1914	10	05	345	30	4	50
1914	10	06	345	28	4	50
1914	10	07	345	25	4	50
1914	10	08	345	23	4	50
1914	10	09	345	21	4	50
1914	10	10	345	18	4	49
1914	10	11	345	16	4	49
1914	10	12	345	14	4	49
1914	10	13	345	12	4	49
1914	10	14	345	10	4	48
1914	10	15	345	07	4	48
1914	10	16	345	05	4	48
1914	10	17	345	03	4	48
1914	10	18	345	01	4	48
1914	10	19	344	59	4	47
1914	10	20	344	57	4	47
1914	10	21	344	56	4	47
1914	10	22	344	54	4	47
1914	10	23	344	52	4	46
1914	10	24	344	50	4	46
1914	10	25	344	48	4	46
1914	10	26	344	47	4	46
1914	10	27	344	45	4	45
1914	10	28	344	44	4	45
1914	10	29	344	42	4	45
1914	10	30	344	40	4	44
1914	10	31	344	39	4	44
1914	11	01	344	38	4	44
1914	11	02	344	36	4	44
1914	11	03	344	35	4	43
1914	11	04	344	34	4	43
1914	11	05	344	33	4	43
1914	11	06	344	31	4	42
1914	11	07	344	30	4	42
1914	11	08	344	29	4	42
1914	11	09	344	28	4	42
1914	11	10	344	27	4	41
1914	11	11	344	27	4	41
1914	11	12	344	26	4	41
1914	11	13	344	25	4	40
1914	11	14	344	24	4	40
1914	11	15	344	24	4	40

1914	11	16	344	23	4	39
1914	11	17	344	23	4	39
1914	11	18	344	22	4	39
1914	11	19	344	22	4	39
1914	11	20	344	21	4	38
1914	11	21	344	21	4	38
1914	11	22	344	21	4	38
1914	11	23	344	20	4	37
1914	11	24	344	20	4	37
1914	11	25	344	20	4	37
1914	11	26	344	20	4	36
1914	11	27	344	20	4	36
1914	11	28	344	20	4	36
1914	11	29	344	20	4	35
1914	11	30	344	21	4	35
1914	12	01	344	21	4	35
1914	12	02	344	21	4	34
1914	12	03	344	22	4	34
1914	12	04	344	22	4	34
1914	12	05	344	23	4	33
1914	12	06	344	23	4	33
1914	12	07	344	24	4	33
1914	12	08	344	24	4	32
1914	12	09	344	25	4	32
1914	12	10	344	26	4	32
1914	12	11	344	27	4	32
1914	12	12	344	28	4	31
1914	12	13	344	28	4	31
1914	12	14	344	29	4	31
1914	12	15	344	30	4	30
1914	12	16	344	32	4	30
1914	12	17	344	33	4	30
1914	12	18	344	34	4	29
1914	12	19	344	35	4	29
1914	12	20	344	37	4	29
1914	12	21	344	38	4	28
1914	12	22	344	39	4	28
1914	12	23	344	41	4	28
1914	12	24	344	42	4	28
1914	12	25	344	44	4	27
1914	12	26	344	46	4	27
1914	12	27	344	47	4	27
1914	12	28	344	49	4	26
1914	12	29	344	51	4	26
1914	12	30	344	53	4	26
1914	12	31	344	54	4	26
1915	01	01	344	56	4	25
1915	01	02	344	58	4	25
1915	01	03	345	00	4	25
1915	01	04	345	02	4	24
1915	01	05	345	05	4	24
1915	01	06	345	07	4	24
1915	01	07	345	09	4	24
1915	01	08	345	11	4	23
1915	01	09	345	14	4	23
1915	01	10	345	16	4	23
1915	01	11	345	18	4	23
1915	01	12	345	21	4	22
1915	01	13	345	23	4	22
1915	01	14	345	26	4	22
1915	01	15	345	28	4	22
1915	01	16	345	31	4	21
1915	01	17	345	33	4	21
1915	01	18	345	36	4	21
1915	01	19	345	39	4	21
1915	01	20	345	42	4	20
1915	01	21	345	44	4	20
1915	01	22	345	47	4	20
1915	01	23	345	50	4	20
1915	01	24	345	53	4	20
1915	01	25	345	56	4	19
1915	01	26	345	59	4	19
1915	01	27	346	02	4	19
1915	01	28	346	05	4	19
1915	01	29	346	08	4	19
1915	01	30	346	11	4	18
1915	01	31	346	14	4	18
1915	02	01	346	17	4	18
1915	02	02	346	20	4	18
1915	02	03	346	24	4	18
1915	02	04	346	27	4	17
1915	02	05	346	30	4	17
1915	02	06	346	33	4	17
1915	02	07	346	37	4	17
1915	02	08	346	40	4	17
1915	02	09	346	43	4	17
1915	02	10	346	47	4	16
1915	02	11	346	50	4	16
1915	02	12	346	54	4	16
1915	02	13	346	57	4	16
1915	02	14	347	01	4	16
1915	02	15	347	04	4	16
1915	02	16	347	07	4	15
1915	02	17	347	11	4	15
1915	02	18	347	15	4	15
1915	02	19	347	18	4	15
1915	02	20	347	22	4	15
1915	02	21	347	25	4	15
1915	02	22	347	29	4	15
1915	02	23	347	32	4	15
1915	02	24	347	36	4	15

⚷ **Chiron**

1915	02	25	347	40	4	14
1915	02	26	347	43	4	14
1915	02	27	347	47	4	14
1915	02	28	347	50	4	14
1915	03	01	347	54	4	14
1915	03	02	347	58	4	14
1915	03	03	348	01	4	14
1915	03	04	348	05	4	14
1915	03	05	348	09	4	14
1915	03	06	348	12	4	14
1915	03	07	348	16	4	14
1915	03	08	348	20	4	13
1915	03	09	348	23	4	13
1915	03	10	348	27	4	13
1915	03	11	348	31	4	13
1915	03	12	348	35	4	13
1915	03	13	348	38	4	13
1915	03	14	348	42	4	13
1915	03	15	348	46	4	13
1915	03	16	348	49	4	13
1915	03	17	348	53	4	13
1915	03	18	348	57	4	13
1915	03	19	349	00	4	13
1915	03	20	349	04	4	13
1915	03	21	349	08	4	13
1915	03	22	349	11	4	13
1915	03	23	349	15	4	13
1915	03	24	349	18	4	13
1915	03	25	349	22	4	13
1915	03	26	349	26	4	13
1915	03	27	349	29	4	13
1915	03	28	349	33	4	13
1915	03	29	349	36	4	13
1915	03	30	349	40	4	13
1915	03	31	349	43	4	13
1915	04	01	349	47	4	13
1915	04	02	349	50	4	13
1915	04	03	349	54	4	13
1915	04	04	349	57	4	13
1915	04	05	350	01	4	13
1915	04	06	350	04	4	13
1915	04	07	350	07	4	13
1915	04	08	350	11	4	13
1915	04	09	350	14	4	13
1915	04	10	350	17	4	13
1915	04	11	350	21	4	13
1915	04	12	350	24	4	13
1915	04	13	350	27	4	13
1915	04	14	350	31	4	14
1915	04	15	350	34	4	14
1915	04	16	350	37	4	14
1915	04	17	350	40	4	14
1915	04	18	350	43	4	14
1915	04	19	350	46	4	14
1915	04	20	350	49	4	14
1915	04	21	350	52	4	14
1915	04	22	350	55	4	14
1915	04	23	350	58	4	14
1915	04	24	351	01	4	14
1915	04	25	351	04	4	14
1915	04	26	351	07	4	15
1915	04	27	351	10	4	15
1915	04	28	351	13	4	15
1915	04	29	351	16	4	15
1915	04	30	351	18	4	15
1915	05	01	351	21	4	15
1915	05	02	351	24	4	15
1915	05	03	351	26	4	15
1915	05	04	351	29	4	15
1915	05	05	351	31	4	16
1915	05	06	351	34	4	16
1915	05	07	351	36	4	16
1915	05	08	351	39	4	16
1915	05	09	351	41	4	16
1915	05	10	351	44	4	16
1915	05	11	351	46	4	16
1915	05	12	351	48	4	16
1915	05	13	351	51	4	17
1915	05	14	351	53	4	17
1915	05	15	351	55	4	17
1915	05	16	351	57	4	17
1915	05	17	351	59	4	17
1915	05	18	352	01	4	17
1915	05	19	352	03	4	17
1915	05	20	352	05	4	18
1915	05	21	352	07	4	18
1915	05	22	352	09	4	18
1915	05	23	352	10	4	18
1915	05	24	352	12	4	18
1915	05	25	352	14	4	18
1915	05	26	352	16	4	19
1915	05	27	352	17	4	19
1915	05	28	352	19	4	19
1915	05	29	352	20	4	19
1915	05	30	352	22	4	19
1915	05	31	352	23	4	19
1915	06	01	352	24	4	20
1915	06	02	352	26	4	20
1915	06	03	352	27	4	20
1915	06	04	352	28	4	20
1915	06	05	352	29	4	20
1915	06	06	352	30	4	21
1915	06	07	352	32	4	21
1915	06	08	352	33	4	21
1915	06	09	352	33	4	21
1915	06	10	352	34	4	21
1915	06	11	352	35	4	21
1915	06	12	352	36	4	22
1915	06	13	352	37	4	22
1915	06	14	352	37	4	22
1915	06	15	352	38	4	22
1915	06	16	352	39	4	22
1915	06	17	352	39	4	23
1915	06	18	352	40	4	23
1915	06	19	352	40	4	23
1915	06	20	352	40	4	23
1915	06	21	352	41	4	23
1915	06	22	352	41	4	23
1915	06	23	352	41	4	24
1915	06	24	352	41	4	24
1915	06	25	352	41	4	24
1915	06	26	352	41	4	24
1915	06	27	352	41	4	24
1915	06	28	352	41	4	25
1915	06	29	352	41	4	25
1915	06	30	352	41	4	25
1915	07	01	352	41	4	25
1915	07	02	352	41	4	25
1915	07	03	352	40	4	25
1915	07	04	352	40	4	26
1915	07	05	352	40	4	26
1915	07	06	352	39	4	26
1915	07	07	352	38	4	26
1915	07	08	352	38	4	26
1915	07	09	352	37	4	26
1915	07	10	352	37	4	27
1915	07	11	352	36	4	27
1915	07	12	352	35	4	27
1915	07	13	352	34	4	27
1915	07	14	352	33	4	27
1915	07	15	352	32	4	27
1915	07	16	352	31	4	28
1915	07	17	352	30	4	28
1915	07	18	352	29	4	28
1915	07	19	352	28	4	28
1915	07	20	352	27	4	28
1915	07	21	352	26	4	28
1915	07	22	352	24	4	29
1915	07	23	352	23	4	29
1915	07	24	352	22	4	29
1915	07	25	352	20	4	29
1915	07	26	352	19	4	29
1915	07	27	352	17	4	29
1915	07	28	352	16	4	29
1915	07	29	352	14	4	30
1915	07	30	352	12	4	30
1915	07	31	352	11	4	30
1915	08	01	352	09	4	30
1915	08	02	352	07	4	30
1915	08	03	352	05	4	30
1915	08	04	352	03	4	30
1915	08	05	352	01	4	30
1915	08	06	352	00	4	30
1915	08	07	351	58	4	31
1915	08	08	351	56	4	31
1915	08	09	351	53	4	31
1915	08	10	351	51	4	31
1915	08	11	351	49	4	31
1915	08	12	351	47	4	31
1915	08	13	351	45	4	31
1915	08	14	351	43	4	31
1915	08	15	351	40	4	31
1915	08	16	351	38	4	31
1915	08	17	351	36	4	31
1915	08	18	351	33	4	31
1915	08	19	351	31	4	31
1915	08	20	351	29	4	32
1915	08	21	351	26	4	32
1915	08	22	351	24	4	32
1915	08	23	351	21	4	32
1915	08	24	351	19	4	32
1915	08	25	351	16	4	32
1915	08	26	351	14	4	32
1915	08	27	351	11	4	32
1915	08	28	351	09	4	32
1915	08	29	351	06	4	32
1915	08	30	351	03	4	32
1915	08	31	351	01	4	32
1915	09	01	350	58	4	32
1915	09	02	350	55	4	32
1915	09	03	350	53	4	32
1915	09	04	350	50	4	32
1915	09	05	350	47	4	32
1915	09	06	350	45	4	32
1915	09	07	350	42	4	32
1915	09	08	350	39	4	32
1915	09	09	350	36	4	32
1915	09	10	350	34	4	32
1915	09	11	350	31	4	32
1915	09	12	350	28	4	32
1915	09	13	350	25	4	31
1915	09	14	350	23	4	31
1915	09	15	350	20	4	31
1915	09	16	350	17	4	31
1915	09	17	350	14	4	31
1915	09	18	350	11	4	31
1915	09	19	350	09	4	31
1915	09	20	350	06	4	31
1915	09	21	350	03	4	31
1915	09	22	350	01	4	31
1915	09	23	349	58	4	31
1915	09	24	349	55	4	31
1915	09	25	349	52	4	30
1915	09	26	349	50	4	30
1915	09	27	349	47	4	30
1915	09	28	349	44	4	30
1915	09	29	349	42	4	30
1915	09	30	349	39	4	30
1915	10	01	349	37	4	30
1915	10	02	349	34	4	29
1915	10	03	349	31	4	29
1915	10	04	349	29	4	29
1915	10	05	349	26	4	29
1915	10	06	349	24	4	29
1915	10	07	349	21	4	29
1915	10	08	349	19	4	29
1915	10	09	349	16	4	28
1915	10	10	349	14	4	28
1915	10	11	349	12	4	28
1915	10	12	349	09	4	28
1915	10	13	349	07	4	28
1915	10	14	349	05	4	27
1915	10	15	349	02	4	27
1915	10	16	349	00	4	27
1915	10	17	348	58	4	27
1915	10	18	348	56	4	27
1915	10	19	348	54	4	26
1915	10	20	348	52	4	26
1915	10	21	348	50	4	26
1915	10	22	348	48	4	26
1915	10	23	348	46	4	25
1915	10	24	348	44	4	25
1915	10	25	348	42	4	25
1915	10	26	348	40	4	25
1915	10	27	348	38	4	25
1915	10	28	348	37	4	24
1915	10	29	348	35	4	24
1915	10	30	348	33	4	24
1915	10	31	348	32	4	24
1915	11	01	348	30	4	23
1915	11	02	348	28	4	23
1915	11	03	348	27	4	23
1915	11	04	348	26	4	23
1915	11	05	348	24	4	22
1915	11	06	348	23	4	22
1915	11	07	348	22	4	22
1915	11	08	348	20	4	21
1915	11	09	348	19	4	21
1915	11	10	348	18	4	21
1915	11	11	348	17	4	21
1915	11	12	348	16	4	20
1915	11	13	348	15	4	20
1915	11	14	348	14	4	20
1915	11	15	348	13	4	20
1915	11	16	348	12	4	19
1915	11	17	348	12	4	19
1915	11	18	348	11	4	19
1915	11	19	348	10	4	18
1915	11	20	348	10	4	18
1915	11	21	348	09	4	18
1915	11	22	348	09	4	18
1915	11	23	348	08	4	17
1915	11	24	348	08	4	17
1915	11	25	348	07	4	17
1915	11	26	348	07	4	16
1915	11	27	348	07	4	16
1915	11	28	348	07	4	16
1915	11	29	348	07	4	15
1915	11	30	348	07	4	15
1915	12	01	348	07	4	15
1915	12	02	348	07	4	15
1915	12	03	348	07	4	14
1915	12	04	348	07	4	14
1915	12	05	348	07	4	14
1915	12	06	348	08	4	13
1915	12	07	348	08	4	13
1915	12	08	348	08	4	13
1915	12	09	348	09	4	13
1915	12	10	348	09	4	12
1915	12	11	348	10	4	12
1915	12	12	348	11	4	12
1915	12	13	348	11	4	11
1915	12	14	348	12	4	11
1915	12	15	348	13	4	11
1915	12	16	348	14	4	10
1915	12	17	348	15	4	10
1915	12	18	348	16	4	10
1915	12	19	348	17	4	10
1915	12	20	348	18	4	09
1915	12	21	348	19	4	09
1915	12	22	348	20	4	09
1915	12	23	348	21	4	08
1915	12	24	348	23	4	08
1915	12	25	348	24	4	08
1915	12	26	348	25	4	08
1915	12	27	348	27	4	07
1915	12	28	348	28	4	07
1915	12	29	348	30	4	07
1915	12	30	348	31	4	07
1915	12	31	348	33	4	06
1916	01	01	348	35	4	06
1916	01	02	348	37	4	06
1916	01	03	348	38	4	05
1916	01	04	348	40	4	05
1916	01	05	348	42	4	05
1916	01	06	348	44	4	05
1916	01	07	348	46	4	04
1916	01	08	348	48	4	04
1916	01	09	348	50	4	04
1916	01	10	348	52	4	04
1916	01	11	348	55	4	03
1916	01	12	348	57	4	03
1916	01	13	348	59	4	03
1916	01	14	349	01	4	03
1916	01	15	349	04	4	02
1916	01	16	349	06	4	02
1916	01	17	349	09	4	02
1916	01	18	349	11	4	02
1916	01	19	349	13	4	01
1916	01	20	349	16	4	01
1916	01	21	349	19	4	01
1916	01	22	349	21	4	01
1916	01	23	349	24	4	01
1916	01	24	349	27	4	00
1916	01	25	349	29	4	00
1916	01	26	349	32	4	00
1916	01	27	349	35	4	00
1916	01	28	349	38	4	00
1916	01	29	349	41	3	59
1916	01	30	349	44	3	59
1916	01	31	349	47	3	59
1916	02	01	349	50	3	59
1916	02	02	349	53	3	59
1916	02	03	349	56	3	58
1916	02	04	349	59	3	58
1916	02	05	350	02	3	58
1916	02	06	350	05	3	58
1916	02	07	350	08	3	58
1916	02	08	350	11	3	57
1916	02	09	350	15	3	57
1916	02	10	350	18	3	57
1916	02	11	350	21	3	57
1916	02	12	350	24	3	57
1916	02	13	350	28	3	57
1916	02	14	350	31	3	57
1916	02	15	350	34	3	56
1916	02	16	350	38	3	56
1916	02	17	350	41	3	56
1916	02	18	350	44	3	56
1916	02	19	350	48	3	56
1916	02	20	350	51	3	56
1916	02	21	350	55	3	56
1916	02	22	350	58	3	55
1916	02	23	351	02	3	55
1916	02	24	351	05	3	55
1916	02	25	351	09	3	55
1916	02	26	351	12	3	55
1916	02	27	351	16	3	55
1916	02	28	351	19	3	55
1916	02	29	351	23	3	55
1916	03	01	351	27	3	55
1916	03	02	351	30	3	54
1916	03	03	351	34	3	54
1916	03	04	351	37	3	54
1916	03	05	351	41	3	54
1916	03	06	351	45	3	54
1916	03	07	351	48	3	54
1916	03	08	351	52	3	54
1916	03	09	351	55	3	54
1916	03	10	351	59	3	54
1916	03	11	352	03	3	54
1916	03	12	352	06	3	54
1916	03	13	352	10	3	54
1916	03	14	352	14	3	54
1916	03	15	352	17	3	53
1916	03	16	352	21	3	53
1916	03	17	352	24	3	53
1916	03	18	352	28	3	53
1916	03	19	352	32	3	53
1916	03	20	352	35	3	53
1916	03	21	352	39	3	53
1916	03	22	352	43	3	53
1916	03	23	352	46	3	53
1916	03	24	352	50	3	53
1916	03	25	352	53	3	53
1916	03	26	352	57	3	53
1916	03	27	353	00	3	53
1916	03	28	353	04	3	53
1916	03	29	353	07	3	53
1916	03	30	353	11	3	53
1916	03	31	353	15	3	53
1916	04	01	353	18	3	53
1916	04	02	353	22	3	53
1916	04	03	353	25	3	53
1916	04	04	353	28	3	53
1916	04	05	353	32	3	53
1916	04	06	353	35	3	53
1916	04	07	353	39	3	53
1916	04	08	353	42	3	53
1916	04	09	353	45	3	53
1916	04	10	353	49	3	53
1916	04	11	353	52	3	53
1916	04	12	353	55	3	53
1916	04	13	353	59	3	53
1916	04	14	354	02	3	53
1916	04	15	354	05	3	53
1916	04	16	354	08	3	53
1916	04	17	354	12	3	54

1916 04 18	354 15	3 54
1916 04 19	354 18	3 54
1916 04 20	354 21	3 54
1916 04 21	354 24	3 54
1916 04 22	354 27	3 54
1916 04 23	354 30	3 54
1916 04 24	354 33	3 54
1916 04 25	354 36	3 54
1916 04 26	354 39	3 54
1916 04 27	354 42	3 54
1916 04 28	354 45	3 54
1916 04 29	354 48	3 54
1916 04 30	354 50	3 54
1916 05 01	354 53	3 55
1916 05 02	354 56	3 55
1916 05 03	354 59	3 55
1916 05 04	355 01	3 55
1916 05 05	355 04	3 55
1916 05 06	355 07	3 55
1916 05 07	355 09	3 55
1916 05 08	355 12	3 55
1916 05 09	355 14	3 55
1916 05 10	355 17	3 55
1916 05 11	355 19	3 56
1916 05 12	355 21	3 56
1916 05 13	355 24	3 56
1916 05 14	355 26	3 56
1916 05 15	355 28	3 56
1916 05 16	355 30	3 56
1916 05 17	355 33	3 56
1916 05 18	355 35	3 56
1916 05 19	355 37	3 57
1916 05 20	355 39	3 57
1916 05 21	355 41	3 57
1916 05 22	355 43	3 57
1916 05 23	355 45	3 57
1916 05 24	355 47	3 57
1916 05 25	355 48	3 57
1916 05 26	355 50	3 57
1916 05 27	355 52	3 58
1916 05 28	355 54	3 58
1916 05 29	355 55	3 58
1916 05 30	355 57	3 58
1916 05 31	355 58	3 58
1916 06 01	356 00	3 58
1916 06 02	356 01	3 58
1916 06 03	356 03	3 59
1916 06 04	356 04	3 59
1916 06 05	356 05	3 59
1916 06 06	356 06	3 59
1916 06 07	356 08	3 59
1916 06 08	356 09	3 59
1916 06 09	356 10	4 00
1916 06 10	356 11	4 00
1916 06 11	356 12	4 00
1916 06 12	356 13	4 00
1916 06 13	356 14	4 00
1916 06 14	356 15	4 00
1916 06 15	356 15	4 00
1916 06 16	356 16	4 01
1916 06 17	356 17	4 01
1916 06 18	356 17	4 01
1916 06 19	356 18	4 01
1916 06 20	356 18	4 01
1916 06 21	356 19	4 01
1916 06 22	356 19	4 02
1916 06 23	356 20	4 02
1916 06 24	356 20	4 02
1916 06 25	356 20	4 02
1916 06 26	356 20	4 02
1916 06 27	356 21	4 02
1916 06 28	356 21	4 03
1916 06 29	356 21	4 03
1916 06 30	356 21	4 03
1916 07 01	356 21	4 03
1916 07 02	356 21	4 03
1916 07 03	356 20	4 03
1916 07 04	356 20	4 04
1916 07 05	356 20	4 04
1916 07 06	356 19	4 04
1916 07 07	356 19	4 04
1916 07 08	356 19	4 04
1916 07 09	356 18	4 04
1916 07 10	356 18	4 04
1916 07 11	356 17	4 05
1916 07 12	356 16	4 05
1916 07 13	356 16	4 05
1916 07 14	356 15	4 05
1916 07 15	356 14	4 05
1916 07 16	356 13	4 05
1916 07 17	356 12	4 05
1916 07 18	356 12	4 06
1916 07 19	356 11	4 06
1916 07 20	356 09	4 06
1916 07 21	356 08	4 06
1916 07 22	356 07	4 06
1916 07 23	356 06	4 06
1916 07 24	356 05	4 06
1916 07 25	356 04	4 07
1916 07 26	356 02	4 07
1916 07 27	356 01	4 07
1916 07 28	355 59	4 07
1916 07 29	355 58	4 07
1916 07 30	355 56	4 07
1916 07 31	355 55	4 07
1916 08 01	355 53	4 07
1916 08 02	355 52	4 07
1916 08 03	355 50	4 08
1916 08 04	355 48	4 08
1916 08 05	355 46	4 08
1916 08 06	355 45	4 08
1916 08 07	355 43	4 08
1916 08 08	355 41	4 08
1916 08 09	355 39	4 08
1916 08 10	355 37	4 08
1916 08 11	355 35	4 08
1916 08 12	355 33	4 08
1916 08 13	355 31	4 08
1916 08 14	355 29	4 09
1916 08 15	355 27	4 09
1916 08 16	355 24	4 09
1916 08 17	355 22	4 09
1916 08 18	355 20	4 09
1916 08 19	355 18	4 09
1916 08 20	355 15	4 09
1916 08 21	355 13	4 09
1916 08 22	355 11	4 09
1916 08 23	355 08	4 09
1916 08 24	355 06	4 09
1916 08 25	355 03	4 09
1916 08 26	355 01	4 09
1916 08 27	354 59	4 09
1916 08 28	354 56	4 09
1916 08 29	354 53	4 09
1916 08 30	354 51	4 09
1916 08 31	354 48	4 09
1916 09 01	354 46	4 09
1916 09 02	354 43	4 09
1916 09 03	354 41	4 09
1916 09 04	354 38	4 09
1916 09 05	354 35	4 09
1916 09 06	354 33	4 09
1916 09 07	354 30	4 09
1916 09 08	354 27	4 09
1916 09 09	354 24	4 09
1916 09 10	354 22	4 09
1916 09 11	354 19	4 09
1916 09 12	354 16	4 09
1916 09 13	354 14	4 09
1916 09 14	354 11	4 09
1916 09 15	354 08	4 09
1916 09 16	354 05	4 09
1916 09 17	354 03	4 09
1916 09 18	354 00	4 09
1916 09 19	353 57	4 09
1916 09 20	353 54	4 09
1916 09 21	353 52	4 08
1916 09 22	353 49	4 08
1916 09 23	353 46	4 08
1916 09 24	353 44	4 08
1916 09 25	353 41	4 08
1916 09 26	353 38	4 08
1916 09 27	353 35	4 08
1916 09 28	353 33	4 08
1916 09 29	353 30	4 08
1916 09 30	353 27	4 08
1916 10 01	353 25	4 07
1916 10 02	353 22	4 07
1916 10 03	353 20	4 07
1916 10 04	353 17	4 07
1916 10 05	353 14	4 07
1916 10 06	353 12	4 07
1916 10 07	353 09	4 07
1916 10 08	353 07	4 06
1916 10 09	353 04	4 06
1916 10 10	353 02	4 06
1916 10 11	352 59	4 06
1916 10 12	352 57	4 06
1916 10 13	352 55	4 06
1916 10 14	352 52	4 05
1916 10 15	352 50	4 05
1916 10 16	352 48	4 05
1916 10 17	352 45	4 05
1916 10 18	352 43	4 05
1916 10 19	352 41	4 05
1916 10 20	352 39	4 04
1916 10 21	352 37	4 04
1916 10 22	352 35	4 04
1916 10 23	352 32	4 04
1916 10 24	352 30	4 04
1916 10 25	352 28	4 03
1916 10 26	352 27	4 03
1916 10 27	352 25	4 03
1916 10 28	352 23	4 03
1916 10 29	352 21	4 02
1916 10 30	352 19	4 02
1916 10 31	352 17	4 02
1916 11 01	352 16	4 02
1916 11 02	352 14	4 02
1916 11 03	352 12	4 01
1916 11 04	352 11	4 01
1916 11 05	352 09	4 01
1916 11 06	352 08	4 01
1916 11 07	352 06	4 00
1916 11 08	352 05	4 00
1916 11 09	352 04	4 00
1916 11 10	352 03	4 00
1916 11 11	352 01	3 59
1916 11 12	352 00	3 59
1916 11 13	351 59	3 59
1916 11 14	351 58	3 59
1916 11 15	351 57	3 58
1916 11 16	351 56	3 58
1916 11 17	351 55	3 58
1916 11 18	351 54	3 58
1916 11 19	351 53	3 57
1916 11 20	351 53	3 57
1916 11 21	351 52	3 57
1916 11 22	351 51	3 56
1916 11 23	351 51	3 56
1916 11 24	351 50	3 56
1916 11 25	351 50	3 56
1916 11 26	351 49	3 55
1916 11 27	351 49	3 55
1916 11 28	351 48	3 55
1916 11 29	351 48	3 55
1916 11 30	351 48	3 54
1916 12 01	351 48	3 54
1916 12 02	351 48	3 54
1916 12 03	351 48	3 53
1916 12 04	351 48	3 53
1916 12 05	351 48	3 53
1916 12 06	351 48	3 53
1916 12 07	351 48	3 52
1916 12 08	351 48	3 52
1916 12 09	351 49	3 52
1916 12 10	351 49	3 52
1916 12 11	351 49	3 51
1916 12 12	351 50	3 51
1916 12 13	351 50	3 51
1916 12 14	351 51	3 50
1916 12 15	351 52	3 50
1916 12 16	351 52	3 50
1916 12 17	351 53	3 50
1916 12 18	351 54	3 49
1916 12 19	351 55	3 49
1916 12 20	351 55	3 49
1916 12 21	351 56	3 49
1916 12 22	351 57	3 48
1916 12 23	351 59	3 48
1916 12 24	352 00	3 48
1916 12 25	352 01	3 47
1916 12 26	352 02	3 47
1916 12 27	352 03	3 47
1916 12 28	352 05	3 47
1916 12 29	352 06	3 46
1916 12 30	352 07	3 46
1916 12 31	352 09	3 46
1917 01 01	352 10	3 46
1917 01 02	352 12	3 45
1917 01 03	352 14	3 45
1917 01 04	352 15	3 45
1917 01 05	352 17	3 45
1917 01 06	352 19	3 44
1917 01 07	352 21	3 44
1917 01 08	352 23	3 44
1917 01 09	352 25	3 44
1917 01 10	352 27	3 43
1917 01 11	352 29	3 43
1917 01 12	352 31	3 43
1917 01 13	352 33	3 43
1917 01 14	352 35	3 42
1917 01 15	352 37	3 42
1917 01 16	352 39	3 42
1917 01 17	352 42	3 42
1917 01 18	352 44	3 42
1917 01 19	352 46	3 41
1917 01 20	352 49	3 41
1917 01 21	352 51	3 41
1917 01 22	352 54	3 41
1917 01 23	352 56	3 41
1917 01 24	352 59	3 40
1917 01 25	353 01	3 40
1917 01 26	353 04	3 40
1917 01 27	353 07	3 40
1917 01 28	353 09	3 39
1917 01 29	353 12	3 39
1917 01 30	353 15	3 39
1917 01 31	353 18	3 39
1917 02 01	353 21	3 39
1917 02 02	353 24	3 39
1917 02 03	353 26	3 38
1917 02 04	353 29	3 38
1917 02 05	353 32	3 38
1917 02 06	353 35	3 38
1917 02 07	353 38	3 38
1917 02 08	353 42	3 37
1917 02 09	353 45	3 37
1917 02 10	353 48	3 37
1917 02 11	353 51	3 37
1917 02 12	353 54	3 37
1917 02 13	353 57	3 37
1917 02 14	354 00	3 37
1917 02 15	354 04	3 36
1917 02 16	354 07	3 36
1917 02 17	354 10	3 36
1917 02 18	354 14	3 36
1917 02 19	354 17	3 36
1917 02 20	354 20	3 36
1917 02 21	354 24	3 36
1917 02 22	354 27	3 35
1917 02 23	354 30	3 35
1917 02 24	354 34	3 35
1917 02 25	354 37	3 35
1917 02 26	354 41	3 35
1917 02 27	354 44	3 35
1917 02 28	354 48	3 35
1917 03 01	354 51	3 35
1917 03 02	354 55	3 34
1917 03 03	354 58	3 34
1917 03 04	355 02	3 34
1917 03 05	355 05	3 34
1917 03 06	355 09	3 34
1917 03 07	355 12	3 34
1917 03 08	355 16	3 34
1917 03 09	355 20	3 34
1917 03 10	355 23	3 34
1917 03 11	355 27	3 34
1917 03 12	355 30	3 34
1917 03 13	355 34	3 33
1917 03 14	355 37	3 33
1917 03 15	355 41	3 33
1917 03 16	355 45	3 33
1917 03 17	355 48	3 33
1917 03 18	355 52	3 33
1917 03 19	355 55	3 33
1917 03 20	355 59	3 33
1917 03 21	356 03	3 33
1917 03 22	356 06	3 33
1917 03 23	356 10	3 33
1917 03 24	356 13	3 33
1917 03 25	356 17	3 33
1917 03 26	356 20	3 33
1917 03 27	356 24	3 33
1917 03 28	356 28	3 33
1917 03 29	356 31	3 33
1917 03 30	356 35	3 33
1917 03 31	356 38	3 33
1917 04 01	356 42	3 33
1917 04 02	356 45	3 33
1917 04 03	356 49	3 33
1917 04 04	356 52	3 33
1917 04 05	356 56	3 33
1917 04 06	356 59	3 33
1917 04 07	357 02	3 33
1917 04 08	357 06	3 33
1917 04 09	357 09	3 33
1917 04 10	357 13	3 33
1917 04 11	357 16	3 33
1917 04 12	357 19	3 33
1917 04 13	357 23	3 33
1917 04 14	357 26	3 33
1917 04 15	357 29	3 33
1917 04 16	357 33	3 33
1917 04 17	357 36	3 33
1917 04 18	357 39	3 33
1917 04 19	357 42	3 33
1917 04 20	357 45	3 33
1917 04 21	357 49	3 33
1917 04 22	357 52	3 33
1917 04 23	357 55	3 33
1917 04 24	357 58	3 33
1917 04 25	358 01	3 33
1917 04 26	358 04	3 33
1917 04 27	358 07	3 33
1917 04 28	358 10	3 33
1917 04 29	358 13	3 33
1917 04 30	358 16	3 33
1917 05 01	358 19	3 34
1917 05 02	358 21	3 34
1917 05 03	358 24	3 34
1917 05 04	358 27	3 34
1917 05 05	358 30	3 34
1917 05 06	358 32	3 34
1917 05 07	358 35	3 34
1917 05 08	358 38	3 34
1917 05 09	358 40	3 34
1917 05 10	358 43	3 34
1917 05 11	358 45	3 34
1917 05 12	358 48	3 34
1917 05 13	358 50	3 34
1917 05 14	358 53	3 35
1917 05 15	358 55	3 35
1917 05 16	358 58	3 35
1917 05 17	359 00	3 35
1917 05 18	359 02	3 35
1917 05 19	359 04	3 35
1917 05 20	359 07	3 35
1917 05 21	359 09	3 35
1917 05 22	359 11	3 35
1917 05 23	359 13	3 35
1917 05 24	359 15	3 35
1917 05 25	359 17	3 36
1917 05 26	359 19	3 36
1917 05 27	359 21	3 36
1917 05 28	359 22	3 36
1917 05 29	359 24	3 36
1917 05 30	359 26	3 36
1917 05 31	359 28	3 36
1917 06 01	359 29	3 36
1917 06 02	359 31	3 37
1917 06 03	359 32	3 37
1917 06 04	359 34	3 37
1917 06 05	359 35	3 37
1917 06 06	359 37	3 37
1917 06 07	359 38	3 37
1917 06 08	359 40	3 37

1917	06	09	359	41	3	37
1917	06	10	359	42	3	38
1917	06	11	359	43	3	38
1917	06	12	359	44	3	38
1917	06	13	359	45	3	38
1917	06	14	359	46	3	38
1917	06	15	359	47	3	38
1917	06	16	359	48	3	38
1917	06	17	359	49	3	39
1917	06	18	359	50	3	39
1917	06	19	359	51	3	39
1917	06	20	359	51	3	39
1917	06	21	359	52	3	39
1917	06	22	359	53	3	39
1917	06	23	359	53	3	39
1917	06	24	359	54	3	40
1917	06	25	359	54	3	40
1917	06	26	359	55	3	40
1917	06	27	359	55	3	40
1917	06	28	359	55	3	40
1917	06	29	359	56	3	40
1917	06	30	359	56	3	40
1917	07	01	359	56	3	40
1917	07	02	359	56	3	41
1917	07	03	359	56	3	41
1917	07	04	359	56	3	41
1917	07	05	359	56	3	41
1917	07	06	359	56	3	41
1917	07	07	359	56	3	41
1917	07	08	359	55	3	41
1917	07	09	359	55	3	42
1917	07	10	359	55	3	42
1917	07	11	359	54	3	42
1917	07	12	359	54	3	42
1917	07	13	359	53	3	42
1917	07	14	359	53	3	42
1917	07	15	359	52	3	42
1917	07	16	359	52	3	42
1917	07	17	359	51	3	43
1917	07	18	359	50	3	43
1917	07	19	359	49	3	43
1917	07	20	359	49	3	43
1917	07	21	359	48	3	43
1917	07	22	359	47	3	43
1917	07	23	359	46	3	43
1917	07	24	359	45	3	43
1917	07	25	359	44	3	44
1917	07	26	359	42	3	44
1917	07	27	359	41	3	44
1917	07	28	359	40	3	44
1917	07	29	359	39	3	44
1917	07	30	359	37	3	44
1917	07	31	359	36	3	44
1917	08	01	359	35	3	44
1917	08	02	359	33	3	44
1917	08	03	359	32	3	45
1917	08	04	359	30	3	45
1917	08	05	359	29	3	45
1917	08	06	359	27	3	45
1917	08	07	359	25	3	45
1917	08	08	359	23	3	45
1917	08	09	359	22	3	45
1917	08	10	359	20	3	45
1917	08	11	359	18	3	45
1917	08	12	359	16	3	45
1917	08	13	359	14	3	45
1917	08	14	359	12	3	45
1917	08	15	359	10	3	45
1917	08	16	359	08	3	46
1917	08	17	359	06	3	46
1917	08	18	359	04	3	46
1917	08	19	359	02	3	46
1917	08	20	359	00	3	46
1917	08	21	358	58	3	46
1917	08	22	358	55	3	46
1917	08	23	358	53	3	46
1917	08	24	358	51	3	46
1917	08	25	358	48	3	46
1917	08	26	358	46	3	46
1917	08	27	358	44	3	46
1917	08	28	358	41	3	46
1917	08	29	358	39	3	46
1917	08	30	358	36	3	46
1917	08	31	358	34	3	46
1917	09	01	358	32	3	46
1917	09	02	358	29	3	46
1917	09	03	358	26	3	46
1917	09	04	358	24	3	46
1917	09	05	358	21	3	46
1917	09	06	358	19	3	46
1917	09	07	358	16	3	46
1917	09	08	358	13	3	46
1917	09	09	358	11	3	46
1917	09	10	358	08	3	46
1917	09	11	358	06	3	46
1917	09	12	358	03	3	46
1917	09	13	358	00	3	46
1917	09	14	357	57	3	46
1917	09	15	357	55	3	46
1917	09	16	357	52	3	46
1917	09	17	357	49	3	46
1917	09	18	357	47	3	46
1917	09	19	357	44	3	46
1917	09	20	357	41	3	46
1917	09	21	357	38	3	46
1917	09	22	357	36	3	46
1917	09	23	357	33	3	45
1917	09	24	357	30	3	45
1917	09	25	357	28	3	45
1917	09	26	357	25	3	45
1917	09	27	357	22	3	45
1917	09	28	357	19	3	45
1917	09	29	357	17	3	45
1917	09	30	357	14	3	45
1917	10	01	357	11	3	45
1917	10	02	357	09	3	45
1917	10	03	357	06	3	44
1917	10	04	357	03	3	44
1917	10	05	357	01	3	44
1917	10	06	356	58	3	44
1917	10	07	356	56	3	44
1917	10	08	356	53	3	44
1917	10	09	356	50	3	44
1917	10	10	356	48	3	44
1917	10	11	356	45	3	43
1917	10	12	356	43	3	43
1917	10	13	356	40	3	43
1917	10	14	356	38	3	43
1917	10	15	356	36	3	43
1917	10	16	356	33	3	43
1917	10	17	356	31	3	43
1917	10	18	356	28	3	42
1917	10	19	356	26	3	42
1917	10	20	356	24	3	42
1917	10	21	356	22	3	42
1917	10	22	356	19	3	42
1917	10	23	356	17	3	42
1917	10	24	356	15	3	41
1917	10	25	356	13	3	41
1917	10	26	356	11	3	41
1917	10	27	356	09	3	41
1917	10	28	356	07	3	41
1917	10	29	356	05	3	40
1917	10	30	356	03	3	40
1917	10	31	356	01	3	40
1917	11	01	355	59	3	40
1917	11	02	355	57	3	40
1917	11	03	355	55	3	39
1917	11	04	355	54	3	39
1917	11	05	355	52	3	39
1917	11	06	355	50	3	39
1917	11	07	355	49	3	39
1917	11	08	355	47	3	38
1917	11	09	355	46	3	38
1917	11	10	355	44	3	38
1917	11	11	355	43	3	38
1917	11	12	355	42	3	37
1917	11	13	355	40	3	37
1917	11	14	355	39	3	37
1917	11	15	355	38	3	37
1917	11	16	355	37	3	36
1917	11	17	355	35	3	36
1917	11	18	355	34	3	36
1917	11	19	355	33	3	36
1917	11	20	355	32	3	36
1917	11	21	355	31	3	35
1917	11	22	355	31	3	35
1917	11	23	355	30	3	35
1917	11	24	355	29	3	35
1917	11	25	355	28	3	34
1917	11	26	355	28	3	34
1917	11	27	355	27	3	34
1917	11	28	355	27	3	34
1917	11	29	355	26	3	33
1917	11	30	355	26	3	33
1917	12	01	355	25	3	33
1917	12	02	355	25	3	33
1917	12	03	355	25	3	32
1917	12	04	355	25	3	32
1917	12	05	355	24	3	32
1917	12	06	355	24	3	31
1917	12	07	355	24	3	31
1917	12	08	355	24	3	31
1917	12	09	355	24	3	31
1917	12	10	355	24	3	30
1917	12	11	355	25	3	30
1917	12	12	355	25	3	30
1917	12	13	355	25	3	30
1917	12	14	355	25	3	29
1917	12	15	355	26	3	29
1917	12	16	355	26	3	29
1917	12	17	355	27	3	29
1917	12	18	355	27	3	28
1917	12	19	355	28	3	28
1917	12	20	355	29	3	28
1917	12	21	355	29	3	28
1917	12	22	355	30	3	27
1917	12	23	355	31	3	27
1917	12	24	355	32	3	27
1917	12	25	355	33	3	27
1917	12	26	355	34	3	26
1917	12	27	355	35	3	26
1917	12	28	355	36	3	26
1917	12	29	355	37	3	26
1917	12	30	355	39	3	25
1917	12	31	355	40	3	25
1918	01	01	355	41	3	25
1918	01	02	355	43	3	25
1918	01	03	355	44	3	24
1918	01	04	355	45	3	24
1918	01	05	355	47	3	24
1918	01	06	355	49	3	24
1918	01	07	355	50	3	24
1918	01	08	355	52	3	23
1918	01	09	355	54	3	23
1918	01	10	355	55	3	23
1918	01	11	355	57	3	23
1918	01	12	355	59	3	22
1918	01	13	356	01	3	22
1918	01	14	356	03	3	22
1918	01	15	356	05	3	22
1918	01	16	356	07	3	22
1918	01	17	356	09	3	21
1918	01	18	356	11	3	21
1918	01	19	356	13	3	21
1918	01	20	356	16	3	21
1918	01	21	356	18	3	20
1918	01	22	356	20	3	20
1918	01	23	356	23	3	20
1918	01	24	356	25	3	20
1918	01	25	356	27	3	20
1918	01	26	356	30	3	19
1918	01	27	356	32	3	19
1918	01	28	356	35	3	19
1918	01	29	356	38	3	19
1918	01	30	356	40	3	19
1918	01	31	356	43	3	18
1918	02	01	356	46	3	18
1918	02	02	356	48	3	18
1918	02	03	356	51	3	18
1918	02	04	356	54	3	18
1918	02	05	356	57	3	18
1918	02	06	357	00	3	17
1918	02	07	357	02	3	17
1918	02	08	357	05	3	17
1918	02	09	357	08	3	17
1918	02	10	357	11	3	17
1918	02	11	357	14	3	17
1918	02	12	357	17	3	16
1918	02	13	357	20	3	16
1918	02	14	357	24	3	16
1918	02	15	357	27	3	16
1918	02	16	357	30	3	16
1918	02	17	357	33	3	16
1918	02	18	357	36	3	15
1918	02	19	357	39	3	15
1918	02	20	357	43	3	15
1918	02	21	357	46	3	15
1918	02	22	357	49	3	15
1918	02	23	357	53	3	15
1918	02	24	357	56	3	15
1918	02	25	357	59	3	15
1918	02	26	358	03	3	14
1918	02	27	358	06	3	14
1918	02	28	358	09	3	14
1918	03	01	358	13	3	14
1918	03	02	358	16	3	14
1918	03	03	358	20	3	14
1918	03	04	358	23	3	14
1918	03	05	358	27	3	14
1918	03	06	358	30	3	14
1918	03	07	358	34	3	13
1918	03	08	358	37	3	13
1918	03	09	358	41	3	13
1918	03	10	358	44	3	13
1918	03	11	358	48	3	13
1918	03	12	358	51	3	13
1918	03	13	358	55	3	13
1918	03	14	358	58	3	13
1918	03	15	359	02	3	13
1918	03	16	359	05	3	13
1918	03	17	359	09	3	13
1918	03	18	359	12	3	13
1918	03	19	359	16	3	12
1918	03	20	359	20	3	12
1918	03	21	359	23	3	12
1918	03	22	359	27	3	12
1918	03	23	359	30	3	12
1918	03	24	359	34	3	12
1918	03	25	359	37	3	12
1918	03	26	359	41	3	12
1918	03	27	359	44	3	12
1918	03	28	359	48	3	12
1918	03	29	359	52	3	12
1918	03	30	359	55	3	12
1918	03	31	359	59	3	12
1918	04	01	00	02	3	12
1918	04	02	00	06	3	12
1918	04	03	00	09	3	12
1918	04	04	00	13	3	12
1918	04	05	00	16	3	12
1918	04	06	00	20	3	12
1918	04	07	00	23	3	12
1918	04	08	00	26	3	12
1918	04	09	00	30	3	12
1918	04	10	00	33	3	12
1918	04	11	00	37	3	12
1918	04	12	00	40	3	12
1918	04	13	00	43	3	12
1918	04	14	00	47	3	12
1918	04	15	00	50	3	12
1918	04	16	00	53	3	12
1918	04	17	00	57	3	12
1918	04	18	01	00	3	12
1918	04	19	01	03	3	12
1918	04	20	01	07	3	12
1918	04	21	01	10	3	12
1918	04	22	01	13	3	12
1918	04	23	01	16	3	12
1918	04	24	01	19	3	12
1918	04	25	01	22	3	12
1918	04	26	01	25	3	12
1918	04	27	01	29	3	12
1918	04	28	01	32	3	12
1918	04	29	01	35	3	12
1918	04	30	01	38	3	12
1918	05	01	01	41	3	12
1918	05	02	01	44	3	12
1918	05	03	01	46	3	12
1918	05	04	01	49	3	12
1918	05	05	01	52	3	12
1918	05	06	01	55	3	12
1918	05	07	01	58	3	12
1918	05	08	02	00	3	12
1918	05	09	02	03	3	12
1918	05	10	02	06	3	13
1918	05	11	02	09	3	13
1918	05	12	02	11	3	13
1918	05	13	02	14	3	13
1918	05	14	02	16	3	13
1918	05	15	02	19	3	13
1918	05	16	02	21	3	13
1918	05	17	02	24	3	13
1918	05	18	02	26	3	13
1918	05	19	02	28	3	13
1918	05	20	02	31	3	13
1918	05	21	02	33	3	13
1918	05	22	02	35	3	13
1918	05	23	02	37	3	13
1918	05	24	02	40	3	14
1918	05	25	02	42	3	14
1918	05	26	02	44	3	14
1918	05	27	02	46	3	14
1918	05	28	02	48	3	14
1918	05	29	02	50	3	14
1918	05	30	02	52	3	14
1918	05	31	02	54	3	14
1918	06	01	02	55	3	14
1918	06	02	02	57	3	14
1918	06	03	02	59	3	14
1918	06	04	03	01	3	15
1918	06	05	03	02	3	15
1918	06	06	03	04	3	15
1918	06	07	03	05	3	15
1918	06	08	03	07	3	15
1918	06	09	03	08	3	15
1918	06	10	03	10	3	15
1918	06	11	03	11	3	15
1918	06	12	03	12	3	15
1918	06	13	03	14	3	16
1918	06	14	03	15	3	16
1918	06	15	03	16	3	16
1918	06	16	03	17	3	16
1918	06	17	03	18	3	16
1918	06	18	03	19	3	16
1918	06	19	03	20	3	16
1918	06	20	03	21	3	16
1918	06	21	03	22	3	16
1918	06	22	03	23	3	17
1918	06	23	03	23	3	17
1918	06	24	03	24	3	17
1918	06	25	03	25	3	17
1918	06	26	03	25	3	17
1918	06	27	03	26	3	17
1918	06	28	03	26	3	17
1918	06	29	03	27	3	17
1918	06	30	03	27	3	17
1918	07	01	03	27	3	18
1918	07	02	03	28	3	18
1918	07	03	03	28	3	18
1918	07	04	03	28	3	18
1918	07	05	03	28	3	18
1918	07	06	03	28	3	18
1918	07	07	03	28	3	18
1918	07	08	03	28	3	18
1918	07	09	03	28	3	18
1918	07	10	03	28	3	19
1918	07	11	03	28	3	19
1918	07	12	03	28	3	19
1918	07	13	03	27	3	19
1918	07	14	03	27	3	19
1918	07	15	03	27	3	19
1918	07	16	03	26	3	19
1918	07	17	03	26	3	19
1918	07	18	03	25	3	19
1918	07	19	03	25	3	20
1918	07	20	03	24	3	20
1918	07	21	03	23	3	20
1918	07	22	03	23	3	20
1918	07	23	03	22	3	20
1918	07	24	03	21	3	20
1918	07	25	03	20	3	20
1918	07	26	03	19	3	20
1918	07	27	03	18	3	20
1918	07	28	03	17	3	21

1918 07 29	03 16	3 21	1918 11 12	359 20	3 15	1919 02 26	01 22	2 53	1919 06 12	06 38	2 53
1918 07 30	03 15	3 21	1918 11 13	359 19	3 15	1919 02 27	01 25	2 53	1919 06 13	06 39	2 53
1918 07 31	03 14	3 21	1918 11 14	359 17	3 15	1919 02 28	01 29	2 53	1919 06 14	06 40	2 53
1918 08 01	03 12	3 21	1918 11 15	359 16	3 14	1919 03 01	01 32	2 53	1919 06 15	06 42	2 53
1918 08 02	03 11	3 21	1918 11 16	359 15	3 14	1919 03 02	01 35	2 53	1919 06 16	06 43	2 53
1918 08 03	03 10	3 21	1918 11 17	359 13	3 14	1919 03 03	01 39	2 53	1919 06 17	06 44	2 53
1918 08 04	03 08	3 21	1918 11 18	359 12	3 14	1919 03 04	01 42	2 53	1919 06 18	06 46	2 53
1918 08 05	03 07	3 21	1918 11 19	359 11	3 14	1919 03 05	01 46	2 53	1919 06 19	06 47	2 53
1918 08 06	03 05	3 21	1918 11 20	359 10	3 13	1919 03 06	01 49	2 52	1919 06 20	06 48	2 53
1918 08 07	03 04	3 21	1918 11 21	359 09	3 13	1919 03 07	01 52	2 52	1919 06 21	06 49	2 53
1918 08 08	03 02	3 21	1918 11 22	359 07	3 13	1919 03 08	01 56	2 52	1919 06 22	06 50	2 53
1918 08 09	03 01	3 22	1918 11 23	359 06	3 13	1919 03 09	01 59	2 52	1919 06 23	06 51	2 54
1918 08 10	02 59	3 22	1918 11 24	359 05	3 12	1919 03 10	02 03	2 52	1919 06 24	06 52	2 54
1918 08 11	02 58	3 22	1918 11 25	359 05	3 12	1919 03 11	02 06	2 52	1919 06 25	06 52	2 54
1918 08 12	02 56	3 22	1918 11 26	359 04	3 12	1919 03 12	02 10	2 52	1919 06 26	06 53	2 54
1918 08 13	02 54	3 22	1918 11 27	359 03	3 12	1919 03 13	02 13	2 52	1919 06 27	06 54	2 54
1918 08 14	02 52	3 22	1918 11 28	359 02	3 11	1919 03 14	02 17	2 52	1919 06 28	06 55	2 54
1918 08 15	02 50	3 22	1918 11 29	359 01	3 11	1919 03 15	02 20	2 52	1919 06 29	06 55	2 54
1918 08 16	02 48	3 22	1918 11 30	359 01	3 11	1919 03 16	02 24	2 52	1919 06 30	06 56	2 54
1918 08 17	02 47	3 22	1918 12 01	359 00	3 11	1919 03 17	02 27	2 51	1919 07 01	06 56	2 54
1918 08 18	02 45	3 22	1918 12 02	359 00	3 11	1919 03 18	02 31	2 51	1919 07 02	06 57	2 54
1918 08 19	02 43	3 22	1918 12 03	358 59	3 10	1919 03 19	02 34	2 51	1919 07 03	06 57	2 54
1918 08 20	02 41	3 22	1918 12 04	358 59	3 10	1919 03 20	02 38	2 51	1919 07 04	06 58	2 55
1918 08 21	02 39	3 22	1918 12 05	358 58	3 10	1919 03 21	02 41	2 51	1919 07 05	06 58	2 55
1918 08 22	02 36	3 22	1918 12 06	358 58	3 10	1919 03 22	02 45	2 51	1919 07 06	06 58	2 55
1918 08 23	02 34	3 22	1918 12 07	358 58	3 09	1919 03 23	02 48	2 51	1919 07 07	06 57	2 55
1918 08 24	02 32	3 22	1918 12 08	358 58	3 09	1919 03 24	02 52	2 51	1919 07 08	06 59	2 55
1918 08 25	02 30	3 22	1918 12 09	358 58	3 09	1919 03 25	02 56	2 51	1919 07 09	06 59	2 55
1918 08 26	02 28	3 22	1918 12 10	358 57	3 09	1919 03 26	02 59	2 51	1919 07 10	06 59	2 55
1918 08 27	02 25	3 22	1918 12 11	358 57	3 08	1919 03 27	03 03	2 51	1919 07 11	06 59	2 55
1918 08 28	02 23	3 22	1918 12 12	358 57	3 08	1919 03 28	03 06	2 51	1919 07 12	06 59	2 55
1918 08 29	02 21	3 22	1918 12 13	358 58	3 08	1919 03 29	03 10	2 51	1919 07 13	06 59	2 55
1918 08 30	02 18	3 23	1918 12 14	358 58	3 08	1919 03 30	03 13	2 51	1919 07 14	06 59	2 56
1918 08 31	02 16	3 23	1918 12 15	358 58	3 08	1919 03 31	03 17	2 51	1919 07 15	06 59	2 56
1918 09 01	02 14	3 23	1918 12 16	358 58	3 07	1919 04 01	03 20	2 51	1919 07 16	06 58	2 56
1918 09 02	02 11	3 23	1918 12 17	358 58	3 07	1919 04 02	03 24	2 50	1919 07 17	06 58	2 56
1918 09 03	02 09	3 23	1918 12 18	358 59	3 07	1919 04 03	03 27	2 50	1919 07 18	06 58	2 56
1918 09 04	02 06	3 23	1918 12 19	358 59	3 07	1919 04 04	03 31	2 50	1919 07 19	06 57	2 56
1918 09 05	02 04	3 23	1918 12 20	359 00	3 06	1919 04 05	03 34	2 50	1919 07 20	06 57	2 56
1918 09 06	02 01	3 23	1918 12 21	359 00	3 06	1919 04 06	03 38	2 50	1919 07 21	06 56	2 56
1918 09 07	01 59	3 23	1918 12 22	359 01	3 06	1919 04 07	03 41	2 50	1919 07 22	06 56	2 56
1918 09 08	01 56	3 23	1918 12 23	359 01	3 06	1919 04 08	03 45	2 50	1919 07 23	06 55	2 56
1918 09 09	01 54	3 23	1918 12 24	359 02	3 05	1919 04 09	03 48	2 50	1919 07 24	06 54	2 56
1918 09 10	01 51	3 23	1918 12 25	359 03	3 05	1919 04 10	03 52	2 50	1919 07 25	06 54	2 56
1918 09 11	01 48	3 23	1918 12 26	359 04	3 05	1919 04 11	03 55	2 50	1919 07 26	06 53	2 57
1918 09 12	01 46	3 22	1918 12 27	359 04	3 05	1919 04 12	03 59	2 50	1919 07 27	06 52	2 57
1918 09 13	01 43	3 22	1918 12 28	359 05	3 04	1919 04 13	04 02	2 50	1919 07 28	06 51	2 57
1918 09 14	01 41	3 22	1918 12 29	359 06	3 04	1919 04 14	04 05	2 50	1919 07 29	06 50	2 57
1918 09 15	01 38	3 22	1918 12 30	359 07	3 04	1919 04 15	04 09	2 50	1919 07 30	06 49	2 57
1918 09 16	01 35	3 22	1918 12 31	359 08	3 04	1919 04 16	04 12	2 50	1919 07 31	06 48	2 57
1918 09 17	01 33	3 22	1919 01 01	359 09	3 04	1919 04 17	04 15	2 50	1919 08 01	06 47	2 57
1918 09 18	01 30	3 22	1919 01 02	359 11	3 03	1919 04 18	04 19	2 50	1919 08 02	06 46	2 57
1918 09 19	01 27	3 22	1919 01 03	359 12	3 03	1919 04 19	04 22	2 50	1919 08 03	06 45	2 57
1918 09 20	01 25	3 22	1919 01 04	359 13	3 03	1919 04 20	04 25	2 50	1919 08 04	06 44	2 57
1918 09 21	01 22	3 22	1919 01 05	359 14	3 03	1919 04 21	04 29	2 50	1919 08 05	06 43	2 57
1918 09 22	01 19	3 22	1919 01 06	359 16	3 02	1919 04 22	04 32	2 50	1919 08 06	06 41	2 57
1918 09 23	01 16	3 22	1919 01 07	359 17	3 02	1919 04 23	04 35	2 50	1919 08 07	06 40	2 57
1918 09 24	01 14	3 22	1919 01 08	359 19	3 02	1919 04 24	04 38	2 50	1919 08 08	06 39	2 58
1918 09 25	01 11	3 22	1919 01 09	359 20	3 02	1919 04 25	04 42	2 50	1919 08 09	06 37	2 58
1918 09 26	01 08	3 22	1919 01 10	359 22	3 02	1919 04 26	04 45	2 50	1919 08 10	06 36	2 58
1918 09 27	01 05	3 22	1919 01 11	359 23	3 01	1919 04 27	04 48	2 50	1919 08 11	06 34	2 58
1918 09 28	01 03	3 22	1919 01 12	359 25	3 01	1919 04 28	04 51	2 50	1919 08 12	06 33	2 58
1918 09 29	01 00	3 22	1919 01 13	359 27	3 01	1919 04 29	04 54	2 50	1919 08 13	06 31	2 58
1918 09 30	00 57	3 22	1919 01 14	359 29	3 01	1919 04 30	04 57	2 50	1919 08 14	06 30	2 58
1918 10 01	00 55	3 21	1919 01 15	359 30	3 01	1919 05 01	05 00	2 50	1919 08 15	06 28	2 58
1918 10 02	00 52	3 21	1919 01 16	359 32	3 00	1919 05 02	05 03	2 50	1919 08 16	06 26	2 58
1918 10 03	00 49	3 21	1919 01 17	359 34	3 00	1919 05 03	05 06	2 50	1919 08 17	06 24	2 58
1918 10 04	00 47	3 21	1919 01 18	359 36	3 00	1919 05 04	05 09	2 50	1919 08 18	06 23	2 58
1918 10 05	00 44	3 21	1919 01 19	359 38	3 00	1919 05 05	05 12	2 50	1919 08 19	06 21	2 58
1918 10 06	00 41	3 21	1919 01 20	359 40	2 59	1919 05 06	05 15	2 50	1919 08 20	06 19	2 58
1918 10 07	00 39	3 21	1919 01 21	359 42	2 59	1919 05 07	05 18	2 50	1919 08 21	06 17	2 58
1918 10 08	00 36	3 21	1919 01 22	359 45	2 59	1919 05 08	05 21	2 50	1919 08 22	06 15	2 58
1918 10 09	00 33	3 21	1919 01 23	359 47	2 59	1919 05 09	05 24	2 50	1919 08 23	06 13	2 58
1918 10 10	00 31	3 20	1919 01 24	359 49	2 59	1919 05 10	05 26	2 51	1919 08 24	06 11	2 58
1918 10 11	00 28	3 20	1919 01 25	359 51	2 59	1919 05 11	05 29	2 51	1919 08 25	06 09	2 58
1918 10 12	00 26	3 20	1919 01 26	359 53	2 58	1919 05 12	05 32	2 51	1919 08 26	06 07	2 58
1918 10 13	00 23	3 20	1919 01 27	359 56	2 58	1919 05 13	05 35	2 51	1919 08 27	06 05	2 58
1918 10 14	00 21	3 20	1919 01 28	359 58	2 58	1919 05 14	05 37	2 51	1919 08 28	06 02	2 58
1918 10 15	00 18	3 20	1919 01 29	00 01	2 58	1919 05 15	05 40	2 51	1919 08 29	06 00	2 58
1918 10 16	00 16	3 20	1919 01 30	00 03	2 58	1919 05 16	05 42	2 51	1919 08 30	05 58	2 58
1918 10 17	00 13	3 20	1919 01 31	00 06	2 57	1919 05 17	05 45	2 51	1919 08 31	05 56	2 58
1918 10 18	00 11	3 19	1919 02 01	00 08	2 57	1919 05 18	05 48	2 51	1919 09 01	05 53	2 58
1918 10 19	00 08	3 19	1919 02 02	00 11	2 57	1919 05 19	05 50	2 51	1919 09 02	05 51	2 58
1918 10 20	00 06	3 19	1919 02 03	00 13	2 57	1919 05 20	05 52	2 51	1919 09 03	05 49	2 58
1918 10 21	00 03	3 19	1919 02 04	00 16	2 57	1919 05 21	05 55	2 51	1919 09 04	05 46	2 58
1918 10 22	00 01	3 19	1919 02 05	00 19	2 57	1919 05 22	05 57	2 51	1919 09 05	05 44	2 58
1918 10 23	359 59	3 19	1919 02 06	00 21	2 56	1919 05 23	06 00	2 51	1919 09 06	05 42	2 58
1918 10 24	359 57	3 19	1919 02 07	00 24	2 56	1919 05 24	06 02	2 51	1919 09 07	05 39	2 58
1918 10 25	359 54	3 18	1919 02 08	00 27	2 56	1919 05 25	06 04	2 51	1919 09 08	05 37	2 58
1918 10 26	359 52	3 18	1919 02 09	00 30	2 56	1919 05 26	06 06	2 51	1919 09 09	05 34	2 58
1918 10 27	359 50	3 18	1919 02 10	00 33	2 56	1919 05 27	06 09	2 51	1919 09 10	05 32	2 58
1918 10 28	359 48	3 18	1919 02 11	00 36	2 56	1919 05 28	06 11	2 51	1919 09 11	05 29	2 58
1918 10 29	359 46	3 18	1919 02 12	00 38	2 55	1919 05 29	06 13	2 52	1919 09 12	05 27	2 58
1918 10 30	359 44	3 17	1919 02 13	00 41	2 55	1919 05 30	06 15	2 52	1919 09 13	05 24	2 58
1918 10 31	359 42	3 17	1919 02 14	00 44	2 55	1919 05 31	06 17	2 52	1919 09 14	05 21	2 58
1918 11 01	359 40	3 17	1919 02 15	00 47	2 55	1919 06 01	06 19	2 52	1919 09 15	05 19	2 58
1918 11 02	359 38	3 17	1919 02 16	00 50	2 55	1919 06 02	06 21	2 52	1919 09 16	05 16	2 58
1918 11 03	359 36	3 17	1919 02 17	00 54	2 55	1919 06 03	06 23	2 52	1919 09 17	05 14	2 58
1918 11 04	359 34	3 17	1919 02 18	00 57	2 54	1919 06 04	06 25	2 52	1919 09 18	05 11	2 58
1918 11 05	359 32	3 16	1919 02 19	01 00	2 54	1919 06 05	06 26	2 52	1919 09 19	05 08	2 58
1918 11 06	359 30	3 16	1919 02 20	01 03	2 54	1919 06 06	06 28	2 52	1919 09 20	05 06	2 58
1918 11 07	359 28	3 16	1919 02 21	01 06	2 54	1919 06 07	06 30	2 52			
1918 11 08	359 27	3 16	1919 02 22	01 09	2 54	1919 06 08	06 31	2 52			
1918 11 09	359 25	3 16	1919 02 23	01 12	2 54	1919 06 09	06 33	2 52			
1918 11 10	359 23	3 15	1919 02 24	01 16	2 54	1919 06 10	06 35	2 52			
1918 11 11	359 22	3 15	1919 02 25	01 19	2 54	1919 06 11	06 36	2 53			

1919 09 21	05 03	2 58
1919 09 22	05 00	2 58
1919 09 23	04 58	2 58
1919 09 24	04 55	2 58
1919 09 25	04 52	2 58
1919 09 26	04 49	2 58
1919 09 27	04 47	2 58
1919 09 28	04 44	2 58
1919 09 29	04 41	2 58
1919 09 30	04 39	2 58
1919 10 01	04 36	2 58
1919 10 02	04 33	2 57
1919 10 03	04 30	2 57
1919 10 04	04 28	2 57
1919 10 05	04 25	2 57
1919 10 06	04 22	2 57
1919 10 07	04 20	2 57
1919 10 08	04 17	2 57
1919 10 09	04 14	2 57
1919 10 10	04 12	2 57
1919 10 11	04 09	2 57
1919 10 12	04 06	2 57
1919 10 13	04 04	2 56
1919 10 14	04 01	2 56
1919 10 15	03 59	2 56
1919 10 16	03 56	2 56
1919 10 17	03 53	2 56
1919 10 18	03 51	2 56
1919 10 19	03 48	2 56
1919 10 20	03 46	2 56
1919 10 21	03 44	2 55
1919 10 22	03 41	2 55
1919 10 23	03 39	2 55
1919 10 24	03 36	2 55
1919 10 25	03 34	2 55
1919 10 26	03 32	2 55
1919 10 27	03 29	2 55
1919 10 28	03 27	2 54
1919 10 29	03 25	2 54
1919 10 30	03 23	2 54
1919 10 31	03 20	2 54
1919 11 01	03 18	2 54
1919 11 02	03 16	2 54
1919 11 03	03 14	2 53
1919 11 04	03 12	2 53
1919 11 05	03 10	2 53
1919 11 06	03 08	2 53
1919 11 07	03 06	2 53
1919 11 08	03 04	2 53
1919 11 09	03 03	2 52
1919 11 10	03 01	2 52
1919 11 11	02 59	2 52
1919 11 12	02 57	2 52
1919 11 13	02 56	2 52
1919 11 14	02 54	2 52
1919 11 15	02 52	2 51
1919 11 16	02 51	2 51
1919 11 17	02 49	2 51
1919 11 18	02 48	2 51
1919 11 19	02 47	2 51
1919 11 20	02 45	2 50
1919 11 21	02 44	2 50
1919 11 22	02 43	2 50
1919 11 23	02 41	2 50
1919 11 24	02 40	2 50
1919 11 25	02 39	2 49
1919 11 26	02 38	2 49
1919 11 27	02 37	2 49
1919 11 28	02 36	2 49
1919 11 29	02 35	2 49
1919 11 30	02 35	2 48
1919 12 01	02 34	2 48
1919 12 02	02 33	2 48
1919 12 03	02 32	2 48
1919 12 04	02 32	2 47
1919 12 05	02 31	2 47
1919 12 06	02 31	2 47
1919 12 07	02 30	2 47
1919 12 08	02 30	2 47
1919 12 09	02 29	2 46
1919 12 10	02 29	2 46
1919 12 11	02 29	2 46
1919 12 12	02 29	2 46
1919 12 13	02 29	2 46
1919 12 14	02 28	2 45
1919 12 15	02 28	2 45
1919 12 16	02 28	2 45
1919 12 17	02 29	2 45
1919 12 18	02 29	2 45
1919 12 19	02 29	2 44
1919 12 20	02 29	2 44
1919 12 21	02 29	2 44
1919 12 22	02 30	2 44
1919 12 23	02 30	2 43
1919 12 24	02 31	2 43
1919 12 25	02 31	2 43
1919 12 26	02 32	2 43
1919 12 27	02 32	2 43
1919 12 28	02 33	2 42
1919 12 29	02 34	2 42

1919 12 30	02 35	2 42
1919 12 31	02 36	2 42
1920 01 01	02 36	2 42
1920 01 02	02 37	2 41
1920 01 03	02 38	2 41
1920 01 04	02 40	2 41
1920 01 05	02 41	2 41
1920 01 06	02 42	2 40
1920 01 07	02 43	2 40
1920 01 08	02 44	2 40
1920 01 09	02 46	2 40
1920 01 10	02 47	2 40
1920 01 11	02 48	2 39
1920 01 12	02 50	2 39
1920 01 13	02 51	2 39
1920 01 14	02 53	2 39
1920 01 15	02 55	2 39
1920 01 16	02 56	2 38
1920 01 17	02 58	2 38
1920 01 18	03 00	2 38
1920 01 19	03 02	2 38
1920 01 20	03 04	2 38
1920 01 21	03 06	2 38
1920 01 22	03 07	2 37
1920 01 23	03 09	2 37
1920 01 24	03 12	2 37
1920 01 25	03 14	2 37
1920 01 26	03 16	2 37
1920 01 27	03 18	2 36
1920 01 28	03 20	2 36
1920 01 29	03 22	2 36
1920 01 30	03 25	2 36
1920 01 31	03 27	2 36
1920 02 01	03 30	2 36
1920 02 02	03 32	2 35
1920 02 03	03 34	2 35
1920 02 04	03 37	2 35
1920 02 05	03 39	2 35
1920 02 06	03 42	2 35
1920 02 07	03 45	2 35
1920 02 08	03 47	2 34
1920 02 09	03 50	2 34
1920 02 10	03 53	2 34
1920 02 11	03 55	2 34
1920 02 12	03 58	2 34
1920 02 13	04 01	2 34
1920 02 14	04 04	2 33
1920 02 15	04 07	2 33
1920 02 16	04 10	2 33
1920 02 17	04 13	2 33
1920 02 18	04 16	2 33
1920 02 19	04 19	2 33
1920 02 20	04 22	2 33
1920 02 21	04 25	2 32
1920 02 22	04 28	2 32
1920 02 23	04 31	2 32
1920 02 24	04 34	2 32
1920 02 25	04 37	2 32
1920 02 26	04 40	2 32
1920 02 27	04 44	2 32
1920 02 28	04 47	2 32
1920 02 29	04 50	2 31
1920 03 01	04 53	2 31
1920 03 02	04 57	2 31
1920 03 03	05 00	2 31
1920 03 04	05 03	2 31
1920 03 05	05 07	2 31
1920 03 06	05 10	2 31
1920 03 07	05 13	2 31
1920 03 08	05 17	2 31
1920 03 09	05 20	2 30
1920 03 10	05 24	2 30
1920 03 11	05 27	2 30
1920 03 12	05 30	2 30
1920 03 13	05 34	2 30
1920 03 14	05 37	2 30
1920 03 15	05 41	2 30
1920 03 16	05 44	2 30
1920 03 17	05 48	2 30
1920 03 18	05 51	2 30
1920 03 19	05 55	2 30
1920 03 20	05 58	2 29
1920 03 21	06 02	2 29
1920 03 22	06 05	2 29
1920 03 23	06 09	2 29
1920 03 24	06 12	2 29
1920 03 25	06 16	2 29
1920 03 26	06 19	2 29
1920 03 27	06 23	2 29
1920 03 28	06 26	2 29
1920 03 29	06 30	2 29
1920 03 30	06 34	2 29
1920 03 31	06 37	2 29
1920 04 01	06 41	2 29
1920 04 02	06 44	2 29
1920 04 03	06 48	2 29
1920 04 04	06 51	2 29
1920 04 05	06 55	2 28
1920 04 06	06 58	2 28
1920 04 07	07 02	2 28
1920 04 08	07 05	2 28
1920 04 09	07 09	2 28
1920 04 10	07 12	2 28
1920 04 11	07 16	2 28
1920 04 12	07 19	2 28

1920 04 13	07 22	2 28
1920 04 14	07 26	2 28
1920 04 15	07 29	2 28
1920 04 16	07 33	2 28
1920 04 17	07 36	2 28
1920 04 18	07 39	2 28
1920 04 19	07 43	2 28
1920 04 20	07 46	2 28
1920 04 21	07 49	2 28
1920 04 22	07 53	2 28
1920 04 23	07 56	2 28
1920 04 24	07 59	2 28
1920 04 25	08 02	2 28
1920 04 26	08 06	2 28
1920 04 27	08 09	2 28
1920 04 28	08 12	2 28
1920 04 29	08 15	2 28
1920 04 30	08 18	2 28
1920 05 01	08 21	2 28
1920 05 02	08 25	2 28
1920 05 03	08 28	2 28
1920 05 04	08 31	2 28
1920 05 05	08 34	2 28
1920 05 06	08 37	2 28
1920 05 07	08 40	2 28
1920 05 08	08 43	2 28
1920 05 09	08 45	2 28
1920 05 10	08 48	2 28
1920 05 11	08 51	2 28
1920 05 12	08 54	2 28
1920 05 13	08 57	2 28
1920 05 14	09 00	2 28
1920 05 15	09 02	2 28
1920 05 16	09 05	2 28
1920 05 17	09 08	2 28
1920 05 18	09 10	2 28
1920 05 19	09 13	2 28
1920 05 20	09 15	2 28
1920 05 21	09 18	2 28
1920 05 22	09 20	2 28
1920 05 23	09 23	2 28
1920 05 24	09 25	2 29
1920 05 25	09 28	2 29
1920 05 26	09 30	2 29
1920 05 27	09 32	2 29
1920 05 28	09 34	2 29
1920 05 29	09 37	2 29
1920 05 30	09 39	2 29
1920 05 31	09 41	2 29
1920 06 01	09 43	2 29
1920 06 02	09 45	2 29
1920 06 03	09 47	2 29
1920 06 04	09 49	2 29
1920 06 05	09 51	2 29
1920 06 06	09 53	2 29
1920 06 07	09 55	2 29
1920 06 08	09 56	2 29
1920 06 09	09 58	2 29
1920 06 10	09 00	2 29
1920 06 11	09 02	2 29
1920 06 12	09 03	2 29
1920 06 13	09 05	2 30
1920 06 14	09 06	2 30
1920 06 15	09 08	2 30
1920 06 16	09 09	2 30
1920 06 17	09 10	2 30
1920 06 18	09 12	2 30
1920 06 19	09 13	2 30
1920 06 20	09 14	2 30
1920 06 21	09 15	2 30
1920 06 22	09 17	2 30
1920 06 23	09 18	2 30
1920 06 24	09 19	2 30
1920 06 25	09 20	2 30
1920 06 26	09 21	2 30
1920 06 27	09 22	2 30
1920 06 28	09 22	2 31
1920 06 29	09 23	2 31
1920 06 30	09 24	2 31
1920 07 01	09 25	2 31
1920 07 02	09 25	2 31
1920 07 03	09 26	2 31
1920 07 04	09 26	2 31
1920 07 05	09 27	2 31
1920 07 06	09 27	2 31
1920 07 07	09 28	2 31
1920 07 08	09 28	2 31
1920 07 09	09 28	2 31
1920 07 10	09 28	2 31
1920 07 11	09 29	2 31
1920 07 12	09 29	2 32
1920 07 13	09 29	2 32
1920 07 14	09 29	2 32
1920 07 15	09 29	2 32
1920 07 16	09 29	2 32
1920 07 17	09 28	2 32
1920 07 18	09 28	2 32
1920 07 19	09 28	2 32
1920 07 20	09 28	2 32
1920 07 21	09 27	2 32
1920 07 22	09 27	2 32
1920 07 23	09 26	2 32
1920 07 24	09 26	2 32
1920 07 25	09 25	2 32
1920 07 26	09 25	2 32

1920 07 27	09 24	2 33
1920 07 28	09 23	2 33
1920 07 29	09 23	2 33
1920 07 30	09 22	2 33
1920 07 31	09 21	2 33
1920 08 01	09 20	2 33
1920 08 02	09 19	2 33
1920 08 03	09 18	2 33
1920 08 04	09 17	2 33
1920 08 05	09 16	2 33
1920 08 06	09 15	2 33
1920 08 07	09 14	2 33
1920 08 08	09 12	2 33
1920 08 09	09 11	2 33
1920 08 10	09 10	2 33
1920 08 11	09 08	2 33
1920 08 12	09 07	2 33
1920 08 13	09 05	2 33
1920 08 14	09 04	2 33
1920 08 15	09 02	2 33
1920 08 16	09 01	2 34
1920 08 17	09 59	2 34
1920 08 18	09 57	2 34
1920 08 19	09 56	2 34
1920 08 20	09 54	2 34
1920 08 21	09 52	2 34
1920 08 22	09 50	2 34
1920 08 23	09 48	2 34
1920 08 24	09 46	2 34
1920 08 25	09 44	2 34
1920 08 26	09 42	2 34
1920 08 27	09 40	2 34
1920 08 28	09 38	2 34
1920 08 29	09 36	2 34
1920 08 30	09 34	2 34
1920 08 31	09 32	2 34
1920 09 01	09 30	2 34
1920 09 02	09 27	2 34
1920 09 03	09 25	2 34
1920 09 04	09 23	2 34
1920 09 05	09 21	2 34
1920 09 06	09 18	2 34
1920 09 07	09 16	2 34
1920 09 08	09 13	2 34
1920 09 09	09 11	2 34
1920 09 10	09 08	2 34
1920 09 11	09 06	2 34
1920 09 12	09 04	2 34
1920 09 13	09 01	2 34
1920 09 14	08 58	2 34
1920 09 15	08 56	2 34
1920 09 16	08 53	2 34
1920 09 17	08 51	2 34
1920 09 18	08 48	2 34
1920 09 19	08 45	2 34
1920 09 20	08 43	2 34
1920 09 21	08 40	2 34
1920 09 22	08 38	2 33
1920 09 23	08 35	2 33
1920 09 24	08 32	2 33
1920 09 25	08 30	2 33
1920 09 26	08 27	2 33
1920 09 27	08 24	2 33
1920 09 28	08 21	2 33
1920 09 29	08 19	2 33
1920 09 30	08 16	2 33
1920 10 01	08 13	2 33
1920 10 02	08 11	2 33
1920 10 03	08 08	2 33
1920 10 04	08 05	2 33
1920 10 05	08 02	2 33
1920 10 06	07 59	2 33
1920 10 07	07 57	2 33
1920 10 08	07 54	2 32
1920 10 09	07 51	2 32
1920 10 10	07 49	2 32
1920 10 11	07 46	2 32
1920 10 12	07 43	2 32
1920 10 13	07 41	2 32
1920 10 14	07 38	2 32
1920 10 15	07 35	2 32
1920 10 16	07 33	2 32
1920 10 17	07 30	2 32
1920 10 18	07 28	2 31
1920 10 19	07 25	2 31
1920 10 20	07 23	2 31
1920 10 21	07 20	2 31
1920 10 22	07 18	2 31
1920 10 23	07 15	2 31
1920 10 24	07 13	2 31
1920 10 25	07 10	2 31
1920 10 26	07 08	2 30
1920 10 27	07 05	2 30
1920 10 28	07 03	2 30
1920 10 29	07 01	2 30
1920 10 30	06 58	2 30
1920 10 31	06 56	2 30
1920 11 01	06 54	2 30
1920 11 02	06 52	2 29
1920 11 03	06 50	2 29
1920 11 04	06 47	2 29
1920 11 05	06 45	2 29
1920 11 06	06 43	2 29
1920 11 07	06 41	2 29
1920 11 08	06 39	2 29

1920	11	09	06	37	2	28
1920	11	10	06	35	2	28
1920	11	11	06	34	2	28
1920	11	12	06	32	2	28
1920	11	13	06	30	2	28
1920	11	14	06	28	2	28
1920	11	15	06	27	2	27
1920	11	16	06	25	2	27
1920	11	17	06	23	2	27
1920	11	18	06	22	2	27
1920	11	19	06	20	2	27
1920	11	20	06	19	2	27
1920	11	21	06	17	2	26
1920	11	22	06	16	2	26
1920	11	23	06	15	2	26
1920	11	24	06	13	2	26
1920	11	25	06	12	2	26
1920	11	26	06	11	2	25
1920	11	27	06	10	2	25
1920	11	28	06	09	2	25
1920	11	29	06	08	2	25
1920	11	30	06	07	2	25
1920	12	01	06	06	2	25
1920	12	02	06	05	2	24
1920	12	03	06	04	2	24
1920	12	04	06	03	2	24
1920	12	05	06	02	2	24
1920	12	06	06	02	2	24
1920	12	07	06	01	2	23
1920	12	08	06	01	2	23
1920	12	09	06	00	2	23
1920	12	10	06	00	2	23
1920	12	11	05	59	2	23
1920	12	12	05	59	2	22
1920	12	13	05	59	2	22
1920	12	14	05	58	2	22
1920	12	15	05	58	2	22
1920	12	16	05	58	2	22
1920	12	17	05	58	2	21
1920	12	18	05	58	2	21
1920	12	19	05	58	2	21
1920	12	20	05	58	2	21
1920	12	21	05	58	2	21
1920	12	22	05	58	2	21
1920	12	23	05	59	2	20
1920	12	24	05	59	2	20
1920	12	25	05	59	2	20
1920	12	26	06	00	2	20
1920	12	27	06	00	2	20
1920	12	28	06	01	2	19
1920	12	29	06	02	2	19
1920	12	30	06	02	2	19
1920	12	31	06	03	2	19
1921	01	01	06	04	2	19
1921	01	02	06	04	2	18
1921	01	03	06	05	2	18
1921	01	04	06	06	2	18
1921	01	05	06	07	2	18
1921	01	06	06	08	2	18
1921	01	07	06	09	2	17
1921	01	08	06	10	2	17
1921	01	09	06	12	2	17
1921	01	10	06	13	2	17
1921	01	11	06	14	2	17
1921	01	12	06	16	2	17
1921	01	13	06	17	2	16
1921	01	14	06	18	2	16
1921	01	15	06	20	2	16
1921	01	16	06	21	2	16
1921	01	17	06	23	2	16
1921	01	18	06	25	2	15
1921	01	19	06	26	2	15
1921	01	20	06	28	2	15
1921	01	21	06	30	2	15
1921	01	22	06	32	2	15
1921	01	23	06	34	2	15
1921	01	24	06	36	2	14
1921	01	25	06	38	2	14
1921	01	26	06	40	2	14
1921	01	27	06	42	2	14
1921	01	28	06	44	2	14
1921	01	29	06	46	2	14
1921	01	30	06	48	2	13
1921	01	31	06	50	2	13
1921	02	01	06	53	2	13
1921	02	02	06	55	2	13
1921	02	03	06	57	2	13
1921	02	04	07	00	2	13
1921	02	05	07	02	2	12
1921	02	06	07	05	2	12
1921	02	07	07	07	2	12
1921	02	08	07	10	2	12
1921	02	09	07	12	2	12
1921	02	10	07	15	2	12
1921	02	11	07	18	2	11
1921	02	12	07	20	2	11
1921	02	13	07	23	2	11
1921	02	14	07	26	2	11
1921	02	15	07	28	2	11
1921	02	16	07	31	2	11
1921	02	17	07	34	2	11
1921	02	18	07	37	2	11
1921	02	19	07	40	2	10
1921	02	20	07	43	2	10
1921	02	21	07	46	2	10
1921	02	22	07	49	2	10

1921	02	23	07	52	2	10
1921	02	24	07	55	2	10
1921	02	25	07	58	2	10
1921	02	26	08	01	2	09
1921	02	27	08	04	2	09
1921	02	28	08	08	2	09
1921	03	01	08	11	2	09
1921	03	02	08	14	2	09
1921	03	03	08	17	2	09
1921	03	04	08	20	2	09
1921	03	05	08	24	2	09
1921	03	06	08	27	2	09
1921	03	07	08	30	2	08
1921	03	08	08	34	2	08
1921	03	09	08	37	2	08
1921	03	10	08	40	2	08
1921	03	11	08	44	2	08
1921	03	12	08	47	2	08
1921	03	13	08	50	2	08
1921	03	14	08	54	2	08
1921	03	15	08	57	2	08
1921	03	16	09	01	2	08
1921	03	17	09	04	2	07
1921	03	18	09	08	2	07
1921	03	19	09	11	2	07
1921	03	20	09	15	2	07
1921	03	21	09	18	2	07
1921	03	22	09	22	2	07
1921	03	23	09	25	2	07
1921	03	24	09	29	2	07
1921	03	25	09	32	2	07
1921	03	26	09	36	2	07
1921	03	27	09	39	2	07
1921	03	28	09	43	2	07
1921	03	29	09	46	2	07
1921	03	30	09	50	2	06
1921	03	31	09	53	2	06
1921	04	01	09	57	2	06
1921	04	02	09	00	2	06
1921	04	03	09	04	2	06
1921	04	04	09	07	2	06
1921	04	05	09	11	2	06
1921	04	06	09	14	2	06
1921	04	07	09	18	2	06
1921	04	08	09	21	2	06
1921	04	09	09	25	2	06
1921	04	10	09	28	2	06
1921	04	11	09	32	2	06
1921	04	12	09	35	2	06
1921	04	13	09	39	2	06
1921	04	14	09	42	2	06
1921	04	15	09	46	2	06
1921	04	16	09	49	2	06
1921	04	17	09	53	2	06
1921	04	18	09	56	2	06
1921	04	19	09	59	2	06
1921	04	20	09	03	2	05
1921	04	21	09	06	2	05
1921	04	22	09	10	2	05
1921	04	23	09	13	2	05
1921	04	24	09	16	2	05
1921	04	25	09	20	2	05
1921	04	26	09	23	2	05
1921	04	27	09	26	2	05
1921	04	28	09	29	2	05
1921	04	29	09	33	2	05
1921	04	30	09	36	2	05
1921	05	01	09	39	2	05
1921	05	02	09	42	2	05
1921	05	03	09	45	2	05
1921	05	04	09	49	2	05
1921	05	05	09	52	2	05
1921	05	06	09	55	2	05
1921	05	07	09	58	2	05
1921	05	08	09	01	2	05
1921	05	09	09	04	2	05
1921	05	10	09	07	2	05
1921	05	11	09	10	2	05
1921	05	12	09	13	2	05
1921	05	13	09	16	2	05
1921	05	14	09	18	2	05
1921	05	15	09	21	2	05
1921	05	16	09	24	2	05
1921	05	17	09	27	2	05
1921	05	18	09	30	2	05
1921	05	19	09	32	2	05
1921	05	20	09	35	2	05
1921	05	21	09	38	2	05
1921	05	22	09	40	2	05
1921	05	23	09	43	2	05
1921	05	24	09	45	2	05
1921	05	25	09	48	2	05
1921	05	26	09	50	2	05
1921	05	27	09	53	2	05
1921	05	28	09	55	2	05
1921	05	29	09	58	2	05
1921	05	30	09	00	2	05
1921	05	31	09	02	2	05
1921	06	01	09	04	2	06
1921	06	02	09	07	2	06
1921	06	03	09	09	2	06
1921	06	04	09	11	2	06
1921	06	05	09	13	2	06
1921	06	06	09	15	2	06
1921	06	07	09	17	2	06
1921	06	08	09	19	2	06

1921	06	09	09	21	2	06
1921	06	10	09	23	2	06
1921	06	11	09	25	2	06
1921	06	12	09	26	2	06
1921	06	13	09	28	2	06
1921	06	14	09	30	2	06
1921	06	15	09	31	2	06
1921	06	16	09	33	2	06
1921	06	17	09	35	2	06
1921	06	18	09	36	2	06
1921	06	19	09	38	2	06
1921	06	20	09	39	2	06
1921	06	21	09	40	2	06
1921	06	22	09	42	2	06
1921	06	23	09	43	2	06
1921	06	24	09	44	2	06
1921	06	25	09	45	2	06
1921	06	26	09	47	2	06
1921	06	27	09	48	2	06
1921	06	28	09	49	2	07
1921	06	29	09	50	2	07
1921	06	30	09	51	2	07
1921	07	01	09	51	2	07
1921	07	02	09	52	2	07
1921	07	03	09	53	2	07
1921	07	04	09	54	2	07
1921	07	05	09	54	2	07
1921	07	06	09	55	2	07
1921	07	07	09	56	2	07
1921	07	08	09	56	2	07
1921	07	09	09	57	2	07
1921	07	10	09	57	2	07
1921	07	11	09	57	2	07
1921	07	12	09	58	2	07
1921	07	13	09	58	2	07
1921	07	14	09	58	2	07
1921	07	15	09	58	2	07
1921	07	16	09	58	2	07
1921	07	17	09	58	2	07
1921	07	18	09	58	2	07
1921	07	19	09	58	2	08
1921	07	20	09	58	2	08
1921	07	21	09	58	2	08
1921	07	22	09	58	2	08
1921	07	23	09	58	2	08
1921	07	24	09	57	2	08
1921	07	25	09	57	2	08
1921	07	26	09	57	2	08
1921	07	27	09	56	2	08
1921	07	28	09	56	2	08
1921	07	29	09	55	2	08
1921	07	30	09	54	2	08
1921	07	31	09	54	2	08
1921	08	01	09	53	2	08
1921	08	02	09	52	2	08
1921	08	03	09	51	2	08
1921	08	04	09	51	2	08
1921	08	05	09	50	2	08
1921	08	06	09	49	2	08
1921	08	07	09	48	2	08
1921	08	08	09	47	2	08
1921	08	09	09	45	2	08
1921	08	10	09	44	2	08
1921	08	11	09	43	2	08
1921	08	12	09	42	2	08
1921	08	13	09	41	2	08
1921	08	14	09	39	2	09
1921	08	15	09	38	2	09
1921	08	16	09	36	2	09
1921	08	17	09	35	2	09
1921	08	18	09	33	2	09
1921	08	19	09	32	2	09
1921	08	20	09	30	2	09
1921	08	21	09	29	2	09
1921	08	22	09	27	2	09
1921	08	23	09	25	2	09
1921	08	24	09	23	2	09
1921	08	25	09	21	2	09
1921	08	26	09	20	2	09
1921	08	27	09	18	2	09
1921	08	28	09	16	2	09
1921	08	29	09	14	2	09
1921	08	30	09	12	2	09
1921	08	31	09	10	2	09
1921	09	01	09	08	2	09
1921	09	02	09	06	2	09
1921	09	03	09	03	2	09
1921	09	04	09	01	2	09
1921	09	05	09	59	2	09
1921	09	06	09	57	2	09
1921	09	07	09	54	2	09
1921	09	08	09	52	2	09
1921	09	09	09	50	2	09
1921	09	10	09	47	2	09
1921	09	11	09	45	2	09
1921	09	12	09	43	2	09
1921	09	13	09	40	2	09
1921	09	14	09	38	2	09
1921	09	15	09	35	2	09
1921	09	16	09	33	2	09
1921	09	17	09	30	2	09
1921	09	18	09	28	2	08
1921	09	19	09	25	2	08
1921	09	20	09	23	2	08
1921	09	21	09	20	2	08
1921	09	22	09	17	2	08

1921	09	23	09	15	2	08
1921	09	24	09	12	2	08
1921	09	25	09	09	2	08
1921	09	26	09	07	2	08
1921	09	27	09	04	2	08
1921	09	28	09	01	2	08
1921	09	29	09	59	2	08
1921	09	30	09	56	2	08
1921	10	01	09	53	2	08
1921	10	02	09	50	2	08
1921	10	03	09	48	2	08
1921	10	04	09	45	2	08
1921	10	05	09	42	2	08
1921	10	06	09	40	2	08
1921	10	07	09	37	2	07
1921	10	08	09	34	2	07
1921	10	09	09	31	2	07
1921	10	10	09	29	2	07
1921	10	11	09	26	2	07
1921	10	12	09	23	2	07
1921	10	13	09	21	2	07
1921	10	14	09	18	2	07
1921	10	15	09	15	2	07
1921	10	16	09	13	2	07
1921	10	17	09	10	2	07
1921	10	18	09	07	2	06
1921	10	19	09	05	2	06
1921	10	20	09	02	2	06
1921	10	21	09	59	2	06
1921	10	22	09	57	2	06
1921	10	23	09	54	2	06
1921	10	24	09	52	2	06
1921	10	25	09	49	2	06
1921	10	26	09	47	2	06
1921	10	27	09	44	2	06
1921	10	28	09	42	2	05
1921	10	29	09	39	2	05
1921	10	30	09	37	2	05
1921	10	31	09	35	2	05
1921	11	01	09	32	2	05
1921	11	02	09	30	2	05
1921	11	03	09	28	2	05
1921	11	04	09	25	2	05
1921	11	05	09	23	2	04
1921	11	06	09	21	2	04
1921	11	07	09	19	2	04
1921	11	08	09	17	2	04
1921	11	09	09	15	2	04
1921	11	10	09	12	2	04
1921	11	11	09	10	2	04
1921	11	12	09	08	2	03
1921	11	13	09	07	2	03
1921	11	14	09	05	2	03
1921	11	15	09	03	2	03
1921	11	16	09	01	2	03
1921	11	17	09	59	2	03
1921	11	18	09	57	2	03
1921	11	19	09	56	2	02
1921	11	20	09	54	2	02
1921	11	21	09	52	2	02
1921	11	22	09	51	2	02
1921	11	23	09	49	2	02
1921	11	24	09	48	2	02
1921	11	25	09	47	2	01
1921	11	26	09	45	2	01
1921	11	27	09	44	2	01
1921	11	28	09	43	2	01
1921	11	29	09	41	2	01
1921	11	30	09	40	2	01
1921	12	01	09	39	2	00
1921	12	02	09	38	2	00
1921	12	03	09	37	2	00
1921	12	04	09	36	2	00
1921	12	05	09	35	2	00
1921	12	06	09	34	2	00
1921	12	07	09	33	1	59
1921	12	08	09	33	1	59
1921	12	09	09	32	1	59
1921	12	10	09	31	1	59
1921	12	11	09	31	1	59
1921	12	12	09	30	1	59
1921	12	13	09	30	1	58
1921	12	14	09	29	1	58
1921	12	15	09	29	1	58
1921	12	16	09	28	1	58
1921	12	17	09	28	1	58
1921	12	18	09	28	1	58
1921	12	19	09	28	1	57
1921	12	20	09	28	1	57
1921	12	21	09	28	1	57
1921	12	22	09	28	1	57
1921	12	23	09	28	1	57
1921	12	24	09	28	1	56
1921	12	25	09	28	1	56
1921	12	26	09	28	1	56
1921	12	27	09	28	1	56
1921	12	28	09	29	1	56
1921	12	29	09	29	1	56
1921	12	30	09	30	1	55
1921	12	31	09	30	1	55
1922	01	01	09	31	1	55

1922	01	02	09 31	1 55
1922	01	03	09 32	1 55
1922	01	04	09 33	1 55
1922	01	05	09 33	1 54
1922	01	06	09 34	1 54
1922	01	07	09 35	1 54
1922	01	08	09 36	1 54
1922	01	09	09 37	1 54
1922	01	10	09 38	1 54
1922	01	11	09 39	1 53
1922	01	12	09 40	1 53
1922	01	13	09 42	1 53
1922	01	14	09 43	1 53
1922	01	15	09 44	1 53
1922	01	16	09 46	1 53
1922	01	17	09 47	1 52
1922	01	18	09 48	1 52
1922	01	19	09 50	1 52
1922	01	20	09 51	1 52
1922	01	21	09 53	1 52
1922	01	22	09 55	1 52
1922	01	23	09 56	1 51
1922	01	24	09 58	1 51
1922	01	25	10 00	1 51
1922	01	26	10 02	1 51
1922	01	27	10 04	1 51
1922	01	28	10 06	1 51
1922	01	29	10 08	1 50
1922	01	30	10 10	1 50
1922	01	31	10 12	1 50
1922	02	01	10 14	1 50
1922	02	02	10 16	1 50
1922	02	03	10 18	1 50
1922	02	04	10 21	1 50
1922	02	05	10 23	1 49
1922	02	06	10 25	1 49
1922	02	07	10 28	1 49
1922	02	08	10 30	1 49
1922	02	09	10 32	1 49
1922	02	10	10 35	1 49
1922	02	11	10 37	1 49
1922	02	12	10 40	1 48
1922	02	13	10 43	1 48
1922	02	14	10 45	1 48
1922	02	15	10 48	1 48
1922	02	16	10 51	1 48
1922	02	17	10 53	1 48
1922	02	18	10 56	1 48
1922	02	19	10 59	1 48
1922	02	20	11 02	1 47
1922	02	21	11 05	1 47
1922	02	22	11 08	1 47
1922	02	23	11 11	1 47
1922	02	24	11 13	1 47
1922	02	25	11 16	1 47
1922	02	26	11 20	1 47
1922	02	27	11 23	1 47
1922	02	28	11 26	1 46
1922	03	01	11 29	1 46
1922	03	02	11 32	1 46
1922	03	03	11 35	1 46
1922	03	04	11 38	1 46
1922	03	05	11 41	1 46
1922	03	06	11 45	1 46
1922	03	07	11 48	1 46
1922	03	08	11 51	1 46
1922	03	09	11 54	1 45
1922	03	10	11 58	1 45
1922	03	11	12 01	1 45
1922	03	12	12 04	1 45
1922	03	13	12 08	1 45
1922	03	14	12 11	1 45
1922	03	15	12 14	1 45
1922	03	16	12 18	1 45
1922	03	17	12 21	1 45
1922	03	18	12 25	1 45
1922	03	19	12 28	1 45
1922	03	20	12 32	1 44
1922	03	21	12 35	1 44
1922	03	22	12 38	1 44
1922	03	23	12 42	1 44
1922	03	24	12 45	1 44
1922	03	25	12 49	1 44
1922	03	26	12 52	1 44
1922	03	27	12 56	1 44
1922	03	28	12 59	1 44
1922	03	29	13 03	1 44
1922	03	30	13 07	1 44
1922	03	31	13 10	1 44
1922	04	01	13 14	1 43
1922	04	02	13 17	1 43
1922	04	03	13 21	1 43
1922	04	04	13 24	1 43
1922	04	05	13 28	1 43
1922	04	06	13 31	1 43
1922	04	07	13 35	1 43
1922	04	08	13 38	1 43
1922	04	09	13 42	1 43
1922	04	10	13 45	1 43
1922	04	11	13 49	1 43
1922	04	12	13 52	1 43
1922	04	13	13 56	1 43
1922	04	14	13 59	1 43
1922	04	15	14 03	1 43
1922	04	16	14 06	1 43
1922	04	17	14 10	1 43
1922	04	18	14 13	1 43
1922	04	19	14 17	1 42
1922	04	20	14 20	1 42
1922	04	21	14 24	1 42
1922	04	22	14 27	1 42
1922	04	23	14 31	1 42
1922	04	24	14 34	1 42
1922	04	25	14 37	1 42
1922	04	26	14 41	1 42
1922	04	27	14 44	1 42
1922	04	28	14 47	1 42
1922	04	29	14 51	1 42
1922	04	30	14 54	1 42
1922	05	01	14 57	1 42
1922	05	02	15 01	1 42
1922	05	03	15 04	1 42
1922	05	04	15 07	1 42
1922	05	05	15 10	1 42
1922	05	06	15 13	1 42
1922	05	07	15 17	1 42
1922	05	08	15 20	1 42
1922	05	09	15 23	1 42
1922	05	10	15 26	1 42
1922	05	11	15 29	1 42
1922	05	12	15 32	1 42
1922	05	13	15 35	1 42
1922	05	14	15 38	1 42
1922	05	15	15 41	1 42
1922	05	16	15 44	1 42
1922	05	17	15 47	1 42
1922	05	18	15 50	1 42
1922	05	19	15 52	1 42
1922	05	20	15 55	1 42
1922	05	21	15 58	1 42
1922	05	22	16 01	1 42
1922	05	23	16 04	1 42
1922	05	24	16 06	1 42
1922	05	25	16 09	1 42
1922	05	26	16 11	1 42
1922	05	27	16 14	1 42
1922	05	28	16 17	1 42
1922	05	29	16 19	1 42
1922	05	30	16 22	1 42
1922	05	31	16 24	1 42
1922	06	01	16 26	1 42
1922	06	02	16 29	1 42
1922	06	03	16 31	1 42
1922	06	04	16 33	1 42
1922	06	05	16 36	1 42
1922	06	06	16 38	1 42
1922	06	07	16 40	1 42
1922	06	08	16 42	1 42
1922	06	09	16 44	1 42
1922	06	10	16 46	1 42
1922	06	11	16 48	1 42
1922	06	12	16 50	1 42
1922	06	13	16 52	1 42
1922	06	14	16 54	1 42
1922	06	15	16 56	1 42
1922	06	16	16 58	1 42
1922	06	17	16 59	1 42
1922	06	18	17 01	1 42
1922	06	19	17 03	1 42
1922	06	20	17 04	1 42
1922	06	21	17 06	1 42
1922	06	22	17 07	1 42
1922	06	23	17 09	1 42
1922	06	24	17 10	1 42
1922	06	25	17 12	1 42
1922	06	26	17 13	1 42
1922	06	27	17 14	1 42
1922	06	28	17 15	1 42
1922	06	29	17 17	1 42
1922	06	30	17 18	1 42
1922	07	01	17 19	1 42
1922	07	02	17 20	1 42
1922	07	03	17 21	1 42
1922	07	04	17 22	1 42
1922	07	05	17 23	1 42
1922	07	06	17 24	1 42
1922	07	07	17 24	1 42
1922	07	08	17 25	1 42
1922	07	09	17 26	1 42
1922	07	10	17 26	1 42
1922	07	11	17 27	1 42
1922	07	12	17 27	1 42
1922	07	13	17 28	1 42
1922	07	14	17 28	1 43
1922	07	15	17 29	1 43
1922	07	16	17 29	1 43
1922	07	17	17 29	1 43
1922	07	18	17 29	1 43
1922	07	19	17 30	1 43
1922	07	20	17 30	1 43
1922	07	21	17 30	1 43
1922	07	22	17 30	1 43
1922	07	23	17 30	1 43
1922	07	24	17 30	1 43
1922	07	25	17 29	1 43
1922	07	26	17 29	1 43
1922	07	27	17 29	1 43
1922	07	28	17 29	1 43
1922	07	29	17 28	1 43
1922	07	30	17 28	1 43
1922	07	31	17 27	1 43
1922	08	01	17 27	1 43
1922	08	02	17 26	1 43
1922	08	03	17 26	1 43
1922	08	04	17 25	1 43
1922	08	05	17 24	1 43
1922	08	06	17 23	1 43
1922	08	07	17 23	1 43
1922	08	08	17 22	1 43
1922	08	09	17 21	1 43
1922	08	10	17 20	1 43
1922	08	11	17 19	1 43
1922	08	12	17 18	1 43
1922	08	13	17 17	1 43
1922	08	14	17 15	1 43
1922	08	15	17 14	1 43
1922	08	16	17 13	1 43
1922	08	17	17 12	1 43
1922	08	18	17 10	1 43
1922	08	19	17 09	1 43
1922	08	20	17 07	1 43
1922	08	21	17 06	1 43
1922	08	22	17 04	1 43
1922	08	23	17 03	1 43
1922	08	24	17 01	1 43
1922	08	25	16 59	1 43
1922	08	26	16 58	1 43
1922	08	27	16 56	1 43
1922	08	28	16 54	1 43
1922	08	29	16 52	1 43
1922	08	30	16 51	1 43
1922	08	31	16 49	1 43
1922	09	01	16 47	1 43
1922	09	02	16 45	1 43
1922	09	03	16 43	1 43
1922	09	04	16 41	1 43
1922	09	05	16 38	1 43
1922	09	06	16 36	1 43
1922	09	07	16 34	1 43
1922	09	08	16 32	1 43
1922	09	09	16 30	1 43
1922	09	10	16 28	1 43
1922	09	11	16 25	1 43
1922	09	12	16 23	1 43
1922	09	13	16 21	1 43
1922	09	14	16 18	1 43
1922	09	15	16 16	1 43
1922	09	16	16 13	1 43
1922	09	17	16 11	1 43
1922	09	18	16 08	1 43
1922	09	19	16 06	1 43
1922	09	20	16 03	1 43
1922	09	21	16 01	1 43
1922	09	22	15 58	1 43
1922	09	23	15 56	1 43
1922	09	24	15 53	1 42
1922	09	25	15 50	1 42
1922	09	26	15 48	1 42
1922	09	27	15 45	1 42
1922	09	28	15 43	1 42
1922	09	29	15 40	1 42
1922	09	30	15 37	1 42
1922	10	01	15 34	1 42
1922	10	02	15 32	1 42
1922	10	03	15 29	1 42
1922	10	04	15 26	1 42
1922	10	05	15 24	1 42
1922	10	06	15 21	1 42
1922	10	07	15 18	1 42
1922	10	08	15 15	1 42
1922	10	09	15 13	1 42
1922	10	10	15 10	1 41
1922	10	11	15 07	1 41
1922	10	12	15 05	1 41
1922	10	13	15 02	1 41
1922	10	14	14 59	1 41
1922	10	15	14 56	1 41
1922	10	16	14 54	1 41
1922	10	17	14 51	1 41
1922	10	18	14 48	1 41
1922	10	19	14 46	1 41
1922	10	20	14 43	1 41
1922	10	21	14 40	1 41
1922	10	22	14 37	1 40
1922	10	23	14 35	1 40
1922	10	24	14 32	1 40
1922	10	25	14 30	1 40
1922	10	26	14 27	1 40
1922	10	27	14 24	1 40
1922	10	28	14 22	1 40
1922	10	29	14 19	1 40
1922	10	30	14 17	1 40
1922	10	31	14 14	1 40
1922	11	01	14 12	1 39
1922	11	02	14 10	1 39
1922	11	03	14 07	1 39
1922	11	04	14 05	1 39
1922	11	05	14 02	1 39
1922	11	06	14 00	1 39
1922	11	07	13 58	1 39
1922	11	08	13 55	1 39
1922	11	09	13 53	1 39
1922	11	10	13 51	1 38
1922	11	11	13 49	1 38
1922	11	12	13 47	1 38
1922	11	13	13 45	1 38
1922	11	14	13 43	1 38
1922	11	15	13 41	1 38
1922	11	16	13 39	1 38
1922	11	17	13 37	1 37
1922	11	18	13 35	1 37
1922	11	19	13 33	1 37
1922	11	20	13 31	1 37
1922	11	21	13 29	1 37
1922	11	22	13 28	1 37
1922	11	23	13 26	1 37
1922	11	24	13 24	1 37
1922	11	25	13 23	1 36
1922	11	26	13 21	1 36
1922	11	27	13 20	1 36
1922	11	28	13 18	1 36
1922	11	29	13 17	1 36
1922	11	30	13 15	1 36
1922	12	01	13 14	1 36
1922	12	02	13 13	1 35
1922	12	03	13 12	1 35
1922	12	04	13 10	1 35
1922	12	05	13 09	1 35
1922	12	06	13 08	1 35
1922	12	07	13 07	1 35
1922	12	08	13 06	1 35
1922	12	09	13 05	1 34
1922	12	10	13 04	1 34
1922	12	11	13 04	1 34
1922	12	12	13 03	1 34
1922	12	13	13 02	1 34
1922	12	14	13 01	1 34
1922	12	15	13 01	1 33
1922	12	16	13 00	1 33
1922	12	17	13 00	1 33
1922	12	18	12 59	1 33
1922	12	19	12 59	1 33
1922	12	20	12 59	1 33
1922	12	21	12 59	1 33
1922	12	22	12 58	1 32
1922	12	23	12 58	1 32
1922	12	24	12 58	1 32
1922	12	25	12 58	1 32
1922	12	26	12 58	1 32
1922	12	27	12 58	1 32
1922	12	28	12 58	1 31
1922	12	29	12 58	1 31
1922	12	30	12 59	1 31
1922	12	31	12 59	1 31
1923	01	01	12 59	1 31
1923	01	02	13 00	1 31
1923	01	03	13 00	1 31
1923	01	04	13 01	1 30
1923	01	05	13 01	1 30
1923	01	06	13 02	1 30
1923	01	07	13 03	1 30
1923	01	08	13 03	1 30
1923	01	09	13 04	1 30
1923	01	10	13 05	1 29
1923	01	11	13 06	1 29
1923	01	12	13 07	1 29
1923	01	13	13 08	1 29
1923	01	14	13 09	1 29
1923	01	15	13 10	1 29
1923	01	16	13 11	1 29
1923	01	17	13 12	1 28
1923	01	18	13 14	1 28
1923	01	19	13 15	1 28
1923	01	20	13 16	1 28
1923	01	21	13 18	1 28
1923	01	22	13 19	1 28
1923	01	23	13 21	1 28
1923	01	24	13 23	1 27
1923	01	25	13 24	1 27
1923	01	26	13 26	1 27
1923	01	27	13 28	1 27
1923	01	28	13 29	1 27
1923	01	29	13 31	1 27
1923	01	30	13 33	1 27
1923	01	31	13 35	1 26
1923	02	01	13 37	1 26
1923	02	02	13 39	1 26
1923	02	03	13 41	1 26
1923	02	04	13 43	1 26
1923	02	05	13 45	1 26
1923	02	06	13 47	1 26
1923	02	07	13 50	1 26
1923	02	08	13 52	1 25
1923	02	09	13 54	1 25
1923	02	10	13 57	1 25
1923	02	11	13 59	1 25
1923	02	12	14 01	1 25
1923	02	13	14 04	1 25
1923	02	14	14 06	1 25
1923	02	15	14 09	1 25
1923	02	16	14 12	1 24
1923	02	17	14 14	1 24
1923	02	18	14 17	1 24
1923	02	19	14 20	1 24
1923	02	20	14 22	1 24

1923 02 21	14 25	1 24
1923 02 22	14 28	1 24
1923 02 23	14 31	1 24
1923 02 24	14 34	1 23
1923 02 25	14 36	1 23
1923 02 26	14 39	1 23
1923 02 27	14 42	1 23
1923 02 28	14 45	1 23
1923 03 01	14 48	1 23
1923 03 02	14 51	1 23
1923 03 03	14 54	1 23
1923 03 04	14 57	1 23
1923 03 05	15 01	1 22
1923 03 06	15 04	1 22
1923 03 07	15 07	1 22
1923 03 08	15 10	1 22
1923 03 09	15 13	1 22
1923 03 10	15 17	1 22
1923 03 11	15 20	1 22
1923 03 12	15 23	1 22
1923 03 13	15 26	1 22
1923 03 14	15 30	1 22
1923 03 15	15 33	1 21
1923 03 16	15 36	1 21
1923 03 17	15 40	1 21
1923 03 18	15 43	1 21
1923 03 19	15 47	1 21
1923 03 20	15 50	1 21
1923 03 21	15 53	1 21
1923 03 22	15 57	1 21
1923 03 23	16 00	1 21
1923 03 24	16 04	1 21
1923 03 25	16 07	1 21
1923 03 26	16 11	1 21
1923 03 27	16 14	1 20
1923 03 28	16 18	1 20
1923 03 29	16 21	1 20
1923 03 30	16 25	1 20
1923 03 31	16 28	1 20
1923 04 01	16 32	1 20
1923 04 02	16 35	1 20
1923 04 03	16 39	1 20
1923 04 04	16 42	1 20
1923 04 05	16 46	1 20
1923 04 06	16 50	1 20
1923 04 07	16 53	1 20
1923 04 08	16 57	1 20
1923 04 09	17 00	1 19
1923 04 10	17 04	1 19
1923 04 11	17 07	1 19
1923 04 12	17 11	1 19
1923 04 13	17 14	1 19
1923 04 14	17 18	1 19
1923 04 15	17 21	1 19
1923 04 16	17 25	1 19
1923 04 17	17 29	1 19
1923 04 18	17 32	1 19
1923 04 19	17 36	1 19
1923 04 20	17 39	1 19
1923 04 21	17 43	1 19
1923 04 22	17 46	1 19
1923 04 23	17 50	1 19
1923 04 24	17 53	1 19
1923 04 25	17 56	1 19
1923 04 26	18 00	1 19
1923 04 27	18 03	1 19
1923 04 28	18 07	1 18
1923 04 29	18 10	1 18
1923 04 30	18 14	1 18
1923 05 01	18 17	1 18
1923 05 02	18 20	1 18
1923 05 03	18 24	1 18
1923 05 04	18 27	1 18
1923 05 05	18 30	1 18
1923 05 06	18 33	1 18
1923 05 07	18 37	1 18
1923 05 08	18 40	1 18
1923 05 09	18 43	1 18
1923 05 10	18 46	1 18
1923 05 11	18 50	1 18
1923 05 12	18 53	1 18
1923 05 13	18 56	1 18
1923 05 14	18 59	1 18
1923 05 15	19 02	1 18
1923 05 16	19 05	1 18
1923 05 17	19 08	1 18
1923 05 18	19 11	1 18
1923 05 19	19 14	1 18
1923 05 20	19 17	1 18
1923 05 21	19 20	1 18
1923 05 22	19 23	1 18
1923 05 23	19 26	1 18
1923 05 24	19 28	1 18
1923 05 25	19 31	1 18
1923 05 26	19 34	1 18
1923 05 27	19 37	1 18
1923 05 28	19 39	1 18
1923 05 29	19 42	1 18
1923 05 30	19 45	1 18
1923 05 31	19 47	1 17
1923 06 01	19 50	1 17
1923 06 02	19 52	1 17
1923 06 03	19 55	1 17
1923 06 04	19 57	1 17
1923 06 05	20 00	1 17

1923 06 06	20 02	1 17
1923 06 07	20 04	1 17
1923 06 08	20 07	1 17
1923 06 09	20 09	1 17
1923 06 10	20 11	1 17
1923 06 11	20 13	1 17
1923 06 12	20 16	1 17
1923 06 13	20 18	1 17
1923 06 14	20 20	1 17
1923 06 15	20 22	1 17
1923 06 16	20 24	1 17
1923 06 17	20 26	1 17
1923 06 18	20 28	1 17
1923 06 19	20 29	1 17
1923 06 20	20 31	1 17
1923 06 21	20 33	1 17
1923 06 22	20 35	1 17
1923 06 23	20 36	1 17
1923 06 24	20 38	1 17
1923 06 25	20 39	1 17
1923 06 26	20 41	1 17
1923 06 27	20 42	1 17
1923 06 28	20 44	1 17
1923 06 29	20 45	1 17
1923 06 30	20 47	1 17
1923 07 01	20 48	1 17
1923 07 02	20 49	1 17
1923 07 03	20 50	1 17
1923 07 04	20 51	1 17
1923 07 05	20 52	1 17
1923 07 06	20 53	1 17
1923 07 07	20 54	1 17
1923 07 08	20 55	1 17
1923 07 09	20 56	1 17
1923 07 10	20 57	1 17
1923 07 11	20 58	1 17
1923 07 12	20 59	1 17
1923 07 13	20 59	1 17
1923 07 14	21 00	1 17
1923 07 15	21 01	1 17
1923 07 16	21 01	1 17
1923 07 17	21 02	1 17
1923 07 18	21 02	1 17
1923 07 19	21 02	1 17
1923 07 20	21 03	1 17
1923 07 21	21 03	1 17
1923 07 22	21 03	1 17
1923 07 23	21 03	1 17
1923 07 24	21 03	1 17
1923 07 25	21 03	1 17
1923 07 26	21 03	1 17
1923 07 27	21 03	1 17
1923 07 28	21 03	1 17
1923 07 29	21 03	1 17
1923 07 30	21 03	1 17
1923 07 31	21 03	1 17
1923 08 01	21 02	1 17
1923 08 02	21 02	1 17
1923 08 03	21 01	1 17
1923 08 04	21 01	1 17
1923 08 05	21 00	1 17
1923 08 06	21 00	1 17
1923 08 07	20 59	1 17
1923 08 08	20 59	1 17
1923 08 09	20 58	1 17
1923 08 10	20 57	1 17
1923 08 11	20 56	1 17
1923 08 12	20 55	1 17
1923 08 13	20 54	1 17
1923 08 14	20 53	1 17
1923 08 15	20 52	1 17
1923 08 16	20 51	1 17
1923 08 17	20 50	1 17
1923 08 18	20 49	1 17
1923 08 19	20 48	1 17
1923 08 20	20 46	1 17
1923 08 21	20 45	1 17
1923 08 22	20 44	1 17
1923 08 23	20 42	1 17
1923 08 24	20 41	1 17
1923 08 25	20 39	1 17
1923 08 26	20 38	1 17
1923 08 27	20 36	1 17
1923 08 28	20 35	1 17
1923 08 29	20 33	1 17
1923 08 30	20 31	1 17
1923 08 31	20 29	1 17
1923 09 01	20 28	1 17
1923 09 02	20 26	1 17
1923 09 03	20 24	1 17
1923 09 04	20 22	1 17
1923 09 05	20 20	1 17
1923 09 06	20 18	1 17
1923 09 07	20 16	1 17
1923 09 08	20 14	1 17
1923 09 09	20 12	1 17
1923 09 10	20 10	1 17
1923 09 11	20 07	1 17
1923 09 12	20 05	1 17
1923 09 13	20 03	1 17
1923 09 14	20 01	1 16
1923 09 15	19 58	1 16
1923 09 16	19 56	1 16
1923 09 17	19 54	1 16
1923 09 18	19 51	1 16

1923 09 19	19 49	1 16
1923 09 20	19 46	1 16
1923 09 21	19 44	1 16
1923 09 22	19 41	1 16
1923 09 23	19 39	1 16
1923 09 24	19 36	1 16
1923 09 25	19 34	1 16
1923 09 26	19 31	1 16
1923 09 27	19 29	1 16
1923 09 28	19 26	1 16
1923 09 29	19 23	1 16
1923 09 30	19 21	1 16
1923 10 01	19 18	1 16
1923 10 02	19 15	1 16
1923 10 03	19 13	1 16
1923 10 04	19 10	1 15
1923 10 05	19 07	1 15
1923 10 06	19 05	1 15
1923 10 07	19 02	1 15
1923 10 08	18 59	1 15
1923 10 09	18 56	1 15
1923 10 10	18 54	1 15
1923 10 11	18 51	1 15
1923 10 12	18 48	1 15
1923 10 13	18 45	1 15
1923 10 14	18 43	1 15
1923 10 15	18 40	1 15
1923 10 16	18 37	1 15
1923 10 17	18 34	1 15
1923 10 18	18 32	1 14
1923 10 19	18 29	1 14
1923 10 20	18 26	1 14
1923 10 21	18 23	1 14
1923 10 22	18 21	1 14
1923 10 23	18 18	1 14
1923 10 24	18 15	1 14
1923 10 25	18 13	1 14
1923 10 26	18 10	1 14
1923 10 27	18 07	1 14
1923 10 28	18 05	1 14
1923 10 29	18 02	1 14
1923 10 30	17 59	1 13
1923 10 31	17 57	1 13
1923 11 01	17 54	1 13
1923 11 02	17 52	1 13
1923 11 03	17 49	1 13
1923 11 04	17 47	1 13
1923 11 05	17 44	1 13
1923 11 06	17 42	1 13
1923 11 07	17 39	1 13
1923 11 08	17 37	1 13
1923 11 09	17 35	1 12
1923 11 10	17 32	1 12
1923 11 11	17 30	1 12
1923 11 12	17 28	1 12
1923 11 13	17 26	1 12
1923 11 14	17 23	1 12
1923 11 15	17 21	1 12
1923 11 16	17 19	1 12
1923 11 17	17 17	1 12
1923 11 18	17 15	1 11
1923 11 19	17 13	1 11
1923 11 20	17 11	1 11
1923 11 21	17 09	1 11
1923 11 22	17 07	1 11
1923 11 23	17 05	1 11
1923 11 24	17 03	1 11
1923 11 25	17 02	1 11
1923 11 26	17 00	1 10
1923 11 27	16 58	1 10
1923 11 28	16 56	1 10
1923 11 29	16 55	1 10
1923 11 30	16 53	1 10
1923 12 01	16 52	1 10
1923 12 02	16 50	1 10
1923 12 03	16 49	1 10
1923 12 04	16 48	1 09
1923 12 05	16 46	1 09
1923 12 06	16 45	1 09
1923 12 07	16 44	1 09
1923 12 08	16 43	1 09
1923 12 09	16 41	1 09
1923 12 10	16 40	1 09
1923 12 11	16 39	1 09
1923 12 12	16 38	1 08
1923 12 13	16 38	1 08
1923 12 14	16 37	1 08
1923 12 15	16 36	1 08
1923 12 16	16 35	1 08
1923 12 17	16 34	1 08
1923 12 18	16 34	1 08
1923 12 19	16 33	1 08
1923 12 20	16 33	1 07
1923 12 21	16 32	1 07
1923 12 22	16 32	1 07
1923 12 23	16 31	1 07
1923 12 24	16 31	1 07
1923 12 25	16 31	1 07
1923 12 26	16 31	1 07
1923 12 27	16 31	1 06
1923 12 28	16 31	1 06
1923 12 29	16 31	1 06
1923 12 30	16 31	1 06
1923 12 31	16 31	1 06
1924 01 01	16 31	1 06

1924 01 02	16 31	1 06
1924 01 03	16 31	1 06
1924 01 04	16 32	1 05
1924 01 05	16 32	1 05
1924 01 06	16 32	1 05
1924 01 07	16 33	1 05
1924 01 08	16 33	1 05
1924 01 09	16 34	1 05
1924 01 10	16 35	1 05
1924 01 11	16 35	1 05
1924 01 12	16 36	1 04
1924 01 13	16 37	1 04
1924 01 14	16 38	1 04
1924 01 15	16 39	1 04
1924 01 16	16 40	1 04
1924 01 17	16 41	1 04
1924 01 18	16 42	1 04
1924 01 19	16 43	1 03
1924 01 20	16 44	1 03
1924 01 21	16 45	1 03
1924 01 22	16 47	1 03
1924 01 23	16 48	1 03
1924 01 24	16 49	1 03
1924 01 25	16 51	1 03
1924 01 26	16 52	1 03
1924 01 27	16 54	1 02
1924 01 28	16 56	1 02
1924 01 29	16 57	1 02
1924 01 30	16 59	1 02
1924 01 31	17 01	1 02
1924 02 01	17 03	1 02
1924 02 02	17 04	1 02
1924 02 03	17 06	1 02
1924 02 04	17 08	1 02
1924 02 05	17 10	1 01
1924 02 06	17 12	1 01
1924 02 07	17 14	1 01
1924 02 08	17 16	1 01
1924 02 09	17 19	1 01
1924 02 10	17 21	1 01
1924 02 11	17 23	1 01
1924 02 12	17 25	1 01
1924 02 13	17 28	1 00
1924 02 14	17 30	1 00
1924 02 15	17 33	1 00
1924 02 16	17 35	1 00
1924 02 17	17 38	1 00
1924 02 18	17 40	1 00
1924 02 19	17 43	1 00
1924 02 20	17 45	1 00
1924 02 21	17 48	1 00
1924 02 22	17 51	0 59
1924 02 23	17 53	0 59
1924 02 24	17 56	0 59
1924 02 25	17 59	0 59
1924 02 26	18 02	0 59
1924 02 27	18 05	0 59
1924 02 28	18 07	0 59
1924 02 29	18 10	0 59
1924 03 01	18 13	0 59
1924 03 02	18 16	0 59
1924 03 03	18 19	0 58
1924 03 04	18 22	0 58
1924 03 05	18 25	0 58
1924 03 06	18 28	0 58
1924 03 07	18 32	0 58
1924 03 08	18 35	0 58
1924 03 09	18 38	0 58
1924 03 10	18 41	0 58
1924 03 11	18 44	0 58
1924 03 12	18 48	0 58
1924 03 13	18 51	0 58
1924 03 14	18 54	0 57
1924 03 15	18 57	0 57
1924 03 16	19 01	0 57
1924 03 17	19 04	0 57
1924 03 18	19 07	0 57
1924 03 19	19 11	0 57
1924 03 20	19 14	0 57
1924 03 21	19 18	0 57
1924 03 22	19 21	0 57
1924 03 23	19 25	0 57
1924 03 24	19 28	0 57
1924 03 25	19 31	0 56
1924 03 26	19 35	0 56
1924 03 27	19 38	0 56
1924 03 28	19 42	0 56
1924 03 29	19 45	0 56
1924 03 30	19 49	0 56
1924 03 31	19 52	0 56
1924 04 01	19 56	0 56
1924 04 02	20 00	0 56
1924 04 03	20 03	0 56
1924 04 04	20 07	0 56
1924 04 05	20 10	0 56
1924 04 06	20 14	0 56
1924 04 07	20 17	0 56
1924 04 08	20 21	0 55
1924 04 09	20 25	0 55
1924 04 10	20 28	0 55
1924 04 11	20 32	0 55

Chiron

1924 04 12	20 35	0 55
1924 04 13	20 39	0 55
1924 04 14	20 42	0 55
1924 04 15	20 46	0 55
1924 04 16	20 50	0 55
1924 04 17	20 53	0 55
1924 04 18	20 57	0 55
1924 04 19	21 00	0 55
1924 04 20	21 04	0 55
1924 04 21	21 07	0 55
1924 04 22	21 11	0 55
1924 04 23	21 14	0 54
1924 04 24	21 18	0 54
1924 04 25	21 21	0 54
1924 04 26	21 25	0 54
1924 04 27	21 28	0 54
1924 04 28	21 32	0 54
1924 04 29	21 35	0 54
1924 04 30	21 39	0 54
1924 05 01	21 42	0 54
1924 05 02	21 46	0 54
1924 05 03	21 49	0 54
1924 05 04	21 53	0 54
1924 05 05	21 56	0 54
1924 05 06	21 59	0 54
1924 05 07	22 03	0 54
1924 05 08	22 06	0 54
1924 05 09	22 09	0 54
1924 05 10	22 13	0 54
1924 05 11	22 16	0 54
1924 05 12	22 19	0 53
1924 05 13	22 22	0 53
1924 05 14	22 25	0 53
1924 05 15	22 29	0 53
1924 05 16	22 32	0 53
1924 05 17	22 35	0 53
1924 05 18	22 38	0 53
1924 05 19	22 41	0 53
1924 05 20	22 44	0 53
1924 05 21	22 47	0 53
1924 05 22	22 50	0 53
1924 05 23	22 53	0 53
1924 05 24	22 56	0 53
1924 05 25	22 59	0 53
1924 05 26	23 02	0 53
1924 05 27	23 05	0 53
1924 05 28	23 07	0 53
1924 05 29	23 10	0 53
1924 05 30	23 13	0 53
1924 05 31	23 16	0 53
1924 06 01	23 18	0 53
1924 06 02	23 21	0 53
1924 06 03	23 24	0 53
1924 06 04	23 26	0 53
1924 06 05	23 29	0 53
1924 06 06	23 31	0 53
1924 06 07	23 34	0 53
1924 06 08	23 36	0 52
1924 06 09	23 39	0 52
1924 06 10	23 41	0 52
1924 06 11	23 43	0 52
1924 06 12	23 46	0 52
1924 06 13	23 48	0 52
1924 06 14	23 50	0 52
1924 06 15	23 52	0 52
1924 06 16	23 54	0 52
1924 06 17	23 56	0 52
1924 06 18	23 58	0 52
1924 06 19	24 00	0 52
1924 06 20	24 02	0 52
1924 06 21	24 04	0 52
1924 06 22	24 06	0 52
1924 06 23	24 08	0 52
1924 06 24	24 10	0 52
1924 06 25	24 11	0 52
1924 06 26	24 13	0 52
1924 06 27	24 15	0 52
1924 06 28	24 16	0 52
1924 06 29	24 18	0 52
1924 06 30	24 19	0 52
1924 07 01	24 21	0 52
1924 07 02	24 22	0 52
1924 07 03	24 23	0 52
1924 07 04	24 25	0 52
1924 07 05	24 26	0 52
1924 07 06	24 27	0 52
1924 07 07	24 28	0 52
1924 07 08	24 29	0 52
1924 07 09	24 31	0 52
1924 07 10	24 32	0 52
1924 07 11	24 32	0 52
1924 07 12	24 33	0 52
1924 07 13	24 34	0 52
1924 07 14	24 35	0 52
1924 07 15	24 36	0 51
1924 07 16	24 36	0 51
1924 07 17	24 37	0 51
1924 07 18	24 38	0 51
1924 07 19	24 38	0 51
1924 07 20	24 39	0 51
1924 07 21	24 39	0 51
1924 07 22	24 39	0 51
1924 07 23	24 40	0 51
1924 07 24	24 40	0 51
1924 07 25	24 40	0 51
1924 07 26	24 40	0 51
1924 07 27	24 41	0 51
1924 07 28	24 41	0 51
1924 07 29	24 41	0 51
1924 07 30	24 41	0 51
1924 07 31	24 40	0 51
1924 08 01	24 40	0 51
1924 08 02	24 40	0 51
1924 08 03	24 40	0 51
1924 08 04	24 39	0 51
1924 08 05	24 39	0 51
1924 08 06	24 39	0 51
1924 08 07	24 38	0 51
1924 08 08	24 38	0 51
1924 08 09	24 37	0 51
1924 08 10	24 36	0 51
1924 08 11	24 36	0 51
1924 08 12	24 35	0 51
1924 08 13	24 34	0 51
1924 08 14	24 33	0 51
1924 08 15	24 33	0 51
1924 08 16	24 32	0 51
1924 08 17	24 31	0 51
1924 08 18	24 30	0 51
1924 08 19	24 28	0 51
1924 08 20	24 27	0 50
1924 08 21	24 26	0 50
1924 08 22	24 25	0 50
1924 08 23	24 24	0 50
1924 08 24	24 22	0 50
1924 08 25	24 21	0 50
1924 08 26	24 19	0 50
1924 08 27	24 18	0 50
1924 08 28	24 17	0 50
1924 08 29	24 15	0 50
1924 08 30	24 13	0 50
1924 08 31	24 12	0 50
1924 09 01	24 10	0 50
1924 09 02	24 08	0 50
1924 09 03	24 06	0 50
1924 09 04	24 05	0 50
1924 09 05	24 03	0 50
1924 09 06	24 01	0 50
1924 09 07	23 59	0 50
1924 09 08	23 57	0 50
1924 09 09	23 55	0 50
1924 09 10	23 53	0 50
1924 09 11	23 51	0 50
1924 09 12	23 49	0 50
1924 09 13	23 46	0 50
1924 09 14	23 44	0 49
1924 09 15	23 42	0 49
1924 09 16	23 40	0 49
1924 09 17	23 38	0 49
1924 09 18	23 35	0 49
1924 09 19	23 33	0 49
1924 09 20	23 30	0 49
1924 09 21	23 28	0 49
1924 09 22	23 26	0 49
1924 09 23	23 23	0 49
1924 09 24	23 21	0 49
1924 09 25	23 18	0 49
1924 09 26	23 16	0 49
1924 09 27	23 13	0 49
1924 09 28	23 10	0 49
1924 09 29	23 08	0 49
1924 09 30	23 05	0 49
1924 10 01	23 03	0 49
1924 10 02	23 00	0 48
1924 10 03	22 57	0 48
1924 10 04	22 55	0 48
1924 10 05	22 52	0 48
1924 10 06	22 49	0 48
1924 10 07	22 46	0 48
1924 10 08	22 44	0 48
1924 10 09	22 41	0 48
1924 10 10	22 38	0 48
1924 10 11	22 35	0 48
1924 10 12	22 33	0 48
1924 10 13	22 30	0 48
1924 10 14	22 27	0 48
1924 10 15	22 24	0 48
1924 10 16	22 22	0 47
1924 10 17	22 19	0 47
1924 10 18	22 16	0 47
1924 10 19	22 13	0 47
1924 10 20	22 10	0 47
1924 10 21	22 08	0 47
1924 10 22	22 05	0 47
1924 10 23	22 02	0 47
1924 10 24	21 59	0 47
1924 10 25	21 57	0 47
1924 10 26	21 54	0 47
1924 10 27	21 51	0 47
1924 10 28	21 49	0 46
1924 10 29	21 46	0 46
1924 10 30	21 43	0 46
1924 10 31	21 41	0 46
1924 11 01	21 38	0 46
1924 11 02	21 35	0 46
1924 11 03	21 33	0 46
1924 11 04	21 30	0 46
1924 11 05	21 28	0 46
1924 11 06	21 25	0 46
1924 11 07	21 22	0 46
1924 11 08	21 20	0 46
1924 11 09	21 18	0 45
1924 11 10	21 15	0 45
1924 11 11	21 13	0 45
1924 11 12	21 10	0 45
1924 11 13	21 08	0 45
1924 11 14	21 06	0 45
1924 11 15	21 03	0 45
1924 11 16	21 01	0 45
1924 11 17	20 59	0 45
1924 11 18	20 57	0 45
1924 11 19	20 55	0 44
1924 11 20	20 52	0 44
1924 11 21	20 50	0 44
1924 11 22	20 48	0 44
1924 11 23	20 46	0 44
1924 11 24	20 44	0 44
1924 11 25	20 42	0 44
1924 11 26	20 41	0 44
1924 11 27	20 39	0 44
1924 11 28	20 37	0 44
1924 11 29	20 35	0 43
1924 11 30	20 34	0 43
1924 12 01	20 32	0 43
1924 12 02	20 30	0 43
1924 12 03	20 29	0 43
1924 12 04	20 27	0 43
1924 12 05	20 26	0 43
1924 12 06	20 24	0 43
1924 12 07	20 23	0 43
1924 12 08	20 22	0 42
1924 12 09	20 20	0 42
1924 12 10	20 19	0 42
1924 12 11	20 18	0 42
1924 12 12	20 17	0 42
1924 12 13	20 16	0 42
1924 12 14	20 15	0 42
1924 12 15	20 14	0 42
1924 12 16	20 13	0 42
1924 12 17	20 12	0 41
1924 12 18	20 11	0 41
1924 12 19	20 11	0 41
1924 12 20	20 10	0 41
1924 12 21	20 09	0 41
1924 12 22	20 09	0 41
1924 12 23	20 08	0 41
1924 12 24	20 08	0 41
1924 12 25	20 07	0 41
1924 12 26	20 07	0 40
1924 12 27	20 07	0 40
1924 12 28	20 06	0 40
1924 12 29	20 06	0 40
1924 12 30	20 06	0 40
1924 12 31	20 06	0 40
1925 01 01	20 06	0 40
1925 01 02	20 06	0 40
1925 01 03	20 06	0 40
1925 01 04	20 06	0 39
1925 01 05	20 07	0 39
1925 01 06	20 07	0 39
1925 01 07	20 07	0 39
1925 01 08	20 08	0 39
1925 01 09	20 08	0 39
1925 01 10	20 09	0 39
1925 01 11	20 09	0 39
1925 01 12	20 10	0 39
1925 01 13	20 10	0 39
1925 01 14	20 11	0 38
1925 01 15	20 12	0 38
1925 01 16	20 13	0 38
1925 01 17	20 14	0 38
1925 01 18	20 15	0 38
1925 01 19	20 16	0 38
1925 01 20	20 17	0 38
1925 01 21	20 18	0 38
1925 01 22	20 19	0 38
1925 01 23	20 20	0 37
1925 01 24	20 22	0 37
1925 01 25	20 23	0 37
1925 01 26	20 24	0 37
1925 01 27	20 26	0 37
1925 01 28	20 27	0 37
1925 01 29	20 29	0 37
1925 01 30	20 30	0 37
1925 01 31	20 32	0 37
1925 02 01	20 34	0 37
1925 02 02	20 35	0 36
1925 02 03	20 37	0 36
1925 02 04	20 39	0 36
1925 02 05	20 41	0 36
1925 02 06	20 43	0 36
1925 02 07	20 45	0 36
1925 02 08	20 47	0 36
1925 02 09	20 49	0 36
1925 02 10	20 51	0 36
1925 02 11	20 53	0 36
1925 02 12	20 55	0 35
1925 02 13	20 57	0 35
1925 02 14	21 00	0 35
1925 02 15	21 02	0 35
1925 02 16	21 04	0 35
1925 02 17	21 07	0 35
1925 02 18	21 09	0 35
1925 02 19	21 12	0 35
1925 02 20	21 14	0 35
1925 02 21	21 17	0 35
1925 02 22	21 20	0 34
1925 02 23	21 22	0 34
1925 02 24	21 25	0 34
1925 02 25	21 28	0 34
1925 02 26	21 30	0 34
1925 02 27	21 33	0 34
1925 02 28	21 36	0 34
1925 03 01	21 39	0 34
1925 03 02	21 42	0 34
1925 03 03	21 45	0 34
1925 03 04	21 48	0 34
1925 03 05	21 51	0 33
1925 03 06	21 54	0 33
1925 03 07	21 57	0 33
1925 03 08	22 00	0 33
1925 03 09	22 03	0 33
1925 03 10	22 06	0 33
1925 03 11	22 09	0 33
1925 03 12	22 12	0 33
1925 03 13	22 15	0 33
1925 03 14	22 19	0 33
1925 03 15	22 22	0 33
1925 03 16	22 25	0 33
1925 03 17	22 29	0 32
1925 03 18	22 32	0 32
1925 03 19	22 35	0 32
1925 03 20	22 39	0 32
1925 03 21	22 42	0 32
1925 03 22	22 45	0 32
1925 03 23	22 49	0 32
1925 03 24	22 52	0 32
1925 03 25	22 56	0 32
1925 03 26	22 59	0 32
1925 03 27	23 03	0 32
1925 03 28	23 06	0 32
1925 03 29	23 10	0 31
1925 03 30	23 13	0 31
1925 03 31	23 17	0 31
1925 04 01	23 20	0 31
1925 04 02	23 24	0 31
1925 04 03	23 27	0 31
1925 04 04	23 31	0 31
1925 04 05	23 34	0 31
1925 04 06	23 38	0 31
1925 04 07	23 42	0 31
1925 04 08	23 45	0 31
1925 04 09	23 49	0 31
1925 04 10	23 52	0 31
1925 04 11	23 56	0 31
1925 04 12	24 00	0 30
1925 04 13	24 03	0 30
1925 04 14	24 07	0 30
1925 04 15	24 10	0 30
1925 04 16	24 14	0 30
1925 04 17	24 18	0 30
1925 04 18	24 21	0 30
1925 04 19	24 25	0 30
1925 04 20	24 29	0 30
1925 04 21	24 32	0 30
1925 04 22	24 36	0 30
1925 04 23	24 39	0 30
1925 04 24	24 43	0 30
1925 04 25	24 46	0 30
1925 04 26	24 50	0 30
1925 04 27	24 54	0 29
1925 04 28	24 57	0 29
1925 04 29	25 01	0 29
1925 04 30	25 04	0 29
1925 05 01	25 08	0 29
1925 05 02	25 11	0 29
1925 05 03	25 15	0 29
1925 05 04	25 18	0 29
1925 05 05	25 22	0 29
1925 05 06	25 25	0 29
1925 05 07	25 29	0 29
1925 05 08	25 32	0 29
1925 05 09	25 36	0 29
1925 05 10	25 39	0 29
1925 05 11	25 42	0 29
1925 05 12	25 46	0 29
1925 05 13	25 49	0 28
1925 05 14	25 52	0 28
1925 05 15	25 56	0 28
1925 05 16	25 59	0 28
1925 05 17	26 02	0 28
1925 05 18	26 05	0 28
1925 05 19	26 09	0 28
1925 05 20	26 12	0 28
1925 05 21	26 15	0 28
1925 05 22	26 18	0 28
1925 05 23	26 21	0 28
1925 05 24	26 24	0 28
1925 05 25	26 27	0 28
1925 05 26	26 30	0 28
1925 05 27	26 33	0 28
1925 05 28	26 36	0 28
1925 05 29	26 39	0 28
1925 05 30	26 42	0 28
1925 05 31	26 45	0 27
1925 06 01	26 48	0 27
1925 06 02	26 51	0 27
1925 06 03	26 54	0 27
1925 06 04	26 56	0 27

1925 06 05	26 59	0 27
1925 06 06	27 02	0 27
1925 06 07	27 04	0 27
1925 06 08	27 07	0 27
1925 06 09	27 10	0 27
1925 06 10	27 12	0 27
1925 06 11	27 15	0 27
1925 06 12	27 17	0 27
1925 06 13	27 19	0 27
1925 06 14	27 22	0 27
1925 06 15	27 24	0 27
1925 06 16	27 26	0 27
1925 06 17	27 29	0 27
1925 06 18	27 31	0 27
1925 06 19	27 33	0 27
1925 06 20	27 35	0 26
1925 06 21	27 37	0 26
1925 06 22	27 40	0 26
1925 06 23	27 42	0 26
1925 06 24	27 43	0 26
1925 06 25	27 45	0 26
1925 06 26	27 47	0 26
1925 06 27	27 49	0 26
1925 06 28	27 51	0 26
1925 06 29	27 53	0 26
1925 06 30	27 54	0 26
1925 07 01	27 56	0 26
1925 07 02	27 58	0 26
1925 07 03	27 59	0 26
1925 07 04	28 01	0 26
1925 07 05	28 02	0 26
1925 07 06	28 04	0 26
1925 07 07	28 05	0 26
1925 07 08	28 06	0 26
1925 07 09	28 08	0 26
1925 07 10	28 09	0 25
1925 07 11	28 10	0 25
1925 07 12	28 11	0 25
1925 07 13	28 12	0 25
1925 07 14	28 13	0 25
1925 07 15	28 14	0 25
1925 07 16	28 15	0 25
1925 07 17	28 16	0 25
1925 07 18	28 17	0 25
1925 07 19	28 17	0 25
1925 07 20	28 18	0 25
1925 07 21	28 19	0 25
1925 07 22	28 19	0 25
1925 07 23	28 20	0 25
1925 07 24	28 20	0 25
1925 07 25	28 21	0 25
1925 07 26	28 21	0 25
1925 07 27	28 22	0 25
1925 07 28	28 22	0 25
1925 07 29	28 22	0 25
1925 07 30	28 22	0 24
1925 07 31	28 22	0 24
1925 08 01	28 23	0 24
1925 08 02	28 23	0 24
1925 08 03	28 22	0 24
1925 08 04	28 22	0 24
1925 08 05	28 22	0 24
1925 08 06	28 22	0 24
1925 08 07	28 22	0 24
1925 08 08	28 21	0 24
1925 08 09	28 21	0 24
1925 08 10	28 21	0 24
1925 08 11	28 20	0 24
1925 08 12	28 20	0 24
1925 08 13	28 19	0 24
1925 08 14	28 19	0 24
1925 08 15	28 18	0 24
1925 08 16	28 17	0 24
1925 08 17	28 16	0 24
1925 08 18	28 15	0 23
1925 08 19	28 15	0 23
1925 08 20	28 14	0 23
1925 08 21	28 13	0 23
1925 08 22	28 12	0 23
1925 08 23	28 11	0 23
1925 08 24	28 09	0 23
1925 08 25	28 08	0 23
1925 08 26	28 07	0 23
1925 08 27	28 06	0 23
1925 08 28	28 04	0 23
1925 08 29	28 03	0 23
1925 08 30	28 01	0 23
1925 08 31	28 00	0 23
1925 09 01	27 58	0 23
1925 09 02	27 57	0 23
1925 09 03	27 55	0 23
1925 09 04	27 54	0 22
1925 09 05	27 52	0 22
1925 09 06	27 50	0 22
1925 09 07	27 48	0 22
1925 09 08	27 47	0 22
1925 09 09	27 45	0 22
1925 09 10	27 43	0 22
1925 09 11	27 41	0 22
1925 09 12	27 39	0 22
1925 09 13	27 37	0 22
1925 09 14	27 35	0 22
1925 09 15	27 33	0 22
1925 09 16	27 30	0 22

1925 09 17	27 28	0 22
1925 09 18	27 26	0 22
1925 09 19	27 24	0 22
1925 09 20	27 22	0 21
1925 09 21	27 19	0 21
1925 09 22	27 17	0 21
1925 09 23	27 14	0 21
1925 09 24	27 12	0 21
1925 09 25	27 10	0 21
1925 09 26	27 07	0 21
1925 09 27	27 05	0 21
1925 09 28	27 02	0 21
1925 09 29	27 00	0 21
1925 09 30	26 57	0 21
1925 10 01	26 54	0 21
1925 10 02	26 52	0 21
1925 10 03	26 49	0 21
1925 10 04	26 47	0 20
1925 10 05	26 44	0 20
1925 10 06	26 41	0 20
1925 10 07	26 39	0 20
1925 10 08	26 36	0 20
1925 10 09	26 33	0 20
1925 10 10	26 30	0 20
1925 10 11	26 28	0 20
1925 10 12	26 25	0 20
1925 10 13	26 22	0 20
1925 10 14	26 19	0 20
1925 10 15	26 16	0 20
1925 10 16	26 14	0 20
1925 10 17	26 11	0 20
1925 10 18	26 08	0 19
1925 10 19	26 05	0 19
1925 10 20	26 02	0 19
1925 10 21	26 00	0 19
1925 10 22	25 57	0 19
1925 10 23	25 54	0 19
1925 10 24	25 51	0 19
1925 10 25	25 48	0 19
1925 10 26	25 46	0 19
1925 10 27	25 43	0 19
1925 10 28	25 40	0 19
1925 10 29	25 37	0 19
1925 10 30	25 35	0 18
1925 10 31	25 32	0 18
1925 11 01	25 29	0 18
1925 11 02	25 26	0 18
1925 11 03	25 24	0 18
1925 11 04	25 21	0 18
1925 11 05	25 18	0 18
1925 11 06	25 16	0 18
1925 11 07	25 13	0 18
1925 11 08	25 11	0 18
1925 11 09	25 08	0 18
1925 11 10	25 05	0 18
1925 11 11	25 03	0 17
1925 11 12	25 00	0 17
1925 11 13	24 58	0 17
1925 11 14	24 55	0 17
1925 11 15	24 53	0 17
1925 11 16	24 51	0 17
1925 11 17	24 48	0 17
1925 11 18	24 46	0 17
1925 11 19	24 44	0 17
1925 11 20	24 41	0 17
1925 11 21	24 39	0 17
1925 11 22	24 37	0 17
1925 11 23	24 35	0 16
1925 11 24	24 33	0 16
1925 11 25	24 30	0 16
1925 11 26	24 28	0 16
1925 11 27	24 26	0 16
1925 11 28	24 24	0 16
1925 11 29	24 22	0 16
1925 11 30	24 21	0 16
1925 12 01	24 19	0 16
1925 12 02	24 17	0 16
1925 12 03	24 15	0 16
1925 12 04	24 13	0 16
1925 12 05	24 12	0 15
1925 12 06	24 10	0 15
1925 12 07	24 09	0 15
1925 12 08	24 07	0 15
1925 12 09	24 06	0 15
1925 12 10	24 04	0 15
1925 12 11	24 03	0 15
1925 12 12	24 02	0 15
1925 12 13	24 00	0 15
1925 12 14	23 59	0 15
1925 12 15	23 58	0 15
1925 12 16	23 57	0 14
1925 12 17	23 56	0 14
1925 12 18	23 55	0 14
1925 12 19	23 54	0 14
1925 12 20	23 53	0 14
1925 12 21	23 52	0 14
1925 12 22	23 51	0 14
1925 12 23	23 50	0 14
1925 12 24	23 50	0 14
1925 12 25	23 49	0 14
1925 12 26	23 49	0 14
1925 12 27	23 48	0 13
1925 12 28	23 48	0 13
1925 12 29	23 47	0 13

1925 12 30	23 47	0 13
1925 12 31	23 47	0 13
1926 01 01	23 46	0 13
1926 01 02	23 46	0 13
1926 01 03	23 46	0 13
1926 01 04	23 46	0 13
1926 01 05	23 46	0 13
1926 01 06	23 46	0 13
1926 01 07	23 46	0 13
1926 01 08	23 46	0 12
1926 01 09	23 47	0 12
1926 01 10	23 47	0 12
1926 01 11	23 47	0 12
1926 01 12	23 48	0 12
1926 01 13	23 48	0 12
1926 01 14	23 49	0 12
1926 01 15	23 49	0 12
1926 01 16	23 50	0 12
1926 01 17	23 51	0 12
1926 01 18	23 51	0 12
1926 01 19	23 52	0 12
1926 01 20	23 53	0 11
1926 01 21	23 54	0 11
1926 01 22	23 55	0 11
1926 01 23	23 56	0 11
1926 01 24	23 57	0 11
1926 01 25	23 58	0 11
1926 01 26	23 59	0 11
1926 01 27	24 01	0 11
1926 01 28	24 02	0 11
1926 01 29	24 03	0 11
1926 01 30	24 05	0 11
1926 01 31	24 06	0 11
1926 02 01	24 08	0 10
1926 02 02	24 09	0 10
1926 02 03	24 11	0 10
1926 02 04	24 13	0 10
1926 02 05	24 14	0 10
1926 02 06	24 16	0 10
1926 02 07	24 18	0 10
1926 02 08	24 20	0 10
1926 02 09	24 22	0 10
1926 02 10	24 24	0 10
1926 02 11	24 26	0 10
1926 02 12	24 28	0 10
1926 02 13	24 30	0 09
1926 02 14	24 32	0 09
1926 02 15	24 34	0 09
1926 02 16	24 36	0 09
1926 02 17	24 39	0 09
1926 02 18	24 41	0 09
1926 02 19	24 43	0 09
1926 02 20	24 46	0 09
1926 02 21	24 48	0 09
1926 02 22	24 51	0 09
1926 02 23	24 53	0 09
1926 02 24	24 56	0 09
1926 02 25	24 58	0 09
1926 02 26	25 01	0 08
1926 02 27	25 04	0 08
1926 02 28	25 06	0 08
1926 03 01	25 09	0 08
1926 03 02	25 12	0 08
1926 03 03	25 15	0 08
1926 03 04	25 18	0 08
1926 03 05	25 20	0 08
1926 03 06	25 23	0 08
1926 03 07	25 26	0 08
1926 03 08	25 29	0 08
1926 03 09	25 32	0 08
1926 03 10	25 35	0 08
1926 03 11	25 39	0 07
1926 03 12	25 42	0 07
1926 03 13	25 45	0 07
1926 03 14	25 48	0 07
1926 03 15	25 51	0 07
1926 03 16	25 54	0 07
1926 03 17	25 58	0 07
1926 03 18	26 01	0 07
1926 03 19	26 04	0 07
1926 03 20	26 07	0 07
1926 03 21	26 11	0 07
1926 03 22	26 14	0 07
1926 03 23	26 18	0 07
1926 03 24	26 21	0 06
1926 03 25	26 24	0 06
1926 03 26	26 28	0 06
1926 03 27	26 31	0 06
1926 03 28	26 35	0 06
1926 03 29	26 38	0 06
1926 03 30	26 42	0 06
1926 03 31	26 45	0 06
1926 04 01	26 49	0 06
1926 04 02	26 52	0 06
1926 04 03	26 56	0 06
1926 04 04	27 00	0 06
1926 04 05	27 03	0 06
1926 04 06	27 07	0 06
1926 04 07	27 10	0 05
1926 04 08	27 14	0 05
1926 04 09	27 18	0 05
1926 04 10	27 21	0 05
1926 04 11	27 25	0 05
1926 04 12	27 28	0 05

1926 04 13	27 32	0 05
1926 04 14	27 36	0 05
1926 04 15	27 39	0 05
1926 04 16	27 43	0 05
1926 04 17	27 47	0 05
1926 04 18	27 50	0 05
1926 04 19	27 54	0 05
1926 04 20	27 58	0 05
1926 04 21	28 01	0 04
1926 04 22	28 05	0 04
1926 04 23	28 09	0 04
1926 04 24	28 12	0 04
1926 04 25	28 16	0 04
1926 04 26	28 20	0 04
1926 04 27	28 23	0 04
1926 04 28	28 27	0 04
1926 04 29	28 31	0 04
1926 04 30	28 34	0 04
1926 05 01	28 38	0 04
1926 05 02	28 41	0 04
1926 05 03	28 45	0 04
1926 05 04	28 49	0 04
1926 05 05	28 52	0 04
1926 05 06	28 56	0 03
1926 05 07	28 59	0 03
1926 05 08	29 03	0 03
1926 05 09	29 06	0 03
1926 05 10	29 10	0 03
1926 05 11	29 13	0 03
1926 05 12	29 17	0 03
1926 05 13	29 20	0 03
1926 05 14	29 24	0 03
1926 05 15	29 27	0 03
1926 05 16	29 31	0 03
1926 05 17	29 34	0 03
1926 05 18	29 37	0 03
1926 05 19	29 41	0 03
1926 05 20	29 44	0 02
1926 05 21	29 47	0 02
1926 05 22	29 51	0 02
1926 05 23	29 54	0 02
1926 05 24	29 57	0 02
1926 05 25	30 00	0 02
1926 05 26	30 03	0 02
1926 05 27	30 07	0 02
1926 05 28	30 10	0 02
1926 05 29	30 13	0 02
1926 05 30	30 16	0 02
1926 05 31	30 19	0 02
1926 06 01	30 22	0 02
1926 06 02	30 25	0 02
1926 06 03	30 28	0 01
1926 06 04	30 31	0 01
1926 06 05	30 34	0 01
1926 06 06	30 37	0 01
1926 06 07	30 39	0 01
1926 06 08	30 42	0 01
1926 06 09	30 45	0 01
1926 06 10	30 48	0 01
1926 06 11	30 50	0 01
1926 06 12	30 53	0 01
1926 06 13	30 56	0 01
1926 06 14	30 58	0 01
1926 06 15	31 01	0 01
1926 06 16	31 03	0 01
1926 06 17	31 06	0 00
1926 06 18	31 08	0 00
1926 06 19	31 11	0 00
1926 06 20	31 13	0 00
1926 06 21	31 15	0 00
1926 06 22	31 18	0 00
1926 06 23	31 20	0 00
1926 06 24	31 22	0 00
1926 06 25	31 24	0 00
1926 06 26	31 26	0 00
1926 06 27	31 28	0 00
1926 06 28	31 30	0 00
1926 06 29	31 32	0 00
1926 06 30	31 34	0 00
1926 07 01	31 36	-0 01
1926 07 02	31 38	-0 01
1926 07 03	31 40	-0 01
1926 07 04	31 41	-0 01
1926 07 05	31 43	-0 01
1926 07 06	31 45	-0 01
1926 07 07	31 46	-0 01
1926 07 08	31 48	-0 01
1926 07 09	31 49	-0 01
1926 07 10	31 51	-0 01
1926 07 11	31 52	-0 01
1926 07 12	31 54	-0 01
1926 07 13	31 55	-0 01
1926 07 14	31 56	-0 02
1926 07 15	31 57	-0 02
1926 07 16	31 59	-0 02
1926 07 17	32 00	-0 02
1926 07 18	32 01	-0 02
1926 07 19	32 02	-0 02
1926 07 20	32 03	-0 02
1926 07 21	32 04	-0 02

1926	07	22	32	04	-0	02
1926	07	23	32	05	-0	02
1926	07	24	32	06	-0	02
1926	07	25	32	07	-0	02
1926	07	26	32	07	-0	02
1926	07	27	32	08	-0	02
1926	07	28	32	08	-0	03
1926	07	29	32	09	-0	03
1926	07	30	32	09	-0	03
1926	07	31	32	10	-0	03
1926	08	01	32	10	-0	03
1926	08	02	32	10	-0	03
1926	08	03	32	10	-0	03
1926	08	04	32	10	-0	03
1926	08	05	32	11	-0	03
1926	08	06	32	11	-0	03
1926	08	07	32	11	-0	03
1926	08	08	32	10	-0	03
1926	08	09	32	10	-0	04
1926	08	10	32	10	-0	04
1926	08	11	32	10	-0	04
1926	08	12	32	10	-0	04
1926	08	13	32	09	-0	04
1926	08	14	32	09	-0	04
1926	08	15	32	08	-0	04
1926	08	16	32	08	-0	04
1926	08	17	32	07	-0	04
1926	08	18	32	07	-0	04
1926	08	19	32	06	-0	04
1926	08	20	32	05	-0	04
1926	08	21	32	05	-0	04
1926	08	22	32	04	-0	05
1926	08	23	32	03	-0	05
1926	08	24	32	02	-0	05
1926	08	25	32	01	-0	05
1926	08	26	32	00	-0	05
1926	08	27	31	59	-0	05
1926	08	28	31	58	-0	05
1926	08	29	31	56	-0	05
1926	08	30	31	55	-0	05
1926	08	31	31	54	-0	05
1926	09	01	31	53	-0	05
1926	09	02	31	51	-0	05
1926	09	03	31	50	-0	06
1926	09	04	31	48	-0	06
1926	09	05	31	47	-0	06
1926	09	06	31	45	-0	06
1926	09	07	31	44	-0	06
1926	09	08	31	42	-0	06
1926	09	09	31	40	-0	06
1926	09	10	31	38	-0	06
1926	09	11	31	37	-0	06
1926	09	12	31	35	-0	06
1926	09	13	31	33	-0	06
1926	09	14	31	31	-0	06
1926	09	15	31	29	-0	07
1926	09	16	31	27	-0	07
1926	09	17	31	25	-0	07
1926	09	18	31	23	-0	07
1926	09	19	31	21	-0	07
1926	09	20	31	18	-0	07
1926	09	21	31	16	-0	07
1926	09	22	31	14	-0	07
1926	09	23	31	12	-0	07
1926	09	24	31	09	-0	07
1926	09	25	31	07	-0	07
1926	09	26	31	05	-0	07
1926	09	27	31	02	-0	08
1926	09	28	31	00	-0	08
1926	09	29	30	57	-0	08
1926	09	30	30	55	-0	08
1926	10	01	30	52	-0	08
1926	10	02	30	50	-0	08
1926	10	03	30	47	-0	08
1926	10	04	30	45	-0	08
1926	10	05	30	42	-0	08
1926	10	06	30	39	-0	08
1926	10	07	30	37	-0	08
1926	10	08	30	34	-0	08
1926	10	09	30	31	-0	09
1926	10	10	30	29	-0	09
1926	10	11	30	26	-0	09
1926	10	12	30	23	-0	09
1926	10	13	30	20	-0	09
1926	10	14	30	18	-0	09
1926	10	15	30	15	-0	09
1926	10	16	30	12	-0	09
1926	10	17	30	09	-0	09
1926	10	18	30	07	-0	09
1926	10	19	30	04	-0	09
1926	10	20	30	01	-0	09
1926	10	21	29	58	-0	09
1926	10	22	29	55	-0	10
1926	10	23	29	52	-0	10
1926	10	24	29	50	-0	10
1926	10	25	29	47	-0	10
1926	10	26	29	44	-0	10
1926	10	27	29	41	-0	10
1926	10	28	29	38	-0	10
1926	10	29	29	35	-0	10
1926	10	30	29	33	-0	10
1926	10	31	29	30	-0	10
1926	11	01	29	27	-0	10
1926	11	02	29	24	-0	10
1926	11	03	29	21	-0	11
1926	11	04	29	19	-0	11
1926	11	05	29	16	-0	11
1926	11	06	29	13	-0	11
1926	11	07	29	10	-0	11
1926	11	08	29	08	-0	11
1926	11	09	29	05	-0	11
1926	11	10	29	02	-0	11
1926	11	11	29	00	-0	11
1926	11	12	28	57	-0	11
1926	11	13	28	54	-0	11
1926	11	14	28	52	-0	11
1926	11	15	28	49	-0	11
1926	11	16	28	47	-0	12
1926	11	17	28	44	-0	12
1926	11	18	28	42	-0	12
1926	11	19	28	39	-0	12
1926	11	20	28	37	-0	12
1926	11	21	28	34	-0	12
1926	11	22	28	32	-0	12
1926	11	23	28	30	-0	12
1926	11	24	28	27	-0	12
1926	11	25	28	25	-0	12
1926	11	26	28	23	-0	12
1926	11	27	28	21	-0	12
1926	11	28	28	18	-0	12
1926	11	29	28	16	-0	12
1926	11	30	28	14	-0	13
1926	12	01	28	12	-0	13
1926	12	02	28	10	-0	13
1926	12	03	28	08	-0	13
1926	12	04	28	06	-0	13
1926	12	05	28	05	-0	13
1926	12	06	28	03	-0	13
1926	12	07	28	01	-0	13
1926	12	08	27	59	-0	13
1926	12	09	27	58	-0	13
1926	12	10	27	56	-0	13
1926	12	11	27	54	-0	13
1926	12	12	27	53	-0	13
1926	12	13	27	51	-0	13
1926	12	14	27	50	-0	13
1926	12	15	27	48	-0	14
1926	12	16	27	47	-0	14
1926	12	17	27	46	-0	14
1926	12	18	27	45	-0	14
1926	12	19	27	43	-0	14
1926	12	20	27	42	-0	14
1926	12	21	27	41	-0	14
1926	12	22	27	40	-0	14
1926	12	23	27	39	-0	14
1926	12	24	27	38	-0	14
1926	12	25	27	38	-0	14
1926	12	26	27	37	-0	14
1926	12	27	27	36	-0	14
1926	12	28	27	35	-0	14
1926	12	29	27	35	-0	14
1926	12	30	27	34	-0	15
1926	12	31	27	34	-0	15
1927	01	01	27	33	-0	15
1927	01	02	27	33	-0	15
1927	01	03	27	32	-0	15
1927	01	04	27	32	-0	15
1927	01	05	27	32	-0	15
1927	01	06	27	32	-0	15
1927	01	07	27	32	-0	15
1927	01	08	27	32	-0	15
1927	01	09	27	32	-0	15
1927	01	10	27	32	-0	15
1927	01	11	27	32	-0	15
1927	01	12	27	32	-0	15
1927	01	13	27	32	-0	15
1927	01	14	27	33	-0	15
1927	01	15	27	33	-0	16
1927	01	16	27	33	-0	16
1927	01	17	27	34	-0	16
1927	01	18	27	34	-0	16
1927	01	19	27	35	-0	16
1927	01	20	27	36	-0	16
1927	01	21	27	36	-0	16
1927	01	22	27	37	-0	16
1927	01	23	27	38	-0	16
1927	01	24	27	39	-0	16
1927	01	25	27	40	-0	16
1927	01	26	27	41	-0	16
1927	01	27	27	42	-0	16
1927	01	28	27	43	-0	16
1927	01	29	27	44	-0	16
1927	01	30	27	45	-0	16
1927	01	31	27	47	-0	17
1927	02	01	27	48	-0	17
1927	02	02	27	49	-0	17
1927	02	03	27	51	-0	17
1927	02	04	27	52	-0	17
1927	02	05	27	54	-0	17
1927	02	06	27	55	-0	17
1927	02	07	27	57	-0	17
1927	02	08	27	59	-0	17
1927	02	09	28	00	-0	17
1927	02	10	28	02	-0	17
1927	02	11	28	04	-0	17
1927	02	12	28	06	-0	17
1927	02	13	28	08	-0	17
1927	02	14	28	10	-0	17
1927	02	15	28	12	-0	17
1927	02	16	28	14	-0	17
1927	02	17	28	16	-0	18
1927	02	18	28	18	-0	18
1927	02	19	28	21	-0	18
1927	02	20	28	23	-0	18
1927	02	21	28	25	-0	18
1927	02	22	28	28	-0	18
1927	02	23	28	30	-0	18
1927	02	24	28	32	-0	18
1927	02	25	28	35	-0	18
1927	02	26	28	37	-0	18
1927	02	27	28	40	-0	18
1927	02	28	28	43	-0	18
1927	03	01	28	45	-0	18
1927	03	02	28	48	-0	18
1927	03	03	28	51	-0	18
1927	03	04	28	53	-0	18
1927	03	05	28	56	-0	18
1927	03	06	28	59	-0	19
1927	03	07	29	02	-0	19
1927	03	08	29	05	-0	19
1927	03	09	29	08	-0	19
1927	03	10	29	11	-0	19
1927	03	11	29	14	-0	19
1927	03	12	29	17	-0	19
1927	03	13	29	20	-0	19
1927	03	14	29	23	-0	19
1927	03	15	29	26	-0	19
1927	03	16	29	29	-0	19
1927	03	17	29	32	-0	19
1927	03	18	29	36	-0	19
1927	03	19	29	39	-0	19
1927	03	20	29	42	-0	19
1927	03	21	29	46	-0	19
1927	03	22	29	49	-0	20
1927	03	23	29	52	-0	20
1927	03	24	29	56	-0	20
1927	03	25	29	59	-0	20
1927	03	26	30	02	-0	20
1927	03	27	30	06	-0	20
1927	03	28	30	09	-0	20
1927	03	29	30	13	-0	20
1927	03	30	30	16	-0	20
1927	03	31	30	20	-0	20
1927	04	01	30	23	-0	20
1927	04	02	30	27	-0	20
1927	04	03	30	30	-0	20
1927	04	04	30	34	-0	20
1927	04	05	30	38	-0	20
1927	04	06	30	41	-0	21
1927	04	07	30	45	-0	21
1927	04	08	30	48	-0	21
1927	04	09	30	52	-0	21
1927	04	10	30	56	-0	21
1927	04	11	30	59	-0	21
1927	04	12	31	03	-0	21
1927	04	13	31	07	-0	21
1927	04	14	31	10	-0	21
1927	04	15	31	14	-0	21
1927	04	16	31	18	-0	21
1927	04	17	31	21	-0	21
1927	04	18	31	25	-0	21
1927	04	19	31	29	-0	21
1927	04	20	31	33	-0	21
1927	04	21	31	36	-0	22
1927	04	22	31	40	-0	22
1927	04	23	31	44	-0	22
1927	04	24	31	47	-0	22
1927	04	25	31	51	-0	22
1927	04	26	31	55	-0	22
1927	04	27	31	59	-0	22
1927	04	28	32	02	-0	22
1927	04	29	32	06	-0	22
1927	04	30	32	10	-0	22
1927	05	01	32	13	-0	22
1927	05	02	32	17	-0	22
1927	05	03	32	21	-0	22
1927	05	04	32	25	-0	22
1927	05	05	32	28	-0	23
1927	05	06	32	32	-0	23
1927	05	07	32	36	-0	23
1927	05	08	32	39	-0	23
1927	05	09	32	43	-0	23
1927	05	10	32	46	-0	23
1927	05	11	32	50	-0	23
1927	05	12	32	54	-0	23
1927	05	13	32	57	-0	23
1927	05	14	33	01	-0	23
1927	05	15	33	04	-0	23
1927	05	16	33	08	-0	23
1927	05	17	33	11	-0	24
1927	05	18	33	15	-0	24
1927	05	19	33	18	-0	24
1927	05	20	33	22	-0	24
1927	05	21	33	25	-0	24
1927	05	22	33	29	-0	24
1927	05	23	33	32	-0	24
1927	05	24	33	36	-0	24
1927	05	25	33	39	-0	24
1927	05	26	33	42	-0	24
1927	05	27	33	46	-0	24
1927	05	28	33	49	-0	24
1927	05	29	33	52	-0	25
1927	05	30	33	55	-0	25
1927	05	31	33	59	-0	25
1927	06	01	34	02	-0	25
1927	06	02	34	05	-0	25
1927	06	03	34	08	-0	25
1927	06	04	34	11	-0	25
1927	06	05	34	14	-0	25
1927	06	06	34	17	-0	25
1927	06	07	34	20	-0	25
1927	06	08	34	23	-0	25
1927	06	09	34	26	-0	25
1927	06	10	34	29	-0	26
1927	06	11	34	32	-0	26
1927	06	12	34	35	-0	26
1927	06	13	34	38	-0	26
1927	06	14	34	41	-0	26
1927	06	15	34	43	-0	26
1927	06	16	34	46	-0	26
1927	06	17	34	49	-0	26
1927	06	18	34	51	-0	26
1927	06	19	34	54	-0	26
1927	06	20	34	57	-0	26
1927	06	21	34	59	-0	27
1927	06	22	35	02	-0	27
1927	06	23	35	04	-0	27
1927	06	24	35	07	-0	27
1927	06	25	35	09	-0	27
1927	06	26	35	11	-0	27
1927	06	27	35	13	-0	27
1927	06	28	35	16	-0	27
1927	06	29	35	18	-0	27
1927	06	30	35	20	-0	27
1927	07	01	35	22	-0	28
1927	07	02	35	24	-0	28
1927	07	03	35	26	-0	28
1927	07	04	35	28	-0	28
1927	07	05	35	30	-0	28
1927	07	06	35	32	-0	28
1927	07	07	35	34	-0	28
1927	07	08	35	36	-0	28
1927	07	09	35	37	-0	28
1927	07	10	35	39	-0	28
1927	07	11	35	41	-0	29
1927	07	12	35	42	-0	29
1927	07	13	35	44	-0	29
1927	07	14	35	45	-0	29
1927	07	15	35	47	-0	29
1927	07	16	35	48	-0	29
1927	07	17	35	50	-0	29
1927	07	18	35	51	-0	29
1927	07	19	35	52	-0	29
1927	07	20	35	53	-0	29
1927	07	21	35	55	-0	30
1927	07	22	35	56	-0	30
1927	07	23	35	57	-0	30
1927	07	24	35	58	-0	30
1927	07	25	35	59	-0	30
1927	07	26	35	59	-0	30
1927	07	27	36	00	-0	30
1927	07	28	36	01	-0	30
1927	07	29	36	02	-0	30
1927	07	30	36	02	-0	30
1927	07	31	36	03	-0	31
1927	08	01	36	04	-0	31
1927	08	02	36	04	-0	31
1927	08	03	36	05	-0	31
1927	08	04	36	05	-0	31
1927	08	05	36	05	-0	31
1927	08	06	36	06	-0	31
1927	08	07	36	06	-0	31
1927	08	08	36	06	-0	31
1927	08	09	36	06	-0	32
1927	08	10	36	06	-0	32
1927	08	11	36	06	-0	32
1927	08	12	36	06	-0	32
1927	08	13	36	06	-0	32
1927	08	14	36	06	-0	32
1927	08	15	36	06	-0	32
1927	08	16	36	05	-0	32
1927	08	17	36	05	-0	32
1927	08	18	36	05	-0	33
1927	08	19	36	04	-0	33
1927	08	20	36	04	-0	33
1927	08	21	36	03	-0	33
1927	08	22	36	03	-0	33
1927	08	23	36	02	-0	33
1927	08	24	36	01	-0	33
1927	08	25	36	00	-0	33
1927	08	26	36	00	-0	33
1927	08	27	35	59	-0	33
1927	08	28	35	58	-0	34
1927	08	29	35	57	-0	34
1927	08	30	35	56	-0	34
1927	08	31	35	55	-0	34
1927	09	01	35	54	-0	34
1927	09	02	35	52	-0	34
1927	09	03	35	51	-0	34
1927	09	04	35	50	-0	34
1927	09	05	35	49	-0	34
1927	09	06	35	47	-0	35
1927	09	07	35	46	-0	35
1927	09	08	35	44	-0	35
1927	09	09	35	43	-0	35
1927	09	10	35	41	-0	35
1927	09	11	35	39	-0	35
1927	09	12	35	38	-0	35
1927	09	13	35	36	-0	35

1927	09	14	35	34	-0	35
1927	09	15	35	32	-0	36
1927	09	16	35	31	-0	36
1927	09	17	35	29	-0	36
1927	09	18	35	27	-0	36
1927	09	19	35	25	-0	36
1927	09	20	35	23	-0	36
1927	09	21	35	21	-0	36
1927	09	22	35	19	-0	36
1927	09	23	35	16	-0	36
1927	09	24	35	14	-0	36
1927	09	25	35	12	-0	37
1927	09	26	35	10	-0	37
1927	09	27	35	07	-0	37
1927	09	28	35	05	-0	37
1927	09	29	35	03	-0	37
1927	09	30	35	00	-0	37
1927	10	01	34	58	-0	37
1927	10	02	34	55	-0	37
1927	10	03	34	53	-0	37
1927	10	04	34	50	-0	37
1927	10	05	34	48	-0	38
1927	10	06	34	45	-0	38
1927	10	07	34	43	-0	38
1927	10	08	34	40	-0	38
1927	10	09	34	37	-0	38
1927	10	10	34	35	-0	38
1927	10	11	34	32	-0	38
1927	10	12	34	29	-0	38
1927	10	13	34	27	-0	38
1927	10	14	34	24	-0	38
1927	10	15	34	21	-0	38
1927	10	16	34	18	-0	39
1927	10	17	34	16	-0	39
1927	10	18	34	13	-0	39
1927	10	19	34	10	-0	39
1927	10	20	34	07	-0	39
1927	10	21	34	04	-0	39
1927	10	22	34	01	-0	39
1927	10	23	33	59	-0	39
1927	10	24	33	56	-0	39
1927	10	25	33	53	-0	39
1927	10	26	33	50	-0	39
1927	10	27	33	47	-0	40
1927	10	28	33	44	-0	40
1927	10	29	33	41	-0	40
1927	10	30	33	38	-0	40
1927	10	31	33	36	-0	40
1927	11	01	33	33	-0	40
1927	11	02	33	30	-0	40
1927	11	03	33	27	-0	40
1927	11	04	33	24	-0	40
1927	11	05	33	21	-0	40
1927	11	06	33	18	-0	40
1927	11	07	33	16	-0	40
1927	11	08	33	13	-0	40
1927	11	09	33	10	-0	41
1927	11	10	33	07	-0	41
1927	11	11	33	04	-0	41
1927	11	12	33	02	-0	41
1927	11	13	32	59	-0	41
1927	11	14	32	56	-0	41
1927	11	15	32	53	-0	41
1927	11	16	32	51	-0	41
1927	11	17	32	48	-0	41
1927	11	18	32	45	-0	41
1927	11	19	32	43	-0	41
1927	11	20	32	40	-0	41
1927	11	21	32	38	-0	41
1927	11	22	32	35	-0	41
1927	11	23	32	33	-0	41
1927	11	24	32	30	-0	42
1927	11	25	32	28	-0	42
1927	11	26	32	25	-0	42
1927	11	27	32	23	-0	42
1927	11	28	32	21	-0	42
1927	11	29	32	18	-0	42
1927	11	30	32	16	-0	42
1927	12	01	32	14	-0	42
1927	12	02	32	12	-0	42
1927	12	03	32	10	-0	42
1927	12	04	32	07	-0	42
1927	12	05	32	05	-0	42
1927	12	06	32	03	-0	42
1927	12	07	32	01	-0	42
1927	12	08	31	59	-0	42
1927	12	09	31	58	-0	42
1927	12	10	31	56	-0	42
1927	12	11	31	54	-0	43
1927	12	12	31	52	-0	43
1927	12	13	31	50	-0	43
1927	12	14	31	49	-0	43
1927	12	15	31	47	-0	43
1927	12	16	31	46	-0	43
1927	12	17	31	44	-0	43
1927	12	18	31	43	-0	43
1927	12	19	31	41	-0	43
1927	12	20	31	40	-0	43
1927	12	21	31	39	-0	43
1927	12	22	31	37	-0	43
1927	12	23	31	36	-0	43
1927	12	24	31	35	-0	43
1927	12	25	31	34	-0	43
1927	12	26	31	33	-0	43
1927	12	27	31	32	-0	43
1927	12	28	31	31	-0	43
1927	12	29	31	30	-0	43
1927	12	30	31	29	-0	43
1927	12	31	31	29	-0	43
1928	01	01	31	28	-0	43
1928	01	02	31	27	-0	43
1928	01	03	31	27	-0	44
1928	01	04	31	26	-0	44
1928	01	05	31	26	-0	44
1928	01	06	31	25	-0	44
1928	01	07	31	25	-0	44
1928	01	08	31	25	-0	44
1928	01	09	31	25	-0	44
1928	01	10	31	24	-0	44
1928	01	11	31	24	-0	44
1928	01	12	31	24	-0	44
1928	01	13	31	24	-0	44
1928	01	14	31	24	-0	44
1928	01	15	31	24	-0	44
1928	01	16	31	25	-0	44
1928	01	17	31	25	-0	44
1928	01	18	31	25	-0	44
1928	01	19	31	26	-0	44
1928	01	20	31	26	-0	44
1928	01	21	31	27	-0	44
1928	01	22	31	27	-0	44
1928	01	23	31	28	-0	44
1928	01	24	31	28	-0	44
1928	01	25	31	29	-0	44
1928	01	26	31	30	-0	44
1928	01	27	31	31	-0	44
1928	01	28	31	32	-0	44
1928	01	29	31	33	-0	44
1928	01	30	31	34	-0	44
1928	01	31	31	35	-0	45
1928	02	01	31	36	-0	45
1928	02	02	31	37	-0	45
1928	02	03	31	38	-0	45
1928	02	04	31	40	-0	45
1928	02	05	31	41	-0	45
1928	02	06	31	42	-0	45
1928	02	07	31	44	-0	45
1928	02	08	31	45	-0	45
1928	02	09	31	47	-0	45
1928	02	10	31	48	-0	45
1928	02	11	31	50	-0	45
1928	02	12	31	52	-0	45
1928	02	13	31	54	-0	45
1928	02	14	31	55	-0	45
1928	02	15	31	57	-0	45
1928	02	16	31	59	-0	45
1928	02	17	32	01	-0	45
1928	02	18	32	03	-0	45
1928	02	19	32	05	-0	45
1928	02	20	32	07	-0	45
1928	02	21	32	10	-0	45
1928	02	22	32	12	-0	45
1928	02	23	32	14	-0	45
1928	02	24	32	16	-0	45
1928	02	25	32	19	-0	45
1928	02	26	32	21	-0	45
1928	02	27	32	24	-0	45
1928	02	28	32	26	-0	46
1928	02	29	32	29	-0	46
1928	03	01	32	31	-0	46
1928	03	02	32	34	-0	46
1928	03	03	32	37	-0	46
1928	03	04	32	39	-0	46
1928	03	05	32	42	-0	46
1928	03	06	32	45	-0	46
1928	03	07	32	48	-0	46
1928	03	08	32	50	-0	46
1928	03	09	32	53	-0	46
1928	03	10	32	56	-0	46
1928	03	11	32	59	-0	46
1928	03	12	33	02	-0	46
1928	03	13	33	05	-0	46
1928	03	14	33	08	-0	46
1928	03	15	33	11	-0	46
1928	03	16	33	14	-0	46
1928	03	17	33	18	-0	46
1928	03	18	33	21	-0	46
1928	03	19	33	24	-0	46
1928	03	20	33	27	-0	46
1928	03	21	33	31	-0	47
1928	03	22	33	34	-0	47
1928	03	23	33	37	-0	47
1928	03	24	33	41	-0	47
1928	03	25	33	44	-0	47
1928	03	26	33	47	-0	47
1928	03	27	33	51	-0	47
1928	03	28	33	54	-0	47
1928	03	29	33	58	-0	47
1928	03	30	34	01	-0	47
1928	03	31	34	05	-0	47
1928	04	01	34	08	-0	47
1928	04	02	34	12	-0	47
1928	04	03	34	15	-0	47
1928	04	04	34	19	-0	47
1928	04	05	34	23	-0	47
1928	04	06	34	26	-0	47
1928	04	07	34	30	-0	47
1928	04	08	34	33	-0	48
1928	04	09	34	37	-0	48
1928	04	10	34	41	-0	48
1928	04	11	34	45	-0	48
1928	04	12	34	48	-0	48
1928	04	13	34	52	-0	48
1928	04	14	34	56	-0	48
1928	04	15	34	59	-0	48
1928	04	16	35	03	-0	48
1928	04	17	35	07	-0	48
1928	04	18	35	11	-0	48
1928	04	19	35	14	-0	48
1928	04	20	35	18	-0	48
1928	04	21	35	22	-0	48
1928	04	22	35	26	-0	48
1928	04	23	35	30	-0	49
1928	04	24	35	33	-0	49
1928	04	25	35	37	-0	49
1928	04	26	35	41	-0	49
1928	04	27	35	45	-0	49
1928	04	28	35	49	-0	49
1928	04	29	35	52	-0	49
1928	04	30	35	56	-0	49
1928	05	01	36	00	-0	49
1928	05	02	36	04	-0	49
1928	05	03	36	07	-0	49
1928	05	04	36	11	-0	49
1928	05	05	36	15	-0	49
1928	05	06	36	19	-0	49
1928	05	07	36	23	-0	50
1928	05	08	36	26	-0	50
1928	05	09	36	30	-0	50
1928	05	10	36	34	-0	50
1928	05	11	36	37	-0	50
1928	05	12	36	41	-0	50
1928	05	13	36	45	-0	50
1928	05	14	36	49	-0	50
1928	05	15	36	52	-0	50
1928	05	16	36	56	-0	50
1928	05	17	37	00	-0	50
1928	05	18	37	03	-0	51
1928	05	19	37	07	-0	51
1928	05	20	37	10	-0	51
1928	05	21	37	14	-0	51
1928	05	22	37	18	-0	51
1928	05	23	37	21	-0	51
1928	05	24	37	25	-0	51
1928	05	25	37	28	-0	51
1928	05	26	37	32	-0	51
1928	05	27	37	35	-0	51
1928	05	28	37	39	-0	51
1928	05	29	37	42	-0	52
1928	05	30	37	45	-0	52
1928	05	31	37	49	-0	52
1928	06	01	37	52	-0	52
1928	06	02	37	55	-0	52
1928	06	03	37	59	-0	52
1928	06	04	38	02	-0	52
1928	06	05	38	05	-0	52
1928	06	06	38	08	-0	52
1928	06	07	38	12	-0	52
1928	06	08	38	15	-0	53
1928	06	09	38	18	-0	53
1928	06	10	38	21	-0	53
1928	06	11	38	24	-0	53
1928	06	12	38	27	-0	53
1928	06	13	38	30	-0	53
1928	06	14	38	33	-0	53
1928	06	15	38	36	-0	53
1928	06	16	38	39	-0	53
1928	06	17	38	42	-0	54
1928	06	18	38	45	-0	54
1928	06	19	38	47	-0	54
1928	06	20	38	50	-0	54
1928	06	21	38	53	-0	54
1928	06	22	38	56	-0	54
1928	06	23	38	58	-0	54
1928	06	24	39	01	-0	54
1928	06	25	39	03	-0	54
1928	06	26	39	06	-0	55
1928	06	27	39	08	-0	55
1928	06	28	39	11	-0	55
1928	06	29	39	13	-0	55
1928	06	30	39	16	-0	55
1928	07	01	39	18	-0	55
1928	07	02	39	20	-0	55
1928	07	03	39	22	-0	55
1928	07	04	39	25	-0	56
1928	07	05	39	27	-0	56
1928	07	06	39	29	-0	56
1928	07	07	39	31	-0	56
1928	07	08	39	33	-0	56
1928	07	09	39	35	-0	56
1928	07	10	39	37	-0	56
1928	07	11	39	39	-0	56
1928	07	12	39	40	-0	57
1928	07	13	39	42	-0	57
1928	07	14	39	44	-0	57
1928	07	15	39	46	-0	57
1928	07	16	39	47	-0	57
1928	07	17	39	49	-0	57
1928	07	18	39	50	-0	57
1928	07	19	39	52	-0	57
1928	07	20	39	53	-0	58
1928	07	21	39	54	-0	58
1928	07	22	39	56	-0	58
1928	07	23	39	57	-0	58
1928	07	24	39	58	-0	58
1928	07	25	39	59	-0	58
1928	07	26	40	00	-0	58
1928	07	27	40	02	-0	59
1928	07	28	40	02	-0	59
1928	07	29	40	03	-0	59
1928	07	30	40	04	-0	59
1928	07	31	40	05	-0	59
1928	08	01	40	06	-0	59
1928	08	02	40	07	-0	59
1928	08	03	40	07	-0	59
1928	08	04	40	08	-1	00
1928	08	05	40	08	-1	00
1928	08	06	40	09	-1	00
1928	08	07	40	09	-1	00
1928	08	08	40	10	-1	00
1928	08	09	40	10	-1	00
1928	08	10	40	10	-1	00
1928	08	11	40	11	-1	01
1928	08	12	40	11	-1	01
1928	08	13	40	11	-1	01
1928	08	14	40	11	-1	01
1928	08	15	40	11	-1	01
1928	08	16	40	11	-1	01
1928	08	17	40	11	-1	01
1928	08	18	40	10	-1	02
1928	08	19	40	10	-1	02
1928	08	20	40	10	-1	02
1928	08	21	40	10	-1	02
1928	08	22	40	09	-1	02
1928	08	23	40	09	-1	02
1928	08	24	40	08	-1	02
1928	08	25	40	08	-1	03
1928	08	26	40	07	-1	03
1928	08	27	40	06	-1	03
1928	08	28	40	05	-1	03
1928	08	29	40	05	-1	03
1928	08	30	40	04	-1	03
1928	08	31	40	03	-1	03
1928	09	01	40	02	-1	03
1928	09	02	40	01	-1	04
1928	09	03	40	00	-1	04
1928	09	04	39	59	-1	04
1928	09	05	39	58	-1	04
1928	09	06	39	56	-1	04
1928	09	07	39	55	-1	04
1928	09	08	39	54	-1	04
1928	09	09	39	52	-1	05
1928	09	10	39	51	-1	05
1928	09	11	39	49	-1	05
1928	09	12	39	48	-1	05
1928	09	13	39	46	-1	05
1928	09	14	39	45	-1	05
1928	09	15	39	43	-1	05
1928	09	16	39	41	-1	06
1928	09	17	39	40	-1	06
1928	09	18	39	38	-1	06
1928	09	19	39	36	-1	06
1928	09	20	39	34	-1	06
1928	09	21	39	32	-1	06
1928	09	22	39	30	-1	06
1928	09	23	39	28	-1	06
1928	09	24	39	26	-1	07
1928	09	25	39	24	-1	07
1928	09	26	39	22	-1	07
1928	09	27	39	19	-1	07
1928	09	28	39	17	-1	07
1928	09	29	39	15	-1	07
1928	09	30	39	13	-1	07
1928	10	01	39	10	-1	07
1928	10	02	39	08	-1	08
1928	10	03	39	05	-1	08
1928	10	04	39	03	-1	08
1928	10	05	39	00	-1	08
1928	10	06	38	58	-1	08
1928	10	07	38	55	-1	08
1928	10	08	38	53	-1	08
1928	10	09	38	50	-1	08
1928	10	10	38	48	-1	08
1928	10	11	38	45	-1	09
1928	10	12	38	42	-1	09
1928	10	13	38	39	-1	09
1928	10	14	38	37	-1	09
1928	10	15	38	34	-1	09
1928	10	16	38	31	-1	09
1928	10	17	38	28	-1	09
1928	10	18	38	26	-1	09
1928	10	19	38	23	-1	09
1928	10	20	38	20	-1	09
1928	10	21	38	17	-1	10
1928	10	22	38	14	-1	10
1928	10	23	38	11	-1	10
1928	10	24	38	08	-1	10
1928	10	25	38	06	-1	10
1928	10	26	38	03	-1	10
1928	10	27	38	00	-1	10
1928	10	28	37	57	-1	10
1928	10	29	37	54	-1	10
1928	10	30	37	51	-1	10
1928	10	31	37	48	-1	10
1928	11	01	37	45	-1	11
1928	11	02	37	42	-1	11

1928	11	03	37	39	-1	11
1928	11	04	37	36	-1	11
1928	11	05	37	33	-1	11
1928	11	06	37	30	-1	11
1928	11	07	37	28	-1	11
1928	11	08	37	25	-1	11
1928	11	09	37	22	-1	11
1928	11	10	37	19	-1	11
1928	11	11	37	16	-1	11
1928	11	12	37	13	-1	11
1928	11	13	37	10	-1	11
1928	11	14	37	07	-1	12
1928	11	15	37	05	-1	12
1928	11	16	37	02	-1	12
1928	11	17	36	59	-1	12
1928	11	18	36	56	-1	12
1928	11	19	36	54	-1	12
1928	11	20	36	51	-1	12
1928	11	21	36	48	-1	12
1928	11	22	36	46	-1	12
1928	11	23	36	43	-1	12
1928	11	24	36	40	-1	12
1928	11	25	36	38	-1	12
1928	11	26	36	35	-1	12
1928	11	27	36	33	-1	12
1928	11	28	36	30	-1	12
1928	11	29	36	28	-1	12
1928	11	30	36	25	-1	12
1928	12	01	36	23	-1	12
1928	12	02	36	21	-1	13
1928	12	03	36	18	-1	13
1928	12	04	36	16	-1	13
1928	12	05	36	14	-1	13
1928	12	06	36	12	-1	13
1928	12	07	36	09	-1	13
1928	12	08	36	07	-1	13
1928	12	09	36	05	-1	13
1928	12	10	36	03	-1	13
1928	12	11	36	01	-1	13
1928	12	12	35	59	-1	13
1928	12	13	35	57	-1	13
1928	12	14	35	56	-1	13
1928	12	15	35	54	-1	13
1928	12	16	35	52	-1	13
1928	12	17	35	50	-1	13
1928	12	18	35	49	-1	13
1928	12	19	35	47	-1	13
1928	12	20	35	46	-1	13
1928	12	21	35	44	-1	13
1928	12	22	35	43	-1	13
1928	12	23	35	41	-1	13
1928	12	24	35	40	-1	13
1928	12	25	35	39	-1	13
1928	12	26	35	38	-1	13
1928	12	27	35	36	-1	13
1928	12	28	35	35	-1	13
1928	12	29	35	34	-1	13
1928	12	30	35	33	-1	13
1928	12	31	35	32	-1	13
1929	01	01	35	31	-1	13
1929	01	02	35	31	-1	13
1929	01	03	35	30	-1	13
1929	01	04	35	29	-1	13
1929	01	05	35	28	-1	13
1929	01	06	35	28	-1	13
1929	01	07	35	27	-1	13
1929	01	08	35	27	-1	13
1929	01	09	35	26	-1	13
1929	01	10	35	26	-1	13
1929	01	11	35	26	-1	13
1929	01	12	35	26	-1	13
1929	01	13	35	25	-1	13
1929	01	14	35	25	-1	13
1929	01	15	35	25	-1	13
1929	01	16	35	25	-1	13
1929	01	17	35	25	-1	13
1929	01	18	35	26	-1	13
1929	01	19	35	26	-1	13
1929	01	20	35	26	-1	13
1929	01	21	35	26	-1	14
1929	01	22	35	27	-1	14
1929	01	23	35	27	-1	14
1929	01	24	35	28	-1	14
1929	01	25	35	28	-1	14
1929	01	26	35	29	-1	14
1929	01	27	35	29	-1	14
1929	01	28	35	30	-1	14
1929	01	29	35	31	-1	14
1929	01	30	35	32	-1	14
1929	01	31	35	33	-1	14
1929	02	01	35	34	-1	14
1929	02	02	35	35	-1	14
1929	02	03	35	36	-1	14
1929	02	04	35	37	-1	14
1929	02	05	35	38	-1	14
1929	02	06	35	39	-1	14
1929	02	07	35	41	-1	14
1929	02	08	35	42	-1	14
1929	02	09	35	44	-1	14
1929	02	10	35	45	-1	14
1929	02	11	35	47	-1	14
1929	02	12	35	48	-1	14
1929	02	13	35	50	-1	14
1929	02	14	35	52	-1	14
1929	02	15	35	53	-1	14
1929	02	16	35	55	-1	14
1929	02	17	35	57	-1	14
1929	02	18	35	59	-1	14
1929	02	19	36	01	-1	14
1929	02	20	36	03	-1	14
1929	02	21	36	05	-1	14
1929	02	22	36	07	-1	14
1929	02	23	36	09	-1	14
1929	02	24	36	11	-1	14
1929	02	25	36	14	-1	14
1929	02	26	36	16	-1	14
1929	02	27	36	18	-1	14
1929	02	28	36	21	-1	14
1929	03	01	36	23	-1	14
1929	03	02	36	26	-1	14
1929	03	03	36	28	-1	14
1929	03	04	36	31	-1	14
1929	03	05	36	33	-1	14
1929	03	06	36	36	-1	14
1929	03	07	36	39	-1	14
1929	03	08	36	42	-1	14
1929	03	09	36	44	-1	14
1929	03	10	36	47	-1	14
1929	03	11	36	50	-1	14
1929	03	12	36	53	-1	14
1929	03	13	36	56	-1	14
1929	03	14	36	59	-1	14
1929	03	15	37	02	-1	14
1929	03	16	37	05	-1	14
1929	03	17	37	08	-1	14
1929	03	18	37	11	-1	14
1929	03	19	37	14	-1	14
1929	03	20	37	18	-1	14
1929	03	21	37	21	-1	14
1929	03	22	37	24	-1	14
1929	03	23	37	27	-1	14
1929	03	24	37	31	-1	15
1929	03	25	37	34	-1	15
1929	03	26	37	37	-1	15
1929	03	27	37	41	-1	15
1929	03	28	37	44	-1	15
1929	03	29	37	48	-1	15
1929	03	30	37	51	-1	15
1929	03	31	37	55	-1	15
1929	04	01	37	58	-1	15
1929	04	02	38	02	-1	15
1929	04	03	38	05	-1	15
1929	04	04	38	09	-1	15
1929	04	05	38	12	-1	15
1929	04	06	38	16	-1	15
1929	04	07	38	20	-1	15
1929	04	08	38	23	-1	15
1929	04	09	38	27	-1	15
1929	04	10	38	31	-1	15
1929	04	11	38	34	-1	15
1929	04	12	38	38	-1	15
1929	04	13	38	42	-1	15
1929	04	14	38	46	-1	15
1929	04	15	38	49	-1	16
1929	04	16	38	53	-1	16
1929	04	17	38	57	-1	16
1929	04	18	39	01	-1	16
1929	04	19	39	05	-1	16
1929	04	20	39	08	-1	16
1929	04	21	39	12	-1	16
1929	04	22	39	16	-1	16
1929	04	23	39	20	-1	16
1929	04	24	39	24	-1	16
1929	04	25	39	28	-1	16
1929	04	26	39	32	-1	16
1929	04	27	39	35	-1	16
1929	04	28	39	39	-1	16
1929	04	29	39	43	-1	16
1929	04	30	39	47	-1	17
1929	05	01	39	51	-1	17
1929	05	02	39	55	-1	17
1929	05	03	39	59	-1	17
1929	05	04	40	03	-1	17
1929	05	05	40	06	-1	17
1929	05	06	40	10	-1	17
1929	05	07	40	14	-1	17
1929	05	08	40	18	-1	17
1929	05	09	40	22	-1	17
1929	05	10	40	26	-1	17
1929	05	11	40	30	-1	17
1929	05	12	40	33	-1	17
1929	05	13	40	37	-1	18
1929	05	14	40	41	-1	18
1929	05	15	40	45	-1	18
1929	05	16	40	49	-1	18
1929	05	17	40	52	-1	18
1929	05	18	40	56	-1	18
1929	05	19	41	00	-1	18
1929	05	20	41	04	-1	18
1929	05	21	41	08	-1	18
1929	05	22	41	11	-1	18
1929	05	23	41	15	-1	19
1929	05	24	41	19	-1	19
1929	05	25	41	22	-1	19
1929	05	26	41	26	-1	19
1929	05	27	41	30	-1	19
1929	05	28	41	33	-1	19
1929	05	29	41	37	-1	19
1929	05	30	41	40	-1	19
1929	05	31	41	44	-1	19
1929	06	01	41	48	-1	19
1929	06	02	41	51	-1	20
1929	06	03	41	55	-1	20
1929	06	04	41	58	-1	20
1929	06	05	42	01	-1	20
1929	06	06	42	05	-1	20
1929	06	07	42	08	-1	20
1929	06	08	42	12	-1	20
1929	06	09	42	15	-1	20
1929	06	10	42	18	-1	21
1929	06	11	42	22	-1	21
1929	06	12	42	25	-1	21
1929	06	13	42	28	-1	21
1929	06	14	42	31	-1	21
1929	06	15	42	34	-1	21
1929	06	16	42	37	-1	21
1929	06	17	42	41	-1	21
1929	06	18	42	44	-1	22
1929	06	19	42	47	-1	22
1929	06	20	42	50	-1	22
1929	06	21	42	53	-1	22
1929	06	22	42	56	-1	22
1929	06	23	42	58	-1	22
1929	06	24	43	01	-1	22
1929	06	25	43	04	-1	22
1929	06	26	43	07	-1	23
1929	06	27	43	10	-1	23
1929	06	28	43	12	-1	23
1929	06	29	43	15	-1	23
1929	06	30	43	18	-1	23
1929	07	01	43	20	-1	23
1929	07	02	43	23	-1	23
1929	07	03	43	25	-1	24
1929	07	04	43	28	-1	24
1929	07	05	43	30	-1	24
1929	07	06	43	32	-1	24
1929	07	07	43	35	-1	24
1929	07	08	43	37	-1	24
1929	07	09	43	39	-1	25
1929	07	10	43	41	-1	25
1929	07	11	43	44	-1	25
1929	07	12	43	46	-1	25
1929	07	13	43	48	-1	25
1929	07	14	43	50	-1	25
1929	07	15	43	52	-1	25
1929	07	16	43	54	-1	26
1929	07	17	43	55	-1	26
1929	07	18	43	57	-1	26
1929	07	19	43	59	-1	26
1929	07	20	44	01	-1	26
1929	07	21	44	02	-1	26
1929	07	22	44	04	-1	27
1929	07	23	44	05	-1	27
1929	07	24	44	07	-1	27
1929	07	25	44	08	-1	27
1929	07	26	44	10	-1	27
1929	07	27	44	11	-1	27
1929	07	28	44	12	-1	28
1929	07	29	44	14	-1	28
1929	07	30	44	15	-1	28
1929	07	31	44	16	-1	28
1929	08	01	44	17	-1	28
1929	08	02	44	18	-1	28
1929	08	03	44	19	-1	29
1929	08	04	44	20	-1	29
1929	08	05	44	21	-1	29
1929	08	06	44	21	-1	29
1929	08	07	44	22	-1	29
1929	08	08	44	23	-1	29
1929	08	09	44	23	-1	30
1929	08	10	44	24	-1	30
1929	08	11	44	24	-1	30
1929	08	12	44	25	-1	30
1929	08	13	44	25	-1	30
1929	08	14	44	26	-1	30
1929	08	15	44	26	-1	31
1929	08	16	44	26	-1	31
1929	08	17	44	26	-1	31
1929	08	18	44	26	-1	31
1929	08	19	44	26	-1	31
1929	08	20	44	26	-1	31
1929	08	21	44	26	-1	32
1929	08	22	44	26	-1	32
1929	08	23	44	26	-1	32
1929	08	24	44	26	-1	32
1929	08	25	44	25	-1	32
1929	08	26	44	25	-1	32
1929	08	27	44	25	-1	33
1929	08	28	44	24	-1	33
1929	08	29	44	24	-1	33
1929	08	30	44	23	-1	33
1929	08	31	44	22	-1	33
1929	09	01	44	22	-1	33
1929	09	02	44	21	-1	34
1929	09	03	44	20	-1	34
1929	09	04	44	19	-1	34
1929	09	05	44	18	-1	34
1929	09	06	44	17	-1	34
1929	09	07	44	16	-1	34
1929	09	08	44	15	-1	35
1929	09	09	44	14	-1	35
1929	09	10	44	13	-1	35
1929	09	11	44	11	-1	35
1929	09	12	44	10	-1	35
1929	09	13	44	09	-1	35
1929	09	14	44	07	-1	36
1929	09	15	44	06	-1	36
1929	09	16	44	04	-1	36
1929	09	17	44	03	-1	36
1929	09	18	44	01	-1	36
1929	09	19	43	59	-1	36
1929	09	20	43	58	-1	37
1929	09	21	43	56	-1	37
1929	09	22	43	54	-1	37
1929	09	23	43	52	-1	37
1929	09	24	43	50	-1	37
1929	09	25	43	48	-1	37
1929	09	26	43	46	-1	38
1929	09	27	43	44	-1	38
1929	09	28	43	42	-1	38
1929	09	29	43	40	-1	38
1929	09	30	43	38	-1	38
1929	10	01	43	36	-1	38
1929	10	02	43	33	-1	38
1929	10	03	43	31	-1	39
1929	10	04	43	29	-1	39
1929	10	05	43	26	-1	39
1929	10	06	43	24	-1	39
1929	10	07	43	21	-1	39
1929	10	08	43	19	-1	39
1929	10	09	43	16	-1	39
1929	10	10	43	14	-1	40
1929	10	11	43	11	-1	40
1929	10	12	43	09	-1	40
1929	10	13	43	06	-1	40
1929	10	14	43	03	-1	40
1929	10	15	43	01	-1	40
1929	10	16	42	58	-1	40
1929	10	17	42	55	-1	40
1929	10	18	42	53	-1	41
1929	10	19	42	50	-1	41
1929	10	20	42	47	-1	41
1929	10	21	42	44	-1	41
1929	10	22	42	41	-1	41
1929	10	23	42	38	-1	41
1929	10	24	42	35	-1	41
1929	10	25	42	33	-1	41
1929	10	26	42	30	-1	41
1929	10	27	42	27	-1	42
1929	10	28	42	24	-1	42
1929	10	29	42	21	-1	42
1929	10	30	42	18	-1	42
1929	10	31	42	15	-1	42
1929	11	01	42	12	-1	42
1929	11	02	42	09	-1	42
1929	11	03	42	06	-1	42
1929	11	04	42	03	-1	42
1929	11	05	42	00	-1	42
1929	11	06	41	57	-1	43
1929	11	07	41	54	-1	43
1929	11	08	41	51	-1	43
1929	11	09	41	48	-1	43
1929	11	10	41	45	-1	43
1929	11	11	41	42	-1	43
1929	11	12	41	39	-1	43
1929	11	13	41	36	-1	43
1929	11	14	41	33	-1	43
1929	11	15	41	30	-1	43
1929	11	16	41	27	-1	43
1929	11	17	41	24	-1	43
1929	11	18	41	22	-1	43
1929	11	19	41	19	-1	43
1929	11	20	41	16	-1	44
1929	11	21	41	13	-1	44
1929	11	22	41	10	-1	44
1929	11	23	41	07	-1	44
1929	11	24	41	05	-1	44
1929	11	25	41	02	-1	44
1929	11	26	40	59	-1	44
1929	11	27	40	56	-1	44
1929	11	28	40	54	-1	44
1929	11	29	40	51	-1	44
1929	11	30	40	48	-1	44
1929	12	01	40	46	-1	44
1929	12	02	40	43	-1	44
1929	12	03	40	41	-1	44
1929	12	04	40	38	-1	44
1929	12	05	40	36	-1	44
1929	12	06	40	34	-1	44
1929	12	07	40	31	-1	44
1929	12	08	40	29	-1	44
1929	12	09	40	27	-1	44
1929	12	10	40	24	-1	44
1929	12	11	40	22	-1	44
1929	12	12	40	20	-1	44
1929	12	13	40	18	-1	44
1929	12	14	40	16	-1	44
1929	12	15	40	14	-1	44
1929	12	16	40	12	-1	44
1929	12	17	40	10	-1	44
1929	12	18	40	08	-1	44
1929	12	19	40	06	-1	44
1929	12	20	40	04	-1	44
1929	12	21	40	03	-1	44
1929	12	22	40	01	-1	44
1929	12	23	39	59	-1	44

1929	12	24	39	58	-1	44
1929	12	25	39	56	-1	44
1929	12	26	39	55	-1	44
1929	12	27	39	53	-1	44
1929	12	28	39	52	-1	44
1929	12	29	39	51	-1	44
1929	12	30	39	49	-1	44
1929	12	31	39	48	-1	44
1930	01	01	39	47	-1	44
1930	01	02	39	46	-1	44
1930	01	03	39	45	-1	44
1930	01	04	39	44	-1	44
1930	01	05	39	43	-1	44
1930	01	06	39	42	-1	44
1930	01	07	39	41	-1	44
1930	01	08	39	41	-1	44
1930	01	09	39	40	-1	44
1930	01	10	39	39	-1	44
1930	01	11	39	39	-1	44
1930	01	12	39	38	-1	44
1930	01	13	39	38	-1	44
1930	01	14	39	37	-1	44
1930	01	15	39	37	-1	44
1930	01	16	39	37	-1	44
1930	01	17	39	37	-1	44
1930	01	18	39	37	-1	44
1930	01	19	39	37	-1	44
1930	01	20	39	37	-1	44
1930	01	21	39	37	-1	44
1930	01	22	39	37	-1	44
1930	01	23	39	37	-1	44
1930	01	24	39	37	-1	44
1930	01	25	39	37	-1	44
1930	01	26	39	38	-1	44
1930	01	27	39	38	-1	44
1930	01	28	39	39	-1	44
1930	01	29	39	39	-1	44
1930	01	30	39	40	-1	44
1930	01	31	39	41	-1	44
1930	02	01	39	41	-1	44
1930	02	02	39	42	-1	44
1930	02	03	39	43	-1	44
1930	02	04	39	44	-1	44
1930	02	05	39	45	-1	44
1930	02	06	39	46	-1	44
1930	02	07	39	47	-1	44
1930	02	08	39	48	-1	44
1930	02	09	39	50	-1	44
1930	02	10	39	51	-1	44
1930	02	11	39	52	-1	44
1930	02	12	39	54	-1	43
1930	02	13	39	55	-1	43
1930	02	14	39	56	-1	43
1930	02	15	39	58	-1	43
1930	02	16	40	00	-1	43
1930	02	17	40	01	-1	43
1930	02	18	40	03	-1	43
1930	02	19	40	05	-1	43
1930	02	20	40	07	-1	43
1930	02	21	40	09	-1	43
1930	02	22	40	11	-1	43
1930	02	23	40	13	-1	43
1930	02	24	40	15	-1	43
1930	02	25	40	17	-1	43
1930	02	26	40	19	-1	43
1930	02	27	40	21	-1	43
1930	02	28	40	23	-1	43
1930	03	01	40	26	-1	43
1930	03	02	40	28	-1	43
1930	03	03	40	30	-1	43
1930	03	04	40	33	-1	43
1930	03	05	40	35	-1	43
1930	03	06	40	38	-1	43
1930	03	07	40	40	-1	43
1930	03	08	40	43	-1	43
1930	03	09	40	46	-1	43
1930	03	10	40	48	-1	43
1930	03	11	40	51	-1	43
1930	03	12	40	54	-1	43
1930	03	13	40	57	-1	43
1930	03	14	41	00	-1	43
1930	03	15	41	03	-1	43
1930	03	16	41	06	-1	43
1930	03	17	41	09	-1	43
1930	03	18	41	12	-1	43
1930	03	19	41	15	-1	43
1930	03	20	41	18	-1	43
1930	03	21	41	21	-1	43
1930	03	22	41	24	-1	43
1930	03	23	41	27	-1	43
1930	03	24	41	31	-1	43
1930	03	25	41	34	-1	43
1930	03	26	41	37	-1	43
1930	03	27	41	41	-1	43
1930	03	28	41	44	-1	43
1930	03	29	41	47	-1	43
1930	03	30	41	51	-1	43
1930	03	31	41	54	-1	43
1930	04	01	41	58	-1	43
1930	04	02	42	01	-1	43
1930	04	03	42	05	-1	43
1930	04	04	42	08	-1	44
1930	04	05	42	12	-1	44
1930	04	06	42	16	-1	44
1930	04	07	42	19	-1	44
1930	04	08	42	23	-1	44
1930	04	09	42	27	-1	44
1930	04	10	42	30	-1	44
1930	04	11	42	34	-1	44
1930	04	12	42	38	-1	44
1930	04	13	42	42	-1	44
1930	04	14	42	45	-1	44
1930	04	15	42	49	-1	44
1930	04	16	42	53	-1	44
1930	04	17	42	57	-1	44
1930	04	18	43	01	-1	44
1930	04	19	43	05	-1	44
1930	04	20	43	08	-1	44
1930	04	21	43	12	-1	44
1930	04	22	43	16	-1	44
1930	04	23	43	20	-1	44
1930	04	24	43	24	-1	44
1930	04	25	43	20	-1	44
1930	04	26	43	32	-1	45
1930	04	27	43	36	-1	45
1930	04	28	43	40	-1	45
1930	04	29	43	44	-1	45
1930	04	30	43	48	-1	45
1930	05	01	43	52	-1	45
1930	05	02	43	56	-1	45
1930	05	03	44	00	-1	45
1930	05	04	44	04	-1	45
1930	05	05	44	08	-1	45
1930	05	06	44	12	-1	45
1930	05	07	44	16	-1	45
1930	05	08	44	20	-1	45
1930	05	09	44	24	-1	45
1930	05	10	44	28	-1	46
1930	05	11	44	32	-1	46
1930	05	12	44	35	-1	46
1930	05	13	44	39	-1	46
1930	05	14	44	43	-1	46
1930	05	15	44	47	-1	46
1930	05	16	44	51	-1	46
1930	05	17	44	55	-1	46
1930	05	18	44	59	-1	46
1930	05	19	45	03	-1	46
1930	05	20	45	07	-1	46
1930	05	21	45	11	-1	47
1930	05	22	45	15	-1	47
1930	05	23	45	19	-1	47
1930	05	24	45	23	-1	47
1930	05	25	45	26	-1	47
1930	05	26	45	30	-1	47
1930	05	27	45	34	-1	47
1930	05	28	45	38	-1	47
1930	05	29	45	42	-1	47
1930	05	30	45	45	-1	48
1930	05	31	45	49	-1	48
1930	06	01	45	53	-1	48
1930	06	02	45	57	-1	48
1930	06	03	46	00	-1	48
1930	06	04	46	04	-1	48
1930	06	05	46	08	-1	48
1930	06	06	46	11	-1	48
1930	06	07	46	15	-1	49
1930	06	08	46	18	-1	49
1930	06	09	46	22	-1	49
1930	06	10	46	26	-1	49
1930	06	11	46	29	-1	49
1930	06	12	46	33	-1	49
1930	06	13	46	36	-1	49
1930	06	14	46	39	-1	49
1930	06	15	46	43	-1	50
1930	06	16	46	46	-1	50
1930	06	17	46	50	-1	50
1930	06	18	46	53	-1	50
1930	06	19	46	56	-1	50
1930	06	20	46	59	-1	50
1930	06	21	47	03	-1	50
1930	06	22	47	06	-1	51
1930	06	23	47	09	-1	51
1930	06	24	47	12	-1	51
1930	06	25	47	15	-1	51
1930	06	26	47	18	-1	51
1930	06	27	47	21	-1	51
1930	06	28	47	24	-1	52
1930	06	29	47	27	-1	52
1930	06	30	47	30	-1	52
1930	07	01	47	33	-1	52
1930	07	02	47	36	-1	52
1930	07	03	47	38	-1	52
1930	07	04	47	41	-1	53
1930	07	05	47	44	-1	53
1930	07	06	47	46	-1	53
1930	07	07	47	49	-1	53
1930	07	08	47	52	-1	53
1930	07	09	47	54	-1	53
1930	07	10	47	57	-1	54
1930	07	11	47	59	-1	54
1930	07	12	48	01	-1	54
1930	07	13	48	04	-1	54
1930	07	14	48	06	-1	54
1930	07	15	48	08	-1	54
1930	07	16	48	10	-1	55
1930	07	17	48	13	-1	55
1930	07	18	48	15	-1	55
1930	07	19	48	17	-1	55
1930	07	20	48	19	-1	55
1930	07	21	48	21	-1	56
1930	07	22	48	23	-1	56
1930	07	23	48	25	-1	56
1930	07	24	48	26	-1	56
1930	07	25	48	28	-1	56
1930	07	26	48	30	-1	57
1930	07	27	48	31	-1	57
1930	07	28	48	33	-1	57
1930	07	29	48	35	-1	57
1930	07	30	48	36	-1	57
1930	07	31	48	37	-1	58
1930	08	01	48	39	-1	58
1930	08	02	48	40	-1	58
1930	08	03	48	41	-1	58
1930	08	04	48	43	-1	58
1930	08	05	48	44	-1	59
1930	08	06	48	45	-1	59
1930	08	07	48	46	-1	59
1930	08	08	48	47	-1	59
1930	08	09	48	48	-1	59
1930	08	10	48	49	-2	00
1930	08	11	48	50	-2	00
1930	08	12	48	50	-2	00
1930	08	13	48	51	-2	00
1930	08	14	48	52	-2	00
1930	08	15	48	52	-2	01
1930	08	16	48	53	-2	01
1930	08	17	48	53	-2	01
1930	08	18	48	54	-2	01
1930	08	19	48	54	-2	01
1930	08	20	48	54	-2	02
1930	08	21	48	54	-2	02
1930	08	22	48	55	-2	02
1930	08	23	48	55	-2	02
1930	08	24	48	55	-2	02
1930	08	25	48	55	-2	03
1930	08	26	48	55	-2	03
1930	08	27	48	55	-2	03
1930	08	28	48	54	-2	03
1930	08	29	48	54	-2	03
1930	08	30	48	54	-2	04
1930	08	31	48	53	-2	04
1930	09	01	48	53	-2	04
1930	09	02	48	52	-2	04
1930	09	03	48	52	-2	05
1930	09	04	48	51	-2	05
1930	09	05	48	51	-2	05
1930	09	06	48	50	-2	05
1930	09	07	48	49	-2	05
1930	09	08	48	48	-2	06
1930	09	09	48	47	-2	06
1930	09	10	48	46	-2	06
1930	09	11	48	45	-2	06
1930	09	12	48	44	-2	06
1930	09	13	48	43	-2	07
1930	09	14	48	42	-2	07
1930	09	15	48	41	-2	07
1930	09	16	48	40	-2	07
1930	09	17	48	38	-2	07
1930	09	18	48	37	-2	08
1930	09	19	48	35	-2	08
1930	09	20	48	34	-2	08
1930	09	21	48	32	-2	08
1930	09	22	48	31	-2	08
1930	09	23	48	29	-2	09
1930	09	24	48	27	-2	09
1930	09	25	48	26	-2	09
1930	09	26	48	24	-2	09
1930	09	27	48	22	-2	09
1930	09	28	48	20	-2	09
1930	09	29	48	18	-2	10
1930	09	30	48	16	-2	10
1930	10	01	48	14	-2	10
1930	10	02	48	12	-2	10
1930	10	03	48	10	-2	10
1930	10	04	48	07	-2	11
1930	10	05	48	05	-2	11
1930	10	06	48	03	-2	11
1930	10	07	48	01	-2	11
1930	10	08	47	58	-2	11
1930	10	09	47	56	-2	11
1930	10	10	47	53	-2	12
1930	10	11	47	51	-2	12
1930	10	12	47	49	-2	12
1930	10	13	47	46	-2	12
1930	10	14	47	43	-2	12
1930	10	15	47	41	-2	12
1930	10	16	47	38	-2	13
1930	10	17	47	35	-2	13
1930	10	18	47	33	-2	13
1930	10	19	47	30	-2	13
1930	10	20	47	27	-2	13
1930	10	21	47	24	-2	13
1930	10	22	47	22	-2	13
1930	10	23	47	19	-2	14
1930	10	24	47	16	-2	14
1930	10	25	47	13	-2	14
1930	10	26	47	10	-2	14
1930	10	27	47	07	-2	14
1930	10	28	47	04	-2	14
1930	10	29	47	01	-2	14
1930	10	30	46	58	-2	14
1930	10	31	46	55	-2	15
1930	11	01	46	52	-2	15
1930	11	02	46	49	-2	15
1930	11	03	46	46	-2	15
1930	11	04	46	43	-2	15
1930	11	05	46	40	-2	15
1930	11	06	46	37	-2	15
1930	11	07	46	34	-2	15
1930	11	08	46	31	-2	15
1930	11	09	46	28	-2	15
1930	11	10	46	25	-2	16
1930	11	11	46	22	-2	16
1930	11	12	46	19	-2	16
1930	11	13	46	16	-2	16
1930	11	14	46	13	-2	16
1930	11	15	46	10	-2	16
1930	11	16	46	07	-2	16
1930	11	17	46	04	-2	16
1930	11	18	46	01	-2	16
1930	11	19	45	58	-2	16
1930	11	20	45	55	-2	16
1930	11	21	45	52	-2	16
1930	11	22	45	49	-2	16
1930	11	23	45	46	-2	16
1930	11	24	45	43	-2	16
1930	11	25	45	40	-2	17
1930	11	26	45	37	-2	17
1930	11	27	45	34	-2	17
1930	11	28	45	31	-2	17
1930	11	29	45	28	-2	17
1930	11	30	45	26	-2	17
1930	12	01	45	23	-2	17
1930	12	02	45	20	-2	17
1930	12	03	45	17	-2	17
1930	12	04	45	15	-2	17
1930	12	05	45	12	-2	17
1930	12	06	45	09	-2	17
1930	12	07	45	07	-2	17
1930	12	08	45	04	-2	17
1930	12	09	45	02	-2	17
1930	12	10	44	59	-2	17
1930	12	11	44	57	-2	17
1930	12	12	44	54	-2	17
1930	12	13	44	52	-2	17
1930	12	14	44	50	-2	17
1930	12	15	44	48	-2	17
1930	12	16	44	45	-2	17
1930	12	17	44	43	-2	17
1930	12	18	44	41	-2	17
1930	12	19	44	39	-2	17
1930	12	20	44	37	-2	17
1930	12	21	44	35	-2	17
1930	12	22	44	33	-2	17
1930	12	23	44	31	-2	17
1930	12	24	44	29	-2	17
1930	12	25	44	27	-2	17
1930	12	26	44	26	-2	17
1930	12	27	44	24	-2	17
1930	12	28	44	22	-2	17
1930	12	29	44	21	-2	17
1930	12	30	44	19	-2	17
1930	12	31	44	18	-2	17
1931	01	01	44	16	-2	17
1931	01	02	44	15	-2	17
1931	01	03	44	13	-2	17
1931	01	04	44	12	-2	17
1931	01	05	44	11	-2	16
1931	01	06	44	10	-2	16
1931	01	07	44	09	-2	16
1931	01	08	44	08	-2	16
1931	01	09	44	07	-2	16
1931	01	10	44	06	-2	16
1931	01	11	44	05	-2	16
1931	01	12	44	04	-2	16
1931	01	13	44	04	-2	16
1931	01	14	44	03	-2	16
1931	01	15	44	02	-2	16
1931	01	16	44	02	-2	16
1931	01	17	44	01	-2	16
1931	01	18	44	01	-2	16
1931	01	19	44	01	-2	16
1931	01	20	44	00	-2	16
1931	01	21	44	00	-2	16
1931	01	22	44	00	-2	16
1931	01	23	44	00	-2	16
1931	01	24	44	00	-2	16
1931	01	25	44	00	-2	16
1931	01	26	44	00	-2	15
1931	01	27	44	00	-2	15
1931	01	28	44	01	-2	15
1931	01	29	44	01	-2	15
1931	01	30	44	01	-2	15
1931	01	31	44	02	-2	15
1931	02	01	44	02	-2	15
1931	02	02	44	03	-2	15
1931	02	03	44	03	-2	15
1931	02	04	44	04	-2	15
1931	02	05	44	05	-2	15
1931	02	06	44	06	-2	15
1931	02	07	44	06	-2	15
1931	02	08	44	07	-2	15
1931	02	09	44	08	-2	15
1931	02	10	44	09	-2	15
1931	02	11	44	10	-2	15
1931	02	12	44	12	-2	15
1931	02	13	44	13	-2	14
1931	02	14	44	14	-2	14

178 30 Lat 2513

1931	02	15	44	15	-2	14
1931	02	16	44	17	-2	14
1931	02	17	44	18	-2	14
1931	02	18	44	20	-2	14
1931	02	19	44	21	-2	14
1931	02	20	44	23	-2	14
1931	02	21	44	25	-2	14
1931	02	22	44	27	-2	14
1931	02	23	44	28	-2	14
1931	02	24	44	30	-2	14
1931	02	25	44	32	-2	14
1931	02	26	44	34	-2	14
1931	02	27	44	36	-2	14
1931	02	28	44	38	-2	14
1931	03	01	44	40	-2	14
1931	03	02	44	43	-2	14
1931	03	03	44	45	-2	14
1931	03	04	44	47	-2	14
1931	03	05	44	50	-2	14
1931	03	06	44	52	-2	13
1931	03	07	44	54	-2	13
1931	03	08	44	57	-2	13
1931	03	09	44	59	-2	13
1931	03	10	45	02	-2	13
1931	03	11	45	05	-2	13
1931	03	12	45	07	-2	13
1931	03	13	45	10	-2	13
1931	03	14	45	13	-2	13
1931	03	15	45	16	-2	13
1931	03	16	45	18	-2	13
1931	03	17	45	21	-2	13
1931	03	18	45	24	-2	13
1931	03	19	45	27	-2	13
1931	03	20	45	30	-2	13
1931	03	21	45	33	-2	13
1931	03	22	45	36	-2	13
1931	03	23	45	40	-2	13
1931	03	24	45	43	-2	13
1931	03	25	45	46	-2	13
1931	03	26	45	49	-2	13
1931	03	27	45	53	-2	13
1931	03	28	45	56	-2	13
1931	03	29	45	59	-2	13
1931	03	30	46	03	-2	13
1931	03	31	46	06	-2	13
1931	04	01	46	10	-2	13
1931	04	02	46	13	-2	13
1931	04	03	46	17	-2	13
1931	04	04	46	20	-2	13
1931	04	05	46	24	-2	13
1931	04	06	46	27	-2	13
1931	04	07	46	31	-2	13
1931	04	08	46	35	-2	13
1931	04	09	46	38	-2	13
1931	04	10	46	42	-2	13
1931	04	11	46	46	-2	13
1931	04	12	46	49	-2	13
1931	04	13	46	53	-2	13
1931	04	14	46	57	-2	13
1931	04	15	47	01	-2	13
1931	04	16	47	05	-2	13
1931	04	17	47	09	-2	13
1931	04	18	47	12	-2	13
1931	04	19	47	16	-2	13
1931	04	20	47	20	-2	13
1931	04	21	47	24	-2	13
1931	04	22	47	28	-2	13
1931	04	23	47	32	-2	13
1931	04	24	47	36	-2	14
1931	04	25	47	40	-2	14
1931	04	26	47	44	-2	14
1931	04	27	47	48	-2	14
1931	04	28	47	52	-2	14
1931	04	29	47	56	-2	14
1931	04	30	48	00	-2	14
1931	05	01	48	04	-2	14
1931	05	02	48	08	-2	14
1931	05	03	48	12	-2	14
1931	05	04	48	17	-2	14
1931	05	05	48	21	-2	14
1931	05	06	48	25	-2	14
1931	05	07	48	29	-2	14
1931	05	08	48	33	-2	14
1931	05	09	48	37	-2	14
1931	05	10	48	41	-2	15
1931	05	11	48	45	-2	15
1931	05	12	48	49	-2	15
1931	05	13	48	53	-2	15
1931	05	14	48	58	-2	15
1931	05	15	49	02	-2	15
1931	05	16	49	06	-2	15
1931	05	17	49	10	-2	15
1931	05	18	49	14	-2	15
1931	05	19	49	18	-2	15
1931	05	20	49	22	-2	15
1931	05	21	49	26	-2	16
1931	05	22	49	30	-2	16
1931	05	23	49	34	-2	16
1931	05	24	49	38	-2	16
1931	05	25	49	42	-2	16
1931	05	26	49	46	-2	16
1931	05	27	49	50	-2	16
1931	05	28	49	54	-2	16
1931	05	29	49	58	-2	16
1931	05	30	50	02	-2	16
1931	05	31	50	06	-2	17
1931	06	01	50	10	-2	17
1931	06	02	50	14	-2	17
1931	06	03	50	18	-2	17
1931	06	04	50	22	-2	17
1931	06	05	50	26	-2	17
1931	06	06	50	30	-2	17
1931	06	07	50	33	-2	18
1931	06	08	50	37	-2	18
1931	06	09	50	41	-2	18
1931	06	10	50	45	-2	18
1931	06	11	50	49	-2	18
1931	06	12	50	52	-2	18
1931	06	13	50	56	-2	18
1931	06	14	51	00	-2	19
1931	06	15	51	03	-2	19
1931	06	16	51	07	-2	19
1931	06	17	51	10	-2	19
1931	06	18	51	14	-2	19
1931	06	19	51	18	-2	19
1931	06	20	51	21	-2	19
1931	06	21	51	25	-2	20
1931	06	22	51	28	-2	20
1931	06	23	51	31	-2	20
1931	06	24	51	35	-2	20
1931	06	25	51	38	-2	20
1931	06	26	51	42	-2	20
1931	06	27	51	45	-2	21
1931	06	28	51	48	-2	21
1931	06	29	51	51	-2	21
1931	06	30	51	54	-2	21
1931	07	01	51	58	-2	21
1931	07	02	52	01	-2	22
1931	07	03	52	04	-2	22
1931	07	04	52	07	-2	22
1931	07	05	52	10	-2	22
1931	07	06	52	13	-2	22
1931	07	07	52	16	-2	22
1931	07	08	52	19	-2	23
1931	07	09	52	21	-2	23
1931	07	10	52	24	-2	23
1931	07	11	52	27	-2	23
1931	07	12	52	30	-2	23
1931	07	13	52	32	-2	24
1931	07	14	52	35	-2	24
1931	07	15	52	37	-2	24
1931	07	16	52	40	-2	24
1931	07	17	52	42	-2	25
1931	07	18	52	45	-2	25
1931	07	19	52	47	-2	25
1931	07	20	52	50	-2	25
1931	07	21	52	52	-2	25
1931	07	22	52	54	-2	26
1931	07	23	52	56	-2	26
1931	07	24	52	58	-2	26
1931	07	25	53	01	-2	26
1931	07	26	53	03	-2	26
1931	07	27	53	05	-2	27
1931	07	28	53	06	-2	27
1931	07	29	53	08	-2	27
1931	07	30	53	10	-2	27
1931	07	31	53	12	-2	28
1931	08	01	53	14	-2	28
1931	08	02	53	15	-2	28
1931	08	03	53	17	-2	28
1931	08	04	53	19	-2	29
1931	08	05	53	20	-2	29
1931	08	06	53	21	-2	29
1931	08	07	53	23	-2	29
1931	08	08	53	24	-2	29
1931	08	09	53	25	-2	30
1931	08	10	53	27	-2	30
1931	08	11	53	28	-2	30
1931	08	12	53	29	-2	30
1931	08	13	53	30	-2	31
1931	08	14	53	31	-2	31
1931	08	15	53	32	-2	31
1931	08	16	53	33	-2	31
1931	08	17	53	34	-2	32
1931	08	18	53	34	-2	32
1931	08	19	53	35	-2	32
1931	08	20	53	36	-2	32
1931	08	21	53	36	-2	33
1931	08	22	53	37	-2	33
1931	08	23	53	37	-2	33
1931	08	24	53	37	-2	33
1931	08	25	53	38	-2	34
1931	08	26	53	38	-2	34
1931	08	27	53	38	-2	34
1931	08	28	53	38	-2	34
1931	08	29	53	38	-2	35
1931	08	30	53	38	-2	35
1931	08	31	53	38	-2	35
1931	09	01	53	38	-2	35
1931	09	02	53	38	-2	36
1931	09	03	53	38	-2	36
1931	09	04	53	38	-2	36
1931	09	05	53	37	-2	36
1931	09	06	53	37	-2	37
1931	09	07	53	36	-2	37
1931	09	08	53	36	-2	37
1931	09	09	53	35	-2	37
1931	09	10	53	35	-2	38
1931	09	11	53	34	-2	38
1931	09	12	53	33	-2	38
1931	09	13	53	32	-2	38
1931	09	14	53	31	-2	39
1931	09	15	53	30	-2	39
1931	09	16	53	29	-2	39
1931	09	17	53	28	-2	39
1931	09	18	53	27	-2	39
1931	09	19	53	26	-2	40
1931	09	20	53	25	-2	40
1931	09	21	53	23	-2	40
1931	09	22	53	22	-2	40
1931	09	23	53	21	-2	41
1931	09	24	53	19	-2	41
1931	09	25	53	18	-2	41
1931	09	26	53	16	-2	41
1931	09	27	53	14	-2	42
1931	09	28	53	13	-2	42
1931	09	29	53	11	-2	42
1931	09	30	53	09	-2	42
1931	10	01	53	07	-2	42
1931	10	02	53	05	-2	43
1931	10	03	53	04	-2	43
1931	10	04	53	02	-2	43
1931	10	05	53	00	-2	43
1931	10	06	52	57	-2	44
1931	10	07	52	55	-2	44
1931	10	08	52	53	-2	44
1931	10	09	52	51	-2	44
1931	10	10	52	49	-2	44
1931	10	11	52	46	-2	45
1931	10	12	52	44	-2	45
1931	10	13	52	41	-2	45
1931	10	14	52	39	-2	45
1931	10	15	52	37	-2	45
1931	10	16	52	34	-2	46
1931	10	17	52	31	-2	46
1931	10	18	52	29	-2	46
1931	10	19	52	26	-2	46
1931	10	20	52	24	-2	46
1931	10	21	52	21	-2	46
1931	10	22	52	18	-2	47
1931	10	23	52	15	-2	47
1931	10	24	52	12	-2	47
1931	10	25	52	10	-2	47
1931	10	26	52	07	-2	47
1931	10	27	52	04	-2	47
1931	10	28	52	01	-2	48
1931	10	29	51	58	-2	48
1931	10	30	51	55	-2	48
1931	10	31	51	52	-2	48
1931	11	01	51	49	-2	48
1931	11	02	51	46	-2	48
1931	11	03	51	43	-2	48
1931	11	04	51	40	-2	49
1931	11	05	51	37	-2	49
1931	11	06	51	34	-2	49
1931	11	07	51	31	-2	49
1931	11	08	51	28	-2	49
1931	11	09	51	25	-2	49
1931	11	10	51	22	-2	49
1931	11	11	51	18	-2	49
1931	11	12	51	15	-2	49
1931	11	13	51	12	-2	50
1931	11	14	51	09	-2	50
1931	11	15	51	06	-2	50
1931	11	16	51	03	-2	50
1931	11	17	51	00	-2	50
1931	11	18	50	56	-2	50
1931	11	19	50	53	-2	50
1931	11	20	50	50	-2	50
1931	11	21	50	47	-2	50
1931	11	22	50	44	-2	50
1931	11	23	50	41	-2	50
1931	11	24	50	38	-2	50
1931	11	25	50	35	-2	50
1931	11	26	50	32	-2	50
1931	11	27	50	29	-2	51
1931	11	28	50	26	-2	51
1931	11	29	50	23	-2	51
1931	11	30	50	20	-2	51
1931	12	01	50	17	-2	51
1931	12	02	50	14	-2	51
1931	12	03	50	11	-2	51
1931	12	04	50	08	-2	51
1931	12	05	50	05	-2	51
1931	12	06	50	02	-2	51
1931	12	07	49	59	-2	51
1931	12	08	49	57	-2	51
1931	12	09	49	54	-2	51
1931	12	10	49	51	-2	51
1931	12	11	49	48	-2	51
1931	12	12	49	46	-2	51
1931	12	13	49	43	-2	51
1931	12	14	49	41	-2	51
1931	12	15	49	38	-2	51
1931	12	16	49	36	-2	51
1931	12	17	49	33	-2	51
1931	12	18	49	31	-2	51
1931	12	19	49	28	-2	51
1931	12	20	49	26	-2	51
1931	12	21	49	24	-2	51
1931	12	22	49	22	-2	51
1931	12	23	49	19	-2	51
1931	12	24	49	17	-2	51
1931	12	25	49	15	-2	51
1931	12	26	49	13	-2	51
1931	12	27	49	11	-2	50
1931	12	28	49	09	-2	50
1931	12	29	49	07	-2	50
1931	12	30	49	05	-2	50
1931	12	31	49	04	-2	50
1932	01	01	49	02	-2	50
1932	01	02	49	00	-2	50
1932	01	03	48	59	-2	50
1932	01	04	48	57	-2	50
1932	01	05	48	56	-2	50
1932	01	06	48	54	-2	50
1932	01	07	48	53	-2	50
1932	01	08	48	51	-2	50
1932	01	09	48	50	-2	50
1932	01	10	48	49	-2	50
1932	01	11	48	48	-2	50
1932	01	12	48	47	-2	50
1932	01	13	48	46	-2	49
1932	01	14	48	45	-2	49
1932	01	15	48	44	-2	49
1932	01	16	48	43	-2	49
1932	01	17	48	42	-2	49
1932	01	18	48	42	-2	49
1932	01	19	48	41	-2	49
1932	01	20	48	40	-2	49
1932	01	21	48	40	-2	49
1932	01	22	48	39	-2	49
1932	01	23	48	39	-2	49
1932	01	24	48	39	-2	49
1932	01	25	48	38	-2	48
1932	01	26	48	38	-2	48
1932	01	27	48	38	-2	48
1932	01	28	48	38	-2	48
1932	01	29	48	38	-2	48
1932	01	30	48	38	-2	48
1932	01	31	48	38	-2	48
1932	02	01	48	39	-2	48
1932	02	02	48	39	-2	48
1932	02	03	48	39	-2	48
1932	02	04	48	40	-2	48
1932	02	05	48	40	-2	47
1932	02	06	48	41	-2	47
1932	02	07	48	41	-2	47
1932	02	08	48	42	-2	47
1932	02	09	48	43	-2	47
1932	02	10	48	43	-2	47
1932	02	11	48	44	-2	47
1932	02	12	48	45	-2	47
1932	02	13	48	46	-2	47
1932	02	14	48	47	-2	47
1932	02	15	48	48	-2	46
1932	02	16	48	49	-2	46
1932	02	17	48	51	-2	46
1932	02	18	48	52	-2	46
1932	02	19	48	53	-2	46
1932	02	20	48	55	-2	46
1932	02	21	48	56	-2	46
1932	02	22	48	58	-2	46
1932	02	23	48	59	-2	46
1932	02	24	49	01	-2	46
1932	02	25	49	03	-2	46
1932	02	26	49	05	-2	46
1932	02	27	49	06	-2	45
1932	02	28	49	08	-2	45
1932	02	29	49	10	-2	45
1932	03	01	49	12	-2	45
1932	03	02	49	14	-2	45
1932	03	03	49	16	-2	45
1932	03	04	49	19	-2	45
1932	03	05	49	21	-2	45
1932	03	06	49	23	-2	45
1932	03	07	49	25	-2	45
1932	03	08	49	28	-2	45
1932	03	09	49	30	-2	45
1932	03	10	49	33	-2	45
1932	03	11	49	35	-2	45
1932	03	12	49	38	-2	44
1932	03	13	49	40	-2	44
1932	03	14	49	43	-2	44
1932	03	15	49	46	-2	44
1932	03	16	49	49	-2	44
1932	03	17	49	51	-2	44
1932	03	18	49	54	-2	44
1932	03	19	49	57	-2	44
1932	03	20	50	00	-2	44
1932	03	21	50	03	-2	44
1932	03	22	50	06	-2	44
1932	03	23	50	09	-2	44
1932	03	24	50	13	-2	44
1932	03	25	50	16	-2	44
1932	03	26	50	19	-2	44
1932	03	27	50	22	-2	44
1932	03	28	50	25	-2	44
1932	03	29	50	29	-2	44
1932	03	30	50	32	-2	44
1932	03	31	50	36	-2	44
1932	04	01	50	39	-2	44
1932	04	02	50	42	-2	44
1932	04	03	50	46	-2	43
1932	04	04	50	50	-2	43

1932 04 05	50 53	-2 43
1932 04 06	50 57	-2 43
1932 04 07	51 00	-2 43
1932 04 08	51 04	-2 43
1932 04 09	51 08	-2 43
1932 04 10	51 11	-2 43
1932 04 11	51 15	-2 43
1932 04 12	51 19	-2 43
1932 04 13	51 23	-2 43
1932 04 14	51 27	-2 43
1932 04 15	51 31	-2 43
1932 04 16	51 34	-2 43
1932 04 17	51 38	-2 43
1932 04 18	51 42	-2 43
1932 04 19	51 46	-2 43
1932 04 20	51 50	-2 43
1932 04 21	51 54	-2 43
1932 04 22	51 58	-2 44
1932 04 23	52 02	-2 44
1932 04 24	52 06	-2 44
1932 04 25	52 10	-2 44
1932 04 26	52 14	-2 44
1932 04 27	52 19	-2 44
1932 04 28	52 23	-2 44
1932 04 29	52 27	-2 44
1932 04 30	52 31	-2 44
1932 05 01	52 35	-2 44
1932 05 02	52 39	-2 44
1932 05 03	52 43	-2 44
1932 05 04	52 48	-2 44
1932 05 05	52 52	-2 44
1932 05 06	52 56	-2 44
1932 05 07	53 00	-2 44
1932 05 08	53 04	-2 44
1932 05 09	53 09	-2 44
1932 05 10	53 13	-2 44
1932 05 11	53 17	-2 44
1932 05 12	53 21	-2 44
1932 05 13	53 26	-2 45
1932 05 14	53 30	-2 45
1932 05 15	53 34	-2 45
1932 05 16	53 38	-2 45
1932 05 17	53 43	-2 45
1932 05 18	53 47	-2 45
1932 05 19	53 51	-2 45
1932 05 20	53 55	-2 45
1932 05 21	53 59	-2 45
1932 05 22	54 04	-2 45
1932 05 23	54 08	-2 45
1932 05 24	54 12	-2 46
1932 05 25	54 16	-2 46
1932 05 26	54 21	-2 46
1932 05 27	54 25	-2 46
1932 05 28	54 29	-2 46
1932 05 29	54 33	-2 46
1932 05 30	54 37	-2 46
1932 05 31	54 41	-2 46
1932 06 01	54 46	-2 46
1932 06 02	54 50	-2 47
1932 06 03	54 54	-2 47
1932 06 04	54 58	-2 47
1932 06 05	55 02	-2 47
1932 06 06	55 06	-2 47
1932 06 07	55 10	-2 47
1932 06 08	55 14	-2 47
1932 06 09	55 18	-2 48
1932 06 10	55 22	-2 48
1932 06 11	55 26	-2 48
1932 06 12	55 30	-2 48
1932 06 13	55 34	-2 48
1932 06 14	55 38	-2 48
1932 06 15	55 42	-2 48
1932 06 16	55 46	-2 49
1932 06 17	55 49	-2 49
1932 06 18	55 53	-2 49
1932 06 19	55 57	-2 49
1932 06 20	56 01	-2 49
1932 06 21	56 05	-2 49
1932 06 22	56 08	-2 50
1932 06 23	56 12	-2 50
1932 06 24	56 16	-2 50
1932 06 25	56 19	-2 50
1932 06 26	56 23	-2 50
1932 06 27	56 26	-2 51
1932 06 28	56 30	-2 51
1932 06 29	56 33	-2 51
1932 06 30	56 37	-2 51
1932 07 01	56 40	-2 51
1932 07 02	56 44	-2 52
1932 07 03	56 47	-2 52
1932 07 04	56 50	-2 52
1932 07 05	56 54	-2 52
1932 07 06	56 57	-2 52
1932 07 07	57 00	-2 53
1932 07 08	57 03	-2 53
1932 07 09	57 06	-2 53
1932 07 10	57 09	-2 53
1932 07 11	57 13	-2 53
1932 07 12	57 16	-2 54
1932 07 13	57 18	-2 54
1932 07 14	57 21	-2 54
1932 07 15	57 24	-2 54
1932 07 16	57 27	-2 55
1932 07 17	57 30	-2 55
1932 07 18	57 33	-2 55
1932 07 19	57 35	-2 55
1932 07 20	57 38	-2 56
1932 07 21	57 41	-2 56
1932 07 22	57 43	-2 56
1932 07 23	57 46	-2 56
1932 07 24	57 48	-2 57
1932 07 25	57 50	-2 57
1932 07 26	57 53	-2 57
1932 07 27	57 55	-2 57
1932 07 28	57 57	-2 58
1932 07 29	58 00	-2 58
1932 07 30	58 02	-2 58
1932 07 31	58 04	-2 58
1932 08 01	58 06	-2 59
1932 08 02	58 08	-2 59
1932 08 03	58 10	-2 59
1932 08 04	58 12	-2 59
1932 08 05	58 14	-3 00
1932 08 06	58 15	-3 00
1932 08 07	58 17	-3 00
1932 08 08	58 19	-3 00
1932 08 09	58 20	-3 01
1932 08 10	58 22	-3 01
1932 08 11	58 23	-3 01
1932 08 12	58 25	-3 02
1932 08 13	58 26	-3 02
1932 08 14	58 27	-3 02
1932 08 15	58 29	-3 02
1932 08 16	58 30	-3 03
1932 08 17	58 31	-3 03
1932 08 18	58 32	-3 03
1932 08 19	58 33	-3 04
1932 08 20	58 34	-3 04
1932 08 21	58 35	-3 04
1932 08 22	58 36	-3 04
1932 08 23	58 36	-3 05
1932 08 24	58 37	-3 05
1932 08 25	58 38	-3 05
1932 08 26	58 38	-3 06
1932 08 27	58 39	-3 06
1932 08 28	58 39	-3 06
1932 08 29	58 40	-3 06
1932 08 30	58 40	-3 07
1932 08 31	58 40	-3 07
1932 09 01	58 40	-3 07
1932 09 02	58 41	-3 08
1932 09 03	58 41	-3 08
1932 09 04	58 41	-3 08
1932 09 05	58 41	-3 08
1932 09 06	58 40	-3 09
1932 09 07	58 40	-3 09
1932 09 08	58 40	-3 09
1932 09 09	58 40	-3 10
1932 09 10	58 39	-3 10
1932 09 11	58 39	-3 10
1932 09 12	58 38	-3 10
1932 09 13	58 38	-3 11
1932 09 14	58 37	-3 11
1932 09 15	58 36	-3 11
1932 09 16	58 36	-3 12
1932 09 17	58 35	-3 12
1932 09 18	58 34	-3 12
1932 09 19	58 33	-3 12
1932 09 20	58 32	-3 13
1932 09 21	58 31	-3 13
1932 09 22	58 30	-3 13
1932 09 23	58 29	-3 14
1932 09 24	58 28	-3 14
1932 09 25	58 26	-3 14
1932 09 26	58 25	-3 14
1932 09 27	58 23	-3 15
1932 09 28	58 22	-3 15
1932 09 29	58 20	-3 15
1932 09 30	58 19	-3 16
1932 10 01	58 17	-3 16
1932 10 02	58 15	-3 16
1932 10 03	58 14	-3 16
1932 10 04	58 12	-3 17
1932 10 05	58 10	-3 17
1932 10 06	58 08	-3 17
1932 10 07	58 06	-3 17
1932 10 08	58 04	-3 18
1932 10 09	58 02	-3 18
1932 10 10	58 00	-3 18
1932 10 11	57 58	-3 18
1932 10 12	57 55	-3 19
1932 10 13	57 53	-3 19
1932 10 14	57 51	-3 19
1932 10 15	57 49	-3 19
1932 10 16	57 46	-3 19
1932 10 17	57 44	-3 20
1932 10 18	57 41	-3 20
1932 10 19	57 39	-3 20
1932 10 20	57 36	-3 20
1932 10 21	57 33	-3 21
1932 10 22	57 31	-3 21
1932 10 23	57 28	-3 21
1932 10 24	57 25	-3 21
1932 10 25	57 23	-3 21
1932 10 26	57 20	-3 22
1932 10 27	57 17	-3 22
1932 10 28	57 14	-3 22
1932 10 29	57 11	-3 22
1932 10 30	57 08	-3 22
1932 10 31	57 05	-3 22
1932 11 01	57 02	-3 23
1932 11 02	56 59	-3 23
1932 11 03	56 56	-3 23
1932 11 04	56 53	-3 23
1932 11 05	56 50	-3 23
1932 11 06	56 47	-3 23
1932 11 07	56 44	-3 24
1932 11 08	56 41	-3 24
1932 11 09	56 38	-3 24
1932 11 10	56 34	-3 24
1932 11 11	56 31	-3 24
1932 11 12	56 28	-3 24
1932 11 13	56 25	-3 24
1932 11 14	56 22	-3 24
1932 11 15	56 19	-3 25
1932 11 16	56 15	-3 25
1932 11 17	56 12	-3 25
1932 11 18	56 09	-3 25
1932 11 19	56 06	-3 25
1932 11 20	56 02	-3 25
1932 11 21	55 59	-3 25
1932 11 22	55 56	-3 25
1932 11 23	55 53	-3 25
1932 11 24	55 50	-3 25
1932 11 25	55 46	-3 25
1932 11 26	55 43	-3 26
1932 11 27	55 40	-3 26
1932 11 28	55 37	-3 26
1932 11 29	55 34	-3 26
1932 11 30	55 30	-3 26
1932 12 01	55 27	-3 26
1932 12 02	55 24	-3 26
1932 12 03	55 21	-3 26
1932 12 04	55 18	-3 26
1932 12 05	55 15	-3 26
1932 12 06	55 12	-3 26
1932 12 07	55 09	-3 26
1932 12 08	55 06	-3 26
1932 12 09	55 03	-3 26
1932 12 10	55 00	-3 26
1932 12 11	54 57	-3 26
1932 12 12	54 54	-3 26
1932 12 13	54 52	-3 26
1932 12 14	54 49	-3 26
1932 12 15	54 46	-3 26
1932 12 16	54 43	-3 26
1932 12 17	54 41	-3 26
1932 12 18	54 38	-3 26
1932 12 19	54 35	-3 26
1932 12 20	54 33	-3 26
1932 12 21	54 30	-3 26
1932 12 22	54 28	-3 26
1932 12 23	54 25	-3 26
1932 12 24	54 23	-3 26
1932 12 25	54 21	-3 26
1932 12 26	54 18	-3 25
1932 12 27	54 16	-3 25
1932 12 28	54 14	-3 25
1932 12 29	54 12	-3 25
1932 12 30	54 10	-3 25
1932 12 31	54 08	-3 25
1933 01 01	54 06	-3 25
1933 01 02	54 04	-3 25
1933 01 03	54 02	-3 25
1933 01 04	54 00	-3 25
1933 01 05	53 58	-3 25
1933 01 06	53 56	-3 25
1933 01 07	53 55	-3 25
1933 01 08	53 53	-3 24
1933 01 09	53 52	-3 24
1933 01 10	53 50	-3 24
1933 01 11	53 49	-3 24
1933 01 12	53 47	-3 24
1933 01 13	53 46	-3 24
1933 01 14	53 45	-3 24
1933 01 15	53 44	-3 24
1933 01 16	53 43	-3 24
1933 01 17	53 42	-3 24
1933 01 18	53 41	-3 23
1933 01 19	53 40	-3 23
1933 01 20	53 39	-3 23
1933 01 21	53 38	-3 23
1933 01 22	53 37	-3 23
1933 01 23	53 37	-3 23
1933 01 24	53 36	-3 23
1933 01 25	53 36	-3 23
1933 01 26	53 35	-3 22
1933 01 27	53 35	-3 22
1933 01 28	53 35	-3 22
1933 01 29	53 34	-3 22
1933 01 30	53 34	-3 22
1933 01 31	53 34	-3 22
1933 02 01	53 34	-3 22
1933 02 02	53 34	-3 22
1933 02 03	53 34	-3 21
1933 02 04	53 34	-3 21
1933 02 05	53 34	-3 21
1933 02 06	53 35	-3 21
1933 02 07	53 35	-3 21
1933 02 08	53 36	-3 21
1933 02 09	53 36	-3 21
1933 02 10	53 37	-3 20
1933 02 11	53 37	-3 20
1933 02 12	53 38	-3 20
1933 02 13	53 39	-3 20
1933 02 14	53 40	-3 20
1933 02 15	53 40	-3 20
1933 02 16	53 41	-3 20
1933 02 17	53 42	-3 20
1933 02 18	53 44	-3 19
1933 02 19	53 45	-3 19
1933 02 20	53 46	-3 19
1933 02 21	53 47	-3 19
1933 02 22	53 49	-3 19
1933 02 23	53 50	-3 19
1933 02 24	53 51	-3 19
1933 02 25	53 53	-3 18
1933 02 26	53 55	-3 18
1933 02 27	53 56	-3 18
1933 02 28	53 58	-3 18
1933 03 01	54 00	-3 18
1933 03 02	54 02	-3 18
1933 03 03	54 04	-3 18
1933 03 04	54 05	-3 18
1933 03 05	54 07	-3 18
1933 03 06	54 10	-3 17
1933 03 07	54 12	-3 17
1933 03 08	54 14	-3 17
1933 03 09	54 16	-3 17
1933 03 10	54 18	-3 17
1933 03 11	54 21	-3 17
1933 03 12	54 23	-3 17
1933 03 13	54 26	-3 17
1933 03 14	54 28	-3 17
1933 03 15	54 31	-3 16
1933 03 16	54 33	-3 16
1933 03 17	54 36	-3 16
1933 03 18	54 39	-3 16
1933 03 19	54 42	-3 16
1933 03 20	54 45	-3 16
1933 03 21	54 47	-3 16
1933 03 22	54 50	-3 16
1933 03 23	54 53	-3 16
1933 03 24	54 56	-3 16
1933 03 25	54 59	-3 16
1933 03 26	55 03	-3 15
1933 03 27	55 06	-3 15
1933 03 28	55 09	-3 15
1933 03 29	55 12	-3 15
1933 03 30	55 15	-3 15
1933 03 31	55 19	-3 15
1933 04 01	55 22	-3 15
1933 04 02	55 26	-3 15
1933 04 03	55 29	-3 15
1933 04 04	55 33	-3 15
1933 04 05	55 36	-3 15
1933 04 06	55 40	-3 15
1933 04 07	55 43	-3 15
1933 04 08	55 47	-3 15
1933 04 09	55 51	-3 15
1933 04 10	55 54	-3 15
1933 04 11	55 58	-3 15
1933 04 12	56 02	-3 15
1933 04 13	56 06	-3 15
1933 04 14	56 09	-3 14
1933 04 15	56 13	-3 14
1933 04 16	56 17	-3 14
1933 04 17	56 21	-3 14
1933 04 18	56 25	-3 14
1933 04 19	56 29	-3 14
1933 04 20	56 33	-3 14
1933 04 21	56 37	-3 14
1933 04 22	56 41	-3 14
1933 04 23	56 45	-3 14
1933 04 24	56 49	-3 14
1933 04 25	56 53	-3 14
1933 04 26	56 57	-3 14
1933 04 27	57 02	-3 14
1933 04 28	57 06	-3 14
1933 04 29	57 10	-3 14
1933 04 30	57 14	-3 14
1933 05 01	57 18	-3 14
1933 05 02	57 23	-3 14
1933 05 03	57 27	-3 14
1933 05 04	57 31	-3 14
1933 05 05	57 36	-3 15
1933 05 06	57 40	-3 15
1933 05 07	57 44	-3 15
1933 05 08	57 49	-3 15
1933 05 09	57 53	-3 15
1933 05 10	57 57	-3 15
1933 05 11	58 02	-3 15
1933 05 12	58 06	-3 15
1933 05 13	58 10	-3 15
1933 05 14	58 15	-3 15
1933 05 15	58 19	-3 15
1933 05 16	58 24	-3 15
1933 05 17	58 28	-3 15
1933 05 18	58 32	-3 15
1933 05 19	58 37	-3 15
1933 05 20	58 41	-3 15
1933 05 21	58 46	-3 15
1933 05 22	58 50	-3 16
1933 05 23	58 54	-3 16
1933 05 24	58 59	-3 16
1933 05 25	59 03	-3 16

Chiron

1933 05 26	59 08	-3 16
1933 05 27	59 12	-3 16
1933 05 28	59 16	-3 16
1933 05 29	59 21	-3 16
1933 05 30	59 25	-3 16
1933 05 31	59 29	-3 16
1933 06 01	59 34	-3 17
1933 06 02	59 38	-3 17
1933 06 03	59 43	-3 17
1933 06 04	59 47	-3 17
1933 06 05	59 51	-3 17
1933 06 06	59 55	-3 17
1933 06 07	60 00	-3 17
1933 06 08	60 04	-3 17
1933 06 09	60 08	-3 18
1933 06 10	60 13	-3 18
1933 06 11	60 17	-3 18
1933 06 12	60 21	-3 18
1933 06 13	60 25	-3 18
1933 06 14	60 29	-3 18
1933 06 15	60 34	-3 19
1933 06 16	60 38	-3 19
1933 06 17	60 42	-3 19
1933 06 18	60 46	-3 19
1933 06 19	60 50	-3 19
1933 06 20	60 54	-3 19
1933 06 21	60 58	-3 20
1933 06 22	61 02	-3 20
1933 06 23	61 06	-3 20
1933 06 24	61 10	-3 20
1933 06 25	61 14	-3 20
1933 06 26	61 18	-3 21
1933 06 27	61 22	-3 21
1933 06 28	61 26	-3 21
1933 06 29	61 30	-3 21
1933 06 30	61 33	-3 21
1933 07 01	61 37	-3 22
1933 07 02	61 41	-3 22
1933 07 03	61 45	-3 22
1933 07 04	61 48	-3 22
1933 07 05	61 52	-3 22
1933 07 06	61 55	-3 23
1933 07 07	61 59	-3 23
1933 07 08	62 03	-3 23
1933 07 09	62 06	-3 23
1933 07 10	62 10	-3 24
1933 07 11	62 13	-3 24
1933 07 12	62 16	-3 24
1933 07 13	62 20	-3 24
1933 07 14	62 23	-3 25
1933 07 15	62 26	-3 25
1933 07 16	62 29	-3 25
1933 07 17	62 33	-3 25
1933 07 18	62 36	-3 26
1933 07 19	62 39	-3 26
1933 07 20	62 42	-3 26
1933 07 21	62 45	-3 26
1933 07 22	62 48	-3 27
1933 07 23	62 51	-3 27
1933 07 24	62 54	-3 27
1933 07 25	62 56	-3 27
1933 07 26	62 59	-3 28
1933 07 27	63 02	-3 28
1933 07 28	63 04	-3 28
1933 07 29	63 07	-3 29
1933 07 30	63 10	-3 29
1933 07 31	63 12	-3 29
1933 08 01	63 15	-3 29
1933 08 02	63 17	-3 30
1933 08 03	63 19	-3 30
1933 08 04	63 22	-3 30
1933 08 05	63 24	-3 31
1933 08 06	63 26	-3 31
1933 08 07	63 28	-3 31
1933 08 08	63 30	-3 32
1933 08 09	63 32	-3 32
1933 08 10	63 34	-3 32
1933 08 11	63 36	-3 32
1933 08 12	63 38	-3 33
1933 08 13	63 40	-3 33
1933 08 14	63 42	-3 33
1933 08 15	63 43	-3 34
1933 08 16	63 45	-3 34
1933 08 17	63 46	-3 34
1933 08 18	63 48	-3 35
1933 08 19	63 49	-3 35
1933 08 20	63 51	-3 35
1933 08 21	63 52	-3 36
1933 08 22	63 53	-3 36
1933 08 23	63 55	-3 36
1933 08 24	63 56	-3 37
1933 08 25	63 57	-3 37
1933 08 26	63 58	-3 37
1933 08 27	63 59	-3 38
1933 08 28	63 59	-3 38
1933 08 29	64 00	-3 38
1933 08 30	64 01	-3 39
1933 08 31	64 02	-3 39
1933 09 01	64 02	-3 39
1933 09 02	64 03	-3 40
1933 09 03	64 03	-3 40
1933 09 04	64 04	-3 40
1933 09 05	64 04	-3 41
1933 09 06	64 04	-3 41
1933 09 07	64 05	-3 41
1933 09 08	64 05	-3 42
1933 09 09	64 05	-3 42
1933 09 10	64 05	-3 42
1933 09 11	64 05	-3 43
1933 09 12	64 05	-3 43
1933 09 13	64 05	-3 43
1933 09 14	64 04	-3 44
1933 09 15	64 04	-3 44
1933 09 16	64 04	-3 44
1933 09 17	64 03	-3 45
1933 09 18	64 03	-3 45
1933 09 19	64 02	-3 45
1933 09 20	64 01	-3 46
1933 09 21	64 01	-3 46
1933 09 22	64 00	-3 46
1933 09 23	63 59	-3 47
1933 09 24	63 58	-3 47
1933 09 25	63 57	-3 47
1933 09 26	63 56	-3 48
1933 09 27	63 55	-3 48
1933 09 28	63 54	-3 48
1933 09 29	63 53	-3 49
1933 09 30	63 52	-3 49
1933 10 01	63 50	-3 49
1933 10 02	63 49	-3 50
1933 10 03	63 47	-3 50
1933 10 04	63 46	-3 50
1933 10 05	63 44	-3 51
1933 10 06	63 43	-3 51
1933 10 07	63 41	-3 51
1933 10 08	63 39	-3 51
1933 10 09	63 37	-3 52
1933 10 10	63 35	-3 52
1933 10 11	63 34	-3 52
1933 10 12	63 32	-3 53
1933 10 13	63 30	-3 53
1933 10 14	63 27	-3 53
1933 10 15	63 25	-3 53
1933 10 16	63 23	-3 54
1933 10 17	63 21	-3 54
1933 10 18	63 19	-3 54
1933 10 19	63 16	-3 55
1933 10 20	63 14	-3 55
1933 10 21	63 11	-3 55
1933 10 22	63 09	-3 55
1933 10 23	63 06	-3 56
1933 10 24	63 04	-3 56
1933 10 25	63 01	-3 56
1933 10 26	62 58	-3 56
1933 10 27	62 56	-3 57
1933 10 28	62 53	-3 57
1933 10 29	62 50	-3 57
1933 10 30	62 47	-3 57
1933 10 31	62 45	-3 57
1933 11 01	62 42	-3 58
1933 11 02	62 39	-3 58
1933 11 03	62 36	-3 58
1933 11 04	62 33	-3 58
1933 11 05	62 30	-3 59
1933 11 06	62 27	-3 59
1933 11 07	62 24	-3 59
1933 11 08	62 21	-3 59
1933 11 09	62 17	-3 59
1933 11 10	62 14	-3 59
1933 11 11	62 11	-4 00
1933 11 12	62 08	-4 00
1933 11 13	62 05	-4 00
1933 11 14	62 01	-4 00
1933 11 15	61 58	-4 00
1933 11 16	61 55	-4 00
1933 11 17	61 52	-4 01
1933 11 18	61 48	-4 01
1933 11 19	61 45	-4 01
1933 11 20	61 42	-4 01
1933 11 21	61 38	-4 01
1933 11 22	61 35	-4 01
1933 11 23	61 32	-4 01
1933 11 24	61 28	-4 01
1933 11 25	61 25	-4 01
1933 11 26	61 22	-4 02
1933 11 27	61 18	-4 02
1933 11 28	61 15	-4 02
1933 11 29	61 12	-4 02
1933 11 30	61 08	-4 02
1933 12 01	61 05	-4 02
1933 12 02	61 02	-4 02
1933 12 03	60 59	-4 02
1933 12 04	60 55	-4 02
1933 12 05	60 52	-4 02
1933 12 06	60 49	-4 02
1933 12 07	60 46	-4 02
1933 12 08	60 42	-4 02
1933 12 09	60 39	-4 02
1933 12 10	60 36	-4 02
1933 12 11	60 33	-4 02
1933 12 12	60 30	-4 02
1933 12 13	60 27	-4 02
1933 12 14	60 24	-4 02
1933 12 15	60 21	-4 02
1933 12 16	60 18	-4 02
1933 12 17	60 15	-4 02
1933 12 18	60 12	-4 02
1933 12 19	60 09	-4 02
1933 12 20	60 06	-4 02
1933 12 21	60 03	-4 02
1933 12 22	60 00	-4 02
1933 12 23	59 58	-4 02
1933 12 24	59 55	-4 02
1933 12 25	59 52	-4 02
1933 12 26	59 50	-4 02
1933 12 27	59 47	-4 02
1933 12 28	59 45	-4 02
1933 12 29	59 42	-4 01
1933 12 30	59 40	-4 01
1933 12 31	59 37	-4 01
1934 01 01	59 35	-4 01
1934 01 02	59 33	-4 01
1934 01 03	59 30	-4 01
1934 01 04	59 28	-4 01
1934 01 05	59 26	-4 01
1934 01 06	59 24	-4 01
1934 01 07	59 22	-4 01
1934 01 08	59 20	-4 00
1934 01 09	59 18	-4 00
1934 01 10	59 16	-4 00
1934 01 11	59 15	-4 00
1934 01 12	59 13	-4 00
1934 01 13	59 11	-4 00
1934 01 14	59 10	-4 00
1934 01 15	59 08	-4 00
1934 01 16	59 07	-3 59
1934 01 17	59 05	-3 59
1934 01 18	59 04	-3 59
1934 01 19	59 03	-3 59
1934 01 20	59 01	-3 59
1934 01 21	59 00	-3 59
1934 01 22	58 59	-3 59
1934 01 23	58 58	-3 58
1934 01 24	58 57	-3 58
1934 01 25	58 56	-3 58
1934 01 26	58 56	-3 58
1934 01 27	58 55	-3 58
1934 01 28	58 54	-3 58
1934 01 29	58 54	-3 57
1934 01 30	58 53	-3 57
1934 01 31	58 53	-3 57
1934 02 01	58 52	-3 57
1934 02 02	58 52	-3 57
1934 02 03	58 52	-3 57
1934 02 04	58 51	-3 56
1934 02 05	58 51	-3 56
1934 02 06	58 51	-3 56
1934 02 07	58 51	-3 56
1934 02 08	58 51	-3 56
1934 02 09	58 51	-3 55
1934 02 10	58 52	-3 55
1934 02 11	58 52	-3 55
1934 02 12	58 52	-3 55
1934 02 13	58 53	-3 55
1934 02 14	58 53	-3 55
1934 02 15	58 54	-3 54
1934 02 16	58 55	-3 54
1934 02 17	58 55	-3 54
1934 02 18	58 56	-3 54
1934 02 19	58 57	-3 54
1934 02 20	58 58	-3 54
1934 02 21	58 59	-3 53
1934 02 22	59 00	-3 53
1934 02 23	59 01	-3 53
1934 02 24	59 02	-3 53
1934 02 25	59 03	-3 53
1934 02 26	59 05	-3 52
1934 02 27	59 06	-3 52
1934 02 28	59 08	-3 52
1934 03 01	59 09	-3 52
1934 03 02	59 11	-3 52
1934 03 03	59 12	-3 52
1934 03 04	59 14	-3 51
1934 03 05	59 16	-3 51
1934 03 06	59 18	-3 51
1934 03 07	59 20	-3 51
1934 03 08	59 22	-3 51
1934 03 09	59 24	-3 51
1934 03 10	59 26	-3 50
1934 03 11	59 28	-3 50
1934 03 12	59 30	-3 50
1934 03 13	59 32	-3 50
1934 03 14	59 35	-3 50
1934 03 15	59 37	-3 50
1934 03 16	59 40	-3 50
1934 03 17	59 42	-3 49
1934 03 18	59 45	-3 49
1934 03 19	59 47	-3 49
1934 03 20	59 50	-3 49
1934 03 21	59 53	-3 49
1934 03 22	59 55	-3 49
1934 03 23	59 58	-3 49
1934 03 24	60 01	-3 48
1934 03 25	60 04	-3 48
1934 03 26	60 07	-3 48
1934 03 27	60 10	-3 48
1934 03 28	60 13	-3 48
1934 03 29	60 16	-3 48
1934 03 30	60 20	-3 48
1934 03 31	60 23	-3 48
1934 04 01	60 26	-3 48
1934 04 02	60 29	-3 47
1934 04 03	60 33	-3 47
1934 04 04	60 36	-3 47
1934 04 05	60 40	-3 47
1934 04 06	60 43	-3 47
1934 04 07	60 47	-3 47
1934 04 08	60 50	-3 47
1934 04 09	60 54	-3 47
1934 04 10	60 58	-3 47
1934 04 11	61 01	-3 47
1934 04 12	61 05	-3 47
1934 04 13	61 09	-3 46
1934 04 14	61 13	-3 46
1934 04 15	61 16	-3 46
1934 04 16	61 20	-3 46
1934 04 17	61 24	-3 46
1934 04 18	61 28	-3 46
1934 04 19	61 32	-3 46
1934 04 20	61 36	-3 46
1934 04 21	61 40	-3 46
1934 04 22	61 44	-3 46
1934 04 23	61 48	-3 46
1934 04 24	61 52	-3 46
1934 04 25	61 57	-3 46
1934 04 26	62 01	-3 46
1934 04 27	62 05	-3 46
1934 04 28	62 09	-3 46
1934 04 29	62 14	-3 46
1934 04 30	62 18	-3 46
1934 05 01	62 22	-3 46
1934 05 02	62 26	-3 46
1934 05 03	62 31	-3 46
1934 05 04	62 35	-3 46
1934 05 05	62 40	-3 46
1934 05 06	62 44	-3 46
1934 05 07	62 48	-3 46
1934 05 08	62 53	-3 46
1934 05 09	62 57	-3 46
1934 05 10	63 02	-3 46
1934 05 11	63 06	-3 46
1934 05 12	63 11	-3 46
1934 05 13	63 15	-3 46
1934 05 14	63 20	-3 46
1934 05 15	63 24	-3 46
1934 05 16	63 29	-3 46
1934 05 17	63 33	-3 46
1934 05 18	63 38	-3 46
1934 05 19	63 43	-3 46
1934 05 20	63 47	-3 46
1934 05 21	63 52	-3 46
1934 05 22	63 56	-3 46
1934 05 23	64 01	-3 46
1934 05 24	64 05	-3 46
1934 05 25	64 10	-3 46
1934 05 26	64 15	-3 47
1934 05 27	64 19	-3 47
1934 05 28	64 24	-3 47
1934 05 29	64 28	-3 47
1934 05 30	64 33	-3 47
1934 05 31	64 38	-3 47
1934 06 01	64 42	-3 47
1934 06 02	64 47	-3 47
1934 06 03	64 51	-3 47
1934 06 04	64 56	-3 47
1934 06 05	65 01	-3 48
1934 06 06	65 05	-3 48
1934 06 07	65 10	-3 48
1934 06 08	65 14	-3 48
1934 06 09	65 19	-3 48
1934 06 10	65 23	-3 48
1934 06 11	65 28	-3 48
1934 06 12	65 32	-3 48
1934 06 13	65 37	-3 49
1934 06 14	65 41	-3 49
1934 06 15	65 46	-3 49
1934 06 16	65 50	-3 49
1934 06 17	65 55	-3 49
1934 06 18	65 59	-3 49
1934 06 19	66 03	-3 50
1934 06 20	66 08	-3 50
1934 06 21	66 12	-3 50
1934 06 22	66 17	-3 50
1934 06 23	66 21	-3 50
1934 06 24	66 25	-3 50
1934 06 25	66 29	-3 51
1934 06 26	66 34	-3 51
1934 06 27	66 38	-3 51
1934 06 28	66 42	-3 51
1934 06 29	66 46	-3 51
1934 06 30	66 50	-3 52
1934 07 01	66 55	-3 52
1934 07 02	66 59	-3 52
1934 07 03	67 03	-3 52
1934 07 04	67 07	-3 53
1934 07 05	67 11	-3 53
1934 07 06	67 15	-3 53
1934 07 07	67 19	-3 53
1934 07 08	67 23	-3 53
1934 07 09	67 27	-3 54
1934 07 10	67 30	-3 54
1934 07 11	67 34	-3 54
1934 07 12	67 38	-3 54
1934 07 13	67 42	-3 55
1934 07 14	67 45	-3 55
1934 07 15	67 49	-3 55
1934 07 16	67 53	-3 56
1934 07 17	67 56	-3 56
1934 07 18	68 00	-3 56

1934	07	19	68	03	-3	56
1934	07	20	68	07	-3	57
1934	07	21	68	10	-3	57
1934	07	22	68	14	-3	57
1934	07	23	68	17	-3	57
1934	07	24	68	20	-3	58
1934	07	25	68	24	-3	58
1934	07	26	68	27	-3	58
1934	07	27	68	30	-3	59
1934	07	28	68	33	-3	59
1934	07	29	68	36	-3	59
1934	07	30	68	39	-4	00
1934	07	31	68	42	-4	00
1934	08	01	68	45	-4	00
1934	08	02	68	48	-4	01
1934	08	03	68	51	-4	01
1934	08	04	68	53	-4	01
1934	08	05	68	56	-4	02
1934	08	06	68	59	-4	02
1934	08	07	69	01	-4	02
1934	08	08	69	04	-4	03
1934	08	09	69	06	-4	03
1934	08	10	69	09	-4	03
1934	08	11	69	11	-4	04
1934	08	12	69	14	-4	04
1934	08	13	69	16	-4	04
1934	08	14	69	18	-4	05
1934	08	15	69	20	-4	05
1934	08	16	69	22	-4	05
1934	08	17	69	24	-4	06
1934	08	18	69	26	-4	06
1934	08	19	69	28	-4	06
1934	08	20	69	30	-4	07
1934	08	21	69	32	-4	07
1934	08	22	69	34	-4	07
1934	08	23	69	35	-4	08
1934	08	24	69	37	-4	08
1934	08	25	69	38	-4	09
1934	08	26	69	40	-4	09
1934	08	27	69	41	-4	09
1934	08	28	69	43	-4	10
1934	08	29	69	44	-4	10
1934	08	30	69	45	-4	10
1934	08	31	69	46	-4	11
1934	09	01	69	48	-4	11
1934	09	02	69	49	-4	12
1934	09	03	69	50	-4	12
1934	09	04	69	50	-4	12
1934	09	05	69	51	-4	13
1934	09	06	69	52	-4	13
1934	09	07	69	53	-4	14
1934	09	08	69	53	-4	14
1934	09	09	69	54	-4	14
1934	09	10	69	54	-4	15
1934	09	11	69	55	-4	15
1934	09	12	69	55	-4	15
1934	09	13	69	55	-4	16
1934	09	14	69	56	-4	16
1934	09	15	69	56	-4	17
1934	09	16	69	56	-4	17
1934	09	17	69	56	-4	17
1934	09	18	69	56	-4	18
1934	09	19	69	56	-4	18
1934	09	20	69	55	-4	19
1934	09	21	69	55	-4	19
1934	09	22	69	55	-4	19
1934	09	23	69	54	-4	20
1934	09	24	69	54	-4	20
1934	09	25	69	53	-4	20
1934	09	26	69	53	-4	21
1934	09	27	69	52	-4	21
1934	09	28	69	51	-4	22
1934	09	29	69	51	-4	22
1934	09	30	69	50	-4	22
1934	10	01	69	49	-4	23
1934	10	02	69	48	-4	23
1934	10	03	69	47	-4	24
1934	10	04	69	45	-4	24
1934	10	05	69	44	-4	24
1934	10	06	69	43	-4	25
1934	10	07	69	42	-4	25
1934	10	08	69	40	-4	25
1934	10	09	69	39	-4	26
1934	10	10	69	37	-4	26
1934	10	11	69	36	-4	26
1934	10	12	69	34	-4	27
1934	10	13	69	32	-4	27
1934	10	14	69	30	-4	27
1934	10	15	69	29	-4	28
1934	10	16	69	27	-4	28
1934	10	17	69	25	-4	28
1934	10	18	69	23	-4	29
1934	10	19	69	21	-4	29
1934	10	20	69	18	-4	29
1934	10	21	69	16	-4	30
1934	10	22	69	14	-4	30
1934	10	23	69	12	-4	30
1934	10	24	69	09	-4	31
1934	10	25	69	07	-4	31
1934	10	26	69	04	-4	31
1934	10	27	69	02	-4	32
1934	10	28	68	59	-4	32
1934	10	29	68	57	-4	32
1934	10	30	68	54	-4	33
1934	10	31	68	51	-4	33
1934	11	01	68	49	-4	33
1934	11	02	68	46	-4	33
1934	11	03	68	43	-4	34
1934	11	04	68	40	-4	34
1934	11	05	68	37	-4	34
1934	11	06	68	34	-4	34
1934	11	07	68	31	-4	35
1934	11	08	68	28	-4	35
1934	11	09	68	25	-4	35
1934	11	10	68	22	-4	35
1934	11	11	68	19	-4	36
1934	11	12	68	16	-4	36
1934	11	13	68	13	-4	36
1934	11	14	68	10	-4	36
1934	11	15	68	06	-4	36
1934	11	16	68	03	-4	37
1934	11	17	68	00	-4	37
1934	11	18	67	56	-4	37
1934	11	19	67	53	-4	37
1934	11	20	67	50	-4	37
1934	11	21	67	46	-4	37
1934	11	22	67	43	-4	38
1934	11	23	67	40	-4	38
1934	11	24	67	36	-4	38
1934	11	25	67	33	-4	38
1934	11	26	67	29	-4	38
1934	11	27	67	26	-4	38
1934	11	28	67	23	-4	38
1934	11	29	67	19	-4	38
1934	11	30	67	16	-4	39
1934	12	01	67	12	-4	39
1934	12	02	67	09	-4	39
1934	12	03	67	05	-4	39
1934	12	04	67	02	-4	39
1934	12	05	66	59	-4	39
1934	12	06	66	55	-4	39
1934	12	07	66	52	-4	39
1934	12	08	66	48	-4	39
1934	12	09	66	45	-4	39
1934	12	10	66	42	-4	39
1934	12	11	66	38	-4	39
1934	12	12	66	35	-4	39
1934	12	13	66	31	-4	39
1934	12	14	66	28	-4	39
1934	12	15	66	25	-4	39
1934	12	16	66	22	-4	39
1934	12	17	66	18	-4	39
1934	12	18	66	15	-4	39
1934	12	19	66	12	-4	39
1934	12	20	66	09	-4	39
1934	12	21	66	06	-4	39
1934	12	22	66	03	-4	39
1934	12	23	66	00	-4	39
1934	12	24	65	57	-4	39
1934	12	25	65	54	-4	39
1934	12	26	65	51	-4	39
1934	12	27	65	48	-4	39
1934	12	28	65	45	-4	39
1934	12	29	65	42	-4	39
1934	12	30	65	39	-4	39
1934	12	31	65	36	-4	39
1935	01	01	65	34	-4	38
1935	01	02	65	31	-4	38
1935	01	03	65	29	-4	38
1935	01	04	65	26	-4	38
1935	01	05	65	23	-4	38
1935	01	06	65	21	-4	38
1935	01	07	65	19	-4	38
1935	01	08	65	16	-4	38
1935	01	09	65	14	-4	37
1935	01	10	65	12	-4	37
1935	01	11	65	10	-4	37
1935	01	12	65	07	-4	37
1935	01	13	65	05	-4	37
1935	01	14	65	03	-4	37
1935	01	15	65	02	-4	37
1935	01	16	65	00	-4	36
1935	01	17	64	58	-4	36
1935	01	18	64	56	-4	36
1935	01	19	64	54	-4	36
1935	01	20	64	53	-4	36
1935	01	21	64	51	-4	36
1935	01	22	64	50	-4	35
1935	01	23	64	48	-4	35
1935	01	24	64	47	-4	35
1935	01	25	64	46	-4	35
1935	01	26	64	44	-4	35
1935	01	27	64	43	-4	34
1935	01	28	64	42	-4	34
1935	01	29	64	41	-4	34
1935	01	30	64	40	-4	34
1935	01	31	64	39	-4	34
1935	02	01	64	39	-4	33
1935	02	02	64	38	-4	33
1935	02	03	64	37	-4	33
1935	02	04	64	37	-4	33
1935	02	05	64	36	-4	32
1935	02	06	64	36	-4	32
1935	02	07	64	35	-4	32
1935	02	08	64	35	-4	32
1935	02	09	64	35	-4	32
1935	02	10	64	35	-4	31
1935	02	11	64	34	-4	31
1935	02	12	64	34	-4	31
1935	02	13	64	34	-4	31
1935	02	14	64	35	-4	30
1935	02	15	64	35	-4	30
1935	02	16	64	35	-4	30
1935	02	17	64	35	-4	30
1935	02	18	64	36	-4	29
1935	02	19	64	36	-4	29
1935	02	20	64	37	-4	29
1935	02	21	64	38	-4	29
1935	02	22	64	38	-4	29
1935	02	23	64	39	-4	28
1935	02	24	64	40	-4	28
1935	02	25	64	41	-4	28
1935	02	26	64	42	-4	28
1935	02	27	64	43	-4	27
1935	02	28	64	44	-4	27
1935	03	01	64	45	-4	27
1935	03	02	64	47	-4	27
1935	03	03	64	48	-4	27
1935	03	04	64	49	-4	26
1935	03	05	64	51	-4	26
1935	03	06	64	52	-4	26
1935	03	07	64	54	-4	26
1935	03	08	64	56	-4	25
1935	03	09	64	58	-4	25
1935	03	10	64	59	-4	25
1935	03	11	65	01	-4	25
1935	03	12	65	03	-4	25
1935	03	13	65	05	-4	24
1935	03	14	65	07	-4	24
1935	03	15	65	09	-4	24
1935	03	16	65	12	-4	24
1935	03	17	65	14	-4	24
1935	03	18	65	16	-4	23
1935	03	19	65	19	-4	23
1935	03	20	65	21	-4	23
1935	03	21	65	24	-4	23
1935	03	22	65	26	-4	23
1935	03	23	65	29	-4	22
1935	03	24	65	32	-4	22
1935	03	25	65	34	-4	22
1935	03	26	65	37	-4	22
1935	03	27	65	40	-4	22
1935	03	28	65	43	-4	21
1935	03	29	65	46	-4	21
1935	03	30	65	49	-4	21
1935	03	31	65	52	-4	21
1935	04	01	65	55	-4	21
1935	04	02	65	58	-4	21
1935	04	03	66	02	-4	20
1935	04	04	66	05	-4	20
1935	04	05	66	08	-4	20
1935	04	06	66	12	-4	20
1935	04	07	66	15	-4	20
1935	04	08	66	19	-4	20
1935	04	09	66	22	-4	20
1935	04	10	66	26	-4	19
1935	04	11	66	29	-4	19
1935	04	12	66	33	-4	19
1935	04	13	66	37	-4	19
1935	04	14	66	41	-4	19
1935	04	15	66	44	-4	19
1935	04	16	66	48	-4	19
1935	04	17	66	52	-4	19
1935	04	18	66	56	-4	18
1935	04	19	67	00	-4	18
1935	04	20	67	04	-4	18
1935	04	21	67	08	-4	18
1935	04	22	67	12	-4	18
1935	04	23	67	16	-4	18
1935	04	24	67	20	-4	18
1935	04	25	67	24	-4	18
1935	04	26	67	29	-4	18
1935	04	27	67	33	-4	18
1935	04	28	67	37	-4	18
1935	04	29	67	41	-4	18
1935	04	30	67	46	-4	17
1935	05	01	67	50	-4	17
1935	05	02	67	54	-4	17
1935	05	03	67	59	-4	17
1935	05	04	68	03	-4	17
1935	05	05	68	08	-4	17
1935	05	06	68	12	-4	17
1935	05	07	68	17	-4	17
1935	05	08	68	21	-4	17
1935	05	09	68	26	-4	17
1935	05	10	68	30	-4	17
1935	05	11	68	35	-4	17
1935	05	12	68	40	-4	17
1935	05	13	68	44	-4	17
1935	05	14	68	49	-4	17
1935	05	15	68	54	-4	17
1935	05	16	68	58	-4	17
1935	05	17	69	03	-4	17
1935	05	18	69	08	-4	17
1935	05	19	69	12	-4	17
1935	05	20	69	17	-4	17
1935	05	21	69	22	-4	17
1935	05	22	69	27	-4	17
1935	05	23	69	31	-4	17
1935	05	24	69	36	-4	17
1935	05	25	69	41	-4	17
1935	05	26	69	46	-4	17
1935	05	27	69	51	-4	17
1935	05	28	69	55	-4	17
1935	05	29	70	00	-4	18
1935	05	30	70	05	-4	18
1935	05	31	70	10	-4	18
1935	06	01	70	15	-4	18
1935	06	02	70	20	-4	18
1935	06	03	70	24	-4	18
1935	06	04	70	29	-4	18
1935	06	05	70	34	-4	18
1935	06	06	70	39	-4	18
1935	06	07	70	44	-4	18
1935	06	08	70	49	-4	18
1935	06	09	70	53	-4	19
1935	06	10	70	58	-4	19
1935	06	11	71	03	-4	19
1935	06	12	71	08	-4	19
1935	06	13	71	13	-4	19
1935	06	14	71	17	-4	19
1935	06	15	71	22	-4	19
1935	06	16	71	27	-4	19
1935	06	17	71	32	-4	20
1935	06	18	71	36	-4	20
1935	06	19	71	41	-4	20
1935	06	20	71	46	-4	20
1935	06	21	71	51	-4	20
1935	06	22	71	55	-4	20
1935	06	23	72	00	-4	21
1935	06	24	72	05	-4	21
1935	06	25	72	09	-4	21
1935	06	26	72	14	-4	21
1935	06	27	72	18	-4	21
1935	06	28	72	23	-4	21
1935	06	29	72	28	-4	22
1935	06	30	72	32	-4	22
1935	07	01	72	37	-4	22
1935	07	02	72	41	-4	22
1935	07	03	72	46	-4	22
1935	07	04	72	50	-4	23
1935	07	05	72	54	-4	23
1935	07	06	72	59	-4	23
1935	07	07	73	03	-4	23
1935	07	08	73	07	-4	24
1935	07	09	73	12	-4	24
1935	07	10	73	16	-4	24
1935	07	11	73	20	-4	24
1935	07	12	73	24	-4	25
1935	07	13	73	29	-4	25
1935	07	14	73	33	-4	25
1935	07	15	73	37	-4	25
1935	07	16	73	41	-4	26
1935	07	17	73	45	-4	26
1935	07	18	73	49	-4	26
1935	07	19	73	53	-4	27
1935	07	20	73	57	-4	27
1935	07	21	74	01	-4	27
1935	07	22	74	05	-4	27
1935	07	23	74	09	-4	28
1935	07	24	74	12	-4	28
1935	07	25	74	16	-4	28
1935	07	26	74	20	-4	29
1935	07	27	74	23	-4	29
1935	07	28	74	27	-4	29
1935	07	29	74	31	-4	30
1935	07	30	74	34	-4	30
1935	07	31	74	38	-4	30
1935	08	01	74	41	-4	31
1935	08	02	74	44	-4	31
1935	08	03	74	48	-4	31
1935	08	04	74	51	-4	32
1935	08	05	74	54	-4	32
1935	08	06	74	57	-4	32
1935	08	07	75	01	-4	33
1935	08	08	75	04	-4	33
1935	08	09	75	07	-4	33
1935	08	10	75	10	-4	34
1935	08	11	75	13	-4	34
1935	08	12	75	15	-4	34
1935	08	13	75	18	-4	35
1935	08	14	75	21	-4	35
1935	08	15	75	24	-4	36
1935	08	16	75	26	-4	36
1935	08	17	75	29	-4	36
1935	08	18	75	31	-4	37
1935	08	19	75	34	-4	37
1935	08	20	75	36	-4	38
1935	08	21	75	39	-4	38
1935	08	22	75	41	-4	38
1935	08	23	75	43	-4	39
1935	08	24	75	45	-4	39
1935	08	25	75	47	-4	40
1935	08	26	75	49	-4	40
1935	08	27	75	51	-4	40
1935	08	28	75	53	-4	41
1935	08	29	75	55	-4	41
1935	08	30	75	57	-4	42
1935	08	31	75	59	-4	42
1935	09	01	76	00	-4	42
1935	09	02	76	02	-4	43
1935	09	03	76	03	-4	43
1935	09	04	76	05	-4	44
1935	09	05	76	06	-4	44
1935	09	06	76	08	-4	45
1935	09	07	76	09	-4	45
1935	09	08	76	10	-4	46
1935	09	09	76	11	-4	46
1935	09	10	76	12	-4	46

1935 09 11	76 13	-4 47
1935 09 12	76 14	-4 47
1935 09 13	76 15	-4 48
1935 09 14	76 16	-4 48
1935 09 15	76 16	-4 49
1935 09 16	76 17	-4 49
1935 09 17	76 17	-4 49
1935 09 18	76 18	-4 50
1935 09 19	76 18	-4 50
1935 09 20	76 19	-4 51
1935 09 21	76 19	-4 51
1935 09 22	76 19	-4 52
1935 09 23	76 19	-4 52
1935 09 24	76 19	-4 53
1935 09 25	76 19	-4 53
1935 09 26	76 19	-4 53
1935 09 27	76 19	-4 54
1935 09 28	76 19	-4 54
1935 09 29	76 18	-4 55
1935 09 30	76 18	-4 55
1935 10 01	76 17	-4 56
1935 10 02	76 17	-4 56
1935 10 03	76 16	-4 57
1935 10 04	76 16	-4 57
1935 10 05	76 15	-4 57
1935 10 06	76 14	-4 58
1935 10 07	76 13	-4 58
1935 10 08	76 12	-4 59
1935 10 09	76 11	-4 59
1935 10 10	76 10	-5 00
1935 10 11	76 09	-5 00
1935 10 12	76 08	-5 00
1935 10 13	76 06	-5 01
1935 10 14	76 05	-5 01
1935 10 15	76 03	-5 02
1935 10 16	76 02	-5 02
1935 10 17	76 00	-5 02
1935 10 18	75 59	-5 03
1935 10 19	75 57	-5 03
1935 10 20	75 55	-5 04
1935 10 21	75 53	-5 04
1935 10 22	75 51	-5 04
1935 10 23	75 49	-5 05
1935 10 24	75 47	-5 05
1935 10 25	75 45	-5 06
1935 10 26	75 43	-5 06
1935 10 27	75 41	-5 06
1935 10 28	75 39	-5 07
1935 10 29	75 36	-5 07
1935 10 30	75 34	-5 07
1935 10 31	75 31	-5 08
1935 11 01	75 29	-5 08
1935 11 02	75 26	-5 08
1935 11 03	75 24	-5 09
1935 11 04	75 21	-5 09
1935 11 05	75 18	-5 09
1935 11 06	75 16	-5 10
1935 11 07	75 13	-5 10
1935 11 08	75 10	-5 10
1935 11 09	75 07	-5 11
1935 11 10	75 04	-5 11
1935 11 11	75 01	-5 11
1935 11 12	74 58	-5 12
1935 11 13	74 55	-5 12
1935 11 14	74 52	-5 12
1935 11 15	74 49	-5 12
1935 11 16	74 46	-5 13
1935 11 17	74 42	-5 13
1935 11 18	74 39	-5 13
1935 11 19	74 36	-5 13
1935 11 20	74 33	-5 14
1935 11 21	74 29	-5 14
1935 11 22	74 26	-5 14
1935 11 23	74 23	-5 14
1935 11 24	74 19	-5 14
1935 11 25	74 16	-5 15
1935 11 26	74 12	-5 15
1935 11 27	74 09	-5 15
1935 11 28	74 05	-5 15
1935 11 29	74 02	-5 15
1935 11 30	73 58	-5 15
1935 12 01	73 55	-5 16
1935 12 02	73 51	-5 16
1935 12 03	73 48	-5 16
1935 12 04	73 44	-5 16
1935 12 05	73 41	-5 16
1935 12 06	73 37	-5 16
1935 12 07	73 33	-5 16
1935 12 08	73 30	-5 16
1935 12 09	73 26	-5 16
1935 12 10	73 23	-5 17
1935 12 11	73 19	-5 17
1935 12 12	73 16	-5 17
1935 12 13	73 12	-5 17
1935 12 14	73 08	-5 17
1935 12 15	73 05	-5 17
1935 12 16	73 01	-5 17
1935 12 17	72 58	-5 17
1935 12 18	72 54	-5 17
1935 12 19	72 51	-5 17
1935 12 20	72 48	-5 17
1935 12 21	72 44	-5 17
1935 12 22	72 41	-5 17
1935 12 23	72 37	-5 17
1935 12 24	72 34	-5 17
1935 12 25	72 31	-5 17
1935 12 26	72 27	-5 17
1935 12 27	72 24	-5 17
1935 12 28	72 21	-5 17
1935 12 29	72 18	-5 16
1935 12 30	72 15	-5 16
1935 12 31	72 12	-5 16
1936 01 01	72 08	-5 16
1936 01 02	72 05	-5 16
1936 01 03	72 02	-5 16
1936 01 04	72 00	-5 16
1936 01 05	71 57	-5 16
1936 01 06	71 54	-5 16
1936 01 07	71 51	-5 16
1936 01 08	71 48	-5 15
1936 01 09	71 46	-5 15
1936 01 10	71 43	-5 15
1936 01 11	71 40	-5 15
1936 01 12	71 38	-5 15
1936 01 13	71 35	-5 15
1936 01 14	71 33	-5 14
1936 01 15	71 30	-5 14
1936 01 16	71 28	-5 14
1936 01 17	71 26	-5 14
1936 01 18	71 24	-5 14
1936 01 19	71 21	-5 14
1936 01 20	71 19	-5 13
1936 01 21	71 17	-5 13
1936 01 22	71 15	-5 13
1936 01 23	71 14	-5 13
1936 01 24	71 12	-5 12
1936 01 25	71 10	-5 12
1936 01 26	71 08	-5 12
1936 01 27	71 07	-5 12
1936 01 28	71 05	-5 12
1936 01 29	71 04	-5 11
1936 01 30	71 02	-5 11
1936 01 31	71 01	-5 11
1936 02 01	71 00	-5 11
1936 02 02	70 58	-5 10
1936 02 03	70 57	-5 10
1936 02 04	70 56	-5 10
1936 02 05	70 55	-5 10
1936 02 06	70 54	-5 09
1936 02 07	70 54	-5 09
1936 02 08	70 53	-5 09
1936 02 09	70 52	-5 08
1936 02 10	70 51	-5 08
1936 02 11	70 51	-5 08
1936 02 12	70 51	-5 08
1936 02 13	70 50	-5 07
1936 02 14	70 50	-5 07
1936 02 15	70 50	-5 07
1936 02 16	70 49	-5 06
1936 02 17	70 49	-5 06
1936 02 18	70 49	-5 06
1936 02 19	70 49	-5 06
1936 02 20	70 50	-5 05
1936 02 21	70 50	-5 05
1936 02 22	70 50	-5 05
1936 02 23	70 50	-5 04
1936 02 24	70 51	-5 04
1936 02 25	70 51	-5 04
1936 02 26	70 52	-5 04
1936 02 27	70 53	-5 03
1936 02 28	70 54	-5 03
1936 02 29	70 54	-5 03
1936 03 01	70 55	-5 02
1936 03 02	70 56	-5 02
1936 03 03	70 57	-5 02
1936 03 04	70 58	-5 02
1936 03 05	71 00	-5 01
1936 03 06	71 01	-5 01
1936 03 07	71 02	-5 01
1936 03 08	71 04	-5 00
1936 03 09	71 05	-5 00
1936 03 10	71 07	-5 00
1936 03 11	71 08	-5 00
1936 03 12	71 10	-4 59
1936 03 13	71 12	-4 59
1936 03 14	71 14	-4 59
1936 03 15	71 16	-4 58
1936 03 16	71 18	-4 58
1936 03 17	71 20	-4 58
1936 03 18	71 22	-4 58
1936 03 19	71 24	-4 57
1936 03 20	71 26	-4 57
1936 03 21	71 29	-4 57
1936 03 22	71 31	-4 57
1936 03 23	71 33	-4 56
1936 03 24	71 36	-4 56
1936 03 25	71 39	-4 56
1936 03 26	71 41	-4 56
1936 03 27	71 44	-4 55
1936 03 28	71 47	-4 55
1936 03 29	71 50	-4 55
1936 03 30	71 52	-4 55
1936 03 31	71 55	-4 54
1936 04 01	71 58	-4 54
1936 04 02	72 01	-4 54
1936 04 03	72 05	-4 54
1936 04 04	72 08	-4 54
1936 04 05	72 11	-4 53
1936 04 06	72 14	-4 53
1936 04 07	72 18	-4 53
1936 04 08	72 21	-4 53
1936 04 09	72 24	-4 53
1936 04 10	72 28	-4 52
1936 04 11	72 32	-4 52
1936 04 12	72 35	-4 52
1936 04 13	72 39	-4 52
1936 04 14	72 43	-4 52
1936 04 15	72 46	-4 51
1936 04 16	72 50	-4 51
1936 04 17	72 54	-4 51
1936 04 18	72 58	-4 51
1936 04 19	73 02	-4 51
1936 04 20	73 06	-4 51
1936 04 21	73 10	-4 50
1936 04 22	73 14	-4 50
1936 04 23	73 18	-4 50
1936 04 24	73 22	-4 50
1936 04 25	73 26	-4 50
1936 04 26	73 31	-4 50
1936 04 27	73 35	-4 50
1936 04 28	73 39	-4 49
1936 04 29	73 43	-4 49
1936 04 30	73 48	-4 49
1936 05 01	73 52	-4 49
1936 05 02	73 57	-4 49
1936 05 03	74 01	-4 49
1936 05 04	74 06	-4 49
1936 05 05	74 10	-4 49
1936 05 06	74 15	-4 49
1936 05 07	74 19	-4 49
1936 05 08	74 24	-4 48
1936 05 09	74 29	-4 48
1936 05 10	74 33	-4 48
1936 05 11	74 38	-4 48
1936 05 12	74 43	-4 48
1936 05 13	74 48	-4 48
1936 05 14	74 52	-4 48
1936 05 15	74 57	-4 48
1936 05 16	75 02	-4 48
1936 05 17	75 07	-4 48
1936 05 18	75 12	-4 48
1936 05 19	75 17	-4 48
1936 05 20	75 21	-4 48
1936 05 21	75 26	-4 48
1936 05 22	75 31	-4 48
1936 05 23	75 36	-4 48
1936 05 24	75 41	-4 48
1936 05 25	75 46	-4 48
1936 05 26	75 51	-4 48
1936 05 27	75 56	-4 48
1936 05 28	76 01	-4 48
1936 05 29	76 06	-4 48
1936 05 30	76 11	-4 48
1936 05 31	76 16	-4 48
1936 06 01	76 22	-4 48
1936 06 02	76 27	-4 48
1936 06 03	76 32	-4 48
1936 06 04	76 37	-4 48
1936 06 05	76 42	-4 48
1936 06 06	76 47	-4 48
1936 06 07	76 52	-4 48
1936 06 08	76 57	-4 49
1936 06 09	77 02	-4 49
1936 06 10	77 07	-4 49
1936 06 11	77 12	-4 49
1936 06 12	77 17	-4 49
1936 06 13	77 23	-4 49
1936 06 14	77 28	-4 49
1936 06 15	77 33	-4 49
1936 06 16	77 38	-4 49
1936 06 17	77 43	-4 49
1936 06 18	77 48	-4 50
1936 06 19	77 53	-4 50
1936 06 20	77 58	-4 50
1936 06 21	78 03	-4 50
1936 06 22	78 08	-4 50
1936 06 23	78 13	-4 50
1936 06 24	78 18	-4 50
1936 06 25	78 23	-4 51
1936 06 26	78 28	-4 51
1936 06 27	78 33	-4 51
1936 06 28	78 38	-4 51
1936 06 29	78 43	-4 51
1936 06 30	78 48	-4 51
1936 07 01	78 53	-4 52
1936 07 02	78 58	-4 52
1936 07 03	79 03	-4 52
1936 07 04	79 07	-4 52
1936 07 05	79 12	-4 53
1936 07 06	79 17	-4 53
1936 07 07	79 22	-4 53
1936 07 08	79 27	-4 53
1936 07 09	79 31	-4 53
1936 07 10	79 36	-4 54
1936 07 11	79 41	-4 54
1936 07 12	79 45	-4 54
1936 07 13	79 50	-4 54
1936 07 14	79 55	-4 55
1936 07 15	79 59	-4 55
1936 07 16	80 04	-4 55
1936 07 17	80 08	-4 55
1936 07 18	80 13	-4 56
1936 07 19	80 17	-4 56
1936 07 20	80 22	-4 56
1936 07 21	80 26	-4 57
1936 07 22	80 30	-4 57
1936 07 23	80 35	-4 57
1936 07 24	80 39	-4 58
1936 07 25	80 43	-4 58
1936 07 26	80 47	-4 58
1936 07 27	80 51	-4 58
1936 07 28	80 56	-4 59
1936 07 29	81 00	-4 59
1936 07 30	81 04	-4 59
1936 07 31	81 08	-5 00
1936 08 01	81 12	-5 00
1936 08 02	81 15	-5 01
1936 08 03	81 19	-5 01
1936 08 04	81 23	-5 01
1936 08 05	81 27	-5 02
1936 08 06	81 31	-5 02
1936 08 07	81 34	-5 02
1936 08 08	81 38	-5 03
1936 08 09	81 41	-5 03
1936 08 10	81 45	-5 03
1936 08 11	81 48	-5 04
1936 08 12	81 52	-5 04
1936 08 13	81 55	-5 05
1936 08 14	81 58	-5 05
1936 08 15	82 02	-5 05
1936 08 16	82 05	-5 06
1936 08 17	82 08	-5 06
1936 08 18	82 11	-5 07
1936 08 19	82 14	-5 07
1936 08 20	82 17	-5 08
1936 08 21	82 20	-5 08
1936 08 22	82 23	-5 08
1936 08 23	82 26	-5 09
1936 08 24	82 28	-5 09
1936 08 25	82 31	-5 10
1936 08 26	82 34	-5 10
1936 08 27	82 36	-5 11
1936 08 28	82 39	-5 11
1936 08 29	82 41	-5 11
1936 08 30	82 44	-5 12
1936 08 31	82 46	-5 12
1936 09 01	82 48	-5 13
1936 09 02	82 50	-5 13
1936 09 03	82 52	-5 14
1936 09 04	82 54	-5 14
1936 09 05	82 56	-5 15
1936 09 06	82 58	-5 15
1936 09 07	83 00	-5 16
1936 09 08	83 02	-5 16
1936 09 09	83 03	-5 17
1936 09 10	83 05	-5 17
1936 09 11	83 07	-5 18
1936 09 12	83 08	-5 18
1936 09 13	83 09	-5 19
1936 09 14	83 11	-5 19
1936 09 15	83 12	-5 20
1936 09 16	83 13	-5 20
1936 09 17	83 14	-5 21
1936 09 18	83 15	-5 21
1936 09 19	83 16	-5 22
1936 09 20	83 17	-5 22
1936 09 21	83 18	-5 23
1936 09 22	83 19	-5 23
1936 09 23	83 19	-5 24
1936 09 24	83 20	-5 24
1936 09 25	83 20	-5 25
1936 09 26	83 21	-5 25
1936 09 27	83 21	-5 26
1936 09 28	83 22	-5 26
1936 09 29	83 22	-5 27
1936 09 30	83 22	-5 27
1936 10 01	83 22	-5 28
1936 10 02	83 22	-5 28
1936 10 03	83 22	-5 29
1936 10 04	83 22	-5 29
1936 10 05	83 21	-5 30
1936 10 06	83 21	-5 30
1936 10 07	83 21	-5 31
1936 10 08	83 20	-5 31
1936 10 09	83 20	-5 32
1936 10 10	83 19	-5 32
1936 10 11	83 18	-5 33
1936 10 12	83 17	-5 33
1936 10 13	83 17	-5 34
1936 10 14	83 16	-5 34
1936 10 15	83 15	-5 35
1936 10 16	83 14	-5 35
1936 10 17	83 12	-5 36
1936 10 18	83 11	-5 36
1936 10 19	83 10	-5 36
1936 10 20	83 08	-5 37
1936 10 21	83 07	-5 37
1936 10 22	83 06	-5 38
1936 10 23	83 04	-5 38
1936 10 24	83 02	-5 39
1936 10 25	83 01	-5 39
1936 10 26	82 59	-5 40
1936 10 27	82 57	-5 40
1936 10 28	82 55	-5 41
1936 10 29	82 53	-5 41
1936 10 30	82 51	-5 41
1936 10 31	82 49	-5 42
1936 11 01	82 47	-5 42
1936 11 02	82 44	-5 43

1936 11 03	82 42	-5 43	1937 02 17	77 45	-5 43	1937 06 03	83 09	-5 17	1937 09 17	90 51	-5 48
1936 11 04	82 40	-5 43	1937 02 18	77 44	-5 42	1937 06 04	83 15	-5 17	1937 09 18	90 53	-5 49
1936 11 05	82 37	-5 44	1937 02 19	77 44	-5 42	1937 06 05	83 20	-5 17	1937 09 19	90 55	-5 50
1936 11 06	82 35	-5 44	1937 02 20	77 43	-5 42	1937 06 06	83 25	-5 17	1937 09 20	90 56	-5 50
1936 11 07	82 32	-5 45	1937 02 21	77 43	-5 41	1937 06 07	83 31	-5 17	1937 09 21	90 58	-5 51
1936 11 08	82 29	-5 45	1937 02 22	77 43	-5 41	1937 06 08	83 36	-5 17	1937 09 22	90 59	-5 51
1936 11 09	82 27	-5 45	1937 02 23	77 43	-5 40	1937 06 09	83 41	-5 17	1937 09 23	91 01	-5 52
1936 11 10	82 24	-5 46	1937 02 24	77 43	-5 40	1937 06 10	83 47	-5 17	1937 09 24	91 02	-5 52
1936 11 11	82 21	-5 46	1937 02 25	77 43	-5 40	1937 06 11	83 52	-5 17	1937 09 25	91 03	-5 53
1936 11 12	82 18	-5 47	1937 02 26	77 44	-5 39	1937 06 12	83 58	-5 17	1937 09 26	91 05	-5 53
1936 11 13	82 16	-5 47	1937 02 27	77 44	-5 39	1937 06 13	84 03	-5 18	1937 09 27	91 06	-5 54
1936 11 14	82 13	-5 47	1937 02 28	77 44	-5 39	1937 06 14	84 08	-5 18	1937 09 28	91 07	-5 55
1936 11 15	82 10	-5 48	1937 03 01	77 45	-5 38	1937 06 15	84 14	-5 18	1937 09 29	91 08	-5 55
1936 11 16	82 07	-5 48	1937 03 02	77 45	-5 38	1937 06 16	84 19	-5 18	1937 09 30	91 09	-5 56
1936 11 17	82 03	-5 48	1937 03 03	77 46	-5 38	1937 06 17	84 25	-5 18	1937 10 01	91 09	-5 56
1936 11 18	82 00	-5 49	1937 03 04	77 46	-5 37	1937 06 18	84 30	-5 18	1937 10 02	91 10	-5 57
1936 11 19	81 57	-5 49	1937 03 05	77 47	-5 37	1937 06 19	84 35	-5 18	1937 10 03	91 11	-5 57
1936 11 20	81 54	-5 49	1937 03 06	77 48	-5 37	1937 06 20	84 41	-5 18	1937 10 04	91 11	-5 58
1936 11 21	81 51	-5 49	1937 03 07	77 49	-5 36	1937 06 21	84 46	-5 18	1937 10 05	91 12	-5 58
1936 11 22	81 47	-5 50	1937 03 08	77 50	-5 36	1937 06 22	84 52	-5 18	1937 10 06	91 12	-5 59
1936 11 23	81 44	-5 50	1937 03 09	77 51	-5 35	1937 06 23	84 57	-5 18	1937 10 07	91 12	-6 00
1936 11 24	81 41	-5 50	1937 03 10	77 52	-5 35	1937 06 24	85 03	-5 19	1937 10 08	91 13	-6 00
1936 11 25	81 37	-5 50	1937 03 11	77 53	-5 35	1937 06 25	85 08	-5 19	1937 10 09	91 13	-6 01
1936 11 26	81 34	-5 51	1937 03 12	77 55	-5 34	1937 06 26	85 13	-5 19	1937 10 10	91 13	-6 01
1936 11 27	81 30	-5 51	1937 03 13	77 56	-5 34	1937 06 27	85 19	-5 19	1937 10 11	91 13	-6 02
1936 11 28	81 27	-5 51	1937 03 14	77 58	-5 34	1937 06 28	85 24	-5 19	1937 10 12	91 13	-6 02
1936 11 29	81 23	-5 51	1937 03 15	77 59	-5 33	1937 06 29	85 29	-5 19	1937 10 13	91 12	-6 03
1936 11 30	81 20	-5 52	1937 03 16	78 01	-5 33	1937 06 30	85 35	-5 19	1937 10 14	91 12	-6 04
1936 12 01	81 16	-5 52	1937 03 17	78 02	-5 33	1937 07 01	85 40	-5 19	1937 10 15	91 12	-6 04
1936 12 02	81 13	-5 52	1937 03 18	78 04	-5 32	1937 07 02	85 45	-5 20	1937 10 16	91 11	-6 05
1936 12 03	81 09	-5 52	1937 03 19	78 06	-5 32	1937 07 03	85 51	-5 20	1937 10 17	91 11	-6 05
1936 12 04	81 06	-5 52	1937 03 20	78 08	-5 32	1937 07 04	85 56	-5 20	1937 10 18	91 10	-6 06
1936 12 05	81 02	-5 53	1937 03 21	78 10	-5 31	1937 07 05	86 01	-5 20	1937 10 19	91 10	-6 06
1936 12 06	80 58	-5 53	1937 03 22	78 12	-5 31	1937 07 06	86 07	-5 20	1937 10 20	91 09	-6 07
1936 12 07	80 55	-5 53	1937 03 23	78 14	-5 31	1937 07 07	86 12	-5 21	1937 10 21	91 08	-6 07
1936 12 08	80 51	-5 53	1937 03 24	78 16	-5 30	1937 07 08	86 17	-5 21	1937 10 22	91 07	-6 08
1936 12 09	80 47	-5 53	1937 03 25	78 19	-5 30	1937 07 09	86 22	-5 21	1937 10 23	91 06	-6 08
1936 12 10	80 44	-5 53	1937 03 26	78 21	-5 30	1937 07 10	86 27	-5 21	1937 10 24	91 05	-6 09
1936 12 11	80 40	-5 53	1937 03 27	78 23	-5 29	1937 07 11	86 33	-5 21	1937 10 25	91 04	-6 10
1936 12 12	80 36	-5 54	1937 03 28	78 26	-5 29	1937 07 12	86 38	-5 22	1937 10 26	91 03	-6 10
1936 12 13	80 32	-5 54	1937 03 29	78 28	-5 29	1937 07 13	86 43	-5 22	1937 10 27	91 02	-6 11
1936 12 14	80 29	-5 54	1937 03 30	78 31	-5 28	1937 07 14	86 48	-5 22	1937 10 28	91 00	-6 11
1936 12 15	80 25	-5 54	1937 03 31	78 34	-5 28	1937 07 15	86 53	-5 22	1937 10 29	90 59	-6 12
1936 12 16	80 21	-5 54	1937 04 01	78 36	-5 28	1937 07 16	86 58	-5 23	1937 10 30	90 57	-6 12
1936 12 17	80 18	-5 54	1937 04 02	78 39	-5 27	1937 07 17	87 03	-5 23	1937 10 31	90 56	-6 13
1936 12 18	80 14	-5 54	1937 04 03	78 42	-5 27	1937 07 18	87 08	-5 23	1937 11 01	90 54	-6 13
1936 12 19	80 10	-5 54	1937 04 04	78 45	-5 27	1937 07 19	87 13	-5 23	1937 11 02	90 52	-6 14
1936 12 20	80 07	-5 54	1937 04 05	78 48	-5 27	1937 07 20	87 18	-5 24	1937 11 03	90 50	-6 14
1936 12 21	80 03	-5 54	1937 04 06	78 51	-5 26	1937 07 21	87 23	-5 24	1937 11 04	90 48	-6 15
1936 12 22	79 59	-5 54	1937 04 07	78 54	-5 26	1937 07 22	87 28	-5 24	1937 11 05	90 46	-6 15
1936 12 23	79 56	-5 54	1937 04 08	78 57	-5 26	1937 07 23	87 33	-5 24	1937 11 06	90 44	-6 16
1936 12 24	79 52	-5 54	1937 04 09	79 01	-5 25	1937 07 24	87 38	-5 25	1937 11 07	90 42	-6 16
1936 12 25	79 48	-5 54	1937 04 10	79 04	-5 25	1937 07 25	87 43	-5 25	1937 11 08	90 40	-6 17
1936 12 26	79 45	-5 54	1937 04 11	79 07	-5 25	1937 07 26	87 47	-5 25	1937 11 09	90 38	-6 17
1936 12 27	79 41	-5 54	1937 04 12	79 11	-5 25	1937 07 27	87 52	-5 26	1937 11 10	90 36	-6 18
1936 12 28	79 38	-5 54	1937 04 13	79 14	-5 24	1937 07 28	87 57	-5 26	1937 11 11	90 33	-6 18
1936 12 29	79 34	-5 54	1937 04 14	79 18	-5 24	1937 07 29	88 01	-5 26	1937 11 12	90 31	-6 18
1936 12 30	79 31	-5 54	1937 04 15	79 22	-5 24	1937 07 30	88 06	-5 27	1937 11 13	90 28	-6 19
1936 12 31	79 27	-5 54	1937 04 16	79 25	-5 24	1937 07 31	88 11	-5 27	1937 11 14	90 26	-6 19
1937 01 01	79 24	-5 54	1937 04 17	79 29	-5 23	1937 08 01	88 15	-5 27	1937 11 15	90 23	-6 20
1937 01 02	79 21	-5 54	1937 04 18	79 33	-5 23	1937 08 02	88 20	-5 28	1937 11 16	90 20	-6 20
1937 01 03	79 17	-5 54	1937 04 19	79 36	-5 23	1937 08 03	88 24	-5 28	1937 11 17	90 17	-6 21
1937 01 04	79 14	-5 53	1937 04 20	79 40	-5 23	1937 08 04	88 29	-5 28	1937 11 18	90 15	-6 21
1937 01 05	79 11	-5 53	1937 04 21	79 44	-5 22	1937 08 05	88 33	-5 29	1937 11 19	90 12	-6 21
1937 01 06	79 07	-5 53	1937 04 22	79 48	-5 22	1937 08 06	88 37	-5 29	1937 11 20	90 09	-6 22
1937 01 07	79 04	-5 53	1937 04 23	79 52	-5 22	1937 08 07	88 42	-5 29	1937 11 21	90 06	-6 22
1937 01 08	79 01	-5 53	1937 04 24	79 56	-5 22	1937 08 08	88 46	-5 30	1937 11 22	90 03	-6 23
1937 01 09	78 58	-5 53	1937 04 25	80 00	-5 22	1937 08 09	88 50	-5 30	1937 11 23	90 00	-6 23
1937 01 10	78 55	-5 53	1937 04 26	80 05	-5 21	1937 08 10	88 54	-5 31	1937 11 24	89 57	-6 23
1937 01 11	78 52	-5 53	1937 04 27	80 09	-5 21	1937 08 11	88 59	-5 31	1937 11 25	89 53	-6 24
1937 01 12	78 49	-5 52	1937 04 28	80 13	-5 21	1937 08 12	89 03	-5 31	1937 11 26	89 50	-6 24
1937 01 13	78 46	-5 52	1937 04 29	80 17	-5 21	1937 08 13	89 07	-5 32	1937 11 27	89 47	-6 24
1937 01 14	78 43	-5 52	1937 04 30	80 22	-5 21	1937 08 14	89 11	-5 32	1937 11 28	89 44	-6 25
1937 01 15	78 40	-5 52	1937 05 01	80 26	-5 20	1937 08 15	89 15	-5 33	1937 11 29	89 40	-6 25
1937 01 16	78 38	-5 52	1937 05 02	80 31	-5 20	1937 08 16	89 18	-5 33	1937 11 30	89 37	-6 25
1937 01 17	78 35	-5 51	1937 05 03	80 35	-5 20	1937 08 17	89 22	-5 33	1937 12 01	89 33	-6 26
1937 01 18	78 32	-5 51	1937 05 04	80 40	-5 20	1937 08 18	89 26	-5 34	1937 12 02	89 30	-6 26
1937 01 19	78 30	-5 51	1937 05 05	80 44	-5 20	1937 08 19	89 30	-5 34	1937 12 03	89 26	-6 26
1937 01 20	78 27	-5 51	1937 05 06	80 49	-5 20	1937 08 20	89 33	-5 35	1937 12 04	89 23	-6 26
1937 01 21	78 25	-5 51	1937 05 07	80 53	-5 19	1937 08 21	89 37	-5 35	1937 12 05	89 19	-6 27
1937 01 22	78 22	-5 50	1937 05 08	80 58	-5 19	1937 08 22	89 41	-5 36	1937 12 06	89 15	-6 27
1937 01 23	78 20	-5 50	1937 05 09	81 03	-5 19	1937 08 23	89 44	-5 36	1937 12 07	89 12	-6 27
1937 01 24	78 18	-5 50	1937 05 10	81 07	-5 19	1937 08 24	89 48	-5 36	1937 12 08	89 08	-6 27
1937 01 25	78 16	-5 50	1937 05 11	81 12	-5 19	1937 08 25	89 51	-5 37	1937 12 09	89 04	-6 28
1937 01 26	78 13	-5 49	1937 05 12	81 17	-5 19	1937 08 26	89 54	-5 37	1937 12 10	89 01	-6 28
1937 01 27	78 11	-5 49	1937 05 13	81 22	-5 19	1937 08 27	89 58	-5 38	1937 12 11	88 57	-6 28
1937 01 28	78 09	-5 49	1937 05 14	81 27	-5 18	1937 08 28	90 01	-5 38	1937 12 12	88 53	-6 28
1937 01 29	78 07	-5 49	1937 05 15	81 32	-5 18	1937 08 29	90 04	-5 39	1937 12 13	88 49	-6 28
1937 01 30	78 05	-5 48	1937 05 16	81 37	-5 18	1937 08 30	90 07	-5 39	1937 12 14	88 46	-6 29
1937 01 31	78 04	-5 48	1937 05 17	81 42	-5 18	1937 08 31	90 10	-5 40	1937 12 15	88 42	-6 29
1937 02 01	78 02	-5 48	1937 05 18	81 47	-5 18	1937 09 01	90 13	-5 40	1937 12 16	88 38	-6 29
1937 02 02	78 00	-5 47	1937 05 19	81 52	-5 18	1937 09 02	90 16	-5 41	1937 12 17	88 34	-6 29
1937 02 03	77 59	-5 47	1937 05 20	81 57	-5 18	1937 09 03	90 19	-5 41	1937 12 18	88 30	-6 29
1937 02 04	77 57	-5 47	1937 05 21	82 02	-5 18	1937 09 04	90 22	-5 42	1937 12 19	88 26	-6 29
1937 02 05	77 56	-5 46	1937 05 22	82 07	-5 18	1937 09 05	90 24	-5 42	1937 12 20	88 23	-6 29
1937 02 06	77 54	-5 46	1937 05 23	82 12	-5 18	1937 09 06	90 27	-5 43	1937 12 21	88 19	-6 29
1937 02 07	77 53	-5 46	1937 05 24	82 17	-5 18	1937 09 07	90 29	-5 43	1937 12 22	88 15	-6 30
1937 02 08	77 52	-5 46	1937 05 25	82 22	-5 18	1937 09 08	90 32	-5 44	1937 12 23	88 11	-6 30
1937 02 09	77 51	-5 45	1937 05 26	82 27	-5 17	1937 09 09	90 34	-5 44	1937 12 24	88 07	-6 30
1937 02 10	77 50	-5 45	1937 05 27	82 33	-5 17	1937 09 10	90 37	-5 45	1937 12 25	88 03	-6 30
1937 02 11	77 49	-5 45	1937 05 28	82 38	-5 17	1937 09 11	90 39	-5 45	1937 12 26	87 59	-6 30
1937 02 12	77 48	-5 44	1937 05 29	82 43	-5 17	1937 09 12	90 41	-5 46			
1937 02 13	77 47	-5 44	1937 05 30	82 48	-5 17	1937 09 13	90 43	-5 46			
1937 02 14	77 46	-5 44	1937 05 31	82 53	-5 17	1937 09 14	90 45	-5 47			
1937 02 15	77 46	-5 43	1937 06 01	82 59	-5 17	1937 09 15	90 47	-5 47			
1937 02 16	77 45	-5 43	1937 06 02	83 04	-5 17	1937 09 16	90 49	-5 48			

Chiron

1937 12 27	87 56	-6 30
1937 12 28	87 52	-6 30
1937 12 29	87 48	-6 30
1937 12 30	87 44	-6 30
1937 12 31	87 40	-6 30
1938 01 01	87 37	-6 30
1938 01 02	87 33	-6 30
1938 01 03	87 29	-6 30
1938 01 04	87 25	-6 30
1938 01 05	87 22	-6 30
1938 01 06	87 18	-6 29
1938 01 07	87 14	-6 29
1938 01 08	87 11	-6 29
1938 01 09	87 07	-6 29
1938 01 10	87 04	-6 29
1938 01 11	87 00	-6 29
1938 01 12	86 57	-6 29
1938 01 13	86 54	-6 29
1938 01 14	86 50	-6 28
1938 01 15	86 47	-6 28
1938 01 16	86 44	-6 28
1938 01 17	86 40	-6 28
1938 01 18	86 37	-6 28
1938 01 19	86 34	-6 27
1938 01 20	86 31	-6 27
1938 01 21	86 28	-6 27
1938 01 22	86 25	-6 27
1938 01 23	86 22	-6 27
1938 01 24	86 19	-6 26
1938 01 25	86 17	-6 26
1938 01 26	86 14	-6 26
1938 01 27	86 11	-6 26
1938 01 28	86 09	-6 25
1938 01 29	86 06	-6 25
1938 01 30	86 04	-6 25
1938 01 31	86 01	-6 24
1938 02 01	85 59	-6 24
1938 02 02	85 57	-6 24
1938 02 03	85 54	-6 23
1938 02 04	85 52	-6 23
1938 02 05	85 50	-6 23
1938 02 06	85 48	-6 22
1938 02 07	85 46	-6 22
1938 02 08	85 45	-6 22
1938 02 09	85 43	-6 21
1938 02 10	85 41	-6 21
1938 02 11	85 40	-6 21
1938 02 12	85 38	-6 20
1938 02 13	85 37	-6 20
1938 02 14	85 35	-6 20
1938 02 15	85 34	-6 19
1938 02 16	85 33	-6 19
1938 02 17	85 32	-6 18
1938 02 18	85 31	-6 18
1938 02 19	85 30	-6 18
1938 02 20	85 29	-6 17
1938 02 21	85 28	-6 17
1938 02 22	85 27	-6 16
1938 02 23	85 27	-6 16
1938 02 24	85 26	-6 16
1938 02 25	85 26	-6 15
1938 02 26	85 25	-6 15
1938 02 27	85 25	-6 14
1938 02 28	85 25	-6 14
1938 03 01	85 25	-6 13
1938 03 02	85 25	-6 13
1938 03 03	85 25	-6 13
1938 03 04	85 25	-6 12
1938 03 05	85 25	-6 12
1938 03 06	85 25	-6 11
1938 03 07	85 26	-6 11
1938 03 08	85 26	-6 10
1938 03 09	85 27	-6 10
1938 03 10	85 27	-6 10
1938 03 11	85 28	-6 09
1938 03 12	85 29	-6 09
1938 03 13	85 30	-6 08
1938 03 14	85 31	-6 08
1938 03 15	85 32	-6 07
1938 03 16	85 33	-6 07
1938 03 17	85 34	-6 06
1938 03 18	85 35	-6 06
1938 03 19	85 37	-6 06
1938 03 20	85 38	-6 05
1938 03 21	85 40	-6 05
1938 03 22	85 41	-6 04
1938 03 23	85 43	-6 04
1938 03 24	85 45	-6 04
1938 03 25	85 47	-6 03
1938 03 26	85 49	-6 03
1938 03 27	85 51	-6 02
1938 03 28	85 53	-6 02
1938 03 29	85 55	-6 01
1938 03 30	85 57	-6 01
1938 03 31	85 59	-6 01
1938 04 01	86 02	-6 00
1938 04 02	86 04	-6 00
1938 04 03	86 07	-5 59
1938 04 04	86 09	-5 59
1938 04 05	86 12	-5 59
1938 04 06	86 15	-5 58
1938 04 07	86 18	-5 58
1938 04 08	86 21	-5 58
1938 04 09	86 24	-5 57
1938 04 10	86 27	-5 57
1938 04 11	86 30	-5 56
1938 04 12	86 33	-5 56
1938 04 13	86 36	-5 56
1938 04 14	86 39	-5 55
1938 04 15	86 43	-5 55
1938 04 16	86 46	-5 55
1938 04 17	86 50	-5 54
1938 04 18	86 53	-5 54
1938 04 19	86 57	-5 54
1938 04 20	87 00	-5 53
1938 04 21	87 04	-5 53
1938 04 22	87 08	-5 53
1938 04 23	87 12	-5 52
1938 04 24	87 16	-5 52
1938 04 25	87 20	-5 52
1938 04 26	87 24	-5 51
1938 04 27	87 28	-5 51
1938 04 28	87 32	-5 51
1938 04 29	87 36	-5 51
1938 04 30	87 40	-5 50
1938 05 01	87 45	-5 50
1938 05 02	87 49	-5 50
1938 05 03	87 54	-5 49
1938 05 04	87 58	-5 49
1938 05 05	88 02	-5 49
1938 05 06	88 07	-5 49
1938 05 07	88 12	-5 48
1938 05 08	88 16	-5 48
1938 05 09	88 21	-5 48
1938 05 10	88 26	-5 48
1938 05 11	88 30	-5 48
1938 05 12	88 35	-5 47
1938 05 13	88 40	-5 47
1938 05 14	88 45	-5 47
1938 05 15	88 50	-5 47
1938 05 16	88 55	-5 47
1938 05 17	89 00	-5 46
1938 05 18	89 05	-5 46
1938 05 19	89 10	-5 46
1938 05 20	89 15	-5 46
1938 05 21	89 20	-5 46
1938 05 22	89 25	-5 45
1938 05 23	89 31	-5 45
1938 05 24	89 36	-5 45
1938 05 25	89 41	-5 45
1938 05 26	89 47	-5 45
1938 05 27	89 52	-5 45
1938 05 28	89 57	-5 45
1938 05 29	90 03	-5 45
1938 05 30	90 08	-5 44
1938 05 31	90 14	-5 44
1938 06 01	90 19	-5 44
1938 06 02	90 24	-5 44
1938 06 03	90 30	-5 44
1938 06 04	90 36	-5 44
1938 06 05	90 41	-5 44
1938 06 06	90 47	-5 44
1938 06 07	90 52	-5 44
1938 06 08	90 58	-5 44
1938 06 09	91 04	-5 44
1938 06 10	91 09	-5 44
1938 06 11	91 15	-5 44
1938 06 12	91 20	-5 44
1938 06 13	91 26	-5 44
1938 06 14	91 32	-5 44
1938 06 15	91 38	-5 44
1938 06 16	91 43	-5 44
1938 06 17	91 49	-5 44
1938 06 18	91 55	-5 44
1938 06 19	92 01	-5 44
1938 06 20	92 06	-5 44
1938 06 21	92 12	-5 44
1938 06 22	92 18	-5 44
1938 06 23	92 24	-5 44
1938 06 24	92 29	-5 44
1938 06 25	92 35	-5 44
1938 06 26	92 41	-5 44
1938 06 27	92 47	-5 44
1938 06 28	92 52	-5 44
1938 06 29	92 58	-5 44
1938 06 30	93 04	-5 44
1938 07 01	93 10	-5 44
1938 07 02	93 16	-5 45
1938 07 03	93 21	-5 45
1938 07 04	93 27	-5 45
1938 07 05	93 33	-5 45
1938 07 06	93 39	-5 45
1938 07 07	93 44	-5 45
1938 07 08	93 50	-5 45
1938 07 09	93 56	-5 45
1938 07 10	94 01	-5 46
1938 07 11	94 07	-5 46
1938 07 12	94 13	-5 46
1938 07 13	94 18	-5 46
1938 07 14	94 24	-5 46
1938 07 15	94 30	-5 47
1938 07 16	94 35	-5 47
1938 07 17	94 41	-5 47
1938 07 18	94 47	-5 47
1938 07 19	94 52	-5 47
1938 07 20	94 58	-5 48
1938 07 21	95 03	-5 48
1938 07 22	95 09	-5 48
1938 07 23	95 14	-5 48
1938 07 24	95 20	-5 49
1938 07 25	95 25	-5 49
1938 07 26	95 30	-5 49
1938 07 27	95 36	-5 49
1938 07 28	95 41	-5 50
1938 07 29	95 46	-5 50
1938 07 30	95 52	-5 50
1938 07 31	95 57	-5 51
1938 08 01	96 02	-5 51
1938 08 02	96 07	-5 51
1938 08 03	96 13	-5 51
1938 08 04	96 18	-5 52
1938 08 05	96 23	-5 52
1938 08 06	96 28	-5 52
1938 08 07	96 33	-5 53
1938 08 08	96 38	-5 53
1938 08 09	96 43	-5 53
1938 08 10	96 48	-5 54
1938 08 11	96 53	-5 54
1938 08 12	96 57	-5 55
1938 08 13	97 02	-5 55
1938 08 14	97 07	-5 55
1938 08 15	97 12	-5 56
1938 08 16	97 16	-5 56
1938 08 17	97 21	-5 57
1938 08 18	97 25	-5 57
1938 08 19	97 30	-5 57
1938 08 20	97 34	-5 58
1938 08 21	97 39	-5 58
1938 08 22	97 43	-5 59
1938 08 23	97 47	-5 59
1938 08 24	97 52	-6 00
1938 08 25	97 56	-6 00
1938 08 26	98 00	-6 00
1938 08 27	98 04	-6 01
1938 08 28	98 08	-6 01
1938 08 29	98 12	-6 02
1938 08 30	98 16	-6 02
1938 08 31	98 20	-6 03
1938 09 01	98 24	-6 03
1938 09 02	98 27	-6 04
1938 09 03	98 31	-6 04
1938 09 04	98 35	-6 05
1938 09 05	98 38	-6 05
1938 09 06	98 42	-6 06
1938 09 07	98 45	-6 06
1938 09 08	98 49	-6 07
1938 09 09	98 52	-6 07
1938 09 10	98 55	-6 08
1938 09 11	98 58	-6 08
1938 09 12	99 01	-6 09
1938 09 13	99 04	-6 09
1938 09 14	99 07	-6 10
1938 09 15	99 10	-6 11
1938 09 16	99 13	-6 11
1938 09 17	99 16	-6 12
1938 09 18	99 19	-6 12
1938 09 19	99 21	-6 13
1938 09 20	99 24	-6 13
1938 09 21	99 26	-6 14
1938 09 22	99 28	-6 15
1938 09 23	99 31	-6 15
1938 09 24	99 33	-6 16
1938 09 25	99 35	-6 16
1938 09 26	99 37	-6 17
1938 09 27	99 39	-6 17
1938 09 28	99 41	-6 18
1938 09 29	99 43	-6 19
1938 09 30	99 45	-6 19
1938 10 01	99 46	-6 20
1938 10 02	99 48	-6 21
1938 10 03	99 50	-6 21
1938 10 04	99 51	-6 22
1938 10 05	99 52	-6 22
1938 10 06	99 54	-6 23
1938 10 07	99 55	-6 24
1938 10 08	99 56	-6 24
1938 10 09	99 57	-6 25
1938 10 10	99 58	-6 25
1938 10 11	99 59	-6 26
1938 10 12	99 59	-6 27
1938 10 13	100 00	-6 27
1938 10 14	100 01	-6 28
1938 10 15	100 01	-6 29
1938 10 16	100 02	-6 29
1938 10 17	100 02	-6 30
1938 10 18	100 02	-6 30
1938 10 19	100 02	-6 31
1938 10 20	100 03	-6 32
1938 10 21	100 02	-6 32
1938 10 22	100 02	-6 33
1938 10 23	100 02	-6 34
1938 10 24	100 02	-6 34
1938 10 25	100 02	-6 35
1938 10 26	100 01	-6 35
1938 10 27	100 01	-6 36
1938 10 28	100 00	-6 37
1938 10 29	99 59	-6 37
1938 10 30	99 59	-6 38
1938 10 31	99 58	-6 38
1938 11 01	99 57	-6 39
1938 11 02	99 56	-6 40
1938 11 03	99 55	-6 40
1938 11 04	99 53	-6 41
1938 11 05	99 52	-6 41
1938 11 06	99 51	-6 42
1938 11 07	99 49	-6 43
1938 11 08	99 48	-6 43
1938 11 09	99 46	-6 44
1938 11 10	99 44	-6 44
1938 11 11	99 43	-6 45
1938 11 12	99 41	-6 45
1938 11 13	99 39	-6 46
1938 11 14	99 37	-6 46
1938 11 15	99 35	-6 47
1938 11 16	99 33	-6 47
1938 11 17	99 30	-6 48
1938 11 18	99 28	-6 48
1938 11 19	99 26	-6 49
1938 11 20	99 23	-6 49
1938 11 21	99 21	-6 50
1938 11 22	99 18	-6 50
1938 11 23	99 16	-6 51
1938 11 24	99 13	-6 51
1938 11 25	99 10	-6 52
1938 11 26	99 07	-6 52
1938 11 27	99 04	-6 53
1938 11 28	99 01	-6 53
1938 11 29	98 58	-6 54
1938 11 30	98 55	-6 54
1938 12 01	98 52	-6 54
1938 12 02	98 49	-6 55
1938 12 03	98 46	-6 55
1938 12 04	98 42	-6 56
1938 12 05	98 39	-6 56
1938 12 06	98 35	-6 56
1938 12 07	98 32	-6 57
1938 12 08	98 28	-6 57
1938 12 09	98 25	-6 57
1938 12 10	98 21	-6 58
1938 12 11	98 18	-6 58
1938 12 12	98 14	-6 58
1938 12 13	98 10	-6 59
1938 12 14	98 07	-6 59
1938 12 15	98 03	-6 59
1938 12 16	97 59	-6 59
1938 12 17	97 55	-7 00
1938 12 18	97 51	-7 00
1938 12 19	97 47	-7 00
1938 12 20	97 43	-7 00
1938 12 21	97 40	-7 00
1938 12 22	97 36	-7 01
1938 12 23	97 32	-7 01
1938 12 24	97 28	-7 01
1938 12 25	97 24	-7 01
1938 12 26	97 20	-7 01
1938 12 27	97 16	-7 01
1938 12 28	97 12	-7 01
1938 12 29	97 07	-7 01
1938 12 30	97 03	-7 02
1938 12 31	96 59	-7 02
1939 01 01	96 55	-7 02
1939 01 02	96 51	-7 02
1939 01 03	96 47	-7 02
1939 01 04	96 43	-7 02
1939 01 05	96 39	-7 02
1939 01 06	96 35	-7 02
1939 01 07	96 31	-7 02
1939 01 08	96 27	-7 02
1939 01 09	96 23	-7 02
1939 01 10	96 20	-7 02
1939 01 11	96 16	-7 01
1939 01 12	96 12	-7 01
1939 01 13	96 08	-7 01
1939 01 14	96 04	-7 01
1939 01 15	96 00	-7 01
1939 01 16	95 57	-7 01
1939 01 17	95 53	-7 01
1939 01 18	95 49	-7 01
1939 01 19	95 45	-7 00
1939 01 20	95 42	-7 00
1939 01 21	95 38	-7 00
1939 01 22	95 35	-7 00
1939 01 23	95 31	-7 00
1939 01 24	95 28	-6 59
1939 01 25	95 25	-6 59
1939 01 26	95 21	-6 59
1939 01 27	95 18	-6 59
1939 01 28	95 15	-6 58
1939 01 29	95 12	-6 58
1939 01 30	95 08	-6 58
1939 01 31	95 05	-6 58
1939 02 01	95 02	-6 57
1939 02 02	95 00	-6 57
1939 02 03	94 57	-6 57
1939 02 04	94 54	-6 56
1939 02 05	94 51	-6 56
1939 02 06	94 48	-6 56
1939 02 07	94 46	-6 55
1939 02 08	94 43	-6 55
1939 02 09	94 41	-6 55
1939 02 10	94 39	-6 54
1939 02 11	94 36	-6 54
1939 02 12	94 34	-6 53
1939 02 13	94 32	-6 53
1939 02 14	94 30	-6 53
1939 02 15	94 28	-6 52
1939 02 16	94 26	-6 52
1939 02 17	94 24	-6 51

1939	02	18	94	22	-6	51
1939	02	19	94	21	-6	50
1939	02	20	94	19	-6	50
1939	02	21	94	17	-6	50
1939	02	22	94	16	-6	49
1939	02	23	94	15	-6	49
1939	02	24	94	13	-6	48
1939	02	25	94	12	-6	48
1939	02	26	94	11	-6	47
1939	02	27	94	10	-6	47
1939	02	28	94	09	-6	46
1939	03	01	94	08	-6	46
1939	03	02	94	08	-6	45
1939	03	03	94	07	-6	45
1939	03	04	94	06	-6	44
1939	03	05	94	06	-6	44
1939	03	06	94	06	-6	43
1939	03	07	94	05	-6	43
1939	03	08	94	05	-6	42
1939	03	09	94	05	-6	42
1939	03	10	94	05	-6	41
1939	03	11	94	05	-6	41
1939	03	12	94	05	-6	40
1939	03	13	94	05	-6	40
1939	03	14	94	06	-6	39
1939	03	15	94	06	-6	39
1939	03	16	94	06	-6	38
1939	03	17	94	07	-6	38
1939	03	18	94	08	-6	37
1939	03	19	94	08	-6	37
1939	03	20	94	09	-6	36
1939	03	21	94	10	-6	36
1939	03	22	94	11	-6	35
1939	03	23	94	12	-6	34
1939	03	24	94	14	-6	34
1939	03	25	94	15	-6	33
1939	03	26	94	16	-6	33
1939	03	27	94	18	-6	32
1939	03	28	94	19	-6	32
1939	03	29	94	21	-6	31
1939	03	30	94	23	-6	31
1939	03	31	94	24	-6	30
1939	04	01	94	26	-6	30
1939	04	02	94	28	-6	29
1939	04	03	94	30	-6	29
1939	04	04	94	32	-6	28
1939	04	05	94	35	-6	28
1939	04	06	94	37	-6	27
1939	04	07	94	39	-6	27
1939	04	08	94	42	-6	26
1939	04	09	94	44	-6	26
1939	04	10	94	47	-6	25
1939	04	11	94	50	-6	25
1939	04	12	94	52	-6	25
1939	04	13	94	55	-6	24
1939	04	14	94	58	-6	24
1939	04	15	95	01	-6	23
1939	04	16	95	04	-6	23
1939	04	17	95	07	-6	22
1939	04	18	95	11	-6	22
1939	04	19	95	14	-6	21
1939	04	20	95	17	-6	21
1939	04	21	95	21	-6	20
1939	04	22	95	24	-6	20
1939	04	23	95	28	-6	20
1939	04	24	95	31	-6	19
1939	04	25	95	35	-6	19
1939	04	26	95	39	-6	18
1939	04	27	95	43	-6	18
1939	04	28	95	47	-6	18
1939	04	29	95	51	-6	17
1939	04	30	95	55	-6	17
1939	05	01	95	59	-6	16
1939	05	02	96	03	-6	16
1939	05	03	96	07	-6	16
1939	05	04	96	11	-6	15
1939	05	05	96	16	-6	15
1939	05	06	96	20	-6	14
1939	05	07	96	24	-6	14
1939	05	08	96	29	-6	14
1939	05	09	96	34	-6	13
1939	05	10	96	38	-6	13
1939	05	11	96	43	-6	13
1939	05	12	96	48	-6	12
1939	05	13	96	52	-6	12
1939	05	14	96	57	-6	12
1939	05	15	97	02	-6	12
1939	05	16	97	07	-6	11
1939	05	17	97	12	-6	11
1939	05	18	97	17	-6	11
1939	05	19	97	22	-6	10
1939	05	20	97	27	-6	10
1939	05	21	97	32	-6	10
1939	05	22	97	37	-6	10
1939	05	23	97	43	-6	09
1939	05	24	97	48	-6	09
1939	05	25	97	53	-6	09
1939	05	26	97	59	-6	09
1939	05	27	98	04	-6	08
1939	05	28	98	10	-6	08
1939	05	29	98	15	-6	08
1939	05	30	98	21	-6	08
1939	05	31	98	26	-6	07
1939	06	01	98	32	-6	07
1939	06	02	98	37	-6	07
1939	06	03	98	43	-6	07
1939	06	04	98	49	-6	07
1939	06	05	98	54	-6	07
1939	06	06	99	00	-6	06
1939	06	07	99	06	-6	06
1939	06	08	99	12	-6	06
1939	06	09	99	17	-6	06
1939	06	10	99	23	-6	06
1939	06	11	99	29	-6	06
1939	06	12	99	35	-6	06
1939	06	13	99	41	-6	05
1939	06	14	99	47	-6	05
1939	06	15	99	53	-6	05
1939	06	16	99	59	-6	05
1939	06	17	100	05	-6	05
1939	06	18	100	11	-6	05
1939	06	19	100	17	-6	05
1939	06	20	100	23	-6	05
1939	06	21	100	29	-6	05
1939	06	22	100	35	-6	05
1939	06	23	100	41	-6	05
1939	06	24	100	48	-6	05
1939	06	25	100	54	-6	05
1939	06	26	101	00	-6	05
1939	06	27	101	06	-6	05
1939	06	28	101	12	-6	05
1939	06	29	101	18	-6	05
1939	06	30	101	25	-6	05
1939	07	01	101	31	-6	05
1939	07	02	101	37	-6	05
1939	07	03	101	43	-6	05
1939	07	04	101	49	-6	05
1939	07	05	101	55	-6	05
1939	07	06	102	02	-6	05
1939	07	07	102	08	-6	05
1939	07	08	102	14	-6	05
1939	07	09	102	20	-6	05
1939	07	10	102	27	-6	05
1939	07	11	102	33	-6	05
1939	07	12	102	39	-6	05
1939	07	13	102	45	-6	05
1939	07	14	102	51	-6	05
1939	07	15	102	57	-6	06
1939	07	16	103	04	-6	06
1939	07	17	103	10	-6	06
1939	07	18	103	16	-6	06
1939	07	19	103	22	-6	06
1939	07	20	103	28	-6	06
1939	07	21	103	34	-6	06
1939	07	22	103	40	-6	07
1939	07	23	103	47	-6	07
1939	07	24	103	53	-6	07
1939	07	25	103	59	-6	07
1939	07	26	104	05	-6	07
1939	07	27	104	11	-6	07
1939	07	28	104	17	-6	08
1939	07	29	104	23	-6	08
1939	07	30	104	29	-6	08
1939	07	31	104	35	-6	08
1939	08	01	104	41	-6	09
1939	08	02	104	46	-6	09
1939	08	03	104	52	-6	09
1939	08	04	104	58	-6	09
1939	08	05	105	04	-6	10
1939	08	06	105	10	-6	10
1939	08	07	105	16	-6	10
1939	08	08	105	21	-6	10
1939	08	09	105	27	-6	11
1939	08	10	105	33	-6	11
1939	08	11	105	38	-6	11
1939	08	12	105	44	-6	12
1939	08	13	105	50	-6	12
1939	08	14	105	55	-6	12
1939	08	15	106	01	-6	13
1939	08	16	106	06	-6	13
1939	08	17	106	11	-6	13
1939	08	18	106	17	-6	14
1939	08	19	106	22	-6	14
1939	08	20	106	27	-6	15
1939	08	21	106	33	-6	15
1939	08	22	106	38	-6	15
1939	08	23	106	43	-6	16
1939	08	24	106	48	-6	16
1939	08	25	106	53	-6	17
1939	08	26	106	58	-6	17
1939	08	27	107	03	-6	17
1939	08	28	107	08	-6	18
1939	08	29	107	13	-6	18
1939	08	30	107	18	-6	19
1939	08	31	107	23	-6	19
1939	09	01	107	28	-6	20
1939	09	02	107	32	-6	20
1939	09	03	107	37	-6	20
1939	09	04	107	41	-6	21
1939	09	05	107	46	-6	21
1939	09	06	107	50	-6	22
1939	09	07	107	55	-6	22
1939	09	08	107	59	-6	23
1939	09	09	108	03	-6	23
1939	09	10	108	08	-6	24
1939	09	11	108	12	-6	24
1939	09	12	108	16	-6	25
1939	09	13	108	20	-6	25
1939	09	14	108	24	-6	26
1939	09	15	108	28	-6	27
1939	09	16	108	32	-6	27
1939	09	17	108	36	-6	28
1939	09	18	108	39	-6	28
1939	09	19	108	43	-6	29
1939	09	20	108	46	-6	29
1939	09	21	108	50	-6	30
1939	09	22	108	53	-6	30
1939	09	23	108	57	-6	31
1939	09	24	109	00	-6	32
1939	09	25	109	03	-6	32
1939	09	26	109	06	-6	33
1939	09	27	109	09	-6	33
1939	09	28	109	12	-6	34
1939	09	29	109	15	-6	35
1939	09	30	109	18	-6	35
1939	10	01	109	21	-6	36
1939	10	02	109	23	-6	36
1939	10	03	109	26	-6	37
1939	10	04	109	29	-6	38
1939	10	05	109	31	-6	38
1939	10	06	109	33	-6	39
1939	10	07	109	36	-6	40
1939	10	08	109	38	-6	40
1939	10	09	109	40	-6	41
1939	10	10	109	42	-6	42
1939	10	11	109	44	-6	42
1939	10	12	109	46	-6	43
1939	10	13	109	47	-6	44
1939	10	14	109	49	-6	44
1939	10	15	109	51	-6	45
1939	10	16	109	52	-6	46
1939	10	17	109	53	-6	46
1939	10	18	109	55	-6	47
1939	10	19	109	56	-6	48
1939	10	20	109	57	-6	48
1939	10	21	109	58	-6	49
1939	10	22	109	59	-6	50
1939	10	23	110	00	-6	50
1939	10	24	110	01	-6	51
1939	10	25	110	01	-6	52
1939	10	26	110	02	-6	52
1939	10	27	110	02	-6	53
1939	10	28	110	03	-6	54
1939	10	29	110	03	-6	54
1939	10	30	110	03	-6	55
1939	10	31	110	04	-6	56
1939	11	01	110	04	-6	56
1939	11	02	110	04	-6	57
1939	11	03	110	03	-6	58
1939	11	04	110	03	-6	58
1939	11	05	110	03	-6	59
1939	11	06	110	02	-7	00
1939	11	07	110	02	-7	00
1939	11	08	110	01	-7	01
1939	11	09	110	01	-7	01
1939	11	10	110	00	-7	02
1939	11	11	109	59	-7	03
1939	11	12	109	58	-7	03
1939	11	13	109	57	-7	04
1939	11	14	109	56	-7	05
1939	11	15	109	54	-7	05
1939	11	16	109	53	-7	06
1939	11	17	109	52	-7	07
1939	11	18	109	50	-7	07
1939	11	19	109	49	-7	08
1939	11	20	109	47	-7	08
1939	11	21	109	45	-7	09
1939	11	22	109	43	-7	10
1939	11	23	109	41	-7	10
1939	11	24	109	39	-7	11
1939	11	25	109	37	-7	11
1939	11	26	109	35	-7	12
1939	11	27	109	33	-7	12
1939	11	28	109	30	-7	13
1939	11	29	109	28	-7	14
1939	11	30	109	26	-7	14
1939	12	01	109	23	-7	15
1939	12	02	109	20	-7	15
1939	12	03	109	18	-7	16
1939	12	04	109	15	-7	16
1939	12	05	109	12	-7	17
1939	12	06	109	09	-7	17
1939	12	07	109	06	-7	18
1939	12	08	109	03	-7	18
1939	12	09	109	00	-7	18
1939	12	10	108	57	-7	19
1939	12	11	108	53	-7	19
1939	12	12	108	50	-7	20
1939	12	13	108	47	-7	20
1939	12	14	108	43	-7	21
1939	12	15	108	40	-7	21
1939	12	16	108	36	-7	21
1939	12	17	108	33	-7	22
1939	12	18	108	29	-7	22
1939	12	19	108	25	-7	22
1939	12	20	108	22	-7	23
1939	12	21	108	18	-7	23
1939	12	22	108	14	-7	23
1939	12	23	108	10	-7	24
1939	12	24	108	06	-7	24
1939	12	25	108	02	-7	24
1939	12	26	107	58	-7	24
1939	12	27	107	54	-7	25
1939	12	28	107	50	-7	25
1939	12	29	107	46	-7	25
1939	12	30	107	42	-7	25
1939	12	31	107	38	-7	25
1940	01	01	107	34	-7	26
1940	01	02	107	30	-7	26
1940	01	03	107	26	-7	26
1940	01	04	107	22	-7	26
1940	01	05	107	17	-7	26
1940	01	06	107	13	-7	26
1940	01	07	107	09	-7	26
1940	01	08	107	05	-7	26
1940	01	09	107	00	-7	26
1940	01	10	106	56	-7	26
1940	01	11	106	52	-7	26
1940	01	12	106	48	-7	26
1940	01	13	106	44	-7	26
1940	01	14	106	39	-7	26
1940	01	15	106	35	-7	26
1940	01	16	106	31	-7	26
1940	01	17	106	27	-7	26
1940	01	18	106	23	-7	26
1940	01	19	106	19	-7	26
1940	01	20	106	15	-7	26
1940	01	21	106	11	-7	26
1940	01	22	106	07	-7	26
1940	01	23	106	03	-7	26
1940	01	24	105	59	-7	26
1940	01	25	105	55	-7	25
1940	01	26	105	51	-7	25
1940	01	27	105	47	-7	25
1940	01	28	105	43	-7	25
1940	01	29	105	39	-7	25
1940	01	30	105	35	-7	24
1940	01	31	105	32	-7	24
1940	02	01	105	28	-7	24
1940	02	02	105	25	-7	23
1940	02	03	105	21	-7	23
1940	02	04	105	17	-7	23
1940	02	05	105	14	-7	23
1940	02	06	105	11	-7	22
1940	02	07	105	07	-7	22
1940	02	08	105	04	-7	22
1940	02	09	105	01	-7	21
1940	02	10	104	58	-7	21
1940	02	11	104	55	-7	21
1940	02	12	104	52	-7	20
1940	02	13	104	49	-7	20
1940	02	14	104	46	-7	19
1940	02	15	104	43	-7	19
1940	02	16	104	40	-7	18
1940	02	17	104	38	-7	18
1940	02	18	104	35	-7	18
1940	02	19	104	32	-7	17
1940	02	20	104	30	-7	17
1940	02	21	104	28	-7	16
1940	02	22	104	25	-7	16
1940	02	23	104	23	-7	15
1940	02	24	104	21	-7	15
1940	02	25	104	19	-7	14
1940	02	26	104	17	-7	14
1940	02	27	104	15	-7	13
1940	02	28	104	13	-7	13
1940	02	29	104	12	-7	12
1940	03	01	104	10	-7	12
1940	03	02	104	09	-7	11
1940	03	03	104	07	-7	11
1940	03	04	104	06	-7	10
1940	03	05	104	05	-7	09
1940	03	06	104	03	-7	09
1940	03	07	104	02	-7	08
1940	03	08	104	01	-7	08
1940	03	09	104	01	-7	07
1940	03	10	104	00	-7	07
1940	03	11	103	59	-7	06
1940	03	12	103	58	-7	05
1940	03	13	103	58	-7	05
1940	03	14	103	58	-7	04
1940	03	15	103	57	-7	04
1940	03	16	103	57	-7	03
1940	03	17	103	57	-7	02
1940	03	18	103	57	-7	02
1940	03	19	103	57	-7	01
1940	03	20	103	57	-7	01
1940	03	21	103	57	-7	00
1940	03	22	103	58	-6	59
1940	03	23	103	58	-6	59
1940	03	24	103	59	-6	58
1940	03	25	103	59	-6	58
1940	03	26	104	00	-6	57
1940	03	27	104	01	-6	56
1940	03	28	104	02	-6	56
1940	03	29	104	03	-6	55
1940	03	30	104	04	-6	55
1940	03	31	104	05	-6	54
1940	04	01	104	06	-6	53
1940	04	02	104	07	-6	53
1940	04	03	104	09	-6	52
1940	04	04	104	10	-6	51
1940	04	05	104	12	-6	51
1940	04	06	104	14	-6	50
1940	04	07	104	16	-6	50
1940	04	08	104	18	-6	49
1940	04	09	104	20	-6	48
1940	04	10	104	22	-6	48

Chiron

1940	04	11	104	24	-6 47
1940	04	12	104	26	-6 47
1940	04	13	104	28	-6 46
1940	04	14	104	31	-6 46
1940	04	15	104	33	-6 45
1940	04	16	104	36	-6 44
1940	04	17	104	39	-6 44
1940	04	18	104	41	-6 43
1940	04	19	104	44	-6 43
1940	04	20	104	47	-6 42
1940	04	21	104	50	-6 42
1940	04	22	104	53	-6 41
1940	04	23	104	56	-6 40
1940	04	24	105	00	-6 40
1940	04	25	105	03	-6 39
1940	04	26	105	06	-6 39
1940	04	27	105	10	-6 38
1940	04	28	105	14	-6 38
1940	04	29	105	17	-6 37
1940	04	30	105	21	-6 37
1940	05	01	105	25	-6 36
1940	05	02	105	29	-6 36
1940	05	03	105	32	-6 35
1940	05	04	105	36	-6 35
1940	05	05	105	41	-6 34
1940	05	06	105	45	-6 34
1940	05	07	105	49	-6 33
1940	05	08	105	53	-6 33
1940	05	09	105	58	-6 32
1940	05	10	106	02	-6 32
1940	05	11	106	06	-6 31
1940	05	12	106	11	-6 31
1940	05	13	106	16	-6 31
1940	05	14	106	20	-6 30
1940	05	15	106	25	-6 30
1940	05	16	106	30	-6 29
1940	05	17	106	35	-6 29
1940	05	18	106	40	-6 28
1940	05	19	106	44	-6 28
1940	05	20	106	49	-6 28
1940	05	21	106	55	-6 27
1940	05	22	107	00	-6 27
1940	05	23	107	05	-6 26
1940	05	24	107	10	-6 26
1940	05	25	107	15	-6 26
1940	05	26	107	21	-6 25
1940	05	27	107	26	-6 25
1940	05	28	107	32	-6 25
1940	05	29	107	37	-6 24
1940	05	30	107	43	-6 24
1940	05	31	107	48	-6 24
1940	06	01	107	54	-6 23
1940	06	02	108	00	-6 23
1940	06	03	108	05	-6 23
1940	06	04	108	11	-6 22
1940	06	05	108	17	-6 22
1940	06	06	108	23	-6 22
1940	06	07	108	29	-6 21
1940	06	08	108	34	-6 21
1940	06	09	108	40	-6 21
1940	06	10	108	46	-6 21
1940	06	11	108	52	-6 20
1940	06	12	108	59	-6 20
1940	06	13	109	05	-6 20
1940	06	14	109	11	-6 20
1940	06	15	109	17	-6 20
1940	06	16	109	23	-6 19
1940	06	17	109	29	-6 19
1940	06	18	109	36	-6 19
1940	06	19	109	42	-6 19
1940	06	20	109	48	-6 19
1940	06	21	109	55	-6 18
1940	06	22	110	01	-6 18
1940	06	23	110	07	-6 18
1940	06	24	110	14	-6 18
1940	06	25	110	20	-6 18
1940	06	26	110	27	-6 18
1940	06	27	110	33	-6 17
1940	06	28	110	40	-6 17
1940	06	29	110	46	-6 17
1940	06	30	110	53	-6 17
1940	07	01	110	59	-6 17
1940	07	02	111	06	-6 17
1940	07	03	111	12	-6 17
1940	07	04	111	19	-6 17
1940	07	05	111	26	-6 17
1940	07	06	111	32	-6 17
1940	07	07	111	39	-6 17
1940	07	08	111	45	-6 17
1940	07	09	111	52	-6 17
1940	07	10	111	59	-6 17
1940	07	11	112	06	-6 17
1940	07	12	112	12	-6 16
1940	07	13	112	19	-6 16
1940	07	14	112	26	-6 16
1940	07	15	112	32	-6 17
1940	07	16	112	39	-6 17
1940	07	17	112	46	-6 17
1940	07	18	112	52	-6 17
1940	07	19	112	59	-6 17
1940	07	20	113	06	-6 17
1940	07	21	113	12	-6 17
1940	07	22	113	19	-6 17
1940	07	23	113	26	-6 17
1940	07	24	113	32	-6 17
1940	07	25	113	39	-6 17
1940	07	26	113	46	-6 17
1940	07	27	113	52	-6 17
1940	07	28	113	59	-6 17
1940	07	29	114	06	-6 17
1940	07	30	114	12	-6 18
1940	07	31	114	19	-6 18
1940	08	01	114	26	-6 18
1940	08	02	114	32	-6 18
1940	08	03	114	39	-6 18
1940	08	04	114	45	-6 18
1940	08	05	114	52	-6 19
1940	08	06	114	58	-6 19
1940	08	07	115	05	-6 19
1940	08	08	115	11	-6 19
1940	08	09	115	18	-6 19
1940	08	10	115	24	-6 20
1940	08	11	115	31	-6 20
1940	08	12	115	37	-6 20
1940	08	13	115	43	-6 20
1940	08	14	115	50	-6 20
1940	08	15	115	56	-6 21
1940	08	16	116	02	-6 21
1940	08	17	116	09	-6 21
1940	08	18	116	15	-6 22
1940	08	19	116	21	-6 22
1940	08	20	116	27	-6 22
1940	08	21	116	33	-6 22
1940	08	22	116	39	-6 23
1940	08	23	116	45	-6 23
1940	08	24	116	51	-6 23
1940	08	25	116	57	-6 24
1940	08	26	117	03	-6 24
1940	08	27	117	09	-6 24
1940	08	28	117	15	-6 25
1940	08	29	117	21	-6 25
1940	08	30	117	27	-6 25
1940	08	31	117	32	-6 26
1940	09	01	117	38	-6 26
1940	09	02	117	44	-6 27
1940	09	03	117	49	-6 27
1940	09	04	117	55	-6 27
1940	09	05	118	00	-6 28
1940	09	06	118	06	-6 28
1940	09	07	118	11	-6 29
1940	09	08	118	17	-6 29
1940	09	09	118	22	-6 30
1940	09	10	118	27	-6 30
1940	09	11	118	32	-6 30
1940	09	12	118	38	-6 31
1940	09	13	118	43	-6 31
1940	09	14	118	48	-6 32
1940	09	15	118	53	-6 32
1940	09	16	118	58	-6 33
1940	09	17	119	02	-6 33
1940	09	18	119	07	-6 34
1940	09	19	119	12	-6 34
1940	09	20	119	17	-6 35
1940	09	21	119	21	-6 35
1940	09	22	119	26	-6 36
1940	09	23	119	30	-6 36
1940	09	24	119	35	-6 37
1940	09	25	119	39	-6 38
1940	09	26	119	43	-6 38
1940	09	27	119	47	-6 39
1940	09	28	119	51	-6 39
1940	09	29	119	56	-6 40
1940	09	30	120	00	-6 40
1940	10	01	120	03	-6 41
1940	10	02	120	07	-6 42
1940	10	03	120	11	-6 42
1940	10	04	120	15	-6 43
1940	10	05	120	18	-6 43
1940	10	06	120	22	-6 44
1940	10	07	120	25	-6 45
1940	10	08	120	29	-6 45
1940	10	09	120	32	-6 46
1940	10	10	120	35	-6 46
1940	10	11	120	38	-6 47
1940	10	12	120	41	-6 48
1940	10	13	120	44	-6 48
1940	10	14	120	47	-6 49
1940	10	15	120	50	-6 50
1940	10	16	120	52	-6 50
1940	10	17	120	55	-6 51
1940	10	18	120	57	-6 52
1940	10	19	121	00	-6 52
1940	10	20	121	02	-6 53
1940	10	21	121	04	-6 54
1940	10	22	121	07	-6 54
1940	10	23	121	09	-6 55
1940	10	24	121	11	-6 56
1940	10	25	121	13	-6 56
1940	10	26	121	14	-6 57
1940	10	27	121	16	-6 58
1940	10	28	121	18	-6 58
1940	10	29	121	19	-6 59
1940	10	30	121	20	-7 00
1940	10	31	121	22	-7 00
1940	11	01	121	23	-7 01
1940	11	02	121	24	-7 02
1940	11	03	121	25	-7 03
1940	11	04	121	26	-7 03
1940	11	05	121	27	-7 04
1940	11	06	121	28	-7 05
1940	11	07	121	28	-7 05
1940	11	08	121	29	-7 06
1940	11	09	121	29	-7 07
1940	11	10	121	29	-7 07
1940	11	11	121	30	-7 08
1940	11	12	121	30	-7 09
1940	11	13	121	30	-7 10
1940	11	14	121	30	-7 10
1940	11	15	121	30	-7 11
1940	11	16	121	29	-7 12
1940	11	17	121	29	-7 12
1940	11	18	121	28	-7 13
1940	11	19	121	28	-7 14
1940	11	20	121	27	-7 14
1940	11	21	121	27	-7 15
1940	11	22	121	26	-7 16
1940	11	23	121	25	-7 16
1940	11	24	121	24	-7 17
1940	11	25	121	23	-7 18
1940	11	26	121	21	-7 18
1940	11	27	121	20	-7 19
1940	11	28	121	19	-7 20
1940	11	29	121	17	-7 20
1940	11	30	121	15	-7 21
1940	12	01	121	14	-7 21
1940	12	02	121	12	-7 22
1940	12	03	121	10	-7 23
1940	12	04	121	08	-7 23
1940	12	05	121	06	-7 24
1940	12	06	121	04	-7 24
1940	12	07	121	02	-7 25
1940	12	08	120	59	-7 26
1940	12	09	120	57	-7 26
1940	12	10	120	54	-7 27
1940	12	11	120	52	-7 27
1940	12	12	120	49	-7 28
1940	12	13	120	46	-7 28
1940	12	14	120	44	-7 29
1940	12	15	120	41	-7 29
1940	12	16	120	38	-7 30
1940	12	17	120	35	-7 30
1940	12	18	120	31	-7 31
1940	12	19	120	28	-7 31
1940	12	20	120	25	-7 32
1940	12	21	120	22	-7 32
1940	12	22	120	18	-7 32
1940	12	23	120	15	-7 33
1940	12	24	120	11	-7 33
1940	12	25	120	08	-7 34
1940	12	26	120	04	-7 34
1940	12	27	120	00	-7 34
1940	12	28	119	57	-7 35
1940	12	29	119	53	-7 35
1940	12	30	119	49	-7 35
1940	12	31	119	45	-7 36
1941	01	01	119	41	-7 36
1941	01	02	119	37	-7 36
1941	01	03	119	33	-7 37
1941	01	04	119	29	-7 37
1941	01	05	119	25	-7 37
1941	01	06	119	21	-7 37
1941	01	07	119	17	-7 37
1941	01	08	119	13	-7 38
1941	01	09	119	08	-7 38
1941	01	10	119	04	-7 38
1941	01	11	119	00	-7 38
1941	01	12	118	55	-7 38
1941	01	13	118	51	-7 38
1941	01	14	118	47	-7 38
1941	01	15	118	42	-7 39
1941	01	16	118	38	-7 39
1941	01	17	118	34	-7 39
1941	01	18	118	29	-7 39
1941	01	19	118	25	-7 39
1941	01	20	118	21	-7 39
1941	01	21	118	16	-7 39
1941	01	22	118	12	-7 39
1941	01	23	118	07	-7 39
1941	01	24	118	03	-7 39
1941	01	25	117	59	-7 38
1941	01	26	117	54	-7 38
1941	01	27	117	50	-7 38
1941	01	28	117	46	-7 38
1941	01	29	117	41	-7 38
1941	01	30	117	37	-7 38
1941	01	31	117	33	-7 38
1941	02	01	117	29	-7 38
1941	02	02	117	25	-7 37
1941	02	03	117	20	-7 37
1941	02	04	117	16	-7 37
1941	02	05	117	12	-7 37
1941	02	06	117	08	-7 36
1941	02	07	117	04	-7 36
1941	02	08	117	00	-7 36
1941	02	09	116	56	-7 36
1941	02	10	116	52	-7 35
1941	02	11	116	49	-7 35
1941	02	12	116	45	-7 35
1941	02	13	116	41	-7 34
1941	02	14	116	38	-7 34
1941	02	15	116	34	-7 33
1941	02	16	116	30	-7 33
1941	02	17	116	27	-7 33
1941	02	18	116	24	-7 32
1941	02	19	116	20	-7 32
1941	02	20	116	17	-7 31
1941	02	21	116	14	-7 31
1941	02	22	116	11	-7 30
1941	02	23	116	08	-7 30
1941	02	24	116	05	-7 29
1941	02	25	116	02	-7 29
1941	02	26	115	59	-7 28
1941	02	27	115	56	-7 28
1941	02	28	115	53	-7 27
1941	03	01	115	51	-7 27
1941	03	02	115	48	-7 26
1941	03	03	115	46	-7 26
1941	03	04	115	43	-7 25
1941	03	05	115	41	-7 25
1941	03	06	115	39	-7 24
1941	03	07	115	37	-7 23
1941	03	08	115	35	-7 23
1941	03	09	115	33	-7 22
1941	03	10	115	31	-7 22
1941	03	11	115	30	-7 21
1941	03	12	115	28	-7 20
1941	03	13	115	26	-7 20
1941	03	14	115	25	-7 19
1941	03	15	115	24	-7 19
1941	03	16	115	22	-7 18
1941	03	17	115	21	-7 17
1941	03	18	115	20	-7 17
1941	03	19	115	19	-7 16
1941	03	20	115	18	-7 15
1941	03	21	115	18	-7 15
1941	03	22	115	17	-7 14
1941	03	23	115	16	-7 13
1941	03	24	115	16	-7 13
1941	03	25	115	15	-7 12
1941	03	26	115	15	-7 11
1941	03	27	115	15	-7 10
1941	03	28	115	15	-7 10
1941	03	29	115	15	-7 09
1941	03	30	115	15	-7 08
1941	03	31	115	15	-7 08
1941	04	01	115	16	-7 07
1941	04	02	115	16	-7 06
1941	04	03	115	17	-7 06
1941	04	04	115	17	-7 05
1941	04	05	115	18	-7 04
1941	04	06	115	19	-7 03
1941	04	07	115	20	-7 03
1941	04	08	115	21	-7 02
1941	04	09	115	22	-7 01
1941	04	10	115	23	-7 01
1941	04	11	115	24	-7 00
1941	04	12	115	26	-6 59
1941	04	13	115	27	-6 59
1941	04	14	115	29	-6 58
1941	04	15	115	31	-6 57
1941	04	16	115	32	-6 56
1941	04	17	115	34	-6 56
1941	04	18	115	36	-6 55
1941	04	19	115	38	-6 54
1941	04	20	115	40	-6 54
1941	04	21	115	43	-6 53
1941	04	22	115	45	-6 52
1941	04	23	115	48	-6 52
1941	04	24	115	50	-6 51
1941	04	25	115	53	-6 50
1941	04	26	115	55	-6 50
1941	04	27	115	58	-6 49
1941	04	28	116	01	-6 48
1941	04	29	116	04	-6 48
1941	04	30	116	07	-6 47
1941	05	01	116	10	-6 46
1941	05	02	116	14	-6 46
1941	05	03	116	17	-6 45
1941	05	04	116	21	-6 44
1941	05	05	116	24	-6 44
1941	05	06	116	28	-6 43
1941	05	07	116	31	-6 43
1941	05	08	116	35	-6 42
1941	05	09	116	39	-6 41
1941	05	10	116	43	-6 41
1941	05	11	116	47	-6 40
1941	05	12	116	51	-6 39
1941	05	13	116	55	-6 39
1941	05	14	116	59	-6 38
1941	05	15	117	04	-6 38
1941	05	16	117	08	-6 37
1941	05	17	117	12	-6 37
1941	05	18	117	17	-6 36
1941	05	19	117	21	-6 35
1941	05	20	117	26	-6 35
1941	05	21	117	31	-6 34
1941	05	22	117	36	-6 34
1941	05	23	117	41	-6 33
1941	05	24	117	45	-6 33
1941	05	25	117	50	-6 32
1941	05	26	117	56	-6 32
1941	05	27	118	01	-6 31
1941	05	28	118	06	-6 31
1941	05	29	118	11	-6 30
1941	05	30	118	16	-6 30
1941	05	31	118	22	-6 29
1941	06	01	118	27	-6 29
1941	06	02	118	33	-6 28
1941	06	03	118	38	-6 28

1941	06	04	118	44	-6	27
1941	06	05	118	50	-6	27
1941	06	06	118	55	-6	27
1941	06	07	119	01	-6	26
1941	06	08	119	07	-6	26
1941	06	09	119	13	-6	25
1941	06	10	119	19	-6	25
1941	06	11	119	25	-6	24
1941	06	12	119	31	-6	24
1941	06	13	119	37	-6	24
1941	06	14	119	43	-6	23
1941	06	15	119	49	-6	23
1941	06	16	119	55	-6	23
1941	06	17	120	02	-6	22
1941	06	18	120	08	-6	22
1941	06	19	120	14	-6	22
1941	06	20	120	21	-6	21
1941	06	21	120	27	-6	21
1941	06	22	120	34	-6	21
1941	06	23	120	40	-6	20
1941	06	24	120	47	-6	20
1941	06	25	120	53	-6	20
1941	06	26	121	00	-6	19
1941	06	27	121	07	-6	19
1941	06	28	121	13	-6	19
1941	06	29	121	20	-6	19
1941	06	30	121	27	-6	18
1941	07	01	121	34	-6	18
1941	07	02	121	40	-6	18
1941	07	03	121	47	-6	18
1941	07	04	121	54	-6	17
1941	07	05	122	01	-6	17
1941	07	06	122	08	-6	17
1941	07	07	122	15	-6	17
1941	07	08	122	22	-6	17
1941	07	09	122	29	-6	16
1941	07	10	122	36	-6	16
1941	07	11	122	43	-6	16
1941	07	12	122	50	-6	16
1941	07	13	122	57	-6	16
1941	07	14	123	04	-6	16
1941	07	15	123	11	-6	15
1941	07	16	123	18	-6	15
1941	07	17	123	25	-6	15
1941	07	18	123	32	-6	15
1941	07	19	123	40	-6	15
1941	07	20	123	47	-6	15
1941	07	21	123	54	-6	15
1941	07	22	124	01	-6	15
1941	07	23	124	08	-6	15
1941	07	24	124	16	-6	15
1941	07	25	124	23	-6	14
1941	07	26	124	30	-6	14
1941	07	27	124	37	-6	14
1941	07	28	124	44	-6	14
1941	07	29	124	52	-6	14
1941	07	30	124	59	-6	14
1941	07	31	125	06	-6	14
1941	08	01	125	13	-6	14
1941	08	02	125	21	-6	14
1941	08	03	125	28	-6	14
1941	08	04	125	35	-6	14
1941	08	05	125	42	-6	14
1941	08	06	125	49	-6	14
1941	08	07	125	57	-6	14
1941	08	08	126	04	-6	15
1941	08	09	126	11	-6	15
1941	08	10	126	18	-6	15
1941	08	11	126	25	-6	15
1941	08	12	126	33	-6	15
1941	08	13	126	40	-6	15
1941	08	14	126	47	-6	15
1941	08	15	126	54	-6	15
1941	08	16	127	01	-6	15
1941	08	17	127	08	-6	15
1941	08	18	127	15	-6	16
1941	08	19	127	22	-6	16
1941	08	20	127	29	-6	16
1941	08	21	127	36	-6	16
1941	08	22	127	43	-6	16
1941	08	23	127	50	-6	16
1941	08	24	127	57	-6	17
1941	08	25	128	04	-6	17
1941	08	26	128	11	-6	17
1941	08	27	128	18	-6	17
1941	08	28	128	25	-6	17
1941	08	29	128	32	-6	18
1941	08	30	128	38	-6	18
1941	08	31	128	45	-6	18
1941	09	01	128	52	-6	18
1941	09	02	128	58	-6	19
1941	09	03	129	05	-6	19
1941	09	04	129	12	-6	19
1941	09	05	129	18	-6	19
1941	09	06	129	25	-6	20
1941	09	07	129	31	-6	20
1941	09	08	129	38	-6	20
1941	09	09	129	44	-6	21
1941	09	10	129	51	-6	21
1941	09	11	129	57	-6	21
1941	09	12	130	03	-6	22
1941	09	13	130	09	-6	22
1941	09	14	130	16	-6	22
1941	09	15	130	22	-6	23
1941	09	16	130	28	-6	23
1941	09	17	130	34	-6	23
1941	09	18	130	40	-6	24
1941	09	19	130	46	-6	24
1941	09	20	130	52	-6	25
1941	09	21	130	58	-6	25
1941	09	22	131	03	-6	25
1941	09	23	131	09	-6	26
1941	09	24	131	15	-6	26
1941	09	25	131	20	-6	27
1941	09	26	131	26	-6	27
1941	09	27	131	31	-6	28
1941	09	28	131	37	-6	28
1941	09	29	131	42	-6	29
1941	09	30	131	48	-6	29
1941	10	01	131	53	-6	29
1941	10	02	131	58	-6	30
1941	10	03	132	03	-6	30
1941	10	04	132	08	-6	31
1941	10	05	132	13	-6	31
1941	10	06	132	18	-6	32
1941	10	07	132	23	-6	32
1941	10	08	132	28	-6	33
1941	10	09	132	32	-6	34
1941	10	10	132	37	-6	34
1941	10	11	132	41	-6	35
1941	10	12	132	46	-6	35
1941	10	13	132	50	-6	36
1941	10	14	132	55	-6	36
1941	10	15	132	59	-6	37
1941	10	16	133	03	-6	37
1941	10	17	133	07	-6	38
1941	10	18	133	11	-6	39
1941	10	19	133	15	-6	39
1941	10	20	133	19	-6	40
1941	10	21	133	23	-6	40
1941	10	22	133	26	-6	41
1941	10	23	133	30	-6	42
1941	10	24	133	33	-6	42
1941	10	25	133	37	-6	43
1941	10	26	133	40	-6	43
1941	10	27	133	43	-6	44
1941	10	28	133	46	-6	45
1941	10	29	133	49	-6	45
1941	10	30	133	52	-6	46
1941	10	31	133	55	-6	47
1941	11	01	133	58	-6	47
1941	11	02	134	00	-6	48
1941	11	03	134	03	-6	49
1941	11	04	134	05	-6	49
1941	11	05	134	08	-6	50
1941	11	06	134	10	-6	51
1941	11	07	134	12	-6	51
1941	11	08	134	14	-6	52
1941	11	09	134	16	-6	52
1941	11	10	134	18	-6	53
1941	11	11	134	20	-6	54
1941	11	12	134	22	-6	55
1941	11	13	134	23	-6	55
1941	11	14	134	25	-6	56
1941	11	15	134	26	-6	57
1941	11	16	134	27	-6	57
1941	11	17	134	28	-6	58
1941	11	18	134	29	-6	59
1941	11	19	134	30	-6	59
1941	11	20	134	31	-7	00
1941	11	21	134	32	-7	01
1941	11	22	134	32	-7	01
1941	11	23	134	33	-7	02
1941	11	24	134	33	-7	03
1941	11	25	134	34	-7	03
1941	11	26	134	34	-7	04
1941	11	27	134	34	-7	05
1941	11	28	134	34	-7	05
1941	11	29	134	34	-7	06
1941	11	30	134	34	-7	07
1941	12	01	134	33	-7	07
1941	12	02	134	33	-7	08
1941	12	03	134	32	-7	09
1941	12	04	134	32	-7	09
1941	12	05	134	31	-7	10
1941	12	06	134	30	-7	11
1941	12	07	134	29	-7	11
1941	12	08	134	28	-7	12
1941	12	09	134	27	-7	12
1941	12	10	134	26	-7	13
1941	12	11	134	24	-7	14
1941	12	12	134	23	-7	14
1941	12	13	134	21	-7	15
1941	12	14	134	20	-7	15
1941	12	15	134	18	-7	16
1941	12	16	134	16	-7	17
1941	12	17	134	14	-7	17
1941	12	18	134	12	-7	18
1941	12	19	134	10	-7	18
1941	12	20	134	08	-7	19
1941	12	21	134	05	-7	19
1941	12	22	134	03	-7	20
1941	12	23	134	00	-7	20
1941	12	24	133	58	-7	21
1941	12	25	133	55	-7	21
1941	12	26	133	52	-7	22
1941	12	27	133	49	-7	22
1941	12	28	133	46	-7	23
1941	12	29	133	43	-7	23
1941	12	30	133	40	-7	24
1941	12	31	133	37	-7	24
1942	01	01	133	34	-7	25
1942	01	02	133	31	-7	25
1942	01	03	133	27	-7	25
1942	01	04	133	24	-7	26
1942	01	05	133	20	-7	26
1942	01	06	133	17	-7	27
1942	01	07	133	13	-7	27
1942	01	08	133	09	-7	27
1942	01	09	133	05	-7	28
1942	01	10	133	01	-7	28
1942	01	11	132	58	-7	28
1942	01	12	132	54	-7	28
1942	01	13	132	50	-7	29
1942	01	14	132	45	-7	29
1942	01	15	132	41	-7	29
1942	01	16	132	37	-7	29
1942	01	17	132	33	-7	30
1942	01	18	132	29	-7	30
1942	01	19	132	24	-7	30
1942	01	20	132	20	-7	30
1942	01	21	132	16	-7	30
1942	01	22	132	11	-7	30
1942	01	23	132	07	-7	30
1942	01	24	132	03	-7	31
1942	01	25	131	58	-7	31
1942	01	26	131	54	-7	31
1942	01	27	131	49	-7	31
1942	01	28	131	45	-7	31
1942	01	29	131	40	-7	31
1942	01	30	131	36	-7	31
1942	01	31	131	31	-7	31
1942	02	01	131	27	-7	31
1942	02	02	131	22	-7	31
1942	02	03	131	17	-7	31
1942	02	04	131	13	-7	30
1942	02	05	131	08	-7	30
1942	02	06	131	04	-7	30
1942	02	07	130	59	-7	30
1942	02	08	130	55	-7	30
1942	02	09	130	50	-7	30
1942	02	10	130	46	-7	30
1942	02	11	130	41	-7	29
1942	02	12	130	37	-7	29
1942	02	13	130	33	-7	29
1942	02	14	130	28	-7	29
1942	02	15	130	24	-7	28
1942	02	16	130	20	-7	28
1942	02	17	130	15	-7	28
1942	02	18	130	11	-7	28
1942	02	19	130	07	-7	27
1942	02	20	130	03	-7	27
1942	02	21	129	59	-7	26
1942	02	22	129	55	-7	26
1942	02	23	129	51	-7	26
1942	02	24	129	47	-7	25
1942	02	25	129	43	-7	25
1942	02	26	129	39	-7	24
1942	02	27	129	35	-7	24
1942	02	28	129	32	-7	24
1942	03	01	129	28	-7	23
1942	03	02	129	25	-7	23
1942	03	03	129	21	-7	22
1942	03	04	129	18	-7	22
1942	03	05	129	14	-7	21
1942	03	06	129	11	-7	21
1942	03	07	129	08	-7	20
1942	03	08	129	05	-7	19
1942	03	09	129	02	-7	19
1942	03	10	128	59	-7	18
1942	03	11	128	56	-7	18
1942	03	12	128	53	-7	17
1942	03	13	128	50	-7	16
1942	03	14	128	48	-7	16
1942	03	15	128	45	-7	15
1942	03	16	128	43	-7	15
1942	03	17	128	40	-7	14
1942	03	18	128	38	-7	13
1942	03	19	128	36	-7	13
1942	03	20	128	34	-7	12
1942	03	21	128	32	-7	11
1942	03	22	128	30	-7	11
1942	03	23	128	28	-7	10
1942	03	24	128	26	-7	09
1942	03	25	128	25	-7	08
1942	03	26	128	23	-7	08
1942	03	27	128	22	-7	07
1942	03	28	128	20	-7	06
1942	03	29	128	19	-7	06
1942	03	30	128	18	-7	05
1942	03	31	128	17	-7	04
1942	04	01	128	16	-7	03
1942	04	02	128	15	-7	03
1942	04	03	128	15	-7	02
1942	04	04	128	14	-7	01
1942	04	05	128	14	-7	00
1942	04	06	128	13	-7	00
1942	04	07	128	13	-6	59
1942	04	08	128	13	-6	58
1942	04	09	128	13	-6	57
1942	04	10	128	13	-6	56
1942	04	11	128	13	-6	56
1942	04	12	128	13	-6	55
1942	04	13	128	13	-6	54
1942	04	14	128	14	-6	53
1942	04	15	128	14	-6	53
1942	04	16	128	15	-6	52
1942	04	17	128	16	-6	51
1942	04	18	128	17	-6	50
1942	04	19	128	18	-6	49
1942	04	20	128	19	-6	49
1942	04	21	128	20	-6	48
1942	04	22	128	21	-6	47
1942	04	23	128	23	-6	46
1942	04	24	128	24	-6	45
1942	04	25	128	26	-6	45
1942	04	26	128	27	-6	44
1942	04	27	128	29	-6	43
1942	04	28	128	31	-6	42
1942	04	29	128	33	-6	42
1942	04	30	128	35	-6	41
1942	05	01	128	37	-6	40
1942	05	02	128	40	-6	39
1942	05	03	128	42	-6	39
1942	05	04	128	45	-6	38
1942	05	05	128	47	-6	37
1942	05	06	128	50	-6	36
1942	05	07	128	53	-6	36
1942	05	08	128	56	-6	35
1942	05	09	128	59	-6	34
1942	05	10	129	02	-6	33
1942	05	11	129	05	-6	33
1942	05	12	129	08	-6	32
1942	05	13	129	12	-6	31
1942	05	14	129	15	-6	30
1942	05	15	129	19	-6	30
1942	05	16	129	22	-6	29
1942	05	17	129	26	-6	28
1942	05	18	129	30	-6	27
1942	05	19	129	34	-6	27
1942	05	20	129	38	-6	26
1942	05	21	129	42	-6	25
1942	05	22	129	46	-6	25
1942	05	23	129	50	-6	24
1942	05	24	129	54	-6	23
1942	05	25	129	59	-6	23
1942	05	26	130	03	-6	22
1942	05	27	130	08	-6	21
1942	05	28	130	12	-6	21
1942	05	29	130	17	-6	20
1942	05	30	130	22	-6	19
1942	05	31	130	27	-6	19
1942	06	01	130	32	-6	18
1942	06	02	130	37	-6	18
1942	06	03	130	42	-6	17
1942	06	04	130	47	-6	16
1942	06	05	130	52	-6	16
1942	06	06	130	57	-6	15
1942	06	07	131	03	-6	15
1942	06	08	131	08	-6	14
1942	06	09	131	14	-6	13
1942	06	10	131	19	-6	13
1942	06	11	131	25	-6	12
1942	06	12	131	31	-6	12
1942	06	13	131	37	-6	11
1942	06	14	131	42	-6	11
1942	06	15	131	48	-6	10
1942	06	16	131	54	-6	10
1942	06	17	132	00	-6	09
1942	06	18	132	06	-6	09
1942	06	19	132	13	-6	08
1942	06	20	132	19	-6	08
1942	06	21	132	25	-6	07
1942	06	22	132	31	-6	07
1942	06	23	132	38	-6	06
1942	06	24	132	44	-6	06
1942	06	25	132	51	-6	05
1942	06	26	132	57	-6	05
1942	06	27	133	04	-6	04
1942	06	28	133	10	-6	04
1942	06	29	133	17	-6	03
1942	06	30	133	24	-6	03
1942	07	01	133	30	-6	02
1942	07	02	133	37	-6	02
1942	07	03	133	44	-6	02
1942	07	04	133	51	-6	01
1942	07	05	133	58	-6	01
1942	07	06	134	05	-6	01
1942	07	07	134	12	-6	00
1942	07	08	134	19	-6	00
1942	07	09	134	26	-5	59
1942	07	10	134	33	-5	59
1942	07	11	134	40	-5	59
1942	07	12	134	47	-5	58
1942	07	13	134	55	-5	58
1942	07	14	135	02	-5	58
1942	07	15	135	09	-5	57
1942	07	16	135	17	-5	57
1942	07	17	135	24	-5	57
1942	07	18	135	31	-5	57
1942	07	19	135	39	-5	56
1942	07	20	135	46	-5	56
1942	07	21	135	54	-5	56
1942	07	22	136	01	-5	55
1942	07	23	136	09	-5	55
1942	07	24	136	16	-5	55
1942	07	25	136	24	-5	55
1942	07	26	136	31	-5	55
1942	07	27	136	39	-5	54

Chiron

1942	07	28	136	46	-5	54
1942	07	29	136	54	-5	54
1942	07	30	137	02	-5	54
1942	07	31	137	09	-5	54
1942	08	01	137	17	-5	53
1942	08	02	137	25	-5	53
1942	08	03	137	32	-5	53
1942	08	04	137	40	-5	53
1942	08	05	137	48	-5	53
1942	08	06	137	56	-5	53
1942	08	07	138	03	-5	52
1942	08	08	138	11	-5	52
1942	08	09	138	19	-5	52
1942	08	10	138	27	-5	52
1942	08	11	138	34	-5	52
1942	08	12	138	42	-5	52
1942	08	13	138	50	-5	52
1942	08	14	138	58	-5	52
1942	08	15	139	06	-5	52
1942	08	16	139	13	-5	52
1942	08	17	139	21	-5	52
1942	08	18	139	29	-5	52
1942	08	19	139	37	-5	52
1942	08	20	139	44	-5	51
1942	08	21	139	52	-5	51
1942	08	22	140	00	-5	51
1942	08	23	140	08	-5	51
1942	08	24	140	15	-5	51
1942	08	25	140	23	-5	51
1942	08	26	140	31	-5	51
1942	08	27	140	39	-5	52
1942	08	28	140	46	-5	52
1942	08	29	140	54	-5	52
1942	08	30	141	02	-5	52
1942	08	31	141	09	-5	52
1942	09	01	141	17	-5	52
1942	09	02	141	24	-5	52
1942	09	03	141	32	-5	52
1942	09	04	141	40	-5	52
1942	09	05	141	47	-5	52
1942	09	06	141	55	-5	52
1942	09	07	142	02	-5	52
1942	09	08	142	10	-5	52
1942	09	09	142	17	-5	53
1942	09	10	142	25	-5	53
1942	09	11	142	32	-5	53
1942	09	12	142	39	-5	53
1942	09	13	142	47	-5	53
1942	09	14	142	54	-5	53
1942	09	15	143	01	-5	54
1942	09	16	143	08	-5	54
1942	09	17	143	16	-5	54
1942	09	18	143	23	-5	54
1942	09	19	143	30	-5	54
1942	09	20	143	37	-5	55
1942	09	21	143	44	-5	55
1942	09	22	143	51	-5	55
1942	09	23	143	58	-5	55
1942	09	24	144	05	-5	56
1942	09	25	144	12	-5	56
1942	09	26	144	19	-5	56
1942	09	27	144	25	-5	56
1942	09	28	144	32	-5	57
1942	09	29	144	39	-5	57
1942	09	30	144	46	-5	57
1942	10	01	144	52	-5	57
1942	10	02	144	59	-5	58
1942	10	03	145	05	-5	58
1942	10	04	145	12	-5	58
1942	10	05	145	18	-5	59
1942	10	06	145	24	-5	59
1942	10	07	145	31	-5	59
1942	10	08	145	37	-6	00
1942	10	09	145	43	-6	00
1942	10	10	145	49	-6	00
1942	10	11	145	55	-6	01
1942	10	12	146	01	-6	01
1942	10	13	146	07	-6	02
1942	10	14	146	13	-6	02
1942	10	15	146	18	-6	02
1942	10	16	146	24	-6	03
1942	10	17	146	30	-6	03
1942	10	18	146	35	-6	04
1942	10	19	146	41	-6	04
1942	10	20	146	46	-6	04
1942	10	21	146	51	-6	05
1942	10	22	146	57	-6	05
1942	10	23	147	02	-6	06
1942	10	24	147	07	-6	06
1942	10	25	147	12	-6	07
1942	10	26	147	17	-6	07
1942	10	27	147	22	-6	08
1942	10	28	147	27	-6	08
1942	10	29	147	31	-6	09
1942	10	30	147	36	-6	09
1942	10	31	147	40	-6	10
1942	11	01	147	45	-6	10
1942	11	02	147	49	-6	11
1942	11	03	147	54	-6	11
1942	11	04	147	58	-6	12
1942	11	05	148	02	-6	12
1942	11	06	148	06	-6	13
1942	11	07	148	10	-6	13
1942	11	08	148	14	-6	14
1942	11	09	148	17	-6	14
1942	11	10	148	21	-6	15
1942	11	11	148	24	-6	15
1942	11	12	148	28	-6	16
1942	11	13	148	31	-6	16
1942	11	14	148	35	-6	17
1942	11	15	148	38	-6	18
1942	11	16	148	41	-6	18
1942	11	17	148	44	-6	19
1942	11	18	148	46	-6	19
1942	11	19	148	49	-6	20
1942	11	20	148	52	-6	20
1942	11	21	148	54	-6	21
1942	11	22	148	57	-6	22
1942	11	23	148	59	-6	22
1942	11	24	149	01	-6	23
1942	11	25	149	03	-6	23
1942	11	26	149	05	-6	24
1942	11	27	149	07	-6	24
1942	11	28	149	09	-6	25
1942	11	29	149	11	-6	26
1942	11	30	149	12	-6	26
1942	12	01	149	14	-6	27
1942	12	02	149	15	-6	27
1942	12	03	149	16	-6	28
1942	12	04	149	18	-6	29
1942	12	05	149	19	-6	29
1942	12	06	149	19	-6	30
1942	12	07	149	20	-6	30
1942	12	08	149	21	-6	31
1942	12	09	149	22	-6	31
1942	12	10	149	22	-6	32
1942	12	11	149	22	-6	33
1942	12	12	149	23	-6	33
1942	12	13	149	23	-6	34
1942	12	14	149	23	-6	34
1942	12	15	149	23	-6	35
1942	12	16	149	22	-6	36
1942	12	17	149	22	-6	36
1942	12	18	149	22	-6	37
1942	12	19	149	21	-6	37
1942	12	20	149	20	-6	38
1942	12	21	149	20	-6	38
1942	12	22	149	19	-6	39
1942	12	23	149	18	-6	39
1942	12	24	149	17	-6	40
1942	12	25	149	15	-6	40
1942	12	26	149	14	-6	41
1942	12	27	149	13	-6	41
1942	12	28	149	11	-6	42
1942	12	29	149	10	-6	42
1942	12	30	149	08	-6	43
1942	12	31	149	06	-6	43
1943	01	01	149	04	-6	44
1943	01	02	149	02	-6	44
1943	01	03	149	00	-6	45
1943	01	04	148	58	-6	45
1943	01	05	148	55	-6	46
1943	01	06	148	53	-6	46
1943	01	07	148	50	-6	47
1943	01	08	148	48	-6	47
1943	01	09	148	45	-6	47
1943	01	10	148	42	-6	48
1943	01	11	148	39	-6	48
1943	01	12	148	36	-6	49
1943	01	13	148	33	-6	49
1943	01	14	148	30	-6	49
1943	01	15	148	27	-6	50
1943	01	16	148	23	-6	50
1943	01	17	148	20	-6	50
1943	01	18	148	17	-6	51
1943	01	19	148	13	-6	51
1943	01	20	148	09	-6	51
1943	01	21	148	06	-6	51
1943	01	22	148	02	-6	52
1943	01	23	147	58	-6	52
1943	01	24	147	54	-6	52
1943	01	25	147	50	-6	52
1943	01	26	147	46	-6	53
1943	01	27	147	42	-6	53
1943	01	28	147	38	-6	53
1943	01	29	147	34	-6	53
1943	01	30	147	30	-6	53
1943	01	31	147	25	-6	53
1943	02	01	147	21	-6	53
1943	02	02	147	17	-6	53
1943	02	03	147	12	-6	54
1943	02	04	147	08	-6	54
1943	02	05	147	03	-6	54
1943	02	06	146	59	-6	54
1943	02	07	146	54	-6	54
1943	02	08	146	50	-6	54
1943	02	09	146	45	-6	54
1943	02	10	146	41	-6	54
1943	02	11	146	36	-6	54
1943	02	12	146	31	-6	54
1943	02	13	146	27	-6	53
1943	02	14	146	22	-6	53
1943	02	15	146	17	-6	53
1943	02	16	146	13	-6	53
1943	02	17	146	08	-6	53
1943	02	18	146	03	-6	53
1943	02	19	145	59	-6	53
1943	02	20	145	54	-6	52
1943	02	21	145	49	-6	52
1943	02	22	145	45	-6	52
1943	02	23	145	40	-6	52
1943	02	24	145	35	-6	51
1943	02	25	145	31	-6	51
1943	02	26	145	26	-6	51
1943	02	27	145	22	-6	51
1943	02	28	145	17	-6	50
1943	03	01	145	13	-6	50
1943	03	02	145	08	-6	50
1943	03	03	145	04	-6	49
1943	03	04	145	00	-6	49
1943	03	05	144	55	-6	48
1943	03	06	144	51	-6	48
1943	03	07	144	47	-6	48
1943	03	08	144	43	-6	47
1943	03	09	144	39	-6	47
1943	03	10	144	35	-6	46
1943	03	11	144	30	-6	46
1943	03	12	144	27	-6	45
1943	03	13	144	23	-6	45
1943	03	14	144	19	-6	44
1943	03	15	144	15	-6	44
1943	03	16	144	11	-6	43
1943	03	17	144	08	-6	43
1943	03	18	144	04	-6	42
1943	03	19	144	01	-6	41
1943	03	20	143	57	-6	41
1943	03	21	143	54	-6	40
1943	03	22	143	51	-6	40
1943	03	23	143	48	-6	39
1943	03	24	143	45	-6	38
1943	03	25	143	42	-6	38
1943	03	26	143	39	-6	37
1943	03	27	143	36	-6	36
1943	03	28	143	33	-6	36
1943	03	29	143	31	-6	35
1943	03	30	143	28	-6	34
1943	03	31	143	26	-6	34
1943	04	01	143	23	-6	33
1943	04	02	143	21	-6	32
1943	04	03	143	19	-6	32
1943	04	04	143	17	-6	31
1943	04	05	143	15	-6	30
1943	04	06	143	13	-6	29
1943	04	07	143	11	-6	29
1943	04	08	143	09	-6	28
1943	04	09	143	08	-6	27
1943	04	10	143	06	-6	26
1943	04	11	143	05	-6	25
1943	04	12	143	04	-6	25
1943	04	13	143	03	-6	24
1943	04	14	143	02	-6	23
1943	04	15	143	01	-6	22
1943	04	16	143	00	-6	22
1943	04	17	142	59	-6	21
1943	04	18	142	59	-6	20
1943	04	19	142	58	-6	19
1943	04	20	142	58	-6	18
1943	04	21	142	58	-6	17
1943	04	22	142	57	-6	17
1943	04	23	142	57	-6	16
1943	04	24	142	57	-6	15
1943	04	25	142	58	-6	14
1943	04	26	142	58	-6	13
1943	04	27	142	58	-6	13
1943	04	28	142	59	-6	12
1943	04	29	142	59	-6	11
1943	04	30	143	00	-6	10
1943	05	01	143	01	-6	09
1943	05	02	143	02	-6	08
1943	05	03	143	03	-6	08
1943	05	04	143	04	-6	07
1943	05	05	143	05	-6	06
1943	05	06	143	07	-6	05
1943	05	07	143	08	-6	04
1943	05	08	143	10	-6	03
1943	05	09	143	11	-6	03
1943	05	10	143	13	-6	02
1943	05	11	143	15	-6	01
1943	05	12	143	17	-6	00
1943	05	13	143	19	-5	59
1943	05	14	143	21	-5	59
1943	05	15	143	24	-5	58
1943	05	16	143	26	-5	57
1943	05	17	143	29	-5	56
1943	05	18	143	31	-5	55
1943	05	19	143	34	-5	55
1943	05	20	143	37	-5	54
1943	05	21	143	40	-5	53
1943	05	22	143	43	-5	52
1943	05	23	143	46	-5	51
1943	05	24	143	49	-5	51
1943	05	25	143	53	-5	50
1943	05	26	143	56	-5	49
1943	05	27	144	00	-5	48
1943	05	28	144	03	-5	48
1943	05	29	144	07	-5	47
1943	05	30	144	11	-5	46
1943	05	31	144	15	-5	45
1943	06	01	144	19	-5	44
1943	06	02	144	23	-5	44
1943	06	03	144	27	-5	43
1943	06	04	144	31	-5	42
1943	06	05	144	36	-5	42
1943	06	06	144	40	-5	41
1943	06	07	144	45	-5	40
1943	06	08	144	49	-5	39
1943	06	09	144	54	-5	39
1943	06	10	144	59	-5	38
1943	06	11	145	04	-5	37
1943	06	12	145	09	-5	37
1943	06	13	145	14	-5	36
1943	06	14	145	19	-5	35
1943	06	15	145	24	-5	35
1943	06	16	145	29	-5	34
1943	06	17	145	35	-5	33
1943	06	18	145	40	-5	33
1943	06	19	145	45	-5	32
1943	06	20	145	51	-5	31
1943	06	21	145	57	-5	31
1943	06	22	146	02	-5	30
1943	06	23	146	08	-5	29
1943	06	24	146	14	-5	29
1943	06	25	146	20	-5	28
1943	06	26	146	26	-5	28
1943	06	27	146	32	-5	27
1943	06	28	146	38	-5	26
1943	06	29	146	45	-5	26
1943	06	30	146	51	-5	25
1943	07	01	146	57	-5	25
1943	07	02	147	04	-5	24
1943	07	03	147	10	-5	23
1943	07	04	147	17	-5	23
1943	07	05	147	23	-5	22
1943	07	06	147	30	-5	22
1943	07	07	147	36	-5	21
1943	07	08	147	43	-5	21
1943	07	09	147	50	-5	20
1943	07	10	147	57	-5	20
1943	07	11	148	04	-5	19
1943	07	12	148	11	-5	19
1943	07	13	148	18	-5	18
1943	07	14	148	25	-5	18
1943	07	15	148	32	-5	17
1943	07	16	148	39	-5	17
1943	07	17	148	46	-5	16
1943	07	18	148	54	-5	16
1943	07	19	149	01	-5	15
1943	07	20	149	08	-5	15
1943	07	21	149	16	-5	15
1943	07	22	149	23	-5	14
1943	07	23	149	31	-5	14
1943	07	24	149	38	-5	13
1943	07	25	149	46	-5	13
1943	07	26	149	53	-5	12
1943	07	27	150	01	-5	12
1943	07	28	150	09	-5	12
1943	07	29	150	16	-5	11
1943	07	30	150	24	-5	11
1943	07	31	150	32	-5	11
1943	08	01	150	40	-5	10
1943	08	02	150	48	-5	10
1943	08	03	150	55	-5	09
1943	08	04	151	03	-5	09
1943	08	05	151	11	-5	09
1943	08	06	151	19	-5	09
1943	08	07	151	27	-5	08
1943	08	08	151	35	-5	08
1943	08	09	151	43	-5	08
1943	08	10	151	51	-5	07
1943	08	11	151	59	-5	07
1943	08	12	152	07	-5	07
1943	08	13	152	15	-5	06
1943	08	14	152	24	-5	06
1943	08	15	152	32	-5	06
1943	08	16	152	40	-5	06
1943	08	17	152	48	-5	05
1943	08	18	152	56	-5	05
1943	08	19	153	04	-5	05
1943	08	20	153	13	-5	05
1943	08	21	153	21	-5	05
1943	08	22	153	29	-5	04
1943	08	23	153	37	-5	04
1943	08	24	153	46	-5	04
1943	08	25	153	54	-5	04
1943	08	26	154	02	-5	04
1943	08	27	154	10	-5	03
1943	08	28	154	19	-5	03
1943	08	29	154	27	-5	03
1943	08	30	154	35	-5	03
1943	08	31	154	44	-5	03
1943	09	01	154	52	-5	03
1943	09	02	155	00	-5	02
1943	09	03	155	08	-5	02
1943	09	04	155	17	-5	02
1943	09	05	155	25	-5	02
1943	09	06	155	33	-5	02
1943	09	07	155	41	-5	02
1943	09	08	155	50	-5	02
1943	09	09	155	58	-5	02
1943	09	10	156	06	-5	02
1943	09	11	156	14	-5	02
1943	09	12	156	23	-5	02
1943	09	13	156	31	-5	01
1943	09	14	156	39	-5	01
1943	09	15	156	47	-5	01
1943	09	16	156	55	-5	01
1943	09	17	157	03	-5	01
1943	09	18	157	11	-5	01
1943	09	19	157	20	-5	01

1943 09 20	157 28	-5 01
1943 09 21	157 36	-5 01
1943 09 22	157 44	-5 01
1943 09 23	157 52	-5 01
1943 09 24	158 00	-5 01
1943 09 25	158 08	-5 01
1943 09 26	158 15	-5 01
1943 09 27	158 23	-5 01
1943 09 28	158 31	-5 02
1943 09 29	158 39	-5 02
1943 09 30	158 47	-5 02
1943 10 01	158 55	-5 02
1943 10 02	159 02	-5 02
1943 10 03	159 10	-5 02
1943 10 04	159 18	-5 02
1943 10 05	159 25	-5 02
1943 10 06	159 33	-5 02
1943 10 07	159 40	-5 02
1943 10 08	159 48	-5 02
1943 10 09	159 55	-5 02
1943 10 10	160 03	-5 03
1943 10 11	160 10	-5 03
1943 10 12	160 17	-5 03
1943 10 13	160 25	-5 03
1943 10 14	160 32	-5 03
1943 10 15	160 39	-5 03
1943 10 16	160 46	-5 04
1943 10 17	160 53	-5 04
1943 10 18	161 00	-5 04
1943 10 19	161 07	-5 04
1943 10 20	161 14	-5 04
1943 10 21	161 21	-5 04
1943 10 22	161 27	-5 05
1943 10 23	161 35	-5 05
1943 10 24	161 41	-5 05
1943 10 25	161 48	-5 05
1943 10 26	161 54	-5 06
1943 10 27	162 01	-5 06
1943 10 28	162 07	-5 06
1943 10 29	162 13	-5 06
1943 10 30	162 20	-5 06
1943 10 31	162 26	-5 07
1943 11 01	162 32	-5 07
1943 11 02	162 38	-5 07
1943 11 03	162 44	-5 08
1943 11 04	162 50	-5 08
1943 11 05	162 56	-5 08
1943 11 06	163 01	-5 08
1943 11 07	163 07	-5 09
1943 11 08	163 13	-5 09
1943 11 09	163 18	-5 09
1943 11 10	163 24	-5 10
1943 11 11	163 29	-5 10
1943 11 12	163 34	-5 10
1943 11 13	163 39	-5 11
1943 11 14	163 45	-5 11
1943 11 15	163 50	-5 11
1943 11 16	163 54	-5 12
1943 11 17	163 59	-5 12
1943 11 18	164 04	-5 12
1943 11 19	164 09	-5 13
1943 11 20	164 13	-5 13
1943 11 21	164 18	-5 13
1943 11 22	164 22	-5 14
1943 11 23	164 26	-5 14
1943 11 24	164 30	-5 14
1943 11 25	164 35	-5 15
1943 11 26	164 39	-5 15
1943 11 27	164 42	-5 16
1943 11 28	164 46	-5 16
1943 11 29	164 50	-5 16
1943 11 30	164 53	-5 17
1943 12 01	164 57	-5 17
1943 12 02	165 00	-5 18
1943 12 03	165 03	-5 18
1943 12 04	165 07	-5 18
1943 12 05	165 10	-5 19
1943 12 06	165 13	-5 19
1943 12 07	165 15	-5 20
1943 12 08	165 18	-5 20
1943 12 09	165 21	-5 20
1943 12 10	165 23	-5 21
1943 12 11	165 26	-5 21
1943 12 12	165 28	-5 22
1943 12 13	165 30	-5 22
1943 12 14	165 32	-5 22
1943 12 15	165 34	-5 23
1943 12 16	165 36	-5 23
1943 12 17	165 38	-5 24
1943 12 18	165 39	-5 24
1943 12 19	165 41	-5 24
1943 12 20	165 42	-5 25
1943 12 21	165 43	-5 25
1943 12 22	165 44	-5 26
1943 12 23	165 45	-5 26
1943 12 24	165 46	-5 26
1943 12 25	165 47	-5 27
1943 12 26	165 48	-5 27
1943 12 27	165 48	-5 28
1943 12 28	165 49	-5 28
1943 12 29	165 49	-5 29
1943 12 30	165 49	-5 29
1943 12 31	165 49	-5 29
1944 01 01	165 49	-5 30
1944 01 02	165 49	-5 30
1944 01 03	165 49	-5 30
1944 01 04	165 48	-5 31
1944 01 05	165 48	-5 31
1944 01 06	165 47	-5 32
1944 01 07	165 46	-5 32
1944 01 08	165 46	-5 32
1944 01 09	165 45	-5 33
1944 01 10	165 43	-5 33
1944 01 11	165 42	-5 33
1944 01 12	165 41	-5 34
1944 01 13	165 40	-5 34
1944 01 14	165 38	-5 34
1944 01 15	165 36	-5 35
1944 01 16	165 35	-5 35
1944 01 17	165 33	-5 35
1944 01 18	165 31	-5 36
1944 01 19	165 29	-5 36
1944 01 20	165 27	-5 36
1944 01 21	165 24	-5 36
1944 01 22	165 22	-5 37
1944 01 23	165 19	-5 37
1944 01 24	165 17	-5 37
1944 01 25	165 14	-5 37
1944 01 26	165 11	-5 38
1944 01 27	165 09	-5 38
1944 01 28	165 06	-5 38
1944 01 29	165 03	-5 38
1944 01 30	164 59	-5 39
1944 01 31	164 56	-5 39
1944 02 01	164 53	-5 39
1944 02 02	164 49	-5 39
1944 02 03	164 46	-5 39
1944 02 04	164 42	-5 39
1944 02 05	164 39	-5 39
1944 02 06	164 35	-5 40
1944 02 07	164 31	-5 40
1944 02 08	164 28	-5 40
1944 02 09	164 24	-5 40
1944 02 10	164 20	-5 40
1944 02 11	164 16	-5 40
1944 02 12	164 12	-5 40
1944 02 13	164 07	-5 40
1944 02 14	164 03	-5 40
1944 02 15	163 59	-5 40
1944 02 16	163 55	-5 40
1944 02 17	163 50	-5 40
1944 02 18	163 46	-5 40
1944 02 19	163 41	-5 40
1944 02 20	163 37	-5 40
1944 02 21	163 32	-5 40
1944 02 22	163 28	-5 40
1944 02 23	163 23	-5 40
1944 02 24	163 18	-5 40
1944 02 25	163 14	-5 39
1944 02 26	163 09	-5 39
1944 02 27	163 04	-5 39
1944 02 28	163 00	-5 39
1944 02 29	162 55	-5 39
1944 03 01	162 50	-5 39
1944 03 02	162 46	-5 38
1944 03 03	162 41	-5 38
1944 03 04	162 36	-5 38
1944 03 05	162 31	-5 38
1944 03 06	162 27	-5 37
1944 03 07	162 22	-5 37
1944 03 08	162 17	-5 37
1944 03 09	162 12	-5 37
1944 03 10	162 08	-5 36
1944 03 11	162 03	-5 36
1944 03 12	161 58	-5 36
1944 03 13	161 54	-5 35
1944 03 14	161 49	-5 35
1944 03 15	161 45	-5 34
1944 03 16	161 40	-5 34
1944 03 17	161 35	-5 34
1944 03 18	161 31	-5 33
1944 03 19	161 27	-5 33
1944 03 20	161 22	-5 32
1944 03 21	161 18	-5 32
1944 03 22	161 13	-5 31
1944 03 23	161 09	-5 31
1944 03 24	161 05	-5 30
1944 03 25	161 01	-5 30
1944 03 26	160 57	-5 29
1944 03 27	160 53	-5 29
1944 03 28	160 49	-5 28
1944 03 29	160 45	-5 28
1944 03 30	160 41	-5 27
1944 03 31	160 37	-5 26
1944 04 01	160 34	-5 26
1944 04 02	160 30	-5 25
1944 04 03	160 26	-5 25
1944 04 04	160 23	-5 24
1944 04 05	160 20	-5 23
1944 04 06	160 16	-5 23
1944 04 07	160 13	-5 22
1944 04 08	160 10	-5 22
1944 04 09	160 07	-5 21
1944 04 10	160 04	-5 20
1944 04 11	160 01	-5 20
1944 04 12	159 58	-5 19
1944 04 13	159 56	-5 18
1944 04 14	159 53	-5 17
1944 04 15	159 51	-5 17
1944 04 16	159 48	-5 16
1944 04 17	159 46	-5 15
1944 04 18	159 44	-5 15
1944 04 19	159 42	-5 14
1944 04 20	159 40	-5 13
1944 04 21	159 38	-5 12
1944 04 22	159 36	-5 12
1944 04 23	159 34	-5 11
1944 04 24	159 33	-5 10
1944 04 25	159 31	-5 09
1944 04 26	159 30	-5 09
1944 04 27	159 29	-5 08
1944 04 28	159 27	-5 07
1944 04 29	159 26	-5 06
1944 04 30	159 26	-5 06
1944 05 01	159 25	-5 05
1944 05 02	159 24	-5 04
1944 05 03	159 23	-5 03
1944 05 04	159 23	-5 02
1944 05 05	159 23	-5 02
1944 05 06	159 22	-5 01
1944 05 07	159 22	-5 00
1944 05 08	159 22	-4 59
1944 05 09	159 22	-4 58
1944 05 10	159 22	-4 58
1944 05 11	159 23	-4 57
1944 05 12	159 23	-4 56
1944 05 13	159 24	-4 55
1944 05 14	159 24	-4 54
1944 05 15	159 25	-4 54
1944 05 16	159 26	-4 53
1944 05 17	159 27	-4 52
1944 05 18	159 28	-4 51
1944 05 19	159 29	-4 50
1944 05 20	159 31	-4 50
1944 05 21	159 32	-4 49
1944 05 22	159 34	-4 48
1944 05 23	159 35	-4 47
1944 05 24	159 37	-4 47
1944 05 25	159 39	-4 46
1944 05 26	159 41	-4 45
1944 05 27	159 43	-4 44
1944 05 28	159 45	-4 43
1944 05 29	159 47	-4 43
1944 05 30	159 50	-4 42
1944 05 31	159 52	-4 41
1944 06 01	159 55	-4 40
1944 06 02	159 58	-4 39
1944 06 03	160 01	-4 39
1944 06 04	160 04	-4 38
1944 06 05	160 07	-4 37
1944 06 06	160 10	-4 36
1944 06 07	160 13	-4 36
1944 06 08	160 16	-4 35
1944 06 09	160 20	-4 34
1944 06 10	160 23	-4 33
1944 06 11	160 27	-4 33
1944 06 12	160 31	-4 32
1944 06 13	160 35	-4 31
1944 06 14	160 39	-4 30
1944 06 15	160 43	-4 30
1944 06 16	160 47	-4 29
1944 06 17	160 51	-4 28
1944 06 18	160 55	-4 28
1944 06 19	161 00	-4 27
1944 06 20	161 04	-4 26
1944 06 21	161 09	-4 25
1944 06 22	161 14	-4 25
1944 06 23	161 18	-4 24
1944 06 24	161 23	-4 23
1944 06 25	161 28	-4 23
1944 06 26	161 33	-4 22
1944 06 27	161 38	-4 21
1944 06 28	161 44	-4 21
1944 06 29	161 49	-4 20
1944 06 30	161 54	-4 19
1944 07 01	162 00	-4 19
1944 07 02	162 05	-4 18
1944 07 03	162 11	-4 17
1944 07 04	162 17	-4 17
1944 07 05	162 22	-4 16
1944 07 06	162 28	-4 16
1944 07 07	162 34	-4 15
1944 07 08	162 40	-4 14
1944 07 09	162 46	-4 14
1944 07 10	162 53	-4 13
1944 07 11	162 59	-4 12
1944 07 12	163 05	-4 12
1944 07 13	163 11	-4 11
1944 07 14	163 18	-4 11
1944 07 15	163 24	-4 10
1944 07 16	163 31	-4 10
1944 07 17	163 38	-4 09
1944 07 18	163 44	-4 08
1944 07 19	163 51	-4 08
1944 07 20	163 58	-4 07
1944 07 21	164 05	-4 07
1944 07 22	164 12	-4 06
1944 07 23	164 19	-4 06
1944 07 24	164 26	-4 05
1944 07 25	164 33	-4 05
1944 07 26	164 40	-4 04
1944 07 27	164 47	-4 04
1944 07 28	164 55	-4 03
1944 07 29	165 02	-4 03
1944 07 30	165 09	-4 02
1944 07 31	165 17	-4 02
1944 08 01	165 24	-4 01
1944 08 02	165 32	-4 01
1944 08 03	165 39	-4 00
1944 08 04	165 47	-4 00
1944 08 05	165 55	-3 59
1944 08 06	166 02	-3 59
1944 08 07	166 10	-3 58
1944 08 08	166 18	-3 58
1944 08 09	166 26	-3 57
1944 08 10	166 34	-3 57
1944 08 11	166 42	-3 57
1944 08 12	166 50	-3 56
1944 08 13	166 58	-3 56
1944 08 14	167 06	-3 55
1944 08 15	167 14	-3 55
1944 08 16	167 22	-3 55
1944 08 17	167 30	-3 54
1944 08 18	167 38	-3 54
1944 08 19	167 46	-3 53
1944 08 20	167 55	-3 53
1944 08 21	168 03	-3 53
1944 08 22	168 11	-3 52
1944 08 23	168 19	-3 52
1944 08 24	168 28	-3 52
1944 08 25	168 36	-3 51
1944 08 26	168 45	-3 51
1944 08 27	168 53	-3 51
1944 08 28	169 01	-3 50
1944 08 29	169 10	-3 50
1944 08 30	169 18	-3 50
1944 08 31	169 27	-3 49
1944 09 01	169 35	-3 49
1944 09 02	169 44	-3 49
1944 09 03	169 52	-3 48
1944 09 04	170 01	-3 48
1944 09 05	170 10	-3 48
1944 09 06	170 18	-3 47
1944 09 07	170 27	-3 47
1944 09 08	170 35	-3 47
1944 09 09	170 44	-3 47
1944 09 10	170 52	-3 46
1944 09 11	171 01	-3 46
1944 09 12	171 10	-3 46
1944 09 13	171 18	-3 46
1944 09 14	171 27	-3 45
1944 09 15	171 36	-3 45
1944 09 16	171 44	-3 45
1944 09 17	171 53	-3 45
1944 09 18	172 02	-3 44
1944 09 19	172 10	-3 44
1944 09 20	172 19	-3 44
1944 09 21	172 27	-3 44
1944 09 22	172 36	-3 44
1944 09 23	172 45	-3 43
1944 09 24	172 53	-3 43
1944 09 25	173 02	-3 43
1944 09 26	173 10	-3 43
1944 09 27	173 19	-3 43
1944 09 28	173 28	-3 43
1944 09 29	173 36	-3 42
1944 09 30	173 45	-3 42
1944 10 01	173 53	-3 42
1944 10 02	174 02	-3 42
1944 10 03	174 10	-3 42
1944 10 04	174 19	-3 42
1944 10 05	174 27	-3 42
1944 10 06	174 35	-3 42
1944 10 07	174 44	-3 41
1944 10 08	174 52	-3 41
1944 10 09	175 01	-3 41
1944 10 10	175 09	-3 41
1944 10 11	175 17	-3 41
1944 10 12	175 25	-3 41
1944 10 13	175 34	-3 41
1944 10 14	175 42	-3 41
1944 10 15	175 50	-3 41
1944 10 16	175 58	-3 41
1944 10 17	176 06	-3 41
1944 10 18	176 14	-3 40
1944 10 19	176 22	-3 40
1944 10 20	176 30	-3 40
1944 10 21	176 38	-3 40
1944 10 22	176 46	-3 40
1944 10 23	176 54	-3 40
1944 10 24	177 02	-3 40
1944 10 25	177 10	-3 40
1944 10 26	177 17	-3 40
1944 10 27	177 25	-3 40
1944 10 28	177 33	-3 40
1944 10 29	177 40	-3 40
1944 10 30	177 48	-3 40
1944 10 31	177 55	-3 40
1944 11 01	178 03	-3 40
1944 11 02	178 10	-3 40
1944 11 03	178 17	-3 40
1944 11 04	178 25	-3 40
1944 11 05	178 32	-3 40
1944 11 06	178 39	-3 40
1944 11 07	178 46	-3 40
1944 11 08	178 53	-3 40
1944 11 09	179 00	-3 40
1944 11 10	179 07	-3 40
1944 11 11	179 14	-3 40

1944 11 12	179 21	-3 40
1944 11 13	179 27	-3 40
1944 11 14	179 34	-3 41
1944 11 15	179 41	-3 41
1944 11 16	179 47	-3 41
1944 11 17	179 53	-3 41
1944 11 18	180 00	-3 41
1944 11 19	180 06	-3 41
1944 11 20	180 12	-3 41
1944 11 21	180 18	-3 41
1944 11 22	180 24	-3 41
1944 11 23	180 30	-3 41
1944 11 24	180 36	-3 41
1944 11 25	180 42	-3 41
1944 11 26	180 48	-3 42
1944 11 27	180 53	-3 42
1944 11 28	180 59	-3 42
1944 11 29	181 04	-3 42
1944 11 30	181 10	-3 42
1944 12 01	181 15	-3 42
1944 12 02	181 20	-3 42
1944 12 03	181 25	-3 42
1944 12 04	181 30	-3 42
1944 12 05	181 35	-3 43
1944 12 06	181 40	-3 43
1944 12 07	181 45	-3 43
1944 12 08	181 49	-3 43
1944 12 09	181 54	-3 43
1944 12 10	181 58	-3 43
1944 12 11	182 02	-3 43
1944 12 12	182 07	-3 43
1944 12 13	182 11	-3 44
1944 12 14	182 15	-3 44
1944 12 15	182 19	-3 44
1944 12 16	182 23	-3 44
1944 12 17	182 26	-3 44
1944 12 18	182 30	-3 44
1944 12 19	182 33	-3 45
1944 12 20	182 37	-3 45
1944 12 21	182 40	-3 45
1944 12 22	182 43	-3 45
1944 12 23	182 46	-3 45
1944 12 24	182 49	-3 45
1944 12 25	182 52	-3 45
1944 12 26	182 55	-3 46
1944 12 27	182 57	-3 46
1944 12 28	183 00	-3 46
1944 12 29	183 02	-3 46
1944 12 30	183 04	-3 46
1944 12 31	183 06	-3 46
1945 01 01	183 08	-3 47
1945 01 02	183 10	-3 47
1945 01 03	183 12	-3 47
1945 01 04	183 14	-3 47
1945 01 05	183 15	-3 47
1945 01 06	183 17	-3 47
1945 01 07	183 18	-3 48
1945 01 08	183 19	-3 48
1945 01 09	183 20	-3 48
1945 01 10	183 21	-3 48
1945 01 11	183 22	-3 48
1945 01 12	183 23	-3 48
1945 01 13	183 23	-3 48
1945 01 14	183 24	-3 49
1945 01 15	183 24	-3 49
1945 01 16	183 24	-3 49
1945 01 17	183 24	-3 49
1945 01 18	183 24	-3 49
1945 01 19	183 24	-3 49
1945 01 20	183 24	-3 49
1945 01 21	183 23	-3 49
1945 01 22	183 23	-3 50
1945 01 23	183 22	-3 50
1945 01 24	183 22	-3 50
1945 01 25	183 21	-3 50
1945 01 26	183 20	-3 50
1945 01 27	183 19	-3 50
1945 01 28	183 18	-3 50
1945 01 29	183 16	-3 50
1945 01 30	183 15	-3 50
1945 01 31	183 13	-3 50
1945 02 01	183 12	-3 51
1945 02 02	183 10	-3 51
1945 02 03	183 08	-3 51
1945 02 04	183 06	-3 51
1945 02 05	183 04	-3 51
1945 02 06	183 02	-3 51
1945 02 07	182 59	-3 51
1945 02 08	182 57	-3 51
1945 02 09	182 55	-3 51
1945 02 10	182 52	-3 51
1945 02 11	182 49	-3 51
1945 02 12	182 46	-3 51
1945 02 13	182 44	-3 51
1945 02 14	182 41	-3 51
1945 02 15	182 38	-3 51
1945 02 16	182 34	-3 51
1945 02 17	182 31	-3 51
1945 02 18	182 28	-3 51
1945 02 19	182 24	-3 51
1945 02 20	182 21	-3 51

1945 02 21	182 17	-3 51
1945 02 22	182 14	-3 51
1945 02 23	182 10	-3 51
1945 02 24	182 06	-3 50
1945 02 25	182 02	-3 50
1945 02 26	181 58	-3 50
1945 02 27	181 54	-3 50
1945 02 28	181 50	-3 50
1945 03 01	181 46	-3 50
1945 03 02	181 42	-3 50
1945 03 03	181 38	-3 50
1945 03 04	181 33	-3 49
1945 03 05	181 29	-3 49
1945 03 06	181 25	-3 49
1945 03 07	181 20	-3 49
1945 03 08	181 16	-3 49
1945 03 09	181 11	-3 48
1945 03 10	181 07	-3 48
1945 03 11	181 02	-3 48
1945 03 12	180 57	-3 48
1945 03 13	180 53	-3 48
1945 03 14	180 48	-3 47
1945 03 15	180 43	-3 47
1945 03 16	180 39	-3 47
1945 03 17	180 34	-3 46
1945 03 18	180 29	-3 46
1945 03 19	180 24	-3 46
1945 03 20	180 20	-3 46
1945 03 21	180 15	-3 45
1945 03 22	180 10	-3 45
1945 03 23	180 05	-3 45
1945 03 24	180 01	-3 44
1945 03 25	179 56	-3 44
1945 03 26	179 51	-3 44
1945 03 27	179 46	-3 43
1945 03 28	179 42	-3 43
1945 03 29	179 37	-3 42
1945 03 30	179 32	-3 42
1945 03 31	179 28	-3 42
1945 04 01	179 23	-3 41
1945 04 02	179 19	-3 41
1945 04 03	179 14	-3 40
1945 04 04	179 09	-3 40
1945 04 05	179 05	-3 39
1945 04 06	179 01	-3 39
1945 04 07	178 56	-3 38
1945 04 08	178 52	-3 38
1945 04 09	178 47	-3 37
1945 04 10	178 43	-3 37
1945 04 11	178 39	-3 36
1945 04 12	178 35	-3 36
1945 04 13	178 31	-3 35
1945 04 14	178 27	-3 35
1945 04 15	178 23	-3 34
1945 04 16	178 19	-3 34
1945 04 17	178 15	-3 33
1945 04 18	178 11	-3 33
1945 04 19	178 08	-3 32
1945 04 20	178 04	-3 32
1945 04 21	178 01	-3 31
1945 04 22	177 57	-3 30
1945 04 23	177 54	-3 30
1945 04 24	177 51	-3 29
1945 04 25	177 47	-3 29
1945 04 26	177 44	-3 28
1945 04 27	177 41	-3 27
1945 04 28	177 38	-3 27
1945 04 29	177 36	-3 26
1945 04 30	177 33	-3 26
1945 05 01	177 30	-3 25
1945 05 02	177 28	-3 24
1945 05 03	177 25	-3 24
1945 05 04	177 23	-3 23
1945 05 05	177 20	-3 23
1945 05 06	177 18	-3 22
1945 05 07	177 16	-3 21
1945 05 08	177 14	-3 21
1945 05 09	177 12	-3 20
1945 05 10	177 11	-3 19
1945 05 11	177 09	-3 19
1945 05 12	177 08	-3 18
1945 05 13	177 06	-3 17
1945 05 14	177 05	-3 17
1945 05 15	177 04	-3 16
1945 05 16	177 02	-3 15
1945 05 17	177 01	-3 15
1945 05 18	177 01	-3 14
1945 05 19	177 00	-3 13
1945 05 20	176 59	-3 13
1945 05 21	176 59	-3 12
1945 05 22	176 58	-3 11
1945 05 23	176 58	-3 11
1945 05 24	176 58	-3 10
1945 05 25	176 58	-3 09
1945 05 26	176 58	-3 09
1945 05 27	176 58	-3 08
1945 05 28	176 58	-3 07
1945 05 29	176 58	-3 07
1945 05 30	176 59	-3 06
1945 05 31	176 59	-3 05
1945 06 01	177 00	-3 05
1945 06 02	177 01	-3 04
1945 06 03	177 02	-3 03
1945 06 04	177 03	-3 03
1945 06 05	177 04	-3 02
1945 06 06	177 05	-3 01

1945 06 07	177 07	-3 01
1945 06 08	177 08	-3 00
1945 06 09	177 10	-2 59
1945 06 10	177 12	-2 59
1945 06 11	177 13	-2 58
1945 06 12	177 15	-2 57
1945 06 13	177 17	-2 57
1945 06 14	177 20	-2 56
1945 06 15	177 22	-2 55
1945 06 16	177 24	-2 55
1945 06 17	177 27	-2 54
1945 06 18	177 29	-2 53
1945 06 19	177 32	-2 53
1945 06 20	177 35	-2 52
1945 06 21	177 38	-2 51
1945 06 22	177 41	-2 51
1945 06 23	177 44	-2 50
1945 06 24	177 47	-2 50
1945 06 25	177 50	-2 49
1945 06 26	177 54	-2 48
1945 06 27	177 57	-2 48
1945 06 28	178 01	-2 47
1945 06 29	178 05	-2 46
1945 06 30	178 09	-2 46
1945 07 01	178 13	-2 45
1945 07 02	178 17	-2 45
1945 07 03	178 21	-2 44
1945 07 04	178 25	-2 43
1945 07 05	178 29	-2 43
1945 07 06	178 34	-2 42
1945 07 07	178 38	-2 42
1945 07 08	178 43	-2 41
1945 07 09	178 47	-2 40
1945 07 10	178 52	-2 40
1945 07 11	178 57	-2 39
1945 07 12	179 02	-2 39
1945 07 13	179 07	-2 38
1945 07 14	179 12	-2 38
1945 07 15	179 18	-2 37
1945 07 16	179 23	-2 36
1945 07 17	179 28	-2 36
1945 07 18	179 34	-2 35
1945 07 19	179 39	-2 35
1945 07 20	179 45	-2 34
1945 07 21	179 51	-2 34
1945 07 22	179 57	-2 33
1945 07 23	180 02	-2 33
1945 07 24	180 08	-2 32
1945 07 25	180 14	-2 31
1945 07 26	180 21	-2 31
1945 07 27	180 27	-2 30
1945 07 28	180 33	-2 30
1945 07 29	180 39	-2 29
1945 07 30	180 46	-2 29
1945 07 31	180 52	-2 28
1945 08 01	180 59	-2 28
1945 08 02	181 05	-2 27
1945 08 03	181 12	-2 27
1945 08 04	181 19	-2 26
1945 08 05	181 26	-2 26
1945 08 06	181 32	-2 25
1945 08 07	181 39	-2 25
1945 08 08	181 46	-2 24
1945 08 09	181 53	-2 24
1945 08 10	182 01	-2 24
1945 08 11	182 08	-2 23
1945 08 12	182 15	-2 23
1945 08 13	182 22	-2 22
1945 08 14	182 30	-2 22
1945 08 15	182 37	-2 21
1945 08 16	182 44	-2 21
1945 08 17	182 52	-2 20
1945 08 18	183 00	-2 20
1945 08 19	183 07	-2 19
1945 08 20	183 15	-2 19
1945 08 21	183 23	-2 19
1945 08 22	183 30	-2 18
1945 08 23	183 38	-2 18
1945 08 24	183 46	-2 17
1945 08 25	183 54	-2 17
1945 08 26	184 02	-2 16
1945 08 27	184 10	-2 16
1945 08 28	184 18	-2 16
1945 08 29	184 26	-2 15
1945 08 30	184 34	-2 15
1945 08 31	184 42	-2 14
1945 09 01	184 50	-2 14
1945 09 02	184 58	-2 14
1945 09 03	185 07	-2 13
1945 09 04	185 15	-2 13
1945 09 05	185 23	-2 13
1945 09 06	185 32	-2 12
1945 09 07	185 40	-2 12
1945 09 08	185 48	-2 11
1945 09 09	185 57	-2 11
1945 09 10	186 05	-2 11
1945 09 11	186 14	-2 10
1945 09 12	186 22	-2 10
1945 09 13	186 31	-2 10
1945 09 14	186 39	-2 09
1945 09 15	186 48	-2 09
1945 09 16	186 56	-2 09
1945 09 17	187 05	-2 08
1945 09 18	187 14	-2 08
1945 09 19	187 22	-2 08
1945 09 20	187 31	-2 07

1945 09 21	187 40	-2 07
1945 09 22	187 48	-2 07
1945 09 23	187 57	-2 06
1945 09 24	188 06	-2 06
1945 09 25	188 14	-2 06
1945 09 26	188 23	-2 05
1945 09 27	188 32	-2 05
1945 09 28	188 41	-2 05
1945 09 29	188 49	-2 05
1945 09 30	188 58	-2 04
1945 10 01	189 07	-2 04
1945 10 02	189 16	-2 04
1945 10 03	189 24	-2 03
1945 10 04	189 33	-2 03
1945 10 05	189 42	-2 03
1945 10 06	189 51	-2 03
1945 10 07	189 59	-2 02
1945 10 08	190 08	-2 02
1945 10 09	190 17	-2 02
1945 10 10	190 26	-2 01
1945 10 11	190 34	-2 01
1945 10 12	190 43	-2 01
1945 10 13	190 52	-2 01
1945 10 14	191 01	-2 00
1945 10 15	191 09	-2 00
1945 10 16	191 18	-2 00
1945 10 17	191 27	-2 00
1945 10 18	191 35	-1 59
1945 10 19	191 44	-1 59
1945 10 20	191 52	-1 59
1945 10 21	192 01	-1 59
1945 10 22	192 10	-1 58
1945 10 23	192 18	-1 58
1945 10 24	192 27	-1 58
1945 10 25	192 35	-1 58
1945 10 26	192 44	-1 58
1945 10 27	192 52	-1 57
1945 10 28	193 01	-1 57
1945 10 29	193 09	-1 57
1945 10 30	193 17	-1 57
1945 10 31	193 26	-1 57
1945 11 01	193 34	-1 56
1945 11 02	193 42	-1 56
1945 11 03	193 50	-1 56
1945 11 04	193 59	-1 56
1945 11 05	194 07	-1 56
1945 11 06	194 15	-1 55
1945 11 07	194 23	-1 55
1945 11 08	194 31	-1 55
1945 11 09	194 39	-1 55
1945 11 10	194 47	-1 55
1945 11 11	194 55	-1 54
1945 11 12	195 03	-1 54
1945 11 13	195 11	-1 54
1945 11 14	195 18	-1 54
1945 11 15	195 26	-1 54
1945 11 16	195 34	-1 54
1945 11 17	195 41	-1 53
1945 11 18	195 49	-1 53
1945 11 19	195 57	-1 53
1945 11 20	196 04	-1 53
1945 11 21	196 11	-1 53
1945 11 22	196 19	-1 53
1945 11 23	196 26	-1 52
1945 11 24	196 33	-1 52
1945 11 25	196 40	-1 52
1945 11 26	196 47	-1 52
1945 11 27	196 54	-1 52
1945 11 28	197 01	-1 52
1945 11 29	197 08	-1 51
1945 11 30	197 15	-1 51
1945 12 01	197 22	-1 51
1945 12 02	197 29	-1 51
1945 12 03	197 35	-1 51
1945 12 04	197 42	-1 51
1945 12 05	197 48	-1 51
1945 12 06	197 55	-1 50
1945 12 07	198 01	-1 50
1945 12 08	198 07	-1 50
1945 12 09	198 13	-1 50
1945 12 10	198 19	-1 50
1945 12 11	198 25	-1 50
1945 12 12	198 31	-1 50
1945 12 13	198 37	-1 50
1945 12 14	198 43	-1 49
1945 12 15	198 49	-1 49
1945 12 16	198 54	-1 49
1945 12 17	199 00	-1 49
1945 12 18	199 05	-1 49
1945 12 19	199 10	-1 49
1945 12 20	199 16	-1 49
1945 12 21	199 21	-1 49
1945 12 22	199 26	-1 48
1945 12 23	199 31	-1 48
1945 12 24	199 35	-1 48
1945 12 25	199 40	-1 48
1945 12 26	199 45	-1 48
1945 12 27	199 49	-1 48
1945 12 28	199 54	-1 48
1945 12 29	199 58	-1 48
1945 12 30	200 02	-1 47
1945 12 31	200 07	-1 47
1946 01 01	200 11	-1 47
1946 01 02	200 14	-1 47
1946 01 03	200 18	-1 47
1946 01 04	200 22	-1 47

1946 01 05	200 26	-1 47
1946 01 06	200 29	-1 47
1946 01 07	200 32	-1 46
1946 01 08	200 36	-1 46
1946 01 09	200 39	-1 46
1946 01 10	200 42	-1 46
1946 01 11	200 45	-1 46
1946 01 12	200 48	-1 46
1946 01 13	200 50	-1 46
1946 01 14	200 53	-1 46
1946 01 15	200 55	-1 45
1946 01 16	200 58	-1 45
1946 01 17	201 00	-1 45
1946 01 18	201 02	-1 45
1946 01 19	201 04	-1 45
1946 01 20	201 06	-1 45
1946 01 21	201 08	-1 45
1946 01 22	201 09	-1 45
1946 01 23	201 11	-1 44
1946 01 24	201 12	-1 44
1946 01 25	201 14	-1 44
1946 01 26	201 15	-1 44
1946 01 27	201 16	-1 44
1946 01 28	201 17	-1 44
1946 01 29	201 18	-1 44
1946 01 30	201 18	-1 44
1946 01 31	201 19	-1 43
1946 02 01	201 19	-1 43
1946 02 02	201 20	-1 43
1946 02 03	201 20	-1 43
1946 02 04	201 20	-1 43
1946 02 05	201 20	-1 43
1946 02 06	201 20	-1 42
1946 02 07	201 20	-1 42
1946 02 08	201 19	-1 42
1946 02 09	201 19	-1 42
1946 02 10	201 18	-1 42
1946 02 11	201 17	-1 42
1946 02 12	201 17	-1 41
1946 02 13	201 16	-1 41
1946 02 14	201 15	-1 41
1946 02 15	201 13	-1 41
1946 02 16	201 12	-1 41
1946 02 17	201 11	-1 41
1946 02 18	201 09	-1 40
1946 02 19	201 07	-1 40
1946 02 20	201 06	-1 40
1946 02 21	201 04	-1 40
1946 02 22	201 02	-1 40
1946 02 23	201 00	-1 39
1946 02 24	200 58	-1 39
1946 02 25	200 55	-1 39
1946 02 26	200 53	-1 39
1946 02 27	200 51	-1 39
1946 02 28	200 48	-1 38
1946 03 01	200 45	-1 38
1946 03 02	200 43	-1 38
1946 03 03	200 40	-1 38
1946 03 04	200 37	-1 37
1946 03 05	200 34	-1 37
1946 03 06	200 31	-1 37
1946 03 07	200 27	-1 37
1946 03 08	200 24	-1 36
1946 03 09	200 21	-1 36
1946 03 10	200 17	-1 36
1946 03 11	200 14	-1 36
1946 03 12	200 10	-1 35
1946 03 13	200 06	-1 35
1946 03 14	200 02	-1 35
1946 03 15	199 59	-1 35
1946 03 16	199 55	-1 34
1946 03 17	199 51	-1 34
1946 03 18	199 47	-1 34
1946 03 19	199 43	-1 33
1946 03 20	199 39	-1 33
1946 03 21	199 34	-1 33
1946 03 22	199 30	-1 33
1946 03 23	199 26	-1 32
1946 03 24	199 21	-1 32
1946 03 25	199 17	-1 32
1946 03 26	199 13	-1 31
1946 03 27	199 08	-1 31
1946 03 28	199 04	-1 31
1946 03 29	198 59	-1 30
1946 03 30	198 55	-1 30
1946 03 31	198 50	-1 30
1946 04 01	198 45	-1 29
1946 04 02	198 41	-1 29
1946 04 03	198 36	-1 29
1946 04 04	198 31	-1 28
1946 04 05	198 27	-1 28
1946 04 06	198 22	-1 28
1946 04 07	198 17	-1 27
1946 04 08	198 12	-1 27
1946 04 09	198 08	-1 26
1946 04 10	198 03	-1 26
1946 04 11	197 58	-1 26
1946 04 12	197 54	-1 25
1946 04 13	197 49	-1 25
1946 04 14	197 44	-1 25
1946 04 15	197 40	-1 24
1946 04 16	197 35	-1 24
1946 04 17	197 30	-1 23
1946 04 18	197 26	-1 23
1946 04 19	197 21	-1 23
1946 04 20	197 17	-1 22

1946 04 21	197 12	-1 22
1946 04 22	197 08	-1 21
1946 04 23	197 03	-1 21
1946 04 24	196 59	-1 20
1946 04 25	196 54	-1 20
1946 04 26	196 50	-1 20
1946 04 27	196 46	-1 19
1946 04 28	196 42	-1 19
1946 04 29	196 37	-1 18
1946 04 30	196 33	-1 18
1946 05 01	196 29	-1 17
1946 05 02	196 25	-1 17
1946 05 03	196 21	-1 17
1946 05 04	196 17	-1 16
1946 05 05	196 14	-1 16
1946 05 06	196 10	-1 15
1946 05 07	196 06	-1 15
1946 05 08	196 03	-1 14
1946 05 09	195 59	-1 14
1946 05 10	195 56	-1 13
1946 05 11	195 52	-1 13
1946 05 12	195 49	-1 13
1946 05 13	195 46	-1 12
1946 05 14	195 43	-1 12
1946 05 15	195 40	-1 11
1946 05 16	195 37	-1 11
1946 05 17	195 34	-1 10
1946 05 18	195 31	-1 10
1946 05 19	195 29	-1 09
1946 05 20	195 26	-1 09
1946 05 21	195 23	-1 08
1946 05 22	195 21	-1 08
1946 05 23	195 19	-1 07
1946 05 24	195 17	-1 07
1946 05 25	195 14	-1 07
1946 05 26	195 13	-1 06
1946 05 27	195 11	-1 06
1946 05 28	195 09	-1 05
1946 05 29	195 07	-1 05
1946 05 30	195 06	-1 04
1946 05 31	195 04	-1 04
1946 06 01	195 03	-1 03
1946 06 02	195 01	-1 03
1946 06 03	195 00	-1 02
1946 06 04	194 59	-1 02
1946 06 05	194 58	-1 01
1946 06 06	194 58	-1 01
1946 06 07	194 57	-1 00
1946 06 08	194 56	-1 00
1946 06 09	194 56	-1 00
1946 06 10	194 55	-0 59
1946 06 11	194 55	-0 59
1946 06 12	194 55	-0 58
1946 06 13	194 55	-0 58
1946 06 14	194 55	-0 57
1946 06 15	194 55	-0 57
1946 06 16	194 55	-0 56
1946 06 17	194 56	-0 56
1946 06 18	194 56	-0 55
1946 06 19	194 57	-0 55
1946 06 20	194 58	-0 55
1946 06 21	194 59	-0 54
1946 06 22	194 59	-0 54
1946 06 23	195 01	-0 53
1946 06 24	195 02	-0 53
1946 06 25	195 03	-0 52
1946 06 26	195 04	-0 52
1946 06 27	195 06	-0 51
1946 06 28	195 08	-0 51
1946 06 29	195 09	-0 51
1946 06 30	195 11	-0 50
1946 07 01	195 13	-0 50
1946 07 02	195 15	-0 49
1946 07 03	195 17	-0 49
1946 07 04	195 20	-0 48
1946 07 05	195 22	-0 48
1946 07 06	195 24	-0 48
1946 07 07	195 27	-0 47
1946 07 08	195 30	-0 47
1946 07 09	195 33	-0 46
1946 07 10	195 36	-0 46
1946 07 11	195 39	-0 45
1946 07 12	195 42	-0 45
1946 07 13	195 45	-0 45
1946 07 14	195 48	-0 44
1946 07 15	195 52	-0 44
1946 07 16	195 55	-0 43
1946 07 17	195 59	-0 43
1946 07 18	196 03	-0 43
1946 07 19	196 06	-0 42
1946 07 20	196 10	-0 42
1946 07 21	196 14	-0 41
1946 07 22	196 18	-0 41
1946 07 23	196 23	-0 40
1946 07 24	196 27	-0 40
1946 07 25	196 31	-0 40
1946 07 26	196 36	-0 39
1946 07 27	196 40	-0 39
1946 07 28	196 45	-0 39
1946 07 29	196 50	-0 38
1946 07 30	196 55	-0 38
1946 07 31	197 00	-0 37
1946 08 01	197 05	-0 37
1946 08 02	197 10	-0 37
1946 08 03	197 15	-0 36
1946 08 04	197 20	-0 36

1946 08 05	197 26	-0 35
1946 08 06	197 31	-0 35
1946 08 07	197 37	-0 35
1946 08 08	197 42	-0 34
1946 08 09	197 48	-0 34
1946 08 10	197 54	-0 34
1946 08 11	198 00	-0 33
1946 08 12	198 05	-0 33
1946 08 13	198 11	-0 32
1946 08 14	198 18	-0 32
1946 08 15	198 24	-0 32
1946 08 16	198 30	-0 31
1946 08 17	198 36	-0 31
1946 08 18	198 43	-0 31
1946 08 19	198 49	-0 30
1946 08 20	198 55	-0 30
1946 08 21	199 02	-0 30
1946 08 22	199 09	-0 29
1946 08 23	199 15	-0 29
1946 08 24	199 22	-0 29
1946 08 25	199 29	-0 28
1946 08 26	199 36	-0 28
1946 08 27	199 43	-0 28
1946 08 28	199 50	-0 27
1946 08 29	199 57	-0 27
1946 08 30	200 04	-0 27
1946 08 31	200 11	-0 26
1946 09 01	200 18	-0 26
1946 09 02	200 26	-0 26
1946 09 03	200 33	-0 25
1946 09 04	200 40	-0 25
1946 09 05	200 48	-0 25
1946 09 06	200 55	-0 24
1946 09 07	201 03	-0 24
1946 09 08	201 10	-0 24
1946 09 09	201 18	-0 23
1946 09 10	201 26	-0 23
1946 09 11	201 34	-0 23
1946 09 12	201 41	-0 22
1946 09 13	201 49	-0 22
1946 09 14	201 57	-0 22
1946 09 15	202 05	-0 21
1946 09 16	202 13	-0 21
1946 09 17	202 21	-0 21
1946 09 18	202 29	-0 20
1946 09 19	202 37	-0 20
1946 09 20	202 45	-0 20
1946 09 21	202 53	-0 19
1946 09 22	203 01	-0 19
1946 09 23	203 09	-0 19
1946 09 24	203 18	-0 18
1946 09 25	203 26	-0 18
1946 09 26	203 34	-0 18
1946 09 27	203 42	-0 17
1946 09 28	203 51	-0 17
1946 09 29	203 59	-0 17
1946 09 30	204 08	-0 17
1946 10 01	204 16	-0 16
1946 10 02	204 24	-0 16
1946 10 03	204 33	-0 16
1946 10 04	204 41	-0 15
1946 10 05	204 50	-0 15
1946 10 06	204 58	-0 15
1946 10 07	205 07	-0 14
1946 10 08	205 15	-0 14
1946 10 09	205 24	-0 14
1946 10 10	205 32	-0 14
1946 10 11	205 41	-0 13
1946 10 12	205 50	-0 13
1946 10 13	205 58	-0 13
1946 10 14	206 07	-0 12
1946 10 15	206 15	-0 12
1946 10 16	206 24	-0 12
1946 10 17	206 33	-0 11
1946 10 18	206 41	-0 11
1946 10 19	206 50	-0 11
1946 10 20	206 59	-0 11
1946 10 21	207 07	-0 10
1946 10 22	207 16	-0 10
1946 10 23	207 24	-0 10
1946 10 24	207 33	-0 09
1946 10 25	207 42	-0 09
1946 10 26	207 50	-0 09
1946 10 27	207 59	-0 08
1946 10 28	208 08	-0 08
1946 10 29	208 16	-0 08
1946 10 30	208 25	-0 08
1946 10 31	208 33	-0 07
1946 11 01	208 42	-0 07
1946 11 02	208 50	-0 07
1946 11 03	208 59	-0 06
1946 11 04	209 07	-0 06
1946 11 05	209 16	-0 06
1946 11 06	209 24	-0 06
1946 11 07	209 33	-0 05
1946 11 08	209 41	-0 05
1946 11 09	209 50	-0 05
1946 11 10	209 58	-0 04
1946 11 11	210 07	-0 04
1946 11 12	210 15	-0 04
1946 11 13	210 23	-0 03
1946 11 14	210 32	-0 03
1946 11 15	210 40	-0 03
1946 11 16	210 48	-0 03
1946 11 17	210 56	-0 02
1946 11 18	211 04	-0 02

1946 11 19	211 13	-0 02
1946 11 20	211 21	-0 01
1946 11 21	211 29	-0 01
1946 11 22	211 37	-0 01
1946 11 23	211 45	-0 01
1946 11 24	211 53	0 00
1946 11 25	212 01	0 00
1946 11 26	212 09	0 00
1946 11 27	212 16	0 01
1946 11 28	212 24	0 01
1946 11 29	212 32	0 01
1946 11 30	212 40	0 02
1946 12 01	212 47	0 02
1946 12 02	212 55	0 02
1946 12 03	213 02	0 02
1946 12 04	213 10	0 03
1946 12 05	213 17	0 03
1946 12 06	213 25	0 03
1946 12 07	213 32	0 04
1946 12 08	213 39	0 04
1946 12 09	213 46	0 04
1946 12 10	213 54	0 05
1946 12 11	214 01	0 05
1946 12 12	214 08	0 05
1946 12 13	214 15	0 06
1946 12 14	214 22	0 06
1946 12 15	214 28	0 06
1946 12 16	214 35	0 07
1946 12 17	214 42	0 07
1946 12 18	214 49	0 07
1946 12 19	214 55	0 07
1946 12 20	215 02	0 08
1946 12 21	215 08	0 08
1946 12 22	215 14	0 08
1946 12 23	215 21	0 09
1946 12 24	215 27	0 09
1946 12 25	215 33	0 09
1946 12 26	215 39	0 10
1946 12 27	215 45	0 10
1946 12 28	215 51	0 10
1946 12 29	215 57	0 11
1946 12 30	216 02	0 11
1946 12 31	216 08	0 11
1947 01 01	216 13	0 12
1947 01 02	216 19	0 12
1947 01 03	216 24	0 12
1947 01 04	216 30	0 13
1947 01 05	216 35	0 13
1947 01 06	216 40	0 13
1947 01 07	216 45	0 14
1947 01 08	216 50	0 14
1947 01 09	216 55	0 14
1947 01 10	216 59	0 15
1947 01 11	217 04	0 15
1947 01 12	217 08	0 15
1947 01 13	217 13	0 16
1947 01 14	217 17	0 16
1947 01 15	217 21	0 16
1947 01 16	217 26	0 17
1947 01 17	217 30	0 17
1947 01 18	217 34	0 17
1947 01 19	217 37	0 18
1947 01 20	217 41	0 18
1947 01 21	217 45	0 19
1947 01 22	217 48	0 19
1947 01 23	217 52	0 19
1947 01 24	217 55	0 20
1947 01 25	217 58	0 20
1947 01 26	218 01	0 20
1947 01 27	218 04	0 21
1947 01 28	218 07	0 21
1947 01 29	218 10	0 21
1947 01 30	218 12	0 22
1947 01 31	218 15	0 22
1947 02 01	218 17	0 23
1947 02 02	218 19	0 23
1947 02 03	218 22	0 23
1947 02 04	218 24	0 24
1947 02 05	218 26	0 24
1947 02 06	218 28	0 24
1947 02 07	218 29	0 25
1947 02 08	218 31	0 25
1947 02 09	218 32	0 26
1947 02 10	218 34	0 26
1947 02 11	218 35	0 26
1947 02 12	218 36	0 27
1947 02 13	218 37	0 27
1947 02 14	218 38	0 28
1947 02 15	218 39	0 28
1947 02 16	218 40	0 28
1947 02 17	218 40	0 29
1947 02 18	218 41	0 29
1947 02 19	218 41	0 30
1947 02 20	218 41	0 30
1947 02 21	218 41	0 30
1947 02 22	218 41	0 31
1947 02 23	218 41	0 31
1947 02 24	218 41	0 31
1947 02 25	218 40	0 32
1947 02 26	218 40	0 32
1947 02 27	218 39	0 33
1947 02 28	218 39	0 33

21 mr 48 Lat 2 01

Chiron

1947 03 01	218 38	0 34
1947 03 02	218 37	0 34
1947 03 03	218 36	0 34
1947 03 04	218 35	0 35
1947 03 05	218 33	0 35
1947 03 06	218 32	0 36
1947 03 07	218 30	0 36
1947 03 08	218 29	0 36
1947 03 09	218 27	0 37
1947 03 10	218 25	0 37
1947 03 11	218 23	0 38
1947 03 12	218 21	0 38
1947 03 13	218 19	0 38
1947 03 14	218 17	0 39
1947 03 15	218 15	0 39
1947 03 16	218 12	0 40
1947 03 17	218 10	0 40
1947 03 18	218 07	0 40
1947 03 19	218 05	0 41
1947 03 20	218 02	0 41
1947 03 21	217 59	0 42
1947 03 22	217 56	0 42
1947 03 23	217 53	0 42
1947 03 24	217 50	0 43
1947 03 25	217 47	0 43
1947 03 26	217 43	0 44
1947 03 27	217 40	0 44
1947 03 28	217 36	0 44
1947 03 29	217 33	0 45
1947 03 30	217 29	0 45
1947 03 31	217 26	0 46
1947 04 01	217 22	0 46
1947 04 02	217 18	0 47
1947 04 03	217 14	0 47
1947 04 04	217 10	0 47
1947 04 05	217 06	0 48
1947 04 06	217 02	0 48
1947 04 07	216 58	0 49
1947 04 08	216 54	0 49
1947 04 09	216 50	0 49
1947 04 10	216 46	0 50
1947 04 11	216 41	0 50
1947 04 12	216 37	0 50
1947 04 13	216 33	0 51
1947 04 14	216 28	0 51
1947 04 15	216 24	0 52
1947 04 16	216 19	0 52
1947 04 17	216 15	0 52
1947 04 18	216 10	0 53
1947 04 19	216 06	0 53
1947 04 20	216 01	0 54
1947 04 21	215 57	0 54
1947 04 22	215 52	0 54
1947 04 23	215 48	0 55
1947 04 24	215 43	0 55
1947 04 25	215 38	0 55
1947 04 26	215 34	0 56
1947 04 27	215 29	0 56
1947 04 28	215 24	0 56
1947 04 29	215 20	0 57
1947 04 30	215 15	0 57
1947 05 01	215 11	0 58
1947 05 02	215 06	0 58
1947 05 03	215 01	0 58
1947 05 04	214 57	0 59
1947 05 05	214 52	0 59
1947 05 06	214 48	0 59
1947 05 07	214 43	1 00
1947 05 08	214 39	1 00
1947 05 09	214 35	1 00
1947 05 10	214 30	1 01
1947 05 11	214 26	1 01
1947 05 12	214 21	1 01
1947 05 13	214 17	1 02
1947 05 14	214 13	1 02
1947 05 15	214 09	1 02
1947 05 16	214 05	1 02
1947 05 17	214 01	1 03
1947 05 18	213 57	1 03
1947 05 19	213 53	1 03
1947 05 20	213 49	1 04
1947 05 21	213 45	1 04
1947 05 22	213 41	1 04
1947 05 23	213 37	1 05
1947 05 24	213 34	1 05
1947 05 25	213 30	1 05
1947 05 26	213 26	1 05
1947 05 27	213 23	1 06
1947 05 28	213 20	1 06
1947 05 29	213 16	1 06
1947 05 30	213 13	1 07
1947 05 31	213 10	1 07
1947 06 01	213 07	1 07
1947 06 02	213 04	1 07
1947 06 03	213 01	1 08
1947 06 04	212 58	1 08
1947 06 05	212 55	1 08
1947 06 06	212 53	1 08
1947 06 07	212 50	1 09
1947 06 08	212 48	1 09
1947 06 09	212 45	1 09
1947 06 10	212 43	1 09
1947 06 11	212 41	1 10
1947 06 12	212 39	1 10
1947 06 13	212 37	1 10
1947 06 14	212 35	1 10
1947 06 15	212 33	1 11
1947 06 16	212 31	1 11
1947 06 17	212 30	1 11
1947 06 18	212 28	1 11
1947 06 19	212 27	1 11
1947 06 20	212 26	1 12
1947 06 21	212 24	1 12
1947 06 22	212 23	1 12
1947 06 23	212 22	1 12
1947 06 24	212 21	1 13
1947 06 25	212 21	1 13
1947 06 26	212 20	1 13
1947 06 27	212 20	1 13
1947 06 28	212 19	1 13
1947 06 29	212 19	1 14
1947 06 30	212 18	1 14
1947 07 01	212 18	1 14
1947 07 02	212 18	1 14
1947 07 03	212 18	1 14
1947 07 04	212 19	1 15
1947 07 05	212 19	1 15
1947 07 06	212 19	1 15
1947 07 07	212 20	1 15
1947 07 08	212 21	1 15
1947 07 09	212 21	1 15
1947 07 10	212 22	1 16
1947 07 11	212 23	1 16
1947 07 12	212 24	1 16
1947 07 13	212 25	1 16
1947 07 14	212 27	1 16
1947 07 15	212 28	1 17
1947 07 16	212 27	1 17
1947 07 17	212 31	1 17
1947 07 18	212 33	1 17
1947 07 19	212 35	1 17
1947 07 20	212 36	1 17
1947 07 21	212 39	1 18
1947 07 22	212 41	1 18
1947 07 23	212 43	1 18
1947 07 24	212 45	1 18
1947 07 25	212 48	1 18
1947 07 26	212 50	1 18
1947 07 27	212 53	1 19
1947 07 28	212 56	1 19
1947 07 29	212 58	1 19
1947 07 30	213 01	1 19
1947 07 31	213 04	1 19
1947 08 01	213 08	1 19
1947 08 02	213 11	1 20
1947 08 03	213 14	1 20
1947 08 04	213 18	1 20
1947 08 05	213 21	1 20
1947 08 06	213 25	1 20
1947 08 07	213 29	1 20
1947 08 08	213 32	1 21
1947 08 09	213 36	1 21
1947 08 10	213 40	1 21
1947 08 11	213 44	1 21
1947 08 12	213 49	1 21
1947 08 13	213 53	1 21
1947 08 14	213 57	1 22
1947 08 15	214 02	1 22
1947 08 16	214 06	1 22
1947 08 17	214 11	1 22
1947 08 18	214 16	1 22
1947 08 19	214 20	1 22
1947 08 20	214 25	1 22
1947 08 21	214 30	1 23
1947 08 22	214 35	1 23
1947 08 23	214 41	1 23
1947 08 24	214 46	1 23
1947 08 25	214 51	1 23
1947 08 26	214 56	1 23
1947 08 27	215 02	1 24
1947 08 28	215 07	1 24
1947 08 29	215 13	1 24
1947 08 30	215 19	1 24
1947 08 31	215 25	1 24
1947 09 01	215 30	1 24
1947 09 02	215 36	1 25
1947 09 03	215 42	1 25
1947 09 04	215 48	1 25
1947 09 05	215 54	1 25
1947 09 06	216 01	1 25
1947 09 07	216 07	1 25
1947 09 08	216 13	1 26
1947 09 09	216 19	1 26
1947 09 10	216 26	1 26
1947 09 11	216 32	1 26
1947 09 12	216 39	1 26
1947 09 13	216 46	1 26
1947 09 14	216 52	1 27
1947 09 15	216 59	1 27
1947 09 16	217 06	1 27
1947 09 17	217 13	1 27
1947 09 18	217 20	1 27
1947 09 19	217 27	1 28
1947 09 20	217 34	1 28
1947 09 21	217 41	1 28
1947 09 22	217 48	1 28
1947 09 23	217 55	1 28
1947 09 24	218 02	1 28
1947 09 25	218 09	1 29
1947 09 26	218 17	1 29
1947 09 27	218 24	1 29
1947 09 28	218 32	1 29
1947 09 29	218 39	1 29
1947 09 30	218 46	1 30
1947 10 01	218 54	1 30
1947 10 02	219 02	1 30
1947 10 03	219 09	1 30
1947 10 04	219 17	1 30
1947 10 05	219 25	1 31
1947 10 06	219 32	1 31
1947 10 07	219 40	1 31
1947 10 08	219 48	1 31
1947 10 09	219 56	1 31
1947 10 10	220 04	1 32
1947 10 11	220 11	1 32
1947 10 12	220 19	1 32
1947 10 13	220 27	1 32
1947 10 14	220 35	1 32
1947 10 15	220 43	1 33
1947 10 16	220 51	1 33
1947 10 17	220 59	1 33
1947 10 18	221 07	1 33
1947 10 19	221 16	1 34
1947 10 20	221 24	1 34
1947 10 21	221 32	1 34
1947 10 22	221 40	1 34
1947 10 23	221 48	1 35
1947 10 24	221 56	1 35
1947 10 25	222 04	1 35
1947 10 26	222 13	1 35
1947 10 27	222 21	1 35
1947 10 28	222 29	1 36
1947 10 29	222 37	1 36
1947 10 30	222 46	1 36
1947 10 31	222 54	1 36
1947 11 01	223 02	1 37
1947 11 02	223 10	1 37
1947 11 03	223 19	1 37
1947 11 04	223 27	1 38
1947 11 05	223 35	1 38
1947 11 06	223 44	1 38
1947 11 07	223 52	1 38
1947 11 08	224 00	1 39
1947 11 09	224 08	1 39
1947 11 10	224 17	1 39
1947 11 11	224 25	1 39
1947 11 12	224 33	1 40
1947 11 13	224 42	1 40
1947 11 14	224 50	1 40
1947 11 15	224 58	1 41
1947 11 16	225 06	1 41
1947 11 17	225 14	1 41
1947 11 18	225 23	1 41
1947 11 19	225 31	1 42
1947 11 20	225 39	1 42
1947 11 21	225 47	1 42
1947 11 22	225 55	1 43
1947 11 23	226 04	1 43
1947 11 24	226 12	1 43
1947 11 25	226 20	1 44
1947 11 26	226 28	1 44
1947 11 27	226 36	1 44
1947 11 28	226 44	1 45
1947 11 29	226 52	1 45
1947 11 30	227 00	1 45
1947 12 01	227 08	1 46
1947 12 02	227 16	1 46
1947 12 03	227 23	1 46
1947 12 04	227 31	1 47
1947 12 05	227 39	1 47
1947 12 06	227 47	1 47
1947 12 07	227 55	1 48
1947 12 08	228 02	1 48
1947 12 09	228 10	1 48
1947 12 10	228 18	1 49
1947 12 11	228 25	1 49
1947 12 12	228 33	1 49
1947 12 13	228 40	1 50
1947 12 14	228 48	1 50
1947 12 15	228 55	1 50
1947 12 16	229 02	1 51
1947 12 17	229 10	1 51
1947 12 18	229 17	1 52
1947 12 19	229 24	1 52
1947 12 20	229 31	1 52
1947 12 21	229 39	1 53
1947 12 22	229 46	1 53
1947 12 23	229 53	1 54
1947 12 24	230 00	1 54
1947 12 25	230 06	1 54
1947 12 26	230 13	1 55
1947 12 27	230 20	1 55
1947 12 28	230 27	1 56
1947 12 29	230 33	1 56
1947 12 30	230 40	1 56
1947 12 31	230 46	1 57
1948 01 01	230 53	1 57
1948 01 02	230 59	1 58
1948 01 03	231 06	1 58
1948 01 04	231 12	1 58
1948 01 05	231 18	1 59
1948 01 06	231 24	1 59
1948 01 07	231 30	2 00
1948 01 08	231 36	2 00
1948 01 09	231 42	2 01
1948 01 10	231 48	2 01
1948 01 11	231 54	2 02
1948 01 12	231 59	2 02
1948 01 13	232 05	2 02
1948 01 14	232 10	2 03
1948 01 15	232 16	2 03
1948 01 16	232 21	2 04
1948 01 17	232 26	2 04
1948 01 18	232 32	2 05
1948 01 19	232 37	2 05
1948 01 20	232 42	2 06
1948 01 21	232 47	2 06
1948 01 22	232 51	2 07
1948 01 23	232 56	2 07
1948 01 24	233 01	2 08
1948 01 25	233 05	2 08
1948 01 26	233 10	2 09
1948 01 27	233 14	2 09
1948 01 28	233 18	2 10
1948 01 29	233 23	2 10
1948 01 30	233 27	2 11
1948 01 31	233 31	2 11
1948 02 01	233 34	2 12
1948 02 02	233 38	2 12
1948 02 03	233 42	2 13
1948 02 04	233 46	2 13
1948 02 05	233 49	2 14
1948 02 06	233 52	2 14
1948 02 07	233 56	2 15
1948 02 08	233 59	2 15
1948 02 09	234 02	2 16
1948 02 10	234 05	2 16
1948 02 11	234 08	2 17
1948 02 12	234 10	2 18
1948 02 13	234 13	2 18
1948 02 14	234 16	2 19
1948 02 15	234 18	2 19
1948 02 16	234 20	2 20
1948 02 17	234 23	2 20
1948 02 18	234 25	2 21
1948 02 19	234 27	2 21
1948 02 20	234 29	2 22
1948 02 21	234 30	2 22
1948 02 22	234 32	2 23
1948 02 23	234 34	2 24
1948 02 24	234 35	2 24
1948 02 25	234 36	2 25
1948 02 26	234 38	2 25
1948 02 27	234 39	2 26
1948 02 28	234 40	2 26
1948 02 29	234 41	2 27
1948 03 01	234 41	2 27
1948 03 02	234 42	2 28
1948 03 03	234 43	2 29
1948 03 04	234 43	2 29
1948 03 05	234 44	2 30
1948 03 06	234 44	2 30
1948 03 07	234 44	2 31
1948 03 08	234 44	2 31
1948 03 09	234 44	2 32
1948 03 10	234 44	2 32
1948 03 11	234 43	2 33
1948 03 12	234 43	2 34
1948 03 13	234 42	2 34
1948 03 14	234 42	2 35
1948 03 15	234 41	2 35
1948 03 16	234 40	2 36
1948 03 17	234 39	2 36
1948 03 18	234 38	2 37
1948 03 19	234 37	2 38
1948 03 20	234 36	2 38
1948 03 21	234 34	2 39
1948 03 22	234 33	2 39
1948 03 23	234 31	2 40
1948 03 24	234 29	2 40
1948 03 25	234 28	2 41
1948 03 26	234 26	2 41
1948 03 27	234 24	2 42
1948 03 28	234 22	2 42
1948 03 29	234 19	2 43
1948 03 30	234 17	2 43
1948 03 31	234 15	2 44
1948 04 01	234 12	2 45
1948 04 02	234 10	2 45
1948 04 03	234 07	2 46
1948 04 04	234 04	2 46
1948 04 05	234 02	2 47
1948 04 06	233 59	2 47
1948 04 07	233 56	2 48
1948 04 08	233 53	2 48
1948 04 09	233 50	2 49
1948 04 10	233 46	2 49
1948 04 11	233 43	2 50
1948 04 12	233 40	2 50
1948 04 13	233 36	2 51
1948 04 14	233 33	2 51
1948 04 15	233 29	2 51
1948 04 16	233 26	2 52
1948 04 17	233 22	2 52
1948 04 18	233 18	2 53
1948 04 19	233 15	2 53
1948 04 20	233 11	2 54
1948 04 21	233 07	2 54
1948 04 22	233 03	2 55
1948 04 23	232 59	2 55

1948	04	24	232	55	2	56
1948	04	25	232	51	2	56
1948	04	26	232	46	2	56
1948	04	27	232	42	2	57
1948	04	28	232	38	2	57
1948	04	29	232	34	2	58
1948	04	30	232	30	2	58
1948	05	01	232	25	2	58
1948	05	02	232	21	2	59
1948	05	03	232	16	2	59
1948	05	04	232	12	2	59
1948	05	05	232	08	3	00
1948	05	06	232	03	3	00
1948	05	07	231	59	3	00
1948	05	08	231	54	3	01
1948	05	09	231	50	3	01
1948	05	10	231	45	3	01
1948	05	11	231	41	3	02
1948	05	12	231	36	3	02
1948	05	13	231	32	3	02
1948	05	14	231	27	3	03
1948	05	15	231	23	3	03
1948	05	16	231	18	3	03
1948	05	17	231	14	3	04
1948	05	18	231	10	3	04
1948	05	19	231	05	3	04
1948	05	20	231	01	3	04
1948	05	21	230	56	3	05
1948	05	22	230	52	3	05
1948	05	23	230	48	3	05
1948	05	24	230	43	3	05
1948	05	25	230	39	3	05
1948	05	26	230	35	3	06
1948	05	27	230	31	3	06
1948	05	28	230	26	3	06
1948	05	29	230	22	3	06
1948	05	30	230	18	3	06
1948	05	31	230	14	3	07
1948	06	01	230	10	3	07
1948	06	02	230	06	3	07
1948	06	03	230	02	3	07
1948	06	04	229	58	3	07
1948	06	05	229	54	3	07
1948	06	06	229	51	3	08
1948	06	07	229	47	3	08
1948	06	08	229	43	3	08
1948	06	09	229	40	3	08
1948	06	10	229	36	3	08
1948	06	11	229	33	3	08
1948	06	12	229	29	3	08
1948	06	13	229	26	3	08
1948	06	14	229	23	3	08
1948	06	15	229	20	3	09
1948	06	16	229	17	3	09
1948	06	17	229	14	3	09
1948	06	18	229	11	3	09
1948	06	19	229	08	3	09
1948	06	20	229	05	3	09
1948	06	21	229	02	3	09
1948	06	22	229	00	3	09
1948	06	23	228	57	3	09
1948	06	24	228	55	3	09
1948	06	25	228	53	3	09
1948	06	26	228	50	3	09
1948	06	27	228	48	3	09
1948	06	28	228	46	3	09
1948	06	29	228	44	3	09
1948	06	30	228	42	3	09
1948	07	01	228	40	3	09
1948	07	02	228	39	3	09
1948	07	03	228	37	3	09
1948	07	04	228	35	3	09
1948	07	05	228	34	3	09
1948	07	06	228	33	3	09
1948	07	07	228	31	3	09
1948	07	08	228	30	3	09
1948	07	09	228	29	3	09
1948	07	10	228	28	3	09
1948	07	11	228	28	3	09
1948	07	12	228	27	3	09
1948	07	13	228	26	3	09
1948	07	14	228	26	3	09
1948	07	15	228	25	3	09
1948	07	16	228	25	3	09
1948	07	17	228	25	3	09
1948	07	18	228	25	3	09
1948	07	19	228	25	3	09
1948	07	20	228	25	3	09
1948	07	21	228	25	3	09
1948	07	22	228	25	3	09
1948	07	23	228	26	3	08
1948	07	24	228	26	3	08
1948	07	25	228	27	3	08
1948	07	26	228	28	3	08
1948	07	27	228	28	3	08
1948	07	28	228	29	3	08
1948	07	29	228	30	3	08
1948	07	30	228	31	3	08
1948	07	31	228	33	3	08
1948	08	01	228	34	3	08
1948	08	02	228	35	3	08
1948	08	03	228	37	3	08
1948	08	04	228	39	3	08
1948	08	05	228	40	3	08
1948	08	06	228	42	3	07
1948	08	07	228	44	3	07
1948	08	08	228	46	3	07
1948	08	09	228	48	3	07
1948	08	10	228	51	3	07
1948	08	11	228	53	3	07
1948	08	12	228	55	3	07
1948	08	13	228	58	3	07
1948	08	14	229	00	3	07
1948	08	15	229	03	3	07
1948	08	16	229	06	3	07
1948	08	17	229	09	3	07
1948	08	18	229	12	3	07
1948	08	19	229	15	3	07
1948	08	20	229	18	3	06
1948	08	21	229	22	3	06
1948	08	22	229	25	3	06
1948	08	23	229	28	3	06
1948	08	24	229	32	3	06
1948	08	25	229	36	3	06
1948	08	26	229	39	3	06
1948	08	27	229	43	3	06
1948	08	28	229	47	3	06
1948	08	29	229	51	3	06
1948	08	30	229	55	3	06
1948	08	31	230	00	3	06
1948	09	01	230	04	3	06
1948	09	02	230	08	3	06
1948	09	03	230	13	3	06
1948	09	04	230	17	3	06
1948	09	05	230	22	3	05
1948	09	06	230	26	3	05
1948	09	07	230	31	3	05
1948	09	08	230	36	3	05
1948	09	09	230	41	3	05
1948	09	10	230	46	3	05
1948	09	11	230	51	3	05
1948	09	12	230	56	3	05
1948	09	13	231	01	3	05
1948	09	14	231	07	3	05
1948	09	15	231	12	3	05
1948	09	16	231	17	3	05
1948	09	17	231	23	3	05
1948	09	18	231	29	3	05
1948	09	19	231	34	3	05
1948	09	20	231	40	3	05
1948	09	21	231	46	3	05
1948	09	22	231	52	3	05
1948	09	23	231	57	3	05
1948	09	24	232	03	3	05
1948	09	25	232	09	3	05
1948	09	26	232	16	3	05
1948	09	27	232	22	3	05
1948	09	28	232	28	3	05
1948	09	29	232	34	3	05
1948	09	30	232	41	3	05
1948	10	01	232	47	3	05
1948	10	02	232	53	3	05
1948	10	03	233	00	3	05
1948	10	04	233	06	3	05
1948	10	05	233	13	3	05
1948	10	06	233	20	3	05
1948	10	07	233	26	3	05
1948	10	08	233	33	3	05
1948	10	09	233	40	3	05
1948	10	10	233	47	3	05
1948	10	11	233	54	3	05
1948	10	12	234	01	3	05
1948	10	13	234	08	3	06
1948	10	14	234	15	3	06
1948	10	15	234	22	3	06
1948	10	16	234	29	3	06
1948	10	17	234	36	3	06
1948	10	18	234	43	3	06
1948	10	19	234	50	3	06
1948	10	20	234	58	3	06
1948	10	21	235	05	3	06
1948	10	22	235	12	3	06
1948	10	23	235	19	3	06
1948	10	24	235	27	3	06
1948	10	25	235	34	3	06
1948	10	26	235	42	3	07
1948	10	27	235	49	3	07
1948	10	28	235	57	3	07
1948	10	29	236	04	3	07
1948	10	30	236	12	3	07
1948	10	31	236	19	3	07
1948	11	01	236	27	3	07
1948	11	02	236	35	3	07
1948	11	03	236	42	3	08
1948	11	04	236	50	3	08
1948	11	05	236	58	3	08
1948	11	06	237	05	3	08
1948	11	07	237	13	3	08
1948	11	08	237	21	3	08
1948	11	09	237	28	3	09
1948	11	10	237	36	3	09
1948	11	11	237	44	3	09
1948	11	12	237	52	3	09
1948	11	13	237	59	3	09
1948	11	14	238	07	3	09
1948	11	15	238	15	3	10
1948	11	16	238	23	3	10
1948	11	17	238	31	3	10
1948	11	18	238	38	3	10
1948	11	19	238	46	3	10
1948	11	20	238	54	3	11
1948	11	21	239	02	3	11
1948	11	22	239	10	3	11
1948	11	23	239	17	3	11
1948	11	24	239	25	3	11
1948	11	25	239	33	3	12
1948	11	26	239	41	3	12
1948	11	27	239	49	3	12
1948	11	28	239	56	3	12
1948	11	29	240	04	3	13
1948	11	30	240	12	3	13
1948	12	01	240	20	3	13
1948	12	02	240	27	3	13
1948	12	03	240	35	3	14
1948	12	04	240	43	3	14
1948	12	05	240	51	3	14
1948	12	06	240	58	3	15
1948	12	07	241	06	3	15
1948	12	08	241	14	3	15
1948	12	09	241	21	3	15
1948	12	10	241	29	3	16
1948	12	11	241	36	3	16
1948	12	12	241	44	3	16
1948	12	13	241	51	3	17
1948	12	14	241	59	3	17
1948	12	15	242	06	3	17
1948	12	16	242	14	3	18
1948	12	17	242	21	3	18
1948	12	18	242	28	3	18
1948	12	19	242	36	3	19
1948	12	20	242	43	3	19
1948	12	21	242	50	3	19
1948	12	22	242	58	3	20
1948	12	23	243	05	3	20
1948	12	24	243	12	3	21
1948	12	25	243	19	3	21
1948	12	26	243	26	3	21
1948	12	27	243	33	3	22
1948	12	28	243	40	3	22
1948	12	29	243	47	3	22
1948	12	30	243	54	3	23
1948	12	31	244	01	3	23
1949	01	01	244	08	3	24
1949	01	02	244	14	3	24
1949	01	03	244	21	3	25
1949	01	04	244	28	3	25
1949	01	05	244	34	3	25
1949	01	06	244	41	3	26
1949	01	07	244	47	3	26
1949	01	08	244	54	3	27
1949	01	09	245	00	3	27
1949	01	10	245	06	3	28
1949	01	11	245	13	3	28
1949	01	12	245	19	3	29
1949	01	13	245	25	3	29
1949	01	14	245	31	3	29
1949	01	15	245	37	3	30
1949	01	16	245	43	3	30
1949	01	17	245	49	3	31
1949	01	18	245	55	3	31
1949	01	19	246	00	3	32
1949	01	20	246	06	3	32
1949	01	21	246	12	3	33
1949	01	22	246	17	3	33
1949	01	23	246	23	3	34
1949	01	24	246	28	3	34
1949	01	25	246	33	3	35
1949	01	26	246	39	3	35
1949	01	27	246	44	3	36
1949	01	28	246	49	3	37
1949	01	29	246	54	3	37
1949	01	30	246	59	3	38
1949	01	31	247	04	3	38
1949	02	01	247	08	3	39
1949	02	02	247	13	3	39
1949	02	03	247	18	3	40
1949	02	04	247	22	3	40
1949	02	05	247	27	3	41
1949	02	06	247	31	3	42
1949	02	07	247	35	3	42
1949	02	08	247	39	3	43
1949	02	09	247	43	3	43
1949	02	10	247	47	3	44
1949	02	11	247	51	3	44
1949	02	12	247	55	3	45
1949	02	13	247	59	3	46
1949	02	14	248	02	3	46
1949	02	15	248	06	3	47
1949	02	16	248	09	3	47
1949	02	17	248	13	3	48
1949	02	18	248	16	3	49
1949	02	19	248	19	3	49
1949	02	20	248	22	3	50
1949	02	21	248	25	3	50
1949	02	22	248	28	3	51
1949	02	23	248	31	3	52
1949	02	24	248	33	3	52
1949	02	25	248	36	3	53
1949	02	26	248	38	3	54
1949	02	27	248	41	3	54
1949	02	28	248	43	3	55
1949	03	01	248	45	3	55
1949	03	02	248	47	3	56
1949	03	03	248	49	3	57
1949	03	04	248	51	3	57
1949	03	05	248	53	3	58
1949	03	06	248	54	3	59
1949	03	07	248	56	3	59
1949	03	08	248	57	4	00
1949	03	09	248	58	4	01
1949	03	10	249	00	4	01
1949	03	11	249	01	4	02
1949	03	12	249	02	4	03
1949	03	13	249	03	4	03
1949	03	14	249	03	4	04
1949	03	15	249	04	4	04
1949	03	16	249	05	4	05
1949	03	17	249	05	4	06
1949	03	18	249	05	4	06
1949	03	19	249	06	4	07
1949	03	20	249	06	4	08
1949	03	21	249	06	4	08
1949	03	22	249	06	4	09
1949	03	23	249	06	4	10
1949	03	24	249	06	4	10
1949	03	25	249	05	4	11
1949	03	26	249	05	4	12
1949	03	27	249	04	4	12
1949	03	28	249	04	4	13
1949	03	29	249	03	4	14
1949	03	30	249	02	4	14
1949	03	31	249	01	4	15
1949	04	01	249	00	4	15
1949	04	02	248	59	4	16
1949	04	03	248	57	4	17
1949	04	04	248	56	4	17
1949	04	05	248	55	4	18
1949	04	06	248	53	4	18
1949	04	07	248	51	4	19
1949	04	08	248	50	4	20
1949	04	09	248	48	4	20
1949	04	10	248	46	4	21
1949	04	11	248	44	4	21
1949	04	12	248	42	4	22
1949	04	13	248	40	4	23
1949	04	14	248	37	4	23
1949	04	15	248	35	4	24
1949	04	16	248	33	4	24
1949	04	17	248	30	4	25
1949	04	18	248	27	4	26
1949	04	19	248	25	4	26
1949	04	20	248	22	4	27
1949	04	21	248	19	4	27
1949	04	22	248	16	4	28
1949	04	23	248	13	4	28
1949	04	24	248	10	4	29
1949	04	25	248	07	4	29
1949	04	26	248	04	4	30
1949	04	27	248	01	4	30
1949	04	28	247	57	4	31
1949	04	29	247	54	4	31
1949	04	30	247	50	4	32
1949	05	01	247	47	4	32
1949	05	02	247	43	4	33
1949	05	03	247	40	4	33
1949	05	04	247	36	4	34
1949	05	05	247	32	4	34
1949	05	06	247	28	4	34
1949	05	07	247	24	4	35
1949	05	08	247	21	4	35
1949	05	09	247	17	4	36
1949	05	10	247	13	4	36
1949	05	11	247	09	4	36
1949	05	12	247	05	4	37
1949	05	13	247	01	4	37
1949	05	14	246	56	4	38
1949	05	15	246	52	4	38
1949	05	16	246	48	4	38
1949	05	17	246	44	4	39
1949	05	18	246	40	4	39
1949	05	19	246	35	4	39
1949	05	20	246	31	4	40
1949	05	21	246	27	4	40
1949	05	22	246	23	4	40
1949	05	23	246	18	4	40
1949	05	24	246	14	4	41
1949	05	25	246	10	4	41
1949	05	26	246	05	4	41
1949	05	27	246	01	4	41
1949	05	28	245	57	4	42
1949	05	29	245	52	4	42
1949	05	30	245	48	4	42
1949	05	31	245	44	4	42
1949	06	01	245	39	4	43
1949	06	02	245	35	4	43
1949	06	03	245	31	4	43
1949	06	04	245	27	4	43
1949	06	05	245	22	4	43
1949	06	06	245	18	4	43
1949	06	07	245	14	4	43
1949	06	08	245	10	4	44
1949	06	09	245	06	4	44
1949	06	10	245	01	4	44
1949	06	11	244	57	4	44
1949	06	12	244	53	4	44
1949	06	13	244	49	4	44
1949	06	14	244	45	4	44
1949	06	15	244	41	4	44
1949	06	16	244	37	4	44
1949	06	17	244	34	4	44

1949	06	18	244	30	4	44
1949	06	19	244	26	4	44
1949	06	20	244	22	4	44
1949	06	21	244	19	4	44
1949	06	22	244	15	4	44
1949	06	23	244	12	4	44
1949	06	24	244	08	4	44
1949	06	25	244	05	4	44
1949	06	26	244	01	4	44
1949	06	27	243	58	4	44
1949	06	28	243	55	4	44
1949	06	29	243	52	4	44
1949	06	30	243	48	4	44
1949	07	01	243	45	4	44
1949	07	02	243	42	4	44
1949	07	03	243	40	4	44
1949	07	04	243	37	4	44
1949	07	05	243	34	4	44
1949	07	06	243	31	4	43
1949	07	07	243	29	4	43
1949	07	08	243	26	4	43
1949	07	09	243	24	4	43
1949	07	10	243	21	4	43
1949	07	11	243	19	4	43
1949	07	12	243	17	4	43
1949	07	13	243	15	4	42
1949	07	14	243	13	4	42
1949	07	15	243	11	4	42
1949	07	16	243	09	4	42
1949	07	17	243	07	4	42
1949	07	18	243	06	4	42
1949	07	19	243	04	4	41
1949	07	20	243	03	4	41
1949	07	21	243	01	4	41
1949	07	22	243	00	4	41
1949	07	23	242	59	4	41
1949	07	24	242	58	4	40
1949	07	25	242	57	4	40
1949	07	26	242	56	4	40
1949	07	27	242	55	4	40
1949	07	28	242	54	4	39
1949	07	29	242	53	4	39
1949	07	30	242	53	4	39
1949	07	31	242	53	4	39
1949	08	01	242	52	4	39
1949	08	02	242	52	4	38
1949	08	03	242	52	4	38
1949	08	04	242	52	4	38
1949	08	05	242	52	4	38
1949	08	06	242	52	4	37
1949	08	07	242	52	4	37
1949	08	08	242	53	4	37
1949	08	09	242	53	4	37
1949	08	10	242	53	4	36
1949	08	11	242	54	4	36
1949	08	12	242	55	4	36
1949	08	13	242	56	4	35
1949	08	14	242	57	4	35
1949	08	15	242	58	4	35
1949	08	16	242	59	4	35
1949	08	17	243	00	4	34
1949	08	18	243	01	4	34
1949	08	19	243	03	4	34
1949	08	20	243	04	4	34
1949	08	21	243	06	4	33
1949	08	22	243	08	4	33
1949	08	23	243	09	4	33
1949	08	24	243	11	4	33
1949	08	25	243	13	4	32
1949	08	26	243	15	4	32
1949	08	27	243	17	4	32
1949	08	28	243	20	4	32
1949	08	29	243	22	4	31
1949	08	30	243	25	4	31
1949	08	31	243	27	4	31
1949	09	01	243	30	4	31
1949	09	02	243	32	4	30
1949	09	03	243	35	4	30
1949	09	04	243	38	4	30
1949	09	05	243	41	4	29
1949	09	06	243	44	4	29
1949	09	07	243	47	4	29
1949	09	08	243	51	4	29
1949	09	09	243	54	4	29
1949	09	10	243	58	4	28
1949	09	11	244	01	4	28
1949	09	12	244	05	4	28
1949	09	13	244	08	4	28
1949	09	14	244	12	4	27
1949	09	15	244	16	4	27
1949	09	16	244	20	4	27
1949	09	17	244	24	4	27
1949	09	18	244	28	4	26
1949	09	19	244	32	4	26
1949	09	20	244	36	4	26
1949	09	21	244	41	4	26
1949	09	22	244	45	4	26
1949	09	23	244	50	4	25
1949	09	24	244	54	4	25
1949	09	25	244	59	4	25
1949	09	26	245	04	4	25
1949	09	27	245	08	4	25

1949	09	28	245	13	4	24
1949	09	29	245	18	4	24
1949	09	30	245	23	4	24
1949	10	01	245	28	4	24
1949	10	02	245	33	4	24
1949	10	03	245	38	4	24
1949	10	04	245	44	4	23
1949	10	05	245	49	4	23
1949	10	06	245	54	4	23
1949	10	07	246	00	4	23
1949	10	08	246	05	4	23
1949	10	09	246	11	4	23
1949	10	10	246	17	4	22
1949	10	11	246	22	4	22
1949	10	12	246	28	4	22
1949	10	13	246	34	4	22
1949	10	14	246	40	4	22
1949	10	15	246	45	4	22
1949	10	16	246	51	4	22
1949	10	17	246	57	4	22
1949	10	18	247	04	4	22
1949	10	19	247	10	4	21
1949	10	20	247	16	4	21
1949	10	21	247	22	4	21
1949	10	22	247	28	4	21
1949	10	23	247	35	4	21
1949	10	24	247	41	4	21
1949	10	25	247	47	4	21
1949	10	26	247	54	4	21
1949	10	27	248	00	4	21
1949	10	28	248	07	4	21
1949	10	29	248	13	4	21
1949	10	30	248	20	4	21
1949	10	31	248	27	4	21
1949	11	01	248	33	4	21
1949	11	02	240	40	4	21
1949	11	03	248	47	4	21
1949	11	04	248	54	4	21
1949	11	05	249	00	4	21
1949	11	06	249	07	4	21
1949	11	07	249	14	4	21
1949	11	08	249	21	4	21
1949	11	09	249	28	4	21
1949	11	10	249	35	4	21
1949	11	11	249	42	4	21
1949	11	12	249	49	4	21
1949	11	13	249	56	4	21
1949	11	14	250	03	4	21
1949	11	15	250	10	4	21
1949	11	16	250	17	4	21
1949	11	17	250	24	4	21
1949	11	18	250	32	4	21
1949	11	19	250	39	4	21
1949	11	20	250	46	4	21
1949	11	21	250	53	4	21
1949	11	22	251	00	4	21
1949	11	23	251	08	4	21
1949	11	24	251	15	4	21
1949	11	25	251	22	4	22
1949	11	26	251	29	4	22
1949	11	27	251	37	4	22
1949	11	28	251	44	4	22
1949	11	29	251	51	4	22
1949	11	30	251	58	4	22
1949	12	01	252	06	4	22
1949	12	02	252	13	4	22
1949	12	03	252	20	4	23
1949	12	04	252	28	4	23
1949	12	05	252	35	4	23
1949	12	06	252	42	4	23
1949	12	07	252	49	4	23
1949	12	08	252	57	4	23
1949	12	09	253	04	4	24
1949	12	10	253	11	4	24
1949	12	11	253	19	4	24
1949	12	12	253	26	4	24
1949	12	13	253	33	4	24
1949	12	14	253	40	4	25
1949	12	15	253	47	4	25
1949	12	16	253	55	4	25
1949	12	17	254	02	4	25
1949	12	18	254	09	4	26
1949	12	19	254	16	4	26
1949	12	20	254	23	4	26
1949	12	21	254	30	4	26
1949	12	22	254	38	4	27
1949	12	23	254	45	4	27
1949	12	24	254	52	4	27
1949	12	25	254	59	4	27
1949	12	26	255	06	4	28
1949	12	27	255	13	4	28
1949	12	28	255	20	4	28
1949	12	29	255	27	4	29
1949	12	30	255	33	4	29
1949	12	31	255	40	4	29
1950	01	01	255	47	4	30
1950	01	02	255	54	4	30
1950	01	03	256	01	4	30
1950	01	04	256	07	4	31
1950	01	05	256	14	4	31
1950	01	06	256	21	4	31
1950	01	07	256	27	4	32
1950	01	08	256	34	4	32
1950	01	09	256	41	4	32
1950	01	10	256	47	4	33
1950	01	11	256	53	4	33

1950	01	12	257	00	4	34
1950	01	13	257	06	4	34
1950	01	14	257	13	4	34
1950	01	15	257	19	4	35
1950	01	16	257	25	4	35
1950	01	17	257	31	4	36
1950	01	18	257	37	4	36
1950	01	19	257	43	4	37
1950	01	20	257	49	4	37
1950	01	21	257	55	4	37
1950	01	22	258	01	4	38
1950	01	23	258	07	4	38
1950	01	24	258	13	4	39
1950	01	25	258	19	4	39
1950	01	26	258	24	4	40
1950	01	27	258	30	4	40
1950	01	28	258	36	4	41
1950	01	29	258	41	4	41
1950	01	30	258	46	4	42
1950	01	31	258	52	4	42
1950	02	01	258	57	4	43
1950	02	02	259	02	4	43
1950	02	03	259	08	4	44
1950	02	04	259	13	4	44
1950	02	05	259	18	4	45
1950	02	06	259	23	4	45
1950	02	07	259	27	4	46
1950	02	08	259	32	4	46
1950	02	09	259	37	4	47
1950	02	10	259	42	4	48
1950	02	11	259	46	4	48
1950	02	12	259	51	4	49
1950	02	13	259	55	4	49
1950	02	14	260	00	4	50
1950	02	15	260	04	4	50
1950	02	16	260	00	4	51
1950	02	17	260	12	4	52
1950	02	18	260	16	4	52
1950	02	19	260	20	4	53
1950	02	20	260	24	4	53
1950	02	21	260	28	4	54
1950	02	22	260	32	4	55
1950	02	23	260	35	4	55
1950	02	24	260	39	4	56
1950	02	25	260	42	4	56
1950	02	26	260	46	4	57
1950	02	27	260	49	4	58
1950	02	28	260	52	4	58
1950	03	01	260	55	4	59
1950	03	02	260	58	5	00
1950	03	03	261	01	5	00
1950	03	04	261	04	5	01
1950	03	05	261	07	5	01
1950	03	06	261	09	5	02
1950	03	07	261	12	5	03
1950	03	08	261	14	5	03
1950	03	09	261	17	5	04
1950	03	10	261	19	5	05
1950	03	11	261	21	5	05
1950	03	12	261	23	5	06
1950	03	13	261	25	5	07
1950	03	14	261	27	5	07
1950	03	15	261	29	5	08
1950	03	16	261	31	5	09
1950	03	17	261	32	5	09
1950	03	18	261	34	5	10
1950	03	19	261	35	5	11
1950	03	20	261	36	5	11
1950	03	21	261	38	5	12
1950	03	22	261	39	5	13
1950	03	23	261	40	5	13
1950	03	24	261	41	5	14
1950	03	25	261	41	5	15
1950	03	26	261	42	5	15
1950	03	27	261	43	5	16
1950	03	28	261	43	5	17
1950	03	29	261	44	5	18
1950	03	30	261	44	5	18
1950	03	31	261	44	5	19
1950	04	01	261	44	5	20
1950	04	02	261	44	5	20
1950	04	03	261	44	5	21
1950	04	04	261	44	5	22
1950	04	05	261	44	5	22
1950	04	06	261	44	5	23
1950	04	07	261	43	5	24
1950	04	08	261	43	5	24
1950	04	09	261	42	5	25
1950	04	10	261	41	5	26
1950	04	11	261	40	5	26
1950	04	12	261	39	5	27
1950	04	13	261	38	5	27
1950	04	14	261	37	5	28
1950	04	15	261	36	5	29
1950	04	16	261	35	5	29
1950	04	17	261	33	5	30
1950	04	18	261	32	5	31
1950	04	19	261	30	5	31
1950	04	20	261	29	5	32
1950	04	21	261	27	5	32
1950	04	22	261	25	5	33
1950	04	23	261	23	5	34
1950	04	24	261	21	5	34
1950	04	25	261	19	5	35
1950	04	26	261	17	5	35
1950	04	27	261	15	5	36

1950	04	28	261	12	5	37
1950	04	29	261	10	5	37
1950	04	30	261	08	5	38
1950	05	01	261	05	5	38
1950	05	02	261	02	5	39
1950	05	03	261	00	5	39
1950	05	04	260	57	5	40
1950	05	05	260	54	5	40
1950	05	06	260	51	5	41
1950	05	07	260	48	5	41
1950	05	08	260	45	5	42
1950	05	09	260	42	5	42
1950	05	10	260	39	5	43
1950	05	11	260	36	5	43
1950	05	12	260	32	5	44
1950	05	13	260	29	5	44
1950	05	14	260	26	5	45
1950	05	15	260	22	5	45
1950	05	16	260	19	5	46
1950	05	17	260	15	5	46
1950	05	18	260	11	5	47
1950	05	19	260	08	5	47
1950	05	20	260	04	5	47
1950	05	21	260	00	5	48
1950	05	22	259	57	5	48
1950	05	23	259	53	5	48
1950	05	24	259	49	5	49
1950	05	25	259	45	5	49
1950	05	26	259	41	5	49
1950	05	27	259	37	5	50
1950	05	28	259	33	5	50
1950	05	29	259	29	5	50
1950	05	30	259	25	5	51
1950	05	31	259	21	5	51
1950	06	01	259	17	5	51
1950	06	02	257	13	5	52
1950	06	03	259	09	5	52
1950	06	04	259	05	5	52
1950	06	05	259	01	5	52
1950	06	06	258	56	5	52
1950	06	07	258	52	5	53
1950	06	08	258	48	5	53
1950	06	09	258	44	5	53
1950	06	10	258	40	5	53
1950	06	11	258	36	5	53
1950	06	12	258	31	5	53
1950	06	13	258	27	5	54
1950	06	14	258	23	5	54
1950	06	15	258	19	5	54
1950	06	16	258	15	5	54
1950	06	17	258	11	5	54
1950	06	18	258	07	5	54
1950	06	19	258	03	5	54
1950	06	20	257	59	5	54
1950	06	21	257	55	5	54
1950	06	22	257	51	5	54
1950	06	23	257	47	5	54
1950	06	24	257	43	5	54
1950	06	25	257	39	5	54
1950	06	26	257	35	5	54
1950	06	27	257	31	5	54
1950	06	28	257	27	5	54
1950	06	29	257	23	5	54
1950	06	30	257	20	5	54
1950	07	01	257	16	5	54
1950	07	02	257	12	5	54
1950	07	03	257	09	5	54
1950	07	04	257	05	5	54
1950	07	05	257	02	5	54
1950	07	06	256	58	5	54
1950	07	07	256	55	5	53
1950	07	08	256	51	5	53
1950	07	09	256	48	5	53
1950	07	10	256	45	5	53
1950	07	11	256	42	5	53
1950	07	12	256	39	5	53
1950	07	13	256	35	5	53
1950	07	14	256	32	5	52
1950	07	15	256	30	5	52
1950	07	16	256	27	5	52
1950	07	17	256	24	5	52
1950	07	18	256	21	5	52
1950	07	19	256	19	5	51
1950	07	20	256	16	5	51
1950	07	21	256	13	5	51
1950	07	22	256	11	5	51
1950	07	23	256	09	5	50
1950	07	24	256	06	5	50
1950	07	25	256	04	5	50
1950	07	26	256	02	5	49
1950	07	27	256	00	5	49
1950	07	28	255	58	5	49
1950	07	29	255	56	5	49
1950	07	30	255	54	5	48
1950	07	31	255	53	5	48
1950	08	01	255	51	5	48
1950	08	02	255	49	5	47
1950	08	03	255	48	5	47
1950	08	04	255	47	5	47
1950	08	05	255	45	5	46
1950	08	06	255	44	5	46
1950	08	07	255	43	5	46
1950	08	08	255	42	5	45
1950	08	09	255	41	5	45
1950	08	10	255	40	5	45
1950	08	11	255	39	5	44

1950	08	12	255	39	5	44
1950	08	13	255	38	5	44
1950	08	14	255	38	5	43
1950	08	15	255	37	5	43
1950	08	16	255	37	5	42
1950	08	17	255	37	5	42
1950	08	18	255	37	5	42
1950	08	19	255	37	5	41
1950	08	20	255	37	5	41
1950	08	21	255	37	5	40
1950	08	22	255	37	5	40
1950	08	23	255	37	5	40
1950	08	24	255	38	5	39
1950	08	25	255	38	5	39
1950	08	26	255	39	5	39
1950	08	27	255	40	5	38
1950	08	28	255	41	5	38
1950	08	29	255	42	5	37
1950	08	30	255	43	5	37
1950	08	31	255	44	5	37
1950	09	01	255	45	5	36
1950	09	02	255	46	5	36
1950	09	03	255	47	5	35
1950	09	04	255	49	5	35
1950	09	05	255	50	5	35
1950	09	06	255	52	5	34
1950	09	07	255	54	5	34
1950	09	08	255	56	5	33
1950	09	09	255	57	5	33
1950	09	10	255	59	5	33
1950	09	11	256	02	5	32
1950	09	12	256	04	5	32
1950	09	13	256	06	5	31
1950	09	14	256	08	5	31
1950	09	15	256	11	5	31
1950	09	16	256	13	5	30
1950	09	17	256	16	5	30
1950	09	18	256	19	5	30
1950	09	19	256	21	5	29
1950	09	20	256	24	5	29
1950	09	21	256	27	5	28
1950	09	22	256	30	5	28
1950	09	23	256	33	5	28
1950	09	24	256	36	5	27
1950	09	25	256	40	5	27
1950	09	26	256	43	5	27
1950	09	27	256	47	5	26
1950	09	28	256	50	5	26
1950	09	29	256	54	5	26
1950	09	30	256	57	5	25
1950	10	01	257	01	5	25
1950	10	02	257	05	5	25
1950	10	03	257	09	5	24
1950	10	04	257	13	5	24
1950	10	05	257	17	5	24
1950	10	06	257	21	5	23
1950	10	07	257	25	5	23
1950	10	08	257	29	5	23
1950	10	09	257	34	5	22
1950	10	10	257	38	5	22
1950	10	11	257	42	5	22
1950	10	12	257	47	5	22
1950	10	13	257	52	5	21
1950	10	14	257	56	5	21
1950	10	15	258	01	5	21
1950	10	16	258	06	5	20
1950	10	17	258	11	5	20
1950	10	18	258	15	5	20
1950	10	19	258	20	5	20
1950	10	20	258	26	5	19
1950	10	21	258	31	5	19
1950	10	22	258	36	5	19
1950	10	23	258	41	5	19
1950	10	24	258	46	5	18
1950	10	25	258	52	5	18
1950	10	26	258	57	5	18
1950	10	27	259	02	5	18
1950	10	28	259	08	5	18
1950	10	29	259	13	5	17
1950	10	30	259	19	5	17
1950	10	31	259	25	5	17
1950	11	01	259	30	5	17
1950	11	02	259	36	5	17
1950	11	03	259	42	5	16
1950	11	04	259	48	5	16
1950	11	05	259	53	5	16
1950	11	06	259	59	5	16
1950	11	07	260	05	5	16
1950	11	08	260	11	5	16
1950	11	09	260	17	5	15
1950	11	10	260	23	5	15
1950	11	11	260	30	5	15
1950	11	12	260	36	5	15
1950	11	13	260	42	5	15
1950	11	14	260	48	5	15
1950	11	15	260	54	5	15
1950	11	16	261	01	5	15
1950	11	17	261	07	5	15
1950	11	18	261	13	5	15
1950	11	19	261	20	5	14
1950	11	20	261	26	5	14
1950	11	21	261	33	5	14
1950	11	22	261	39	5	14
1950	11	23	261	46	5	14
1950	11	24	261	52	5	14
1950	11	25	261	59	5	14

1950	11	26	262	05	5	14
1950	11	27	262	12	5	14
1950	11	28	262	18	5	14
1950	11	29	262	25	5	14
1950	11	30	262	32	5	14
1950	12	01	262	38	5	14
1950	12	02	262	45	5	14
1950	12	03	262	52	5	14
1950	12	04	262	58	5	14
1950	12	05	263	05	5	14
1950	12	06	263	12	5	14
1950	12	07	263	19	5	14
1950	12	08	263	25	5	14
1950	12	09	263	32	5	14
1950	12	10	263	39	5	14
1950	12	11	263	46	5	14
1950	12	12	263	52	5	15
1950	12	13	263	59	5	15
1950	12	14	264	06	5	15
1950	12	15	264	13	5	15
1950	12	16	264	19	5	15
1950	12	17	264	26	5	15
1950	12	18	264	33	5	15
1950	12	19	264	40	5	15
1950	12	20	264	47	5	15
1950	12	21	264	53	5	16
1950	12	22	265	00	5	16
1950	12	23	265	07	5	16
1950	12	24	265	14	5	16
1950	12	25	265	20	5	16
1950	12	26	265	27	5	16
1950	12	27	265	34	5	17
1950	12	28	265	40	5	17
1950	12	29	265	47	5	17
1950	12	30	265	54	5	17
1950	12	31	266	00	5	17
1951	01	01	266	07	5	18
1951	01	02	266	14	5	18
1951	01	03	266	20	5	18
1951	01	04	266	27	5	18
1951	01	05	266	33	5	19
1951	01	06	266	40	5	19
1951	01	07	266	46	5	19
1951	01	08	266	53	5	19
1951	01	09	266	59	5	20
1951	01	10	267	06	5	20
1951	01	11	267	12	5	20
1951	01	12	267	18	5	20
1951	01	13	267	25	5	21
1951	01	14	267	31	5	21
1951	01	15	267	37	5	21
1951	01	16	267	44	5	22
1951	01	17	267	50	5	22
1951	01	18	267	56	5	22
1951	01	19	268	02	5	23
1951	01	20	268	08	5	23
1951	01	21	268	14	5	23
1951	01	22	268	20	5	24
1951	01	23	268	26	5	24
1951	01	24	268	32	5	25
1951	01	25	268	38	5	25
1951	01	26	268	44	5	25
1951	01	27	268	49	5	26
1951	01	28	268	55	5	26
1951	01	29	269	01	5	26
1951	01	30	269	07	5	27
1951	01	31	269	12	5	27
1951	02	01	269	18	5	28
1951	02	02	269	23	5	28
1951	02	03	269	29	5	29
1951	02	04	269	34	5	29
1951	02	05	269	39	5	30
1951	02	06	269	45	5	30
1951	02	07	269	50	5	30
1951	02	08	269	55	5	31
1951	02	09	270	00	5	31
1951	02	10	270	05	5	32
1951	02	11	270	10	5	32
1951	02	12	270	15	5	33
1951	02	13	270	20	5	33
1951	02	14	270	25	5	34
1951	02	15	270	29	5	34
1951	02	16	270	34	5	35
1951	02	17	270	39	5	35
1951	02	18	270	43	5	36
1951	02	19	270	47	5	36
1951	02	20	270	52	5	37
1951	02	21	270	56	5	38
1951	02	22	271	00	5	38
1951	02	23	271	05	5	39
1951	02	24	271	09	5	39
1951	02	25	271	13	5	40
1951	02	26	271	17	5	40
1951	02	27	271	21	5	41
1951	02	28	271	24	5	41
1951	03	01	271	28	5	42
1951	03	02	271	32	5	43
1951	03	03	271	35	5	43
1951	03	04	271	39	5	44
1951	03	05	271	42	5	44
1951	03	06	271	45	5	45
1951	03	07	271	49	5	46
1951	03	08	271	52	5	46
1951	03	09	271	55	5	47
1951	03	10	271	58	5	47
1951	03	11	272	01	5	48

1951	03	12	272	04	5	49
1951	03	13	272	07	5	49
1951	03	14	272	09	5	50
1951	03	15	272	12	5	51
1951	03	16	272	14	5	51
1951	03	17	272	17	5	52
1951	03	18	272	19	5	53
1951	03	19	272	21	5	53
1951	03	20	272	23	5	54
1951	03	21	272	25	5	54
1951	03	22	272	27	5	55
1951	03	23	272	29	5	56
1951	03	24	272	31	5	56
1951	03	25	272	33	5	57
1951	03	26	272	34	5	58
1951	03	27	272	36	5	58
1951	03	28	272	37	5	59
1951	03	29	272	39	6	00
1951	03	30	272	40	6	00
1951	03	31	272	41	6	01
1951	04	01	272	42	6	02
1951	04	02	272	43	6	02
1951	04	03	272	44	6	03
1951	04	04	272	45	6	04
1951	04	05	272	45	6	04
1951	04	06	272	46	6	05
1951	04	07	272	47	6	06
1951	04	08	272	47	6	06
1951	04	09	272	47	6	07
1951	04	10	272	48	6	08
1951	04	11	272	48	6	08
1951	04	12	272	48	6	09
1951	04	13	272	48	6	10
1951	04	14	272	48	6	10
1951	04	15	272	47	6	11
1951	04	16	272	47	6	12
1951	04	17	272	47	6	12
1951	04	18	272	46	6	13
1951	04	19	272	46	6	14
1951	04	20	272	45	6	14
1951	04	21	272	44	6	15
1951	04	22	272	43	6	16
1951	04	23	272	42	6	16
1951	04	24	272	41	6	17
1951	04	25	272	40	6	17
1951	04	26	272	39	6	18
1951	04	27	272	38	6	19
1951	04	28	272	36	6	19
1951	04	29	272	35	6	20
1951	04	30	272	33	6	21
1951	05	01	272	32	6	21
1951	05	02	272	30	6	22
1951	05	03	272	28	6	22
1951	05	04	272	27	6	23
1951	05	05	272	25	6	23
1951	05	06	272	22	6	24
1951	05	07	272	20	6	25
1951	05	08	272	18	6	25
1951	05	09	272	16	6	26
1951	05	10	272	14	6	26
1951	05	11	272	11	6	27
1951	05	12	272	09	6	27
1951	05	13	272	06	6	28
1951	05	14	272	04	6	28
1951	05	15	272	01	6	29
1951	05	16	271	58	6	29
1951	05	17	271	56	6	30
1951	05	18	271	53	6	30
1951	05	19	271	50	6	31
1951	05	20	271	47	6	31
1951	05	21	271	44	6	32
1951	05	22	271	41	6	32
1951	05	23	271	38	6	33
1951	05	24	271	35	6	33
1951	05	25	271	31	6	33
1951	05	26	271	28	6	34
1951	05	27	271	25	6	34
1951	05	28	271	21	6	35
1951	05	29	271	18	6	35
1951	05	30	271	14	6	35
1951	05	31	271	11	6	36
1951	06	01	271	07	6	36
1951	06	02	271	04	6	36
1951	06	03	271	00	6	37
1951	06	04	270	56	6	37
1951	06	05	270	53	6	37
1951	06	06	270	49	6	38
1951	06	07	270	45	6	38
1951	06	08	270	41	6	38
1951	06	09	270	37	6	39
1951	06	10	270	33	6	39
1951	06	11	270	30	6	39
1951	06	12	270	26	6	39
1951	06	13	270	22	6	39
1951	06	14	270	18	6	40
1951	06	15	270	14	6	40
1951	06	16	270	10	6	40
1951	06	17	270	06	6	40
1951	06	18	270	02	6	40
1951	06	19	269	58	6	40
1951	06	20	269	54	6	41
1951	06	21	269	50	6	41
1951	06	22	269	46	6	41
1951	06	23	269	42	6	41
1951	06	24	269	38	6	41
1951	06	25	269	34	6	41

1951	06	26	269	30	6	41
1951	06	27	269	26	6	41
1951	06	28	269	22	6	41
1951	06	29	269	18	6	41
1951	06	30	269	14	6	41
1951	07	01	269	10	6	41
1951	07	02	269	06	6	41
1951	07	03	269	03	6	41
1951	07	04	268	59	6	41
1951	07	05	268	55	6	41
1951	07	06	268	51	6	41
1951	07	07	268	47	6	41
1951	07	08	268	44	6	41
1951	07	09	268	40	6	41
1951	07	10	268	36	6	41
1951	07	11	268	33	6	41
1951	07	12	268	29	6	41
1951	07	13	268	25	6	40
1951	07	14	268	22	6	40
1951	07	15	268	18	6	40
1951	07	16	268	15	6	40
1951	07	17	268	12	6	40
1951	07	18	268	08	6	40
1951	07	19	268	05	6	39
1951	07	20	268	02	6	39
1951	07	21	267	59	6	39
1951	07	22	267	55	6	39
1951	07	23	267	52	6	38
1951	07	24	267	49	6	38
1951	07	25	267	46	6	38
1951	07	26	267	44	6	38
1951	07	27	267	41	6	37
1951	07	28	267	38	6	37
1951	07	29	267	35	6	37
1951	07	30	267	33	6	37
1951	07	31	267	30	6	36
1951	08	01	267	27	6	36
1951	08	02	267	25	6	36
1951	08	03	267	23	6	35
1951	08	04	267	20	6	35
1951	08	05	267	18	6	35
1951	08	06	267	16	6	34
1951	08	07	267	14	6	34
1951	08	08	267	12	6	34
1951	08	09	267	10	6	33
1951	08	10	267	08	6	33
1951	08	11	267	06	6	32
1951	08	12	267	05	6	32
1951	08	13	267	03	6	32
1951	08	14	267	01	6	31
1951	08	15	267	00	6	31
1951	08	16	266	58	6	30
1951	08	17	266	57	6	30
1951	08	18	266	56	6	30
1951	08	19	266	55	6	29
1951	08	20	266	54	6	29
1951	08	21	266	53	6	28
1951	08	22	266	52	6	28
1951	08	23	266	51	6	27
1951	08	24	266	50	6	27
1951	08	25	266	50	6	27
1951	08	26	266	49	6	26
1951	08	27	266	49	6	26
1951	08	28	266	48	6	25
1951	08	29	266	48	6	25
1951	08	30	266	48	6	24
1951	08	31	266	48	6	24
1951	09	01	266	48	6	23
1951	09	02	266	48	6	23
1951	09	03	266	48	6	22
1951	09	04	266	48	6	22
1951	09	05	266	48	6	21
1951	09	06	266	49	6	21
1951	09	07	266	49	6	21
1951	09	08	266	50	6	20
1951	09	09	266	51	6	20
1951	09	10	266	51	6	19
1951	09	11	266	52	6	19
1951	09	12	266	53	6	18
1951	09	13	266	54	6	18
1951	09	14	266	55	6	17
1951	09	15	266	57	6	17
1951	09	16	266	58	6	16
1951	09	17	266	59	6	16
1951	09	18	267	01	6	15
1951	09	19	267	02	6	15
1951	09	20	267	04	6	14
1951	09	21	267	06	6	14
1951	09	22	267	07	6	13
1951	09	23	267	09	6	13
1951	09	24	267	11	6	12
1951	09	25	267	13	6	12
1951	09	26	267	15	6	12
1951	09	27	267	18	6	11
1951	09	28	267	20	6	11
1951	09	29	267	22	6	10
1951	09	30	267	25	6	10
1951	10	01	267	27	6	09
1951	10	02	267	30	6	09
1951	10	03	267	33	6	08
1951	10	04	267	35	6	08
1951	10	05	267	38	6	08

27 ♐ 56
Lat 5 22

1951	10	06	267	41	6	07
1951	10	07	267	44	6	07
1951	10	08	267	47	6	06
1951	10	09	267	50	6	06
1951	10	10	267	54	6	05
1951	10	11	267	57	6	05
1951	10	12	268	00	6	05
1951	10	13	268	04	6	04
1951	10	14	268	07	6	04
1951	10	15	268	11	6	03
1951	10	16	268	15	6	03
1951	10	17	268	18	6	03
1951	10	18	268	22	6	02
1951	10	19	268	26	6	02
1951	10	20	268	30	6	01
1951	10	21	268	34	6	01
1951	10	22	268	38	6	01
1951	10	23	268	42	6	00
1951	10	24	268	46	6	00
1951	10	25	268	51	6	00
1951	10	26	268	55	5	59
1951	10	27	268	59	5	59
1951	10	28	269	04	5	59
1951	10	29	269	08	5	58
1951	10	30	269	13	5	58
1951	10	31	269	18	5	58
1951	11	01	269	22	5	57
1951	11	02	269	27	5	57
1951	11	03	269	32	5	57
1951	11	04	269	37	5	56
1951	11	05	269	42	5	56
1951	11	06	269	47	5	56
1951	11	07	269	52	5	56
1951	11	08	269	57	5	55
1951	11	09	270	02	5	55
1951	11	10	270	07	5	55
1951	11	11	270	12	5	55
1951	11	12	270	18	5	54
1951	11	13	270	23	5	54
1951	11	14	270	28	5	54
1951	11	15	270	34	5	54
1951	11	16	270	39	5	53
1951	11	17	270	45	5	53
1951	11	18	270	50	5	53
1951	11	19	270	56	5	53
1951	11	20	271	01	5	53
1951	11	21	271	07	5	52
1951	11	22	271	13	5	52
1951	11	23	271	18	5	52
1951	11	24	271	24	5	52
1951	11	25	271	30	5	52
1951	11	26	271	36	5	52
1951	11	27	271	41	5	51
1951	11	28	271	47	5	51
1951	11	29	271	53	5	51
1951	11	30	271	59	5	51
1951	12	01	272	05	5	51
1951	12	02	272	11	5	51
1951	12	03	272	17	5	51
1951	12	04	272	23	5	51
1951	12	05	272	29	5	50
1951	12	06	272	35	5	50
1951	12	07	272	41	5	50
1951	12	08	272	48	5	50
1951	12	09	272	54	5	50
1951	12	10	273	00	5	50
1951	12	11	273	06	5	50
1951	12	12	273	12	5	50
1951	12	13	273	18	5	50
1951	12	14	273	25	5	50
1951	12	15	273	31	5	50
1951	12	16	273	37	5	50
1951	12	17	273	43	5	50
1951	12	18	273	50	5	50
1951	12	19	273	56	5	50
1951	12	20	274	02	5	50
1951	12	21	274	09	5	50
1951	12	22	274	15	5	50
1951	12	23	274	21	5	50
1951	12	24	274	27	5	50
1951	12	25	274	34	5	50
1951	12	26	274	40	5	50
1951	12	27	274	46	5	50
1951	12	28	274	53	5	50
1951	12	29	274	59	5	50
1951	12	30	275	05	5	50
1951	12	31	275	12	5	51
1952	01	01	275	18	5	51
1952	01	02	275	24	5	51
1952	01	03	275	30	5	51
1952	01	04	275	37	5	51
1952	01	05	275	43	5	51
1952	01	06	275	49	5	51
1952	01	07	275	55	5	51
1952	01	08	276	02	5	52
1952	01	09	276	08	5	52
1952	01	10	276	14	5	52
1952	01	11	276	20	5	52
1952	01	12	276	26	5	52
1952	01	13	276	32	5	53
1952	01	14	276	39	5	53
1952	01	15	276	45	5	53
1952	01	16	276	51	5	53
1952	01	17	276	57	5	53
1952	01	18	277	03	5	54
1952	01	19	277	09	5	54
1952	01	20	277	15	5	54
1952	01	21	277	21	5	54
1952	01	22	277	27	5	55
1952	01	23	277	33	5	55
1952	01	24	277	38	5	55
1952	01	25	277	44	5	55
1952	01	26	277	50	5	56
1952	01	27	277	56	5	56
1952	01	28	278	02	5	56
1952	01	29	278	07	5	57
1952	01	30	278	13	5	57
1952	01	31	278	19	5	57
1952	02	01	278	24	5	58
1952	02	02	278	30	5	58
1952	02	03	278	35	5	58
1952	02	04	278	41	5	59
1952	02	05	278	46	5	59
1952	02	06	278	51	5	59
1952	02	07	278	57	6	00
1952	02	08	279	02	6	00
1952	02	09	279	07	6	01
1952	02	10	279	12	6	01
1952	02	11	279	17	6	01
1952	02	12	279	23	6	02
1952	02	13	279	28	6	02
1952	02	14	279	33	6	03
1952	02	15	279	38	6	03
1952	02	16	279	42	6	03
1952	02	17	279	47	6	04
1952	02	18	279	52	6	04
1952	02	19	279	57	6	05
1952	02	20	280	01	6	05
1952	02	21	280	06	6	06
1952	02	22	280	11	6	06
1952	02	23	280	15	6	07
1952	02	24	280	19	6	07
1952	02	25	280	24	6	08
1952	02	26	280	28	6	08
1952	02	27	280	32	6	09
1952	02	28	280	36	6	09
1952	02	29	280	41	6	10
1952	03	01	280	45	6	10
1952	03	02	280	49	6	11
1952	03	03	280	53	6	11
1952	03	04	280	56	6	12
1952	03	05	281	00	6	12
1952	03	06	281	04	6	13
1952	03	07	281	07	6	13
1952	03	08	281	11	6	14
1952	03	09	281	14	6	14
1952	03	10	281	18	6	15
1952	03	11	281	21	6	15
1952	03	12	281	25	6	16
1952	03	13	281	28	6	17
1952	03	14	281	31	6	17
1952	03	15	281	34	6	18
1952	03	16	281	37	6	18
1952	03	17	281	40	6	19
1952	03	18	281	43	6	19
1952	03	19	281	45	6	20
1952	03	20	281	48	6	21
1952	03	21	281	51	6	21
1952	03	22	281	53	6	22
1952	03	23	281	55	6	22
1952	03	24	281	58	6	23
1952	03	25	282	00	6	24
1952	03	26	282	02	6	24
1952	03	27	282	04	6	25
1952	03	28	282	06	6	26
1952	03	29	282	08	6	26
1952	03	30	282	10	6	27
1952	03	31	282	12	6	27
1952	04	01	282	14	6	28
1952	04	02	282	15	6	29
1952	04	03	282	17	6	29
1952	04	04	282	18	6	30
1952	04	05	282	19	6	31
1952	04	06	282	21	6	31
1952	04	07	282	22	6	32
1952	04	08	282	23	6	32
1952	04	09	282	24	6	33
1952	04	10	282	25	6	34
1952	04	11	282	26	6	34
1952	04	12	282	26	6	35
1952	04	13	282	27	6	36
1952	04	14	282	28	6	36
1952	04	15	282	28	6	37
1952	04	16	282	28	6	38
1952	04	17	282	29	6	38
1952	04	18	282	29	6	39
1952	04	19	282	29	6	39
1952	04	20	282	29	6	40
1952	04	21	282	29	6	41
1952	04	22	282	29	6	41
1952	04	23	282	29	6	42
1952	04	24	282	29	6	43
1952	04	25	282	28	6	43
1952	04	26	282	28	6	44
1952	04	27	282	27	6	44
1952	04	28	282	27	6	45
1952	04	29	282	26	6	46
1952	04	30	282	25	6	46
1952	05	01	282	24	6	47
1952	05	02	282	23	6	47
1952	05	03	282	22	6	48
1952	05	04	282	21	6	49
1952	05	05	282	20	6	49
1952	05	06	282	19	6	50
1952	05	07	282	17	6	50
1952	05	08	282	16	6	51
1952	05	09	282	14	6	52
1952	05	10	282	13	6	52
1952	05	11	282	11	6	53
1952	05	12	282	09	6	53
1952	05	13	282	07	6	54
1952	05	14	282	06	6	54
1952	05	15	282	04	6	55
1952	05	16	282	02	6	55
1952	05	17	282	00	6	56
1952	05	18	281	57	6	56
1952	05	19	281	55	6	57
1952	05	20	281	53	6	57
1952	05	21	281	50	6	58
1952	05	22	281	48	6	58
1952	05	23	281	46	6	59
1952	05	24	281	43	6	59
1952	05	25	281	40	7	00
1952	05	26	281	38	7	00
1952	05	27	281	35	7	01
1952	05	28	281	32	7	01
1952	05	29	281	29	7	02
1952	05	30	281	26	7	02
1952	05	31	281	23	7	02
1952	06	01	281	20	7	03
1952	06	02	281	17	7	03
1952	06	03	281	14	7	04
1952	06	04	281	11	7	04
1952	06	05	281	08	7	04
1952	06	06	281	04	7	05
1952	06	07	281	01	7	05
1952	06	08	280	58	7	05
1952	06	09	280	54	7	06
1952	06	10	280	51	7	06
1952	06	11	280	48	7	06
1952	06	12	280	44	7	07
1952	06	13	280	41	7	07
1952	06	14	280	37	7	07
1952	06	15	280	33	7	07
1952	06	16	280	30	7	08
1952	06	17	280	26	7	08
1952	06	18	280	22	7	08
1952	06	19	280	19	7	08
1952	06	20	280	15	7	08
1952	06	21	280	11	7	09
1952	06	22	280	08	7	09
1952	06	23	280	04	7	09
1952	06	24	280	00	7	09
1952	06	25	279	56	7	09
1952	06	26	279	52	7	09
1952	06	27	279	49	7	09
1952	06	28	279	45	7	10
1952	06	29	279	41	7	10
1952	06	30	279	37	7	10
1952	07	01	279	33	7	10
1952	07	02	279	29	7	10
1952	07	03	279	26	7	10
1952	07	04	279	22	7	10
1952	07	05	279	18	7	10
1952	07	06	279	14	7	10
1952	07	07	279	10	7	10
1952	07	08	279	06	7	10
1952	07	09	279	03	7	10
1952	07	10	278	59	7	10
1952	07	11	278	55	7	10
1952	07	12	278	51	7	10
1952	07	13	278	48	7	10
1952	07	14	278	44	7	10
1952	07	15	278	40	7	10
1952	07	16	278	37	7	09
1952	07	17	278	33	7	09
1952	07	18	278	30	7	09
1952	07	19	278	26	7	09
1952	07	20	278	23	7	09
1952	07	21	278	19	7	09
1952	07	22	278	16	7	09
1952	07	23	278	12	7	08
1952	07	24	278	09	7	08
1952	07	25	278	06	7	08
1952	07	26	278	02	7	08
1952	07	27	277	59	7	08
1952	07	28	277	56	7	07
1952	07	29	277	53	7	07
1952	07	30	277	49	7	07
1952	07	31	277	46	7	07
1952	08	01	277	43	7	06
1952	08	02	277	40	7	06
1952	08	03	277	38	7	06
1952	08	04	277	35	7	05
1952	08	05	277	32	7	05
1952	08	06	277	29	7	05
1952	08	07	277	27	7	04
1952	08	08	277	24	7	04
1952	08	09	277	21	7	04
1952	08	10	277	19	7	03
1952	08	11	277	17	7	03
1952	08	12	277	14	7	03
1952	08	13	277	12	7	02
1952	08	14	277	10	7	02
1952	08	15	277	07	7	02
1952	08	16	277	05	7	01
1952	08	17	277	03	7	01
1952	08	18	277	01	7	00
1952	08	19	277	00	7	00
1952	08	20	276	58	6	59
1952	08	21	276	56	6	59
1952	08	22	276	54	6	59
1952	08	23	276	53	6	58
1952	08	24	276	51	6	58
1952	08	25	276	50	6	57
1952	08	26	276	48	6	57
1952	08	27	276	47	6	56
1952	08	28	276	46	6	56
1952	08	29	276	45	6	55
1952	08	30	276	44	6	55
1952	08	31	276	43	6	54
1952	09	01	276	42	6	54
1952	09	02	276	41	6	53
1952	09	03	276	40	6	53
1952	09	04	276	40	6	53
1952	09	05	276	39	6	52
1952	09	06	276	39	6	52
1952	09	07	276	38	6	51
1952	09	08	276	38	6	51
1952	09	09	276	38	6	50
1952	09	10	276	38	6	50
1952	09	11	276	38	6	49
1952	09	12	276	38	6	49
1952	09	13	276	38	6	48
1952	09	14	276	38	6	47
1952	09	15	276	38	6	47
1952	09	16	276	39	6	46
1952	09	17	276	39	6	46
1952	09	18	276	39	6	45
1952	09	19	276	40	6	45
1952	09	20	276	41	6	44
1952	09	21	276	42	6	44
1952	09	22	276	42	6	43
1952	09	23	276	43	6	43
1952	09	24	276	44	6	42
1952	09	25	276	45	6	42
1952	09	26	276	47	6	41
1952	09	27	276	48	6	41
1952	09	28	276	49	6	40
1952	09	29	276	51	6	40
1952	09	30	276	52	6	39
1952	10	01	276	54	6	39
1952	10	02	276	55	6	38
1952	10	03	276	57	6	38
1952	10	04	276	59	6	37
1952	10	05	277	01	6	37
1952	10	06	277	03	6	36
1952	10	07	277	05	6	36
1952	10	08	277	07	6	35
1952	10	09	277	09	6	35
1952	10	10	277	12	6	34
1952	10	11	277	14	6	34
1952	10	12	277	16	6	33
1952	10	13	277	19	6	33
1952	10	14	277	21	6	32
1952	10	15	277	24	6	32
1952	10	16	277	27	6	31
1952	10	17	277	30	6	31
1952	10	18	277	33	6	30
1952	10	19	277	36	6	30
1952	10	20	277	39	6	30
1952	10	21	277	42	6	29
1952	10	22	277	45	6	29
1952	10	23	277	48	6	28
1952	10	24	277	51	6	28
1952	10	25	277	55	6	27
1952	10	26	277	58	6	27
1952	10	27	278	02	6	26
1952	10	28	278	05	6	26
1952	10	29	278	09	6	26
1952	10	30	278	13	6	25
1952	10	31	278	16	6	25
1952	11	01	278	20	6	24
1952	11	02	278	24	6	24
1952	11	03	278	28	6	24
1952	11	04	278	32	6	23
1952	11	05	278	36	6	23
1952	11	06	278	40	6	22
1952	11	07	278	45	6	22
1952	11	08	278	49	6	22
1952	11	09	278	53	6	21
1952	11	10	278	57	6	21
1952	11	11	279	02	6	21
1952	11	12	279	06	6	20
1952	11	13	279	11	6	20
1952	11	14	279	15	6	20
1952	11	15	279	20	6	19
1952	11	16	279	25	6	19
1952	11	17	279	29	6	19
1952	11	18	279	34	6	18
1952	11	19	279	39	6	18
1952	11	20	279	44	6	18
1952	11	21	279	49	6	18
1952	11	22	279	54	6	17
1952	11	23	279	59	6	17
1952	11	24	280	04	6	17
1952	11	25	280	09	6	17
1952	11	26	280	14	6	16
1952	11	27	280	19	6	16
1952	11	28	280	24	6	16

12♑29
LAT 6 41

1952	11	29	280	30	6	16
1952	11	30	280	35	6	15
1952	12	01	280	40	6	15
1952	12	02	280	45	6	15
1952	12	03	280	51	6	15
1952	12	04	280	56	6	15
1952	12	05	281	02	6	14
1952	12	06	281	07	6	14
1952	12	07	281	13	6	14
1952	12	08	281	18	6	14
1952	12	09	281	24	6	14
1952	12	10	281	29	6	14
1952	12	11	281	35	6	13
1952	12	12	281	40	6	13
1952	12	13	281	46	6	13
1952	12	14	281	52	6	13
1952	12	15	281	57	6	13
1952	12	16	282	03	6	13
1952	12	17	282	09	6	13
1952	12	18	282	15	6	13
1952	12	19	282	20	6	12
1952	12	20	282	26	6	12
1952	12	21	282	32	6	12
1952	12	22	282	38	6	12
1952	12	23	282	44	6	12
1952	12	24	282	49	6	12
1952	12	25	282	55	6	12
1952	12	26	283	01	6	12
1952	12	27	283	07	6	12
1952	12	28	283	13	6	12
1952	12	29	283	19	6	12
1952	12	30	283	25	6	12
1952	12	31	283	31	6	12
1953	01	01	283	36	6	12
1953	01	02	283	42	6	12
1953	01	03	283	48	6	12
1953	01	04	283	54	6	12
1953	01	05	284	00	6	12
1953	01	06	284	06	6	12
1953	01	07	284	12	6	12
1953	01	08	284	18	6	12
1953	01	09	284	23	6	12
1953	01	10	284	29	6	13
1953	01	11	284	35	6	13
1953	01	12	284	41	6	13
1953	01	13	284	47	6	13
1953	01	14	284	53	6	13
1953	01	15	284	59	6	13
1953	01	16	285	04	6	13
1953	01	17	285	10	6	13
1953	01	18	285	16	6	13
1953	01	19	285	22	6	14
1953	01	20	285	27	6	14
1953	01	21	285	33	6	14
1953	01	22	285	39	6	14
1953	01	23	285	45	6	14
1953	01	24	285	50	6	14
1953	01	25	285	56	6	15
1953	01	26	286	01	6	15
1953	01	27	286	07	6	15
1953	01	28	286	13	6	15
1953	01	29	286	18	6	15
1953	01	30	286	24	6	16
1953	01	31	286	29	6	16
1953	02	01	286	35	6	16
1953	02	02	286	40	6	16
1953	02	03	286	45	6	17
1953	02	04	286	51	6	17
1953	02	05	286	56	6	17
1953	02	06	287	02	6	18
1953	02	07	287	07	6	18
1953	02	08	287	12	6	18
1953	02	09	287	17	6	18
1953	02	10	287	22	6	19
1953	02	11	287	28	6	19
1953	02	12	287	33	6	19
1953	02	13	287	38	6	20
1953	02	14	287	43	6	20
1953	02	15	287	48	6	20
1953	02	16	287	52	6	21
1953	02	17	287	57	6	21
1953	02	18	288	02	6	21
1953	02	19	288	07	6	22
1953	02	20	288	12	6	22
1953	02	21	288	16	6	23
1953	02	22	288	21	6	23
1953	02	23	288	26	6	23
1953	02	24	288	30	6	24
1953	02	25	288	35	6	24
1953	02	26	288	39	6	24
1953	02	27	288	43	6	25
1953	02	28	288	48	6	25
1953	03	01	288	52	6	26
1953	03	02	288	56	6	26
1953	03	03	289	00	6	27
1953	03	04	289	04	6	27
1953	03	05	289	08	6	28
1953	03	06	289	12	6	28
1953	03	07	289	16	6	28
1953	03	08	289	20	6	29
1953	03	09	289	24	6	29
1953	03	10	289	28	6	30
1953	03	11	289	31	6	30
1953	03	12	289	35	6	31
1953	03	13	289	39	6	31
1953	03	14	289	42	6	32
1953	03	15	289	45	6	32
1953	03	16	289	49	6	33
1953	03	17	289	52	6	33
1953	03	18	289	55	6	34
1953	03	19	289	58	6	34
1953	03	20	290	02	6	35
1953	03	21	290	05	6	35
1953	03	22	290	07	6	36
1953	03	23	290	10	6	37
1953	03	24	290	13	6	37
1953	03	25	290	16	6	38
1953	03	26	290	18	6	38
1953	03	27	290	21	6	39
1953	03	28	290	24	6	39
1953	03	29	290	26	6	40
1953	03	30	290	28	6	40
1953	03	31	290	31	6	41
1953	04	01	290	33	6	42
1953	04	02	290	35	6	42
1953	04	03	290	37	6	43
1953	04	04	290	39	6	43
1953	04	05	290	41	6	44
1953	04	06	290	43	6	44
1953	04	07	290	44	6	45
1953	04	08	290	46	6	46
1953	04	09	290	48	6	46
1953	04	10	290	49	6	47
1953	04	11	290	51	6	47
1953	04	12	290	52	6	48
1953	04	13	290	53	6	49
1953	04	14	290	54	6	49
1953	04	15	290	55	6	50
1953	04	16	290	56	6	50
1953	04	17	290	57	6	51
1953	04	18	290	58	6	51
1953	04	19	290	59	6	52
1953	04	20	291	00	6	53
1953	04	21	291	00	6	53
1953	04	22	291	01	6	54
1953	04	23	291	01	6	54
1953	04	24	291	02	6	55
1953	04	25	291	02	6	56
1953	04	26	291	02	6	56
1953	04	27	291	02	6	57
1953	04	28	291	02	6	57
1953	04	29	291	02	6	58
1953	04	30	291	02	6	59
1953	05	01	291	02	6	59
1953	05	02	291	02	7	00
1953	05	03	291	01	7	00
1953	05	04	291	01	7	01
1953	05	05	291	00	7	02
1953	05	06	291	00	7	02
1953	05	07	290	59	7	03
1953	05	08	290	58	7	03
1953	05	09	290	58	7	04
1953	05	10	290	57	7	04
1953	05	11	290	56	7	05
1953	05	12	290	55	7	05
1953	05	13	290	54	7	06
1953	05	14	290	52	7	07
1953	05	15	290	51	7	07
1953	05	16	290	50	7	08
1953	05	17	290	48	7	08
1953	05	18	290	47	7	09
1953	05	19	290	45	7	09
1953	05	20	290	44	7	10
1953	05	21	290	42	7	10
1953	05	22	290	40	7	11
1953	05	23	290	38	7	11
1953	05	24	290	36	7	12
1953	05	25	290	34	7	12
1953	05	26	290	32	7	13
1953	05	27	290	30	7	13
1953	05	28	290	28	7	14
1953	05	29	290	26	7	14
1953	05	30	290	24	7	15
1953	05	31	290	21	7	15
1953	06	01	290	19	7	15
1953	06	02	290	16	7	16
1953	06	03	290	14	7	16
1953	06	04	290	11	7	17
1953	06	05	290	08	7	17
1953	06	06	290	06	7	17
1953	06	07	290	03	7	18
1953	06	08	290	00	7	18
1953	06	09	289	57	7	19
1953	06	10	289	54	7	19
1953	06	11	289	51	7	19
1953	06	12	289	48	7	20
1953	06	13	289	45	7	20
1953	06	14	289	42	7	20
1953	06	15	289	39	7	21
1953	06	16	289	36	7	21
1953	06	17	289	33	7	21
1953	06	18	289	29	7	22
1953	06	19	289	26	7	22
1953	06	20	289	23	7	22
1953	06	21	289	19	7	22
1953	06	22	289	16	7	23
1953	06	23	289	13	7	23
1953	06	24	289	09	7	23
1953	06	25	289	06	7	23
1953	06	26	289	02	7	23
1953	06	27	288	59	7	24
1953	06	28	288	55	7	24
1953	06	29	288	52	7	24
1953	06	30	288	48	7	24
1953	07	01	288	44	7	24
1953	07	02	288	41	7	24
1953	07	03	288	37	7	24
1953	07	04	288	33	7	25
1953	07	05	288	30	7	25
1953	07	06	288	26	7	25
1953	07	07	288	22	7	25
1953	07	08	288	19	7	25
1953	07	09	288	15	7	25
1953	07	10	288	11	7	25
1953	07	11	288	08	7	25
1953	07	12	288	04	7	25
1953	07	13	288	00	7	25
1953	07	14	287	57	7	25
1953	07	15	287	53	7	25
1953	07	16	287	49	7	25
1953	07	17	287	46	7	25
1953	07	18	287	42	7	25
1953	07	19	287	38	7	25
1953	07	20	287	35	7	25
1953	07	21	287	31	7	25
1953	07	22	287	28	7	25
1953	07	23	287	24	7	24
1953	07	24	287	21	7	24
1953	07	25	287	17	7	24
1953	07	26	287	14	7	24
1953	07	27	287	10	7	24
1953	07	28	287	07	7	24
1953	07	29	287	03	7	24
1953	07	30	287	00	7	23
1953	07	31	286	57	7	23
1953	08	01	286	53	7	23
1953	08	02	286	50	7	23
1953	08	03	286	47	7	23
1953	08	04	286	44	7	22
1953	08	05	286	41	7	22
1953	08	06	286	37	7	22
1953	08	07	286	34	7	22
1953	08	08	286	31	7	21
1953	08	09	286	28	7	21
1953	08	10	286	26	7	21
1953	08	11	286	23	7	20
1953	08	12	286	20	7	20
1953	08	13	286	17	7	20
1953	08	14	286	14	7	19
1953	08	15	286	12	7	19
1953	08	16	286	09	7	19
1953	08	17	286	07	7	18
1953	08	18	286	04	7	18
1953	08	19	286	02	7	18
1953	08	20	285	59	7	17
1953	08	21	285	57	7	17
1953	08	22	285	55	7	16
1953	08	23	285	52	7	16
1953	08	24	285	50	7	16
1953	08	25	285	48	7	15
1953	08	26	285	46	7	15
1953	08	27	285	44	7	14
1953	08	28	285	42	7	14
1953	08	29	285	41	7	14
1953	08	30	285	39	7	13
1953	08	31	285	37	7	13
1953	09	01	285	36	7	12
1953	09	02	285	34	7	12
1953	09	03	285	33	7	11
1953	09	04	285	31	7	11
1953	09	05	285	30	7	10
1953	09	06	285	29	7	10
1953	09	07	285	28	7	09
1953	09	08	285	27	7	09
1953	09	09	285	26	7	08
1953	09	10	285	25	7	08
1953	09	11	285	24	7	07
1953	09	12	285	23	7	07
1953	09	13	285	22	7	06
1953	09	14	285	22	7	06
1953	09	15	285	21	7	05
1953	09	16	285	21	7	05
1953	09	17	285	20	7	04
1953	09	18	285	20	7	04
1953	09	19	285	20	7	03
1953	09	20	285	20	7	03
1953	09	21	285	19	7	02
1953	09	22	285	19	7	02
1953	09	23	285	20	7	01
1953	09	24	285	20	7	01
1953	09	25	285	20	7	00
1953	09	26	285	20	7	00
1953	09	27	285	21	6	59
1953	09	28	285	21	6	58
1953	09	29	285	22	6	58
1953	09	30	285	22	6	57
1953	10	01	285	23	6	57
1953	10	02	285	24	6	56
1953	10	03	285	25	6	56
1953	10	04	285	26	6	55
1953	10	05	285	27	6	55
1953	10	06	285	28	6	54
1953	10	07	285	29	6	54
1953	10	08	285	30	6	53
1953	10	09	285	32	6	53
1953	10	10	285	33	6	52
1953	10	11	285	34	6	52
1953	10	12	285	36	6	51
1953	10	13	285	38	6	51
1953	10	14	285	39	6	50
1953	10	15	285	41	6	49
1953	10	16	285	43	6	49
1953	10	17	285	45	6	48
1953	10	18	285	47	6	48
1953	10	19	285	49	6	47
1953	10	20	285	51	6	47
1953	10	21	285	54	6	46
1953	10	22	285	56	6	46
1953	10	23	285	58	6	45
1953	10	24	286	01	6	45
1953	10	25	286	03	6	44
1953	10	26	286	06	6	44
1953	10	27	286	09	6	44
1953	10	28	286	11	6	43
1953	10	29	286	14	6	43
1953	10	30	286	17	6	42
1953	10	31	286	20	6	42
1953	11	01	286	23	6	41
1953	11	02	286	26	6	41
1953	11	03	286	29	6	40
1953	11	04	286	32	6	40
1953	11	05	286	36	6	39
1953	11	06	286	39	6	39
1953	11	07	286	42	6	39
1953	11	08	286	46	6	38
1953	11	09	286	49	6	38
1953	11	10	286	53	6	37
1953	11	11	286	56	6	37
1953	11	12	287	00	6	36
1953	11	13	287	04	6	36
1953	11	14	287	08	6	36
1953	11	15	287	12	6	35
1953	11	16	287	15	6	35
1953	11	17	287	19	6	34
1953	11	18	287	23	6	34
1953	11	19	287	28	6	34
1953	11	20	287	32	6	33
1953	11	21	287	36	6	33
1953	11	22	287	40	6	33
1953	11	23	287	44	6	32
1953	11	24	287	49	6	32
1953	11	25	287	53	6	32
1953	11	26	287	57	6	31
1953	11	27	288	02	6	31
1953	11	28	288	06	6	31
1953	11	29	288	11	6	30
1953	11	30	288	16	6	30
1953	12	01	288	20	6	30
1953	12	02	288	25	6	30
1953	12	03	288	30	6	29
1953	12	04	288	34	6	29
1953	12	05	288	39	6	29
1953	12	06	288	44	6	28
1953	12	07	288	49	6	28
1953	12	08	288	54	6	28
1953	12	09	288	59	6	28
1953	12	10	289	04	6	27
1953	12	11	289	09	6	27
1953	12	12	289	14	6	27
1953	12	13	289	19	6	27
1953	12	14	289	24	6	27
1953	12	15	289	29	6	26
1953	12	16	289	34	6	26
1953	12	17	289	39	6	26
1953	12	18	289	45	6	26
1953	12	19	289	50	6	26
1953	12	20	289	55	6	26
1953	12	21	290	00	6	25
1953	12	22	290	06	6	25
1953	12	23	290	11	6	25
1953	12	24	290	16	6	25
1953	12	25	290	22	6	25
1953	12	26	290	27	6	25
1953	12	27	290	33	6	25
1953	12	28	290	38	6	25
1953	12	29	290	43	6	24
1953	12	30	290	49	6	24
1953	12	31	290	54	6	24
1954	01	01	291	00	6	24
1954	01	02	291	05	6	24
1954	01	03	291	11	6	24
1954	01	04	291	16	6	24
1954	01	05	291	22	6	24
1954	01	06	291	27	6	24
1954	01	07	291	33	6	24
1954	01	08	291	38	6	24
1954	01	09	291	44	6	24
1954	01	10	291	49	6	24
1954	01	11	291	55	6	24
1954	01	12	292	00	6	24
1954	01	13	292	06	6	24
1954	01	14	292	11	6	24
1954	01	15	292	17	6	24
1954	01	16	292	22	6	24
1954	01	17	292	28	6	24
1954	01	18	292	33	6	24
1954	01	19	292	39	6	24
1954	01	20	292	44	6	24
1954	01	21	292	50	6	24

1954	01	22	292	55	6	24
1954	01	23	293	01	6	24
1954	01	24	293	06	6	25
1954	01	25	293	12	6	25
1954	01	26	293	17	6	25
1954	01	27	293	22	6	25
1954	01	28	293	28	6	25
1954	01	29	293	33	6	25
1954	01	30	293	39	6	25
1954	01	31	293	44	6	25
1954	02	01	293	49	6	26
1954	02	02	293	55	6	26
1954	02	03	294	00	6	26
1954	02	04	294	05	6	26
1954	02	05	294	10	6	26
1954	02	06	294	16	6	26
1954	02	07	294	21	6	27
1954	02	08	294	26	6	27
1954	02	09	294	31	6	27
1954	02	10	294	36	6	27
1954	02	11	294	41	6	28
1954	02	12	294	46	6	28
1954	02	13	294	51	6	28
1954	02	14	294	56	6	28
1954	02	15	295	01	6	29
1954	02	16	295	06	6	29
1954	02	17	295	11	6	29
1954	02	18	295	16	6	29
1954	02	19	295	20	6	30
1954	02	20	295	25	6	30
1954	02	21	295	30	6	30
1954	02	22	295	35	6	31
1954	02	23	295	39	6	31
1954	02	24	295	44	6	31
1954	02	25	295	48	6	31
1954	02	26	295	53	6	32
1954	02	27	295	57	6	32
1954	02	28	296	02	6	32
1954	03	01	296	06	6	33
1954	03	02	296	11	6	33
1954	03	03	296	15	6	34
1954	03	04	296	19	6	34
1954	03	05	296	23	6	34
1954	03	06	296	27	6	35
1954	03	07	296	31	6	35
1954	03	08	296	36	6	35
1954	03	09	296	39	6	36
1954	03	10	296	43	6	36
1954	03	11	296	47	6	37
1954	03	12	296	51	6	37
1954	03	13	296	55	6	37
1954	03	14	296	59	6	38
1954	03	15	297	02	6	38
1954	03	16	297	06	6	39
1954	03	17	297	09	6	39
1954	03	18	297	13	6	40
1954	03	19	297	16	6	40
1954	03	20	297	20	6	41
1954	03	21	297	23	6	41
1954	03	22	297	26	6	41
1954	03	23	297	29	6	42
1954	03	24	297	32	6	42
1954	03	25	297	35	6	43
1954	03	26	297	38	6	43
1954	03	27	297	41	6	44
1954	03	28	297	44	6	44
1954	03	29	297	47	6	45
1954	03	30	297	50	6	45
1954	03	31	297	52	6	46
1954	04	01	297	55	6	46
1954	04	02	297	57	6	47
1954	04	03	298	00	6	47
1954	04	04	298	02	6	48
1954	04	05	298	05	6	48
1954	04	06	298	07	6	49
1954	04	07	298	09	6	49
1954	04	08	298	11	6	50
1954	04	09	298	13	6	50
1954	04	10	298	15	6	51
1954	04	11	298	17	6	51
1954	04	12	298	19	6	52
1954	04	13	298	20	6	53
1954	04	14	298	22	6	53
1954	04	15	298	24	6	54
1954	04	16	298	25	6	54
1954	04	17	298	27	6	55
1954	04	18	298	28	6	55
1954	04	19	298	29	6	56
1954	04	20	298	30	6	56
1954	04	21	298	32	6	57
1954	04	22	298	33	6	57
1954	04	23	298	34	6	58
1954	04	24	298	34	6	59
1954	04	25	298	35	6	59
1954	04	26	298	36	7	00
1954	04	27	298	37	7	00
1954	04	28	298	37	7	01
1954	04	29	298	38	7	01
1954	04	30	298	38	7	02
1954	05	01	298	39	7	02
1954	05	02	298	39	7	03
1954	05	03	298	39	7	04
1954	05	04	298	39	7	04
1954	05	05	298	39	7	05
1954	05	06	298	39	7	05
1954	05	07	298	39	7	06
1954	05	08	298	39	7	06
1954	05	09	298	39	7	07
1954	05	10	298	39	7	07
1954	05	11	298	38	7	08
1954	05	12	298	38	7	08
1954	05	13	298	37	7	09
1954	05	14	298	37	7	09
1954	05	15	298	36	7	10
1954	05	16	298	35	7	11
1954	05	17	298	34	7	11
1954	05	18	298	33	7	12
1954	05	19	298	32	7	12
1954	05	20	298	31	7	13
1954	05	21	298	30	7	13
1954	05	22	298	29	7	14
1954	05	23	298	28	7	14
1954	05	24	298	26	7	15
1954	05	25	298	25	7	15
1954	05	26	298	23	7	16
1954	05	27	298	22	7	16
1954	05	28	298	20	7	17
1954	05	29	298	19	7	17
1954	05	30	298	17	7	17
1954	05	31	298	15	7	18
1954	06	01	298	13	7	18
1954	06	02	298	11	7	19
1954	06	03	298	09	7	19
1954	06	04	298	07	7	20
1954	06	05	298	05	7	20
1954	06	06	298	03	7	20
1954	06	07	298	01	7	21
1954	06	08	297	58	7	21
1954	06	09	297	56	7	22
1954	06	10	297	54	7	22
1954	06	11	297	51	7	22
1954	06	12	297	49	7	23
1954	06	13	297	46	7	23
1954	06	14	297	44	7	24
1954	06	15	297	41	7	24
1954	06	16	297	38	7	24
1954	06	17	297	35	7	25
1954	06	18	297	33	7	25
1954	06	19	297	30	7	25
1954	06	20	297	27	7	26
1954	06	21	297	24	7	26
1954	06	22	297	21	7	26
1954	06	23	297	18	7	26
1954	06	24	297	15	7	27
1954	06	25	297	12	7	27
1954	06	26	297	09	7	27
1954	06	27	297	05	7	27
1954	06	28	297	02	7	28
1954	06	29	296	59	7	28
1954	06	30	296	56	7	28
1954	07	01	296	52	7	28
1954	07	02	296	49	7	28
1954	07	03	296	46	7	29
1954	07	04	296	42	7	29
1954	07	05	296	39	7	29
1954	07	06	296	36	7	29
1954	07	07	296	32	7	29
1954	07	08	296	29	7	29
1954	07	09	296	25	7	30
1954	07	10	296	22	7	30
1954	07	11	296	18	7	30
1954	07	12	296	15	7	30
1954	07	13	296	11	7	30
1954	07	14	296	08	7	30
1954	07	15	296	04	7	30
1954	07	16	296	01	7	30
1954	07	17	295	57	7	30
1954	07	18	295	54	7	30
1954	07	19	295	50	7	30
1954	07	20	295	46	7	30
1954	07	21	295	43	7	30
1954	07	22	295	39	7	30
1954	07	23	295	36	7	30
1954	07	24	295	32	7	30
1954	07	25	295	29	7	30
1954	07	26	295	25	7	30
1954	07	27	295	22	7	30
1954	07	28	295	18	7	30
1954	07	29	295	15	7	30
1954	07	30	295	11	7	29
1954	07	31	295	08	7	29
1954	08	01	295	05	7	29
1954	08	02	295	01	7	29
1954	08	03	294	58	7	29
1954	08	04	294	54	7	29
1954	08	05	294	51	7	28
1954	08	06	294	48	7	28
1954	08	07	294	45	7	28
1954	08	08	294	41	7	28
1954	08	09	294	38	7	28
1954	08	10	294	35	7	27
1954	08	11	294	32	7	27
1954	08	12	294	29	7	27
1954	08	13	294	26	7	27
1954	08	14	294	23	7	26
1954	08	15	294	20	7	26
1954	08	16	294	17	7	26
1954	08	17	294	14	7	26
1954	08	18	294	11	7	25
1954	08	19	294	08	7	25
1954	08	20	294	06	7	25
1954	08	21	294	03	7	24
1954	08	22	294	00	7	24
1954	08	23	293	58	7	24
1954	08	24	293	55	7	23
1954	08	25	293	53	7	23
1954	08	26	293	50	7	23
1954	08	27	293	48	7	22
1954	08	28	293	45	7	22
1954	08	29	293	43	7	21
1954	08	30	293	41	7	21
1954	08	31	293	39	7	21
1954	09	01	293	37	7	20
1954	09	02	293	35	7	20
1954	09	03	293	33	7	19
1954	09	04	293	31	7	19
1954	09	05	293	29	7	19
1954	09	06	293	27	7	18
1954	09	07	293	25	7	18
1954	09	08	293	24	7	17
1954	09	09	293	22	7	17
1954	09	10	293	21	7	16
1954	09	11	293	19	7	16
1954	09	12	293	18	7	15
1954	09	13	293	16	7	15
1954	09	14	293	15	7	14
1954	09	15	293	14	7	14
1954	09	16	293	13	7	13
1954	09	17	293	12	7	13
1954	09	18	293	11	7	12
1954	09	19	293	10	7	12
1954	09	20	293	09	7	11
1954	09	21	293	08	7	11
1954	09	22	293	08	7	10
1954	09	23	293	07	7	10
1954	09	24	293	07	7	09
1954	09	25	293	06	7	09
1954	09	26	293	06	7	08
1954	09	27	293	05	7	08
1954	09	28	293	05	7	07
1954	09	29	293	05	7	07
1954	09	30	293	05	7	06
1954	10	01	293	05	7	06
1954	10	02	293	05	7	05
1954	10	03	293	05	7	05
1954	10	04	293	05	7	04
1954	10	05	293	06	7	04
1954	10	06	293	06	7	03
1954	10	07	293	07	7	03
1954	10	08	293	07	7	02
1954	10	09	293	08	7	01
1954	10	10	293	08	7	01
1954	10	11	293	09	7	00
1954	10	12	293	10	7	00
1954	10	13	293	11	6	59
1954	10	14	293	12	6	59
1954	10	15	293	13	6	58
1954	10	16	293	14	6	58
1954	10	17	293	15	6	57
1954	10	18	293	17	6	57
1954	10	19	293	18	6	56
1954	10	20	293	19	6	56
1954	10	21	293	21	6	55
1954	10	22	293	22	6	55
1954	10	23	293	24	6	54
1954	10	24	293	26	6	54
1954	10	25	293	27	6	53
1954	10	26	293	29	6	53
1954	10	27	293	31	6	52
1954	10	28	293	33	6	52
1954	10	29	293	35	6	51
1954	10	30	293	37	6	51
1954	10	31	293	40	6	50
1954	11	01	293	42	6	50
1954	11	02	293	44	6	49
1954	11	03	293	47	6	49
1954	11	04	293	49	6	48
1954	11	05	293	52	6	48
1954	11	06	293	54	6	47
1954	11	07	293	57	6	47
1954	11	08	294	00	6	46
1954	11	09	294	03	6	46
1954	11	10	294	05	6	45
1954	11	11	294	08	6	45
1954	11	12	294	11	6	44
1954	11	13	294	14	6	44
1954	11	14	294	17	6	44
1954	11	15	294	21	6	43
1954	11	16	294	24	6	43
1954	11	17	294	27	6	42
1954	11	18	294	30	6	42
1954	11	19	294	34	6	41
1954	11	20	294	37	6	41
1954	11	21	294	41	6	41
1954	11	22	294	44	6	40
1954	11	23	294	48	6	40
1954	11	24	294	52	6	39
1954	11	25	294	55	6	39
1954	11	26	294	59	6	39
1954	11	27	295	03	6	38
1954	11	28	295	07	6	38
1954	11	29	295	11	6	38
1954	11	30	295	15	6	37
1954	12	01	295	19	6	37
1954	12	02	295	23	6	36
1954	12	03	295	27	6	36
1954	12	04	295	31	6	36
1954	12	05	295	35	6	35
1954	12	06	295	40	6	35
1954	12	07	295	44	6	35
1954	12	08	295	48	6	35
1954	12	09	295	53	6	34
1954	12	10	295	57	6	34
1954	12	11	296	02	6	34
1954	12	12	296	06	6	33
1954	12	13	296	11	6	33
1954	12	14	296	15	6	33
1954	12	15	296	20	6	33
1954	12	16	296	24	6	32
1954	12	17	296	29	6	32
1954	12	18	296	34	6	32
1954	12	19	296	38	6	32
1954	12	20	296	43	6	31
1954	12	21	296	48	6	31
1954	12	22	296	53	6	31
1954	12	23	296	58	6	31
1954	12	24	297	02	6	31
1954	12	25	297	07	6	30
1954	12	26	297	12	6	30
1954	12	27	297	17	6	30
1954	12	28	297	22	6	30
1954	12	29	297	27	6	30
1954	12	30	297	32	6	30
1954	12	31	297	37	6	29
1955	01	01	297	42	6	29
1955	01	02	297	47	6	29
1955	01	03	297	52	6	29
1955	01	04	297	57	6	29
1955	01	05	298	03	6	29
1955	01	06	298	08	6	29
1955	01	07	298	13	6	29
1955	01	08	298	18	6	28
1955	01	09	298	23	6	28
1955	01	10	298	28	6	28
1955	01	11	298	33	6	28
1955	01	12	298	39	6	28
1955	01	13	298	44	6	28
1955	01	14	298	49	6	28
1955	01	15	298	54	6	28
1955	01	16	298	59	6	28
1955	01	17	299	05	6	28
1955	01	18	299	10	6	28
1955	01	19	299	15	6	28
1955	01	20	299	20	6	28
1955	01	21	299	25	6	28
1955	01	22	299	31	6	28
1955	01	23	299	36	6	28
1955	01	24	299	41	6	28
1955	01	25	299	46	6	28
1955	01	26	299	51	6	28
1955	01	27	299	57	6	28
1955	01	28	300	02	6	28
1955	01	29	300	07	6	28
1955	01	30	300	12	6	28
1955	01	31	300	17	6	28
1955	02	01	300	22	6	28
1955	02	02	300	27	6	28
1955	02	03	300	33	6	29
1955	02	04	300	38	6	29
1955	02	05	300	43	6	29
1955	02	06	300	48	6	29
1955	02	07	300	53	6	29
1955	02	08	300	58	6	29
1955	02	09	301	03	6	29
1955	02	10	301	08	6	29
1955	02	11	301	13	6	30
1955	02	12	301	18	6	30
1955	02	13	301	23	6	30
1955	02	14	301	28	6	30
1955	02	15	301	32	6	30
1955	02	16	301	37	6	30
1955	02	17	301	42	6	31
1955	02	18	301	47	6	31
1955	02	19	301	52	6	31
1955	02	20	301	56	6	31
1955	02	21	302	01	6	31
1955	02	22	302	06	6	32
1955	02	23	302	10	6	32
1955	02	24	302	15	6	32
1955	02	25	302	19	6	32
1955	02	26	302	24	6	33
1955	02	27	302	28	6	33
1955	02	28	302	33	6	33
1955	03	01	302	37	6	33
1955	03	02	302	42	6	34
1955	03	03	302	46	6	34
1955	03	04	302	50	6	34
1955	03	05	302	55	6	35
1955	03	06	302	59	6	35
1955	03	07	303	03	6	35
1955	03	08	303	07	6	36
1955	03	09	303	11	6	36
1955	03	10	303	15	6	36
1955	03	11	303	19	6	37
1955	03	12	303	23	6	37
1955	03	13	303	27	6	37
1955	03	14	303	31	6	38
1955	03	15	303	35	6	38
1955	03	16	303	38	6	38
1955	03	17	303	42	6	39

27 ♑ 47 Lat 6 29

1955	03	18	303	46	6	39
1955	03	19	303	49	6	39
1955	03	20	303	53	6	40
1955	03	21	303	56	6	40
1955	03	22	304	00	6	41
1955	03	23	304	03	6	41
1955	03	24	304	07	6	41
1955	03	25	304	10	6	42
1955	03	26	304	13	6	42
1955	03	27	304	16	6	43
1955	03	28	304	19	6	43
1955	03	29	304	22	6	43
1955	03	30	304	25	6	44
1955	03	31	304	28	6	44
1955	04	01	304	31	6	45
1955	04	02	304	34	6	45
1955	04	03	304	37	6	46
1955	04	04	304	39	6	46
1955	04	05	304	42	6	46
1955	04	06	304	44	6	47
1955	04	07	304	47	6	47
1955	04	08	304	49	6	48
1955	04	09	304	52	6	48
1955	04	10	304	54	6	49
1955	04	11	304	56	6	49
1955	04	12	304	58	6	50
1955	04	13	305	00	6	50
1955	04	14	305	02	6	51
1955	04	15	305	04	6	51
1955	04	16	305	06	6	52
1955	04	17	305	08	6	52
1955	04	18	305	10	6	53
1955	04	19	305	12	6	53
1955	04	20	305	13	6	54
1955	04	21	305	15	6	54
1955	04	22	305	16	6	55
1955	04	23	305	18	6	55
1955	04	24	305	19	6	56
1955	04	25	305	20	6	56
1955	04	26	305	21	6	57
1955	04	27	305	22	6	57
1955	04	28	305	23	6	58
1955	04	29	305	24	6	58
1955	04	30	305	25	6	59
1955	05	01	305	26	6	59
1955	05	02	305	27	7	00
1955	05	03	305	28	7	00
1955	05	04	305	28	7	01
1955	05	05	305	29	7	01
1955	05	06	305	29	7	02
1955	05	07	305	30	7	02
1955	05	08	305	30	7	03
1955	05	09	305	30	7	03
1955	05	10	305	30	7	04
1955	05	11	305	30	7	04
1955	05	12	305	30	7	05
1955	05	13	305	30	7	05
1955	05	14	305	30	7	06
1955	05	15	305	30	7	06
1955	05	16	305	30	7	07
1955	05	17	305	29	7	07
1955	05	18	305	29	7	08
1955	05	19	305	29	7	08
1955	05	20	305	28	7	09
1955	05	21	305	27	7	09
1955	05	22	305	27	7	10
1955	05	23	305	26	7	10
1955	05	24	305	25	7	11
1955	05	25	305	24	7	11
1955	05	26	305	23	7	12
1955	05	27	305	22	7	12
1955	05	28	305	21	7	13
1955	05	29	305	20	7	13
1955	05	30	305	19	7	13
1955	05	31	305	17	7	14
1955	06	01	305	16	7	14
1955	06	02	305	15	7	15
1955	06	03	305	13	7	15
1955	06	04	305	12	7	16
1955	06	05	305	10	7	16
1955	06	06	305	08	7	17
1955	06	07	305	07	7	17
1955	06	08	305	05	7	17
1955	06	09	305	03	7	18
1955	06	10	305	01	7	18
1955	06	11	304	59	7	19
1955	06	12	304	57	7	19
1955	06	13	304	55	7	19
1955	06	14	304	53	7	20
1955	06	15	304	50	7	20
1955	06	16	304	48	7	20
1955	06	17	304	46	7	21
1955	06	18	304	43	7	21
1955	06	19	304	41	7	21
1955	06	20	304	39	7	22
1955	06	21	304	36	7	22
1955	06	22	304	34	7	22
1955	06	23	304	31	7	23
1955	06	24	304	28	7	23
1955	06	25	304	26	7	23
1955	06	26	304	23	7	24
1955	06	27	304	20	7	24
1955	06	28	304	17	7	24
1955	06	29	304	14	7	24
1955	06	30	304	11	7	25
1955	07	01	304	08	7	25

1955	07	02	304	05	7	25
1955	07	03	304	02	7	25
1955	07	04	303	59	7	26
1955	07	05	303	56	7	26
1955	07	06	303	53	7	26
1955	07	07	303	50	7	26
1955	07	08	303	47	7	26
1955	07	09	303	44	7	27
1955	07	10	303	40	7	27
1955	07	11	303	37	7	27
1955	07	12	303	34	7	27
1955	07	13	303	31	7	27
1955	07	14	303	27	7	27
1955	07	15	303	24	7	27
1955	07	16	303	21	7	27
1955	07	17	303	17	7	27
1955	07	18	303	14	7	28
1955	07	19	303	11	7	28
1955	07	20	303	07	7	28
1955	07	21	303	04	7	28
1955	07	22	303	00	7	28
1955	07	23	302	57	7	28
1955	07	24	302	54	7	28
1955	07	25	302	50	7	28
1955	07	26	302	47	7	28
1955	07	27	302	43	7	28
1955	07	28	302	40	7	28
1955	07	29	302	36	7	28
1955	07	30	302	33	7	28
1955	07	31	302	30	7	28
1955	08	01	302	26	7	28
1955	08	02	302	23	7	27
1955	08	03	302	19	7	27
1955	08	04	302	16	7	27
1955	08	05	302	13	7	27
1955	08	06	302	09	7	27
1955	08	07	302	06	7	27
1955	08	08	302	03	7	27
1955	08	09	301	59	7	27
1955	08	10	301	56	7	26
1955	08	11	301	53	7	26
1955	08	12	301	50	7	26
1955	08	13	301	47	7	26
1955	08	14	301	43	7	26
1955	08	15	301	40	7	26
1955	08	16	301	37	7	25
1955	08	17	301	34	7	25
1955	08	18	301	31	7	25
1955	08	19	301	28	7	25
1955	08	20	301	25	7	24
1955	08	21	301	22	7	24
1955	08	22	301	19	7	24
1955	08	23	301	16	7	24
1955	08	24	301	14	7	23
1955	08	25	301	11	7	23
1955	08	26	301	08	7	23
1955	08	27	301	05	7	22
1955	08	28	301	03	7	22
1955	08	29	301	00	7	22
1955	08	30	300	58	7	21
1955	08	31	300	55	7	21
1955	09	01	300	53	7	21
1955	09	02	300	50	7	20
1955	09	03	300	48	7	20
1955	09	04	300	46	7	20
1955	09	05	300	43	7	19
1955	09	06	300	41	7	19
1955	09	07	300	39	7	18
1955	09	08	300	37	7	18
1955	09	09	300	35	7	18
1955	09	10	300	33	7	17
1955	09	11	300	31	7	17
1955	09	12	300	29	7	16
1955	09	13	300	27	7	16
1955	09	14	300	26	7	15
1955	09	15	300	24	7	15
1955	09	16	300	22	7	15
1955	09	17	300	21	7	14
1955	09	18	300	19	7	14
1955	09	19	300	18	7	13
1955	09	20	300	17	7	13
1955	09	21	300	15	7	12
1955	09	22	300	14	7	12
1955	09	23	300	13	7	11
1955	09	24	300	12	7	11
1955	09	25	300	11	7	10
1955	09	26	300	10	7	10
1955	09	27	300	09	7	09
1955	09	28	300	08	7	09
1955	09	29	300	08	7	08
1955	09	30	300	07	7	08
1955	10	01	300	06	7	07
1955	10	02	300	06	7	07
1955	10	03	300	05	7	06
1955	10	04	300	05	7	06
1955	10	05	300	05	7	05
1955	10	06	300	05	7	05
1955	10	07	300	04	7	04
1955	10	08	300	04	7	04
1955	10	09	300	04	7	03
1955	10	10	300	04	7	03
1955	10	11	300	04	7	02
1955	10	12	300	05	7	02
1955	10	13	300	05	7	01
1955	10	14	300	05	7	01
1955	10	15	300	06	7	00

1955	10	16	300	06	7	00
1955	10	17	300	07	6	59
1955	10	18	300	07	6	59
1955	10	19	300	08	6	58
1955	10	20	300	09	6	57
1955	10	21	300	10	6	57
1955	10	22	300	11	6	56
1955	10	23	300	12	6	56
1955	10	24	300	13	6	55
1955	10	25	300	14	6	55
1955	10	26	300	15	6	54
1955	10	27	300	16	6	54
1955	10	28	300	18	6	53
1955	10	29	300	19	6	53
1955	10	30	300	21	6	52
1955	10	31	300	22	6	52
1955	11	01	300	24	6	51
1955	11	02	300	26	6	51
1955	11	03	300	27	6	50
1955	11	04	300	29	6	50
1955	11	05	300	31	6	49
1955	11	06	300	33	6	49
1955	11	07	300	35	6	48
1955	11	08	300	37	6	48
1955	11	09	300	39	6	47
1955	11	10	300	42	6	47
1955	11	11	300	44	6	46
1955	11	12	300	46	6	46
1955	11	13	300	49	6	46
1955	11	14	300	51	6	45
1955	11	15	300	54	6	45
1955	11	16	300	56	6	44
1955	11	17	300	59	6	44
1955	11	18	301	02	6	43
1955	11	19	301	05	6	43
1955	11	20	301	07	6	42
1955	11	21	301	10	6	42
1955	11	22	301	13	6	41
1955	11	23	301	16	6	41
1955	11	24	301	19	6	41
1955	11	25	301	23	6	40
1955	11	26	301	26	6	40
1955	11	27	301	29	6	39
1955	11	28	301	32	6	39
1955	11	29	301	36	6	39
1955	11	30	301	39	6	38
1955	12	01	301	42	6	38
1955	12	02	301	46	6	37
1955	12	03	301	50	6	37
1955	12	04	301	53	6	37
1955	12	05	301	57	6	36
1955	12	06	302	01	6	36
1955	12	07	302	04	6	36
1955	12	08	302	08	6	35
1955	12	09	302	12	6	35
1955	12	10	302	16	6	35
1955	12	11	302	20	6	34
1955	12	12	302	24	6	34
1955	12	13	302	28	6	34
1955	12	14	302	32	6	33
1955	12	15	302	36	6	33
1955	12	16	302	40	6	33
1955	12	17	302	44	6	32
1955	12	18	302	48	6	32
1955	12	19	302	53	6	32
1955	12	20	302	57	6	32
1955	12	21	303	01	6	31
1955	12	22	303	06	6	31
1955	12	23	303	10	6	31
1955	12	24	303	14	6	31
1955	12	25	303	19	6	30
1955	12	26	303	23	6	30
1955	12	27	303	28	6	30
1955	12	28	303	32	6	30
1955	12	29	303	37	6	29
1955	12	30	303	41	6	29
1955	12	31	303	46	6	29
1956	01	01	303	51	6	29
1956	01	02	303	55	6	29
1956	01	03	304	00	6	28
1956	01	04	304	05	6	28
1956	01	05	304	09	6	28
1956	01	06	304	14	6	28
1956	01	07	304	19	6	28
1956	01	08	304	24	6	28
1956	01	09	304	28	6	27
1956	01	10	304	33	6	27
1956	01	11	304	38	6	27
1956	01	12	304	43	6	27
1956	01	13	304	48	6	27
1956	01	14	304	53	6	27
1956	01	15	304	58	6	27
1956	01	16	305	02	6	27
1956	01	17	305	07	6	27
1956	01	18	305	12	6	27
1956	01	19	305	17	6	26
1956	01	20	305	22	6	26
1956	01	21	305	27	6	26
1956	01	22	305	32	6	26
1956	01	23	305	37	6	26
1956	01	24	305	42	6	26
1956	01	25	305	47	6	26
1956	01	26	305	52	6	26
1956	01	27	305	57	6	26
1956	01	28	306	02	6	26
1956	01	29	306	06	6	26

1956	01	30	306	11	6	26
1956	01	31	306	16	6	26
1956	02	01	306	21	6	26
1956	02	02	306	26	6	26
1956	02	03	306	31	6	26
1956	02	04	306	36	6	26
1956	02	05	306	41	6	26
1956	02	06	306	46	6	26
1956	02	07	306	51	6	26
1956	02	08	306	55	6	26
1956	02	09	307	00	6	27
1956	02	10	307	05	6	27
1956	02	11	307	10	6	27
1956	02	12	307	15	6	27
1956	02	13	307	20	6	27
1956	02	14	307	24	6	27
1956	02	15	307	29	6	27
1956	02	16	307	34	6	27
1956	02	17	307	39	6	27
1956	02	18	307	43	6	27
1956	02	19	307	48	6	28
1956	02	20	307	53	6	28
1956	02	21	307	57	6	28
1956	02	22	308	02	6	28
1956	02	23	308	06	6	28
1956	02	24	308	11	6	28
1956	02	25	308	15	6	29
1956	02	26	308	20	6	29
1956	02	27	308	24	6	29
1956	02	28	308	29	6	29
1956	02	29	308	33	6	29
1956	03	01	308	38	6	30
1956	03	02	308	42	6	30
1956	03	03	308	46	6	30
1956	03	04	308	50	6	30
1956	03	05	308	55	6	30
1956	03	06	308	59	6	31
1956	03	07	309	03	6	31
1956	03	08	309	07	6	31
1956	03	09	309	11	6	31
1956	03	10	309	15	6	32
1956	03	11	309	19	6	32
1956	03	12	309	23	6	32
1956	03	13	309	27	6	33
1956	03	14	309	31	6	33
1956	03	15	309	35	6	33
1956	03	16	309	39	6	33
1956	03	17	309	43	6	34
1956	03	18	309	46	6	34
1956	03	19	309	50	6	34
1956	03	20	309	54	6	35
1956	03	21	309	57	6	35
1956	03	22	310	01	6	35
1956	03	23	310	04	6	36
1956	03	24	310	08	6	36
1956	03	25	310	11	6	36
1956	03	26	310	14	6	37
1956	03	27	310	17	6	37
1956	03	28	310	21	6	37
1956	03	29	310	24	6	38
1956	03	30	310	27	6	38
1956	03	31	310	30	6	39
1956	04	01	310	33	6	39
1956	04	02	310	36	6	39
1956	04	03	310	39	6	40
1956	04	04	310	42	6	40
1956	04	05	310	45	6	40
1956	04	06	310	47	6	41
1956	04	07	310	50	6	41
1956	04	08	310	53	6	42
1956	04	09	310	55	6	42
1956	04	10	310	58	6	42
1956	04	11	311	00	6	43
1956	04	12	311	02	6	43
1956	04	13	311	05	6	44
1956	04	14	311	07	6	44
1956	04	15	311	09	6	45
1956	04	16	311	11	6	45
1956	04	17	311	13	6	45
1956	04	18	311	15	6	46
1956	04	19	311	17	6	46
1956	04	20	311	19	6	47
1956	04	21	311	21	6	47
1956	04	22	311	23	6	48
1956	04	23	311	24	6	48
1956	04	24	311	26	6	49
1956	04	25	311	27	6	49
1956	04	26	311	29	6	49
1956	04	27	311	30	6	50
1956	04	28	311	32	6	50
1956	04	29	311	33	6	51
1956	04	30	311	34	6	51
1956	05	01	311	35	6	52
1956	05	02	311	36	6	52
1956	05	03	311	37	6	53
1956	05	04	311	38	6	53
1956	05	05	311	39	6	54
1956	05	06	311	40	6	54
1956	05	07	311	40	6	55
1956	05	08	311	41	6	55
1956	05	09	311	42	6	56
1956	05	10	311	42	6	56

1956	05	11	311	43	6	56
1956	05	12	311	43	6	57
1956	05	13	311	43	6	57
1956	05	14	311	44	6	58
1956	05	15	311	44	6	58
1956	05	16	311	44	6	59
1956	05	17	311	44	6	59
1956	05	18	311	44	7	00
1956	05	19	311	44	7	00
1956	05	20	311	43	7	01
1956	05	21	311	43	7	01
1956	05	22	311	43	7	02
1956	05	23	311	43	7	02
1956	05	24	311	42	7	02
1956	05	25	311	42	7	03
1956	05	26	311	41	7	03
1956	05	27	311	40	7	04
1956	05	28	311	40	7	04
1956	05	29	311	39	7	05
1956	05	30	311	38	7	05
1956	05	31	311	37	7	06
1956	06	01	311	36	7	06
1956	06	02	311	35	7	06
1956	06	03	311	34	7	07
1956	06	04	311	33	7	07
1956	06	05	311	31	7	08
1956	06	06	311	30	7	08
1956	06	07	311	29	7	08
1956	06	08	311	27	7	09
1956	06	09	311	26	7	09
1956	06	10	311	24	7	10
1956	06	11	311	23	7	10
1956	06	12	311	21	7	10
1956	06	13	311	19	7	11
1956	06	14	311	18	7	11
1956	06	15	311	16	7	12
1956	06	16	311	14	7	12
1956	06	17	311	12	7	12
1956	06	18	311	10	7	13
1956	06	19	311	08	7	13
1956	06	20	311	06	7	13
1956	06	21	311	03	7	14
1956	06	22	311	01	7	14
1956	06	23	310	59	7	14
1956	06	24	310	57	7	15
1956	06	25	310	54	7	15
1956	06	26	310	52	7	15
1956	06	27	310	49	7	15
1956	06	28	310	47	7	16
1956	06	29	310	44	7	16
1956	06	30	310	42	7	16
1956	07	01	310	39	7	17
1956	07	02	310	36	7	17
1956	07	03	310	34	7	17
1956	07	04	310	31	7	17
1956	07	05	310	28	7	18
1956	07	06	310	25	7	18
1956	07	07	310	23	7	18
1956	07	08	310	20	7	18
1956	07	09	310	17	7	18
1956	07	10	310	14	7	19
1956	07	11	310	11	7	19
1956	07	12	310	08	7	19
1956	07	13	310	05	7	19
1956	07	14	310	02	7	19
1956	07	15	309	58	7	19
1956	07	16	309	55	7	19
1956	07	17	309	52	7	20
1956	07	18	309	49	7	20
1956	07	19	309	46	7	20
1956	07	20	309	43	7	20
1956	07	21	309	39	7	20
1956	07	22	309	36	7	20
1956	07	23	309	33	7	20
1956	07	24	309	30	7	20
1956	07	25	309	26	7	20
1956	07	26	309	23	7	20
1956	07	27	309	20	7	20
1956	07	28	309	17	7	20
1956	07	29	309	13	7	20
1956	07	30	309	10	7	20
1956	07	31	309	07	7	20
1956	08	01	309	03	7	20
1956	08	02	309	00	7	20
1956	08	03	308	57	7	20
1956	08	04	308	53	7	20
1956	08	05	308	50	7	20
1956	08	06	308	47	7	20
1956	08	07	308	43	7	20
1956	08	08	308	40	7	20
1956	08	09	308	37	7	20
1956	08	10	308	34	7	20
1956	08	11	308	30	7	19
1956	08	12	308	27	7	19
1956	08	13	308	24	7	19
1956	08	14	308	21	7	19
1956	08	15	308	18	7	19
1956	08	16	308	14	7	19
1956	08	17	308	11	7	19
1956	08	18	308	08	7	18
1956	08	19	308	05	7	18
1956	08	20	308	02	7	18
1956	08	21	307	59	7	18
1956	08	22	307	56	7	18
1956	08	23	307	53	7	17
1956	08	24	307	50	7	17
1956	08	25	307	47	7	17
1956	08	26	307	44	7	17
1956	08	27	307	41	7	16
1956	08	28	307	39	7	16
1956	08	29	307	36	7	16
1956	08	30	307	33	7	15
1956	08	31	307	30	7	15
1956	09	01	307	28	7	15
1956	09	02	307	25	7	15
1956	09	03	307	23	7	14
1956	09	04	307	20	7	14
1956	09	05	307	18	7	14
1956	09	06	307	15	7	13
1956	09	07	307	13	7	13
1956	09	08	307	11	7	13
1956	09	09	307	08	7	12
1956	09	10	307	06	7	12
1956	09	11	307	04	7	11
1956	09	12	307	02	7	11
1956	09	13	307	00	7	11
1956	09	14	306	58	7	10
1956	09	15	306	56	7	10
1956	09	16	306	54	7	10
1956	09	17	306	52	7	09
1956	09	18	306	50	7	09
1956	09	19	306	48	7	08
1956	09	20	306	47	7	08
1956	09	21	306	45	7	07
1956	09	22	306	43	7	07
1956	09	23	306	42	7	07
1956	09	24	306	41	7	06
1956	09	25	306	39	7	06
1956	09	26	306	38	7	05
1956	09	27	306	37	7	05
1956	09	28	306	35	7	04
1956	09	29	306	34	7	04
1956	09	30	306	33	7	03
1956	10	01	306	32	7	03
1956	10	02	306	31	7	02
1956	10	03	306	30	7	02
1956	10	04	306	30	7	01
1956	10	05	306	29	7	01
1956	10	06	306	28	7	00
1956	10	07	306	28	7	00
1956	10	08	306	27	6	59
1956	10	09	306	27	6	59
1956	10	10	306	26	6	59
1956	10	11	306	26	6	58
1956	10	12	306	26	6	58
1956	10	13	306	26	6	57
1956	10	14	306	26	6	57
1956	10	15	306	25	6	56
1956	10	16	306	26	6	56
1956	10	17	306	26	6	55
1956	10	18	306	26	6	55
1956	10	19	306	26	6	54
1956	10	20	306	26	6	53
1956	10	21	306	27	6	53
1956	10	22	306	27	6	52
1956	10	23	306	28	6	52
1956	10	24	306	28	6	51
1956	10	25	306	29	6	51
1956	10	26	306	30	6	50
1956	10	27	306	30	6	50
1956	10	28	306	31	6	49
1956	10	29	306	32	6	49
1956	10	30	306	33	6	48
1956	10	31	306	34	6	48
1956	11	01	306	36	6	47
1956	11	02	306	37	6	47
1956	11	03	306	38	6	46
1956	11	04	306	39	6	46
1956	11	05	306	41	6	46
1956	11	06	306	42	6	45
1956	11	07	306	44	6	45
1956	11	08	306	45	6	44
1956	11	09	306	47	6	44
1956	11	10	306	49	6	43
1956	11	11	306	51	6	43
1956	11	12	306	52	6	42
1956	11	13	306	54	6	42
1956	11	14	306	56	6	41
1956	11	15	306	58	6	41
1956	11	16	307	01	6	40
1956	11	17	307	03	6	40
1956	11	18	307	05	6	39
1956	11	19	307	07	6	39
1956	11	20	307	10	6	38
1956	11	21	307	12	6	38
1956	11	22	307	15	6	38
1956	11	23	307	17	6	37
1956	11	24	307	20	6	37
1956	11	25	307	22	6	36
1956	11	26	307	25	6	36
1956	11	27	307	28	6	35
1956	11	28	307	31	6	35
1956	11	29	307	34	6	35
1956	11	30	307	37	6	34
1956	12	01	307	40	6	34
1956	12	02	307	43	6	33
1956	12	03	307	46	6	33
1956	12	04	307	49	6	33
1956	12	05	307	52	6	32
1956	12	06	307	55	6	32
1956	12	07	307	59	6	31
1956	12	08	308	02	6	31
1956	12	09	308	05	6	31
1956	12	10	308	09	6	30
1956	12	11	308	12	6	30
1956	12	12	308	16	6	30
1956	12	13	308	19	6	29
1956	12	14	308	23	6	29
1956	12	15	308	27	6	29
1956	12	16	308	30	6	28
1956	12	17	308	34	6	28
1956	12	18	308	38	6	28
1956	12	19	308	42	6	27
1956	12	20	308	46	6	27
1956	12	21	308	50	6	27
1956	12	22	308	53	6	27
1956	12	23	308	57	6	26
1956	12	24	309	01	6	26
1956	12	25	309	06	6	26
1956	12	26	309	10	6	25
1956	12	27	309	14	6	25
1956	12	28	309	18	6	25
1956	12	29	309	22	6	25
1956	12	30	309	26	6	24
1956	12	31	309	31	6	24
1957	01	01	309	35	6	24
1957	01	02	309	39	6	24
1957	01	03	309	43	6	23
1957	01	04	309	48	6	23
1957	01	05	309	52	6	23
1957	01	06	309	57	6	23
1957	01	07	310	01	6	23
1957	01	08	310	05	6	22
1957	01	09	310	10	6	22
1957	01	10	310	14	6	22
1957	01	11	310	19	6	22
1957	01	12	310	23	6	22
1957	01	13	310	28	6	22
1957	01	14	310	33	6	22
1957	01	15	310	37	6	21
1957	01	16	310	42	6	21
1957	01	17	310	46	6	21
1957	01	18	310	51	6	21
1957	01	19	310	56	6	21
1957	01	20	311	00	6	21
1957	01	21	311	05	6	21
1957	01	22	311	10	6	21
1957	01	23	311	14	6	20
1957	01	24	311	19	6	20
1957	01	25	311	24	6	20
1957	01	26	311	28	6	20
1957	01	27	311	33	6	20
1957	01	28	311	38	6	20
1957	01	29	311	42	6	20
1957	01	30	311	47	6	20
1957	01	31	311	52	6	20
1957	02	01	311	56	6	20
1957	02	02	312	01	6	20
1957	02	03	312	06	6	20
1957	02	04	312	11	6	20
1957	02	05	312	15	6	20
1957	02	06	312	20	6	20
1957	02	07	312	25	6	20
1957	02	08	312	29	6	20
1957	02	09	312	34	6	20
1957	02	10	312	39	6	20
1957	02	11	312	43	6	20
1957	02	12	312	48	6	20
1957	02	13	312	53	6	20
1957	02	14	312	57	6	20
1957	02	15	313	02	6	20
1957	02	16	313	06	6	20
1957	02	17	313	11	6	20
1957	02	18	313	16	6	20
1957	02	19	313	20	6	21
1957	02	20	313	25	6	21
1957	02	21	313	29	6	21
1957	02	22	313	34	6	21
1957	02	23	313	38	6	21
1957	02	24	313	43	6	21
1957	02	25	313	47	6	21
1957	02	26	313	51	6	21
1957	02	27	313	56	6	22
1957	02	28	314	00	6	22
1957	03	01	314	04	6	22
1957	03	02	314	09	6	22
1957	03	03	314	13	6	22
1957	03	04	314	17	6	22
1957	03	05	314	21	6	22
1957	03	06	314	26	6	23
1957	03	07	314	30	6	23
1957	03	08	314	34	6	23
1957	03	09	314	38	6	23
1957	03	10	314	42	6	23
1957	03	11	314	46	6	24
1957	03	12	314	50	6	24
1957	03	13	314	54	6	24
1957	03	14	314	58	6	24
1957	03	15	315	02	6	25
1957	03	16	315	06	6	25
1957	03	17	315	10	6	25
1957	03	18	315	13	6	25
1957	03	19	315	17	6	26
1957	03	20	315	21	6	26
1957	03	21	315	25	6	26
1957	03	22	315	28	6	26
1957	03	23	315	32	6	27
1957	03	24	315	35	6	27
1957	03	25	315	39	6	27
1957	03	26	315	42	6	27
1957	03	27	315	46	6	28
1957	03	28	315	49	6	28
1957	03	29	315	52	6	28
1957	03	30	315	55	6	29
1957	03	31	315	59	6	29
1957	04	01	316	02	6	29
1957	04	02	316	05	6	30
1957	04	03	316	08	6	30
1957	04	04	316	11	6	30
1957	04	05	316	14	6	31
1957	04	06	316	17	6	31
1957	04	07	316	20	6	31
1957	04	08	316	23	6	32
1957	04	09	316	25	6	32
1957	04	10	316	28	6	32
1957	04	11	316	31	6	33
1957	04	12	316	33	6	33
1957	04	13	316	36	6	33
1957	04	14	316	38	6	34
1957	04	15	316	41	6	34
1957	04	16	316	43	6	35
1957	04	17	316	45	6	35
1957	04	18	316	47	6	35
1957	04	19	316	50	6	36
1957	04	20	316	52	6	36
1957	04	21	316	54	6	37
1957	04	22	316	56	6	37
1957	04	23	316	58	6	37
1957	04	24	317	00	6	38
1957	04	25	317	01	6	38
1957	04	26	317	03	6	39
1957	04	27	317	05	6	39
1957	04	28	317	07	6	39
1957	04	29	317	08	6	40
1957	04	30	317	10	6	40
1957	05	01	317	11	6	41
1957	05	02	317	12	6	41
1957	05	03	317	14	6	41
1957	05	04	317	15	6	42
1957	05	05	317	16	6	42
1957	05	06	317	17	6	43
1957	05	07	317	18	6	43
1957	05	08	317	19	6	44
1957	05	09	317	20	6	44
1957	05	10	317	21	6	44
1957	05	11	317	22	6	45
1957	05	12	317	23	6	45
1957	05	13	317	23	6	46
1957	05	14	317	24	6	46
1957	05	15	317	24	6	47
1957	05	16	317	25	6	47
1957	05	17	317	25	6	47
1957	05	18	317	26	6	48
1957	05	19	317	26	6	48
1957	05	20	317	26	6	49
1957	05	21	317	26	6	49
1957	05	22	317	26	6	49
1957	05	23	317	26	6	50
1957	05	24	317	26	6	50
1957	05	25	317	26	6	51
1957	05	26	317	26	6	51
1957	05	27	317	26	6	52
1957	05	28	317	25	6	52
1957	05	29	317	25	6	52
1957	05	30	317	24	6	53
1957	05	31	317	24	6	53
1957	06	01	317	23	6	54
1957	06	02	317	23	6	54
1957	06	03	317	22	6	54
1957	06	04	317	21	6	55
1957	06	05	317	20	6	55
1957	06	06	317	19	6	56
1957	06	07	317	18	6	56
1957	06	08	317	17	6	56
1957	06	09	317	16	6	57
1957	06	10	317	15	6	57
1957	06	11	317	14	6	58
1957	06	12	317	13	6	58
1957	06	13	317	11	6	58
1957	06	14	317	10	6	59
1957	06	15	317	08	6	59
1957	06	16	317	07	6	59
1957	06	17	317	05	7	00
1957	06	18	317	04	7	00
1957	06	19	317	02	7	00
1957	06	20	317	00	7	01
1957	06	21	316	59	7	01
1957	06	22	316	57	7	01
1957	06	23	316	55	7	02
1957	06	24	316	53	7	02
1957	06	25	316	51	7	02
1957	06	26	316	49	7	03
1957	06	27	316	47	7	03
1957	06	28	316	44	7	03
1957	06	29	316	42	7	04
1957	06	30	316	40	7	04
1957	07	01	316	38	7	04
1957	07	02	316	35	7	04
1957	07	03	316	33	7	05

1957	07	04	316	31	7	05
1957	07	05	316	28	7	05
1957	07	06	316	26	7	05
1957	07	07	316	23	7	06
1957	07	08	316	20	7	06
1957	07	09	316	18	7	06
1957	07	10	316	15	7	06
1957	07	11	316	12	7	07
1957	07	12	316	10	7	07
1957	07	13	316	07	7	07
1957	07	14	316	04	7	07
1957	07	15	316	01	7	07
1957	07	16	315	58	7	07
1957	07	17	315	56	7	08
1957	07	18	315	53	7	08
1957	07	19	315	50	7	08
1957	07	20	315	47	7	08
1957	07	21	315	44	7	08
1957	07	22	315	41	7	08
1957	07	23	315	38	7	08
1957	07	24	315	34	7	08
1957	07	25	315	31	7	08
1957	07	26	315	28	7	09
1957	07	27	315	25	7	09
1957	07	28	315	22	7	09
1957	07	29	315	19	7	09
1957	07	30	315	16	7	09
1957	07	31	315	13	7	09
1957	08	01	315	09	7	09
1957	08	02	315	06	7	09
1957	08	03	315	03	7	09
1957	08	04	315	00	7	09
1957	08	05	314	57	7	09
1957	08	06	314	53	7	09
1957	08	07	314	50	7	09
1957	08	08	314	47	7	09
1957	08	09	314	44	7	09
1957	08	10	314	40	7	09
1957	08	11	314	37	7	09
1957	08	12	314	34	7	09
1957	08	13	314	31	7	08
1957	08	14	314	28	7	08
1957	08	15	314	25	7	08
1957	08	16	314	21	7	08
1957	08	17	314	18	7	08
1957	08	18	314	15	7	08
1957	08	19	314	12	7	08
1957	08	20	314	09	7	08
1957	08	21	314	06	7	07
1957	08	22	314	03	7	07
1957	08	23	314	00	7	07
1957	08	24	313	57	7	07
1957	08	25	313	54	7	07
1957	08	26	313	51	7	07
1957	08	27	313	48	7	06
1957	08	28	313	45	7	06
1957	08	29	313	42	7	06
1957	08	30	313	39	7	06
1957	08	31	313	36	7	05
1957	09	01	313	33	7	05
1957	09	02	313	31	7	05
1957	09	03	313	28	7	05
1957	09	04	313	25	7	04
1957	09	05	313	22	7	04
1957	09	06	313	20	7	04
1957	09	07	313	17	7	04
1957	09	08	313	15	7	03
1957	09	09	313	12	7	03
1957	09	10	313	10	7	03
1957	09	11	313	07	7	02
1957	09	12	313	05	7	02
1957	09	13	313	03	7	02
1957	09	14	313	00	7	01
1957	09	15	312	58	7	01
1957	09	16	312	56	7	01
1957	09	17	312	54	7	00
1957	09	18	312	52	7	00
1957	09	19	312	50	7	00
1957	09	20	312	48	6	59
1957	09	21	312	46	6	59
1957	09	22	312	44	6	58
1957	09	23	312	42	6	58
1957	09	24	312	40	6	58
1957	09	25	312	38	6	57
1957	09	26	312	37	6	57
1957	09	27	312	35	6	56
1957	09	28	312	34	6	56
1957	09	29	312	32	6	56
1957	09	30	312	31	6	55
1957	10	01	312	29	6	55
1957	10	02	312	28	6	54
1957	10	03	312	27	6	54
1957	10	04	312	26	6	53
1957	10	05	312	24	6	53
1957	10	06	312	23	6	52
1957	10	07	312	22	6	52
1957	10	08	312	21	6	52
1957	10	09	312	21	6	51
1957	10	10	312	20	6	51
1957	10	11	312	19	6	50
1957	10	12	312	18	6	50
1957	10	13	312	18	6	49
1957	10	14	312	17	6	49
1957	10	15	312	17	6	48
1957	10	16	312	16	6	48
1957	10	17	312	16	6	47

1957	10	18	312	16	6	47
1957	10	19	312	15	6	46
1957	10	20	312	15	6	46
1957	10	21	312	15	6	45
1957	10	22	312	15	6	45
1957	10	23	312	15	6	44
1957	10	24	312	15	6	44
1957	10	25	312	15	6	43
1957	10	26	312	16	6	43
1957	10	27	312	16	6	43
1957	10	28	312	16	6	42
1957	10	29	312	17	6	42
1957	10	30	312	17	6	41
1957	10	31	312	18	6	41
1957	11	01	312	19	6	40
1957	11	02	312	19	6	40
1957	11	03	312	20	6	39
1957	11	04	312	21	6	39
1957	11	05	312	22	6	38
1957	11	06	312	23	6	38
1957	11	07	312	24	6	37
1957	11	08	312	25	6	37
1957	11	09	312	26	6	36
1957	11	10	312	28	6	36
1957	11	11	312	29	6	35
1957	11	12	312	30	6	35
1957	11	13	312	32	6	34
1957	11	14	312	33	6	34
1957	11	15	312	35	6	33
1957	11	16	312	36	6	33
1957	11	17	312	38	6	33
1957	11	18	312	40	6	32
1957	11	19	312	42	6	32
1957	11	20	312	44	6	31
1957	11	21	312	46	6	31
1957	11	22	312	48	6	30
1957	11	23	312	50	6	30
1957	11	24	312	52	6	29
1957	11	25	312	54	6	29
1957	11	26	312	56	6	29
1957	11	27	312	58	6	28
1957	11	28	313	01	6	28
1957	11	29	313	03	6	27
1957	11	30	313	06	6	27
1957	12	01	313	08	6	26
1957	12	02	313	11	6	26
1957	12	03	313	13	6	26
1957	12	04	313	16	6	25
1957	12	05	313	19	6	25
1957	12	06	313	22	6	24
1957	12	07	313	25	6	24
1957	12	08	313	27	6	24
1957	12	09	313	30	6	23
1957	12	10	313	33	6	23
1957	12	11	313	36	6	23
1957	12	12	313	40	6	22
1957	12	13	313	43	6	22
1957	12	14	313	46	6	21
1957	12	15	313	49	6	21
1957	12	16	313	52	6	21
1957	12	17	313	56	6	20
1957	12	18	313	59	6	20
1957	12	19	314	03	6	20
1957	12	20	314	06	6	19
1957	12	21	314	10	6	19
1957	12	22	314	13	6	19
1957	12	23	314	17	6	19
1957	12	24	314	20	6	18
1957	12	25	314	24	6	18
1957	12	26	314	28	6	18
1957	12	27	314	31	6	17
1957	12	28	314	35	6	17
1957	12	29	314	39	6	17
1957	12	30	314	43	6	16
1957	12	31	314	47	6	16
1958	01	01	314	51	6	16
1958	01	02	314	55	6	16
1958	01	03	314	59	6	15
1958	01	04	315	03	6	15
1958	01	05	315	07	6	15
1958	01	06	315	11	6	15
1958	01	07	315	15	6	15
1958	01	08	315	19	6	14
1958	01	09	315	23	6	14
1958	01	10	315	27	6	14
1958	01	11	315	31	6	14
1958	01	12	315	36	6	13
1958	01	13	315	40	6	13
1958	01	14	315	44	6	13
1958	01	15	315	48	6	13
1958	01	16	315	53	6	13
1958	01	17	315	57	6	13
1958	01	18	316	01	6	12
1958	01	19	316	06	6	12
1958	01	20	316	10	6	12
1958	01	21	316	14	6	12
1958	01	22	316	19	6	12
1958	01	23	316	23	6	12
1958	01	24	316	28	6	12
1958	01	25	316	32	6	11
1958	01	26	316	37	6	11
1958	01	27	316	41	6	11
1958	01	28	316	45	6	11
1958	01	29	316	50	6	11
1958	01	30	316	54	6	11
1958	01	31	316	59	6	11

1958	02	01	317	03	6	11
1958	02	02	317	08	6	11
1958	02	03	317	12	6	11
1958	02	04	317	17	6	11
1958	02	05	317	21	6	11
1958	02	06	317	26	6	11
1958	02	07	317	30	6	11
1958	02	08	317	35	6	10
1958	02	09	317	39	6	10
1958	02	10	317	44	6	10
1958	02	11	317	48	6	10
1958	02	12	317	53	6	10
1958	02	13	317	57	6	10
1958	02	14	318	02	6	10
1958	02	15	318	06	6	10
1958	02	16	318	11	6	10
1958	02	17	318	15	6	11
1958	02	18	318	20	6	11
1958	02	19	318	24	6	11
1958	02	20	318	28	6	11
1958	02	21	318	33	6	11
1958	02	22	318	37	6	11
1958	02	23	318	42	6	11
1958	02	24	318	46	6	11
1958	02	25	318	50	6	11
1958	02	26	318	55	6	11
1958	02	27	318	59	6	11
1958	02	28	319	03	6	11
1958	03	01	319	08	6	11
1958	03	02	319	12	6	11
1958	03	03	319	16	6	12
1958	03	04	319	20	6	12
1958	03	05	319	24	6	12
1958	03	06	319	29	6	12
1958	03	07	319	33	6	12
1958	03	08	319	37	6	12
1958	03	09	319	41	6	12
1958	03	10	319	45	6	12
1958	03	11	319	49	6	13
1958	03	12	319	53	6	13
1958	03	13	319	57	6	13
1958	03	14	320	01	6	13
1958	03	15	320	05	6	13
1958	03	16	320	09	6	14
1958	03	17	320	13	6	14
1958	03	18	320	16	6	14
1958	03	19	320	20	6	14
1958	03	20	320	24	6	14
1958	03	21	320	28	6	15
1958	03	22	320	31	6	15
1958	03	23	320	35	6	15
1958	03	24	320	39	6	15
1958	03	25	320	42	6	15
1958	03	26	320	46	6	16
1958	03	27	320	49	6	16
1958	03	28	320	53	6	16
1958	03	29	320	56	6	16
1958	03	30	320	59	6	17
1958	03	31	321	03	6	17
1958	04	01	321	06	6	17
1958	04	02	321	09	6	17
1958	04	03	321	12	6	18
1958	04	04	321	15	6	18
1958	04	05	321	19	6	18
1958	04	06	321	22	6	19
1958	04	07	321	25	6	19
1958	04	08	321	28	6	19
1958	04	09	321	30	6	19
1958	04	10	321	33	6	20
1958	04	11	321	36	6	20
1958	04	12	321	39	6	20
1958	04	13	321	42	6	21
1958	04	14	321	44	6	21
1958	04	15	321	47	6	21
1958	04	16	321	49	6	22
1958	04	17	321	52	6	22
1958	04	18	321	54	6	22
1958	04	19	321	57	6	23
1958	04	20	321	59	6	23
1958	04	21	322	01	6	23
1958	04	22	322	04	6	24
1958	04	23	322	06	6	24
1958	04	24	322	08	6	24
1958	04	25	322	10	6	25
1958	04	26	322	12	6	25
1958	04	27	322	14	6	25
1958	04	28	322	16	6	26
1958	04	29	322	17	6	26
1958	04	30	322	19	6	27
1958	05	01	322	21	6	27
1958	05	02	322	23	6	27
1958	05	03	322	24	6	28
1958	05	04	322	26	6	28
1958	05	05	322	27	6	28
1958	05	06	322	29	6	29
1958	05	07	322	30	6	29
1958	05	08	322	31	6	30
1958	05	09	322	32	6	30
1958	05	10	322	34	6	30
1958	05	11	322	35	6	31
1958	05	12	322	36	6	31
1958	05	13	322	37	6	31
1958	05	14	322	37	6	32
1958	05	15	322	38	6	32
1958	05	16	322	39	6	33
1958	05	17	322	40	6	33

1958	05	18	322	40	6	33
1958	05	19	322	41	6	34
1958	05	20	322	42	6	34
1958	05	21	322	42	6	35
1958	05	22	322	42	6	35
1958	05	23	322	43	6	35
1958	05	24	322	43	6	36
1958	05	25	322	43	6	36
1958	05	26	322	43	6	37
1958	05	27	322	43	6	37
1958	05	28	322	43	6	37
1958	05	29	322	43	6	38
1958	05	30	322	43	6	38
1958	05	31	322	43	6	38
1958	06	01	322	43	6	39
1958	06	02	322	43	6	39
1958	06	03	322	42	6	40
1958	06	04	322	42	6	40
1958	06	05	322	41	6	40
1958	06	06	322	41	6	41
1958	06	07	322	40	6	41
1958	06	08	322	39	6	41
1958	06	09	322	39	6	42
1958	06	10	322	38	6	42
1958	06	11	322	37	6	43
1958	06	12	322	36	6	43
1958	06	13	322	35	6	43
1958	06	14	322	34	6	44
1958	06	15	322	33	6	44
1958	06	16	322	32	6	44
1958	06	17	322	31	6	45
1958	06	18	322	29	6	45
1958	06	19	322	28	6	45
1958	06	20	322	27	6	46
1958	06	21	322	25	6	46
1958	06	22	322	24	6	46
1958	06	23	322	22	6	47
1958	06	24	322	20	6	47
1958	06	25	322	19	6	47
1958	06	26	322	17	6	48
1958	06	27	322	15	6	48
1958	06	28	322	13	6	48
1958	06	29	322	12	6	48
1958	06	30	322	10	6	49
1958	07	01	322	08	6	49
1958	07	02	322	06	6	49
1958	07	03	322	04	6	50
1958	07	04	322	02	6	50
1958	07	05	321	59	6	50
1958	07	06	321	57	6	50
1958	07	07	321	55	6	51
1958	07	08	321	53	6	51
1958	07	09	321	50	6	51
1958	07	10	321	48	6	51
1958	07	11	321	45	6	52
1958	07	12	321	43	6	52
1958	07	13	321	41	6	52
1958	07	14	321	38	6	52
1958	07	15	321	35	6	52
1958	07	16	321	33	6	53
1958	07	17	321	30	6	53
1958	07	18	321	27	6	53
1958	07	19	321	25	6	53
1958	07	20	321	22	6	53
1958	07	21	321	19	6	53
1958	07	22	321	16	6	53
1958	07	23	321	14	6	54
1958	07	24	321	11	6	54
1958	07	25	321	08	6	54
1958	07	26	321	05	6	54
1958	07	27	321	02	6	54
1958	07	28	320	59	6	54
1958	07	29	320	56	6	54
1958	07	30	320	53	6	54
1958	07	31	320	50	6	54
1958	08	01	320	47	6	54
1958	08	02	320	44	6	54
1958	08	03	320	41	6	55
1958	08	04	320	38	6	55
1958	08	05	320	35	6	55
1958	08	06	320	32	6	55
1958	08	07	320	29	6	55
1958	08	08	320	26	6	55
1958	08	09	320	22	6	55
1958	08	10	320	19	6	55
1958	08	11	320	16	6	55
1958	08	12	320	13	6	55
1958	08	13	320	10	6	55
1958	08	14	320	07	6	54
1958	08	15	320	04	6	54
1958	08	16	320	01	6	54
1958	08	17	319	57	6	54
1958	08	18	319	54	6	54
1958	08	19	319	51	6	54
1958	08	20	319	48	6	54
1958	08	21	319	45	6	54
1958	08	22	319	42	6	54
1958	08	23	319	39	6	54
1958	08	24	319	36	6	54
1958	08	25	319	33	6	53
1958	08	26	319	30	6	53
1958	08	27	319	27	6	53

Chiron

1958	08	28	319	24	6	53
1958	08	29	319	21	6	53
1958	08	30	319	18	6	53
1958	08	31	319	15	6	52
1958	09	01	319	12	6	52
1958	09	02	319	09	6	52
1958	09	03	319	06	6	52
1958	09	04	319	04	6	52
1958	09	05	319	01	6	51
1958	09	06	318	58	6	51
1958	09	07	318	55	6	51
1958	09	08	318	53	6	51
1958	09	09	318	50	6	50
1958	09	10	318	47	6	50
1958	09	11	318	45	6	50
1958	09	12	318	42	6	50
1958	09	13	318	40	6	49
1958	09	14	318	37	6	49
1958	09	15	318	35	6	49
1958	09	16	318	32	6	48
1958	09	17	318	30	6	48
1958	09	18	318	28	6	48
1958	09	19	318	25	6	47
1958	09	20	318	23	6	47
1958	09	21	318	21	6	47
1958	09	22	318	19	6	46
1958	09	23	318	17	6	46
1958	09	24	318	15	6	46
1958	09	25	318	13	6	45
1958	09	26	318	11	6	45
1958	09	27	318	09	6	45
1958	09	28	318	07	6	44
1958	09	29	318	05	6	44
1958	09	30	318	03	6	44
1958	10	01	318	02	6	43
1958	10	02	318	00	6	43
1958	10	03	317	59	6	42
1958	10	04	317	57	6	42
1958	10	05	317	56	6	42
1958	10	06	317	54	6	41
1958	10	07	317	53	6	41
1958	10	08	317	52	6	40
1958	10	09	317	50	6	40
1958	10	10	317	49	6	39
1958	10	11	317	48	6	39
1958	10	12	317	47	6	39
1958	10	13	317	46	6	38
1958	10	14	317	45	6	38
1958	10	15	317	44	6	37
1958	10	16	317	44	6	37
1958	10	17	317	43	6	36
1958	10	18	317	42	6	36
1958	10	19	317	42	6	36
1958	10	20	317	41	6	35
1958	10	21	317	40	6	35
1958	10	22	317	40	6	34
1958	10	23	317	40	6	34
1958	10	24	317	39	6	33
1958	10	25	317	39	6	33
1958	10	26	317	39	6	32
1958	10	27	317	39	6	32
1958	10	28	317	39	6	31
1958	10	29	317	39	6	31
1958	10	30	317	39	6	31
1958	10	31	317	39	6	30
1958	11	01	317	39	6	30
1958	11	02	317	40	6	29
1958	11	03	317	40	6	29
1958	11	04	317	41	6	28
1958	11	05	317	41	6	28
1958	11	06	317	42	6	27
1958	11	07	317	42	6	27
1958	11	08	317	43	6	26
1958	11	09	317	44	6	26
1958	11	10	317	44	6	25
1958	11	11	317	45	6	25
1958	11	12	317	46	6	25
1958	11	13	317	47	6	24
1958	11	14	317	48	6	24
1958	11	15	317	50	6	23
1958	11	16	317	51	6	23
1958	11	17	317	52	6	22
1958	11	18	317	53	6	22
1958	11	19	317	55	6	21
1958	11	20	317	56	6	21
1958	11	21	317	58	6	21
1958	11	22	317	59	6	20
1958	11	23	318	01	6	20
1958	11	24	318	03	6	19
1958	11	25	318	04	6	19
1958	11	26	318	06	6	18
1958	11	27	318	08	6	18
1958	11	28	318	10	6	18
1958	11	29	318	12	6	17
1958	11	30	318	14	6	17
1958	12	01	318	16	6	16
1958	12	02	318	18	6	16
1958	12	03	318	20	6	15
1958	12	04	318	23	6	15
1958	12	05	318	25	6	15
1958	12	06	318	27	6	14

1958	12	07	318	30	6	14
1958	12	08	318	32	6	13
1958	12	09	318	35	6	13
1958	12	10	318	38	6	13
1958	12	11	318	40	6	12
1958	12	12	318	43	6	12
1958	12	13	318	46	6	12
1958	12	14	318	48	6	11
1958	12	15	318	51	6	11
1958	12	16	318	54	6	10
1958	12	17	318	57	6	10
1958	12	18	319	00	6	10
1958	12	19	319	03	6	09
1958	12	20	319	06	6	09
1958	12	21	319	09	6	09
1958	12	22	319	12	6	08
1958	12	23	319	16	6	08
1958	12	24	319	19	6	08
1958	12	25	319	22	6	07
1958	12	26	319	26	6	07
1958	12	27	319	29	6	07
1958	12	28	319	32	6	07
1958	12	29	319	36	6	06
1958	12	30	319	39	6	06
1958	12	31	319	43	6	06
1959	01	01	319	46	6	05
1959	01	02	319	50	6	05
1959	01	03	319	54	6	05
1959	01	04	319	57	6	05
1959	01	05	320	01	6	04
1959	01	06	320	05	6	04
1959	01	07	320	09	6	04
1959	01	08	320	12	6	04
1959	01	09	320	16	6	03
1959	01	10	320	20	6	03
1959	01	11	320	24	6	03
1959	01	12	320	28	6	03
1959	01	13	320	32	6	02
1959	01	14	320	36	6	02
1959	01	15	320	40	6	02
1959	01	16	320	44	6	02
1959	01	17	320	48	6	02
1959	01	18	320	52	6	01
1959	01	19	320	56	6	01
1959	01	20	321	00	6	01
1959	01	21	321	04	6	01
1959	01	22	321	08	6	01
1959	01	23	321	12	6	01
1959	01	24	321	17	6	00
1959	01	25	321	21	6	00
1959	01	26	321	25	6	00
1959	01	27	321	29	6	00
1959	01	28	321	33	6	00
1959	01	29	321	38	6	00
1959	01	30	321	42	6	00
1959	01	31	321	46	5	59
1959	02	01	321	51	5	59
1959	02	02	321	55	5	59
1959	02	03	321	59	5	59
1959	02	04	322	03	5	59
1959	02	05	322	08	5	59
1959	02	06	322	12	5	59
1959	02	07	322	16	5	59
1959	02	08	322	21	5	59
1959	02	09	322	25	5	59
1959	02	10	322	29	5	59
1959	02	11	322	34	5	59
1959	02	12	322	38	5	59
1959	02	13	322	42	5	59
1959	02	14	322	47	5	59
1959	02	15	322	51	5	58
1959	02	16	322	55	5	58
1959	02	17	323	00	5	58
1959	02	18	323	04	5	58
1959	02	19	323	08	5	58
1959	02	20	323	13	5	58
1959	02	21	323	17	5	58
1959	02	22	323	21	5	58
1959	02	23	323	25	5	59
1959	02	24	323	30	5	59
1959	02	25	323	34	5	59
1959	02	26	323	38	5	59
1959	02	27	323	42	5	59
1959	02	28	323	47	5	59
1959	03	01	323	51	5	59
1959	03	02	323	55	5	59
1959	03	03	323	59	5	59
1959	03	04	324	03	5	59
1959	03	05	324	07	5	59
1959	03	06	324	12	5	59
1959	03	07	324	16	5	59
1959	03	08	324	20	5	59
1959	03	09	324	24	5	59
1959	03	10	324	28	6	00
1959	03	11	324	32	6	00
1959	03	12	324	36	6	00
1959	03	13	324	40	6	00
1959	03	14	324	44	6	00
1959	03	15	324	48	6	00
1959	03	16	324	51	6	00
1959	03	17	324	55	6	00
1959	03	18	324	59	6	01
1959	03	19	325	03	6	01
1959	03	20	325	07	6	01
1959	03	21	325	10	6	01
1959	03	22	325	14	6	01

1959	03	23	325	18	6	01
1959	03	24	325	21	6	02
1959	03	25	325	25	6	02
1959	03	26	325	29	6	02
1959	03	27	325	32	6	02
1959	03	28	325	36	6	02
1959	03	29	325	39	6	03
1959	03	30	325	43	6	03
1959	03	31	325	46	6	03
1959	04	01	325	49	6	03
1959	04	02	325	53	6	03
1959	04	03	325	56	6	04
1959	04	04	325	59	6	04
1959	04	05	326	02	6	04
1959	04	06	326	06	6	04
1959	04	07	326	09	6	05
1959	04	08	326	12	6	05
1959	04	09	326	15	6	05
1959	04	10	326	18	6	05
1959	04	11	326	21	6	06
1959	04	12	326	24	6	06
1959	04	13	326	26	6	06
1959	04	14	326	29	6	06
1959	04	15	326	32	6	07
1959	04	16	326	35	6	07
1959	04	17	326	37	6	07
1959	04	18	326	40	6	07
1959	04	19	326	42	6	08
1959	04	20	326	45	6	08
1959	04	21	326	47	6	08
1959	04	22	326	50	6	09
1959	04	23	326	52	6	09
1959	04	24	326	54	6	09
1959	04	25	326	57	6	10
1959	04	26	326	59	6	10
1959	04	27	327	01	6	10
1959	04	28	327	03	6	10
1959	04	29	327	05	6	11
1959	04	30	327	07	6	11
1959	05	01	327	09	6	11
1959	05	02	327	11	6	12
1959	05	03	327	13	6	12
1959	05	04	327	14	6	12
1959	05	05	327	16	6	13
1959	05	06	327	18	6	13
1959	05	07	327	19	6	13
1959	05	08	327	21	6	14
1959	05	09	327	22	6	14
1959	05	10	327	24	6	14
1959	05	11	327	25	6	15
1959	05	12	327	26	6	15
1959	05	13	327	28	6	16
1959	05	14	327	29	6	16
1959	05	15	327	30	6	16
1959	05	16	327	31	6	17
1959	05	17	327	32	6	17
1959	05	18	327	33	6	17
1959	05	19	327	34	6	18
1959	05	20	327	35	6	18
1959	05	21	327	35	6	18
1959	05	22	327	36	6	19
1959	05	23	327	37	6	19
1959	05	24	327	37	6	19
1959	05	25	327	38	6	20
1959	05	26	327	38	6	20
1959	05	27	327	38	6	20
1959	05	28	327	39	6	21
1959	05	29	327	39	6	21
1959	05	30	327	39	6	22
1959	05	31	327	39	6	22
1959	06	01	327	39	6	22
1959	06	02	327	39	6	23
1959	06	03	327	39	6	23
1959	06	04	327	39	6	23
1959	06	05	327	39	6	24
1959	06	06	327	39	6	24
1959	06	07	327	39	6	24
1959	06	08	327	38	6	25
1959	06	09	327	38	6	25
1959	06	10	327	37	6	25
1959	06	11	327	37	6	26
1959	06	12	327	36	6	26
1959	06	13	327	36	6	26
1959	06	14	327	35	6	27
1959	06	15	327	34	6	27
1959	06	16	327	33	6	27
1959	06	17	327	32	6	28
1959	06	18	327	31	6	28
1959	06	19	327	30	6	28
1959	06	20	327	29	6	29
1959	06	21	327	28	6	29
1959	06	22	327	27	6	29
1959	06	23	327	26	6	30
1959	06	24	327	24	6	30
1959	06	25	327	23	6	30
1959	06	26	327	22	6	31
1959	06	27	327	20	6	31
1959	06	28	327	19	6	31
1959	06	29	327	17	6	31
1959	06	30	327	16	6	32
1959	07	01	327	14	6	32
1959	07	02	327	12	6	32
1959	07	03	327	10	6	33
1959	07	04	327	09	6	33
1959	07	05	327	07	6	33
1959	07	06	327	05	6	33

1959	07	07	327	03	6	34
1959	07	08	327	01	6	34
1959	07	09	326	59	6	34
1959	07	10	326	57	6	34
1959	07	11	326	55	6	34
1959	07	12	326	52	6	35
1959	07	13	326	50	6	35
1959	07	14	326	48	6	35
1959	07	15	326	46	6	35
1959	07	16	326	43	6	36
1959	07	17	326	41	6	36
1959	07	18	326	38	6	36
1959	07	19	326	36	6	36
1959	07	20	326	33	6	36
1959	07	21	326	31	6	36
1959	07	22	326	28	6	37
1959	07	23	326	26	6	37
1959	07	24	326	23	6	37
1959	07	25	326	20	6	37
1959	07	26	326	18	6	37
1959	07	27	326	15	6	37
1959	07	28	326	12	6	37
1959	07	29	326	09	6	38
1959	07	30	326	07	6	38
1959	07	31	326	04	6	38
1959	08	01	326	01	6	38
1959	08	02	325	58	6	38
1959	08	03	325	55	6	38
1959	08	04	325	52	6	38
1959	08	05	325	49	6	38
1959	08	06	325	46	6	38
1959	08	07	325	43	6	38
1959	08	08	325	40	6	38
1959	08	09	325	38	6	38
1959	08	10	325	35	6	38
1959	08	11	325	31	6	38
1959	08	12	325	28	6	38
1959	08	13	325	25	6	38
1959	08	14	325	22	6	38
1959	08	15	325	19	6	38
1959	08	16	325	16	6	38
1959	08	17	325	13	6	38
1959	08	18	325	10	6	38
1959	08	19	325	07	6	38
1959	08	20	325	04	6	38
1959	08	21	325	01	6	38
1959	08	22	324	58	6	38
1959	08	23	324	55	6	38
1959	08	24	324	52	6	38
1959	08	25	324	49	6	38
1959	08	26	324	46	6	38
1959	08	27	324	43	6	37
1959	08	28	324	40	6	37
1959	08	29	324	37	6	37
1959	08	30	324	34	6	37
1959	08	31	324	31	6	37
1959	09	01	324	28	6	37
1959	09	02	324	25	6	37
1959	09	03	324	22	6	36
1959	09	04	324	19	6	36
1959	09	05	324	17	6	36
1959	09	06	324	14	6	36
1959	09	07	324	11	6	36
1959	09	08	324	08	6	35
1959	09	09	324	05	6	35
1959	09	10	324	03	6	35
1959	09	11	324	00	6	35
1959	09	12	323	57	6	35
1959	09	13	323	55	6	34
1959	09	14	323	52	6	34
1959	09	15	323	49	6	34
1959	09	16	323	47	6	34
1959	09	17	323	44	6	33
1959	09	18	323	42	6	33
1959	09	19	323	39	6	33
1959	09	20	323	37	6	33
1959	09	21	323	35	6	32
1959	09	22	323	32	6	32
1959	09	23	323	30	6	32
1959	09	24	323	28	6	31
1959	09	25	323	26	6	31
1959	09	26	323	23	6	31
1959	09	27	323	21	6	30
1959	09	28	323	19	6	30
1959	09	29	323	17	6	30
1959	09	30	323	15	6	29
1959	10	01	323	13	6	29
1959	10	02	323	11	6	29
1959	10	03	323	10	6	28
1959	10	04	323	08	6	28
1959	10	05	323	06	6	28
1959	10	06	323	04	6	27
1959	10	07	323	03	6	27
1959	10	08	323	01	6	27
1959	10	09	323	00	6	26
1959	10	10	322	58	6	26
1959	10	11	322	57	6	25
1959	10	12	322	55	6	25
1959	10	13	322	54	6	25
1959	10	14	322	53	6	24
1959	10	15	322	52	6	24
1959	10	16	322	51	6	23
1959	10	17	322	50	6	23
1959	10	18	322	49	6	23
1959	10	19	322	48	6	22
1959	10	20	322	47	6	22

1959 10 21	322 46	6 21
1959 10 22	322 45	6 21
1959 10 23	322 45	6 21
1959 10 24	322 44	6 20
1959 10 25	322 43	6 20
1959 10 26	322 43	6 19
1959 10 27	322 42	6 19
1959 10 28	322 42	6 18
1959 10 29	322 42	6 18
1959 10 30	322 41	6 18
1959 10 31	322 41	6 17
1959 11 01	322 41	6 17
1959 11 02	322 41	6 16
1959 11 03	322 41	6 16
1959 11 04	322 41	6 15
1959 11 05	322 41	6 15
1959 11 06	322 41	6 14
1959 11 07	322 42	6 14
1959 11 08	322 42	6 14
1959 11 09	322 42	6 13
1959 11 10	322 43	6 13
1959 11 11	322 43	6 12
1959 11 12	322 44	6 12
1959 11 13	322 44	6 11
1959 11 14	322 45	6 11
1959 11 15	322 46	6 11
1959 11 16	322 47	6 10
1959 11 17	322 47	6 10
1959 11 18	322 48	6 09
1959 11 19	322 49	6 09
1959 11 20	322 50	6 08
1959 11 21	322 52	6 08
1959 11 22	322 53	6 08
1959 11 23	322 54	6 07
1959 11 24	322 55	6 07
1959 11 25	322 57	6 06
1959 11 26	322 58	6 06
1959 11 27	323 00	6 05
1959 11 28	323 01	6 05
1959 11 29	323 03	6 05
1959 11 30	323 04	6 04
1959 12 01	323 06	6 04
1959 12 02	323 08	6 03
1959 12 03	323 10	6 03
1959 12 04	323 12	6 03
1959 12 05	323 13	6 02
1959 12 06	323 15	6 02
1959 12 07	323 18	6 01
1959 12 08	323 20	6 01
1959 12 09	323 22	6 01
1959 12 10	323 24	6 00
1959 12 11	323 26	6 00
1959 12 12	323 29	5 59
1959 12 13	323 31	5 59
1959 12 14	323 33	5 59
1959 12 15	323 36	5 58
1959 12 16	323 38	5 58
1959 12 17	323 41	5 58
1959 12 18	323 44	5 57
1959 12 19	323 46	5 57
1959 12 20	323 49	5 57
1959 12 21	323 52	5 56
1959 12 22	323 55	5 56
1959 12 23	323 58	5 56
1959 12 24	324 00	5 55
1959 12 25	324 03	5 55
1959 12 26	324 06	5 55
1959 12 27	324 09	5 54
1959 12 28	324 13	5 54
1959 12 29	324 16	5 54
1959 12 30	324 19	5 53
1959 12 31	324 22	5 53
1960 01 01	324 25	5 53
1960 01 02	324 29	5 52
1960 01 03	324 32	5 52
1960 01 04	324 35	5 52
1960 01 05	324 39	5 52
1960 01 06	324 42	5 51
1960 01 07	324 46	5 51
1960 01 08	324 49	5 51
1960 01 09	324 53	5 51
1960 01 10	324 56	5 50
1960 01 11	325 00	5 50
1960 01 12	325 03	5 50
1960 01 13	325 07	5 50
1960 01 14	325 11	5 49
1960 01 15	325 14	5 49
1960 01 16	325 18	5 49
1960 01 17	325 22	5 49
1960 01 18	325 26	5 49
1960 01 19	325 30	5 48
1960 01 20	325 33	5 48
1960 01 21	325 37	5 48
1960 01 22	325 41	5 48
1960 01 23	325 45	5 48
1960 01 24	325 49	5 47
1960 01 25	325 53	5 47
1960 01 26	325 57	5 47
1960 01 27	326 01	5 47
1960 01 28	326 05	5 47
1960 01 29	326 09	5 47
1960 01 30	326 13	5 46
1960 01 31	326 17	5 46
1960 02 01	326 21	5 46
1960 02 02	326 25	5 46
1960 02 03	326 29	5 46

1960 02 04	326 34	5 46
1960 02 05	326 38	5 46
1960 02 06	326 42	5 46
1960 02 07	326 46	5 45
1960 02 08	326 50	5 45
1960 02 09	326 54	5 45
1960 02 10	326 58	5 45
1960 02 11	327 03	5 45
1960 02 12	327 07	5 45
1960 02 13	327 11	5 45
1960 02 14	327 15	5 45
1960 02 15	327 19	5 45
1960 02 16	327 23	5 45
1960 02 17	327 28	5 45
1960 02 18	327 32	5 45
1960 02 19	327 36	5 45
1960 02 20	327 40	5 45
1960 02 21	327 44	5 45
1960 02 22	327 48	5 45
1960 02 23	327 53	5 45
1960 02 24	327 57	5 45
1960 02 25	328 01	5 45
1960 02 26	328 05	5 45
1960 02 27	328 09	5 45
1960 02 28	328 13	5 45
1960 02 29	328 17	5 45
1960 03 01	328 22	5 45
1960 03 02	328 26	5 45
1960 03 03	328 30	5 45
1960 03 04	328 34	5 45
1960 03 05	328 38	5 45
1960 03 06	328 42	5 45
1960 03 07	328 46	5 45
1960 03 08	328 50	5 45
1960 03 09	328 54	5 45
1960 03 10	328 58	5 45
1960 03 11	329 02	5 45
1960 03 12	329 06	5 45
1960 03 13	329 10	5 45
1960 03 14	329 14	5 45
1960 03 15	329 17	5 45
1960 03 16	329 21	5 46
1960 03 17	329 25	5 46
1960 03 18	329 29	5 46
1960 03 19	329 33	5 46
1960 03 20	329 36	5 46
1960 03 21	329 40	5 46
1960 03 22	329 44	5 46
1960 03 23	329 48	5 46
1960 03 24	329 51	5 47
1960 03 25	329 55	5 47
1960 03 26	329 58	5 47
1960 03 27	330 02	5 47
1960 03 28	330 05	5 47
1960 03 29	330 09	5 47
1960 03 30	330 12	5 47
1960 03 31	330 16	5 48
1960 04 01	330 19	5 48
1960 04 02	330 23	5 48
1960 04 03	330 26	5 48
1960 04 04	330 29	5 48
1960 04 05	330 32	5 49
1960 04 06	330 36	5 49
1960 04 07	330 39	5 49
1960 04 08	330 42	5 49
1960 04 09	330 45	5 49
1960 04 10	330 48	5 50
1960 04 11	330 51	5 50
1960 04 12	330 54	5 50
1960 04 13	330 57	5 50
1960 04 14	331 00	5 51
1960 04 15	331 02	5 51
1960 04 16	331 05	5 51
1960 04 17	331 08	5 51
1960 04 18	331 11	5 51
1960 04 19	331 13	5 52
1960 04 20	331 16	5 52
1960 04 21	331 19	5 52
1960 04 22	331 21	5 52
1960 04 23	331 23	5 53
1960 04 24	331 26	5 53
1960 04 25	331 28	5 53
1960 04 26	331 31	5 54
1960 04 27	331 33	5 54
1960 04 28	331 35	5 54
1960 04 29	331 37	5 54
1960 04 30	331 39	5 55
1960 05 01	331 41	5 55
1960 05 02	331 43	5 55
1960 05 03	331 45	5 56
1960 05 04	331 47	5 56
1960 05 05	331 49	5 56
1960 05 06	331 51	5 56
1960 05 07	331 53	5 57
1960 05 08	331 54	5 57
1960 05 09	331 56	5 57
1960 05 10	331 57	5 58
1960 05 11	331 59	5 58
1960 05 12	332 00	5 58
1960 05 13	332 02	5 59
1960 05 14	332 03	5 59
1960 05 15	332 04	5 59
1960 05 16	332 06	6 00
1960 05 17	332 07	6 00
1960 05 18	332 08	6 00
1960 05 19	332 09	6 00

1960 05 20	332 10	6 01
1960 05 21	332 11	6 01
1960 05 22	332 12	6 01
1960 05 23	332 13	6 02
1960 05 24	332 13	6 02
1960 05 25	332 14	6 02
1960 05 26	332 15	6 03
1960 05 27	332 15	6 03
1960 05 28	332 16	6 03
1960 05 29	332 16	6 04
1960 05 30	332 17	6 04
1960 05 31	332 17	6 04
1960 06 01	332 17	6 05
1960 06 02	332 18	6 05
1960 06 03	332 18	6 05
1960 06 04	332 18	6 06
1960 06 05	332 18	6 06
1960 06 06	332 18	6 06
1960 06 07	332 18	6 07
1960 06 08	332 18	6 07
1960 06 09	332 18	6 07
1960 06 10	332 17	6 08
1960 06 11	332 17	6 08
1960 06 12	332 17	6 08
1960 06 13	332 16	6 08
1960 06 14	332 16	6 09
1960 06 15	332 15	6 09
1960 06 16	332 15	6 09
1960 06 17	332 14	6 10
1960 06 18	332 13	6 10
1960 06 19	332 12	6 10
1960 06 20	332 12	6 11
1960 06 21	332 11	6 11
1960 06 22	332 10	6 11
1960 06 23	332 09	6 12
1960 06 24	332 08	6 12
1960 06 25	332 07	6 12
1960 06 26	332 05	6 12
1960 06 27	332 04	6 13
1960 06 28	332 03	6 13
1960 06 29	332 02	6 13
1960 06 30	332 00	6 13
1960 07 01	331 59	6 14
1960 07 02	331 57	6 14
1960 07 03	331 56	6 14
1960 07 04	331 54	6 15
1960 07 05	331 53	6 15
1960 07 06	331 51	6 15
1960 07 07	331 49	6 15
1960 07 08	331 47	6 15
1960 07 09	331 46	6 16
1960 07 10	331 44	6 16
1960 07 11	331 42	6 16
1960 07 12	331 40	6 16
1960 07 13	331 38	6 17
1960 07 14	331 36	6 17
1960 07 15	331 34	6 17
1960 07 16	331 32	6 17
1960 07 17	331 29	6 17
1960 07 18	331 27	6 18
1960 07 19	331 25	6 18
1960 07 20	331 23	6 18
1960 07 21	331 20	6 18
1960 07 22	331 18	6 18
1960 07 23	331 15	6 18
1960 07 24	331 13	6 19
1960 07 25	331 11	6 19
1960 07 26	331 08	6 19
1960 07 27	331 05	6 19
1960 07 28	331 03	6 19
1960 07 29	331 00	6 19
1960 07 30	330 58	6 19
1960 07 31	330 55	6 20
1960 08 01	330 52	6 20
1960 08 02	330 50	6 20
1960 08 03	330 47	6 20
1960 08 04	330 44	6 20
1960 08 05	330 41	6 20
1960 08 06	330 38	6 20
1960 08 07	330 36	6 20
1960 08 08	330 33	6 20
1960 08 09	330 30	6 20
1960 08 10	330 27	6 20
1960 08 11	330 24	6 20
1960 08 12	330 21	6 20
1960 08 13	330 18	6 20
1960 08 14	330 15	6 20
1960 08 15	330 12	6 20
1960 08 16	330 10	6 20
1960 08 17	330 07	6 20
1960 08 18	330 04	6 20
1960 08 19	330 01	6 20
1960 08 20	329 58	6 20
1960 08 21	329 55	6 20
1960 08 22	329 52	6 20
1960 08 23	329 49	6 20
1960 08 24	329 46	6 20
1960 08 25	329 43	6 20
1960 08 26	329 40	6 20
1960 08 27	329 37	6 20
1960 08 28	329 34	6 20
1960 08 29	329 31	6 20
1960 08 30	329 28	6 20
1960 08 31	329 25	6 19
1960 09 01	329 22	6 19
1960 09 02	329 19	6 19

1960 09 03	329 16	6 19
1960 09 04	329 13	6 19
1960 09 05	329 10	6 19
1960 09 06	329 08	6 19
1960 09 07	329 05	6 18
1960 09 08	329 02	6 18
1960 09 09	328 59	6 18
1960 09 10	328 56	6 18
1960 09 11	328 54	6 18
1960 09 12	328 51	6 18
1960 09 13	328 48	6 17
1960 09 14	328 45	6 17
1960 09 15	328 43	6 17
1960 09 16	328 40	6 17
1960 09 17	328 38	6 16
1960 09 18	328 35	6 16
1960 09 19	328 32	6 16
1960 09 20	328 30	6 16
1960 09 21	328 28	6 16
1960 09 22	328 25	6 15
1960 09 23	328 23	6 15
1960 09 24	328 20	6 15
1960 09 25	328 18	6 14
1960 09 26	328 16	6 14
1960 09 27	328 13	6 14
1960 09 28	328 11	6 14
1960 09 29	328 09	6 13
1960 09 30	328 07	6 13
1960 10 01	328 05	6 13
1960 10 02	328 03	6 12
1960 10 03	328 01	6 12
1960 10 04	327 59	6 12
1960 10 05	327 57	6 11
1960 10 06	327 55	6 11
1960 10 07	327 53	6 11
1960 10 08	327 52	6 10
1960 10 09	327 50	6 10
1960 10 10	327 48	6 10
1960 10 11	327 47	6 09
1960 10 12	327 45	6 09
1960 10 13	327 44	6 09
1960 10 14	327 42	6 08
1960 10 15	327 41	6 08
1960 10 16	327 39	6 08
1960 10 17	327 38	6 07
1960 10 18	327 37	6 07
1960 10 19	327 36	6 06
1960 10 20	327 35	6 06
1960 10 21	327 34	6 06
1960 10 22	327 33	6 05
1960 10 23	327 32	6 05
1960 10 24	327 31	6 05
1960 10 25	327 30	6 04
1960 10 26	327 29	6 04
1960 10 27	327 29	6 03
1960 10 28	327 28	6 03
1960 10 29	327 27	6 03
1960 10 30	327 27	6 02
1960 10 31	327 26	6 02
1960 11 01	327 26	6 01
1960 11 02	327 26	6 01
1960 11 03	327 25	6 01
1960 11 04	327 25	6 00
1960 11 05	327 25	6 00
1960 11 06	327 25	5 59
1960 11 07	327 25	5 59
1960 11 08	327 25	5 58
1960 11 09	327 25	5 58
1960 11 10	327 25	5 58
1960 11 11	327 25	5 57
1960 11 12	327 26	5 57
1960 11 13	327 26	5 56
1960 11 14	327 26	5 56
1960 11 15	327 27	5 56
1960 11 16	327 27	5 55
1960 11 17	327 28	5 55
1960 11 18	327 28	5 54
1960 11 19	327 29	5 54
1960 11 20	327 30	5 53
1960 11 21	327 31	5 53
1960 11 22	327 32	5 53
1960 11 23	327 33	5 52
1960 11 24	327 34	5 52
1960 11 25	327 35	5 51
1960 11 26	327 36	5 51
1960 11 27	327 37	5 51
1960 11 28	327 38	5 50
1960 11 29	327 40	5 50
1960 11 30	327 41	5 49
1960 12 01	327 42	5 49
1960 12 02	327 44	5 49
1960 12 03	327 45	5 48
1960 12 04	327 47	5 48
1960 12 05	327 49	5 48
1960 12 06	327 50	5 47
1960 12 07	327 52	5 47
1960 12 08	327 54	5 46
1960 12 09	327 56	5 46
1960 12 10	327 58	5 46
1960 12 11	328 00	5 45
1960 12 12	328 02	5 45
1960 12 13	328 04	5 45

Chiron

1960	12	14	328	06	5	44
1960	12	15	328	08	5	44
1960	12	16	328	10	5	43
1960	12	17	328	13	5	43
1960	12	18	328	15	5	43
1960	12	19	328	17	5	42
1960	12	20	328	20	5	42
1960	12	21	328	22	5	42
1960	12	22	328	25	5	41
1960	12	23	328	28	5	41
1960	12	24	328	30	5	41
1960	12	25	328	33	5	40
1960	12	26	328	36	5	40
1960	12	27	328	38	5	40
1960	12	28	328	41	5	39
1960	12	29	328	44	5	39
1960	12	30	328	47	5	39
1960	12	31	328	50	5	39
1961	01	01	328	53	5	38
1961	01	02	328	56	5	38
1961	01	03	328	59	5	38
1961	01	04	329	02	5	37
1961	01	05	329	05	5	37
1961	01	06	329	08	5	37
1961	01	07	329	12	5	37
1961	01	08	329	15	5	36
1961	01	09	329	18	5	36
1961	01	10	329	22	5	36
1961	01	11	329	25	5	35
1961	01	12	329	28	5	35
1961	01	13	329	32	5	35
1961	01	14	329	35	5	35
1961	01	15	329	39	5	34
1961	01	16	329	42	5	34
1961	01	17	329	46	5	34
1961	01	18	329	49	5	34
1961	01	19	329	53	5	34
1961	01	20	329	57	5	33
1961	01	21	330	00	5	33
1961	01	22	330	04	5	33
1961	01	23	330	08	5	33
1961	01	24	330	11	5	33
1961	01	25	330	15	5	32
1961	01	26	330	19	5	32
1961	01	27	330	23	5	32
1961	01	28	330	26	5	32
1961	01	29	330	30	5	32
1961	01	30	330	34	5	32
1961	01	31	330	38	5	31
1961	02	01	330	42	5	31
1961	02	02	330	46	5	31
1961	02	03	330	50	5	31
1961	02	04	330	54	5	31
1961	02	05	330	58	5	31
1961	02	06	331	02	5	31
1961	02	07	331	06	5	30
1961	02	08	331	10	5	30
1961	02	09	331	14	5	30
1961	02	10	331	18	5	30
1961	02	11	331	22	5	30
1961	02	12	331	26	5	30
1961	02	13	331	30	5	30
1961	02	14	331	34	5	30
1961	02	15	331	38	5	30
1961	02	16	331	42	5	30
1961	02	17	331	46	5	29
1961	02	18	331	50	5	29
1961	02	19	331	54	5	29
1961	02	20	331	58	5	29
1961	02	21	332	02	5	29
1961	02	22	332	06	5	29
1961	02	23	332	10	5	29
1961	02	24	332	14	5	29
1961	02	25	332	18	5	29
1961	02	26	332	22	5	29
1961	02	27	332	26	5	29
1961	02	28	332	30	5	29
1961	03	01	332	34	5	29
1961	03	02	332	38	5	29
1961	03	03	332	42	5	29
1961	03	04	332	46	5	29
1961	03	05	332	50	5	29
1961	03	06	332	54	5	29
1961	03	07	332	58	5	29
1961	03	08	333	02	5	29
1961	03	09	333	06	5	29
1961	03	10	333	10	5	29
1961	03	11	333	14	5	29
1961	03	12	333	18	5	29
1961	03	13	333	22	5	29
1961	03	14	333	26	5	29
1961	03	15	333	29	5	29
1961	03	16	333	33	5	30
1961	03	17	333	37	5	30
1961	03	18	333	41	5	30
1961	03	19	333	45	5	30
1961	03	20	333	48	5	30
1961	03	21	333	52	5	30
1961	03	22	333	56	5	30
1961	03	23	333	59	5	30
1961	03	24	334	03	5	30
1961	03	25	334	07	5	30
1961	03	26	334	10	5	30
1961	03	27	334	14	5	31
1961	03	28	334	17	5	31
1961	03	29	334	21	5	31
1961	03	30	334	24	5	31
1961	03	31	334	28	5	31
1961	04	01	334	31	5	31
1961	04	02	334	35	5	31
1961	04	03	334	38	5	31
1961	04	04	334	41	5	32
1961	04	05	334	45	5	32
1961	04	06	334	48	5	32
1961	04	07	334	51	5	32
1961	04	08	334	54	5	32
1961	04	09	334	58	5	32
1961	04	10	335	01	5	33
1961	04	11	335	04	5	33
1961	04	12	335	07	5	33
1961	04	13	335	10	5	33
1961	04	14	335	13	5	33
1961	04	15	335	16	5	34
1961	04	16	335	19	5	34
1961	04	17	335	22	5	34
1961	04	18	335	24	5	34
1961	04	19	335	27	5	34
1961	04	20	335	30	5	35
1961	04	21	335	33	5	35
1961	04	22	335	35	5	35
1961	04	23	335	38	5	35
1961	04	24	335	40	5	35
1961	04	25	335	43	5	36
1961	04	26	335	45	5	36
1961	04	27	335	48	5	36
1961	04	28	335	50	5	36
1961	04	29	335	52	5	37
1961	04	30	335	55	5	37
1961	05	01	335	57	5	37
1961	05	02	335	59	5	37
1961	05	03	336	01	5	38
1961	05	04	336	03	5	38
1961	05	05	336	05	5	38
1961	05	06	336	07	5	38
1961	05	07	336	09	5	39
1961	05	08	336	11	5	39
1961	05	09	336	13	5	39
1961	05	10	336	15	5	39
1961	05	11	336	16	5	40
1961	05	12	336	18	5	40
1961	05	13	336	20	5	40
1961	05	14	336	21	5	41
1961	05	15	336	23	5	41
1961	05	16	336	24	5	41
1961	05	17	336	26	5	41
1961	05	18	336	27	5	42
1961	05	19	336	28	5	42
1961	05	20	336	29	5	42
1961	05	21	336	31	5	43
1961	05	22	336	32	5	43
1961	05	23	336	33	5	43
1961	05	24	336	34	5	43
1961	05	25	336	35	5	44
1961	05	26	336	36	5	44
1961	05	27	336	36	5	44
1961	05	28	336	37	5	45
1961	05	29	336	38	5	45
1961	05	30	336	38	5	45
1961	05	31	336	39	5	45
1961	06	01	336	40	5	46
1961	06	02	336	40	5	46
1961	06	03	336	41	5	46
1961	06	04	336	41	5	47
1961	06	05	336	41	5	47
1961	06	06	336	41	5	47
1961	06	07	336	42	5	47
1961	06	08	336	42	5	48
1961	06	09	336	42	5	48
1961	06	10	336	42	5	48
1961	06	11	336	42	5	49
1961	06	12	336	42	5	49
1961	06	13	336	42	5	49
1961	06	14	336	41	5	50
1961	06	15	336	41	5	50
1961	06	16	336	41	5	50
1961	06	17	336	40	5	50
1961	06	18	336	40	5	51
1961	06	19	336	39	5	51
1961	06	20	336	39	5	51
1961	06	21	336	38	5	52
1961	06	22	336	38	5	52
1961	06	23	336	37	5	52
1961	06	24	336	36	5	52
1961	06	25	336	35	5	53
1961	06	26	336	34	5	53
1961	06	27	336	33	5	53
1961	06	28	336	32	5	53
1961	06	29	336	31	5	54
1961	06	30	336	30	5	54
1961	07	01	336	29	5	54
1961	07	02	336	28	5	54
1961	07	03	336	27	5	55
1961	07	04	336	25	5	55
1961	07	05	336	24	5	55
1961	07	06	336	23	5	55
1961	07	07	336	21	5	56
1961	07	08	336	20	5	56
1961	07	09	336	18	5	56
1961	07	10	336	16	5	56
1961	07	11	336	15	5	57
1961	07	12	336	13	5	57
1961	07	13	336	11	5	57
1961	07	14	336	09	5	57
1961	07	15	336	08	5	57
1961	07	16	336	06	5	58
1961	07	17	336	04	5	58
1961	07	18	336	02	5	58
1961	07	19	336	00	5	58
1961	07	20	335	58	5	58
1961	07	21	335	55	5	59
1961	07	22	335	53	5	59
1961	07	23	335	51	5	59
1961	07	24	335	49	5	59
1961	07	25	335	47	5	59
1961	07	26	335	44	5	59
1961	07	27	335	42	5	59
1961	07	28	335	40	6	00
1961	07	29	335	37	6	00
1961	07	30	335	35	6	00
1961	07	31	335	32	6	00
1961	08	01	335	30	6	00
1961	08	02	335	27	6	00
1961	08	03	335	25	6	00
1961	08	04	335	22	6	00
1961	08	05	335	20	6	01
1961	08	06	335	17	6	01
1961	08	07	335	14	6	01
1961	08	08	335	12	6	01
1961	08	09	335	09	6	01
1961	08	10	335	06	6	01
1961	08	11	335	03	6	01
1961	08	12	335	01	6	01
1961	08	13	334	58	6	01
1961	08	14	334	55	6	01
1961	08	15	334	52	6	01
1961	08	16	334	49	6	01
1961	08	17	334	46	6	01
1961	08	18	334	44	6	01
1961	08	19	334	41	6	01
1961	08	20	334	38	6	01
1961	08	21	334	35	6	01
1961	08	22	334	32	6	01
1961	08	23	334	29	6	01
1961	08	24	334	26	6	01
1961	08	25	334	23	6	01
1961	08	26	334	20	6	01
1961	08	27	334	17	6	01
1961	08	28	334	15	6	01
1961	08	29	334	12	6	01
1961	08	30	334	09	6	01
1961	08	31	334	06	6	01
1961	09	01	334	03	6	01
1961	09	02	334	00	6	01
1961	09	03	333	57	6	00
1961	09	04	333	54	6	00
1961	09	05	333	51	6	00
1961	09	06	333	48	6	00
1961	09	07	333	46	6	00
1961	09	08	333	43	6	00
1961	09	09	333	40	6	00
1961	09	10	333	37	6	00
1961	09	11	333	34	5	59
1961	09	12	333	31	5	59
1961	09	13	333	29	5	59
1961	09	14	333	26	5	59
1961	09	15	333	23	5	59
1961	09	16	333	21	5	59
1961	09	17	333	18	5	58
1961	09	18	333	15	5	58
1961	09	19	333	13	5	58
1961	09	20	333	10	5	58
1961	09	21	333	07	5	58
1961	09	22	333	05	5	57
1961	09	23	333	02	5	57
1961	09	24	333	00	5	57
1961	09	25	332	57	5	57
1961	09	26	332	55	5	56
1961	09	27	332	53	5	56
1961	09	28	332	50	5	56
1961	09	29	332	48	5	56
1961	09	30	332	46	5	55
1961	10	01	332	43	5	55
1961	10	02	332	41	5	55
1961	10	03	332	39	5	55
1961	10	04	332	37	5	54
1961	10	05	332	35	5	54
1961	10	06	332	33	5	54
1961	10	07	332	31	5	53
1961	10	08	332	29	5	53
1961	10	09	332	27	5	53
1961	10	10	332	25	5	53
1961	10	11	332	23	5	52
1961	10	12	332	21	5	52
1961	10	13	332	20	5	52
1961	10	14	332	18	5	51
1961	10	15	332	16	5	51
1961	10	16	332	15	5	51
1961	10	17	332	13	5	50
1961	10	18	332	12	5	50
1961	10	19	332	11	5	50
1961	10	20	332	09	5	49
1961	10	21	332	08	5	49
1961	10	22	332	07	5	49
1961	10	23	332	05	5	4
1961	10	24	332	04	5	48
1961	10	25	332	03	5	47
1961	10	26	332	02	5	47
1961	10	27	332	01	5	47
1961	10	28	332	00	5	46
1961	10	29	331	59	5	46
1961	10	30	331	59	5	46
1961	10	31	331	58	5	45
1961	11	01	331	57	5	45
1961	11	02	331	56	5	44
1961	11	03	331	56	5	44
1961	11	04	331	55	5	44
1961	11	05	331	55	5	43
1961	11	06	331	55	5	43
1961	11	07	331	54	5	43
1961	11	08	331	54	5	42
1961	11	09	331	54	5	42
1961	11	10	331	54	5	41
1961	11	11	331	53	5	41
1961	11	12	331	53	5	41
1961	11	13	331	53	5	40
1961	11	14	331	53	5	40
1961	11	15	331	54	5	39
1961	11	16	331	54	5	39
1961	11	17	331	54	5	39
1961	11	18	331	54	5	38
1961	11	19	331	55	5	38
1961	11	20	331	55	5	38
1961	11	21	331	56	5	37
1961	11	22	331	56	5	37
1961	11	23	331	57	5	36
1961	11	24	331	58	5	36
1961	11	25	331	58	5	36
1961	11	26	331	59	5	35
1961	11	27	332	00	5	35
1961	11	28	332	01	5	34
1961	11	29	332	02	5	34
1961	11	30	332	03	5	34
1961	12	01	332	04	5	33
1961	12	02	332	05	5	33
1961	12	03	332	06	5	33
1961	12	04	332	08	5	32
1961	12	05	332	09	5	32
1961	12	06	332	10	5	31
1961	12	07	332	12	5	31
1961	12	08	332	13	5	31
1961	12	09	332	15	5	30
1961	12	10	332	17	5	30
1961	12	11	332	18	5	30
1961	12	12	332	20	5	29
1961	12	13	332	22	5	29
1961	12	14	332	24	5	28
1961	12	15	332	25	5	28
1961	12	16	332	27	5	28
1961	12	17	332	29	5	27
1961	12	18	332	31	5	27
1961	12	19	332	34	5	27
1961	12	20	332	36	5	26
1961	12	21	332	38	5	26
1961	12	22	332	40	5	26
1961	12	23	332	42	5	25
1961	12	24	332	45	5	25
1961	12	25	332	47	5	25
1961	12	26	332	50	5	24
1961	12	27	332	52	5	24
1961	12	28	332	55	5	24
1961	12	29	332	57	5	23
1961	12	30	333	00	5	23
1961	12	31	333	02	5	23
1962	01	01	333	05	5	23
1962	01	02	333	08	5	22
1962	01	03	333	11	5	22
1962	01	04	333	14	5	22
1962	01	05	333	16	5	21
1962	01	06	333	19	5	21
1962	01	07	333	22	5	21
1962	01	08	333	25	5	21
1962	01	09	333	28	5	20
1962	01	10	333	31	5	20
1962	01	11	333	34	5	20
1962	01	12	333	38	5	20
1962	01	13	333	41	5	19
1962	01	14	333	44	5	19
1962	01	15	333	47	5	19
1962	01	16	333	51	5	19
1962	01	17	333	54	5	18
1962	01	18	333	57	5	18
1962	01	19	334	01	5	18
1962	01	20	334	04	5	18
1962	01	21	334	07	5	17
1962	01	22	334	11	5	17
1962	01	23	334	14	5	17
1962	01	24	334	18	5	17
1962	01	25	334	21	5	17
1962	01	26	334	25	5	16
1962	01	27	334	29	5	16
1962	01	28	334	32	5	16
1962	01	29	334	36	5	16
1962	01	30	334	39	5	16
1962	01	31	334	43	5	15
1962	02	01	334	47	5	15
1962	02	02	334	51	5	15
1962	02	03	334	54	5	15
1962	02	04	334	58	5	15
1962	02	05	335	02	5	15

1962	02	06	335	06	5	15
1962	02	07	335	09	5	14
1962	02	08	335	13	5	14
1962	02	09	335	17	5	14
1962	02	10	335	21	5	14
1962	02	11	335	25	5	14
1962	02	12	335	29	5	14
1962	02	13	335	32	5	14
1962	02	14	335	36	5	14
1962	02	15	335	40	5	13
1962	02	16	335	44	5	13
1962	02	17	335	48	5	13
1962	02	18	335	52	5	13
1962	02	19	335	56	5	13
1962	02	20	336	00	5	13
1962	02	21	336	04	5	13
1962	02	22	336	08	5	13
1962	02	23	336	12	5	13
1962	02	24	336	16	5	13
1962	02	25	336	20	5	13
1962	02	26	336	23	5	13
1962	02	27	336	27	5	13
1962	02	28	336	31	5	13
1962	03	01	336	35	5	12
1962	03	02	336	39	5	12
1962	03	03	336	43	5	12
1962	03	04	336	47	5	12
1962	03	05	336	51	5	12
1962	03	06	336	55	5	12
1962	03	07	336	59	5	12
1962	03	08	337	03	5	12
1962	03	09	337	07	5	12
1962	03	10	337	10	5	12
1962	03	11	337	14	5	12
1962	03	12	337	18	5	12
1962	03	13	337	22	5	12
1962	03	14	337	26	5	12
1962	03	15	337	30	5	12
1962	03	16	337	33	5	13
1962	03	17	337	37	5	13
1962	03	18	337	41	5	13
1962	03	19	337	45	5	13
1962	03	20	337	49	5	13
1962	03	21	337	52	5	13
1962	03	22	337	56	5	13
1962	03	23	338	00	5	13
1962	03	24	338	03	5	13
1962	03	25	338	07	5	13
1962	03	26	338	11	5	13
1962	03	27	338	14	5	13
1962	03	28	338	18	5	13
1962	03	29	338	21	5	13
1962	03	30	338	25	5	13
1962	03	31	338	28	5	14
1962	04	01	338	32	5	14
1962	04	02	338	35	5	14
1962	04	03	338	39	5	14
1962	04	04	338	42	5	14
1962	04	05	338	45	5	14
1962	04	06	338	49	5	14
1962	04	07	338	52	5	14
1962	04	08	338	55	5	15
1962	04	09	338	58	5	15
1962	04	10	339	02	5	15
1962	04	11	339	05	5	15
1962	04	12	339	08	5	15
1962	04	13	339	11	5	15
1962	04	14	339	14	5	15
1962	04	15	339	17	5	16
1962	04	16	339	20	5	16
1962	04	17	339	23	5	16
1962	04	18	339	26	5	16
1962	04	19	339	29	5	16
1962	04	20	339	32	5	16
1962	04	21	339	34	5	17
1962	04	22	339	37	5	17
1962	04	23	339	40	5	17
1962	04	24	339	42	5	17
1962	04	25	339	45	5	17
1962	04	26	339	48	5	17
1962	04	27	339	50	5	18
1962	04	28	339	53	5	18
1962	04	29	339	55	5	18
1962	04	30	339	58	5	18
1962	05	01	340	00	5	19
1962	05	02	340	02	5	19
1962	05	03	340	05	5	19
1962	05	04	340	07	5	19
1962	05	05	340	09	5	19
1962	05	06	340	11	5	20
1962	05	07	340	13	5	20
1962	05	08	340	15	5	20
1962	05	09	340	17	5	20
1962	05	10	340	19	5	21
1962	05	11	340	21	5	21
1962	05	12	340	23	5	21
1962	05	13	340	25	5	21
1962	05	14	340	26	5	21
1962	05	15	340	28	5	22
1962	05	16	340	30	5	22
1962	05	17	340	31	5	22
1962	05	18	340	33	5	22
1962	05	19	340	34	5	23
1962	05	20	340	36	5	23
1962	05	21	340	37	5	23
1962	05	22	340	39	5	23
1962	05	23	340	40	5	24
1962	05	24	340	41	5	24
1962	05	25	340	42	5	24
1962	05	26	340	43	5	24
1962	05	27	340	44	5	25
1962	05	28	340	45	5	25
1962	05	29	340	46	5	25
1962	05	30	340	47	5	26
1962	05	31	340	48	5	26
1962	06	01	340	49	5	26
1962	06	02	340	49	5	26
1962	06	03	340	50	5	27
1962	06	04	340	51	5	27
1962	06	05	340	51	5	27
1962	06	06	340	52	5	27
1962	06	07	340	52	5	28
1962	06	08	340	53	5	28
1962	06	09	340	53	5	28
1962	06	10	340	53	5	28
1962	06	11	340	53	5	29
1962	06	12	340	53	5	29
1962	06	13	340	54	5	29
1962	06	14	340	54	5	30
1962	06	15	340	54	5	30
1962	06	16	340	54	5	30
1962	06	17	340	53	5	30
1962	06	18	340	53	5	31
1962	06	19	340	53	5	31
1962	06	20	340	53	5	31
1962	06	21	340	52	5	31
1962	06	22	340	52	5	32
1962	06	23	340	51	5	32
1962	06	24	340	51	5	32
1962	06	25	340	50	5	32
1962	06	26	340	50	5	33
1962	06	27	340	49	5	33
1962	06	28	340	48	5	33
1962	06	29	340	47	5	33
1962	06	30	340	47	5	34
1962	07	01	340	46	5	34
1962	07	02	340	45	5	34
1962	07	03	340	44	5	34
1962	07	04	340	43	5	35
1962	07	05	340	41	5	35
1962	07	06	340	40	5	35
1962	07	07	340	39	5	35
1962	07	08	340	38	5	35
1962	07	09	340	36	5	36
1962	07	10	340	35	5	36
1962	07	11	340	34	5	36
1962	07	12	340	32	5	36
1962	07	13	340	31	5	37
1962	07	14	340	29	5	37
1962	07	15	340	28	5	37
1962	07	16	340	26	5	37
1962	07	17	340	24	5	37
1962	07	18	340	22	5	37
1962	07	19	340	21	5	38
1962	07	20	340	19	5	38
1962	07	21	340	17	5	38
1962	07	22	340	15	5	38
1962	07	23	340	13	5	38
1962	07	24	340	11	5	39
1962	07	25	340	09	5	39
1962	07	26	340	07	5	39
1962	07	27	340	05	5	39
1962	07	28	340	03	5	39
1962	07	29	340	00	5	39
1962	07	30	339	58	5	39
1962	07	31	339	56	5	40
1962	08	01	339	53	5	40
1962	08	02	339	51	5	40
1962	08	03	339	49	5	40
1962	08	04	339	46	5	40
1962	08	05	339	44	5	40
1962	08	06	339	41	5	40
1962	08	07	339	39	5	40
1962	08	08	339	36	5	40
1962	08	09	339	34	5	40
1962	08	10	339	31	5	41
1962	08	11	339	29	5	41
1962	08	12	339	26	5	41
1962	08	13	339	23	5	41
1962	08	14	339	21	5	41
1962	08	15	339	18	5	41
1962	08	16	339	15	5	41
1962	08	17	339	13	5	41
1962	08	18	339	10	5	41
1962	08	19	339	07	5	41
1962	08	20	339	04	5	41
1962	08	21	339	01	5	41
1962	08	22	338	59	5	41
1962	08	23	338	56	5	41
1962	08	24	338	53	5	41
1962	08	25	338	50	5	41
1962	08	26	338	47	5	41
1962	08	27	338	44	5	41
1962	08	28	338	42	5	41
1962	08	29	338	39	5	41
1962	08	30	338	36	5	41
1962	08	31	338	33	5	41
1962	09	01	338	30	5	41
1962	09	02	338	27	5	41
1962	09	03	338	24	5	41
1962	09	04	338	22	5	41
1962	09	05	338	19	5	40
1962	09	06	338	16	5	40
1962	09	07	338	13	5	40
1962	09	08	338	10	5	40
1962	09	09	338	07	5	40
1962	09	10	338	04	5	40
1962	09	11	338	02	5	40
1962	09	12	337	59	5	40
1962	09	13	337	56	5	40
1962	09	14	337	53	5	39
1962	09	15	337	50	5	39
1962	09	16	337	48	5	39
1962	09	17	337	45	5	39
1962	09	18	337	42	5	39
1962	09	19	337	40	5	39
1962	09	20	337	37	5	39
1962	09	21	337	34	5	38
1962	09	22	337	32	5	38
1962	09	23	337	29	5	38
1962	09	24	337	26	5	38
1962	09	25	337	24	5	38
1962	09	26	337	21	5	37
1962	09	27	337	19	5	37
1962	09	28	337	16	5	37
1962	09	29	337	14	5	37
1962	09	30	337	12	5	37
1962	10	01	337	09	5	36
1962	10	02	337	07	5	36
1962	10	03	337	05	5	36
1962	10	04	337	02	5	36
1962	10	05	337	00	5	35
1962	10	06	336	58	5	35
1962	10	07	336	56	5	35
1962	10	08	336	54	5	35
1962	10	09	336	51	5	34
1962	10	10	336	49	5	34
1962	10	11	336	47	5	34
1962	10	12	336	46	5	33
1962	10	13	336	44	5	33
1962	10	14	336	42	5	33
1962	10	15	336	40	5	33
1962	10	16	336	38	5	32
1962	10	17	336	36	5	32
1962	10	18	336	35	5	32
1962	10	19	336	33	5	31
1962	10	20	336	32	5	31
1962	10	21	336	30	5	31
1962	10	22	336	29	5	30
1962	10	23	336	27	5	30
1962	10	24	336	26	5	30
1962	10	25	336	24	5	29
1962	10	26	336	23	5	29
1962	10	27	336	22	5	29
1962	10	28	336	21	5	28
1962	10	29	336	20	5	28
1962	10	30	336	19	5	28
1962	10	31	336	18	5	27
1962	11	01	336	17	5	27
1962	11	02	336	16	5	27
1962	11	03	336	15	5	26
1962	11	04	336	14	5	26
1962	11	05	336	13	5	26
1962	11	06	336	13	5	25
1962	11	07	336	12	5	25
1962	11	08	336	12	5	25
1962	11	09	336	11	5	24
1962	11	10	336	11	5	24
1962	11	11	336	10	5	24
1962	11	12	336	10	5	23
1962	11	13	336	10	5	23
1962	11	14	336	09	5	22
1962	11	15	336	09	5	22
1962	11	16	336	09	5	22
1962	11	17	336	09	5	21
1962	11	18	336	09	5	21
1962	11	19	336	09	5	21
1962	11	20	336	09	5	20
1962	11	21	336	10	5	20
1962	11	22	336	10	5	20
1962	11	23	336	10	5	19
1962	11	24	336	11	5	19
1962	11	25	336	11	5	18
1962	11	26	336	12	5	18
1962	11	27	336	12	5	18
1962	11	28	336	13	5	17
1962	11	29	336	14	5	17
1962	11	30	336	14	5	17
1962	12	01	336	15	5	16
1962	12	02	336	16	5	16
1962	12	03	336	17	5	16
1962	12	04	336	18	5	15
1962	12	05	336	19	5	15
1962	12	06	336	20	5	14
1962	12	07	336	21	5	14
1962	12	08	336	22	5	14
1962	12	09	336	24	5	13
1962	12	10	336	25	5	13
1962	12	11	336	26	5	13
1962	12	12	336	28	5	12
1962	12	13	336	29	5	12
1962	12	14	336	31	5	12
1962	12	15	336	32	5	11
1962	12	16	336	34	5	11
1962	12	17	336	36	5	11
1962	12	18	336	37	5	10
1962	12	19	336	39	5	10
1962	12	20	336	41	5	10
1962	12	21	336	43	5	09
1962	12	22	336	45	5	09
1962	12	23	336	47	5	09
1962	12	24	336	49	5	08
1962	12	25	336	51	5	08
1962	12	26	336	53	5	08
1962	12	27	336	55	5	07
1962	12	28	336	58	5	07
1962	12	29	337	00	5	07
1962	12	30	337	02	5	06
1962	12	31	337	05	5	06
1963	01	01	337	07	5	06
1963	01	02	337	10	5	06
1963	01	03	337	12	5	05
1963	01	04	337	15	5	05
1963	01	05	337	17	5	05
1963	01	06	337	20	5	04
1963	01	07	337	23	5	04
1963	01	08	337	25	5	04
1963	01	09	337	28	5	04
1963	01	10	337	31	5	03
1963	01	11	337	34	5	03
1963	01	12	337	37	5	03
1963	01	13	337	40	5	03
1963	01	14	337	43	5	02
1963	01	15	337	46	5	02
1963	01	16	337	49	5	02
1963	01	17	337	52	5	02
1963	01	18	337	55	5	01
1963	01	19	337	58	5	01
1963	01	20	338	01	5	01
1963	01	21	338	05	5	01
1963	01	22	338	08	5	00
1963	01	23	338	11	5	00
1963	01	24	338	14	5	00
1963	01	25	338	18	5	00
1963	01	26	338	21	5	00
1963	01	27	338	24	4	59
1963	01	28	338	28	4	59
1963	01	29	338	31	4	59
1963	01	30	338	35	4	59
1963	01	31	338	38	4	59
1963	02	01	338	42	4	58
1963	02	02	338	45	4	58
1963	02	03	338	49	4	58
1963	02	04	338	52	4	58
1963	02	05	338	56	4	58
1963	02	06	339	00	4	58
1963	02	07	339	03	4	57
1963	02	08	339	07	4	57
1963	02	09	339	11	4	57
1963	02	10	339	14	4	57
1963	02	11	339	18	4	57
1963	02	12	339	22	4	57
1963	02	13	339	26	4	57
1963	02	14	339	29	4	56
1963	02	15	339	33	4	56
1963	02	16	339	37	4	56
1963	02	17	339	41	4	56
1963	02	18	339	44	4	56
1963	02	19	339	48	4	56
1963	02	20	339	52	4	56
1963	02	21	339	56	4	56
1963	02	22	340	00	4	56
1963	02	23	340	03	4	55
1963	02	24	340	07	4	55
1963	02	25	340	11	4	55
1963	02	26	340	15	4	55
1963	02	27	340	19	4	55
1963	02	28	340	23	4	55
1963	03	01	340	27	4	55
1963	03	02	340	30	4	55
1963	03	03	340	34	4	55
1963	03	04	340	38	4	55
1963	03	05	340	42	4	55
1963	03	06	340	46	4	55
1963	03	07	340	50	4	55
1963	03	08	340	53	4	55
1963	03	09	340	57	4	55
1963	03	10	341	01	4	55
1963	03	11	341	05	4	55
1963	03	12	341	09	4	55
1963	03	13	341	12	4	55
1963	03	14	341	16	4	55
1963	03	15	341	20	4	55
1963	03	16	341	24	4	55
1963	03	17	341	28	4	55
1963	03	18	341	31	4	55
1963	03	19	341	35	4	55
1963	03	20	341	39	4	55
1963	03	21	341	42	4	55
1963	03	22	341	46	4	55
1963	03	23	341	50	4	55
1963	03	24	341	53	4	55
1963	03	25	341	57	4	55
1963	03	26	342	01	4	55
1963	03	27	342	04	4	55
1963	03	28	342	08	4	55
1963	03	29	342	11	4	55
1963	03	30	342	15	4	55
1963	03	31	342	18	4	55
1963	04	01	342	22	4	55

Chiron

1963 04 02	342 25	4 55
1963 04 03	342 29	4 56
1963 04 04	342 32	4 56
1963 04 05	342 36	4 56
1963 04 06	342 39	4 56
1963 04 07	342 42	4 56
1963 04 08	342 46	4 56
1963 04 09	342 49	4 56
1963 04 10	342 52	4 56
1963 04 11	342 55	4 56
1963 04 12	342 59	4 56
1963 04 13	343 02	4 57
1963 04 14	343 05	4 57
1963 04 15	343 08	4 57
1963 04 16	343 11	4 57
1963 04 17	343 14	4 57
1963 04 18	343 17	4 57
1963 04 19	343 20	4 57
1963 04 20	343 23	4 58
1963 04 21	343 26	4 58
1963 04 22	343 29	4 58
1963 04 23	343 32	4 58
1963 04 24	343 34	4 58
1963 04 25	343 37	4 58
1963 04 26	343 40	4 58
1963 04 27	343 42	4 59
1963 04 28	343 45	4 59
1963 04 29	343 48	4 59
1963 04 30	343 50	4 59
1963 05 01	343 53	4 59
1963 05 02	343 55	4 59
1963 05 03	343 58	5 00
1963 05 04	344 00	5 00
1963 05 05	344 02	5 00
1963 05 06	344 05	5 00
1963 05 07	344 07	5 00
1963 05 08	344 09	5 01
1963 05 09	344 11	5 01
1963 05 10	344 13	5 01
1963 05 11	344 15	5 01
1963 05 12	344 17	5 01
1963 05 13	344 19	5 02
1963 05 14	344 21	5 02
1963 05 15	344 23	5 02
1963 05 16	344 25	5 02
1963 05 17	344 27	5 02
1963 05 18	344 28	5 03
1963 05 19	344 30	5 03
1963 05 20	344 32	5 03
1963 05 21	344 33	5 03
1963 05 22	344 35	5 04
1963 05 23	344 36	5 04
1963 05 24	344 37	5 04
1963 05 25	344 39	5 04
1963 05 26	344 40	5 04
1963 05 27	344 41	5 05
1963 05 28	344 43	5 05
1963 05 29	344 44	5 05
1963 05 30	344 45	5 05
1963 05 31	344 46	5 06
1963 06 01	344 47	5 06
1963 06 02	344 48	5 06
1963 06 03	344 49	5 06
1963 06 04	344 49	5 07
1963 06 05	344 50	5 07
1963 06 06	344 51	5 07
1963 06 07	344 52	5 07
1963 06 08	344 52	5 07
1963 06 09	344 53	5 08
1963 06 10	344 53	5 08
1963 06 11	344 54	5 08
1963 06 12	344 54	5 08
1963 06 13	344 54	5 09
1963 06 14	344 55	5 09
1963 06 15	344 55	5 09
1963 06 16	344 55	5 09
1963 06 17	344 55	5 10
1963 06 18	344 55	5 10
1963 06 19	344 55	5 10
1963 06 20	344 55	5 10
1963 06 21	344 55	5 11
1963 06 22	344 55	5 11
1963 06 23	344 55	5 11
1963 06 24	344 54	5 11
1963 06 25	344 54	5 12
1963 06 26	344 53	5 12
1963 06 27	344 53	5 12
1963 06 28	344 53	5 12
1963 06 29	344 52	5 12
1963 06 30	344 51	5 13
1963 07 01	344 51	5 13
1963 07 02	344 50	5 13
1963 07 03	344 49	5 13
1963 07 04	344 48	5 14
1963 07 05	344 47	5 14
1963 07 06	344 47	5 14
1963 07 07	344 46	5 14
1963 07 08	344 45	5 14
1963 07 09	344 43	5 15
1963 07 10	344 42	5 15
1963 07 11	344 41	5 15
1963 07 12	344 40	5 15
1963 07 13	344 39	5 15
1963 07 14	344 37	5 16
1963 07 15	344 36	5 16
1963 07 16	344 34	5 16
1963 07 17	344 33	5 16
1963 07 18	344 31	5 16
1963 07 19	344 30	5 17
1963 07 20	344 28	5 17
1963 07 21	344 27	5 17
1963 07 22	344 25	5 17
1963 07 23	344 23	5 17
1963 07 24	344 21	5 17
1963 07 25	344 19	5 18
1963 07 26	344 18	5 18
1963 07 27	344 16	5 18
1963 07 28	344 14	5 18
1963 07 29	344 12	5 18
1963 07 30	344 10	5 18
1963 07 31	344 08	5 18
1963 08 01	344 05	5 19
1963 08 02	344 03	5 19
1963 08 03	344 01	5 19
1963 08 04	343 59	5 19
1963 08 05	343 57	5 19
1963 08 06	343 54	5 19
1963 08 07	343 52	5 19
1963 08 08	343 50	5 19
1963 08 09	343 47	5 19
1963 08 10	343 45	5 19
1963 08 11	343 42	5 20
1963 08 12	343 40	5 20
1963 08 13	343 37	5 20
1963 08 14	343 35	5 20
1963 08 15	343 32	5 20
1963 08 16	343 30	5 20
1963 08 17	343 27	5 20
1963 08 18	343 24	5 20
1963 08 19	343 22	5 20
1963 08 20	343 19	5 20
1963 08 21	343 16	5 20
1963 08 22	343 14	5 20
1963 08 23	343 11	5 20
1963 08 24	343 08	5 20
1963 08 25	343 05	5 20
1963 08 26	343 03	5 20
1963 08 27	343 00	5 20
1963 08 28	342 57	5 20
1963 08 29	342 54	5 20
1963 08 30	342 52	5 20
1963 08 31	342 49	5 20
1963 09 01	342 46	5 20
1963 09 02	342 43	5 20
1963 09 03	342 40	5 20
1963 09 04	342 37	5 20
1963 09 05	342 35	5 20
1963 09 06	342 32	5 20
1963 09 07	342 29	5 20
1963 09 08	342 26	5 20
1963 09 09	342 23	5 20
1963 09 10	342 20	5 20
1963 09 11	342 18	5 19
1963 09 12	342 15	5 19
1963 09 13	342 12	5 19
1963 09 14	342 09	5 19
1963 09 15	342 06	5 19
1963 09 16	342 04	5 19
1963 09 17	342 01	5 19
1963 09 18	341 58	5 19
1963 09 19	341 55	5 19
1963 09 20	341 53	5 18
1963 09 21	341 50	5 18
1963 09 22	341 47	5 18
1963 09 23	341 45	5 18
1963 09 24	341 42	5 18
1963 09 25	341 39	5 18
1963 09 26	341 37	5 17
1963 09 27	341 34	5 17
1963 09 28	341 32	5 17
1963 09 29	341 29	5 17
1963 09 30	341 27	5 17
1963 10 01	341 24	5 16
1963 10 02	341 22	5 16
1963 10 03	341 19	5 16
1963 10 04	341 17	5 16
1963 10 05	341 15	5 16
1963 10 06	341 12	5 15
1963 10 07	341 10	5 15
1963 10 08	341 08	5 15
1963 10 09	341 06	5 15
1963 10 10	341 03	5 14
1963 10 11	341 01	5 14
1963 10 12	340 59	5 14
1963 10 13	340 57	5 14
1963 10 14	340 55	5 13
1963 10 15	340 53	5 13
1963 10 16	340 51	5 13
1963 10 17	340 49	5 13
1963 10 18	340 47	5 12
1963 10 19	340 45	5 12
1963 10 20	340 44	5 12
1963 10 21	340 42	5 12
1963 10 22	340 40	5 11
1963 10 23	340 39	5 11
1963 10 24	340 37	5 11
1963 10 25	340 36	5 10
1963 10 26	340 34	5 10
1963 10 27	340 33	5 10
1963 10 28	340 31	5 10
1963 10 29	340 30	5 09
1963 10 30	340 29	5 09
1963 10 31	340 27	5 09
1963 11 01	340 26	5 08
1963 11 02	340 25	5 08
1963 11 03	340 24	5 08
1963 11 04	340 23	5 07
1963 11 05	340 22	5 07
1963 11 06	340 21	5 07
1963 11 07	340 20	5 06
1963 11 08	340 19	5 06
1963 11 09	340 19	5 06
1963 11 10	340 18	5 05
1963 11 11	340 17	5 05
1963 11 12	340 17	5 05
1963 11 13	340 16	5 04
1963 11 14	340 16	5 04
1963 11 15	340 15	5 04
1963 11 16	340 15	5 03
1963 11 17	340 15	5 03
1963 11 18	340 15	5 03
1963 11 19	340 14	5 02
1963 11 20	340 14	5 02
1963 11 21	340 14	5 02
1963 11 22	340 14	5 01
1963 11 23	340 14	5 01
1963 11 24	340 14	5 01
1963 11 25	340 15	5 00
1963 11 26	340 15	5 00
1963 11 27	340 15	5 00
1963 11 28	340 15	4 59
1963 11 29	340 16	4 59
1963 11 30	340 16	4 59
1963 12 01	340 17	4 58
1963 12 02	340 17	4 58
1963 12 03	340 18	4 57
1963 12 04	340 19	4 57
1963 12 05	340 19	4 57
1963 12 06	340 20	4 56
1963 12 07	340 21	4 56
1963 12 08	340 22	4 56
1963 12 09	340 23	4 55
1963 12 10	340 24	4 55
1963 12 11	340 25	4 55
1963 12 12	340 26	4 54
1963 12 13	340 28	4 54
1963 12 14	340 29	4 54
1963 12 15	340 30	4 53
1963 12 16	340 31	4 53
1963 12 17	340 33	4 53
1963 12 18	340 34	4 52
1963 12 19	340 36	4 52
1963 12 20	340 38	4 52
1963 12 21	340 39	4 52
1963 12 22	340 41	4 51
1963 12 23	340 43	4 51
1963 12 24	340 44	4 51
1963 12 25	340 46	4 50
1963 12 26	340 48	4 50
1963 12 27	340 50	4 50
1963 12 28	340 52	4 49
1963 12 29	340 54	4 49
1963 12 30	340 56	4 49
1963 12 31	340 58	4 48
1964 01 01	341 01	4 48
1964 01 02	341 03	4 48
1964 01 03	341 05	4 48
1964 01 04	341 07	4 47
1964 01 05	341 10	4 47
1964 01 06	341 12	4 47
1964 01 07	341 15	4 46
1964 01 08	341 17	4 46
1964 01 09	341 20	4 46
1964 01 10	341 22	4 46
1964 01 11	341 25	4 45
1964 01 12	341 28	4 45
1964 01 13	341 30	4 45
1964 01 14	341 33	4 45
1964 01 15	341 36	4 44
1964 01 16	341 39	4 44
1964 01 17	341 41	4 44
1964 01 18	341 44	4 44
1964 01 19	341 47	4 43
1964 01 20	341 50	4 43
1964 01 21	341 53	4 43
1964 01 22	341 56	4 43
1964 01 23	341 59	4 42
1964 01 24	342 03	4 42
1964 01 25	342 06	4 42
1964 01 26	342 09	4 42
1964 01 27	342 12	4 42
1964 01 28	342 15	4 41
1964 01 29	342 18	4 41
1964 01 30	342 22	4 41
1964 01 31	342 25	4 41
1964 02 01	342 28	4 41
1964 02 02	342 32	4 40
1964 02 03	342 35	4 40
1964 02 04	342 39	4 40
1964 02 05	342 42	4 40
1964 02 06	342 45	4 40
1964 02 07	342 49	4 40
1964 02 08	342 52	4 39
1964 02 09	342 56	4 39
1964 02 10	343 00	4 39
1964 02 11	343 03	4 39
1964 02 12	343 07	4 39
1964 02 13	343 10	4 39
1964 02 14	343 14	4 39
1964 02 15	343 17	4 38
1964 02 16	343 21	4 38
1964 02 17	343 25	4 38
1964 02 18	343 28	4 38
1964 02 19	343 32	4 38
1964 02 20	343 36	4 38
1964 02 21	343 40	4 38
1964 02 22	343 43	4 38
1964 02 23	343 47	4 37
1964 02 24	343 51	4 37
1964 02 25	343 54	4 37
1964 02 26	343 58	4 37
1964 02 27	344 02	4 37
1964 02 28	344 06	4 37
1964 02 29	344 09	4 37
1964 03 01	344 13	4 37
1964 03 02	344 17	4 37
1964 03 03	344 21	4 37
1964 03 04	344 24	4 37
1964 03 05	344 28	4 37
1964 03 06	344 32	4 37
1964 03 07	344 36	4 37
1964 03 08	344 40	4 36
1964 03 09	344 43	4 36
1964 03 10	344 47	4 36
1964 03 11	344 51	4 36
1964 03 12	344 55	4 36
1964 03 13	344 58	4 36
1964 03 14	345 02	4 36
1964 03 15	345 06	4 36
1964 03 16	345 09	4 36
1964 03 17	345 13	4 36
1964 03 18	345 17	4 36
1964 03 19	345 21	4 36
1964 03 20	345 24	4 36
1964 03 21	345 28	4 36
1964 03 22	345 32	4 36
1964 03 23	345 35	4 36
1964 03 24	345 39	4 36
1964 03 25	345 42	4 36
1964 03 26	345 46	4 36
1964 03 27	345 50	4 36
1964 03 28	345 53	4 36
1964 03 29	345 57	4 36
1964 03 30	346 00	4 36
1964 03 31	346 04	4 37
1964 04 01	346 07	4 37
1964 04 02	346 11	4 37
1964 04 03	346 14	4 37
1964 04 04	346 18	4 37
1964 04 05	346 21	4 37
1964 04 06	346 24	4 37
1964 04 07	346 28	4 37
1964 04 08	346 31	4 37
1964 04 09	346 34	4 37
1964 04 10	346 38	4 37
1964 04 11	346 41	4 37
1964 04 12	346 44	4 37
1964 04 13	346 47	4 37
1964 04 14	346 50	4 38
1964 04 15	346 54	4 38
1964 04 16	346 57	4 38
1964 04 17	347 00	4 38
1964 04 18	347 03	4 38
1964 04 19	347 06	4 38
1964 04 20	347 09	4 38
1964 04 21	347 12	4 38
1964 04 22	347 15	4 38
1964 04 23	347 18	4 39
1964 04 24	347 20	4 39
1964 04 25	347 23	4 39
1964 04 26	347 26	4 39
1964 04 27	347 29	4 39
1964 04 28	347 31	4 39
1964 04 29	347 34	4 39
1964 04 30	347 37	4 40
1964 05 01	347 39	4 40
1964 05 02	347 42	4 40
1964 05 03	347 44	4 40
1964 05 04	347 47	4 40
1964 05 05	347 49	4 40
1964 05 06	347 51	4 40
1964 05 07	347 54	4 41
1964 05 08	347 56	4 41
1964 05 09	347 58	4 41
1964 05 10	348 00	4 41
1964 05 11	348 03	4 41
1964 05 12	348 05	4 41
1964 05 13	348 07	4 42
1964 05 14	348 09	4 42
1964 05 15	348 11	4 42
1964 05 16	348 13	4 42
1964 05 17	348 15	4 42
1964 05 18	348 16	4 43
1964 05 19	348 18	4 43
1964 05 20	348 20	4 43
1964 05 21	348 22	4 43
1964 05 22	348 23	4 43
1964 05 23	348 25	4 43
1964 05 24	348 26	4 44

1964	05	25	348	28	4	44
1964	05	26	348	29	4	44
1964	05	27	348	31	4	44
1964	05	28	348	32	4	44
1964	05	29	348	33	4	45
1964	05	30	348	35	4	45
1964	05	31	348	36	4	45
1964	06	01	348	37	4	45
1964	06	02	348	38	4	46
1964	06	03	348	39	4	46
1964	06	04	348	40	4	46
1964	06	05	348	41	4	46
1964	06	06	348	42	4	46
1964	06	07	348	43	4	47
1964	06	08	348	43	4	47
1964	06	09	348	44	4	47
1964	06	10	348	45	4	47
1964	06	11	348	45	4	47
1964	06	12	348	46	4	48
1964	06	13	348	46	4	48
1964	06	14	348	47	4	48
1964	06	15	348	47	4	48
1964	06	16	348	47	4	48
1964	06	17	348	48	4	49
1964	06	18	348	48	4	49
1964	06	19	348	48	4	49
1964	06	20	348	48	4	49
1964	06	21	348	48	4	50
1964	06	22	348	48	4	50
1964	06	23	348	48	4	50
1964	06	24	348	48	4	50
1964	06	25	348	48	4	50
1964	06	26	348	48	4	51
1964	06	27	348	47	4	51
1964	06	28	348	47	4	51
1964	06	29	348	47	4	51
1964	06	30	348	46	4	51
1964	07	01	348	46	4	52
1964	07	02	348	45	4	52
1964	07	03	348	44	4	52
1964	07	04	348	44	4	52
1964	07	05	348	43	4	52
1964	07	06	348	42	4	53
1964	07	07	348	42	4	53
1964	07	08	348	41	4	53
1964	07	09	348	40	4	53
1964	07	10	348	39	4	53
1964	07	11	348	38	4	54
1964	07	12	348	37	4	54
1964	07	13	348	36	4	54
1964	07	14	348	34	4	54
1964	07	15	348	33	4	54
1964	07	16	348	32	4	54
1964	07	17	348	31	4	55
1964	07	18	348	29	4	55
1964	07	19	348	28	4	55
1964	07	20	348	26	4	55
1964	07	21	348	25	4	55
1964	07	22	348	23	4	55
1964	07	23	348	22	4	56
1964	07	24	348	20	4	56
1964	07	25	348	18	4	56
1964	07	26	348	17	4	56
1964	07	27	348	15	4	56
1964	07	28	348	13	4	56
1964	07	29	348	11	4	57
1964	07	30	348	09	4	57
1964	07	31	348	07	4	57
1964	08	01	348	05	4	57
1964	08	02	348	03	4	57
1964	08	03	348	01	4	57
1964	08	04	347	59	4	57
1964	08	05	347	57	4	57
1964	08	06	347	55	4	57
1964	08	07	347	53	4	58
1964	08	08	347	51	4	58
1964	08	09	347	48	4	58
1964	08	10	347	46	4	58
1964	08	11	347	44	4	58
1964	08	12	347	41	4	58
1964	08	13	347	39	4	58
1964	08	14	347	37	4	58
1964	08	15	347	34	4	58
1964	08	16	347	32	4	58
1964	08	17	347	29	4	58
1964	08	18	347	27	4	58
1964	08	19	347	24	4	58
1964	08	20	347	22	4	58
1964	08	21	347	19	4	59
1964	08	22	347	16	4	59
1964	08	23	347	14	4	59
1964	08	24	347	11	4	59
1964	08	25	347	08	4	59
1964	08	26	347	06	4	59
1964	08	27	347	03	4	59
1964	08	28	347	00	4	59
1964	08	29	346	58	4	59
1964	08	30	346	55	4	59
1964	08	31	346	52	4	59
1964	09	01	346	49	4	59
1964	09	02	346	47	4	59
1964	09	03	346	44	4	59
1964	09	04	346	41	4	59
1964	09	05	346	38	4	58
1964	09	06	346	35	4	58
1964	09	07	346	33	4	58
1964	09	08	346	30	4	58
1964	09	09	346	27	4	58
1964	09	10	346	24	4	58
1964	09	11	346	21	4	58
1964	09	12	346	19	4	58
1964	09	13	346	16	4	58
1964	09	14	346	13	4	58
1964	09	15	346	10	4	58
1964	09	16	346	08	4	58
1964	09	17	346	05	4	58
1964	09	18	346	02	4	57
1964	09	19	345	59	4	57
1964	09	20	345	57	4	57
1964	09	21	345	54	4	57
1964	09	22	345	51	4	57
1964	09	23	345	48	4	57
1964	09	24	345	46	4	57
1964	09	25	345	43	4	57
1964	09	26	345	40	4	56
1964	09	27	345	38	4	56
1964	09	28	345	35	4	56
1964	09	29	345	33	4	56
1964	09	30	345	30	4	56
1964	10	01	345	28	4	56
1964	10	02	345	25	4	55
1964	10	03	345	23	4	55
1964	10	04	345	20	4	55
1964	10	05	345	18	4	55
1964	10	06	345	15	4	55
1964	10	07	345	13	4	54
1964	10	08	345	11	4	54
1964	10	09	345	08	4	54
1964	10	10	345	06	4	54
1964	10	11	345	04	4	54
1964	10	12	345	02	4	53
1964	10	13	344	59	4	53
1964	10	14	344	57	4	53
1964	10	15	344	55	4	53
1964	10	16	344	53	4	52
1964	10	17	344	51	4	52
1964	10	18	344	49	4	52
1964	10	19	344	47	4	52
1964	10	20	344	45	4	52
1964	10	21	344	43	4	51
1964	10	22	344	42	4	51
1964	10	23	344	40	4	51
1964	10	24	344	38	4	50
1964	10	25	344	37	4	50
1964	10	26	344	35	4	50
1964	10	27	344	33	4	50
1964	10	28	344	32	4	49
1964	10	29	344	30	4	49
1964	10	30	344	29	4	49
1964	10	31	344	27	4	49
1964	11	01	344	26	4	48
1964	11	02	344	25	4	48
1964	11	03	344	24	4	48
1964	11	04	344	22	4	47
1964	11	05	344	21	4	47
1964	11	06	344	20	4	47
1964	11	07	344	19	4	46
1964	11	08	344	18	4	46
1964	11	09	344	17	4	46
1964	11	10	344	16	4	46
1964	11	11	344	16	4	45
1964	11	12	344	15	4	45
1964	11	13	344	14	4	45
1964	11	14	344	13	4	44
1964	11	15	344	13	4	44
1964	11	16	344	12	4	44
1964	11	17	344	12	4	43
1964	11	18	344	11	4	43
1964	11	19	344	11	4	43
1964	11	20	344	11	4	42
1964	11	21	344	11	4	42
1964	11	22	344	10	4	42
1964	11	23	344	10	4	41
1964	11	24	344	10	4	41
1964	11	25	344	10	4	41
1964	11	26	344	10	4	40
1964	11	27	344	10	4	40
1964	11	28	344	10	4	40
1964	11	29	344	11	4	40
1964	11	30	344	11	4	39
1964	12	01	344	11	4	39
1964	12	02	344	12	4	39
1964	12	03	344	12	4	38
1964	12	04	344	12	4	38
1964	12	05	344	13	4	38
1964	12	06	344	14	4	37
1964	12	07	344	14	4	37
1964	12	08	344	15	4	37
1964	12	09	344	16	4	36
1964	12	10	344	17	4	36
1964	12	11	344	17	4	36
1964	12	12	344	18	4	35
1964	12	13	344	19	4	35
1964	12	14	344	20	4	35
1964	12	15	344	22	4	34
1964	12	16	344	23	4	34
1964	12	17	344	24	4	34
1964	12	18	344	25	4	33
1964	12	19	344	27	4	33
1964	12	20	344	28	4	33
1964	12	21	344	29	4	33
1964	12	22	344	31	4	32
1964	12	23	344	32	4	32
1964	12	24	344	34	4	32
1964	12	25	344	36	4	31
1964	12	26	344	37	4	31
1964	12	27	344	39	4	31
1964	12	28	344	41	4	30
1964	12	29	344	43	4	30
1964	12	30	344	45	4	30
1964	12	31	344	47	4	30
1965	01	01	344	49	4	29
1965	01	02	344	51	4	29
1965	01	03	344	53	4	29
1965	01	04	344	55	4	28
1965	01	05	344	57	4	28
1965	01	06	344	59	4	28
1965	01	07	345	02	4	28
1965	01	08	345	04	4	27
1965	01	09	345	06	4	27
1965	01	10	345	09	4	27
1965	01	11	345	11	4	27
1965	01	12	345	14	4	26
1965	01	13	345	16	4	26
1965	01	14	345	19	4	26
1965	01	15	345	21	4	26
1965	01	16	345	24	4	25
1965	01	17	345	27	4	25
1965	01	18	345	29	4	25
1965	01	19	345	32	4	25
1965	01	20	345	35	4	24
1965	01	21	345	38	4	24
1965	01	22	345	41	4	24
1965	01	23	345	44	4	24
1965	01	24	345	47	4	24
1965	01	25	345	49	4	23
1965	01	26	345	52	4	23
1965	01	27	345	56	4	23
1965	01	28	345	59	4	23
1965	01	29	346	02	4	23
1965	01	30	346	05	4	22
1965	01	31	346	08	4	22
1965	02	01	346	11	4	22
1965	02	02	346	14	4	22
1965	02	03	346	18	4	22
1965	02	04	346	21	4	21
1965	02	05	346	24	4	21
1965	02	06	346	28	4	21
1965	02	07	346	31	4	21
1965	02	08	346	34	4	21
1965	02	09	346	38	4	21
1965	02	10	346	41	4	20
1965	02	11	346	45	4	20
1965	02	12	346	48	4	20
1965	02	13	346	51	4	20
1965	02	14	346	55	4	20
1965	02	15	346	58	4	20
1965	02	16	347	02	4	20
1965	02	17	347	06	4	19
1965	02	18	347	09	4	19
1965	02	19	347	13	4	19
1965	02	20	347	16	4	19
1965	02	21	347	20	4	19
1965	02	22	347	23	4	19
1965	02	23	347	27	4	19
1965	02	24	347	31	4	19
1965	02	25	347	34	4	18
1965	02	26	347	38	4	18
1965	02	27	347	42	4	18
1965	02	28	347	45	4	18
1965	03	01	347	49	4	18
1965	03	02	347	53	4	18
1965	03	03	347	56	4	18
1965	03	04	348	00	4	18
1965	03	05	348	04	4	18
1965	03	06	348	07	4	18
1965	03	07	348	11	4	18
1965	03	08	348	15	4	18
1965	03	09	348	19	4	17
1965	03	10	348	22	4	17
1965	03	11	348	26	4	17
1965	03	12	348	30	4	17
1965	03	13	348	33	4	17
1965	03	14	348	37	4	17
1965	03	15	348	41	4	17
1965	03	16	348	44	4	17
1965	03	17	348	48	4	17
1965	03	18	348	52	4	17
1965	03	19	348	55	4	17
1965	03	20	348	59	4	17
1965	03	21	349	03	4	17
1965	03	22	349	06	4	17
1965	03	23	349	10	4	17
1965	03	24	349	14	4	17
1965	03	25	349	17	4	17
1965	03	26	349	21	4	17
1965	03	27	349	24	4	17
1965	03	28	349	28	4	17
1965	03	29	349	31	4	17
1965	03	30	349	35	4	17
1965	03	31	349	39	4	17
1965	04	01	349	42	4	17
1965	04	02	349	46	4	17
1965	04	03	349	49	4	17
1965	04	04	349	52	4	17
1965	04	05	349	56	4	17
1965	04	06	349	59	4	17
1965	04	07	350	03	4	17
1965	04	08	350	06	4	17
1965	04	09	350	09	4	17
1965	04	10	350	13	4	18
1965	04	11	350	16	4	18
1965	04	12	350	19	4	18
1965	04	13	350	23	4	18
1965	04	14	350	26	4	18
1965	04	15	350	29	4	18
1965	04	16	350	32	4	18
1965	04	17	350	35	4	18
1965	04	18	350	38	4	18
1965	04	19	350	41	4	18
1965	04	20	350	44	4	18
1965	04	21	350	47	4	18
1965	04	22	350	50	4	18
1965	04	23	350	53	4	19
1965	04	24	350	56	4	19
1965	04	25	350	59	4	19
1965	04	26	351	02	4	19
1965	04	27	351	05	4	19
1965	04	28	351	08	4	19
1965	04	29	351	10	4	19
1965	04	30	351	13	4	19
1965	05	01	351	16	4	19
1965	05	02	351	19	4	20
1965	05	03	351	21	4	20
1965	05	04	351	24	4	20
1965	05	05	351	26	4	20
1965	05	06	351	29	4	20
1965	05	07	351	31	4	20
1965	05	08	351	34	4	20
1965	05	09	351	36	4	20
1965	05	10	351	38	4	21
1965	05	11	351	41	4	21
1965	05	12	351	43	4	21
1965	05	13	351	45	4	21
1965	05	14	351	47	4	21
1965	05	15	351	49	4	21
1965	05	16	351	51	4	21
1965	05	17	351	53	4	22
1965	05	18	351	55	4	22
1965	05	19	351	57	4	22
1965	05	20	351	59	4	22
1965	05	21	352	01	4	22
1965	05	22	352	03	4	22
1965	05	23	352	05	4	23
1965	05	24	352	06	4	23
1965	05	25	352	08	4	23
1965	05	26	352	10	4	23
1965	05	27	352	11	4	23
1965	05	28	352	13	4	23
1965	05	29	352	14	4	24
1965	05	30	352	16	4	24
1965	05	31	352	17	4	24
1965	06	01	352	18	4	24
1965	06	02	352	19	4	24
1965	06	03	352	21	4	24
1965	06	04	352	22	4	25
1965	06	05	352	23	4	25
1965	06	06	352	24	4	25
1965	06	07	352	25	4	25
1965	06	08	352	26	4	25
1965	06	09	352	27	4	26
1965	06	10	352	28	4	26
1965	06	11	352	29	4	26
1965	06	12	352	29	4	26
1965	06	13	352	30	4	26
1965	06	14	352	31	4	27
1965	06	15	352	31	4	27
1965	06	16	352	32	4	27
1965	06	17	352	32	4	27
1965	06	18	352	33	4	27
1965	06	19	352	33	4	28
1965	06	20	352	33	4	28
1965	06	21	352	34	4	28
1965	06	22	352	34	4	28
1965	06	23	352	34	4	28
1965	06	24	352	34	4	28
1965	06	25	352	34	4	29
1965	06	26	352	34	4	29
1965	06	27	352	34	4	29
1965	06	28	352	34	4	29
1965	06	29	352	34	4	29
1965	06	30	352	33	4	30
1965	07	01	352	33	4	30
1965	07	02	352	33	4	30
1965	07	03	352	32	4	30
1965	07	04	352	32	4	30
1965	07	05	352	32	4	30
1965	07	06	352	31	4	31
1965	07	07	352	30	4	31
1965	07	08	352	30	4	31
1965	07	09	352	29	4	31
1965	07	10	352	28	4	31
1965	07	11	352	28	4	32
1965	07	12	352	27	4	32
1965	07	13	352	26	4	32
1965	07	14	352	25	4	32
1965	07	15	352	24	4	32
1965	07	16	352	23	4	32
1965	07	17	352	22	4	33
1965	07	18	352	21	4	33
1965	07	19	352	19	4	33

Chiron

1965	07	20	352	18	4	33
1965	07	21	352	17	4	33
1965	07	22	352	15	4	33
1965	07	23	352	14	4	33
1965	07	24	352	13	4	34
1965	07	25	352	11	4	34
1965	07	26	352	10	4	34
1965	07	27	352	08	4	34
1965	07	28	352	06	4	34
1965	07	29	352	05	4	34
1965	07	30	352	03	4	34
1965	07	31	352	01	4	35
1965	08	01	351	59	4	35
1965	08	02	351	58	4	35
1965	08	03	351	56	4	35
1965	08	04	351	54	4	35
1965	08	05	351	52	4	35
1965	08	06	351	50	4	35
1965	08	07	351	48	4	35
1965	08	08	351	46	4	35
1965	08	09	351	44	4	36
1965	08	10	351	42	4	36
1965	08	11	351	39	4	36
1965	08	12	351	37	4	36
1965	08	13	351	35	4	36
1965	08	14	351	33	4	36
1965	08	15	351	30	4	36
1965	08	16	351	28	4	36
1965	08	17	351	26	4	36
1965	08	18	351	23	4	36
1965	08	19	351	21	4	36
1965	08	20	351	18	4	36
1965	08	21	351	16	4	36
1965	08	22	351	14	4	36
1965	08	23	351	11	4	36
1965	08	24	351	08	4	36
1965	08	25	351	06	4	36
1965	08	26	351	03	4	36
1965	08	27	351	01	4	37
1965	08	28	350	58	4	37
1965	08	29	350	55	4	37
1965	08	30	350	53	4	37
1965	08	31	350	50	4	37
1965	09	01	350	47	4	37
1965	09	02	350	45	4	37
1965	09	03	350	42	4	37
1965	09	04	350	39	4	36
1965	09	05	350	37	4	36
1965	09	06	350	34	4	36
1965	09	07	350	31	4	36
1965	09	08	350	28	4	36
1965	09	09	350	26	4	36
1965	09	10	350	23	4	36
1965	09	11	350	20	4	36
1965	09	12	350	17	4	36
1965	09	13	350	15	4	36
1965	09	14	350	12	4	36
1965	09	15	350	09	4	36
1965	09	16	350	06	4	36
1965	09	17	350	03	4	36
1965	09	18	350	01	4	36
1965	09	19	349	58	4	36
1965	09	20	349	55	4	36
1965	09	21	349	52	4	35
1965	09	22	349	50	4	35
1965	09	23	349	47	4	35
1965	09	24	349	44	4	35
1965	09	25	349	42	4	35
1965	09	26	349	39	4	35
1965	09	27	349	36	4	35
1965	09	28	349	34	4	35
1965	09	29	349	31	4	34
1965	09	30	349	28	4	34
1965	10	01	349	26	4	34
1965	10	02	349	23	4	34
1965	10	03	349	21	4	34
1965	10	04	349	18	4	34
1965	10	05	349	16	4	34
1965	10	06	349	13	4	33
1965	10	07	349	11	4	33
1965	10	08	349	08	4	33
1965	10	09	349	06	4	33
1965	10	10	349	03	4	33
1965	10	11	349	01	4	32
1965	10	12	348	59	4	32
1965	10	13	348	57	4	32
1965	10	14	348	54	4	32
1965	10	15	348	52	4	32
1965	10	16	348	50	4	31
1965	10	17	348	48	4	31
1965	10	18	348	46	4	31
1965	10	19	348	43	4	31
1965	10	20	348	41	4	31
1965	10	21	348	39	4	30
1965	10	22	348	37	4	30
1965	10	23	348	36	4	30
1965	10	24	348	34	4	30
1965	10	25	348	32	4	29
1965	10	26	348	30	4	29
1965	10	27	348	28	4	29
1965	10	28	348	27	4	29

1965	10	29	348	25	4	28
1965	10	30	348	23	4	28
1965	10	31	348	22	4	28
1965	11	01	348	20	4	28
1965	11	02	348	19	4	27
1965	11	03	348	17	4	27
1965	11	04	348	16	4	27
1965	11	05	348	15	4	27
1965	11	06	348	13	4	26
1965	11	07	348	12	4	26
1965	11	08	348	11	4	26
1965	11	09	348	10	4	26
1965	11	10	348	09	4	25
1965	11	11	348	08	4	25
1965	11	12	348	07	4	25
1965	11	13	348	06	4	24
1965	11	14	348	05	4	24
1965	11	15	348	04	4	24
1965	11	16	348	03	4	24
1965	11	17	348	03	4	23
1965	11	18	348	02	4	23
1965	11	19	348	01	4	23
1965	11	20	348	01	4	22
1965	11	21	348	00	4	22
1965	11	22	348	00	4	22
1965	11	23	347	59	4	21
1965	11	24	347	59	4	21
1965	11	25	347	59	4	21
1965	11	26	347	59	4	21
1965	11	27	347	59	4	20
1965	11	28	347	58	4	20
1965	11	29	347	58	4	20
1965	11	30	347	58	4	19
1965	12	01	347	58	4	19
1965	12	02	347	59	4	19
1965	12	03	347	59	4	18
1965	12	04	347	59	4	18
1965	12	05	347	59	4	18
1965	12	06	348	00	4	18
1965	12	07	348	00	4	17
1965	12	08	348	01	4	17
1965	12	09	348	01	4	17
1965	12	10	348	02	4	16
1965	12	11	348	02	4	16
1965	12	12	348	03	4	16
1965	12	13	348	04	4	15
1965	12	14	348	05	4	15
1965	12	15	348	05	4	15
1965	12	16	348	06	4	15
1965	12	17	348	07	4	14
1965	12	18	348	08	4	14
1965	12	19	348	10	4	14
1965	12	20	348	11	4	13
1965	12	21	348	12	4	13
1965	12	22	348	13	4	13
1965	12	23	348	14	4	13
1965	12	24	348	16	4	12
1965	12	25	348	17	4	12
1965	12	26	348	19	4	12
1965	12	27	348	20	4	11
1965	12	28	348	22	4	11
1965	12	29	348	23	4	11
1965	12	30	348	25	4	11
1965	12	31	348	27	4	10
1966	01	01	348	28	4	10
1966	01	02	348	30	4	10
1966	01	03	348	32	4	09
1966	01	04	348	34	4	09
1966	01	05	348	36	4	09
1966	01	06	348	38	4	09
1966	01	07	348	40	4	08
1966	01	08	348	42	4	08
1966	01	09	348	44	4	08
1966	01	10	348	46	4	08
1966	01	11	348	49	4	07
1966	01	12	348	51	4	07
1966	01	13	348	53	4	07
1966	01	14	348	56	4	07
1966	01	15	348	58	4	06
1966	01	16	349	01	4	06
1966	01	17	349	03	4	06
1966	01	18	349	06	4	06
1966	01	19	349	08	4	06
1966	01	20	349	11	4	05
1966	01	21	349	13	4	05
1966	01	22	349	16	4	05
1966	01	23	349	19	4	05
1966	01	24	349	22	4	04
1966	01	25	349	24	4	04
1966	01	26	349	27	4	04
1966	01	27	349	30	4	04
1966	01	28	349	33	4	04
1966	01	29	349	36	4	03
1966	01	30	349	39	4	03
1966	01	31	349	42	4	03
1966	02	01	349	45	4	03
1966	02	02	349	48	4	03
1966	02	03	349	51	4	02
1966	02	04	349	54	4	02
1966	02	05	349	57	4	02
1966	02	06	350	00	4	02
1966	02	07	350	04	4	02
1966	02	08	350	07	4	02
1966	02	09	350	10	4	01
1966	02	10	350	13	4	01
1966	02	11	350	17	4	01

1966	02	12	350	20	4	01
1966	02	13	350	23	4	01
1966	02	14	350	27	4	01
1966	02	15	350	30	4	00
1966	02	16	350	33	4	00
1966	02	17	350	37	4	00
1966	02	18	350	40	4	00
1966	02	19	350	44	4	00
1966	02	20	350	47	4	00
1966	02	21	350	51	4	00
1966	02	22	350	54	3	59
1966	02	23	350	58	3	59
1966	02	24	351	01	3	59
1966	02	25	351	05	3	59
1966	02	26	351	08	3	59
1966	02	27	351	12	3	59
1966	02	28	351	16	3	59
1966	03	01	351	19	3	59
1966	03	02	351	23	3	59
1966	03	03	351	26	3	58
1966	03	04	351	30	3	58
1966	03	05	351	34	3	58
1966	03	06	351	37	3	58
1966	03	07	351	41	3	58
1966	03	08	351	44	3	58
1966	03	09	351	48	3	58
1966	03	10	351	52	3	58
1966	03	11	351	55	3	58
1966	03	12	351	59	3	58
1966	03	13	352	03	3	58
1966	03	14	352	06	3	58
1966	03	15	352	10	3	58
1966	03	16	352	14	3	58
1966	03	17	352	17	3	58
1966	03	18	352	21	3	57
1966	03	19	352	24	3	57
1966	03	20	352	28	3	57
1966	03	21	352	32	3	57
1966	03	22	352	35	3	57
1966	03	23	352	39	3	57
1966	03	24	352	43	3	57
1966	03	25	352	46	3	57
1966	03	26	352	50	3	57
1966	03	27	352	53	3	57
1966	03	28	352	57	3	57
1966	03	29	353	00	3	57
1966	03	30	353	04	3	57
1966	03	31	353	07	3	57
1966	04	01	353	11	3	57
1966	04	02	353	15	3	57
1966	04	03	353	18	3	57
1966	04	04	353	21	3	57
1966	04	05	353	25	3	57
1966	04	06	353	28	3	57
1966	04	07	353	32	3	57
1966	04	08	353	35	3	57
1966	04	09	353	39	3	57
1966	04	10	353	42	3	57
1966	04	11	353	45	3	57
1966	04	12	353	49	3	57
1966	04	13	353	52	3	58
1966	04	14	353	55	3	58
1966	04	15	353	58	3	58
1966	04	16	354	02	3	58
1966	04	17	354	05	3	58
1966	04	18	354	08	3	58
1966	04	19	354	11	3	58
1966	04	20	354	14	3	58
1966	04	21	354	17	3	58
1966	04	22	354	20	3	58
1966	04	23	354	23	3	58
1966	04	24	354	26	3	58
1966	04	25	354	29	3	58
1966	04	26	354	32	3	58
1966	04	27	354	35	3	58
1966	04	28	354	38	3	58
1966	04	29	354	41	3	59
1966	04	30	354	44	3	59
1966	05	01	354	47	3	59
1966	05	02	354	49	3	59
1966	05	03	354	52	3	59
1966	05	04	354	55	3	59
1966	05	05	354	57	3	59
1966	05	06	355	00	3	59
1966	05	07	355	03	3	59
1966	05	08	355	05	3	59
1966	05	09	355	08	4	00
1966	05	10	355	10	4	00
1966	05	11	355	12	4	00
1966	05	12	355	15	4	00
1966	05	13	355	17	4	00
1966	05	14	355	19	4	00
1966	05	15	355	22	4	00
1966	05	16	355	24	4	00
1966	05	17	355	26	4	01
1966	05	18	355	28	4	01
1966	05	19	355	30	4	01
1966	05	20	355	32	4	01
1966	05	21	355	34	4	01
1966	05	22	355	36	4	01
1966	05	23	355	38	4	01
1966	05	24	355	40	4	01
1966	05	25	355	42	4	02
1966	05	26	355	44	4	02
1966	05	27	355	45	4	02
1966	05	28	355	47	4	02

1966	05	29	355	49	4	02
1966	05	30	355	50	4	02
1966	05	31	355	52	4	02
1966	06	01	355	53	4	03
1966	06	02	355	55	4	03
1966	06	03	355	56	4	03
1966	06	04	355	57	4	03
1966	06	05	355	59	4	03
1966	06	06	356	00	4	03
1966	06	07	356	01	4	04
1966	06	08	356	02	4	04
1966	06	09	356	03	4	04
1966	06	10	356	04	4	04
1966	06	11	356	05	4	04
1966	06	12	356	06	4	04
1966	06	13	356	07	4	05
1966	06	14	356	08	4	05
1966	06	15	356	09	4	05
1966	06	16	356	10	4	05
1966	06	17	356	10	4	05
1966	06	18	356	11	4	05
1966	06	19	356	11	4	06
1966	06	20	356	12	4	06
1966	06	21	356	12	4	06
1966	06	22	356	13	4	06
1966	06	23	356	13	4	06
1966	06	24	356	14	4	06
1966	06	25	356	14	4	07
1966	06	26	356	14	4	07
1966	06	27	356	14	4	07
1966	06	28	356	14	4	07
1966	06	29	356	14	4	07
1966	06	30	356	14	4	07
1966	07	01	356	14	4	08
1966	07	02	356	14	4	08
1966	07	03	356	14	4	08
1966	07	04	356	14	4	08
1966	07	05	356	13	4	08
1966	07	06	356	13	4	08
1966	07	07	356	13	4	08
1966	07	08	356	12	4	09
1966	07	09	356	12	4	09
1966	07	10	356	11	4	09
1966	07	11	356	11	4	09
1966	07	12	356	10	4	09
1966	07	13	356	09	4	09
1966	07	14	356	09	4	10
1966	07	15	356	08	4	10
1966	07	16	356	07	4	10
1966	07	17	356	06	4	10
1966	07	18	356	05	4	10
1966	07	19	356	04	4	10
1966	07	20	356	03	4	10
1966	07	21	356	02	4	11
1966	07	22	356	01	4	11
1966	07	23	356	00	4	11
1966	07	24	355	58	4	11
1966	07	25	355	57	4	11
1966	07	26	355	56	4	11
1966	07	27	355	54	4	11
1966	07	28	355	53	4	11
1966	07	29	355	51	4	12
1966	07	30	355	50.	4	12
1966	07	31	355	48	4	12
1966	08	01	355	47	4	12
1966	08	02	355	45	4	12
1966	08	03	355	43	4	12
1966	08	04	355	42	4	12
1966	08	05	355	40	4	12
1966	08	06	355	38	4	12
1966	08	07	355	36	4	13
1966	08	08	355	34	4	13
1966	08	09	355	32	4	13
1966	08	10	355	30	4	13
1966	08	11	355	28	4	13
1966	08	12	355	26	4	13
1966	08	13	355	24	4	13
1966	08	14	355	22	4	13
1966	08	15	355	20	4	13
1966	08	16	355	18	4	13
1966	08	17	355	16	4	13
1966	08	18	355	13	4	13
1966	08	19	355	11	4	14
1966	08	20	355	09	4	14
1966	08	21	355	06	4	14
1966	08	22	355	04	4	14
1966	08	23	355	02	4	14
1966	08	24	354	59	4	14
1966	08	25	354	57	4	14
1966	08	26	354	54	4	14
1966	08	27	354	52	4	14
1966	08	28	354	49	4	14
1966	08	29	354	47	4	14
1966	08	30	354	44	4	14
1966	08	31	354	42	4	14
1966	09	01	354	39	4	14
1966	09	02	354	36	4	14
1966	09	03	354	34	4	14
1966	09	04	354	31	4	14
1966	09	05	354	28	4	14
1966	09	06	354	26	4	14
1966	09	07	354	23	4	14
1966	09	08	354	20	4	14
1966	09	09	354	18	4	14
1966	09	10	354	15	4	14
1966	09	11	354	12	4	14

1966	09	12	354	10	4	14
1966	09	13	354	07	4	14
1966	09	14	354	04	4	14
1966	09	15	354	01	4	14
1966	09	16	353	59	4	13
1966	09	17	353	56	4	13
1966	09	18	353	53	4	13
1966	09	19	353	50	4	13
1966	09	20	353	48	4	13
1966	09	21	353	45	4	13
1966	09	22	353	42	4	13
1966	09	23	353	39	4	13
1966	09	24	353	37	4	13
1966	09	25	353	34	4	13
1966	09	26	353	31	4	13
1966	09	27	353	29	4	13
1966	09	28	353	26	4	12
1966	09	29	353	23	4	12
1966	09	30	353	20	4	12
1966	10	01	353	18	4	12
1966	10	02	353	15	4	12
1966	10	03	353	13	4	12
1966	10	04	353	10	4	12
1966	10	05	353	07	4	12
1966	10	06	353	05	4	11
1966	10	07	353	02	4	11
1966	10	08	353	00	4	11
1966	10	09	352	57	4	11
1966	10	10	352	55	4	11
1966	10	11	352	52	4	11
1966	10	12	352	50	4	10
1966	10	13	352	48	4	10
1966	10	14	352	45	4	10
1966	10	15	352	43	4	10
1966	10	16	352	41	4	10
1966	10	17	352	38	4	10
1966	10	18	352	36	4	09
1966	10	19	352	34	4	09
1966	10	20	352	32	4	09
1966	10	21	352	30	4	09
1966	10	22	352	27	4	09
1966	10	23	352	25	4	08
1966	10	24	352	23	4	08
1966	10	25	352	21	4	08
1966	10	26	352	19	4	08
1966	10	27	352	18	4	08
1966	10	28	352	16	4	07
1966	10	29	352	14	4	07
1966	10	30	352	12	4	07
1966	10	31	352	10	4	07
1966	11	01	352	09	4	06
1966	11	02	352	07	4	06
1966	11	03	352	05	4	06
1966	11	04	352	04	4	06
1966	11	05	352	02	4	05
1966	11	06	352	01	4	05
1966	11	07	351	59	4	05
1966	11	08	351	58	4	05
1966	11	09	351	57	4	04
1966	11	10	351	55	4	04
1966	11	11	351	54	4	04
1966	11	12	351	53	4	04
1966	11	13	351	52	4	03
1966	11	14	351	51	4	03
1966	11	15	351	50	4	03
1966	11	16	351	49	4	03
1966	11	17	351	48	4	02
1966	11	18	351	47	4	02
1966	11	19	351	46	4	02
1966	11	20	351	45	4	02
1966	11	21	351	45	4	01
1966	11	22	351	44	4	01
1966	11	23	351	43	4	01
1966	11	24	351	43	4	00
1966	11	25	351	42	4	00
1966	11	26	351	42	4	00
1966	11	27	351	42	4	00
1966	11	28	351	41	3	59
1966	11	29	351	41	3	59
1966	11	30	351	41	3	59
1966	12	01	351	41	3	59
1966	12	02	351	41	3	58
1966	12	03	351	41	3	58
1966	12	04	351	41	3	58
1966	12	05	351	41	3	57
1966	12	06	351	41	3	57
1966	12	07	351	41	3	57
1966	12	08	351	41	3	57
1966	12	09	351	41	3	56
1966	12	10	351	42	3	56
1966	12	11	351	42	3	56
1966	12	12	351	43	3	55
1966	12	13	351	43	3	55
1966	12	14	351	44	3	55
1966	12	15	351	44	3	55
1966	12	16	351	45	3	54
1966	12	17	351	46	3	54
1966	12	18	351	47	3	54
1966	12	19	351	47	3	54
1966	12	20	351	48	3	53
1966	12	21	351	49	3	53
1966	12	22	351	50	3	53
1966	12	23	351	51	3	52
1966	12	24	351	53	3	52
1966	12	25	351	54	3	52
1966	12	26	351	55	3	52
1966	12	27	351	56	3	51
1966	12	28	351	58	3	51
1966	12	29	351	59	3	51
1966	12	30	352	00	3	51
1966	12	31	352	02	3	50
1967	01	01	352	03	3	50
1967	01	02	352	05	3	50
1967	01	03	352	07	3	50
1967	01	04	352	08	3	49
1967	01	05	352	10	3	49
1967	01	06	352	12	3	49
1967	01	07	352	14	3	48
1967	01	08	352	16	3	48
1967	01	09	352	18	3	48
1967	01	10	352	20	3	48
1967	01	11	352	22	3	48
1967	01	12	352	24	3	47
1967	01	13	352	26	3	47
1967	01	14	352	28	3	47
1967	01	15	352	30	3	47
1967	01	16	352	32	3	46
1967	01	17	352	35	3	46
1967	01	18	352	37	3	46
1967	01	19	352	39	3	46
1967	01	20	352	42	3	45
1967	01	21	352	44	3	45
1967	01	22	352	47	3	45
1967	01	23	352	49	3	45
1967	01	24	352	52	3	45
1967	01	25	352	54	3	44
1967	01	26	352	57	3	44
1967	01	27	353	00	3	44
1967	01	28	353	03	3	44
1967	01	29	353	05	3	44
1967	01	30	353	08	3	43
1967	01	31	353	11	3	43
1967	02	01	353	14	3	43
1967	02	02	353	17	3	43
1967	02	03	353	20	3	43
1967	02	04	353	23	3	42
1967	02	05	353	26	3	42
1967	02	06	353	29	3	42
1967	02	07	353	32	3	42
1967	02	08	353	35	3	42
1967	02	09	353	38	3	42
1967	02	10	353	41	3	41
1967	02	11	353	44	3	41
1967	02	12	353	47	3	41
1967	02	13	353	50	3	41
1967	02	14	353	54	3	41
1967	02	15	353	57	3	41
1967	02	16	354	00	3	40
1967	02	17	354	04	3	40
1967	02	18	354	07	3	40
1967	02	19	354	10	3	40
1967	02	20	354	14	3	40
1967	02	21	354	17	3	40
1967	02	22	354	20	3	40
1967	02	23	354	24	3	39
1967	02	24	354	27	3	39
1967	02	25	354	31	3	39
1967	02	26	354	34	3	39
1967	02	27	354	38	3	39
1967	02	28	354	41	3	39
1967	03	01	354	45	3	39
1967	03	02	354	48	3	39
1967	03	03	354	52	3	39
1967	03	04	354	55	3	38
1967	03	05	354	59	3	38
1967	03	06	355	02	3	38
1967	03	07	355	06	3	38
1967	03	08	355	09	3	38
1967	03	09	355	13	3	38
1967	03	10	355	17	3	38
1967	03	11	355	20	3	38
1967	03	12	355	24	3	38
1967	03	13	355	27	3	38
1967	03	14	355	31	3	38
1967	03	15	355	35	3	38
1967	03	16	355	38	3	37
1967	03	17	355	42	3	37
1967	03	18	355	45	3	37
1967	03	19	355	49	3	37
1967	03	20	355	53	3	37
1967	03	21	355	56	3	37
1967	03	22	356	00	3	37
1967	03	23	356	03	3	37
1967	03	24	356	07	3	37
1967	03	25	356	10	3	37
1967	03	26	356	14	3	37
1967	03	27	356	18	3	37
1967	03	28	356	21	3	37
1967	03	29	356	25	3	37
1967	03	30	356	28	3	37
1967	03	31	356	32	3	37
1967	04	01	356	35	3	37
1967	04	02	356	39	3	37
1967	04	03	356	42	3	37
1967	04	04	356	46	3	37
1967	04	05	356	49	3	37
1967	04	06	356	53	3	37
1967	04	07	356	56	3	37
1967	04	08	357	00	3	37
1967	04	09	357	03	3	37
1967	04	10	357	06	3	37
1967	04	11	357	10	3	37
1967	04	12	357	13	3	37
1967	04	13	357	16	3	37
1967	04	14	357	20	3	37
1967	04	15	357	23	3	37
1967	04	16	357	26	3	37
1967	04	17	357	30	3	37
1967	04	18	357	33	3	37
1967	04	19	357	36	3	37
1967	04	20	357	39	3	37
1967	04	21	357	42	3	37
1967	04	22	357	45	3	37
1967	04	23	357	49	3	37
1967	04	24	357	52	3	37
1967	04	25	357	55	3	37
1967	04	26	357	58	3	37
1967	04	27	358	01	3	37
1967	04	28	358	04	3	38
1967	04	29	358	07	3	38
1967	04	30	358	10	3	38
1967	05	01	358	12	3	38
1967	05	02	358	15	3	38
1967	05	03	358	18	3	38
1967	05	04	358	21	3	38
1967	05	05	358	24	3	38
1967	05	06	358	26	3	38
1967	05	07	358	29	3	38
1967	05	08	358	32	3	38
1967	05	09	358	34	3	38
1967	05	10	358	37	3	38
1967	05	11	358	39	3	38
1967	05	12	358	42	3	39
1967	05	13	358	44	3	39
1967	05	14	358	47	3	39
1967	05	15	358	49	3	39
1967	05	16	358	51	3	39
1967	05	17	358	54	3	39
1967	05	18	358	56	3	39
1967	05	19	358	58	3	39
1967	05	20	359	00	3	39
1967	05	21	359	03	3	39
1967	05	22	359	05	3	40
1967	05	23	359	07	3	40
1967	05	24	359	09	3	40
1967	05	25	359	11	3	40
1967	05	26	359	13	3	40
1967	05	27	359	15	3	40
1967	05	28	359	16	3	40
1967	05	29	359	18	3	40
1967	05	30	359	20	3	41
1967	05	31	359	22	3	41
1967	06	01	359	23	3	41
1967	06	02	359	25	3	41
1967	06	03	359	26	3	41
1967	06	04	359	28	3	41
1967	06	05	359	29	3	41
1967	06	06	359	31	3	41
1967	06	07	359	32	3	42
1967	06	08	359	34	3	42
1967	06	09	359	35	3	42
1967	06	10	359	36	3	42
1967	06	11	359	37	3	42
1967	06	12	359	38	3	42
1967	06	13	359	39	3	42
1967	06	14	359	40	3	43
1967	06	15	359	41	3	43
1967	06	16	359	42	3	43
1967	06	17	359	43	3	43
1967	06	18	359	44	3	43
1967	06	19	359	45	3	43
1967	06	20	359	45	3	43
1967	06	21	359	46	3	43
1967	06	22	359	47	3	44
1967	06	23	359	47	3	44
1967	06	24	359	48	3	44
1967	06	25	359	48	3	44
1967	06	26	359	49	3	44
1967	06	27	359	49	3	44
1967	06	28	359	49	3	44
1967	06	29	359	50	3	45
1967	06	30	359	50	3	45
1967	07	01	359	50	3	45
1967	07	02	359	50	3	45
1967	07	03	359	50	3	45
1967	07	04	359	50	3	45
1967	07	05	359	50	3	45
1967	07	06	359	50	3	46
1967	07	07	359	50	3	46
1967	07	08	359	49	3	46
1967	07	09	359	49	3	46
1967	07	10	359	49	3	46
1967	07	11	359	48	3	46
1967	07	12	359	48	3	46
1967	07	13	359	47	3	47
1967	07	14	359	47	3	47
1967	07	15	359	46	3	47
1967	07	16	359	46	3	47
1967	07	17	359	45	3	47
1967	07	18	359	44	3	47
1967	07	19	359	43	3	47
1967	07	20	359	43	3	47
1967	07	21	359	42	3	48
1967	07	22	359	41	3	48
1967	07	23	359	40	3	48
1967	07	24	359	39	3	48
1967	07	25	359	38	3	48
1967	07	26	359	36	3	48
1967	07	27	359	35	3	48
1967	07	28	359	34	3	48
1967	07	29	359	33	3	49
1967	07	30	359	31	3	49
1967	07	31	359	30	3	49
1967	08	01	359	29	3	49
1967	08	02	359	27	3	49
1967	08	03	359	26	3	49
1967	08	04	359	24	3	49
1967	08	05	359	22	3	49
1967	08	06	359	21	3	49
1967	08	07	359	19	3	49
1967	08	08	359	17	3	50
1967	08	09	359	16	3	50
1967	08	10	359	14	3	50
1967	08	11	359	12	3	50
1967	08	12	359	10	3	50
1967	08	13	359	08	3	50
1967	08	14	359	06	3	50
1967	08	15	359	04	3	50
1967	08	16	359	02	3	50
1967	08	17	359	00	3	50
1967	08	18	358	58	3	50
1967	08	19	358	56	3	50
1967	08	20	358	54	3	50
1967	08	21	358	51	3	50
1967	08	22	358	49	3	50
1967	08	23	358	47	3	51
1967	08	24	358	45	3	51
1967	08	25	358	42	3	51
1967	08	26	358	40	3	51
1967	08	27	358	38	3	51
1967	08	28	358	35	3	51
1967	08	29	358	33	3	51
1967	08	30	358	30	3	51
1967	08	31	358	28	3	51
1967	09	01	358	25	3	51
1967	09	02	358	23	3	51
1967	09	03	358	20	3	51
1967	09	04	358	18	3	51
1967	09	05	358	15	3	51
1967	09	06	358	13	3	51
1967	09	07	358	10	3	51
1967	09	08	358	07	3	51
1967	09	09	358	05	3	51
1967	09	10	358	02	3	51
1967	09	11	357	59	3	51
1967	09	12	357	57	3	51
1967	09	13	357	54	3	51
1967	09	14	357	51	3	51
1967	09	15	357	48	3	51
1967	09	16	357	46	3	51
1967	09	17	357	43	3	50
1967	09	18	357	40	3	50
1967	09	19	357	38	3	50
1967	09	20	357	35	3	50
1967	09	21	357	32	3	50
1967	09	22	357	29	3	50
1967	09	23	357	27	3	50
1967	09	24	357	24	3	50
1967	09	25	357	21	3	50
1967	09	26	357	19	3	50
1967	09	27	357	16	3	50
1967	09	28	357	13	3	50
1967	09	29	357	10	3	50
1967	09	30	357	08	3	49
1967	10	01	357	05	3	49
1967	10	02	357	02	3	49
1967	10	03	357	00	3	49
1967	10	04	356	57	3	49
1967	10	05	356	54	3	49
1967	10	06	356	52	3	49
1967	10	07	356	49	3	49
1967	10	08	356	47	3	49
1967	10	09	356	44	3	48
1967	10	10	356	42	3	48
1967	10	11	356	39	3	48
1967	10	12	356	36	3	48
1967	10	13	356	34	3	48
1967	10	14	356	32	3	48
1967	10	15	356	29	3	48
1967	10	16	356	27	3	47
1967	10	17	356	24	3	47
1967	10	18	356	22	3	47
1967	10	19	356	20	3	47
1967	10	20	356	17	3	47
1967	10	21	356	15	3	47
1967	10	22	356	13	3	46
1967	10	23	356	11	3	46
1967	10	24	356	09	3	46
1967	10	25	356	06	3	46
1967	10	26	356	04	3	46
1967	10	27	356	02	3	45
1967	10	28	356	00	3	45
1967	10	29	355	58	3	45
1967	10	30	355	56	3	45
1967	10	31	355	55	3	45
1967	11	01	355	53	3	44
1967	11	02	355	51	3	44
1967	11	03	355	49	3	44
1967	11	04	355	47	3	44
1967	11	05	355	46	3	44

Chiron

1967	11	06	355	44	3	43
1967	11	07	355	42	3	43
1967	11	08	355	41	3	43
1967	11	09	355	39	3	43
1967	11	10	355	38	3	42
1967	11	11	355	36	3	42
1967	11	12	355	35	3	42
1967	11	13	355	34	3	42
1967	11	14	355	33	3	41
1967	11	15	355	31	3	41
1967	11	16	355	30	3	41
1967	11	17	355	29	3	41
1967	11	18	355	28	3	41
1967	11	19	355	27	3	40
1967	11	20	355	26	3	40
1967	11	21	355	25	3	40
1967	11	22	355	24	3	40
1967	11	23	355	23	3	39
1967	11	24	355	23	3	39
1967	11	25	355	22	3	39
1967	11	26	355	21	3	39
1967	11	27	355	21	3	38
1967	11	28	355	20	3	38
1967	11	29	355	20	3	38
1967	11	30	355	19	3	38
1967	12	01	355	19	3	37
1967	12	02	355	18	3	37
1967	12	03	355	18	3	37
1967	12	04	355	18	3	36
1967	12	05	355	18	3	36
1967	12	06	355	18	3	36
1967	12	07	355	18	3	36
1967	12	08	355	18	3	35
1967	12	09	355	18	3	35
1967	12	10	355	18	3	35
1967	12	11	355	18	3	35
1967	12	12	355	18	3	34
1967	12	13	355	19	3	34
1967	12	14	355	19	3	34
1967	12	15	355	19	3	34
1967	12	16	355	20	3	33
1967	12	17	355	20	3	33
1967	12	18	355	21	3	33
1967	12	19	355	22	3	33
1967	12	20	355	22	3	32
1967	12	21	355	23	3	32
1967	12	22	355	24	3	32
1967	12	23	355	25	3	32
1967	12	24	355	26	3	31
1967	12	25	355	27	3	31
1967	12	26	355	28	3	31
1967	12	27	355	29	3	31
1967	12	28	355	30	3	30
1967	12	29	355	31	3	30
1967	12	30	355	32	3	30
1967	12	31	355	33	3	30
1968	01	01	355	35	3	29
1968	01	02	355	36	3	29
1968	01	03	355	37	3	29
1968	01	04	355	39	3	29
1968	01	05	355	41	3	28
1968	01	06	355	42	3	28
1968	01	07	355	44	3	28
1968	01	08	355	45	3	28
1968	01	09	355	47	3	27
1968	01	10	355	49	3	27
1968	01	11	355	51	3	27
1968	01	12	355	53	3	27
1968	01	13	355	55	3	26
1968	01	14	355	56	3	26
1968	01	15	355	59	3	26
1968	01	16	356	01	3	26
1968	01	17	356	03	3	26
1968	01	18	356	05	3	25
1968	01	19	356	07	3	25
1968	01	20	356	09	3	25
1968	01	21	356	11	3	25
1968	01	22	356	14	3	24
1968	01	23	356	16	3	24
1968	01	24	356	19	3	24
1968	01	25	356	21	3	24
1968	01	26	356	23	3	24
1968	01	27	356	26	3	23
1968	01	28	356	29	3	23
1968	01	29	356	31	3	23
1968	01	30	356	34	3	23
1968	01	31	356	36	3	23
1968	02	01	356	39	3	22
1968	02	02	356	42	3	22
1968	02	03	356	45	3	22
1968	02	04	356	47	3	22
1968	02	05	356	50	3	22
1968	02	06	356	53	3	22
1968	02	07	356	56	3	21
1968	02	08	356	59	3	21
1968	02	09	357	02	3	21
1968	02	10	357	05	3	21
1968	02	11	357	08	3	21
1968	02	12	357	11	3	21
1968	02	13	357	14	3	20
1968	02	14	357	17	3	20
1968	02	15	357	20	3	20
1968	02	16	357	24	3	20
1968	02	17	357	27	3	20
1968	02	18	357	30	3	20
1968	02	19	357	33	3	20
1968	02	20	357	36	3	19
1968	02	21	357	40	3	19
1968	02	22	357	43	3	19
1968	02	23	357	46	3	19
1968	02	24	357	50	3	19
1968	02	25	357	53	3	19
1968	02	26	357	56	3	19
1968	02	27	358	00	3	18
1968	02	28	358	03	3	18
1968	02	29	358	07	3	18
1968	03	01	358	10	3	18
1968	03	02	358	13	3	18
1968	03	03	358	17	3	18
1968	03	04	358	20	3	18
1968	03	05	358	24	3	18
1968	03	06	358	27	3	18
1968	03	07	358	31	3	17
1968	03	08	358	34	3	17
1968	03	09	358	38	3	17
1968	03	10	358	41	3	17
1968	03	11	358	45	3	17
1968	03	12	358	48	3	17
1968	03	13	358	52	3	17
1968	03	14	358	56	3	17
1968	03	15	358	59	3	17
1968	03	16	359	03	3	17
1968	03	17	359	06	3	17
1968	03	18	359	10	3	17
1968	03	19	359	13	3	17
1968	03	20	359	17	3	16
1968	03	21	359	21	3	16
1968	03	22	359	24	3	16
1968	03	23	359	28	3	16
1968	03	24	359	31	3	16
1968	03	25	359	35	3	16
1968	03	26	359	38	3	16
1968	03	27	359	42	3	16
1968	03	28	359	45	3	16
1968	03	29	359	49	3	16
1968	03	30	359	52	3	16
1968	03	31	359	56	3	16
1968	04	01	00	00	3	16
1968	04	02	00	03	3	16
1968	04	03	00	07	3	16
1968	04	04	00	10	3	16
1968	04	05	00	13	3	16
1968	04	06	00	17	3	16
1968	04	07	00	20	3	16
1968	04	08	00	24	3	16
1968	04	09	00	27	3	16
1968	04	10	00	31	3	16
1968	04	11	00	34	3	16
1968	04	12	00	37	3	16
1968	04	13	00	41	3	16
1968	04	14	00	44	3	16
1968	04	15	00	47	3	16
1968	04	16	00	51	3	16
1968	04	17	00	54	3	16
1968	04	18	00	57	3	16
1968	04	19	01	01	3	16
1968	04	20	01	04	3	16
1968	04	21	01	07	3	16
1968	04	22	01	10	3	16
1968	04	23	01	13	3	16
1968	04	24	01	16	3	16
1968	04	25	01	19	3	16
1968	04	26	01	23	3	16
1968	04	27	01	26	3	16
1968	04	28	01	29	3	16
1968	04	29	01	32	3	16
1968	04	30	01	35	3	16
1968	05	01	01	38	3	16
1968	05	02	01	40	3	16
1968	05	03	01	43	3	16
1968	05	04	01	46	3	16
1968	05	05	01	49	3	16
1968	05	06	01	52	3	17
1968	05	07	01	55	3	17
1968	05	08	01	57	3	17
1968	05	09	02	00	3	17
1968	05	10	02	03	3	17
1968	05	11	02	05	3	17
1968	05	12	02	08	3	17
1968	05	13	02	10	3	17
1968	05	14	02	13	3	17
1968	05	15	02	15	3	17
1968	05	16	02	18	3	17
1968	05	17	02	20	3	17
1968	05	18	02	22	3	17
1968	05	19	02	25	3	17
1968	05	20	02	27	3	18
1968	05	21	02	29	3	18
1968	05	22	02	32	3	18
1968	05	23	02	34	3	18
1968	05	24	02	36	3	18
1968	05	25	02	38	3	18
1968	05	26	02	40	3	18
1968	05	27	02	42	3	18
1968	05	28	02	44	3	18
1968	05	29	02	46	3	18
1968	05	30	02	48	3	18
1968	05	31	02	49	3	19
1968	06	01	02	51	3	19
1968	06	02	02	53	3	19
1968	06	03	02	55	3	19
1968	06	04	02	56	3	19
1968	06	05	02	58	3	19
1968	06	06	02	59	3	19
1968	06	07	03	01	3	19
1968	06	08	03	02	3	19
1968	06	09	03	04	3	20
1968	06	10	03	05	3	20
1968	06	11	03	06	3	20
1968	06	12	03	08	3	20
1968	06	13	03	09	3	20
1968	06	14	03	10	3	20
1968	06	15	03	11	3	20
1968	06	16	03	12	3	20
1968	06	17	03	13	3	20
1968	06	18	03	14	3	21
1968	06	19	03	15	3	21
1968	06	20	03	16	3	21
1968	06	21	03	17	3	21
1968	06	22	03	17	3	21
1968	06	23	03	18	3	21
1968	06	24	03	19	3	21
1968	06	25	03	19	3	21
1968	06	26	03	20	3	21
1968	06	27	03	20	3	22
1968	06	28	03	21	3	22
1968	06	29	03	21	3	22
1968	06	30	03	22	3	22
1968	07	01	03	22	3	22
1968	07	02	03	22	3	22
1968	07	03	03	22	3	22
1968	07	04	03	22	3	22
1968	07	05	03	22	3	23
1968	07	06	03	22	3	23
1968	07	07	03	22	3	23
1968	07	08	03	22	3	23
1968	07	09	03	22	3	23
1968	07	10	03	22	3	23
1968	07	11	03	22	3	23
1968	07	12	03	21	3	23
1968	07	13	03	21	3	23
1968	07	14	03	21	3	24
1968	07	15	03	20	3	24
1968	07	16	03	20	3	24
1968	07	17	03	19	3	24
1968	07	18	03	19	3	24
1968	07	19	03	18	3	24
1968	07	20	03	17	3	24
1968	07	21	03	17	3	24
1968	07	22	03	16	3	24
1968	07	23	03	15	3	25
1968	07	24	03	14	3	25
1968	07	25	03	13	3	25
1968	07	26	03	12	3	25
1968	07	27	03	11	3	25
1968	07	28	03	10	3	25
1968	07	29	03	09	3	25
1968	07	30	03	08	3	25
1968	07	31	03	06	3	25
1968	08	01	03	05	3	25
1968	08	02	03	04	3	26
1968	08	03	03	02	3	26
1968	08	04	03	01	3	26
1968	08	05	02	59	3	26
1968	08	06	02	58	3	26
1968	08	07	02	56	3	26
1968	08	08	02	55	3	26
1968	08	09	02	53	3	26
1968	08	10	02	51	3	26
1968	08	11	02	50	3	26
1968	08	12	02	48	3	26
1968	08	13	02	46	3	26
1968	08	14	02	44	3	26
1968	08	15	02	42	3	27
1968	08	16	02	41	3	27
1968	08	17	02	39	3	27
1968	08	18	02	37	3	27
1968	08	19	02	35	3	27
1968	08	20	02	33	3	27
1968	08	21	02	30	3	27
1968	08	22	02	28	3	27
1968	08	23	02	26	3	27
1968	08	24	02	24	3	27
1968	08	25	02	22	3	27
1968	08	26	02	19	3	27
1968	08	27	02	17	3	27
1968	08	28	02	15	3	27
1968	08	29	02	12	3	27
1968	08	30	02	10	3	27
1968	08	31	02	08	3	27
1968	09	01	02	05	3	27
1968	09	02	02	03	3	27
1968	09	03	02	00	3	27
1968	09	04	01	58	3	27
1968	09	05	01	55	3	27
1968	09	06	01	53	3	27
1968	09	07	01	50	3	27
1968	09	08	01	48	3	27
1968	09	09	01	45	3	27
1968	09	10	01	42	3	27
1968	09	11	01	40	3	27
1968	09	12	01	37	3	27
1968	09	13	01	35	3	27
1968	09	14	01	32	3	27
1968	09	15	01	29	3	27
1968	09	16	01	27	3	27
1968	09	17	01	24	3	27
1968	09	18	01	21	3	27
1968	09	19	01	18	3	27
1968	09	20	01	16	3	27
1968	09	21	01	13	3	27
1968	09	22	01	10	3	27
1968	09	23	01	08	3	27
1968	09	24	01	05	3	27
1968	09	25	01	02	3	26
1968	09	26	00	59	3	26
1968	09	27	00	57	3	26
1968	09	28	00	54	3	26
1968	09	29	00	51	3	26
1968	09	30	00	49	3	26
1968	10	01	00	46	3	26
1968	10	02	00	43	3	26
1968	10	03	00	41	3	26
1968	10	04	00	38	3	26
1968	10	05	00	35	3	26
1968	10	06	00	33	3	25
1968	10	07	00	30	3	25
1968	10	08	00	27	3	25
1968	10	09	00	25	3	25
1968	10	10	00	22	3	25
1968	10	11	00	20	3	25
1968	10	12	00	17	3	25
1968	10	13	00	14	3	25
1968	10	14	00	12	3	24
1968	10	15	00	09	3	24
1968	10	16	00	07	3	24
1968	10	17	00	05	3	24
1968	10	18	00	02	3	24
1968	10	19	00	00	3	24
1968	10	20	359	57	3	24
1968	10	21	359	55	3	23
1968	10	22	359	53	3	23
1968	10	23	359	50	3	23
1968	10	24	359	48	3	23
1968	10	25	359	46	3	23
1968	10	26	359	44	3	23
1968	10	27	359	42	3	22
1968	10	28	359	40	3	22
1968	10	29	359	38	3	22
1968	10	30	359	35	3	22
1968	10	31	359	33	3	22
1968	11	01	359	32	3	22
1968	11	02	359	30	3	21
1968	11	03	359	28	3	21
1968	11	04	359	26	3	21
1968	11	05	359	24	3	21
1968	11	06	359	22	3	21
1968	11	07	359	21	3	20
1968	11	08	359	19	3	20
1968	11	09	359	17	3	20
1968	11	10	359	16	3	20
1968	11	11	359	14	3	20
1968	11	12	359	13	3	19
1968	11	13	359	11	3	19
1968	11	14	359	10	3	19
1968	11	15	359	08	3	19
1968	11	16	359	07	3	18
1968	11	17	359	06	3	18
1968	11	18	359	05	3	18
1968	11	19	359	03	3	18
1968	11	20	359	02	3	18
1968	11	21	359	01	3	17
1968	11	22	359	00	3	17
1968	11	23	358	59	3	17
1968	11	24	358	58	3	17
1968	11	25	358	58	3	16
1968	11	26	358	57	3	16
1968	11	27	358	56	3	16
1968	11	28	358	55	3	16
1968	11	29	358	55	3	16
1968	11	30	358	54	3	15
1968	12	01	358	54	3	15
1968	12	02	358	53	3	15
1968	12	03	358	53	3	15
1968	12	04	358	52	3	14
1968	12	05	358	52	3	14
1968	12	06	358	52	3	14
1968	12	07	358	52	3	14
1968	12	08	358	51	3	13
1968	12	09	358	51	3	13
1968	12	10	358	51	3	13
1968	12	11	358	51	3	13
1968	12	12	358	51	3	12
1968	12	13	358	52	3	12
1968	12	14	358	52	3	12
1968	12	15	358	52	3	12
1968	12	16	358	52	3	11
1968	12	17	358	53	3	11
1968	12	18	358	53	3	11
1968	12	19	358	53	3	11
1968	12	20	358	54	3	11
1968	12	21	358	55	3	10
1968	12	22	358	55	3	10
1968	12	23	358	56	3	10
1968	12	24	358	57	3	10
1968	12	25	358	57	3	09
1968	12	26	358	58	3	09
1968	12	27	358	59	3	09
1968	12	28	359	00	3	09

1968 12 29	359 01	3 08
1968 12 30	359 02	3 08
1968 12 31	359 03	3 08
1969 01 01	359 04	3 08
1969 01 02	359 06	3 07
1969 01 03	359 07	3 07
1969 01 04	359 08	3 07
1969 01 05	359 10	3 07
1969 01 06	359 11	3 07
1969 01 07	359 13	3 06
1969 01 08	359 14	3 06
1969 01 09	359 16	3 06
1969 01 10	359 17	3 06
1969 01 11	359 19	3 05
1969 01 12	359 21	3 05
1969 01 13	359 22	3 05
1969 01 14	359 24	3 05
1969 01 15	359 26	3 05
1969 01 16	359 28	3 04
1969 01 17	359 30	3 04
1969 01 18	359 32	3 04
1969 01 19	359 34	3 04
1969 01 20	359 36	3 04
1969 01 21	359 38	3 03
1969 01 22	359 41	3 03
1969 01 23	359 43	3 03
1969 01 24	359 45	3 03
1969 01 25	359 47	3 03
1969 01 26	359 50	3 02
1969 01 27	359 52	3 02
1969 01 28	359 54	3 02
1969 01 29	359 57	3 02
1969 01 30	359 59	3 02
1969 01 31	00 02	3 01
1969 02 01	00 05	3 01
1969 02 02	00 07	3 01
1969 02 03	00 10	3 01
1969 02 04	00 13	3 01
1969 02 05	00 15	3 01
1969 02 06	00 18	3 00
1969 02 07	00 21	3 00
1969 02 08	00 24	3 00
1969 02 09	00 27	3 00
1969 02 10	00 29	3 00
1969 02 11	00 32	3 00
1969 02 12	00 35	2 59
1969 02 13	00 38	2 59
1969 02 14	00 41	2 59
1969 02 15	00 44	2 59
1969 02 16	00 47	2 59
1969 02 17	00 50	2 59
1969 02 18	00 54	2 58
1969 02 19	00 57	2 58
1969 02 20	01 00	2 58
1969 02 21	01 03	2 58
1969 02 22	01 06	2 58
1969 02 23	01 09	2 58
1969 02 24	01 13	2 58
1969 02 25	01 16	2 58
1969 02 26	01 19	2 57
1969 02 27	01 23	2 57
1969 02 28	01 26	2 57
1969 03 01	01 29	2 57
1969 03 02	01 33	2 57
1969 03 03	01 36	2 57
1969 03 04	01 39	2 57
1969 03 05	01 43	2 57
1969 03 06	01 46	2 57
1969 03 07	01 50	2 56
1969 03 08	01 53	2 56
1969 03 09	01 57	2 56
1969 03 10	02 00	2 56
1969 03 11	02 04	2 56
1969 03 12	02 07	2 56
1969 03 13	02 11	2 56
1969 03 14	02 14	2 56
1969 03 15	02 18	2 56
1969 03 16	02 21	2 56
1969 03 17	02 25	2 56
1969 03 18	02 28	2 55
1969 03 19	02 32	2 55
1969 03 20	02 35	2 55
1969 03 21	02 39	2 55
1969 03 22	02 42	2 55
1969 03 23	02 46	2 55
1969 03 24	02 49	2 55
1969 03 25	02 53	2 55
1969 03 26	02 56	2 55
1969 03 27	03 00	2 55
1969 03 28	03 04	2 55
1969 03 29	03 07	2 55
1969 03 30	03 11	2 55
1969 03 31	03 14	2 55
1969 04 01	03 18	2 55
1969 04 02	03 21	2 55
1969 04 03	03 25	2 55
1969 04 04	03 28	2 55
1969 04 05	03 32	2 54
1969 04 06	03 35	2 54
1969 04 07	03 39	2 54
1969 04 08	03 42	2 54
1969 04 09	03 46	2 54
1969 04 10	03 49	2 54
1969 04 11	03 52	2 54
1969 04 12	03 56	2 54
1969 04 13	03 59	2 54

1969 04 14	04 03	2 54
1969 04 15	04 06	2 54
1969 04 16	04 09	2 54
1969 04 17	04 13	2 54
1969 04 18	04 16	2 54
1969 04 19	04 19	2 54
1969 04 20	04 23	2 54
1969 04 21	04 26	2 54
1969 04 22	04 29	2 54
1969 04 23	04 32	2 54
1969 04 24	04 35	2 54
1969 04 25	04 39	2 54
1969 04 26	04 42	2 54
1969 04 27	04 45	2 54
1969 04 28	04 48	2 54
1969 04 29	04 51	2 54
1969 04 30	04 54	2 54
1969 05 01	04 57	2 54
1969 05 02	05 00	2 54
1969 05 03	05 03	2 54
1969 05 04	05 06	2 54
1969 05 05	05 09	2 55
1969 05 06	05 12	2 55
1969 05 07	05 15	2 55
1969 05 08	05 18	2 55
1969 05 09	05 20	2 55
1969 05 10	05 23	2 55
1969 05 11	05 26	2 55
1969 05 12	05 28	2 55
1969 05 13	05 31	2 55
1969 05 14	05 34	2 55
1969 05 15	05 36	2 55
1969 05 16	05 39	2 55
1969 05 17	05 41	2 55
1969 05 18	05 44	2 55
1969 05 19	05 46	2 55
1969 05 20	05 49	2 55
1969 05 21	05 51	2 55
1969 05 22	05 54	2 55
1969 05 23	05 56	2 55
1969 05 24	05 58	2 55
1969 05 25	06 00	2 56
1969 05 26	06 02	2 56
1969 05 27	06 05	2 56
1969 05 28	06 07	2 56
1969 05 29	06 09	2 56
1969 05 30	06 11	2 56
1969 05 31	06 13	2 56
1969 06 01	06 15	2 56
1969 06 02	06 17	2 56
1969 06 03	06 18	2 56
1969 06 04	06 20	2 56
1969 06 05	06 22	2 56
1969 06 06	06 24	2 56
1969 06 07	06 25	2 57
1969 06 08	06 27	2 57
1969 06 09	06 29	2 57
1969 06 10	06 30	2 57
1969 06 11	06 32	2 57
1969 06 12	06 33	2 57
1969 06 13	06 34	2 57
1969 06 14	06 36	2 57
1969 06 15	06 37	2 57
1969 06 16	06 38	2 57
1969 06 17	06 39	2 57
1969 06 18	06 41	2 58
1969 06 19	06 42	2 58
1969 06 20	06 43	2 58
1969 06 21	06 44	2 58
1969 06 22	06 45	2 58
1969 06 23	06 45	2 58
1969 06 24	06 46	2 58
1969 06 25	06 47	2 58
1969 06 26	06 48	2 58
1969 06 27	06 49	2 58
1969 06 28	06 49	2 58
1969 06 29	06 50	2 59
1969 06 30	06 50	2 59
1969 07 01	06 51	2 59
1969 07 02	06 51	2 59
1969 07 03	06 52	2 59
1969 07 04	06 52	2 59
1969 07 05	06 52	2 59
1969 07 06	06 52	2 59
1969 07 07	06 53	2 59
1969 07 08	06 53	2 59
1969 07 09	06 53	3 00
1969 07 10	06 53	3 00
1969 07 11	06 53	3 00
1969 07 12	06 53	3 00
1969 07 13	06 53	3 00
1969 07 14	06 52	3 00
1969 07 15	06 52	3 00
1969 07 16	06 52	3 00
1969 07 17	06 51	3 00
1969 07 18	06 51	3 00
1969 07 19	06 51	3 00
1969 07 20	06 50	3 01
1969 07 21	06 50	3 01
1969 07 22	06 49	3 01
1969 07 23	06 48	3 01
1969 07 24	06 48	3 01
1969 07 25	06 47	3 01
1969 07 26	06 46	3 01
1969 07 27	06 45	3 01
1969 07 28	06 44	3 01

1969 07 29	06 43	3 01
1969 07 30	06 42	3 01
1969 07 31	06 41	3 01
1969 08 01	06 40	3 02
1969 08 02	06 39	3 02
1969 08 03	06 38	3 02
1969 08 04	06 37	3 02
1969 08 05	06 35	3 02
1969 08 06	06 34	3 02
1969 08 07	06 33	3 02
1969 08 08	06 31	3 02
1969 08 09	06 30	3 02
1969 08 10	06 28	3 02
1969 08 11	06 27	3 02
1969 08 12	06 25	3 02
1969 08 13	06 23	3 02
1969 08 14	06 22	3 02
1969 08 15	06 20	3 02
1969 08 16	06 18	3 03
1969 08 17	06 16	3 03
1969 08 18	06 14	3 03
1969 08 19	06 13	3 03
1969 08 20	06 11	3 03
1969 08 21	06 09	3 03
1969 08 22	06 07	3 03
1969 08 23	06 05	3 03
1969 08 24	06 03	3 03
1969 08 25	06 01	3 03
1969 08 26	05 58	3 03
1969 08 27	05 56	3 03
1969 08 28	05 54	3 03
1969 08 29	05 52	3 03
1969 08 30	05 50	3 03
1969 08 31	05 47	3 03
1969 09 01	05 45	3 03
1969 09 02	05 43	3 03
1969 09 03	05 40	3 03
1969 09 04	05 38	3 03
1969 09 05	05 35	3 03
1969 09 06	05 33	3 03
1969 09 07	05 30	3 03
1969 09 08	05 28	3 03
1969 09 09	05 25	3 03
1969 09 10	05 23	3 03
1969 09 11	05 20	3 03
1969 09 12	05 18	3 03
1969 09 13	05 15	3 03
1969 09 14	05 13	3 03
1969 09 15	05 10	3 03
1969 09 16	05 07	3 03
1969 09 17	05 05	3 03
1969 09 18	05 02	3 03
1969 09 19	04 59	3 03
1969 09 20	04 57	3 03
1969 09 21	04 54	3 03
1969 09 22	04 51	3 03
1969 09 23	04 49	3 03
1969 09 24	04 46	3 03
1969 09 25	04 43	3 02
1969 09 26	04 41	3 02
1969 09 27	04 38	3 02
1969 09 28	04 35	3 02
1969 09 29	04 32	3 02
1969 09 30	04 30	3 02
1969 10 01	04 27	3 02
1969 10 02	04 24	3 02
1969 10 03	04 22	3 02
1969 10 04	04 19	3 02
1969 10 05	04 16	3 02
1969 10 06	04 13	3 02
1969 10 07	04 11	3 02
1969 10 08	04 08	3 01
1969 10 09	04 06	3 01
1969 10 10	04 03	3 01
1969 10 11	04 00	3 01
1969 10 12	03 58	3 01
1969 10 13	03 55	3 01
1969 10 14	03 52	3 01
1969 10 15	03 50	3 01
1969 10 16	03 47	3 01
1969 10 17	03 45	3 00
1969 10 18	03 42	3 00
1969 10 19	03 40	3 00
1969 10 20	03 37	3 00
1969 10 21	03 35	3 00
1969 10 22	03 33	3 00
1969 10 23	03 30	3 00
1969 10 24	03 28	2 59
1969 10 25	03 26	2 59
1969 10 26	03 23	2 59
1969 10 27	03 21	2 59
1969 10 28	03 19	2 59
1969 10 29	03 17	2 59
1969 10 30	03 14	2 59
1969 10 31	03 12	2 58
1969 11 01	03 10	2 58
1969 11 02	03 08	2 58
1969 11 03	03 06	2 58
1969 11 04	03 04	2 58
1969 11 05	03 02	2 58
1969 11 06	03 00	2 57
1969 11 07	02 58	2 57
1969 11 08	02 56	2 57
1969 11 09	02 55	2 57
1969 11 10	02 53	2 57
1969 11 11	02 51	2 56

1969 11 12	02 50	2 56
1969 11 13	02 48	2 56
1969 11 14	02 46	2 56
1969 11 15	02 45	2 56
1969 11 16	02 43	2 55
1969 11 17	02 42	2 55
1969 11 18	02 41	2 55
1969 11 19	02 39	2 55
1969 11 20	02 38	2 55
1969 11 21	02 37	2 54
1969 11 22	02 35	2 54
1969 11 23	02 34	2 54
1969 11 24	02 33	2 54
1969 11 25	02 32	2 54
1969 11 26	02 31	2 53
1969 11 27	02 30	2 53
1969 11 28	02 29	2 53
1969 11 29	02 28	2 53
1969 11 30	02 28	2 53
1969 12 01	02 27	2 52
1969 12 02	02 26	2 52
1969 12 03	02 26	2 52
1969 12 04	02 25	2 52
1969 12 05	02 25	2 52
1969 12 06	02 24	2 51
1969 12 07	02 24	2 51
1969 12 08	02 23	2 51
1969 12 09	02 23	2 51
1969 12 10	02 23	2 50
1969 12 11	02 23	2 50
1969 12 12	02 22	2 50
1969 12 13	02 22	2 50
1969 12 14	02 22	2 50
1969 12 15	02 22	2 49
1969 12 16	02 22	2 49
1969 12 17	02 23	2 49
1969 12 18	02 23	2 49
1969 12 19	02 23	2 48
1969 12 20	02 23	2 48
1969 12 21	02 24	2 48
1969 12 22	02 24	2 48
1969 12 23	02 25	2 48
1969 12 24	02 25	2 47
1969 12 25	02 26	2 47
1969 12 26	02 26	2 47
1969 12 27	02 27	2 47
1969 12 28	02 28	2 47
1969 12 29	02 29	2 46
1969 12 30	02 29	2 46
1969 12 31	02 30	2 46
1970 01 01	02 31	2 46
1970 01 02	02 32	2 45
1970 01 03	02 33	2 45
1970 01 04	02 35	2 45
1970 01 05	02 36	2 45
1970 01 06	02 37	2 45
1970 01 07	02 38	2 44
1970 01 08	02 40	2 44
1970 01 09	02 41	2 44
1970 01 10	02 42	2 44
1970 01 11	02 44	2 44
1970 01 12	02 45	2 43
1970 01 13	02 47	2 43
1970 01 14	02 49	2 43
1970 01 15	02 50	2 43
1970 01 16	02 52	2 43
1970 01 17	02 54	2 42
1970 01 18	02 56	2 42
1970 01 19	02 57	2 42
1970 01 20	02 59	2 42
1970 01 21	03 01	2 42
1970 01 22	03 03	2 41
1970 01 23	03 05	2 41
1970 01 24	03 07	2 41
1970 01 25	03 10	2 41
1970 01 26	03 12	2 41
1970 01 27	03 14	2 40
1970 01 28	03 16	2 40
1970 01 29	03 19	2 40
1970 01 30	03 21	2 40
1970 01 31	03 23	2 40
1970 02 01	03 26	2 40
1970 02 02	03 28	2 39
1970 02 03	03 31	2 39
1970 02 04	03 33	2 39
1970 02 05	03 36	2 39
1970 02 06	03 38	2 39
1970 02 07	03 41	2 39
1970 02 08	03 44	2 38
1970 02 09	03 47	2 38
1970 02 10	03 49	2 38
1970 02 11	03 52	2 38
1970 02 12	03 55	2 38
1970 02 13	03 58	2 38
1970 02 14	04 01	2 37
1970 02 15	04 04	2 37
1970 02 16	04 06	2 37
1970 02 17	04 09	2 37
1970 02 18	04 12	2 37
1970 02 19	04 15	2 37
1970 02 20	04 19	2 37
1970 02 21	04 22	2 36

Chiron

1970 02 22	04 25	2 36
1970 02 23	04 28	2 36
1970 02 24	04 31	2 36
1970 02 25	04 34	2 36
1970 02 26	04 37	2 36
1970 02 27	04 41	2 36
1970 02 28	04 44	2 36
1970 03 01	04 47	2 35
1970 03 02	04 50	2 35
1970 03 03	04 54	2 35
1970 03 04	04 57	2 35
1970 03 05	05 00	2 35
1970 03 06	05 04	2 35
1970 03 07	05 07	2 35
1970 03 08	05 10	2 35
1970 03 09	05 14	2 35
1970 03 10	05 17	2 34
1970 03 11	05 21	2 34
1970 03 12	05 24	2 34
1970 03 13	05 28	2 34
1970 03 14	05 31	2 34
1970 03 15	05 35	2 34
1970 03 16	05 38	2 34
1970 03 17	05 41	2 34
1970 03 18	05 45	2 34
1970 03 19	05 48	2 34
1970 03 20	05 52	2 34
1970 03 21	05 55	2 34
1970 03 22	05 59	2 33
1970 03 23	06 03	2 33
1970 03 24	06 06	2 33
1970 03 25	06 10	2 33
1970 03 26	06 13	2 33
1970 03 27	06 17	2 33
1970 03 28	06 20	2 33
1970 03 29	06 24	2 33
1970 03 30	06 27	2 33
1970 03 31	06 31	2 33
1970 04 01	06 34	2 33
1970 04 02	06 38	2 33
1970 04 03	06 41	2 33
1970 04 04	06 45	2 33
1970 04 05	06 48	2 33
1970 04 06	06 52	2 33
1970 04 07	06 55	2 33
1970 04 08	06 59	2 32
1970 04 09	07 02	2 32
1970 04 10	07 06	2 32
1970 04 11	07 09	2 32
1970 04 12	07 13	2 32
1970 04 13	07 16	2 32
1970 04 14	07 19	2 32
1970 04 15	07 23	2 32
1970 04 16	07 26	2 32
1970 04 17	07 30	2 32
1970 04 18	07 33	2 32
1970 04 19	07 36	2 32
1970 04 20	07 40	2 32
1970 04 21	07 43	2 32
1970 04 22	07 46	2 32
1970 04 23	07 50	2 32
1970 04 24	07 53	2 32
1970 04 25	07 56	2 32
1970 04 26	07 59	2 32
1970 04 27	08 03	2 32
1970 04 28	08 06	2 32
1970 04 29	08 09	2 32
1970 04 30	08 12	2 32
1970 05 01	08 15	2 32
1970 05 02	08 18	2 32
1970 05 03	08 21	2 32
1970 05 04	08 24	2 32
1970 05 05	08 27	2 32
1970 05 06	08 30	2 32
1970 05 07	08 33	2 32
1970 05 08	08 36	2 32
1970 05 09	08 39	2 32
1970 05 10	08 42	2 32
1970 05 11	08 45	2 32
1970 05 12	08 48	2 32
1970 05 13	08 50	2 32
1970 05 14	08 53	2 32
1970 05 15	08 56	2 32
1970 05 16	08 58	2 32
1970 05 17	09 01	2 32
1970 05 18	09 04	2 32
1970 05 19	09 06	2 33
1970 05 20	09 09	2 33
1970 05 21	09 11	2 33
1970 05 22	09 14	2 33
1970 05 23	09 16	2 33
1970 05 24	09 19	2 33
1970 05 25	09 21	2 33
1970 05 26	09 23	2 33
1970 05 27	09 26	2 33
1970 05 28	09 28	2 33
1970 05 29	09 30	2 33
1970 05 30	09 32	2 33
1970 05 31	09 34	2 33
1970 06 01	09 36	2 33
1970 06 02	09 39	2 33
1970 06 03	09 41	2 33
1970 06 04	09 42	2 33
1970 06 05	09 44	2 33
1970 06 06	09 46	2 33
1970 06 07	09 48	2 33
1970 06 08	09 50	2 34
1970 06 09	09 52	2 34
1970 06 10	09 53	2 34
1970 06 11	09 55	2 34
1970 06 12	09 57	2 34
1970 06 13	09 58	2 34
1970 06 14	10 00	2 34
1970 06 15	10 01	2 34
1970 06 16	10 03	2 34
1970 06 17	10 04	2 34
1970 06 18	10 05	2 34
1970 06 19	10 06	2 34
1970 06 20	10 08	2 34
1970 06 21	10 09	2 34
1970 06 22	10 10	2 34
1970 06 23	10 11	2 35
1970 06 24	10 12	2 35
1970 06 25	10 13	2 35
1970 06 26	10 14	2 35
1970 06 27	10 15	2 35
1970 06 28	10 16	2 35
1970 06 29	10 17	2 35
1970 06 30	10 17	2 35
1970 07 01	10 18	2 35
1970 07 02	10 19	2 35
1970 07 03	10 19	2 35
1970 07 04	10 20	2 35
1970 07 05	10 20	2 35
1970 07 06	10 21	2 35
1970 07 07	10 21	2 36
1970 07 08	10 21	2 36
1970 07 09	10 22	2 36
1970 07 10	10 22	2 36
1970 07 11	10 22	2 36
1970 07 12	10 22	2 36
1970 07 13	10 22	2 36
1970 07 14	10 22	2 36
1970 07 15	10 22	2 36
1970 07 16	10 22	2 36
1970 07 17	10 22	2 36
1970 07 18	10 22	2 36
1970 07 19	10 21	2 36
1970 07 20	10 21	2 36
1970 07 21	10 21	2 37
1970 07 22	10 20	2 37
1970 07 23	10 20	2 37
1970 07 24	10 19	2 37
1970 07 25	10 19	2 37
1970 07 26	10 18	2 37
1970 07 27	10 17	2 37
1970 07 28	10 17	2 37
1970 07 29	10 16	2 37
1970 07 30	10 15	2 37
1970 07 31	10 14	2 37
1970 08 01	10 13	2 37
1970 08 02	10 12	2 37
1970 08 03	10 11	2 37
1970 08 04	10 10	2 37
1970 08 05	10 09	2 38
1970 08 06	10 08	2 38
1970 08 07	10 07	2 38
1970 08 08	10 06	2 38
1970 08 09	10 04	2 38
1970 08 10	10 03	2 38
1970 08 11	10 02	2 38
1970 08 12	10 00	2 38
1970 08 13	09 59	2 38
1970 08 14	09 57	2 38
1970 08 15	09 56	2 38
1970 08 16	09 54	2 38
1970 08 17	09 52	2 38
1970 08 18	09 51	2 38
1970 08 19	09 49	2 38
1970 08 20	09 47	2 38
1970 08 21	09 45	2 38
1970 08 22	09 44	2 38
1970 08 23	09 42	2 38
1970 08 24	09 40	2 38
1970 08 25	09 38	2 38
1970 08 26	09 36	2 38
1970 08 27	09 34	2 38
1970 08 28	09 32	2 38
1970 08 29	09 30	2 38
1970 08 30	09 27	2 38
1970 08 31	09 25	2 38
1970 09 01	09 23	2 38
1970 09 02	09 21	2 38
1970 09 03	09 19	2 38
1970 09 04	09 16	2 38
1970 09 05	09 14	2 38
1970 09 06	09 12	2 38
1970 09 07	09 09	2 38
1970 09 08	09 07	2 38
1970 09 09	09 04	2 38
1970 09 10	09 02	2 38
1970 09 11	08 59	2 38
1970 09 12	08 57	2 38
1970 09 13	08 54	2 38
1970 09 14	08 52	2 38
1970 09 15	08 49	2 38
1970 09 16	08 47	2 38
1970 09 17	08 44	2 38
1970 09 18	08 42	2 38
1970 09 19	08 39	2 38
1970 09 20	08 36	2 38
1970 09 21	08 34	2 38
1970 09 22	08 31	2 38
1970 09 23	08 28	2 38
1970 09 24	08 26	2 38
1970 09 25	08 23	2 38
1970 09 26	08 20	2 38
1970 09 27	08 18	2 38
1970 09 28	08 15	2 38
1970 09 29	08 12	2 38
1970 09 30	08 09	2 38
1970 10 01	08 07	2 38
1970 10 02	08 04	2 38
1970 10 03	08 01	2 37
1970 10 04	07 59	2 37
1970 10 05	07 56	2 37
1970 10 06	07 53	2 37
1970 10 07	07 51	2 37
1970 10 08	07 48	2 37
1970 10 09	07 45	2 37
1970 10 10	07 42	2 37
1970 10 11	07 40	2 37
1970 10 12	07 37	2 37
1970 10 13	07 34	2 37
1970 10 14	07 32	2 36
1970 10 15	07 29	2 36
1970 10 16	07 27	2 36
1970 10 17	07 24	2 36
1970 10 18	07 21	2 36
1970 10 19	07 19	2 36
1970 10 20	07 16	2 36
1970 10 21	07 14	2 36
1970 10 22	07 11	2 36
1970 10 23	07 09	2 35
1970 10 24	07 06	2 35
1970 10 25	07 04	2 35
1970 10 26	07 02	2 35
1970 10 27	06 59	2 35
1970 10 28	06 57	2 35
1970 10 29	06 55	2 35
1970 10 30	06 52	2 34
1970 10 31	06 50	2 34
1970 11 01	06 48	2 34
1970 11 02	06 46	2 34
1970 11 03	06 43	2 34
1970 11 04	06 41	2 34
1970 11 05	06 39	2 34
1970 11 06	06 37	2 33
1970 11 07	06 35	2 33
1970 11 08	06 33	2 33
1970 11 09	06 31	2 33
1970 11 10	06 29	2 33
1970 11 11	06 27	2 33
1970 11 12	06 26	2 32
1970 11 13	06 24	2 32
1970 11 14	06 22	2 32
1970 11 15	06 20	2 32
1970 11 16	06 19	2 32
1970 11 17	06 17	2 32
1970 11 18	06 16	2 31
1970 11 19	06 14	2 31
1970 11 20	06 13	2 31
1970 11 21	06 11	2 31
1970 11 22	06 10	2 31
1970 11 23	06 08	2 31
1970 11 24	06 07	2 30
1970 11 25	06 06	2 30
1970 11 26	06 05	2 30
1970 11 27	06 04	2 30
1970 11 28	06 03	2 30
1970 11 29	06 02	2 29
1970 11 30	06 01	2 29
1970 12 01	06 00	2 29
1970 12 02	05 59	2 29
1970 12 03	05 58	2 29
1970 12 04	05 57	2 28
1970 12 05	05 56	2 28
1970 12 06	05 56	2 28
1970 12 07	05 55	2 28
1970 12 08	05 55	2 28
1970 12 09	05 54	2 28
1970 12 10	05 54	2 27
1970 12 11	05 53	2 27
1970 12 12	05 53	2 27
1970 12 13	05 53	2 27
1970 12 14	05 52	2 27
1970 12 15	05 52	2 26
1970 12 16	05 52	2 26
1970 12 17	05 52	2 26
1970 12 18	05 52	2 26
1970 12 19	05 52	2 26
1970 12 20	05 52	2 25
1970 12 21	05 52	2 25
1970 12 22	05 52	2 25
1970 12 23	05 53	2 25
1970 12 24	05 53	2 25
1970 12 25	05 53	2 24
1970 12 26	05 54	2 24
1970 12 27	05 54	2 24
1970 12 28	05 55	2 24
1970 12 29	05 55	2 24
1970 12 30	05 56	2 23
1970 12 31	05 57	2 23
1971 01 01	05 58	2 23
1971 01 02	05 58	2 23
1971 01 03	05 59	2 23
1971 01 04	06 00	2 22
1971 01 05	06 01	2 22
1971 01 06	06 02	2 22
1971 01 07	06 03	2 22
1971 01 08	06 04	2 22
1971 01 09	06 06	2 21
1971 01 10	06 07	2 21
1971 01 11	06 08	2 21
1971 01 12	06 09	2 21
1971 01 13	06 11	2 21
1971 01 14	06 12	2 20
1971 01 15	06 14	2 20
1971 01 16	06 15	2 20
1971 01 17	06 17	2 20
1971 01 18	06 19	2 20
1971 01 19	06 20	2 20
1971 01 20	06 22	2 19
1971 01 21	06 24	2 19
1971 01 22	06 26	2 19
1971 01 23	06 27	2 19
1971 01 24	06 29	2 19
1971 01 25	06 31	2 19
1971 01 26	06 33	2 18
1971 01 27	06 35	2 18
1971 01 28	06 38	2 18
1971 01 29	06 40	2 18
1971 01 30	06 42	2 18
1971 01 31	06 44	2 17
1971 02 01	06 46	2 17
1971 02 02	06 49	2 17
1971 02 03	06 51	2 17
1971 02 04	06 53	2 17
1971 02 05	06 56	2 17
1971 02 06	06 58	2 17
1971 02 07	07 01	2 16
1971 02 08	07 03	2 16
1971 02 09	07 06	2 16
1971 02 10	07 09	2 16
1971 02 11	07 11	2 16
1971 02 12	07 14	2 16
1971 02 13	07 17	2 15
1971 02 14	07 19	2 15
1971 02 15	07 22	2 15
1971 02 16	07 25	2 15
1971 02 17	07 28	2 15
1971 02 18	07 31	2 15
1971 02 19	07 34	2 15
1971 02 20	07 37	2 14
1971 02 21	07 40	2 14
1971 02 22	07 43	2 14
1971 02 23	07 46	2 14
1971 02 24	07 49	2 14
1971 02 25	07 52	2 14
1971 02 26	07 55	2 14
1971 02 27	07 58	2 14
1971 02 28	08 01	2 13
1971 03 01	08 04	2 13
1971 03 02	08 08	2 13
1971 03 03	08 11	2 13
1971 03 04	08 14	2 13
1971 03 05	08 17	2 13
1971 03 06	08 21	2 13
1971 03 07	08 24	2 13
1971 03 08	08 27	2 13
1971 03 09	08 31	2 12
1971 03 10	08 34	2 12
1971 03 11	08 37	2 12
1971 03 12	08 40	2 12
1971 03 13	08 44	2 12
1971 03 14	08 47	2 12
1971 03 15	08 51	2 12
1971 03 16	08 54	2 12
1971 03 17	08 58	2 12
1971 03 18	09 01	2 12
1971 03 19	09 04	2 12
1971 03 20	09 08	2 11
1971 03 21	09 11	2 11
1971 03 22	09 15	2 11
1971 03 23	09 18	2 11
1971 03 24	09 22	2 11
1971 03 25	09 25	2 11
1971 03 26	09 29	2 11
1971 03 27	09 32	2 11
1971 03 28	09 36	2 11
1971 03 29	09 40	2 11
1971 03 30	09 43	2 11
1971 03 31	09 47	2 11
1971 04 01	09 50	2 11
1971 04 02	09 54	2 10
1971 04 03	09 57	2 10
1971 04 04	10 01	2 10
1971 04 05	10 04	2 10
1971 04 06	10 08	2 10
1971 04 07	10 11	2 10
1971 04 08	10 15	2 10
1971 04 09	10 18	2 10
1971 04 10	10 22	2 10
1971 04 11	10 25	2 10
1971 04 12	10 29	2 10
1971 04 13	10 32	2 10
1971 04 14	10 36	2 10
1971 04 15	10 39	2 10
1971 04 16	10 42	2 10
1971 04 17	10 46	2 10

1971 04 18	10 49	2 10
1971 04 19	10 53	2 10
1971 04 20	10 56	2 10
1971 04 21	10 59	2 10
1971 04 22	11 03	2 10
1971 04 23	11 06	2 10
1971 04 24	11 09	2 10
1971 04 25	11 13	2 10
1971 04 26	11 16	2 10
1971 04 27	11 19	2 10
1971 04 28	11 23	2 10
1971 04 29	11 26	2 09
1971 04 30	11 29	2 09
1971 05 01	11 32	2 09
1971 05 02	11 35	2 09
1971 05 03	11 39	2 09
1971 05 04	11 42	2 09
1971 05 05	11 45	2 09
1971 05 06	11 48	2 09
1971 05 07	11 51	2 09
1971 05 08	11 54	2 09
1971 05 09	11 57	2 09
1971 05 10	12 00	2 09
1971 05 11	12 03	2 09
1971 05 12	12 06	2 09
1971 05 13	12 09	2 09
1971 05 14	12 12	2 09
1971 05 15	12 14	2 09
1971 05 16	12 17	2 09
1971 05 17	12 20	2 09
1971 05 18	12 23	2 10
1971 05 19	12 25	2 10
1971 05 20	12 28	2 10
1971 05 21	12 31	2 10
1971 05 22	12 33	2 10
1971 05 23	12 36	2 10
1971 05 24	12 38	2 10
1971 05 25	12 41	2 10
1971 05 26	12 43	2 10
1971 05 27	12 46	2 10
1971 05 28	12 48	2 10
1971 05 29	12 51	2 10
1971 05 30	12 53	2 10
1971 05 31	12 55	2 10
1971 06 01	12 57	2 10
1971 06 02	13 00	2 10
1971 06 03	13 02	2 10
1971 06 04	13 04	2 10
1971 06 05	13 06	2 10
1971 06 06	13 08	2 10
1971 06 07	13 10	2 10
1971 06 08	13 12	2 10
1971 06 09	13 14	2 10
1971 06 10	13 16	2 10
1971 06 11	13 17	2 10
1971 06 12	13 19	2 10
1971 06 13	13 21	2 10
1971 06 14	13 23	2 10
1971 06 15	13 24	2 10
1971 06 16	13 26	2 10
1971 06 17	13 27	2 10
1971 06 18	13 29	2 10
1971 06 19	13 30	2 11
1971 06 20	13 32	2 11
1971 06 21	13 33	2 11
1971 06 22	13 35	2 11
1971 06 23	13 36	2 11
1971 06 24	13 37	2 11
1971 06 25	13 38	2 11
1971 06 26	13 39	2 11
1971 06 27	13 40	2 11
1971 06 28	13 41	2 11
1971 06 29	13 42	2 11
1971 06 30	13 43	2 11
1971 07 01	13 44	2 11
1971 07 02	13 45	2 11
1971 07 03	13 46	2 11
1971 07 04	13 46	2 11
1971 07 05	13 47	2 11
1971 07 06	13 48	2 11
1971 07 07	13 48	2 11
1971 07 08	13 49	2 11
1971 07 09	13 49	2 11
1971 07 10	13 50	2 12
1971 07 11	13 50	2 12
1971 07 12	13 50	2 12
1971 07 13	13 51	2 12
1971 07 14	13 51	2 12
1971 07 15	13 51	2 12
1971 07 16	13 51	2 12
1971 07 17	13 51	2 12
1971 07 18	13 51	2 12
1971 07 19	13 51	2 12
1971 07 20	13 51	2 12
1971 07 21	13 51	2 12
1971 07 22	13 51	2 12
1971 07 23	13 50	2 12
1971 07 24	13 50	2 12
1971 07 25	13 50	2 12
1971 07 26	13 49	2 12
1971 07 27	13 49	2 12
1971 07 28	13 48	2 12
1971 07 29	13 48	2 12
1971 07 30	13 47	2 13
1971 07 31	13 46	2 13
1971 08 01	13 46	2 13
1971 08 02	13 45	2 13
1971 08 03	13 44	2 13
1971 08 04	13 43	2 13
1971 08 05	13 42	2 13
1971 08 06	13 41	2 13
1971 08 07	13 40	2 13
1971 08 08	13 39	2 13
1971 08 09	13 38	2 13
1971 08 10	13 37	2 13
1971 08 11	13 36	2 13
1971 08 12	13 35	2 13
1971 08 13	13 33	2 13
1971 08 14	13 32	2 13
1971 08 15	13 31	2 13
1971 08 16	13 29	2 13
1971 08 17	13 28	2 13
1971 08 18	13 26	2 13
1971 08 19	13 25	2 13
1971 08 20	13 23	2 13
1971 08 21	13 21	2 13
1971 08 22	13 20	2 13
1971 08 23	13 18	2 13
1971 08 24	13 16	2 13
1971 08 25	13 14	2 13
1971 08 26	13 12	2 13
1971 08 27	13 10	2 13
1971 08 28	13 09	2 13
1971 08 29	13 07	2 13
1971 08 30	13 05	2 13
1971 08 31	13 03	2 13
1971 09 01	13 00	2 13
1971 09 02	12 58	2 13
1971 09 03	12 56	2 13
1971 09 04	12 54	2 13
1971 09 05	12 52	2 13
1971 09 06	12 50	2 13
1971 09 07	12 47	2 13
1971 09 08	12 45	2 13
1971 09 09	12 43	2 13
1971 09 10	12 40	2 13
1971 09 11	12 38	2 13
1971 09 12	12 36	2 13
1971 09 13	12 33	2 13
1971 09 14	12 31	2 13
1971 09 15	12 28	2 13
1971 09 16	12 26	2 13
1971 09 17	12 23	2 13
1971 09 18	12 21	2 13
1971 09 19	12 18	2 13
1971 09 20	12 15	2 13
1971 09 21	12 13	2 13
1971 09 22	12 10	2 13
1971 09 23	12 08	2 13
1971 09 24	12 05	2 13
1971 09 25	12 02	2 13
1971 09 26	12 00	2 13
1971 09 27	11 57	2 13
1971 09 28	11 54	2 13
1971 09 29	11 52	2 13
1971 09 30	11 49	2 13
1971 10 01	11 46	2 13
1971 10 02	11 43	2 12
1971 10 03	11 41	2 12
1971 10 04	11 38	2 12
1971 10 05	11 35	2 12
1971 10 06	11 33	2 12
1971 10 07	11 30	2 12
1971 10 08	11 27	2 12
1971 10 09	11 25	2 12
1971 10 10	11 22	2 12
1971 10 11	11 19	2 12
1971 10 12	11 16	2 12
1971 10 13	11 14	2 12
1971 10 14	11 11	2 12
1971 10 15	11 08	2 11
1971 10 16	11 06	2 11
1971 10 17	11 03	2 11
1971 10 18	11 00	2 11
1971 10 19	10 58	2 11
1971 10 20	10 55	2 11
1971 10 21	10 53	2 11
1971 10 22	10 50	2 11
1971 10 23	10 47	2 11
1971 10 24	10 45	2 10
1971 10 25	10 42	2 10
1971 10 26	10 40	2 10
1971 10 27	10 37	2 10
1971 10 28	10 35	2 10
1971 10 29	10 33	2 10
1971 10 30	10 30	2 10
1971 10 31	10 28	2 10
1971 11 01	10 25	2 10
1971 11 02	10 23	2 09
1971 11 03	10 21	2 09
1971 11 04	10 19	2 09
1971 11 05	10 16	2 09
1971 11 06	10 14	2 09
1971 11 07	10 12	2 09
1971 11 08	10 10	2 09
1971 11 09	10 08	2 09
1971 11 10	10 06	2 08
1971 11 11	10 04	2 08
1971 11 12	10 02	2 08
1971 11 13	10 00	2 08
1971 11 14	09 58	2 08
1971 11 15	09 56	2 08
1971 11 16	09 54	2 07
1971 11 17	09 53	2 07
1971 11 18	09 51	2 07
1971 11 19	09 49	2 07
1971 11 20	09 47	2 07
1971 11 21	09 46	2 07
1971 11 22	09 44	2 07
1971 11 23	09 43	2 06
1971 11 24	09 41	2 06
1971 11 25	09 40	2 06
1971 11 26	09 39	2 06
1971 11 27	09 37	2 06
1971 11 28	09 36	2 06
1971 11 29	09 35	2 05
1971 11 30	09 34	2 05
1971 12 01	09 32	2 05
1971 12 02	09 31	2 05
1971 12 03	09 30	2 05
1971 12 04	09 29	2 05
1971 12 05	09 28	2 04
1971 12 06	09 28	2 04
1971 12 07	09 27	2 04
1971 12 08	09 26	2 04
1971 12 09	09 25	2 04
1971 12 10	09 25	2 03
1971 12 11	09 24	2 03
1971 12 12	09 23	2 03
1971 12 13	09 23	2 03
1971 12 14	09 23	2 03
1971 12 15	09 22	2 03
1971 12 16	09 22	2 02
1971 12 17	09 22	2 02
1971 12 18	09 21	2 02
1971 12 19	09 21	2 02
1971 12 20	09 21	2 02
1971 12 21	09 21	2 02
1971 12 22	09 21	2 01
1971 12 23	09 21	2 01
1971 12 24	09 21	2 01
1971 12 25	09 21	2 01
1971 12 26	09 22	2 01
1971 12 27	09 22	2 00
1971 12 28	09 22	2 00
1971 12 29	09 23	2 00
1971 12 30	09 23	2 00
1971 12 31	09 24	2 00
1972 01 01	09 24	2 00
1972 01 02	09 25	1 59
1972 01 03	09 25	1 59
1972 01 04	09 26	1 59
1972 01 05	09 27	1 59
1972 01 06	09 28	1 59
1972 01 07	09 29	1 59
1972 01 08	09 30	1 58
1972 01 09	09 31	1 58
1972 01 10	09 32	1 58
1972 01 11	09 33	1 58
1972 01 12	09 34	1 58
1972 01 13	09 35	1 58
1972 01 14	09 36	1 57
1972 01 15	09 38	1 57
1972 01 16	09 39	1 57
1972 01 17	09 40	1 57
1972 01 18	09 42	1 57
1972 01 19	09 43	1 57
1972 01 20	09 45	1 56
1972 01 21	09 46	1 56
1972 01 22	09 48	1 56
1972 01 23	09 50	1 56
1972 01 24	09 52	1 56
1972 01 25	09 53	1 56
1972 01 26	09 55	1 55
1972 01 27	09 57	1 55
1972 01 28	09 59	1 55
1972 01 29	10 01	1 55
1972 01 30	10 03	1 55
1972 01 31	10 05	1 55
1972 02 01	10 07	1 54
1972 02 02	10 09	1 54
1972 02 03	10 12	1 54
1972 02 04	10 14	1 54
1972 02 05	10 16	1 54
1972 02 06	10 18	1 54
1972 02 07	10 21	1 54
1972 02 08	10 23	1 53
1972 02 09	10 26	1 53
1972 02 10	10 28	1 53
1972 02 11	10 31	1 53
1972 02 12	10 33	1 53
1972 02 13	10 36	1 53
1972 02 14	10 38	1 53
1972 02 15	10 41	1 52
1972 02 16	10 44	1 52
1972 02 17	10 47	1 52
1972 02 18	10 49	1 52
1972 02 19	10 52	1 52
1972 02 20	10 55	1 52
1972 02 21	10 58	1 52
1972 02 22	11 01	1 52
1972 02 23	11 04	1 51
1972 02 24	11 07	1 51
1972 02 25	11 10	1 51
1972 02 26	11 13	1 51
1972 02 27	11 16	1 51
1972 02 28	11 19	1 51
1972 02 29	11 22	1 51
1972 03 01	11 25	1 51
1972 03 02	11 28	1 50
1972 03 03	11 31	1 50
1972 03 04	11 34	1 50
1972 03 05	11 38	1 50
1972 03 06	11 41	1 50
1972 03 07	11 44	1 50
1972 03 08	11 47	1 50
1972 03 09	11 51	1 50
1972 03 10	11 54	1 50
1972 03 11	11 57	1 49
1972 03 12	12 01	1 49
1972 03 13	12 04	1 49
1972 03 14	12 07	1 49
1972 03 15	12 11	1 49
1972 03 16	12 14	1 49
1972 03 17	12 18	1 49
1972 03 18	12 21	1 49
1972 03 19	12 24	1 49
1972 03 20	12 28	1 49
1972 03 21	12 31	1 49
1972 03 22	12 35	1 48
1972 03 23	12 38	1 48
1972 03 24	12 42	1 48
1972 03 25	12 45	1 48
1972 03 26	12 49	1 48
1972 03 27	12 52	1 48
1972 03 28	12 56	1 48
1972 03 29	12 59	1 48
1972 03 30	13 03	1 48
1972 03 31	13 06	1 48
1972 04 01	13 10	1 48
1972 04 02	13 13	1 48
1972 04 03	13 17	1 48
1972 04 04	13 20	1 48
1972 04 05	13 24	1 47
1972 04 06	13 28	1 47
1972 04 07	13 31	1 47
1972 04 08	13 35	1 47
1972 04 09	13 38	1 47
1972 04 10	13 42	1 47
1972 04 11	13 45	1 47
1972 04 12	13 49	1 47
1972 04 13	13 52	1 47
1972 04 14	13 56	1 47
1972 04 15	13 59	1 47
1972 04 16	14 03	1 47
1972 04 17	14 06	1 47
1972 04 18	14 09	1 47
1972 04 19	14 13	1 47
1972 04 20	14 16	1 47
1972 04 21	14 20	1 47
1972 04 22	14 23	1 47
1972 04 23	14 27	1 47
1972 04 24	14 30	1 47
1972 04 25	14 33	1 47
1972 04 26	14 37	1 46
1972 04 27	14 40	1 46
1972 04 28	14 43	1 46
1972 04 29	14 46	1 46
1972 04 30	14 50	1 46
1972 05 01	14 53	1 46
1972 05 02	14 56	1 46
1972 05 03	14 59	1 46
1972 05 04	15 03	1 46
1972 05 05	15 06	1 46
1972 05 06	15 09	1 46
1972 05 07	15 12	1 46
1972 05 08	15 15	1 46
1972 05 09	15 18	1 46
1972 05 10	15 21	1 46
1972 05 11	15 24	1 46
1972 05 12	15 27	1 46
1972 05 13	15 30	1 46
1972 05 14	15 33	1 46
1972 05 15	15 36	1 46
1972 05 16	15 39	1 46
1972 05 17	15 42	1 46
1972 05 18	15 45	1 46
1972 05 19	15 48	1 46
1972 05 20	15 50	1 46
1972 05 21	15 53	1 46
1972 05 22	15 56	1 46
1972 05 23	15 58	1 46
1972 05 24	16 01	1 46
1972 05 25	16 04	1 46
1972 05 26	16 06	1 46
1972 05 27	16 09	1 46
1972 05 28	16 11	1 46
1972 05 29	16 14	1 46
1972 05 30	16 16	1 46
1972 05 31	16 19	1 46
1972 06 01	16 21	1 46
1972 06 02	16 23	1 46
1972 06 03	16 26	1 46
1972 06 04	16 28	1 46
1972 06 05	16 30	1 46
1972 06 06	16 32	1 46
1972 06 07	16 34	1 46
1972 06 08	16 36	1 46
1972 06 09	16 38	1 46

Chiron

1972 06 10	16 40	1 46
1972 06 11	16 42	1 46
1972 06 12	16 44	1 46
1972 06 13	16 46	1 46
1972 06 14	16 48	1 46
1972 06 15	16 50	1 46
1972 06 16	16 51	1 46
1972 06 17	16 53	1 46
1972 06 18	16 55	1 46
1972 06 19	16 56	1 46
1972 06 20	16 58	1 46
1972 06 21	16 59	1 46
1972 06 22	17 01	1 46
1972 06 23	17 02	1 47
1972 06 24	17 04	1 47
1972 06 25	17 05	1 47
1972 06 26	17 06	1 47
1972 06 27	17 07	1 47
1972 06 28	17 09	1 47
1972 06 29	17 10	1 47
1972 06 30	17 11	1 47
1972 07 01	17 12	1 47
1972 07 02	17 13	1 47
1972 07 03	17 14	1 47
1972 07 04	17 15	1 47
1972 07 05	17 15	1 47
1972 07 06	17 16	1 47
1972 07 07	17 17	1 47
1972 07 08	17 18	1 47
1972 07 09	17 18	1 47
1972 07 10	17 19	1 47
1972 07 11	17 19	1 47
1972 07 12	17 20	1 47
1972 07 13	17 20	1 47
1972 07 14	17 21	1 47
1972 07 15	17 21	1 47
1972 07 16	17 21	1 47
1972 07 17	17 21	1 47
1972 07 18	17 21	1 47
1972 07 19	17 22	1 47
1972 07 20	17 22	1 47
1972 07 21	17 22	1 47
1972 07 22	17 21	1 47
1972 07 23	17 21	1 47
1972 07 24	17 21	1 47
1972 07 25	17 21	1 47
1972 07 26	17 21	1 47
1972 07 27	17 20	1 47
1972 07 28	17 20	1 47
1972 07 29	17 20	1 47
1972 07 30	17 19	1 48
1972 07 31	17 19	1 48
1972 08 01	17 18	1 48
1972 08 02	17 17	1 48
1972 08 03	17 17	1 48
1972 08 04	17 16	1 48
1972 08 05	17 15	1 48
1972 08 06	17 14	1 48
1972 08 07	17 14	1 48
1972 08 08	17 13	1 48
1972 08 09	17 12	1 48
1972 08 10	17 11	1 48
1972 08 11	17 10	1 48
1972 08 12	17 08	1 48
1972 08 13	17 07	1 48
1972 08 14	17 06	1 48
1972 08 15	17 05	1 48
1972 08 16	17 03	1 48
1972 08 17	17 02	1 48
1972 08 18	17 01	1 48
1972 08 19	16 59	1 48
1972 08 20	16 58	1 48
1972 08 21	16 56	1 48
1972 08 22	16 55	1 48
1972 08 23	16 53	1 48
1972 08 24	16 51	1 48
1972 08 25	16 50	1 48
1972 08 26	16 48	1 48
1972 08 27	16 46	1 48
1972 08 28	16 44	1 48
1972 08 29	16 42	1 48
1972 08 30	16 41	1 48
1972 08 31	16 39	1 48
1972 09 01	16 37	1 48
1972 09 02	16 35	1 48
1972 09 03	16 33	1 48
1972 09 04	16 30	1 48
1972 09 05	16 28	1 48
1972 09 06	16 26	1 48
1972 09 07	16 24	1 48
1972 09 08	16 22	1 48
1972 09 09	16 19	1 48
1972 09 10	16 17	1 48
1972 09 11	16 15	1 48
1972 09 12	16 13	1 48
1972 09 13	16 10	1 48
1972 09 14	16 08	1 48
1972 09 15	16 05	1 48
1972 09 16	16 03	1 48
1972 09 17	16 00	1 48
1972 09 18	15 58	1 47
1972 09 19	15 55	1 47
1972 09 20	15 53	1 47
1972 09 21	15 50	1 47
1972 09 22	15 48	1 47
1972 09 23	15 45	1 47
1972 09 24	15 43	1 47
1972 09 25	15 40	1 47
1972 09 26	15 37	1 47
1972 09 27	15 35	1 47
1972 09 28	15 32	1 47
1972 09 29	15 29	1 47
1972 09 30	15 27	1 47
1972 10 01	15 24	1 47
1972 10 02	15 21	1 47
1972 10 03	15 19	1 47
1972 10 04	15 16	1 47
1972 10 05	15 13	1 47
1972 10 06	15 10	1 47
1972 10 07	15 08	1 46
1972 10 08	15 05	1 46
1972 10 09	15 02	1 46
1972 10 10	15 00	1 46
1972 10 11	14 57	1 46
1972 10 12	14 54	1 46
1972 10 13	14 51	1 46
1972 10 14	14 49	1 46
1972 10 15	14 46	1 46
1972 10 16	14 43	1 46
1972 10 17	14 41	1 46
1972 10 18	14 38	1 46
1972 10 19	14 35	1 45
1972 10 20	14 33	1 45
1972 10 21	14 30	1 45
1972 10 22	14 27	1 45
1972 10 23	14 25	1 45
1972 10 24	14 22	1 45
1972 10 25	14 20	1 45
1972 10 26	14 17	1 45
1972 10 27	14 14	1 45
1972 10 28	14 12	1 45
1972 10 29	14 09	1 44
1972 10 30	14 07	1 44
1972 10 31	14 05	1 44
1972 11 01	14 02	1 44
1972 11 02	14 00	1 44
1972 11 03	13 57	1 44
1972 11 04	13 55	1 44
1972 11 05	13 53	1 44
1972 11 06	13 50	1 44
1972 11 07	13 48	1 43
1972 11 08	13 46	1 43
1972 11 09	13 44	1 43
1972 11 10	13 42	1 43
1972 11 11	13 39	1 43
1972 11 12	13 37	1 43
1972 11 13	13 35	1 43
1972 11 14	13 33	1 43
1972 11 15	13 31	1 42
1972 11 16	13 29	1 42
1972 11 17	13 27	1 42
1972 11 18	13 26	1 42
1972 11 19	13 24	1 42
1972 11 20	13 22	1 42
1972 11 21	13 20	1 42
1972 11 22	13 19	1 41
1972 11 23	13 17	1 41
1972 11 24	13 15	1 41
1972 11 25	13 14	1 41
1972 11 26	13 12	1 41
1972 11 27	13 11	1 41
1972 11 28	13 09	1 41
1972 11 29	13 08	1 40
1972 11 30	13 07	1 40
1972 12 01	13 06	1 40
1972 12 02	13 04	1 40
1972 12 03	13 03	1 40
1972 12 04	13 02	1 40
1972 12 05	13 01	1 40
1972 12 06	13 00	1 39
1972 12 07	12 59	1 39
1972 12 08	12 58	1 39
1972 12 09	12 57	1 39
1972 12 10	12 56	1 39
1972 12 11	12 56	1 39
1972 12 12	12 55	1 38
1972 12 13	12 54	1 38
1972 12 14	12 54	1 38
1972 12 15	12 53	1 38
1972 12 16	12 53	1 38
1972 12 17	12 52	1 38
1972 12 18	12 52	1 38
1972 12 19	12 52	1 37
1972 12 20	12 51	1 37
1972 12 21	12 51	1 37
1972 12 22	12 51	1 37
1972 12 23	12 51	1 37
1972 12 24	12 51	1 37
1972 12 25	12 51	1 36
1972 12 26	12 51	1 36
1972 12 27	12 51	1 36
1972 12 28	12 51	1 36
1972 12 29	12 52	1 36
1972 12 30	12 52	1 36
1972 12 31	12 52	1 36
1973 01 01	12 53	1 35
1973 01 02	12 53	1 35
1973 01 03	12 54	1 35
1973 01 04	12 54	1 35
1973 01 05	12 55	1 35
1973 01 06	12 56	1 35
1973 01 07	12 56	1 34
1973 01 08	12 57	1 34
1973 01 09	12 58	1 34
1973 01 10	12 59	1 34
1973 01 11	13 00	1 34
1973 01 12	13 01	1 34
1973 01 13	13 02	1 34
1973 01 14	13 03	1 33
1973 01 15	13 04	1 33
1973 01 16	13 05	1 33
1973 01 17	13 07	1 33
1973 01 18	13 08	1 33
1973 01 19	13 09	1 33
1973 01 20	13 11	1 32
1973 01 21	13 12	1 32
1973 01 22	13 14	1 32
1973 01 23	13 15	1 32
1973 01 24	13 17	1 32
1973 01 25	13 19	1 32
1973 01 26	13 20	1 32
1973 01 27	13 22	1 31
1973 01 28	13 24	1 31
1973 01 29	13 26	1 31
1973 01 30	13 28	1 31
1973 01 31	13 30	1 31
1973 02 01	13 32	1 31
1973 02 02	13 34	1 31
1973 02 03	13 36	1 30
1973 02 04	13 38	1 30
1973 02 05	13 40	1 30
1973 02 06	13 42	1 30
1973 02 07	13 45	1 30
1973 02 08	13 47	1 30
1973 02 09	13 49	1 30
1973 02 10	13 52	1 30
1973 02 11	13 54	1 29
1973 02 12	13 57	1 29
1973 02 13	13 59	1 29
1973 02 14	14 02	1 29
1973 02 15	14 04	1 29
1973 02 16	14 07	1 29
1973 02 17	14 09	1 29
1973 02 18	14 12	1 29
1973 02 19	14 15	1 28
1973 02 20	14 18	1 28
1973 02 21	14 20	1 28
1973 02 22	14 23	1 28
1973 02 23	14 26	1 28
1973 02 24	14 29	1 28
1973 02 25	14 32	1 28
1973 02 26	14 35	1 28
1973 02 27	14 38	1 27
1973 02 28	14 41	1 27
1973 03 01	14 44	1 27
1973 03 02	14 47	1 27
1973 03 03	14 50	1 27
1973 03 04	14 53	1 27
1973 03 05	14 56	1 27
1973 03 06	14 59	1 27
1973 03 07	15 02	1 27
1973 03 08	15 06	1 27
1973 03 09	15 09	1 26
1973 03 10	15 12	1 26
1973 03 11	15 15	1 26
1973 03 12	15 19	1 26
1973 03 13	15 22	1 26
1973 03 14	15 25	1 26
1973 03 15	15 29	1 26
1973 03 16	15 32	1 26
1973 03 17	15 35	1 26
1973 03 18	15 39	1 26
1973 03 19	15 42	1 25
1973 03 20	15 46	1 25
1973 03 21	15 49	1 25
1973 03 22	15 52	1 25
1973 03 23	15 56	1 25
1973 03 24	15 59	1 25
1973 03 25	16 03	1 25
1973 03 26	16 06	1 25
1973 03 27	16 10	1 25
1973 03 28	16 13	1 25
1973 03 29	16 17	1 25
1973 03 30	16 20	1 25
1973 03 31	16 24	1 24
1973 04 01	16 27	1 24
1973 04 02	16 31	1 24
1973 04 03	16 34	1 24
1973 04 04	16 38	1 24
1973 04 05	16 42	1 24
1973 04 06	16 45	1 24
1973 04 07	16 49	1 24
1973 04 08	16 52	1 24
1973 04 09	16 56	1 24
1973 04 10	16 59	1 24
1973 04 11	17 03	1 24
1973 04 12	17 06	1 24
1973 04 13	17 10	1 24
1973 04 14	17 13	1 24
1973 04 15	17 17	1 24
1973 04 16	17 20	1 23
1973 04 17	17 24	1 23
1973 04 18	17 27	1 23
1973 04 19	17 31	1 23
1973 04 20	17 34	1 23
1973 04 21	17 38	1 23
1973 04 22	17 41	1 23
1973 04 23	17 45	1 23
1973 04 24	17 48	1 23
1973 04 25	17 52	1 23
1973 04 26	17 55	1 23
1973 04 27	17 58	1 23
1973 04 28	18 02	1 23
1973 04 29	18 05	1 23
1973 04 30	18 08	1 23
1973 05 01	18 12	1 23
1973 05 02	18 15	1 23
1973 05 03	18 18	1 23
1973 05 04	18 22	1 23
1973 05 05	18 25	1 23
1973 05 06	18 28	1 23
1973 05 07	18 31	1 23
1973 05 08	18 35	1 22
1973 05 09	18 38	1 22
1973 05 10	18 41	1 22
1973 05 11	18 44	1 22
1973 05 12	18 47	1 22
1973 05 13	18 50	1 22
1973 05 14	18 53	1 22
1973 05 15	18 56	1 22
1973 05 16	18 59	1 22
1973 05 17	19 02	1 22
1973 05 18	19 05	1 22
1973 05 19	19 08	1 22
1973 05 20	19 11	1 22
1973 05 21	19 14	1 22
1973 05 22	19 17	1 22
1973 05 23	19 20	1 22
1973 05 24	19 23	1 22
1973 05 25	19 25	1 22
1973 05 26	19 28	1 22
1973 05 27	19 31	1 22
1973 05 28	19 33	1 22
1973 05 29	19 36	1 22
1973 05 30	19 39	1 22
1973 05 31	19 41	1 22
1973 06 01	19 44	1 22
1973 06 02	19 46	1 22
1973 06 03	19 48	1 22
1973 06 04	19 51	1 22
1973 06 05	19 53	1 22
1973 06 06	19 56	1 22
1973 06 07	19 58	1 22
1973 06 08	20 00	1 22
1973 06 09	20 02	1 22
1973 06 10	20 04	1 22
1973 06 11	20 07	1 22
1973 06 12	20 09	1 22
1973 06 13	20 11	1 22
1973 06 14	20 13	1 22
1973 06 15	20 15	1 22
1973 06 16	20 17	1 22
1973 06 17	20 18	1 22
1973 06 18	20 20	1 22
1973 06 19	20 22	1 22
1973 06 20	20 24	1 22
1973 06 21	20 25	1 22
1973 06 22	20 27	1 22
1973 06 23	20 29	1 22
1973 06 24	20 30	1 22
1973 06 25	20 32	1 22
1973 06 26	20 33	1 22
1973 06 27	20 35	1 22
1973 06 28	20 36	1 22
1973 06 29	20 37	1 22
1973 06 30	20 39	1 22
1973 07 01	20 40	1 22
1973 07 02	20 41	1 22
1973 07 03	20 42	1 22
1973 07 04	20 43	1 22
1973 07 05	20 44	1 22
1973 07 06	20 45	1 22
1973 07 07	20 46	1 22
1973 07 08	20 47	1 22
1973 07 09	20 48	1 22
1973 07 10	20 49	1 22
1973 07 11	20 49	1 22
1973 07 12	20 50	1 22
1973 07 13	20 51	1 22
1973 07 14	20 51	1 22
1973 07 15	20 52	1 22
1973 07 16	20 52	1 22
1973 07 17	20 53	1 22
1973 07 18	20 53	1 22
1973 07 19	20 53	1 22
1973 07 20	20 54	1 22
1973 07 21	20 54	1 22
1973 07 22	20 54	1 22
1973 07 23	20 54	1 22
1973 07 24	20 54	1 22
1973 07 25	20 54	1 22
1973 07 26	20 54	1 22
1973 07 27	20 54	1 22
1973 07 28	20 54	1 22
1973 07 29	20 53	1 22
1973 07 30	20 53	1 22
1973 07 31	20 53	1 22
1973 08 01	20 53	1 22
1973 08 02	20 52	1 22
1973 08 03	20 52	1 22

1973 08 04	20 51	1 22
1973 08 05	20 50	1 22
1973 08 06	20 50	1 22
1973 08 07	20 49	1 22
1973 08 08	20 48	1 22
1973 08 09	20 48	1 22
1973 08 10	20 47	1 22
1973 08 11	20 46	1 22
1973 08 12	20 45	1 22
1973 08 13	20 44	1 22
1973 08 14	20 43	1 22
1973 08 15	20 42	1 22
1973 08 16	20 41	1 22
1973 08 17	20 40	1 22
1973 08 18	20 38	1 22
1973 08 19	20 37	1 22
1973 08 20	20 36	1 22
1973 08 21	20 34	1 22
1973 08 22	20 33	1 22
1973 08 23	20 32	1 22
1973 08 24	20 30	1 22
1973 08 25	20 29	1 22
1973 08 26	20 27	1 22
1973 08 27	20 25	1 22
1973 08 28	20 24	1 22
1973 08 29	20 22	1 22
1973 08 30	20 20	1 22
1973 08 31	20 18	1 22
1973 09 01	20 16	1 22
1973 09 02	20 15	1 22
1973 09 03	20 13	1 22
1973 09 04	20 11	1 22
1973 09 05	20 09	1 22
1973 09 06	20 07	1 22
1973 09 07	20 05	1 22
1973 09 08	20 03	1 22
1973 09 09	20 00	1 22
1973 09 10	19 58	1 22
1973 09 11	19 56	1 22
1973 09 12	19 54	1 21
1973 09 13	19 52	1 21
1973 09 14	19 49	1 21
1973 09 15	19 47	1 21
1973 09 16	19 45	1 21
1973 09 17	19 42	1 21
1973 09 18	19 40	1 21
1973 09 19	19 37	1 21
1973 09 20	19 35	1 21
1973 09 21	19 32	1 21
1973 09 22	19 30	1 21
1973 09 23	19 27	1 21
1973 09 24	19 25	1 21
1973 09 25	19 22	1 21
1973 09 26	19 20	1 21
1973 09 27	19 17	1 21
1973 09 28	19 14	1 21
1973 09 29	19 12	1 21
1973 09 30	19 09	1 21
1973 10 01	19 06	1 21
1973 10 02	19 04	1 21
1973 10 03	19 01	1 20
1973 10 04	18 58	1 20
1973 10 05	18 56	1 20
1973 10 06	18 53	1 20
1973 10 07	18 50	1 20
1973 10 08	18 48	1 20
1973 10 09	18 45	1 20
1973 10 10	18 42	1 20
1973 10 11	18 39	1 20
1973 10 12	18 37	1 20
1973 10 13	18 34	1 20
1973 10 14	18 31	1 20
1973 10 15	18 28	1 20
1973 10 16	18 26	1 20
1973 10 17	18 23	1 20
1973 10 18	18 20	1 19
1973 10 19	18 17	1 19
1973 10 20	18 15	1 19
1973 10 21	18 12	1 19
1973 10 22	18 09	1 19
1973 10 23	18 07	1 19
1973 10 24	18 04	1 19
1973 10 25	18 01	1 19
1973 10 26	17 59	1 19
1973 10 27	17 56	1 19
1973 10 28	17 54	1 19
1973 10 29	17 51	1 18
1973 10 30	17 48	1 18
1973 10 31	17 46	1 18
1973 11 01	17 43	1 18
1973 11 02	17 41	1 18
1973 11 03	17 38	1 18
1973 11 04	17 36	1 18
1973 11 05	17 33	1 18
1973 11 06	17 31	1 18
1973 11 07	17 29	1 18
1973 11 08	17 26	1 17
1973 11 09	17 24	1 17
1973 11 10	17 22	1 17
1973 11 11	17 19	1 17
1973 11 12	17 17	1 17
1973 11 13	17 15	1 17
1973 11 14	17 13	1 17
1973 11 15	17 11	1 17
1973 11 16	17 09	1 17
1973 11 17	17 07	1 16
1973 11 18	17 05	1 16
1973 11 19	17 03	1 16
1973 11 20	17 01	1 16
1973 11 21	16 59	1 16
1973 11 22	16 57	1 16
1973 11 23	16 55	1 16
1973 11 24	16 53	1 16
1973 11 25	16 52	1 15
1973 11 26	16 50	1 15
1973 11 27	16 48	1 15
1973 11 28	16 47	1 15
1973 11 29	16 45	1 15
1973 11 30	16 44	1 15
1973 12 01	16 42	1 15
1973 12 02	16 41	1 15
1973 12 03	16 39	1 14
1973 12 04	16 38	1 14
1973 12 05	16 37	1 14
1973 12 06	16 36	1 14
1973 12 07	16 35	1 14
1973 12 08	16 33	1 14
1973 12 09	16 32	1 14
1973 12 10	16 31	1 14
1973 12 11	16 30	1 13
1973 12 12	16 29	1 13
1973 12 13	16 29	1 13
1973 12 14	16 28	1 13
1973 12 15	16 27	1 13
1973 12 16	16 26	1 13
1973 12 17	16 26	1 13
1973 12 18	16 25	1 12
1973 12 19	16 25	1 12
1973 12 20	16 24	1 12
1973 12 21	16 24	1 12
1973 12 22	16 23	1 12
1973 12 23	16 23	1 12
1973 12 24	16 23	1 12
1973 12 25	16 23	1 11
1973 12 26	16 23	1 11
1973 12 27	16 23	1 11
1973 12 28	16 23	1 11
1973 12 29	16 23	1 11
1973 12 30	16 23	1 11
1973 12 31	16 23	1 11
1974 01 01	16 23	1 11
1974 01 02	16 23	1 10
1974 01 03	16 24	1 10
1974 01 04	16 24	1 10
1974 01 05	16 24	1 10
1974 01 06	16 25	1 10
1974 01 07	16 25	1 10
1974 01 08	16 26	1 10
1974 01 09	16 27	1 09
1974 01 10	16 27	1 09
1974 01 11	16 28	1 09
1974 01 12	16 29	1 09
1974 01 13	16 30	1 09
1974 01 14	16 31	1 09
1974 01 15	16 32	1 09
1974 01 16	16 33	1 09
1974 01 17	16 34	1 08
1974 01 18	16 35	1 08
1974 01 19	16 36	1 08
1974 01 20	16 37	1 08
1974 01 21	16 39	1 08
1974 01 22	16 40	1 08
1974 01 23	16 41	1 08
1974 01 24	16 43	1 07
1974 01 25	16 44	1 07
1974 01 26	16 46	1 07
1974 01 27	16 48	1 07
1974 01 28	16 49	1 07
1974 01 29	16 51	1 07
1974 01 30	16 53	1 07
1974 01 31	16 54	1 07
1974 02 01	16 56	1 06
1974 02 02	16 58	1 06
1974 02 03	17 00	1 06
1974 02 04	17 02	1 06
1974 02 05	17 04	1 06
1974 02 06	17 06	1 06
1974 02 07	17 08	1 06
1974 02 08	17 10	1 06
1974 02 09	17 13	1 06
1974 02 10	17 15	1 05
1974 02 11	17 17	1 05
1974 02 12	17 19	1 05
1974 02 13	17 22	1 05
1974 02 14	17 24	1 05
1974 02 15	17 27	1 05
1974 02 16	17 29	1 05
1974 02 17	17 32	1 05
1974 02 18	17 34	1 04
1974 02 19	17 37	1 04
1974 02 20	17 40	1 04
1974 02 21	17 42	1 04
1974 02 22	17 45	1 04
1974 02 23	17 48	1 04
1974 02 24	17 50	1 04
1974 02 25	17 53	1 04
1974 02 26	17 56	1 04
1974 02 27	17 59	1 04
1974 02 28	18 02	1 03
1974 03 01	18 05	1 03
1974 03 02	18 08	1 03
1974 03 03	18 11	1 03
1974 03 04	18 14	1 03
1974 03 05	18 17	1 03
1974 03 06	18 20	1 03
1974 03 07	18 23	1 03
1974 03 08	18 26	1 03
1974 03 09	18 29	1 03
1974 03 10	18 32	1 02
1974 03 11	18 36	1 02
1974 03 12	18 39	1 02
1974 03 13	18 42	1 02
1974 03 14	18 45	1 02
1974 03 15	18 49	1 02
1974 03 16	18 52	1 02
1974 03 17	18 55	1 02
1974 03 18	18 59	1 02
1974 03 19	19 02	1 02
1974 03 20	19 05	1 02
1974 03 21	19 09	1 01
1974 03 22	19 12	1 01
1974 03 23	19 16	1 01
1974 03 24	19 19	1 01
1974 03 25	19 23	1 01
1974 03 26	19 26	1 01
1974 03 27	19 30	1 01
1974 03 28	19 33	1 01
1974 03 29	19 36	1 01
1974 03 30	19 40	1 01
1974 03 31	19 44	1 01
1974 04 01	19 47	1 01
1974 04 02	19 51	1 00
1974 04 03	19 54	1 00
1974 04 04	19 58	1 00
1974 04 05	20 01	1 00
1974 04 06	20 05	1 00
1974 04 07	20 08	1 00
1974 04 08	20 12	1 00
1974 04 09	20 15	1 00
1974 04 10	20 19	1 00
1974 04 11	20 23	1 00
1974 04 12	20 26	1 00
1974 04 13	20 30	1 00
1974 04 14	20 33	1 00
1974 04 15	20 37	1 00
1974 04 16	20 40	1 00
1974 04 17	20 44	0 59
1974 04 18	20 47	0 59
1974 04 19	20 51	0 59
1974 04 20	20 54	0 59
1974 04 21	20 58	0 59
1974 04 22	21 02	0 59
1974 04 23	21 05	0 59
1974 04 24	21 09	0 59
1974 04 25	21 12	0 59
1974 04 26	21 16	0 59
1974 04 27	21 19	0 59
1974 04 28	21 22	0 59
1974 04 29	21 26	0 59
1974 04 30	21 29	0 59
1974 05 01	21 33	0 59
1974 05 02	21 36	0 59
1974 05 03	21 40	0 59
1974 05 04	21 43	0 59
1974 05 05	21 46	0 58
1974 05 06	21 50	0 58
1974 05 07	21 53	0 58
1974 05 08	21 56	0 58
1974 05 09	22 00	0 58
1974 05 10	22 03	0 58
1974 05 11	22 06	0 58
1974 05 12	22 09	0 58
1974 05 13	22 12	0 58
1974 05 14	22 16	0 58
1974 05 15	22 19	0 58
1974 05 16	22 22	0 58
1974 05 17	22 25	0 58
1974 05 18	22 28	0 58
1974 05 19	22 31	0 58
1974 05 20	22 34	0 58
1974 05 21	22 37	0 58
1974 05 22	22 40	0 58
1974 05 23	22 43	0 58
1974 05 24	22 46	0 58
1974 05 25	22 49	0 58
1974 05 26	22 52	0 58
1974 05 27	22 55	0 58
1974 05 28	22 57	0 58
1974 05 29	23 00	0 58
1974 05 30	23 03	0 57
1974 05 31	23 06	0 57
1974 06 01	23 08	0 57
1974 06 02	23 11	0 57
1974 06 03	23 13	0 57
1974 06 04	23 16	0 57
1974 06 05	23 19	0 57
1974 06 06	23 21	0 57
1974 06 07	23 24	0 57
1974 06 08	23 26	0 57
1974 06 09	23 28	0 57
1974 06 10	23 31	0 57
1974 06 11	23 33	0 57
1974 06 12	23 35	0 57
1974 06 13	23 37	0 57
1974 06 14	23 40	0 57
1974 06 15	23 42	0 57
1974 06 16	23 44	0 57
1974 06 17	23 46	0 57
1974 06 18	23 48	0 57
1974 06 19	23 50	0 57
1974 06 20	23 52	0 57
1974 06 21	23 54	0 57
1974 06 22	23 56	0 57
1974 06 23	23 57	0 57
1974 06 24	23 59	0 57
1974 06 25	24 01	0 57
1974 06 26	24 03	0 57
1974 06 27	24 04	0 57
1974 06 28	24 06	0 57
1974 06 29	24 07	0 57
1974 06 30	24 09	0 57
1974 07 01	24 10	0 57
1974 07 02	24 11	0 57
1974 07 03	24 13	0 57
1974 07 04	24 14	0 57
1974 07 05	24 15	0 57
1974 07 06	24 17	0 57
1974 07 07	24 18	0 57
1974 07 08	24 19	0 57
1974 07 09	24 20	0 57
1974 07 10	24 21	0 56
1974 07 11	24 22	0 56
1974 07 12	24 23	0 56
1974 07 13	24 23	0 56
1974 07 14	24 24	0 56
1974 07 15	24 25	0 56
1974 07 16	24 26	0 56
1974 07 17	24 26	0 56
1974 07 18	24 27	0 56
1974 07 19	24 27	0 56
1974 07 20	24 28	0 56
1974 07 21	24 28	0 56
1974 07 22	24 29	0 56
1974 07 23	24 29	0 56
1974 07 24	24 29	0 56
1974 07 25	24 29	0 56
1974 07 26	24 29	0 56
1974 07 27	24 30	0 56
1974 07 28	24 30	0 56
1974 07 29	24 30	0 56
1974 07 30	24 30	0 56
1974 07 31	24 29	0 56
1974 08 01	24 29	0 56
1974 08 02	24 29	0 56
1974 08 03	24 29	0 56
1974 08 04	24 29	0 56
1974 08 05	24 28	0 56
1974 08 06	24 28	0 56
1974 08 07	24 27	0 56
1974 08 08	24 27	0 56
1974 08 09	24 26	0 56
1974 08 10	24 25	0 56
1974 08 11	24 25	0 56
1974 08 12	24 24	0 56
1974 08 13	24 23	0 56
1974 08 14	24 22	0 56
1974 08 15	24 22	0 56
1974 08 16	24 21	0 56
1974 08 17	24 20	0 56
1974 08 18	24 19	0 56
1974 08 19	24 18	0 56
1974 08 20	24 16	0 56
1974 08 21	24 15	0 56
1974 08 22	24 14	0 56
1974 08 23	24 13	0 56
1974 08 24	24 11	0 55
1974 08 25	24 10	0 55
1974 08 26	24 09	0 55
1974 08 27	24 07	0 55
1974 08 28	24 06	0 55
1974 08 29	24 04	0 55
1974 08 30	24 02	0 55
1974 08 31	24 01	0 55
1974 09 01	23 59	0 55
1974 09 02	23 57	0 55
1974 09 03	23 56	0 55
1974 09 04	23 54	0 55
1974 09 05	23 52	0 55
1974 09 06	23 50	0 55
1974 09 07	23 48	0 55
1974 09 08	23 46	0 55
1974 09 09	23 44	0 55
1974 09 10	23 42	0 55
1974 09 11	23 40	0 55
1974 09 12	23 38	0 55
1974 09 13	23 36	0 55
1974 09 14	23 34	0 55
1974 09 15	23 31	0 55
1974 09 16	23 29	0 55
1974 09 17	23 27	0 55
1974 09 18	23 24	0 54
1974 09 19	23 22	0 54
1974 09 20	23 20	0 54
1974 09 21	23 17	0 54
1974 09 22	23 15	0 54
1974 09 23	23 12	0 54
1974 09 24	23 10	0 54
1974 09 25	23 07	0 54
1974 09 26	23 05	0 54
1974 09 27	23 02	0 54

1974 09 28	23 00	0 54
1974 09 29	22 57	0 54
1974 09 30	22 55	0 54
1974 10 01	22 52	0 54
1974 10 02	22 49	0 54
1974 10 03	22 47	0 54
1974 10 04	22 44	0 54
1974 10 05	22 41	0 54
1974 10 06	22 39	0 53
1974 10 07	22 36	0 53
1974 10 08	22 33	0 53
1974 10 09	22 30	0 53
1974 10 10	22 28	0 53
1974 10 11	22 25	0 53
1974 10 12	22 22	0 53
1974 10 13	22 20	0 53
1974 10 14	22 17	0 53
1974 10 15	22 14	0 53
1974 10 16	22 11	0 53
1974 10 17	22 08	0 53
1974 10 18	22 06	0 53
1974 10 19	22 03	0 53
1974 10 20	22 00	0 52
1974 10 21	21 57	0 52
1974 10 22	21 55	0 52
1974 10 23	21 52	0 52
1974 10 24	21 49	0 52
1974 10 25	21 47	0 52
1974 10 26	21 44	0 52
1974 10 27	21 41	0 52
1974 10 28	21 38	0 52
1974 10 29	21 36	0 52
1974 10 30	21 33	0 52
1974 10 31	21 30	0 52
1974 11 01	21 28	0 51
1974 11 02	21 25	0 51
1974 11 03	21 23	0 51
1974 11 04	21 20	0 51
1974 11 05	21 18	0 51
1974 11 06	21 15	0 51
1974 11 07	21 13	0 51
1974 11 08	21 10	0 51
1974 11 09	21 08	0 51
1974 11 10	21 05	0 51
1974 11 11	21 03	0 50
1974 11 12	21 00	0 50
1974 11 13	20 58	0 50
1974 11 14	20 56	0 50
1974 11 15	20 54	0 50
1974 11 16	20 51	0 50
1974 11 17	20 49	0 50
1974 11 18	20 47	0 50
1974 11 19	20 45	0 50
1974 11 20	20 43	0 50
1974 11 21	20 41	0 49
1974 11 22	20 39	0 49
1974 11 23	20 37	0 49
1974 11 24	20 35	0 49
1974 11 25	20 33	0 49
1974 11 26	20 31	0 49
1974 11 27	20 29	0 49
1974 11 28	20 27	0 49
1974 11 29	20 26	0 49
1974 11 30	20 24	0 49
1974 12 01	20 22	0 48
1974 12 02	20 21	0 48
1974 12 03	20 19	0 48
1974 12 04	20 18	0 48
1974 12 05	20 16	0 48
1974 12 06	20 15	0 48
1974 12 07	20 13	0 48
1974 12 08	20 12	0 48
1974 12 09	20 11	0 48
1974 12 10	20 10	0 47
1974 12 11	20 09	0 47
1974 12 12	20 07	0 47
1974 12 13	20 06	0 47
1974 12 14	20 05	0 47
1974 12 15	20 04	0 47
1974 12 16	20 04	0 47
1974 12 17	20 03	0 47
1974 12 18	20 02	0 47
1974 12 19	20 01	0 46
1974 12 20	20 01	0 46
1974 12 21	20 00	0 46
1974 12 22	19 59	0 46
1974 12 23	19 59	0 46
1974 12 24	19 58	0 46
1974 12 25	19 58	0 46
1974 12 26	19 58	0 46
1974 12 27	19 57	0 46
1974 12 28	19 57	0 45
1974 12 29	19 57	0 45
1974 12 30	19 57	0 45
1974 12 31	19 57	0 45
1975 01 01	19 57	0 45
1975 01 02	19 57	0 45
1975 01 03	19 57	0 45
1975 01 04	19 57	0 45
1975 01 05	19 57	0 44
1975 01 06	19 58	0 44
1975 01 07	19 58	0 44
1975 01 08	19 58	0 44
1975 01 09	19 59	0 44
1975 01 10	19 59	0 44
1975 01 11	20 00	0 44
1975 01 12	20 00	0 44
1975 01 13	20 01	0 44
1975 01 14	20 02	0 43
1975 01 15	20 03	0 43
1975 01 16	20 03	0 43
1975 01 17	20 04	0 43
1975 01 18	20 05	0 43
1975 01 19	20 06	0 43
1975 01 20	20 07	0 43
1975 01 21	20 08	0 43
1975 01 22	20 10	0 43
1975 01 23	20 11	0 42
1975 01 24	20 12	0 42
1975 01 25	20 13	0 42
1975 01 26	20 15	0 42
1975 01 27	20 16	0 42
1975 01 28	20 18	0 42
1975 01 29	20 19	0 42
1975 01 30	20 21	0 42
1975 01 31	20 22	0 42
1975 02 01	20 24	0 42
1975 02 02	20 26	0 41
1975 02 03	20 28	0 41
1975 02 04	20 29	0 41
1975 02 05	20 31	0 41
1975 02 06	20 33	0 41
1975 02 07	20 35	0 41
1975 02 08	20 37	0 41
1975 02 09	20 39	0 41
1975 02 10	20 41	0 41
1975 02 11	20 43	0 40
1975 02 12	20 46	0 40
1975 02 13	20 40	0 40
1975 02 14	20 50	0 40
1975 02 15	20 52	0 40
1975 02 16	20 55	0 40
1975 02 17	20 57	0 40
1975 02 18	21 00	0 40
1975 02 19	21 02	0 40
1975 02 20	21 05	0 40
1975 02 21	21 07	0 39
1975 02 22	21 10	0 39
1975 02 23	21 12	0 39
1975 02 24	21 15	0 39
1975 02 25	21 18	0 39
1975 02 26	21 21	0 39
1975 02 27	21 23	0 39
1975 02 28	21 26	0 39
1975 03 01	21 29	0 39
1975 03 02	21 32	0 39
1975 03 03	21 35	0 39
1975 03 04	21 38	0 38
1975 03 05	21 41	0 38
1975 03 06	21 44	0 38
1975 03 07	21 47	0 38
1975 03 08	21 50	0 38
1975 03 09	21 53	0 38
1975 03 10	21 56	0 38
1975 03 11	21 59	0 38
1975 03 12	22 02	0 38
1975 03 13	22 05	0 38
1975 03 14	22 09	0 38
1975 03 15	22 12	0 37
1975 03 16	22 15	0 37
1975 03 17	22 18	0 37
1975 03 18	22 22	0 37
1975 03 19	22 25	0 37
1975 03 20	22 28	0 37
1975 03 21	22 32	0 37
1975 03 22	22 35	0 37
1975 03 23	22 38	0 37
1975 03 24	22 42	0 37
1975 03 25	22 45	0 37
1975 03 26	22 49	0 37
1975 03 27	22 52	0 37
1975 03 28	22 56	0 36
1975 03 29	22 59	0 36
1975 03 30	23 03	0 36
1975 03 31	23 06	0 36
1975 04 01	23 10	0 36
1975 04 02	23 13	0 36
1975 04 03	23 17	0 36
1975 04 04	23 20	0 36
1975 04 05	23 24	0 36
1975 04 06	23 27	0 36
1975 04 07	23 31	0 36
1975 04 08	23 35	0 36
1975 04 09	23 38	0 36
1975 04 10	23 42	0 35
1975 04 11	23 45	0 35
1975 04 12	23 49	0 35
1975 04 13	23 52	0 35
1975 04 14	23 56	0 35
1975 04 15	24 00	0 35
1975 04 16	24 03	0 35
1975 04 17	24 07	0 35
1975 04 18	24 10	0 35
1975 04 19	24 14	0 35
1975 04 20	24 18	0 35
1975 04 21	24 21	0 35
1975 04 22	24 25	0 35
1975 04 23	24 28	0 35
1975 04 24	24 32	0 35
1975 04 25	24 35	0 34
1975 04 26	24 39	0 34
1975 04 27	24 43	0 34
1975 04 28	24 46	0 34
1975 04 29	24 50	0 34
1975 04 30	24 53	0 34
1975 05 01	24 57	0 34
1975 05 02	25 00	0 34
1975 05 03	25 04	0 34
1975 05 04	25 07	0 34
1975 05 05	25 11	0 34
1975 05 06	25 14	0 34
1975 05 07	25 17	0 34
1975 05 08	25 21	0 34
1975 05 09	25 24	0 34
1975 05 10	25 28	0 34
1975 05 11	25 31	0 34
1975 05 12	25 34	0 33
1975 05 13	25 38	0 33
1975 05 14	25 41	0 33
1975 05 15	25 44	0 33
1975 05 16	25 47	0 33
1975 05 17	25 51	0 33
1975 05 18	25 54	0 33
1975 05 19	25 57	0 33
1975 05 20	26 00	0 33
1975 05 21	26 03	0 33
1975 05 22	26 06	0 33
1975 05 23	26 09	0 33
1975 05 24	26 13	0 33
1975 05 25	26 16	0 33
1975 05 26	26 19	0 33
1975 05 27	26 22	0 33
1975 05 28	26 25	0 33
1975 05 29	26 27	0 33
1975 05 30	26 30	0 33
1975 05 31	26 33	0 32
1975 06 01	26 36	0 32
1975 06 02	26 39	0 32
1975 06 03	26 42	0 32
1975 06 04	26 44	0 32
1975 06 05	26 47	0 32
1975 06 06	26 50	0 32
1975 06 07	26 52	0 32
1975 06 08	26 55	0 32
1975 06 09	26 57	0 32
1975 06 10	27 00	0 32
1975 06 11	27 02	0 32
1975 06 12	27 05	0 32
1975 06 13	27 07	0 32
1975 06 14	27 10	0 32
1975 06 15	27 12	0 32
1975 06 16	27 14	0 32
1975 06 17	27 17	0 32
1975 06 18	27 19	0 32
1975 06 19	27 21	0 32
1975 06 20	27 23	0 31
1975 06 21	27 25	0 31
1975 06 22	27 27	0 31
1975 06 23	27 29	0 31
1975 06 24	27 31	0 31
1975 06 25	27 33	0 31
1975 06 26	27 35	0 31
1975 06 27	27 37	0 31
1975 06 28	27 38	0 31
1975 06 29	27 40	0 31
1975 06 30	27 42	0 31
1975 07 01	27 43	0 31
1975 07 02	27 45	0 31
1975 07 03	27 47	0 31
1975 07 04	27 48	0 31
1975 07 05	27 50	0 31
1975 07 06	27 51	0 31
1975 07 07	27 52	0 31
1975 07 08	27 54	0 31
1975 07 09	27 55	0 31
1975 07 10	27 56	0 31
1975 07 11	27 57	0 31
1975 07 12	27 58	0 31
1975 07 13	27 59	0 30
1975 07 14	28 00	0 30
1975 07 15	28 01	0 30
1975 07 16	28 02	0 30
1975 07 17	28 03	0 30
1975 07 18	28 04	0 30
1975 07 19	28 05	0 30
1975 07 20	28 05	0 30
1975 07 21	28 06	0 30
1975 07 22	28 07	0 30
1975 07 23	28 07	0 30
1975 07 24	28 08	0 30
1975 07 25	28 08	0 30
1975 07 26	28 08	0 30
1975 07 27	28 09	0 30
1975 07 28	28 09	0 30
1975 07 29	28 09	0 30
1975 07 30	28 09	0 30
1975 07 31	28 09	0 30
1975 08 01	28 10	0 30
1975 08 02	28 10	0 30
1975 08 03	28 09	0 30
1975 08 04	28 09	0 29
1975 08 05	28 09	0 29
1975 08 06	28 09	0 29
1975 08 07	28 09	0 29
1975 08 08	28 08	0 29
1975 08 09	28 08	0 29
1975 08 10	28 08	0 29
1975 08 11	28 07	0 29
1975 08 12	28 07	0 29
1975 08 13	28 06	0 29
1975 08 14	28 05	0 29
1975 08 15	28 05	0 29
1975 08 16	28 04	0 29
1975 08 17	28 03	0 29
1975 08 18	28 02	0 29
1975 08 19	28 01	0 29
1975 08 20	28 01	0 29
1975 08 21	28 00	0 29
1975 08 22	27 58	0 29
1975 08 23	27 57	0 29
1975 08 24	27 56	0 29
1975 08 25	27 55	0 28
1975 08 26	27 54	0 28
1975 08 27	27 53	0 28
1975 08 28	27 51	0 28
1975 08 29	27 50	0 28
1975 08 30	27 48	0 28
1975 08 31	27 47	0 28
1975 09 01	27 45	0 28
1975 09 02	27 44	0 28
1975 09 03	27 42	0 28
1975 09 04	27 41	0 28
1975 09 05	27 39	0 28
1975 09 06	27 37	0 28
1975 09 07	27 35	0 28
1975 09 08	27 33	0 28
1975 09 09	27 32	0 28
1975 09 10	27 30	0 28
1975 09 11	27 28	0 28
1975 09 12	27 26	0 27
1975 09 13	27 24	0 27
1975 09 14	27 22	0 27
1975 09 15	27 20	0 27
1975 09 16	27 17	0 27
1975 09 17	27 15	0 27
1975 09 18	27 13	0 27
1975 09 19	27 11	0 27
1975 09 20	27 09	0 27
1975 09 21	27 06	0 27
1975 09 22	27 04	0 27
1975 09 23	27 02	0 27
1975 09 24	26 59	0 27
1975 09 25	26 57	0 27
1975 09 26	26 54	0 27
1975 09 27	26 52	0 27
1975 09 28	26 49	0 26
1975 09 29	26 47	0 26
1975 09 30	26 44	0 26
1975 10 01	26 42	0 26
1975 10 02	26 39	0 26
1975 10 03	26 36	0 26
1975 10 04	26 34	0 26
1975 10 05	26 31	0 26
1975 10 06	26 29	0 26
1975 10 07	26 26	0 26
1975 10 08	26 23	0 26
1975 10 09	26 20	0 26
1975 10 10	26 18	0 26
1975 10 11	26 15	0 26
1975 10 12	26 12	0 25
1975 10 13	26 09	0 25
1975 10 14	26 07	0 25
1975 10 15	26 04	0 25
1975 10 16	26 01	0 25
1975 10 17	25 58	0 25
1975 10 18	25 56	0 25
1975 10 19	25 53	0 25
1975 10 20	25 50	0 25
1975 10 21	25 47	0 25
1975 10 22	25 44	0 25
1975 10 23	25 42	0 25
1975 10 24	25 39	0 25
1975 10 25	25 36	0 24
1975 10 26	25 33	0 24
1975 10 27	25 31	0 24
1975 10 28	25 28	0 24
1975 10 29	25 25	0 24
1975 10 30	25 22	0 24
1975 10 31	25 20	0 24
1975 11 01	25 17	0 24
1975 11 02	25 14	0 24
1975 11 03	25 12	0 24
1975 11 04	25 09	0 24
1975 11 05	25 06	0 24
1975 11 06	25 04	0 24
1975 11 07	25 01	0 23
1975 11 08	24 58	0 23
1975 11 09	24 56	0 23
1975 11 10	24 53	0 23
1975 11 11	24 51	0 23
1975 11 12	24 48	0 23
1975 11 13	24 46	0 23
1975 11 14	24 43	0 23
1975 11 15	24 41	0 23
1975 11 16	24 39	0 23
1975 11 17	24 36	0 23
1975 11 18	24 34	0 22
1975 11 19	24 32	0 22
1975 11 20	24 29	0 22
1975 11 21	24 27	0 22

1975	11	22	24	25	0	22
1975	11	23	24	23	0	22
1975	11	24	24	21	0	22
1975	11	25	24	19	0	22
1975	11	26	24	17	0	22
1975	11	27	24	15	0	22
1975	11	28	24	13	0	22
1975	11	29	24	11	0	22
1975	11	30	24	09	0	21
1975	12	01	24	07	0	21
1975	12	02	24	05	0	21
1975	12	03	24	04	0	21
1975	12	04	24	02	0	21
1975	12	05	24	00	0	21
1975	12	06	23	59	0	21
1975	12	07	23	57	0	21
1975	12	08	23	56	0	21
1975	12	09	23	54	0	21
1975	12	10	23	53	0	21
1975	12	11	23	51	0	20
1975	12	12	23	50	0	20
1975	12	13	23	49	0	20
1975	12	14	23	48	0	20
1975	12	15	23	46	0	20
1975	12	16	23	45	0	20
1975	12	17	23	44	0	20
1975	12	18	23	43	0	20
1975	12	19	23	42	0	20
1975	12	20	23	41	0	20
1975	12	21	23	41	0	20
1975	12	22	23	40	0	19
1975	12	23	23	39	0	19
1975	12	24	23	38	0	19
1975	12	25	23	38	0	19
1975	12	26	23	37	0	19
1975	12	27	23	37	0	19
1975	12	28	23	36	0	19
1975	12	29	23	36	0	19
1975	12	30	23	36	0	19
1975	12	31	23	35	0	19
1976	01	01	23	35	0	19
1976	01	02	23	35	0	18
1976	01	03	23	35	0	18
1976	01	04	23	35	0	18
1976	01	05	23	35	0	18
1976	01	06	23	35	0	18
1976	01	07	23	35	0	18
1976	01	08	23	35	0	18
1976	01	09	23	35	0	18
1976	01	10	23	36	0	18
1976	01	11	23	36	0	18
1976	01	12	23	36	0	18
1976	01	13	23	37	0	17
1976	01	14	23	37	0	17
1976	01	15	23	38	0	17
1976	01	16	23	39	0	17
1976	01	17	23	39	0	17
1976	01	18	23	40	0	17
1976	01	19	23	41	0	17
1976	01	20	23	42	0	17
1976	01	21	23	43	0	17
1976	01	22	23	44	0	17
1976	01	23	23	45	0	17
1976	01	24	23	46	0	16
1976	01	25	23	47	0	16
1976	01	26	23	48	0	16
1976	01	27	23	49	0	16
1976	01	28	23	51	0	16
1976	01	29	23	52	0	16
1976	01	30	23	53	0	16
1976	01	31	23	55	0	16
1976	02	01	23	56	0	16
1976	02	02	23	58	0	16
1976	02	03	23	59	0	16
1976	02	04	24	01	0	15
1976	02	05	24	03	0	15
1976	02	06	24	04	0	15
1976	02	07	24	06	0	15
1976	02	08	24	08	0	15
1976	02	09	24	10	0	15
1976	02	10	24	12	0	15
1976	02	11	24	14	0	15
1976	02	12	24	16	0	15
1976	02	13	24	18	0	15
1976	02	14	24	20	0	15
1976	02	15	24	22	0	15
1976	02	16	24	25	0	14
1976	02	17	24	27	0	14
1976	02	18	24	29	0	14
1976	02	19	24	32	0	14
1976	02	20	24	34	0	14
1976	02	21	24	36	0	14
1976	02	22	24	39	0	14
1976	02	23	24	41	0	14
1976	02	24	24	44	0	14
1976	02	25	24	46	0	14
1976	02	26	24	49	0	14
1976	02	27	24	52	0	14
1976	02	28	24	54	0	14
1976	02	29	24	57	0	13
1976	03	01	25	00	0	13
1976	03	02	25	03	0	13
1976	03	03	25	06	0	13
1976	03	04	25	09	0	13
1976	03	05	25	11	0	13
1976	03	06	25	14	0	13

1976	03	07	25	17	0	13
1976	03	08	25	20	0	13
1976	03	09	25	23	0	13
1976	03	10	25	26	0	13
1976	03	11	25	30	0	13
1976	03	12	25	33	0	12
1976	03	13	25	36	0	12
1976	03	14	25	39	0	12
1976	03	15	25	42	0	12
1976	03	16	25	45	0	12
1976	03	17	25	49	0	12
1976	03	18	25	52	0	12
1976	03	19	25	55	0	12
1976	03	20	25	59	0	12
1976	03	21	26	02	0	12
1976	03	22	26	05	0	12
1976	03	23	26	09	0	12
1976	03	24	26	12	0	12
1976	03	25	26	15	0	12
1976	03	26	26	19	0	11
1976	03	27	26	22	0	11
1976	03	28	26	26	0	11
1976	03	29	26	29	0	11
1976	03	30	26	33	0	11
1976	03	31	26	36	0	11
1976	04	01	26	40	0	11
1976	04	02	26	43	0	11
1976	04	03	26	47	0	11
1976	04	04	26	50	0	11
1976	04	05	26	54	0	11
1976	04	06	26	58	0	11
1976	04	07	27	01	0	11
1976	04	08	27	05	0	10
1976	04	09	27	08	0	10
1976	04	10	27	12	0	10
1976	04	11	27	16	0	10
1976	04	12	27	19	0	10
1976	04	13	27	23	0	10
1976	04	14	27	27	0	10
1976	04	15	27	30	0	10
1976	04	16	27	34	0	10
1976	04	17	27	37	0	10
1976	04	18	27	41	0	10
1976	04	19	27	45	0	10
1976	04	20	27	48	0	10
1976	04	21	27	52	0	10
1976	04	22	27	56	0	10
1976	04	23	27	59	0	09
1976	04	24	28	03	0	09
1976	04	25	28	06	0	09
1976	04	26	28	10	0	09
1976	04	27	28	14	0	09
1976	04	28	28	17	0	09
1976	04	29	28	21	0	09
1976	04	30	28	24	0	09
1976	05	01	28	28	0	09
1976	05	02	28	32	0	09
1976	05	03	28	35	0	09
1976	05	04	28	39	0	09
1976	05	05	28	42	0	09
1976	05	06	28	46	0	09
1976	05	07	28	49	0	08
1976	05	08	28	53	0	08
1976	05	09	28	56	0	08
1976	05	10	29	00	0	08
1976	05	11	29	03	0	08
1976	05	12	29	07	0	08
1976	05	13	29	10	0	08
1976	05	14	29	13	0	08
1976	05	15	29	17	0	08
1976	05	16	29	20	0	08
1976	05	17	29	23	0	08
1976	05	18	29	27	0	08
1976	05	19	29	30	0	08
1976	05	20	29	33	0	08
1976	05	21	29	37	0	08
1976	05	22	29	40	0	07
1976	05	23	29	43	0	07
1976	05	24	29	46	0	07
1976	05	25	29	49	0	07
1976	05	26	29	52	0	07
1976	05	27	29	56	0	07
1976	05	28	29	59	0	07
1976	05	29	30	02	0	07
1976	05	30	30	05	0	07
1976	05	31	30	08	0	07
1976	06	01	30	11	0	07
1976	06	02	30	14	0	07
1976	06	03	30	17	0	07
1976	06	04	30	19	0	07
1976	06	05	30	22	0	07
1976	06	06	30	25	0	06
1976	06	07	30	28	0	06
1976	06	08	30	31	0	06
1976	06	09	30	33	0	06
1976	06	10	30	36	0	06
1976	06	11	30	38	0	06
1976	06	12	30	41	0	06
1976	06	13	30	44	0	06
1976	06	14	30	46	0	06
1976	06	15	30	49	0	06
1976	06	16	30	51	0	06
1976	06	17	30	53	0	06
1976	06	18	30	56	0	06
1976	06	19	30	58	0	06
1976	06	20	31	00	0	06

1976	06	21	31	03	0	05
1976	06	22	31	05	0	05
1976	06	23	31	07	0	05
1976	06	24	31	09	0	05
1976	06	25	31	11	0	05
1976	06	26	31	13	0	05
1976	06	27	31	15	0	05
1976	06	28	31	17	0	05
1976	06	29	31	19	0	05
1976	06	30	31	21	0	05
1976	07	01	31	23	0	05
1976	07	02	31	25	0	05
1976	07	03	31	26	0	05
1976	07	04	31	28	0	05
1976	07	05	31	30	0	05
1976	07	06	31	31	0	04
1976	07	07	31	33	0	04
1976	07	08	31	34	0	04
1976	07	09	31	36	0	04
1976	07	10	31	37	0	04
1976	07	11	31	38	0	04
1976	07	12	31	40	0	04
1976	07	13	31	41	0	04
1976	07	14	31	42	0	04
1976	07	15	31	43	0	04
1976	07	16	31	44	0	04
1976	07	17	31	45	0	04
1976	07	18	31	46	0	04
1976	07	19	31	47	0	04
1976	07	20	31	48	0	03
1976	07	21	31	49	0	03
1976	07	22	31	50	0	03
1976	07	23	31	50	0	03
1976	07	24	31	51	0	03
1976	07	25	31	52	0	03
1976	07	26	31	52	0	03
1976	07	27	31	53	0	03
1976	07	28	31	53	0	03
1976	07	29	31	53	0	03
1976	07	30	31	54	0	03
1976	07	31	31	54	0	03
1976	08	01	31	54	0	03
1976	08	02	31	55	0	03
1976	08	03	31	55	0	02
1976	08	04	31	55	0	02
1976	08	05	31	55	0	02
1976	08	06	31	55	0	02
1976	08	07	31	55	0	02
1976	08	08	31	54	0	02
1976	08	09	31	54	0	02
1976	08	10	31	54	0	02
1976	08	11	31	54	0	02
1976	08	12	31	53	0	02
1976	08	13	31	53	0	02
1976	08	14	31	52	0	02
1976	08	15	31	52	0	02
1976	08	16	31	51	0	02
1976	08	17	31	51	0	01
1976	08	18	31	50	0	01
1976	08	19	31	49	0	01
1976	08	20	31	49	0	01
1976	08	21	31	48	0	01
1976	08	22	31	47	0	01
1976	08	23	31	46	0	01
1976	08	24	31	45	0	01
1976	08	25	31	44	0	01
1976	08	26	31	43	0	01
1976	08	27	31	42	0	01
1976	08	28	31	40	0	01
1976	08	29	31	39	0	01
1976	08	30	31	38	0	00
1976	08	31	31	37	0	00
1976	09	01	31	35	0	00
1976	09	02	31	34	0	00
1976	09	03	31	32	0	00
1976	09	04	31	31	0	00
1976	09	05	31	29	0	00
1976	09	06	31	27	0	00
1976	09	07	31	26	0	00
1976	09	08	31	24	0	00
1976	09	09	31	22	0	00
1976	09	10	31	21	0	00
1976	09	11	31	19	0	00
1976	09	12	31	17	-0	01
1976	09	13	31	15	-0	01
1976	09	14	31	13	-0	01
1976	09	15	31	11	-0	01
1976	09	16	31	09	-0	01
1976	09	17	31	07	-0	01
1976	09	18	31	05	-0	01
1976	09	19	31	03	-0	01
1976	09	20	31	00	-0	01
1976	09	21	30	58	-0	01
1976	09	22	30	56	-0	01
1976	09	23	30	54	-0	01
1976	09	24	30	51	-0	01
1976	09	25	30	49	-0	02
1976	09	26	30	46	-0	02
1976	09	27	30	44	-0	02
1976	09	28	30	42	-0	02
1976	09	29	30	39	-0	02
1976	09	30	30	37	-0	02
1976	10	01	30	34	-0	02
1976	10	02	30	32	-0	02
1976	10	03	30	29	-0	02
1976	10	04	30	26	-0	02

1976	10	05	30	24	-0	02
1976	10	06	30	21	-0	02
1976	10	07	30	18	-0	02
1976	10	08	30	16	-0	03
1976	10	09	30	13	-0	03
1976	10	10	30	10	-0	03
1976	10	11	30	08	-0	03
1976	10	12	30	05	-0	03
1976	10	13	30	02	-0	03
1976	10	14	29	59	-0	03
1976	10	15	29	57	-0	03
1976	10	16	29	54	-0	03
1976	10	17	29	51	-0	03
1976	10	18	29	48	-0	03
1976	10	19	29	45	-0	03
1976	10	20	29	43	-0	04
1976	10	21	29	40	-0	04
1976	10	22	29	37	-0	04
1976	10	23	29	34	-0	04
1976	10	24	29	31	-0	04
1976	10	25	29	28	-0	04
1976	10	26	29	26	-0	04
1976	10	27	29	23	-0	04
1976	10	28	29	20	-0	04
1976	10	29	29	17	-0	04
1976	10	30	29	14	-0	04
1976	10	31	29	12	-0	04
1976	11	01	29	09	-0	04
1976	11	02	29	06	-0	05
1976	11	03	29	03	-0	05
1976	11	04	29	01	-0	05
1976	11	05	28	58	-0	05
1976	11	06	28	55	-0	05
1976	11	07	28	52	-0	05
1976	11	08	28	50	-0	05
1976	11	09	28	47	-0	05
1976	11	10	28	45	-0	05
1976	11	11	28	42	-0	05
1976	11	12	28	39	-0	05
1976	11	13	28	37	-0	05
1976	11	14	28	34	-0	05
1976	11	15	28	32	-0	06
1976	11	16	28	29	-0	06
1976	11	17	28	27	-0	06
1976	11	18	28	24	-0	06
1976	11	19	28	22	-0	06
1976	11	20	28	19	-0	06
1976	11	21	28	17	-0	06
1976	11	22	28	15	-0	06
1976	11	23	28	13	-0	06
1976	11	24	28	10	-0	06
1976	11	25	28	08	-0	06
1976	11	26	28	06	-0	06
1976	11	27	28	04	-0	06
1976	11	28	28	02	-0	06
1976	11	29	28	00	-0	07
1976	11	30	27	58	-0	07
1976	12	01	27	56	-0	07
1976	12	02	27	54	-0	07
1976	12	03	27	52	-0	07
1976	12	04	27	50	-0	07
1976	12	05	27	48	-0	07
1976	12	06	27	46	-0	07
1976	12	07	27	45	-0	07
1976	12	08	27	43	-0	07
1976	12	09	27	41	-0	07
1976	12	10	27	40	-0	07
1976	12	11	27	38	-0	07
1976	12	12	27	37	-0	08
1976	12	13	27	36	-0	08
1976	12	14	27	34	-0	08
1976	12	15	27	33	-0	08
1976	12	16	27	32	-0	08
1976	12	17	27	30	-0	08
1976	12	18	27	29	-0	08
1976	12	19	27	28	-0	08
1976	12	20	27	27	-0	08
1976	12	21	27	26	-0	08
1976	12	22	27	25	-0	08
1976	12	23	27	24	-0	08
1976	12	24	27	23	-0	08
1976	12	25	27	23	-0	08
1976	12	26	27	22	-0	08
1976	12	27	27	21	-0	09
1976	12	28	27	21	-0	09
1976	12	29	27	20	-0	09
1976	12	30	27	19	-0	09
1976	12	31	27	19	-0	09
1977	01	01	27	19	-0	09
1977	01	02	27	18	-0	09
1977	01	03	27	18	-0	09
1977	01	04	27	18	-0	09
1977	01	05	27	18	-0	09
1977	01	06	27	18	-0	09
1977	01	07	27	18	-0	09
1977	01	08	27	18	-0	09
1977	01	09	27	18	-0	09
1977	01	10	27	18	-0	10
1977	01	11	27	18	-0	10
1977	01	12	27	18	-0	10
1977	01	13	27	19	-0	10
1977	01	14	27	19	-0	10

1977	01	15	27	19	-0	10
1977	01	16	27	20	-0	10
1977	01	17	27	20	-0	10
1977	01	18	27	21	-0	10
1977	01	19	27	22	-0	10
1977	01	20	27	22	-0	10
1977	01	21	27	23	-0	10
1977	01	22	27	24	-0	10
1977	01	23	27	25	-0	10
1977	01	24	27	26	-0	10
1977	01	25	27	27	-0	10
1977	01	26	27	28	-0	11
1977	01	27	27	29	-0	11
1977	01	28	27	30	-0	11
1977	01	29	27	31	-0	11
1977	01	30	27	32	-0	11
1977	01	31	27	34	-0	11
1977	02	01	27	35	-0	11
1977	02	02	27	37	-0	11
1977	02	03	27	38	-0	11
1977	02	04	27	40	-0	11
1977	02	05	27	41	-0	11
1977	02	06	27	43	-0	11
1977	02	07	27	44	-0	11
1977	02	08	27	46	0	11
1977	02	09	27	48	-0	11
1977	02	10	27	50	-0	12
1977	02	11	27	52	-0	12
1977	02	12	27	54	-0	12
1977	02	13	27	56	-0	12
1977	02	14	27	58	-0	12
1977	02	15	28	00	-0	12
1977	02	16	28	02	-0	12
1977	02	17	28	04	-0	12
1977	02	18	28	06	-0	12
1977	02	19	28	08	-0	12
1977	02	20	28	11	-0	12
1977	02	21	28	13	-0	12
1977	02	22	28	15	-0	12
1977	02	23	28	18	-0	12
1977	02	24	28	20	-0	12
1977	02	25	28	23	-0	12
1977	02	26	28	25	-0	13
1977	02	27	28	28	-0	13
1977	02	28	28	31	-0	13
1977	03	01	28	33	-0	13
1977	03	02	28	36	-0	13
1977	03	03	28	39	-0	13
1977	03	04	28	42	-0	13
1977	03	05	28	44	-0	13
1977	03	06	28	47	-0	13
1977	03	07	28	50	-0	13
1977	03	08	28	53	-0	13
1977	03	09	28	56	-0	13
1977	03	10	28	59	-0	13
1977	03	11	29	02	-0	13
1977	03	12	29	05	-0	13
1977	03	13	29	08	-0	13
1977	03	14	29	11	-0	14
1977	03	15	29	14	-0	14
1977	03	16	29	17	-0	14
1977	03	17	29	21	-0	14
1977	03	18	29	24	-0	14
1977	03	19	29	27	-0	14
1977	03	20	29	30	-0	14
1977	03	21	29	34	-0	14
1977	03	22	29	37	-0	14
1977	03	23	29	40	-0	14
1977	03	24	29	44	-0	14
1977	03	25	29	47	-0	14
1977	03	26	29	51	-0	14
1977	03	27	29	54	-0	14
1977	03	28	29	57	-0	14
1977	03	29	30	01	-0	15
1977	03	30	30	04	-0	15
1977	03	31	30	08	-0	15
1977	04	01	30	11	-0	15
1977	04	02	30	15	-0	15
1977	04	03	30	18	-0	15
1977	04	04	30	22	-0	15
1977	04	05	30	26	-0	15
1977	04	06	30	29	-0	15
1977	04	07	30	33	-0	15
1977	04	08	30	36	-0	15
1977	04	09	30	40	-0	15
1977	04	10	30	44	-0	15
1977	04	11	30	47	-0	15
1977	04	12	30	51	-0	15
1977	04	13	30	55	-0	16
1977	04	14	30	58	-0	16
1977	04	15	31	02	-0	16
1977	04	16	31	06	-0	16
1977	04	17	31	09	-0	16
1977	04	18	31	13	-0	16
1977	04	19	31	17	-0	16
1977	04	20	31	20	-0	16
1977	04	21	31	24	-0	16
1977	04	22	31	28	-0	16
1977	04	23	31	31	-0	16
1977	04	24	31	35	-0	16
1977	04	25	31	39	-0	16
1977	04	26	31	42	-0	16
1977	04	27	31	46	-0	17
1977	04	28	31	50	-0	17
1977	04	29	31	53	-0	17
1977	04	30	31	57	-0	17
1977	05	01	32	01	-0	17
1977	05	02	32	04	-0	17
1977	05	03	32	08	-0	17
1977	05	04	32	12	-0	17
1977	05	05	32	15	-0	17
1977	05	06	32	19	-0	17
1977	05	07	32	23	-0	17
1977	05	08	32	26	-0	17
1977	05	09	32	30	-0	17
1977	05	10	32	33	-0	18
1977	05	11	32	37	-0	18
1977	05	12	32	40	-0	18
1977	05	13	32	44	-0	18
1977	05	14	32	48	-0	18
1977	05	15	32	51	-0	18
1977	05	16	32	55	-0	18
1977	05	17	32	58	-0	18
1977	05	18	33	01	-0	18
1977	05	19	33	05	-0	18
1977	05	20	33	08	-0	18
1977	05	21	33	12	-0	18
1977	05	22	33	15	-0	18
1977	05	23	33	18	-0	19
1977	05	24	33	22	-0	19
1977	05	25	33	25	-0	19
1977	05	26	33	28	-0	19
1977	05	27	33	32	-0	19
1977	05	28	33	35	-0	19
1977	05	29	33	38	-0	19
1977	05	30	33	41	-0	19
1977	05	31	33	44	-0	19
1977	06	01	33	47	-0	19
1977	06	02	33	51	-0	19
1977	06	03	33	54	-0	19
1977	06	04	33	57	-0	20
1977	06	05	34	00	-0	20
1977	06	06	34	03	-0	20
1977	06	07	34	06	-0	20
1977	06	08	34	09	-0	20
1977	06	09	34	11	-0	20
1977	06	10	34	14	-0	20
1977	06	11	34	17	-0	20
1977	06	12	34	20	-0	20
1977	06	13	34	23	-0	20
1977	06	14	34	25	-0	20
1977	06	15	34	28	-0	20
1977	06	16	34	31	-0	21
1977	06	17	34	33	-0	21
1977	06	18	34	36	-0	21
1977	06	19	34	38	-0	21
1977	06	20	34	41	-0	21
1977	06	21	34	43	-0	21
1977	06	22	34	46	-0	21
1977	06	23	34	48	-0	21
1977	06	24	34	51	-0	21
1977	06	25	34	53	-0	21
1977	06	26	34	55	-0	21
1977	06	27	34	57	-0	22
1977	06	28	34	59	-0	22
1977	06	29	35	02	-0	22
1977	06	30	35	04	-0	22
1977	07	01	35	06	-0	22
1977	07	02	35	08	-0	22
1977	07	03	35	10	-0	22
1977	07	04	35	12	-0	22
1977	07	05	35	13	-0	22
1977	07	06	35	15	-0	22
1977	07	07	35	17	-0	22
1977	07	08	35	19	-0	23
1977	07	09	35	20	-0	23
1977	07	10	35	22	-0	23
1977	07	11	35	24	-0	23
1977	07	12	35	25	-0	23
1977	07	13	35	26	-0	23
1977	07	14	35	28	-0	23
1977	07	15	35	29	-0	23
1977	07	16	35	31	-0	23
1977	07	17	35	32	-0	23
1977	07	18	35	33	-0	23
1977	07	19	35	34	-0	24
1977	07	20	35	35	-0	24
1977	07	21	35	36	-0	24
1977	07	22	35	37	-0	24
1977	07	23	35	38	-0	24
1977	07	24	35	39	-0	24
1977	07	25	35	40	-0	24
1977	07	26	35	41	-0	24
1977	07	27	35	42	-0	24
1977	07	28	35	42	-0	24
1977	07	29	35	43	-0	25
1977	07	30	35	44	-0	25
1977	07	31	35	44	-0	25
1977	08	01	35	45	-0	25
1977	08	02	35	45	-0	25
1977	08	03	35	45	-0	25
1977	08	04	35	46	-0	25
1977	08	05	35	46	-0	25
1977	08	06	35	46	-0	25
1977	08	07	35	46	-0	25
1977	08	08	35	46	-0	26
1977	08	09	35	47	-0	26
1977	08	10	35	46	-0	26
1977	08	11	35	46	-0	26
1977	08	12	35	46	-0	26
1977	08	13	35	46	-0	26
1977	08	14	35	46	-0	26
1977	08	15	35	46	-0	26
1977	08	16	35	45	-0	26
1977	08	17	35	45	-0	26
1977	08	18	35	44	-0	27
1977	08	19	35	44	-0	27
1977	08	20	35	43	-0	27
1977	08	21	35	43	-0	27
1977	08	22	35	42	-0	27
1977	08	23	35	41	-0	27
1977	08	24	35	41	-0	27
1977	08	25	35	40	-0	27
1977	08	26	35	39	-0	27
1977	08	27	35	38	-0	27
1977	08	28	35	37	-0	28
1977	08	29	35	36	-0	28
1977	08	30	35	35	-0	28
1977	08	31	35	34	-0	28
1977	09	01	35	32	-0	28
1977	09	02	35	31	-0	28
1977	09	03	35	30	-0	28
1977	09	04	35	29	-0	28
1977	09	05	35	27	-0	28
1977	09	06	35	26	-0	28
1977	09	07	35	24	-0	29
1977	09	08	35	23	-0	29
1977	09	09	35	21	-0	29
1977	09	10	35	19	-0	29
1977	09	11	35	18	-0	29
1977	09	12	35	16	-0	29
1977	09	13	35	14	-0	29
1977	09	14	35	12	-0	29
1977	09	15	35	11	-0	29
1977	09	16	35	09	-0	29
1977	09	17	35	07	-0	30
1977	09	18	35	05	-0	30
1977	09	19	35	03	-0	30
1977	09	20	35	01	-0	30
1977	09	21	34	59	-0	30
1977	09	22	34	56	-0	30
1977	09	23	34	54	-0	30
1977	09	24	34	52	-0	30
1977	09	25	34	50	-0	30
1977	09	26	34	48	-0	30
1977	09	27	34	45	-0	31
1977	09	28	34	43	-0	31
1977	09	29	34	40	-0	31
1977	09	30	34	38	-0	31
1977	10	01	34	36	-0	31
1977	10	02	34	33	-0	31
1977	10	03	34	31	-0	31
1977	10	04	34	28	-0	31
1977	10	05	34	26	-0	31
1977	10	06	34	23	-0	31
1977	10	07	34	20	-0	31
1977	10	08	34	18	-0	32
1977	10	09	34	15	-0	32
1977	10	10	34	12	-0	32
1977	10	11	34	10	-0	32
1977	10	12	34	07	-0	32
1977	10	13	34	04	-0	32
1977	10	14	34	02	-0	32
1977	10	15	33	59	-0	32
1977	10	16	33	56	-0	32
1977	10	17	33	53	-0	32
1977	10	18	33	50	-0	32
1977	10	19	33	48	-0	33
1977	10	20	33	45	-0	33
1977	10	21	33	42	-0	33
1977	10	22	33	39	-0	33
1977	10	23	33	36	-0	33
1977	10	24	33	33	-0	33
1977	10	25	33	30	-0	33
1977	10	26	33	28	-0	33
1977	10	27	33	25	-0	33
1977	10	28	33	22	-0	33
1977	10	29	33	19	-0	33
1977	10	30	33	16	-0	33
1977	10	31	33	13	-0	34
1977	11	01	33	11	-0	34
1977	11	02	33	08	-0	34
1977	11	03	33	05	-0	34
1977	11	04	33	02	-0	34
1977	11	05	32	59	-0	34
1977	11	06	32	56	-0	34
1977	11	07	32	54	-0	34
1977	11	08	32	51	-0	34
1977	11	09	32	48	-0	34
1977	11	10	32	45	-0	34
1977	11	11	32	43	-0	34
1977	11	12	32	40	-0	34
1977	11	13	32	37	-0	34
1977	11	14	32	34	-0	35
1977	11	15	32	32	-0	35
1977	11	16	32	29	-0	35
1977	11	17	32	27	-0	35
1977	11	18	32	24	-0	35
1977	11	19	32	21	-0	35
1977	11	20	32	19	-0	35
1977	11	21	32	16	-0	35
1977	11	22	32	14	-0	35
1977	11	23	32	11	-0	35
1977	11	24	32	09	-0	35
1977	11	25	32	07	-0	35
1977	11	26	32	04	-0	35
1977	11	27	32	02	-0	35
1977	11	28	32	00	-0	35
1977	11	29	31	58	-0	36
1977	11	30	31	55	-0	36
1977	12	01	31	53	-0	36
1977	12	02	31	51	-0	36
1977	12	03	31	49	-0	36
1977	12	04	31	47	-0	36
1977	12	05	31	45	-0	36
1977	12	06	31	43	-0	36
1977	12	07	31	41	-0	36
1977	12	08	31	39	-0	36
1977	12	09	31	37	-0	36
1977	12	10	31	36	-0	36
1977	12	11	31	34	-0	36
1977	12	12	31	32	-0	36
1977	12	13	31	30	-0	36
1977	12	14	31	29	-0	36
1977	12	15	31	27	-0	36
1977	12	16	31	26	-0	36
1977	12	17	31	24	-0	37
1977	12	18	31	23	-0	37
1977	12	19	31	22	-0	37
1977	12	20	31	20	-0	37
1977	12	21	31	19	-0	37
1977	12	22	31	18	-0	37
1977	12	23	31	17	-0	37
1977	12	24	31	16	-0	37
1977	12	25	31	15	-0	37
1977	12	26	31	14	-0	37
1977	12	27	31	13	-0	37
1977	12	28	31	12	-0	37
1977	12	29	31	11	-0	37
1977	12	30	31	11	-0	37
1977	12	31	31	10	-0	37
1978	01	01	31	09	-0	37
1978	01	02	31	09	-0	37
1978	01	03	31	08	-0	37
1978	01	04	31	08	-0	37
1978	01	05	31	07	-0	37
1978	01	06	31	07	-0	37
1978	01	07	31	07	-0	37
1978	01	08	31	07	-0	38
1978	01	09	31	06	-0	38
1978	01	10	31	06	-0	38
1978	01	11	31	06	-0	38
1978	01	12	31	06	-0	38
1978	01	13	31	06	-0	38
1978	01	14	31	07	-0	38
1978	01	15	31	07	-0	38
1978	01	16	31	07	-0	38
1978	01	17	31	07	-0	38
1978	01	18	31	08	-0	38
1978	01	19	31	08	-0	38
1978	01	20	31	09	-0	38
1978	01	21	31	09	-0	38
1978	01	22	31	10	-0	38
1978	01	23	31	10	-0	38
1978	01	24	31	11	-0	38
1978	01	25	31	12	-0	38
1978	01	26	31	13	-0	38
1978	01	27	31	14	-0	38
1978	01	28	31	15	-0	38
1978	01	29	31	16	-0	38
1978	01	30	31	17	-0	38
1978	01	31	31	18	-0	38
1978	02	01	31	19	-0	38
1978	02	02	31	20	-0	39
1978	02	03	31	22	-0	39
1978	02	04	31	23	-0	39
1978	02	05	31	24	-0	39
1978	02	06	31	26	-0	39
1978	02	07	31	27	-0	39
1978	02	08	31	29	-0	39
1978	02	09	31	30	-0	39
1978	02	10	31	32	-0	39
1978	02	11	31	34	-0	39
1978	02	12	31	36	-0	39
1978	02	13	31	37	-0	39
1978	02	14	31	39	-0	39
1978	02	15	31	41	-0	39
1978	02	16	31	43	-0	39
1978	02	17	31	45	-0	39
1978	02	18	31	47	-0	39
1978	02	19	31	49	-0	39
1978	02	20	31	51	-0	39
1978	02	21	31	54	-0	39
1978	02	22	31	56	-0	39
1978	02	23	31	58	-0	39
1978	02	24	32	01	-0	39
1978	02	25	32	03	-0	39
1978	02	26	32	05	-0	40
1978	02	27	32	08	-0	40
1978	02	28	32	10	-0	40
1978	03	01	32	13	-0	40
1978	03	02	32	15	-0	40
1978	03	03	32	18	-0	40
1978	03	04	32	21	-0	40
1978	03	05	32	24	-0	40
1978	03	06	32	26	-0	40
1978	03	07	32	29	-0	40
1978	03	08	32	32	-0	40
1978	03	09	32	35	-0	40
1978	03	10	32	38	-0	40

1978 03 11	32 41	−0 40
1978 03 12	32 44	−0 40
1978 03 13	32 47	−0 40
1978 03 14	32 50	−0 40
1978 03 15	32 53	−0 40
1978 03 16	32 56	−0 40
1978 03 17	32 59	−0 40
1978 03 18	33 02	−0 40
1978 03 19	33 05	−0 41
1978 03 20	33 08	−0 41
1978 03 21	33 12	−0 41
1978 03 22	33 15	−0 41
1978 03 23	33 18	−0 41
1978 03 24	33 22	−0 41
1978 03 25	33 25	−0 41
1978 03 26	33 28	−0 41
1978 03 27	33 32	−0 41
1978 03 28	33 35	−0 41
1978 03 29	33 39	−0 41
1978 03 30	33 42	−0 41
1978 03 31	33 46	−0 41
1978 04 01	33 49	−0 41
1978 04 02	33 53	−0 41
1978 04 03	33 56	−0 41
1978 04 04	34 00	−0 41
1978 04 05	34 03	−0 41
1978 04 06	34 07	−0 42
1978 04 07	34 10	−0 42
1978 04 08	34 14	−0 42
1978 04 09	34 18	−0 42
1978 04 10	34 21	−0 42
1978 04 11	34 25	−0 42
1978 04 12	34 29	−0 42
1978 04 13	34 32	−0 42
1978 04 14	34 36	−0 42
1978 04 15	34 40	−0 42
1978 04 16	34 43	−0 42
1978 04 17	34 47	−0 42
1978 04 18	34 51	−0 42
1978 04 19	34 55	−0 42
1978 04 20	34 58	−0 42
1978 04 21	35 02	−0 43
1978 04 22	35 06	−0 43
1978 04 23	35 10	−0 43
1978 04 24	35 13	−0 43
1978 04 25	35 17	−0 43
1978 04 26	35 21	−0 43
1978 04 27	35 25	−0 43
1978 04 28	35 28	−0 43
1978 04 29	35 32	−0 43
1978 04 30	35 36	−0 43
1978 05 01	35 40	−0 43
1978 05 02	35 43	−0 43
1978 05 03	35 47	−0 43
1978 05 04	35 51	−0 43
1978 05 05	35 55	−0 44
1978 05 06	35 58	−0 44
1978 05 07	36 02	−0 44
1978 05 08	36 06	−0 44
1978 05 09	36 09	−0 44
1978 05 10	36 13	−0 44
1978 05 11	36 17	−0 44
1978 05 12	36 20	−0 44
1978 05 13	36 24	−0 44
1978 05 14	36 28	−0 44
1978 05 15	36 31	−0 44
1978 05 16	36 35	−0 44
1978 05 17	36 39	−0 45
1978 05 18	36 42	−0 45
1978 05 19	36 46	−0 45
1978 05 20	36 49	−0 45
1978 05 21	36 53	−0 45
1978 05 22	36 56	−0 45
1978 05 23	37 00	−0 45
1978 05 24	37 03	−0 45
1978 05 25	37 07	−0 45
1978 05 26	37 10	−0 45
1978 05 27	37 14	−0 45
1978 05 28	37 17	−0 46
1978 05 29	37 20	−0 46
1978 05 30	37 24	−0 46
1978 05 31	37 27	−0 46
1978 06 01	37 30	−0 46
1978 06 02	37 34	−0 46
1978 06 03	37 37	−0 46
1978 06 04	37 40	−0 46
1978 06 05	37 43	−0 46
1978 06 06	37 47	−0 46
1978 06 07	37 50	−0 47
1978 06 08	37 53	−0 47
1978 06 09	37 56	−0 47
1978 06 10	37 59	−0 47
1978 06 11	38 02	−0 47
1978 06 12	38 05	−0 47
1978 06 13	38 08	−0 47
1978 06 14	38 11	−0 47
1978 06 15	38 14	−0 47
1978 06 16	38 17	−0 47
1978 06 17	38 19	−0 48
1978 06 18	38 22	−0 48
1978 06 19	38 25	−0 48
1978 06 20	38 28	−0 48
1978 06 21	38 30	−0 48
1978 06 22	38 33	−0 48
1978 06 23	38 36	−0 48
1978 06 24	38 38	−0 48

1978 06 25	38 41	−0 48
1978 06 26	38 43	−0 49
1978 06 27	38 46	−0 49
1978 06 28	38 48	−0 49
1978 06 29	38 50	−0 49
1978 06 30	38 53	−0 49
1978 07 01	38 55	−0 49
1978 07 02	38 57	−0 49
1978 07 03	38 59	−0 49
1978 07 04	39 01	−0 49
1978 07 05	39 04	−0 50
1978 07 06	39 06	−0 50
1978 07 07	39 08	−0 50
1978 07 08	39 10	−0 50
1978 07 09	39 11	−0 50
1978 07 10	39 13	−0 50
1978 07 11	39 15	−0 50
1978 07 12	39 17	−0 50
1978 07 13	39 19	−0 51
1978 07 14	39 20	−0 51
1978 07 15	39 22	−0 51
1978 07 16	39 24	−0 51
1978 07 17	39 25	−0 51
1978 07 18	39 27	−0 51
1978 07 19	39 28	−0 51
1978 07 20	39 29	−0 51
1978 07 21	39 31	−0 51
1978 07 22	39 32	−0 52
1978 07 23	39 33	−0 52
1978 07 24	39 34	−0 52
1978 07 25	39 35	−0 52
1978 07 26	39 36	−0 52
1978 07 27	39 37	−0 52
1978 07 28	39 38	−0 52
1978 07 29	39 39	−0 53
1978 07 30	39 40	−0 53
1978 07 31	39 41	−0 53
1978 08 01	39 42	−0 53
1978 08 02	39 42	−0 53
1978 08 03	39 43	−0 53
1978 08 04	39 44	−0 53
1978 08 05	39 44	−0 53
1978 08 06	39 45	−0 54
1978 08 07	39 45	−0 54
1978 08 08	39 45	−0 54
1978 08 09	39 46	−0 54
1978 08 10	39 46	−0 54
1978 08 11	39 46	−0 54
1978 08 12	39 46	−0 54
1978 08 13	39 46	−0 54
1978 08 14	39 46	−0 55
1978 08 15	39 46	−0 55
1978 08 16	39 46	−0 55
1978 08 17	39 46	−0 55
1978 08 18	39 46	−0 55
1978 08 19	39 46	−0 55
1978 08 20	39 45	−0 55
1978 08 21	39 45	−0 55
1978 08 22	39 44	−0 56
1978 08 23	39 44	−0 56
1978 08 24	39 43	−0 56
1978 08 25	39 43	−0 56
1978 08 26	39 42	−0 56
1978 08 27	39 41	−0 56
1978 08 28	39 41	−0 56
1978 08 29	39 40	−0 57
1978 08 30	39 39	−0 57
1978 08 31	39 38	−0 57
1978 09 01	39 37	−0 57
1978 09 02	39 36	−0 57
1978 09 03	39 35	−0 57
1978 09 04	39 34	−0 57
1978 09 05	39 33	−0 57
1978 09 06	39 31	−0 58
1978 09 07	39 30	−0 58
1978 09 08	39 29	−0 58
1978 09 09	39 27	−0 58
1978 09 10	39 26	−0 58
1978 09 11	39 24	−0 58
1978 09 12	39 23	−0 58
1978 09 13	39 21	−0 58
1978 09 14	39 20	−0 59
1978 09 15	39 18	−0 59
1978 09 16	39 16	−0 59
1978 09 17	39 14	−0 59
1978 09 18	39 13	−0 59
1978 09 19	39 11	−0 59
1978 09 20	39 09	−0 59
1978 09 21	39 07	−0 59
1978 09 22	39 05	−1 00
1978 09 23	39 03	−1 00
1978 09 24	39 01	−1 00
1978 09 25	38 59	−1 00
1978 09 26	38 57	−1 00
1978 09 27	38 54	−1 00
1978 09 28	38 52	−1 00
1978 09 29	38 50	−1 00
1978 09 30	38 47	−1 01
1978 10 01	38 45	−1 01
1978 10 02	38 43	−1 01
1978 10 03	38 40	−1 01
1978 10 04	38 38	−1 01
1978 10 05	38 35	−1 01
1978 10 06	38 33	−1 01
1978 10 07	38 30	−1 01
1978 10 08	38 28	−1 01

1978 10 09	38 25	−1 02
1978 10 10	38 23	−1 02
1978 10 11	38 20	−1 02
1978 10 12	38 17	−1 02
1978 10 13	38 15	−1 02
1978 10 14	38 12	−1 02
1978 10 15	38 09	−1 02
1978 10 16	38 06	−1 02
1978 10 17	38 04	−1 02
1978 10 18	38 01	−1 02
1978 10 19	37 58	−1 03
1978 10 20	37 55	−1 03
1978 10 21	37 52	−1 03
1978 10 22	37 50	−1 03
1978 10 23	37 47	−1 03
1978 10 24	37 44	−1 03
1978 10 25	37 41	−1 03
1978 10 26	37 38	−1 03
1978 10 27	37 35	−1 03
1978 10 28	37 32	−1 03
1978 10 29	37 29	−1 03
1978 10 30	37 26	−1 04
1978 10 31	37 24	−1 04
1978 11 01	37 21	−1 04
1978 11 02	37 18	−1 04
1978 11 03	37 15	−1 04
1978 11 04	37 12	−1 04
1978 11 05	37 09	−1 04
1978 11 06	37 06	−1 04
1978 11 07	37 03	−1 04
1978 11 08	37 00	−1 04
1978 11 09	36 57	−1 04
1978 11 10	36 55	−1 04
1978 11 11	36 52	−1 04
1978 11 12	36 49	−1 05
1978 11 13	36 46	−1 05
1978 11 14	36 43	−1 05
1978 11 15	36 41	−1 05
1978 11 16	36 38	−1 05
1978 11 17	36 35	−1 05
1978 11 18	36 32	−1 05
1978 11 19	36 30	−1 05
1978 11 20	36 27	−1 05
1978 11 21	36 24	−1 05
1978 11 22	36 22	−1 05
1978 11 23	36 19	−1 05
1978 11 24	36 16	−1 05
1978 11 25	36 14	−1 05
1978 11 26	36 11	−1 05
1978 11 27	36 09	−1 05
1978 11 28	36 06	−1 05
1978 11 29	36 04	−1 05
1978 11 30	36 02	−1 06
1978 12 01	35 59	−1 06
1978 12 02	35 57	−1 06
1978 12 03	35 55	−1 06
1978 12 04	35 52	−1 06
1978 12 05	35 50	−1 06
1978 12 06	35 48	−1 06
1978 12 07	35 46	−1 06
1978 12 08	35 44	−1 06
1978 12 09	35 42	−1 06
1978 12 10	35 40	−1 06
1978 12 11	35 38	−1 06
1978 12 12	35 36	−1 06
1978 12 13	35 34	−1 06
1978 12 14	35 32	−1 06
1978 12 15	35 31	−1 06
1978 12 16	35 29	−1 06
1978 12 17	35 27	−1 06
1978 12 18	35 26	−1 06
1978 12 19	35 24	−1 06
1978 12 20	35 22	−1 06
1978 12 21	35 21	−1 06
1978 12 22	35 20	−1 06
1978 12 23	35 18	−1 06
1978 12 24	35 17	−1 06
1978 12 25	35 16	−1 06
1978 12 26	35 14	−1 06
1978 12 27	35 13	−1 06
1978 12 28	35 12	−1 06
1978 12 29	35 11	−1 06
1978 12 30	35 10	−1 07
1978 12 31	35 09	−1 07
1979 01 01	35 08	−1 07
1979 01 02	35 08	−1 07
1979 01 03	35 07	−1 07
1979 01 04	35 06	−1 07
1979 01 05	35 06	−1 07
1979 01 06	35 05	−1 07
1979 01 07	35 05	−1 07
1979 01 08	35 04	−1 07
1979 01 09	35 04	−1 07
1979 01 10	35 03	−1 07
1979 01 11	35 03	−1 07
1979 01 12	35 03	−1 07
1979 01 13	35 03	−1 07
1979 01 14	35 03	−1 07
1979 01 15	35 03	−1 07
1979 01 16	35 03	−1 07
1979 01 17	35 03	−1 07
1979 01 18	35 03	−1 07
1979 01 19	35 03	−1 07
1979 01 20	35 03	−1 07
1979 01 21	35 04	−1 07
1979 01 22	35 04	−1 07

1979 01 23	35 04	−1 07
1979 01 24	35 05	−1 07
1979 01 25	35 05	−1 07
1979 01 26	35 06	−1 07
1979 01 27	35 07	−1 07
1979 01 28	35 07	−1 07
1979 01 29	35 08	−1 07
1979 01 30	35 09	−1 07
1979 01 31	35 10	−1 07
1979 02 01	35 11	−1 07
1979 02 02	35 12	−1 07
1979 02 03	35 13	−1 07
1979 02 04	35 14	−1 07
1979 02 05	35 15	−1 07
1979 02 06	35 17	−1 07
1979 02 07	35 18	−1 07
1979 02 08	35 19	−1 07
1979 02 09	35 21	−1 07
1979 02 10	35 22	−1 07
1979 02 11	35 24	−1 07
1979 02 12	35 25	−1 07
1979 02 13	35 27	−1 07
1979 02 14	35 29	−1 07
1979 02 15	35 31	−1 07
1979 02 16	35 32	−1 07
1979 02 17	35 34	−1 07
1979 02 18	35 36	−1 07
1979 02 19	35 38	−1 07
1979 02 20	35 40	−1 07
1979 02 21	35 42	−1 07
1979 02 22	35 44	−1 07
1979 02 23	35 46	−1 07
1979 02 24	35 49	−1 07
1979 02 25	35 51	−1 07
1979 02 26	35 53	−1 07
1979 02 27	35 55	−1 07
1979 02 28	35 58	−1 07
1979 03 01	36 00	−1 08
1979 03 02	36 03	−1 08
1979 03 03	36 05	−1 08
1979 03 04	36 08	−1 08
1979 03 05	36 10	−1 08
1979 03 06	36 13	−1 08
1979 03 07	36 16	−1 08
1979 03 08	36 18	−1 08
1979 03 09	36 21	−1 08
1979 03 10	36 24	−1 08
1979 03 11	36 27	−1 08
1979 03 12	36 30	−1 08
1979 03 13	36 33	−1 08
1979 03 14	36 36	−1 08
1979 03 15	36 39	−1 08
1979 03 16	36 42	−1 08
1979 03 17	36 45	−1 08
1979 03 18	36 48	−1 08
1979 03 19	36 51	−1 08
1979 03 20	36 54	−1 08
1979 03 21	36 57	−1 08
1979 03 22	37 00	−1 08
1979 03 23	37 04	−1 08
1979 03 24	37 07	−1 08
1979 03 25	37 10	−1 08
1979 03 26	37 14	−1 08
1979 03 27	37 17	−1 08
1979 03 28	37 20	−1 08
1979 03 29	37 24	−1 08
1979 03 30	37 27	−1 08
1979 03 31	37 31	−1 09
1979 04 01	37 34	−1 09
1979 04 02	37 38	−1 09
1979 04 03	37 41	−1 09
1979 04 04	37 45	−1 09
1979 04 05	37 48	−1 09
1979 04 06	37 52	−1 09
1979 04 07	37 55	−1 09
1979 04 08	37 59	−1 09
1979 04 09	38 03	−1 09
1979 04 10	38 06	−1 09
1979 04 11	38 10	−1 09
1979 04 12	38 14	−1 09
1979 04 13	38 17	−1 09
1979 04 14	38 21	−1 09
1979 04 15	38 25	−1 09
1979 04 16	38 29	−1 09
1979 04 17	38 32	−1 09
1979 04 18	38 36	−1 09
1979 04 19	38 40	−1 10
1979 04 20	38 44	−1 10
1979 04 21	38 48	−1 10
1979 04 22	38 51	−1 10
1979 04 23	38 55	−1 10
1979 04 24	38 59	−1 10
1979 04 25	39 03	−1 10
1979 04 26	39 07	−1 10
1979 04 27	39 10	−1 10
1979 04 28	39 14	−1 10
1979 04 29	39 18	−1 10
1979 04 30	39 22	−1 10
1979 05 01	39 26	−1 10
1979 05 02	39 30	−1 10
1979 05 03	39 33	−1 11
1979 05 04	39 37	−1 11

Chiron

1979	05	05	39	41	-1	11
1979	05	06	39	45	-1	11
1979	05	07	39	49	-1	11
1979	05	08	39	53	-1	11
1979	05	09	39	56	-1	11
1979	05	10	40	00	-1	11
1979	05	11	40	04	-1	11
1979	05	12	40	08	-1	11
1979	05	13	40	11	-1	11
1979	05	14	40	15	-1	11
1979	05	15	40	19	-1	12
1979	05	16	40	23	-1	12
1979	05	17	40	26	-1	12
1979	05	18	40	30	-1	12
1979	05	19	40	34	-1	12
1979	05	20	40	38	-1	12
1979	05	21	40	41	-1	12
1979	05	22	40	45	-1	12
1979	05	23	40	49	-1	12
1979	05	24	40	52	-1	12
1979	05	25	40	56	-1	12
1979	05	26	41	00	-1	13
1979	05	27	41	03	-1	13
1979	05	28	41	07	-1	13
1979	05	29	41	10	-1	13
1979	05	30	41	14	-1	13
1979	05	31	41	17	-1	13
1979	06	01	41	21	-1	13
1979	06	02	41	24	-1	13
1979	06	03	41	28	-1	13
1979	06	04	41	31	-1	14
1979	06	05	41	34	-1	14
1979	06	06	41	38	-1	14
1979	06	07	41	41	-1	14
1979	06	08	41	44	-1	14
1979	06	09	41	48	-1	14
1979	06	10	41	51	-1	14
1979	06	11	41	54	-1	14
1979	06	12	41	57	-1	14
1979	06	13	42	01	-1	15
1979	06	14	42	04	-1	15
1979	06	15	42	07	-1	15
1979	06	16	42	10	-1	15
1979	06	17	42	13	-1	15
1979	06	18	42	16	-1	15
1979	06	19	42	19	-1	15
1979	06	20	42	22	-1	15
1979	06	21	42	25	-1	16
1979	06	22	42	28	-1	16
1979	06	23	42	30	-1	16
1979	06	24	42	33	-1	16
1979	06	25	42	36	-1	16
1979	06	26	42	39	-1	16
1979	06	27	42	41	-1	16
1979	06	28	42	44	-1	16
1979	06	29	42	47	-1	17
1979	06	30	42	49	-1	17
1979	07	01	42	52	-1	17
1979	07	02	42	54	-1	17
1979	07	03	42	57	-1	17
1979	07	04	42	59	-1	17
1979	07	05	43	01	-1	17
1979	07	06	43	04	-1	18
1979	07	07	43	06	-1	18
1979	07	08	43	08	-1	18
1979	07	09	43	10	-1	18
1979	07	10	43	13	-1	18
1979	07	11	43	15	-1	18
1979	07	12	43	17	-1	18
1979	07	13	43	19	-1	19
1979	07	14	43	21	-1	19
1979	07	15	43	22	-1	19
1979	07	16	43	24	-1	19
1979	07	17	43	26	-1	19
1979	07	18	43	28	-1	19
1979	07	19	43	30	-1	19
1979	07	20	43	31	-1	20
1979	07	21	43	33	-1	20
1979	07	22	43	34	-1	20
1979	07	23	43	36	-1	20
1979	07	24	43	37	-1	20
1979	07	25	43	39	-1	20
1979	07	26	43	40	-1	21
1979	07	27	43	41	-1	21
1979	07	28	43	43	-1	21
1979	07	29	43	44	-1	21
1979	07	30	43	45	-1	21
1979	07	31	43	46	-1	21
1979	08	01	43	47	-1	21
1979	03	02	43	48	-1	22
1979	08	03	43	49	-1	22
1979	08	04	43	50	-1	22
1979	08	05	43	50	-1	22
1979	08	06	43	51	-1	22
1979	08	07	43	52	-1	22
1979	08	08	43	53	-1	23
1979	08	09	43	53	-1	23
1979	08	10	43	54	-1	23
1979	08	11	43	54	-1	23
1979	08	12	43	54	-1	23
1979	08	13	43	55	-1	23
1979	08	14	43	55	-1	24
1979	08	15	43	55	-1	24
1979	08	16	43	56	-1	24
1979	08	17	43	56	-1	24
1979	08	18	43	56	-1	24
1979	08	19	43	56	-1	24
1979	08	20	43	56	-1	25
1979	08	21	43	56	-1	25
1979	08	22	43	55	-1	25
1979	08	23	43	55	-1	25
1979	08	24	43	55	-1	25
1979	08	25	43	55	-1	25
1979	08	26	43	54	-1	26
1979	08	27	43	54	-1	26
1979	08	28	43	53	-1	26
1979	08	29	43	53	-1	26
1979	08	30	43	52	-1	26
1979	08	31	43	51	-1	26
1979	09	01	43	51	-1	27
1979	09	02	43	50	-1	27
1979	09	03	43	49	-1	27
1979	09	04	43	48	-1	27
1979	09	05	43	47	-1	27
1979	09	06	43	46	-1	27
1979	09	07	43	45	-1	27
1979	09	08	43	44	-1	28
1979	09	09	43	43	-1	28
1979	09	10	43	41	-1	28
1979	09	11	43	40	-1	28
1979	09	12	43	39	-1	28
1979	09	13	43	37	-1	28
1979	09	14	43	36	-1	29
1979	09	15	43	35	-1	29
1979	09	16	43	33	-1	29
1979	09	17	43	31	-1	29
1979	09	18	43	30	-1	29
1979	09	19	43	28	-1	29
1979	09	20	43	26	-1	29
1979	09	21	43	25	-1	30
1979	09	22	43	23	-1	30
1979	09	23	43	21	-1	30
1979	09	24	43	19	-1	30
1979	09	25	43	17	-1	30
1979	09	26	43	15	-1	30
1979	09	27	43	13	-1	31
1979	09	28	43	11	-1	31
1979	09	29	43	09	-1	31
1979	09	30	43	06	-1	31
1979	10	01	43	04	-1	31
1979	10	02	43	02	-1	31
1979	10	03	43	00	-1	31
1979	10	04	42	57	-1	31
1979	10	05	42	55	-1	32
1979	10	06	42	53	-1	32
1979	10	07	42	50	-1	32
1979	10	08	42	48	-1	32
1979	10	09	42	45	-1	32
1979	10	10	42	43	-1	32
1979	10	11	42	40	-1	32
1979	10	12	42	37	-1	33
1979	10	13	42	35	-1	33
1979	10	14	42	32	-1	33
1979	10	15	42	30	-1	33
1979	10	16	42	27	-1	33
1979	10	17	42	24	-1	33
1979	10	18	42	21	-1	33
1979	10	19	42	19	-1	33
1979	10	20	42	16	-1	33
1979	10	21	42	13	-1	34
1979	10	22	42	10	-1	34
1979	10	23	42	07	-1	34
1979	10	24	42	04	-1	34
1979	10	25	42	02	-1	34
1979	10	26	41	59	-1	34
1979	10	27	41	56	-1	34
1979	10	28	41	53	-1	34
1979	10	29	41	50	-1	34
1979	10	30	41	47	-1	35
1979	10	31	41	44	-1	35
1979	11	01	41	41	-1	35
1979	11	02	41	38	-1	35
1979	11	03	41	35	-1	35
1979	11	04	41	32	-1	35
1979	11	05	41	29	-1	35
1979	11	06	41	26	-1	35
1979	11	07	41	23	-1	35
1979	11	08	41	20	-1	35
1979	11	09	41	17	-1	35
1979	11	10	41	14	-1	35
1979	11	11	41	11	-1	36
1979	11	12	41	09	-1	36
1979	11	13	41	06	-1	36
1979	11	14	41	03	-1	36
1979	11	15	41	00	-1	36
1979	11	16	40	57	-1	36
1979	11	17	40	54	-1	36
1979	11	18	40	51	-1	36
1979	11	19	40	48	-1	36
1979	11	20	40	45	-1	36
1979	11	21	40	43	-1	36
1979	11	22	40	40	-1	36
1979	11	23	40	37	-1	36
1979	11	24	40	34	-1	36
1979	11	25	40	32	-1	36
1979	11	26	40	29	-1	36
1979	11	27	40	26	-1	36
1979	11	28	40	24	-1	36
1979	11	29	40	21	-1	37
1979	11	30	40	18	-1	37
1979	12	01	40	16	-1	37
1979	12	02	40	13	-1	37
1979	12	03	40	11	-1	37
1979	12	04	40	09	-1	37
1979	12	05	40	06	-1	37
1979	12	06	40	04	-1	37
1979	12	07	40	01	-1	37
1979	12	08	39	59	-1	37
1979	12	09	39	57	-1	37
1979	12	10	39	55	-1	37
1979	12	11	39	52	-1	37
1979	12	12	39	50	-1	37
1979	12	13	39	48	-1	37
1979	12	14	39	46	-1	37
1979	12	15	39	44	-1	37
1979	12	16	39	42	-1	37
1979	12	17	39	40	-1	37
1979	12	18	39	38	-1	37
1979	12	19	39	37	-1	37
1979	12	20	39	35	-1	37
1979	12	21	39	33	-1	37
1979	12	22	39	32	-1	37
1979	12	23	39	30	-1	37
1979	12	24	39	28	-1	37
1979	12	25	39	27	-1	37
1979	12	26	39	25	-1	37
1979	12	27	39	24	-1	37
1979	12	28	39	23	-1	37
1979	12	29	39	21	-1	37
1979	12	30	39	20	-1	37
1979	12	31	39	19	-1	37
1980	01	01	39	18	-1	37
1980	01	02	39	17	-1	37
1980	01	03	39	16	-1	37
1980	01	04	39	15	-1	37
1980	01	05	39	14	-1	37
1980	01	06	39	13	-1	37
1980	01	07	39	12	-1	37
1980	01	08	39	12	-1	37
1980	01	09	39	11	-1	37
1980	01	10	39	10	-1	37
1980	01	11	39	10	-1	37
1980	01	12	39	09	-1	37
1980	01	13	39	09	-1	37
1980	01	14	39	09	-1	37
1980	01	15	39	08	-1	37
1980	01	16	39	08	-1	37
1980	01	17	39	08	-1	37
1980	01	18	39	08	-1	37
1980	01	19	39	08	-1	37
1980	01	20	39	08	-1	37
1980	01	21	39	08	-1	37
1980	01	22	39	08	-1	37
1980	01	23	39	08	-1	37
1980	01	24	39	09	-1	37
1980	01	25	39	09	-1	37
1980	01	26	39	09	-1	37
1980	01	27	39	10	-1	37
1980	01	28	39	10	-1	37
1980	01	29	39	11	-1	37
1980	01	30	39	11	-1	37
1980	01	31	39	12	-1	37
1980	02	01	39	13	-1	37
1980	02	02	39	14	-1	37
1980	02	03	39	14	-1	37
1980	02	04	39	15	-1	37
1980	02	05	39	16	-1	37
1980	02	06	39	17	-1	37
1980	02	07	39	19	-1	37
1980	02	08	39	20	-1	37
1980	02	09	39	21	-1	37
1980	02	10	39	22	-1	37
1980	02	11	39	24	-1	37
1980	02	12	39	25	-1	36
1980	02	13	39	26	-1	36
1980	02	14	39	28	-1	36
1980	02	15	39	29	-1	36
1980	02	16	39	31	-1	36
1980	02	17	39	33	-1	36
1980	02	18	39	34	-1	36
1980	02	19	39	36	-1	36
1980	02	20	39	38	-1	36
1980	02	21	39	40	-1	36
1980	02	22	39	42	-1	36
1980	02	23	39	44	-1	36
1980	02	24	39	46	-1	36
1980	02	25	39	48	-1	36
1980	02	26	39	50	-1	36
1980	02	27	39	52	-1	36
1980	02	28	39	55	-1	36
1980	02	29	39	57	-1	36
1980	03	01	39	59	-1	36
1980	03	02	40	02	-1	36
1980	03	03	40	04	-1	36
1980	03	04	40	06	-1	36
1980	03	05	40	09	-1	36
1980	03	06	40	12	-1	36
1980	03	07	40	14	-1	36
1980	03	08	40	17	-1	36
1980	03	09	40	19	-1	36
1980	03	10	40	22	-1	36
1980	03	11	40	25	-1	36
1980	03	12	40	28	-1	36
1980	03	13	40	31	-1	36
1980	03	14	40	34	-1	36
1980	03	15	40	36	-1	36
1980	03	16	40	39	-1	36
1980	03	17	40	42	-1	36
1980	03	18	40	46	-1	36
1980	03	19	40	49	-1	36
1980	03	20	40	52	-1	36
1980	03	21	40	55	-1	36
1980	03	22	40	58	-1	37
1980	03	23	41	01	-1	37
1980	03	24	41	05	-1	37
1980	03	25	41	08	-1	37
1980	03	26	41	11	-1	37
1980	03	27	41	14	-1	37
1980	03	28	41	18	-1	37
1980	03	29	41	21	-1	37
1980	03	30	41	25	-1	37
1980	03	31	41	28	-1	37
1980	04	01	41	32	-1	37
1980	04	02	41	35	-1	37
1980	04	03	41	39	-1	37
1980	04	04	41	42	-1	37
1980	04	05	41	46	-1	37
1980	04	06	41	49	-1	37
1980	04	07	41	53	-1	37
1980	04	08	41	57	-1	37
1980	04	09	42	00	-1	37
1980	04	10	42	04	-1	37
1980	04	11	42	08	-1	37
1980	04	12	42	11	-1	37
1980	04	13	42	15	-1	37
1980	04	14	42	19	-1	37
1980	04	15	42	23	-1	37
1980	04	16	42	27	-1	37
1980	04	17	42	30	-1	37
1980	04	18	42	34	-1	37
1980	04	19	42	38	-1	38
1980	04	20	42	42	-1	38
1980	04	21	42	46	-1	38
1980	04	22	42	50	-1	38
1980	04	23	42	53	-1	38
1980	04	24	42	57	-1	38
1980	04	25	43	01	-1	38
1980	04	26	43	05	-1	38
1980	04	27	43	09	-1	38
1980	04	28	43	13	-1	38
1980	04	29	43	17	-1	38
1980	04	30	43	21	-1	38
1980	05	01	43	25	-1	38
1980	05	02	43	29	-1	38
1980	05	03	43	32	-1	38
1980	05	04	43	36	-1	38
1980	05	05	43	40	-1	39
1980	05	06	43	44	-1	39
1980	05	07	43	48	-1	39
1980	05	08	43	52	-1	39
1980	05	09	43	56	-1	39
1980	05	10	44	00	-1	39
1980	05	11	44	04	-1	39
1980	05	12	44	08	-1	39
1980	05	13	44	12	-1	39
1980	05	14	44	16	-1	39
1980	05	15	44	19	-1	39
1980	05	16	44	23	-1	40
1980	05	17	44	27	-1	40
1980	05	18	44	31	-1	40
1980	05	19	44	35	-1	40
1980	05	20	44	39	-1	40
1980	05	21	44	43	-1	40
1980	05	22	44	46	-1	40
1980	05	23	44	50	-1	40
1980	05	24	44	54	-1	40
1980	05	25	44	58	-1	40
1980	05	26	45	01	-1	41
1980	05	27	45	05	-1	41
1980	05	28	45	09	-1	41
1980	05	29	45	13	-1	41
1980	05	30	45	16	-1	41
1980	05	31	45	20	-1	41
1980	06	01	45	24	-1	41
1980	06	02	45	27	-1	41
1980	06	03	45	31	-1	41
1980	06	04	45	35	-1	42
1980	06	05	45	38	-1	42
1980	06	06	45	42	-1	42
1980	06	07	45	45	-1	42
1980	06	08	45	49	-1	42
1980	06	09	45	52	-1	42
1980	06	10	45	56	-1	42
1980	06	11	45	59	-1	42
1980	06	12	46	02	-1	43
1980	06	13	46	06	-1	43
1980	06	14	46	09	-1	43
1980	06	15	46	12	-1	43
1980	06	16	46	16	-1	43
1980	06	17	46	19	-1	43
1980	06	18	46	22	-1	43
1980	06	19	46	25	-1	44
1980	06	20	46	28	-1	44
1980	06	21	46	32	-1	44
1980	06	22	46	35	-1	44
1980	06	23	46	38	-1	44
1980	06	24	46	41	-1	44
1980	06	25	46	44	-1	44
1980	06	26	46	47	-1	45
1980	06	27	46	49	-1	45

1980	06	28	46	52	-1	45
1980	06	29	46	55	-1	45
1980	06	30	46	58	-1	45
1980	07	01	47	01	-1	45
1980	07	02	47	03	-1	46
1980	07	03	47	06	-1	46
1980	07	04	47	09	-1	46
1980	07	05	47	11	-1	46
1980	07	06	47	14	-1	46
1980	07	07	47	16	-1	46
1980	07	08	47	19	-1	47
1980	07	09	47	21	-1	47
1980	07	10	47	24	-1	47
1980	07	11	47	26	-1	47
1980	07	12	47	28	-1	47
1980	07	13	47	30	-1	47
1980	07	14	47	33	-1	48
1980	07	15	47	35	-1	48
1980	07	16	47	37	-1	48
1980	07	17	47	39	-1	48
1980	07	18	47	41	-1	48
1980	07	19	47	43	-1	48
1980	07	20	47	45	-1	49
1980	07	21	47	46	-1	49
1980	07	22	47	48	-1	49
1980	07	23	47	50	-1	49
1980	07	24	47	52	-1	49
1980	07	25	47	53	-1	50
1980	07	26	47	55	-1	50
1980	07	27	47	56	-1	50
1980	07	28	47	58	-1	50
1980	07	29	47	59	-1	50
1980	07	30	48	01	-1	50
1980	07	31	48	02	-1	51
1980	08	01	48	03	-1	51
1980	08	02	48	05	-1	51
1980	08	03	48	06	-1	51
1980	08	04	48	07	-1	51
1980	08	05	48	08	-1	52
1980	08	06	48	09	-1	52
1980	08	07	48	10	-1	52
1980	08	08	48	11	-1	52
1980	08	09	48	11	-1	52
1980	08	10	48	12	-1	53
1980	08	11	48	13	-1	53
1980	08	12	48	14	-1	53
1980	08	13	48	14	-1	53
1980	08	14	48	15	-1	53
1980	08	15	48	15	-1	54
1980	08	16	48	16	-1	54
1980	08	17	48	16	-1	54
1980	08	18	48	16	-1	54
1980	08	19	48	16	-1	54
1980	08	20	48	17	-1	55
1980	08	21	48	17	-1	55
1980	08	22	48	17	-1	55
1980	08	23	48	17	-1	55
1980	08	24	48	17	-1	55
1980	08	25	48	17	-1	56
1980	08	26	48	16	-1	56
1980	08	27	48	16	-1	56
1980	08	28	48	16	-1	56
1980	08	29	48	16	-1	56
1980	08	30	48	15	-1	56
1980	08	31	48	15	-1	57
1980	09	01	48	14	-1	57
1980	09	02	48	14	-1	57
1980	09	03	48	13	-1	57
1980	09	04	48	12	-1	57
1980	09	05	48	11	-1	58
1980	09	06	48	11	-1	58
1980	09	07	48	10	-1	58
1980	09	08	48	09	-1	58
1980	09	09	48	08	-1	58
1980	09	10	48	07	-1	59
1980	09	11	48	06	-1	59
1980	09	12	48	05	-1	59
1980	09	13	48	03	-1	59
1980	09	14	48	02	-1	59
1980	09	15	48	01	-2	00
1980	09	16	47	59	-2	00
1980	09	17	47	58	-2	00
1980	09	18	47	57	-2	00
1980	09	19	47	55	-2	00
1980	09	20	47	53	-2	01
1980	09	21	47	52	-2	01
1980	09	22	47	50	-2	01
1980	09	23	47	48	-2	01
1980	09	24	47	47	-2	01
1980	09	25	47	45	-2	01
1980	09	26	47	43	-2	02
1980	09	27	47	41	-2	02
1980	09	28	47	39	-2	02
1980	09	29	47	37	-2	02
1980	09	30	47	35	-2	02
1980	10	01	47	33	-2	02
1980	10	02	47	31	-2	03
1980	10	03	47	29	-2	03
1980	10	04	47	26	-2	03
1980	10	05	47	24	-2	03
1980	10	06	47	22	-2	03
1980	10	07	47	19	-2	03
1980	10	08	47	17	-2	04
1980	10	09	47	15	-2	04
1980	10	10	47	12	-2	04
1980	10	11	47	10	-2	04
1980	10	12	47	07	-2	04
1980	10	13	47	04	-2	04
1980	10	14	47	02	-2	04
1980	10	15	46	59	-2	05
1980	10	16	46	57	-2	05
1980	10	17	46	54	-2	05
1980	10	18	46	51	-2	05
1980	10	19	46	48	-2	05
1980	10	20	46	46	-2	05
1980	10	21	46	43	-2	05
1980	10	22	46	40	-2	06
1980	10	23	46	37	-2	06
1980	10	24	46	34	-2	06
1980	10	25	46	31	-2	06
1980	10	26	46	28	-2	06
1980	10	27	46	26	-2	06
1980	10	28	46	23	-2	06
1980	10	29	46	20	-2	06
1980	10	30	46	17	-2	07
1980	10	31	46	14	-2	07
1980	11	01	46	11	-2	07
1980	11	02	46	08	-2	07
1980	11	03	46	05	-2	07
1980	11	04	46	02	-2	07
1980	11	05	45	59	-2	07
1980	11	06	45	56	-2	07
1980	11	07	45	53	-2	07
1980	11	08	45	50	-2	07
1980	11	09	45	47	-2	08
1980	11	10	45	44	-2	08
1980	11	11	45	41	-2	08
1980	11	12	45	38	-2	08
1980	11	13	45	35	-2	08
1980	11	14	45	32	-2	08
1980	11	15	45	29	-2	08
1980	11	16	45	26	-2	08
1980	11	17	45	23	-2	08
1980	11	18	45	20	-2	08
1980	11	19	45	17	-2	08
1980	11	20	45	14	-2	08
1980	11	21	45	11	-2	08
1980	11	22	45	08	-2	08
1980	11	23	45	05	-2	08
1980	11	24	45	02	-2	09
1980	11	25	44	59	-2	09
1980	11	26	44	56	-2	09
1980	11	27	44	54	-2	09
1980	11	28	44	51	-2	09
1980	11	29	44	48	-2	09
1980	11	30	44	45	-2	09
1980	12	01	44	43	-2	09
1980	12	02	44	40	-2	09
1980	12	03	44	37	-2	09
1980	12	04	44	35	-2	09
1980	12	05	44	32	-2	09
1980	12	06	44	30	-2	09
1980	12	07	44	27	-2	09
1980	12	08	44	25	-2	09
1980	12	09	44	22	-2	09
1980	12	10	44	20	-2	09
1980	12	11	44	17	-2	09
1980	12	12	44	15	-2	09
1980	12	13	44	13	-2	09
1980	12	14	44	10	-2	09
1980	12	15	44	08	-2	09
1980	12	16	44	06	-2	09
1980	12	17	44	04	-2	09
1980	12	18	44	02	-2	09
1980	12	19	44	00	-2	09
1980	12	20	43	58	-2	09
1980	12	21	43	56	-2	09
1980	12	22	43	54	-2	09
1980	12	23	43	52	-2	09
1980	12	24	43	51	-2	09
1980	12	25	43	49	-2	09
1980	12	26	43	47	-2	09
1980	12	27	43	46	-2	09
1980	12	28	43	44	-2	09
1980	12	29	43	43	-2	09
1980	12	30	43	41	-2	09
1980	12	31	43	40	-2	09
1981	01	01	43	38	-2	09
1981	01	02	43	37	-2	09
1981	01	03	43	36	-2	09
1981	01	04	43	35	-2	09
1981	01	05	43	34	-2	09
1981	01	06	43	33	-2	09
1981	01	07	43	32	-2	09
1981	01	08	43	31	-2	08
1981	01	09	43	30	-2	08
1981	01	10	43	29	-2	08
1981	01	11	43	28	-2	08
1981	01	12	43	28	-2	08
1981	01	13	43	27	-2	08
1981	01	14	43	26	-2	08
1981	01	15	43	26	-2	08
1981	01	16	43	26	-2	08
1981	01	17	43	25	-2	08
1981	01	18	43	25	-2	08
1981	01	19	43	25	-2	08
1981	01	20	43	24	-2	08
1981	01	21	43	24	-2	08
1981	01	22	43	24	-2	08
1981	01	23	43	24	-2	08
1981	01	24	43	24	-2	08
1981	01	25	43	24	-2	08
1981	01	26	43	25	-2	08
1981	01	27	43	25	-2	08
1981	01	28	43	25	-2	08
1981	01	29	43	26	-2	08
1981	01	30	43	26	-2	08
1981	01	31	43	26	-2	07
1981	02	01	43	27	-2	07
1981	02	02	43	28	-2	07
1981	02	03	43	28	-2	07
1981	02	04	43	29	-2	07
1981	02	05	43	30	-2	07
1981	02	06	43	31	-2	07
1981	02	07	43	32	-2	07
1981	02	08	43	33	-2	07
1981	02	09	43	34	-2	07
1981	02	10	43	35	-2	07
1981	02	11	43	36	-2	07
1981	02	12	43	37	-2	07
1981	02	13	43	39	-2	07
1981	02	14	43	40	-2	07
1981	02	15	43	41	-2	07
1981	02	16	43	43	-2	07
1981	02	17	43	44	-2	07
1981	02	18	43	46	-2	07
1981	02	19	43	48	-2	07
1981	02	20	43	49	-2	07
1981	02	21	43	51	-2	07
1981	02	22	43	53	-2	06
1981	02	23	43	55	-2	06
1981	02	24	43	57	-2	06
1981	02	25	43	59	-2	06
1981	02	26	44	01	-2	06
1981	02	27	44	03	-2	06
1981	02	28	44	05	-2	06
1981	03	01	44	07	-2	06
1981	03	02	44	09	-2	06
1981	03	03	44	11	-2	06
1981	03	04	44	14	-2	06
1981	03	05	44	16	-2	06
1981	03	06	44	19	-2	06
1981	03	07	44	21	-2	06
1981	03	08	44	24	-2	06
1981	03	09	44	26	-2	06
1981	03	10	44	29	-2	06
1981	03	11	44	31	-2	06
1981	03	12	44	34	-2	06
1981	03	13	44	37	-2	06
1981	03	14	44	40	-2	06
1981	03	15	44	42	-2	06
1981	03	16	44	45	-2	06
1981	03	17	44	48	-2	06
1981	03	18	44	51	-2	06
1981	03	19	44	54	-2	06
1981	03	20	44	57	-2	06
1981	03	21	45	00	-2	06
1981	03	22	45	03	-2	06
1981	03	23	45	07	-2	06
1981	03	24	45	10	-2	06
1981	03	25	45	13	-2	06
1981	03	26	45	16	-2	06
1981	03	27	45	20	-2	06
1981	03	28	45	23	-2	06
1981	03	29	45	26	-2	06
1981	03	30	45	30	-2	06
1981	03	31	45	33	-2	06
1981	04	01	45	37	-2	06
1981	04	02	45	40	-2	06
1981	04	03	45	43	-2	06
1981	04	04	45	47	-2	06
1981	04	05	45	51	-2	06
1981	04	06	45	54	-2	06
1981	04	07	45	58	-2	06
1981	04	08	46	01	-2	06
1981	04	09	46	05	-2	06
1981	04	10	46	09	-2	06
1981	04	11	46	13	-2	06
1981	04	12	46	16	-2	06
1981	04	13	46	20	-2	06
1981	04	14	46	24	-2	06
1981	04	15	46	28	-2	06
1981	04	16	46	31	-2	06
1981	04	17	46	35	-2	06
1981	04	18	46	39	-2	06
1981	04	19	46	43	-2	06
1981	04	20	46	47	-2	06
1981	04	21	46	51	-2	06
1981	04	22	46	55	-2	06
1981	04	23	46	59	-2	06
1981	04	24	47	03	-2	06
1981	04	25	47	06	-2	07
1981	04	26	47	10	-2	07
1981	04	27	47	14	-2	07
1981	04	28	47	18	-2	07
1981	04	29	47	22	-2	07
1981	04	30	47	26	-2	07
1981	05	01	47	30	-2	07
1981	05	02	47	34	-2	07
1981	05	03	47	38	-2	07
1981	05	04	47	42	-2	07
1981	05	05	47	46	-2	07
1981	05	06	47	51	-2	07
1981	05	07	47	55	-2	07
1981	05	08	47	59	-2	07
1981	05	09	48	03	-2	07
1981	05	10	48	07	-2	08
1981	05	11	48	11	-2	08
1981	05	12	48	15	-2	08
1981	05	13	48	19	-2	08
1981	05	14	48	23	-2	08
1981	05	15	48	27	-2	08
1981	05	16	48	31	-2	08
1981	05	17	48	35	-2	08
1981	05	18	48	39	-2	08
1981	05	19	48	43	-2	08
1981	05	20	48	47	-2	08
1981	05	21	48	51	-2	09
1981	05	22	48	55	-2	09
1981	05	23	48	59	-2	09
1981	05	24	49	03	-2	09
1981	05	25	49	07	-2	09
1981	05	26	49	11	-2	09
1981	05	27	49	15	-2	09
1981	05	28	49	18	-2	09
1981	05	29	49	22	-2	09
1981	05	30	49	26	-2	09
1981	05	31	49	30	-2	10
1981	06	01	49	34	-2	10
1981	06	02	49	38	-2	10
1981	06	03	49	42	-2	10
1981	06	04	49	45	-2	10
1981	06	05	49	49	-2	10
1981	06	06	49	53	-2	10
1981	06	07	49	57	-2	11
1981	06	08	50	00	-2	11
1981	06	09	50	04	-2	11
1981	06	10	50	08	-2	11
1981	06	11	50	11	-2	11
1981	06	12	50	15	-2	11
1981	06	13	50	19	-2	11
1981	06	14	50	22	-2	11
1981	06	15	50	26	-2	12
1981	06	16	50	29	-2	12
1981	06	17	50	33	-2	12
1981	06	18	50	36	-2	12
1981	06	19	50	40	-2	12
1981	06	20	50	43	-2	12
1981	06	21	50	46	-2	13
1981	06	22	50	50	-2	13
1981	06	23	50	53	-2	13
1981	06	24	50	56	-2	13
1981	06	25	51	00	-2	13
1981	06	26	51	03	-2	13
1981	06	27	51	06	-2	14
1981	06	28	51	09	-2	14
1981	06	29	51	12	-2	14
1981	06	30	51	15	-2	14
1981	07	01	51	18	-2	14
1981	07	02	51	21	-2	14
1981	07	03	51	24	-2	15
1981	07	04	51	27	-2	15
1981	07	05	51	30	-2	15
1981	07	06	51	33	-2	15
1981	07	07	51	36	-2	15
1981	07	08	51	38	-2	16
1981	07	09	51	41	-2	16
1981	07	10	51	44	-2	16
1981	07	11	51	46	-2	16
1981	07	12	51	49	-2	16
1981	07	13	51	52	-2	17
1981	07	14	51	54	-2	17
1981	07	15	51	56	-2	17
1981	07	16	51	59	-2	17
1981	07	17	52	01	-2	17
1981	07	18	52	04	-2	18
1981	07	19	52	06	-2	18
1981	07	20	52	08	-2	18
1981	07	21	52	10	-2	18
1981	07	22	52	12	-2	18
1981	07	23	52	14	-2	19
1981	07	24	52	16	-2	19
1981	07	25	52	18	-2	19
1981	07	26	52	20	-2	19
1981	07	27	52	22	-2	19
1981	07	28	52	24	-2	20
1981	07	29	52	26	-2	20
1981	07	30	52	27	-2	20
1981	07	31	52	29	-2	20
1981	08	01	52	31	-2	21
1981	08	02	52	32	-2	21
1981	08	03	52	34	-2	21
1981	08	04	52	35	-2	21
1981	08	05	52	36	-2	21
1981	08	06	52	38	-2	22
1981	08	07	52	39	-2	22
1981	08	08	52	40	-2	22
1981	08	09	52	41	-2	22
1981	08	10	52	42	-2	23
1981	08	11	52	43	-2	23
1981	08	12	52	44	-2	23
1981	08	13	52	45	-2	23
1981	08	14	52	46	-2	23
1981	08	15	52	47	-2	24
1981	08	16	52	48	-2	24
1981	08	17	52	48	-2	24
1981	08	18	52	49	-2	24
1981	08	19	52	50	-2	25
1981	08	20	52	50	-2	25
1981	08	21	52	50	-2	25

Chiron

1981	08	22	52	51	-2	25
1981	08	23	52	51	-2	26
1981	08	24	52	51	-2	26
1981	08	25	52	52	-2	26
1981	08	26	52	52	-2	26
1981	08	27	52	52	-2	27
1981	08	28	52	52	-2	27
1981	08	29	52	52	-2	27
1981	08	30	52	52	-2	27
1981	08	31	52	52	-2	27
1981	09	01	52	51	-2	28
1981	09	02	52	51	-2	28
1981	09	03	52	51	-2	28
1981	09	04	52	50	-2	28
1981	09	05	52	50	-2	29
1981	09	06	52	49	-2	29
1981	09	07	52	49	-2	29
1981	09	08	52	48	-2	29
1981	09	09	52	47	-2	30
1981	09	10	52	47	-2	30
1981	09	11	52	46	-2	30
1981	09	12	52	45	-2	30
1981	09	13	52	44	-2	30
1981	09	14	52	43	-2	31
1981	09	15	52	42	-2	31
1981	09	16	52	41	-2	31
1981	09	17	52	40	-2	31
1981	09	18	52	38	-2	32
1981	09	19	52	37	-2	32
1981	09	20	52	36	-2	32
1981	09	21	52	34	-2	32
1981	09	22	52	33	-2	32
1981	09	23	52	32	-2	33
1981	09	24	52	30	-2	33
1981	09	25	52	28	-2	33
1981	09	26	52	27	-2	33
1981	09	27	52	25	-2	34
1981	09	28	52	23	-2	34
1981	09	29	52	21	-2	34
1981	09	30	52	20	-2	34
1981	10	01	52	18	-2	34
1981	10	02	52	16	-2	35
1981	10	03	52	14	-2	35
1981	10	04	52	12	-2	35
1981	10	05	52	09	-2	35
1981	10	06	52	07	-2	35
1981	10	07	52	05	-2	36
1981	10	08	52	03	-2	36
1981	10	09	52	01	-2	36
1981	10	10	51	58	-2	36
1981	10	11	51	56	-2	36
1981	10	12	51	53	-2	37
1981	10	13	51	51	-2	37
1981	10	14	51	49	-2	37
1981	10	15	51	46	-2	37
1981	10	16	51	43	-2	37
1981	10	17	51	41	-2	37
1981	10	18	51	38	-2	38
1981	10	19	51	36	-2	38
1981	10	20	51	33	-2	38
1981	10	21	51	30	-2	38
1981	10	22	51	27	-2	38
1981	10	23	51	25	-2	38
1981	10	24	51	22	-2	39
1981	10	25	51	19	-2	39
1981	10	26	51	16	-2	39
1981	10	27	51	13	-2	39
1981	10	28	51	10	-2	39
1981	10	29	51	07	-2	39
1981	10	30	51	04	-2	39
1981	10	31	51	01	-2	40
1981	11	01	50	58	-2	40
1981	11	02	50	55	-2	40
1981	11	03	50	52	-2	40
1981	11	04	50	49	-2	40
1981	11	05	50	46	-2	40
1981	11	06	50	43	-2	40
1981	11	07	50	40	-2	40
1981	11	08	50	37	-2	40
1981	11	09	50	34	-2	41
1981	11	10	50	31	-2	41
1981	11	11	50	28	-2	41
1981	11	12	50	25	-2	41
1981	11	13	50	22	-2	41
1981	11	14	50	18	-2	41
1981	11	15	50	15	-2	41
1981	11	16	50	12	-2	41
1981	11	17	50	09	-2	41
1981	11	18	50	06	-2	41
1981	11	19	50	03	-2	41
1981	11	20	50	00	-2	42
1981	11	21	49	57	-2	42
1981	11	22	49	54	-2	42
1981	11	23	49	51	-2	42
1981	11	24	49	48	-2	42
1981	11	25	49	45	-2	42
1981	11	26	49	42	-2	42
1981	11	27	49	39	-2	42
1981	11	28	49	36	-2	42
1981	11	29	49	33	-2	42
1981	11	30	49	30	-2	42
1981	12	01	49	27	-2	42
1981	12	02	49	24	-2	42
1981	12	03	49	21	-2	42
1981	12	04	49	19	-2	42
1981	12	05	49	16	-2	42
1981	12	06	49	13	-2	42
1981	12	07	49	10	-2	42
1981	12	08	49	08	-2	42
1981	12	09	49	05	-2	42
1981	12	10	49	02	-2	42
1981	12	11	49	00	-2	42
1981	12	12	48	57	-2	42
1981	12	13	48	55	-2	42
1981	12	14	48	52	-2	42
1981	12	15	48	50	-2	42
1981	12	16	48	47	-2	42
1981	12	17	48	45	-2	42
1981	12	18	48	43	-2	42
1981	12	19	48	40	-2	42
1981	12	20	48	38	-2	42
1981	12	21	48	36	-2	42
1981	12	22	48	34	-2	42
1981	12	23	48	32	-2	42
1981	12	24	48	30	-2	42
1981	12	25	48	28	-2	42
1981	12	26	48	26	-2	42
1981	12	27	48	24	-2	42
1981	12	28	48	22	-2	42
1981	12	29	48	20	-2	42
1981	12	30	48	18	-2	42
1981	12	31	48	17	-2	42
1982	01	01	48	15	-2	42
1982	01	02	48	14	-2	42
1982	01	03	48	12	-2	42
1982	01	04	48	11	-2	41
1982	01	05	48	09	-2	41
1982	01	06	48	08	-2	41
1982	01	07	48	07	-2	41
1982	01	08	48	05	-2	41
1982	01	09	48	04	-2	41
1982	01	10	48	03	-2	41
1982	01	11	48	02	-2	41
1982	01	12	48	01	-2	41
1982	01	13	48	00	-2	41
1982	01	14	47	59	-2	41
1982	01	15	47	59	-2	41
1982	01	16	47	58	-2	41
1982	01	17	47	57	-2	41
1982	01	18	47	57	-2	41
1982	01	19	47	56	-2	40
1982	01	20	47	56	-2	40
1982	01	21	47	55	-2	40
1982	01	22	47	55	-2	40
1982	01	23	47	55	-2	40
1982	01	24	47	54	-2	40
1982	01	25	47	54	-2	40
1982	01	26	47	54	-2	40
1982	01	27	47	54	-2	40
1982	01	28	47	54	-2	40
1982	01	29	47	54	-2	40
1982	01	30	47	54	-2	40
1982	01	31	47	55	-2	39
1982	02	01	47	55	-2	39
1982	02	02	47	55	-2	39
1982	02	03	47	56	-2	39
1982	02	04	47	56	-2	39
1982	02	05	47	57	-2	39
1982	02	06	47	57	-2	39
1982	02	07	47	58	-2	39
1982	02	08	47	59	-2	39
1982	02	09	48	00	-2	39
1982	02	10	48	00	-2	39
1982	02	11	48	01	-2	39
1982	02	12	48	02	-2	38
1982	02	13	48	03	-2	38
1982	02	14	48	04	-2	38
1982	02	15	48	06	-2	38
1982	02	16	48	07	-2	38
1982	02	17	48	08	-2	38
1982	02	18	48	10	-2	38
1982	02	19	48	11	-2	38
1982	02	20	48	12	-2	38
1982	02	21	48	14	-2	38
1982	02	22	48	16	-2	38
1982	02	23	48	17	-2	38
1982	02	24	48	19	-2	38
1982	02	25	48	21	-2	37
1982	02	26	48	23	-2	37
1982	02	27	48	24	-2	37
1982	02	28	48	26	-2	37
1982	03	01	48	28	-2	37
1982	03	02	48	30	-2	37
1982	03	03	48	33	-2	37
1982	03	04	48	35	-2	37
1982	03	05	48	37	-2	37
1982	03	06	48	39	-2	37
1982	03	07	48	42	-2	37
1982	03	08	48	44	-2	37
1982	03	09	48	46	-2	37
1982	03	10	48	49	-2	37
1982	03	11	48	51	-2	37
1982	03	12	48	54	-2	37
1982	03	13	48	57	-2	36
1982	03	14	48	59	-2	36
1982	03	15	49	02	-2	36
1982	03	16	49	05	-2	36
1982	03	17	49	07	-2	36
1982	03	18	49	10	-2	36
1982	03	19	49	13	-2	36
1982	03	20	49	16	-2	36
1982	03	21	49	19	-2	36
1982	03	22	49	22	-2	36
1982	03	23	49	25	-2	36
1982	03	24	49	28	-2	36
1982	03	25	49	31	-2	36
1982	03	26	49	35	-2	36
1982	03	27	49	38	-2	36
1982	03	28	49	41	-2	36
1982	03	29	49	44	-2	36
1982	03	30	49	48	-2	36
1982	03	31	49	51	-2	36
1982	04	01	49	55	-2	36
1982	04	02	49	58	-2	36
1982	04	03	50	01	-2	36
1982	04	04	50	05	-2	36
1982	04	05	50	08	-2	36
1982	04	06	50	12	-2	36
1982	04	07	50	16	-2	36
1982	04	08	50	19	-2	36
1982	04	09	50	23	-2	36
1982	04	10	50	27	-2	36
1982	04	11	50	30	-2	36
1982	04	12	50	34	-2	36
1982	04	13	50	38	-2	36
1982	04	14	50	42	-2	36
1982	04	15	50	45	-2	36
1982	04	16	50	49	-2	36
1982	04	17	50	53	-2	36
1982	04	18	50	57	-2	36
1982	04	19	51	01	-2	36
1982	04	20	51	05	-2	36
1982	04	21	51	09	-2	36
1982	04	22	51	13	-2	36
1982	04	23	51	17	-2	36
1982	04	24	51	21	-2	36
1982	04	25	51	25	-2	36
1982	04	26	51	29	-2	36
1982	04	27	51	33	-2	36
1982	04	28	51	37	-2	36
1982	04	29	51	41	-2	36
1982	04	30	51	45	-2	36
1982	05	01	51	49	-2	36
1982	05	02	51	53	-2	36
1982	05	03	51	57	-2	36
1982	05	04	52	01	-2	36
1982	05	05	52	05	-2	36
1982	05	06	52	10	-2	36
1982	05	07	52	14	-2	37
1982	05	08	52	18	-2	37
1982	05	09	52	22	-2	37
1982	05	10	52	26	-2	37
1982	05	11	52	30	-2	37
1982	05	12	52	35	-2	37
1982	05	13	52	39	-2	37
1982	05	14	52	43	-2	37
1982	05	15	52	47	-2	37
1982	05	16	52	51	-2	37
1982	05	17	52	55	-2	37
1982	05	18	53	00	-2	37
1982	05	19	53	04	-2	37
1982	05	20	53	08	-2	38
1982	05	21	53	12	-2	38
1982	05	22	53	16	-2	38
1982	05	23	53	20	-2	38
1982	05	24	53	24	-2	38
1982	05	25	53	29	-2	38
1982	05	26	53	33	-2	38
1982	05	27	53	37	-2	38
1982	05	28	53	41	-2	38
1982	05	29	53	45	-2	39
1982	05	30	53	49	-2	39
1982	05	31	53	53	-2	39
1982	06	01	53	57	-2	39
1982	06	02	54	01	-2	39
1982	06	03	54	05	-2	39
1982	06	04	54	09	-2	39
1982	06	05	54	13	-2	39
1982	06	06	54	17	-2	40
1982	06	07	54	21	-2	40
1982	06	08	54	25	-2	40
1982	06	09	54	29	-2	40
1982	06	10	54	33	-2	40
1982	06	11	54	37	-2	40
1982	06	12	54	41	-2	40
1982	06	13	54	45	-2	41
1982	06	14	54	48	-2	41
1982	06	15	54	52	-2	41
1982	06	16	54	56	-2	41
1982	06	17	55	00	-2	41
1982	06	18	55	03	-2	41
1982	06	19	55	07	-2	41
1982	06	20	55	11	-2	42
1982	06	21	55	14	-2	42
1982	06	22	55	18	-2	42
1982	06	23	55	22	-2	42
1982	06	24	55	25	-2	42
1982	06	25	55	29	-2	43
1982	06	26	55	32	-2	43
1982	06	27	55	36	-2	43
1982	06	28	55	39	-2	43
1982	06	29	55	43	-2	43
1982	06	30	55	46	-2	43
1982	07	01	55	49	-2	44
1982	07	02	55	53	-2	44
1982	07	03	55	56	-2	44
1982	07	04	55	59	-2	44
1982	07	05	56	02	-2	44
1982	07	06	56	05	-2	45
1982	07	07	56	08	-2	45
1982	07	08	56	12	-2	45
1982	07	09	56	15	-2	45
1982	07	10	56	18	-2	45
1982	07	11	56	21	-2	46
1982	07	12	56	23	-2	46
1982	07	13	56	26	-2	46
1982	07	14	56	29	-2	46
1982	07	15	56	32	-2	47
1982	07	16	56	35	-2	47
1982	07	17	56	37	-2	47
1982	07	18	56	40	-2	47
1982	07	19	56	43	-2	47
1982	07	20	56	45	-2	48
1982	07	21	56	48	-2	48
1982	07	22	56	50	-2	48
1982	07	23	56	52	-2	48
1982	07	24	56	55	-2	49
1982	07	25	56	57	-2	49
1982	07	26	56	59	-2	49
1982	07	27	57	02	-2	49
1982	07	28	57	04	-2	50
1982	07	29	57	06	-2	50
1982	07	30	57	08	-2	50
1982	07	31	57	10	-2	50
1982	08	01	57	12	-2	51
1982	08	02	57	14	-2	51
1982	08	03	57	16	-2	51
1982	08	04	57	17	-2	51
1982	08	05	57	19	-2	52
1982	08	06	57	21	-2	52
1982	08	07	57	22	-2	52
1982	08	08	57	24	-2	52
1982	08	09	57	26	-2	53
1982	08	10	57	27	-2	53
1982	08	11	57	28	-2	53
1982	08	12	57	30	-2	53
1982	08	13	57	31	-2	54
1982	08	14	57	32	-2	54
1982	08	15	57	33	-2	54
1982	08	16	57	34	-2	55
1982	08	17	57	36	-2	55
1982	08	18	57	37	-2	55
1982	08	19	57	37	-2	55
1982	08	20	57	38	-2	56
1982	08	21	57	39	-2	56
1982	08	22	57	40	-2	56
1982	08	23	57	41	-2	56
1982	08	24	57	41	-2	57
1982	08	25	57	42	-2	57
1982	08	26	57	42	-2	57
1982	08	27	57	43	-2	58
1982	08	28	57	43	-2	58
1982	08	29	57	43	-2	58
1982	08	30	57	44	-2	58
1982	08	31	57	44	-2	59
1982	09	01	57	44	-2	59
1982	09	02	57	44	-2	59
1982	09	03	57	44	-2	59
1982	09	04	57	44	-3	00
1982	09	05	57	44	-3	00
1982	09	06	57	44	-3	00
1982	09	07	57	43	-3	01
1982	09	08	57	43	-3	01
1982	09	09	57	43	-3	01
1982	09	10	57	42	-3	01
1982	09	11	57	42	-3	02
1982	09	12	57	41	-3	02
1982	09	13	57	40	-3	02
1982	09	14	57	40	-3	03
1982	09	15	57	39	-3	03
1982	09	16	57	38	-3	03
1982	09	17	57	37	-3	03
1982	09	18	57	36	-3	04
1982	09	19	57	35	-3	04
1982	09	20	57	34	-3	04
1982	09	21	57	33	-3	04
1982	09	22	57	32	-3	05
1982	09	23	57	31	-3	05
1982	09	24	57	30	-3	05
1982	09	25	57	28	-3	05
1982	09	26	57	27	-3	06
1982	09	27	57	25	-3	06
1982	09	28	57	24	-3	06
1982	09	29	57	22	-3	06
1982	09	30	57	21	-3	07
1982	10	01	57	19	-3	07
1982	10	02	57	17	-3	07
1982	10	03	57	15	-3	07
1982	10	04	57	14	-3	08
1982	10	05	57	12	-3	08
1982	10	06	57	10	-3	08
1982	10	07	57	08	-3	08
1982	10	08	57	06	-3	09
1982	10	09	57	04	-3	09
1982	10	10	57	01	-3	09
1982	10	11	56	59	-3	09
1982	10	12	56	57	-3	10
1982	10	13	56	55	-3	10
1982	10	14	56	52	-3	10
1982	10	15	56	50	-3	10

1982 10 16	56 48	-3 10
1982 10 17	56 45	-3 11
1982 10 18	56 43	-3 11
1982 10 19	56 40	-3 11
1982 10 20	56 37	-3 11
1982 10 21	56 35	-3 11
1982 10 22	56 32	-3 12
1982 10 23	56 29	-3 12
1982 10 24	56 27	-3 12
1982 10 25	56 24	-3 12
1982 10 26	56 21	-3 12
1982 10 27	56 18	-3 13
1982 10 28	56 16	-3 13
1982 10 29	56 13	-3 13
1982 10 30	56 10	-3 13
1982 10 31	56 07	-3 13
1982 11 01	56 04	-3 13
1982 11 02	56 01	-3 14
1982 11 03	55 58	-3 14
1982 11 04	55 55	-3 14
1982 11 05	55 52	-3 14
1982 11 06	55 49	-3 14
1982 11 07	55 46	-3 14
1982 11 08	55 43	-3 14
1982 11 09	55 39	-3 15
1982 11 10	55 36	-3 15
1982 11 11	55 33	-3 15
1982 11 12	55 30	-3 15
1982 11 13	55 27	-3 15
1982 11 14	55 24	-3 15
1982 11 15	55 20	-3 15
1982 11 16	55 17	-3 15
1982 11 17	55 14	-3 15
1982 11 18	55 11	-3 16
1982 11 19	55 08	-3 16
1982 11 20	55 05	-3 16
1982 11 21	55 01	-3 16
1982 11 22	54 58	-3 16
1982 11 23	54 55	-3 16
1982 11 24	54 52	-3 16
1982 11 25	54 49	-3 16
1982 11 26	54 46	-3 16
1982 11 27	54 42	-3 16
1982 11 28	54 39	-3 16
1982 11 29	54 36	-3 16
1982 11 30	54 33	-3 16
1982 12 01	54 30	-3 16
1982 12 02	54 27	-3 16
1982 12 03	54 24	-3 16
1982 12 04	54 21	-3 17
1982 12 05	54 18	-3 17
1982 12 06	54 15	-3 17
1982 12 07	54 12	-3 17
1982 12 08	54 09	-3 17
1982 12 09	54 06	-3 17
1982 12 10	54 03	-3 17
1982 12 11	54 00	-3 17
1982 12 12	53 58	-3 17
1982 12 13	53 55	-3 17
1982 12 14	53 52	-3 17
1982 12 15	53 49	-3 17
1982 12 16	53 47	-3 17
1982 12 17	53 44	-3 17
1982 12 18	53 42	-3 16
1982 12 19	53 39	-3 16
1982 12 20	53 37	-3 16
1982 12 21	53 34	-3 16
1982 12 22	53 32	-3 16
1982 12 23	53 29	-3 16
1982 12 24	53 27	-3 16
1982 12 25	53 25	-3 16
1982 12 26	53 22	-3 16
1982 12 27	53 20	-3 16
1982 12 28	53 18	-3 16
1982 12 29	53 16	-3 16
1982 12 30	53 14	-3 16
1982 12 31	53 12	-3 16
1983 01 01	53 10	-3 16
1983 01 02	53 08	-3 16
1983 01 03	53 06	-3 16
1983 01 04	53 05	-3 16
1983 01 05	53 03	-3 15
1983 01 06	53 01	-3 15
1983 01 07	53 00	-3 15
1983 01 08	52 58	-3 15
1983 01 09	52 57	-3 15
1983 01 10	52 55	-3 15
1983 01 11	52 54	-3 15
1983 01 12	52 53	-3 15
1983 01 13	52 51	-3 15
1983 01 14	52 50	-3 15
1983 01 15	52 49	-3 15
1983 01 16	52 48	-3 14
1983 01 17	52 47	-3 14
1983 01 18	52 46	-3 14
1983 01 19	52 45	-3 14
1983 01 20	52 45	-3 14
1983 01 21	52 44	-3 14
1983 01 22	52 43	-3 14
1983 01 23	52 43	-3 14
1983 01 24	52 42	-3 14
1983 01 25	52 42	-3 13
1983 01 26	52 41	-3 13
1983 01 27	52 41	-3 13
1983 01 28	52 41	-3 13
1983 01 29	52 40	-3 13
1983 01 30	52 40	-3 13
1983 01 31	52 40	-3 13
1983 02 01	52 40	-3 13
1983 02 02	52 40	-3 13
1983 02 03	52 40	-3 12
1983 02 04	52 40	-3 12
1983 02 05	52 41	-3 12
1983 02 06	52 41	-3 12
1983 02 07	52 41	-3 12
1983 02 08	52 42	-3 12
1983 02 09	52 42	-3 12
1983 02 10	52 43	-3 12
1983 02 11	52 44	-3 11
1983 02 12	52 44	-3 11
1983 02 13	52 45	-3 11
1983 02 14	52 46	-3 11
1983 02 15	52 47	-3 11
1983 02 16	52 48	-3 11
1983 02 17	52 49	-3 11
1983 02 18	52 50	-3 11
1983 02 19	52 51	-3 10
1983 02 20	52 53	-3 10
1983 02 21	52 54	-3 10
1983 02 22	52 55	-3 10
1983 02 23	52 57	-3 10
1983 02 24	52 58	-3 10
1983 02 25	53 00	-3 10
1983 02 26	53 01	-3 10
1983 02 27	53 03	-3 10
1983 02 28	53 05	-3 09
1983 03 01	53 06	-3 09
1983 03 02	53 08	-3 09
1983 03 03	53 10	-3 09
1983 03 04	53 12	-3 09
1983 03 05	53 14	-3 09
1983 03 06	53 16	-3 09
1983 03 07	53 18	-3 09
1983 03 08	53 21	-3 09
1983 03 09	53 23	-3 09
1983 03 10	53 25	-3 08
1983 03 11	53 28	-3 08
1983 03 12	53 30	-3 08
1983 03 13	53 32	-3 08
1983 03 14	53 35	-3 08
1983 03 15	53 37	-3 08
1983 03 16	53 40	-3 08
1983 03 17	53 43	-3 08
1983 03 18	53 45	-3 08
1983 03 19	53 48	-3 08
1983 03 20	53 51	-3 08
1983 03 21	53 54	-3 07
1983 03 22	53 57	-3 07
1983 03 23	54 00	-3 07
1983 03 24	54 03	-3 07
1983 03 25	54 06	-3 07
1983 03 26	54 09	-3 07
1983 03 27	54 12	-3 07
1983 03 28	54 15	-3 07
1983 03 29	54 18	-3 07
1983 03 30	54 22	-3 07
1983 03 31	54 25	-3 07
1983 04 01	54 28	-3 07
1983 04 02	54 32	-3 07
1983 04 03	54 35	-3 07
1983 04 04	54 39	-3 07
1983 04 05	54 42	-3 07
1983 04 06	54 46	-3 07
1983 04 07	54 49	-3 06
1983 04 08	54 53	-3 06
1983 04 09	54 56	-3 06
1983 04 10	55 00	-3 06
1983 04 11	55 04	-3 06
1983 04 12	55 07	-3 06
1983 04 13	55 11	-3 06
1983 04 14	55 15	-3 06
1983 04 15	55 19	-3 06
1983 04 16	55 23	-3 06
1983 04 17	55 27	-3 06
1983 04 18	55 30	-3 06
1983 04 19	55 34	-3 06
1983 04 20	55 38	-3 06
1983 04 21	55 42	-3 06
1983 04 22	55 46	-3 06
1983 04 23	55 50	-3 06
1983 04 24	55 54	-3 06
1983 04 25	55 58	-3 06
1983 04 26	56 02	-3 06
1983 04 27	56 07	-3 06
1983 04 28	56 11	-3 06
1983 04 29	56 15	-3 06
1983 04 30	56 19	-3 06
1983 05 01	56 23	-3 06
1983 05 02	56 27	-3 06
1983 05 03	56 32	-3 06
1983 05 04	56 36	-3 06
1983 05 05	56 40	-3 06
1983 05 06	56 44	-3 06
1983 05 07	56 48	-3 07
1983 05 08	56 53	-3 07
1983 05 09	56 57	-3 07
1983 05 10	57 01	-3 07
1983 05 11	57 06	-3 07
1983 05 12	57 10	-3 07
1983 05 13	57 14	-3 07
1983 05 14	57 18	-3 07
1983 05 15	57 23	-3 07
1983 05 16	57 27	-3 07
1983 05 17	57 31	-3 07
1983 05 18	57 36	-3 07
1983 05 19	57 40	-3 07
1983 05 20	57 44	-3 07
1983 05 21	57 49	-3 07
1983 05 22	57 53	-3 08
1983 05 23	57 57	-3 08
1983 05 24	58 02	-3 08
1983 05 25	58 06	-3 08
1983 05 26	58 10	-3 08
1983 05 27	58 15	-3 08
1983 05 28	58 19	-3 08
1983 05 29	58 23	-3 08
1983 05 30	58 27	-3 08
1983 05 31	58 32	-3 08
1983 06 01	58 36	-3 09
1983 06 02	58 40	-3 09
1983 06 03	58 44	-3 09
1983 06 04	58 49	-3 09
1983 06 05	58 53	-3 09
1983 06 06	58 57	-3 09
1983 06 07	59 01	-3 09
1983 06 08	59 06	-3 09
1983 06 09	59 10	-3 10
1983 06 10	59 14	-3 10
1983 06 11	59 18	-3 10
1983 06 12	59 22	-3 10
1983 06 13	59 26	-3 10
1983 06 14	59 30	-3 10
1983 06 15	59 34	-3 11
1983 06 16	59 38	-3 11
1983 06 17	59 42	-3 11
1983 06 18	59 46	-3 11
1983 06 19	59 50	-3 11
1983 06 20	59 54	-3 11
1983 06 21	59 58	-3 12
1983 06 22	60 02	-3 12
1983 06 23	60 06	-3 12
1983 06 24	60 10	-3 12
1983 06 25	60 14	-3 12
1983 06 26	60 18	-3 12
1983 06 27	60 21	-3 13
1983 06 28	60 25	-3 13
1983 06 29	60 29	-3 13
1983 06 30	60 32	-3 13
1983 07 01	60 36	-3 13
1983 07 02	60 40	-3 14
1983 07 03	60 43	-3 14
1983 07 04	60 47	-3 14
1983 07 05	60 50	-3 14
1983 07 06	60 54	-3 15
1983 07 07	60 57	-3 15
1983 07 08	61 01	-3 15
1983 07 09	61 04	-3 15
1983 07 10	61 08	-3 15
1983 07 11	61 11	-3 16
1983 07 12	61 14	-3 16
1983 07 13	61 17	-3 16
1983 07 14	61 20	-3 16
1983 07 15	61 24	-3 17
1983 07 16	61 27	-3 17
1983 07 17	61 30	-3 17
1983 07 18	61 33	-3 17
1983 07 19	61 36	-3 18
1983 07 20	61 39	-3 18
1983 07 21	61 42	-3 18
1983 07 22	61 44	-3 18
1983 07 23	61 47	-3 19
1983 07 24	61 50	-3 19
1983 07 25	61 53	-3 19
1983 07 26	61 55	-3 19
1983 07 27	61 58	-3 20
1983 07 28	62 00	-3 20
1983 07 29	62 03	-3 20
1983 07 30	62 05	-3 20
1983 07 31	62 08	-3 21
1983 08 01	62 10	-3 21
1983 08 02	62 12	-3 21
1983 08 03	62 15	-3 22
1983 08 04	62 17	-3 22
1983 08 05	62 19	-3 22
1983 08 06	62 21	-3 22
1983 08 07	62 23	-3 23
1983 08 08	62 25	-3 23
1983 08 09	62 27	-3 23
1983 08 10	62 29	-3 24
1983 08 11	62 31	-3 24
1983 08 12	62 32	-3 24
1983 08 13	62 34	-3 25
1983 08 14	62 36	-3 25
1983 08 15	62 37	-3 25
1983 08 16	62 39	-3 25
1983 08 17	62 40	-3 26
1983 08 18	62 42	-3 26
1983 08 19	62 43	-3 26
1983 08 20	62 44	-3 27
1983 08 21	62 45	-3 27
1983 08 22	62 46	-3 27
1983 08 23	62 48	-3 28
1983 08 24	62 49	-3 28
1983 08 25	62 50	-3 28
1983 08 26	62 50	-3 29
1983 08 27	62 51	-3 29
1983 08 28	62 52	-3 29
1983 08 29	62 53	-3 30
1983 08 30	62 53	-3 30
1983 08 31	62 54	-3 30
1983 09 01	62 54	-3 30
1983 09 02	62 55	-3 31
1983 09 03	62 55	-3 31
1983 09 04	62 56	-3 31
1983 09 05	62 56	-3 32
1983 09 06	62 56	-3 32
1983 09 07	62 56	-3 32
1983 09 08	62 56	-3 33
1983 09 09	62 56	-3 33
1983 09 10	62 56	-3 33
1983 09 11	62 56	-3 34
1983 09 12	62 56	-3 34
1983 09 13	62 56	-3 34
1983 09 14	62 55	-3 35
1983 09 15	62 55	-3 35
1983 09 16	62 54	-3 35
1983 09 17	62 54	-3 36
1983 09 18	62 53	-3 36
1983 09 19	62 53	-3 36
1983 09 20	62 52	-3 37
1983 09 21	62 51	-3 37
1983 09 22	62 50	-3 37
1983 09 23	62 49	-3 38
1983 09 24	62 48	-3 38
1983 09 25	62 47	-3 38
1983 09 26	62 46	-3 38
1983 09 27	62 45	-3 39
1983 09 28	62 44	-3 39
1983 09 29	62 43	-3 39
1983 09 30	62 41	-3 40
1983 10 01	62 40	-3 40
1983 10 02	62 39	-3 40
1983 10 03	62 37	-3 41
1983 10 04	62 35	-3 41
1983 10 05	62 34	-3 41
1983 10 06	62 32	-3 41
1983 10 07	62 30	-3 42
1983 10 08	62 29	-3 42
1983 10 09	62 27	-3 42
1983 10 10	62 25	-3 43
1983 10 11	62 23	-3 43
1983 10 12	62 21	-3 43
1983 10 13	62 19	-3 43
1983 10 14	62 17	-3 44
1983 10 15	62 14	-3 44
1983 10 16	62 12	-3 44
1983 10 17	62 10	-3 44
1983 10 18	62 08	-3 45
1983 10 19	62 05	-3 45
1983 10 20	62 03	-3 45
1983 10 21	62 00	-3 45
1983 10 22	61 58	-3 46
1983 10 23	61 55	-3 46
1983 10 24	61 53	-3 46
1983 10 25	61 50	-3 46
1983 10 26	61 47	-3 47
1983 10 27	61 45	-3 47
1983 10 28	61 42	-3 47
1983 10 29	61 39	-3 47
1983 10 30	61 36	-3 47
1983 10 31	61 34	-3 48
1983 11 01	61 31	-3 48
1983 11 02	61 28	-3 48
1983 11 03	61 25	-3 48
1983 11 04	61 22	-3 48
1983 11 05	61 19	-3 49
1983 11 06	61 16	-3 49
1983 11 07	61 13	-3 49
1983 11 08	61 10	-3 49
1983 11 09	61 07	-3 49
1983 11 10	61 03	-3 50
1983 11 11	61 00	-3 50
1983 11 12	60 57	-3 50
1983 11 13	60 54	-3 50
1983 11 14	60 51	-3 50
1983 11 15	60 47	-3 50
1983 11 16	60 44	-3 50
1983 11 17	60 41	-3 51
1983 11 18	60 38	-3 51
1983 11 19	60 34	-3 51
1983 11 20	60 31	-3 51
1983 11 21	60 28	-3 51
1983 11 22	60 25	-3 51
1983 11 23	60 21	-3 51
1983 11 24	60 18	-3 51
1983 11 25	60 15	-3 51
1983 11 26	60 12	-3 51
1983 11 27	60 08	-3 52
1983 11 28	60 05	-3 52
1983 11 29	60 02	-3 52
1983 11 30	59 58	-3 52
1983 12 01	59 55	-3 52
1983 12 02	59 52	-3 52
1983 12 03	59 49	-3 52
1983 12 04	59 46	-3 52
1983 12 05	59 42	-3 52
1983 12 06	59 39	-3 52
1983 12 07	59 36	-3 52
1983 12 08	59 33	-3 52
1983 12 09	59 30	-3 52

Chiron

1983 12 10	59 27	-3 52
1983 12 11	59 24	-3 52
1983 12 12	59 21	-3 52
1983 12 13	59 18	-3 52
1983 12 14	59 15	-3 52
1983 12 15	59 12	-3 52
1983 12 16	59 09	-3 52
1983 12 17	59 06	-3 52
1983 12 18	59 03	-3 52
1983 12 19	59 00	-3 52
1983 12 20	58 57	-3 52
1983 12 21	58 55	-3 52
1983 12 22	58 52	-3 52
1983 12 23	58 49	-3 52
1983 12 24	58 47	-3 52
1983 12 25	58 44	-3 52
1983 12 26	58 42	-3 52
1983 12 27	58 39	-3 52
1983 12 28	58 37	-3 51
1983 12 29	58 34	-3 51
1983 12 30	58 32	-3 51
1983 12 31	58 30	-3 51
1984 01 01	58 27	-3 51
1984 01 02	58 25	-3 51
1984 01 03	58 23	-3 51
1984 01 04	58 21	-3 51
1984 01 05	58 19	-3 51
1984 01 06	58 17	-3 51
1984 01 07	58 15	-3 51
1984 01 08	58 13	-3 50
1984 01 09	58 11	-3 50
1984 01 10	58 09	-3 50
1984 01 11	58 08	-3 50
1984 01 12	58 06	-3 50
1984 01 13	58 04	-3 50
1984 01 14	58 03	-3 50
1984 01 15	58 01	-3 50
1984 01 16	58 00	-3 49
1984 01 17	57 59	-3 49
1984 01 18	57 57	-3 49
1984 01 19	57 56	-3 49
1984 01 20	57 55	-3 49
1984 01 21	57 54	-3 49
1984 01 22	57 53	-3 49
1984 01 23	57 52	-3 49
1984 01 24	57 51	-3 48
1984 01 25	57 50	-3 48
1984 01 26	57 50	-3 48
1984 01 27	57 49	-3 48
1984 01 28	57 48	-3 48
1984 01 29	57 48	-3 48
1984 01 30	57 47	-3 47
1984 01 31	57 47	-3 47
1984 02 01	57 47	-3 47
1984 02 02	57 46	-3 47
1984 02 03	57 46	-3 47
1984 02 04	57 46	-3 47
1984 02 05	57 46	-3 46
1984 02 06	57 46	-3 46
1984 02 07	57 46	-3 46
1984 02 08	57 46	-3 46
1984 02 09	57 46	-3 46
1984 02 10	57 47	-3 46
1984 02 11	57 47	-3 46
1984 02 12	57 47	-3 45
1984 02 13	57 48	-3 45
1984 02 14	57 48	-3 45
1984 02 15	57 49	-3 45
1984 02 16	57 50	-3 45
1984 02 17	57 50	-3 45
1984 02 18	57 51	-3 44
1984 02 19	57 52	-3 44
1984 02 20	57 53	-3 44
1984 02 21	57 54	-3 44
1984 02 22	57 55	-3 44
1984 02 23	57 56	-3 44
1984 02 24	57 58	-3 43
1984 02 25	57 59	-3 43
1984 02 26	58 00	-3 43
1984 02 27	58 02	-3 43
1984 02 28	58 03	-3 43
1984 02 29	58 05	-3 43
1984 03 01	58 06	-3 42
1984 03 02	58 08	-3 42
1984 03 03	58 10	-3 42
1984 03 04	58 11	-3 42
1984 03 05	58 13	-3 42
1984 03 06	58 15	-3 42
1984 03 07	58 17	-3 42
1984 03 08	58 19	-3 41
1984 03 09	58 21	-3 41
1984 03 10	58 24	-3 41
1984 03 11	58 26	-3 41
1984 03 12	58 28	-3 41
1984 03 13	58 30	-3 41
1984 03 14	58 33	-3 41
1984 03 15	58 35	-3 40
1984 03 16	58 38	-3 40
1984 03 17	58 40	-3 40
1984 03 18	58 43	-3 40
1984 03 19	58 46	-3 40
1984 03 20	58 48	-3 40
1984 03 21	58 51	-3 40
1984 03 22	58 54	-3 40
1984 03 23	58 57	-3 39
1984 03 24	59 00	-3 39
1984 03 25	59 03	-3 39
1984 03 26	59 06	-3 39
1984 03 27	59 09	-3 39
1984 03 28	59 12	-3 39
1984 03 29	59 15	-3 39
1984 03 30	59 18	-3 39
1984 03 31	59 21	-3 39
1984 04 01	59 25	-3 38
1984 04 02	59 28	-3 38
1984 04 03	59 31	-3 38
1984 04 04	59 35	-3 38
1984 04 05	59 38	-3 38
1984 04 06	59 42	-3 38
1984 04 07	59 45	-3 38
1984 04 08	59 49	-3 38
1984 04 09	59 53	-3 38
1984 04 10	59 56	-3 38
1984 04 11	60 00	-3 38
1984 04 12	60 04	-3 38
1984 04 13	60 07	-3 38
1984 04 14	60 11	-3 38
1984 04 15	60 15	-3 37
1984 04 16	60 19	-3 37
1984 04 17	60 23	-3 37
1984 04 18	60 27	-3 37
1984 04 19	60 31	-3 37
1984 04 20	60 35	-3 37
1984 04 21	60 39	-3 37
1984 04 22	60 43	-3 37
1984 04 23	60 47	-3 37
1984 04 24	60 51	-3 37
1984 04 25	60 55	-3 37
1984 04 26	60 59	-3 37
1984 04 27	61 03	-3 37
1984 04 28	61 07	-3 37
1984 04 29	61 12	-3 37
1984 04 30	61 16	-3 37
1984 05 01	61 20	-3 37
1984 05 02	61 24	-3 37
1984 05 03	61 29	-3 37
1984 05 04	61 33	-3 37
1984 05 05	61 37	-3 37
1984 05 06	61 42	-3 37
1984 05 07	61 46	-3 37
1984 05 08	61 50	-3 37
1984 05 09	61 55	-3 37
1984 05 10	61 59	-3 37
1984 05 11	62 04	-3 37
1984 05 12	62 08	-3 37
1984 05 13	62 13	-3 37
1984 05 14	62 17	-3 37
1984 05 15	62 21	-3 37
1984 05 16	62 26	-3 37
1984 05 17	62 30	-3 38
1984 05 18	62 35	-3 38
1984 05 19	62 39	-3 38
1984 05 20	62 44	-3 38
1984 05 21	62 48	-3 38
1984 05 22	62 53	-3 38
1984 05 23	62 57	-3 38
1984 05 24	63 02	-3 38
1984 05 25	63 06	-3 38
1984 05 26	63 11	-3 38
1984 05 27	63 15	-3 38
1984 05 28	63 20	-3 38
1984 05 29	63 24	-3 38
1984 05 30	63 29	-3 39
1984 05 31	63 33	-3 39
1984 06 01	63 38	-3 39
1984 06 02	63 42	-3 39
1984 06 03	63 47	-3 39
1984 06 04	63 51	-3 39
1984 06 05	63 56	-3 39
1984 06 06	64 00	-3 39
1984 06 07	64 05	-3 39
1984 06 08	64 09	-3 40
1984 06 09	64 13	-3 40
1984 06 10	64 18	-3 40
1984 06 11	64 22	-3 40
1984 06 12	64 27	-3 40
1984 06 13	64 31	-3 40
1984 06 14	64 35	-3 40
1984 06 15	64 40	-3 41
1984 06 16	64 44	-3 41
1984 06 17	64 48	-3 41
1984 06 18	64 52	-3 41
1984 06 19	64 57	-3 41
1984 06 20	65 01	-3 41
1984 06 21	65 05	-3 42
1984 06 22	65 09	-3 42
1984 06 23	65 14	-3 42
1984 06 24	65 18	-3 42
1984 06 25	65 22	-3 42
1984 06 26	65 26	-3 43
1984 06 27	65 30	-3 43
1984 06 28	65 34	-3 43
1984 06 29	65 38	-3 43
1984 06 30	65 42	-3 43
1984 07 01	65 46	-3 44
1984 07 02	65 50	-3 44
1984 07 03	65 54	-3 44
1984 07 04	65 58	-3 44
1984 07 05	66 02	-3 45
1984 07 06	66 05	-3 45
1984 07 07	66 09	-3 45
1984 07 08	66 13	-3 45
1984 07 09	66 17	-3 45
1984 07 10	66 20	-3 46
1984 07 11	66 24	-3 46
1984 07 12	66 28	-3 46
1984 07 13	66 31	-3 46
1984 07 14	66 35	-3 47
1984 07 15	66 38	-3 47
1984 07 16	66 42	-3 47
1984 07 17	66 45	-3 47
1984 07 18	66 48	-3 48
1984 07 19	66 52	-3 48
1984 07 20	66 55	-3 48
1984 07 21	66 58	-3 49
1984 07 22	67 02	-3 49
1984 07 23	67 05	-3 49
1984 07 24	67 08	-3 49
1984 07 25	67 11	-3 50
1984 07 26	67 14	-3 50
1984 07 27	67 17	-3 50
1984 07 28	67 20	-3 51
1984 07 29	67 23	-3 51
1984 07 30	67 25	-3 51
1984 07 31	67 28	-3 52
1984 08 01	67 31	-3 52
1984 08 02	67 34	-3 52
1984 08 03	67 36	-3 52
1984 08 04	67 39	-3 53
1984 08 05	67 41	-3 53
1984 08 06	67 44	-3 53
1984 08 07	67 46	-3 54
1984 08 08	67 49	-3 54
1984 08 09	67 51	-3 54
1984 08 10	67 53	-3 55
1984 08 11	67 55	-3 55
1984 08 12	67 57	-3 55
1984 08 13	68 00	-3 56
1984 08 14	68 02	-3 56
1984 08 15	68 04	-3 56
1984 08 16	68 05	-3 57
1984 08 17	68 07	-3 57
1984 08 18	68 09	-3 57
1984 08 19	68 11	-3 58
1984 08 20	68 12	-3 58
1984 08 21	68 14	-3 58
1984 08 22	68 16	-3 59
1984 08 23	68 17	-3 59
1984 08 24	68 18	-4 00
1984 08 25	68 20	-4 00
1984 08 26	68 21	-4 00
1984 08 27	68 22	-4 01
1984 08 28	68 24	-4 01
1984 08 29	68 25	-4 01
1984 08 30	68 26	-4 02
1984 08 31	68 27	-4 02
1984 09 01	68 28	-4 02
1984 09 02	68 28	-4 03
1984 09 03	68 29	-4 03
1984 09 04	68 30	-4 04
1984 09 05	68 30	-4 04
1984 09 06	68 31	-4 04
1984 09 07	68 32	-4 05
1984 09 08	68 32	-4 05
1984 09 09	68 32	-4 05
1984 09 10	68 33	-4 06
1984 09 11	68 33	-4 06
1984 09 12	68 33	-4 06
1984 09 13	68 33	-4 07
1984 09 14	68 33	-4 07
1984 09 15	68 33	-4 08
1984 09 16	68 33	-4 08
1984 09 17	68 33	-4 08
1984 09 18	68 33	-4 09
1984 09 19	68 32	-4 09
1984 09 20	68 32	-4 09
1984 09 21	68 32	-4 10
1984 09 22	68 31	-4 10
1984 09 23	68 30	-4 11
1984 09 24	68 30	-4 11
1984 09 25	68 29	-4 11
1984 09 26	68 28	-4 12
1984 09 27	68 28	-4 12
1984 09 28	68 27	-4 12
1984 09 29	68 26	-4 13
1984 09 30	68 25	-4 13
1984 10 01	68 23	-4 13
1984 10 02	68 22	-4 14
1984 10 03	68 21	-4 14
1984 10 04	68 20	-4 14
1984 10 05	68 18	-4 15
1984 10 06	68 17	-4 15
1984 10 07	68 16	-4 15
1984 10 08	68 14	-4 16
1984 10 09	68 12	-4 16
1984 10 10	68 11	-4 16
1984 10 11	68 09	-4 17
1984 10 12	68 07	-4 17
1984 10 13	68 05	-4 17
1984 10 14	68 03	-4 18
1984 10 15	68 02	-4 18
1984 10 16	68 00	-4 18
1984 10 17	67 57	-4 19
1984 10 18	67 55	-4 19
1984 10 19	67 53	-4 19
1984 10 20	67 51	-4 20
1984 10 21	67 49	-4 20
1984 10 22	67 46	-4 20
1984 10 23	67 44	-4 21
1984 10 24	67 41	-4 21
1984 10 25	67 39	-4 21
1984 10 26	67 36	-4 21
1984 10 27	67 34	-4 22
1984 10 28	67 31	-4 22
1984 10 29	67 29	-4 22
1984 10 30	67 26	-4 22
1984 10 31	67 23	-4 23
1984 11 01	67 20	-4 23
1984 11 02	67 17	-4 23
1984 11 03	67 15	-4 23
1984 11 04	67 12	-4 24
1984 11 05	67 09	-4 24
1984 11 06	67 06	-4 24
1984 11 07	67 03	-4 24
1984 11 08	67 00	-4 25
1984 11 09	66 57	-4 25
1984 11 10	66 53	-4 25
1984 11 11	66 50	-4 25
1984 11 12	66 47	-4 25
1984 11 13	66 44	-4 26
1984 11 14	66 41	-4 26
1984 11 15	66 38	-4 26
1984 11 16	66 34	-4 26
1984 11 17	66 31	-4 26
1984 11 18	66 28	-4 26
1984 11 19	66 24	-4 27
1984 11 20	66 21	-4 27
1984 11 21	66 18	-4 27
1984 11 22	66 14	-4 27
1984 11 23	66 11	-4 27
1984 11 24	66 08	-4 27
1984 11 25	66 04	-4 27
1984 11 26	66 01	-4 27
1984 11 27	65 58	-4 28
1984 11 28	65 54	-4 28
1984 11 29	65 51	-4 28
1984 11 30	65 47	-4 28
1984 12 01	65 44	-4 28
1984 12 02	65 41	-4 28
1984 12 03	65 37	-4 28
1984 12 04	65 34	-4 28
1984 12 05	65 31	-4 28
1984 12 06	65 27	-4 28
1984 12 07	65 24	-4 28
1984 12 08	65 21	-4 28
1984 12 09	65 17	-4 28
1984 12 10	65 14	-4 28
1984 12 11	65 11	-4 28
1984 12 12	65 07	-4 28
1984 12 13	65 04	-4 28
1984 12 14	65 01	-4 28
1984 12 15	64 58	-4 28
1984 12 16	64 55	-4 28
1984 12 17	64 52	-4 28
1984 12 18	64 48	-4 28
1984 12 19	64 45	-4 28
1984 12 20	64 42	-4 28
1984 12 21	64 39	-4 28
1984 12 22	64 36	-4 28
1984 12 23	64 33	-4 28
1984 12 24	64 31	-4 28
1984 12 25	64 28	-4 28
1984 12 26	64 25	-4 28
1984 12 27	64 22	-4 28
1984 12 28	64 19	-4 28
1984 12 29	64 17	-4 28
1984 12 30	64 14	-4 28
1984 12 31	64 11	-4 28
1985 01 01	64 09	-4 27
1985 01 02	64 06	-4 27
1985 01 03	64 04	-4 27
1985 01 04	64 01	-4 27
1985 01 05	63 59	-4 27
1985 01 06	63 57	-4 27
1985 01 07	63 55	-4 27
1985 01 08	63 52	-4 27
1985 01 09	63 50	-4 27
1985 01 10	63 48	-4 26
1985 01 11	63 46	-4 26
1985 01 12	63 44	-4 26
1985 01 13	63 42	-4 26
1985 01 14	63 40	-4 26
1985 01 15	63 39	-4 26
1985 01 16	63 37	-4 26
1985 01 17	63 35	-4 25
1985 01 18	63 34	-4 25
1985 01 19	63 32	-4 25
1985 01 20	63 31	-4 25
1985 01 21	63 29	-4 25
1985 01 22	63 28	-4 24
1985 01 23	63 27	-4 24
1985 01 24	63 25	-4 24
1985 01 25	63 24	-4 24
1985 01 26	63 23	-4 24
1985 01 27	63 22	-4 24
1985 01 28	63 21	-4 23
1985 01 29	63 20	-4 23
1985 01 30	63 20	-4 23
1985 01 31	63 19	-4 23
1985 02 01	63 18	-4 23

1985	02	02	63	18	−4	22
1985	02	03	63	17	−4	22
1985	02	04	63	17	−4	22
1985	02	05	63	16	−4	22
1985	02	06	63	16	−4	22
1985	02	07	63	16	−4	21
1985	02	08	63	16	−4	21
1985	02	09	63	16	−4	21
1985	02	10	63	16	−4	21
1985	02	11	63	16	−4	20
1985	02	12	63	16	−4	20
1985	02	13	63	16	−4	20
1985	02	14	63	16	−4	20
1985	02	15	63	17	−4	20
1985	02	16	63	17	−4	19
1985	02	17	63	17	−4	19
1985	02	18	63	18	−4	19
1985	02	19	63	19	−4	19
1985	02	20	63	19	−4	19
1985	02	21	63	20	−4	18
1985	02	22	63	21	−4	18
1985	02	23	63	22	−4	18
1985	02	24	63	23	−4	18
1985	02	25	63	24	−4	18
1985	02	26	63	25	−4	17
1985	02	27	63	26	−4	17
1985	02	28	63	27	−4	17
1985	03	01	63	29	−4	17
1985	03	02	63	30	−4	16
1985	03	03	63	32	−4	16
1985	03	04	63	33	−4	16
1985	03	05	63	35	−4	16
1985	03	06	63	36	−4	16
1985	03	07	63	38	−4	15
1985	03	08	63	40	−4	15
1985	03	09	63	42	−4	15
1985	03	10	63	44	−4	15
1985	03	11	63	46	−4	15
1985	03	12	63	48	−4	14
1985	03	13	63	50	−4	14
1985	03	14	63	52	−4	14
1985	03	15	63	54	−4	14
1985	03	16	63	56	−4	14
1985	03	17	63	59	−4	14
1985	03	18	64	01	−4	13
1985	03	19	64	04	−4	13
1985	03	20	64	06	−4	13
1985	03	21	64	09	−4	13
1985	03	22	64	11	−4	13
1985	03	23	64	14	−4	12
1985	03	24	64	17	−4	12
1985	03	25	64	20	−4	12
1985	03	26	64	23	−4	12
1985	03	27	64	25	−4	12
1985	03	28	64	28	−4	12
1985	03	29	64	31	−4	12
1985	03	30	64	35	−4	11
1985	03	31	64	38	−4	11
1985	04	01	64	41	−4	11
1985	04	02	64	44	−4	11
1985	04	03	64	47	−4	11
1985	04	04	64	51	−4	11
1985	04	05	64	54	−4	11
1985	04	06	64	57	−4	10
1985	04	07	65	01	−4	10
1985	04	08	65	04	−4	10
1985	04	09	65	08	−4	10
1985	04	10	65	12	−4	10
1985	04	11	65	15	−4	10
1985	04	12	65	19	−4	10
1985	04	13	65	23	−4	10
1985	04	14	65	26	−4	09
1985	04	15	65	30	−4	09
1985	04	16	65	34	−4	09
1985	04	17	65	38	−4	09
1985	04	18	65	42	−4	09
1985	04	19	65	46	−4	09
1985	04	20	65	50	−4	09
1985	04	21	65	54	−4	09
1985	04	22	65	58	−4	09
1985	04	23	66	02	−4	09
1985	04	24	66	06	−4	09
1985	04	25	66	10	−4	09
1985	04	26	66	14	−4	09
1985	04	27	66	18	−4	08
1985	04	28	66	23	−4	08
1985	04	29	66	27	−4	08
1985	04	30	66	31	−4	08
1985	05	01	66	35	−4	08
1985	05	02	66	40	−4	08
1985	05	03	66	44	−4	08
1985	05	04	66	49	−4	08
1985	05	05	66	53	−4	08
1985	05	06	66	57	−4	08
1985	05	07	67	02	−4	08
1985	05	08	67	06	−4	08
1985	05	09	67	11	−4	08
1985	05	10	67	15	−4	08
1985	05	11	67	20	−4	08
1985	05	12	67	24	−4	08
1985	05	13	67	29	−4	08
1985	05	14	67	34	−4	08
1985	05	15	67	38	−4	08
1985	05	16	67	43	−4	08
1985	05	17	67	47	−4	08
1985	05	18	67	52	−4	08
1985	05	19	67	57	−4	08
1985	05	20	68	01	−4	08
1985	05	21	68	06	−4	08
1985	05	22	68	11	−4	08
1985	05	23	68	15	−4	08
1985	05	24	68	20	−4	08
1985	05	25	68	25	−4	09
1985	05	26	68	29	−4	09
1985	05	27	68	34	−4	09
1985	05	28	68	39	−4	09
1985	05	29	68	44	−4	09
1985	05	30	68	48	−4	09
1985	05	31	68	53	−4	09
1985	06	01	68	58	−4	09
1985	06	02	69	02	−4	09
1985	06	03	69	07	−4	09
1985	06	04	69	12	−4	09
1985	06	05	69	16	−4	09
1985	06	06	69	21	−4	10
1985	06	07	69	26	−4	10
1985	06	08	69	31	−4	10
1985	06	09	69	35	−4	10
1985	06	10	69	40	−4	10
1985	06	11	69	45	−4	10
1985	06	12	69	49	−4	10
1985	06	13	69	54	−4	10
1985	06	14	69	59	−4	11
1985	06	15	70	03	−4	11
1985	06	16	70	08	−4	11
1985	06	17	70	12	−4	11
1985	06	18	70	17	−4	11
1985	06	19	70	22	−4	11
1985	06	20	70	26	−4	11
1985	06	21	70	31	−4	12
1985	06	22	70	35	−4	12
1985	06	23	70	40	−4	12
1985	06	24	70	44	−4	12
1985	06	25	70	49	−4	12
1985	06	26	70	53	−4	13
1985	06	27	70	58	−4	13
1985	06	28	71	02	−4	13
1985	06	29	71	06	−4	13
1985	06	30	71	11	−4	13
1985	07	01	71	15	−4	14
1985	07	02	71	19	−4	14
1985	07	03	71	24	−4	14
1985	07	04	71	28	−4	14
1985	07	05	71	32	−4	14
1985	07	06	71	36	−4	15
1985	07	07	71	41	−4	15
1985	07	08	71	45	−4	15
1985	07	09	71	49	−4	15
1985	07	10	71	53	−4	16
1985	07	11	71	57	−4	16
1985	07	12	72	01	−4	16
1985	07	13	72	05	−4	16
1985	07	14	72	09	−4	17
1985	07	15	72	13	−4	17
1985	07	16	72	17	−4	17
1985	07	17	72	21	−4	17
1985	07	18	72	24	−4	18
1985	07	19	72	28	−4	18
1985	07	20	72	32	−4	18
1985	07	21	72	36	−4	19
1985	07	22	72	39	−4	19
1985	07	23	72	43	−4	19
1985	07	24	72	46	−4	19
1985	07	25	72	50	−4	20
1985	07	26	72	53	−4	20
1985	07	27	72	57	−4	20
1985	07	28	73	00	−4	21
1985	07	29	73	04	−4	21
1985	07	30	73	07	−4	21
1985	07	31	73	10	−4	22
1985	08	01	73	13	−4	22
1985	08	02	73	17	−4	22
1985	08	03	73	20	−4	23
1985	08	04	73	23	−4	23
1985	08	05	73	26	−4	23
1985	08	06	73	29	−4	24
1985	08	07	73	32	−4	24
1985	08	08	73	35	−4	24
1985	08	09	73	37	−4	25
1985	08	10	73	40	−4	25
1985	08	11	73	43	−4	25
1985	08	12	73	45	−4	26
1985	08	13	73	48	−4	26
1985	08	14	73	51	−4	27
1985	08	15	73	53	−4	27
1985	08	16	73	55	−4	27
1985	08	17	73	58	−4	28
1985	08	18	74	00	−4	28
1985	08	19	74	02	−4	28
1985	08	20	74	04	−4	29
1985	08	21	74	07	−4	29
1985	08	22	74	09	−4	30
1985	08	23	74	11	−4	30
1985	08	24	74	13	−4	30
1985	08	25	74	14	−4	31
1985	08	26	74	16	−4	31
1985	08	27	74	18	−4	32
1985	08	28	74	20	−4	32
1985	08	29	74	21	−4	32
1985	08	30	74	23	−4	33
1985	08	31	74	24	−4	33
1985	09	01	74	26	−4	34
1985	09	02	74	27	−4	34
1985	09	03	74	28	−4	34
1985	09	04	74	30	−4	35
1985	09	05	74	31	−4	35
1985	09	06	74	32	−4	36
1985	09	07	74	33	−4	36
1985	09	08	74	34	−4	36
1985	09	09	74	35	−4	37
1985	09	10	74	36	−4	37
1985	09	11	74	36	−4	38
1985	09	12	74	37	−4	38
1985	09	13	74	38	−4	39
1985	09	14	74	38	−4	39
1985	09	15	74	39	−4	39
1985	09	16	74	39	−4	40
1985	09	17	74	39	−4	40
1985	09	18	74	40	−4	41
1985	09	19	74	40	−4	41
1985	09	20	74	40	−4	42
1985	09	21	74	40	−4	42
1985	09	22	74	40	−4	42
1985	09	23	74	40	−4	43
1985	09	24	74	40	−4	43
1985	09	25	74	39	−4	44
1985	09	26	74	39	−4	44
1985	09	27	74	39	−4	44
1985	09	28	74	38	−4	45
1985	09	29	74	38	−4	45
1985	09	30	74	37	−4	46
1985	10	01	74	36	−4	46
1985	10	02	74	36	−4	47
1985	10	03	74	35	−4	47
1985	10	04	74	34	−4	47
1985	10	05	74	33	−4	48
1985	10	06	74	32	−4	48
1985	10	07	74	31	−4	49
1985	10	08	74	30	−4	49
1985	10	09	74	29	−4	49
1985	10	10	74	27	−4	50
1985	10	11	74	26	−4	50
1985	10	12	74	25	−4	51
1985	10	13	74	23	−4	51
1985	10	14	74	22	−4	51
1985	10	15	74	20	−4	52
1985	10	16	74	18	−4	52
1985	10	17	74	17	−4	53
1985	10	18	74	15	−4	53
1985	10	19	74	13	−4	53
1985	10	20	74	11	−4	54
1985	10	21	74	09	−4	54
1985	10	22	74	07	−4	54
1985	10	23	74	05	−4	55
1985	10	24	74	03	−4	55
1985	10	25	74	00	−4	55
1985	10	26	73	58	−4	56
1985	10	27	73	56	−4	56
1985	10	28	73	53	−4	56
1985	10	29	73	51	−4	57
1985	10	30	73	49	−4	57
1985	10	31	73	46	−4	57
1985	11	01	73	43	−4	58
1985	11	02	73	41	−4	58
1985	11	03	73	38	−4	58
1985	11	04	73	35	−4	59
1985	11	05	73	33	−4	59
1985	11	06	73	30	−4	59
1985	11	07	73	27	−5	00
1985	11	08	73	24	−5	00
1985	11	09	73	21	−5	00
1985	11	10	73	18	−5	00
1985	11	11	73	15	−5	01
1985	11	12	73	12	−5	01
1985	11	13	73	09	−5	01
1985	11	14	73	06	−5	01
1985	11	15	73	02	−5	02
1985	11	16	72	59	−5	02
1985	11	17	72	56	−5	02
1985	11	18	72	53	−5	02
1985	11	19	72	49	−5	02
1985	11	20	72	46	−5	03
1985	11	21	72	43	−5	03
1985	11	22	72	39	−5	03
1985	11	23	72	36	−5	03
1985	11	24	72	33	−5	03
1985	11	25	72	29	−5	04
1985	11	26	72	26	−5	04
1985	11	27	72	22	−5	04
1985	11	28	72	19	−5	04
1985	11	29	72	15	−5	04
1985	11	30	72	12	−5	04
1985	12	01	72	08	−5	04
1985	12	02	72	05	−5	05
1985	12	03	72	02	−5	05
1985	12	04	71	58	−5	05
1985	12	05	71	54	−5	05
1985	12	06	71	51	−5	05
1985	12	07	71	47	−5	05
1985	12	08	71	44	−5	05
1985	12	09	71	41	−5	05
1985	12	10	71	37	−5	05
1985	12	11	71	34	−5	05
1985	12	12	71	30	−5	05
1985	12	13	71	27	−5	05
1985	12	14	71	23	−5	05
1985	12	15	71	20	−5	05
1985	12	16	71	16	−5	05
1985	12	17	71	13	−5	05
1985	12	18	71	10	−5	05
1985	12	19	71	06	−5	05
1985	12	20	71	03	−5	05
1985	12	21	71	00	−5	05
1985	12	22	70	56	−5	05
1985	12	23	70	53	−5	05
1985	12	24	70	50	−5	05
1985	12	25	70	47	−5	05
1985	12	26	70	44	−5	05
1985	12	27	70	40	−5	05
1985	12	28	70	37	−5	05
1985	12	29	70	34	−5	05
1985	12	30	70	31	−5	05
1985	12	31	70	28	−5	05
1986	01	01	70	25	−5	05
1986	01	02	70	23	−5	05
1986	01	03	70	20	−5	04
1986	01	04	70	17	−5	04
1986	01	05	70	14	−5	04
1986	01	06	70	12	−5	04
1986	01	07	70	09	−5	04
1986	01	08	70	06	−5	04
1986	01	09	70	04	−5	04
1986	01	10	70	01	−5	03
1986	01	11	69	59	−5	03
1986	01	12	69	56	−5	03
1986	01	13	69	54	−5	03
1986	01	14	69	52	−5	03
1986	01	15	69	50	−5	03
1986	01	16	69	48	−5	02
1986	01	17	69	45	−5	02
1986	01	18	69	43	−5	02
1986	01	19	69	42	−5	02
1986	01	20	69	40	−5	02
1986	01	21	69	38	−5	02
1986	01	22	69	36	−5	01
1986	01	23	69	34	−5	01
1986	01	24	69	33	−5	01
1986	01	25	69	31	−5	01
1986	01	26	69	30	−5	00
1986	01	27	69	28	−5	00
1986	01	28	69	27	−5	00
1986	01	29	69	25	−5	00
1986	01	30	69	24	−5	00
1986	01	31	69	23	−4	59
1986	02	01	69	22	−4	59
1986	02	02	69	21	−4	59
1986	02	03	69	20	−4	59
1986	02	04	69	19	−4	58
1986	02	05	69	18	−4	58
1986	02	06	69	18	−4	58
1986	02	07	69	17	−4	58
1986	02	08	69	16	−4	57
1986	02	09	69	16	−4	57
1986	02	10	69	15	−4	57
1986	02	11	69	15	−4	57
1986	02	12	69	15	−4	56
1986	02	13	69	15	−4	56
1986	02	14	69	14	−4	56
1986	02	15	69	14	−4	55
1986	02	16	69	14	−4	55
1986	02	17	69	15	−4	55
1986	02	18	69	15	−4	55
1986	02	19	69	15	−4	54
1986	02	20	69	15	−4	54
1986	02	21	69	16	−4	54
1986	02	22	69	16	−4	54
1986	02	23	69	17	−4	53
1986	02	24	69	17	−4	53
1986	02	25	69	18	−4	53
1986	02	26	69	19	−4	53
1986	02	27	69	19	−4	52
1986	02	28	69	20	−4	52
1986	03	01	69	21	−4	52
1986	03	02	69	22	−4	51
1986	03	03	69	23	−4	51
1986	03	04	69	25	−4	51
1986	03	05	69	26	−4	51
1986	03	06	69	27	−4	50
1986	03	07	69	29	−4	50
1986	03	08	69	30	−4	50
1986	03	09	69	32	−4	50
1986	03	10	69	33	−4	49
1986	03	11	69	35	−4	49
1986	03	12	69	37	−4	49
1986	03	13	69	39	−4	49
1986	03	14	69	40	−4	48
1986	03	15	69	42	−4	48
1986	03	16	69	44	−4	48
1986	03	17	69	47	−4	48
1986	03	18	69	49	−4	47
1986	03	19	69	51	−4	47
1986	03	20	69	53	−4	47
1986	03	21	69	56	−4	47
1986	03	22	69	58	−4	46
1986	03	23	70	00	−4	46
1986	03	24	70	03	−4	46
1986	03	25	70	06	−4	46
1986	03	26	70	08	−4	46
1986	03	27	70	11	−4	45
1986	03	28	70	14	−4	45

20II45

K Chiron

CAO TIMES
Page 92

1986 03 29	70 17	-4 45	
1986 03 30	70 19	-4 45	
1986 03 31	70 22	-4 44	
1986 04 01	70 25	-4 44	
1986 04 02	70 28	-4 44	
1986 04 03	70 32	-4 44	
1986 04 04	70 35	-4 44	
1986 04 05	70 38	-4 43	
1986 04 06	70 41	-4 43	
1986 04 07	70 45	-4 43	
1986 04 08	70 48	-4 43	
1986 04 09	70 51	-4 43	
1986 04 10	70 55	-4 43	
1986 04 11	70 58	-4 42	
1986 04 12	71 02	-4 42	
1986 04 13	71 06	-4 42	
1986 04 14	71 09	-4 42	
1986 04 15	71 13	-4 42	
1986 04 16	71 17	-4 42	
1986 04 17	71 21	-4 41	
1986 04 18	71 24	-4 41	
1986 04 19	71 28	-4 41	
1986 04 20	71 32	-4 41	
1986 04 21	71 36	-4 41	
1986 04 22	71 40	--4 41	
1986 04 23	71 44	-4 41	
1986 04 24	71 48	-4 40	
1986 04 25	71 53	-4 40	
1986 04 26	71 57	-4 40	
1986 04 27	72 01	-4 40	
1986 04 28	72 05	-4 40	
1986 04 29	72 09	-4 40	
1986 04 30	72 14	-4 40	
1986 05 01	72 18	-4 40	
1986 05 02	72 22	-4 40	
1986 05 03	72 27	-4 40	
1986 05 04	72 31	-4 39	
1986 05 05	72 36	-4 39	
1986 05 06	72 40	-4 39	
1986 05 07	72 45	-4 39	
1986 05 08	72 49	-4 39	
1986 05 09	72 54	-4 39	
1986 05 10	72 59	-4 39	
1986 05 11	73 03	-4 39	
1986 05 12	73 08	-4 39	
1986 05 13	73 13	-4 39	
1986 05 14	73 17	-4 39	
1986 05 15	73 22	-4 39	
1986 05 16	73 27	-4 39	
1986 05 17	73 31	-4 39	
1986 05 18	73 36	-4 39	
1986 05 19	73 41	-4 39	
1986 05 20	73 46	-4 39	
1986 05 21	73 51	-4 39	
1986 05 22	73 55	-4 39	
1986 05 23	74 00	-4 39	
1986 05 24	74 05	-4 39	
1986 05 25	74 10	-4 39	
1986 05 26	74 15	-4 39	
1986 05 27	74 20	-4 39	
1986 05 28	74 25	-4 39	
1986 05 29	74 30	-4 39	
1986 05 30	74 35	-4 39	
1986 05 31	74 39	-4 39	
1986 06 01	74 44	-4 39	
1986 06 02	74 49	-4 39	
1986 06 03	74 54	-4 39	
1986 06 04	74 59	-4 39	
1986 06 05	75 04	-4 39	
1986 06 06	75 09	-4 39	
1986 06 07	75 14	-4 40	
1986 06 08	75 19	-4 40	
1986 06 09	75 24	-4 40	
1986 06 10	75 29	-4 40	
1986 06 11	75 34	-4 40	
1986 06 12	75 39	-4 40	
1986 06 13	75 44	-4 40	
1986 06 14	75 49	-4 40	
1986 06 15	75 54	-4 40	
1986 06 16	75 59	-4 40	
1986 06 17	76 04	-4 41	
1986 06 18	76 09	-4 41	
1986 06 19	76 13	-4 41	
1986 06 20	76 18	-4 41	
1986 06 21	76 23	-4 41	
1986 06 22	76 28	-4 41	
1986 06 23	76 33	-4 41	
1986 06 24	76 38	-4 42	
1986 06 25	76 43	-4 42	
1986 06 26	76 47	-4 42	
1986 06 27	76 52	-4 42	
1986 06 28	76 57	-4 42	
1986 06 29	77 02	-4 43	
1986 06 30	77 07	-4 43	
1986 07 01	77 11	-4 43	
1986 07 02	77 16	-4 43	
1986 07 03	77 21	-4 43	
1986 07 04	77 25	-4 44	
1986 07 05	77 30	-4 44	
1986 07 06	77 35	-4 44	
1986 07 07	77 39	-4 44	
1986 07 08	77 44	-4 44	
1986 07 09	77 48	-4 45	
1986 07 10	77 53	-4 45	
1986 07 11	77 57	-4 45	
1986 07 12	78 02	-4 45	
1986 07 13	78 06	-4 46	
1986 07 14	78 11	-4 46	
1986 07 15	78 15	-4 46	
1986 07 16	78 20	-4 46	
1986 07 17	78 24	-4 47	
1986 07 18	78 28	-4 47	
1986 07 19	78 32	-4 47	
1986 07 20	78 37	-4 48	
1986 07 21	78 41	-4 48	
1986 07 22	78 45	-4 48	
1986 07 23	78 49	-4 48	
1986 07 24	78 53	-4 49	
1986 07 25	78 57	-4 49	
1986 07 26	79 01	-4 49	
1986 07 27	79 05	-4 50	
1986 07 28	79 09	-4 50	
1986 07 29	79 13	-4 50	
1986 07 30	79 17	-4 51	
1986 07 31	79 21	-4 51	
1986 08 01	79 24	-4 51	
1986 08 02	79 28	-4 52	
1986 08 03	79 32	-4 52	
1986 08 04	79 35	-4 52	
1986 08 05	79 39	-4 53	
1986 08 06	79 42	-4 53	
1986 08 07	79 46	-4 53	
1986 08 08	79 49	-4 54	
1986 08 09	79 53	-4 54	
1986 08 10	79 56	-4 55	
1986 08 11	79 59	-4 55	
1986 08 12	80 02	-4 55	
1986 08 13	80 05	-4 56	
1986 08 14	80 09	-4 56	
1986 08 15	80 12	-4 56	
1986 08 16	80 15	-4 57	
1986 08 17	80 18	-4 57	
1986 08 18	80 20	-4 58	
1986 08 19	80 23	-4 58	
1986 08 20	80 26	-4 59	
1986 08 21	80 29	-4 59	
1986 08 22	80 31	-4 59	
1986 08 23	80 34	-5 00	
1986 08 24	80 36	-5 00	
1986 08 25	80 39	-5 01	
1986 08 26	80 41	-5 01	
1986 08 27	80 44	-5 01	
1986 08 28	80 46	-5 02	
1986 08 29	80 48	-5 02	
1986 08 30	80 50	-5 03	
1986 08 31	80 52	-5 03	
1986 09 01	80 54	-5 04	
1986 09 02	80 56	-5 04	
1986 09 03	80 58	-5 05	
1986 09 04	81 00	-5 05	
1986 09 05	81 02	-5 05	
1986 09 06	81 04	-5 06	
1986 09 07	81 05	-5 06	
1986 09 08	81 07	-5 07	
1986 09 09	81 08	-5 07	
1986 09 10	81 10	-5 08	
1986 09 11	81 11	-5 08	
1986 09 12	81 12	-5 09	
1986 09 13	81 13	-5 09	
1986 09 14	81 15	-5 10	
1986 09 15	81 16	-5 10	
1986 09 16	81 17	-5 11	
1986 09 17	81 17	-5 11	
1986 09 18	81 18	-5 12	
1986 09 19	81 19	-5 12	
1986 09 20	81 20	-5 13	
1986 09 21	81 20	-5 13	
1986 09 22	81 21	-5 13	
1986 09 23	81 21	-5 14	
1986 09 24	81 22	-5 14	
1986 09 25	81 22	-5 15	
1986 09 26	81 22	-5 15	
1986 09 27	81 23	-5 16	
1986 09 28	81 23	-5 16	
1986 09 29	81 23	-5 17	
1986 09 30	81 23	-5 17	
1986 10 01	81 23	-5 18	
1986 10 02	81 22	-5 18	
1986 10 03	81 22	-5 19	
1986 10 04	81 22	-5 19	
1986 10 05	81 21	-5 20	
1986 10 06	81 21	-5 20	
1986 10 07	81 20	-5 21	
1986 10 08	81 20	-5 21	
1986 10 09	81 19	-5 22	
1986 10 10	81 18	-5 22	
1986 10 11	81 17	-5 23	
1986 10 12	81 16	-5 23	
1986 10 13	81 15	-5 23	
1986 10 14	81 14	-5 24	
1986 10 15	81 13	-5 24	
1986 10 16	81 12	-5 25	
1986 10 17	81 11	-5 25	
1986 10 18	81 09	-5 26	
1986 10 19	81 08	-5 26	
1986 10 20	81 06	-5 27	
1986 10 21	81 05	-5 27	
1986 10 22	81 03	-5 27	
1986 10 23	81 01	-5 28	
1986 10 24	81 00	-5 28	Rx
1986 10 25	80 58	-5 29	
1986 10 26	80 56	-5 29	
1986 10 27	80 54	-5 30	
1986 10 28	80 52	-5 30	
1986 10 29	80 50	-5 30	
1986 10 30	80 48	-5 31	
1986 10 31	80 45	-5 31	
1986 11 01	80 43	-5 32	
1986 11 02	80 41	-5 32	
1986 11 03	80 38	-5 32	
1986 11 04	80 36	-5 33	
1986 11 05	80 33	-5 33	
1986 11 06	80 31	-5 33	
1986 11 07	80 28	-5 34	
1986 11 08	80 26	-5 34	
1986 11 09	80 23	-5 35	
1986 11 10	80 20	-5 35	
1986 11 11	80 17	-5 35	
1986 11 12	80 14	-5 36	
1986 11 13	80 11	-5 36	
1986 11 14	80 08	-5 36	
1986 11 15	80 05	-5 36	
1986 11 16	80 02	-5 37	
1986 11 17	79 59	-5 37	
1986 11 18	79 56	-5 37	
1986 11 19	79 53	-5 38	
1986 11 20	79 50	-5 38	
1986 11 21	79 47	-5 38	
1986 11 22	79 43	-5 38	
1986 11 23	79 40	-5 39	
1986 11 24	79 37	-5 39	
1986 11 25	79 33	-5 39	
1986 11 26	79 30	-5 39	
1986 11 27	79 26	-5 40	
1986 11 28	79 23	-5 40	
1986 11 29	79 19	-5 40	
1986 11 30	79 16	-5 40	
1986 12 01	79 12	-5 40	
1986 12 02	79 09	-5 41	
1986 12 03	79 05	-5 41	
1986 12 04	79 02	-5 41	
1986 12 05	78 58	-5 41	
1986 12 06	78 54	-5 41	
1986 12 07	78 51	-5 41	
1986 12 08	78 47	-5 41	
1986 12 09	78 44	-5 42	
1986 12 10	78 40	-5 42	
1986 12 11	78 36	-5 42	
1986 12 12	78 33	-5 42	
1986 12 13	78 29	-5 42	
1986 12 14	78 25	-5 42	
1986 12 15	78 22	-5 42	
1986 12 16	78 18	-5 42	
1986 12 17	78 15	-5 42	
1986 12 18	78 11	-5 42	
1986 12 19	78 07	-5 42	
1986 12 20	78 04	-5 42	
1986 12 21	78 00	-5 42	
1986 12 22	77 57	-5 42	
1986 12 23	77 53	-5 42	
1986 12 24	77 50	-5 42	
1986 12 25	77 46	-5 42	
1986 12 26	77 43	-5 42	
1986 12 27	77 39	-5 42	
1986 12 28	77 36	-5 42	
1986 12 29	77 32	-5 42	
1986 12 30	77 29	-5 42	
1986 12 31	77 26	-5 42	
1987 01 01	77 22	-5 42	
1987 01 02	77 19	-5 42	
1987 01 03	77 16	-5 42	
1987 01 04	77 13	-5 42	
1987 01 05	77 10	-5 41	
1987 01 06	77 07	-5 41	
1987 01 07	77 03	-5 41	
1987 01 08	77 00	-5 41	
1987 01 09	76 58	-5 41	
1987 01 10	76 55	-5 41	
1987 01 11	76 52	-5 41	
1987 01 12	76 49	-5 40	
1987 01 13	76 46	-5 40	
1987 01 14	76 43	-5 40	
1987 01 15	76 41	-5 40	
1987 01 16	76 38	-5 40	
1987 01 17	76 36	-5 40	
1987 01 18	76 33	-5 39	
1987 01 19	76 31	-5 39	
1987 01 20	76 28	-5 39	
1987 01 21	76 26	-5 39	
1987 01 22	76 24	-5 39	
1987 01 23	76 22	-5 38	
1987 01 24	76 19	-5 38	
1987 01 25	76 17	-5 38	
1987 01 26	76 15	-5 38	
1987 01 27	76 13	-5 37	
1987 01 28	76 12	-5 37	
1987 01 29	76 10	-5 37	
1987 01 30	76 08	-5 37	
1987 01 31	76 06	-5 36	
1987 02 01	76 05	-5 36	
1987 02 02	76 03	-5 36	
1987 02 03	76 02	-5 35	
1987 02 04	76 01	-5 35	
1987 02 05	75 59	-5 35	
1987 02 06	75 58	-5 35	
1987 02 07	75 57	-5 34	
1987 02 08	75 56	-5 34	
1987 02 09	75 55	-5 34	
1987 02 10	75 54	-5 33	
1987 02 11	75 53	-5 33	
1987 02 12	75 52	-5 33	
1987 02 13	75 52	-5 32	
1987 02 14	75 51	-5 32	
1987 02 15	75 50	-5 32	
1987 02 16	75 50	-5 31	
1987 02 17	75 50	-5 31	
1987 02 18	75 49	-5 31	
1987 02 19	75 49	-5 31	
1987 02 20	75 49	-5 30	
1987 02 21	75 49	-5 30	
1987 02 22	75 49	-5 30	
1987 02 23	75 49	-5 29	
1987 02 24	75 49	-5 29	
1987 02 25	75 49	-5 29	
1987 02 26	75 50	-5 28	
1987 02 27	75 50	-5 28	
1987 02 28	75 50	-5 28	D
1987 03 01	75 51	-5 27	
1987 03 02	75 52	-5 27	
1987 03 03	75 52	-5 27	
1987 03 04	75 53	-5 26	
1987 03 05	75 54	-5 26	
1987 03 06	75 55	-5 26	
1987 03 07	75 56	-5 25	
1987 03 08	75 57	-5 25	
1987 03 09	75 58	-5 25	
1987 03 10	75 59	-5 24	
1987 03 11	76 01	-5 24	
1987 03 12	76 02	-5 24	
1987 03 13	76 04	-5 23	
1987 03 14	76 05	-5 23	
1987 03 15	76 07	-5 23	
1987 03 16	76 08	-5 22	
1987 03 17	76 10	-5 22	
1987 03 18	76 12	-5 22	
1987 03 19	76 14	-5 21	
1987 03 20	76 16	-5 21	
1987 03 21	76 18	-5 21	
1987 03 22	76 20	-5 20	
1987 03 23	76 22	-5 20	
1987 03 24	76 24	-5 20	
1987 03 25	76 27	-5 20	
1987 03 26	76 29	-5 19	
1987 03 27	76 32	-5 19	
1987 03 28	76 34	-5 19	
1987 03 29	76 37	-5 18	
1987 03 30	76 39	-5 18	
1987 03 31	76 42	-5 18	
1987 04 01	76 45	-5 17	
1987 04 02	76 48	-5 17	
1987 04 03	76 50	-5 17	
1987 04 04	76 53	-5 17	
1987 04 05	76 56	-5 16	
1987 04 06	77 00	-5 16	
1987 04 07	77 03	-5 16	
1987 04 08	77 06	-5 16	
1987 04 09	77 09	-5 15	
1987 04 10	77 12	-5 15	
1987 04 11	77 16	-5 15	
1987 04 12	77 19	-5 15	
1987 04 13	77 23	-5 14	
1987 04 14	77 26	-5 14	
1987 04 15	77 30	-5 14	
1987 04 16	77 34	-5 14	
1987 04 17	77 37	-5 13	
1987 04 18	77 41	-5 13	
1987 04 19	77 45	-5 13	
1987 04 20	77 49	-5 13	
1987 04 21	77 53	-5 13	
1987 04 22	77 56	-5 12	
1987 04 23	78 00	-5 12	
1987 04 24	78 05	-5 12	
1987 04 25	78 09	-5 12	
1987 04 26	78 13	-5 12	
1987 04 27	78 17	-5 11	
1987 04 28	78 21	-5 11	
1987 04 29	78 25	-5 11	
1987 04 30	78 30	-5 11	
1987 05 01	78 34	-5 11	
1987 05 02	78 38	-5 11	
1987 05 03	78 43	-5 11	
1987 05 04	78 47	-5 10	
1987 05 05	78 52	-5 10	
1987 05 06	78 56	-5 10	
1987 05 07	79 01	-5 10	
1987 05 08	79 05	-5 10	
1987 05 09	79 10	-5 10	
1987 05 10	79 15	-5 10	
1987 05 11	79 19	-5 10	
1987 05 12	79 24	-5 09	
1987 05 13	79 29	-5 09	
1987 05 14	79 34	-5 09	
1987 05 15	79 38	-5 09	
1987 05 16	79 43	-5 09	
1987 05 17	79 48	-5 09	
1987 05 18	79 53	-5 09	
1987 05 19	79 58	-5 09	
1987 05 20	80 03	-5 09	
1987 05 21	80 08	-5 09	
1987 05 22	80 13	-5 09	

1987	05	23	80	18	-5	09
1987	05	24	80	23	-5	09
1987	05	25	80	28	-5	09
1987	05	26	80	33	-5	08
1987	05	27	80	38	-5	08
1987	05	28	80	43	-5	08
1987	05	29	80	48	-5	08
1987	05	30	80	53	-5	08
1987	05	31	80	59	-5	08
1987	06	01	81	04	-5	08
1987	06	02	81	09	-5	08
1987	06	03	81	14	-5	08
1987	06	04	81	19	-5	08
1987	06	05	81	24	-5	08
1987	06	06	81	30	-5	08
1987	06	07	81	35	-5	09
1987	06	08	81	40	-5	09
1987	06	09	81	45	-5	09
1987	06	10	81	51	-5	09
1987	06	11	81	56	-5	09
1987	06	12	82	01	-5	09
1987	06	13	82	06	-5	09
1987	06	14	82	12	-5	09
1987	06	15	82	17	-5	09
1987	06	16	82	22	-5	09
1987	06	17	82	27	-5	09
1987	06	18	82	33	-5	09
1987	06	19	82	38	-5	09
1987	06	20	82	43	-5	09
1987	06	21	82	48	-5	10
1987	06	22	82	54	-5	10
1987	06	23	82	59	-5	10
1987	06	24	83	04	-5	10
1987	06	25	83	09	-5	10
1987	06	26	83	14	-5	10
1987	06	27	83	20	-5	10
1987	06	28	83	25	-5	11
1987	06	29	83	30	-5	11
1987	06	30	83	35	-5	11
1987	07	01	83	40	-5	11
1987	07	02	83	45	-5	11
1987	07	03	83	51	-5	11
1987	07	04	83	56	-5	12
1987	07	05	84	01	-5	12
1987	07	06	84	06	-5	12
1987	07	07	84	11	-5	12
1987	07	08	84	16	-5	12
1987	07	09	84	21	-5	13
1987	07	10	84	26	-5	13
1987	07	11	84	31	-5	13
1987	07	12	84	36	-5	13
1987	07	13	84	41	-5	13
1987	07	14	84	46	-5	14
1987	07	15	84	51	-5	14
1987	07	16	84	55	-5	14
1987	07	17	85	00	-5	14
1987	07	18	85	05	-5	15
1987	07	19	85	10	-5	15
1987	07	20	85	15	-5	15
1987	07	21	85	19	-5	16
1987	07	22	85	24	-5	16
1987	07	23	85	29	-5	16
1987	07	24	85	33	-5	16
1987	07	25	85	38	-5	17
1987	07	26	85	42	-5	17
1987	07	27	85	47	-5	17
1987	07	28	85	51	-5	18
1987	07	29	85	56	-5	18
1987	07	30	86	00	-5	18
1987	07	31	86	05	-5	19
1987	08	01	86	09	-5	19
1987	08	02	86	13	-5	19
1987	08	03	86	17	-5	20
1987	08	04	86	22	-5	20
1987	08	05	86	26	-5	20
1987	08	06	86	30	-5	21
1987	08	07	86	34	-5	21
1987	08	08	86	38	-5	21
1987	08	09	86	42	-5	22
1987	08	10	86	46	-5	22
1987	08	11	86	50	-5	23
1987	08	12	86	54	-5	23
1987	08	13	86	57	-5	23
1987	08	14	87	01	-5	24
1987	08	15	87	05	-5	24
1987	08	16	87	08	-5	25
1987	08	17	87	12	-5	25
1987	08	18	87	16	-5	25
1987	08	19	87	19	-5	26
1987	08	20	87	22	-5	26
1987	08	21	87	26	-5	27
1987	08	22	87	29	-5	27
1987	08	23	87	32	-5	28
1987	08	24	87	36	-5	28
1987	08	25	87	39	-5	28
1987	08	26	87	42	-5	29
1987	08	27	87	45	-5	29
1987	08	28	87	48	-5	30
1987	08	29	87	51	-5	30
1987	08	30	87	54	-5	31
1987	08	31	87	56	-5	31
1987	09	01	87	59	-5	32
1987	09	02	88	02	-5	32
1987	09	03	88	04	-5	33
1987	09	04	88	07	-5	33
1987	09	05	88	09	-5	34
1987	09	06	88	12	-5	34
1987	09	07	88	14	-5	35
1987	09	08	88	16	-5	35
1987	09	09	88	18	-5	36
1987	09	10	88	20	-5	36
1987	09	11	88	22	-5	37
1987	09	12	88	24	-5	37
1987	09	13	88	26	-5	38
1987	09	14	88	28	-5	38
1987	09	15	88	30	-5	39
1987	09	16	88	32	-5	39
1987	09	17	88	33	-5	40
1987	09	18	88	35	-5	40
1987	09	19	88	36	-5	41
1987	09	20	88	38	-5	41
1987	09	21	88	39	-5	42
1987	09	22	88	40	-5	42
1987	09	23	88	41	-5	43
1987	09	24	88	42	-5	43
1987	09	25	88	43	-5	44
1987	09	26	88	44	-5	44
1987	09	27	88	45	-5	45
1987	09	28	88	46	-5	46
1987	09	29	88	47	-5	46
1987	09	30	88	47	-5	47
1987	10	01	88	48	-5	47
1987	10	02	88	48	-5	48
1987	10	03	88	49	-5	48
1987	10	04	88	49	-5	49
1987	10	05	88	49	-5	49
1987	10	06	88	49	-5	50
1987	10	07	88	50	-5	50
1987	10	08	88	50	-5	51
1987	10	09	88	50	-5	51
1987	10	10	88	49	-5	52
1987	10	11	88	49	-5	53
1987	10	12	88	49	-5	53
1987	10	13	88	48	-5	54
1987	10	14	88	48	-5	54
1987	10	15	88	47	-5	55
1987	10	16	88	47	-5	55
1987	10	17	88	46	-5	56
1987	10	18	88	45	-5	56
1987	10	19	88	44	-5	57
1987	10	20	88	44	-5	57
1987	10	21	88	42	-5	58
1987	10	22	88	41	-5	58
1987	10	23	88	40	-5	59
1987	10	24	88	39	-5	59
1987	10	25	88	38	-6	00
1987	10	26	88	36	-6	00
1987	10	27	88	35	-6	01
1987	10	28	88	33	-6	01
1987	10	29	88	32	-6	02
1987	10	30	88	30	-6	02
1987	10	31	88	28	-6	03
1987	11	01	88	26	-6	03
1987	11	02	88	25	-6	04
1987	11	03	88	23	-6	04
1987	11	04	88	21	-6	05
1987	11	05	88	18	-6	05
1987	11	06	88	16	-6	06
1987	11	07	88	14	-6	06
1987	11	08	88	12	-6	06
1987	11	09	88	09	-6	07
1987	11	10	88	07	-6	07
1987	11	11	88	04	-6	08
1987	11	12	88	02	-6	08
1987	11	13	87	59	-6	09
1987	11	14	87	57	-6	09
1987	11	15	87	54	-6	09
1987	11	16	87	51	-6	10
1987	11	17	87	48	-6	10
1987	11	18	87	45	-6	11
1987	11	19	87	42	-6	11
1987	11	20	87	39	-6	11
1987	11	21	87	36	-6	12
1987	11	22	87	33	-6	12
1987	11	23	87	30	-6	12
1987	11	24	87	27	-6	13
1987	11	25	87	24	-6	13
1987	11	26	87	20	-6	13
1987	11	27	87	17	-6	14
1987	11	28	87	14	-6	14
1987	11	29	87	10	-6	14
1987	11	30	87	07	-6	14
1987	12	01	87	03	-6	15
1987	12	02	87	00	-6	15
1987	12	03	86	56	-6	15
1987	12	04	86	53	-6	15
1987	12	05	86	49	-6	16
1987	12	06	86	46	-6	16
1987	12	07	86	42	-6	16
1987	12	08	86	38	-6	16
1987	12	09	86	35	-6	16
1987	12	10	86	31	-6	17
1987	12	11	86	27	-6	17
1987	12	12	86	24	-6	17
1987	12	13	86	20	-6	17
1987	12	14	86	16	-6	17
1987	12	15	86	12	-6	17
1987	12	16	86	09	-6	18
1987	12	17	86	05	-6	18
1987	12	18	86	01	-6	18
1987	12	19	85	57	-6	18
1987	12	20	85	53	-6	18
1987	12	21	85	50	-6	18
1987	12	22	85	46	-6	18
1987	12	23	85	42	-6	18
1987	12	24	85	38	-6	18
1987	12	25	85	35	-6	18
1987	12	26	85	31	-6	18
1987	12	27	85	27	-6	18
1987	12	28	85	23	-6	18
1987	12	29	85	20	-6	18
1987	12	30	85	16	-6	18
1987	12	31	85	12	-6	18
1988	01	01	85	09	-6	18
1988	01	02	85	05	-6	18
1988	01	03	85	01	-6	18
1988	01	04	84	58	-6	18
1988	01	05	84	54	-6	18
1988	01	06	84	51	-6	18
1988	01	07	84	47	-6	18
1988	01	08	84	44	-6	18
1988	01	09	84	41	-6	17
1988	01	10	84	37	-6	17
1988	01	11	84	34	-6	17
1988	01	12	84	31	-6	17
1988	01	13	84	27	-6	17
1988	01	14	84	24	-6	17
1988	01	15	84	21	-6	17
1988	01	16	84	18	-6	16
1988	01	17	84	15	-6	16
1988	01	18	84	12	-6	16
1988	01	19	84	09	-6	16
1988	01	20	84	06	-6	16
1988	01	21	84	03	-6	15
1988	01	22	84	01	-6	15
1988	01	23	83	58	-6	15
1988	01	24	83	55	-6	15
1988	01	25	83	53	-6	14
1988	01	26	83	50	-6	14
1988	01	27	83	48	-6	14
1988	01	28	83	45	-6	14
1988	01	29	83	43	-6	13
1988	01	30	83	40	-6	13
1988	01	31	83	38	-6	13
1988	02	01	83	36	-6	12
1988	02	02	83	34	-6	12
1988	02	03	83	32	-6	12
1988	02	04	83	30	-6	11
1988	02	05	83	28	-6	11
1988	02	06	83	26	-6	11
1988	02	07	83	25	-6	10
1988	02	08	83	23	-6	10
1988	02	09	83	22	-6	10
1988	02	10	83	20	-6	09
1988	02	11	83	19	-6	09
1988	02	12	83	17	-6	09
1988	02	13	83	16	-6	08
1988	02	14	83	15	-6	08
1988	02	15	83	14	-6	08
1988	02	16	83	13	-6	07
1988	02	17	83	12	-6	07
1988	02	18	83	11	-6	07
1988	02	19	83	10	-6	06
1988	02	20	83	09	-6	06
1988	02	21	83	09	-6	05
1988	02	22	83	08	-6	05
1988	02	23	83	08	-6	05
1988	02	24	83	07	-6	04
1988	02	25	83	07	-6	04
1988	02	26	83	07	-6	03
1988	02	27	83	07	-6	03
1988	02	28	83	07	-6	03
1988	02	29	83	07	-6	02
1988	03	01	83	07	-6	02
1988	03	02	83	07	-6	01
1988	03	03	83	07	-6	01
1988	03	04	83	08	-6	01
1988	03	05	83	08	-6	00
1988	03	06	83	08	-6	00
1988	03	07	83	09	-5	59
1988	03	08	83	10	-5	59
1988	03	09	83	11	-5	59
1988	03	10	83	11	-5	58
1988	03	11	83	12	-5	58
1988	03	12	83	13	-5	57
1988	03	13	83	14	-5	57
1988	03	14	83	16	-5	57
1988	03	15	83	17	-5	56
1988	03	16	83	18	-5	56
1988	03	17	83	19	-5	55
1988	03	18	83	21	-5	55
1988	03	19	83	22	-5	55
1988	03	20	83	24	-5	54
1988	03	21	83	26	-5	54
1988	03	22	83	28	-5	53
1988	03	23	83	29	-5	53
1988	03	24	83	31	-5	53
1988	03	25	83	33	-5	52
1988	03	26	83	36	-5	52
1988	03	27	83	38	-5	52
1988	03	28	83	40	-5	51
1988	03	29	83	42	-5	51
1988	03	30	83	45	-5	50
1988	03	31	83	47	-5	50
1988	04	01	83	50	-5	50
1988	04	02	83	52	-5	49
1988	04	03	83	55	-5	49
1988	04	04	83	58	-5	49
1988	04	05	84	00	-5	48
1988	04	06	84	03	-5	48
1988	04	07	84	06	-5	48
1988	04	08	84	09	-5	47
1988	04	09	84	12	-5	47
1988	04	10	84	15	-5	47
1988	04	11	84	19	-5	46
1988	04	12	84	22	-5	46
1988	04	13	84	25	-5	46
1988	04	14	84	29	-5	45
1988	04	15	84	32	-5	45
1988	04	16	84	36	-5	45
1988	04	17	84	39	-5	44
1988	04	18	84	43	-5	44
1988	04	19	84	46	-5	44
1988	04	20	84	50	-5	43
1988	04	21	84	54	-5	43
1988	04	22	84	58	-5	43
1988	04	23	85	02	-5	43
1988	04	24	85	06	-5	42
1988	04	25	85	10	-5	42
1988	04	26	85	14	-5	42
1988	04	27	85	18	-5	42
1988	04	28	85	22	-5	41
1988	04	29	85	26	-5	41
1988	04	30	85	31	-5	41
1988	05	01	85	35	-5	41
1988	05	02	85	39	-5	40
1988	05	03	85	44	-5	40
1988	05	04	85	48	-5	40
1988	05	05	85	53	-5	40
1988	05	06	85	57	-5	39
1988	05	07	86	02	-5	39
1988	05	08	86	06	-5	39
1988	05	09	86	11	-5	39
1988	05	10	86	16	-5	39
1988	05	11	86	20	-5	39
1988	05	12	86	25	-5	38
1988	05	13	86	30	-5	38
1988	05	14	86	35	-5	38
1988	05	15	86	40	-5	38
1988	05	16	86	45	-5	38
1988	05	17	86	50	-5	38
1988	05	18	86	55	-5	37
1988	05	19	87	00	-5	37
1988	05	20	87	05	-5	37
1988	05	21	87	10	-5	37
1988	05	22	87	15	-5	37
1988	05	23	87	20	-5	37
1988	05	24	87	25	-5	37
1988	05	25	87	31	-5	37
1988	05	26	87	36	-5	36
1988	05	27	87	41	-5	36
1988	05	28	87	46	-5	36
1988	05	29	87	52	-5	36
1988	05	30	87	57	-5	36
1988	05	31	88	02	-5	36
1988	06	01	88	08	-5	36
1988	06	02	88	13	-5	36
1988	06	03	88	19	-5	36
1988	06	04	88	24	-5	36
1988	06	05	88	29	-5	36
1988	06	06	88	35	-5	36
1988	06	07	88	40	-5	36
1988	06	08	88	46	-5	36
1988	06	09	88	51	-5	36
1988	06	10	88	57	-5	36
1988	06	11	89	02	-5	36
1988	06	12	89	08	-5	36
1988	06	13	89	13	-5	36
1988	06	14	89	19	-5	36
1988	06	15	89	25	-5	36
1988	06	16	89	30	-5	36
1988	06	17	89	36	-5	36
1988	06	18	89	41	-5	36
1988	06	19	89	47	-5	36
1988	06	20	89	52	-5	36
1988	06	21	89	58	-5	36
1988	06	22	90	04	-5	36
1988	06	23	90	09	-5	36
1988	06	24	90	15	-5	36
1988	06	25	90	20	-5	36
1988	06	26	90	26	-5	36
1988	06	27	90	32	-5	37
1988	06	28	90	37	-5	37
1988	06	29	90	43	-5	37
1988	06	30	90	48	-5	37
1988	07	01	90	54	-5	37
1988	07	02	90	59	-5	37
1988	07	03	91	05	-5	37
1988	07	04	91	11	-5	37
1988	07	05	91	16	-5	38
1988	07	06	91	22	-5	38
1988	07	07	91	27	-5	38
1988	07	08	91	33	-5	38
1988	07	09	91	38	-5	38
1988	07	10	91	44	-5	38
1988	07	11	91	49	-5	39
1988	07	12	91	54	-5	39
1988	07	13	92	00	-5	39
1988	07	14	92	05	-5	39
1988	07	15	92	11	-5	39

Chiron

1988	07	16	92	16	-5	40
1988	07	17	92	21	-5	40
1988	07	18	92	27	-5	40
1988	07	19	92	32	-5	40
1988	07	20	92	37	-5	41
1988	07	21	92	43	-5	41
1988	07	22	92	48	-5	41
1988	07	23	92	53	-5	41
1988	07	24	92	58	-5	42
1988	07	25	93	03	-5	42
1988	07	26	93	08	-5	42
1988	07	27	93	13	-5	42
1988	07	28	93	18	-5	43
1988	07	29	93	24	-5	43
1988	07	30	93	29	-5	43
1988	07	31	93	33	-5	44
1988	08	01	93	38	-5	44
1988	08	02	93	43	-5	44
1988	08	03	93	48	-5	45
1988	08	04	93	53	-5	45
1988	08	05	93	58	-5	45
1988	08	06	94	02	-5	46
1988	08	07	94	07	-5	46
1988	08	08	94	12	-5	46
1988	08	09	94	16	-5	47
1988	08	10	94	21	-5	47
1988	08	11	94	26	-5	48
1988	08	12	94	30	-5	48
1988	08	13	94	35	-5	48
1988	08	14	94	39	-5	49
1988	08	15	94	43	-5	49
1988	08	16	94	48	-5	49
1988	08	17	94	52	-5	50
1988	08	18	94	56	-5	50
1988	08	19	95	00	-5	51
1988	08	20	95	04	-5	51
1988	08	21	95	08	-5	52
1988	08	22	95	12	-5	52
1988	08	23	95	16	-5	52
1988	08	24	95	20	-5	53
1988	08	25	95	24	-5	53
1988	08	26	95	28	-5	54
1988	08	27	95	32	-5	54
1988	08	28	95	35	-5	55
1988	08	29	95	39	-5	55
1988	08	30	95	42	-5	56
1988	08	31	95	46	-5	56
1988	09	01	95	49	-5	57
1988	09	02	95	53	-5	57
1988	09	03	95	56	-5	58
1988	09	04	95	59	-5	58
1988	09	05	96	02	-5	59
1988	09	06	96	06	-5	59
1988	09	07	96	09	-6	00
1988	09	08	96	12	-6	00
1988	09	09	96	15	-6	01
1988	09	10	96	17	-6	01
1988	09	11	96	20	-6	02
1988	09	12	96	23	-6	02
1988	09	13	96	26	-6	03
1988	09	14	96	28	-6	03
1988	09	15	96	31	-6	04
1988	09	16	96	33	-6	05
1988	09	17	96	35	-6	05
1988	09	18	96	38	-6	06
1988	09	19	96	40	-6	06
1988	09	20	96	42	-6	07
1988	09	21	96	44	-6	07
1988	09	22	96	46	-6	08
1988	09	23	96	48	-6	08
1988	09	24	96	50	-6	09
1988	09	25	96	52	-6	10
1988	09	26	96	53	-6	10
1988	09	27	96	55	-6	11
1988	09	28	96	56	-6	11
1988	09	29	96	58	-6	12
1988	09	30	96	59	-6	13
1988	10	01	97	01	-6	13
1988	10	02	97	02	-6	14
1988	10	03	97	03	-6	14
1988	10	04	97	04	-6	15
1988	10	05	97	05	-6	15
1988	10	06	97	06	-6	16
1988	10	07	97	07	-6	17
1988	10	08	97	07	-6	17
1988	10	09	97	08	-6	18
1988	10	10	97	09	-6	18
1988	10	11	97	09	-6	19
1988	10	12	97	09	-6	20
1988	10	13	97	10	-6	20
1988	10	14	97	10	-6	21
1988	10	15	97	10	-6	21
1988	10	16	97	10	-6	22
1988	10	17	97	10	-6	23
1988	10	18	97	10	-6	23
1988	10	19	97	10	-6	24
1988	10	20	97	09	-6	24
1988	10	21	97	09	-6	25
1988	10	22	97	09	-6	26
1988	10	23	97	08	-6	26
1988	10	24	97	07	-6	27
1988	10	25	97	07	-6	27

1988	10	26	97	06	-6	28
1988	10	27	97	05	-6	29
1988	10	28	97	04	-6	29
1988	10	29	97	03	-6	30
1988	10	30	97	02	-6	30
1988	10	31	97	01	-6	31
1988	11	01	97	00	-6	31
1988	11	02	96	58	-6	32
1988	11	03	96	57	-6	32
1988	11	04	96	55	-6	33
1988	11	05	96	54	-6	34
1988	11	06	96	52	-6	34
1988	11	07	96	50	-6	35
1988	11	08	96	49	-6	35
1988	11	09	96	47	-6	36
1988	11	10	96	45	-6	36
1988	11	11	96	43	-6	37
1988	11	12	96	41	-6	37
1988	11	13	96	38	-6	38
1988	11	14	96	36	-6	38
1988	11	15	96	34	-6	39
1988	11	16	96	31	-6	39
1988	11	17	96	29	-6	40
1988	11	18	96	26	-6	40
1988	11	19	96	24	-6	41
1988	11	20	96	21	-6	41
1988	11	21	96	18	-6	42
1988	11	22	96	16	-6	42
1988	11	23	96	13	-6	42
1988	11	24	96	10	-6	43
1988	11	25	96	07	-6	43
1988	11	26	96	04	-6	44
1988	11	27	96	01	-6	44
1988	11	28	95	58	-6	44
1988	11	29	95	55	-6	45
1988	11	30	95	51	-6	45
1988	12	01	95	48	-6	46
1988	12	02	95	45	-6	46
1988	12	03	95	41	-6	46
1988	12	04	95	38	-6	47
1988	12	05	95	34	-6	47
1988	12	06	95	31	-6	47
1988	12	07	95	27	-6	47
1988	12	08	95	24	-6	48
1988	12	09	95	20	-6	48
1988	12	10	95	16	-6	48
1988	12	11	95	13	-6	49
1988	12	12	95	09	-6	49
1988	12	13	95	05	-6	49
1988	12	14	95	02	-6	49
1988	12	15	94	58	-6	50
1988	12	16	94	54	-6	50
1988	12	17	94	50	-6	50
1988	12	18	94	46	-6	50
1988	12	19	94	42	-6	50
1988	12	20	94	38	-6	50
1988	12	21	94	35	-6	51
1988	12	22	94	31	-6	51
1988	12	23	94	27	-6	51
1988	12	24	94	23	-6	51
1988	12	25	94	19	-6	51
1988	12	26	94	15	-6	51
1988	12	27	94	11	-6	51
1988	12	28	94	07	-6	51
1988	12	29	94	03	-6	51
1988	12	30	93	59	-6	51
1988	12	31	93	55	-6	51
1989	01	01	93	51	-6	51
1989	01	02	93	47	-6	51
1989	01	03	93	43	-6	51
1989	01	04	93	40	-6	51
1989	01	05	93	36	-6	51
1989	01	06	93	32	-6	51
1989	01	07	93	28	-6	51
1989	01	08	93	24	-6	51
1989	01	09	93	20	-6	51
1989	01	10	93	17	-6	51
1989	01	11	93	13	-6	51
1989	01	12	93	09	-6	51
1989	01	13	93	06	-6	51
1989	01	14	93	02	-6	50
1989	01	15	92	58	-6	50
1989	01	16	92	55	-6	50
1989	01	17	92	51	-6	50
1989	01	18	92	48	-6	50
1989	01	19	92	44	-6	50
1989	01	20	92	41	-6	49
1989	01	21	92	38	-6	49
1989	01	22	92	34	-6	49
1989	01	23	92	31	-6	49
1989	01	24	92	28	-6	49
1989	01	25	92	25	-6	48
1989	01	26	92	22	-6	48
1989	01	27	92	19	-6	48
1989	01	28	92	16	-6	48
1989	01	29	92	13	-6	47
1989	01	30	92	10	-6	47
1989	01	31	92	07	-6	47
1989	02	01	92	05	-6	46
1989	02	02	92	02	-6	46
1989	02	03	92	00	-6	46
1989	02	04	91	57	-6	45
1989	02	05	91	55	-6	45
1989	02	06	91	52	-6	45
1989	02	07	91	50	-6	44
1989	02	08	91	48	-6	44
1989	02	09	91	46	-6	44

1989	02	10	91	43	-6	43
1989	02	11	91	41	-6	43
1989	02	12	91	40	-6	42
1989	02	13	91	38	-6	42
1989	02	14	91	36	-6	42
1989	02	15	91	34	-6	41
1989	02	16	91	33	-6	41
1989	02	17	91	31	-6	40
1989	02	18	91	30	-6	40
1989	02	19	91	28	-6	40
1989	02	20	91	27	-6	39
1989	02	21	91	26	-6	39
1989	02	22	91	25	-6	38
1989	02	23	91	24	-6	38
1989	02	24	91	23	-6	37
1989	02	25	91	22	-6	37
1989	02	26	91	21	-6	36
1989	02	27	91	20	-6	36
1989	02	28	91	20	-6	35
1989	03	01	91	19	-6	35
1989	03	02	91	19	-6	35
1989	03	03	91	18	-6	34
1989	03	04	91	18	-6	34
1989	03	05	91	18	-6	33
1989	03	06	91	18	-6	33
1989	03	07	91	18	-6	32
1989	03	08	91	18	-6	32
1989	03	09	91	18	-6	31
1989	03	10	91	18	-6	31
1989	03	11	91	18	-6	30
1989	03	12	91	19	-6	30
1989	03	13	91	19	-6	29
1989	03	14	91	20	-6	29
1989	03	15	91	21	-6	28
1989	03	16	91	21	-6	28
1989	03	17	91	22	-6	27
1989	03	18	91	23	-6	27
1989	03	19	91	24	-6	26
1989	03	20	91	25	-6	26
1989	03	21	91	26	-6	25
1989	03	22	91	28	-6	25
1989	03	23	91	29	-6	24
1989	03	24	91	30	-6	24
1989	03	25	91	32	-6	24
1989	03	26	91	34	-6	23
1989	03	27	91	35	-6	23
1989	03	28	91	37	-6	22
1989	03	29	91	39	-6	22
1989	03	30	91	41	-6	21
1989	03	31	91	43	-6	21
1989	04	01	91	45	-6	20
1989	04	02	91	47	-6	20
1989	04	03	91	49	-6	19
1989	04	04	91	52	-6	19
1989	04	05	91	54	-6	18
1989	04	06	91	56	-6	18
1989	04	07	91	59	-6	18
1989	04	08	92	02	-6	17
1989	04	09	92	04	-6	17
1989	04	10	92	07	-6	16
1989	04	11	92	10	-6	16
1989	04	12	92	13	-6	15
1989	04	13	92	16	-6	15
1989	04	14	92	19	-6	15
1989	04	15	92	22	-6	14
1989	04	16	92	25	-6	14
1989	04	17	92	29	-6	13
1989	04	18	92	32	-6	13
1989	04	19	92	35	-6	12
1989	04	20	92	39	-6	12
1989	04	21	92	42	-6	12
1989	04	22	92	46	-6	11
1989	04	23	92	50	-6	11
1989	04	24	92	53	-6	11
1989	04	25	92	57	-6	10
1989	04	26	93	01	-6	10
1989	04	27	93	05	-6	09
1989	04	28	93	09	-6	09
1989	04	29	93	13	-6	09
1989	04	30	93	17	-6	08
1989	05	01	93	21	-6	08
1989	05	02	93	26	-6	08
1989	05	03	93	30	-6	07
1989	05	04	93	34	-6	07
1989	05	05	93	39	-6	07
1989	05	06	93	43	-6	06
1989	05	07	93	47	-6	06
1989	05	08	93	52	-6	06
1989	05	09	93	57	-6	06
1989	05	10	94	01	-6	05
1989	05	11	94	06	-6	05
1989	05	12	94	11	-6	05
1989	05	13	94	16	-6	04
1989	05	14	94	20	-6	04
1989	05	15	94	25	-6	04
1989	05	16	94	30	-6	04
1989	05	17	94	35	-6	03
1989	05	18	94	40	-6	03
1989	05	19	94	45	-6	03
1989	05	20	94	50	-6	03
1989	05	21	94	55	-6	02
1989	05	22	95	01	-6	02
1989	05	23	95	06	-6	02
1989	05	24	95	11	-6	02
1989	05	25	95	16	-6	02
1989	05	26	95	22	-6	01

1989	05	27	95	27	-6	01
1989	05	28	95	32	-6	01
1989	05	29	95	38	-6	01
1989	05	30	95	43	-6	01
1989	05	31	95	49	-6	01
1989	06	01	95	54	-6	00
1989	06	02	96	00	-6	00
1989	06	03	96	05	-6	00
1989	06	04	96	11	-6	00
1989	06	05	96	17	-6	00
1989	06	06	96	22	-6	00
1989	06	07	96	28	-6	00
1989	06	08	96	34	-5	59
1989	06	09	96	39	-5	59
1989	06	10	96	45	-5	59
1989	06	11	96	51	-5	59
1989	06	12	96	57	-5	59
1989	06	13	97	03	-5	59
1989	06	14	97	08	-5	59
1989	06	15	97	14	-5	59
1989	06	16	97	20	-5	59
1989	06	17	97	26	-5	59
1989	06	18	97	32	-5	59
1989	06	19	97	38	-5	59
1989	06	20	97	44	-5	59
1989	06	21	97	50	-5	59
1989	06	22	97	55	-5	59
1989	06	23	98	01	-5	59
1989	06	24	98	07	-5	59
1989	06	25	98	13	-5	59
1989	06	26	98	19	-5	59
1989	06	27	98	25	-5	59
1989	06	28	98	31	-5	59
1989	06	29	98	37	-5	59
1989	06	30	98	43	-5	59
1989	07	01	98	49	-5	59
1989	07	02	98	55	-5	59
1989	07	03	99	01	-5	59
1989	07	04	99	07	-5	59
1989	07	05	99	13	-5	59
1989	07	06	99	19	-5	59
1989	07	07	99	25	-5	59
1989	07	08	99	31	-5	59
1989	07	09	99	37	-6	00
1989	07	10	99	43	-6	00
1989	07	11	99	49	-6	00
1989	07	12	99	55	-6	00
1989	07	13	100	01	-6	00
1989	07	14	100	07	-6	00
1989	07	15	100	13	-6	00
1989	07	16	100	19	-6	01
1989	07	17	100	25	-6	01
1989	07	18	100	30	-6	01
1989	07	19	100	36	-6	01
1989	07	20	100	42	-6	01
1989	07	21	100	48	-6	01
1989	07	22	100	54	-6	02
1989	07	23	101	00	-6	02
1989	07	24	101	05	-6	02
1989	07	25	101	11	-6	02
1989	07	26	101	17	-6	02
1989	07	27	101	23	-6	03
1989	07	28	101	28	-6	03
1989	07	29	101	34	-6	03
1989	07	30	101	40	-6	03
1989	07	31	101	45	-6	04
1989	08	01	101	51	-6	04
1989	08	02	101	57	-6	04
1989	08	03	102	02	-6	05
1989	08	04	102	08	-6	05
1989	08	05	102	13	-6	05
1989	08	06	102	19	-6	05
1989	08	07	102	24	-6	06
1989	08	08	102	29	-6	06
1989	08	09	102	35	-6	06
1989	08	10	102	40	-6	07
1989	08	11	102	45	-6	07
1989	08	12	102	51	-6	07
1989	08	13	102	56	-6	08
1989	08	14	103	01	-6	08
1989	08	15	103	06	-6	08
1989	08	16	103	11	-6	09
1989	08	17	103	16	-6	09
1989	08	18	103	21	-6	10
1989	08	19	103	26	-6	10
1989	08	20	103	31	-6	10
1989	08	21	103	36	-6	11
1989	08	22	103	41	-6	11
1989	08	23	103	46	-6	12
1989	08	24	103	50	-6	12
1989	08	25	103	55	-6	12
1989	08	26	104	00	-6	13
1989	08	27	104	04	-6	13
1989	08	28	104	09	-6	14
1989	08	29	104	13	-6	14
1989	08	30	104	18	-6	15
1989	08	31	104	22	-6	15
1989	09	01	104	27	-6	16
1989	09	02	104	31	-6	16
1989	09	03	104	35	-6	17
1989	09	04	104	39	-6	17
1989	09	05	104	43	-6	18
1989	09	06	104	47	-6	18
1989	09	07	104	51	-6	19
1989	09	08	104	55	-6	19
1989	09	09	104	59	-6	20

1989	09	10	105	03	-6	20
1989	09	11	105	06	-6	21
1989	09	12	105	10	-6	21
1989	09	13	105	14	-6	22
1989	09	14	105	17	-6	22
1989	09	15	105	21	-6	23
1989	09	16	105	24	-6	23
1989	09	17	105	27	-6	24
1989	09	18	105	31	-6	24
1989	09	19	105	34	-6	25
1989	09	20	105	37	-6	26
1989	09	21	105	40	-6	26
1989	09	22	105	43	-6	27
1989	09	23	105	46	-6	27
1989	09	24	105	49	-6	28
1989	09	25	105	51	-6	29
1989	09	26	105	54	-6	29
1989	09	27	105	57	-6	30
1989	09	28	105	59	-6	30
1989	09	29	106	02	-6	31
1989	09	30	106	04	-6	32
1989	10	01	106	06	-6	32
1989	10	02	106	08	-6	33
1989	10	03	106	10	-6	33
1989	10	04	106	13	-6	34
1989	10	05	106	14	-6	35
1989	10	06	106	16	-6	35
1989	10	07	106	18	-6	36
1989	10	08	106	20	-6	37
1989	10	09	106	21	-6	37
1989	10	10	106	23	-6	38
1989	10	11	106	24	-6	38
1989	10	12	106	26	-6	39
1989	10	13	106	27	-6	40
1989	10	14	106	28	-6	40
1989	10	15	106	29	-6	41
1989	10	16	106	30	-6	42
1989	10	17	106	31	-6	42
1989	10	18	106	32	-6	43
1989	10	19	106	33	-6	44
1989	10	20	106	34	-6	44
1989	10	21	106	34	-6	45
1989	10	22	106	35	-6	46
1989	10	23	106	35	-6	46
1989	10	24	106	35	-6	47
1989	10	25	106	36	-6	48
1989	10	26	106	36	-6	48
1989	10	27	106	36	-6	49
1989	10	28	106	36	-6	49
1989	10	29	106	36	-6	50
1989	10	30	106	35	-6	51
1989	10	31	106	35	-6	51
1989	11	01	106	35	-6	52
1989	11	02	106	34	-6	53
1989	11	03	106	34	-6	53
1989	11	04	106	33	-6	54
1989	11	05	106	32	-6	55
1989	11	06	106	31	-6	55
1989	11	07	106	30	-6	56
1989	11	08	106	29	-6	56
1989	11	09	106	28	-6	57
1989	11	10	106	27	-6	58
1989	11	11	106	26	-6	58
1989	11	12	106	24	-6	59
1989	11	13	106	23	-7	00
1989	11	14	106	21	-7	00
1989	11	15	106	20	-7	01
1989	11	16	106	18	-7	01
1989	11	17	106	16	-7	02
1989	11	18	106	14	-7	02
1989	11	19	106	12	-7	03
1989	11	20	106	10	-7	04
1989	11	21	106	08	-7	04
1989	11	22	106	06	-7	05
1989	11	23	106	04	-7	05
1989	11	24	106	02	-7	06
1989	11	25	105	59	-7	06
1989	11	26	105	57	-7	07
1989	11	27	105	54	-7	07
1989	11	28	105	51	-7	08
1989	11	29	105	49	-7	08
1989	11	30	105	46	-7	09
1989	12	01	105	43	-7	09
1989	12	02	105	40	-7	10
1989	12	03	105	37	-7	10
1989	12	04	105	34	-7	11
1989	12	05	105	31	-7	11
1989	12	06	105	28	-7	11
1989	12	07	105	25	-7	12
1989	12	08	105	21	-7	12
1989	12	09	105	18	-7	13
1989	12	10	105	15	-7	13
1989	12	11	105	11	-7	13
1989	12	12	105	08	-7	14
1989	12	13	105	04	-7	14
1989	12	14	105	01	-7	15
1989	12	15	104	57	-7	15
1989	12	16	104	53	-7	15
1989	12	17	104	50	-7	15
1989	12	18	104	46	-7	16
1989	12	19	104	42	-7	16
1989	12	20	104	38	-7	16
1989	12	21	104	35	-7	17
1989	12	22	104	31	-7	17
1989	12	23	104	27	-7	17
1989	12	24	104	23	-7	17
1989	12	25	104	19	-7	18
1989	12	26	104	15	-7	18
1989	12	27	104	11	-7	18
1989	12	28	104	07	-7	18
1989	12	29	104	03	-7	18
1989	12	30	103	59	-7	18
1989	12	31	103	54	-7	18
1990	01	01	103	50	-7	19
1990	01	02	103	46	-7	19
1990	01	03	103	42	-7	19
1990	01	04	103	38	-7	19
1990	01	05	103	34	-7	19
1990	01	06	103	30	-7	19
1990	01	07	103	26	-7	19
1990	01	08	103	22	-7	19
1990	01	09	103	17	-7	19
1990	01	10	103	13	-7	19
1990	01	11	103	09	-7	19
1990	01	12	103	05	-7	19
1990	01	13	103	01	-7	19
1990	01	14	102	57	-7	19
1990	01	15	102	53	-7	19
1990	01	16	102	49	-7	19
1990	01	17	102	45	-7	19
1990	01	18	102	41	-7	18
1990	01	19	102	37	-7	18
1990	01	20	102	33	-7	18
1990	01	21	102	30	-7	18
1990	01	22	102	26	-7	18
1990	01	23	102	22	-7	18
1990	01	24	102	18	-7	18
1990	01	25	102	14	-7	17
1990	01	26	102	11	-7	17
1990	01	27	102	07	-7	17
1990	01	28	102	04	-7	17
1990	01	29	102	00	-7	16
1990	01	30	101	57	-7	16
1990	01	31	101	53	-7	16
1990	02	01	101	50	-7	16
1990	02	02	101	46	-7	15
1990	02	03	101	43	-7	15
1990	02	04	101	40	-7	15
1990	02	05	101	37	-7	14
1990	02	06	101	34	-7	14
1990	02	07	101	31	-7	14
1990	02	08	101	28	-7	13
1990	02	09	101	25	-7	13
1990	02	10	101	22	-7	13
1990	02	11	101	19	-7	12
1990	02	12	101	17	-7	12
1990	02	13	101	14	-7	11
1990	02	14	101	12	-7	11
1990	02	15	101	09	-7	10
1990	02	16	101	07	-7	10
1990	02	17	101	04	-7	10
1990	02	18	101	02	-7	09
1990	02	19	101	00	-7	09
1990	02	20	100	58	-7	08
1990	02	21	100	56	-7	08
1990	02	22	100	54	-7	07
1990	02	23	100	52	-7	07
1990	02	24	100	50	-7	06
1990	02	25	100	49	-7	06
1990	02	26	100	47	-7	05
1990	02	27	100	46	-7	05
1990	02	28	100	44	-7	04
1990	03	01	100	43	-7	04
1990	03	02	100	42	-7	03
1990	03	03	100	41	-7	03
1990	03	04	100	39	-7	02
1990	03	05	100	39	-7	02
1990	03	06	100	38	-7	01
1990	03	07	100	37	-7	01
1990	03	08	100	36	-7	00
1990	03	09	100	36	-7	00
1990	03	10	100	35	-6	59
1990	03	11	100	35	-6	58
1990	03	12	100	34	-6	58
1990	03	13	100	34	-6	57
1990	03	14	100	34	-6	57
1990	03	15	100	34	-6	56
1990	03	16	100	34	-6	56
1990	03	17	100	34	-6	55
1990	03	18	100	34	-6	55
1990	03	19	100	34	-6	54
1990	03	20	100	35	-6	53
1990	03	21	100	35	-6	53
1990	03	22	100	36	-6	52
1990	03	23	100	37	-6	52
1990	03	24	100	37	-6	51
1990	03	25	100	38	-6	51
1990	03	26	100	39	-6	50
1990	03	27	100	40	-6	49
1990	03	28	100	41	-6	49
1990	03	29	100	42	-6	48
1990	03	30	100	44	-6	48
1990	03	31	100	45	-6	47
1990	04	01	100	47	-6	47
1990	04	02	100	48	-6	46
1990	04	03	100	50	-6	45
1990	04	04	100	52	-6	45
1990	04	05	100	53	-6	44
1990	04	06	100	55	-6	44
1990	04	07	100	57	-6	43
1990	04	08	100	59	-6	43
1990	04	09	101	02	-6	42
1990	04	10	101	04	-6	42
1990	04	11	101	06	-6	41
1990	04	12	101	09	-6	40
1990	04	13	101	11	-6	40
1990	04	14	101	14	-6	39
1990	04	15	101	16	-6	39
1990	04	16	101	19	-6	38
1990	04	17	101	22	-6	38
1990	04	18	101	25	-6	37
1990	04	19	101	28	-6	37
1990	04	20	101	31	-6	36
1990	04	21	101	34	-6	36
1990	04	22	101	37	-6	35
1990	04	23	101	41	-6	35
1990	04	24	101	44	-6	34
1990	04	25	101	47	-6	34
1990	04	26	101	51	-6	33
1990	04	27	101	54	-6	33
1990	04	28	101	58	-6	32
1990	04	29	102	02	-6	32
1990	04	30	102	06	-6	31
1990	05	01	102	10	-6	31
1990	05	02	102	13	-6	30
1990	05	03	102	17	-6	30
1990	05	04	102	22	-6	30
1990	05	05	102	26	-6	29
1990	05	06	102	30	-6	29
1990	05	07	102	34	-6	28
1990	05	08	102	38	-6	28
1990	05	09	102	43	-6	27
1990	05	10	102	47	-6	27
1990	05	11	102	52	-6	27
1990	05	12	102	56	-6	26
1990	05	13	103	01	-6	26
1990	05	14	103	06	-6	25
1990	05	15	103	10	-6	25
1990	05	16	103	15	-6	25
1990	05	17	103	20	-6	24
1990	05	18	103	25	-6	24
1990	05	19	103	30	-6	23
1990	05	20	103	35	-6	23
1990	05	21	103	40	-6	23
1990	05	22	103	45	-6	22
1990	05	23	103	50	-6	22
1990	05	24	103	56	-6	22
1990	05	25	104	01	-6	21
1990	05	26	104	06	-6	21
1990	05	27	104	11	-6	21
1990	05	28	104	17	-6	21
1990	05	29	104	22	-6	20
1990	05	30	104	28	-6	20
1990	05	31	104	33	-6	20
1990	06	01	104	39	-6	19
1990	06	02	104	45	-6	19
1990	06	03	104	50	-6	19
1990	06	04	104	56	-6	19
1990	06	05	105	02	-6	18
1990	06	06	105	07	-6	18
1990	06	07	105	13	-6	18
1990	06	08	105	19	-6	18
1990	06	09	105	25	-6	18
1990	06	10	105	31	-6	17
1990	06	11	105	37	-6	17
1990	06	12	105	43	-6	17
1990	06	13	105	49	-6	17
1990	06	14	105	55	-6	17
1990	06	15	106	01	-6	16
1990	06	16	106	07	-6	16
1990	06	17	106	13	-6	16
1990	06	18	106	19	-6	16
1990	06	19	106	25	-6	16
1990	06	20	106	31	-6	16
1990	06	21	106	38	-6	15
1990	06	22	106	44	-6	15
1990	06	23	106	50	-6	15
1990	06	24	106	56	-6	15
1990	06	25	107	03	-6	15
1990	06	26	107	09	-6	15
1990	06	27	107	15	-6	15
1990	06	28	107	22	-6	15
1990	06	29	107	28	-6	15
1990	06	30	107	34	-6	15
1990	07	01	107	41	-6	15
1990	07	02	107	47	-6	15
1990	07	03	107	53	-6	15
1990	07	04	108	00	-6	15
1990	07	05	108	06	-6	14
1990	07	06	108	13	-6	14
1990	07	07	108	19	-6	14
1990	07	08	108	25	-6	14
1990	07	09	108	32	-6	14
1990	07	10	108	38	-6	14
1990	07	11	108	45	-6	15
1990	07	12	108	51	-6	15
1990	07	13	108	58	-6	15
1990	07	14	109	04	-6	15
1990	07	15	109	11	-6	15
1990	07	16	109	17	-6	15
1990	07	17	109	24	-6	15
1990	07	18	109	30	-6	15
1990	07	19	109	36	-6	15
1990	07	20	109	43	-6	15
1990	07	21	109	49	-6	15
1990	07	22	109	56	-6	15
1990	07	23	110	02	-6	15
1990	07	24	110	09	-6	15
1990	07	25	110	15	-6	16
1990	07	26	110	21	-6	16
1990	07	27	110	28	-6	16
1990	07	28	110	34	-6	16
1990	07	29	110	40	-6	16
1990	07	30	110	47	-6	16
1990	07	31	110	53	-6	17
1990	08	01	110	59	-6	17
1990	08	02	111	06	-6	17
1990	08	03	111	12	-6	17
1990	08	04	111	18	-6	17
1990	08	05	111	24	-6	18
1990	08	06	111	30	-6	18
1990	08	07	111	37	-6	18
1990	08	08	111	43	-6	18
1990	08	09	111	49	-6	18
1990	08	10	111	55	-6	19
1990	08	11	112	01	-6	19
1990	08	12	112	07	-6	19
1990	08	13	112	13	-6	20
1990	08	14	112	19	-6	20
1990	08	15	112	25	-6	20
1990	08	16	112	31	-6	20
1990	08	17	112	37	-6	21
1990	08	18	112	43	-6	21
1990	08	19	112	49	-6	21
1990	08	20	112	54	-6	22
1990	08	21	113	00	-6	22
1990	08	22	113	06	-6	22
1990	08	23	113	12	-6	23
1990	08	24	113	17	-6	23
1990	08	25	113	23	-6	23
1990	08	26	113	28	-6	24
1990	08	27	113	34	-6	24
1990	08	28	113	39	-6	25
1990	08	29	113	45	-6	25
1990	08	30	113	50	-6	25
1990	08	31	113	56	-6	26
1990	09	01	114	01	-6	26
1990	09	02	114	06	-6	27
1990	09	03	114	11	-6	27
1990	09	04	114	16	-6	27
1990	09	05	114	21	-6	28
1990	09	06	114	27	-6	28
1990	09	07	114	32	-6	29
1990	09	08	114	36	-6	29
1990	09	09	114	41	-6	30
1990	09	10	114	46	-6	30
1990	09	11	114	51	-6	31
1990	09	12	114	56	-6	31
1990	09	13	115	00	-6	32
1990	09	14	115	05	-6	32
1990	09	15	115	09	-6	33
1990	09	16	115	14	-6	33
1990	09	17	115	18	-6	34
1990	09	18	115	23	-6	34
1990	09	19	115	27	-6	35
1990	09	20	115	31	-6	35
1990	09	21	115	35	-6	36
1990	09	22	115	39	-6	36
1990	09	23	115	43	-6	37
1990	09	24	115	47	-6	37
1990	09	25	115	51	-6	38
1990	09	26	115	55	-6	39
1990	09	27	115	59	-6	39
1990	09	28	116	02	-6	40
1990	09	29	116	06	-6	40
1990	09	30	116	09	-6	41
1990	10	01	116	13	-6	42
1990	10	02	116	16	-6	42
1990	10	03	116	19	-6	43
1990	10	04	116	23	-6	43
1990	10	05	116	26	-6	44
1990	10	06	116	29	-6	45
1990	10	07	116	32	-6	45
1990	10	08	116	34	-6	46
1990	10	09	116	37	-6	47
1990	10	10	116	40	-6	47
1990	10	11	116	43	-6	48
1990	10	12	116	45	-6	48
1990	10	13	116	48	-6	49
1990	10	14	116	50	-6	50
1990	10	15	116	52	-6	50
1990	10	16	116	54	-6	51
1990	10	17	116	57	-6	52
1990	10	18	116	59	-6	52
1990	10	19	117	00	-6	53
1990	10	20	117	02	-6	54
1990	10	21	117	04	-6	54
1990	10	22	117	06	-6	55
1990	10	23	117	07	-6	56
1990	10	24	117	09	-6	56
1990	10	25	117	10	-6	57
1990	10	26	117	11	-6	58
1990	10	27	117	13	-6	59
1990	10	28	117	14	-6	59
1990	10	29	117	15	-7	00
1990	10	30	117	16	-7	01
1990	10	31	117	17	-7	01
1990	11	01	117	17	-7	02
1990	11	02	117	18	-7	03
1990	11	03	117	18	-7	03

⚷ Chiron

1990	11	04	117	19	-7	04
1990	11	05	117	19	-7	05
1990	11	06	117	19	-7	05
1990	11	07	117	20	-7	06
1990	11	08	117	20	-7	07
1990	11	09	117	20	-7	07
1990	11	10	117	20	-7	08
1990	11	11	117	19	-7	09
1990	11	12	117	19	-7	09
1990	11	13	117	19	-7	10
1990	11	14	117	18	-7	11
1990	11	15	117	17	-7	11
1990	11	16	117	17	-7	12
1990	11	17	117	16	-7	13
1990	11	18	117	15	-7	13
1990	11	19	117	14	-7	14
1990	11	20	117	13	-7	15
1990	11	21	117	12	-7	15
1990	11	22	117	11	-7	16
1990	11	23	117	09	-7	17
1990	11	24	117	08	-7	17
1990	11	25	117	06	-7	18
1990	11	26	117	05	-7	19
1990	11	27	117	03	-7	19
1990	11	28	117	01	-7	20
1990	11	29	116	59	-7	20
1990	11	30	116	57	-7	21
1990	12	01	116	55	-7	22
1990	12	02	116	53	-7	22
1990	12	03	116	51	-7	23
1990	12	04	116	49	-7	23
1990	12	05	116	46	-7	24
1990	12	06	116	44	-7	24
1990	12	07	116	41	-7	25
1990	12	08	116	39	-7	25
1990	12	09	116	36	-7	26
1990	12	10	116	33	-7	26
1990	12	11	116	30	-7	27
1990	12	12	116	27	-7	27
1990	12	13	116	24	-7	28
1990	12	14	116	21	-7	28
1990	12	15	116	18	-7	29
1990	12	16	116	15	-7	29
1990	12	17	116	12	-7	30
1990	12	18	116	08	-7	30
1990	12	19	116	05	-7	31
1990	12	20	116	01	-7	31
1990	12	21	115	58	-7	31
1990	12	22	115	54	-7	32
1990	12	23	115	51	-7	32
1990	12	24	115	47	-7	32
1990	12	25	115	43	-7	33
1990	12	26	115	39	-7	33
1990	12	27	115	36	-7	33
1990	12	28	115	32	-7	34
1990	12	29	115	28	-7	34
1990	12	30	115	24	-7	34
1990	12	31	115	20	-7	35
1991	01	01	115	16	-7	35
1991	01	02	115	12	-7	35
1991	01	03	115	08	-7	35
1991	01	04	115	04	-7	35
1991	01	05	114	59	-7	36
1991	01	06	114	55	-7	36
1991	01	07	114	51	-7	36
1991	01	08	114	47	-7	36
1991	01	09	114	43	-7	36
1991	01	10	114	38	-7	36
1991	01	11	114	34	-7	36
1991	01	12	114	30	-7	37
1991	01	13	114	26	-7	37
1991	01	14	114	21	-7	37
1991	01	15	114	17	-7	37
1991	01	16	114	13	-7	37
1991	01	17	114	08	-7	37
1991	01	18	114	04	-7	37
1991	01	19	114	00	-7	37
1991	01	20	113	56	-7	37
1991	01	21	113	51	-7	37
1991	01	22	113	47	-7	37
1991	01	23	113	43	-7	36
1991	01	24	113	39	-7	36
1991	01	25	113	34	-7	36
1991	01	26	113	30	-7	36
1991	01	27	113	26	-7	36
1991	01	28	113	22	-7	36
1991	01	29	113	18	-7	36
1991	01	30	113	14	-7	35
1991	01	31	113	10	-7	35
1991	02	01	113	06	-7	35
1991	02	02	113	02	-7	35
1991	02	03	112	58	-7	35
1991	02	04	112	54	-7	34
1991	02	05	112	50	-7	34
1991	02	06	112	46	-7	34
1991	02	07	112	42	-7	34
1991	02	08	112	39	-7	33
1991	02	09	112	35	-7	33
1991	02	10	112	32	-7	33
1991	02	11	112	28	-7	32
1991	02	12	112	25	-7	32
1991	02	13	112	21	-7	31
1991	02	14	112	18	-7	31
1991	02	15	112	14	-7	31
1991	02	16	112	11	-7	30
1991	02	17	112	08	-7	30
1991	02	18	112	05	-7	29
1991	02	19	112	02	-7	29
1991	02	20	111	59	-7	29
1991	02	21	111	56	-7	28
1991	02	22	111	53	-7	28
1991	02	23	111	51	-7	27
1991	02	24	111	48	-7	27
1991	02	25	111	45	-7	26
1991	02	26	111	43	-7	26
1991	02	27	111	40	-7	25
1991	02	28	111	38	-7	25
1991	03	01	111	36	-7	24
1991	03	02	111	34	-7	24
1991	03	03	111	32	-7	23
1991	03	04	111	30	-7	22
1991	03	05	111	28	-7	22
1991	03	06	111	26	-7	21
1991	03	07	111	24	-7	21
1991	03	08	111	23	-7	20
1991	03	09	111	21	-7	20
1991	03	10	111	19	-7	19
1991	03	11	111	18	-7	18
1991	03	12	111	17	-7	18
1991	03	13	111	16	-7	17
1991	03	14	111	15	-7	16
1991	03	15	111	14	-7	16
1991	03	16	111	13	-7	15
1991	03	17	111	12	-7	15
1991	03	18	111	11	-7	14
1991	03	19	111	11	-7	13
1991	03	20	111	10	-7	13
1991	03	21	111	10	-7	12
1991	03	22	111	09	-7	11
1991	03	23	111	09	-7	11
1991	03	24	111	09	-7	10
1991	03	25	111	09	-7	09
1991	03	26	111	09	-7	09
1991	03	27	111	09	-7	08
1991	03	28	111	09	-7	07
1991	03	29	111	10	-7	07
1991	03	30	111	10	-7	06
1991	03	31	111	11	-7	05
1991	04	01	111	11	-7	05
1991	04	02	111	12	-7	04
1991	04	03	111	13	-7	03
1991	04	04	111	14	-7	03
1991	04	05	111	15	-7	02
1991	04	06	111	16	-7	01
1991	04	07	111	17	-7	01
1991	04	08	111	19	-7	00
1991	04	09	111	20	-6	59
1991	04	10	111	21	-6	59
1991	04	11	111	23	-6	58
1991	04	12	111	25	-6	58
1991	04	13	111	27	-6	57
1991	04	14	111	28	-6	56
1991	04	15	111	30	-6	56
1991	04	16	111	32	-6	55
1991	04	17	111	35	-6	54
1991	04	18	111	37	-6	54
1991	04	19	111	39	-6	53
1991	04	20	111	42	-6	52
1991	04	21	111	44	-6	52
1991	04	22	111	47	-6	51
1991	04	23	111	49	-6	50
1991	04	24	111	52	-6	50
1991	04	25	111	55	-6	49
1991	04	26	111	58	-6	49
1991	04	27	112	01	-6	48
1991	04	28	112	04	-6	47
1991	04	29	112	07	-6	47
1991	04	30	112	11	-6	46
1991	05	01	112	14	-6	46
1991	05	02	112	17	-6	45
1991	05	03	112	21	-6	44
1991	05	04	112	24	-6	44
1991	05	05	112	28	-6	43
1991	05	06	112	32	-6	43
1991	05	07	112	36	-6	42
1991	05	08	112	40	-6	41
1991	05	09	112	44	-6	41
1991	05	10	112	48	-6	40
1991	05	11	112	52	-6	40
1991	05	12	112	56	-6	39
1991	05	13	113	00	-6	39
1991	05	14	113	05	-6	38
1991	05	15	113	09	-6	38
1991	05	16	113	14	-6	37
1991	05	17	113	18	-6	37
1991	05	18	113	23	-6	36
1991	05	19	113	27	-6	36
1991	05	20	113	32	-6	35
1991	05	21	113	37	-6	35
1991	05	22	113	42	-6	34
1991	05	23	113	47	-6	34
1991	05	24	113	52	-6	33
1991	05	25	113	57	-6	33
1991	05	26	114	02	-6	32
1991	05	27	114	07	-6	32
1991	05	28	114	13	-6	31
1991	05	29	114	18	-6	31
1991	05	30	114	23	-6	31
1991	05	31	114	29	-6	30
1991	06	01	114	34	-6	30
1991	06	02	114	40	-6	29
1991	06	03	114	45	-6	29
1991	06	04	114	51	-6	29
1991	06	05	114	56	-6	28
1991	06	06	115	02	-6	28
1991	06	07	115	08	-6	27
1991	06	08	115	14	-6	27
1991	06	09	115	20	-6	27
1991	06	10	115	26	-6	26
1991	06	11	115	32	-6	26
1991	06	12	115	38	-6	26
1991	06	13	115	44	-6	25
1991	06	14	115	50	-6	25
1991	06	15	115	56	-6	25
1991	06	16	116	02	-6	24
1991	06	17	116	08	-6	24
1991	06	18	116	14	-6	24
1991	06	19	116	21	-6	24
1991	06	20	116	27	-6	23
1991	06	21	116	33	-6	23
1991	06	22	116	40	-6	23
1991	06	23	116	46	-6	22
1991	06	24	116	53	-6	22
1991	06	25	116	59	-6	22
1991	06	26	117	06	-6	22
1991	06	27	117	12	-6	22
1991	06	28	117	19	-6	21
1991	06	29	117	25	-6	21
1991	06	30	117	32	-6	21
1991	07	01	117	39	-6	21
1991	07	02	117	45	-6	21
1991	07	03	117	52	-6	20
1991	07	04	117	59	-6	20
1991	07	05	118	05	-6	20
1991	07	06	118	12	-6	20
1991	07	07	118	19	-6	20
1991	07	08	118	26	-6	20
1991	07	09	118	33	-6	19
1991	07	10	118	40	-6	19
1991	07	11	118	46	-6	19
1991	07	12	118	53	-6	19
1991	07	13	119	00	-6	19
1991	07	14	119	07	-6	19
1991	07	15	119	14	-6	19
1991	07	16	119	21	-6	19
1991	07	17	119	28	-6	19
1991	07	18	119	35	-6	19
1991	07	19	119	42	-6	19
1991	07	20	119	49	-6	19
1991	07	21	119	56	-6	19
1991	07	22	120	02	-6	19
1991	07	23	120	09	-6	19
1991	07	24	120	16	-6	19
1991	07	25	120	23	-6	19
1991	07	26	120	30	-6	19
1991	07	27	120	37	-6	19
1991	07	28	120	44	-6	19
1991	07	29	120	51	-6	19
1991	07	30	120	58	-6	19
1991	07	31	121	05	-6	19
1991	08	01	121	12	-6	19
1991	08	02	121	19	-6	19
1991	08	03	121	26	-6	19
1991	08	04	121	33	-6	19
1991	08	05	121	40	-6	19
1991	08	06	121	47	-6	19
1991	08	07	121	54	-6	19
1991	08	08	122	01	-6	19
1991	08	09	122	07	-6	20
1991	08	10	122	14	-6	20
1991	08	11	122	21	-6	20
1991	08	12	122	28	-6	20
1991	08	13	122	35	-6	20
1991	08	14	122	42	-6	20
1991	08	15	122	48	-6	20
1991	08	16	122	55	-6	21
1991	08	17	123	02	-6	21
1991	08	18	123	09	-6	21
1991	08	19	123	15	-6	21
1991	08	20	123	22	-6	21
1991	08	21	123	29	-6	22
1991	08	22	123	35	-6	22
1991	08	23	123	42	-6	22
1991	08	24	123	48	-6	22
1991	08	25	123	55	-6	23
1991	08	26	124	01	-6	23
1991	08	27	124	08	-6	23
1991	08	28	124	14	-6	23
1991	08	29	124	21	-6	24
1991	08	30	124	27	-6	24
1991	08	31	124	33	-6	24
1991	09	01	124	40	-6	25
1991	09	02	124	46	-6	25
1991	09	03	124	52	-6	25
1991	09	04	124	58	-6	25
1991	09	05	125	04	-6	26
1991	09	06	125	11	-6	26
1991	09	07	125	17	-6	27
1991	09	08	125	23	-6	27
1991	09	09	125	29	-6	27
1991	09	10	125	35	-6	28
1991	09	11	125	40	-6	28
1991	09	12	125	46	-6	28
1991	09	13	125	52	-6	29
1991	09	14	125	58	-6	29
1991	09	15	126	03	-6	30
1991	09	16	126	09	-6	30
1991	09	17	126	15	-6	30
1991	09	18	126	20	-6	31
1991	09	19	126	26	-6	31
1991	09	20	126	31	-6	32
1991	09	21	126	36	-6	32
1991	09	22	126	42	-6	33
1991	09	23	126	47	-6	33
1991	09	24	126	52	-6	34
1991	09	25	126	57	-6	34
1991	09	26	127	02	-6	35
1991	09	27	127	07	-6	35
1991	09	28	127	12	-6	36
1991	09	29	127	17	-6	36
1991	09	30	127	22	-6	37
1991	10	01	127	26	-6	37
1991	10	02	127	31	-6	38
1991	10	03	127	36	-6	38
1991	10	04	127	40	-6	39
1991	10	05	127	45	-6	39
1991	10	06	127	49	-6	40
1991	10	07	127	53	-6	40
1991	10	08	127	57	-6	41
1991	10	09	128	02	-6	42
1991	10	10	128	06	-6	42
1991	10	11	128	10	-6	43
1991	10	12	128	13	-6	43
1991	10	13	128	17	-6	44
1991	10	14	128	21	-6	44
1991	10	15	128	25	-6	45
1991	10	16	128	28	-6	46
1991	10	17	128	32	-6	46
1991	10	18	128	35	-6	47
1991	10	19	128	38	-6	48
1991	10	20	128	42	-6	48
1991	10	21	128	45	-6	49
1991	10	22	128	48	-6	49
1991	10	23	128	51	-6	50
1991	10	24	128	54	-6	51
1991	10	25	128	57	-6	51
1991	10	26	128	59	-6	52
1991	10	27	129	02	-6	53
1991	10	28	129	04	-6	53
1991	10	29	129	07	-6	54
1991	10	30	129	09	-6	55
1991	10	31	129	11	-6	55
1991	11	01	129	14	-6	56
1991	11	02	129	16	-6	57
1991	11	03	129	18	-6	57
1991	11	04	129	19	-6	58
1991	11	05	129	21	-6	59
1991	11	06	129	23	-6	59
1991	11	07	129	24	-7	00
1991	11	08	129	26	-7	01
1991	11	09	129	27	-7	01
1991	11	10	129	29	-7	02
1991	11	11	129	30	-7	03
1991	11	12	129	31	-7	04
1991	11	13	129	32	-7	04
1991	11	14	129	33	-7	05
1991	11	15	129	33	-7	06
1991	11	16	129	34	-7	06
1991	11	17	129	35	-7	07
1991	11	18	129	35	-7	08
1991	11	19	129	35	-7	08
1991	11	20	129	36	-7	09
1991	11	21	129	36	-7	10
1991	11	22	129	36	-7	10
1991	11	23	129	36	-7	11
1991	11	24	129	36	-7	12
1991	11	25	129	35	-7	12
1991	11	26	129	35	-7	13
1991	11	27	129	35	-7	14
1991	11	28	129	34	-7	14
1991	11	29	129	33	-7	15
1991	11	30	129	33	-7	16
1991	12	01	129	32	-7	16
1991	12	02	129	31	-7	17
1991	12	03	129	30	-7	18
1991	12	04	129	28	-7	18
1991	12	05	129	27	-7	19
1991	12	06	129	26	-7	20
1991	12	07	129	24	-7	20
1991	12	08	129	23	-7	21
1991	12	09	129	21	-7	22
1991	12	10	129	19	-7	22
1991	12	11	129	18	-7	23
1991	12	12	129	16	-7	23
1991	12	13	129	14	-7	24
1991	12	14	129	11	-7	24
1991	12	15	129	09	-7	25
1991	12	16	129	07	-7	26
1991	12	17	129	04	-7	26
1991	12	18	129	02	-7	27
1991	12	19	128	59	-7	27
1991	12	20	128	57	-7	28
1991	12	21	128	54	-7	28
1991	12	22	128	51	-7	29
1991	12	23	128	48	-7	29
1991	12	24	128	45	-7	30
1991	12	25	128	42	-7	30
1991	12	26	128	39	-7	31
1991	12	27	128	36	-7	31
1991	12	28	128	33	-7	31

1991 12 29	128 29	-7 32
1991 12 30	128 26	-7 32
1991 12 31	128 23	-7 33
1992 01 01	128 19	-7 33
1992 01 02	128 15	-7 33
1992 01 03	128 12	-7 34
1992 01 04	128 08	-7 34
1992 01 05	128 04	-7 35
1992 01 06	128 00	-7 35
1992 01 07	127 56	-7 35
1992 01 08	127 52	-7 35
1992 01 09	127 48	-7 36
1992 01 10	127 44	-7 36
1992 01 11	127 40	-7 36
1992 01 12	127 36	-7 36
1992 01 13	127 32	-7 37
1992 01 14	127 28	-7 37
1992 01 15	127 24	-7 37
1992 01 16	127 19	-7 37
1992 01 17	127 15	-7 37
1992 01 18	127 11	-7 37
1992 01 19	127 06	-7 38
1992 01 20	127 02	-7 38
1992 01 21	126 58	-7 38
1992 01 22	126 53	-7 38
1992 01 23	126 49	-7 38
1992 01 24	126 44	-7 38
1992 01 25	126 40	-7 38
1992 01 26	126 35	-7 38
1992 01 27	126 31	-7 38
1992 01 28	126 26	-7 38
1992 01 29	126 22	-7 38
1992 01 30	126 17	-7 38
1992 01 31	126 13	-7 38
1992 02 01	126 09	-7 38
1992 02 02	126 04	-7 38
1992 02 03	126 00	-7 37
1992 02 04	125 55	-7 37
1992 02 05	125 51	-7 37
1992 02 06	125 47	-7 37
1992 02 07	125 42	-7 37
1992 02 08	125 38	-7 37
1992 02 09	125 34	-7 36
1992 02 10	125 29	-7 36
1992 02 11	125 25	-7 36
1992 02 12	125 21	-7 36
1992 02 13	125 17	-7 35
1992 02 14	125 13	-7 35
1992 02 15	125 08	-7 35
1992 02 16	125 04	-7 34
1992 02 17	125 00	-7 34
1992 02 18	124 57	-7 34
1992 02 19	124 53	-7 33
1992 02 20	124 49	-7 33
1992 02 21	124 45	-7 33
1992 02 22	124 41	-7 32
1992 02 23	124 38	-7 32
1992 02 24	124 34	-7 31
1992 02 25	124 30	-7 31
1992 02 26	124 27	-7 30
1992 02 27	124 24	-7 30
1992 02 28	124 20	-7 29
1992 02 29	124 17	-7 29
1992 03 01	124 14	-7 28
1992 03 02	124 11	-7 28
1992 03 03	124 08	-7 27
1992 03 04	124 05	-7 27
1992 03 05	124 02	-7 26
1992 03 06	123 59	-7 26
1992 03 07	123 56	-7 25
1992 03 08	123 54	-7 25
1992 03 09	123 51	-7 24
1992 03 10	123 49	-7 23
1992 03 11	123 46	-7 23
1992 03 12	123 44	-7 22
1992 03 13	123 42	-7 22
1992 03 14	123 40	-7 21
1992 03 15	123 38	-7 20
1992 03 16	123 36	-7 20
1992 03 17	123 34	-7 19
1992 03 18	123 32	-7 18
1992 03 19	123 30	-7 18
1992 03 20	123 29	-7 17
1992 03 21	123 27	-7 16
1992 03 22	123 26	-7 16
1992 03 23	123 25	-7 15
1992 03 24	123 24	-7 14
1992 03 25	123 23	-7 13
1992 03 26	123 22	-7 13
1992 03 27	123 21	-7 12
1992 03 28	123 20	-7 11
1992 03 29	123 19	-7 11
1992 03 30	123 19	-7 10
1992 03 31	123 18	-7 09
1992 04 01	123 18	-7 08
1992 04 02	123 18	-7 08
1992 04 03	123 17	-7 07
1992 04 04	123 17	-7 06
1992 04 05	123 17	-7 05
1992 04 06	123 18	-7 05
1992 04 07	123 18	-7 04
1992 04 08	123 18	-7 03
1992 04 09	123 19	-7 02
1992 04 10	123 19	-7 02
1992 04 11	123 20	-7 01
1992 04 12	123 21	-7 00

1992 04 13	123 22	-6 59
1992 04 14	123 23	-6 59
1992 04 15	123 24	-6 58
1992 04 16	123 25	-6 57
1992 04 17	123 26	-6 56
1992 04 18	123 27	-6 56
1992 04 19	123 29	-6 55
1992 04 20	123 31	-6 54
1992 04 21	123 32	-6 53
1992 04 22	123 34	-6 53
1992 04 23	123 36	-6 52
1992 04 24	123 38	-6 51
1992 04 25	123 40	-6 50
1992 04 26	123 42	-6 50
1992 04 27	123 44	-6 49
1992 04 28	123 47	-6 48
1992 04 29	123 49	-6 48
1992 04 30	123 52	-6 47
1992 05 01	123 54	-6 46
1992 05 02	123 57	-6 45
1992 05 03	124 00	-6 45
1992 05 04	124 03	-6 44
1992 05 05	124 06	-6 43
1992 05 06	124 09	-6 43
1992 05 07	124 12	-6 42
1992 05 08	124 15	-6 41
1992 05 09	124 19	-6 40
1992 05 10	124 22	-6 40
1992 05 11	124 26	-6 39
1992 05 12	124 29	-6 38
1992 05 13	124 33	-6 38
1992 05 14	124 37	-6 37
1992 05 15	124 41	-6 36
1992 05 16	124 45	-6 36
1992 05 17	124 49	-6 35
1992 05 18	124 53	-6 34
1992 05 19	124 57	-6 34
1992 05 20	125 02	-6 33
1992 05 21	125 06	-6 33
1992 05 22	125 10	-6 32
1992 05 23	125 15	-6 31
1992 05 24	125 20	-6 31
1992 05 25	125 24	-6 30
1992 05 26	125 29	-6 29
1992 05 27	125 34	-6 29
1992 05 28	125 39	-6 28
1992 05 29	125 44	-6 28
1992 05 30	125 49	-6 27
1992 05 31	125 54	-6 27
1992 06 01	125 59	-6 26
1992 06 02	126 04	-6 25
1992 06 03	126 10	-6 25
1992 06 04	126 15	-6 24
1992 06 05	126 20	-6 24
1992 06 06	126 26	-6 23
1992 06 07	126 31	-6 23
1992 06 08	126 37	-6 22
1992 06 09	126 43	-6 22
1992 06 10	126 49	-6 21
1992 06 11	126 54	-6 21
1992 06 12	127 00	-6 20
1992 06 13	127 06	-6 20
1992 06 14	127 12	-6 19
1992 06 15	127 18	-6 19
1992 06 16	127 24	-6 18
1992 06 17	127 30	-6 18
1992 06 18	127 37	-6 17
1992 06 19	127 43	-6 17
1992 06 20	127 49	-6 17
1992 06 21	127 55	-6 16
1992 06 22	128 02	-6 16
1992 06 23	128 08	-6 15
1992 06 24	128 15	-6 15
1992 06 25	128 21	-6 15
1992 06 26	128 28	-6 14
1992 06 27	128 35	-6 14
1992 06 28	128 41	-6 13
1992 06 29	128 48	-6 13
1992 06 30	128 55	-6 13
1992 07 01	129 01	-6 12
1992 07 02	129 08	-6 12
1992 07 03	129 15	-6 12
1992 07 04	129 22	-6 11
1992 07 05	129 29	-6 11
1992 07 06	129 36	-6 11
1992 07 07	129 43	-6 10
1992 07 08	129 50	-6 10
1992 07 09	129 57	-6 10
1992 07 10	130 04	-6 10
1992 07 11	130 11	-6 09
1992 07 12	130 18	-6 09
1992 07 13	130 25	-6 09
1992 07 14	130 33	-6 09
1992 07 15	130 40	-6 08
1992 07 16	130 47	-6 08
1992 07 17	130 54	-6 08
1992 07 18	131 02	-6 08
1992 07 19	131 09	-6 07
1992 07 20	131 16	-6 07
1992 07 21	131 24	-6 07
1992 07 22	131 31	-6 07
1992 07 23	131 38	-6 07
1992 07 24	131 46	-6 07
1992 07 25	131 53	-6 06
1992 07 26	132 01	-6 06
1992 07 27	132 08	-6 06

1992 07 28	132 16	-6 06
1992 07 29	132 23	-6 06
1992 07 30	132 30	-6 06
1992 07 31	132 38	-6 06
1992 08 01	132 45	-6 06
1992 08 02	132 53	-6 05
1992 08 03	133 00	-6 05
1992 08 04	133 08	-6 05
1992 08 05	133 16	-6 05
1992 08 06	133 23	-6 05
1992 08 07	133 31	-6 05
1992 08 08	133 38	-6 05
1992 08 09	133 46	-6 05
1992 08 10	133 53	-6 05
1992 08 11	134 01	-6 05
1992 08 12	134 08	-6 05
1992 08 13	134 16	-6 05
1992 08 14	134 23	-6 05
1992 08 15	134 31	-6 05
1992 08 16	134 38	-6 05
1992 08 17	134 46	-6 05
1992 08 18	134 53	-6 05
1992 08 19	135 01	-6 05
1992 08 20	135 08	-6 05
1992 08 21	135 15	-6 05
1992 08 22	135 23	-6 05
1992 08 23	135 30	-6 05
1992 08 24	135 38	-6 05
1992 08 25	135 45	-6 06
1992 08 26	135 52	-6 06
1992 08 27	136 00	-6 06
1992 08 28	136 07	-6 06
1992 08 29	136 14	-6 06
1992 08 30	136 22	-6 06
1992 08 31	136 29	-6 06
1992 09 01	136 36	-6 06
1992 09 02	136 43	-6 07
1992 09 03	136 51	-6 07
1992 09 04	136 58	-6 07
1992 09 05	137 05	-6 07
1992 09 06	137 12	-6 07
1992 09 07	137 19	-6 08
1992 09 08	137 26	-6 08
1992 09 09	137 33	-6 08
1992 09 10	137 40	-6 08
1992 09 11	137 47	-6 08
1992 09 12	137 54	-6 09
1992 09 13	138 01	-6 09
1992 09 14	138 07	-6 09
1992 09 15	138 14	-6 09
1992 09 16	138 21	-6 10
1992 09 17	138 28	-6 10
1992 09 18	138 34	-6 10
1992 09 19	138 41	-6 11
1992 09 20	138 48	-6 11
1992 09 21	138 54	-6 11
1992 09 22	139 01	-6 11
1992 09 23	139 07	-6 12
1992 09 24	139 13	-6 12
1992 09 25	139 20	-6 12
1992 09 26	139 26	-6 13
1992 09 27	139 32	-6 13
1992 09 28	139 38	-6 14
1992 09 29	139 44	-6 14
1992 09 30	139 51	-6 14
1992 10 01	139 57	-6 15
1992 10 02	140 02	-6 15
1992 10 03	140 08	-6 15
1992 10 04	140 14	-6 16
1992 10 05	140 20	-6 16
1992 10 06	140 26	-6 17
1992 10 07	140 31	-6 17
1992 10 08	140 37	-6 18
1992 10 09	140 42	-6 18
1992 10 10	140 48	-6 18
1992 10 11	140 53	-6 19
1992 10 12	140 58	-6 19
1992 10 13	141 04	-6 20
1992 10 14	141 09	-6 20
1992 10 15	141 14	-6 21
1992 10 16	141 19	-6 21
1992 10 17	141 24	-6 22
1992 10 18	141 29	-6 22
1992 10 19	141 34	-6 23
1992 10 20	141 38	-6 23
1992 10 21	141 43	-6 24
1992 10 22	141 47	-6 24
1992 10 23	141 52	-6 25
1992 10 24	141 56	-6 25
1992 10 25	142 01	-6 26
1992 10 26	142 05	-6 26
1992 10 27	142 09	-6 27
1992 10 28	142 13	-6 27
1992 10 29	142 17	-6 28
1992 10 30	142 21	-6 29
1992 10 31	142 25	-6 29
1992 11 01	142 28	-6 30
1992 11 02	142 32	-6 30
1992 11 03	142 35	-6 31
1992 11 04	142 39	-6 31
1992 11 05	142 42	-6 32
1992 11 06	142 45	-6 33
1992 11 07	142 48	-6 33
1992 11 08	142 52	-6 34
1992 11 09	142 54	-6 34
1992 11 10	142 57	-6 35

1992 11 11	143 00	-6 36
1992 11 12	143 03	-6 36
1992 11 13	143 05	-6 37
1992 11 14	143 08	-6 37
1992 11 15	143 10	-6 38
1992 11 16	143 12	-6 39
1992 11 17	143 14	-6 39
1992 11 18	143 16	-6 40
1992 11 19	143 18	-6 41
1992 11 20	143 20	-6 41
1992 11 21	143 22	-6 42
1992 11 22	143 24	-6 43
1992 11 23	143 25	-6 43
1992 11 24	143 26	-6 44
1992 11 25	143 28	-6 44
1992 11 26	143 29	-6 45
1992 11 27	143 30	-6 46
1992 11 28	143 31	-6 46
1992 11 29	143 32	-6 47
1992 11 30	143 33	-6 48
1992 12 01	143 33	-6 48
1992 12 02	143 34	-6 49
1992 12 03	143 34	-6 49
1992 12 04	143 34	-6 50
1992 12 05	143 35	-6 51
1992 12 06	143 35	-6 51
1992 12 07	143 35	-6 52
1992 12 08	143 35	-6 53
1992 12 09	143 34	-6 53
1992 12 10	143 34	-6 54
1992 12 11	143 34	-6 54
1992 12 12	143 33	-6 55
1992 12 13	143 32	-6 56
1992 12 14	143 32	-6 56
1992 12 15	143 31	-6 57
1992 12 16	143 30	-6 57
1992 12 17	143 29	-6 58
1992 12 18	143 27	-6 59
1992 12 19	143 26	-6 59
1992 12 20	143 25	-7 00
1992 12 21	143 23	-7 00
1992 12 22	143 22	-7 01
1992 12 23	143 20	-7 01
1992 12 24	143 18	-7 02
1992 12 25	143 16	-7 02
1992 12 26	143 14	-7 03
1992 12 27	143 12	-7 03
1992 12 28	143 10	-7 04
1992 12 29	143 08	-7 04
1992 12 30	143 05	-7 05
1992 12 31	143 03	-7 05
1993 01 01	143 00	-7 06
1993 01 02	142 57	-7 06
1993 01 03	142 55	-7 07
1993 01 04	142 52	-7 07
1993 01 05	142 49	-7 08
1993 01 06	142 46	-7 08
1993 01 07	142 43	-7 08
1993 01 08	142 40	-7 09
1993 01 09	142 36	-7 09
1993 01 10	142 33	-7 10
1993 01 11	142 30	-7 10
1993 01 12	142 26	-7 10
1993 01 13	142 22	-7 11
1993 01 14	142 19	-7 11
1993 01 15	142 15	-7 11
1993 01 16	142 11	-7 12
1993 01 17	142 08	-7 12
1993 01 18	142 04	-7 12
1993 01 19	142 00	-7 12
1993 01 20	141 56	-7 13
1993 01 21	141 52	-7 13
1993 01 22	141 48	-7 13
1993 01 23	141 43	-7 13
1993 01 24	141 39	-7 13
1993 01 25	141 35	-7 14
1993 01 26	141 31	-7 14
1993 01 27	141 26	-7 14
1993 01 28	141 22	-7 14
1993 01 29	141 17	-7 14
1993 01 30	141 13	-7 14
1993 01 31	141 09	-7 14
1993 02 01	141 04	-7 14
1993 02 02	141 00	-7 14
1993 02 03	140 55	-7 14
1993 02 04	140 50	-7 14
1993 02 05	140 46	-7 14
1993 02 06	140 41	-7 14
1993 02 07	140 37	-7 14
1993 02 08	140 32	-7 14
1993 02 09	140 27	-7 14
1993 02 10	140 23	-7 14
1993 02 11	140 18	-7 14
1993 02 12	140 14	-7 14
1993 02 13	140 09	-7 13
1993 02 14	140 04	-7 13
1993 02 15	140 00	-7 13
1993 02 16	139 55	-7 13
1993 02 17	139 51	-7 13
1993 02 18	139 46	-7 12
1993 02 19	139 42	-7 12
1993 02 20	139 37	-7 12

1993	02	21	139	33	-7	12
1993	02	22	139	28	-7	11
1993	02	23	139	24	-7	11
1993	02	24	139	19	-7	11
1993	02	25	139	15	-7	10
1993	02	26	139	11	-7	10
1993	02	27	139	07	-7	10
1993	02	28	139	02	-7	09
1993	03	01	138	58	-7	09
1993	03	02	138	54	-7	08
1993	03	03	138	50	-7	08
1993	03	04	138	46	-7	08
1993	03	05	138	42	-7	07
1993	03	06	138	38	-7	07
1993	03	07	138	34	-7	06
1993	03	08	138	31	-7	06
1993	03	09	138	27	-7	05
1993	03	10	138	23	-7	05
1993	03	11	138	20	-7	04
1993	03	12	138	16	-7	04
1993	03	13	138	13	-7	03
1993	03	14	138	10	-7	02
1993	03	15	138	06	-7	02
1993	03	16	138	03	-7	01
1993	03	17	138	00	-7	01
1993	03	18	137	57	-7	00
1993	03	19	137	54	-6	59
1993	03	20	137	51	-6	59
1993	03	21	137	49	-6	58
1993	03	22	137	46	-6	57
1993	03	23	137	43	-6	57
1993	03	24	137	41	-6	56
1993	03	25	137	38	-6	55
1993	03	26	137	36	-6	55
1993	03	27	137	34	-6	54
1993	03	28	137	32	-6	53
1993	03	29	137	30	-6	53
1993	03	30	137	28	-6	52
1993	03	31	137	26	-6	51
1993	04	01	137	24	-6	50
1993	04	02	137	23	-6	50
1993	04	03	137	21	-6	49
1993	04	04	137	20	-6	48
1993	04	05	137	18	-6	47
1993	04	06	137	17	-6	47
1993	04	07	137	16	-6	46
1993	04	08	137	15	-6	45
1993	04	09	137	14	-6	44
1993	04	10	137	14	-6	43
1993	04	11	137	13	-6	43
1993	04	12	137	12	-6	42
1993	04	13	137	12	-6	41
1993	04	14	137	11	-6	40
1993	04	15	137	11	-6	40
1993	04	16	137	11	-6	39
1993	04	17	137	11	-6	38
1993	04	18	137	11	-6	37
1993	04	19	137	11	-6	36
1993	04	20	137	11	-6	35
1993	04	21	137	12	-6	35
1993	04	22	137	12	-6	34
1993	04	23	137	13	-6	33
1993	04	24	137	14	-6	32
1993	04	25	137	14	-6	31
1993	04	26	137	15	-6	31
1993	04	27	137	16	-6	30
1993	04	28	137	18	-6	29
1993	04	29	137	19	-6	28
1993	04	30	137	20	-6	27
1993	05	01	137	22	-6	27
1993	05	02	137	23	-6	26
1993	05	03	137	25	-6	25
1993	05	04	137	27	-6	24
1993	05	05	137	29	-6	23
1993	05	06	137	31	-6	22
1993	05	07	137	33	-6	22
1993	05	08	137	35	-6	21
1993	05	09	137	37	-6	20
1993	05	10	137	40	-6	19
1993	05	11	137	42	-6	19
1993	05	12	137	45	-6	18
1993	05	13	137	47	-6	17
1993	05	14	137	50	-6	16
1993	05	15	137	53	-6	15
1993	05	16	137	56	-6	15
1993	05	17	137	59	-6	14
1993	05	18	138	02	-6	13
1993	05	19	138	06	-6	12
1993	05	20	138	09	-6	12
1993	05	21	138	12	-6	11
1993	05	22	138	16	-6	10
1993	05	23	138	20	-6	09
1993	05	24	138	23	-6	09
1993	05	25	138	27	-6	08
1993	05	26	138	31	-6	07
1993	05	27	138	35	-6	06
1993	05	28	138	39	-6	06
1993	05	29	138	43	-6	05
1993	05	30	138	48	-6	04
1993	05	31	138	52	-6	03
1993	06	01	138	57	-6	03
1993	06	02	139	01	-6	02
1993	06	03	139	06	-6	01
1993	06	04	139	10	-6	01
1993	06	05	139	15	-6	00
1993	06	06	139	20	-5	59
1993	06	07	139	25	-5	59
1993	06	08	139	30	-5	58
1993	06	09	139	35	-5	57
1993	06	10	139	40	-5	57
1993	06	11	139	46	-5	56
1993	06	12	139	51	-5	55
1993	06	13	139	56	-5	55
1993	06	14	140	02	-5	54
1993	06	15	140	07	-5	53
1993	06	16	140	13	-5	53
1993	06	17	140	19	-5	52
1993	06	18	140	24	-5	52
1993	06	19	140	30	-5	51
1993	06	20	140	36	-5	50
1993	06	21	140	42	-5	50
1993	06	22	140	48	-5	49
1993	06	23	140	54	-5	49
1993	06	24	141	00	-5	48
1993	06	25	141	07	-5	48
1993	06	26	141	13	-5	47
1993	06	27	141	19	-5	47
1993	06	28	141	26	-5	46
1993	06	29	141	32	-5	45
1993	06	30	141	38	-5	45
1993	07	01	141	45	-5	44
1993	07	02	141	52	-5	44
1993	07	03	141	58	-5	43
1993	07	04	142	05	-5	43
1993	07	05	142	12	-5	42
1993	07	06	142	19	-5	42
1993	07	07	142	26	-5	42
1993	07	08	142	32	-5	41
1993	07	09	142	39	-5	41
1993	07	10	142	46	-5	40
1993	07	11	142	53	-5	40
1993	07	12	143	01	-5	39
1993	07	13	143	08	-5	39
1993	07	14	143	15	-5	38
1993	07	15	143	22	-5	38
1993	07	16	143	29	-5	38
1993	07	17	143	37	-5	37
1993	07	18	143	44	-5	37
1993	07	19	143	52	-5	36
1993	07	20	143	59	-5	36
1993	07	21	144	06	-5	36
1993	07	22	144	14	-5	35
1993	07	23	144	21	-5	35
1993	07	24	144	29	-5	35
1993	07	25	144	37	-5	34
1993	07	26	144	44	-5	34
1993	07	27	144	52	-5	34
1993	07	28	145	00	-5	33
1993	07	29	145	07	-5	33
1993	07	30	145	15	-5	33
1993	07	31	145	23	-5	32
1993	08	01	145	31	-5	32
1993	08	02	145	38	-5	32
1993	08	03	145	46	-5	32
1993	08	04	145	54	-5	31
1993	08	05	146	02	-5	31
1993	08	06	146	10	-5	31
1993	08	07	146	18	-5	31
1993	08	08	146	26	-5	30
1993	08	09	146	34	-5	30
1993	08	10	146	42	-5	30
1993	08	11	146	50	-5	30
1993	08	12	146	58	-5	30
1993	08	13	147	06	-5	29
1993	08	14	147	14	-5	29
1993	08	15	147	22	-5	29
1993	08	16	147	30	-5	29
1993	08	17	147	38	-5	29
1993	08	18	147	46	-5	28
1993	08	19	147	54	-5	28
1993	08	20	148	02	-5	28
1993	08	21	148	10	-5	28
1993	08	22	148	18	-5	28
1993	08	23	148	26	-5	28
1993	08	24	148	34	-5	28
1993	08	25	148	42	-5	28
1993	08	26	148	50	-5	27
1993	08	27	148	58	-5	27
1993	08	28	149	06	-5	27
1993	08	29	149	14	-5	27
1993	08	30	149	22	-5	27
1993	08	31	149	30	-5	27
1993	09	01	149	38	-5	27
1993	09	02	149	46	-5	27
1993	09	03	149	54	-5	27
1993	09	04	150	02	-5	27
1993	09	05	150	10	-5	27
1993	09	06	150	18	-5	27
1993	09	07	150	26	-5	27
1993	09	08	150	34	-5	27
1993	09	09	150	42	-5	27
1993	09	10	150	50	-5	27
1993	09	11	150	58	-5	27
1993	09	12	151	06	-5	27
1993	09	13	151	14	-5	27
1993	09	14	151	21	-5	27
1993	09	15	151	29	-5	27
1993	09	16	151	37	-5	27
1993	09	17	151	45	-5	27
1993	09	18	151	52	-5	27
1993	09	19	152	00	-5	27
1993	09	20	152	08	-5	28
1993	09	21	152	15	-5	28
1993	09	22	152	23	-5	28
1993	09	23	152	31	-5	28
1993	09	24	152	38	-5	28
1993	09	25	152	46	-5	28
1993	09	26	152	53	-5	28
1993	09	27	153	01	-5	28
1993	09	28	153	08	-5	29
1993	09	29	153	15	-5	29
1993	09	30	153	23	-5	29
1993	10	01	153	30	-5	29
1993	10	02	153	37	-5	29
1993	10	03	153	44	-5	29
1993	10	04	153	51	-5	30
1993	10	05	153	59	-5	30
1993	10	06	154	06	-5	30
1993	10	07	154	13	-5	30
1993	10	08	154	20	-5	30
1993	10	09	154	26	-5	31
1993	10	10	154	33	-5	31
1993	10	11	154	40	-5	31
1993	10	12	154	47	-5	31
1993	10	13	154	54	-5	32
1993	10	14	155	00	-5	32
1993	10	15	155	07	-5	32
1993	10	16	155	13	-5	32
1993	10	17	155	20	-5	33
1993	10	18	155	26	-5	33
1993	10	19	155	32	-5	33
1993	10	20	155	39	-5	34
1993	10	21	155	45	-5	34
1993	10	22	155	51	-5	34
1993	10	23	155	57	-5	34
1993	10	24	156	03	-5	35
1993	10	25	156	09	-5	35
1993	10	26	156	15	-5	35
1993	10	27	156	21	-5	36
1993	10	28	156	26	-5	36
1993	10	29	156	32	-5	37
1993	10	30	156	37	-5	37
1993	10	31	156	43	-5	37
1993	11	01	156	48	-5	38
1993	11	02	156	54	-5	38
1993	11	03	156	59	-5	38
1993	11	04	157	04	-5	39
1993	11	05	157	09	-5	39
1993	11	06	157	14	-5	40
1993	11	07	157	19	-5	40
1993	11	08	157	24	-5	40
1993	11	09	157	29	-5	41
1993	11	10	157	33	-5	41
1993	11	11	157	38	-5	42
1993	11	12	157	42	-5	42
1993	11	13	157	47	-5	42
1993	11	14	157	51	-5	43
1993	11	15	157	55	-5	43
1993	11	16	157	59	-5	44
1993	11	17	158	03	-5	44
1993	11	18	158	07	-5	45
1993	11	19	158	11	-5	45
1993	11	20	158	15	-5	46
1993	11	21	158	18	-5	46
1993	11	22	158	22	-5	47
1993	11	23	158	25	-5	47
1993	11	24	158	29	-5	47
1993	11	25	158	32	-5	48
1993	11	26	158	35	-5	48
1993	11	27	158	38	-5	49
1993	11	28	158	41	-5	49
1993	11	29	158	44	-5	50
1993	11	30	158	46	-5	50
1993	12	01	158	49	-5	51
1993	12	02	158	51	-5	51
1993	12	03	158	54	-5	52
1993	12	04	158	56	-5	52
1993	12	05	158	58	-5	53
1993	12	06	159	00	-5	53
1993	12	07	159	02	-5	54
1993	12	08	159	04	-5	54
1993	12	09	159	06	-5	55
1993	12	10	159	07	-5	55
1993	12	11	159	09	-5	56
1993	12	12	159	10	-5	56
1993	12	13	159	11	-5	57
1993	12	14	159	12	-5	57
1993	12	15	159	13	-5	58
1993	12	16	159	14	-5	58
1993	12	17	159	15	-5	59
1993	12	18	159	16	-5	59
1993	12	19	159	16	-6	00
1993	12	20	159	17	-6	00
1993	12	21	159	17	-6	01
1993	12	22	159	17	-6	01
1993	12	23	159	17	-6	02
1993	12	24	159	17	-6	02
1993	12	25	159	17	-6	03
1993	12	26	159	17	-6	03
1993	12	27	159	17	-6	04
1993	12	28	159	16	-6	04
1993	12	29	159	16	-6	05
1993	12	30	159	15	-6	05
1993	12	31	159	14	-6	05
1994	01	01	159	13	-6	06
1994	01	02	159	12	-6	06
1994	01	03	159	11	-6	07
1994	01	04	159	10	-6	07
1994	01	05	159	08	-6	08
1994	01	06	159	07	-6	08
1994	01	07	159	05	-6	08
1994	01	08	159	04	-6	09
1994	01	09	159	02	-6	09
1994	01	10	159	00	-6	10
1994	01	11	158	58	-6	10
1994	01	12	158	56	-6	10
1994	01	13	158	54	-6	11
1994	01	14	158	51	-6	11
1994	01	15	158	49	-6	11
1994	01	16	158	46	-6	12
1994	01	17	158	44	-6	12
1994	01	18	158	41	-6	12
1994	01	19	158	38	-6	13
1994	01	20	158	35	-6	13
1994	01	21	158	32	-6	13
1994	01	22	158	29	-6	14
1994	01	23	158	26	-6	14
1994	01	24	158	23	-6	14
1994	01	25	158	20	-6	14
1994	01	26	158	16	-6	15
1994	01	27	158	13	-6	15
1994	01	28	158	09	-6	15
1994	01	29	158	05	-6	15
1994	01	30	158	02	-6	15
1994	01	31	157	58	-6	16
1994	02	01	157	54	-6	16
1994	02	02	157	50	-6	16
1994	02	03	157	46	-6	16
1994	02	04	157	42	-6	16
1994	02	05	157	38	-6	16
1994	02	06	157	34	-6	16
1994	02	07	157	30	-6	16
1994	02	08	157	25	-6	17
1994	02	09	157	21	-6	17
1994	02	10	157	17	-6	17
1994	02	11	157	12	-6	17
1994	02	12	157	08	-6	17
1994	02	13	157	03	-6	17
1994	02	14	156	59	-6	17
1994	02	15	156	54	-6	17
1994	02	16	156	50	-6	17
1994	02	17	156	45	-6	16
1994	02	18	156	41	-6	16
1994	02	19	156	36	-6	16
1994	02	20	156	31	-6	16
1994	02	21	156	27	-6	16
1994	02	22	156	22	-6	16
1994	02	23	156	17	-6	16
1994	02	24	156	12	-6	16
1994	02	25	156	08	-6	15
1994	02	26	156	03	-6	15
1994	02	27	155	58	-6	15
1994	02	28	155	54	-6	15
1994	03	01	155	49	-6	15
1994	03	02	155	44	-6	14
1994	03	03	155	40	-6	14
1994	03	04	155	35	-6	14
1994	03	05	155	30	-6	13
1994	03	06	155	26	-6	13
1994	03	07	155	21	-6	13
1994	03	08	155	16	-6	12
1994	03	09	155	12	-6	12
1994	03	10	155	07	-6	12
1994	03	11	155	03	-6	11
1994	03	12	154	58	-6	11
1994	03	13	154	54	-6	10
1994	03	14	154	50	-6	10
1994	03	15	154	45	-6	10
1994	03	16	154	41	-6	09
1994	03	17	154	37	-6	09
1994	03	18	154	33	-6	08
1994	03	19	154	29	-6	08
1994	03	20	154	24	-6	07
1994	03	21	154	21	-6	07
1994	03	22	154	17	-6	06
1994	03	23	154	13	-6	05
1994	03	24	154	09	-6	05
1994	03	25	154	05	-6	04
1994	03	26	154	02	-6	04
1994	03	27	153	58	-6	03
1994	03	28	153	54	-6	03
1994	03	29	153	51	-6	02
1994	03	30	153	48	-6	01
1994	03	31	153	44	-6	01
1994	04	01	153	41	-6	00
1994	04	02	153	38	-5	59
1994	04	03	153	35	-5	59
1994	04	04	153	32	-5	58
1994	04	05	153	29	-5	57
1994	04	06	153	27	-5	57
1994	04	07	153	24	-5	56
1994	04	08	153	21	-5	55
1994	04	09	153	19	-5	55
1994	04	10	153	17	-5	54
1994	04	11	153	14	-5	53
1994	04	12	153	12	-5	52
1994	04	13	153	10	-5	52
1994	04	14	153	08	-5	51
1994	04	15	153	06	-5	50
1994	04	16	153	04	-5	49

1994	04	17	153	03	-5	49
1994	04	18	153	01	-5	48
1994	04	19	153	00	-5	47
1994	04	20	152	58	-5	46
1994	04	21	152	57	-5	46
1994	04	22	152	56	-5	45
1994	04	23	152	55	-5	44
1994	04	24	152	54	-5	43
1994	04	25	152	53	-5	42
1994	04	26	152	53	-5	42
1994	04	27	152	52	-5	41
1994	04	28	152	52	-5	40
1994	04	29	152	51	-5	39
1994	04	30	152	51	-5	38
1994	05	01	152	51	-5	38
1994	05	02	152	51	-5	37
1994	05	03	152	51	-5	36
1994	05	04	152	51	-5	35
1994	05	05	152	51	-5	34
1994	05	06	152	52	-5	33
1994	05	07	152	52	-5	33
1994	05	08	152	53	-5	32
1994	05	09	152	54	-5	31
1994	05	10	152	55	-5	30
1994	05	11	152	56	-5	29
1994	05	12	152	57	-5	29
1994	05	13	152	58	-5	28
1994	05	14	152	59	-5	27
1994	05	15	153	01	-5	26
1994	05	16	153	02	-5	25
1994	05	17	153	04	-5	24
1994	05	18	153	06	-5	24
1994	05	19	153	07	-5	23
1994	05	20	153	09	-5	22
1994	05	21	153	11	-5	21
1994	05	22	153	14	-5	20
1994	05	23	153	16	-5	20
1994	05	24	153	18	-5	19
1994	05	25	153	21	-5	18
1994	05	26	153	23	-5	17
1994	05	27	153	26	-5	16
1994	05	28	153	29	-5	16
1994	05	29	153	32	-5	15
1994	05	30	153	35	-5	14
1994	05	31	153	38	-5	13
1994	06	01	153	41	-5	12
1994	06	02	153	45	-5	12
1994	06	03	153	48	-5	11
1994	06	04	153	52	-5	10
1994	06	05	153	55	-5	09
1994	06	06	153	59	-5	09
1994	06	07	154	03	-5	08
1994	06	08	154	07	-5	07
1994	06	09	154	11	-5	06
1994	06	10	154	15	-5	06
1994	06	11	154	19	-5	05
1994	06	12	154	23	-5	04
1994	06	13	154	28	-5	03
1994	06	14	154	32	-5	03
1994	06	15	154	37	-5	02
1994	06	16	154	41	-5	01
1994	06	17	154	46	-5	01
1994	06	18	154	51	-5	00
1994	06	19	154	56	-4	59
1994	06	20	155	01	-4	58
1994	06	21	155	06	-4	58
1994	06	22	155	11	-4	57
1994	06	23	155	16	-4	56
1994	06	24	155	22	-4	56
1994	06	25	155	27	-4	55
1994	06	26	155	32	-4	54
1994	06	27	155	38	-4	54
1994	06	28	155	44	-4	53
1994	06	29	155	49	-4	52
1994	06	30	155	55	-4	52
1994	07	01	156	01	-4	51
1994	07	02	156	07	-4	50
1994	07	03	156	13	-4	50
1994	07	04	156	19	-4	49
1994	07	05	156	25	-4	49
1994	07	06	156	31	-4	48
1994	07	07	156	38	-4	47
1994	07	08	156	44	-4	47
1994	07	09	156	50	-4	46
1994	07	10	156	57	-4	46
1994	07	11	157	03	-4	45
1994	07	12	157	10	-4	44
1994	07	13	157	17	-4	44
1994	07	14	157	24	-4	43
1994	07	15	157	30	-4	43
1994	07	16	157	37	-4	42
1994	07	17	157	44	-4	42
1994	07	18	157	51	-4	41
1994	07	19	157	58	-4	41
1994	07	20	158	05	-4	40
1994	07	21	158	12	-4	40
1994	07	22	158	20	-4	39
1994	07	23	158	27	-4	39
1994	07	24	158	34	-4	38
1994	07	25	158	41	-4	38
1994	07	26	158	49	-4	37
1994	07	27	158	56	-4	37
1994	07	28	159	04	-4	36
1994	07	29	159	11	-4	36
1994	07	30	159	19	-4	35
1994	07	31	159	26	-4	35

1994	08	01	159	34	-4	34
1994	08	02	159	42	-4	34
1994	08	03	159	50	-4	34
1994	08	04	159	57	-4	33
1994	08	05	160	05	-4	33
1994	08	06	160	13	-4	32
1994	08	07	160	21	-4	32
1994	08	08	160	29	-4	31
1994	08	09	160	37	-4	31
1994	08	10	160	45	-4	31
1994	08	11	160	53	-4	30
1994	08	12	161	01	-4	30
1994	08	13	161	09	-4	30
1994	08	14	161	17	-4	29
1994	08	15	161	25	-4	29
1994	08	16	161	33	-4	28
1994	08	17	161	42	-4	28
1994	08	18	161	50	-4	28
1994	08	19	161	58	-4	27
1994	08	20	162	06	-4	27
1994	08	21	162	15	-4	27
1994	08	22	162	23	-4	27
1994	08	23	162	31	-4	26
1994	08	24	162	40	-4	26
1994	08	25	162	48	-4	26
1994	08	26	162	56	-4	25
1994	08	27	163	05	-4	25
1994	08	28	163	13	-4	25
1994	08	29	163	22	-4	25
1994	08	30	163	30	-4	24
1994	08	31	163	39	-4	24
1994	09	01	163	47	-4	24
1994	09	02	163	55	-4	24
1994	09	03	164	04	-4	23
1994	09	04	164	12	-4	23
1994	09	05	164	21	-4	23
1994	09	06	164	29	-4	23
1994	09	07	164	38	-4	22
1994	09	08	164	46	-4	22
1994	09	09	164	55	-4	22
1994	09	10	165	03	-4	22
1994	09	11	165	12	-4	22
1994	09	12	165	20	-4	21
1994	09	13	165	29	-4	21
1994	09	14	165	37	-4	21
1994	09	15	165	46	-4	21
1994	09	16	165	54	-4	21
1994	09	17	166	03	-4	21
1994	09	18	166	11	-4	20
1994	09	19	166	20	-4	20
1994	09	20	166	28	-4	20
1994	09	21	166	37	-4	20
1994	09	22	166	45	-4	20
1994	09	23	166	53	-4	20
1994	09	24	167	02	-4	20
1994	09	25	167	10	-4	20
1994	09	26	167	19	-4	20
1994	09	27	167	27	-4	19
1994	09	28	167	35	-4	19
1994	09	29	167	43	-4	19
1994	09	30	167	52	-4	19
1994	10	01	168	00	-4	19
1994	10	02	168	08	-4	19
1994	10	03	168	16	-4	19
1994	10	04	168	25	-4	19
1994	10	05	168	33	-4	19
1994	10	06	168	41	-4	19
1994	10	07	168	49	-4	19
1994	10	08	168	57	-4	19
1994	10	09	169	05	-4	19
1994	10	10	169	13	-4	19
1994	10	11	169	21	-4	19
1994	10	12	169	29	-4	19
1994	10	13	169	37	-4	19
1994	10	14	169	45	-4	19
1994	10	15	169	52	-4	19
1994	10	16	170	00	-4	19
1994	10	17	170	08	-4	19
1994	10	18	170	16	-4	19
1994	10	19	170	23	-4	19
1994	10	20	170	31	-4	19
1994	10	21	170	38	-4	19
1994	10	22	170	46	-4	19
1994	10	23	170	53	-4	19
1994	10	24	171	01	-4	19
1994	10	25	171	08	-4	19
1994	10	26	171	15	-4	19
1994	10	27	171	22	-4	20
1994	10	28	171	30	-4	20
1994	10	29	171	37	-4	20
1994	10	30	171	44	-4	20
1994	10	31	171	51	-4	20
1994	11	01	171	58	-4	20
1994	11	02	172	05	-4	20
1994	11	03	172	11	-4	20
1994	11	04	172	18	-4	20
1994	11	05	172	25	-4	21
1994	11	06	172	32	-4	21
1994	11	07	172	38	-4	21
1994	11	08	172	45	-4	21
1994	11	09	172	51	-4	21
1994	11	10	172	57	-4	21
1994	11	11	173	04	-4	21
1994	11	12	173	10	-4	22
1994	11	13	173	16	-4	22
1994	11	14	173	22	-4	22

1994	11	15	173	28	-4	22
1994	11	16	173	34	-4	22
1994	11	17	173	40	-4	22
1994	11	18	173	45	-4	23
1994	11	19	173	51	-4	23
1994	11	20	173	57	-4	23
1994	11	21	174	02	-4	23
1994	11	22	174	07	-4	23
1994	11	23	174	13	-4	24
1994	11	24	174	18	-4	24
1994	11	25	174	23	-4	24
1994	11	26	174	28	-4	24
1994	11	27	174	33	-4	25
1994	11	28	174	38	-4	25
1994	11	29	174	43	-4	25
1994	11	30	174	47	-4	25
1994	12	01	174	52	-4	25
1994	12	02	174	56	-4	26
1994	12	03	175	01	-4	26
1994	12	04	175	05	-4	26
1994	12	05	175	09	-4	26
1994	12	06	175	13	-4	27
1994	12	07	175	17	-4	27
1994	12	08	175	21	-4	27
1994	12	09	175	25	-4	27
1994	12	10	175	29	-4	28
1994	12	11	175	32	-4	28
1994	12	12	175	36	-4	28
1994	12	13	175	39	-4	28
1994	12	14	175	42	-4	29
1994	12	15	175	45	-4	29
1994	12	16	175	48	-4	29
1994	12	17	175	51	-4	30
1994	12	18	175	54	-4	30
1994	12	19	175	57	-4	30
1994	12	20	175	59	-4	30
1994	12	21	176	02	-4	31
1994	12	22	176	04	-4	31
1994	12	23	176	06	-4	31
1994	12	24	176	09	-4	31
1994	12	25	176	11	-4	32
1994	12	26	176	12	-4	32
1994	12	27	176	14	-4	32
1994	12	28	176	16	-4	33
1994	12	29	176	17	-4	33
1994	12	30	176	19	-4	33
1994	12	31	176	20	-4	33
1995	01	01	176	21	-4	34
1995	01	02	176	22	-4	34
1995	01	03	176	23	-4	34
1995	01	04	176	24	-4	34
1995	01	05	176	25	-4	35
1995	01	06	176	25	-4	35
1995	01	07	176	26	-4	35
1995	01	08	176	26	-4	36
1995	01	09	176	26	-4	36
1995	01	10	176	26	-4	36
1995	01	11	176	26	-4	36
1995	01	12	176	26	-4	37
1995	01	13	176	26	-4	37
1995	01	14	176	26	-4	37
1995	01	15	176	25	-4	37
1995	01	16	176	25	-4	37
1995	01	17	176	24	-4	38
1995	01	18	176	23	-4	38
1995	01	19	176	22	-4	38
1995	01	20	176	21	-4	38
1995	01	21	176	20	-4	39
1995	01	22	176	19	-4	39
1995	01	23	176	17	-4	39
1995	01	24	176	16	-4	39
1995	01	25	176	14	-4	39
1995	01	26	176	12	-4	39
1995	01	27	176	10	-4	40
1995	01	28	176	08	-4	40
1995	01	29	176	06	-4	40
1995	01	30	176	04	-4	40
1995	01	31	176	02	-4	40
1995	02	01	175	59	-4	40
1995	02	02	175	57	-4	41
1995	02	03	175	54	-4	41
1995	02	04	175	52	-4	41
1995	02	05	175	49	-4	41
1995	02	06	175	46	-4	41
1995	02	07	175	43	-4	41
1995	02	08	175	40	-4	41
1995	02	09	175	37	-4	41
1995	02	10	175	34	-4	41
1995	02	11	175	30	-4	41
1995	02	12	175	27	-4	41
1995	02	13	175	23	-4	41
1995	02	14	175	20	-4	41
1995	02	15	175	16	-4	42
1995	02	16	175	13	-4	42
1995	02	17	175	09	-4	42
1995	02	18	175	05	-4	42
1995	02	19	175	01	-4	41
1995	02	20	174	57	-4	41
1995	02	21	174	53	-4	41
1995	02	22	174	49	-4	41
1995	02	23	174	45	-4	41
1995	02	24	174	40	-4	41
1995	02	25	174	36	-4	41
1995	02	26	174	32	-4	41
1995	02	27	174	27	-4	41
1995	02	28	174	23	-4	41

1995	03	01	174	18	-4	41
1995	03	02	174	14	-4	41
1995	03	03	174	09	-4	40
1995	03	04	174	05	-4	40
1995	03	05	174	00	-4	40
1995	03	06	173	56	-4	40
1995	03	07	173	51	-4	40
1995	03	08	173	46	-4	39
1995	03	09	173	41	-4	39
1995	03	10	173	37	-4	39
1995	03	11	173	32	-4	39
1995	03	12	173	27	-4	38
1995	03	13	173	22	-4	38
1995	03	14	173	18	-4	38
1995	03	15	173	13	-4	38
1995	03	16	173	08	-4	37
1995	03	17	173	03	-4	37
1995	03	18	172	59	-4	37
1995	03	19	172	54	-4	36
1995	03	20	172	49	-4	36
1995	03	21	172	44	-4	36
1995	03	22	172	40	-4	35
1995	03	23	172	35	-4	35
1995	03	24	172	30	-4	34
1995	03	25	172	26	-4	34
1995	03	26	172	21	-4	34
1995	03	27	172	17	-4	33
1995	03	28	172	12	-4	33
1995	03	29	172	08	-4	32
1995	03	30	172	03	-4	32
1995	03	31	171	59	-4	31
1995	04	01	171	54	-4	31
1995	04	02	171	50	-4	30
1995	04	03	171	46	-4	30
1995	04	04	171	42	-4	29
1995	04	05	171	38	-4	29
1995	04	06	171	33	-4	28
1995	04	07	171	29	-4	28
1995	04	08	171	25	-4	27
1995	04	09	171	22	-4	27
1995	04	10	171	18	-4	26
1995	04	11	171	14	-4	26
1995	04	12	171	10	-4	25
1995	04	13	171	07	-4	24
1995	04	14	171	03	-4	24
1995	04	15	171	00	-4	23
1995	04	16	170	56	-4	23
1995	04	17	170	53	-4	22
1995	04	18	170	50	-4	21
1995	04	19	170	47	-4	21
1995	04	20	170	44	-4	20
1995	04	21	170	41	-4	19
1995	04	22	170	38	-4	19
1995	04	23	170	35	-4	18
1995	04	24	170	32	-4	17
1995	04	25	170	30	-4	17
1995	04	26	170	27	-4	16
1995	04	27	170	25	-4	15
1995	04	28	170	23	-4	15
1995	04	29	170	20	-4	14
1995	04	30	170	18	-4	13
1995	05	01	170	16	-4	13
1995	05	02	170	14	-4	12
1995	05	03	170	13	-4	11
1995	05	04	170	11	-4	11
1995	05	05	170	09	-4	10
1995	05	06	170	08	-4	09
1995	05	07	170	07	-4	08
1995	05	08	170	05	-4	08
1995	05	09	170	04	-4	07
1995	05	10	170	03	-4	06
1995	05	11	170	02	-4	06
1995	05	12	170	02	-4	05
1995	05	13	170	01	-4	04
1995	05	14	170	00	-4	03
1995	05	15	170	00	-4	03
1995	05	16	170	00	-4	02
1995	05	17	169	59	-4	01
1995	05	18	169	59	-4	00
1995	05	19	169	59	-4	00
1995	05	20	169	59	-3	59
1995	05	21	170	00	-3	58
1995	05	22	170	00	-3	57
1995	05	23	170	00	-3	57
1995	05	24	170	01	-3	56
1995	05	25	170	02	-3	55
1995	05	26	170	02	-3	54
1995	05	27	170	03	-3	54
1995	05	28	170	04	-3	53
1995	05	29	170	05	-3	52
1995	05	30	170	07	-3	52
1995	05	31	170	08	-3	51
1995	06	01	170	10	-3	50
1995	06	02	170	11	-3	49
1995	06	03	170	13	-3	49
1995	06	04	170	15	-3	48
1995	06	05	170	17	-3	47
1995	06	06	170	19	-3	46
1995	06	07	170	21	-3	46
1995	06	08	170	23	-3	45
1995	06	09	170	25	-3	44

Chiron

1995 06 10	170 28	-3 44
1995 06 11	170 30	-3 43
1995 06 12	170 33	-3 42
1995 06 13	170 36	-3 41
1995 06 14	170 39	-3 41
1995 06 15	170 42	-3 40
1995 06 16	170 45	-3 39
1995 06 17	170 48	-3 39
1995 06 18	170 51	-3 38
1995 06 19	170 55	-3 37
1995 06 20	170 58	-3 36
1995 06 21	171 02	-3 36
1995 06 22	171 06	-3 35
1995 06 23	171 09	-3 34
1995 06 24	171 13	-3 34
1995 06 25	171 17	-3 33
1995 06 26	171 21	-3 32
1995 06 27	171 26	-3 32
1995 06 28	171 30	-3 31
1995 06 29	171 34	-3 30
1995 06 30	171 39	-3 30
1995 07 01	171 43	-3 29
1995 07 02	171 48	-3 28
1995 07 03	171 53	-3 28
1995 07 04	171 58	-3 27
1995 07 05	172 03	-3 27
1995 07 06	172 08	-3 26
1995 07 07	172 13	-3 25
1995 07 08	172 18	-3 25
1995 07 09	172 23	-3 24
1995 07 10	172 29	-3 23
1995 07 11	172 34	-3 23
1995 07 12	172 40	-3 22
1995 07 13	172 45	-3 22
1995 07 14	172 51	-3 21
1995 07 15	172 57	-3 20
1995 07 16	173 03	-3 20
1995 07 17	173 09	-3 19
1995 07 18	173 15	-3 19
1995 07 19	173 21	-3 18
1995 07 20	173 27	-3 17
1995 07 21	173 33	-3 17
1995 07 22	173 39	-3 16
1995 07 23	173 46	-3 16
1995 07 24	173 52	-3 15
1995 07 25	173 59	-3 15
1995 07 26	174 05	-3 14
1995 07 27	174 12	-3 14
1995 07 28	174 19	-3 13
1995 07 29	174 25	-3 13
1995 07 30	174 32	-3 12
1995 07 31	174 39	-3 11
1995 08 01	174 46	-3 11
1995 08 02	174 53	-3 10
1995 08 03	175 00	-3 10
1995 08 04	175 07	-3 09
1995 08 05	175 15	-3 09
1995 08 06	175 22	-3 08
1995 08 07	175 29	-3 08
1995 08 08	175 37	-3 07
1995 08 09	175 44	-3 07
1995 08 10	175 52	-3 07
1995 08 11	175 59	-3 06
1995 08 12	176 07	-3 06
1995 08 13	176 14	-3 05
1995 08 14	176 22	-3 05
1995 08 15	176 30	-3 04
1995 08 16	176 37	-3 04
1995 08 17	176 45	-3 03
1995 08 18	176 53	-3 03
1995 08 19	177 01	-3 02
1995 08 20	177 09	-3 02
1995 08 21	177 17	-3 02
1995 08 22	177 25	-3 01
1995 08 23	177 33	-3 01
1995 08 24	177 41	-3 00
1995 08 25	177 49	-3 00
1995 08 26	177 58	-2 59
1995 08 27	178 06	-2 59
1995 08 28	178 14	-2 59
1995 08 29	178 22	-2 58
1995 08 30	178 31	-2 58
1995 08 31	178 39	-2 58
1995 09 01	178 47	-2 57
1995 09 02	178 56	-2 57
1995 09 03	179 04	-2 56
1995 09 04	179 13	-2 56
1995 09 05	179 21	-2 56
1995 09 06	179 30	-2 55
1995 09 07	179 38	-2 55
1995 09 08	179 47	-2 55
1995 09 09	179 55	-2 54
1995 09 10	180 04	-2 54
1995 09 11	180 12	-2 54
1995 09 12	180 21	-2 53
1995 09 13	180 30	-2 53
1995 09 14	180 38	-2 53
1995 09 15	180 47	-2 52
1995 09 16	180 56	-2 52
1995 09 17	181 04	-2 52
1995 09 18	181 13	-2 51
1995 09 19	181 22	-2 51

1995 09 20	181 30	-2 51
1995 09 21	181 39	-2 51
1995 09 22	181 48	-2 50
1995 09 23	181 57	-2 50
1995 09 24	182 05	-2 50
1995 09 25	182 14	-2 49
1995 09 26	182 23	-2 49
1995 09 27	182 32	-2 49
1995 09 28	182 40	-2 49
1995 09 29	182 49	-2 48
1995 09 30	182 58	-2 48
1995 10 01	183 07	-2 48
1995 10 02	183 15	-2 48
1995 10 03	183 24	-2 47
1995 10 04	183 33	-2 47
1995 10 05	183 41	-2 47
1995 10 06	183 50	-2 47
1995 10 07	183 59	-2 46
1995 10 08	184 07	-2 46
1995 10 09	184 16	-2 46
1995 10 10	184 25	-2 46
1995 10 11	184 33	-2 46
1995 10 12	184 42	-2 45
1995 10 13	184 51	-2 45
1995 10 14	184 59	-2 45
1995 10 15	185 08	-2 45
1995 10 16	185 16	-2 45
1995 10 17	185 25	-2 44
1995 10 18	185 33	-2 44
1995 10 19	185 42	-2 44
1995 10 20	185 50	-2 44
1995 10 21	185 59	-2 44
1995 10 22	186 07	-2 44
1995 10 23	186 15	-2 43
1995 10 24	186 24	-2 43
1995 10 25	186 32	-2 43
1995 10 26	186 40	-2 43
1995 10 27	186 49	-2 43
1995 10 28	186 57	-2 43
1995 10 29	187 05	-2 42
1995 10 30	187 13	-2 42
1995 10 31	187 21	-2 42
1995 11 01	187 29	-2 42
1995 11 02	187 37	-2 42
1995 11 03	187 45	-2 42
1995 11 04	187 53	-2 42
1995 11 05	188 01	-2 42
1995 11 06	188 09	-2 41
1995 11 07	188 17	-2 41
1995 11 08	188 24	-2 41
1995 11 09	188 32	-2 41
1995 11 10	188 40	-2 41
1995 11 11	188 47	-2 41
1995 11 12	188 55	-2 41
1995 11 13	189 02	-2 41
1995 11 14	189 10	-2 41
1995 11 15	189 17	-2 41
1995 11 16	189 24	-2 40
1995 11 17	189 32	-2 40
1995 11 18	189 39	-2 40
1995 11 19	189 46	-2 40
1995 11 20	189 53	-2 40
1995 11 21	190 00	-2 40
1995 11 22	190 07	-2 40
1995 11 23	190 14	-2 40
1995 11 24	190 20	-2 40
1995 11 25	190 27	-2 40
1995 11 26	190 34	-2 40
1995 11 27	190 40	-2 40
1995 11 28	190 47	-2 40
1995 11 29	190 53	-2 40
1995 11 30	191 00	-2 40
1995 12 01	191 06	-2 40
1995 12 02	191 12	-2 39
1995 12 03	191 18	-2 39
1995 12 04	191 24	-2 39
1995 12 05	191 30	-2 39
1995 12 06	191 36	-2 39
1995 12 07	191 42	-2 39
1995 12 08	191 47	-2 39
1995 12 09	191 53	-2 39
1995 12 10	191 59	-2 39
1995 12 11	192 04	-2 39
1995 12 12	192 09	-2 39
1995 12 13	192 15	-2 39
1995 12 14	192 20	-2 39
1995 12 15	192 25	-2 39
1995 12 16	192 30	-2 39
1995 12 17	192 35	-2 39
1995 12 18	192 39	-2 39
1995 12 19	192 44	-2 39
1995 12 20	192 49	-2 39
1995 12 21	192 53	-2 39
1995 12 22	192 58	-2 39
1995 12 23	193 02	-2 39
1995 12 24	193 06	-2 39
1995 12 25	193 10	-2 39
1995 12 26	193 14	-2 39
1995 12 27	193 18	-2 39
1995 12 28	193 22	-2 39
1995 12 29	193 25	-2 39
1995 12 30	193 29	-2 39
1995 12 31	193 32	-2 39
1996 01 01	193 36	-2 39
1996 01 02	193 39	-2 39
1996 01 03	193 42	-2 39

1996 01 04	193 45	-2 39
1996 01 05	193 48	-2 39
1996 01 06	193 50	-2 39
1996 01 07	193 53	-2 39
1996 01 08	193 56	-2 39
1996 01 09	193 58	-2 39
1996 01 10	194 00	-2 39
1996 01 11	194 02	-2 39
1996 01 12	194 04	-2 39
1996 01 13	194 06	-2 39
1996 01 14	194 08	-2 39
1996 01 15	194 10	-2 39
1996 01 16	194 12	-2 39
1996 01 17	194 13	-2 39
1996 01 18	194 14	-2 39
1996 01 19	194 16	-2 39
1996 01 20	194 17	-2 39
1996 01 21	194 18	-2 39
1996 01 22	194 18	-2 39
1996 01 23	194 19	-2 39
1996 01 24	194 20	-2 39
1996 01 25	194 20	-2 39
1996 01 26	194 21	-2 39
1996 01 27	194 21	-2 39
1996 01 28	194 21	-2 39
1996 01 29	194 21	-2 39
1996 01 30	194 21	-2 39
1996 01 31	194 21	-2 39
1996 02 01	194 20	-2 39
1996 02 02	194 20	-2 38
1996 02 03	194 19	-2 38
1996 02 04	194 19	-2 38
1996 02 05	194 18	-2 38
1996 02 06	194 17	-2 38
1996 02 07	194 16	-2 38
1996 02 08	194 15	-2 38
1996 02 09	194 13	-2 38
1996 02 10	194 12	-2 38
1996 02 11	194 10	-2 38
1996 02 12	194 09	-2 38
1996 02 13	194 07	-2 38
1996 02 14	194 05	-2 38
1996 02 15	194 03	-2 38
1996 02 16	194 01	-2 37
1996 02 17	193 59	-2 37
1996 02 18	193 57	-2 37
1996 02 19	193 55	-2 37
1996 02 20	193 52	-2 37
1996 02 21	193 49	-2 37
1996 02 22	193 47	-2 37
1996 02 23	193 44	-2 37
1996 02 24	193 41	-2 37
1996 02 25	193 38	-2 36
1996 02 26	193 35	-2 36
1996 02 27	193 32	-2 36
1996 02 28	193 29	-2 36
1996 02 29	193 26	-2 36
1996 03 01	193 22	-2 36
1996 03 02	193 19	-2 35
1996 03 03	193 15	-2 35
1996 03 04	193 12	-2 35
1996 03 05	193 08	-2 35
1996 03 06	193 04	-2 35
1996 03 07	193 00	-2 34
1996 03 08	192 56	-2 34
1996 03 09	192 52	-2 34
1996 03 10	192 48	-2 34
1996 03 11	192 44	-2 34
1996 03 12	192 40	-2 33
1996 03 13	192 36	-2 33
1996 03 14	192 32	-2 33
1996 03 15	192 27	-2 33
1996 03 16	192 23	-2 32
1996 03 17	192 18	-2 32
1996 03 18	192 14	-2 32
1996 03 19	192 09	-2 32
1996 03 20	192 05	-2 31
1996 03 21	192 00	-2 31
1996 03 22	191 56	-2 31
1996 03 23	191 51	-2 30
1996 03 24	191 46	-2 30
1996 03 25	191 42	-2 30
1996 03 26	191 37	-2 29
1996 03 27	191 32	-2 29
1996 03 28	191 28	-2 29
1996 03 29	191 23	-2 28
1996 03 30	191 18	-2 28
1996 03 31	191 13	-2 28
1996 04 01	191 09	-2 27
1996 04 02	191 04	-2 27
1996 04 03	190 59	-2 27
1996 04 04	190 54	-2 26
1996 04 05	190 50	-2 26
1996 04 06	190 45	-2 25
1996 04 07	190 40	-2 25
1996 04 08	190 36	-2 25
1996 04 09	190 31	-2 24
1996 04 10	190 26	-2 24
1996 04 11	190 22	-2 23
1996 04 12	190 17	-2 23
1996 04 13	190 13	-2 23
1996 04 14	190 08	-2 22
1996 04 15	190 04	-2 22
1996 04 16	189 59	-2 21
1996 04 17	189 55	-2 21
1996 04 18	189 50	-2 20

1996 04 19	189 46	-2 20
1996 04 20	189 42	-2 19
1996 04 21	189 38	-2 19
1996 04 22	189 33	-2 18
1996 04 23	189 29	-2 18
1996 04 24	189 25	-2 18
1996 04 25	189 21	-2 17
1996 04 26	189 18	-2 17
1996 04 27	189 14	-2 16
1996 04 28	189 10	-2 16
1996 04 29	189 06	-2 15
1996 04 30	189 03	-2 15
1996 05 01	188 59	-2 14
1996 05 02	188 56	-2 14
1996 05 03	188 52	-2 13
1996 05 04	188 49	-2 12
1996 05 05	188 46	-2 12
1996 05 06	188 43	-2 11
1996 05 07	188 40	-2 11
1996 05 08	188 37	-2 10
1996 05 09	188 34	-2 10
1996 05 10	188 31	-2 09
1996 05 11	188 28	-2 09
1996 05 12	188 26	-2 08
1996 05 13	188 23	-2 08
1996 05 14	188 21	-2 07
1996 05 15	188 19	-2 07
1996 05 16	188 16	-2 06
1996 05 17	188 14	-2 05
1996 05 18	188 12	-2 05
1996 05 19	188 10	-2 04
1996 05 20	188 09	-2 04
1996 05 21	188 07	-2 03
1996 05 22	188 05	-2 03
1996 05 23	188 04	-2 02
1996 05 24	188 03	-2 02
1996 05 25	188 01	-2 01
1996 05 26	188 00	-2 00
1996 05 27	187 59	-2 00
1996 05 28	187 58	-1 59
1996 05 29	187 57	-1 59
1996 05 30	187 57	-1 58
1996 05 31	187 56	-1 58
1996 06 01	187 56	-1 57
1996 06 02	187 55	-1 57
1996 06 03	187 55	-1 56
1996 06 04	187 55	-1 55
1996 06 05	187 55	-1 55
1996 06 06	187 55	-1 54
1996 06 07	187 55	-1 54
1996 06 08	187 55	-1 53
1996 06 09	187 56	-1 53
1996 06 10	187 56	-1 52
1996 06 11	187 57	-1 52
1996 06 12	187 58	-1 51
1996 06 13	187 59	-1 50
1996 06 14	188 00	-1 50
1996 06 15	188 01	-1 49
1996 06 16	188 02	-1 49
1996 06 17	188 03	-1 48
1996 06 18	188 05	-1 48
1996 06 19	188 06	-1 47
1996 06 20	188 08	-1 47
1996 06 21	188 10	-1 46
1996 06 22	188 11	-1 46
1996 06 23	188 13	-1 45
1996 06 24	188 16	-1 44
1996 06 25	188 18	-1 44
1996 06 26	188 20	-1 43
1996 06 27	188 23	-1 43
1996 06 28	188 25	-1 42
1996 06 29	188 28	-1 42
1996 06 30	188 30	-1 41
1996 07 01	188 33	-1 41
1996 07 02	188 36	-1 40
1996 07 03	188 39	-1 40
1996 07 04	188 43	-1 39
1996 07 05	188 46	-1 39
1996 07 06	188 49	-1 38
1996 07 07	188 53	-1 38
1996 07 08	188 56	-1 37
1996 07 09	189 00	-1 37
1996 07 10	189 04	-1 36
1996 07 11	189 08	-1 36
1996 07 12	189 12	-1 35
1996 07 13	189 16	-1 35
1996 07 14	189 20	-1 34
1996 07 15	189 24	-1 34
1996 07 16	189 28	-1 33
1996 07 17	189 33	-1 33
1996 07 18	189 37	-1 32
1996 07 19	189 42	-1 32
1996 07 20	189 47	-1 31
1996 07 21	189 52	-1 31
1996 07 22	189 57	-1 30
1996 07 23	190 02	-1 30
1996 07 24	190 07	-1 29
1996 07 25	190 12	-1 29
1996 07 26	190 17	-1 28
1996 07 27	190 22	-1 28
1996 07 28	190 28	-1 27
1996 07 29	190 33	-1 27
1996 07 30	190 39	-1 26
1996 07 31	190 45	-1 26
1996 08 01	190 50	-1 26
1996 08 02	190 56	-1 25

1996 08 03	191 02	-1 25
1996 08 04	191 08	-1 24
1996 08 05	191 14	-1 24
1996 08 06	191 20	-1 23
1996 08 07	191 26	-1 23
1996 08 08	191 33	-1 22
1996 08 09	191 39	-1 22
1996 08 10	191 46	-1 22
1996 08 11	191 52	-1 21
1996 08 12	191 59	-1 21
1996 08 13	192 05	-1 20
1996 08 14	192 12	-1 20
1996 08 15	192 19	-1 19
1996 08 16	192 26	-1 19
1996 08 17	192 32	-1 19
1996 08 18	192 39	-1 18
1996 08 19	192 46	-1 18
1996 08 20	192 53	-1 17
1996 08 21	193 01	-1 17
1996 08 22	193 08	-1 17
1996 08 23	193 15	-1 16
1996 08 24	193 22	-1 16
1996 08 25	193 30	-1 15
1996 08 26	193 37	-1 15
1996 08 27	193 45	-1 15
1996 08 28	193 52	-1 14
1996 08 29	194 00	-1 14
1996 08 30	194 07	-1 13
1996 08 31	194 15	-1 13
1996 09 01	194 23	-1 13
1996 09 02	194 30	-1 12
1996 09 03	194 38	-1 12
1996 09 04	194 46	-1 12
1996 09 05	194 54	-1 11
1996 09 06	195 02	-1 11
1996 09 07	195 10	-1 10
1996 09 08	195 18	-1 10
1996 09 09	195 26	-1 10
1996 09 10	195 34	-1 09
1996 09 11	195 42	-1 09
1996 09 12	195 50	-1 09
1996 09 13	195 59	-1 08
1996 09 14	196 07	-1 08
1996 09 15	196 15	-1 08
1996 09 16	196 23	-1 07
1996 09 17	196 32	-1 07
1996 09 18	196 40	-1 07
1996 09 19	196 48	-1 06
1996 09 20	196 57	-1 06
1996 09 21	197 05	-1 06
1996 09 22	197 14	-1 05
1996 09 23	197 22	-1 05
1996 09 24	197 31	-1 05
1996 09 25	197 39	-1 04
1996 09 26	197 48	-1 04
1996 09 27	197 56	-1 04
1996 09 28	198 05	-1 03
1996 09 29	198 14	-1 03
1996 09 30	198 22	-1 03
1996 10 01	198 31	-1 02
1996 10 02	198 40	-1 02
1996 10 03	198 48	-1 02
1996 10 04	198 57	-1 01
1996 10 05	199 06	-1 01
1996 10 06	199 14	-1 01
1996 10 07	199 23	-1 00
1996 10 08	199 32	-1 00
1996 10 09	199 40	-1 00
1996 10 10	199 49	-1 00
1996 10 11	199 58	-0 59
1996 10 12	200 07	-0 59
1996 10 13	200 15	-0 59
1996 10 14	200 24	-0 58
1996 10 15	200 33	-0 58
1996 10 16	200 42	-0 58
1996 10 17	200 50	-0 57
1996 10 18	200 59	-0 57
1996 10 19	201 08	-0 57
1996 10 20	201 16	-0 57
1996 10 21	201 25	-0 56
1996 10 22	201 34	-0 56
1996 10 23	201 42	-0 56
1996 10 24	201 51	-0 55
1996 10 25	202 00	-0 55
1996 10 26	202 08	-0 55
1996 10 27	202 17	-0 55
1996 10 28	202 26	-0 54
1996 10 29	202 34	-0 54
1996 10 30	202 43	-0 54
1996 10 31	202 51	-0 54
1996 11 01	203 00	-0 53
1996 11 02	203 08	-0 53
1996 11 03	203 17	-0 53
1996 11 04	203 25	-0 52
1996 11 05	203 34	-0 52
1996 11 06	203 42	-0 52
1996 11 07	203 51	-0 52
1996 11 08	203 59	-0 51
1996 11 09	204 07	-0 51
1996 11 10	204 16	-0 51
1996 11 11	204 24	-0 51
1996 11 12	204 32	-0 50
1996 11 13	204 40	-0 50
1996 11 14	204 49	-0 50
1996 11 15	204 57	-0 49
1996 11 16	205 05	-0 49
1996 11 17	205 13	-0 49
1996 11 18	205 21	-0 49
1996 11 19	205 29	-0 48
1996 11 20	205 37	-0 48
1996 11 21	205 44	-0 48
1996 11 22	205 52	-0 48
1996 11 23	206 00	-0 47
1996 11 24	206 08	-0 47
1996 11 25	206 15	-0 47
1996 11 26	206 23	-0 47
1996 11 27	206 31	-0 46
1996 11 28	206 38	-0 46
1996 11 29	206 46	-0 46
1996 11 30	206 53	-0 46
1996 12 01	207 00	-0 45
1996 12 02	207 08	-0 45
1996 12 03	207 15	-0 45
1996 12 04	207 22	-0 45
1996 12 05	207 29	-0 44
1996 12 06	207 36	-0 44
1996 12 07	207 43	-0 44
1996 12 08	207 50	-0 44
1996 12 09	207 57	-0 43
1996 12 10	208 04	-0 43
1996 12 11	208 10	-0 43
1996 12 12	208 17	-0 43
1996 12 13	208 24	-0 42
1996 12 14	208 30	-0 42
1996 12 15	208 37	-0 42
1996 12 16	208 43	-0 42
1996 12 17	208 49	-0 41
1996 12 18	208 55	-0 41
1996 12 19	209 01	-0 41
1996 12 20	209 07	-0 41
1996 12 21	209 13	-0 40
1996 12 22	209 19	-0 40
1996 12 23	209 25	-0 40
1996 12 24	209 31	-0 40
1996 12 25	209 36	-0 39
1996 12 26	209 42	-0 39
1996 12 27	209 47	-0 39
1996 12 28	209 53	-0 39
1996 12 29	209 58	-0 38
1996 12 30	210 03	-0 38
1996 12 31	210 08	-0 38
1997 01 01	210 13	-0 38
1997 01 02	210 18	-0 37
1997 01 03	210 23	-0 37
1997 01 04	210 27	-0 37
1997 01 05	210 32	-0 37
1997 01 06	210 36	-0 36
1997 01 07	210 41	-0 36
1997 01 08	210 45	-0 36
1997 01 09	210 49	-0 35
1997 01 10	210 53	-0 35
1997 01 11	210 57	-0 35
1997 01 12	211 01	-0 35
1997 01 13	211 05	-0 34
1997 01 14	211 09	-0 34
1997 01 15	211 12	-0 34
1997 01 16	211 16	-0 34
1997 01 17	211 19	-0 33
1997 01 18	211 22	-0 33
1997 01 19	211 25	-0 33
1997 01 20	211 28	-0 33
1997 01 21	211 31	-0 32
1997 01 22	211 34	-0 32
1997 01 23	211 36	-0 32
1997 01 24	211 39	-0 31
1997 01 25	211 41	-0 31
1997 01 26	211 44	-0 31
1997 01 27	211 46	-0 31
1997 01 28	211 48	-0 30
1997 01 29	211 50	-0 30
1997 01 30	211 52	-0 30
1997 01 31	211 54	-0 30
1997 02 01	211 55	-0 29
1997 02 02	211 57	-0 29
1997 02 03	211 58	-0 29
1997 02 04	211 59	-0 28
1997 02 05	212 00	-0 28
1997 02 06	212 01	-0 28
1997 02 07	212 02	-0 28
1997 02 08	212 03	-0 27
1997 02 09	212 04	-0 27
1997 02 10	212 04	-0 27
1997 02 11	212 05	-0 26
1997 02 12	212 05	-0 26
1997 02 13	212 05	-0 26
1997 02 14	212 05	-0 25
1997 02 15	212 05	-0 25
1997 02 16	212 05	-0 25
1997 02 17	212 05	-0 25
1997 02 18	212 04	-0 24
1997 02 19	212 04	-0 24
1997 02 20	212 03	-0 24
1997 02 21	212 03	-0 23
1997 02 22	212 02	-0 23
1997 02 23	212 01	-0 23
1997 02 24	212 00	-0 22
1997 02 25	211 58	-0 22
1997 02 26	211 57	-0 22
1997 02 27	211 56	-0 21
1997 02 28	211 54	-0 21
1997 03 01	211 53	-0 21
1997 03 02	211 51	-0 20
1997 03 03	211 49	-0 20
1997 03 04	211 47	-0 20
1997 03 05	211 45	-0 19
1997 03 06	211 43	-0 19
1997 03 07	211 41	-0 19
1997 03 08	211 38	-0 18
1997 03 09	211 36	-0 18
1997 03 10	211 33	-0 18
1997 03 11	211 30	-0 17
1997 03 12	211 28	-0 17
1997 03 13	211 25	-0 17
1997 03 14	211 22	-0 16
1997 03 15	211 19	-0 16
1997 03 16	211 16	-0 16
1997 03 17	211 13	-0 15
1997 03 18	211 09	-0 15
1997 03 19	211 06	-0 15
1997 03 20	211 03	-0 14
1997 03 21	210 59	-0 14
1997 03 22	210 55	-0 14
1997 03 23	210 52	-0 13
1997 03 24	210 48	-0 13
1997 03 25	210 44	-0 13
1997 03 26	210 40	-0 12
1997 03 27	210 36	-0 12
1997 03 28	210 32	-0 11
1997 03 29	210 28	-0 11
1997 03 30	210 24	-0 11
1997 03 31	210 20	-0 10
1997 04 01	210 16	-0 10
1997 04 02	210 12	-0 10
1997 04 03	210 07	-0 09
1997 04 04	210 03	-0 09
1997 04 05	209 59	-0 09
1997 04 06	209 54	-0 08
1997 04 07	209 50	-0 08
1997 04 08	209 45	-0 07
1997 04 09	209 41	-0 07
1997 04 10	209 36	-0 07
1997 04 11	209 32	-0 06
1997 04 12	209 27	-0 06
1997 04 13	209 22	-0 06
1997 04 14	209 18	-0 05
1997 04 15	209 13	-0 05
1997 04 16	209 08	-0 04
1997 04 17	209 04	-0 04
1997 04 18	208 59	-0 04
1997 04 19	208 54	-0 03
1997 04 20	208 50	-0 03
1997 04 21	208 45	-0 03
1997 04 22	208 40	-0 02
1997 04 23	208 36	-0 02
1997 04 24	208 31	-0 01
1997 04 25	208 26	-0 01
1997 04 26	208 22	-0 01
1997 04 27	208 17	0 00
1997 04 28	208 13	0 00
1997 04 29	208 08	0 00
1997 04 30	208 04	0 01
1997 05 01	207 59	0 01
1997 05 02	207 55	0 01
1997 05 03	207 50	0 02
1997 05 04	207 46	0 02
1997 05 05	207 41	0 03
1997 05 06	207 37	0 03
1997 05 07	207 33	0 03
1997 05 08	207 29	0 04
1997 05 09	207 25	0 04
1997 05 10	207 20	0 04
1997 05 11	207 16	0 05
1997 05 12	207 12	0 05
1997 05 13	207 09	0 06
1997 05 14	207 05	0 06
1997 05 15	207 01	0 06
1997 05 16	206 57	0 07
1997 05 17	206 54	0 07
1997 05 18	206 50	0 07
1997 05 19	206 46	0 08
1997 05 20	206 43	0 08
1997 05 21	206 40	0 08
1997 05 22	206 36	0 09
1997 05 23	206 33	0 09
1997 05 24	206 30	0 09
1997 05 25	206 27	0 10
1997 05 26	206 24	0 10
1997 05 27	206 21	0 11
1997 05 28	206 18	0 11
1997 05 29	206 16	0 11
1997 05 30	206 13	0 12
1997 05 31	206 11	0 12
1997 06 01	206 08	0 12
1997 06 02	206 06	0 13
1997 06 03	206 04	0 13
1997 06 04	206 02	0 13
1997 06 05	205 59	0 14
1997 06 06	205 58	0 14
1997 06 07	205 56	0 14
1997 06 08	205 54	0 15
1997 06 09	205 52	0 15
1997 06 10	205 51	0 15
1997 06 11	205 49	0 16
1997 06 12	205 48	0 16
1997 06 13	205 47	0 16
1997 06 14	205 46	0 17
1997 06 15	205 45	0 17
1997 06 16	205 44	0 17
1997 06 17	205 43	0 18
1997 06 18	205 43	0 18
1997 06 19	205 42	0 18
1997 06 20	205 42	0 18
1997 06 21	205 41	0 19
1997 06 22	205 41	0 19
1997 06 23	205 41	0 19
1997 06 24	205 41	0 20
1997 06 25	205 41	0 20
1997 06 26	205 41	0 20
1997 06 27	205 41	0 21
1997 06 28	205 42	0 21
1997 06 29	205 42	0 21
1997 06 30	205 43	0 22
1997 07 01	205 44	0 22
1997 07 02	205 45	0 22
1997 07 03	205 46	0 22
1997 07 04	205 47	0 23
1997 07 05	205 48	0 23
1997 07 06	205 49	0 23
1997 07 07	205 51	0 24
1997 07 08	205 52	0 24
1997 07 09	205 54	0 24
1997 07 10	205 56	0 24
1997 07 11	205 57	0 25
1997 07 12	205 59	0 25
1997 07 13	206 01	0 25
1997 07 14	206 04	0 26
1997 07 15	206 06	0 26
1997 07 16	206 08	0 26
1997 07 17	206 11	0 26
1997 07 18	206 13	0 27
1997 07 19	206 16	0 27
1997 07 20	206 19	0 27
1997 07 21	206 22	0 28
1997 07 22	206 25	0 28
1997 07 23	206 28	0 28
1997 07 24	206 31	0 28
1997 07 25	206 34	0 29
1997 07 26	206 38	0 29
1997 07 27	206 41	0 29
1997 07 28	206 45	0 29
1997 07 29	206 49	0 30
1997 07 30	206 52	0 30
1997 07 31	206 56	0 30
1997 08 01	207 00	0 31
1997 08 02	207 04	0 31
1997 08 03	207 09	0 31
1997 08 04	207 13	0 31
1997 08 05	207 17	0 32
1997 08 06	207 22	0 32
1997 08 07	207 26	0 32
1997 08 08	207 31	0 32
1997 08 09	207 36	0 33
1997 08 10	207 40	0 33
1997 08 11	207 45	0 33
1997 08 12	207 50	0 33
1997 08 13	207 55	0 34
1997 08 14	208 00	0 34
1997 08 15	208 06	0 34
1997 08 16	208 11	0 34
1997 08 17	208 16	0 35
1997 08 18	208 22	0 35
1997 08 19	208 27	0 35
1997 08 20	208 33	0 35
1997 08 21	208 39	0 36
1997 08 22	208 45	0 36
1997 08 23	208 50	0 36
1997 08 24	208 56	0 36
1997 08 25	209 02	0 37
1997 08 26	209 08	0 37
1997 08 27	209 15	0 37
1997 08 28	209 21	0 37
1997 08 29	209 27	0 38
1997 08 30	209 33	0 38
1997 08 31	209 40	0 38
1997 09 01	209 46	0 38
1997 09 02	209 53	0 39
1997 09 03	209 59	0 39
1997 09 04	210 06	0 39
1997 09 05	210 13	0 39
1997 09 06	210 20	0 40
1997 09 07	210 27	0 40
1997 09 08	210 34	0 40
1997 09 09	210 40	0 40
1997 09 10	210 48	0 41
1997 09 11	210 55	0 41
1997 09 12	211 02	0 41
1997 09 13	211 09	0 41
1997 09 14	211 16	0 42
1997 09 15	211 24	0 42
1997 09 16	211 31	0 42
1997 09 17	211 38	0 42
1997 09 18	211 46	0 43
1997 09 19	211 53	0 43
1997 09 20	212 01	0 43
1997 09 21	212 08	0 43
1997 09 22	212 16	0 44
1997 09 23	212 24	0 44
1997 09 24	212 31	0 44
1997 09 25	212 39	0 44
1997 09 26	212 47	0 45

1997	09	27	212	55	0	45
1997	09	28	213	03	0	45
1997	09	29	213	10	0	45
1997	09	30	213	18	0	46
1997	10	01	213	26	0	46
1997	10	02	213	34	0	46
1997	10	03	213	42	0	47
1997	10	04	213	51	0	47
1997	10	05	213	59	0	47
1997	10	06	214	07	0	47
1997	10	07	214	15	0	48
1997	10	08	214	23	0	48
1997	10	09	214	31	0	48
1997	10	10	214	40	0	48
1997	10	11	214	48	0	49
1997	10	12	214	56	0	49
1997	10	13	215	04	0	49
1997	10	14	215	13	0	49
1997	10	15	215	21	0	50
1997	10	16	215	29	0	50
1997	10	17	215	38	0	50
1997	10	18	215	46	0	50
1997	10	19	215	54	0	51
1997	10	20	216	03	0	51
1997	10	21	216	11	0	51
1997	10	22	216	20	0	52
1997	10	23	216	28	0	52
1997	10	24	216	37	0	52
1997	10	25	216	45	0	52
1997	10	26	216	53	0	53
1997	10	27	217	02	0	53
1997	10	28	217	10	0	53
1997	10	29	217	19	0	54
1997	10	30	217	27	0	54
1997	10	31	217	36	0	54
1997	11	01	217	44	0	54
1997	11	02	217	53	0	55
1997	11	03	218	01	0	55
1997	11	04	218	10	0	55
1997	11	05	218	18	0	56
1997	11	06	218	27	0	56
1997	11	07	218	35	0	56
1997	11	08	218	43	0	56
1997	11	09	218	52	0	57
1997	11	10	219	00	0	57
1997	11	11	219	09	0	57
1997	11	12	219	17	0	58
1997	11	13	219	25	0	58
1997	11	14	219	34	0	58
1997	11	15	219	42	0	59
1997	11	16	219	50	0	59
1997	11	17	219	59	0	59
1997	11	18	220	07	0	59
1997	11	19	220	15	1	00
1997	11	20	220	23	1	00
1997	11	21	220	32	1	00
1997	11	22	220	40	1	01
1997	11	23	220	48	1	01
1997	11	24	220	56	1	01
1997	11	25	221	04	1	02
1997	11	26	221	12	1	02
1997	11	27	221	20	1	02
1997	11	28	221	28	1	03
1997	11	29	221	36	1	03
1997	11	30	221	44	1	03
1997	12	01	221	52	1	04
1997	12	02	222	00	1	04
1997	12	03	222	08	1	04
1997	12	04	222	15	1	05
1997	12	05	222	23	1	05
1997	12	06	222	31	1	05
1997	12	07	222	38	1	06
1997	12	08	222	46	1	06
1997	12	09	222	53	1	06
1997	12	10	223	01	1	07
1997	12	11	223	08	1	07
1997	12	12	223	16	1	07
1997	12	13	223	23	1	08
1997	12	14	223	30	1	08
1997	12	15	223	38	1	09
1997	12	16	223	45	1	09
1997	12	17	223	52	1	09
1997	12	18	223	59	1	10
1997	12	19	224	06	1	10
1997	12	20	224	13	1	10
1997	12	21	224	20	1	11
1997	12	22	224	27	1	11
1997	12	23	224	33	1	12
1997	12	24	224	40	1	12
1997	12	25	224	47	1	12
1997	12	26	224	53	1	13
1997	12	27	225	00	1	13
1997	12	28	225	06	1	13
1997	12	29	225	13	1	14
1997	12	30	225	19	1	14
1997	12	31	225	25	1	15
1998	01	01	225	31	1	15
1998	01	02	225	37	1	15
1998	01	03	225	43	1	16
1998	01	04	225	49	1	16
1998	01	05	225	55	1	17
1998	01	06	226	01	1	17
1998	01	07	226	07	1	18
1998	01	08	226	12	1	18
1998	01	09	226	18	1	18
1998	01	10	226	23	1	19
1998	01	11	226	28	1	19
1998	01	12	226	34	1	20
1998	01	13	226	39	1	20
1998	01	14	226	44	1	21
1998	01	15	226	49	1	21
1998	01	16	226	54	1	21
1998	01	17	226	59	1	22
1998	01	18	227	03	1	22
1998	01	19	227	08	1	23
1998	01	20	227	12	1	23
1998	01	21	227	17	1	24
1998	01	22	227	21	1	24
1998	01	23	227	25	1	24
1998	01	24	227	29	1	25
1998	01	25	227	34	1	25
1998	01	26	227	37	1	26
1998	01	27	227	41	1	26
1998	01	28	227	45	1	27
1998	01	29	227	49	1	27
1998	01	30	227	52	1	28
1998	01	31	227	56	1	28
1998	02	01	227	59	1	29
1998	02	02	228	02	1	29
1998	02	03	228	05	1	30
1998	02	04	228	08	1	30
1998	02	05	228	11	1	30
1998	02	06	228	14	1	31
1998	02	07	228	16	1	31
1998	02	08	228	19	1	32
1998	02	09	228	22	1	32
1998	02	10	228	24	1	33
1998	02	11	228	26	1	33
1998	02	12	228	28	1	34
1998	02	13	228	30	1	34
1998	02	14	228	32	1	35
1998	02	15	228	34	1	35
1998	02	16	228	36	1	36
1998	02	17	228	37	1	36
1998	02	18	228	39	1	37
1998	02	19	228	40	1	37
1998	02	20	228	41	1	38
1998	02	21	228	42	1	38
1998	02	22	228	43	1	39
1998	02	23	228	44	1	39
1998	02	24	228	45	1	40
1998	02	25	228	45	1	40
1998	02	26	228	46	1	41
1998	02	27	228	46	1	41
1998	02	28	228	47	1	42
1998	03	01	228	47	1	42
1998	03	02	228	47	1	43
1998	03	03	228	47	1	43
1998	03	04	228	47	1	44
1998	03	05	228	46	1	44
1998	03	06	228	46	1	45
1998	03	07	228	46	1	45
1998	03	08	228	45	1	46
1998	03	09	228	44	1	46
1998	03	10	228	43	1	47
1998	03	11	228	43	1	47
1998	03	12	228	42	1	48
1998	03	13	228	40	1	48
1998	03	14	228	39	1	49
1998	03	15	228	38	1	49
1998	03	16	228	36	1	50
1998	03	17	228	35	1	50
1998	03	18	228	33	1	51
1998	03	19	228	31	1	51
1998	03	20	228	29	1	52
1998	03	21	228	27	1	52
1998	03	22	228	25	1	53
1998	03	23	228	23	1	53
1998	03	24	228	21	1	54
1998	03	25	228	19	1	54
1998	03	26	228	16	1	55
1998	03	27	228	14	1	55
1998	03	28	228	11	1	56
1998	03	29	228	08	1	56
1998	03	30	228	05	1	57
1998	03	31	228	02	1	57
1998	04	01	228	00	1	58
1998	04	02	227	56	1	58
1998	04	03	227	53	1	59
1998	04	04	227	50	1	59
1998	04	05	227	47	2	00
1998	04	06	227	43	2	00
1998	04	07	227	40	2	00
1998	04	08	227	36	2	01
1998	04	09	227	33	2	01
1998	04	10	227	29	2	02
1998	04	11	227	25	2	02
1998	04	12	227	22	2	03
1998	04	13	227	18	2	03
1998	04	14	227	14	2	04
1998	04	15	227	10	2	04
1998	04	16	227	06	2	04
1998	04	17	227	02	2	05
1998	04	18	226	58	2	05
1998	04	19	226	54	2	06
1998	04	20	226	49	2	06
1998	04	21	226	45	2	06
1998	04	22	226	41	2	07
1998	04	23	226	37	2	07
1998	04	24	226	32	2	08
1998	04	25	226	28	2	08
1998	04	26	226	23	2	08
1998	04	27	226	19	2	09
1998	04	28	226	14	2	09
1998	04	29	226	10	2	10
1998	04	30	226	05	2	10
1998	05	01	226	01	2	10
1998	05	02	225	56	2	11
1998	05	03	225	52	2	11
1998	05	04	225	47	2	11
1998	05	05	225	43	2	12
1998	05	06	225	38	2	12
1998	05	07	225	34	2	12
1998	05	08	225	29	2	13
1998	05	09	225	25	2	13
1998	05	10	225	20	2	13
1998	05	11	225	15	2	14
1998	05	12	225	11	2	14
1998	05	13	225	06	2	14
1998	05	14	225	02	2	15
1998	05	15	224	58	2	15
1998	05	16	224	53	2	15
1998	05	17	224	49	2	15
1998	05	18	224	44	2	16
1998	05	19	224	40	2	16
1998	05	20	224	36	2	16
1998	05	21	224	31	2	16
1998	05	22	224	27	2	17
1998	05	23	224	23	2	17
1998	05	24	224	19	2	17
1998	05	25	224	15	2	17
1998	05	26	224	10	2	18
1998	05	27	224	06	2	18
1998	05	28	224	02	2	18
1998	05	29	223	59	2	18
1998	05	30	223	55	2	19
1998	05	31	223	51	2	19
1998	06	01	223	47	2	19
1998	06	02	223	43	2	19
1998	06	03	223	40	2	19
1998	06	04	223	36	2	20
1998	06	05	223	33	2	20
1998	06	06	223	29	2	20
1998	06	07	223	26	2	20
1998	06	08	223	23	2	20
1998	06	09	223	20	2	20
1998	06	10	223	17	2	21
1998	06	11	223	14	2	21
1998	06	12	223	11	2	21
1998	06	13	223	08	2	21
1998	06	14	223	05	2	21
1998	06	15	223	02	2	21
1998	06	16	223	00	2	21
1998	06	17	222	57	2	21
1998	06	18	222	55	2	22
1998	06	19	222	52	2	22
1998	06	20	222	50	2	22
1998	06	21	222	48	2	22
1998	06	22	222	46	2	22
1998	06	23	222	44	2	22
1998	06	24	222	42	2	22
1998	06	25	222	40	2	22
1998	06	26	222	38	2	22
1998	06	27	222	37	2	23
1998	06	28	222	35	2	23
1998	06	29	222	34	2	23
1998	06	30	222	33	2	23
1998	07	01	222	31	2	23
1998	07	02	222	30	2	23
1998	07	03	222	29	2	23
1998	07	04	222	28	2	23
1998	07	05	222	28	2	23
1998	07	06	222	27	2	23
1998	07	07	222	26	2	23
1998	07	08	222	26	2	23
1998	07	09	222	26	2	23
1998	07	10	222	25	2	23
1998	07	11	222	25	2	23
1998	07	12	222	25	2	24
1998	07	13	222	25	2	24
1998	07	14	222	25	2	24
1998	07	15	222	26	2	24
1998	07	16	222	26	2	24
1998	07	17	222	26	2	24
1998	07	18	222	27	2	24
1998	07	19	222	28	2	24
1998	07	20	222	28	2	24
1998	07	21	222	29	2	24
1998	07	22	222	30	2	24
1998	07	23	222	32	2	24
1998	07	24	222	33	2	24
1998	07	25	222	34	2	24
1998	07	26	222	35	2	24
1998	07	27	222	37	2	24
1998	07	28	222	39	2	24
1998	07	29	222	40	2	24
1998	07	30	222	42	2	24
1998	07	31	222	44	2	24
1998	08	01	222	46	2	24
1998	08	02	222	48	2	24
1998	08	03	222	51	2	24
1998	08	04	222	53	2	24
1998	08	05	222	55	2	24
1998	08	06	222	58	2	24
1998	08	07	223	01	2	24
1998	08	08	223	03	2	24
1998	08	09	223	06	2	24
1998	08	10	223	09	2	24
1998	08	11	223	12	2	24
1998	08	12	223	15	2	24
1998	08	13	223	19	2	24
1998	08	14	223	22	2	24
1998	08	15	223	25	2	25
1998	08	16	223	29	2	25
1998	08	17	223	32	2	25
1998	08	18	223	36	2	25
1998	08	19	223	40	2	25
1998	08	20	223	44	2	25
1998	08	21	223	48	2	25
1998	08	22	223	52	2	25
1998	08	23	223	56	2	25
1998	08	24	224	00	2	25
1998	08	25	224	05	2	25
1998	08	26	224	09	2	25
1998	08	27	224	13	2	25
1998	08	28	224	18	2	25
1998	08	29	224	23	2	25
1998	08	30	224	27	2	25
1998	08	31	224	32	2	25
1998	09	01	224	37	2	25
1998	09	02	224	42	2	25
1998	09	03	224	47	2	25
1998	09	04	224	52	2	25
1998	09	05	224	58	2	25
1998	09	06	225	03	2	25
1998	09	07	225	08	2	25
1998	09	08	225	14	2	25
1998	09	09	225	19	2	25
1998	09	10	225	25	2	25
1998	09	11	225	31	2	25
1998	09	12	225	36	2	26
1998	09	13	225	42	2	26
1998	09	14	225	48	2	26
1998	09	15	225	54	2	26
1998	09	16	226	00	2	26
1998	09	17	226	06	2	26
1998	09	18	226	12	2	26
1998	09	19	226	18	2	26
1998	09	20	226	25	2	26
1998	09	21	226	31	2	26
1998	09	22	226	37	2	26
1998	09	23	226	44	2	26
1998	09	24	226	50	2	26
1998	09	25	226	57	2	26
1998	09	26	227	03	2	27
1998	09	27	227	10	2	27
1998	09	28	227	17	2	27
1998	09	29	227	24	2	27
1998	09	30	227	31	2	27
1998	10	01	227	37	2	27
1998	10	02	227	44	2	27
1998	10	03	227	51	2	27
1998	10	04	227	58	2	27
1998	10	05	228	05	2	27
1998	10	06	228	13	2	28
1998	10	07	228	20	2	28
1998	10	08	228	27	2	28
1998	10	09	228	34	2	28
1998	10	10	228	41	2	28
1998	10	11	228	49	2	28
1998	10	12	228	56	2	28
1998	10	13	229	04	2	28
1998	10	14	229	11	2	28
1998	10	15	229	18	2	29
1998	10	16	229	26	2	29
1998	10	17	229	34	2	29
1998	10	18	229	41	2	29
1998	10	19	229	49	2	29
1998	10	20	229	56	2	29
1998	10	21	230	04	2	30
1998	10	22	230	12	2	30
1998	10	23	230	19	2	30
1998	10	24	230	27	2	30
1998	10	25	230	35	2	30
1998	10	26	230	43	2	30
1998	10	27	230	51	2	30
1998	10	28	230	58	2	31
1998	10	29	231	06	2	31
1998	10	30	231	14	2	31
1998	10	31	231	22	2	31
1998	11	01	231	30	2	31
1998	11	02	231	38	2	32
1998	11	03	231	46	2	32
1998	11	04	231	54	2	32
1998	11	05	232	02	2	32
1998	11	06	232	10	2	32
1998	11	07	232	18	2	33
1998	11	08	232	26	2	33
1998	11	09	232	34	2	33
1998	11	10	232	42	2	33
1998	11	11	232	50	2	33
1998	11	12	232	58	2	34
1998	11	13	233	06	2	34
1998	11	14	233	14	2	34
1998	11	15	233	22	2	34
1998	11	16	233	30	2	35
1998	11	17	233	38	2	35
1998	11	18	233	46	2	35
1998	11	19	233	54	2	35
1998	11	20	234	02	2	36

1998	11	21	234	10	2	36
1998	11	22	234	18	2	36
1998	11	23	234	26	2	36
1998	11	24	234	34	2	37
1998	11	25	234	42	2	37
1998	11	26	234	50	2	37
1998	11	27	234	58	2	38
1998	11	28	235	06	2	38
1998	11	29	235	14	2	38
1998	11	30	235	22	2	38
1998	12	01	235	30	2	39
1998	12	02	235	37	2	39
1998	12	03	235	45	2	39
1998	12	04	235	53	2	40
1998	12	05	236	01	2	40
1998	12	06	236	09	2	40
1998	12	07	236	16	2	41
1998	12	08	236	24	2	41
1998	12	09	236	32	2	41
1998	12	10	236	40	2	42
1998	12	11	236	47	2	42
1998	12	12	236	55	2	42
1998	12	13	237	02	2	43
1998	12	14	237	10	2	43
1998	12	15	237	17	2	43
1998	12	16	237	25	2	44
1998	12	17	237	32	2	44
1998	12	18	237	40	2	44
1998	12	19	237	47	2	45
1998	12	20	237	54	2	45
1998	12	21	238	02	2	46
1998	12	22	238	09	2	46
1998	12	23	238	16	2	46
1998	12	24	238	23	2	47
1998	12	25	238	30	2	47
1998	12	26	238	37	2	48
1998	12	27	238	44	2	48
1998	12	28	238	51	2	48
1998	12	29	238	58	2	49
1998	12	30	239	05	2	49
1998	12	31	239	12	2	50
1999	01	01	239	19	2	50
1999	01	02	239	25	2	50
1999	01	03	239	32	2	51
1999	01	04	239	38	2	51
1999	01	05	239	45	2	52
1999	01	06	239	51	2	52
1999	01	07	239	58	2	53
1999	01	08	240	04	2	53
1999	01	09	240	10	2	54
1999	01	10	240	17	2	54
1999	01	11	240	23	2	54
1999	01	12	240	29	2	55
1999	01	13	240	35	2	55
1999	01	14	240	41	2	56
1999	01	15	240	46	2	56
1999	01	16	240	52	2	57
1999	01	17	240	58	2	57
1999	01	18	241	04	2	58
1999	01	19	241	09	2	58
1999	01	20	241	15	2	59
1999	01	21	241	20	2	59
1999	01	22	241	25	3	00
1999	01	23	241	31	3	00
1999	01	24	241	36	3	01
1999	01	25	241	41	3	01
1999	01	26	241	46	3	02
1999	01	27	241	51	3	02
1999	01	28	241	56	3	03
1999	01	29	242	00	3	04
1999	01	30	242	05	3	04
1999	01	31	242	10	3	05
1999	02	01	242	14	3	05
1999	02	02	242	18	3	06
1999	02	03	242	23	3	06
1999	02	04	242	27	3	07
1999	02	05	242	31	3	07
1999	02	06	242	35	3	08
1999	02	07	242	39	3	08
1999	02	08	242	43	3	09
1999	02	09	242	47	3	10
1999	02	10	242	50	3	10
1999	02	11	242	54	3	11
1999	02	12	242	57	3	11
1999	02	13	243	01	3	12
1999	02	14	243	04	3	13
1999	02	15	243	07	3	13
1999	02	16	243	10	3	14
1999	02	17	243	13	3	14
1999	02	18	243	16	3	15
1999	02	19	243	19	3	15
1999	02	20	243	21	3	16
1999	02	21	243	24	3	17
1999	02	22	243	26	3	17
1999	02	23	243	29	3	18
1999	02	24	243	31	3	18
1999	02	25	243	33	3	19
1999	02	26	243	35	3	20
1999	02	27	243	37	3	20
1999	02	28	243	39	3	21
1999	03	01	243	41	3	22
1999	03	02	243	42	3	22
1999	03	03	243	44	3	23
1999	03	04	243	45	3	23
1999	03	05	243	46	3	24
1999	03	06	243	48	3	25
1999	03	07	243	49	3	25
1999	03	08	243	50	3	26
1999	03	09	243	50	3	26
1999	03	10	243	51	3	27
1999	03	11	243	52	3	28
1999	03	12	243	52	3	28
1999	03	13	243	53	3	29
1999	03	14	243	53	3	30
1999	03	15	243	53	3	30
1999	03	16	243	53	3	31
1999	03	17	243	53	3	31
1999	03	18	243	53	3	32
1999	03	19	243	53	3	33
1999	03	20	243	53	3	33
1999	03	21	243	52	3	34
1999	03	22	243	52	3	35
1999	03	23	243	51	3	35
1999	03	24	243	50	3	36
1999	03	25	243	49	3	36
1999	03	26	243	49	3	37
1999	03	27	243	47	3	38
1999	03	28	243	46	3	38
1999	03	29	243	45	3	39
1999	03	30	243	44	3	39
1999	03	31	243	42	3	40
1999	04	01	243	41	3	41
1999	04	02	243	39	3	41
1999	04	03	243	37	3	42
1999	04	04	243	35	3	42
1999	04	05	243	33	3	43
1999	04	06	243	31	3	44
1999	04	07	243	29	3	44
1999	04	08	243	27	3	45
1999	04	09	243	25	3	45
1999	04	10	243	22	3	46
1999	04	11	243	20	3	46
1999	04	12	243	17	3	47
1999	04	13	243	15	3	47
1999	04	14	243	12	3	48
1999	04	15	243	09	3	49
1999	04	16	243	06	3	49
1999	04	17	243	03	3	50
1999	04	18	243	00	3	50
1999	04	19	242	57	3	51
1999	04	20	242	54	3	51
1999	04	21	242	51	3	52
1999	04	22	242	47	3	52
1999	04	23	242	44	3	53
1999	04	24	242	40	3	53
1999	04	25	242	37	3	54
1999	04	26	242	33	3	54
1999	04	27	242	30	3	55
1999	04	28	242	26	3	55
1999	04	29	242	22	3	55
1999	04	30	242	18	3	56
1999	05	01	242	15	3	56
1999	05	02	242	11	3	57
1999	05	03	242	07	3	57
1999	05	04	242	03	3	58
1999	05	05	241	59	3	58
1999	05	06	241	54	3	58
1999	05	07	241	50	3	59
1999	05	08	241	46	3	59
1999	05	09	241	42	4	00
1999	05	10	241	38	4	00
1999	05	11	241	34	4	00
1999	05	12	241	29	4	01
1999	05	13	241	25	4	01
1999	05	14	241	21	4	01
1999	05	15	241	16	4	02
1999	05	16	241	12	4	02
1999	05	17	241	07	4	02
1999	05	18	241	03	4	03
1999	05	19	240	59	4	03
1999	05	20	240	54	4	03
1999	05	21	240	50	4	04
1999	05	22	240	45	4	04
1999	05	23	240	41	4	04
1999	05	24	240	37	4	04
1999	05	25	240	32	4	05
1999	05	26	240	28	4	05
1999	05	27	240	23	4	05
1999	05	28	240	19	4	05
1999	05	29	240	15	4	05
1999	05	30	240	10	4	06
1999	05	31	240	06	4	06
1999	06	01	240	02	4	06
1999	06	02	239	58	4	06
1999	06	03	239	53	4	06
1999	06	04	239	49	4	06
1999	06	05	239	45	4	07
1999	06	06	239	41	4	07
1999	06	07	239	37	4	07
1999	06	08	239	33	4	07
1999	06	09	239	29	4	07
1999	06	10	239	25	4	07
1999	06	11	239	21	4	07
1999	06	12	239	17	4	07
1999	06	13	239	13	4	07
1999	06	14	239	09	4	08
1999	06	15	239	05	4	08
1999	06	16	239	02	4	08
1999	06	17	238	58	4	08
1999	06	18	238	54	4	08
1999	06	19	238	51	4	08
1999	06	20	238	47	4	08
1999	06	21	238	44	4	08
1999	06	22	238	41	4	08
1999	06	23	238	37	4	08
1999	06	24	238	34	4	08
1999	06	25	238	31	4	08
1999	06	26	238	28	4	08
1999	06	27	238	25	4	08
1999	06	28	238	22	4	08
1999	06	29	238	19	4	08
1999	06	30	238	17	4	08
1999	07	01	238	14	4	08
1999	07	02	238	11	4	08
1999	07	03	238	09	4	07
1999	07	04	238	07	4	07
1999	07	05	238	04	4	07
1999	07	06	238	02	4	07
1999	07	07	238	00	4	07
1999	07	08	237	58	4	07
1999	07	09	237	56	4	07
1999	07	10	237	54	4	07
1999	07	11	237	52	4	07
1999	07	12	237	50	4	07
1999	07	13	237	49	4	07
1999	07	14	237	47	4	06
1999	07	15	237	46	4	06
1999	07	16	237	44	4	06
1999	07	17	237	43	4	06
1999	07	18	237	42	4	06
1999	07	19	237	41	4	06
1999	07	20	237	40	4	06
1999	07	21	237	39	4	05
1999	07	22	237	38	4	05
1999	07	23	237	38	4	05
1999	07	24	237	37	4	05
1999	07	25	237	37	4	05
1999	07	26	237	36	4	05
1999	07	27	237	36	4	04
1999	07	28	237	36	4	04
1999	07	29	237	36	4	04
1999	07	30	237	36	4	04
1999	07	31	237	36	4	04
1999	08	01	237	36	4	04
1999	08	02	237	37	4	03
1999	08	03	237	37	4	03
1999	08	04	237	38	4	03
1999	08	05	237	38	4	03
1999	08	06	237	39	4	03
1999	08	07	237	40	4	02
1999	08	08	237	41	4	02
1999	08	09	237	42	4	02
1999	08	10	237	43	4	02
1999	08	11	237	44	4	02
1999	08	12	237	45	4	02
1999	08	13	237	47	4	01
1999	08	14	237	48	4	01
1999	08	15	237	50	4	01
1999	08	16	237	52	4	01
1999	08	17	237	54	4	01
1999	08	18	237	56	4	00
1999	08	19	237	58	4	00
1999	08	20	238	00	4	00
1999	08	21	238	02	4	00
1999	08	22	238	04	4	00
1999	08	23	238	07	3	59
1999	08	24	238	09	3	59
1999	08	25	238	12	3	59
1999	08	26	238	14	3	59
1999	08	27	238	17	3	59
1999	08	28	238	20	3	58
1999	08	29	238	23	3	58
1999	08	30	238	26	3	58
1999	08	31	238	29	3	58
1999	09	01	238	32	3	58
1999	09	02	238	36	3	58
1999	09	03	238	39	3	57
1999	09	04	238	43	3	57
1999	09	05	238	46	3	57
1999	09	06	238	50	3	57
1999	09	07	238	54	3	57
1999	09	08	238	58	3	57
1999	09	09	239	02	3	56
1999	09	10	239	06	3	56
1999	09	11	239	10	3	56
1999	09	12	239	14	3	56
1999	09	13	239	18	3	56
1999	09	14	239	22	3	56
1999	09	15	239	27	3	55
1999	09	16	239	31	3	55
1999	09	17	239	36	3	55
1999	09	18	239	41	3	55
1999	09	19	239	45	3	55
1999	09	20	239	50	3	55
1999	09	21	239	55	3	55
1999	09	22	240	00	3	54
1999	09	23	240	05	3	54
1999	09	24	240	10	3	54
1999	09	25	240	15	3	54
1999	09	26	240	21	3	54
1999	09	27	240	26	3	54
1999	09	28	240	31	3	54
1999	09	29	240	37	3	54
1999	09	30	240	42	3	54
1999	10	01	240	48	3	53
1999	10	02	240	53	3	53
1999	10	03	240	59	3	53
1999	10	04	241	05	3	53
1999	10	05	241	11	3	53
1999	10	06	241	17	3	53
1999	10	07	241	22	3	53
1999	10	08	241	28	3	53
1999	10	09	241	35	3	53
1999	10	10	241	41	3	53
1999	10	11	241	47	3	53
1999	10	12	241	53	3	53
1999	10	13	241	59	3	53
1999	10	14	242	06	3	53
1999	10	15	242	12	3	52
1999	10	16	242	18	3	52
1999	10	17	242	25	3	52
1999	10	18	242	31	3	52
1999	10	19	242	38	3	52
1999	10	20	242	45	3	52
1999	10	21	242	51	3	52
1999	10	22	242	58	3	52
1999	10	23	243	05	3	52
1999	10	24	243	11	3	52
1999	10	25	243	18	3	52
1999	10	26	243	25	3	52
1999	10	27	243	32	3	52
1999	10	28	243	39	3	52
1999	10	29	243	46	3	52
1999	10	30	243	53	3	52
1999	10	31	244	00	3	52
1999	11	01	244	07	3	52
1999	11	02	244	14	3	52
1999	11	03	244	21	3	53
1999	11	04	244	28	3	53
1999	11	05	244	36	3	53
1999	11	06	244	43	3	53
1999	11	07	244	50	3	53
1999	11	08	244	57	3	53
1999	11	09	245	05	3	53
1999	11	10	245	12	3	53
1999	11	11	245	19	3	53
1999	11	12	245	27	3	53
1999	11	13	245	34	3	53
1999	11	14	245	41	3	53
1999	11	15	245	49	3	53
1999	11	16	245	56	3	54
1999	11	17	246	04	3	54
1999	11	18	246	11	3	54
1999	11	19	246	18	3	54
1999	11	20	246	26	3	54
1999	11	21	246	33	3	54
1999	11	22	246	41	3	54
1999	11	23	246	48	3	54
1999	11	24	246	56	3	55
1999	11	25	247	03	3	55
1999	11	26	247	11	3	55
1999	11	27	247	18	3	55
1999	11	28	247	26	3	55
1999	11	29	247	33	3	55
1999	11	30	247	41	3	56
1999	12	01	247	48	3	56
1999	12	02	247	56	3	56
1999	12	03	248	03	3	56
1999	12	04	248	11	3	56
1999	12	05	248	18	3	57
1999	12	06	248	26	3	57
1999	12	07	248	33	3	57
1999	12	08	248	41	3	57
1999	12	09	248	48	3	58
1999	12	10	248	56	3	58
1999	12	11	249	03	3	58
1999	12	12	249	11	3	58
1999	12	13	249	18	3	59
1999	12	14	249	25	3	59
1999	12	15	249	33	3	59
1999	12	16	249	40	3	59
1999	12	17	249	48	4	00
1999	12	18	249	55	4	00
1999	12	19	250	02	4	00
1999	12	20	250	09	4	01
1999	12	21	250	17	4	01
1999	12	22	250	24	4	01
1999	12	23	250	31	4	01
1999	12	24	250	38	4	02
1999	12	25	250	45	4	02
1999	12	26	250	52	4	02
1999	12	27	250	59	4	03
1999	12	28	251	07	4	03
1999	12	29	251	14	4	03
1999	12	30	251	20	4	04
1999	12	31	251	27	4	04
2000	01	01	251	34	4	05
2000	01	02	251	41	4	05
2000	01	03	251	48	4	05
2000	01	04	251	55	4	06
2000	01	05	252	01	4	06
2000	01	06	252	08	4	06
2000	01	07	252	15	4	07
2000	01	08	252	21	4	07
2000	01	09	252	28	4	08
2000	01	10	252	34	4	08
2000	01	11	252	41	4	08
2000	01	12	252	47	4	09
2000	01	13	252	54	4	09
2000	01	14	253	00	4	10

⚷ Chiron

2000	01	15	253	06	4	10
2000	01	16	253	12	4	11
2000	01	17	253	19	4	11
2000	01	18	253	25	4	12
2000	01	19	253	31	4	12
2000	01	20	253	37	4	12
2000	01	21	253	43	4	13
2000	01	22	253	48	4	13
2000	01	23	253	54	4	14
2000	01	24	254	00	4	14
2000	01	25	254	06	4	15
2000	01	26	254	11	4	15
2000	01	27	254	17	4	16
2000	01	28	254	22	4	16
2000	01	29	254	28	4	17
2000	01	30	254	33	4	17
2000	01	31	254	38	4	18
2000	02	01	254	43	4	19
2000	02	02	254	48	4	19
2000	02	03	254	53	4	20
2000	02	04	254	58	4	20
2000	02	05	255	03	4	21
2000	02	06	255	08	4	21
2000	02	07	255	13	4	22
2000	02	08	255	17	4	22
2000	02	09	255	22	4	23
2000	02	10	255	27	4	23
2000	02	11	255	31	4	24
2000	02	12	255	35	4	25
2000	02	13	255	40	4	25
2000	02	14	255	44	4	26
2000	02	15	255	48	4	26
2000	02	16	255	52	4	27
2000	02	17	255	56	4	28
2000	02	18	255	59	4	28
2000	02	19	256	03	4	29
2000	02	20	256	07	4	29
2000	02	21	256	10	4	30
2000	02	22	256	14	4	31
2000	02	23	256	17	4	31
2000	02	24	256	21	4	32
2000	02	25	256	24	4	33
2000	02	26	256	27	4	33
2000	02	27	256	30	4	34
2000	02	28	256	33	4	34
2000	02	29	256	36	4	35
2000	03	01	256	38	4	36
2000	03	02	256	41	4	36
2000	03	03	256	43	4	37
2000	03	04	256	46	4	38
2000	03	05	256	48	4	38
2000	03	06	256	51	4	39
2000	03	07	256	53	4	40
2000	03	08	256	55	4	40
2000	03	09	256	57	4	41
2000	03	10	256	59	4	42
2000	03	11	257	00	4	42
2000	03	12	257	02	4	43
2000	03	13	257	03	4	44
2000	03	14	257	05	4	44
2000	03	15	257	06	4	45
2000	03	16	257	07	4	46
2000	03	17	257	09	4	46
2000	03	18	257	10	4	47
2000	03	19	257	11	4	48
2000	03	20	257	11	4	48
2000	03	21	257	12	4	49
2000	03	22	257	13	4	50
2000	03	23	257	13	4	50
2000	03	24	257	14	4	51
2000	03	25	257	14	4	52
2000	03	26	257	14	4	52
2000	03	27	257	15	4	53
2000	03	28	257	15	4	54
2000	03	29	257	15	4	54
2000	03	30	257	14	4	55
2000	03	31	257	14	4	56
2000	04	01	257	14	4	56
2000	04	02	257	13	4	57
2000	04	03	257	13	4	58
2000	04	04	257	12	4	58
2000	04	05	257	11	4	59
2000	04	06	257	10	5	00
2000	04	07	257	09	5	00
2000	04	08	257	08	5	01
2000	04	09	257	07	5	02
2000	04	10	257	06	5	02
2000	04	11	257	05	5	03
2000	04	12	257	03	5	03
2000	04	13	257	02	5	04
2000	04	14	257	00	5	05
2000	04	15	256	58	5	05
2000	04	16	256	57	5	06
2000	04	17	256	55	5	07
2000	04	18	256	53	5	07
2000	04	19	256	51	5	08
2000	04	20	256	49	5	08
2000	04	21	256	46	5	09
2000	04	22	256	44	5	10
2000	04	23	256	42	5	10
2000	04	24	256	39	5	11
2000	04	25	256	37	5	11
2000	04	26	256	34	5	12
2000	04	27	256	31	5	12
2000	04	28	256	29	5	13
2000	04	29	256	26	5	13
2000	04	30	256	23	5	14
2000	05	01	256	20	5	14
2000	05	02	256	17	5	15
2000	05	03	256	14	5	16
2000	05	04	256	11	5	16
2000	05	05	256	07	5	16
2000	05	06	256	04	5	17
2000	05	07	256	01	5	17
2000	05	08	255	57	5	18
2000	05	09	255	54	5	18
2000	05	10	255	50	5	19
2000	05	11	255	47	5	19
2000	05	12	255	43	5	20
2000	05	13	255	39	5	20
2000	05	14	255	36	5	21
2000	05	15	255	32	5	21
2000	05	16	255	28	5	21
2000	05	17	255	24	5	22
2000	05	18	255	20	5	22
2000	05	19	255	16	5	22
2000	05	20	255	12	5	23
2000	05	21	255	08	5	23
2000	05	22	255	04	5	24
2000	05	23	255	00	5	24
2000	05	24	254	56	5	24
2000	05	25	254	52	5	24
2000	05	26	254	48	5	25
2000	05	27	254	44	5	25
2000	05	28	254	39	5	25
2000	05	29	254	35	5	26
2000	05	30	254	31	5	26
2000	05	31	254	27	5	26
2000	06	01	254	22	5	26
2000	06	02	254	18	5	27
2000	06	03	254	14	5	27
2000	06	04	254	10	5	27
2000	06	05	254	06	5	27
2000	06	06	254	01	5	27
2000	06	07	253	57	5	27
2000	06	08	253	53	5	28
2000	06	09	253	49	5	28
2000	06	10	253	44	5	28
2000	06	11	253	40	5	28
2000	06	12	253	36	5	28
2000	06	13	253	32	5	28
2000	06	14	253	28	5	28
2000	06	15	253	24	5	28
2000	06	16	253	20	5	28
2000	06	17	253	15	5	29
2000	06	18	253	11	5	29
2000	06	19	253	07	5	29
2000	06	20	253	03	5	29
2000	06	21	252	59	5	29
2000	06	22	252	56	5	29
2000	06	23	252	52	5	29
2000	06	24	252	48	5	29
2000	06	25	252	44	5	29
2000	06	26	252	40	5	29
2000	06	27	252	37	5	29
2000	06	28	252	33	5	28
2000	06	29	252	29	5	28
2000	06	30	252	26	5	28
2000	07	01	252	22	5	28
2000	07	02	252	19	5	28
2000	07	03	252	16	5	28
2000	07	04	252	12	5	28
2000	07	05	252	09	5	28
2000	07	06	252	06	5	28
2000	07	07	252	03	5	28
2000	07	08	252	00	5	27
2000	07	09	251	57	5	27
2000	07	10	251	54	5	27
2000	07	11	251	51	5	27
2000	07	12	251	48	5	27
2000	07	13	251	46	5	27
2000	07	14	251	43	5	26
2000	07	15	251	40	5	26
2000	07	16	251	38	5	26
2000	07	17	251	35	5	26
2000	07	18	251	33	5	26
2000	07	19	251	31	5	25
2000	07	20	251	29	5	25
2000	07	21	251	27	5	25
2000	07	22	251	25	5	25
2000	07	23	251	23	5	24
2000	07	24	251	21	5	24
2000	07	25	251	19	5	24
2000	07	26	251	17	5	24
2000	07	27	251	16	5	23
2000	07	28	251	14	5	23
2000	07	29	251	13	5	23
2000	07	30	251	12	5	22
2000	07	31	251	10	5	22
2000	08	01	251	09	5	22
2000	08	02	251	08	5	22
2000	08	03	251	07	5	21
2000	08	04	251	06	5	21
2000	08	05	251	06	5	21
2000	08	06	251	05	5	20
2000	08	07	251	04	5	20
2000	08	08	251	04	5	20
2000	08	09	251	04	5	19
2000	08	10	251	03	5	19
2000	08	11	251	03	5	19
2000	08	12	251	03	5	18
2000	08	13	251	03	5	18
2000	08	14	251	03	5	18
2000	08	15	251	03	5	17
2000	08	16	251	04	5	17
2000	08	17	251	04	5	17
2000	08	18	251	04	5	16
2000	08	19	251	05	5	16
2000	08	20	251	06	5	16
2000	08	21	251	06	5	15
2000	08	22	251	07	5	15
2000	08	23	251	08	5	15
2000	08	24	251	09	5	14
2000	08	25	251	10	5	14
2000	08	26	251	11	5	14
2000	08	27	251	13	5	13
2000	08	28	251	14	5	13
2000	08	29	251	16	5	13
2000	08	30	251	17	5	12
2000	08	31	251	19	5	12
2000	09	01	251	21	5	12
2000	09	02	251	23	5	11
2000	09	03	251	25	5	11
2000	09	04	251	27	5	10
2000	09	05	251	29	5	10
2000	09	06	251	31	5	10
2000	09	07	251	33	5	09
2000	09	08	251	36	5	09
2000	09	09	251	38	5	09
2000	09	10	251	41	5	08
2000	09	11	251	44	5	08
2000	09	12	251	46	5	08
2000	09	13	251	49	5	07
2000	09	14	251	52	5	07
2000	09	15	251	55	5	07
2000	09	16	251	58	5	06
2000	09	17	252	01	5	06
2000	09	18	252	05	5	06
2000	09	19	252	08	5	06
2000	09	20	252	12	5	05
2000	09	21	252	15	5	05
2000	09	22	252	19	5	05
2000	09	23	252	22	5	04
2000	09	24	252	26	5	04
2000	09	25	252	30	5	04
2000	09	26	252	34	5	03
2000	09	27	252	38	5	03
2000	09	28	252	42	5	03
2000	09	29	252	46	5	03
2000	09	30	252	50	5	02
2000	10	01	252	55	5	02
2000	10	02	252	59	5	02

DECLINATIONS

10 - day intervals

0 h Ephemeris Time

Chiron

DECLINATION

1891	03	09	+12	58
1891	03	19	+13	08
1891	03	29	+13	17
1891	04	08	+13	23
1891	04	18	+13	28
1891	04	28	+13	30
1891	05	08	+13	30
1891	05	18	+13	28
1891	05	28	+13	23
1891	06	07	+13	16
1891	06	17	+13	07
1891	06	27	+12	55
1891	07	07	+12	42
1891	07	17	+12	26
1891	07	27	+12	09
1891	08	06	+11	50
1891	08	16	+11	30
1891	08	26	+11	09
1891	09	05	+10	48
1891	09	15	+10	26
1891	09	25	+10	05
1891	10	05	+09	44
1891	10	15	+09	24
1891	10	25	+09	06
1891	11	04	+08	50
1891	11	14	+08	37
1891	11	24	+08	26
1891	12	04	+08	19
1891	12	14	+08	15
1891	12	24	+08	15
1892	01	03	+08	19
1892	01	13	+08	26
1892	01	23	+08	36
1892	02	02	+08	49
1892	02	12	+09	03
1892	02	22	+09	18
1892	03	03	+09	34
1892	03	13	+09	49
1892	03	23	+10	02
1892	04	02	+10	13
1892	04	12	+10	22
1892	04	22	+10	28
1892	05	02	+10	32
1892	05	12	+10	32
1892	05	22	+10	29
1892	06	01	+10	23
1892	06	11	+10	14
1892	06	21	+10	01
1892	07	01	+09	47
1892	07	11	+09	29
1892	07	21	+09	10
1892	07	31	+08	48
1892	08	10	+08	25
1892	08	20	+07	60
1892	08	30	+07	34
1892	09	09	+07	07
1892	09	19	+06	40
1892	09	29	+06	13
1892	10	09	+05	47
1892	10	19	+05	22
1892	10	29	+04	59
1892	11	08	+04	38
1892	11	18	+04	20
1892	11	28	+04	05
1892	12	08	+03	54
1892	12	18	+03	47
1892	12	28	+03	44
1893	01	07	+03	46
1893	01	17	+03	52
1893	01	27	+04	03
1893	02	06	+04	17
1893	02	16	+04	33
1893	02	26	+04	52
1893	03	08	+05	11
1893	03	18	+05	30
1893	03	28	+05	47
1893	04	07	+06	03
1893	04	17	+06	15
1893	04	27	+06	25
1893	05	07	+06	30
1893	05	17	+06	32
1893	05	27	+06	30
1893	06	06	+06	24
1893	06	16	+06	15
1893	06	26	+06	01
1893	07	06	+05	45
1893	07	16	+05	25
1893	07	26	+05	03
1893	08	05	+04	38
1893	08	15	+04	11
1893	08	25	+03	43
1893	09	04	+03	13
1893	09	14	+02	43
1893	09	24	+02	11
1893	10	04	+01	40
1893	10	14	+01	10
1893	10	24	+00	41
1893	11	03	+00	13
1893	11	13	-00	13
1893	11	23	-00	36
1893	12	03	-00	55
1893	12	13	-01	11
1893	12	23	-01	22
1894	01	02	-01	29
1894	01	12	-01	31
1894	01	22	-01	27
1894	02	01	-01	19
1894	02	11	-01	07
1894	02	21	-00	50
1894	03	03	-00	31
1894	03	13	-00	10
1894	03	23	+00	12
1894	04	02	+00	33
1894	04	12	+00	53
1894	04	22	+01	09
1894	05	02	+01	23
1894	05	12	+01	33
1894	05	22	+01	38
1894	06	01	+01	39
1894	06	11	+01	36
1894	06	21	+01	28
1894	07	01	+01	16
1894	07	11	+01	00
1894	07	21	+00	41
1894	07	31	+00	18
1894	08	10	-00	07
1894	08	20	-00	35
1894	08	30	-01	04
1894	09	09	-01	35
1894	09	19	-02	07
1894	09	29	-02	40
1894	10	09	-03	13
1894	10	19	-03	45
1894	10	29	-04	17
1894	11	08	-04	47
1894	11	18	-05	15
1894	11	28	-05	40
1894	12	08	-06	03
1894	12	18	-06	22
1894	12	28	-06	37
1895	01	07	-06	47
1895	01	17	-06	53
1895	01	27	-06	54
1895	02	06	-06	50
1895	02	16	-06	41
1895	02	26	-06	28
1895	03	08	-06	11
1895	03	18	-05	51
1895	03	28	-05	29
1895	04	07	-05	06
1895	04	17	-04	44
1895	04	27	-04	24
1895	05	07	-04	07
1895	05	17	-03	53
1895	05	27	-03	43
1895	06	06	-03	38
1895	06	16	-03	38
1895	06	26	-03	41
1895	07	06	-03	50
1895	07	16	-04	02
1895	07	26	-04	19
1895	08	05	-04	38
1895	08	15	-05	01
1895	08	25	-05	26
1895	09	04	-05	54
1895	09	14	-06	23
1895	09	24	-06	53
1895	10	04	-07	24
1895	10	14	-07	55
1895	10	24	-08	26
1895	11	03	-08	56
1895	11	13	-09	25
1895	11	23	-09	53
1895	12	03	-10	18
1895	12	13	-10	40
1895	12	23	-10	60
1896	01	02	-11	16
1896	01	12	-11	28
1896	01	22	-11	36
1896	02	01	-11	40
1896	02	11	-11	40
1896	02	21	-11	35
1896	03	02	-11	25
1896	03	12	-11	12
1896	03	22	-10	56
1896	04	01	-10	37
1896	04	11	-10	17
1896	04	21	-09	56
1896	05	01	-09	36
1896	05	11	-09	17
1896	05	21	-09	01
1896	05	31	-08	48
1896	06	10	-08	39
1896	06	20	-08	35
1896	06	30	-08	34
1896	07	10	-08	38
1896	07	20	-08	46
1896	07	30	-08	57
1896	08	09	-09	12
1896	08	19	-09	30
1896	08	29	-09	51
1896	09	08	-10	14
1896	09	18	-10	38
1896	09	28	-11	04
1896	10	08	-11	30
1896	10	18	-11	57
1896	10	28	-12	23
1896	11	07	-12	49
1896	11	17	-13	14
1896	11	27	-13	37
1896	12	07	-13	58
1896	12	17	-14	18
1896	12	27	-14	34
1897	01	06	-14	48
1897	01	16	-14	59
1897	01	26	-15	07
1897	02	05	-15	11
1897	02	15	-15	12
1897	02	25	-15	10
1897	03	07	-15	04
1897	03	17	-14	54
1897	03	27	-14	42
1897	04	06	-14	28
1897	04	16	-14	12
1897	04	26	-13	54
1897	05	06	-13	37
1897	05	16	-13	20
1897	05	26	-13	05
1897	06	05	-12	52
1897	06	15	-12	42
1897	06	25	-12	35
1897	07	05	-12	32
1897	07	15	-12	32
1897	07	25	-12	36
1897	08	04	-12	43
1897	08	14	-12	53
1897	08	24	-13	06
1897	09	03	-13	21
1897	09	13	-13	38
1897	09	23	-13	56
1897	10	03	-14	16
1897	10	13	-14	36
1897	10	23	-14	56
1897	11	02	-15	17
1897	11	12	-15	36
1897	11	22	-15	55
1897	12	02	-16	12
1897	12	12	-16	28
1897	12	22	-16	42
1898	01	01	-16	54
1898	01	11	-17	04
1898	01	21	-17	11
1898	01	31	-17	16
1898	02	10	-17	19
1898	02	20	-17	19
1898	03	02	-17	16
1898	03	12	-17	11
1898	03	22	-17	04
1898	04	01	-16	55
1898	04	11	-16	45
1898	04	21	-16	33
1898	05	01	-16	20
1898	05	11	-16	07
1898	05	21	-15	54
1898	05	31	-15	42
1898	06	10	-15	32
1898	06	20	-15	23
1898	06	30	-15	17
1898	07	10	-15	13
1898	07	20	-15	12
1898	07	30	-15	13
1898	08	09	-15	17
1898	08	19	-15	23
1898	08	29	-15	32
1898	09	08	-15	43
1898	09	18	-15	54
1898	09	28	-16	07
1898	10	08	-16	21
1898	10	18	-16	35
1898	10	28	-16	50
1898	11	07	-17	03
1898	11	17	-17	16
1898	11	27	-17	29
1898	12	07	-17	40
1898	12	17	-17	49
1898	12	27	-17	57
1899	01	06	-18	04
1899	01	16	-18	09
1899	01	26	-18	12
1899	02	05	-18	13
1899	02	15	-18	12
1899	02	25	-18	10
1899	03	07	-18	06
1899	03	17	-18	01
1899	03	27	-17	55
1899	04	06	-17	48
1899	04	16	-17	40
1899	04	26	-17	31
1899	05	06	-17	22
1899	05	16	-17	13
1899	05	26	-17	05
1899	06	05	-16	57
1899	06	15	-16	50
1899	06	25	-16	44
1899	07	05	-16	40
1899	07	15	-16	37
1899	07	25	-16	37
1899	08	04	-16	38
1899	08	14	-16	41
1899	08	24	-16	46
1899	09	03	-16	52
1899	09	13	-16	59
1899	09	23	-17	07
1899	10	03	-17	16
1899	10	13	-17	25
1899	10	23	-17	34
1899	11	02	-17	43
1899	11	12	-17	51
1899	11	22	-17	59
1899	12	02	-18	05
1899	12	12	-18	11
1899	12	22	-18	15
1900	01	01	-18	18
1900	01	11	-18	19
1900	01	21	-18	19
1900	01	31	-18	18
1900	02	10	-18	15
1900	02	20	-18	11
1900	03	02	-18	07
1900	03	12	-18	01
1900	03	22	-17	55
1900	04	01	-17	49
1900	04	11	-17	42
1900	04	21	-17	35
1900	05	01	-17	29
1900	05	11	-17	23
1900	05	21	-17	17
1900	05	31	-17	12
1900	06	10	-17	07
1900	06	20	-17	04
1900	06	30	-17	02
1900	07	10	-17	00
1900	07	20	-17	00
1900	07	30	-17	01
1900	08	09	-17	04
1900	08	19	-17	07
1900	08	29	-17	11
1900	09	08	-17	16
1900	09	18	-17	22
1900	09	28	-17	27
1900	10	08	-17	33
1900	10	18	-17	39
1900	10	28	-17	45
1900	11	07	-17	49
1900	11	17	-17	53
1900	11	27	-17	57
1900	12	07	-17	59
1900	12	17	-17	59
1900	12	27	-17	59
1901	01	06	-17	57
1901	01	16	-17	55
1901	01	26	-17	51
1901	02	05	-17	46
1901	02	15	-17	40
1901	02	25	-17	34
1901	03	07	-17	27
1901	03	17	-17	19
1901	03	27	-17	12
1901	04	06	-17	05
1901	04	16	-16	59
1901	04	26	-16	53
1901	05	06	-16	47
1901	05	16	-16	43
1901	05	26	-16	39
1901	06	05	-16	37
1901	06	15	-16	35
1901	06	25	-16	35
1901	07	05	-16	36
1901	07	15	-16	37
1901	07	25	-16	39
1901	08	04	-16	42
1901	08	14	-16	46
1901	08	24	-16	51
1901	09	03	-16	55
1901	09	13	-16	60
1901	09	23	-17	05
1901	10	03	-17	09
1901	10	13	-17	14
1901	10	23	-17	17
1901	11	02	-17	20
1901	11	12	-17	22
1901	11	22	-17	23
1901	12	02	-17	23
1901	12	12	-17	22
1901	12	22	-17	19
1902	01	01	-17	15
1902	01	11	-17	10
1902	01	21	-17	04
1902	01	31	-16	57
1902	02	10	-16	49
1902	02	20	-16	41
1902	03	02	-16	33
1902	03	12	-16	24
1902	03	22	-16	15
1902	04	01	-16	07
1902	04	11	-15	59
1902	04	21	-15	53
1902	05	01	-15	47
1902	05	11	-15	42
1902	05	21	-15	39
1902	05	31	-15	37
1902	06	10	-15	36
1902	06	20	-15	37
1902	06	30	-15	39
1902	07	10	-15	42
1902	07	20	-15	46
1902	07	30	-15	50
1902	08	09	-15	55
1902	08	19	-16	00
1902	08	29	-16	06
1902	09	08	-16	11
1902	09	18	-16	17
1902	09	28	-16	21
1902	10	08	-16	25
1902	10	18	-16	29
1902	10	28	-16	31
1902	11	07	-16	32
1902	11	17	-16	32
1902	11	27	-16	31
1902	12	07	-16	29
1902	12	17	-16	25
1902	12	27	-16	20
1903	01	06	-16	13
1903	01	16	-16	06
1903	01	26	-15	57
1903	02	05	-15	48
1903	02	15	-15	38
1903	02	25	-15	28
1903	03	07	-15	18
1903	03	17	-15	08
1903	03	27	-14	58
1903	04	06	-14	49
1903	04	16	-14	41
1903	04	26	-14	34
1903	05	06	-14	28
1903	05	16	-14	24
1903	05	26	-14	22
1903	06	05	-14	21
1903	06	15	-14	22
1903	06	25	-14	24
1903	07	05	-14	27
1903	07	15	-14	32
1903	07	25	-14	38
1903	08	04	-14	44
1903	08	14	-14	51
1903	08	24	-14	57
1903	09	03	-15	04
1903	09	13	-15	10
1903	09	23	-15	16
1903	10	03	-15	21
1903	10	13	-15	25
1903	10	23	-15	28
1903	11	02	-15	29
1903	11	12	-15	29
1903	11	22	-15	28
1903	12	02	-15	25
1903	12	12	-15	21
1903	12	22	-15	15
1904	01	01	-15	08
1904	01	11	-15	00
1904	01	21	-14	51
1904	01	31	-14	41
1904	02	10	-14	30
1904	02	20	-14	19
1904	03	01	-14	07
1904	03	11	-13	56
1904	03	21	-13	44
1904	03	31	-13	34
1904	04	10	-13	24
1904	04	20	-13	16
1904	04	30	-13	09
1904	05	10	-13	04
1904	05	20	-13	00
1904	05	30	-12	58
1904	06	09	-12	58
1904	06	19	-12	60
1904	06	29	-13	03
1904	07	09	-13	08
1904	07	19	-13	14
1904	07	29	-13	21
1904	08	08	-13	28
1904	08	18	-13	36
1904	08	28	-13	44
1904	09	07	-13	52
1904	09	17	-13	59
1904	09	27	-14	05
1904	10	07	-14	10
1904	10	17	-14	14
1904	10	27	-14	17
1904	11	06	-14	18
1904	11	16	-14	17
1904	11	26	-14	15
1904	12	06	-14	11
1904	12	16	-14	06
1904	12	26	-13	59
1905	01	05	-13	51
1905	01	15	-13	41
1905	01	25	-13	30

Chiron

1905 02 04	-13 19
1905 02 14	-13 07
1905 02 24	-12 55
1905 03 06	-12 42
1905 03 16	-12 30
1905 03 26	-12 18
1905 04 05	-12 07
1905 04 15	-11 57
1905 04 25	-11 49
1905 05 05	-11 42
1905 05 15	-11 37
1905 05 25	-11 33
1905 06 04	-11 32
1905 06 14	-11 32
1905 06 24	-11 35
1905 07 04	-11 39
1905 07 14	-11 45
1905 07 24	-11 52
1905 08 03	-11 60
1905 08 13	-12 09
1905 08 23	-12 18
1905 09 02	-12 26
1905 09 12	-12 35
1905 09 22	-12 43
1905 10 02	-12 49
1905 10 12	-12 55
1905 10 22	-12 59
1905 11 01	-13 01
1905 11 11	-13 02
1905 11 21	-13 00
1905 12 01	-12 58
1905 12 11	-12 53
1905 12 21	-12 47
1905 12 31	-12 39
1906 01 10	-12 30
1906 01 20	-12 19
1906 01 30	-12 08
1906 02 09	-11 55
1906 02 19	-11 42
1906 03 01	-11 29
1906 03 11	-11 16
1906 03 21	-11 03
1906 03 31	-10 51
1906 04 10	-10 40
1906 04 20	-10 30
1906 04 30	-10 22
1906 05 10	-10 15
1906 05 20	-10 10
1906 05 30	-10 07
1906 06 09	-10 06
1906 06 19	-10 07
1906 06 29	-10 10
1906 07 09	-10 15
1906 07 19	-10 21
1906 07 29	-10 29
1906 08 08	-10 38
1906 08 18	-10 47
1906 08 28	-10 57
1906 09 07	-11 07
1906 09 17	-11 16
1906 09 27	-11 24
1906 10 07	-11 31
1906 10 17	-11 36
1906 10 27	-11 40
1906 11 06	-11 43
1906 11 16	-11 43
1906 11 26	-11 41
1906 12 06	-11 38
1906 12 16	-11 33
1906 12 26	-11 26
1907 01 05	-11 17
1907 01 15	-11 07
1907 01 25	-10 56
1907 02 04	-10 44
1907 02 14	-10 31
1907 02 24	-10 18
1907 03 06	-10 04
1907 03 16	-09 51
1907 03 26	-09 38
1907 04 05	-09 25
1907 04 15	-09 14
1907 04 25	-09 04
1907 05 05	-08 56
1907 05 15	-08 49
1907 05 25	-08 44
1907 06 04	-08 41
1907 06 14	-08 41
1907 06 24	-08 42
1907 07 04	-08 46
1907 07 14	-08 52
1907 07 24	-08 59
1907 08 03	-09 07
1907 08 13	-09 17
1907 08 23	-09 27
1907 09 02	-09 37
1907 09 12	-09 47
1907 09 22	-09 56
1907 10 02	-10 05
1907 10 12	-10 12
1907 10 22	-10 18
1907 11 01	-10 22
1907 11 11	-10 24
1907 11 21	-10 24
1907 12 01	-10 22
1907 12 11	-10 18
1907 12 21	-10 12
1907 12 31	-10 05
1908 01 10	-09 56
1908 01 20	-09 45
1908 01 30	-09 34
1908 02 09	-09 21
1908 02 19	-09 08
1908 02 29	-08 54
1908 03 10	-08 40
1908 03 20	-08 26
1908 03 30	-08 13
1908 04 09	-08 01
1908 04 19	-07 49
1908 04 29	-07 40
1908 05 09	-07 31
1908 05 19	-07 25
1908 05 29	-07 21
1908 06 08	-07 18
1908 06 18	-07 18
1908 06 28	-07 20
1908 07 08	-07 24
1908 07 18	-07 30
1908 07 28	-07 38
1908 08 07	-07 47
1908 08 17	-07 57
1908 08 27	-08 07
1908 09 06	-08 18
1908 09 16	-08 28
1908 09 26	-08 38
1908 10 06	-08 47
1908 10 16	-08 54
1908 10 26	-08 60
1908 11 05	-09 04
1908 11 15	-09 06
1908 11 25	-09 05
1908 12 05	-09 03
1908 12 15	-08 59
1908 12 25	-08 53
1909 01 04	-08 45
1909 01 14	-08 35
1909 01 24	-08 24
1909 02 03	-08 12
1909 02 13	-07 59
1909 02 23	-07 45
1909 03 05	-07 31
1909 03 15	-07 17
1909 03 25	-07 04
1909 04 04	-06 50
1909 04 14	-06 38
1909 04 24	-06 27
1909 05 04	-06 17
1909 05 14	-06 09
1909 05 24	-06 03
1909 06 03	-05 59
1909 06 13	-05 57
1909 06 23	-05 58
1909 07 03	-06 00
1909 07 13	-06 05
1909 07 23	-06 11
1909 08 02	-06 19
1909 08 12	-06 29
1909 08 22	-06 39
1909 09 01	-06 50
1909 09 11	-07 01
1909 09 21	-07 11
1909 10 01	-07 21
1909 10 11	-07 30
1909 10 21	-07 37
1909 10 31	-07 43
1909 11 10	-07 47
1909 11 20	-07 48
1909 11 30	-07 48
1909 12 10	-07 45
1909 12 20	-07 41
1909 12 30	-07 34
1910 01 09	-07 26
1910 01 19	-07 16
1910 01 29	-07 05
1910 02 08	-06 52
1910 02 18	-06 39
1910 02 28	-06 25
1910 03 10	-06 11
1910 03 20	-05 57
1910 03 30	-05 43
1910 04 09	-05 30
1910 04 19	-05 18
1910 04 29	-05 07
1910 05 09	-04 58
1910 05 19	-04 50
1910 05 29	-04 44
1910 06 08	-04 40
1910 06 18	-04 39
1910 06 28	-04 40
1910 07 08	-04 43
1910 07 18	-04 47
1910 07 28	-04 54
1910 08 07	-05 03
1910 08 17	-05 12
1910 08 27	-05 23
1910 09 06	-05 34
1910 09 16	-05 45
1910 09 26	-05 56
1910 10 06	-06 06
1910 10 16	-06 15
1910 10 26	-06 22
1910 11 05	-06 28
1910 11 15	-06 31
1910 11 25	-06 33
1910 12 05	-06 32
1910 12 15	-06 29
1910 12 25	-06 24
1911 01 04	-06 17
1911 01 14	-06 08
1911 01 24	-05 58
1911 02 03	-05 47
1911 02 13	-05 34
1911 02 23	-05 20
1911 03 05	-05 06
1911 03 15	-04 52
1911 03 25	-04 38
1911 04 04	-04 24
1911 04 14	-04 12
1911 04 24	-03 60
1911 05 04	-03 49
1911 05 14	-03 40
1911 05 24	-03 33
1911 06 03	-03 27
1911 06 13	-03 24
1911 06 23	-03 23
1911 07 03	-03 24
1911 07 13	-03 27
1911 07 23	-03 33
1911 08 02	-03 40
1911 08 12	-03 49
1911 08 22	-03 59
1911 09 01	-04 10
1911 09 11	-04 21
1911 09 21	-04 32
1911 10 01	-04 43
1911 10 11	-04 53
1911 10 21	-05 02
1911 10 31	-05 09
1911 11 10	-05 14
1911 11 20	-05 17
1911 11 30	-05 18
1911 12 10	-05 17
1911 12 20	-05 14
1911 12 30	-05 09
1912 01 09	-05 02
1912 01 19	-04 53
1912 01 29	-04 42
1912 02 08	-04 30
1912 02 18	-04 17
1912 02 28	-04 04
1912 03 09	-03 50
1912 03 19	-03 35
1912 03 29	-03 21
1912 04 08	-03 08
1912 04 18	-02 55
1912 04 28	-02 44
1912 05 08	-02 33
1912 05 18	-02 25
1912 05 28	-02 18
1912 06 07	-02 13
1912 06 17	-02 10
1912 06 27	-02 09
1912 07 07	-02 11
1912 07 17	-02 14
1912 07 27	-02 20
1912 08 06	-02 28
1912 08 16	-02 37
1912 08 26	-02 47
1912 09 05	-02 58
1912 09 15	-03 09
1912 09 25	-03 21
1912 10 05	-03 32
1912 10 15	-03 42
1912 10 25	-03 50
1912 11 04	-03 57
1912 11 14	-04 02
1912 11 24	-04 05
1912 12 04	-04 06
1912 12 14	-04 04
1912 12 24	-04 01
1913 01 03	-03 55
1913 01 13	-03 48
1913 01 23	-03 38
1913 02 02	-03 28
1913 02 12	-03 16
1913 02 22	-03 03
1913 03 04	-02 49
1913 03 14	-02 35
1913 03 24	-02 21
1913 04 03	-02 07
1913 04 13	-01 53
1913 04 23	-01 41
1913 05 03	-01 29
1913 05 13	-01 20
1913 05 23	-01 11
1913 06 02	-01 05
1913 06 12	-01 00
1913 06 22	-00 58
1913 07 02	-00 57
1913 07 12	-00 59
1913 07 22	-01 04
1913 08 01	-01 10
1913 08 11	-01 17
1913 08 21	-01 27
1913 08 31	-01 37
1913 09 10	-01 48
1913 09 20	-02 00
1913 09 30	-02 11
1913 10 10	-02 22
1913 10 20	-02 32
1913 10 30	-02 40
1913 11 09	-02 47
1913 11 19	-02 52
1913 11 29	-02 54
1913 12 09	-02 55
1913 12 19	-02 53
1913 12 29	-02 49
1914 01 08	-02 43
1914 01 18	-02 35
1914 01 28	-02 26
1914 02 07	-02 15
1914 02 17	-02 02
1914 02 27	-01 49
1914 03 09	-01 36
1914 03 19	-01 22
1914 03 29	-01 07
1914 04 08	-00 54
1914 04 18	-00 41
1914 04 28	-00 28
1914 05 08	-00 17
1914 05 18	-00 08
1914 05 28	+00 00
1914 06 07	+00 06
1914 06 17	+00 10
1914 06 27	+00 12
1914 07 07	+00 12
1914 07 17	+00 10
1914 07 27	+00 05
1914 08 06	-00 01
1914 08 16	-00 09
1914 08 26	-00 19
1914 09 05	-00 29
1914 09 15	-00 41
1914 09 25	-00 52
1914 10 05	-01 04
1914 10 15	-01 14
1914 10 25	-01 24
1914 11 04	-01 32
1914 11 14	-01 39
1914 11 24	-01 43
1914 12 04	-01 45
1914 12 14	-01 45
1914 12 24	-01 43
1915 01 03	-01 39
1915 01 13	-01 33
1915 01 23	-01 24
1915 02 02	-01 15
1915 02 12	-01 03
1915 02 22	-00 51
1915 03 04	-00 38
1915 03 14	-00 24
1915 03 24	-00 10
1915 04 03	+00 04
1915 04 13	+00 18
1915 04 23	+00 30
1915 05 03	+00 42
1915 05 13	+00 53
1915 05 23	+01 02
1915 06 02	+01 10
1915 06 12	+01 16
1915 06 22	+01 19
1915 07 02	+01 21
1915 07 12	+01 20
1915 07 22	+01 17
1915 08 01	+01 12
1915 08 11	+01 06
1915 08 21	+00 57
1915 08 31	+00 47
1915 09 10	+00 37
1915 09 20	+00 25
1915 09 30	+00 14
1915 10 10	+00 02
1915 10 20	-00 08
1915 10 30	-00 18
1915 11 09	-00 26
1915 11 19	-00 32
1915 11 29	-00 36
1915 12 09	-00 38
1915 12 19	-00 37
1915 12 29	-00 35
1916 01 08	-00 30
1916 01 18	-00 23
1916 01 28	-00 15
1916 02 07	-00 05
1916 02 17	+00 07
1916 02 27	+00 19
1916 03 08	+00 32
1916 03 18	+00 46
1916 03 28	+01 00
1916 04 07	+01 14
1916 04 17	+01 27
1916 04 27	+01 40
1916 05 07	+01 51
1916 05 17	+02 02
1916 05 27	+02 11
1916 06 06	+02 18
1916 06 16	+02 23
1916 06 26	+02 26
1916 07 06	+02 27
1916 07 16	+02 26
1916 07 26	+02 23
1916 08 05	+02 18
1916 08 15	+02 11
1916 08 25	+02 02
1916 09 04	+01 52
1916 09 14	+01 41
1916 09 24	+01 29
1916 10 04	+01 18
1916 10 14	+01 07
1916 10 24	+00 56
1916 11 03	+00 47
1916 11 13	+00 40
1916 11 23	+00 34
1916 12 03	+00 30
1916 12 13	+00 29
1916 12 23	+00 29
1917 01 02	+00 32
1917 01 12	+00 37
1917 01 22	+00 44
1917 02 01	+00 53
1917 02 11	+01 04
1917 02 21	+01 15
1917 03 03	+01 28
1917 03 13	+01 41
1917 03 23	+01 55
1917 04 02	+02 09
1917 04 12	+02 22
1917 04 22	+02 35
1917 05 02	+02 48
1917 05 12	+02 59
1917 05 22	+03 09
1917 06 01	+03 17
1917 06 11	+03 24
1917 06 21	+03 29
1917 07 01	+03 31
1917 07 11	+03 32
1917 07 21	+03 31
1917 07 31	+03 27
1917 08 10	+03 21
1917 08 20	+03 14
1917 08 30	+03 05
1917 09 09	+02 55
1917 09 19	+02 44
1917 09 29	+02 32
1917 10 09	+02 21
1917 10 19	+02 10
1917 10 29	+01 59
1917 11 08	+01 51
1917 11 18	+01 43
1917 11 28	+01 38
1917 12 08	+01 35
1917 12 18	+01 34
1917 12 28	+01 35
1918 01 07	+01 38
1918 01 17	+01 44
1918 01 27	+01 51
1918 02 06	+01 60
1918 02 16	+02 11
1918 02 26	+02 22
1918 03 08	+02 35
1918 03 18	+02 48
1918 03 28	+03 02
1918 04 07	+03 16
1918 04 17	+03 29
1918 04 27	+03 42
1918 05 07	+03 54
1918 05 17	+04 05
1918 05 27	+04 14
1918 06 06	+04 22
1918 06 16	+04 29
1918 06 26	+04 33
1918 07 06	+04 35
1918 07 16	+04 35
1918 07 26	+04 33
1918 08 05	+04 29
1918 08 15	+04 23
1918 08 25	+04 16
1918 09 04	+04 07
1918 09 14	+03 56
1918 09 24	+03 45
1918 10 04	+03 33
1918 10 14	+03 22
1918 10 24	+03 11
1918 11 03	+03 01
1918 11 13	+02 53
1918 11 23	+02 46
1918 12 03	+02 41
1918 12 13	+02 38
1918 12 23	+02 37
1919 01 02	+02 39
1919 01 12	+02 43
1919 01 22	+02 48
1919 02 01	+02 56
1919 02 11	+03 05
1919 02 21	+03 16
1919 03 03	+03 28
1919 03 13	+03 41
1919 03 23	+03 54
1919 04 02	+04 08
1919 04 12	+04 21
1919 04 22	+04 34

1919	05	02	+04	47
1919	05	12	+04	59
1919	05	22	+05	09
1919	06	01	+05	18
1919	06	11	+05	26
1919	06	21	+05	32
1919	07	01	+05	36
1919	07	11	+05	37
1919	07	21	+05	37
1919	07	31	+05	35
1919	08	10	+05	30
1919	08	20	+05	24
1919	08	30	+05	16
1919	09	09	+05	07
1919	09	19	+04	56
1919	09	29	+04	45
1919	10	09	+04	33
1919	10	19	+04	22
1919	10	29	+04	11
1919	11	08	+04	02
1919	11	18	+03	54
1919	11	28	+03	47
1919	12	08	+03	42
1919	12	18	+03	40
1919	12	28	+03	40
1920	01	07	+03	42
1920	01	17	+03	46
1920	01	27	+03	52
1920	02	06	+04	00
1920	02	16	+04	10
1920	02	26	+04	21
1920	03	07	+04	33
1920	03	17	+04	45
1920	03	27	+04	59
1920	04	06	+05	12
1920	04	16	+05	26
1920	04	26	+05	38
1920	05	06	+05	51
1920	05	16	+06	02
1920	05	26	+06	12
1920	06	05	+06	21
1920	06	15	+06	28
1920	06	25	+06	33
1920	07	05	+06	37
1920	07	15	+06	38
1920	07	25	+06	37
1920	08	04	+06	35
1920	08	14	+06	30
1920	08	24	+06	23
1920	09	03	+06	15
1920	09	13	+06	06
1920	09	23	+05	55
1920	10	03	+05	44
1920	10	13	+05	32
1920	10	23	+05	21
1920	11	02	+05	10
1920	11	12	+05	01
1920	11	22	+04	53
1920	12	02	+04	47
1920	12	12	+04	43
1920	12	22	+04	41
1921	01	01	+04	41
1921	01	11	+04	44
1921	01	21	+04	48
1921	01	31	+04	55
1921	02	10	+05	03
1921	02	20	+05	13
1921	03	02	+05	24
1921	03	12	+05	36
1921	03	22	+05	49
1921	04	01	+06	02
1921	04	11	+06	15
1921	04	21	+06	29
1921	05	01	+06	41
1921	05	11	+06	53
1921	05	21	+07	04
1921	05	31	+07	14
1921	06	10	+07	22
1921	06	20	+07	29
1921	06	30	+07	34
1921	07	10	+07	37
1921	07	20	+07	38
1921	07	30	+07	36
1921	08	09	+07	33
1921	08	19	+07	28
1921	08	29	+07	21
1921	09	08	+07	13
1921	09	18	+07	03
1921	09	28	+06	52
1921	10	08	+06	41
1921	10	18	+06	30
1921	10	28	+06	19
1921	11	07	+06	08
1921	11	17	+05	59
1921	11	27	+05	52
1921	12	07	+05	46
1921	12	17	+05	43
1921	12	27	+05	41
1922	01	06	+05	42
1922	01	16	+05	45
1922	01	26	+05	50
1922	02	05	+05	57
1922	02	15	+06	05
1922	02	25	+06	15
1922	03	07	+06	26
1922	03	17	+06	38
1922	03	27	+06	51
1922	04	06	+07	04
1922	04	16	+07	17
1922	04	26	+07	30
1922	05	06	+07	43
1922	05	16	+07	54
1922	05	26	+08	05
1922	06	05	+08	14
1922	06	15	+08	22
1922	06	25	+08	28
1922	07	05	+08	33
1922	07	15	+08	35
1922	07	25	+08	36
1922	08	04	+08	34
1922	08	14	+08	31
1922	08	24	+08	25
1922	09	03	+08	18
1922	09	13	+08	09
1922	09	23	+07	60
1922	10	03	+07	49
1922	10	13	+07	38
1922	10	23	+07	26
1922	11	02	+07	16
1922	11	12	+07	06
1922	11	22	+06	57
1922	12	02	+06	50
1922	12	12	+06	45
1922	12	22	+06	41
1923	01	01	+06	40
1923	01	11	+06	42
1923	01	21	+06	45
1923	01	31	+06	50
1923	02	10	+06	57
1923	02	20	+07	06
1923	03	02	+07	16
1923	03	12	+07	28
1923	03	22	+07	40
1923	04	01	+07	53
1923	04	11	+08	06
1923	04	21	+08	18
1923	05	01	+08	31
1923	05	11	+08	43
1923	05	21	+08	54
1923	05	31	+09	05
1923	06	10	+09	14
1923	06	20	+09	21
1923	06	30	+09	27
1923	07	10	+09	31
1923	07	20	+09	33
1923	07	30	+09	33
1923	08	09	+09	31
1923	08	19	+09	27
1923	08	29	+09	21
1923	09	08	+09	14
1923	09	18	+09	05
1923	09	28	+08	55
1923	10	08	+08	44
1923	10	18	+08	33
1923	10	28	+08	22
1923	11	07	+08	11
1923	11	17	+08	02
1923	11	27	+07	53
1923	12	07	+07	47
1923	12	17	+07	42
1923	12	27	+07	39
1924	01	06	+07	39
1924	01	16	+07	40
1924	01	26	+07	44
1924	02	05	+07	50
1924	02	15	+07	57
1924	02	25	+08	06
1924	03	06	+08	17
1924	03	16	+08	28
1924	03	26	+08	40
1924	04	05	+08	53
1924	04	15	+09	06
1924	04	25	+09	18
1924	05	05	+09	31
1924	05	15	+09	43
1924	05	25	+09	53
1924	06	04	+10	03
1924	06	14	+10	12
1924	06	24	+10	19
1924	07	04	+10	24
1924	07	14	+10	27
1924	07	24	+10	29
1924	08	03	+10	29
1924	08	13	+10	26
1924	08	23	+10	22
1924	09	02	+10	16
1924	09	12	+10	09
1924	09	22	+09	60
1924	10	02	+09	49
1924	10	12	+09	39
1924	10	22	+09	28
1924	11	01	+09	17
1924	11	11	+09	06
1924	11	21	+08	57
1924	12	01	+08	49
1924	12	11	+08	43
1924	12	21	+08	39
1924	12	31	+08	36
1925	01	10	+08	36
1925	01	20	+08	38
1925	01	30	+08	43
1925	02	09	+08	49
1925	02	19	+08	56
1925	03	01	+09	06
1925	03	11	+09	16
1925	03	21	+09	27
1925	03	31	+09	40
1925	04	10	+09	52
1925	04	20	+10	05
1925	04	30	+10	17
1925	05	10	+10	29
1925	05	20	+10	41
1925	05	30	+10	51
1925	06	09	+11	00
1925	06	19	+11	08
1925	06	29	+11	15
1925	07	09	+11	20
1925	07	19	+11	23
1925	07	29	+11	24
1925	08	08	+11	23
1925	08	18	+11	21
1925	08	28	+11	16
1925	09	07	+11	10
1925	09	17	+11	02
1925	09	27	+10	53
1925	10	07	+10	43
1925	10	17	+10	32
1925	10	27	+10	21
1925	11	06	+10	11
1925	11	16	+10	01
1925	11	26	+09	52
1925	12	06	+09	44
1925	12	16	+09	38
1925	12	26	+09	35
1926	01	05	+09	33
1926	01	15	+09	33
1926	01	25	+09	36
1926	02	04	+09	40
1926	02	14	+09	47
1926	02	24	+09	55
1926	03	06	+10	04
1926	03	16	+10	14
1926	03	26	+10	26
1926	04	05	+10	38
1926	04	15	+10	50
1926	04	25	+11	03
1926	05	05	+11	15
1926	05	15	+11	27
1926	05	25	+11	38
1926	06	04	+11	48
1926	06	14	+11	56
1926	06	24	+12	04
1926	07	04	+12	10
1926	07	14	+12	14
1926	07	24	+12	17
1926	08	03	+12	18
1926	08	13	+12	17
1926	08	23	+12	14
1926	09	02	+12	09
1926	09	12	+12	02
1926	09	22	+11	55
1926	10	02	+11	45
1926	10	12	+11	35
1926	10	22	+11	25
1926	11	01	+11	14
1926	11	11	+11	04
1926	11	21	+10	54
1926	12	01	+10	45
1926	12	11	+10	38
1926	12	21	+10	33
1926	12	31	+10	30
1927	01	10	+10	29
1927	01	20	+10	29
1927	01	30	+10	32
1927	02	09	+10	37
1927	02	19	+10	44
1927	03	01	+10	52
1927	03	11	+11	01
1927	03	21	+11	12
1927	03	31	+11	23
1927	04	10	+11	35
1927	04	20	+11	47
1927	04	30	+11	59
1927	05	10	+12	11
1927	05	20	+12	23
1927	05	30	+12	33
1927	06	09	+12	43
1927	06	19	+12	51
1927	06	29	+12	58
1927	07	09	+13	04
1927	07	19	+13	07
1927	07	29	+13	10
1927	08	08	+13	10
1927	08	18	+13	09
1927	08	28	+13	05
1927	09	07	+13	00
1927	09	17	+12	54
1927	09	27	+12	46
1927	10	07	+12	36
1927	10	17	+12	26
1927	10	27	+12	16
1927	11	06	+12	06
1927	11	16	+11	56
1927	11	26	+11	46
1927	12	06	+11	38
1927	12	16	+11	32
1927	12	26	+11	27
1928	01	05	+11	24
1928	01	15	+11	23
1928	01	25	+11	24
1928	02	04	+11	28
1928	02	14	+11	33
1928	02	24	+11	40
1928	03	05	+11	48
1928	03	15	+11	58
1928	03	25	+12	08
1928	04	04	+12	19
1928	04	14	+12	31
1928	04	24	+12	43
1928	05	04	+12	55
1928	05	14	+13	06
1928	05	24	+13	17
1928	06	03	+13	27
1928	06	13	+13	36
1928	06	23	+13	44
1928	07	03	+13	50
1928	07	13	+13	55
1928	07	23	+13	59
1928	08	02	+14	00
1928	08	12	+14	00
1928	08	22	+13	59
1928	09	01	+13	55
1928	09	11	+13	50
1928	09	21	+13	43
1928	10	01	+13	35
1928	10	11	+13	26
1928	10	21	+13	16
1928	10	31	+13	06
1928	11	10	+12	56
1928	11	20	+12	46
1928	11	30	+12	37
1928	12	10	+12	30
1928	12	20	+12	24
1928	12	30	+12	19
1929	01	09	+12	17
1929	01	19	+12	17
1929	01	29	+12	18
1929	02	08	+12	22
1929	02	18	+12	27
1929	02	28	+12	34
1929	03	10	+12	43
1929	03	20	+12	52
1929	03	30	+13	03
1929	04	09	+13	14
1929	04	19	+13	25
1929	04	29	+13	37
1929	05	09	+13	48
1929	05	19	+13	59
1929	05	29	+14	09
1929	06	08	+14	19
1929	06	18	+14	27
1929	06	28	+14	34
1929	07	08	+14	40
1929	07	18	+14	45
1929	07	28	+14	48
1929	08	07	+14	49
1929	08	17	+14	49
1929	08	27	+14	46
1929	09	06	+14	43
1929	09	16	+14	37
1929	09	26	+14	31
1929	10	06	+14	22
1929	10	16	+14	14
1929	10	26	+14	04
1929	11	05	+13	54
1929	11	15	+13	44
1929	11	25	+13	35
1929	12	05	+13	27
1929	12	15	+13	20
1929	12	25	+13	14
1930	01	04	+13	10
1930	01	14	+13	08
1930	01	24	+13	09
1930	02	03	+13	11
1930	02	13	+13	15
1930	02	23	+13	20
1930	03	05	+13	27
1930	03	15	+13	36
1930	03	25	+13	45
1930	04	04	+13	55
1930	04	14	+14	06
1930	04	24	+14	17
1930	05	04	+14	28
1930	05	14	+14	39
1930	05	24	+14	49
1930	06	03	+14	59
1930	06	13	+15	08
1930	06	23	+15	16
1930	07	03	+15	22
1930	07	13	+15	28
1930	07	23	+15	32
1930	08	02	+15	34
1930	08	12	+15	35
1930	08	22	+15	34
1930	09	01	+15	32
1930	09	11	+15	28
1930	09	21	+15	22
1930	10	01	+15	15
1930	10	11	+15	07
1930	10	21	+14	59
1930	10	31	+14	49
1930	11	10	+14	40
1930	11	20	+14	30
1930	11	30	+14	22
1930	12	10	+14	14
1930	12	20	+14	07
1930	12	30	+14	02
1931	01	09	+13	59
1931	01	19	+13	58
1931	01	29	+13	58
1931	02	08	+14	01
1931	02	18	+14	05
1931	02	28	+14	11
1931	03	10	+14	18
1931	03	20	+14	26
1931	03	30	+14	36
1931	04	09	+14	46
1931	04	19	+14	56
1931	04	29	+15	07
1931	05	09	+15	17
1931	05	19	+15	27
1931	05	29	+15	37
1931	06	08	+15	46
1931	06	18	+15	54
1931	06	28	+16	01
1931	07	08	+16	07
1931	07	18	+16	12
1931	07	28	+16	15
1931	08	07	+16	17
1931	08	17	+16	17
1931	08	27	+16	16
1931	09	06	+16	13
1931	09	16	+16	09
1931	09	26	+16	03
1931	10	06	+15	57
1931	10	16	+15	49
1931	10	26	+15	40
1931	11	05	+15	31
1931	11	15	+15	22
1931	11	25	+15	14
1931	12	05	+15	05
1931	12	15	+14	58
1931	12	25	+14	52
1932	01	04	+14	48
1932	01	14	+14	45
1932	01	24	+14	45
1932	02	03	+14	46
1932	02	13	+14	48
1932	02	23	+14	53
1932	03	04	+14	59
1932	03	14	+15	06
1932	03	24	+15	14
1932	04	03	+15	23
1932	04	13	+15	33
1932	04	23	+15	43
1932	05	03	+15	53
1932	05	13	+16	02
1932	05	23	+16	12
1932	06	02	+16	21
1932	06	12	+16	29
1932	06	22	+16	36
1932	07	02	+16	42
1932	07	12	+16	47
1932	07	22	+16	51
1932	08	01	+16	54
1932	08	11	+16	55
1932	08	21	+16	54
1932	08	31	+16	53
1932	09	10	+16	50
1932	09	20	+16	45
1932	09	30	+16	40
1932	10	10	+16	33
1932	10	20	+16	26
1932	10	30	+16	18
1932	11	09	+16	09
1932	11	19	+16	01
1932	11	29	+15	53
1932	12	09	+15	45
1932	12	19	+15	39
1932	12	29	+15	34
1933	01	08	+15	30
1933	01	18	+15	28
1933	01	28	+15	28
1933	02	07	+15	29
1933	02	17	+15	32
1933	02	27	+15	37
1933	03	09	+15	43
1933	03	19	+15	50
1933	03	29	+15	58
1933	04	08	+16	07
1933	04	18	+16	16
1933	04	28	+16	25
1933	05	08	+16	34
1933	05	18	+16	43
1933	05	28	+16	51
1933	06	07	+16	59
1933	06	17	+17	06
1933	06	27	+17	13
1933	07	07	+17	18
1933	07	17	+17	22
1933	07	27	+17	25
1933	08	06	+17	26
1933	08	16	+17	27
1933	08	26	+17	26
1933	09	05	+17	24
1933	09	15	+17	20

1933	09	25	+17	16
1933	10	05	+17	10
1933	10	15	+17	04
1933	10	25	+16	57
1933	11	04	+16	49
1933	11	14	+16	42
1933	11	24	+16	34
1933	12	04	+16	27
1933	12	14	+16	20
1933	12	24	+16	15
1934	01	03	+16	10
1934	01	13	+16	07
1934	01	23	+16	06
1934	02	02	+16	06
1934	02	12	+16	08
1934	02	22	+16	12
1934	03	04	+16	16
1934	03	14	+16	22
1934	03	24	+16	29
1934	04	03	+16	37
1934	04	13	+16	45
1934	04	23	+16	53
1934	05	03	+17	01
1934	05	13	+17	09
1934	05	23	+17	17
1934	06	02	+17	25
1934	06	12	+17	31
1934	06	22	+17	37
1934	07	02	+17	42
1934	07	12	+17	46
1934	07	22	+17	49
1934	08	01	+17	51
1934	08	11	+17	51
1934	08	21	+17	51
1934	08	31	+17	49
1934	09	10	+17	46
1934	09	20	+17	43
1934	09	30	+17	38
1934	10	10	+17	33
1934	10	20	+17	27
1934	10	30	+17	20
1934	11	09	+17	13
1934	11	19	+17	06
1934	11	29	+16	60
1934	12	09	+16	53
1934	12	19	+16	48
1934	12	29	+16	43
1935	01	08	+16	40
1935	01	18	+16	38
1935	01	28	+16	38
1935	02	07	+16	38
1935	02	17	+16	41
1935	02	27	+16	44
1935	03	09	+16	49
1935	03	19	+16	55
1935	03	29	+17	01
1935	04	08	+17	08
1935	04	18	+17	15
1935	04	28	+17	23
1935	05	08	+17	30
1935	05	18	+17	37
1935	05	28	+17	44
1935	06	07	+17	50
1935	06	17	+17	55
1935	06	27	+17	59
1935	07	07	+18	02
1935	07	17	+18	05
1935	07	27	+18	06
1935	08	06	+18	06
1935	08	16	+18	06
1935	08	26	+18	04
1935	09	05	+18	02
1935	09	15	+17	58
1935	09	25	+17	54
1935	10	05	+17	49
1935	10	15	+17	44
1935	10	25	+17	38
1935	11	04	+17	32
1935	11	14	+17	26
1935	11	24	+17	20
1935	12	04	+17	15
1935	12	14	+17	10
1935	12	24	+17	06
1936	01	03	+17	03
1936	01	13	+17	00
1936	01	23	+17	00
1936	02	02	+17	00
1936	02	12	+17	02
1936	02	22	+17	04
1936	03	03	+17	08
1936	03	13	+17	13
1936	03	23	+17	18
1936	04	02	+17	24
1936	04	12	+17	31
1936	04	22	+17	37
1936	05	02	+17	43
1936	05	12	+17	49
1936	05	22	+17	54
1936	06	01	+17	59
1936	06	11	+18	03
1936	06	21	+18	07
1936	07	01	+18	09
1936	07	11	+18	10
1936	07	21	+18	11
1936	07	31	+18	10
1936	08	10	+18	09
1936	08	20	+18	07
1936	08	30	+18	04
1936	09	09	+18	00
1936	09	19	+17	56
1936	09	29	+17	51
1936	10	09	+17	46
1936	10	19	+17	41
1936	10	29	+17	35
1936	11	08	+17	30
1936	11	18	+17	25
1936	11	28	+17	20
1936	12	08	+17	16
1936	12	18	+17	13
1936	12	28	+17	10
1937	01	07	+17	09
1937	01	17	+17	08
1937	01	27	+17	08
1937	02	06	+17	10
1937	02	16	+17	12
1937	02	26	+17	16
1937	03	08	+17	20
1937	03	18	+17	24
1937	03	28	+17	30
1937	04	07	+17	35
1937	04	17	+17	40
1937	04	27	+17	45
1937	05	07	+17	50
1937	05	17	+17	54
1937	05	27	+17	58
1937	06	06	+18	01
1937	06	16	+18	02
1937	06	26	+18	03
1937	07	06	+18	03
1937	07	16	+18	02
1937	07	26	+18	00
1937	08	05	+17	58
1937	08	15	+17	54
1937	08	25	+17	50
1937	09	04	+17	45
1937	09	14	+17	40
1937	09	24	+17	34
1937	10	04	+17	28
1937	10	14	+17	23
1937	10	24	+17	17
1937	11	03	+17	12
1937	11	13	+17	08
1937	11	23	+17	04
1937	12	03	+17	01
1937	12	13	+16	58
1937	12	23	+16	57
1938	01	02	+16	56
1938	01	12	+16	56
1938	01	22	+16	57
1938	02	01	+16	59
1938	02	11	+17	02
1938	02	21	+17	06
1938	03	03	+17	10
1938	03	13	+17	14
1938	03	23	+17	19
1938	04	02	+17	24
1938	04	12	+17	28
1938	04	22	+17	33
1938	05	02	+17	36
1938	05	12	+17	39
1938	05	22	+17	41
1938	06	01	+17	42
1938	06	11	+17	43
1938	06	21	+17	42
1938	07	01	+17	40
1938	07	11	+17	37
1938	07	21	+17	33
1938	07	31	+17	28
1938	08	10	+17	22
1938	08	20	+17	16
1938	08	30	+17	09
1938	09	09	+17	02
1938	09	19	+16	54
1938	09	29	+16	47
1938	10	09	+16	40
1938	10	19	+16	33
1938	10	29	+16	27
1938	11	08	+16	22
1938	11	18	+16	18
1938	11	28	+16	15
1938	12	08	+16	14
1938	12	18	+16	13
1938	12	28	+16	14
1939	01	07	+16	15
1939	01	17	+16	18
1939	01	27	+16	22
1939	02	06	+16	26
1939	02	16	+16	30
1939	02	26	+16	36
1939	03	08	+16	41
1939	03	18	+16	46
1939	03	28	+16	51
1939	04	07	+16	55
1939	04	17	+16	59
1939	04	27	+17	01
1939	05	07	+17	03
1939	05	17	+17	04
1939	05	27	+17	04
1939	06	06	+17	02
1939	06	16	+16	59
1939	06	26	+16	55
1939	07	06	+16	50
1939	07	16	+16	43
1939	07	26	+16	36
1939	08	05	+16	27
1939	08	15	+16	18
1939	08	25	+16	08
1939	09	04	+15	58
1939	09	14	+15	47
1939	09	24	+15	37
1939	10	04	+15	27
1939	10	14	+15	18
1939	10	24	+15	09
1939	11	03	+15	02
1939	11	13	+14	57
1939	11	23	+14	53
1939	12	03	+14	51
1939	12	13	+14	51
1939	12	23	+14	52
1940	01	02	+14	55
1940	01	12	+14	59
1940	01	22	+15	05
1940	02	01	+15	11
1940	02	11	+15	18
1940	02	21	+15	25
1940	03	02	+15	32
1940	03	12	+15	39
1940	03	22	+15	45
1940	04	01	+15	50
1940	04	11	+15	54
1940	04	21	+15	57
1940	05	01	+15	59
1940	05	11	+15	59
1940	05	21	+15	57
1940	05	31	+15	54
1940	06	10	+15	50
1940	06	20	+15	43
1940	06	30	+15	35
1940	07	10	+15	26
1940	07	20	+15	15
1940	07	30	+15	03
1940	08	09	+14	50
1940	08	19	+14	37
1940	08	29	+14	22
1940	09	08	+14	08
1940	09	18	+13	53
1940	09	28	+13	39
1940	10	08	+13	26
1940	10	18	+13	13
1940	10	28	+13	02
1940	11	07	+12	53
1940	11	17	+12	46
1940	11	27	+12	42
1940	12	07	+12	40
1940	12	17	+12	40
1940	12	27	+12	43
1941	01	06	+12	48
1941	01	16	+12	56
1941	01	26	+13	04
1941	02	05	+13	14
1941	02	15	+13	24
1941	02	25	+13	34
1941	03	07	+13	44
1941	03	17	+13	53
1941	03	27	+14	01
1941	04	06	+14	07
1941	04	16	+14	11
1941	04	26	+14	14
1941	05	06	+14	15
1941	05	16	+14	13
1941	05	26	+14	09
1941	06	05	+14	03
1941	06	15	+13	56
1941	06	25	+13	46
1941	07	05	+13	34
1941	07	15	+13	20
1941	07	25	+13	05
1941	08	04	+12	48
1941	08	14	+12	30
1941	08	24	+12	11
1941	09	03	+11	52
1941	09	13	+11	32
1941	09	23	+11	13
1941	10	03	+10	54
1941	10	13	+10	36
1941	10	23	+10	19
1941	11	02	+10	05
1941	11	12	+09	53
1941	11	22	+09	43
1941	12	02	+09	36
1941	12	12	+09	33
1941	12	22	+09	33
1942	01	01	+09	37
1942	01	11	+09	44
1942	01	21	+09	53
1942	01	31	+10	04
1942	02	10	+10	17
1942	02	20	+10	31
1942	03	02	+10	45
1942	03	12	+10	59
1942	03	22	+11	11
1942	04	01	+11	21
1942	04	11	+11	29
1942	04	21	+11	35
1942	05	01	+11	38
1942	05	11	+11	39
1942	05	21	+11	36
1942	05	31	+11	31
1942	06	10	+11	23
1942	06	20	+11	12
1942	06	30	+10	58
1942	07	10	+10	43
1942	07	20	+10	25
1942	07	30	+10	05
1942	08	09	+09	43
1942	08	19	+09	20
1942	08	29	+08	56
1942	09	08	+08	32
1942	09	18	+08	07
1942	09	28	+07	42
1942	10	08	+07	18
1942	10	18	+06	55
1942	10	28	+06	34
1942	11	07	+06	14
1942	11	17	+05	58
1942	11	27	+05	44
1942	12	07	+05	34
1942	12	17	+05	28
1942	12	27	+05	26
1943	01	06	+05	29
1943	01	16	+05	35
1943	01	26	+05	45
1943	02	05	+05	59
1943	02	15	+06	14
1943	02	25	+06	32
1943	03	07	+06	49
1943	03	17	+07	07
1943	03	27	+07	23
1943	04	06	+07	37
1943	04	16	+07	48
1943	04	26	+07	57
1943	05	06	+08	02
1943	05	16	+08	03
1943	05	26	+08	01
1943	06	05	+07	55
1943	06	15	+07	46
1943	06	25	+07	34
1943	07	05	+07	18
1943	07	15	+07	00
1943	07	25	+06	38
1943	08	04	+06	15
1943	08	14	+05	50
1943	08	24	+05	23
1943	09	03	+04	54
1943	09	13	+04	25
1943	09	23	+03	56
1943	10	03	+03	26
1943	10	13	+02	57
1943	10	23	+02	29
1943	11	02	+02	03
1943	11	12	+01	39
1943	11	22	+01	18
1943	12	02	+01	00
1943	12	12	+00	45
1943	12	22	+00	35
1944	01	01	+00	30
1944	01	11	+00	29
1944	01	21	+00	33
1944	01	31	+00	42
1944	02	10	+00	55
1944	02	20	+01	11
1944	03	01	+01	30
1944	03	11	+01	50
1944	03	21	+02	11
1944	03	31	+02	31
1944	04	10	+02	49
1944	04	20	+03	05
1944	04	30	+03	17
1944	05	10	+03	26
1944	05	20	+03	30
1944	05	30	+03	30
1944	06	09	+03	26
1944	06	19	+03	18
1944	06	29	+03	06
1944	07	09	+02	50
1944	07	19	+02	31
1944	07	29	+02	08
1944	08	08	+01	43
1944	08	18	+01	16
1944	08	28	+00	47
1944	09	07	+00	17
1944	09	17	-00	15
1944	09	27	-00	47
1944	10	07	-01	19
1944	10	17	-01	51
1944	10	27	-02	22
1944	11	06	-02	51
1944	11	16	-03	19
1944	11	26	-03	44
1944	12	06	-04	06
1944	12	16	-04	24
1944	12	26	-04	38
1945	01	05	-04	48
1945	01	15	-04	53
1945	01	25	-04	52
1945	02	04	-04	47
1945	02	14	-04	37
1945	02	24	-04	23
1945	03	06	-04	05
1945	03	16	-03	45
1945	03	26	-03	23
1945	04	05	-03	01
1945	04	15	-02	40
1945	04	25	-02	20
1945	05	05	-02	04
1945	05	15	-01	51
1945	05	25	-01	43
1945	06	04	-01	39
1945	06	14	-01	39
1945	06	24	-01	44
1945	07	04	-01	54
1945	07	14	-02	07
1945	07	24	-02	24
1945	08	03	-02	45
1945	08	13	-03	08
1945	08	23	-03	35
1945	09	02	-04	03
1945	09	12	-04	33
1945	09	22	-05	04
1945	10	02	-05	35
1945	10	12	-06	07
1945	10	22	-06	39
1945	11	01	-07	10
1945	11	11	-07	40
1945	11	21	-08	07
1945	12	01	-08	33
1945	12	11	-08	56
1945	12	21	-09	16
1945	12	31	-09	32
1946	01	10	-09	45
1946	01	20	-09	53
1946	01	30	-09	56
1946	02	09	-09	55
1946	02	19	-09	49
1946	03	01	-09	38
1946	03	11	-09	24
1946	03	21	-09	07
1946	03	31	-08	47
1946	04	10	-08	26
1946	04	20	-08	04
1946	04	30	-07	44
1946	05	10	-07	25
1946	05	20	-07	09
1946	05	30	-06	57
1946	06	09	-06	49
1946	06	19	-06	45
1946	06	29	-06	46
1946	07	09	-06	51
1946	07	19	-07	00
1946	07	29	-07	13
1946	08	08	-07	30
1946	08	18	-07	49
1946	08	28	-08	12
1946	09	07	-08	36
1946	09	17	-09	02
1946	09	27	-09	30
1946	10	07	-09	58
1946	10	17	-10	26
1946	10	27	-10	54
1946	11	06	-11	22
1946	11	16	-11	49
1946	11	26	-12	14
1946	12	06	-12	37
1946	12	16	-12	58
1946	12	26	-13	16
1947	01	05	-13	32
1947	01	15	-13	44
1947	01	25	-13	52
1947	02	04	-13	57
1947	02	14	-13	58
1947	02	24	-13	55
1947	03	06	-13	48
1947	03	16	-13	38
1947	03	26	-13	25
1947	04	05	-13	09
1947	04	15	-12	51
1947	04	25	-12	33
1947	05	05	-12	14
1947	05	15	-11	57
1947	05	25	-11	41
1947	06	04	-11	27
1947	06	14	-11	17
1947	06	24	-11	10
1947	07	04	-11	07
1947	07	14	-11	08
1947	07	24	-11	13
1947	08	03	-11	21
1947	08	13	-11	33
1947	08	23	-11	48
1947	09	02	-12	04
1947	09	12	-12	23
1947	09	22	-12	44
1947	10	02	-13	06
1947	10	12	-13	28
1947	10	22	-13	51
1947	11	01	-14	14
1947	11	11	-14	36
1947	11	21	-14	57
1947	12	01	-15	16
1947	12	11	-15	35
1947	12	21	-15	51
1947	12	31	-16	05
1948	01	10	-16	17
1948	01	20	-16	26
1948	01	30	-16	32
1948	02	09	-16	36

1948	02	19	−16	37
1948	02	29	−16	34
1948	03	10	−16	30
1948	03	20	−16	22
1948	03	30	−16	13
1948	04	09	−16	01
1948	04	19	−15	48
1948	04	29	−15	34
1948	05	09	−15	19
1948	05	19	−15	05
1948	05	29	−14	51
1948	06	08	−14	40
1948	06	18	−14	30
1948	06	28	−14	23
1948	07	08	−14	19
1948	07	18	−14	18
1948	07	28	−14	19
1948	08	07	−14	24
1948	08	17	−14	32
1948	08	27	−14	41
1948	09	06	−14	53
1948	09	16	−15	07
1948	09	26	−15	22
1948	10	06	−15	37
1948	10	16	−15	54
1948	10	26	−16	10
1948	11	05	−16	26
1948	11	15	−16	42
1948	11	25	−16	56
1948	12	05	−17	10
1948	12	15	−17	22
1948	12	25	−17	32
1949	01	04	−17	41
1949	01	14	−17	48
1949	01	24	−17	52
1949	02	03	−17	55
1949	02	13	−17	56
1949	02	23	−17	55
1949	03	05	−17	52
1949	03	15	−17	47
1949	03	25	−17	41
1949	04	04	−17	34
1949	04	14	−17	25
1949	04	24	−17	15
1949	05	04	−17	05
1949	05	14	−16	55
1949	05	24	−16	45
1949	06	03	−16	35
1949	06	13	−16	27
1949	06	23	−16	20
1949	07	03	−16	15
1949	07	13	−16	11
1949	07	23	−16	10
1949	08	02	−16	11
1949	08	12	−16	14
1949	08	22	−16	19
1949	09	01	−16	26
1949	09	11	−16	34
1949	09	21	−16	43
1949	10	01	−16	53
1949	10	11	−17	04
1949	10	21	−17	15
1949	10	31	−17	26
1949	11	10	−17	36
1949	11	20	−17	45
1949	11	30	−17	54
1949	12	10	−18	01
1949	12	20	−18	08
1949	12	30	−18	12
1950	01	09	−18	16
1950	01	19	−18	17
1950	01	29	−18	18
1950	02	08	−18	16
1950	02	18	−18	14
1950	02	28	−18	10
1950	03	10	−18	06
1950	03	20	−18	00
1950	03	30	−17	54
1950	04	09	−17	47
1950	04	19	−17	40
1950	04	29	−17	33
1950	05	09	−17	25
1950	05	19	−17	19
1950	05	29	−17	12
1950	06	08	−17	07
1950	06	18	−17	02
1950	06	28	−16	58
1950	07	08	−16	56
1950	07	18	−16	55
1950	07	28	−16	55
1950	08	07	−16	57
1950	08	17	−17	00
1950	08	27	−17	04
1950	09	06	−17	09
1950	09	16	−17	15
1950	09	26	−17	22
1950	10	06	−17	29
1950	10	16	−17	36
1950	10	26	−17	42
1950	11	05	−17	48
1950	11	15	−17	54
1950	11	25	−17	59
1950	12	05	−18	02
1950	12	15	−18	05
1950	12	25	−18	06
1951	01	04	−18	06
1951	01	14	−18	04
1951	01	24	−18	02
1951	02	03	−17	58
1951	02	13	−17	53
1951	02	23	−17	48
1951	03	05	−17	42
1951	03	15	−17	35
1951	03	25	−17	28
1951	04	04	−17	21
1951	04	14	−17	15
1951	04	24	−17	08
1951	05	04	−17	03
1951	05	14	−16	58
1951	05	24	−16	53
1951	06	03	−16	50
1951	06	13	−16	47
1951	06	23	−16	46
1951	07	03	−16	45
1951	07	13	−16	46
1951	07	23	−16	47
1951	08	02	−16	50
1951	08	12	−16	53
1951	08	22	−16	57
1951	09	01	−17	01
1951	09	11	−17	06
1951	09	21	−17	11
1951	10	01	−17	16
1951	10	11	−17	21
1951	10	21	−17	25
1951	10	31	−17	29
1951	11	10	−17	32
1951	11	20	−17	34
1951	11	30	−17	35
1951	12	10	−17	35
1951	12	20	−17	33
1951	12	30	−17	31
1952	01	09	−17	27
1952	01	19	−17	22
1952	01	29	−17	16
1952	02	08	−17	09
1952	02	18	−17	02
1952	02	28	−16	54
1952	03	09	−16	45
1952	03	19	−16	37
1952	03	29	−16	29
1952	04	08	−16	21
1952	04	18	−16	15
1952	04	28	−16	09
1952	05	08	−16	04
1952	05	18	−16	00
1952	05	28	−15	57
1952	06	07	−15	56
1952	06	17	−15	56
1952	06	27	−15	57
1952	07	07	−15	59
1952	07	17	−16	02
1952	07	27	−16	06
1952	08	06	−16	10
1952	08	16	−16	15
1952	08	26	−16	20
1952	09	05	−16	25
1952	09	15	−16	30
1952	09	25	−16	35
1952	10	05	−16	40
1952	10	15	−16	43
1952	10	25	−16	46
1952	11	04	−16	48
1952	11	14	−16	49
1952	11	24	−16	48
1952	12	04	−16	47
1952	12	14	−16	44
1952	12	24	−16	39
1953	01	03	−16	34
1953	01	13	−16	27
1953	01	23	−16	20
1953	02	02	−16	11
1953	02	12	−16	02
1953	02	22	−15	52
1953	03	04	−15	42
1953	03	14	−15	32
1953	03	24	−15	23
1953	04	03	−15	14
1953	04	13	−15	06
1953	04	23	−14	59
1953	05	03	−14	53
1953	05	13	−14	48
1953	05	23	−14	46
1953	06	02	−14	44
1953	06	12	−14	44
1953	06	22	−14	46
1953	07	02	−14	49
1953	07	12	−14	53
1953	07	22	−14	58
1953	08	01	−15	03
1953	08	11	−15	10
1953	08	21	−15	16
1953	08	31	−15	22
1953	09	10	−15	29
1953	09	20	−15	34
1953	09	30	−15	39
1953	10	10	−15	43
1953	10	20	−15	46
1953	10	30	−15	48
1953	11	09	−15	49
1953	11	19	−15	48
1953	11	29	−15	46
1953	12	09	−15	42
1953	12	19	−15	38
1953	12	29	−15	31
1954	01	08	−15	24
1954	01	18	−15	15
1954	01	28	−15	05
1954	02	07	−14	55
1954	02	17	−14	44
1954	02	27	−14	33
1954	03	09	−14	22
1954	03	19	−14	11
1954	03	29	−14	00
1954	04	08	−13	51
1954	04	18	−13	42
1954	04	28	−13	35
1954	05	08	−13	29
1954	05	18	−13	25
1954	05	28	−13	23
1954	06	07	−13	22
1954	06	17	−13	23
1954	06	27	−13	26
1954	07	07	−13	30
1954	07	17	−13	36
1954	07	27	−13	42
1954	08	06	−13	50
1954	08	16	−13	57
1954	08	26	−14	05
1954	09	05	−14	12
1954	09	15	−14	19
1954	09	25	−14	26
1954	10	05	−14	31
1954	10	15	−14	35
1954	10	25	−14	38
1954	11	04	−14	39
1954	11	14	−14	39
1954	11	24	−14	37
1954	12	04	−14	34
1954	12	14	−14	29
1954	12	24	−14	23
1955	01	03	−14	15
1955	01	13	−14	06
1955	01	23	−13	56
1955	02	02	−13	45
1955	02	12	−13	33
1955	02	22	−13	21
1955	03	04	−13	09
1955	03	14	−12	56
1955	03	24	−12	45
1955	04	03	−12	34
1955	04	13	−12	24
1955	04	23	−12	15
1955	05	03	−12	08
1955	05	13	−12	02
1955	05	23	−11	58
1955	06	02	−11	57
1955	06	12	−11	57
1955	06	22	−11	59
1955	07	02	−12	02
1955	07	12	−12	08
1955	07	22	−12	14
1955	08	01	−12	22
1955	08	11	−12	30
1955	08	21	−12	39
1955	08	31	−12	48
1955	09	10	−12	56
1955	09	20	−13	04
1955	09	30	−13	10
1955	10	10	−13	16
1955	10	20	−13	20
1955	10	30	−13	23
1955	11	09	−13	24
1955	11	19	−13	23
1955	11	29	−13	21
1955	12	09	−13	16
1955	12	19	−13	11
1955	12	29	−13	03
1956	01	08	−12	54
1956	01	18	−12	44
1956	01	28	−12	33
1956	02	07	−12	21
1956	02	17	−12	08
1956	02	27	−11	55
1956	03	08	−11	42
1956	03	18	−11	30
1956	03	28	−11	17
1956	04	07	−11	06
1956	04	17	−10	56
1956	04	27	−10	47
1956	05	07	−10	40
1956	05	17	−10	35
1956	05	27	−10	31
1956	06	06	−10	30
1956	06	16	−10	30
1956	06	26	−10	33
1956	07	06	−10	37
1956	07	16	−10	44
1956	07	26	−10	51
1956	08	05	−11	00
1956	08	15	−11	09
1956	08	25	−11	18
1956	09	04	−11	28
1956	09	14	−11	37
1956	09	24	−11	45
1956	10	04	−11	52
1956	10	14	−11	58
1956	10	24	−12	02
1956	11	03	−12	05
1956	11	13	−12	05
1956	11	23	−12	04
1956	12	03	−12	01
1956	12	13	−11	56
1956	12	23	−11	50
1957	01	02	−11	42
1957	01	12	−11	32
1957	01	22	−11	21
1957	02	01	−11	09
1957	02	11	−10	56
1957	02	21	−10	43
1957	03	03	−10	30
1957	03	13	−10	16
1957	03	23	−10	03
1957	04	02	−09	51
1957	04	12	−09	39
1957	04	22	−09	29
1957	05	02	−09	20
1957	05	12	−09	13
1957	05	22	−09	08
1957	06	01	−09	05
1957	06	11	−09	04
1957	06	21	−09	05
1957	07	01	−09	08
1957	07	11	−09	13
1957	07	21	−09	20
1957	07	31	−09	28
1957	08	10	−09	37
1957	08	20	−09	47
1957	08	30	−09	57
1957	09	09	−10	07
1957	09	19	−10	17
1957	09	29	−10	25
1957	10	09	−10	33
1957	10	19	−10	39
1957	10	29	−10	43
1957	11	08	−10	45
1957	11	18	−10	46
1957	11	28	−10	44
1957	12	08	−10	41
1957	12	18	−10	36
1957	12	28	−10	28
1958	01	07	−10	20
1958	01	17	−10	09
1958	01	27	−09	58
1958	02	06	−09	45
1958	02	16	−09	32
1958	02	26	−09	18
1958	03	08	−09	05
1958	03	18	−08	51
1958	03	28	−08	38
1958	04	07	−08	25
1958	04	17	−08	14
1958	04	27	−08	03
1958	05	07	−07	55
1958	05	17	−07	48
1958	05	27	−07	43
1958	06	06	−07	40
1958	06	16	−07	40
1958	06	26	−07	41
1958	07	06	−07	45
1958	07	16	−07	51
1958	07	26	−07	58
1958	08	05	−08	07
1958	08	15	−08	16
1958	08	25	−08	27
1958	09	04	−08	37
1958	09	14	−08	48
1958	09	24	−08	58
1958	10	04	−09	06
1958	10	14	−09	14
1958	10	24	−09	20
1958	11	03	−09	24
1958	11	13	−09	26
1958	11	23	−09	27
1958	12	03	−09	25
1958	12	13	−09	21
1958	12	23	−09	15
1959	01	02	−09	08
1959	01	12	−08	58
1959	01	22	−08	48
1959	02	01	−08	36
1959	02	11	−08	23
1959	02	21	−08	09
1959	03	03	−07	55
1959	03	13	−07	41
1959	03	23	−07	27
1959	04	02	−07	14
1959	04	12	−07	01
1959	04	22	−06	50
1959	05	02	−06	40
1959	05	12	−06	32
1959	05	22	−06	25
1959	06	01	−06	21
1959	06	11	−06	18
1959	06	21	−06	18
1959	07	01	−06	20
1959	07	11	−06	24
1959	07	21	−06	30
1959	07	31	−06	38
1959	08	10	−06	47
1959	08	20	−06	57
1959	08	30	−07	08
1959	09	09	−07	19
1959	09	19	−07	30
1959	09	29	−07	40
1959	10	09	−07	49
1959	10	19	−07	56
1959	10	29	−08	02
1959	11	08	−08	06
1959	11	18	−08	08
1959	11	28	−08	08
1959	12	08	−08	06
1959	12	18	−08	02
1959	12	28	−07	56
1960	01	07	−07	48
1960	01	17	−07	38
1960	01	27	−07	27
1960	02	06	−07	15
1960	02	16	−07	02
1960	02	26	−06	48
1960	03	07	−06	34
1960	03	17	−06	19
1960	03	27	−06	06
1960	04	06	−05	52
1960	04	16	−05	40
1960	04	26	−05	29
1960	05	06	−05	19
1960	05	16	−05	11
1960	05	26	−05	05
1960	06	05	−05	01
1960	06	15	−04	59
1960	06	25	−04	59
1960	07	05	−05	01
1960	07	15	−05	06
1960	07	25	−05	12
1960	08	04	−05	20
1960	08	14	−05	30
1960	08	24	−05	40
1960	09	03	−05	51
1960	09	13	−06	02
1960	09	23	−06	13
1960	10	03	−06	23
1960	10	13	−06	32
1960	10	23	−06	40
1960	11	02	−06	46
1960	11	12	−06	50
1960	11	22	−06	52
1960	12	02	−06	51
1960	12	12	−06	49
1960	12	22	−06	44
1961	01	01	−06	38
1961	01	11	−06	29
1961	01	21	−06	19
1961	01	31	−06	08
1961	02	10	−05	55
1961	02	20	−05	42
1961	03	02	−05	28
1961	03	12	−05	14
1961	03	22	−05	00
1961	04	01	−04	46
1961	04	11	−04	33
1961	04	21	−04	21
1961	05	01	−04	10
1961	05	11	−04	00
1961	05	21	−03	52
1961	05	31	−03	47
1961	06	10	−03	43
1961	06	20	−03	41
1961	06	30	−03	42
1961	07	10	−03	45
1961	07	20	−03	50
1961	07	30	−03	57
1961	08	09	−04	05
1961	08	19	−04	15
1961	08	29	−04	25
1961	09	08	−04	37
1961	09	18	−04	48
1961	09	28	−04	59
1961	10	08	−05	09
1961	10	18	−05	18
1961	10	28	−05	26
1961	11	07	−05	31
1961	11	17	−05	35
1961	11	27	−05	36
1961	12	07	−05	36
1961	12	17	−05	33
1961	12	27	−05	28
1962	01	06	−05	21
1962	01	16	−05	13
1962	01	26	−05	02
1962	02	05	−04	51
1962	02	15	−04	38
1962	02	25	−04	24
1962	03	07	−04	10
1962	03	17	−03	56
1962	03	27	−03	42
1962	04	06	−03	28
1962	04	16	−03	15
1962	04	26	−03	03
1962	05	06	−02	53
1962	05	16	−02	44
1962	05	26	−02	36
1962	06	05	−02	31
1962	06	15	−02	28
1962	06	25	−02	26
1962	07	05	−02	27

1962	07	15	-02	31
1962	07	25	-02	36
1962	08	04	-02	43
1962	08	14	-02	52
1962	08	24	-03	02
1962	09	03	-03	13
1962	09	13	-03	24
1962	09	23	-03	36
1962	10	03	-03	47
1962	10	13	-03	57
1962	10	23	-04	06
1962	11	02	-04	13
1962	11	12	-04	18
1962	11	22	-04	22
1962	12	02	-04	23
1962	12	12	-04	22
1962	12	22	-04	19
1963	01	01	-04	14
1963	01	11	-04	07
1963	01	21	-03	58
1963	01	31	-03	47
1963	02	10	-03	35
1963	02	20	-03	22
1963	03	02	-03	09
1963	03	12	-02	55
1963	03	22	-02	40
1963	04	01	-02	26
1963	04	11	-02	13
1963	04	21	-02	00
1963	05	01	-01	48
1963	05	11	-01	38
1963	05	21	-01	29
1963	05	31	-01	22
1963	06	10	-01	17
1963	06	20	-01	14
1963	06	30	-01	14
1963	07	10	-01	15
1963	07	20	-01	19
1963	07	30	-01	25
1963	08	09	-01	32
1963	08	19	-01	41
1963	08	29	-01	51
1963	09	08	-02	02
1963	09	18	-02	14
1963	09	28	-02	25
1963	10	08	-02	36
1963	10	18	-02	46
1963	10	28	-02	55
1963	11	07	-03	02
1963	11	17	-03	07
1963	11	27	-03	10
1963	12	07	-03	11
1963	12	17	-03	10
1963	12	27	-03	07
1964	01	06	-03	01
1964	01	16	-02	53
1964	01	26	-02	44
1964	02	05	-02	33
1964	02	15	-02	21
1964	02	25	-02	08
1964	03	06	-01	55
1964	03	16	-01	41
1964	03	26	-01	27
1964	04	05	-01	13
1964	04	15	-00	59
1964	04	25	-00	47
1964	05	05	-00	35
1964	05	15	-00	26
1964	05	25	-00	17
1964	06	04	-00	11
1964	06	14	-00	06
1964	06	24	-00	04
1964	07	04	-00	03
1964	07	14	-00	05
1964	07	24	-00	09
1964	08	03	-00	15
1964	08	13	-00	23
1964	08	23	-00	32
1964	09	02	-00	43
1964	09	12	-00	54
1964	09	22	-01	06
1964	10	02	-01	17
1964	10	12	-01	28
1964	10	22	-01	38
1964	11	01	-01	46
1964	11	11	-01	53
1964	11	21	-01	58
1964	12	01	-02	01
1964	12	11	-02	01
1964	12	21	-02	00
1964	12	31	-01	56
1965	01	10	-01	50
1965	01	20	-01	42
1965	01	30	-01	33
1965	02	09	-01	22
1965	02	19	-01	09
1965	03	01	-00	56
1965	03	11	-00	43
1965	03	21	-00	29
1965	03	31	-00	15
1965	04	10	-00	01
1965	04	20	+00	12
1965	04	30	+00	24
1965	05	10	+00	35
1965	05	20	+00	45
1965	05	30	+00	53
1965	06	09	+00	59
1965	06	19	+01	03
1965	06	29	+01	05
1965	07	09	+01	05
1965	07	19	+01	03
1965	07	29	+00	58
1965	08	08	+00	52
1965	08	18	+00	44
1965	08	28	+00	34
1965	09	07	+00	24
1965	09	17	+00	12
1965	09	27	+00	01
1965	10	07	-00	11
1965	10	17	-00	22
1965	10	27	-00	31
1965	11	06	-00	39
1965	11	16	-00	46
1965	11	26	-00	50
1965	12	06	-00	53
1965	12	16	-00	53
1965	12	26	-00	51
1966	01	05	-00	47
1966	01	15	-00	40
1966	01	25	-00	32
1966	02	04	-00	22
1966	02	14	-00	11
1966	02	24	+00	01
1966	03	06	+00	14
1966	03	16	+00	28
1966	03	26	+00	42
1966	04	05	+00	56
1966	04	15	+01	09
1966	04	25	+01	22
1966	05	05	+01	34
1966	05	15	+01	44
1966	05	25	+01	54
1966	06	04	+02	01
1966	06	14	+02	07
1966	06	24	+02	11
1966	07	04	+02	12
1966	07	14	+02	12
1966	07	24	+02	09
1966	08	03	+02	04
1966	08	13	+01	57
1966	08	23	+01	49
1966	09	02	+01	39
1966	09	12	+01	28
1966	09	22	+01	17
1966	10	02	+01	05
1966	10	12	+00	54
1966	10	22	+00	43
1966	11	01	+00	34
1966	11	11	+00	26
1966	11	21	+00	20
1966	12	01	+00	16
1966	12	11	+00	14
1966	12	21	+00	14
1966	12	31	+00	16
1967	01	10	+00	21
1967	01	20	+00	28
1967	01	30	+00	36
1967	02	09	+00	46
1967	02	19	+00	57
1967	03	01	+01	10
1967	03	11	+01	23
1967	03	21	+01	37
1967	03	31	+01	50
1967	04	10	+02	04
1967	04	20	+02	17
1967	04	30	+02	30
1967	05	10	+02	41
1967	05	20	+02	52
1967	05	30	+03	01
1967	06	09	+03	08
1967	06	19	+03	13
1967	06	29	+03	16
1967	07	09	+03	17
1967	07	19	+03	16
1967	07	29	+03	13
1967	08	08	+03	08
1967	08	18	+03	01
1967	08	28	+02	52
1967	09	07	+02	42
1967	09	17	+02	31
1967	09	27	+02	20
1967	10	07	+02	08
1967	10	17	+01	57
1967	10	27	+01	46
1967	11	06	+01	37
1967	11	16	+01	30
1967	11	26	+01	24
1967	12	06	+01	20
1967	12	16	+01	19
1967	12	26	+01	19
1968	01	05	+01	22
1968	01	15	+01	27
1968	01	25	+01	34
1968	02	04	+01	43
1968	02	14	+01	53
1968	02	24	+02	05
1968	03	05	+02	17
1968	03	15	+02	30
1968	03	25	+02	44
1968	04	04	+02	58
1968	04	14	+03	11
1968	04	24	+03	24
1968	05	04	+03	36
1968	05	14	+03	47
1968	05	24	+03	57
1968	06	03	+04	06
1968	06	13	+04	12
1968	06	23	+04	17
1968	07	03	+04	20
1968	07	13	+04	21
1968	07	23	+04	19
1968	08	02	+04	15
1968	08	12	+04	10
1968	08	22	+04	03
1968	09	01	+03	54
1968	09	11	+03	43
1968	09	21	+03	32
1968	10	01	+03	21
1968	10	11	+03	09
1968	10	21	+02	58
1968	10	31	+02	48
1968	11	10	+02	39
1968	11	20	+02	32
1968	11	30	+02	27
1968	12	10	+02	23
1968	12	20	+02	22
1968	12	30	+02	23
1969	01	09	+02	27
1969	01	19	+02	32
1969	01	29	+02	39
1969	02	08	+02	48
1969	02	18	+02	59
1969	02	28	+03	10
1969	03	10	+03	23
1969	03	20	+03	36
1969	03	30	+03	50
1969	04	09	+04	03
1969	04	19	+04	17
1969	04	29	+04	29
1969	05	09	+04	41
1969	05	19	+04	52
1969	05	29	+05	01
1969	06	08	+05	09
1969	06	18	+05	16
1969	06	28	+05	20
1969	07	08	+05	22
1969	07	18	+05	22
1969	07	28	+05	20
1969	08	07	+05	16
1969	08	17	+05	11
1969	08	27	+05	03
1969	09	06	+04	54
1969	09	16	+04	43
1969	09	26	+04	32
1969	10	06	+04	21
1969	10	16	+04	09
1969	10	26	+03	59
1969	11	05	+03	49
1969	11	15	+03	40
1969	11	25	+03	33
1969	12	05	+03	28
1969	12	15	+03	25
1969	12	25	+03	25
1970	01	04	+03	26
1970	01	14	+03	30
1970	01	24	+03	36
1970	02	03	+03	43
1970	02	13	+03	52
1970	02	23	+04	03
1970	03	05	+04	15
1970	03	15	+04	28
1970	03	25	+04	41
1970	04	04	+04	54
1970	04	14	+05	08
1970	04	24	+05	21
1970	05	04	+05	33
1970	05	14	+05	45
1970	05	24	+05	55
1970	06	03	+06	04
1970	06	13	+06	12
1970	06	23	+06	17
1970	07	03	+06	21
1970	07	13	+06	23
1970	07	23	+06	23
1970	08	02	+06	20
1970	08	12	+06	16
1970	08	22	+06	10
1970	09	01	+06	02
1970	09	11	+05	53
1970	09	21	+05	42
1970	10	01	+05	31
1970	10	11	+05	20
1970	10	21	+05	08
1970	10	31	+04	58
1970	11	10	+04	48
1970	11	20	+04	40
1970	11	30	+04	33
1970	12	10	+04	29
1970	12	20	+04	26
1970	12	30	+04	26
1971	01	09	+04	28
1971	01	19	+04	32
1971	01	29	+04	38
1971	02	08	+04	46
1971	02	18	+04	56
1971	02	28	+05	06
1971	03	10	+05	18
1971	03	20	+05	31
1971	03	30	+05	44
1971	04	09	+05	57
1971	04	19	+06	11
1971	04	29	+06	23
1971	05	09	+06	36
1971	05	19	+06	47
1971	05	29	+06	57
1971	06	08	+07	05
1971	06	18	+07	13
1971	06	28	+07	18
1971	07	08	+07	21
1971	07	18	+07	23
1971	07	28	+07	22
1971	08	07	+07	19
1971	08	17	+07	14
1971	08	27	+07	08
1971	09	06	+07	00
1971	09	16	+06	50
1971	09	26	+06	40
1971	10	06	+06	28
1971	10	16	+06	17
1971	10	26	+06	06
1971	11	05	+05	56
1971	11	15	+05	46
1971	11	25	+05	38
1971	12	05	+05	32
1971	12	15	+05	28
1971	12	25	+05	26
1972	01	04	+05	27
1972	01	14	+05	29
1972	01	24	+05	33
1972	02	03	+05	40
1972	02	13	+05	48
1972	02	23	+05	58
1972	03	04	+06	09
1972	03	14	+06	21
1972	03	24	+06	33
1972	04	03	+06	46
1972	04	13	+07	00
1972	04	23	+07	13
1972	05	03	+07	25
1972	05	13	+07	37
1972	05	23	+07	48
1972	06	02	+07	57
1972	06	12	+08	06
1972	06	22	+08	12
1972	07	02	+08	17
1972	07	12	+08	20
1972	07	22	+08	21
1972	08	01	+08	20
1972	08	11	+08	17
1972	08	21	+08	12
1972	08	31	+08	05
1972	09	10	+07	56
1972	09	20	+07	47
1972	09	30	+07	36
1972	10	10	+07	25
1972	10	20	+07	14
1972	10	30	+07	03
1972	11	09	+06	53
1972	11	19	+06	44
1972	11	29	+06	36
1972	12	09	+06	31
1972	12	19	+06	27
1972	12	29	+06	26
1973	01	08	+06	26
1973	01	18	+06	29
1973	01	28	+06	34
1973	02	07	+06	41
1973	02	17	+06	49
1973	02	27	+06	59
1973	03	09	+07	10
1973	03	19	+07	22
1973	03	29	+07	35
1973	04	08	+07	48
1973	04	18	+08	01
1973	04	28	+08	14
1973	05	08	+08	26
1973	05	18	+08	37
1973	05	28	+08	48
1973	06	07	+08	57
1973	06	17	+09	05
1973	06	27	+09	11
1973	07	07	+09	15
1973	07	17	+09	18
1973	07	27	+09	18
1973	08	06	+09	17
1973	08	16	+09	13
1973	08	26	+09	08
1973	09	05	+09	01
1973	09	15	+08	52
1973	09	25	+08	42
1973	10	05	+08	32
1973	10	15	+08	21
1973	10	25	+08	09
1973	11	04	+07	59
1973	11	14	+07	49
1973	11	24	+07	40
1973	12	04	+07	33
1973	12	14	+07	28
1973	12	24	+07	25
1974	01	03	+07	24
1974	01	13	+07	25
1974	01	23	+07	28
1974	02	02	+07	34
1974	02	12	+07	41
1974	02	22	+07	49
1974	03	04	+08	00
1974	03	14	+08	11
1974	03	24	+08	23
1974	04	03	+08	35
1974	04	13	+08	48
1974	04	23	+09	01
1974	05	03	+09	13
1974	05	13	+09	25
1974	05	23	+09	36
1974	06	02	+09	46
1974	06	12	+09	55
1974	06	22	+10	02
1974	07	02	+10	08
1974	07	12	+10	12
1974	07	22	+10	14
1974	08	01	+10	14
1974	08	11	+10	12
1974	08	21	+10	08
1974	08	31	+10	03
1974	09	10	+09	55
1974	09	20	+09	47
1974	09	30	+09	37
1974	10	10	+09	26
1974	10	20	+09	15
1974	10	30	+09	04
1974	11	09	+08	54
1974	11	19	+08	44
1974	11	29	+08	36
1974	12	09	+08	30
1974	12	19	+08	25
1974	12	29	+08	22
1975	01	08	+08	22
1975	01	18	+08	23
1975	01	28	+08	27
1975	02	07	+08	32
1975	02	17	+08	40
1975	02	27	+08	49
1975	03	09	+08	59
1975	03	19	+09	10
1975	03	29	+09	22
1975	04	08	+09	35
1975	04	18	+09	47
1975	04	28	+10	00
1975	05	08	+10	12
1975	05	18	+10	24
1975	05	28	+10	34
1975	06	07	+10	44
1975	06	17	+10	52
1975	06	27	+10	59
1975	07	07	+11	04
1975	07	17	+11	08
1975	07	27	+11	09
1975	08	06	+11	09
1975	08	16	+11	07
1975	08	26	+11	03
1975	09	05	+10	57
1975	09	15	+10	49
1975	09	25	+10	40
1975	10	05	+10	30
1975	10	15	+10	20
1975	10	25	+10	09
1975	11	04	+09	58
1975	11	14	+09	48
1975	11	24	+09	39
1975	12	04	+09	31
1975	12	14	+09	25
1975	12	24	+09	21
1976	01	03	+09	18
1976	01	13	+09	18
1976	01	23	+09	20
1976	02	02	+09	24
1976	02	12	+09	30
1976	02	22	+09	38
1976	03	03	+09	47
1976	03	13	+09	57
1976	03	23	+10	09
1976	04	02	+10	21
1976	04	12	+10	33
1976	04	22	+10	45
1976	05	02	+10	58
1976	05	12	+11	09
1976	05	22	+11	21
1976	06	01	+11	31
1976	06	11	+11	40
1976	06	21	+11	48
1976	07	01	+11	54
1976	07	11	+11	59
1976	07	21	+12	02
1976	07	31	+12	03
1976	08	10	+12	02
1976	08	20	+12	00
1976	08	30	+11	55
1976	09	09	+11	49
1976	09	19	+11	42
1976	09	29	+11	33
1976	10	09	+11	23
1976	10	19	+11	12
1976	10	29	+11	01
1976	11	08	+10	51
1976	11	18	+10	41

1976	11	28	+10	32
1976	12	08	+10	25
1976	12	18	+10	19
1976	12	28	+10	16
1977	01	07	+10	14
1977	01	17	+10	14
1977	01	27	+10	17
1977	02	06	+10	21
1977	02	16	+10	27
1977	02	26	+10	35
1977	03	08	+10	44
1977	03	18	+10	55
1977	03	28	+11	06
1977	04	07	+11	18
1977	04	17	+11	30
1977	04	27	+11	42
1977	05	07	+11	54
1977	05	17	+12	05
1977	05	27	+12	16
1977	06	06	+12	26
1977	06	16	+12	35
1977	06	26	+12	42
1977	07	06	+12	48
1977	07	16	+12	52
1977	07	26	+12	55
1977	08	05	+12	55
1977	08	15	+12	54
1977	08	25	+12	51
1977	09	04	+12	47
1977	09	14	+12	40
1977	09	24	+12	33
1977	10	04	+12	24
1977	10	14	+12	14
1977	10	24	+12	03
1977	11	03	+11	53
1977	11	13	+11	43
1977	11	23	+11	33
1977	12	03	+11	25
1977	12	13	+11	18
1977	12	23	+11	13
1978	01	02	+11	09
1978	01	12	+11	08
1978	01	22	+11	09
1978	02	01	+11	12
1978	02	11	+11	17
1978	02	21	+11	23
1978	03	03	+11	31
1978	03	13	+11	40
1978	03	23	+11	51
1978	04	02	+12	02
1978	04	12	+12	14
1978	04	22	+12	25
1978	05	02	+12	37
1978	05	12	+12	49
1978	05	22	+13	00
1978	06	01	+13	10
1978	06	11	+13	19
1978	06	21	+13	27
1978	07	01	+13	34
1978	07	11	+13	40
1978	07	21	+13	43
1978	07	31	+13	45
1978	08	10	+13	46
1978	08	20	+13	44
1978	08	30	+13	41
1978	09	09	+13	36
1978	09	19	+13	30
1978	09	29	+13	22
1978	10	09	+13	13
1978	10	19	+13	03
1978	10	29	+12	53
1978	11	08	+12	43
1978	11	18	+12	33
1978	11	28	+12	24
1978	12	08	+12	16
1978	12	18	+12	10
1978	12	28	+12	05
1979	01	07	+12	02
1979	01	17	+12	01
1979	01	27	+12	03
1979	02	06	+12	06
1979	02	16	+12	11
1979	02	26	+12	17
1979	03	08	+12	26
1979	03	18	+12	35
1979	03	28	+12	45
1979	04	07	+12	56
1979	04	17	+13	08
1979	04	27	+13	19
1979	05	07	+13	31
1979	05	17	+13	42
1979	05	27	+13	52
1979	06	06	+14	02
1979	06	16	+14	11
1979	06	26	+14	18
1979	07	06	+14	24
1979	07	16	+14	29
1979	07	26	+14	32
1979	08	05	+14	34
1979	08	15	+14	34
1979	08	25	+14	32
1979	09	04	+14	29
1979	09	14	+14	24
1979	09	24	+14	17
1979	10	04	+14	09
1979	10	14	+14	00
1979	10	24	+13	51
1979	11	03	+13	41
1979	11	13	+13	31
1979	11	23	+13	21
1979	12	03	+13	13
1979	12	13	+13	05
1979	12	23	+13	00
1980	01	02	+12	55
1980	01	12	+12	53
1980	01	22	+12	53
1980	02	01	+12	54
1980	02	11	+12	58
1980	02	21	+13	03
1980	03	02	+13	10
1980	03	12	+13	18
1980	03	22	+13	28
1980	04	01	+13	38
1980	04	11	+13	49
1980	04	21	+14	00
1980	05	01	+14	11
1980	05	11	+14	22
1980	05	21	+14	32
1980	05	31	+14	42
1980	06	10	+14	51
1980	06	20	+14	59
1980	06	30	+15	06
1980	07	10	+15	12
1980	07	20	+15	16
1980	07	30	+15	19
1980	08	09	+15	20
1980	08	19	+15	20
1980	08	29	+15	17
1980	09	08	+15	14
1980	09	18	+15	08
1980	09	28	+15	02
1980	10	08	+14	54
1980	10	18	+14	45
1980	10	28	+14	36
1980	11	07	+14	26
1980	11	17	+14	17
1980	11	27	+14	08
1980	12	07	+14	00
1980	12	17	+13	53
1980	12	27	+13	48
1981	01	06	+13	44
1981	01	16	+13	42
1981	01	26	+13	42
1981	02	05	+13	45
1981	02	15	+13	48
1981	02	25	+13	54
1981	03	07	+14	01
1981	03	17	+14	09
1981	03	27	+14	18
1981	04	06	+14	28
1981	04	16	+14	39
1981	04	26	+14	49
1981	05	06	+15	00
1981	05	16	+15	10
1981	05	26	+15	20
1981	06	05	+15	29
1981	06	15	+15	38
1981	06	25	+15	45
1981	07	05	+15	51
1981	07	15	+15	56
1981	07	25	+16	00
1981	08	04	+16	02
1981	08	14	+16	03
1981	08	24	+16	02
1981	09	03	+15	59
1981	09	13	+15	55
1981	09	23	+15	50
1981	10	03	+15	43
1981	10	13	+15	36
1981	10	23	+15	27
1981	11	02	+15	18
1981	11	12	+15	09
1981	11	22	+15	00
1981	12	02	+14	52
1981	12	12	+14	44
1981	12	22	+14	38
1982	01	01	+14	33
1982	01	11	+14	30
1982	01	21	+14	29
1982	01	31	+14	30
1982	02	10	+14	32
1982	02	20	+14	36
1982	03	02	+14	42
1982	03	12	+14	49
1982	03	22	+14	57
1982	04	01	+15	06
1982	04	11	+15	16
1982	04	21	+15	25
1982	05	01	+15	36
1982	05	11	+15	46
1982	05	21	+15	55
1982	05	31	+16	04
1982	06	10	+16	13
1982	06	20	+16	20
1982	06	30	+16	27
1982	07	10	+16	32
1982	07	20	+16	37
1982	07	30	+16	40
1982	08	09	+16	41
1982	08	19	+16	41
1982	08	29	+16	40
1982	09	08	+16	37
1982	09	18	+16	33
1982	09	28	+16	27
1982	10	08	+16	21
1982	10	18	+16	14
1982	10	28	+16	05
1982	11	07	+15	57
1982	11	17	+15	48
1982	11	27	+15	40
1982	12	07	+15	32
1982	12	17	+15	25
1982	12	27	+15	20
1983	01	06	+15	16
1983	01	16	+15	13
1983	01	26	+15	13
1983	02	05	+15	14
1983	02	15	+15	17
1983	02	25	+15	21
1983	03	07	+15	27
1983	03	17	+15	34
1983	03	27	+15	41
1983	04	06	+15	50
1983	04	16	+15	59
1983	04	26	+16	09
1983	05	06	+16	18
1983	05	16	+16	27
1983	05	26	+16	36
1983	06	05	+16	44
1983	06	15	+16	52
1983	06	25	+16	58
1983	07	05	+17	04
1983	07	15	+17	09
1983	07	25	+17	12
1983	08	04	+17	14
1983	08	14	+17	15
1983	08	24	+17	14
1983	09	03	+17	12
1983	09	13	+17	09
1983	09	23	+17	05
1983	10	03	+17	00
1983	10	13	+16	53
1983	10	23	+16	46
1983	11	02	+16	38
1983	11	12	+16	31
1983	11	22	+16	23
1983	12	02	+16	15
1983	12	12	+16	08
1983	12	22	+16	02
1984	01	01	+15	58
1984	01	11	+15	54
1984	01	21	+15	52
1984	01	31	+15	52
1984	02	10	+15	54
1984	02	20	+15	57
1984	03	01	+16	01
1984	03	11	+16	07
1984	03	21	+16	14
1984	03	31	+16	21
1984	04	10	+16	30
1984	04	20	+16	38
1984	04	30	+16	47
1984	05	10	+16	55
1984	05	20	+17	04
1984	05	30	+17	11
1984	06	09	+17	18
1984	06	19	+17	25
1984	06	29	+17	30
1984	07	09	+17	35
1984	07	19	+17	38
1984	07	29	+17	40
1984	08	08	+17	41
1984	08	18	+17	41
1984	08	28	+17	40
1984	09	07	+17	38
1984	09	17	+17	34
1984	09	27	+17	30
1984	10	07	+17	25
1984	10	17	+17	18
1984	10	27	+17	12
1984	11	06	+17	05
1984	11	16	+16	58
1984	11	26	+16	50
1984	12	06	+16	44
1984	12	16	+16	38
1984	12	26	+16	33
1985	01	05	+16	29
1985	01	15	+16	27
1985	01	25	+16	26
1985	02	04	+16	26
1985	02	14	+16	28
1985	02	24	+16	32
1985	03	06	+16	36
1985	03	16	+16	42
1985	03	26	+16	48
1985	04	05	+16	55
1985	04	15	+17	03
1985	04	25	+17	11
1985	05	05	+17	18
1985	05	15	+17	26
1985	05	25	+17	33
1985	06	04	+17	39
1985	06	14	+17	45
1985	06	24	+17	50
1985	07	04	+17	54
1985	07	14	+17	57
1985	07	24	+17	59
1985	08	03	+18	00
1985	08	13	+18	00
1985	08	23	+17	59
1985	09	02	+17	57
1985	09	12	+17	54
1985	09	22	+17	50
1985	10	02	+17	45
1985	10	12	+17	40
1985	10	22	+17	34
1985	11	01	+17	28
1985	11	11	+17	22
1985	11	21	+17	15
1985	12	01	+17	10
1985	12	11	+17	04
1985	12	21	+16	59
1985	12	31	+16	56
1986	01	10	+16	53
1986	01	20	+16	51
1986	01	30	+16	51
1986	02	09	+16	53
1986	02	19	+16	55
1986	03	01	+16	59
1986	03	11	+17	03
1986	03	21	+17	09
1986	03	31	+17	15
1986	04	10	+17	21
1986	04	20	+17	28
1986	04	30	+17	35
1986	05	10	+17	41
1986	05	20	+17	47
1986	05	30	+17	53
1986	06	09	+17	57
1986	06	19	+18	01
1986	06	29	+18	05
1986	07	09	+18	07
1986	07	19	+18	08
1986	07	29	+18	09
1986	08	08	+18	08
1986	08	18	+18	06
1986	08	28	+18	04
1986	09	07	+18	01
1986	09	17	+17	57
1986	09	27	+17	53
1986	10	07	+17	48
1986	10	17	+17	43
1986	10	27	+17	37
1986	11	06	+17	32
1986	11	16	+17	26
1986	11	26	+17	21
1986	12	06	+17	16
1986	12	16	+17	12
1986	12	26	+17	09
1987	01	05	+17	07
1987	01	15	+17	05
1987	01	25	+17	05
1987	02	04	+17	06
1987	02	14	+17	08
1987	02	24	+17	11
1987	03	06	+17	15
1987	03	16	+17	20
1987	03	26	+17	25
1987	04	05	+17	30
1987	04	15	+17	36
1987	04	25	+17	42
1987	05	05	+17	47
1987	05	15	+17	52
1987	05	25	+17	56
1987	06	04	+18	00
1987	06	14	+18	03
1987	06	24	+18	05
1987	07	04	+18	06
1987	07	14	+18	06
1987	07	24	+18	05
1987	08	03	+18	03
1987	08	13	+18	01
1987	08	23	+17	57
1987	09	02	+17	53
1987	09	12	+17	49
1987	09	22	+17	44
1987	10	02	+17	38
1987	10	12	+17	33
1987	10	22	+17	28
1987	11	01	+17	23
1987	11	11	+17	18
1987	11	21	+17	13
1987	12	01	+17	09
1987	12	11	+17	06
1987	12	21	+17	04
1987	12	31	+17	02
1988	01	10	+17	02
1988	01	20	+17	02
1988	01	30	+17	04
1988	02	09	+17	06
1988	02	19	+17	09
1988	02	29	+17	13
1988	03	10	+17	17
1988	03	20	+17	21
1988	03	30	+17	26
1988	04	09	+17	31
1988	04	19	+17	36
1988	04	29	+17	40
1988	05	09	+17	44
1988	05	19	+17	47
1988	05	29	+17	49
1988	06	08	+17	50
1988	06	18	+17	51
1988	06	28	+17	50
1988	07	08	+17	48
1988	07	18	+17	46
1988	07	28	+17	42
1988	08	07	+17	38
1988	08	17	+17	33
1988	08	27	+17	27
1988	09	06	+17	21
1988	09	16	+17	14
1988	09	26	+17	08
1988	10	06	+17	01
1988	10	16	+16	55
1988	10	26	+16	50
1988	11	05	+16	44
1988	11	15	+16	40
1988	11	25	+16	37
1988	12	05	+16	34
1988	12	15	+16	33
1988	12	25	+16	33
1989	01	04	+16	33
1989	01	14	+16	35
1989	01	24	+16	37
1989	02	03	+16	41
1989	02	13	+16	44
1989	02	23	+16	49
1989	03	05	+16	53
1989	03	15	+16	58
1989	03	25	+17	03
1989	04	04	+17	07
1989	04	14	+17	12
1989	04	24	+17	15
1989	05	04	+17	18
1989	05	14	+17	20
1989	05	24	+17	20
1989	06	03	+17	20
1989	06	13	+17	19
1989	06	23	+17	16
1989	07	03	+17	12
1989	07	13	+17	07
1989	07	23	+17	01
1989	08	02	+16	54
1989	08	12	+16	47
1989	08	22	+16	38
1989	09	01	+16	30
1989	09	11	+16	21
1989	09	21	+16	12
1989	10	01	+16	03
1989	10	11	+15	54
1989	10	21	+15	47
1989	10	31	+15	40
1989	11	10	+15	35
1989	11	20	+15	31
1989	11	30	+15	29
1989	12	10	+15	28
1989	12	20	+15	28
1989	12	30	+15	30
1990	01	09	+15	33
1990	01	19	+15	37
1990	01	29	+15	42
1990	02	08	+15	48
1990	02	18	+15	54
1990	02	28	+16	00
1990	03	10	+16	06
1990	03	20	+16	12
1990	03	30	+16	17
1990	04	09	+16	21
1990	04	19	+16	24
1990	04	29	+16	27
1990	05	09	+16	28
1990	05	19	+16	27
1990	05	29	+16	25
1990	06	08	+16	22
1990	06	18	+16	18
1990	06	28	+16	11
1990	07	08	+16	04
1990	07	18	+15	55
1990	07	28	+15	45
1990	08	07	+15	34
1990	08	17	+15	22
1990	08	27	+15	10
1990	09	06	+14	57
1990	09	16	+14	45
1990	09	26	+14	32
1990	10	06	+14	20
1990	10	16	+14	09
1990	10	26	+14	00
1990	11	05	+13	52
1990	11	15	+13	45
1990	11	25	+13	41
1990	12	05	+13	39
1990	12	15	+13	39
1990	12	25	+13	41
1991	01	04	+13	45
1991	01	14	+13	51
1991	01	24	+13	58
1991	02	03	+14	06
1991	02	13	+14	15
1991	02	23	+14	24
1991	03	05	+14	32
1991	03	15	+14	40
1991	03	25	+14	47
1991	04	04	+14	53
1991	04	14	+14	58

Chiron

1991	04	24	+15	01
1991	05	04	+15	02
1991	05	14	+15	01
1991	05	24	+14	58
1991	06	03	+14	54
1991	06	13	+14	47
1991	06	23	+14	39
1991	07	03	+14	29
1991	07	13	+14	17
1991	07	23	+14	04
1991	08	02	+13	50
1991	08	12	+13	34
1991	08	22	+13	18
1991	09	01	+13	00
1991	09	11	+12	43
1991	09	21	+12	26
1991	10	01	+12	09
1991	10	11	+11	53
1991	10	21	+11	38
1991	10	31	+11	25
1991	11	10	+11	15
1991	11	20	+11	06
1991	11	30	+11	00
1991	12	10	+10	58
1991	12	20	+10	58
1991	12	30	+11	01
1992	01	09	+11	07
1992	01	19	+11	15
1992	01	29	+11	26
1992	02	08	+11	37
1992	02	18	+11	49
1992	02	28	+12	02
1992	03	09	+12	14
1992	03	19	+12	24
1992	03	29	+12	34
1992	04	08	+12	41
1992	04	18	+12	46
1992	04	28	+12	49
1992	05	08	+12	50
1992	05	18	+12	48
1992	05	28	+12	43
1992	06	07	+12	36
1992	06	17	+12	27
1992	06	27	+12	15
1992	07	07	+12	01
1992	07	17	+11	45
1992	07	27	+11	27
1992	08	06	+11	08
1992	08	16	+10	47
1992	08	26	+10	26
1992	09	05	+10	03
1992	09	15	+09	41
1992	09	25	+09	18
1992	10	05	+08	56
1992	10	15	+08	36
1992	10	25	+08	16
1992	11	04	+07	59
1992	11	14	+07	44
1992	11	24	+07	32
1992	12	04	+07	24
1992	12	14	+07	19
1992	12	24	+07	18
1993	01	03	+07	21
1993	01	13	+07	27
1993	01	23	+07	37
1993	02	02	+07	49
1993	02	12	+08	04
1993	02	22	+08	20
1993	03	04	+08	36
1993	03	14	+08	52
1993	03	24	+09	06
1993	04	03	+09	19
1993	04	13	+09	29
1993	04	23	+09	36
1993	05	03	+09	41
1993	05	13	+09	42
1993	05	23	+09	40
1993	06	02	+09	34
1993	06	12	+09	25
1993	06	22	+09	14
1993	07	02	+08	59
1993	07	12	+08	42
1993	07	22	+08	22
1993	08	01	+08	00
1993	08	11	+07	36
1993	08	21	+07	11
1993	08	31	+06	45
1993	09	10	+06	17
1993	09	20	+05	50
1993	09	30	+05	22
1993	10	10	+04	55
1993	10	20	+04	29
1993	10	30	+04	05
1993	11	09	+03	43
1993	11	19	+03	23
1993	11	29	+03	07
1993	12	09	+02	54
1993	12	19	+02	46
1993	12	29	+02	42
1994	01	08	+02	42
1994	01	18	+02	47
1994	01	28	+02	56
1994	02	07	+03	09
1994	02	17	+03	25
1994	02	27	+03	44
1994	03	09	+04	03
1994	03	19	+04	23
1994	03	29	+04	41
1994	04	08	+04	58
1994	04	18	+05	12
1994	04	28	+05	23
1994	05	08	+05	30
1994	05	18	+05	33
1994	05	28	+05	33
1994	06	07	+05	28
1994	06	17	+05	19
1994	06	27	+05	07
1994	07	07	+04	51
1994	07	17	+04	32
1994	07	27	+04	10
1994	08	06	+03	46
1994	08	16	+03	20
1994	08	26	+02	51
1994	09	05	+02	21
1994	09	15	+01	51
1994	09	25	+01	19
1994	10	05	+00	48
1994	10	15	+00	17
1994	10	25	-00	13
1994	11	04	-00	41
1994	11	14	-01	08
1994	11	24	-01	32
1994	12	04	-01	52
1994	12	14	-02	09
1994	12	24	-02	22
1995	01	03	-02	30
1995	01	13	-02	34
1995	01	23	-02	32
1995	02	02	-02	26
1995	02	12	-02	15
1995	02	22	-02	00
1995	03	04	-01	41
1995	03	14	-01	21
1995	03	24	-00	59
1995	04	03	-00	37
1995	04	13	-00	17
1995	04	23	+00	01
1995	05	03	+00	16
1995	05	13	+00	28
1995	05	23	+00	35
1995	06	02	+00	37
1995	06	12	+00	35
1995	06	22	+00	29
1995	07	02	+00	19
1995	07	12	+00	04
1995	07	22	-00	14
1995	08	01	-00	35
1995	08	11	-01	00
1995	08	21	-01	27
1995	08	31	-01	55
1995	09	10	-02	26
1995	09	20	-02	57
1995	09	30	-03	30
1995	10	10	-04	02
1995	10	20	-04	34
1995	10	30	-05	06
1995	11	09	-05	36
1995	11	19	-06	04
1995	11	29	-06	30
1995	12	09	-06	53
1995	12	19	-07	13
1995	12	29	-07	29
1996	01	08	-07	41
1996	01	18	-07	48
1996	01	28	-07	51
1996	02	07	-07	48
1996	02	17	-07	41
1996	02	27	-07	29
1996	03	08	-07	14
1996	03	18	-06	55
1996	03	28	-06	34
1996	04	07	-06	12
1996	04	17	-05	50
1996	04	27	-05	29
1996	05	07	-05	11
1996	05	17	-04	56
1996	05	27	-04	45
1996	06	06	-04	38
1996	06	16	-04	36
1996	06	26	-04	38
1996	07	06	-04	45
1996	07	16	-04	55
1996	07	26	-05	10
1996	08	05	-05	28
1996	08	15	-05	50
1996	08	25	-06	14
1996	09	04	-06	40
1996	09	14	-07	08
1996	09	24	-07	37
1996	10	04	-08	07
1996	10	14	-08	38
1996	10	24	-09	08
1996	11	03	-09	37
1996	11	13	-10	06
1996	11	23	-10	33
1996	12	03	-10	57
1996	12	13	-11	20
1996	12	23	-11	39
1997	01	02	-11	56
1997	01	12	-12	09
1997	01	22	-12	18
1997	02	01	-12	22
1997	02	11	-12	23
1997	02	21	-12	19
1997	03	03	-12	12
1997	03	13	-12	00
1997	03	23	-11	45
1997	04	02	-11	28
1997	04	12	-11	08
1997	04	22	-10	48
1997	05	02	-10	28
1997	05	12	-10	10
1997	05	22	-09	53
1997	06	01	-09	40
1997	06	11	-09	30
1997	06	21	-09	24
1997	07	01	-09	22
1997	07	11	-09	24
1997	07	21	-09	30
1997	07	31	-09	40
1997	08	10	-09	54
1997	08	20	-10	10
1997	08	30	-10	29
1997	09	09	-10	51
1997	09	19	-11	14
1997	09	29	-11	38
1997	10	09	-12	03
1997	10	19	-12	28
1997	10	29	-12	54
1997	11	08	-13	18
1997	11	18	-13	42
1997	11	28	-14	05
1997	12	08	-14	25
1997	12	18	-14	44
1997	12	28	-15	00
1998	01	07	-15	14
1998	01	17	-15	25
1998	01	27	-15	33
1998	02	06	-15	37
1998	02	16	-15	39
1998	02	26	-15	37
1998	03	08	-15	31
1998	03	18	-15	23
1998	03	28	-15	13
1998	04	07	-14	59
1998	04	17	-14	44
1998	04	27	-14	28
1998	05	07	-14	12
1998	05	17	-13	56
1998	05	27	-13	41
1998	06	06	-13	28
1998	06	16	-13	18
1998	06	26	-13	10
1998	07	06	-13	06
1998	07	16	-13	05
1998	07	26	-13	08
1998	08	05	-13	13
1998	08	15	-13	22
1998	08	25	-13	34
1998	09	04	-13	47
1998	09	14	-14	03
1998	09	24	-14	20
1998	10	04	-14	39
1998	10	14	-14	57
1998	10	24	-15	17
1998	11	03	-15	35
1998	11	13	-15	54
1998	11	23	-16	11
1998	12	03	-16	28
1998	12	13	-16	42
1998	12	23	-16	55
1999	01	02	-17	07
1999	01	12	-17	16
1999	01	22	-17	23
1999	02	01	-17	27
1999	02	11	-17	29
1999	02	21	-17	29
1999	03	03	-17	27
1999	03	13	-17	23
1999	03	23	-17	16
1999	04	02	-17	08
1999	04	12	-16	59
1999	04	22	-16	48
1999	05	02	-16	36
1999	05	12	-16	24
1999	05	22	-16	12
1999	06	01	-16	01
1999	06	11	-15	51
1999	06	21	-15	42
1999	07	01	-15	36
1999	07	11	-15	32
1999	07	21	-15	30
1999	07	31	-15	31
1999	08	10	-15	34
1999	08	20	-15	40
1999	08	30	-15	48
1999	09	09	-15	57
1999	09	19	-16	08
1999	09	29	-16	20
1999	10	09	-16	32
1999	10	19	-16	46
1999	10	29	-16	59
1999	11	08	-17	11
1999	11	18	-17	23
1999	11	28	-17	34
1999	12	08	-17	44
1999	12	18	-17	53
1999	12	28	-18	00
2000	01	07	-18	06
2000	01	17	-18	10
2000	01	27	-18	12
2000	02	06	-18	13
2000	02	16	-18	12
2000	02	26	-18	09
2000	03	07	-18	05
2000	03	17	-18	00
2000	03	27	-17	54
2000	04	06	-17	47
2000	04	16	-17	40
2000	04	26	-17	32
2000	05	06	-17	23
2000	05	16	-17	15
2000	05	26	-17	07
2000	06	05	-17	00
2000	06	15	-16	54
2000	06	25	-16	49
2000	07	05	-16	45
2000	07	15	-16	43
2000	07	25	-16	42
2000	08	04	-16	43
2000	08	14	-16	46
2000	08	24	-16	50
2000	09	03	-16	56

The Meaning Of Chiron

ZANE B. STEIN

*Text of a lecture given by Mr. Stein 16 December 1979 in New York City.

1977 was a big year for astronomers, with many discoveries altering our conceptions of the solar system. In March, for example, rings were found around Uranus. This meant that Saturn had lost its monopoly on rings, but it also meant that Uranus and Saturn have something in common.

It was an especially big year for one astronomer in particular, named Charles T. Kowal. He started off the year discovering a comet and an asteroid, and rediscovering two bodies that had been lost. But the biggest discovery of all took place that Fall.

Kowal routinely photographs an area of the heavens each month, near the opposition point of the Sun. Then the photos are carefully examined in an apparatus called a "Blink Microscope"—which shows a segment of first one plate, then another, in rapid alternation. Stars appear to be stationary, but moving object appear to jump from side to side.

In October, he was only able to obtain one set of plates—on the nights of October 18th and 19th. He did not have a chance to make a thorough examination of the plates then, nor for several days. But when he returned to his office on November 1st, he was able to use the Blink Microscope, and with it spotted an object on the photos inside the orbit of Uranus. This was Object Kowal, which he soon named Chiron. Upon further study, photos of it turned up as far back as 1895; one plate from 1941 even had Chiron's trail marked on it, but this was not followed up. Mankind had to await the specific moment—Nov. 1, 1977—with Chiron at 3 TAU 08, before it was ready for the news.

Astronomers are not sure what Chiron is, although they have several theories. The one theory that seems the most likely is that Chiron was captured from outside the solar system, and eventually will be thrown out again.

No matter what it turns out to be for astronomers, for astrologers it is a major tool. Webster's defines the word tool as, "Any instrument or device necessary to one's profession or occupation." The important word here is *necessary*. For now that Chiron's principle is awakening in mankind's consciousness, its use becomes essential to the astrologer to understand mankind's present problems.

Over the past two years since the discovery, we have begun to get a handle on this new tool; certain overall themes have begun to emerge. Of course, much more research is needed; we don't even know everything about Pluto, although that planet was discovered almost fifty years ago. But I'd like to share with you what we have already discovered about Chiron.

To begin with, Chiron has a definite connection with pregnancy and birth. But this connection seems so far to function only when the birth will result in a major change in someone's life. THere also seems to be some connection to the fetus itself. In one case, natal Chiron was located in a woman's sixth house. When Pluto transitted in square aspect to this position, she suffered a violent miscarriage. The doctor said, however, that it was for the better; had the child lived it would have been defective. We have many cases when Chiron transits the midheaven or fourth house of only children, and the children suddenly find out that they are going to have a new brother or sister. We also have many cases of Chiron passing over an adult's midheaven, or Jupiter, and that person discovers he/she is to become a parent. My wife is due to have a baby next June. Chiron will conjunct her Jupiter June 4th, so we will see how close it comes. Chiron conjuncted *my* Jupiter when our daughter was born.

In addition, Chiron has occurred in many solar return fifth houses of people who became parents within the following year. Louise Brown, the first "Artificial Inovulation Baby," or "test tube" baby, was conceived almost to the day of Chiron's discovery. Chiron was rising at her birth, and her natal ascendant is conjunct Chiron in her conception chart.

There may be a connection between Chiron and Libra, either through a partial rulership, or through the fact that Chiron reaches its perihelion in that sign. Through research, we have dug up the fact that the sign Libra was also called by the ancient name Zugon, meaning that which joins together. Zugon comes from the root word Zugos, from which we also get the biological term zygote—that is, the stage of the embryo where the sperm and egg first join in conception—the actual biological union which forms the fetus. There are also a few other connections to Libra, which I will mention later.

Chiron also has a great deal to do with relationships, but not in the same sense as in the seventh house. Chiron focuses more deeply—upon the very basis of the relationship itself. Ever since Pluto entered Libra, we have all observed relationships changing on every level; in fact, the very definitions of relationships have altered. Chiron has come as a tool to discover the foundation each relationship is built upon; it focuses on whatever common ground people share which can unite them. And we can see by discovering the foundation, exactly what in the relationship needs to change. By example, I'll mention a couple who I'll call Jill and Paul. Jill describes her early relationship with Paul (who later became her husband) as one of companionship, based on common interests like theater and religion. They felt they could talk about ideas. They met when Chiron was square to her Jupiter, ruler of her fifth house—and Jupiter is religion and philosophy, while the fifth house is theater. In Paul's chart, at this time, Chiron sextiled his Jupiter, but more importantly, it opposed his fifth house Sun.

There are many other cases when Chiron forms an aspect, denoting the common ground people share. Then, of course, other aspects between the charts add to, and change the relationship further. But Chiron is the initial basis. This too could relate to Libra.

Another side of Chiron is as a key. For this, I must explain a bit about its relationship to Saturn and Uranus.

Chiron's orbit is extremely eccentric, even more so than Pluto s, which is the most elliptical orbit of all the planets.

In this it has much in common with Pluto. But anyway, when Chiron reaches perihelion, it crosses Saturn's orbit, for a short time being closer to us than Saturn. At aphelion, it touches Uranus' orbit. So, by contacting both of these orbits, it functions as a link, or bridge between these two extremes.

Now, there are many times when some aspect of Saturn will go to an extreme, acting as a wall to keep us closed off from another world. Some impasse situation will exist, blocking off any action in any direction. Maybe it is restrictions which have outlived their usefulness; maybe it is fears which are no longer valid. But we need some way to go beyond that wall, so we can grow and evolve. Chiron comes along, and alters the situation that kept things at a standstill. Chiron often discovers a doorway in the wall, and unlocks it, giving us access to a larger, unexplored world beyond, which is represented by Uranus. It is up to us, then, to make the effort to step through the doorway.

At other times, Chiron opens the door, letting Uranus force its way in, and removing Saturn's protection. But in any event, we do not remain unchanged, for Chiron has brought us the awareness that another world exists beyond the walls—an awareness we cannot ignore.

Uranus can take us out of our Saturn walls by itself, but in a much different manner. For Uranus totally shatters the existing structure, leaving us to fend for ourselves, unprotected, in a new world. Chiron, on the other hand, often allows us the freedom to step through the door at our own speed. But even when it doesn't, it brings us out of the Saturnian without destroying the Saturn itself.

Astrologers often define Saturn as major lessons one has to learn, which restrict us until we learn them. Chiron brings lessons which teach us to go beyond our limitations, break out of ruts, and open up to some new field when we have outgrown the status of a child, and are no longer number one.

Chiron has much to do with the pupil/teacher relationship. It often represents the teacher's desire to open new worlds to the student, and kindle a spark in him to *want* to learn. Closely related to this, it describes much about the early education your parents gave you, especially how they approached each *new step* of your education.

Chiron can act as an actual mediator between the forces of Saturn and Uranus, filtering and interpreting the attitudes of each, in terms the other can understand. Here too is an aspect of Saturn. For example, Chiron can represent a go-between mediating a dispute between a traditional viewpoint steeped in ideas of the past, and an unconventional viewpoint looking towards the future. For Chiron does not belong to either extreme. In fact, Chiron is a true independent, not aligning himself with any party or group.

Which brings us to another use for Chiron as a tool—it shows us who is truly a maverick. In fact, maverick is an excellent keyword for this body. If you think of Saturn as a conservative, oriented to the establishment, and Uranus as an iconoclast or revolutionary, then Chiron is midway between—not belonging to the establishment, but not desirous of destroying it either.

Chiron was on the Midheaven when Anwar Sadat went to Israel. He definitely took a stand apart from his associates, the rest of the Arab world. Of course, this did produce many enemies, for his associates took the view, "If you are not with us, you are against us." And this is another side to Chiron—often producing many enemies by refusing to align itself with a particular side.

Chiron can be a tool to show us how best to use the energy represented by the Saturn/Uranus midpoint. Where the midpoint falls is the maximum expression of these two planets' interrelations. But it is often very difficult energy to tap. Where Chiron falls, we can actively integrate the two forces, and tap their energy to consciously evolve and grow.

Chiron's greatest use as a tool, I feel, is through understanding its effects in aspect to other planets. Some astrologers feel, due to Chiron's small size which is about that of a large asteroid, that we should limit the orb of the aspect to one degree. I disagree with this view, having seen the effects in aspects with even larger orbs. But for the research, I have confined my study to this orb, since such aspects would be the strongest, and the clearest to perceive.

At present, our research has focused on the conjunction, sextile, square, trine, and opposition. But I feel that future research will also reveal that other aspects are significant.

I'll start with the square, which seems to produce the most easily observable effects. Chiron, by square, produces a need to constantly rebalance whatever the other planet signifies. There is a tendency in the squared planet to shift back and forth to extremes. The reason for this is that, in some way, the planet is in a rut, and not growing. So Chiron throws it off balance, forcing the individual to search for something that is missing, or some quality that needs to be added on. Only then can a person succeed in bringing back a state of equilibrium. Once a person has learned to allow for continual growth with the squared planet, he succeeds in maintaining a steady balance.

Paul, whom I mentioned earlier, has Saturn in his first house. He had a very strict upbringing, giving him a very serious attitude towards life. But it also closed off many areas of life to him, which were taboo as far as his parents were concerned. Chiron is square Paul's Saturn. Suddenly he finds himself going through a period of irresponsibility, unable to buckle down to work, and unable to stick to necessary tasks. Then he discovers that some part of his life's structure, with roots in his childhood, is really not valid. He replaces it with a healthier, more realistic attitude, and soon becomes the hardworking, responsible Saturn rising again.

Robin Williams, TV's zany character Mork from the planet Ork, also has Saturn square Chiron. He is just as zany off camera as on. He has somewhat resolved his square by not accepting any definition of reality as absolute—by not seeing any structure as permanent, but allowing things to change whenever change is needed. His unusual brand of humor is partly a result of this square, for he thinks of concepts the average person could not, due to a rigid sense of reality.

Next, the opposition: A need is produced in the opposed planet to constantly search for alternative methods of expression. Positively, this produces the ability to surmount ordinary obstacles by finding a non-ordinary way around them. Negatively, there is a great deal of difficulty working within any rules or limits, for the planet constantly wants to go beyond and and all such walls.

Mercury opposing Chiron is a very good example. Positively, the people with this aspect have an unusual ability to perceive connections other miss. They believe no problem is unsolvable, and always see a way beyond any obstacle. They are great at picking up new skills, learning quickly, not letting things stand in their way. And their thinking patterns are unlike anyone else's, following no school of thought. But negatively, they find a great difficulty when they *must* work in an organized way; their minds constantly drift outside the structure to the many, many other possibilities, and they feel those are wasted by staying within the structure.

Much different is the case when Chiron is conjunct a planet. Here, the maverick nature of Chiron comes out in full force. The principles of the planet refuse to align themselves with any one style, but work independently. There is an ability, as well as a desire, to use the planet principles to open doors to new worlds—both for the self and others. This entails maverick methods as well. The tendency to develop enemies can surface here, especially among those who feel that the normal methods are the best. There is also a desire to equalize extremes in some way.

Ted Mack was born with a very close Chiron–Mercury conjunction. He had a number of talents, such as clarinetist, saxophonist, and even band leader. In each of these areas he had his own unique and independent style. But his Chiron really showed through when he met Major Edward Bowes, and became the talent scout for his radio show, "The Original Amateur Hour." As talent scout, and later as host when Bowes died, he opened the door for over 10,000 amateurs to get a chance to perform and be recognized. About 500 of these became professionals, including Frank Sinatra, Ann Margret, and Pat Boone.

Huey P. Long was a maverick all his life. He passed the Louisiana bar exam, even though he did not attend college for the full law course, but only a few semesters. In fact, he acquired much of his legal knowledge as a traveling salesman.

Chiron was only a few minutes away from his Mars, which was also conjunct his Sun. He was Senator and Governor of Louisiana with unimaginable popularity among the common people. He claimed to represent the poor, the dispossessed, and the rural folk. Politically he led a very unconventional campaign, perfectly attuned to the mounting grievances of the majority of people outside the cities. He attacked the Standard Oil Company, and was convicted of libel, but this only broadened his popularity. People felt that here was someone who was not a member of any group; they felt they were, for the first time, exercising their own power over the traditional enemies—the rich and the urban business establishment. He used his Mars to fight to open doors for people. He formulated a "Share the Wealth" program, wanting to equalize the rich and the poor, saying such maverick things as, "Every man would be a king."

In August 1935, he announced his intention to run for President against FDR. Roosevelt's supporters were alarmed, for he was uniting many small minority interests into a large, powerful bloc. Then, a month later, he was shot and killed by the son of one of his political enemies.

Another popular figure, with dreams of opening the doors of racial integration, was Martin Luther King, Jr. He had Chiron conjunct his ascendant, and was filling thousands of people with his dreams of racial harmony and non-violence. He wanted to equalize the races. He, too, was killed, because he was rocking too many boats.

Next, I'd like to describe Chiron trining a planet. A trine is typified in most books as an easy aspect, with little effort necessary on the individual's part to get the two planets working together. Chiron trine a planet produces a maverick talent, which is perfectly natural to the person. He needs to make no adjustment to express his independent views; often he flaunts them.

For example, Frank Zappa is a rock musician who is well known for his independent, unconventional music and style. He is an innovator, trying new things, yet integrating them with a traditional style. He had a group in the sixties called the Mothers of Invention. His lyrics were often beyond any sense of ordinary reality, such as a line from a song, "Ask any vegetable, and the chances are good it will answer you." His Chiron is in close trine to his Venus, which is aesthetic tastes, including music.

Two comedians with styles totally unique in the entertainment world are Peter Sellers and Phyllis Diller. There is no one like them. Both have Chiron trine Mercury.

The last aspect to be studied in detail is the sextile. The major difference between this and a trine is that the person with Chiron sextile a planet uses the planet as a tool to try to open doors, and go beyond established pathways. It is the aspect where the most positive expression of Chiron emerges, with the least amount of friction.

Alan Watts is a psychologist who could not stand the rigid views of traditional psychology such as Freud's. He has gone into many unconventional areas such as Eastern Mysticism, and has tried to open doorways for the mind and ego to go beyond traditional views of reality. He has Chiron sextile his Sun and Mercury.

Joe McDonald, better known as Country Joe, was a rock musician of the sixties. He tried to use his music as a tool to get his beliefs against the Vietnam War to the people. Many people were converted to an anti-war viewpoint after hearing some of his musical philosophy, such as one song which went, "Be the first one on your block to have your boy come home in a box." He has a close Chiron sextile Jupiter.

I'd also like to mention Neil Michelsen's company, Astro Computing Services. Chiron is sextile Saturn in that company's chart, and the company truly uses conventional business practices and machines in unique ways. Recently he added, free, the option of including Chiron in any computer chart you order. He utilizes the Chiron symbol of the "K" over the ellipse, which has been adopted all over the world. This should interest many more people in involving themselves in Chiron research.

There is a vast field of study in the other aspects. For instance, what did Jack Benny and Ava Gardner have in common? They both had Chiron quincunx their Mercuries. And was Chiron semi-sextile Uranus in any way responsible for both Hugh Hefner and Howard Hughes having rich "playboy" images?

Another field of research that should prove a good tool is when Chiron is the first planet to rise before the Sun. Other planets have shown major significance here as special skills the individual has in dealing with everyday life. Chiron seems to produce unique skills; an ability to break new ground others have not; unusual methods of dealing with people; even the ability to manipulate people. A number of famous people have this, including Neil Michelsen and such diverse individuals as Jim Jones of the Peoples Temple, Patricia Hearst, Judy Garland, Jean Harlow, Audrey Hepburn, and William Holden. Much more research is needed here.

Another area in which to make good use of this tool is house position. However, good research is difficult due to two problems. First, the accuracy of birth times is often in question. Second, different house systems will move Chiron from one house to another. So I have tried to restrict my research to birth times that are fairly certain, and house positions that stay the same in different systems.

As I mentioned before, Chiron's house position shows us how we can best tap the energy of the Saturn/Uranus midpoint. It is also the area of life a person can turn to to get out of ruts and outgrow his limitations. Here, too, is the area of life where one searches for others with similar interests —others with something in common. And it is a house of lessons.

I'd like to delve into just a few of the houses, to give you a better idea of Chiron's influence.

Chiron in the third house has relationships on his mind almost all the time. The more highly evolved souls seem to focus on companionship, while the more physically oriented types have sex on their minds constantly. There seems to be a rawness here—feelings, passions, and emotions are all near the surface. Often they are libertarians. Both Hugh Hefner, who publishes *Playboy*, and Larry Flynt, who publishes *Hustler*, have Chiron here. So do both Betty Davis and Joan Crawford.

Chiron in the seventh house causes a lot of trouble dealing with everyday people. Yet they cannot be loners—they need people. There is a strong urge to be "macho" in the males; and "ideal" women in the females—to prove they are equal to the best of their own sex. Marriage for these people often changes their lives much more drastically than for others. Grace Kelly, for example, has Chiron here, and she married to become Princess Grace of Monaco. Others with Chiron here include Fidel Castro, Gary Cooper, Charles De Gaulle, Charlton Heston, Joe Namath, and John Wayne.

Chiron in the ninth house searches for people with his philosophy. They are capable of using their beliefs as tools, even weapons. There is often a great deal of intolerance of others' beliefs, for they search for people with equal or similar ways of thinking. They have many lessons to learn about how closed their minds are compared to the opposite third house. Adolf Hitler had Chiron here, as well as J. Edgar Hoover, Ronald Reagan, George Wallace, Dane Rudyhar, and Alfred Hitchcock.

Last, I want to mention Chiron in the tenth house. This particularly interests me, because it is my position. It is also Charles Kowal's position, and that of a number of others responsible for getting the Chiron ephemeris computed and printed. There is a strong need to be accepted by the world at large as being equal, especially by those of the same sex. The individual has many lessons to learn about his status in the eyes of the world. Others with this position are Judy Garland, Gina Lollabrigida, Marlon Brando, and Truman Capote.

One aspect of this tool which needs much research is how Chiron's nature varies from sign to sign, especially since, like Pluto, it is in some signs much longer than in others. Pluto spends barely 12 years in Scorpio—its own sign—and over 31 in Taurus. But Chiron is even more unusual. When last in Libra, it spent a total of only 12½ months, while it was in Aries five times that—a total of 8¼ years! If Chiron follows Pluto's pattern, it should have some rulership over Libra. Of course, this will have to be researched, for there is also some evidence that it affects Sagittarius as well.

But no matter what its rulership—and it may have none at all—there is already some evidence that Chiron shapes the tide of world events depending on whether it is moving from Saturn towards Uranus, as it did after World War II, or the reverse, as it has been doing seen November 1970. A brief look at the past 25 years is especially revealing.

From 1955 to 1960 was a time of beatniks, mergers of vast unions such as the AFL and CIO, and exploring the sky with the first satellites. All of these fit the sign Aquarius, which Chiron then occupied.

The sixties were largely under Chiron in Pisces. It was an extremely chaotic time with such Piscean things as a major drug culture, the search for spiritual truths, an influx of mystical religion from the East, and the confusion of fighting a war that divided our country and brought disillusionment.

In 1969, however, Chiron entered Aries, and we began a period which has been called the "Me" decade. That in itself is a good Aries picture.

In 1977, Chiron entered Taurus, and there were shifts in man's attitude from "Me" to "My." People became concerned with major shortages; money became much tighter; and economizing became a household word. By the way, the stock market crash of 1929 came right in the midst of the last Chiron in Taurus period; then we had depression.

Obviously, if Chiron's sign is representative of the times, it must also influence children born in those times. This must be a major priority in our research, discovering how Chiron changes in each sign, before we can truly make best use of this tool.

Chiron's period may shed more light on its nature, especially if we relate it to Saturn and Uranus. Right now, its period is 50.7 years, but this ordinarily changes and averages out to 49 years. Forty-nine years is the life span of a vulture!

Seriously, though, 49 is seven times seven. Uranus is twelve times seven. And Saturn is four times seven. All three bodies, then, have seven as a major part of their nature. What is more, whenever Chiron makes a return, Saturn is not far from squaring its natal position. So this makes the Saturn square around age 49 especially significant.

One final point. Many years ago, Charles Jayne speculated about a body he called Jason, with an orbit similar to that of Chiron. It ruled things that were "up in the air." Could this be similar to Percival Lowell's prediction of the discovery of Pluto 15 years earlier? In mythology, Jason was one of Chiron's most famous pupils. Could Mr. Jayne have tuned into one particular aspect of Chiron, long before its discovery—that of teacher/pupil?

As I've mentioned a number of times, much more research is needed. For example, Chiron may be related to the major news events that occurred at the time of its discovery, such as the first National Women's Conference, which emphasized the concept of equality. I would like to invite each of you to join the Association for Studying Chiron and help with the investigation.

the Association for Studying Chiron

Born: November 13, 1978
7:27 pm
40°12'N 75°08'W

For information:

Zane B. Stein
158 Poplar Street
Ambler PA 19002

DIE BEDEUTUNG VON CHIRON

ZANE B. STEIN

[Text eines Vortrages gehalten am 16. Dezember 1979, Astrologers' Guild of America, in New York City]

1977 war fuer die Astronomen ein wichtiges Jahr mit vielen Neuendeckungen, welche unsere Vorstellungen vom Sonnensystem veraendert haben. Im Maerz fand man beispielsweise Ringe um Uranus. Dies bedeutete, dass Saturn sein Monopol auf ein Ringsystem verloren hat, es bedeutete aber auch, dass Uranus und Saturn etwas gemeinsam haben.

Es war ein ganz besonders wichtiges Jahr fuer den Astronomen Charles T. Kowal. Er begann das Jahr mit der Endeckung eines Kometen und eines Asteroiden, dann entdeckte er zwei Himmelskoerper wieder, welche verloren waren. Aber die groesste Endeckung gelang ihm im Herbst jenes Jahres.

Kowal photographiert routinemaessig jeden Monat einen Himmelsabschnitt in der Naehe des Oppositionspunktes der Sonne.Anschliessend werden die Aufnamen sorgfaeltig mit einem Geraet untersucht, das 'Blink-Microscope' heisst, welches in sehr schnellem Wechsel ein Segment der ersten Photoplatte zeigt, dann eines der anderen. Sterne erscheinen dabei stationaer, waehrend bewegende Objekte von einer Seite zur anderen zu huepfen scheinen.

Im Oktober konnte er nur eine Serie von Aufnahmen erlangen - in den Naechten des 18. und 19. Oktober. Er hatte zunaechst mehrere Tage lang keine Gelegenheit die Platten einer eingehenden Pruefung zu unterziehen. Als er dann aber am 1. November wieder in sein Buero zurueckkehrte, konnte er mit dem Mikróskop arbeiten and machte damit ein Objekt innerhalb der Uranusbahn auf den Fotos ausfindig. Dies war das Objekt Kowal, welchem er bald den Namen Chiron gab. Nach weiteren Studien tauchten Fotos von Chiron auf, wobei die fruehesten schon aus dem Jahre 1895 stammten. Auf einer Platte von 1941 war sogar Chirons Schweif markiert worden, aber man hatte dies nicht weiter verfolgt. Die Menscheit musste noch auf ein spezifischen Augenblick warten - den 1. November 1977 - mit Chiron auf 3°08' Stier, bis sie fuer diese Neuigkeit bereit war.

Die Astronomen sind sich nicht ganz in Klaren darueber, was Chiron ist, obwohl sie verschiedene Theorien haben Die eine Theorie, welche auch die neheliegenste zu sein scheint, besagt, dass Chiron durch unser Sonnensystem von ausserhalb eingefangen wurde und vielleicht irgenwann wieder hinausgeworfen wird.

Einerlei als was er sich fuer die Astronomen erweisen wird, fuer die Astrologen ist er ein bedeutendes Werkzeug. Webster's definiert das Wort Werkzeug as 'jedes Instrument oder Vorrichtung, die fuer jemanden im Beruf oder Beschaeftigung notwendig ist.' Das wichtigste Wort hier ist notwendig. Denn jetzt, da Chirons Prinzip im Bewusstsein der Menschheit erwacht, wird seine Verwendung fuer den Astrologen essentiell, um die gegenwaertige Probleme der Menschheit zu Verstehen.

In den vergangen zwei Jahren seit der Entdeckung haben wir damit begonnen, dieses neue Werkzeug zu handhaben; gewisse Gesamtthematiken fingen an, zum Vorschein zu kommen. Selbstverstaendlich ist aber noch sehr viel mehr Forschung von noeten; wir wissen noch nicht einmal alles ueber Pluto, obwohl er schon vor beinahe 50 Jahren entdeckt wurde. Aber ich moechte mit Ihnen teilen, was wir schon alles ueber Chiron herausgefunden haben.

Zunaechst hat Chiron eine eindeutige Beziehung zu Schwangerschaft und Geburt. Aber dieser Zusammenhang scheint soweit nur dann zu funktionieren, wenn de Geburt auf eine wichtige Veraenderung im Leben des Betreffenden hinauslaeuft. Es scheint auch eine gewisse Verbindung zu dem Foetus selber vorhanden zu sein. Bei einem Fall befand sich der Natal-Chiron einer Frau in Sechsten Haus. Als Pluto auf diese Stellung einen Transit im Quadrat hatte, erlitt sie eine gewaltsame Fehlgeburt. Der Arzt meinte allerdings, dass es besser war so, denn wenn das Kind ueberlebt haette, waere es behindert gewesen. Wir kennen zahlreiche Faelle von Einzelkindern, die ploetzlich herausfinden, das sie einen neuen Bruder oder eine neue Schwester bekommen, wenn Chiron ihre Himmelsmitte oder ihr Fuenftes Haus transitiert. Ebenso haeufig sind die Faelle in denen Chiron ueber die Himmelsmitte oder demn Jupiter eines Erwachsenen laeuft and wo diese Person festgestellt, dass er/sie Nachwuchs erhaelt. Meine Frau erwartet naechsten Juni ein Baby. Chiron steht am 4. Juni in Konjunktion zu ihrem Jupiter; wollen wir mal sehen wie exakt das Ereignis entritt. Chiron stand in Konjunction zu meinem Jupiter, als unsere erste Tochter geboren wurde.

Zudem war Chiron in vielen Solarhoroskopen im Fuenften Haus bei Leuten, die innerhalb des naechsten Jahres Eltern wurden. Louise Brown, das erste Retortenbaby wurde ungefaehr um den Tag von Chirons Entdeckung herum empfangen. Chiron ging bei ihrer Geburt gerade auf und ihr Natal-Aszendent steht in Konjunktion zum Chiron ihres Empfaengnishoroskopes.

Es kann auch eine Verbindung zwischen Chiron und dem Zeichen Waage vorliegen, entweder dadurch, dass er teilweise in diesem Zeichen herrscht, oder aufgrund der Tatsache, dass Chiron sein Perihel in diesem Zeichen erreicht. Durch unsere Nachforschungen haben wir folgende Tatsache ausgegraben: das Zeichen Waage wurde auch mit dem antiken Namen Zugon benannt, der all das bedeutet, was zusammen verbindet. Zugon kommt von dem Grundwort Zugos, von dem auch der biologische Ausdruck Zygote abstammt - das ist jenes embryonale Stadium, in dem sich Same und Ei bei der Empfaengnis verbinden - tatsaechliche biologische Vereinigung, welche den Foetus bildet. Es gibt auch noch ein paar andere Zusammenhaenge mit der Waage, auf die ich spaeter eingehen werde.

Chiron hat auch sehr viel mit Beziehungen zu tun, aber nicht auf dieselbe Weise wie das Siebte Haus. Chiron konzentriert sich sehr viel tiefer auf die entscheidene Basis der Beziehung selber. Seit Pluto in Waage eingetreten ist, haben wir alle beobachtet, dass sich Beziehungen auf jeder Stufe veraendert haben; tatsaechlich haben sich gerade die Definitionen von Beziehungen veraendert. Chiron ist als ein Werkzeug gekommen, mit dem wir das Fundament, auf dem jede Beziehung aufgebaut ist, endecken koennen: er konzentriert sich ueberhaupt auf den von Menschen geteilten gemeinsame Grund, welcher sie vereinigen kann. Und wir koennen durch die Aufdeckung des Fundaments genau erkennen, was in einer Partnerschaft der Veraenderung bedarf. Als Beispiel moechte ich ein Paar erwaehnen, das ich Jill und Paul nennen werde. Jill beschreibtk ihre fruehek Beziehung zu Paul [der spaeter ihr Ehemann wurde] als eine Kameradschaft, die sich auf gemeinsame Interesse wie Theater und Religion stuetzte. Sie fuehlten, dass sie ueber Ideen sprechen konnten. Sie trafen sich als Chiron im Quadrat zu ihrem Jupiter stand, dem Herrscherk ihres Fuenften Hauses - und Jupiter steht fuer Philosophie und Religion waehrend das Fuenfte Haus dem Theater enspricht. In Pauls Horoskop hatte Chiron zu dieser Zeit gerade ein Sextil zu Jupiter, aber was noch bedeutsamer ist, er stand in Opposition zu seiner Sonne im Fuenften Haus.

Es gibt zahlreiche andere Faelle, bei denen Chiron einen Aspekt bildet, welcher die von Menschen geteilte gemeinsame Grundlage bezeichnet. Dann tragen selbstverstaendlich auch die anderen Aspekte zwischen den Horoskopbildern ihren Teil dazu bei and und veraendern die Beziehung weiter. Aber Chiron ist die anfaengliche Basis. Dies koennte sich ebenfalls auf die Waage beziehen.

Ein anderer Gesichtpunkt Chirons ist der des Schluessels. Dazu muss ich etwas von seiner Beziehung zu Saturn und Uranus erklaeren.

Chirons Umlaufbahn ist sehr exzentrisch, sogar noch staerker, als die von Pluto, welche die am meisten elliptische aller anderen Planeten ist.

Diesbezueglich hat er sehr viel mit Pluto gemeinsam. Aber wenn Chiron sein Perihel erreicht, ueberquert er die Saturnbahn and kommt uns dadurch naeher als Saturn. Im Aphel beruehrt er die Uranusbahn. Indem er also mit beiden Umlaufbahnen in Kontact tritt, arbeitet er als ein Vebindungslied oder Bruecke zwischen zwei Extremen.

Nun kommt es haeufig vor, dass ein Saturnaspekt bis an das aeusserste geht un wie eine Mauer wirkt, welche uns von einer anderen Welt ausschliesst. Eine Sackgassen-Situation wird vorhanden sein, welche jede Handlung in eine bestimmte Richtung abblockt. Vielleicht sind es Einschraenkungen, deren Nuetzlichkeit sich ueberlebt haben; vielleicht sind es Aengste, die nicht mehr laenger stichhaltig sind. Aber wir brauchen eine Methode, um hinter diese Mauer zu gelangen, damit wir wachsen und uns entwicklen koennen. Chiron kommt und veraendert die Situation, welche die Dinge in einem Stillstand hielt. Chiron entdeckt oft eine Tueroeffnung in der Mauer, schliesst sie auf und ermoeglicht uns den Zutritt zu einer groesseren, unerforschten Welt dahinter, welche von Uranus repraesentiert wird. Danach liegt es an uns die Anstrengung aufzubringen, um durch die Oeffnung zu schreiten.

Zu anderen Zeiten oeffnet Chiron das Tor, laesst die Uranusenergie sich ihren Weg bahnen und rueckt Saturns Schutz beiseite. Aber wir bleiben sowieso nicht unveraendert, denn Chiron hat uns das Bewusstsein vermittelt, dass hinter der Mauer eine andere Welt existiert - ein Bewusstsein, das wir nicht ignorien koennen.

Auch Uranus kann uns aus unseren saturnalen Einschraenkungen herausfuehren, aber auf eine ganz andere Art. Denn Uranus erschuettert die bestehenden Strukturen total und laesst uns unbeschuetzt in einer neuen Welt zurueck, damit wir fuer uns selber sorgen. Chiron laesst uns dagegen die Freiheit mit unserer eigenen Geschwindigkeitdurch die Pforte zu schreiten. Aber selbst wenn dem nicht so ist, dann bringt er uns aus dem Saturnalen heraus ohne Saturns Strukturen zu vernichten.

Astrologen definieren Saturn oft als die Hauptlektion, welche uns solange einschraenkt, bis wir sie gelernt haben. Chiron bringt uns Lektionen, die uns lehren, unsere Beschraenkungen zu Ueberwinden, aus den Gleisen auszubrechen und uns irgendein Feld zu erschliessen, wenn wir dem Kindsein entwachsen un nicht mehr Nummer eins sind.

Chiron hat viel mit der Schueler/Lehrer-Beziehung zu tun. Chiron repraesentieren oft den Wunsch des Lehrers, dem Student neue Welten zu eroeffnen und einem Funken zu entfachen, dass er lernen will. Eng damit verknuepft schildert er viel ueber die fruehe Erziehung, die deine Eltern dir vermittelt haben, besonders wie sie sich jedem neuen Schritt in deiner Erziehung angenaehert haben.

Chiron kann als ein Vermittler zwischen den Saturn- und Uranus - kraeften wirken, indem er die Haltungen eines jeden filtert und in Begriffen auslegt, die der andere jeweils versteht. Hier gibt es auch einen saturnalen Gesichtspunkt. Zum Beispiel kann Chiron einen eingreifenden Vermittler verkoerpern bei einer Auseinandersetzung zwischen einem traditionellen, in den Ideen der Vergangenheit getraenkten Standpunkt und einem unkonventionellen, auf die Zukunft ausgerichteten Standpunkt. Chiron gehoert jedoch zu keinem der Extreme. Chiron ist vielmehr ein Unabhaengiger, der sich mit keiner Partei oder Gruppe verbindet.

Dies bringt uns zu einer weiteren Verwendungsweise von Chiron als Werkzeug - er zeigt uns, wer wirklich ein Einzelgaenger ist. In der Tat ist Einzelgaenger ein augezeichnetes Schluesselwort fuer diesen Himmelskoerper. Wenn man Saturn fuer einen Konservativen haelt, der nach dem Establishment ausgerichtet ist, und Uranus fuer einen Bilderstuermer oder Revolutionaer haelt, dann befindet sich Chiron genau in der Mitte dazwischen - nicht zum Establishment gehoerig, aber auch nicht begierig es zu zerstoeren.

Chiron stand an der Himmelsmitte, als Sadat nach Israel ging. Er nahm dadurch deutlich eine Aussenseiterposition ein unter seinen Gesinnungsgenossen, dem Rest der arabischen Welt. Selbstverstaendlich schuf er sich dadurch viele Feinde, denn seine Verbuenten waren der Ansicht, 'wenn Du nicht fuer uns bist, dann bist Du gegen uns'. Und genau dies ist noch eine andere Seite von Chiron - erloest oft Feindschaften aus, weil sich weigert, sich mit einer bestimmten Seite zu verbuenden.

Chiron kann auch ein Werkzeug sein, das uns zeigt, wie wir die Energie, welche durch die Uranus/Saturn -Halbsumme faellt, kommt die Wechselbeziehung dieser zweier Planeten am staerksten zum Ausdruck. Aber es handelt sich meistens um eine sehr schwer anzapfbare Energie. Dort wo Chiron steht, koennen wir diese zwei Kraefte aktiv integrieren und ihre Energie anzapfen, um uns bewusst zu entwickeln und zu wachsen.

Ich meine, dass wir Chirons wichtigste Bedeutung als ein Werkzeug erkennen, wenn wir seine Auswirkungen bei Aspekten zu anderen Planeten verstehen. Einige Astrologen sind der Meinung, dass wir aufgrund des geringen Umfanges von Chiron, welcher etwas einem grossen Asteroiden entspricht, den Orbis auf 1° einscharenken sollten. Ich stimme nicht mit dieser Ansicht ueberein, weil ich die Wirkung schon bei wesentlich groesseren Orben gesehen habe. Aber zum Zwecke der Forschung habe ich meine Studien mit diesem eingeschraenkten Orbis gemacht, denn dies sind die am staerksten und klarsten wahrnehmbaren Aspekte.

Gegenwaertig konzentrieren wir uns auf die Erforschung von Konjunktion, Sextil, Quadrat, Trigon und Opposition. Ich vermute aber, dass die zukuenftigen Untersuchungen auch die Signifikanz der uebrigen Aspekte enthuellen werden.

Ich werde mit dem Quadrat beginnen, welches die am ehesten beobachtbaren Effekte zu bewirken scheint. Chiron im Quadrat erzeugt ein Beduerfnis nach konstantem Wiederausgleich dessen, was von dem anderen Planeten angedeutet wird. Es gibt bei dem aspektierten Planeten eine Tendenz, sich zwischen den Extremen hin-und-her zu verlagern.

Die Ursache dessen liegt in gewisser Weise darin, dass der Planet auf einem Gleis befindet und sich nicht entwickeln kann. Also wirft Chiron ihn aus dem Gleichgewicht and zwingt das Individuum dazu, nach etwas Fehlenden oder noch einer gewissen Qualitaet, welche hinsugefuegt werden muss, zu suchen. Nur dann kann eine Person erfolgreich in den Zustand des Ausgleiches zurueckgelangen. Wenn man gelernt hat das staendige Wachstum mit dem aspektierten Planeten zu beruecksichtigen, dann gelingt es, das stetige Gleichgewicht beizubehalten.

Paul, den ich schon weiter oben erwaehnt habe, hat Saturn im Ersten Haus. Er genoss eine strenge Erziehung, welche bei ihm auch einer sehr ernsten Lebenshaltung fuehrte. Aber man enthielt ihm auch viele Lebensbereich vor, die tabu waren, insoweit siene Eltern betroffen wurden. Chiron steht im Quadrat zu Pauls Saturn. Ploetzlich bemerkt er, wie er durch eine Phase der Unverantwortlichkeit geht, unfaehig sich an die Arbeit zu machen und unfaehig an notwendigen Aufgaben zu bleiben. Schliesslich endeckt er, dass ein Teil seiner Lebensstruktur, der in der Kindheit wurzelte, fuer ihn nicht meher gueltig ist. Er ersetzte ihn durch eine gesuendere und realistischere Einstellung und wurde bald wieder der hart arbeitende und verantwortungsvolle Saturn-Aufsteiger.

Der Schauspieler Robin Williams, der die dummkoepfige Figur Mork vom Planeten Ork mimte, hatte ebenfalls Chiron Quadrat Saturn. Ob vor der Kamera oder nicht, er ismmer gleich 'dummkoepfig'. Er hat sein Quadrat ziemlich geloest, da er keine Definition der Realitaet als absolut akzeptiert - indem er keine Struktur als andauernd sieht, sondern die Dinge sich veraendern laesst, wann immer eine Veraenderung noetig ist. Seine ungewoehnliche Art von Humor ist teilweweise ein Ergebnis dieses Quadrates, denn er besinnt sich auf Vorstellungen, auf welche der Durchschnittsmensch aufgrund eines rigiden Wirklichkeitssinnes nicht kommt.

Nun zur Opposition. Der Planet in Oppositiion entwickelt das Beduerfnis staendig nact alternativen Ausdrucksmoeglichkeiten zu suchen. Im positiven Fall erzeugt dies die Faehigkeit einfache Hindernisse zu ueberwinden, indem man einen unkonventionellen Weg findet, diese zu umgehen. In unguengstigien Fall gibt es sehr viele Schwierigkeiten innerhalb irgenwelcher Regeln oder Grenzen zu arbeiten, denn der Planet moechte immer auf die andere Seite und ueber all Mauern hinausgehen.

Merkur Opposition Chiron ist ein sehr gutes Beispiel. Das Positive daran ist, dass Menschen mit diesem Aspekt eine aussergewoehnliche Faehigkeit haben, dort Verbindungen wahrzunehmen, wo andere sie uebersehen. Sie halten kein Problem fuer unloesbar, and sehen immer einen Wege hinter jedem Hindernis. Sie sind grossartig, wenn es darum geht sich neue Fertigkeiten anzueignen, sie lernen schnell und lassen die Dinge nicht auf sich beruehen. Ihre Denkmuster sind anders und sie folgen keiner bestimmten Denkrichtung. Aber im negativen Sinne befinden sie sich in einer grossen Schwierigkeit, wenn sie auf organisierte Art und Weise arbeiten muessen. Ihr Verstand treibt staendig aus der Struktur hinaus zu den vielen, vielen anderen Moeglichkeiten und sie meinen, dass diese verwuesstet werden, wenn man innerhalb der Strukturen verbleibt.

Ganz anders ist die Situation dagegen, wenn Chiron in Konjunktion zu einem Planet steht. Hier tritt die Enzelgaengernatur Chirons mit ganzer Kraft zutage. Die planetaren Prinzipien weigern sich mit irgendeinem Stil eine Verbindung einzugehen, wirken indessen aber viel lieber unabhaengig voneinander. Es besteht eine Moeglichkeit, sowie auch ein Wunsch, die planetaren Prinzipien zum Oeffnen der Pforten in neue Welten zu verwenden - sowohl fuer sich selber, als auch fuer andere. Das bringt auch einzelgaengerische Methoden mit sich. Die Tendenz sich Feinde zu schaffen kann hier auftauchen, besonders in den Reihen derjenigen, die meinen, normale Methoden waeren die besten. Es besteht ferner auch ein Wunsch Extreme auf gewisse Weise auszugleichen.

Ted Mack wurde mit einer sehr exakten Chiron-Merkur-Konjunktion geboren. Er hatte zahlreiche Faehigkeiten, so spielte er Klarinette, Saxophon und war sogar Bandleader. In jedem dieser Bereiche hatte er seinen einmaligen und unabhaengigen Stil. Aber sein Chiron drang erst richtig durch, als er Major Edward Bowes traf, und Talentsucher fuer dessen Radiosendung 'The Original Amateur Hour' wurde. Als Talentsucher und spaeter, nach Bowes Tod als Gastgeber der Sendung, oeffnete er fuer zehntausende Amateure die Tore, die dadurch eine Chance zum Auftreten erhielten und Anerkennung fanden. Ueber 500 von ihnen wurden spaeter Profis, darunter waren auch Frank Sinatra, Ann Margret und Pat Boone.

Huey P. Long war sein ganzes Leben lang ein Aussenseiter. Er erwarb das Anwaltsexamen in Louisiana, obwohl er nicht regelmaessig an Juraseminaren teilnahm, sondern nur ein paar Semester lang am College war. Das meiste seine juristischen Wissens erwarb er tatsaechlich als Vertreter.

Chiron war nur ein paar Minuten weit von seinem Mars entfernt, der ausserdem in exakter Konjunktion zu der Sonne stand. Er war Senator und Gouverneur von Louisiana mit unverstellbar Popularitaet unter dem einfachen Volk. Er nahm fuer sich in Anspruch die Armen, die Enteigneten und die Landbevoelkerung zu vertreten. Politische fuehrte er eine sehr unkonventionelle Kampagne durch, die voellig auf die wachsenden Misstaenda der Bevoelkerungsmehrheit ausserhalb der Staedt abgestimmt war. Er griff die Standard Oil Company an und wurde der Verleumdung fuer schuldig erklaert, aber das vergroesssert nur seine Popularitaet. Die Menschen spuerten, dass es sich hier um jemanden handelte, der zu keiner Gruppe gehoert; sie spuerten, dass sie durch ihn zum ersten Mal ihre eigene Macht ueber ihre traditionelle Feinde ausuebten - das reiche und staedtische Geschaeftsestablishment. Er benutzte seinen Mars, um fuer das Volk eine Oeffnung der Pforten zu erkaempfen. Ein 'Teilt den Wohlstand' - wurde von ihm ausgearbeitet und er sagte solche aussenseiterische Dinge wie: 'Jeder wuerde Koenig sein.'

Im August 1935 gab er seine Absicht kund, bei den Praesidenschaftswahlen gegen Roosevelt anzutreten. Roosevelts Mitarbeiterstab war alarmiert, denn Long vereinigte viele kleine Minoritaetsinteressen zu einem grossen Block. Dann, einen Monat spaeter, wurde er vondem Sohn eines politischen Gegners angeschossen und umgebracht.

Eine andere populaere Person mit den Traeumen, die Tore fuer eine Rassenintegration zu oeffnen, war Martin Luther King Jr. Sein Chiron war in Konjunktion zu seinem AC, und er efuellte tausende von Menschen mit seinen Traeumen von der Harmonie und Gewaltlosigkeit der Rassen. Er wollte die Rassen einander angleichen. Auch er wurde getoetet, weil er zuviele Boote ins Wanken brachte.

Als naechstes moechte ich Chiron im Trigon beschreiben.

In den meisten Buechern wird das Trigon als ein leichter Aspekt typisiert, bei dem die beiden Planeten zusammenarbeiten, ohne dass Individuum viel Muehe afwenden muesste. Chiron im Trigon erzeugt ein einzelgaengerisches Talent, das fuer die betreffende Person voellig natuerlich ist. Sie braucht keine Aenderungen vorzunehmen, um ihre unabhaengigen Standpunkte zum Ausdruck zu bringen: haeufig zeigt sie sie offen.

Frank Zappa ist zum Beispiel ein Rockmusiker, der sehr bekannt fuer seinen unabhaengigen und unkonventionellen Musikstil ist. Er ist ein Innovator, er versucht Neues und integrier es jedoch in den traditionellen Stil. In den Sechziger Jahren hatte er eine Gruppe mit dem Namen 'The Mothers of Invention'. Seine Texte gehen oft ueber jeden herkoemmlichen Wirklichkeitssinn hinaus, wie etwa diese Zeile aus einem Lied: 'Frage irgendein Gemuese und die Chancen stehen gut, dass es antwortet'. Sein Chiron hat ein exaktes Trigon zu seiner Venus, was fuer den aesthetischen Geschmack einschliesslich der Musik steht.

Zwei Komiker mit voellig einzigartigem Stil in der Unterhaltungsbranche sind Peter Sellers und Phyllis Diller. Niemand ist so wie sie. Beide haben Chiron Trigon Merkur.

Der letzte Aspekt auf den ich naeher eingehen moechte, ist das Sextil. Der groesste Unterschied zwischen diesem and dem Trigon liegt darin, dass die Person mit Chiron-Sextil den anderen Planeten als ein Mittel benuetzt, um Tueren zu oeffnen und die establierten Wege zu verlassen. Es ist der Aspekt, bei dem der positivste Ausdruck von Chiron mit der geringsten Reibung zum Vorschein kommt.

Alan Watts war ein Psychologue, der die rigiden Standpunkte der traditionellen Psychologie beispielweise Freuds nicht ertrug. Er drang in sehr viele unkonventionelle Bereiche, wie etwa die oestliche Mystik vor, und hat versucht dem Verstand und dem Ich Wege zu eroeffnen, um die herkoemmlichen Gesichtspunkte der Wirklichkeit zu ueberwinden. Er hat Chiron im Sextil zu Sonne und Merkur.

Joe McDonald, besser bekannt als Country Joe, war ein Rockmusiker der Sechziger Jahre. Er versuchte seine Musik als ein Mittel einzusetzen, um den Leuten seine Ansichten gegen den Vietnamekrieg nahezubringen. Viele Menschen wurden zu einer Anti-Kriegsbehaltung bekehrt, nachdem sie etwas von seiner musikalischen Philosophie gehoert hatten, so wie zum Beispiel den Song mit der folgende Zeile: 'Sei der erste in Deinem Block, der seinen Jungen in einer Kiste wieder nach Hause bekommt'. Er hat eine exaktes Chiron-Jupiter-Sextil.

Ich moechte auch Neil Michelsens Gesellschaft 'Astro Computing Service' erwaehnen. Chiron hat im Horoskop dieser Firma ein Sextil zum Saturn, und tatsaechlich verwendet die Gesellschaft konventionelle Geschaefts-pratiken und Maschinen auf einmalige Weise. Seit kuerzem enthaelt jede bestellte Computerberechnung auch die Daten von Chiron. Er benuewtzt das Symbol des 'K' ueber der Ellipse, das auf der ganzen Welt angenommen wurde. Dieses duerfte bei wesentlich mehr Leuten das Interesse wecken, sich der Chiron-Forschung anzuschliessen

Es gibt noch den riesigen Bereich der anderen Aspekte zu studieren. Was haben beispielweised Jack Benny und Ava Gardner gemeinsam? Nun, beide haben Chiron-Merkur-Quincunx. Und war vielleicht das Chiron-Uranus-Halbsextil irgendwie dafuer verantwortlich, dass Hugh Hefner und Howard Hughes beide das Image des reichen Playboys hatten?

Einen anderen Forschungsbereich, welcher sich als ein gutes Arbeitsmittel erweisen sollte, haben wir, wen Chiron als erster Planet vor der Sonne aufgeht. Andere Planeten haben sich hier also von grosser Bedeutung erwiesen, weil der Einzelne dann ueber spezielle Fertigkeiten im Umgang mit taeglich Leben verfuegt; Chiron scheint einmalige Faehigkeiten zu bewirken: eine Faehigkeit in ein neues Gebiet durchzubrechen, welche anderen fehlt: aussergewoehnliche Methoden beim Umgang mit Menschen, sogar die Faehigkeit Menschen zu manipulieren. Dies finden wir bei einer ganzen Reihe von Persoenlichkeiten, einschliesslich Neil Michelsen un so unterschiedlichen Personen wie Jim Jones vom 'Peoples Temple', Patricia Hearst, Judy Garland, Jean Harlow, Audrey Hepburn und William Holden. Hier muessten noch mehr Untersuchungen gemacht werden.

Nochmals ein anderer Bereich, bei dem wir Chiron gut benuetzen koennen ist auf die Haeuserposition. Allerdings sind gute Untersuchungen aufgrund zweier Probleme schwierig. Erstens ist die Genauigkeit von Geburtsdaten oft fraglich. Zweitens verschieben die unterschiedlichen Haeusersysteme Chiron mal in das eine, mal in das andere Haus. So habe it also versucht meine Untersuchungen auf die Geburtsdaten einzuschraenken, die einigermassen genau sind, und auf solche Haeuserstellungen, die in den verschiedene Systemen gleich bleiben.

Wie ich schon weiter oben ausgefuehrt habe, zeigt uns die Hausstellung, wie wir am besten die Energie der Uranus/Saturn-Halbsumme anzapfen koennen. Es ist auch der Lebensbereich, in dem eine Person sich daran machen kann, aus den Gleisen herauszutreten, und seinen Beschraenkungen zu entwachsen. Hier haben wir ebenfalls den Lebensbereich, in dem man andere mit aehlichen Interessen sucht - andere, mit denen man etwas gemeinsam hat. Und es ist das Haus der Lektionen.

Ich Moechte nun gerne einfach in ein paar Haeuser vordringen, um Ihnen eine bessere Verstellung von Chirons Einfluessen zu geben.

Chiron in Dritten Haus has fast immer Lust an Beziehungen. Die hoeher entwickelteren Seelen scheinen sich auf Kameradschaften zu konzentrieren, waehrend der eher koerperlich ausgerichtete Typus immer nur Sex im kopf hat. Es scheint hier eine gewisse Rohheit vorzuliegen - Gefuehle, Leidenschaften und Erregnung sind alle ganz nahe an der Oberflaeche. Sie sind freizuegig. Sowohl Hugh Hefner, der den Playboy herausgibt, als auch Larry Flint, der den Hustler publiziert, haben Chiron hier. Ebenso Bette Davis und Joan Crawford.

Chiron im Siebten Haus verursacht jede Menge Verwirrungen in bezug auf alltaegliche Menschen. Allerdings koennen diese Geborene nicht alleine sein - sie brauchen Menschen. Maenner haben den starken Drang 'Macho' zu sein, and die Frauen moechten 'Ideal' sein, um zu beweisen, dass sie gleichrangig mit den besten ihres eigenen Geschlechts sind. Heirat veraendert das Leben dieser Menschen oft drastischer, als bei anderen. Grace Kelly hatte zum Beispiel Chiron hier und sie heiratete, um Prinzessin Gracia von Monaco zu werden. Andere mit Chiron in diesem Haus sind Fidel Castro, Gary Cooper, Charles de Gaulle, Charlton Heston, Joe Namath und John Wayne.

Chiron im Neunten Haus sucht nach Menschen mit seiner Philosophie. Sie sind faehig ihren Glauben als Instrumente zu benuetzen, sogar als Waffen. Es gibt oft sehr viel Intoleranz dem Glauben anderer gegenueber, denn sie suchen Menschen mit gleichen oder aehnlichen Denkweisen. Sie muessen viele Lektionen darueber lernen, wie eng verschlossen ihr Geist im Vergleich zum entgegensetzten Dritten Haus ist. Adolf Hitler hatte Chiron hier, sowie Edgar J. Hoover, George Wallace, Ronald Reagan, Dane Rudhyar und Alfred Hitchcock.

Zuletzt moechte ich noch Chiron im Zehnten Haus besprechen. Dies interessiert mich besonders, weil dort mein eigener Chiron steht. Es ist auch die Positionen von Charles Kowal, sowie vieler anderer, die mitverantwortlich fuer das Zustandekommen der Chiron-Ephemeride waren. Es liegt ein starkes Verlangen vor, von der Welt akzeptiert zu werden, besonders von denen des eigenen Geschlechts. Der Einzelne muss viele lektionen lernen ueber seinen Status in den Augen der Welt. Andere mit dieser Stellung sind Judy Garlan, Gina Lollobrigida, Marlon Brando und Truman Capote.

Eine weitere Gesichtpunkt von Chiron, der noch vieler Forschung bedarf, ist die Frage, wie sich Chirons Wesen von Zeichen zu Zeichen veraendert, vor allem, weil er, wie Pluto, in eigenen Zeichen viel laenger verweilt als in anderen. Pluto bleibt kaum 12 Jahre in Skorpion, seinem eigenen Zeichen, und ueber 31 Jahre im Stier. Aber Chiron ist sogar noch ungewoehnlicher. Als er das letzte Mal in der Waage war blieb er dort nur ingesamt 12½ Monate, waehrend er sich in Widder fuenfmal solange aufhielt, naemlich insgesamt 8¼ Jahre. Falls Chiron Plutos Muster folgt, dann muesste er in der Waage herrschen. Selbsverstaendlich wird man das noch untersuchen muessen, denn es gibt auch einige Belege dafuer, das er genauso noch den Schuetzen beeinflusst.

Aber ganz egal, wo Chiron nun herrscht - und vielleicht herrscht er auch gar nirgends - es gibt jedenfalls schon einige Anzeichen dafuer, dass Chiron den Gezeitenwechsel des Weltgeschehens formt. Das ist jeweils davon abhaengig, ob er sich von Saturn zu Uranus hin bewegt, wie es etwa nach dem Zeiten Weltkrieg der Fall war, oder umgekehrt, was seit November 1970 beobachtet werden kann. Ein kurzer Blick auf die vergangenen 25 Jahre ist besonders enthuelllend.

Von 1955 bis 1960 war die Zeit der Beatniks, der Fusionen grosser Gesellschaften wie AFL und CIO und der erforschung des Himmels mit den ersten Satelliten. All dies passt zum Zeichen Wasserman, welches Chiron damals gerade besetzte.

In den Sechziger Jahren war Chiron weitgehenst in den Fischen. Es war eine extrem chaotische Zeit, mit solch 'fischigen' Dingen wie einer bedeutenden Drogenkultur, der Suche nach spirituellen Wahrheiten, einem Zustrom von mysterischen Religionen aus dem Osten und der Verwirrung durch einen Krieg [Anm. Vietnam], der die USA aufspaltete und enttaeuschung brachte.

1969 jedoch trat Chiron in den Widder ein, und wir begannen eine Periode, die mand die "Ich"-Dekade nannte. Dies ist sich selber schon ein sehr gutes Widderbild.

1977 trat Chiron in den Stier ein, und es kam zu Verschiebungen vom "Ich" zu "Mein" in der Einstellung des Menschen. Die Leute wurden mehr und mehr von groesseren Verlusten Betroffend: Geld wurde knapper und Sparsamkeit wurde ein Haushaltswort. Uebrigens der Boersenkrach 1929 genau dann ein, als Chiron das letzte Mal in der Mitte des Zeichens Stier war; danach hatten wir die Depression.

Es ist offensichtlich, dass wenn das Zeichen Chiron fuer bestimmte Zeitraeume repraesentative ist, dass es dann auch die Kinder beeinflussen muss, die in dier jeweiligen Zeit geboren werden. Den groessten Vorrang in undserer Forschung muss die Entdeckung einnehmen, wie sich Chiron in jedem Zeichen aendert.

Chirons Umlaufperiode kann mehr Licht und sein Weisen werfen, vor allem wenn wir sie auf Saturn und Uranus beziehen. Gerade jetzt betraegt seine Umlaufzeit 50.7 Jahre, aber diese veraendert sich normalerweise und betraegt durschnittlich 49 Jahre. Neunundvierzig is genau die Lebensspanne eines Geiers!

Aber wieder im Ernst, 49 ist sieben mal sieben. Der Uranusumlauf betraegt zwoelf mal sieben. Und Saturns Periode ist vier mal sieben. Alle drei Himmelskoerper haben also die Sieben als seinen wichtigen Bestandteil ihres Wesens. Mehr noch, wann immer Chiron eine Rundlauf beendet, steht Saturn nich weit weg von einem Quadrat zum Natal-Saturn. Dadurch wird das Saturn-Quadrat um das 49. Lebensjahr herum besonders wichtig.

Ein letzter Punkt. Vor vielen Jahren stellte Charles Jayne Spekulationen ueber einen Himmelskoerper an, den er Jason nannte, und der eine Umlaufbahn hatte, die der von Chiron ziemlich aehnlich war. Er herrschte ueber Dinge, die 'in der Luft lagen'. Koennte dies etwas aehnliches gewesen sein wie Percival Lowells Vorhersage von der Entdeckung Plutos 15 Jahre bevor es soweit war? In der Mythologie war Jason einer von Chirons Schuelern. Koennte es sein dass Charles Jayne, lange vor Chirons Entdeckung, schon auf seinen bestimmten Gesichtspunkt seines Wesens eingestimmt war - naemlich das Schueler/Lehrer-Prinzip?

Wie ich Schon des oefteren angefuehrt habe, ist noch sehr viel mehr Forschung von noeten. Zum Beispiel koennte Chiron auch in Beziehung stehen zu den Ereignissen um die Zeit entdeckung herum, wo etwa die Erste Nationale Frauenkonferenz tagte, welche nachdruecklich das Konzept der Gleichheit betonte. Ich moechte jeden von Ihnen dazu einladen der Association for Studying Chiron beizutraten und bei der Untersuchungsarbeit zu helfen.

[Uebersetzung Reinhardt Stiehle.]

THE ASSOCIATION FOR STUDYING CHIRON
Gegruendet: 13. November 1978, 19 h 27
40°12'N 75°08'W

Naehere Information bei
Association for Studying Chiron
Zane B. Stein
158 Poplar Street
Ambler PA 19002

BOOK REVIEW:

The Continuing Discovery of CHIRON

Erminie Lantero
M.Div., Ph.D.

$8.95

In a style that speaks to both the serious student and professional astrologer, THE CONTINUING DISCOVERY OF CHIRON engages the reader in a rare opportunity—a chance to witness the way in which astrologers come to assign meaning to a new planetary body. Erminie Lantero presents the only comprehensive study of the recently discovered Chiron, and lets the reader participate in the astronomical research leading up to its sighting, its background in mythology, its literary referents, and its use as an indispensable tool in astrological charts. Through the use of case studies, the author exhaustively documents Chiron's first four years in our consciousness, and goes on to pinpoint how Chiron can be used by astrologers to better understand certain facets of personality in the natal chart.

> "Lantero is exploring some fascinating terrain when she talks about Chiron transits as healing crises whose quality is one of transition. I suspect most literature on healing makes unconscious Neptunian and/or Plutonian assumptions about the process: that a healing crisis is either of the whole-making, detoxifying, definitely disorienting and confusing Neptunian variety, or the intense death and re-birth Plutonian melodrama. She is encompassing something which has great subtlety and complexity when she is discussing the healing possibilities inherent in the nature of transition."

ABOUT THE AUTHOR: Erminie Lantero came to astrology rather late in life. A Ph.D. in Philosophy from Radcliffe, she began her religious studies at Mount Holyoke College and received a M.Div. from Union Theological Seminary in New York. She has been on the faculties of Sweet Briar and Wellesley Colleges, and served as an editor and participant at Pendle Hill, an experimental Center for Religious and Social Studies near Philadelphia. In the late 1960's she served as research assistant for a two-volume history of the Ecumenical Movement in the American Churches. Her official "retirement" led her to a long-delayed exploration of the occult, and finally (some fifty years late) she discovered astrology as the life work she would have preferred all along. Since finishing her book on Chiron, she has retired to a community run according to the principles of Rudolf Steiner.

Samuel Weiser, Inc. • Box 612 • York Beach, ME 03910

Cover design by Alden Cole ISBN 0-87728-549-7